CONCEPTS & CASES

Strategic Management

COMPETITIVENESS & GLOBALIZATION

11e

Michael A. Hitt
Texas A&M University

R. Duane Ireland
Texas A&M University

Robert E. Hoskisson
Rice University

CENGAGE
Learning·

Australia • Brazil • Japan • Korea • Mexico • Singapore • Spain • United Kingdom • United States

CENGAGE
Learning®

Strategic Management: Competitiveness & Globalization: Concepts and Cases, **Eleventh Edition**

Michael A. Hitt, R. Duane Ireland, and Robert E. Hoskisson

Senior Vice President, Global Product Manager, Higher Education:
Jack W. Calhoun

Vice President, General Manager, Social Science & Qualitative Business:
Erin Joyner

Product Director:
Mike Schenk

Sr. Product Manager:
Scott Person

Sr. Content Developer:
Julia Chase

Product Assistant:
Tamara Grega

Sr. Content Project Manager:
Holly Henjum

Media Developer:
Courtney Bavaro

Manufacturing Planner:
Ron Montgomery

Production Service:
Cenveo Publisher Services

Sr. Art Director:
Stacy Jenkins Shirley

Rights Acquisitions Specialist:
Amber Hosea

Cover and Internal Designer:
Lou Ann Thesing

Cover Images:
© leonello calvetti/Shutterstock.com

For product information and technology assistance, contact us at Cengage Learning Customer & Sales Support, 1-800-354-9706

For permission to use material from this text or product, submit all requests online at **www.cengage.com/permissions**
Further permissions questions can be emailed to
permissionrequest@cengage.com

Library of Congress Control Number: 2013951199

ISBN-13: 978-1-285-42517-7
ISBN-10: 1-285-42517-0

Cengage Learning
200 First Stamford Place, 4th Floor
Stamford, CT 06902
USA

Cengage Learning is a leading provider of customized learning solutions with office locations around the globe, including Singapore, the United Kingdom, Australia, Mexico, Brazil, and Japan. Locate your local office at:
www.cengage.com/global

Cengage Learning products are represented in Canada by **Nelson Education, Ltd.**

To learn more about Cengage Learning Solutions, visit **www.cengage.com**

Purchase any of our products at your local college store or at our preferred online store **www.cengagebrain.com**

With each edition of this book, our goal has been to develop an effective learning tool for students and an effective teaching tool for instructors. Accordingly, we dedicate this 11th edition to all students and instructors past and present who have used or currently use this book. We sincerely hope that it proves to be of value as you learn about and successfully use the strategic management process.

—MICHAEL A. HITT, R. DUANE IRELAND, ROBERT E. HOSKISSON

Printed in Canada
2 3 4 5 6 7 17 16 15

Brief Contents

Contents

©Bikeworldtravel / Shutterstock.com

© Vividfour / Shutterstock.com

Contentsv

2: The External Environment: Opportunities, Threats, Industry Competition, and Competitor Analysis 36

Opening Case: The Coca-Cola Co. and Pepsico: Rivals Competing in a Challenging Environment 37

Photo ITAR-TASS Itar-Tass Photos/Newscom

2-1   The General, Industry, and Competitor Environments 38

2-2   External Environmental Analysis 40

2-2a   Scanning 41

2-2b   Monitoring 42

2-2c   Forecasting 42

2-2d   Assessing 43

2-3   Segments of the General Environment 43

2-3a   The Demographic Segment 43

Population Size 43

Age Structure 44

Geographic Distribution 44

Ethnic Mix 45

Income Distribution 45

2-3b   The Economic Segment 46

2-3c   The Political/Legal Segment 46

2-3d   The Sociocultural Segment 47

2-3e   The Technological Segment 48

2-3f   The Global Segment 49

2-3g   The Physical Environment Segment 50

Strategic Focus: The Informal Economy: What It Is and Why It Is Important 51

2-4   Industry Environment Analysis 52

2-4a   Threat of New Entrants 53

Barriers to Entry 53

Expected Retaliation 55

2-4b   Bargaining Power of Suppliers 56

2-4c   Bargaining Power of Buyers 56

2-4d   Threat of Substitute Products 57

2-4e   Intensity of Rivalry among Competitors 57

Numerous or Equally Balanced Competitors 57

Slow Industry Growth 58

High Fixed Costs or High Storage Costs 58

Lack of Differentiation or Low Switching Costs 58

High Strategic Stakes 58

High Exit Barriers 59

2-5   Interpreting Industry Analyses 59

2-6   Strategic Groups 60

2-7   Competitor Analysis 60

Strategic Focus: German Performance/Luxury Cars: If You Have Seen One, Have You Seen Them All? 61

2-8   Ethical Considerations 63

Summary 64 • Review Questions 65 • Experiential Exercises 65 • Video Case 66 • Notes 66

5: Competitive Rivalry and Competitive Dynamics 134

Yanice Idir/Alamy

Alessia Pierdomenico/Bloomberg/Getty Images

VINCENZO PINTO/AFP/Getty Images

8: International Strategy 226

Opening Case: An International Strategy Powers ABB's Future 227

© Torsten Lorenz/Shutterstock.com

WOLFGANG RATTAY/Reuters/Landov

9: Cooperative Strategy 262

Part 3: Strategic Actions: Strategy Implementation

10: Corporate Governance 294

Opening Case: The Imperial CEO, JPMorgan Chase's Jamie Dimon: Is It the End of Corporate Governance? 295

11: Organizational Structure and Controls 328

Opening Case: Big-Box Retailers Struggle to Change Their Strategies and Structures in the Face of Online Competition 329

Tom Williams/CQ Roll Call/Getty Images

Justin Sullivan/Getty Images

AP Photo/Al Behrman

13: Strategic Entrepreneurship 398

Opening Case: Innovation's Importance to Competitive Success 399

AP Photo/Procter & Gamble Co.

Part 4: Cases

Our goal in writing each edition of this book is to present a new, up-to-date standard for explaining the strategic management process. To reach this goal with the 11th edition of our market-leading text, we again present you with an intellectually rich yet thoroughly practical analysis of strategic management.

With each new edition, we are challenged and invigorated by the goal of maintaining the standard that we established for presenting strategic management knowledge in a readable style. To prepare for each new edition, we carefully study the most recent academic research to ensure that the strategic management content we present to you is highly current and relevant. In addition, we continuously read articles appearing in many different and widely read business publications (e.g., *Wall Street Journal, Bloomberg Businessweek, Fortune, Financial Times, Fast Company*, and *Forbes*, to name a few). We also study postings through social media (such as blogs), given their increasing use as channels of information distribution. By studying a wide array of sources, we are able to identify valuable examples of how companies are using (or not using) the strategic management process. Though many of the hundreds of companies we discuss in the book will be quite familiar, some will likely be new to you. One reason for this is that we use examples of companies from around the world to demonstrate how globalized business has become. To maximize your opportunities to learn as you read and think about how actual companies use strategic management tools, techniques, and concepts (based on the most current research), we emphasize a lively and user-friendly writing style.

Several *characteristics* of this 11th edition of our book will enhance your learning opportunities:

- This book presents you with the most comprehensive and thorough coverage of strategic management that is available on the market.
- The research used in this book is drawn from the "classics" as well as the most recent contributions to the strategic management literature. The historically significant "classic" research provides the foundation for much of what is known about strategic management, while the most recent contributions reveal insights about how to effectively use strategic management in the complex, global business environment in which firms now compete. Our book also presents you with many up-to-date examples of how firms use the strategic management tools, techniques, and concepts developed by leading researchers. Indeed, although this book is grounded in relevant theory and current research, it also is strongly application-oriented and presents you, our readers, with a vast number of examples and applications of strategic management concepts, techniques, and tools. In this edition, for example, we examine more than 500 companies to describe the use of strategic management. Collectively, no other strategic management book presents you with the *combination* of useful and insightful *research* and *applications* in a wide variety of organizations as does this text.

  Company examples range from the large U.S.-based firms such as Apple, Amazon.com, Boeing, Starbucks, Walmart, Walt Disney, General Electric, Dell, Campbell Soup, Coca-Cola, Hewlett-Packard, Ford, United Parcel Service, JPMorgan Chase, and Merck, to major foreign-based firms such as Carrefour, Nestlé, Ericsson, Nokia, Virgin Group,

Tokyo Electric Power, Rio Tinto, CEMEX, Cadbury, IKEA, FEMSA, Takeda, Publicis, Sany Heavy Equipment, Hutchison Whampoa, and Zara. As this list suggests, the firms examined in this book compete in a wide range of industries and produce a diverse set of goods and services.

- We use the ideas of prominent scholars (e.g., Ron Adner, Rajshree Agarwal, Gautam Ahuja, Raffi Amit, Africa Arino, Jay Barney, Paul Beamish, Peter Buckley, Ming-Jer Chen, Russ Coff, Rich D'Aveni, Kathy Eisenhardt, Gerry George, Javier Gimeno, Luis Gomez-Mejia, Melissa Graebner, Ranjay Gulati, Don Hambrick, Connie Helfat, Amy Hillman, Tomas Hult, Dave Ketchen, Dovev Lavie, Michael Lennox, , Yadong Luo, Shige Makino, Costas Markides, Danny Miller, Will Mitchell, Margie Peteraf, Michael Porter, Nandini Rajagopalan, Jeff Reuer, Joan Ricart, Alan Rugman, Richard Rumelt, David Sirmon, Ken Smith, Steve Tallman, David Teece, Michael Tushman, Margarethe Wiersema, Oliver Williamson, Mike Wright, Anthea Zhang, and Ed Zajac) to shape the discussion of *what* strategic management is. We describe the practices of prominent executives and practitioners (e.g., Michael Corbat, Jamie Dimon, Carlos Ghosn, Heinrich Hiesinger, Marilyn Hewson, Jeff Immelt, Elon Musk, Paul Pullman, and many others) to help us describe *how* strategic management is used in many types of organizations.

The authors of this book are also active scholars. We conduct research on different strategic management topics. Our interest in doing so is to contribute to the strategic management literature and to better understand how to effectively apply strategic management tools, techniques, and concepts to increase organizational performance. Thus, our own research is integrated in the appropriate chapters along with the research of numerous other scholars, some of whom are noted above.

In addition to our book's *characteristics*, there are some specific *features* and *revisions* that we have made in this 11th edition that we are pleased to highlight for you:

- **New Opening Cases and Strategic Focus Segments.** We continue our tradition of providing all-new Opening Cases and Strategic Focus segments (a few are on the same company[ies] but are substantially updated). Many of these deal with companies located outside North America. In addition, virtually all of the company-specific examples included in each chapter are new or substantially updated. Through all of these venues, we present you with a wealth of examples of how actual organizations, most of which compete internationally as well as in their home markets, use the strategic management process for the purpose of outperforming rivals and increasing their performance.

- **New Strategy Right Now Callouts.** Each chapter contains four Strategy Right Now icons (up from three in the last edition) that direct the student to the CourseMate site. There students can find out how to access the Gale Business Insights: Essentials content. This material includes recent articles covering most of the concepts and companies highlighted in each of the Opening Cases, Strategic Focus segments, and other important areas in the chapter. In addition, online quizzes are associated with all of the BIE content in CengageNow.

- **Thirty All-New Cases** with an effective mix of organizations headquartered or based in the United States and a number of other countries. Many of the cases have full financial data (the analyses of which are in the Case Notes that are available to instructors). These timely cases present active learners with opportunities to apply the strategic management process and understand organizational conditions and contexts and to make appropriate recommendations to deal with critical concerns. These cases can also be found in CengageNow.

- **More than 1000 New References** (2012, 2013) are included in the chapters' endnotes to support new material added or current strategic management concepts used in the book. In addition to demonstrating the classic and recent research from which we draw our material, these data support the fact that this book references the current cutting-edge research and thinking in the field.

- **New Concepts** were added in several chapters. Examples include executive ambidexterity and ambicultural executives (Chapter 1), the informal economy (Chapter 2), private-public partnerships in strategic alliances such as those found in industrial clusters (Chapter 9), and strategic change (Chapter 12).

- **New Content** was added to several chapters. Examples include the Analysis-Strategy-Performance framework (Chapter 1 and referenced in several other chapters), the importance of emerging economies and influence of emerging economy multinationals (Chapters 1 and 8), the size and scope of the informal economy (Chapter 2), innovators' dilemma (Chapter 4), the use of TQM in cost leadership and differentiation strategies (Chapter 4), and intra-industry diversification (Chapter 6).

- **New Information** was provided in several chapters. Examples include the stakeholder host communities (Chapter 1), all-new and current demographic data (e.g., ethnic mix, geographic distribution) and on the economic environment (Chapter 2), the general partner strategies of private equity firms (Chapter 7), information from the *World Economic Forum Competitiveness Report* regarding political risks of international investments (Chapter 8), examples of industrial clusters or districts of geographic concentrations of a set of interconnected companies and public organizations (Chapter 9), new and updated information on corporate governance in different countries (Chapter 10), discussion of how online retailers are changing the structures of big box retailers (Chapter 11), and updated data about the number of internal and external CEO selections occurring in companies today (Chapter 12).

- **New and Revised Experiential Exercises** are at the end of each chapter to support individuals' efforts to understand the use of the strategic management process. These exercises place active learners in a variety of situations requiring application of some part of the strategic management process.

- **An Exceptional Balance** between current research and up-to-date applications of it in actual organizations. The content has not only the best research documentation but also the largest number of effective real-world examples to help active learners understand the different types of strategies that organizations use to achieve their vision and mission.

- **Access to Harvard Business School (HBS) Cases.** We have developed a set of assignment sheets and AACSB International assessment rubrics to accompany 10 of the best-selling HBS cases. Instructors can customize the text to include these cases (www.cengage.com/custom/makeityours/hitt11e) and utilize the accompanying set of teaching notes and assessment rubrics to formalize assurance of learning efforts in the capstone Strategic Management/Business Policy course. Contact your Cengage Learning representative for more information.

Supplements to Accompany This Text

Instructor Web site. Access important teaching resources on this companion Web site. For your convenience, you can download electronic versions of the instructor supplements from the password-protected section of the site, including Instructor's Resource Manual, Comprehensive Case Notes, Cognero Testing, Word Test Bank files, PowerPoint® slides, and Video Segments and Guide. To access these additional course materials and companion resources, please visit www.cengagebrain.com. On the Cengagebrain.com homepage, use the search box at the top of the page to search for the ISBN of your title (from the back cover of your book). This will take you to the product page where free companion resources can be found.

- **Instructor's Resource Manual.** The Instructor's Resource Manual, organized around each chapter's knowledge objectives, includes teaching ideas for each chapter and how to reinforce essential principles with extra examples. This support product includes lecture outlines, detailed answers to end-of-chapter review questions, instructions for using each chapter's experiential exercises and video cases, and additional assignments.
- **Case Notes.** These notes include directed assignments, financial analyses, and thorough discussion and exposition of issues in the case. Select cases also have assessment rubrics tied to National Standards (AACSB outcomes) that can be used for grading each case. The Case Notes provide consistent and thorough support for instructors, following the method espoused by the author team for preparing an effective case analysis.
- **Cengage Learning Testing Powered by Cognero.** This is a flexible, online system that allows you to author, edit, and manage test bank content from multiple Cengage Learning solutions; create multiple test versions in an instant; and deliver tests from your LMS, your classroom, or wherever you want. Cengage Learning Testing Powered by Cognero works on any operating system or browser, no special installs or downloads needed. You can create tests from school, home, the coffee shop—anywhere with Internet access and enhanced, test bank questions are linked to each chapter's knowledge objectives and are ranked by difficulty and question type. We provide an ample number of application questions throughout, and we have also retained scenario-based questions as a means of adding in-depth problem-solving questions. The questions are also tagged to National Standards (AACSB outcomes), Bloom's Taxonomy, and the Dierdorff/Rubin metrics.
- **PowerPoints®.** An all-new PowerPoint presentation, created for the 11th edition, provides support for lectures, emphasizing key concepts, key terms, and instructive graphics.
- **Video Segments.** A collection of 13 BBC videos have been included in the end-of-chapter material. These new videos are short, compelling, and timely illustrations of today's management world. Topics include Brazil's growing global economy, the aftermath of BP's oil spill, Zappos.com, the Southwest merger with AirTrans, and more. Available on the DVD and Instructor Web site. Detailed case write-ups including questions and suggested answers appear in the Instructor's Resource Manual and Video Guide.

CengageNow. This robust online course management system gives you more control in less time and delivers better student outcomes—NOW. CengageNow includes teaching and learning resources organized around lecturing, creating assignments, casework, quizzing, and gradework to track student progress and performance. The 30 comprehensive cases appear in CengageNow. There are 13 Guided Cases that bring students to a higher level of understanding in preparation for in-class activities. Multiple types of quizzes, including BBC video quizzes and YouTube video quizzes, are assignable and gradable. We also include assignable and gradable Business Insights: Essentials (BIE) quizzes that direct students to Gale articles to find expansive, current event coverage for companies, including a wealth of daily updated articles and company financials. Flexible assignments, automatic grading, and a gradebook option provide more control while saving you valuable time. A Personalized Study diagnostic tool empowers students to master concepts, prepare for exams, and become more involved in class.

Cengage Learning Write Experience 2.0. This new technology is the first in higher education to offer students the opportunity to improve their writing and analytical skills without adding to your workload. Offered through an exclusive agreement with Vantage Learning, creator of the software used for GMAT essay grading, Write Experience evaluates students' answers to a select set of writing assignments for voice, style, format, and originality. We have trained new prompts for this edition!

The Business Insights: Essentials Resource Center (BIE). Put a complete business library at your students' fingertips! This premier online business research tool allows you and your students to search thousands of periodicals, journals, references, financial data, industry reports, and more. This powerful research tool saves time for students—whether they are preparing for a presentation or writing a reaction paper. You can use the BIE to quickly and easily assign readings or research projects.

Micromatic Strategic Management Simulation (for bundles only). The Micromatic Business Simulation Game allows students to decide their company's mission, goals, policies, and strategies. Student teams make their decisions on a quarter-by-quarter basis, determining price, sales and promotion budgets, operations decisions, and financing requirements. Each decision round requires students to make approximately 100 decisions. Students can play in teams or play alone, compete against other players or the computer, or use Micromatic for practice, tournaments, or assessment. You can control any business simulation element you wish, leaving the rest alone if you desire. Because of the number and type of decisions the student users must make, Micromatic is classified as a medium to complex business simulation game. This helps students understand how the functional areas of a business fit together without being bogged down in needless detail and provides students with an excellent capstone experience in decision making.

Smartsims (for bundles only). MikesBikes Advanced is a premier strategy simulation, providing students with the unique opportunity to evaluate, plan, and implement strategy as they manage their own company while competing online against other students within their course. Students from the management team of a bicycle manufacturing company make all the key functional decisions involving price, marketing, distribution, finance, operations, HR, and R&D. They formulate a comprehensive strategy, starting with their existing product, and then adapt the strategy as they develop new products for emerging markets. Through the Smartsims easy-to-use interface, students are taught the cross-functional disciplines of business and how the development and implementation of strategy involves these disciplines. The competitive nature of MikesBikes encourages involvement and learning in a way that no other teaching methodology can, and your students will have fun in the process!

MindTap. MindTap is a fully online digital learning platform of authoritative Cengage Learning content, assignments, and services that engages your students with interactivity while also offering you choice in the configuration of coursework and enhancement of the curriculum via complimentary Web apps known as MindApps. MindApps range from ReadSpeaker (which reads the text out loud to students), to Kaltura (allowing you to insert inline video and audio into your curriculum), to ConnectYard (allowing you to create digital "yards" through social media—all without "friending" your students). This is well beyond an eBook, a homework solution or digital supplement, a resource center website, a course delivery platform or a Learning Management System. It is the first in a new category—the Personal Learning Experience.

Make It Yours—Custom Case Selection

Cengage Learning is dedicated to making the educational experience unique for all learners by creating custom materials that best suit your course needs. With our Make It Yours program, you can easily select a unique set of cases for your course from providers such as Harvard Business School Publishing, Darden, and Ivey. See http://www.custom.cengage.com/makeityours/hitt11e for more details.

Acknowledgments

We express our appreciation for the excellent support received from our editorial and production team at Cengage Learning. We especially wish to thank Scott Person, our Senior Product Manager; and Julia Chase, our Senior Content Developer. We are grateful for their dedication, commitment, and outstanding contributions to the development and publication of this book and its package of support materials.

We are highly indebted to all of the reviewers of past editions. Their comments have provided much insight in the preparation of this current edition:

Jay Azriel
York College of Pennsylvania

Lana Belousova
Suffolk University

Ruben Boling
North Georgia University

Matthias Bollmus
Carroll University

Erich Brockmann
University of New Orleans

David Cadden
Quinnipiac University

Ken Chadwick
Nicholls State University

Bruce H. Charnov
Hofstra University

Jay Chok
USC Marshall

Peter Clement
State University of New York – Delhi

Terry Coalter
Northwest Missouri University

James Cordeiro
SUNY Brockport

Deborah de Lange
Suffolk University

Irem Demirkan
Northeastern University

Dev Dutta
University of New Hampshire

Scott Elston
Iowa State University

Harold Fraser
California State University, Fullerton

Robert Goldberg
Northeastern University

Monica Gordillo
Iowa State University

George Griffin
Spring Arbor University

Susan Hansen
University of Wisconsin-Platteville

Glenn Hoetker
Arizona State University

James Hoyt
Troy University

Miriam Huddleston
Harford Community College

Carol Jacobson
Purdue University

James Katzenstein
California State University, Dominguez Hills

Robert Keidel
Drexel University

Nancy E. Landrum
University of Arkansas at Little Rock

Mina Lee
Xavier University

Patrice Luoma
Quinnipiac University

Mzamo Mangaliso
University of Massachusetts – Amherst

Michele K. Masterfano
Drexel University

James McClain
California State University, Fullerton

Jean McGuire
Louisiana State University

John McIntyre
Georgia Tech

Rick McPherson
University of Washington

Karen Middleton
Texas A&M–Corpus Christi

Raza Mir
William Paterson University

Martina Musteen
San Diego State University

Louise Nemanich
Arizona State University

Frank Novakowski
Davenport University

Consuelo M. Ramirez
University of Texas at San Antonio

Barbara Ribbens
Western Illinois University

Jason Ridge
Clemson University

William Roering
Michigan State University

Manjula S. Salimath
University of North Texas

Deepak Sethi
Old Dominion University

Manisha Singal
Virginia Tech

Warren Stone
University of Arkansas at Little Rock

Elisabeth Teal
University of North Georgia

Jill Thomas Jorgensen
Lewis and Clark State College

Len J. Trevino
Washington State University

Edward Ward
Saint Cloud State University

Marta Szabo White
Georgia State University

Michael L. Williams
Michigan State University

Diana J. Wong-MingJi
Eastern Michigan University

Patricia A. Worsham
California State Polytechnic University, Pomona

William J. Worthington
Baylor University

Wilson Zehr
Concordia University

Finally, we are very appreciative of the following people for the time and care that went into preparing the supplements to accompany this edition:

Charlie Cook

Richard H. Lester
Texas A&M University

Susan Leshnower
Midland College

Paul Mallette
University of West Alabama

Kristi L. Marshall

Patricia A. Worsham
California State Polytechnic University, Pomona

Michael A. Hitt
R. Duane Ireland
Robert E. Hoskisson

About the Authors

Michael A. Hitt

Michael A. Hitt is a University Distinguished Professor and holds the Joe B. Foster Chair in Business Leadership at Texas A&M University. He received his Ph.D. from the University of Colorado. He has more than 260 publications including 26 co-authored or co-edited books and was cited as one of the 10 most-cited scholars in management over a 25-year period in an article published in the 2008 volume of the *Journal of Management*. In 2010, *Times Higher Education* listed him as one of the top scholars in economics, finance, and management.

Some of his books are *Downscoping: How to Tame the Diversified Firm* (Oxford University Press, 1994); *Mergers and Acquisitions: A Guide to Creating Value for Stakeholders* (Oxford University Press, 2001); *Competing for Advantage*, 3rd edition (South-Western, 2013); and *Understanding Business Strategy*, 3rd edition (South-Western Cengage Learning, 2012). He is co-editor of several books including the following: *Managing Strategically in an Interconnected World* (1998); *New Managerial Mindsets: Organizational Transformation and Strategy Implementation* (1998); *Dynamic Strategic Resources: Development, Diffusion, and Integration* (1999); *Winning Strategies in a Deconstructing World* (John Wiley & Sons, 2000); *Handbook of Strategic Management* (2001); *Strategic Entrepreneurship: Creating a New Integrated Mindset* (2002); *Creating Value: Winners in the New Business Environment* (Blackwell Publishers, 2002); *Managing Knowledge for Sustained Competitive Advantage* (Jossey-Bass, 2003); *Great Minds in Management: The Process of Theory Development* (Oxford University Press, 2005); and *The Global Mindset* (Elsevier, 2007). He has served on the editorial review boards of multiple journals, including the *Academy of Management Journal*, *Academy of Management Executive*, *Journal of Applied Psychology*, *Journal of Management*, *Journal of World Business*, and *Journal of Applied Behavioral Sciences*. Furthermore, he has served as consulting editor and editor of the *Academy of Management Journal*. He was a founding co-editor and currently a consulting editor for the *Strategic Entrepreneurship Journal*. He is a past president of the Strategic Management Society and of the Academy of Management.

He is a Fellow in the Academy of Management and in the Strategic Management Society. He received an honorary doctorate from the Universidad Carlos III de Madrid and is an Honorary Professor and Honorary Dean at Xi'an Jiao Tong University. He has been acknowledged with several awards for his scholarly research and he received the Irwin Outstanding Educator Award and the Distinguished Service Award from the Academy of Management. He has received best paper awards for articles published in the *Academy of Management Journal*, *Academy of Management Executive*, *Journal of Management, and Family Business Review*.

R. Duane Ireland

R. Duane Ireland is a University Distinguished Professor and holds the Conn Chair in New Ventures Leadership in the Mays Business School, Texas A&M University where he previously served as head of the management department. He teaches strategic management courses at all levels (undergraduate, masters, doctoral, and executive). He has over 200 publications including more than a dozen books. His research, which focuses on diversification, innovation, corporate entrepreneurship, and strategic entrepreneurship, has been published in a number of journals, including *Academy of Management Journal, Academy of Management Review, Academy of Management Executive, Administrative Science Quarterly, Strategic Management Journal, Journal of Management, Strategic Entrepreneurship Journal, Human Relations, Entrepreneurship Theory and Practice, Journal of Business Venturing,* and *Journal of Management Studies,* among others. His recently published books include *Understanding Business Strategy,* 3rd edition (SouthWestern Cengage Learning, 2012), *Entrepreneurship: Successfully Launching New Ventures,* 4th edition (Prentice-Hall, 2012), and *Competing for Advantage,* 3rd edition (South-Western, 2013). He is serving or has served as a member of the editorial review boards for a number of journals, including *Academy of Management Journal, Academy of Management Review, Academy of Management Executive, Journal of Management, Strategic Entrepreneurship Journal, Journal of Business Venturing, Entrepreneurship Theory and Practice, Journal of Business Strategy, Academy of Management Perspectives,* and *European Management Journal.* He recently completed a term as editor of the *Academy of Management Journal.* He has completed terms as an associate editor for *Academy of Management Journal,* as an associate editor for *Academy of Management Executive,* and as a consulting editor for *Entrepreneurship Theory and Practice.* He has co-edited special issues of *Academy of Management Review, Academy of Management Executive, Journal of Business Venturing, Strategic Management Journal, Journal of High Technology and Engineering Management,* and *Organizational Research Methods.* He received awards for the best article published in *Academy of Management Executive* (1999) and *Academy of Management Journal* (2000). In 2001, his co-authored article published in *Academy of Management Executive* won the Best Journal Article in Corporate Entrepreneurship Award from the U.S. Association for Small Business & Entrepreneurship (USASBE).

He is a Fellow of the Academy of Management, a Fellow of the Strategic Management Society, and a 21st Century Entrepreneurship Research Scholar. He is the current President of the Academy of Management. He received the 1999 Award for Outstanding Intellectual Contributions to Competitiveness Research from the American Society for Competitiveness and the USASBE Scholar in Corporate Entrepreneurship Award (2004).

Robert E. Hoskisson

Robert E. Hoskisson is the George R. Brown Chair of Strategic Management at the Jesse H. Jones Graduate School of Business, Rice University. He received his Ph.D. from the University of California-Irvine. Professor Hoskisson's research topics focus on corporate governance, acquisitions and divestitures, corporate and international diversification, corporate entrepreneurship, privatization, and cooperative strategy. He teaches courses in corporate and international strategic management, cooperative strategy, and strategy consulting, among others. Professor Hoskisson's research has appeared in over 120 publications, including articles in the *Academy of Management Journal, Academy of Management Review, Strategic Management Journal, Organization Science, Journal of Management, Journal of International Business Studies, Journal of Management Studies, Organization Research Methods, Journal of Business Venturing, Entrepreneurship Theory and Practice, Academy of Management*

Perspectives, Academy of Management Executive, Journal of World Business, California Management Review, and 26 co-authored books. In 2010, *Times Higher Education* listed him as one of the most highly cited scholars in economics, finance, and management. He is currently an associate editor of the *Strategic Management Journal* and serves on the Editorial Review board of the *Academy of Management Journal.* Professor Hoskisson has served on several editorial boards for such publications as the *Academy of Management Journal* (including consulting editor and guest editor of a special issue), *Journal of Management* (including associate editor), *Organization Science, Journal of International Business Studies* (including consulting editor), *Journal of Management Studies* (guest editor of a special issue), and *Entrepreneurship Theory and Practice.* He has co-authored several books including *Understanding Business Strategy*, 3rd Edition (South-Western Cengage Learning, 2012), *Competing for Advantage*, 3rd edition (South-Western, 2013), and *Downscoping: How to Tame the Diversified Firm* (Oxford University Press, 1994).

He has an appointment as a Special Professor at the University of Nottingham and as an Honorary Professor at Xi'an Jiao Tong University. He is a Fellow of the Academy of Management and a charter member of the Academy of Management Journals Hall of Fame. He is also a Fellow of the Strategic Management Society. In 1998, he received an award for Outstanding Academic Contributions to Competitiveness, American Society for Competitiveness. He also received the William G. Dyer Distinguished Alumni Award given at the Marriott School of Management, Brigham Young University. He completed three years of service as a representative at large on the Board of Governors of the Academy of Management and currently is President of the Strategic Management Society.

Case Title	Manufacturing	Service	Consumer Goods	Food/Retail	High Technology	Internet	Transportation/Communication	International Perspective	Social/Ethical Issues	Industry Perspective
Ally Bank		•				•				•
AstraZeneca										
Avon			•	•				•	•	
Black Canyon				•				•		
Blue Nile			•	•		•		•		•
Campbell		•		•						
Chick-fil-A		•		•					•	
Chipotle				•						•
Columbia Sportswear	•		•						•	•
Common Ground	•								•	
Equal Exchange		•		•				•	•	•
Facebook					•	•				
Glencore, Xstrata	•							•		•
Harley-Davidson	•		•				•	•		
Herman Miller	•		•	•					•	
Itaipu Binacional	•							•	•	
J.C. Penney			•	•				•		
Kipp Schools		•								
Krispy Kreme	•			•					•	•
Lockheed Martin	•							•	•	•
Logitech	•				•			•		•
lululemon		•		•				•	•	
Movie Exhibition Industry		•								•
Phase Separation	•				•			•	•	•
RIM					•	•		•		
Sirius		•			•	•	•	•		•
Tata Motors	•						•	•		
TEOCO		•			•	•		•	•	
Tesla	•						•			
Yahoo!					•	•				

Case Title	1	2	3	4	5	6	7	8	9	10	11	12	13
Ally Bank		●			●	●					●		●
AstraZeneca	●	●			●								●
Avon	●			●				●		●			
Black Canyon		●	●	●	●								
Blue Nile		●	●	●	●			●					
Campbell				●	●	●					●	●	
Chick-fil-A	●				●	●							
Chipotle			●	●	●								
Columbia Sportswear		●	●	●	●							●	
Common Ground	●	●										●	●
Equal Exchange	●		●							●		●	●
Facebook	●		●						●			●	●
Glencore, Xstrata	●	●				●	●	●					
Harley-Davidson		●	●	●	●	●	●						
Herman Miller		●	●	●								●	●
Itaipu Binacional							●	●	●			●	●
J.C. Penney		●	●	●	●						●		
Kipp Schools		●	●										●
Krispy Kreme		●	●	●								●	●
Lockheed Martin	●	●				●	●	●				●	
Logitech		●			●	●	●	●					●
lululemon	●	●	●	●				●					●
Movie Exhibition Industry		●		●	●								
Phase Separation		●				●	●	●			●		●
RIM					●				●			●	●
Sirius						●	●	●			●		●
Tata Motors						●		●					
TEOCO								●	●		●	●	●
Tesla		●		●							●		●
Yahoo!	●									●		●	

1

Strategic Management and Strategic Competitiveness

Studying this chapter should provide you with the strategic management knowledge needed to:

1 Define strategic competitiveness, strategy, competitive advantage, above-average returns, and the strategic management process.

2 Describe the competitive landscape and explain how globalization and technological changes shape it.

3 Use the industrial organization (I/O) model to explain how firms can earn above-average returns.

4 Use the resource-based model to explain how firms can earn above-average returns.

5 Describe vision and mission and discuss their value.

6 Define stakeholders and describe their ability to influence organizations.

7 Describe the work of strategic leaders.

8 Explain the strategic management process.

THE GLOBAL IMPACT OF THE GOLDEN ARCHES

McDonald's has achieved substantial success over the years, which is exemplified by its impact throughout the world. Many people know about and are customers of McDonald's. For example, a recent survey found that 88 percent of people recognize the golden arches and associate them with McDonald's. This is likely because McDonald's touches a lot of people in a year. Each day, about 68 million people eat at a McDonald's, which equates to almost one percent of the world's population. In the United States alone, McDonald's hires approximately one million employees per year. Approximately 12 to 13 percent of all U.S. workers have been employed at McDonald's at one time (including such famous people as actress Sharon Stone, singer, Shania Twain and comedian Jay Leno). Given that McDonald's includes a toy in about 20 percent of its sales, it is the world's largest distributor of toys.

Finally, McDonald's serves about one billion pounds of beef annually in the United States, which requires approximately 5.5 million head of cattle.

McDonald's is larger and has been more successful in the market than its close competitors, Burger King and Wendy's, as well as other large competitors for the fast food customer, such as Subway and Starbucks. It has been estimated that McDonald's has about 17 percent of the limited service restaurants in the United States. Its success against competitors is demonstrated by the results of a recent review of the specialty coffees offered by fast food outlets. McDonald's McCafé was rated higher than the "gourmet" coffees sold by Burger King (a new entrant in this product category), Wendy's, Subway, and 7-Eleven. In fact, McCafé even stole some customers from Starbucks when it was first offered by McDonald's.

McDonald's made a decision early to move into international markets and now one can find the golden arches

in many countries across the world. However, its success has created a company of such size and reach that it is also easy to criticize. For example, in 2012 it created an advertisement that received acclaim because it included farmers and ranchers who supplied the food to McDonald's. The evaluations showed that it was perceived to be authentic. Early responses from the public were positive but over time the tweets became more negative with people voicing criticisms of the company and its food. It especially has been criticized because of its supposed contribution to the obesity problems in the United States.

McDonald's has tried to respond to this criticism and the public's concerns about obesity by offering more healthy food alternatives such as salads, chicken, and fish and by providing the amount of calories in its foods on their packaging. McDonald's now serves more Happy Meals with Chicken McNuggets than with hamburgers.

It also offers apple slices in place of French fries. It recently has introduced Fish McBites following its popular entry of Chicken McBites. In addition to providing new food products for customers, McDonald's now offers Wi-Fi, which has been particularly popular with students.

Even with all of its success and rapid responses to criticism, McDonald's must always be prepared to react to negative outcomes. For example, while its global sales revenue in 2012 increased by 6.7 percent over 2011 sales, early sales in 2013 have been discouraging. Sales in January dropped significantly in Asia, the Middle East, and Africa. It also has experienced recent sales declines in Europe, especially Germany and France. Some of these reductions in sales reflect general economic conditions with which McDonald's must regularly cope with intensifying competition from regional and global rivals. These results suggest that its global reach has helped the firm in many ways (massive economies of scope, recognition in the market) but also means that it must deal with geographic economic differences and varying competitive forces across the globe.

Sources: K. Mayo & V. Wong, 2013, Who serves the best fast-food coffee? *Bloomberg Businessweek*, March 4, 76–77; C. Choi, 2013, McDonald's sales fall with tough year ahead, *Bloomberg Businessweek*, www.businessweek.com, February 8; C. Choi, McDonald's to put "Fish McBites" in happy meals, *Bloomberg Businessweek*, www.businessweek.com, February 4; A. Troianovovski, 2013, The web-deprived study at McDonald's, *Wall Street Journal*, www.wsj.com, January, 28; G. Lubin & M. Badkar, 2012, 17 facts about McDonald's that will blow your mind, *Yahoo! Finance*, http://finance.yahoo.com, December 7; K. O'Brien, 2012, How McDonald's came back bigger than ever, *New York Times*, www.nytimes.com, May 4.

Learn more about **B**urger King, a large competitor of McDonald's.
www.cengagebrain.com

As we see from the Opening Case, McDonald's is highly successful because of its strategy to grow globally and gain massive economies of scale (keeping costs low) that provide widespread name/brand recognition. These attributes along with other critical strategic decisions (e.g., adding new food and drink products such as salads, Chicken and Fish McBites, and McCafé) have enhanced its ability to compete against other major fast food restaurants. Therefore, we can conclude that McDonald's has achieved *strategic competitiveness*. It clearly has been able to earn *above-average returns*. Yet McDonald's has received its share of criticism because of its perceived contribution to the childhood obesity problem in the United States. In addition, it continues to cope with global economic problems and fierce competition. For example, Burger King and Wendy's now serve gourmet coffee in response to the success of McDonald's McCafé. The top management of McDonald's has used the strategic management process (see Figure 1.1) as the foundation for the commitments, decisions, and actions they took to pursue strategic competitiveness and above-average terms. The strategic management process is fully explained in this book. We introduce you to this process in the next few paragraphs.

Strategic competitiveness is achieved when a firm successfully formulates and implements a value-creating strategy. A **strategy** is an integrated and coordinated set of commitments and actions designed to exploit core competencies and gain a competitive advantage. When choosing a strategy, firms make choices among competing alternatives as the pathway for deciding how they will pursue strategic competitiveness.[1] In this sense, the chosen strategy indicates what the firm *will do* as well as what the firm *will not do*.

As explained in the Opening Case, McDonald's has been a leader in its industry as one of the first fast food companies to enter global markets and is now a highly global business. However, it continues to change its product line in response to a changing environment. In fact, to adapt to local environments, it sometimes makes major changes. For example, it has changed its name to Macca in Australia because people there often abbreviate names to avoid pronouncing multiple syllables. So, McDonald's shortened its name to two syllables (from three) and used its highly recognizable golden arches as the symbol of the firm.[2]

A recent study conducted to identify the factors that contribute to the success of top corporate performers showed why McDonald's has been successful. This study found that the top performers were entrepreneurial, market oriented (effective knowledge of the customers' needs), used valuable competencies, and offered innovative products and services.[3] McDonald's displays several of these attributes. It clearly understands its market and

Strategic competitiveness is achieved when a firm successfully formulates and implements a value-creating strategy.

A **strategy** is an integrated and coordinated set of commitments and actions designed to exploit core competencies and gain a competitive advantage.

M. Stasy

customers and is innovative. Therefore, its success is not surprising. A firm's strategy also demonstrates how it differs from its competitors. Recently, Ford Motor Company devoted efforts to explain to stakeholders how the company differs from its competitors. The main idea is that Ford claims that it is "greener" and more technically advanced than its competitors, such as General Motors and Chrysler Group LLC (with majority ownership held by Fiat SpA).[4]

A firm has a **competitive advantage** when it implements a strategy that creates superior value for customers and that its competitors are unable to duplicate or find too costly to imitate.[5] An organization can be confident that its strategy has resulted in one or more useful competitive advantages only after competitors' efforts to duplicate its strategy have ceased or failed. In addition, firms must understand that no competitive advantage is permanent.[6] The speed with which competitors are able to acquire the skills needed to duplicate the benefits of a firm's value-creating strategy determines how long the competitive advantage will last.[7]

Above-average returns are returns in excess of what an investor expects to earn from other investments with a similar amount of risk. **Risk** is an investor's uncertainty about the economic gains or losses that will result from a particular investment.[8] The most successful companies learn how to effectively manage risk. Effectively managing risks reduces investors' uncertainty about the results of their investment.[9] Returns are often measured in terms of accounting figures, such as return on assets, return on equity, or return on sales. Alternatively, returns can be measured on the basis of stock market returns, such as monthly returns (the end-of-the-period stock price minus the beginning stock price, divided by the beginning stock price, yielding a percentage return). In smaller, new venture firms, returns are sometimes measured in terms of the amount and speed of growth (e.g., in annual sales) rather than more traditional profitability measures[10] because new ventures require time to earn acceptable returns (in the form of return on assets and so forth) on investors' investments.[11]

Understanding how to exploit a competitive advantage is important for firms seeking to earn above-average returns.[12] Firms without a competitive advantage or that are not competing in an attractive industry earn, at best, average returns. **Average returns** are returns equal to those an investor expects to earn from other investments with a similar amount of risk. In the long run, an inability to earn at least average returns results first in decline and, eventually, failure.[13] Failure occurs because investors withdraw their investments from those firms earning less-than-average returns.

As previously noted, there are no guarantees of permanent success. For example, American Airlines was very successful at one time earning above average returns. But in recent years, it has performed very poorly and had to declare bankruptcy. As a result it is being acquired by US Airways. Companies that are prospering must not become overconfident. For example, even considering Apple's excellent current performance, it still must be careful not to become overconfident and continue its quest to be the leader for its markets.

The **strategic management process** (see Figure 1.1) is the full set of commitments, decisions, and actions required for a firm to achieve strategic competitiveness and earn above-average returns.[14] The process involves analysis, strategy and performance (the A-S-P model—see Figure 1.1). The firm's first step in the process is to *analyze* its external environment and internal organization to determine its resources, capabilities, and core competencies—on which its strategy likely will be based. McDonald's has excelled in using this process over the years. The *strategy* portion of the model entails strategy formulation and strategy implementation.

With the information gained from external and internal analyses, the firm develops its vision and mission and formulates one or more *strategies*. To implement its strategies, the firm takes actions to enact each strategy with the intent of achieving strategic

A firm has a **competitive advantage** when it implements a strategy that creates superior value for customers and competitors are unable to duplicate or find too costly to try to imitate.

Above-average returns are returns in excess of what an investor expects to earn from other investments with a similar amount of risk.

Risk is an investor's uncertainty about the economic gains or losses that will result from a particular investment.

Average returns are returns equal to those an investor expects to earn from other investments with a similar amount of risk.

The **strategic management process** is the full set of commitment, decisions, and actions required for a firm to achieve strategic competitiveness and earn above-average returns.

Figure 1.1 The Strategic Management Process

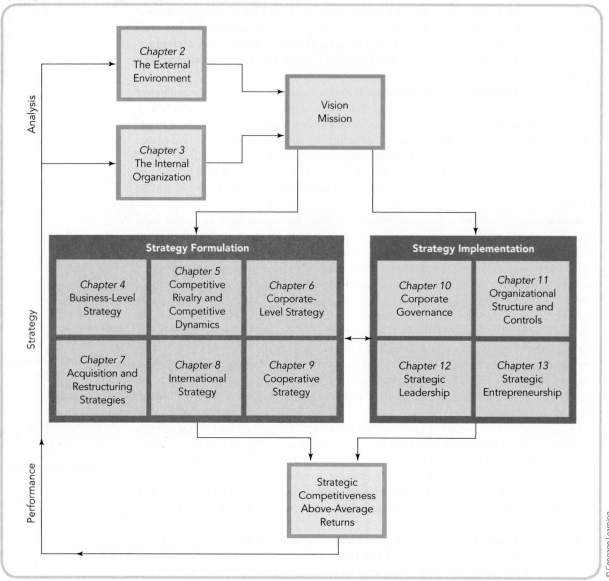

competitiveness and above-average returns (*performance*). Effective strategic actions that take place in the context of carefully integrated strategy formulation and implementation efforts result in positive performance. This dynamic strategic management process must be maintained as ever-changing markets and competitive structures are coordinated with a firm's continuously evolving strategic inputs.[15]

In the remaining chapters of this book, we use the strategic management process to explain what firms do to achieve strategic competitiveness and earn above-average returns. We demonstrate why some firms consistently achieve competitive success while others fail to do so.[16] As you will see, the reality of global competition is a critical part of the strategic management process and significantly influences firms' performances.[17] Indeed, learning how to successfully compete in the globalized world is one of the most significant challenges for firms competing in the current century.[18]

Several topics will be discussed in this chapter. First, we describe the current competitive landscape. This challenging landscape is being created primarily by the emergence of a global economy, globalization resulting from that economy, and rapid technological changes. Next, we examine two models that firms use to gather the information and knowledge required to choose and then effectively implement their strategies. The insights gained from these models also serve as the foundation for forming the firm's vision and mission. The first model (the industrial organization or I/O model) suggests that the external environment is the primary determinant of a firm's strategic actions. According to this model, identifying and then operating effectively in an attractive (i.e., profitable) industry or segment of an industry are the keys to competitive success.[19] The second model (resource-based) suggests that a firm's unique resources and capabilities are the critical link to strategic competitiveness.[20] Thus, the first model is concerned primarily with the firm's external environment while the second model is concerned primarily with the firm's internal organization. After discussing vision and mission, direction-setting statements that influence the choice and use of strategies, we describe the stakeholders that organizations serve. The degree to which stakeholders' needs can be met increases when firms achieve strategic competitiveness and earn above-average returns. Closing the chapter are introductions to strategic leaders and the elements of the strategic management process.

1-1 The Competitive Landscape

The fundamental nature of competition in many of the world's industries is changing. The reality is that financial capital continues to be scarce and markets are increasingly volatile.[21] Because of this, the pace of change is relentless and ever-increasing. Even determining the boundaries of an industry has become challenging. Consider, for example, how advances in interactive computer networks and telecommunications have blurred the boundaries of the entertainment industry. Today, not only do cable companies and satellite networks compete for entertainment revenue from television, but telecommunication companies are moving into the entertainment business through significant improvements in fiber-optic lines.[22] Partnerships among firms in different segments of the entertainment industry further blur industry boundaries. For example, MSNBC is co-owned by NBC Universal and Microsoft. At one time, General Electric owned 49 percent of NBC Universal while Comcast owned the remaining 51 percent. In March 2013, Comcast acquired the remaining shares in the firm.[23]

Other characteristics of the current competitive landscape are noteworthy. Conventional sources of competitive advantage such as economies of scale and huge advertising budgets are not as effective as they once were in terms of helping firms earn above-average returns. Moreover, the traditional managerial mind-set is unlikely to lead a firm to strategic competitiveness. Managers must adopt a new mind-set that values flexibility, speed, innovation, integration, and the challenges that evolve from constantly changing conditions.[24] The conditions of the competitive landscape result in a perilous business world, one in which the investments that are required to compete on a global scale are enormous and the consequences of failure are severe.[25] Effective use of the strategic management process reduces the likelihood of failure for firms as they encounter the conditions of today's competitive landscape.

Hypercompetition is a term often used to capture the realities of the competitive landscape. Under conditions of hypercompetition, assumptions of market stability are replaced by notions of inherent instability and change.[26] Hypercompetition results from the dynamics of strategic maneuvering among global and innovative combatants.[27] It is a condition of rapidly escalating competition based on price-quality positioning, competition to create new know-how and establish first-mover advantage, and competition to protect or invade established product or geographic markets.[28] In a hypercompetitive market, firms often aggressively challenge their competitors in the hopes of improving their competitive position and ultimately their performance.[29]

Several factors create hypercompetitive environments and influence the nature of the current competitive landscape. The emergence of a global economy and technology, specifically rapid technological change, are the two primary drivers of hypercompetitive environments and the nature of today's competitive landscape.

1-1a The Global Economy

A **global economy** is one in which goods, services, people, skills, and ideas move freely across geographic borders. Relatively unfettered by artificial constraints, such as tariffs, the global economy significantly expands and complicates a firm's competitive environment.[30]

Interesting opportunities and challenges are associated with the emergence of the global economy.[31] For example, the European Union (composed of several countries) has become one of the world's largest markets, with 700 million potential customers. "In the past, China was generally seen as a low-competition market and a low-cost producer. Today, China is an extremely competitive market in which local market-seeking MNCs [multinational corporations] must fiercely compete against other MNCs and against those local companies that are more cost effective and faster in product development. While China has been viewed as a country from which to source low-cost goods, lately, many MNCs, such as P&G [Procter and Gamble], are actually net exporters of local management talent; they have been dispatching more Chinese abroad than bringing foreign expatriates to China."[32] China has become the second-largest economy in the world, surpassing Japan. India, the world's largest democracy, has an economy that also is growing rapidly and now ranks as the fourth largest in the world.[33] Simultaneously, many firms in these emerging economies are moving into international markets and are now regarded as multinational firms. This fact is demonstrated by the case of Huawei, a Chinese company that has entered the U.S. market. Barriers to entering foreign markets still exist and Huawei has encountered several, such as the inability to gain the U.S. government's approval for acquisition of U.S. firms. Essentially, Huawei must build credibility in the U.S. market, and especially build a positive relationship with stakeholders such as the U.S. government.

The nature of the global economy reflects the realities of a hypercompetitive business environment and challenges individual firms to seriously evaluate the markets in which they will compete. This is reflected in Starbucks' actions and outcomes. While Starbucks has enjoyed substantial success in North America and Asia, it is struggling in Europe. It has substantial competition there. Alternatively, the fact that a company that sells cups of coffee is a multinational firm suggests the reach and influence of the global economy.

Consider the case of General Electric (GE). Although headquartered in the United States, GE expects that as much as 60 percent of its revenue growth through 2015 will be generated by competing in rapidly developing economies (e.g., China and India). The decision to count on revenue growth in emerging economies instead of in developed countries such as the United States and in Europe seems quite reasonable in the global economy. GE achieved significant growth in 2010 partly because of signing contracts for large infrastructure projects in China and Russia. GE's CEO, Jeffrey Immelt, argues that we have entered a new economic era in which the global economy will be more volatile and that most of the growth will come from emerging economies such as Brazil, China, and India.[34] Therefore, GE is investing significantly in these emerging economies, in order to improve its competitive position in vital geographic sources of revenue and profitability.

Find out more about Evolution Fresh, a Starbucks acquisition.
www.cengagebrain.com

A **global economy** is one in which goods, services, people, skills, and ideas move freely across geographic borders.

M. Stasy

Strategic Focus

GLOBALIZATION

Starbucks is a New Economy Multinational

Starbucks is not an ordinary purveyor of a cup of coffee. It is a large and innovative multinational firm that engages in major strategic actions to enter new international and product markets (e.g., acquisitions). It is a multibillion-dollar company with many stores operating in multiple countries. By 2015, Starbucks plans to have more than 12,500 stores in the United States, up from 11,128 in 2012. For example, Starbucks has become a major player in Asian markets, which is interesting because it took on a largely tea-drinking culture. By 2015, Starbucks expects to have 1,500 stores operating in China, a major increase over its 700 stores there in 2012. Starbucks adapts to local market tastes by developing larger stores where, for example, the Chinese can lounge and meet with friends. It also has introduced flavors specifically for the Chinese market, such as red-bean frappuccinos. It also has products that cater to tea drinkers as well. Starbucks' success in China is reflected by the fact that China is expected to become the company's second largest market by 2014. The average annual single store sales in China have increased by almost 75 percent since 2008 to $886,000 at the end of 2012.

Starbucks has also entered Vietnam and India with high expectations. In 2013 it opened its first store in Vietnam. Interestingly, Vietnam is the second largest producer of coffee beans in the world behind only Brazil. Starbucks hopes to work with local Vietnamese farmers to grow a high-quality Arabica coffee bean. In partnership with the Tata Group, Starbucks also recently opened its first stores (three) in India with plans to have 50 stores there within a year.

Although Starbucks has experienced significant success in Asia, its experience in Europe has been mixed. It has had some success but has also encountered a different coffee culture. At first, it tried to have Europeans adapt to the Starbucks approach. Now, because of the importance Starbucks places on its future in Europe, the company is adapting to the European café culture. This means that Starbucks is building larger stores with additional seating to allow people to meet and spend time in their stores, as they have done in Asia. It has implemented other practices and products that adapt even more to local (country) cultures and tastes (e.g., France, England).

Customers line up to purchase drinks on the opening day of the first Starbucks outlet in Ho Chi Minh City on February 1, 2013. Starbucks opened its first store in coffee-loving Vietnam, seeking to compete with local rivals in a country known for its strong café culture.

In addition to Starbucks' international thrust, it also engages in significant innovation and strategic actions to add to its product line. In recent years, it has introduced Via, an instant coffee, and a single-cup coffee maker (named the Verismo) that allows customers to make their own lattes at home. Another attempt to add to its product line is evidenced in its recent acquisition of the tea chain, Teavana. In fact, it paid $620 million to acquire the Atlanta-based company. In recent times it also acquired a juice maker, Evolution Fresh, and Bay Bread, the operator of La Boulange bakeries.

Starbucks' strategic actions have enjoyed much success. In fact, Starbucks announced major increases in stores' sales open at least 13 months (7 percent in the Americas and 11 percent in China) and in profits (13 percent overall) in the last quarter of 2012.

Sources: J. Gertner, 2013, For infusing a steady stream of new ideas to revive its business, *Fast Company*, www.fastcompany.com, accessed on January 30; A. Gasparro, 2013, Starbucks enjoys sales jolt from its U.S., China stores, *Wall Street Journal*, www.wsj.com, January 24; J. Noble, 2013, Starbucks takes on Vietnam coffee culture, *Financial Times*, www.ft.com, January 3; A. Gasparro, 2012, Starbucks: China to become no. 2 market, *Wall Street Journal*, www.wsj.com, December 6; 2012, A look at Starbucks' U.S. presence over the years, *Bloomberg Businessweek*, www.businessweek.com, December 5; L. Burkitt, 2012, Starbucks plays to local Chinese tastes, *Wall Street Journal*, www.wsj.com, November 26; J. Jargon, 2012, Starbucks CEO: 'We will do for tea what we did for coffee,' *Wall Street Journal*, www.wsj.com, November 14; V. Bajaj, 2012, Starbucks opens in India with pomp and tempered ambition, *New York Times*, www.nytimes.com, October 19; S. Strom, 2012, Starbucks to introduce single-serve coffee maker, *New York Times*, www.nytimes.com, September 20; L. Alderman, 2012, In Europe, Starbucks adjusts to a café culture, *New York Times*, www.nytimes.com, March 30.

The March of Globalization

Globalization is the increasing economic interdependence among countries and their organizations as reflected in the flow of goods and services, financial capital, and knowledge across country borders.[35] Globalization is a product of a large number of firms competing against one another in an increasing number of global economies.

In globalized markets and industries, financial capital might be obtained in one national market and used to buy raw materials in another. Manufacturing equipment bought from a third national market can then be used to produce products that are sold in yet a fourth market. Thus, globalization increases the range of opportunities for companies competing in the current competitive landscape.[36]

Firms engaging in globalization of their operations must make culturally sensitive decisions when using the strategic management process, as is the case in Starbucks' operations in European countries. Additionally, highly globalized firms must anticipate ever-increasing complexity in their operations as goods, services, people, and so forth move freely across geographic borders and throughout different economic markets.

Overall, it is important to note that globalization has led to higher performance standards in many competitive dimensions, including those of quality, cost, productivity, product introduction time, and operational efficiency. In addition to firms competing in the global economy, these standards affect firms competing on a domestic-only basis. The reason is that customers will purchase from a global competitor rather than a domestic firm is that the global company's good or service is superior. Workers now flow rather freely among global economies, and employees are a key source of competitive advantage.[37] Thus, managers have to learn how to operate effectively in a "multi-polar" world with many important countries having unique interests and environments.[38] Firms must learn how to deal with the reality that in the competitive landscape of the twenty-first century, only companies capable of meeting, if not exceeding, global standards typically have the capability to earn above-average returns.

Although globalization offers potential benefits to firms, it is not without risks. Collectively, the risks of participating outside of a firm's domestic markets in the global economy are labeled a "liability of foreignness."[39]

One risk of entering the global market is the amount of time typically required for firms to learn how to compete in markets that are new to them. A firm's performance can suffer until this knowledge is either developed locally or transferred from the home market to the newly established global location.[40] Additionally, a firm's performance may suffer with substantial amounts of globalization. In this instance, firms may overdiversify internationally beyond their ability to manage these extended operations.[41] Overdiversification can have strong negative effects on a firm's overall performance.

A major factor in the global economy in recent years has been the growth in the influence of emerging economies. The important emerging economies include not only the BRIC countries (Brazil, Russia, India and China) but also the VISTA countries (Vietnam, Indonesia, South Africa, Turkey, and Argentina). Mexico and Thailand also have become increasingly important markets.[42] Obviously, as these economies have grown, their markets have become targets for entry by large multinational firms. Emerging economy firms have also began to compete in global markets, some with increasing success.[43] For example, there are now more than 1,000 multinational firms home-based in emerging economies with more than $1 billion in annual sales.[44] In fact, the emergence of emerging-market multinational firms in international markets has forced large multinational firms based in developed markets to enrich their own capabilities to compete effectively in global markets.[45]

Thus, entry into international markets, even for firms with substantial experience in the global economy, requires effective use of the strategic management process. It is also

Learn more about the emerging economies of the BRIC countries (Brazil, Russia, India, & China).

www.cengagebrain.com

M. Stasy

important to note that even though global markets are an attractive strategic option for some companies, they are not the only source of strategic competitiveness. In fact, for most companies, even for those capable of competing successfully in global markets, it is critical to remain committed to and strategically competitive in both domestic and international markets by staying attuned to technological opportunities and potential competitive disruptions that innovations create.[46]

1-1b Technology and Technological Changes

Technology-related trends and conditions can be placed into three categories: technology diffusion and disruptive technologies, the information age, and increasing knowledge intensity. Through these categories, technology is significantly altering the nature of competition and contributing to highly dynamic competitive environments as a result of doing so.

Technology Diffusion and Disruptive Technologies

The rate of technology diffusion, which is the speed at which new technologies become available and are used, has increased substantially over the past 15 to 20 years. Consider the following rates of technology diffusion:

It took the telephone 35 years to get into 25 percent of all homes in the United States. It took TV 26 years. It took radio 22 years. It took PCs 16 years. It took the Internet 7 years.[47]

The impact of technological changes on individual firms and industries has been broad and significant. For example, in the not-too-distant-past, people rented movies on videotapes at retail stores. Now, movie rentals are almost entirely electronic. The publishing industry (books, journals, magazines, newspapers) is moving rapidly from hard copy to electronic form. Many firms in these industries operating with a more traditional business model are suffering. These changes are also affecting other industries, from trucking to mail services (public and private).

Perpetual innovation is a term used to describe how rapidly and consistently new, information-intensive technologies replace older ones. The shorter product life cycles resulting from these rapid diffusions of new technologies place a competitive premium on being able to quickly introduce new, innovative goods and services into the marketplace.[48]

In fact, when products become somewhat indistinguishable because of the widespread and rapid diffusion of technologies, speed to market with innovative products may be the primary source of competitive advantage (see Chapter 5).[49] Indeed, some argue that the global economy is increasingly driven by constant innovations. Not surprisingly, such innovations must be derived from an understanding of global standards and expectations of product functionality.[50] Although some argue that large established firms may have trouble innovating, evidence suggests that today these firms are developing radically new technologies that transform old industries or create new ones.[51] Apple is an excellent example of a large established firm capable of radical innovation. Also, in order to diffuse the technology and enhance the value of an innovation, additional firms need to be innovative in their use of the new technology, building it into their products.[52]

Another indicator of rapid technology diffusion is that it now may take only 12 to 18 months for firms to gather information about their competitors' research and development and product decisions.[53] In the global economy, competitors can sometimes imitate a firm's successful competitive actions within a few days. In this sense, the rate of technological diffusion has reduced the competitive benefits of patents. Today, patents may be an effective way of protecting proprietary technology in a small number of industries such as pharmaceuticals. Indeed, many firms competing in the electronics industry often do not apply for

Iain Masterton / Alamy

Reading a book on an iPad. In recent years Apple has brought to market several disruptive technologies that create new markets and change existing industries.

patents to prevent competitors from gaining access to the technological knowledge included in the patent application.

Disruptive technologies—technologies that destroy the value of an existing technology and create new markets[54]—surface frequently in today's competitive markets. Think of the new markets created by the technologies underlying the development of products such as iPods, iPads, Wi-Fi, and the browser. These types of products are thought by some to represent radical or breakthrough innovations.[55] (We discuss more about radical innovations in Chapter 13.) A disruptive or radical technology can create what is essentially a new industry or can harm industry incumbents. However, some incumbents are able to adapt based on their superior resources, experience, and ability to gain access to the new technology through multiple sources (e.g., alliances, acquisitions, and ongoing internal research).[56]

Clearly, Apple has developed and introduced "disruptive technologies" such as the iPod, and in so doing changed several industries. For example, the iPod and its complementary iTunes revolutionized how music is sold to and used by consumers. In conjunction with other complementary and competitive products (e.g., Amazon's Kindle), Apple's iPad is contributing to and speeding major changes in the publishing industry, moving from hard copies to electronic books. Apple's new technologies and products are also contributing to the new "information age." Thus, Apple provides an example of entrepreneurship through technology emergence across multiple industries.[57]

The Information Age

Dramatic changes in information technology have occurred in recent years. Personal computers, cellular phones, artificial intelligence, virtual reality, massive databases, and multiple social networking sites are only a few examples of how information is used differently as a result of technological developments. An important outcome of these changes is that the ability to effectively and efficiently access and use information has become an important source of competitive advantage in virtually all industries. Information technology advances have given small firms more flexibility in competing with large firms, if that technology can be efficiently used.[58]

Both the pace of change in information technology and its diffusion will continue to increase. For instance, the number of personal computers in use globally is expected to surpass 2.3 billion by 2015. More than 372 million were sold globally in 2011. This number is expected to increase to about 518 million in 2015.[59] The declining costs of information technologies and the increased accessibility to them are also evident in the current competitive landscape. The global proliferation of relatively inexpensive computing power and its linkage on a global scale via computer networks combine to increase the speed and diffusion of information technologies. Thus, the competitive potential of information technologies is now available to companies of all sizes throughout the world, including those in emerging economies.[60]

The Internet is another technological innovation contributing to hypercompetition. Available to an increasing number of people throughout the world, the Internet provides an infrastructure that allows the delivery of information to computers in any location. Access to the Internet on smaller devices such as cell phones is having an ever-growing impact on competition in a number of industries. However, possible changes to Internet Service Providers' (ISPs) pricing structures could affect the rate of growth of Internet-based applications. Users downloading or streaming high-definition movies, playing video games online, and so forth would be affected the most if ISPs were to base their pricing structure around total usage.

Increasing Knowledge Intensity

Knowledge (information, intelligence, and expertise) is the basis of technology and its application. In the competitive landscape of the twenty-first century, knowledge is a critical organizational resource and an increasingly valuable source of competitive advantage.[61]

Indeed, starting in the 1980s, the basis of competition shifted from hard assets to intangible resources. For example, "Wal-Mart transformed retailing through its proprietary approach to supply chain management and its information-rich relationships with customers and suppliers."[62] Relationships with customers and suppliers are an example of an intangible resource.

Knowledge is gained through experience, observation, and inference and is an intangible resource (tangible and intangible resources are fully described in Chapter 3). The value of intangible resources, including knowledge, is growing as a proportion of total shareholder value in today's competitive landscape.[63] In fact, the Brookings Institution estimates that intangible resources contribute approximately 85 percent of that value.[64] The probability of achieving strategic competitiveness is enhanced for the firm that develops the ability to capture intelligence, transform it into usable knowledge, and diffuse it rapidly throughout the company.[65] Therefore, firms must develop (e.g., through training programs) and acquire (e.g., by hiring educated and experienced employees) knowledge, integrate it into the organization to create capabilities, and then apply it to gain a competitive advantage.[66]

A strong knowledge base is necessary to create innovations. In fact, firms lacking the appropriate internal knowledge resources are less likely to invest money in research and development.[67] Firms must continue to learn (building their knowledge stock) because knowledge spillovers to competitors are common. There are several ways in which knowledge spillovers occur, including the hiring of professional staff and managers by competitors.[68] Because of the potential for spillovers, firms must move quickly to use their knowledge in productive ways. In addition, firms must build routines that facilitate the diffusion of local knowledge throughout the organization for use everywhere that it has value.[69] Firms are better able to do these things when they have strategic flexibility.

Strategic flexibility is a set of capabilities used to respond to various demands and opportunities existing in a dynamic and uncertain competitive environment. Thus, strategic flexibility involves coping with uncertainty and its accompanying risks.[70] Firms should try to develop strategic flexibility in all areas of their operations. However, those working within firms to develop strategic flexibility should understand that the task is not easy, largely because of inertia that can build up over time. A firm's focus and past core competencies may actually slow change and strategic flexibility.[71]

To be strategically flexible on a continuing basis and to gain the competitive benefits of such flexibility, a firm has to develop the capacity to learn. Continuous learning provides the firm with new and up-to-date skill sets, which allow it to adapt to its environment as it encounters changes.[72] Firms capable of rapidly and broadly applying what they have learned exhibit the strategic flexibility and the capacity to change in ways that will increase the probability of successfully dealing with uncertain, hypercompetitive environments.

Strategic flexibility is a set of capabilities used to respond to various demands and opportunities existing in a dynamic and uncertain competitive environment.

1-2 The I/O Model of Above-Average Returns

From the 1960s through the 1980s, the external environment was thought to be the primary determinant of strategies that firms selected to be successful.[73] The industrial organization model of above-average returns explains the external environment's dominant influence on a firm's strategic actions. The model specifies that the industry or segment of an industry in which a company chooses to compete has a stronger influence on performance than do the choices managers make inside their organizations.[74] The firm's performance is believed to be determined primarily by a range of industry properties, including economies of scale, barriers to market entry, diversification, product differentiation, the degree of concentration of firms in the industry, and market frictions.[75] We examine these industry characteristics in Chapter 2.

Grounded in economics, the I/O model has four underlying assumptions. First, the external environment is assumed to impose pressures and constraints that determine the strategies that would result in above-average returns. Second, most firms competing within an industry or within a segment of that industry are assumed to control similar strategically relevant resources and to pursue similar strategies in light of those resources. Third, resources used to implement strategies are assumed to be highly mobile across firms, so any resource differences that might develop between firms will be short-lived. Fourth, organizational decision makers are assumed to be rational and committed to acting in the firm's best interests, as shown by their profit-maximizing behaviors.[76] The I/O model challenges firms to find the most attractive industry in which to compete. Because most firms are assumed to have similar valuable resources that are mobile across companies, their performance generally can be increased only when they operate in the industry with the highest profit potential and learn how to use their resources to implement the strategy required by the industry's structural characteristics. To do so, they must imitate each other.[77]

The five forces model of competition is an analytical tool used to help firms find the industry that is the most attractive for them. The model (explained in Chapter 2) encompasses several variables and tries to capture the complexity of competition. The five forces model suggests that an industry's profitability (i.e., its rate of return on invested capital relative to its cost of capital) is a function of interactions among five forces: suppliers, buyers, competitive rivalry among firms currently in the industry, product substitutes, and potential entrants to the industry.[78]

Firms use the five forces model to identify the attractiveness of an industry (as measured by its profitability potential) as well as the most advantageous position for the firm to take in that industry, given the industry's structural characteristics.[79] Typically, the model suggests that firms can earn above-average returns by producing either standardized goods or services at costs below those of competitors (a cost leadership strategy) or by producing differentiated goods or services for which customers are willing to pay a price premium (a differentiation strategy). (The cost leadership and product differentiation strategies are discussed in Chapter 4.) The fact that "… the fast food industry is becoming a 'zero-sum industry' as companies battle for the same pool of customers"[80] suggests that fast food giant McDonald's is competing in a relatively unattractive industry. And, its problems in dealing with competitors as described in the Opening Case exemplify these facts. However, by focusing on product innovations and enhancing existing facilities while increasing its presence in international markets, McDonald's has earned above-average returns over time.

As shown in Figure 1.2, the I/O model suggests that above-average returns are earned when firms are able to effectively study the external environment as the foundation for identifying an attractive industry and implementing the appropriate strategy. For example,

Figure 1.2 The I/O Model of Above-Average Returns

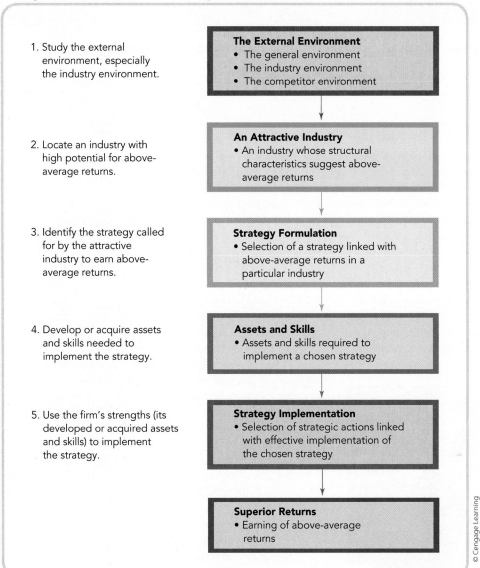

1. Study the external environment, especially the industry environment.

The External Environment
- The general environment
- The industry environment
- The competitor environment

2. Locate an industry with high potential for above-average returns.

An Attractive Industry
- An industry whose structural characteristics suggest above-average returns

3. Identify the strategy called for by the attractive industry to earn above-average returns.

Strategy Formulation
- Selection of a strategy linked with above-average returns in a particular industry

4. Develop or acquire assets and skills needed to implement the strategy.

Assets and Skills
- Assets and skills required to implement a chosen strategy

5. Use the firm's strengths (its developed or acquired assets and skills) to implement the strategy.

Strategy Implementation
- Selection of strategic actions linked with effective implementation of the chosen strategy

Superior Returns
- Earning of above-average returns

© Cengage Learning

in some industries, firms can reduce competitive rivalry and erect barriers to entry by forming joint ventures. Because of these outcomes, the joint ventures increase profitability in the industry.[81] Companies that develop or acquire the internal skills needed to implement strategies required by the external environment are likely to succeed, while those that do not are likely to fail.[82] Hence, this model suggests that returns are determined primarily by external characteristics rather than by the firm's unique internal resources and capabilities.

Research findings support the I/O model in that approximately 20 percent of a firm's profitability is explained by the industry in which it chooses to compete. However, this research also shows that 36 percent of the variance in firm profitability can be attributed to the firm's characteristics and actions.[83] Thus, managers' strategic actions affect the firm's performance in addition to or in conjunction with external environmental influences.[84]

Strategic Focus   TECHNOLOGY

The Airlines Industry Exemplifies the I/O Model Imitation and Poor Performance

The airline industry is a living example of the I/O model. For many years, the airline industry was highly regulated, which resulted in most airlines acting like each other by definition. However, the similarities among the large airline companies remained after the industry was partially deregulated more than 30 years ago. These similarities in services, routes and performance have persisted even to the present time. For example, airlines often offer a new service (e.g., Wi-Fi availability on flights) but these services are easily imitated; therefore, any differentiation in offerings is only temporary.

In recent times, consolidation has occurred in both the European and U.S. airline industries. In particular, poor performance led US Airways and America West to merge. Additionally, much for the same reasons, Northwest Airlines and Delta merged. More recently, United and Continental merged to create the largest airline in the industry. Finally, American Airlines and US Air have announced that they plan to merge. All of these mergers have not created highly differentiated services (or prices). All of them largely provide the same type of services and prices do not differ greatly among the large "full-service" carriers. In fact, it

A passenger using WiFi on a plane. Innovations in the airline industry that create differentiation are often easily copied by rivals.

seems that the primary competition is in trying to make fewer mistakes. Positive industry reports focus on reductions in lost bags, fewer cancellations of flights, and fewer delays. What this suggests is that all of these areas still represent a major problem. It looks pretty bad when the most positive statement one can make is that lately fewer bags have been lost.

Obviously, there are differences between airlines across time. United, the largest airline, which was created to provide more financial efficiencies and to offer greater travel options to customers, has had significant problems making the merger of the two systems work effectively. In fact, it announced a major net loss for 2012 because of these problems. In November 2012, a computer malfunction (software problem) caused the delay of 250 of United's flights globally for almost two hours. Its reservation system failed twice during 2012, which shut down its Web site and stranded passengers as flights were then delayed or cancelled. United's on-time performance suffered and was one of the worst in the industry for 2012. The number of customer complaints for United was much higher than in the past. In short, it is relatively easy to determine why the airline suffered a serious net loss in 2012. Yet Delta, which performed very poorly a few years earlier, performed better in 2012. It made a net profit for the third year in a row. Its on-time performance was about 10 percentage points higher than United's. While United is eliminating flights and furloughing employees to cuts costs (trying to make a profit), in 2012 Delta purchased a 49 percent share of Virgin Atlantic to gain access to the highly valuable New York–London routes and gates in both locations. Delta was also one of the first airlines to introduce Wi-Fi to passengers during flights.

Certainly, some reduced-service airlines, such as Southwest Airlines, have fared much better in most of these categories (e.g., profits, on-time flights, customer complaints). Interestingly, while it started as a low-price airline (and maintained that feature over time), it also has generally offered superior service compared to the full-service airlines. The large airlines tried but were unable to imitate Southwest Airlines. In effect, Southwest developed its resources and capabilities over time, allowing it to provide service much more effectively and at a lower price than its full-service rivals.

Sources: 2013, Anatomy of 99.5%, Delta Airlines Web site, http://blog.delta.com, February 15; S. McCartney, 2013, Believe it or not, flying is improving, *Wall Street Journal*, www.wsj.com, January 9; J. Freed, 2012, Delta grabs bigger share of key NY-London route, *Bloomberg Businessweek*, www.businessweek.com, December 11; D. Benoit, 2012, Delta lands London space with Virgin joint venture, *Wall Street Journal*, http://blogs.wsj.com/deals, December 11; J. Mouawad, 2012, For United, big problems at biggest airline, *New York Times*, www.nytimes.com, November 28; C. Negroni, 2012, Good airlines news: Losing fewer bags, *New York Times*, www.nytimes.com, August 6.

These findings suggest that the external environment and a firm's resources, capabilities, core competencies, and competitive advantages (see Chapter 3) influence the company's ability to achieve strategic competitiveness and earn above-average returns.

The Strategic Focus explains how most of the firms in the airline industry are similar in services offered and in performance. They largely imitate each other and have performed poorly over the years. The few airlines which have not followed in the mode of trying to imitate others, such as Southwest Airlines, have developed unique and valuable resources and capabilities on which they have relied to provide a superior product (better service at a lower price) than major rivals.

As shown in Figure 1.2, the I/O model assumes that a firm's strategy is a set of commitments and actions flowing from the characteristics of the industry in which the firm has decided to compete. The resource-based model, discussed next, takes a different view of the major influences on a firm's choice of strategy.

1-3 The Resource-Based Model of Above-Average Returns

The resource-based model assumes that each organization is a collection of unique resources and capabilities. The *uniqueness* of its resources and capabilities is the basis of a firm's strategy and its ability to earn above-average returns.[85]

Resources are inputs into a firm's production process, such as capital equipment, the skills of individual employees, patents, finances, and talented managers. In general, a firm's resources are classified into three categories: physical, human, and organizational capital. Described fully in Chapter 3, resources are either tangible or intangible in nature.

Individual resources alone may not yield a competitive advantage.[86] In fact, resources have a greater likelihood of being a source of competitive advantage when they are formed into a capability. A **capability** is the capacity for a set of resources to perform a task or an activity in an integrative manner. Capabilities evolve over time and must be managed dynamically in pursuit of above-average returns.[87] **Core competencies** are resources and capabilities that serve as a source of competitive advantage for a firm over its rivals. Core competencies are often visible in the form of organizational functions. For example, Apple's R&D function is one of its core competencies, as its ability to produce innovative new products that are perceived as valuable in the marketplace is a critical reason for Apple's success.

According to the resource-based model, differences in firms' performances across time are due primarily to their unique resources and capabilities rather than the industry's structural characteristics. This model also assumes that firms acquire different resources and develop unique capabilities based on how they combine and use the resources; that resources and certainly capabilities are not highly mobile across firms; and that the differences in resources and capabilities are the basis of competitive advantage.[88] Through continued use, capabilities become stronger and more difficult for competitors to understand and imitate. As a source of competitive advantage, a capability must not be easily imitated but also not too complex to understand and manage.[89]

The resource-based model of superior returns is shown in Figure 1.3. This model suggests that the strategy the firm chooses should allow it to use its competitive advantages in an attractive industry (the I/O model is used to identify an attractive industry).

Not all of a firm's resources and capabilities have the potential to be the foundation for a competitive advantage. This potential is realized when resources and capabilities are valuable, rare, costly to imitate, and nonsubstitutable.[90] Resources are *valuable* when they allow a firm to take advantage of opportunities or neutralize threats in its external environment. They are *rare* when possessed by few, if any, current and potential competitors.

Strategy Right NOW

Learn about the merger of American Airlines and US Airways.
www.cengagebrain.com

Resources are inputs into a firm's production process, such as capital equipment, the skills of individual employees, patents, finances, and talented managers.

A **Capability** is the capacity for a set of resources to perform a task or an activity in an integrative manner.

Core competencies are capabilities that serve as a source of competitive advantage for a firm over its rivals.

M. Stasy

Figure 1.3 The Resource-Based Model of Above-Average Returns

1. Identify the firm's resources. Study its strengths and weaknesses compared with those of competitors.

Resources
- Inputs into a firm's production process

2. Determine the firm's capabilities. What do the capabilities allow the firm to do better than its competitors?

Capability
- Capacity of an integrated set of resources to integratively perform a task or activity

3. Determine the potential of the firm's resources and capabilities in terms of a competitive advantage.

Competitive Advantage
- Ability of a firm to outperform its rivals

4. Locate an attractive industry.

An Attractive Industry
- An industry with opportunities that can be exploited by the firm's resources and capabilities

5. Select a strategy that best allows the firm to utilize its resources and capabilities relative to opportunities in the external environment.

Strategy Formulation and Implementation
- Strategic actions taken to earn above-average returns

Superior Returns
- Earning of above-average returns

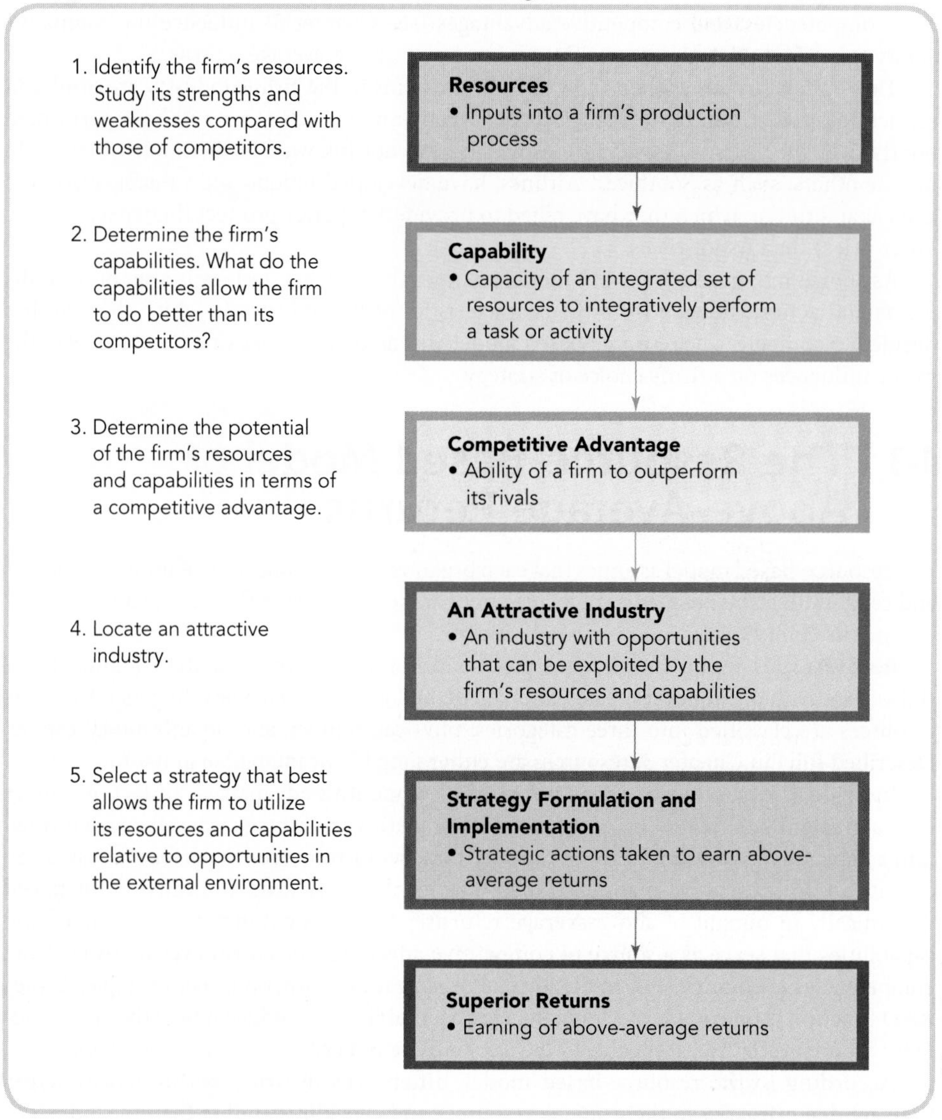

© Cengage Learning

Resources are *costly to imitate* when other firms either cannot obtain them or are at a cost disadvantage in obtaining them compared with the firm that already possesses them. And they are *nonsubstitutable* when they have no structural equivalents. Many resources can either be imitated or substituted over time. Therefore, it is difficult to achieve and sustain a competitive advantage based on resources alone.[91] Individual resources are often integrated to produce configurations in order to build capabilities. These capabilities are more likely to have these four attributes.[92] When these four criteria are met, however, resources and capabilities become core competencies.

As noted previously, research shows that both the industry environment and a firm's internal assets affect that firm's performance over time.[93] Thus, to form a vision and mission, and subsequently to select one or more strategies and determine how to implement them, firms use both the I/O and resource-based models.[94] In fact, these models complement each other in that one (I/O) focuses outside the firm while the other (resource-based) focuses inside the firm. Next, we discuss the formation of a firm's vision and mission—actions taken after the firm understands the realities of its external environment (Chapter 2) and internal organization (Chapter 3).

1-4 Vision and Mission

After studying the external environment and the internal organization, the firm has the information it needs to form its vision and a mission (see Figure 1.1). Stakeholders (those who affect or are affected by a firm's performance, as explained later in the chapter) learn a great deal about a firm by studying its vision and mission. Indeed, a key purpose of vision and mission statements is to inform stakeholders of what the firm is, what it seeks to accomplish, and who it seeks to serve.

1-4a Vision

Vision is a picture of what the firm wants to be and, in broad terms, what it wants to ultimately achieve.[95] Thus, a vision statement articulates the ideal description of an organization and gives shape to its intended future. In other words, a vision statement points the firm in the direction of where it would like to be in the years to come.[96] An effective vision stretches and challenges people as well. In her book about Steve Jobs, Apple's phenomenally successful CEO, Carmine Gallo argues that one of the reasons that Apple is so innovative was Jobs' vision for the company. She suggests that he thought bigger and differently than most people. To be innovative, she explains that one has to think differently about the firm's products and customers—"sell dreams not products"—and differently about the story to "create great expectations."[97] With Steve Jobs' death, Apple will be challenged to remain highly innovative. Interestingly, similar to Jobs, many new entrepreneurs are highly optimistic when they develop their ventures.[98] However, very few are able to develop and successfully implement a vision in the manner that Jobs did.

It is also important to recognize that vision statements reflect a firm's values and aspirations and are intended to capture the heart and mind of each employee and, hopefully, many of its other stakeholders. A firm's vision tends to be enduring while its mission can change with new environmental conditions. A vision statement tends to be relatively short and concise, making it easily remembered. Examples of vision statements include the following:

Our vision is to be the world's best quick service restaurant. (McDonald's)

To make the automobile accessible to every American. (Ford Motor Company's vision when established by Henry Ford)

As a firm's most important and prominent strategic leader, the CEO is responsible for working with others to form the firm's vision. Experience shows that the most effective vision statement results when the chief executive officer (CEO) involves a host of stakeholders (e.g., other top-level managers, employees working in different parts of the organization, suppliers, and customers) to develop it. In short, they need to develop a shared vision for it to be successful.[99] In addition, to help the firm reach its desired future state, a vision statement should be clearly tied to the conditions in the firm's external environment and internal organization. Moreover, the decisions and actions of those involved with developing the vision, especially the CEO and the other top-level managers, must be consistent with that vision.

1-4b Mission

The vision is the foundation for the firm's mission. A **mission** specifies the business or businesses in which the firm intends to compete and the customers it intends to serve.[100] The firm's mission is more concrete than its vision. However, similar to the vision,

Vision is a picture of what the firm wants to be and, in broad terms, what it wants to ultimately achieve.

A **mission** specifies the businesses in which the film intends to compete and the customers it intends to serve.

a mission should establish a firm's individuality and should be inspiring and relevant to all stakeholders.[101] Together, the vision and mission provide the foundation that the firm needs to choose and implement one or more strategies. The probability of forming an effective mission increases when employees have a strong sense of the ethical standards that guide their behaviors as they work to help the firm reach its vision.[102] Thus, business ethics are a vital part of the firm's discussions to decide what it wants to become (its vision) as well as who it intends to serve and how it desires to serve those individuals and groups (its mission).[103]

Even though the final responsibility for forming the firm's mission rests with the CEO, the CEO and other top-level managers often involve more people in developing the mission. The main reason is that the mission deals more directly with product markets and customers, and middle- and first-level managers and other employees have more direct contact with customers and the markets in which they are served. Examples of mission statements include the following:

Be the best employer for our people in each community around the world and deliver operational excellence to our customers in each of our restaurants. (McDonald's)

Our mission is to be recognized by our customers as the leader in applications engineering. We always focus on the activities customers desire; we are highly motivated and strive to advance our technical knowledge in the areas of material, part design and fabrication technology. (LNP, a GE Plastics Company)

McDonald's mission statement flows from its vision of being the world's best quick-service restaurant. LNP's mission statement describes the business areas (material, part design, and fabrication technology) in which the firm intends to compete.

Clearly, vision and mission statements that are poorly developed do not provide the direction a firm needs to take appropriate strategic actions. Still, as shown in Figure 1.1, a firm's vision and mission are critical aspects of the *analysis* and the base required to engage in *strategic actions* that help to achieve strategic competitiveness and earn above-average returns. Therefore, firms must accept the challenge of forming effective vision and mission statements.

1-5   Stakeholders

Every organization involves a system of primary stakeholder groups with whom it establishes and manages relationships.[104] **Stakeholders** are the individuals, groups, and organizations who can affect the firm's vision and mission, are affected by the strategic outcomes achieved, and have enforceable claims on the firm's performance.[105] Claims on a firm's performance are enforced through the stakeholders' ability to withhold participation essential to the organization's survival, competitiveness, and profitability.[106] Stakeholders continue to support an organization when its performance meets or exceeds their expectations.[107] Also, research suggests that firms that effectively manage stakeholder relationships outperform those that do not. Stakeholder relationships can therefore be managed to be a source of competitive advantage.[108]

Although organizations have dependency relationships with their stakeholders, they are not equally dependent on all stakeholders at all times; as a consequence, not every stakeholder has the same level of influence.[109] The more critical and valued a stakeholder's participation, the greater a firm's dependency on it. Greater dependence, in turn, gives the stakeholder more potential influence over a firm's commitments, decisions, and actions. Managers must find ways to either accommodate or insulate the organization from the demands of stakeholders controlling critical resources.[110]

Stakeholders are the individuals, groups, and organizations that can affect the firm's vision and mission, are affected by the strategic outcomes achieved, and have enforceable claims on the firm's performance.

1-5a Classifications of Stakeholders

The parties involved with a firm's operations can be separated into at least three groups.[111] As shown in Figure 1.4, these groups are the capital market stakeholders (shareholders and the major suppliers of a firm's capital), the product market stakeholders (the firm's primary customers, suppliers, host communities, and unions representing the workforce), and the organizational stakeholders (all of a firm's employees, including both nonmanagerial and managerial personnel).

Each stakeholder group expects those making strategic decisions in a firm to provide the leadership through which its valued objectives will be reached.[112] The objectives of the various stakeholder groups often differ from one another, sometimes placing those involved with a firm's strategic management process in situations where trade-offs have to be made. The most obvious stakeholders, at least in U.S. organizations, are *shareholders*—individuals and groups who have invested capital in a firm in the expectation of earning a positive return on their investments. These stakeholders' rights are grounded in laws governing private property and private enterprise.

In contrast to shareholders, another group of stakeholders—the firm's customers—prefers that investors receive a minimum return on their investments. Customers could have their interests maximized when the quality and reliability of a firm's products are improved, but without high prices. High returns to customers, therefore, might come at the expense of lower returns for capital market stakeholders.

Because of potential conflicts, each firm must carefully manage its stakeholders. First, a firm must thoroughly identify and understand all important stakeholders. Second, it must prioritize them in case it cannot satisfy all of them. Power is the most critical criterion in

Figure 1.4 The Three Stakeholder Groups

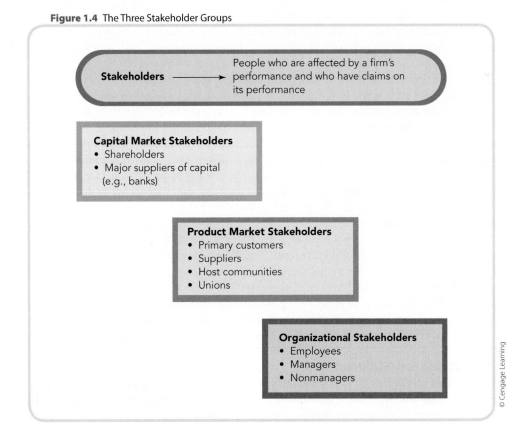

Stakeholders ⟶ People who are affected by a firm's performance and who have claims on its performance

Capital Market Stakeholders
- Shareholders
- Major suppliers of capital (e.g., banks)

Product Market Stakeholders
- Primary customers
- Suppliers
- Host communities
- Unions

Organizational Stakeholders
- Employees
- Managers
- Nonmanagers

© Cengage Learning

prioritizing stakeholders. Other criteria might include the urgency of satisfying each particular stakeholder group and the degree of importance of each to the firm.[113]

When the firm earns above-average returns, the challenge of effectively managing stakeholder relationships is lessened substantially. With the capability and flexibility provided by above-average returns, a firm can more easily satisfy multiple stakeholders simultaneously. When the firm earns only average returns, it is unable to maximize the interests of all stakeholders. The objective then becomes one of at least minimally satisfying each stakeholder.

Trade-off decisions are made in light of how important the support of each stakeholder group is to the firm. For example, environmental groups may be very important to firms in the energy industry but less important to professional service firms.[114] A firm earning below-average returns does not have the capacity to minimally satisfy all stakeholders. The managerial challenge in this case is to make trade-offs that minimize the amount of support lost from stakeholders. Societal values also influence the general weightings allocated among the three stakeholder groups shown in Figure 1.4. Although all three groups are served by and, in turn, influence firms in the major industrialized nations, the priorities in their service and influence vary because of cultural and institutional differences. Next, we present additional details about each of the three major stakeholder groups.

Capital Market Stakeholders

Shareholders and lenders both expect a firm to preserve and enhance the wealth they have entrusted to it. The returns they expect are commensurate with the degree of risk they accept with those investments (i.e., lower returns are expected with low-risk investments while higher returns are expected with high-risk investments). Dissatisfied lenders may impose stricter covenants on subsequent borrowing of capital. Dissatisfied shareholders may reflect their concerns through several means, including selling their stock. Institutional investors (e.g., pension funds, mutual funds) often are willing to sell their stock if the returns are not what they desire, or take actions to improve the firm's performance such as pressuring top managers and members of boards of directors to improve the strategic decisions and governance oversight. Some institutions owning major shares of a firm's stock may have conflicting views of the actions needed, which can be challenging for managers. This is because some may want an increase in returns in the short term while the others desire a focus on building long-term competitiveness.[115] Managers may have to balance their desires with those of other shareholders or prioritize the importance of the institutional owners with different goals. Clearly shareholders who hold a large share of stock (sometimes referred to as blockholders—see Chapter 10 for more explanation) are influential, especially in the determination of the firm's capital structure (i.e., the amount of equity versus the amount of debt used). Large shareholders often prefer that the firm minimize its use of debt because of the risk of debt, its cost, and the possibility that debt holders have first call on the firm's assets over the shareholders in case of default.[116]

When a firm is aware of potential or actual dissatisfactions among capital market stakeholders, it may respond to their concerns. The firm's response to stakeholders who are dissatisfied is affected by the nature of its dependence on them (which, as noted earlier, is also influenced by a society's values). The greater and more significant the dependency is, the more likely the firm is to provide a significant response. Sometimes firms are unable to satisfy key stakeholders such as creditors and have to file for bankruptcy (e.g., American Airlines filed for Chapter 11 bankruptcy in November 2011, as noted in the Strategic Focus).

Product Market Stakeholders

Some might think that product market stakeholders (customers, suppliers, host communities, and unions) share few common interests. However, all four groups can benefit as firms engage in competitive battles. For example, depending on product and industry characteristics, marketplace competition may result in lower product prices being charged to a firm's customers and higher prices being paid to its suppliers (the firm might be willing to pay higher supplier prices to ensure delivery of the types of goods and services that are linked with its competitive success).[117]

Customers, as stakeholders, demand reliable products at the lowest possible prices. Suppliers seek loyal customers who are willing to pay the highest sustainable prices for the goods and services they receive. Although all product market stakeholders are important, without customers, the other product market stakeholders are of little value. Therefore, the firm must try to learn about and understand current and potential customers.[118]

Host communities are represented by national (home and abroad), state/province, and local government entities with which the firm must deal. Governments want companies willing to be long-term employers and providers of tax revenue without placing excessive demands on public support services. These stakeholders also influence the firm through laws and regulations. In fact, firms must deal with laws and regulations developed and enforced at the national, state, and local levels (the influence is polycentric—multiple levels of power and influence).[119]

Union officials are interested in secure jobs, under highly desirable working conditions, for employees they represent. Thus, product market stakeholders are generally satisfied when a firm's profit margin reflects at least a balance between the returns to capital market stakeholders (i.e., the returns lenders and shareholders will accept and still retain their interests in the firm) and the returns in which they share.

Organizational Stakeholders

Employees—the firm's organizational stakeholders—expect the firm to provide a dynamic, stimulating, and rewarding work environment. Employees generally prefer to work for a company that is growing and actively developing their skills, especially those skills required to be effective team members and to meet or exceed global work standards. Workers who learn how to use new knowledge productively are critical to organizational success. In a collective sense, the education and skills of a firm's workforce are competitive weapons affecting strategy implementation and firm performance.[120] Strategic leaders are ultimately responsible for serving the needs of organizational stakeholders on a day-to-day basis. In fact, to be successful, strategic leaders must effectively use the firm's human capital.[121] The importance of human capital to their success is likely why outside directors are more likely to propose layoffs compared to inside strategic leaders, while such insiders are likely to use preventative cost-cutting measures and seek to protect incumbent employees.[122] A highly important means of building employee skills for the global competitive landscape is through international assignments. The process of managing expatriate employees and helping them build knowledge can have significant effects over time on the firm's ability to compete in global markets.[123]

1-6 Strategic Leaders

Strategic leaders are people located in different areas and levels of the firm using the strategic management process to select strategic actions that help the firm achieve its vision and fulfill its mission. Regardless of their location in the firm, successful strategic leaders are decisive, committed to nurturing those around them, and committed to helping the firm create value for all stakeholder groups.[124] In this vein, research evidence suggests that employees who perceive that their CEO is a visionary leader also believe that the CEO leads the firm to operate in ways that are consistent with the values of all stakeholder groups rather than emphasizing only maximizing profits for shareholders. In turn, visionary leadership motivates employees to expend extra effort, thereby helping to increase firm performance.

Strategic leaders are people located in different areas and levels of the firm using the strategic management process to select strategic actions that help the firm achieve its vision and fulfill its mission.

Moment/Cultura/Getty Images

Strategic leaders shape the organization's culture. Culture affects how work gets done and people interact with each other.

When identifying strategic leaders, most of us tend to think of CEOs and other top-level managers. Clearly, these people are strategic leaders. In the final analysis, CEOs are responsible for making certain their firm effectively uses the strategic management process. Indeed, the pressure on CEOs to manage strategically is stronger than ever.[125] However, many other people help choose a firm's strategy and then determine the actions for successfully implementing it.[126] The main reason is that the realities of twenty-first-century competition that we discussed earlier in this chapter (e.g., the global economy, globalization, rapid technological change, and the increasing importance of knowledge and people as sources of competitive advantage) are creating a need for those "closest to the action" to be making decisions and determining the actions to be taken. In fact, all managers (as strategic leaders) must think globally and act locally.[127] Thus, the most effective CEOs and top-level managers understand how to delegate strategic responsibilities to people throughout the firm who influence the use of organizational resources. Delegation also helps to avoid too much managerial hubris at the top and the problems it causes, especially in situations allowing significant managerial discretion.[128]

Organizational culture also affects strategic leaders and their work. In turn, strategic leaders' decisions and actions shape a firm's culture. **Organizational culture** refers to the complex set of ideologies, symbols, and core values that are shared throughout the firm and that influence how the firm conducts business. It is the social energy that drives—or fails to drive—the organization.[129] For example, Southwest Airlines is known for having a unique and valuable culture. Its culture encourages employees to work hard but also to have fun while doing so. Moreover, its culture entails respect for others—employees and customers alike. The firm also places a premium on service, as suggested by its commitment to provide POS (Positively Outrageous Service) to each customer.

1-6a The Work of Effective Strategic Leaders

Perhaps not surprisingly, hard work, thorough analyses, a willingness to be brutally honest, a penchant for wanting the firm and its people to accomplish more, and tenacity are prerequisites to an individual's success as a strategic leader. The top strategic leaders are chosen on the basis of their capabilities (their accumulation of human capital over time). Potent top management teams (human capital, management skills, and cognitive abilities) make better strategic decisions.[130] In addition, strategic leaders must have a strong strategic orientation while simultaneously embracing change in the dynamic competitive landscape we have discussed.[131] In order to deal with this change effectively, strategic leaders must be innovative thinkers and promote innovation in their organization.[132] Promoting innovation is facilitated by a diverse top management team representing different types of expertise and leveraging relationships with external parties.[133] Strategic leaders can best leverage partnerships with external parties and organizations when their organizations are ambidextrous. That is, the organizations simultaneously promote exploratory learning of new and unique forms of knowledge and exploitative learning that adds incremental knowledge to existing knowledge bases, allowing them to better understand and use their existing products.[134] In addition, strategic leaders need to have a global mind-set, or what some refer to as an ambicultural approach to management.[135]

Organizational culture refers to the complex set of ideologies, symbols, and core values that are shared throughout the firm and that influence how the firm conducts business.

Strategic leaders, regardless of their location in the organization, often work long hours, and their work is filled with ambiguous decision situations. However, the opportunities afforded by this work are appealing and offer exciting chances to dream and to act. The following words, given as advice to the late Time Warner chair and co-CEO Steven J. Ross by his father, describe the opportunities in a strategic leader's work:

There are three categories of people—the person who goes into the office, puts his feet up on his desk, and dreams for 12 hours; the person who arrives at 5 A.M. and works for 16 hours, never once stopping to dream; and the person who puts his feet up, dreams for one hour, then does something about those dreams.[136]

The operational term used for a dream that challenges and energizes a company is vision. The most effective strategic leaders provide a vision as the foundation for the firm's mission and subsequent choice and use of one or more strategies.

1-6b Predicting Outcomes of Strategic Decisions: Profit Pools

Strategic leaders attempt to predict the outcomes of their decisions before taking efforts to implement them, which is difficult to do. Many decisions that are a part of the strategic management process are concerned with an uncertain future and the firm's place in that future. As such, managers try to predict the effects on the firm's profits of strategic decisions that they are considering.[137]

Mapping an industry's profit pool is something strategic leaders can do to anticipate the possible outcomes of different decisions and to focus on growth in profits rather than strictly growth in revenues. A **profit pool** entails the total profits earned in an industry at all points along the value chain.[138] (We explain the value chain in Chapter 3 and discuss it further in Chapter 4.) Analyzing the profit pool in the industry may help a firm see something others are unable to see and to understand the primary sources of profits in an industry. There are four steps to identifying profit pools: (1) define the pool's boundaries, (2) estimate the pool's overall size, (3) estimate the size of the value-chain activity in the pool, and (4) reconcile the calculations.[139]

For example, McDonald's might desire to map the quick-service restaurant industry's profit pools. First, McDonald's would need to define the industry's boundaries and, second, estimate its size (which is large because McDonald's operates in markets across the globe, as noted in the Opening Case). The net result of this is that McDonald's tries to take market share away from competitors such as Burger King and Wendy's, and growth is more likely in international markets. Armed with information about its industry, McDonald's could then estimate the amount of profit potential in each part of the value chain (step 3). In the quick-service restaurant industry, marketing campaigns and customer service are likely more important sources of potential profits than are inbound logistics' activities (see Chapter 3). With an understanding of where the greatest amount of profits are likely to be earned, McDonald's would then be ready to select the strategy to use to be successful where the largest profit pools are located in the value chain.[140] As this brief discussion shows, profit pools are a

A **profit pool** entails the total profits earned in an industry at all points along the value chain.

McDonald's customer service gives it an advantage over its rivals.

Justin Sullivan/Getty Images

potentially useful tool to help strategic leaders recognize the actions to take to increase the likelihood of increasing profits. Of course, profits made by a firm and in an industry can be partially interdependent on the profits earned in adjacent industries.[141] For example, profits earned in the energy industry can affect profits in other industries (e.g., airlines). When oil prices are high, it can reduce the profits earned in industries that must use a lot of energy to provide their goods or services.

1-7   The Strategic Management Process

As suggested by Figure 1.1, the strategic management process is a rational approach firms use to achieve strategic competitiveness and earn above-average returns. Figure 1.1 also features the topics we examine in this book to present the strategic management process to you.

This book is divided into three parts aligned with the A-S-P process explained in the beginning of the chapter. In Part 1, we describe the *analyses* (A) necessary for developing strategies. Specifically, we explain what firms do to analyze their external environment (Chapter 2) and internal organization (Chapter 3). These analyses are completed to identify marketplace opportunities and threats in the external environment (Chapter 2) and to decide how to use the resources, capabilities, core competencies, and competitive advantages in the firm's internal organization to pursue opportunities and overcome threats (Chapter 3). The analyses explained in Chapters 2 and 3 are the well-known SWOT analyses (strengths, weaknesses, opportunities, threats).[142] With knowledge about its external environment and internal organization, the firm formulates its strategy taking into account the firm's vision and mission.

The firm's analyses (see Figure 1.1) provide the foundation for choosing one or more *strategies* (S) and deciding how to implement them. As suggested in Figure 1.1 by the horizontal arrow linking the two types of strategic actions, formulation and implementation must be simultaneously integrated for a successful strategic management process. Integration occurs as decision makers think about implementation issues when choosing strategies and as they think about possible changes to the firm's strategies while implementing a current strategy.

In Part 2 of this book, we discuss the different strategies firms may choose to use. First, we examine business-level strategies (Chapter 4). A business-level strategy describes the actions a firm takes to exploit its competitive advantage over rivals. A company competing in a single product market (e.g., a locally owned grocery store operating in only one location) has but one business-level strategy while a diversified firm competing in multiple product markets (e.g., General Electric) forms a business-level strategy for each of its businesses. In Chapter 5, we describe the actions and reactions that occur among firms in marketplace competition. Competitors typically respond to and try to anticipate each other's actions. The dynamics of competition affect the strategies firms choose as well as how they try to implement the chosen strategies.[143]

For the diversified firm, corporate-level strategy (Chapter 6) is concerned with determining the businesses in which the company intends to compete as well as how to manage its different businesses. Other topics vital to strategy formulation, particularly in the diversified company, include acquiring other businesses and, as appropriate, restructuring the firm's portfolio of businesses (Chapter 7) and selecting an international strategy (Chapter 8). With cooperative strategies (Chapter 9), firms form a partnership to share their resources and capabilities in order to develop a competitive advantage. Cooperative strategies are becoming increasingly important as firms seek ways to compete in the global economy's array of different markets.[144]

To examine actions taken to implement strategies, we consider several topics in Part 3 of the book. First, we examine the different mechanisms used to govern firms (Chapter 10).

With demands for improved corporate governance being voiced by many stakeholders in the current business environment, organizations are challenged to learn how to simultaneously satisfy their stakeholders' different interests.[145] Finally, the organizational structure and actions needed to control a firm's operations (Chapter 11), the patterns of strategic leadership appropriate for today's firms and competitive environments (Chapter 12), and strategic entrepreneurship (Chapter 13) as a path to continuous innovation are addressed.

It is important to emphasize that primarily because they are related to how a firm interacts with its stakeholders, almost all strategic management process decisions have ethical dimensions.[146] Organizational ethics are revealed by an organization's culture; that is to say, a firm's decisions are a product of the core values that are shared by most or all of a company's managers and employees. Especially in the turbulent and often ambiguous competitive landscape in the global economy, those making decisions as a part of the strategic management process must understand how their decisions affect capital market, product market, and organizational stakeholders differently and regularly evaluate the ethical implications of their decisions.[147] Decision makers failing to recognize these realities accept the risk of placing their firm at a competitive disadvantage.[148]

As you will discover, the strategic management process examined in this book calls for disciplined approaches to serve as the foundation for developing a competitive advantage. Therefore, it has a major effect on the *performance* (P) of the firm.[149] Performance is reflected in the firm's ability to achieve strategic competitiveness and earn above-average returns. Mastery of this strategic management process will effectively serve you, our readers, and the organizations for which you will choose to work.

SUMMARY

- Firms use the strategic management process to achieve strategic competitiveness and earn above-average returns. Firms *analyze* the external environment and their internal organization, then formulate and implement a *strategy* to achieve a desired level of *performance* (A-S-P). Performance is reflected by the firm's level of strategic competitiveness and the extent to which it earns above-average returns. Strategic competitiveness is achieved when a firm develops and implements a value-creating strategy. Above-average returns (in excess of what investors expect to earn from other investments with similar levels of risk) provide the foundation needed to simultaneously satisfy all of a firm's stakeholders.

- The fundamental nature of competition is different in the current competitive landscape. As a result, those making strategic decisions must adopt a different mind-set, one that allows them to learn how to compete in highly turbulent and chaotic environments that produce a great deal of uncertainty. The globalization of industries and their markets and rapid and significant technological changes are the two primary factors contributing to the turbulence of the competitive landscape.

- Firms use two major models to help develop their vision and mission and then choose one or more strategies in pursuit of strategic competitiveness and above-average returns. The core assumption of the I/O model is that the firm's external

environment has a large influence on the choice of strategies more than do the firm's internal resources, capabilities, and core competencies. Thus, the I/O model is used to understand the effects an industry's characteristics can have on a firm when deciding what strategy or strategies to use in competing against rivals. The logic supporting the I/O model suggests that above-average returns are earned when the firm locates an attractive industry or part of an industry and successfully implements the strategy dictated by that industry's characteristics. The core assumption of the resource-based model is that the firm's unique resources, capabilities, and core competencies have more of an influence on selecting and using strategies than does the firm's external environment. Above-average returns are earned when the firm uses its valuable, rare, costly-to-imitate, and nonsubstitutable resources and capabilities to compete against its rivals in one or more industries. Evidence indicates that both models yield insights that are linked to successfully selecting and using strategies. Thus, firms want to use their unique resources, capabilities, and core competencies as the foundation to engage in one or more strategies that allow them to effectively compete against rivals in their industry.

- Vision and mission are formed to guide the selection of strategies based on the information from the analyses of the firm's internal organization and external environment. Vision is a picture of what the firm wants to be and, in broad terms, what it wants to ultimately achieve. Flowing from the vision, the mission specifies the business or businesses in which the firm intends to compete and the customers it intends to serve. Vision and mission provide direction to the firm and signal important descriptive information to stakeholders.

■ Stakeholders are those who can affect, and are affected by, a firm's performance. Because a firm is dependent on the continuing support of stakeholders (shareholders, customers, suppliers, employees, host communities, etc.), they have enforceable claims on the company's performance. When earning above-average returns, a firm generally has the resources it needs to satisfy the interests of all stakeholders. However, when earning only average returns, the firm must carefully manage its stakeholders in order to retain their support. A firm earning below-average returns must minimize the amount of support it loses from unsatisfied stakeholders.

■ Strategic leaders are people located in different areas and levels of the firm using the strategic management process to help the firm achieve its vision and fulfill its mission. In general, CEOs are responsible for making certain that their firms properly use the strategic management process. The effectiveness of the strategic management process is increased when it is grounded in ethical intentions and behaviors. The strategic leader's work demands decision trade-offs, often among attractive alternatives. It is important for all strategic leaders and especially the CEO and other members of the top-management team to conduct thorough analyses of conditions facing the firm, be brutally and consistently honest, and work jointly to select and implement the correct strategies.

■ Strategic leaders predict the potential outcomes of their strategic decisions. To do this, they must first calculate profit pools in their industry (and adjacent industries as appropriate) that are linked to value chain activities. Predicting the potential outcomes of their strategic decisions reduces the likelihood of the firm formulating and implementing ineffective strategies.

REVIEW QUESTIONS

1. What are strategic competitiveness, strategy, competitive advantage, above-average returns, and the strategic management process?

2. What are the characteristics of the current competitive landscape? What two factors are the primary drivers of this landscape?

3. According to the I/O model, what should a firm do to earn above-average returns?

4. What does the resource-based model suggest a firm should do to earn above-average returns?

5. What are vision and mission? What is their value for the strategic management process?

6. What are stakeholders? How do the three primary stakeholder groups influence organizations?

7. How would you describe the work of strategic leaders?

8. What are the elements of the strategic management process? How are they interrelated?

EXPERIENTIAL EXERCISES

EXERCISE 1: STAKEHOLDER ANALYSIS, STRATEGIC PLANNING, AND STRATEGIC LEADERSHIP

Every organization relies on its own unique bundle of organizational stakeholders. Each one of the relationships between the organization and its stakeholders is influential in its ability to serve its mission and achieve above-average profits in the for-profit sector, or to create value in the not-for-profit sector. However, there are many ways that stakeholder management differs between the for-profit and not-for-profit worlds. It is easy to think of a for-profit firm that has product market stakeholders, such as customers, who can add or subtract their support by their decision of whether or not to purchase the firm's products or services. But who is the customer for a not-for-profit, and are the

categories of product, market, organization, and capital market stakeholders very different from the for-profit arena? This exercise challenges you to uncover some of the more influential ways in which this is so.

Part One

In this exercise, you will be working in teams of approximately four students per team.

1. Decide which not-for-profit organization you wish to analyze. If you would like assistance in identifying a not-for-profit organization, a good Web source is the IRS. You may search for charities at http://www.irs.gov/app/pub-78/.

2. Determine two or three key strategic initiatives of this not-for-profit organization. Most not-for-profits, particularly well-known ones, are good about posting their strategic plans on their Web sites.

3. Now perform a macro environmental analysis, and list all known or expected stakeholders for the organization. You should place them in the context of product, market, and organizational stakeholders.

Part Two

Now you are ready to start thinking critically about the organization and the challenges it faces among its stakeholders as it attempts to roll out its strategic initiatives.

1. For each strategic initiative that the organization has announced, analyze each stakeholder for the organization, and list areas in which the proposed strategy is likely to be supported, or not, by that particular stakeholder.

2. For the purpose of presenting to the class, organize your list so as to be able to present those strategies upon which expected support is likely to be gained and those strategies upon which support is likely to be discouraged.

3. Present to the class your recommendation for how the organization should proceed. For instance, if perceived support is critical to the successful strategic initiative but the strategy is likely to be viewed negatively by the stakeholder, provide some potential actions that the organization might take to mitigate the negative reaction or, alternatively, that might gain the stakeholders' support.

Conflicts are normal among organizational stakeholders, and deciding which must be attended to and at which time for which strategic action is a critical strategic leadership activity for every firm.

EXERCISE 2: PUTTING ABOVE AVERAGE RETURNS TO THE I/O MODEL TEST

For some time, the Industrial Organization (I/O) model of above-average returns has adopted as principal that the primary source of above average returns rested with the industry in which a firm competed. However, the strength of this model has been brought into question with the rise of rapid technological and business model innovation. Additionally the link between leadership effectiveness and the I/O model seems incomplete.

Working in teams, pick one firm from the *Fortune* 500 "Top Companies: Most Profitable Firm" annually published in CNNMoney (http://money.cnn.com/). Pick a firm you find of interest that represents as close as possible a single industry (i.e., automobiles, oil and gas, telecommunications) and avoid conglomerates (i.e., General Electric).

Following your text descriptions of the I/O model, identify:

1. Identify the external environment pressures and constraints.

2. List the similar strategically and relevant resources available to other firms competing in the industry.

3. What resources are highly mobile across firms and think through those that you believe will be short-lived.

4. Identify the strategies of your most profitable firm in the industry and decide if each of these are signals that management is committed to acting in the firm's best interests as shown by their profit-maximizing behavior.

Be prepared to present in class your findings. Pay particular attention to performance of closely related competitors. Does the I/O model explain well the firm's above average returns?

VIDEO CASE ▶

BRAZIL: AN EMERGING ECONOMY WITH STRATEGIC COMPETITIVENESS

Brazil had the lowest GDP growth rate among BRICS countries (Brazil, Russia, India, China and South Africa) in 2012, according to by the Organization for Economic Cooperation and Development (OECD). The OECD said Brazil's economy grew by only 1.3 percent. A country rich in natural resources and sophisticated in hydropower and biofuels, Brazil has emerged with strategic competitiveness. Being one of the greenest economies, Brazil is one of the largest producers of iron ore and one of the leading exporters of many popular commodities. After surviving historic financial collapse, Brazil has risen to have a strong manufacturing base, and the country's poor now have more purchasing power. (Please note that Brazil's current president is Dilma Rousseff.)

Be prepared to discuss the following concepts and questions in class:

Concepts

- Strategic competitiveness
- Strategy
- Hypercompetition
- Global economy
- Resources
- Capabilities
- Core competencies
- Stakeholders
- Strategic leaders

Questions

1. How is Brazil a strategic competitor?

2. What is Brazil's strategy?

3. Is Brazil a hypercompetitor?

4. What impact does Brazil have on the global economy?

5. What resources, capabilities, and core competencies does Brazil have?

6. What are the stakeholders associated with Brazil's thriving economy? Explain their significance.

NOTES

1. J. McGregor, 2009, Smart management for tough times, *Businessweek*, www.businessweek.com, March 12.

2. M. Wembridge, 2013, McDonald's goes native down under, *Financial Times*, www.ft.com, January 21.

3. K. Matzler, F. Bailom, M. Anschober, & S. Richardson, 2010, Sustaining corporate success: What drives the top performers? *Journal of Business Strategy*, 31(5): 4–13.

4. Chrysler, 2013, Wikipedia, http://en.wikipedia.org, accessed on March 8; D. Kiley, 2009, Ford heats out on a road of its own, *Businessweek*, January 19, 47–49.

5. C. Sialas & V. P. Economou, 2013, Revisiting the concept of competitive advantage, *Journal of Strategy and Management*, 6: 61–80; D. G. Sirmon, M. A. Hitt, R. D. Ireland, & B. A. Gilbert, 2011, Resource orchestration to create competitive advantage: Breadth, depth and life cycle effects, *Journal of Management*, 37: 1390–1412; D. G. Sirmon, M. A. Hitt, & R. D. Ireland, 2007, Managing firm resources in dynamic environments to create value: Looking inside the black box, *Academy of Management Review*, 32: 273–292.

6. R. D'Aveni, G. B. Dagnino, & K. G. Smith, 2010, The age of temporary advantage, *Strategic Management Journal*, 31: 1371–1385; R. D. Ireland & J. W. Webb, 2009, Crossing the great divide of strategic entrepreneurship: Transitioning between exploration and exploitation, *Business Horizons*, 52(5): 469–479.

7. J. A. Lamberg, H. Tikkanen, T. Nokelainen, & H. Suur-Inkeroinen, 2009, Competitive dynamics, strategic consistency, and organizational survival, *Strategic Management Journal*, 30: 45–60; G. Pacheco-de-Almeida & P. Zemsky, 2007, The timing of resource development and sustainable competitive advantage, *Management Science*, 53: 651–666.

8. K. D. Miller, 2007, Risk and rationality in entrepreneurial processes, *Strategic Entrepreneurship Journal*, 1: 57–74.

9. R. M. Stulz, 2009, 6 ways companies mismanage risk, *Harvard Business Review*, 87(3): 86–94.

10. P. Steffens, P. Davidsson, & J. Fitzsimmons, 2009, Performance configurations over time: Implications for growth- and profit-oriented strategies, *Entrepreneurship Theory and Practice*, 33: 125–148.

11. E. Karniouchina, S. J. Carson, J. C. Short, & D. J. Ketchen, 2013, Extending the firm vs. industry debate: Does industry life cycle stage matter? *Strategic Management Journal*, in press; J. C. Short, A. McKelvie, D. J. Ketchen, Jr., & G. N. Chandler, 2009, Firm and industry effects on firm performance: A generalization and extension for new ventures, *Strategic Entrepreneurship Journal*, 3: 47–65.

12. D. G. Sirmon, M. A. Hitt, J.-L. Arregle, & J. T. Campbell, 2010, The dynamic interplay of capability strengths and weaknesses: Investigating the bases of temporary competitive advantage, *Strategic Management Journal*, 31: 1386–1409; A. M. McGahan & M. E. Porter, 2003, The emergence and sustainability of abnormal profits, *Strategic Organization*, 1: 79–108.

13. D. Ucbasaran, D. A. Shepherd, A. Lockett, & S. J. Lyon, 2013, Life after business failure: The process and consequences of business failure for entrepreneurs, *Journal of Management*, 39: 163–202.

14. Y. Zhang & J. Gimeno, 2010, Earnings pressure and competitive behavior: Evidence from the U.S. electronics industry, *Academy of Management Journal*, 53: 743–768; T. R. Crook, D. J. Ketchen, Jr., J. G. Combs, & S. Y. Todd, 2008, Strategic resources and performance: A meta-analysis, *Strategic Management Journal*, 29: 1141–1154.

15. A. J. Bock, T. Opsahl, G. George, & D. M. Gann, 2012, The effects of culture and structure on strategic flexibility during business model innovation, *Journal of Management Studies*, 49: 275–305; J. Barthelemy, 2008, Opportunism, knowledge, and the performance of franchise chains, *Strategic Management Journal*, 29: 1451–1463.

16. Bock, Opsahl, George, & Gann, The effects of culture and structure on strategic flexibility; J. Li, 2008, Asymmetric interactions between foreign and domestic banks: Effects on market entry, *Strategic Management Journal*, 29: 873–893.

17. R. G. Bell, I. Filatotchev, & A. A. Rasheed, 2012, The liability of foreignness in capital markets: Sources and remedies, *Journal of International Business Studies*, 43: 107–122; L. Nachum, 2010, When is foreignness an asset or a liability? Explaining the performance differential between foreign and local firms, *Journal of Management*, 36: 714–739.

18. J. H. Fisch, 2012, Information costs and internationalization performance, *Global Strategy Journal*, 2: 296–312.

19. Karniouchina, Carson, Short, & Ketchen, Extending the firm vs. industry debate; M. A. Delmas & M. W. Toffel, 2008, Organizational responses to environmental demands: Opening the black box, *Strategic Management Journal*, 29: 1027–1055.

20. J. Barney, D. J. Ketchen, & M. Wright, 2011, The future of resource-based theory: Revitalization or decline? *Journal of Management*, 37: 37: 1299–1315; T. R. Holcomb, R. M. Holmes, Jr., & B. L. Connelly, 2009, Making the most of what you have: Managerial ability as a source of resource value creation, *Strategic Management Journal*, 30: 457–485.

21. M. Statman, 2011, Calm investment behavior in turbulent investment times, in *What's Next 2011*, New York: McGraw-Hill Professional, E-Book; E. Thornton, 2009, The new rules, *Businessweek*, January 19, 30–34; T. Friedman, 2005, *The World is Flat: A Brief History of the 21st Century*, New York: Farrar, Strauss and Giroux.

22. D. Searcey, 2006, Beyond cable. Beyond DSL. *Wall Street Journal*, July 24, R9.

23. 2013, NBC Universal, Wikipedia, http://en.wikipedia.org/wiki/NBC Universal, accessed March 8.

24. B. Agypt & B. A. Rubin, 2012, Time in the new economy: The impact of the interaction of individual and structural temporalities and job satisfaction, *Journal of Management*, 49: 403–428; D. F. Kuratko & D. B. Audretsch, 2009, Strategic entrepreneurship: Exploring different perspectives of an emerging concept, *Entrepreneurship Theory and Practice*, 33: 1–17.

25. J. Hagel, III, J. S. Brown, & L. Davison, 2008, Shaping strategy in a world of constant disruption, *Harvard Business Review*, 86(10): 81–89; G. Probst & S. Raisch, 2005, Organizational crisis: The logic of failure, *Academy of Management Executive*, 19(1): 90–105.

26. D'Aveni, Dagnino, & Smith, The age of temporary advantage; A. V. Izosimov, 2008, Managing hypergrowth, *Harvard Business Review*, 86(4): 121–127; J. W. Selsky, J. Goes, & O. N. Babüroglu, 2007, Contrasting perspectives of strategy making: Applications in "Hyper" environments, *Organization Studies*, 28(1): 71–94.

27. D'Aveni, Dagnino, & Smith, The age of temporary advantage; R. A. D'Aveni, 1995, Coping with hyper-competition: Utilizing the new 7S's framework, *Academy of Management Executive*, 9(3): 46.

28. D'Aveni, Dagnino, & Smith, The age of temporary advantage.

29. D. J. Bryce & J. H. Dyer, 2007, Strategies to crack well-guarded markets, *Harvard Business Review* 85(5): 84–92.

30. S. H. Lee & M. Makhija, 2009, Flexibility in internationalization: Is it valuable during an economic crisis? *Strategic Management Journal*, 30: 537–555; S. J. Chang & S. Park, 2005, Types of firms generating network externalities and MNCs' co-location decisions, *Strategic Management Journal*, 26: 595–615.

31. Y. Luo & S. L. Wang, 2012, foreign direct investment strategies by developing country multinationals: A diagnostic model for home country effects, *Global Strategy Journal*, 2: 244–261; S. E. Feinberg & A. K. Gupta, 2009, MNC subsidiaries and country risk: Internalization as a safeguard against weak external institutions, *Academy of Management Journal*, 52: 381–399.

32. Y. Luo, 2007, From foreign investors to strategic insiders: Shifting parameters, prescriptions and paradigms for MNCs in China, *Journal of World Business*, 42(1): 14–34.

33. M. A. Hitt & X. He, 2008, Firm strategies in a changing global competitive landscape, *Business Horizons*, 51: 363–369; A. Ratanpal, 2008, Indian economy and Indian private equity, *Thunderbird International Business Review*, 50: 353–358.

34. J.-F. Hennart, 2012, Emerging market multinationals and the theory of the multinational enterprise, *Global Strategy Journal*, 2: 168–187; S. Malone, 2011, GE's Immelt sees new economic era for globe, *Financial Post*, www.financialpost.com, March 13.

35. R. M. Holmes, T. Miller, M. A. Hitt, & M. P. Salmador, 2013, The interrelationships among informal institutions, formal institutions, and inward foreign direct investment, *Journal of Management*, 39: 531–566; K. D. Brouthers, 2013, A retrospective on: Institutions, cultural and transaction cost influences on entry mode choice and performance, *Journal of International Business Studies*, 44: 14–22.

36. A. H. Kirca, G. T. Hult, S. Deligonul, M. Z. Perry, & S. T. Cavusgil, 2012, A multilevel examination of the drivers of firm multinationality: A meta-analysis, *Journal of Management*, 38: 502–530; A. Ciarione, P. Piselli, & G. Trebeschi, 2009, Emerging markets' spreads and global financial conditions, *Journal of International Financial Markets, Institutions and Money*, 19: 222–239.

37. Y.-Y. Chang, Y. Gong, & M. W. Peng, 2012, Expatriate knowledge transfer, subsidiary absorptive capacity, and subsidiary performance, *Academy of Management Journal*, 55: 927–948.

38. J. P. Quinlan, 2011, Speeding towards a messy, multi-polar world, in *What's Next 2011*, New York: McGraw-Hill Professional, E-Book.

39. B. Elango, 2009, Minimizing effects of "liability of foreignness": Response strategies of foreign firms in the United States, *Journal of World Business*, 44: 51–62; D. B. Fuller, 2010, How law, politics and transnational networks affect technology entrepreneurship: Explaining divergent venture capital investing strategies in China, *Asia Pacific Journal of Management*, 27: 445–459.

40. J. Mata & E. Freitas, 2012, Foreignness and exit over the life cycle of firms, *Journal of International Business Studies*, 43: 615–630.

41. M. A. Hitt, R. E. Hoskisson, & H. Kim, 1997, International diversification: Effects on innovation and firm performance in product-diversified firms, *Academy of Management Journal*, 40: 767–798.

42. Hennart, Emerging market multinationals.

43. R. Ramamurti, 2012, What is really different about emerging market multinationals? *Global Strategy Journal*, 2: 41–47.

44. M. Naim, 2013, Power outage, *Bloomberg Businessweek*, March 3: 4–5.

45. G. McDermott, R. Mudambi, & R. Parente, 2013, Strategic modularity and the architecture of the multinational firm, *Global Strategy Journal*, 3: 1–7.

46. R. D. Ireland & J. W. Webb, 2007, Strategic entrepreneurship: Creating competitive advantage through streams of innovation, *Business Horizons*, 50(1): 49–59; G. Hamel, 2001, Revolution vs. evolution: You need both, *Harvard Business Review*, 79(5): 150–156.

47. K. H. Hammonds, 2001, What is the state of the new economy? *Fast Company*, September, 101–104.

48. S. W. Bradley, J. S. McMullen, K. W. Artz, & E. M. Simiyu, 2012, Capital is not enough: Innovation in developing economies, *Journal of Management Studies*, 49: 684–717; D. Dunlap-Hinkler, M. Kotabe, & R. Mudambi, 2010, A story of breakthrough versus incremental innovation: Corporate entrepreneurship in the global pharmaceutical industry, *Strategic Entrepreneurship Journal*, 4: 106–127.

49. C. Beckman, K. Eisenhardt, S. Kotha, A. Meyer, & N. Rajagopalan, 2012, Technology entrepreneurship, *Strategic Entrepreneurship Journal*, 6: 89–93; K. Z. Zhou & F. Wu, 2010, Technological capability, strategic flexibility and product innovation, *Strategic Management Journal*, 31: 547–561.

50. J. Kao, 2009, Tapping the world's innovation hot spots, *Harvard Business Review*, 87(3): 109–117.

51. N. Furr, F. Cavarretta, & S. Garg, 2012, Who changes course? The role of domain knowledge and novel framing in making technological changes, *Strategic Entrepreneurship Journal*, 6: 236–256; L. Jiang, J. Tan, & M. Thursby, 2011, Incumbent firm invention in emerging fields: Evidence from the semiconductor industry, *Strategic Management Journal*, 32: 55–75.

52. R. Adner & R. Kapoor, 2010, Value creation in innovation ecosystems: How the structure of technological interdependence affects firm performance in new technology generations, *Strategic Management Journal*, 31: 306–333.

53. J. L. Funk, 2008, Components, systems and technological discontinuities: Lessons from the IT sector, *Long Range Planning*, 41: 555–573; C. M. Christensen, 1997, *The Innovator's Dilemma*, Boston: Harvard Business School Press.

54. A. Kaul, 2012, Technology and corporate scope: Firm and rival innovation as antecedents of corporate transactions, *Strategic Management Journal*, 33: 347–367; Dunlap-Hinkler, Kotabe, & Mudambi, A story of breakthrough versus incremental innovation.

55. C. M. Christensen, 2006, The ongoing process of building a theory of disruption, *Journal of Product Innovation Management*, 23(1): 39–55.

56. H. K. Steensma, M. Howard, M. Lyles, & C Dhanaraj, 2012, The compensatory relationship between technological relatedness, social interaction, and knowledge flow between firms, *Strategic Entrepreneurship Journal*, 6: 291–306; A. Phene, S. Tallman, & P. Almeida, 2012, When do acquisitions facilitate technological exploration and exploitation? *Journal of Management*, 38: 753–783; M. Makri, M. A. Hitt, & P. J. Lane, 2010, Complementary technologies, knowledge relatedness and invention outcomes in high technology mergers and acquisitions, *Strategic Management Journal*, 31: 602–628.

57. R. Kapoor & J. M. Lee, 2013, Coordinating and competing in ecosystems: How organizational forms shape new technology investments, *Strategic Management Journal*, 34: 274–296; J. Woolley, 2010, Technology emergence through entrepreneurship across multiple industries, *Strategic Entrepreneurship Journal*, 4: 1–21.

58.   K. Celuch, G. B. Murphy, & S. K. Callaway, 2007, More bang for your buck: Small firms and the importance of aligned information technology capabilities and strategic flexibility, *Journal of High Technology Management Research*, 17: 187–197.

59.   2013, Worldwide PC Market, eTForecasts, www.etforecasts.com, accessed on March 10, 2013.

60.   M. S. Giarratana & S. Torrisi, 2010, Foreign entry and survival in a knowledge-intensive market: Emerging economy countries' international linkages, technology competences and firm experience, *Strategic Entrepreneurship Journal*, 4: 85–104.

61.   C. Phelps, R. Heidl, & A., Wadhwa, 2012, Knowledge, networks, and knowledge networks: A review and research agenda, *Journal of Management*, 38: 1115–1166; R. Agarwal, D. Audretsch, & M. B. Sarkar, 2010, Knowledge spillovers and strategic entrepreneurship, *Strategic Entrepreneurship Journal*, 4: 271–283.

62.   M. Gottfredson, R. Puryear, & S. Phillips, 2005, Strategic sourcing: From periphery to the core, *Harvard Business Review*, 83(2): 132–139.

63.   J. T. Macher & C. Boerner, 2012, Technological development at the boundary of the firm: A knowledge-based examination in drug development, *Strategic Managment Journal*, 33: 1016–1036; K. G. Smith, C. J. Collins, & K. D. Clark, 2005, Existing knowledge, knowledge creation capability, and the rate of new product introduction in high-technology firms, *Academy of Management Journal*, 48: 346–357.

64.   E. Sherman, 2010, Climbing the corporate ladder, *Continental Magazine*, November, 54–56.

65.   K. Z. Zhou & C. B. Li, 2012, How knowledge affects radical innovation: Knowledge base, market knowledge acquisition, and internal knowledge sharing, *Strategic Management Journal*, 33: 1090–1102; A. Capaldo, 2007, Network structure and innovation: The leveraging of a dual network as a distinctive relational capability, *Strategic Management Journal*, 28: 585–608.

66.   C. A. Siren, M. Kohtamaki, & A. Kuckertz, 2012, Exploration and exploitation strategies, profit performance and the mediating role of strategic learning: Escaping the exploitation trap, *Strategic Entrepreneurship Journal*, 6: 18–41; Sirmon, Hitt, & Ireland, Managing firm resources.

67.   A. Cuervo-Cazurra & C. A. Un, 2010, Why some firms never invest in formal R&D, *Strategic Management Journal*, 31: 759–779.

68.   H. Yang, C. Phelps, & H. K. Steensma, 2010, Learning from what others have learned from you: The effects of knowledge spillovers on originating firms, *Academy of Management Journal*, 53: 371–389.

69.   A. C. Inkpen, 2008, Knowledge transfer and international joint ventures: The case of NUMMI and General Motors, *Strategic Management Journal*, 29: 447–453; P. L. Robertson & P. R. Patel, 2007, New wine in old bottles: Technological diffusion in developed economies, *Research Policy*, 36: 708–721.

70.   R. E. Hoskisson, M. A. Hitt, R. D. Ireland, & J. S. Harrison, 2013, *Competing for Advantage*, 3rd ed., Mason, OH: South-Western Cengage Learning; K. R. Harrigan, 2001, Strategic flexibility in old and new economies, in M. A. Hitt, R. E. Freeman, & J. S. Harrison (eds.), *Handbook of Strategic Management*, Oxford, UK: Blackwell Publishers, 97–123.

71.   S. Nadkarni & P. Herrmann, 2010, CEO personality, strategic flexibility, and firm performance: The case of the Indian business process outsourcing industry, *Academy of Management Journal*, 53: 1050–1073; S. Nadkarni & V. K. Narayanan, 2007, Strategic schemas, strategic flexibility, and firm performance: The moderating role of industry clockspeed, *Strategic Management Journal*, 28: 243–270.

72.   M. L. Santos-Vijande, J. A. Lopez-Sanchez, & J. A. Trespalacios, 2011, How organizational learning affects a firm's flexibility, competitive strategy and performance, *Journal of Business Research*, 65: 1079–1089; A. C. Edmondson, 2008, The competitive imperative of learning, *Harvard Business Review*, 86(7/8): 60–67; K. Shimizu & M. A. Hitt, 2004, Strategic flexibility: Organizational preparedness to reverse ineffective strategic decisions, *Academy of Management Executive*, 18(4): 44–59.

73.   R. E. Hoskisson, M. A. Hitt, W. P. Wan, & D. Yiu, 1999, Swings of a pendulum: Theory and research in strategic management, *Journal of Management*, 25: 417–456.

74.   E. H. Bowman & C. E. Helfat, 2001, Does corporate strategy matter? *Strategic Management Journal*, 22: 1–23.

75.   J. T. Mahoney & L. Qian, 2013, Market frictions as building blocks of an organizational economics approach to strategic management, *Strategic Management Journal*, in press; M. A. Delmas & M. W. Toffel, 2008, Organizational responses to environmental demands: Opening the black box, *Strategic Management Journal*, 29: 1027–1055.

76.   J. Galbreath & P. Galvin, 2008, Firm factors, industry structure and performance variation: New empirical evidence to a classic debate, *Journal of Business Research*, 61: 109–117.

77.   H. E. Posen, J. Lee, & S. Yi, 2013, The power of imperfect imitation, *Strategic Management Journal*, 34: 149–164; M. F. Brauer & M. F. Wiersema, 2012, Industry divestiture waves: How a firm's position influences investor returns, *Academy of Management Journal*, 55: 1472–1492; M. B. Lieberman & S. Asaba, 2006, Why do firms imitate each other? *Academy of Management Journal*, 31: 366–385.

78.   M. E. Porter, 1985, *Competitive Advantage*, New York: Free Press; M. E. Porter, 1980, *Competitive Strategy*, New York: Free Press.

79.   J. C. Short, D. J. Ketchen, Jr., T. B. Palmer, & G. T. M. Hult, 2007, Firm, strategic group, and industry influences on performance, *Strategic Management Journal*, 28: 147–167.

80.   P. Ziobro, 2009, McDonald's pounds out good quarter, *Wall Street Journal*, www.wsj.com, April 23.

81.   T. W. Tong and J. J. Reuer, 2010, Competitive consequences of interfirm collaboration: How joint ventures shape industry profitability, *Journal of International Business Studies*, 41: 1056–1073.

82.   C. Moschieri, 2011, The implementation and structuring of divestitures: The unit's perspective, *Strategic Management Journal*, 32: 368–401.

83.   A. M. McGahan, 1999, Competition, strategy and business performance, *California Management Review*, 41(3): 74–101; McGahan & Porter, How much does industry matter, really?

84.   M. Schijven & M. A. Hitt, 2012, The vicarious wisdom of crowds: Toward a behavioral perspective of investor reactions to acquisition announcements, *Strategic Management Journal*, 33: 1247–1268; J. W. Upson, D. J. Ketchen, B. L. Connelly, & A. L. Ranft, 2012, Competitor analysis and foothold moves, *Academy of Management Journal*, 55: 93–110; A. Zavyalova, M. D. Pfarrer, R. K. Reger, & D. K. Shapiro, 2012, Managing the message: The effects of firm actions and industry spillovers on media coverage following wrongdoing, *Academy of Management Journal*, 55: 1079–1101.

85.   M. G. Jacobides, S. G. Winter, & S. M. Kassberger, 2012, The dynamics of wealth, profit and sustainable advantage, *Strategic Management Journal*, 33: 1384–1410; J. Kraaijenbrink, J.-C. Spender, & A. J. Groen, 2010, The resource-based view: A review and assessment of its critiques, *Journal of Management*, 38: 349–372.

86.   A. Arora & A. Nandkumar, 2012, Insecure advantage? Markets for technology and the value of resources for entrepreneurial ventures, *Strategic Management Journal*, 33: 231–251; S. L. Newbert, 2008, Value, rareness, competitive advantage, and performance: A conceptual-level empirical investigation of the resource-based view of the firm, *Strategic Management Journal*, 29: 745–768.

87.   Kraaijenbrink, Spender, & Groen, The resource-based view; E. Verwall, H. Commandeur, & W. Verbeke, 2009, Value creation and value claiming in strategic outsourcing decisions: A resource contingency perspective, *Journal of Management*, 35: 420–444.

88.   H. Wang & K. F. E. Wong, 2012, The effect of managerial bias on employees' specific human capital investments, *Journal of Management Studies*, 49: 1435–1458; P. L. Drnevich & A. P. Kriauciunas, 2011, Clarifying the conditions and limits of the contributions of ordinary and dynamic capabilities to relative firm performance, *Strategic Management Journal*, 32: 254–279.

89. C. Weigelt, 2013, Leveraging supplier capabilities: The role of locus of capability development, *Strategic Management Journal*, 34: 1–21; S. L. Newbert, 2007, Empirical research on the resource-based view of the firm: An assessment and suggestions for future research, *Strategic Management Journal*, 28: 121–146.

90. R. Nag & D. A. Gioia, 2012, From common to uncommon knowledge: Foundations of firm-specific use of knowledge as a resource, *Academy of Management Journal*, 55: 421–455; D. M. DeCarolis, 2003, Competencies and imitability in the pharmaceutical industry: An analysis of their relationship with firm performance, *Journal of Management*, 29: 27–50.

91. C. Zott, 2003, Dynamic capabilities and the emergence of intraindustry differential firm performance: Insights from a simulation study, *Strategic Management Journal*, 24: 97–125.

92. M. Gruber, F. Heinemann, & M. Brettel, 2010, Configurations of resources and capabilities and their performance implications: An exploratory study on technology ventures, *Strategic Management Journal*, 31: 1337–1356.

93. E. Levitas & H. A. Ndofor, 2006, What to do with the resource-based view: A few suggestions for what ails the RBV that supporters and opponents might accept, *Journal of Management Inquiry*, 15(2): 135–144; G. Hawawini, V. Subramanian, & P. Verdin, 2003, Is performance driven by industry- or firm-specific factors? A new look at the evidence, *Strategic Management Journal*, 24: 1–16.

94. M. Makhija, 2003, Comparing the source-based and market-based views of the firm: Empirical evidence from Czech privatization, *Strategic Management Journal*, 24: 433–451; T. J. Douglas & J. A. Ryman, 2003, Understanding competitive advantage in the general hospital industry: Evaluating strategic competencies, *Strategic Management Journal*, 24: 333–347.

95. R. D. Ireland, R. E. Hoskisson, & M. A. Hitt. 2012, *Understanding Business Strategy*, 3rd ed., Mason, OH: South-Western Cengage Learning.

96. S. Ward, 2009, Vision statement, *About.com*, www.sbinfocanada.about.com, April 22; R. Zolli, 2006, Recognizing tomorrow's hot ideas today, *Businessweek*, September 25: 12.

97. C. Gallo, 2010, *The Innovation Secrets of Steve Jobs*, NY: McGraw-Hill.

98. G. Cassar, 2010, Are individuals entering self-employment overly optimistic? An empirical test of plans and projections on nascent entrepreneur expectations, *Strategic Management Journal*, 31: 822–840.

99. O. R. Mihalache, J. J. P. Jansen, F. A. J. Van Den Bosch, & H. W. Volberda, 2012, Offshoring and firm innovation: The role of top management team attributes, *Strategic Management Journal*, 33: 1480–1498.

100. S. Kemp & L. Dwyer, 2003, Mission statements of international airlines: A content analysis, *Tourism Management*, 24: 635–653; R. D. Ireland & M. A. Hitt, 1992, Mission statements: Importance, challenge, and recommendations for development, *Business Horizons*, 35(3): 34–42.

101. A. S. Khalifa, 2012, Mission, purpose, and ambition: Redefining the mission statement, *Journal of Business and Strategy*, 5: 236–251; J. I. Siciliano, 2008, A comparison of CEO and director perceptions of board involvement in strategy, *Nonprofit and Voluntary Sector Quarterly*, 27: 152–162.

102. J. H. Davis, J. A. Ruhe, M. Lee, & U. Rajadhyaksha, 2007, Mission possible: Do school mission statements work? *Journal of Business Ethics*, 70: 99–110.

103. L. W. Fry & J. W. Slocum, Jr., 2008, Maximizing the triple bottom line through spiritual leadership, *Organizational Dynamics*, 37: 86–96; A. J. Ward, M. J. Lankau, A. C. Amason, J. A. Sonnenfeld, & B. A. Agle, 2007, Improving the performance of top management teams, *MIT Sloan Management Review*, 48(3): 85–90.

104. K. Basu & G. Palazzo, 2008, Corporate social responsibility: A process model of sensemaking, *Academy of Management Review*, 33: 122–136.

105. G. Kenny, 2012, From a stakeholder viewpoint: Designing measurable objectives, *Journal of Business Strategy*, 33(6): 40–46; D. A. Bosse, R. A. Phillips, & J. S. Harrison, 2009, Stakeholders, reciprocity, and firm performance, *Strategic Management Journal*, 30: 447–456.

106. N. Darnell, I. Henrique, & P. Sadorsky, 2010, Adopting proactive environmental strategy: The influence of stakeholders and firm size, *Journal of Management Studies*, 47: 1072–1122; G. Donaldson & J. W. Lorsch, 1983, *Decision Making at the Top: The Shaping of Strategic Direction*, New York: Basic Books, 37–40.

107. S. Sharma & I. Henriques, 2005, Stakeholder influences on sustainability practices in the Canadian forest products industry, *Strategic Management Journal*, 26: 159–180.

108. D. Crilly & P. Sloan, 2012, Enterprise logic: Explaining corporate attention to stakeholders from the 'inside-out', *Strategic Management Journal*, 33: 1174–1193.

109. G. Van der Laan, H. Van Ees, & A. Van Witteloostuijn, 2008, Corporate social and financial performance: An extended stakeholder theory, and empirical test with accounting measures, *Journal of Business Ethics*, 79: 299–310; M. L. Barnett & R. M. Salomon, 2006, Beyond dichotomy: The curvilinear relationship between social responsibility and financial performance, *Strategic Management Journal*, 27: 1101–1122.

110. G. Pandher & R. Currie, 2013, CEO compensation: A resource advantage and stakeholder-bargaining perspective, *Strategic Management Journal*, 34: 22–41; T. Kuhn, 2008, A communicative theory of the firm: Developing an alternative perspective on intra-organizational power

and stakeholder relationships, *Organization Studies*, 29: 1227–1254.

111. D. Bush & B. D. Gelb, 2012, Antitrust enforcement: An inflection point? *Journal of Business Strategy*, 33(6): 15–21; J. P. Doh, T. C. Lawton, & T. Rajwani, 2012, *Academy of Management Perspectives*, 26(3): 22–39; J. L. Murrillo-Luna, C. Garces-Ayerbe, & P. Rivera-Torres, 2008, Why do patterns of environmental response differ? A stakeholders' pressure approach, Strategic *Management Journal*, 29: 1225–1240.

112. R. Boutilier, 2009, *Stakeholder Politics: Social Capital, Sustainable Development, and the Corporation*, Sheffield, UK: Greenleaf Publishing; C. Caldwell & R. Karri, 2005, Organizational governance and ethical systems: A conventional approach to building trust, *Journal of Business Ethics*, 58: 249–267.

113. F. G. A. de Bakker & F. den Hond, 2008, Introducing the politics of stakeholder influence, *Business & Society*, 47: 8–20.

114. Darnell, Henrique, & Sadorsky, Adopting proactive environmental strategy; P. Berrone & L. R. Gomez-Meija, 2009, Environmental performance and executive compensation: An integrated agency-institutional perspective, *Academy of Management Journal*, 52: 103–126.

115. B. L. Connelly, L. Tihanyi, S. T. Certo, & M. A. Hitt, 2010, Marching to the beat of different drummers: The influence of institutional owners on competitive actions, *Academy of Management Journal*, 53: 723–742.

116. X. Zuoping, 2010, Large shareholders, legal institution and capital structure decision, *Nankai Business Review International*, 1: 59–86.

117. L. Pierce, 2009, Big losses in ecosystems niches: How core firm decisions drive complementary product shakeouts, *Strategic Management Journal*, 30: 323–347; B. A. Neville & B. Menguc, 2006, Stakeholder multiplicity: Toward an understanding of the interactions between stakeholders, *Journal of Business Ethics*, 66: 377–391.

118. O. D. Fjeldstad & A. Sasson, 2010, Membership matters: On the value of being embedded in customer networks, *Journal of Management Studies*, 47: 944–966.

119. B. Batjargal, M. A. Hitt, A. S. Tsui, J.-L. Arregle, J. Webb, & T. Miller, 2013, Institutional polycentrism, entrepreneurs' social networks and new venture growth, *Academy of Management Journal*, in press.

120. D. A. Ready, L. A. Hill, & J. A. Conger, 2008, Winning the race for talent in emerging markets, *Harvard Business* Review, 86(11): 62–70; A. M. Grant, J. E. Dutton, & B. D. Rosso, 2008, Giving commitment: Employee support programs and the prosocial sensemaking process, *Academy of Management Journal*, 51: 898–918.

121. T. R. Crook, S.Y. Todd, J. G. Combs, D. J. Woehr & D. J. Ketchen, 2011, Does human capital matter? A meta-analysis of the relationship between human capital

and firm performance, *Journal of Applied Psychology*, 96: 443–456; M. A. Hitt, K. T. Haynes, & R. Serpa, 2010, Strategic leadership for the 21st century, *Business Horizons*, 53: 437–444.

122. J. I. Hancock, D. G. Allen, F. A. Bosco, K. R. McDaniel, & C. A. Pierce, 2013, Meta-analytic review of employee turnover as a predictor of firm performance, *Journal of Management*, 39: 573–603; N. Abe & S. Shimizutani, 2007, Employment policy and corporate governance—An empirical comparison of the stakeholder and the profit-maximization model, *Journal of Comparative Economics*, 35: 346–368.

123. R. Takeuchi, 2010, A critical review of expatriate adjustment research through a multiple stakeholder view: Progress, emerging trends and prospects, *Journal of Management*, 36: 1040–1064.

124. Hitt, Haynes, & Serpa, Strategic leadership for the 21st century; J. P. Jansen, D. Vera, & M. Crossan, 2008, Strategic leadership for exploration and exploitation: The moderating role of environmental dynamism, *The Leadership Quarterly*, 20: 5–18.

125. E. F. Goldman, 2012, Leadership practices that encourage strategic thinking, *Journal of Strategy and Management*, 5: 25–40; D. C. Hambrick, 2007, Upper echelons theory: An update, *Academy of Management Review*, 32: 334–339.

126. J. C. Camillus, 2008, Strategy as a wicked problem, *Harvard Business Review* 86(5): 99–106; A. Priestland & T. R. Hanig, 2005, Developing first-level managers, *Harvard Business Review*, 83(6): 113–120.

127. B. Gutierrez, S. M. Spencer, & G. Zhu, 2012, Thinking globally, leading locally: Chinese, Indian, and Western leadership, *Cross Cultural Management*, 19: 67–89; R. J. Harrington & A. K. Tjan, 2008, Transforming strategy one customer at a time, *Harvard Business Review*, 86(3): 62–72.

128. J. Li & Y. Tang, 2010, CEO hubris and firm risk taking in China: The moderating role of managerial discretion, *Academy of Management Journal*, 53: 45–68; Y. L. Doz & M. Kosonen, 2007, The new deal at the top, *Harvard Business Review*, 85(6): 98–104.

129. B. Stevens, 2008, Corporate ethical codes: Effective instruments for influencing behavior, *Journal of Business Ethics*, 78: 601–609; D. Lavie, 2006, The competitive advantage of interconnected firms: An extension of the resource-based view, *Academy of Management Review*, 31: 638–658.

130. K. D. Clark & P. G. Maggitti, 2012, TMT potency and strategic decision making in high technology firms, *Journal of Management Studies*, 49: 1168–1193; C. Salvato, A. Minichilli, & R. Piccarreta, 2012, *Family Business Review*, 25: 206–224; H. Ibarra & O. Obodru, 2009, Women and the vision thing, *Harvard Business Review*, 87(1): 62–70.

131. R. Shambaugh, 2011, Leading in today's economy: The transformational leadership model, in *What's Next 2011*, NY: McGraw-Hill.

132. S. Khavul & G. D. Bruton, 2013, Harnessing innovation for change: Sustainability and poverty in developing countries, *Journal of Management Studies*, 50: 285–306; A. Leiponen & C. E. Helfat, 2010, Innovation objectives, knowledge sources and the benefits of breadth, *Strategic Management Journal*, 31: 224–236.

133. T. Buyl, C. Boone, W. Hendriks, & P. Matthyssens, 2011, Top management team functional diversity and firm performance: The moderating role of CEO characteristics, *Journal of Management Studies*, 48: 151–177; S. Nadkarni & P. Hermann, 2010, CEO personality, strategic flexibility and firm performance: The case of Indian business process outsourcing industry, *Academy of Management Journal*, 53: 1050–1073.

134. Q. Cao, Z. Simsek, & H. Zhang, 2010, Modelling the joint impact of the CEO and the TMT on organizational ambidexterity, *Journal of Management Studies*, 47: 1272–1296.

135. M.-J. Chen & D. Miller, 2010, West meets east: Toward an ambicultural approach to management, *Academy of Management Perspectives*, 24(4): 17–37.

136. M. Loeb, 1993, Steven J. Ross, 1927–1992, *Fortune*, January 25, 4.

137. Y.-C. Tang & F.-M. Liou, 2010, Does firm performance reveal its own causes? The role of Bayesian inference, *Strategic Management Journal*, 31: 39–57.

138. O. Gadiesh & J. L. Gilbert, 1998, Profit pools: A fresh look at strategy, *Harvard Business Review*, 76(3): 139–147.

139. O. Gadiesh & J. L. Gilbert, 1998, How to map your industry's profit pool, *Harvard Business Review*, 76(3): 149–162.

140. C. Zook, 2007, Finding your next CORE business, *Harvard Business Review*, 85(4): 66–75; M. J. Epstein & R. A. Westbrook, 2001, Linking actions to profits in strategic decision making, *Sloan Management Review*, 42(3): 39–49.

141. M. J. Lenox, S. F. Rockart, & A. Y. Lewin, 2010, Does interdependency affect firm and industry profitability? An empirical test, *Strategic Management Journal*, 31: 121–139.

142. M. M. Helms & J. Nixon, 2010, Exploring SWOT analysis—where are we now? A review of the academic research from the last decade, *Journal of Strategy and Management*, 3: 215–251.

143. T. Yu, M. Subramaniam, & A. A. Cannella, Jr., 2009, Rivalry deterrence in international markets: Contingencies governing the mutual forbearance hypothesis, *Academy of Management Journal*, 52: 127–147; D. J. Ketchen, C. C. Snow, & V. L. Street, 2004, Improving firm performance by matching strategic decision-making processes to competitive dynamics, *Academy of Management Executive*, 18(4): 29–43.

144. D. Li, L. Eden, M. A. Hitt, R. D. Ireland, & R. P. Garrett, 2012, Governance in multilateral R&D alliances, *Organization Science*, 23: 1191–1210; D. Li, S. R. Miller, L. Eden, & M. A. Hitt, 2012, The impact of rule of law on market value creation for local alliance partners in BRIC countries, *Journal of International Management*, 18: 305–321.

145. S. D. Julian, J. C. Ofori-Dankwa, & R. T. Justis, 2008, Understanding strategic responses to interest group pressures, *Strategic Management Journal*, 29: 963–984; C. Eesley & M. J. Lenox, 2006, Firm responses to secondary stakeholder action, *Strategic Management Journal*, 27: 765–781.

146. Y. Luo, 2008, Procedural fairness and interfirm cooperation in strategic alliances, *Strategic Management Journal*, 29: 27–46; S. J. Reynolds, F. C. Schultz, & D. R. Hekman, 2006, Stakeholder theory and managerial decision-making: Constraints and implications of balancing stakeholder interests, *Journal of Business Ethics*, 64: 285–301; L. K. Trevino & G. R. Weaver, 2003, *Managing Ethics in Business Organizations*, Stanford, CA: Stanford University Press.

147. D. Pastoriza, M. A. Arino, & J. E. Ricart, 2008, Ethical managerial behavior as an antecedent of organizational social capital, *Journal of Business Ethics*, 78: 329–341.

148. B. W. Heineman Jr., 2007, Avoiding integrity land mines, *Harvard Business Review*, 85(4): 100–108.

149. P. Klarner & S. Raisch, 2013, Move to the beat—Rhythms of change and firm performance, *Academy of Management Journal*, 56: 160–184.

2

The External Environment: Opportunities, Threats, Industry Competition, and Competitor Analysis

Studying this chapter should provide you with the strategic management knowledge needed to:

1 Explain the importance of analyzing and understanding the firm's external environment.

2 Define and describe the general environment and the industry environment.

3 Discuss the four parts of the external environmental analysis process.

4 Name and describe the general environment's seven segments.

5 Identify the five competitive forces and explain how they determine an industry's profitability potential.

6 Define strategic groups and describe their influence on firms.

7 Describe what firms need to know about their competitors and different methods (including ethical standards) used to collect intelligence about them.

THE COCA-COLA CO. AND PEPSICO: RIVALS COMPETING IN A CHALLENGING ENVIRONMENT

Recognized throughout the world, Coca-Cola and Pepsi-Co are both successful companies. At least historically, these firms are best known for their soft drinks or sodas. Interestingly, some believe that the United States "has been defined by soda in the same way France defined its empire on wine, Germany on beer, and Britain on tea."

Even though they differ in the total set of products they offer, the rivalry between these companies remains intense, particularly in terms of both carbonated and noncarbonated beverages. These competitions play out in many nations and regions of the world.

Of the two companies, PepsiCo is more diversified in that, through its Frito-Lay business unit, it is a leader in the global snack industry. The importance of this unit to PepsiCo is shown by the fact that it recently accounted for 21 percent of the firm's sales

revenue but 35 percent of its operating profits. In contrast, Coca-Cola is the world's largest producer of soft drink concentrates and syrups and is also the world's largest producer of juice and juice-related products; however, it does not have a snack business unit.

Changing conditions in the external environment are affecting these firms' competitive choices. Overall declining sales in the soda category in the United States in particular but in other parts of the world as well are one reason for this. Soda sales appear to be declining partly as a result of changes in societies' attitudes toward the "value" associated with consuming soda products, particularly full-calorie versions of them. In response, Coca-Cola is finding ways to generate more returns through its juice products. To ensure access to the supply of oranges it needs, the firm recently established long-term leases with two large Florida growers. This deal gives Coca-Cola access

to the production of 5 million orange trees for a period of 20 years. PepsiCo's recent competitive actions include paying $4.2 billion for Russian yogurt giant Wimm-Bill-Dann Foods. This is PepsiCo's largest-ever foreign acquisition and is seen as a path to reach consumers in neighboring countries such as Ukraine, Turkmenistan, and Kyrgyzstan for the purpose of successfully distributing its Frito-Lay products.

In addition, these firms continue competing aggressively against each other in sodas. Each firm has developed fountain machines that allow customers to create a variety of flavor combinations, such as strawberry Mountain Dew (a Pepsi-Cola product). To better attract younger consumers, PepsiCo completed an endorsement deal with pop star Beyoncé. And both firms are competing against each other to gain market share in noncarbonated beverage products such as waters, juices, and sports drinks.

Suggested links between obesity and some of these firms' products is another condition in the external environment that is affecting these firms, causing them to compete against each other to find ways to most effectively respond to this threat. Coca-Cola has announced that it is committed to contributing to individuals' health on a global basis. Supporting physical activities programs in every country where the firm competes is one action it is taking to demonstrate this commitment. In addition to committing to sell healthier products through its Quaker Oats, Gatorade, and Tropicana divisions, PepsiCo has established the "Global Nutrition Group" for the purpose of developing breakthrough products that will satisfy customers' needs for enjoyable but healthy products.

Sources: 2013, Coca-Cola Co, *Standard & Poor's Stock Report*, www.standardandpoors.com, May 17; 2013, PepsiCo Inc., *Standard & Poor's Stock Report*, www.standardandpoors.com, May 17; A. Cardenal, 2013, The battle of the soda giants: Coke vs. Pepsi, www.beta.fool.com, April 10; C. Passy, 2013, Why soda is the great American beverage, *Wall Street Journal*, www.wsj.com, March 12; D. Stanford, 2013, Cola-Cola expands calorie labels and emphasizes no-cals, *Bloomberg Business-week*, www.businessweek.com, May 9; D. Stanford, 2013, PepsiCo's East European snack attack, *Bloomberg Businessweek*, www.businessweek.com, February 28; K. Stock, 2013, Coke's sweet $2 billion orange juice deal, *Bloomberg Businessweek*, www.businessweek.com, May 8.

Strategy Right NOW

Learn more about Tropicana, a company acquired by Coca-Cola.

www.cengagebrain.com

As described in the Opening Case and suggested by research, the external environment (which includes the industry in which a firm competes as well as those against whom it competes) affects the competition actions and responses firms take to outperform competitors and earn above-average returns.[1] For example, Coca-Cola and PepsiCo are trying to effectively address the allegation that some and perhaps many of their products contribute to obesity. The socio-cultural segment of the general environment (discussed in this chapter) is the source of this allegation and the threat it represents to the two firms. The Opening Case also describes some of the ways these two firms compete against each other in markets throughout the world.

As noted in Chapter 1, the characteristics of today's external environment differ from historical conditions. For example, technological changes and the continuing growth of information gathering and processing capabilities increase the need for firms to develop effective competitive actions and responses on a timely basis.[2] (We fully discuss competitive actions and responses in Chapter 5.) Additionally, the rapid sociological changes occurring in many countries affect labor practices and the nature of products that increasingly diverse consumers demand. Governmental policies and laws also affect where and how firms choose to compete.[3] And, changes to a number of nations' financial regulatory systems that have been enacted since 2010 are expected to increase the complexity of organizations' financial transactions.[4]

Firms understand the external environment by acquiring information about competitors, customers, and other stakeholders to build their own base of knowledge and capabilities.[5] On the basis of the new information, firms take actions, such as building new capabilities and core competencies, in hopes of buffering themselves from any negative environmental effects and to pursue opportunities as the basis for better serving their stakeholders' needs.[6]

In summary, a firm's competitive actions and responses are influenced by the conditions in the three parts (the general, industry, and competitor) of its external environment (see Figure 2.1) and its understanding of those conditions. Next, we fully describe each part of the firm's external environment.

2-1 The General, Industry, and Competitor Environments

The **general environment** is composed of dimensions in the broader society that influence an industry and the firms within it.

The **general environment** is composed of dimensions in the broader society that influence an industry and the firms within it.[7] We group these dimensions into seven environmental *segments:* demographic, economic, political/legal, sociocultural, technological, global, and physical. Examples of *elements* analyzed in each of these segments are shown in Table 2.1.

M. Stasy

Figure 2.1 The External Environment

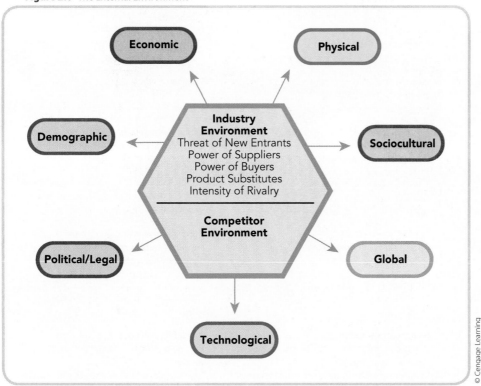

© Cengage Learning

Firms cannot directly control the general environment's segments. Accordingly, what a company seeks to do is recognize trends in each segment of the general environment and then *predict* each trend's effect on it. For example, some believe that over the next 10 to 20 years, millions of people living in emerging market countries will join the middle class. Of course no firm, including large multinationals, is able to control where growth in potential customers may take place in the next decade or two. Nonetheless, firms must study this anticipated trend as a foundation for predicting its effects on their ability to identify strategies to use that will allow them to remain successful as market conditions change.[8]

The **industry environment** is the set of factors that directly influences a firm and its competitive actions and responses:[9] the threat of new entrants, the power of suppliers, the power of buyers, the threat of product substitutes, and the intensity of rivalry among competing firms. In total, the interactions among these five factors determine an industry's profitability potential; in turn, the industry's profitability potential influences the choices each firm makes about its competitive actions and responses. The challenge for a firm is to locate a position within an industry where it can favorably influence the five factors or where it can successfully defend itself against their influence. The greater a firm's capacity to favorably influence its industry environment, the greater the likelihood it will earn above-average returns.

How companies gather and interpret information about their competitors is called **competitor analysis**. Understanding the firm's competitor environment complements the insights provided by studying the general and industry environments.[10] This means, for example, that Coca-Cola and PepsiCo want to learn as much about each other as they can while each company simultaneously seeks to understand its general and industry environments.

The **industry environment** is the set of factors that directly influences a firm and its competitive actions and responses: the threat of new entrants, the power of suppliers, the power of buyers, the threat of product substitutes, and the intensity of rivalry among competing firms.

How companies gather and interpret information about their competitors is called **competitor analysis**.

Table 2.1 The General Environment: Segments and Elements

Demographic segment	• Population size • Age structure • Geographic distribution	• Ethnic mix • Income distribution
Economic segment	• Inflation rates • Interest rates • Trade deficits or surpluses • Budget deficits or surpluses	• Personal savings rate • Business savings rates • Gross domestic product
Political/Legal segment	• Antitrust laws • Taxation laws • Deregulation philosophies	• Labor training laws • Educational philosophies and policies
Sociocultural segment	• Women in the workforce • Workforce diversity • Attitudes about the quality of work life	• Shifts in work and career preferences • Shifts in preferences regarding product and service characteristics
Technological segment	• Product innovations • Applications of knowledge	• Focus of private and government-supported R&D expenditures • New communication technologies
Global segment	• Important political events • Critical global markets	• Newly industrialized countries • Different cultural and institutional attributes
Physical environment segment	• Energy consumption • Practices used to develop energy sources • Renewable energy efforts • Minimizing a firm's environmental footprint	• Availability of water as a resource • Producing environmentally friendly products • Reacting to natural or man-made disasters

© Cengage Learning

An analysis of the general environment focuses on environmental trends and their implications, an analysis of the industry environment focuses on the factors and conditions influencing an industry's profitability potential, and an analysis of competitors is focused on predicting competitors' actions, responses, and intentions. In combination, the results of these three analyses influence the firm's vision, mission, its choice of strategies, and the competitive actions and responses it will take to implement those strategies. Although we discuss each analysis separately, performance improves when the firm effectively integrates the insights provided by analyses of the general environment, the industry environment, and the competitor environment.

2-2 External Environmental Analysis

Most firms face external environments that are turbulent, complex, and global—conditions that make interpreting those environments difficult.[11] To cope with often ambiguous and incomplete environmental data and to increase understanding of the general environment, firms complete an *external environmental analysis*. This analysis has four parts: scanning, monitoring, forecasting, and assessing (see Table 2.2).

Identifying opportunities and threats is an important objective of studying the general environment. An **opportunity** is a condition in the general environment that, if exploited effectively, helps a company reach strategic competitiveness. Most companies—and certainly large ones—continuously encounter multiple opportunities as well as threats.

An **opportunity** is a condition in the general environment that, if exploited effectively, helps a company reach strategic competitiveness.

Table 2.2 Parts of the External Environment Analysis

Scanning	• Identifying early signals of environmental changes and trends
Monitoring	• Detecting meaning through ongoing observations of environmental changes and trends
Forecasting	• Developing projections of anticipated outcomes based on monitored changes and trends
Assessing	• Determining the timing and importance of environmental changes and trends for firms' strategies and their management

© Cengage Learning

In terms of possible opportunities, we can note that a combination of cultural, political, and economic factors is resulting in rapid retail growth in Africa and the Middle East as well as in Latin America. Accordingly Walmart, the world's largest retailer, and the next three largest global giants (France's Carrefour, U.K.–based Tesco, and Germany's Metro) are planning to expand in these regions. "Walmart is expanding its horizon to Chile, India and South Africa; Carrefour will open stores in Bulgaria, India and Iran. Tesco is also opening stores in India, and Metro will open in Egypt and Kazakhstan."[12] Similarly, Google intends to partner with local telecommunications firms and equipment providers to help build and operate wireless networks in emerging markets such as sub-Saharan Africa and Southeast Asia. Pursuing these opportunities is part of Google's goal of connecting a billion or more new users to the Internet.[13]

A **threat** is a condition in the general environment that may hinder a company's efforts to achieve strategic competitiveness.[14] Finnish-based Nokia Corp. is dealing with threats including one regarding its intellectual property rights. In roughly mid-2013, the company filed two additional complaints against competitor HTC Corp. alleging that the Taiwanese smartphone manufacturer had infringed on nine of Nokia's patents.[15] This threat obviously deals with the political/legal segment. From the technological segment, Nokia is facing a potential threat from a new device called Jolla. Created by former Nokia executives and developers who founded their own firm in Helsinki in 2011, its manufacturer believes that the Jolla operating system is "a truly independent and open alternative in mobile."[16] While its competitive success is yet to be determined, this product does appear to represent a technological threat for Nokia and others smartphone manufacturers as well.

Firms use multiple sources to analyze the general environment through scanning, monitoring, forecasting, and assessing. Examples of these sources include a wide variety of printed materials (such as trade publications, newspapers, business publications, and the results of academic research and public polls), trade shows and suppliers, customers, and employees of public-sector organizations. Of course, the information available from Internet sources is of increasing importance to a firm's efforts to study the general environment.

2-2a Scanning

Scanning entails the study of all segments in the general environment. Although challenging, scanning is critically important to firms' efforts to understand trends in the general environment and predict their implications. This is particularly the case for companies competing in highly volatile environments.[17]

Through scanning, firms identify early signals of potential changes in the general environment and detect changes that are already under way.[18] Scanning activities must be aligned with the organizational context; a scanning system designed for a volatile environment is inappropriate for a firm in a stable environment.[19] Scanning often reveals ambiguous, incomplete, or unconnected data and information that require careful analysis.

Many firms use special software to help them identify events that are taking place in the environment and that are announced in public sources. For example, news event detection

A **threat** is a condition in the general environment that may hinder a company's efforts to achieve strategic competitiveness.

uses information-based systems to categorize text and reduce the trade-off between an important missed event and false alarm rates. Increasingly, these systems are used to study social media outlets as sources of information.[20]

Broadly speaking, the Internet provides a wealth of opportunities for scanning. Amazon.com, for example, records information about individuals visiting its Web site, particularly if a purchase is made. Amazon then welcomes these customers by name when they visit the Web site again. The firm sends messages to customers about specials and new products similar to those they purchased in previous visits. A number of other companies, such as Netflix, also collect demographic data about their customers in an attempt to identify their unique preferences (demographics is one of the segments in the general environment).

2-2b Monitoring

When *monitoring*, analysts observe environmental changes to see if an important trend is emerging from among those spotted through scanning.[21] Critical to successful monitoring is the firm's ability to detect meaning in environmental events and trends. For example, those monitoring retirement trends in the United States learned in 2013 that 57 percent of U.S. workers surveyed reported that excluding the value of their home, they have only $25,000 or less in savings and investments set aside for their retirement. This particular survey also discovered "that 28% of Americans have no confidence they will have enough money to retire comfortably—the highest level in the (survey's) 23-year history."[22] Historically, U.S. workers saved larger percentages of their earned income as a foundation for retirement. Firms seeking to serve retirees' financial needs will continue monitoring this change in workers' savings and investment patterns to see if a trend is developing. Once convinced that saving less for retirement is indeed a trend, these firms will seek to understand its competitive implications.

Effective monitoring requires the firm to identify important stakeholders and understand its reputation among these stakeholders as the foundation for serving their unique needs.[23] (Stakeholders' unique needs are described in Chapter 1.) Scanning and monitoring are particularly important when a firm competes in an industry with high technological uncertainty.[24] Scanning and monitoring can provide the firm with information; these activities also serve as a means of importing knowledge about markets and about how to successfully commercialize the new technologies the firm has developed.[25]

A variety of microprocessors are displayed at the Mobile World Congress in Barcelona, Spain. The global showcase for the mobile technology industry draws 1,500 exhibitors to discuss the future of wireless communication.

Bloomberg/Getty Images

2-2c Forecasting

Scanning and monitoring are concerned with events and trends in the general environment at a point in time. When *forecasting*, analysts develop feasible projections of what might happen, and how quickly, as a result of the events and trends detected through scanning and monitoring.[26] For example, analysts might forecast the time that will be required for a new technology to reach the marketplace, the length of time before different corporate training procedures are required to deal with anticipated changes in the composition of the workforce, or how much time will elapse before changes in governmental taxation policies affect consumers' purchasing patterns.

Forecasting events and outcomes accurately is challenging. Forecasting demand for new technological products is difficult because technology trends are continually driving product life cycles shorter. This is particularly difficult for a firm such as Intel, whose products go into many customers' technological products, which are consistently updated. Increasing the difficulty, each new wafer fabrication or silicon chip technology production plant in which Intel invests becomes significantly more expensive for each generation of chip products. In this instance, having access to tools that allow better forecasting of electronic product demand is of value to Intel as the firm studies conditions in its external environment.[27]

2-2d Assessing

When *assessing*, the objective is to determine the timing and significance of the effects of environmental changes and trends that have been identified.[28] Through scanning, monitoring, and forecasting, analysts are able to understand the general environment. Going a step further, the intent of assessment is to specify the implications of that understanding. Without assessment, the firm is left with data that may be interesting but of unknown competitive relevance. Even if formal assessment is inadequate, the appropriate interpretation of that information is important.

Accurately assessing the trends expected to take place in the segments of a firm's general environment is important. However, accurately interpreting the meaning of those trends is even more important. In slightly different words, although gathering and organizing information is important, appropriately interpreting the intelligence the collected information provides to determine if an identified trend in the general environment is an opportunity or threat is critical.[29]

2-3 Segments of the General Environment

The general environment is composed of segments that are external to the firm (see Table 2.1). Although the degree of impact varies, these environmental segments affect all industries and the firms competing in them. The challenge to each firm is to scan, monitor, forecast, and assess the elements in each segment to predict their effects on it. Effective scanning, monitoring, forecasting, and assessing are vital to the firm's efforts to recognize and evaluate opportunities and threats.

2-3a The Demographic Segment

The **demographic segment** is concerned with a population's size, age structure, geographic distribution, ethnic mix, and income distribution.[30] Demographic segments are commonly analyzed on a global basis because of their potential effects across countries' borders and because many firms compete in global markets.

Population Size

The world's population doubled (from 3 billion to 6 billion) between 1959 and 1999. Current projections suggest that population growth will continue in the twenty-first century, but at a slower pace. The U.S. Census Bureau projects that the world's population will be 9 billion by 2042 and roughly 9.25 billion by 2050.[31] In 2012, China was the world's largest country by population with over 1.3 billion people. By 2050, however, India is expected to be the most populous nation in the world (approximately 1.69 billion). China (1.3 billion), the United States (439 million), Indonesia (313 million), and Pakistan (276 million) are expected to be the next four most populous countries in 2050.[32] Firms seeking to find growing markets in which to sell their goods and services want to recognize the market potential that may exist for them in these five nations.

The **demographic segment** is concerned with a population's size, age structure, geographic distribution, ethnic mix, and income distribution.

While observing the population of nations and regions of the world, firms also want to study changes occurring within different populations to assess their strategic implications. For example, in 2011, 23 percent of Japan's citizens were 65 or older, while the United States and China will not reach this level until 2036.[33] Aging populations are a significant problem for countries because of the need for workers and the burden of supporting retirement programs. In Japan and some other countries, employees are urged to work longer to overcome these problems.

Age Structure

The most noteworthy aspect of this element of the demographic segment is that the world's population is rapidly aging. For example, predictions are that, "By 2050, over one-fifth of the U.S. population will be 65 or older up from the current figure (in 2012) of one-seventh. The number of centenarians worldwide will double by 2023 and double again by 2035. Projections suggest life expectancy will surpass 100 in some industrialized countries by the second half of this century—roughly triple the lifespan that prevailed worldwide throughout most of human history."[34] In China, the 65 and over population is expected to reach roughly 330 million by 2050, which will be close to one-fourth of the nation's total population.[35] In the 1950s, Japan's population was one of the youngest in the world. However, 45 is now the median age in Japan, with the projection that it will be 55 by 2040. With a fertility rate that is below replacement value, another prediction is that by 2040, there will be almost as many Japanese people 100 years old or older as there are newborns.[36]

These predictions lead to different possibilities. In Japan, an expectation that the working age population will shrink from 81 million in 2012 to about 57 million in 2040 seems to threaten companies' ability to operate. On the other hand, is there an opportunity for Japanese firms to find ways to increase the productivity of their workers and/or to establish additional operations in other nations? From an opportunity perspective, delayed retirements of baby boomers (those born between 1947 and 1965) that are expected in the United States (and perhaps other countries as well) create the possibility of helping companies "avoid or defer the baby-boomer brain drain that has been looming for so long." In this sense, "organizations now have a fresh opportunity to address the talent gap created by a shortage of critical skills in the marketplace as well as the experience gap created by multiple waves of downsizing over the past decade."[37] Having those delaying their retirement use their knowledge to help younger employees quickly gain valuable skills is another opportunity that the age structure element suggests firms should consider.

Geographic Distribution

How a population is distributed within countries and regions is subject to change over time. For example, the last few decades have seen the U.S. population shifting from states in the Northeast and Great Lakes region to states in the west (California), south (Florida), and southwest (Texas). These changes can be seen as moving from the "Frost Belt" to the "Sun Belt." Outcomes from these shifts include the facts that the gross domestic product (GDP) of California in 2011 was just under $2 trillion, an amount that makes California the ninth-largest economy in the world. In this same year, at a value of $1.3 trillion, Texas' GDP was second to that of California.[38]

Recent shifts show that New Jersey had the highest ratio of people moving out compared to the number of people moving into the state in 2012. Illinois, New York, Michigan, Maine, Connecticut, and Wisconsin are additional states for which a large net migration occurred in 2012. In a shift in the pattern witnessed for the first decade-plus of the twenty-first century, Washington, D.C., was the most popular destination for relocation in 2012 with Oregon being the second most popular. Washington, D.C., seemed to be popular because of its somewhat recession-proof economic opportunities that are generated by a maturing high-tech sector and federal government jobs. In particular, the city of Portland appears to capture the allure of Oregon in terms of its mix of economic growth, cutting edge urban planning, and scenic landscapes.[39]

Firms want to carefully study the patterns of population distributions in countries and regions to identify opportunities and threats. Thus in the United States, current patterns suggest the possibility of opportunities in Washington, D.C., as well as in states on the West Coast including Oregon and those in the South and Southwest. In contrast, firms competing in the Northeast and Great Lakes areas may concentrate on identifying threats to their ability to operate profitably in those areas.

Of course, geographic distribution patterns differ throughout the world. For example, in China, the majority of the population still lives in rural areas; however, today's growth patterns are toward urban communities such as Shanghai and Beijing.[40] Shifts that occurred between 2011 and 2012 in Europe show net (but small) population gains for countries such as France, Germany, and the United Kingdom while Greece experienced a net (again, small) population decline. Overall, the geographic distribution patterns at least for this year in Europe were quite stable.[41] This fact too has relevance for firms studying this segment of their general environment.

Ethnic Mix

The ethnic mix of countries' populations continues to change, creating opportunities and threats for many companies as a result. For example, Hispanics are now the largest ethnic minority in the United States.[42] In fact, the U.S. Hispanic market is the third largest "Latin American" economy behind Brazil and Mexico. Spanish is now the dominant language in parts of U.S. states such as Texas, California, Florida, and New Mexico. Given these facts, some firms might want to assess the degree to which their goods or services could be adapted to serve the unique needs of Hispanic consumers.

Additional evidence is of interest to firms when examining this segment. For example, African countries are the most ethnically diverse in the world, with Uganda having the highest ethnic diversity rating with Liberia second. In contrast, Japan and the Koreas are the least diversified from the perspective of a mix of ethnicities in their populations. European countries are ethnically homogeneous while the Americas are often diverse. "From the United States through Central America down to Brazil, the 'new world' countries, maybe in part because of their histories of relatively open immigration (and, in some cases, intermingling between natives and new arrivals) tend to be pretty diverse."[43]

Income Distribution

Understanding how income is distributed within and across populations informs firms of different groups' purchasing power and discretionary income. Of particular interest to firms are the average incomes of households and individuals. For instance, the increase in dual-career couples has had a notable effect on average incomes. Although real income has been declining in general in some nations, the household income of dual-career couples has increased, especially in the United States. These figures yield strategically relevant information for firms. For instance, research indicates that whether an employee is part of a dual-career couple can strongly influence the willingness of the employee to accept an international assignment. However, because of recent global

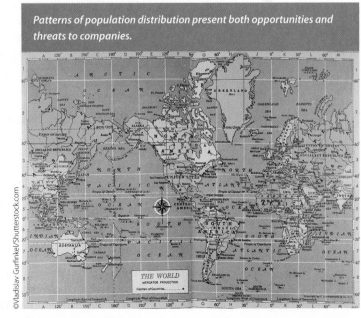

Patterns of population distribution present both opportunities and threats to companies.

©Vladislav Gurfinkel/Shutterstock.com

economic conditions, many companies were still pursuing international assignments but changing them to avoid some of the additional costs of funding expatriates abroad.[44]

The growth of the economy in China has drawn many firms, not only for the low-cost production, but also because of the large potential demand for products, given its large population base. However, in recent times, the amount of China's gross domestic product that makes up domestic consumption is the lowest of any major economy at less than one-third. In comparison, India's domestic consumption of consumer goods accounts for two-thirds of its economy, or twice China's level. As such, many western multinationals are considering entering India as a consumption market as its middle class grows extensively. Although India as a nation has poor infrastructure, its consumers are in a better position to spend. Furthermore, the urban-rural income difference has been declining in India more rapidly than in China. Because of situations such as this, paying attention to the differences between markets based on income distribution can be very important.[45]

2-3b   The Economic Segment

The **economic environment** refers to the nature and direction of the economy in which a firm competes or may compete.[46] In general, firms seek to compete in relatively stable economies with strong growth potential. Because nations are interconnected as a result of the global economy, firms must scan, monitor, forecast, and assess the health of their host nation as well as the health of the economies outside it.

For firms studying the economic environment today for purposes of being able to predict trends that may occur in this segment of the general environment and their effects on them, the picture remains unclear and challenging. There are at least two reasons for this. First, the global recession of 2008 and 2009 created numerous problems for companies throughout the world, including those of reduced consumer demand, increases in firms' inventory levels, development of additional governmental regulations, and a tightening of access to financial resources. The second reason to consider is that the global recovery from the 2008 and 2009 recession remains persistently slow and relatively weak compared to previous recoveries. Some argue that enhanced *economic uncertainty* (which refers to an environment in which relatively little and perhaps nothing at all is known about the future state of an economy) is a major cause of the "less-than-robust-recovery" that was experienced at least through mid-2013. Of likely concern to firms studying the economic segment today is the fact that historically, high degrees of economic uncertainty coincide with periods of lower growth. And again, according to some research, "it is clear that (economic) uncertainty has increased in recent times."[47] This increase suggests the possibility of slower growth in the foreseeable future.

When facing economic uncertainty, firms want to be certain to study the economic environment in multiple regions and countries throughout the world. Although economic growth remains relatively weak and economic uncertainty has been strong in Europe and the United States in recent times, this was not the case in other settings. In 2013, for example, growth was projected to increase by 8.2 percent in China, by 4 percent in Brazil, and by 3.5 percent in Mexico. From a regional perspective, 2013 projections were for growth of 5.8 percent in Southeast Asia and 5.7 percent in sub-Saharan Africa, estimates that highlight the anticipation of the continuing development of emerging economies.[48] Ideally, firms will be able to pursue growth opportunities in regions and nations where they exist while avoiding the threats of slow growth periods in other settings.

2-3c   The Political/Legal Segment

The **political/legal segment** is the arena in which organizations and interest groups compete for attention, resources, and a voice in overseeing the body of laws and regulations guiding interactions among nations as well as between firms and various local governmental agencies.[49] Essentially, this segment is concerned with how organizations try to influence

The **economic environment** refers to the nature and direction of the economy in which a firm competes or may compete.

The **political/legal segment** is the arena in which organizations and interest groups compete for attention, resources, and a voice in overseeing the body of laws and regulations guiding interactions among nations as well as between firms and various local governmental agencies.

governments and how they try to understand the influences (current and projected) of those governments on their competitive actions and responses. Commonly, firms develop a political strategy to specify how they will study the political/legal segment as well as approaches they might take (such as lobbying efforts) in order to successfully deal with opportunities and threats that surface within this segment at different points in time.[50]

Regulations formed in response to new national, regional, state, and/or local laws that are legislated often influence a firm's competitive actions and responses. For example, the state of Nevada in the United States recently legalized the business of online poker/gambling. New Jersey and Delaware quickly took the same action. In response to Nevada's regulatory change, firms such as MGM Resorts International were trying to decide the degree to which these decisions represented a viable opportunity. According to a MGM official, the immediate concern with respect to Nevada is that "the state may be too small to provide a lucrative online market on a standalone basis."[51]

At a regional level, changes in the laws regarding the appropriate regulation of European banks are still being actively debated.[52] For interactive, technology-based firms such as Facebook, Google, and Amazon, among others, "the effort in Europe to adopt the world's strongest data protection law has drawn the attention of dozens of lobbyists from U.S. technology and advertising companies."[53] Highly restrictive laws about consumer privacy could threaten how these firms conduct business in the European Union. Finally, in a comprehensive sense, recent transformations from state-owned to private firms occurring in multiple nations have substantial implications for the competitive landscapes in a number of countries and across multiple industries.[54]

2-3d The Sociocultural Segment

The **sociocultural segment** is concerned with a society's attitudes and cultural values. Because attitudes and values form the cornerstone of a society, they often drive demographic, economic, political/legal, and technological conditions and changes.

Individual societies' attitudes and cultural orientations are anything other than stable, meaning that firms must carefully scan, monitor, forecast, and assess them to recognize and study associated opportunities and threats. Another way of thinking about this is to note that companies do not exist in an isolated state. Because of this, even successful firms must have an awareness of changes taking place in the societies and their associated cultures in which they are competing. Indeed, societal and culture changes challenge firms to find ways to "adapt to stay ahead of their competitors and stay relevant in the minds of their consumers."[55]

Attitudes about and approaches to health care are issues being considered in nations and regions throughout the world. For Europe, the European Commission has developed a health care strategy for all of Europe that is oriented to preventing diseases while tackling lifestyle factors influencing health such as nutrition, working conditions, and physical activity. This Commission argues that promoting attitudes to take care of one's health is especially important in the context of an aging Europe as shown by the projection that the proportion of people over 65 living in Europe will increase from 17 percent in 2010 to almost 30 percent by 2060.[56]

In the United States, costs remain at the forefront of discussions about health care. Recent surveys show that consumers are dissatisfied with the cost of health care and do not understand why these costs continue to increase. Simultaneously though, most patients (as many as 80 percent of women and 85 percent of men) fail to compare the costs of doctors and recommended procedures.[57] At issue for business firms is that attitudes and values about health care can affect them; accordingly, they must carefully examine trends regarding health care in order to anticipate the effects on their operations.

As the U.S. labor force has increased, it has become more diverse, as significantly more women and minorities from a variety of cultures enter the workplace. In 1993, the total U.S. workforce was slightly less than 130 million; in 2005, it was slightly greater than 148 million. It is predicted to grow to more than 192 million by 2050.

The **sociocultural segment** is concerned with a society's attitudes and cultural values.

Chris Sattlberger/Photographer's Choice RF/Getty Images

Greater workforce diversity has become the norm in many industries. These changes have forced many companies to challenge the notion of traditional organizational roles for men and women.

However, the rate of growth in the U.S. labor force has declined over the past two decades largely as a result of slower growth of the nation's population and because of a downward trend in the labor force participation rate. More specifically, data show that "after nearly five decades of steady growth, the overall participation rate—defined as the proportion of the civilian noninstitutional population in the labor force—peaked at an annual average of 67.1 percent for each year from 1997 to 2000… By September 2012, the rate had dropped to 63.6 percent"[58] and is expected to fall to 58.5 percent by 2050. Other changes in the U.S. labor force between 2010 and 2050 are expected. During this time period, the Asian labor force is projected to more than double in size while the growth in the white labor force is predicted to be much slower compared to other racial groups. In contrast, people of Hispanic origin are expected to account for roughly 80 percent of the total growth in the labor force. Finally, "it is projected that the higher growth rate of the female labor force relative to that of men will end by 2020 and the growth rates for men and women will be similar for the 2020–2050 period."[59]

Greater diversity in the workforce creates challenges and opportunities, including combining the best of both men's and women's traditional leadership styles. Although diversity in the workforce has the potential to improve performance, research indicates that diversity initiatives must be successfully managed in order to reap these organizational benefits. Human resource practitioners are trained to successfully manage diversity issues to enhance positive outcomes.[60] In an overall sense though, learning how to effectively manage a firm's workforce is increasingly important in that "many companies recognize today, more than ever, their people have become their most critical competitive asset."[61]

Although the lifestyle and workforce changes referenced previously reflect the attitudes and values of the U.S. population, each country is unique with respect to these sociocultural indicators. National cultural values affect behavior in organizations and thus also influence organizational outcomes such as differences in CEO compensation.[62] Likewise, the national culture influences to a large extent the internationalization strategy that firms pursue relative to one's home country.[63] Knowledge sharing is important for dispersing new knowledge in organizations and increasing the speed in implementing innovations. Personal relationships are especially important in China as *guanxi* (personal relationships or good connections) has become a way of doing business within the country and for individuals to advance their careers in what is becoming a more open market society. Understanding the importance of guanxi is critical for foreign firms doing business in China.[64]

2-3e The Technological Segment

Pervasive and diversified in scope, technological changes affect many parts of societies. These effects occur primarily through new products, processes, and materials. The **technological segment** includes the institutions and activities involved in creating new knowledge and translating that knowledge into new outputs, products, processes, and materials.

Given the rapid pace of technological change and risk of disruption, it is vital for firms to thoroughly study the technological segment.[65] The importance of these efforts is suggested

The **technological segment** includes the institutions and activities involved in creating new knowledge and translating that knowledge into new outputs, products, processes, and materials.

by the finding that early adopters of new technology often achieve higher market shares and earn higher returns. Thus, both large and small firms should continuously scan the general environment to identify potential substitutes for technologies that are in current use, as well as to identify newly emerging technologies from which their firm could derive competitive advantage.[66]

As a significant technological development, the Internet offers firms a remarkable capability in terms of their efforts to scan, monitor, forecast, and assess conditions in their general environment. Companies continue to study the Internet's capabilities to anticipate how it may allow them to create more value for customers in the future and to anticipate future trends.

Additionally, the Internet generates a significant number of opportunities and threats for firms across the world. Predictions about Internet usage in the years to come are one reason for this. By 2016, the estimate is that there will be 3 billion Internet users globally. This is almost one-half of the world's population. Moreover, "the Internet economy will reach $4.2 trillion in the G-20 economies. If it were a national economy, the Internet economy would rank in the world's top five, behind only the U.S., China, Japan, and India, and ahead of Germany."[67] Overall, firms can expect that the future is a time period in which the Internet "will have more users (especially in developing markets), more mobile users, more users using various devices throughout the day, and many more people engaged in an increasingly participatory medium."[68]

In spite of the Internet's far-reaching effects and the opportunities and threats associated with its potential, wireless communication technology is becoming a significant technological opportunity for companies to pursue. Handheld devices and other wireless communications equipment are used to access a variety of network-based services. The use of handheld computers with wireless network connectivity, Web-enabled mobile phone handsets, and other emerging platforms (e.g., consumer Internet-access devices such as the iPhone, iPad, and Kindle) has increased substantially and may soon become the dominant form of communication and commerce. In fact, with each new version of these products, additional functionalities and software applications are generating multiple opportunities—and potential threats—for companies of all types.

2-3f The Global Segment

The **global segment** includes relevant new global markets, existing markets that are changing, important international political events, and critical cultural and institutional characteristics of global markets.[69] For example, firms competing in the automobile industry must study the global segment. The fact that consumers in multiple nations are willing to buy cars and trucks "from whatever area of the world"[70] supports this position.

When studying the global segment, firms (including automobile manufacturers) should recognize that globalization of business markets may create opportunities to enter new markets as well as threats that new competitors from other economies may also enter their market. In terms of an opportunity for automobile manufacturers, the possibility for these firms to sell their products outside of their home market would seem attractive. But what markets might firms choose to enter? Currently, Brazil, Russia, India, China, and to a lesser extent Indonesia and Malaysia are nations in which automobile and truck sales are expected to increase. In contract, sales are expected to decline, at least in the near term, in Europe and Japan. These expectations suggest the most and least attractive markets for automobile manufacturers desiring to sell outside their domestic market. At the same time, from the perspective of a threat, Japan, Germany, Korea, Spain, France, and the United States are nations in which there appears to be excess production capacity in the automobile manufacturing industry. In turn, overcapacity signals the possibility that companies based in markets where this is the case will simultaneously attempt to increase their exports as well

The **global segment** includes relevant new global markets, existing markets that are changing, important international political events, and critical cultural and institutional characteristics of global markets.

as sales in their domestic market.[71] Thus, global automobile manufacturers should carefully examine the global segment in order to precisely identify all opportunities and threats.

In light of threats associated with participating in international markets, some firms choose to take a more cautious approach to globalization. These firms participate in what some refer to as *globalfocusing*. Globalfocusing often is used by firms with moderate levels of international operations who increase their internationalization by focusing on global niche markets.[72] This approach allows firms to build on and use their core competencies while limiting their risks within the niche market. Another way in which firms limit their risks in international markets is to focus their operations and sales in one region of the world.[73] Success with these efforts finds a firm building relationships in and knowledge of its markets. As the firm builds these strengths, rivals find it more difficult to enter its markets and compete successfully.

Firms competing in global markets should recognize each market's sociocultural and institutional attributes. For example, Korean ideology emphasizes communitarianism, a characteristic of many Asian countries. Alternatively, the ideology in China calls for an emphasis on *guanxi*—personal connections—while in Japan, the focus is on *wa*, or group harmony and social cohesion.[74] The institutional context of China suggests a major emphasis on centralized planning by the government. The Chinese government provides incentives to firms to develop alliances with foreign firms having sophisticated technology in hopes of building knowledge and introducing new technologies to the Chinese markets over time.[75] As such, it is important to analyze the strategic intent of foreign firms when pursuing alliances and joint ventures abroad, especially where the local partners are receiving technology which may in the long run reduce the foreign firms' advantages.[76]

Increasingly, the *informal economy* as it exits throughout the world is another aspect of the global segment requiring analysis. Growing in size, this economy has implications for firms' competitive actions and responses in that increasingly firms competing in the formal economy (defined in the Strategic Focus) will find that they are competing against informal economy companies as well. We provide additional insights about the informal economy in the Strategic Focus.

2-3g The Physical Environment Segment

The **physical environment segment** refers to potential and actual changes in the physical environment and business practices that are intended to positively respond to and deal with those changes.[77] Concerned with trends oriented to sustaining the world's physical environment, firms recognize that ecological, social, and economic systems interactively influence what happens in this particular segment and that they are part of an interconnected global society.[78]

Companies across the globe are concerned about the physical environment and many record the actions they are taking in reports with names such as "Sustainability" and "Corporate Social Responsibility." Moreover and in a comprehensive sense, an increasing number of companies are interested in sustainable development, which is "the development that meets the needs of the present without compromising the ability of future generations to meet their own needs."[79]

There are many parts or attributes of the physical environment that firms consider as they try to identify trends in the physical environment segment.[80] For example, McDonald's seeks to become a sustainable influence on the global food industry. Receiving certification from the Marine Stewardship Council (MCS) for its U.S. supply signals that the company is sourcing fish from "suppliers that follow strict MSC standards for ecosystem impact, management, and health of fish stock."[81] As the world's largest retailer, Walmart's environmental footprint is huge, meaning that trends in the physical environment can significantly affect this firm and how it chooses to operate. Perhaps in light of trends occurring in the physical environment, Walmart has announced that its goal is to produce zero waste and to use 100 percent renewable energy to power its operations.[82]

Strategy Right NOW

Learn more about Spain's Informal Economy.
www.cengagebrain.com

The **physical environment segment** refers to potential and actual changes in the physical environment and business practices that are intended to positively respond to and deal with those changes.

M. Stasy

Strategic Focus   GLOBALIZATION

The Informal Economy: What It Is and Why It Is Important

The informal economy refers to commercial activities that occur at least partly outside a governing body's observation, taxation, and regulation. In slightly different words, sociologists Manuel Castells and Alejandro Portes suggest that the "informal economy is characterized by one central feature: it is unregulated by the institutions of society in a legal and social environment in which similar activities are regulated." Firms located in the informal economy are typically thought of as businesses that are unregistered but that are producing and selling legal products. In contrast to the informal economy, the formal economy is comprised of commercial activities that a governing body taxes and monitors for society's benefit and whose outputs are included in a country's gross domestic product.

For some, working in the informal economy is a choice, such as is the case when individuals decide to supplement the income they are earning through employment in the formal economy with a second job in the informal economy. However, for most people working in the informal economy is a necessity rather than a choice—a reality that contributes to the informal economy's size and significance. Although generalizing about the quality of informal employment is difficult, evidence suggests that it typically means poor employment conditions and greater poverty for workers.

Estimates of the informal economy's size across countries and regions vary. In developing countries, the informal economy accounts for as much as three-quarters of all nonagricultural employment, and perhaps as much as 90 percent in some countries in South Asia and sub-Saharan Africa. But the informal economy is also prominent in developed countries such as Finland, Germany, and France (where this economy is estimated to account for 18.3 percent, 16.3 percent, and 15.3 percent, respectively, of these nations' total economic activity). In the United States, recent estimates are that the informal economy is now generating as much as $2 trillion in economic activity on an annual basis. This is double the size of the U.S. informal economy

in 2009. In terms of the number of people working in an informal economy, we can consider the suggestion that "India's informal economy…(includes) hundreds of millions of shopkeepers, farmers, construction workers, taxi drivers, street vendors, rag pickers, tailors, repairmen, middlemen, black marketers and more."

There are various causes of the informal economy's growth, including an inability of a nation's economic environment to create a significant number of jobs relative to available workers. This has been a particularly acute problem during the recent global recession. In the words of a person living in Spain: "Without the underground (informal) economy, we would be in a situation of probably violent social unrest." Governments' inability to facilitate growth efforts in their nation's economic environment is another issue. In this regard, another Spanish citizen suggests that "What the government should focus on is reforming the formal economy to make it more efficient and competitive."

In a general sense, the informal economy yields threats and opportunities for formal economy firms. One threat is that informal businesses may have a cost advantage when competing against formal economy firms in that they do not pay taxes or incur the costs of regulations. But the informal economy surfaces opportunities as well. For example, formal economy firms can try to understand the needs of customers that informal economy firms are satisfying and then find ways to better meet their needs. Another valuable opportunity is to attract some of the informal economy's talented human capital to accept positions of employment in formal economy firms.

Sources: A. Picchi, 2013, A shadow economy may be keeping the US afloat, *MSN Money*, www.msn.com, May 3; 2013, Meeting on informal economy statistics: Country experience, international recommendations, and application, *United Nations Economic Commission for Africa*, www.uneca.org, April; 2013, About the informal economy, *Women in informal employment: Globalizing and organizing*, www.wiego.org, May; G. Bruton, R. D. Ireland, & D. J. Ketchen, Jr., 2012, Toward a research agenda on the informal economy, *Academy of Management Perspectives*, 26(3): 1–11; R. D. Ireland, 2012, 2012 program theme: The informal economy, *Academy of Management*, www.meeting. aomonline.org, March; R. Minder, 2012, In Spain, jobless find a refuge off the books, *New York Times*, www.nytimes.com, May 18.

As our discussion of the general environment shows, identifying anticipated changes and trends among segments and their elements is a key objective of analyzing this environment. With a focus on the future, the analysis of the general environment allows firms to identify opportunities and threats. It is necessary to have a top management team with the experience, knowledge, and sensitivity required to effectively analyze a firm's general environment.[83] Also critical to a firm's choices of strategies and their associated competitive actions and responses is an understanding of its industry environment and its competitors; next, we discuss the analyses firms complete to gain such an understanding.

2-4 Industry Environment Analysis

An **industry** is a group of firms producing products that are close substitutes. In the course of competition, these firms influence one another. Typically, companies use a rich mix of different competitive strategies to pursue above-average returns when competing in a particular industry. An industry's structural characteristics influence a firm's choice of strategies.[84]

Compared with the general environment, the industry environment (measured primarily in the form of its characteristics) has a more direct effect on the competitive actions and responses a firm takes to succeed.[85] To study an industry, the firm examines five forces that affect the ability of all firms to operate profitably within a given industry. Shown in Figure 2.2, the five forces are: the threats posed by new entrants, the power of suppliers, the power of buyers, product substitutes, and the intensity of rivalry among competitors.

The five forces of competition model depicted in Figure 2.2 expands the scope of a firm's competitive analysis. Historically, when studying the competitive environment, firms concentrated on companies with which they directly competed. However, firms must search more broadly to recognize current and potential competitors by identifying potential customers as well as the firms serving them. For example, the communications industry is now broadly defined as encompassing media companies, telecoms, entertainment companies, and companies producing devices such as smartphones.[86] In such an environment, firms must study many other industries to identify companies with capabilities (especially technology-based capabilities) that might be the foundation for producing a good or a service that can compete against what they are producing.

When studying the industry environment, firms must also recognize that suppliers can become a firm's competitors (by integrating forward) as can buyers (by integrating

Figure 2.2 The Five Forces of Competition Model

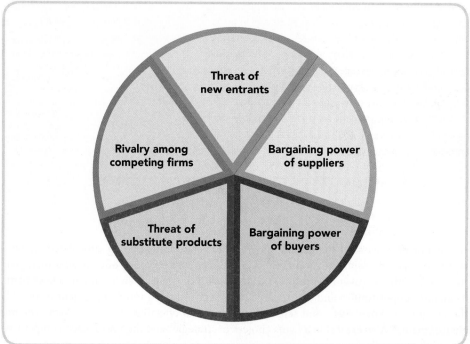

An **industry** is a group of firms producing products that are close substitutes.

© Cengage Learning

backward). For example, several firms have integrated forward in the pharmaceutical industry by acquiring distributors or wholesalers. In addition, firms choosing to enter a new market and those producing products that are adequate substitutes for existing products can become a company's competitors.

Next, we examine the five forces the firm analyzes to understand the profitability potential within an industry (or a segment of an industry) in which it competes or may choose to compete.

2-4a Threat of New Entrants

Identifying new entrants is important because they can threaten the market share of existing competitors.[87] One reason new entrants pose such a threat is that they bring additional production capacity. Unless the demand for a good or service is increasing, additional capacity holds consumers' costs down, resulting in less revenue and lower returns for competing firms. Often, new entrants have a keen interest in gaining a large market share. As a result, new competitors may force existing firms to be more efficient and to learn how to compete in new dimensions (e.g., using an Internet-based distribution channel).

The likelihood that firms will enter an industry is a function of two factors: barriers to entry and the retaliation expected from current industry participants. Entry barriers make it difficult for new firms to enter an industry and often place them at a competitive disadvantage even when they are able to enter. As such, high entry barriers tend to increase the returns for existing firms in the industry and may allow some firms to dominate the industry.[88] Thus, firms competing successfully in an industry want to maintain high entry barriers in order to discourage potential competitors from deciding to enter the industry.

Barriers to Entry

Firms competing in an industry (and especially those earning above-average returns) try to develop entry barriers to thwart potential competitors. In general, more is known about entry barriers (with respect to how they are developed as well as paths firms can pursue to overcome them) in industrialized countries such as those in North America and Western Europe. In contrast, relatively little is known about barriers to entry in the rapidly emerging markets such as those in China. However, recent research suggests that Chinese executives perceive that advertising effects are the most significant of seven barriers to China while capital requirements are viewed as the least important.[89]

There are different kinds of barriers to entering a market that firms study when examining an industry environment. Companies competing within a particular industry study these barriers to determine the degree to which their competitive position reduces the likelihood of new competitors being able to enter the industry for the purpose of competing against them. Firms considering entering an industry study entry barriers to determine the likelihood of being able to identify an attractive competitive position within the industry being analyzed. Next, we discuss several significant entry barriers that may discourage competitors from entering a market and that may facilitate a firm's ability to remain competitive in a market in which it currently competes.

Economies of Scale *Economies of scale* are derived from incremental efficiency improvements through experience as a firm grows larger. Therefore, the cost of producing each unit declines as the quantity of a product produced during a given period increases. A new entrant is unlikely to quickly generate the level of demand for its product that in turn would allow it to develop economies of scale.

Economies of scale can be developed in most business functions, such as marketing, manufacturing, research and development, and purchasing.[90] Firms sometimes form strategic alliances or joint ventures to gain scale economies. This is the case for Mitsubishi Heavy Industries Ltd. and Hitachi Ltd., as these companies "merged their operations for fossil-fuel-based power systems into a joint venture aimed at gaining scale to compete against global rivals."[91]

Becoming more flexible in terms of being able to meet shifts in customer demand is another benefit for an industry incumbent and another possible entry barrier for the firm thinking of entering an industry. For example, a firm may choose to reduce its price with the intention of capturing a larger share of the market. Alternatively, it may keep its price constant to increase profits. In so doing, it likely will increase its free cash flow, which is very helpful during financially challenging times.

Some competitive conditions reduce the ability of economies of scale to create an entry barrier. Many companies now customize their products for large numbers of small customer groups. In these cases, customized products are not manufactured in the volumes necessary to achieve economies of scale. Customization is made possible by several factors including flexible manufacturing systems (this point is discussed further in Chapter 4). In fact, the new manufacturing technology facilitated by advanced information systems has allowed the development of mass customization in an increasing number of industries. Although it is not appropriate for all products and implementing it can be challenging, mass customization has become increasingly common in manufacturing products.[92] Online ordering has enhanced customers' ability to buy customized products. Companies manufacturing customized products learn how to respond quickly to customers' needs in lieu of developing scale economies.

Product Differentiation Over time, customers may come to believe that a firm's product is unique. This belief can result from the firm's service to the customer, effective advertising campaigns, or being the first to market a good or service. Greater levels of perceived product uniqueness create customers who consistently purchase a firm's products. To combat the perception of uniqueness, new entrants frequently offer products at lower prices. This decision, however, may result in lower profits or even losses.

As noted in the Opening Case, Coca-Cola Company and PepsiCo have established strong brands in the markets in which they compete, and these companies compete against each other in countries throughout the world. Because each of these competitors has allocated a significant amount of resources over many decades to build its brands, customer loyalty is strong for each firm. When considering entry into the soft drink market, a potential entrant would be well advised to pause to determine actions it would take for the purpose of trying to overcome the brand image and consumer loyalty each of these giants possess.

Capital Requirements Competing in a new industry requires a firm to have resources to invest. In addition to physical facilities, capital is needed for inventories, marketing activities, and other critical business functions. Even when a new industry is attractive, the capital required for successful market entry may not be available to pursue the market opportunity.[93] For example, defense industries are difficult to enter because of the substantial resource investments required to be competitive. In addition, because of the high knowledge requirements of the defense industry, a firm might acquire an existing company as a means of entering this industry, but it must have access to the capital necessary to do this.

Switching Costs Switching costs are the one-time costs customers incur when they buy from a different supplier. The costs of buying new ancillary equipment and of retraining employees, and even the psychic costs of ending a relationship, may be incurred in switching to a new supplier. In some cases, switching costs are low, such as when the consumer switches to a different brand of soft drink. Switching costs can vary as a function of time as shown by the fact that in terms of credit hours toward graduation, the cost to a student to transfer from one university to another as a freshman is much lower than it is when the student is entering the senior year.

Occasionally, a decision made by manufacturers to produce a new, innovative product creates high switching costs for customers. Customer loyalty programs, such as airlines' frequent flyer miles, are intended to increase the customer's switching costs. If switching costs are high, a new entrant must offer either a sub-stantially lower price or a much better product to attract buyers. Usually, the more established the relationships between parties, the greater the switching costs.

Access to Distribution Channels   Over time, industry participants commonly learn how to effectively distribute their products. Once a relationship with its distributors has been built a firm will nurture it, thus creating switching costs for the distributors. Access to distribution channels can be a strong entry barrier for new entrants, particularly in consumer nondurable goods industries (e.g., in grocery stores where shelf space is limited) and in international markets. New entrants have to persuade distributors to carry their products, either in addition to or in place of those currently distributed. Price breaks and cooperative advertising allowances may be used for this purpose; however, those practices reduce the new entrant's profit potential. Interestingly, access to distribution is less of a barrier for products that can be sold on the Internet.

The Naked Grocer provides boxes of assorted, locally sourced vegetables to order. By offering locally-sourced produce the company is trying to reduce the strategic relevance of advantages possessed by established firms.

Cost Disadvantages Independent of Scale   Sometimes, established competitors have cost advantages that new entrants cannot duplicate. Proprietary product technology, favor-able access to raw materials, desirable locations, and government subsidies are examples. Successful competition requires new entrants to reduce the strategic relevance of these fac-tors. For example, delivering purchases directly to the buyer can counter the advantage of a desirable location; new food establishments in an undesirable location often follow this practice. Zara is owned by Inditex, the largest fashion clothing retailer in the world.[94] From the time of its launching, Spanish clothing company Zara relied on classy, well-tailored, and relatively inexpensive items that were produced and sold by adhering to ethical practices to successfully enter the highly competitive global clothing market and overcome that market's entry barriers.[95]

Government Policy   Through their decisions about issues such as the granting of licenses and permits, governments can also control entry into an industry. Liquor retail-ing, radio and TV broadcasting, banking, and trucking are examples of industries in which government decisions and actions affect entry possibilities. Also, governments often restrict entry into some industries because of the need to provide quality service or the desire to protect jobs. Alternatively, deregulating industries such as the airline and utilities industries in the United States, generally results in additional firms choosing to enter and compete within an industry.[96] Governmental decisions and policies regarding antitrust issues also affect entry barriers. For example, in the United States, the Antitrust Division of the Justice Department or the Federal Trade Commission will sometimes disallow a proposed merger because officials conclude that approving it would create a firm that is too dominant in an industry and would thus create unfair competition.[97] Such a negative ruling would obviously be an entry barrier for an acquiring firm.

Expected Retaliation

Companies seeking to enter an industry also anticipate the reactions of firms in the indus-try. An expectation of swift and vigorous competitive responses reduces the likelihood of entry. Vigorous retaliation can be expected when the existing firm has a major stake in the industry (e.g., it has fixed assets with few, if any, alternative uses), when it has substantial resources, and when industry growth is slow or constrained. For example, any firm attempting to enter the airline industry can expect significant retaliation from existing competitors due to overcapacity.

Locating market niches not being served by incumbents allows the new entrant to avoid entry barriers. Small entrepreneurial firms are generally best suited for identifying and serving neglected market segments. When Honda first entered the U.S. motorcycle market, it concentrated on small-engine motorcycles, a market that firms such as Harley-Davidson ignored. By targeting this neglected niche, Honda initially avoided a significant amount of head-to-head competition with well-established competitors. After consolidating its position, Honda used its strength to attack rivals by introducing larger motorcycles and competing in the broader market.

2-4b Bargaining Power of Suppliers

Increasing prices and reducing the quality of their products are potential means suppliers use to exert power over firms competing within an industry. If a firm is unable to recover cost increases by its suppliers through its own pricing structure, its profitability is reduced by its suppliers' actions. A supplier group is powerful when

- It is dominated by a few large companies and is more concentrated than the industry to which it sells.
- Satisfactory substitute products are not available to industry firms.
- Industry firms are not a significant customer for the supplier group.
- Suppliers' goods are critical to buyers' marketplace success.
- The effectiveness of suppliers' products has created high switching costs for industry firms.
- It poses a credible threat to integrate forward into the buyers' industry. Credibility is enhanced when suppliers have substantial resources and provide a highly differentiated product.

The airline industry is one in which suppliers' bargaining power is changing. Though the number of suppliers is low, the demand for major aircraft is also relatively low. Boeing and Airbus aggressively compete for orders of major aircraft, creating more power for buyers in the process. When a large airline signals that it might place a "significant" order for wide-body airliners that either Airbus or Boeing might produce, both companies are likely to battle for the business and include a financing arrangement, highlighting the buyer's power in the potential transaction.

2-4c Bargaining Power of Buyers

Firms seek to maximize the return on their invested capital. Alternatively, buyers (customers of an industry or a firm) want to buy products at the lowest possible price—the point at which the industry earns the lowest acceptable rate of return on its invested capital. To reduce their costs, buyers bargain for higher quality, greater levels of service, and lower prices.[98] These outcomes are achieved by encouraging competitive battles among the industry's firms. Customers (buyer groups) are powerful when

- They purchase a large portion of an industry's total output.
- The sales of the product being purchased account for a significant portion of the seller's annual revenues.
- They could switch to another product at little, if any, cost.
- The industry's products are undifferentiated or standardized, and the buyers pose a credible threat if they were to integrate backward into the sellers' industry.

Consumers armed with greater amounts of information about the manufacturer's costs and the power of the Internet as a shopping and distribution alternative have increased bargaining power in many industries.

2-4d Threat of Substitute Products

Substitute products are goods or services from outside a given industry that perform similar or the same functions as a product that the industry produces. For example, as a sugar substitute, NutraSweet (and other sugar substitutes) places an upper limit on sugar manufacturers' prices—NutraSweet and sugar perform the same function, though with different characteristics. Other product substitutes include e-mail and fax machines instead of overnight deliveries, plastic containers rather than glass jars, and tea instead of coffee.

Newspaper firms have experienced significant circulation declines over the past decade or more. The declines are a result of the ready availability of substitute outlets for news including Internet sources, cable television news channels, and e-mail and cell phone alerts. Likewise, satellite TV and cable and telecommunication companies provide substitute services for basic media services such as television, Internet, and phone. Tablets such as the iPad are reducing the number of PCs sold as suggested by the fact that worldwide shipments of PCs declined 14 percent during the first quarter of 2013 compared to the same quarter a year earlier. At the same time, "tablets like Apple's iPad flew off the shelves."[99]

In general, product substitutes present a strong threat to a firm when customers face few if any switching costs and when the substitute product's price is lower or its quality and performance capabilities are equal to or greater than those of the competing product. Differentiating a product along dimensions that are valuable to customers (such as quality, service after the sale, and location) reduces a substitute's attractiveness.

Learn more about Substitute Products.
www.cengagebrain.com

2-4e Intensity of Rivalry among Competitors

Because an industry's firms are mutually dependent, actions taken by one company usually invite responses. In many industries, firms actively compete against one another. Competitive rivalry intensifies when a firm is challenged by a competitor's actions or when a company recognizes an opportunity to improve its market position.

Firms within industries are rarely homogeneous; they differ in resources and capabilities and seek to differentiate themselves from competitors. Typically, firms seek to differentiate their products from competitors' offerings in ways that customers value and in which the firms have a competitive advantage. Common dimensions on which rivalry is based include price, service after the sale, and innovation.

Next, we discuss the most prominent factors that experience shows affect the intensity of rivalries among firms.

Numerous or Equally Balanced Competitors

Intense rivalries are common in industries with many companies. With multiple competitors, it is common for a few firms to believe they can act without eliciting a response. However, evidence suggests that other firms generally are aware of competitors' actions, often choosing to respond to them. At the other extreme, industries with only a few firms of equivalent size and power also tend to have strong rivalries. The large and often similar-sized resource bases of these firms permit vigorous actions and responses. The competitive battles between Airbus and Boeing exemplify intense rivalry between relatively equal competitors, especially as airlines place bids for the new wide-body planes they are producing. As discussed in the Opening Case, Coca-Cola Company and PepsiCo have a strong rivalry in an array of liquid drinks as consumers demand great taste and real health benefits.[100]

M. Stasy

Slow Industry Growth

When a market is growing, firms try to effectively use resources to serve an expanding customer base. Markets increasing in size reduce the pressure to take customers from competitors. However, rivalry in no-growth or slow-growth markets becomes more intense as firms battle to increase their market shares by attracting competitors' customers. Certainly, this has been the case in the fast-food industry as McDonald's, Wendy's, and Burger King use their resources, capabilities, and core competencies to try to win each other's customers.[101] The instability in the market that results from these competitive engagements may reduce the profitability for all firms engaging in such battles.

High Fixed Costs or High Storage Costs

When fixed costs account for a large part of total costs, companies try to maximize the use of their productive capacity. Doing so allows the firm to spread costs across a larger volume of output. However, when many firms attempt to maximize their productive capacity, excess capacity is created on an industry-wide basis. To then reduce inventories, individual companies typically cut the price of their product and offer rebates and other special discounts to customers. However, doing this often intensifies competition. The pattern of excess capacity at the industry level followed by intense rivalry at the firm level is frequently observed in industries with high storage costs. Perishable products, for example, lose their value rapidly with the passage of time. As their inventories grow, producers of perishable goods often use pricing strategies to sell products quickly.

Lack of Differentiation or Low Switching Costs

When buyers find a differentiated product that satisfies their needs, they frequently purchase the product loyally over time. Industries with many companies that have successfully differentiated their products have less rivalry, resulting in lower competition for individual firms. Firms that develop and sustain a differentiated product that cannot be easily imitated by competitors often earn higher returns. However, when buyers view products as commodities (i.e., as products with few differentiated features or capabilities), rivalry intensifies. In these instances, buyers' purchasing decisions are based primarily on price and, to a lesser degree, service. Personal computers are a commodity product and the cost to switch from a computer manufactured by one firm to another is low. Thus, the rivalry among Dell, Hewlett-Packard, Lenovo, and other computer manufacturers is strong as these companies consistently seek to find ways to differentiate their offerings.

High Strategic Stakes

Competitive rivalry is likely to be high when it is important for several of the competitors to perform well in the market. Competing in diverse businesses (such as semiconductors, petrochemicals, fashion, medicine, and skyscraper and plant construction, among others), Samsung has now become a formidable foe for Apple in the global smartphone market. Samsung has committed a significant amount of resources to develop innovative products as the foundation for its efforts to try to outperform Apple in selling this particular product. The fact that the end of the first quarter of 2013 found Samsung holding 33 percent of the global smartphone market compared to an 18 percent share for Apple seemed to suggest that the firm's commitment was yielding desirable outcomes.[102] However, this market is extremely important to Apple as well, suggesting that the smartphone rivalry between these two firms (along with others) will remain quite intense.

High strategic stakes can also exist in terms of geographic locations. For example, a number of automobile manufacturers have committed or are committing to establishing manufacturing facilities in China, which has been the world's largest car market since 2009.[103] General Motors recently announced that it received permission from Chinese authorities to build an 8 billion yuan ($1.3 billion) factory to manufacture its Cadillac brand. The Shanghai GM joint venture is to build this facility.[104] Because of the high stakes involved in China for both General Motors and other firms producing luxury cars (including Audi, BMW, and Mercedes-Benz), rivalry among these firms in this market is quite intense.

High Exit Barriers

Sometimes companies continue competing in an industry even though the returns on their invested capital are low or negative. Firms making this choice likely face high exit barriers, which include economic, strategic, and emotional factors causing them to remain in an industry when the profitability of doing so is questionable.

Exit barriers are especially high in the airline industry. Profitability in this industry has been very difficult to achieve since the start of the latest global financial crisis (beginning in roughly late 2007 or early 2008). However, profits in the airline industry were expected to increase by approximately 40 percent in 2013 compared to 2012. Industry consolidation and efficiency enhancements to how airline alliances integrate their activities helped reduce airline companies' costs while improving economic conditions in a number of countries. This resulted in a greater demand for travel. These are positive signs, at least in the short run, for these firms given that they do indeed face very high barriers if they were to contemplate leaving the airline travel industry.[105] Common exit barriers that firms face include the following:

- Specialized assets (assets with values linked to a particular business or location)
- Fixed costs of exit (such as labor agreements)
- Strategic interrelationships (relationships of mutual dependence, such as those between one business and other parts of a company's operations, including shared facilities and access to financial markets)
- Emotional barriers (aversion to economically justified business decisions because of fear for one's own career, loyalty to employees, and so forth)
- Government and social restrictions (often based on government concerns for job losses and regional economic effects; more common outside the United States).

2-5 Interpreting Industry Analyses

Effective industry analyses are products of careful study and interpretation of data and information from multiple sources. A wealth of industry-specific data is available for firms to analyze for the purpose of better understanding an industry's competitive realities. Because of globalization, international markets and rivalries must be included in the firm's analyses. And, because of the development of global markets, a country's borders no longer restrict industry structures. In fact, in general, entering international markets enhances the chances of success for new ventures as well as more established firms.[106]

Analysis of the five forces within a given industry allows the firm to determine the industry's attractiveness in terms of the potential to earn average or above-average returns. In general, the stronger the competitive forces, the lower the potential for firms to generate profits by implementing their strategies. An unattractive industry has low entry barriers, suppliers and buyers with strong bargaining positions, strong competitive threats from product substitutes, and intense rivalry among competitors. These industry characteristics make it difficult for firms to achieve strategic competitiveness and earn above-average returns. Alternatively, an attractive industry has high entry barriers, suppliers and buyers with little bargaining power, few competitive threats from product substitutes, and relatively moderate rivalry.[107] Next, we explain strategic groups as an aspect of industry competition.

**Find out more
about Mercedes.**
www.cengagebrain.com

2-6   Strategic Groups

A set of firms emphasizing similar strategic dimensions and using a similar strategy is called a **strategic group**.[108] The competition between firms within a strategic group is greater than the competition between a member of a strategic group and companies outside that strategic group. Therefore, intra-strategic group competition is more intense than is inter-strategic group competition. In fact, more heterogeneity is evident in the performance of firms within strategic groups than across the groups. The performance leaders within groups are able to follow strategies similar to those of other firms in the group and yet maintain strategic distinctiveness as a foundation for earning above-average returns.[109]

The extent of technological leadership, product quality, pricing policies, distribution channels, and customer service are examples of strategic dimensions that firms in a strategic group may treat similarly. Thus, membership in a particular strategic group defines the essential characteristics of the firm's strategy.[110]

The notion of strategic groups can be useful for analyzing an industry's competitive structure. Such analyses can be helpful in diagnosing competition, positioning, and the profitability of firms competing within an industry.[111] High mobility barriers, high rivalry, and low resources among the firms within an industry limit the formation of strategic groups.[112] However, after strategic groups are formed, their membership remains relatively stable over time.[113] Using strategic groups to understand an industry's competitive structure requires the firm to plot companies' competitive actions and responses along strategic dimensions such as pricing decisions, product quality, distribution channels, and so forth. This type of analysis shows the firm how certain companies are competing similarly in terms of how they use similar strategic dimensions.

Strategic groups have several implications. First, because firms within a group offer similar products to the same customers, the competitive rivalry among them can be intense. The more intense the rivalry, the greater the threat to each firm's profitability. Second, the strengths of the five forces differ across strategic groups. Third, the closer the strategic groups are in terms of their strategies, the greater is the likelihood of rivalry between the groups.

German-based car manufacturers Audi (a part of the Volkswagen group), Bayerische Motoren Werke AG (BMW), and Daimler-Benz (Mercedes-Benz) implement similar strategies (based on the differentiation business-level strategy), emphasize similar strategic dimensions, and compete aggressively against each other. These three firms constitute a strategic group (in the performance/luxury segment) as do Maruti-Suzuki, Tata Motors, and Skoda (these three firms form a passenger car strategic group with the distinctive feature that they sell their products primarily in their domestic markets and very little internationally). We describe the strategic group featuring the three German companies in the Strategic Focus.

2-7   Competitor Analysis

The competitor environment is the final part of the external environment requiring study. Competitor analysis focuses on each company against which a firm competes directly. Coca-Cola Company and PepsiCo, Home Depot and Lowe's, Carrefour SA and Tesco PLC, and Boeing and Airbus are examples of competitors who are keenly interested in understanding each other's objectives, strategies, assumptions, and capabilities. Indeed, intense rivalry creates a strong need to understand competitors.[114] In a competitor analysis, the firm seeks to understand the following:

▪   What drives the competitor, as shown by its *future objectives*
▪   What the competitor is doing and can do, as revealed by its *current strategy*

A set of firms emphasizing similar strategic dimensions and using a similar strategy is called a **strategic group**.

M. Stasy

Strategic Focus　　　　GLOBALIZATION

German Performance/Luxury Cars: If You Have Seen One, Have You Seen Them All?

Audi, BMW, and Mercedes-Benz (Mercedes) have long competed against each other in the performance/luxury segment of the automobile industry. Given that they implement similar strategies in many of the same markets throughout the world and emphasize similar dimensions to do so, these firms form a strategic group. This means that the rivalry within this group is more intense than is the rivalry between members of this group and companies offering products that are intended to functionally serve and satisfy a mass-market appeal among large customer groups. One could even argue that three sub-strategic groups exist for these firms in that each offers products in the large, mid-size, and small parts of the performance/luxury segment. (Think of the Audi S8 versus the BMW 7 series versus the S Mercedes series as products through which these firms compete against each other in terms of large performance/luxury cars.)

The similarities among these firms as they compete are extensive. For example, the Chinese and U.S. markets are critical to their success. With respect to China, an analyst recently noted that "BMW, Audi and Daimler's Mercedes-Benz units have benefited as China's fast-growing wealthy population has flocked to high-end cars in recent years." In response to this growth in demand for their products, all three firms are investing billions of dollars to expand production and their sales operations in China.

For the U.S. market, the firms are introducing new models that are intended to significantly expand their sales. One way these competitors are doing this is to offer "lower priced models that would draw younger, less affluent U.S. customers away from mass market brands such as Ford Motor Co., Honda Motor Co., and Toyota Motor Corp." A lower-cost version of the A3 sedan is Audi's initial offering to reach this objective. BMW has developed a new version of its top-selling 3 series sedan (the 320) that will have a base price roughly $4,000 below the currently least expensive car in this series. Similarly, Mercedes intends to offer the CLA, which is a 4-cyclinder car with a base price just below $30,000. Essentially, introducing these products is a strong attempt by the three firms to lower price as an entry barrier to their products among consumers in their 20s, 30s, and early 40s.

These firms are emphasizing similar dimensions or product features to produce these new models as well as some existing ones. For example, diesel engines are important to the companies and their efforts to sell more cars in China, the United

The 2014 CLA 45 AMG Mercedes-Benz is presented at the New York International Auto Show in New York's Javits Center in March 2013. The new addition to Mercedes-Benz' product mix is aimed at customers typically targeted by mass market brands.

States, and other countries as well. Because of this, the three of them recently joined a few other companies to develop a Web site (www.clearlybetterdiesel.org) that touts diesel's benefits of superior fuel economy and a reduced environmental impact. To better serve the needs of younger consumers, all three companies are "re-thinking everything from dashboard entertainment systems to the relative importance of mileage over horsepower to fundamental marketing strategies." An initial outcome from these evaluation processes is a decision to include smartly presented, smartphone-driven multimedia systems in models being developed for the U.S. market.

As is often the case with strategic groups, the one among Audi, BMW, and Mercedes has remained stable over the years. As such, we can anticipate that the rivalry among them will remain intense as they rely on similar strategic dimensions to implement similar strategies.

Sources: C. Carroll, 2013, Audi plans to attract more U.S. buyers with diesels, *Wall Street Journal*, www.wsj.com, February 8; V. Fuhrmans, 2013, Europe bets U.S. auto demand to stay high, *Wall Street Journal*, www.wsj.com, January 16; V. Fuhrmans, 2013, German auto makers to shake up luxury market, *Wall Street Journal*, www.wsj.com, January 14; V. Fuhrmans & F. Geiger, 2013, VW to bolster its output in China, *Wall Street Journal*, www.wsj.com, March 14; F. Geiger, 2013, Daimler boosts investment in China, *Wall Street Journal*, www.wsj.com, February 1; J. W. White, 2013, Beyond boomer buyers: Car makers seek younger crop of customers, *Wall Street Journal*, www.wsj.com, January 16.

© Vividfour / Shutterstock.com; AP Photo/Richard Drew

■ What the competitor believes about the industry, as shown by its *assumptions*

■ What the competitor's capabilities are, as shown by its *strengths* and *weaknesses*.[115]

Knowledge about these four dimensions helps the firm prepare an anticipated response profile for each competitor (see Figure 2.3). The results of an effective competitor analysis help a firm understand, interpret, and predict its competitors' actions and responses. Understanding competitors' actions and responses clearly contributes to the firm's ability to compete successfully within the industry.[116] Interestingly, research suggests that executives often fail to analyze competitors' possible reactions to competitive actions their firm takes,[117] placing their firm at a potential competitive disadvantage as a result.

Critical to an effective competitor analysis is gathering data and information that can help the firm understand its competitors' intentions and the strategic implications resulting from them.[118] Useful data and information combine to form **competitor intelligence**, the set of data and information the firm gathers to better understand and anticipate competitors' objectives, strategies, assumptions, and capabilities. In competitor analysis, the firm gathers intelligence not only about its competitors, but also regarding public policies in countries around the world. Such intelligence facilitates an understanding of the strategic posture of foreign competitors. Through effective competitive and public policy intelligence, the firm gains the insights needed to make effective strategic decisions regarding how to compete against rivals.

When asked to describe competitive intelligence, phrases such as "competitive spying" and "corporate espionage" come to my mind for some. These phrases denote the fact that

Competitor intelligence is the set of data and information the firm gathers to better understand and anticipate competitors' objectives, strategies, assumptions, and capabilities.

Figure 2.3 Competitor Analysis Components

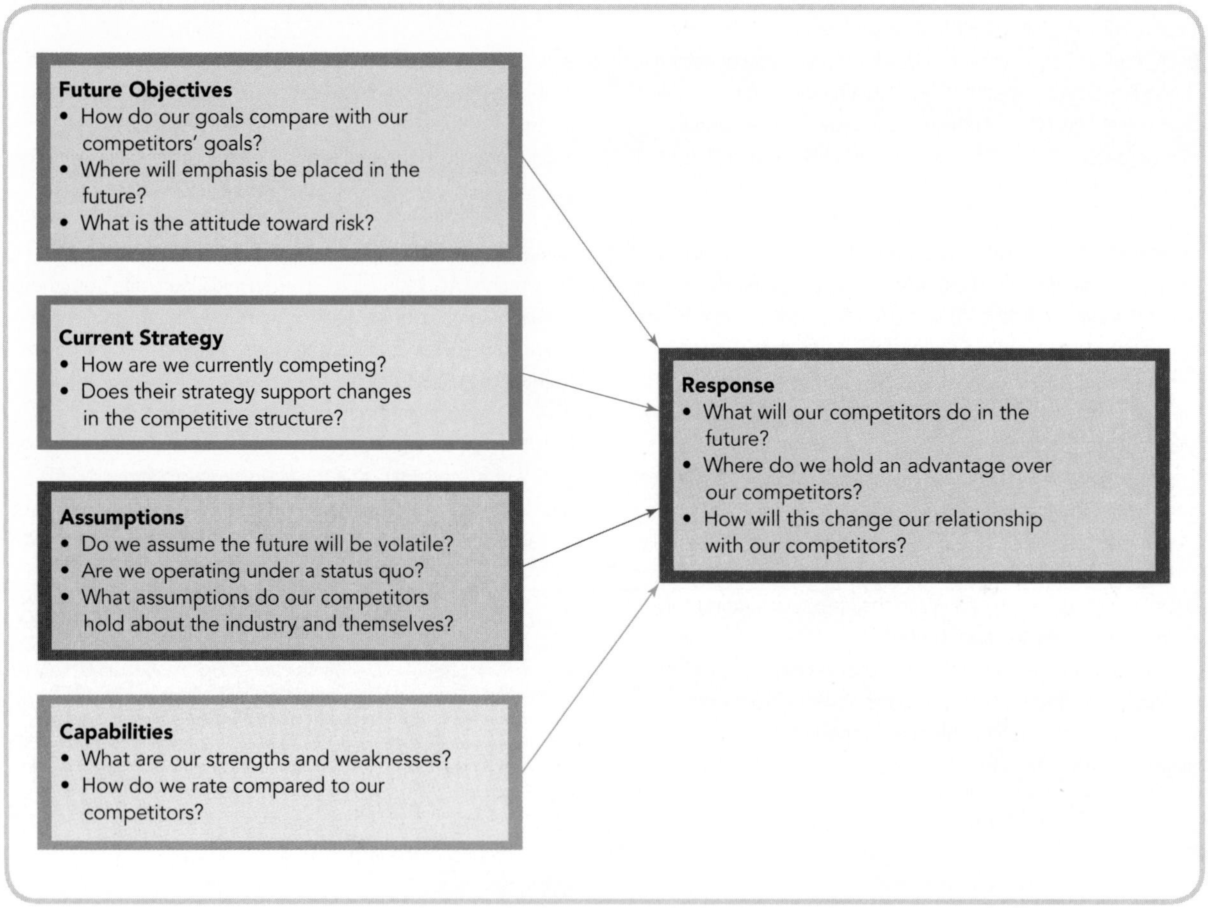

Future Objectives
• How do our goals compare with our competitors' goals?
• Where will emphasis be placed in the future?
• What is the attitude toward risk?

Current Strategy
• How are we currently competing?
• Does their strategy support changes in the competitive structure?

Assumptions
• Do we assume the future will be volatile?
• Are we operating under a status quo?
• What assumptions do our competitors hold about the industry and themselves?

Capabilities
• What are our strengths and weaknesses?
• How do we rate compared to our competitors?

Response
• What will our competitors do in the future?
• Where do we hold an advantage over our competitors?
• How will this change our relationship with our competitors?

© Cengage Learning

competitive intelligence is an activity that appears to involve trade-offs.[119] The reason for this is that "what is ethical in one country is different from what is ethical in other countries." This position implies that the rules of engagement to follow when gathering competitive intelligence change in different contexts.[120] However, firms avoid the possibility of legal entanglements and ethical quandaries only when their competitive intelligence gathering methods are governed by a strict set of legal and ethical guidelines.[121] This means that ethical behavior and actions as well as the mandates of relevant laws and regulations should be the foundation on which a firm's competitive intelligence-gathering process is formed.

When gathering competitive intelligence, firms must also pay attention to the complementors of its products and strategy.[122] **Complementors** are companies or networks of companies that sell goods or services that are compatible with the focal firm's good or service. When a complementor's good or service contributes to the functionality of a focal firm's good or service, it in turn creates additional value for that firm.

There are many examples of firms whose good or service complements other companies' offerings. For example, firms manufacturing affordable home photo printers complement other companies' efforts to sell digital cameras. Intel and Microsoft are perhaps the most widely recognized complementors. The Microsoft slogan "Intel Inside" demonstrates the relationship between two firms who do not directly buy from or sell to each other but whose products have a strong complementary relationship. Gasoline and automobiles are obvious complementors in that gasoline-powered cars are useless without gas while the price of gasoline would decline significantly without cars.

Alliances among airline companies such as Oneworld and Star find member companies sharing their route structures and customer loyalty programs as a means of complementing each other's operations. (Alliances and other cooperative strategies are described in Chapter 9.) In the example we are considering here, each of the two alliances is a network of complementors. American Airlines, British Airways, Finnair, Japan Airlines, and Royal Jordanian are among the airlines forming the Oneworld alliance. Air Canada, Brussels Airlines, Croatia Airlines, Lufthansa, and United Airlines are five of the total of 27 members forming the Star alliance. Both of these alliances constantly adjust their members and services offered to better meet customers' needs. For example, SriLankan Airlines is scheduled to join Oneworld in 2014 while Qatar Airways is to join the alliance in late 2013 or early 2014. In terms of services, the Star alliance announced in May of 2013 that it was expanding its mobile device capabilities by introducing a customized Navigator application for iPads.

As our discussion shows, complementors expand the set of competitors firms must evaluate when completing a competitor analysis. In this sense, American Airlines and United Airlines examine each other both as direct competitors on multiple routes but also as complementors who are part of different alliances (Oneworld for American and Star for United). In all cases though, ethical commitments and actions should be the foundation on which competitor analyses are developed.

2-8 Ethical Considerations

Firms must follow relevant laws and regulations as well as carefully articulated ethical guidelines when gathering competitor intelligence. Industry associations often develop lists of these practices that firms can adopt. Practices considered both legal and ethical include (1) obtaining publicly available information (e.g., court records, competitors' help-wanted advertisements, annual reports, financial reports of publicly held corporations, and Uniform Commercial Code filings) and (2) attending trade fairs and shows to obtain competitors' brochures, view their exhibits, and listen to discussions about their products. In contrast,

Complementors are companies or networks of companies that sell complementary goods or services that are compatible with the focal firm's good or service.

certain practices (including blackmail, trespassing, eavesdropping, and stealing drawings, samples, or documents) are widely viewed as unethical and often are illegal as well.

Some competitor intelligence practices may be legal, but a firm must decide whether they are also ethical, given the image it desires as a corporate citizen. Especially with electronic transmissions, the line between legal and ethical practices can be difficult to determine. For example, a firm may develop Web site addresses that are similar to those of its competitors and thus occasionally receive e-mail transmissions that were intended for those competitors. The practice is an example of the challenges companies face in deciding how to gather intelligence about competitors while simultaneously determining how to prevent competitors from learning too much about them. To deal with these challenges, firms should establish principles and take actions that are consistent with them.

Professional associations are available to firms as sources of information regarding competitive intelligence practices. For example, while pursuing its mission to help firms make "better decisions through competitive intelligence," the association known as the Strategy and Competitive Intelligence Professionals offers codes of professional practice and ethics to firms for their possible use when deciding how to gather competitive intelligence.[123]

Open discussions of intelligence-gathering techniques can help a firm ensure that employees, customers, suppliers, and even potential competitors understand its convictions to follow ethical practices when gathering intelligence about its competitors. An appropriate guideline for competitor intelligence practices is to respect the principles of common morality and the right of competitors not to reveal certain information about their products, operations, and intentions.[124]

SUMMARY

- The firm's external environment is challenging and complex. Because of its effect on performance, the firm must develop the skills required to identify opportunities and threats that are a part of its external environment.

- The external environment has three major parts: (1) the general environment (segments and elements in the broader society that affect industries and the firms competing in them), (2) the industry environment (factors that influence a firm, its competitive actions and responses, and the industry's profitability potential), and (3) the competitor environment (in which the firm analyzes each major competitor's future objectives, current strategies, assumptions, and capabilities).

- Scanning, monitoring, forecasting, and assessing are the four parts of the external environmental analysis process. Effectively using this process helps the firm in its efforts to identify opportunities and threats.

- The general environment has seven segments: demographic, economic, political/legal, sociocultural, technological, global, and physical. For each segment, the firm has to determine the strategic relevance of environmental changes and trends.

- Compared with the general environment, the industry environment has a more direct effect on the firm's competitive actions and responses. The five forces model of competition includes the threat of entry, the power of suppliers, the power of buyers, product substitutes, and the intensity of rivalry among competitors. By studying these forces, the firm finds a position in an industry where it can influence the forces in its favor or where it can buffer itself from the power of the forces to achieve strategic competitiveness and earn above-average returns.

- Industries are populated with different strategic groups. A strategic group is a collection of firms following similar strategies along similar dimensions. Competitive rivalry is greater within a strategic group than between strategic groups.

- Competitor analysis informs the firm about the future objectives, current strategies, assumptions, and capabilities of the companies with which it competes directly. A thorough competitor analysis examines complementors that support forming and implementing rivals' strategies.

- Different techniques are used to create competitor intelligence: the set of data, information, and knowledge that allows the firm to better understand its competitors and thereby predict their likely competitive actions and responses. Firms absolutely should use only legal and ethical practices to gather intelligence. The Internet enhances firms' ability to gather insights about competitors and their strategic intentions.

REVIEW QUESTIONS

1. Why is it important for a firm to study and understand the external environment?

2. What are the differences between the general environment and the industry environment? Why are these differences important?

3. What is the external environmental analysis process (four parts)? What does the firm want to learn when using this process?

4. What are the seven segments of the general environment? Explain the differences among them.

5. How do the five forces of competition in an industry affect its profitability potential? Explain.

6. What is a strategic group? Of what value is knowledge of the firm's strategic group in formulating that firm's strategy?

7. What is the importance of collecting and interpreting data and information about competitors? What practices should a firm use to gather competitor intelligence and why?

EXPERIENTIAL EXERCISES

EXERCISE 1: CREATING A FIVE FORCES INDUSTRY MODEL

The five forces model is designed to better understand the competitive forces in an industry in which a firm competes. For example, if the combination of forces in an industry serves to restrict or reduce profitability, the industry is said to be unattractive. Naturally the inverse is true—if the combined forces serve to improve or increase the firm's chances for profitability, this is said to be an attractive industry in which to compete.

Michael Porter's analysis explores the three horizontal forces (threat of new entrants, threat of substitutes, and threat from rivals) and two vertical forces (bargaining power of buyers and bargaining power of suppliers).

The following exercise asks you to work in teams to evaluate the U.S. automotive industry. Bear in mind you are evaluating an industry and not a particular firm, and your analysis should be positioned to evaluate the industry in which rivals compete in manufacturing and selling cars and trucks. This exercise will be all the more compelling since the industry has undergone some relatively significant economic shifts in the past few years as well as the potential for disruption due to new technology.

Each team will be required to present a summary of its analysis using the following table. As you will note after completing the exercise, a five forces model requires some solid research but also requires judgment and intuition as to how the forces interact. There are relatively few concrete answers to any of the forces. Your team should fill out and hand in the accompanying table along with your supporting analysis.

Once your team has identified and supported its rating for each force, summarize the results and indicate your assessment that the industry is either attractive or unattractive with respect to its profitability potential. Also, be prepared to examine the impact of your analysis on an individual firm in the industry.

EXERCISE 2: WHAT DOES THE FUTURE LOOK LIKE?

A critical ingredient to studying the general environment is identifying opportunities and threats. An opportunity is a condition in the environment that, if exploited, helps a company achieve strategic competitiveness. In order to identify opportunities, you must be aware of trends that affect the world around us now or that are projected to do so in the future.

Thomas Fry, executive director and senior futurist at the DaVinci Institute, believes that the chaotic nature of interconnecting trends and the vast array of possibilities that arise from them are somewhat akin to watching a spinning compass needle. From the way we use phones or e-mail, or how we recruit new workers to organizations, the climate for business is changing and shifting dramatically, and at rapidly increasing rates. Sorting these trends out and making sense of them provides the basis for opportunity decision making. Which ones will dominate and which ones will fade? Understanding this is crucial for business success.

Your challenge (either individually or as a group) is to identify a trend, technology, entertainment mode, or design that is likely to

Overall Rating	Favorable	Team Rating	Unfavorable
Threat of New Entrants	10		1
Intensity of Rivalry	10		1
Threat of Substitutes	10		1
Bargaining Power of Buyers	10		1
Bargaining Power of Suppliers	10		1

alter the way in which business is conducted in the future. Once you have identified this, be prepared to discuss:

- Which of the seven dimensions of the general environment will this affect (may be more than one)?

  - Describe the effect.

  - List some business opportunities that will come from this.

  - Identify some existing organizations that stand to benefit.

  - What, if any, are the ethical implications?

You should consult a wide variety of sources. For example, the Gartner Group and McKinsey & Company both produce market research and forecasts for business. There are also many Web forecasting tools and addresses such as TED (technology, entertainment, design, where you can find videos of their discussions; see www.ted.com), that host an annual conference for path-breaking new ideas. Similarly, the DaVinci Institute and the Institute for Global Futures as well as many others have their own unique vision for tomorrow's environment.

VIDEO CASE ▶

THE NEED TO EXAMINE THE EXTERNAL ENVIRONMENT: DISASTER IN THE GULF THREE-PLUS YEARS LATER

The Gulf Coast oil spill disaster not only resulted in oil and tar balls washing up on local beaches but contributed to the evaporation of the wedding business on the beach. In one family business, 85 percent of the business and $90,000 were lost while the firm received only $20,000 in emergency payments. The first year after the spill, resentful wedding business owners were still living day to day. They contended that British Petroleum (BP), which owned the Deepwater Horizon oil rig where the explosion and subsequent leak occurred, had not fulfilled its obligations to them and their true losses would never be recovered. With government intervention, the $20 billion fund established by BP had paid out only $3.8 billion at the end of the first year. Government attorney Kenneth Feinberg emphasized at that time that 200,000 claimants had been compensated in nine months.

Be prepared to discuss the following concepts and questions in class:

Concepts

- The external environment
- External environmental analysis

- Five forces of competition
- Strategic groups
- Competitor analysis

Questions

1. What parts of the external environment (general, industry, and competitive) do you believe BP considered or didn't consider prior to drilling off the Gulf Coast? What should the wedding business owners now consider in their external environment?

2. How should BP have handled an external environmental analysis and what environmental changes and trends (opportunities and threats) might the firm have discovered?

3. Analyze BP using the five forces of competition model to determine the industry's current attractiveness in terms of profitability potential.

4. Who might be in BP's strategic group and why?

5. What would a competitor of BP now discover about the firm by completing a competitor analysis?

NOTES

1. R. Krause, M. Semadeni, & A. A. Cannella, 2013, External COO/presidents as expert directors: A new look at the service of role of boards, *Strategic Management Journal*, 34: in press; Y. Y. Kor & A. Mesko, 2013, Dynamic managerial capabilities: Configuration and orchestration of top executives' capabilities and the firm's dominant logic, *Strategic Management Journal*, 34: 233–234.

2. R. Kapoor & J. M. Lee, 2013, Coordinating and competing in ecosystems: How organizational forms shape new technology investments, *Strategic Management Journal*, 34: 274–296; M. J. Benner & R. Ranganathan, 2012, Offsetting illegitimacy? How pressures from securities analysts influence incumbents in the face of new technologies, *Academy of Management Journal*, 55: 213–233.

3. A. R. Fremeth & J. M. Shaver, 2013, Strategic rationale for responding to extra-jurisdictional regulation: Evidence from firm adoption of renewable power in the US, *Strategic Management Journal*, 34: in press; E.-H. Kim, 2013, Deregulation and differentiation: Incumbent investment in green technologies, *Strategic Management Journal*, 34: in press.

4. R. J. Sawant, 2012, Asset specificity and corporate political activity in regulated industries, *Academy of Management Review*, 37: 194–210; S. Hanson, A. Kashyap, & J. Stein, 2011, A macroprudential approach to financial regulation. *Journal of Economic Perspectives*, 25(1): 3–28.

5. S. Garg, 2013, Venture boards: Distinctive monitoring and implications for firm performance, *Academy of Management Review*, 38: 90–108; J. Harrison, D. Bosse, & R. Phillips, 2010, Managing for stakeholders, stakeholder utility functions, and competitive advantage, *Strategic Management Journal*, 31(1): 58–74.

6. S. C. Schleimer & T. Pedersen, 2013, The driving forces of subsidiary absorptive capacity, *Journal of Management Studies*, 50: 646–672; M. T. Lucas & O. M. Kirillova, 2011, Reconciling the resource-based and competitive positioning perspectives on manufacturing flexibility, *Journal of Manufacturing Technology Management*, 22(2): 189–203.

7. C. Qian, Q. Cao, & R. Takeuchi, 2013, Top management team functional diversity and organizational innovation in China: The moderating effects of environment, *Strategic Management Journal*, 34: 110–120; L. Fahey, 1999, *Competitors*, New York: John Wiley & Sons.

8. Z. Lindgardt, C. Nettesheim, & T. Chen, 2012, Unlocking growth in the middle, *bcg. perspectives*, www.bcgperspectives.com, May 9.

9. E. V. Karniouchina, S. J. Carson, J. C. Short, & D. J. Ketchen, 2013, Extending the firm vs. industry debate: Does industry life cycle stage matter? *Strategic Management Journal*, 34: in press; B. Larraneta, S. A. Zahra, & J. L. Gonzalez, 2013, Strategic repertoire variety and new venture growth: The moderating effects of origin and industry dynamism, *Strategic Management Journal*, 34: in press.

10. R. B. MacKay & R. Chia, 2013, Choice, chance, and unintended consequences in strategic change: A process understanding of the rise and fall of NorthCo Automotive, *Academy of Management Journal*, 56: 208–230; J. P. Murmann, 2013, The coevolution of industries and important features of their environments, *Organization Science*, 24: 58–78; G. J. Kilduff, H. A. Elfenbein, & B. M. Staw, 2010, The psychology of rivalry: A relationally dependent analysis of competition, *Academy of Management Journal*, 53: 943–969.

11. A. Hecker & A. Ganter, 2013, The influence of product market competition on technological and management innovation: Firm-level evidence from a large-scale survey, *European Management Review*, 10: 17–33; W. K. Smith & M. W. Lewis, 2011, Toward a theory of paradox: A dynamic equilibrium model of organizing, *Academy of Management Review*, 36(2): 381–403.

12. W. Loeb, 2013, Successful global growers: What we can learn from Walmart, Carrefour, Tesco, Metro, *Forbes*, www.forbes.com, March 7.

13. A. Efrati, 2013, Google to fund, develop wireless in networks in emerging markets, *Wall Street Journal*, www.wsj.com, May 24.

14. F. Bridoux & J. W. Stoelhorst, 2013, Microfoundations for stakeholder theory: Managing stakeholders with heterogeneous motives, *Strategic Management Journal*, in press; B. Gilad, 2011, The power of blindspots. What companies don't know, surprises them. What they don't want to know, kills them, *Strategic Direction*, 27(4): 3–4.

15. A. Poon & J. Rossi, 2013, Patent battle between Nokia, HTC heats up, *Wall Street Journal*, www.wsj.com, May 24.

16. J. Rossi, 2013, Jolla set to join global smartphone market, *Wall Street Journal*, www.wsj.com, May 21.

17. D. Li, 2013, Multilateral R&D alliances by new ventures, *Journal of Business Venturing*, 28: 241–260; A. Graefe, S. Luckner, & C. Weinhardt, 2010, Prediction markets for foresight, *Futures*, 42(4): 394–404.

18. J. Tang, K. M. Kacmar, & L. Busenitz, 2012, Entrepreneurial alertness in the pursuit of new opportunities, *Journal of Business Venturing*, 27: 77–94; D. Chrusciel, 2011, Environmental scan: Influence on strategic direction, *Journal of Facilities Management*, 9(1): 7–15.

19. D. E. Hughes, J. Le Bon, & A. Rapp, 2013, Gaining and leveraging customer-based competitive intelligence: The pivotal role of social capital and salesperson adaptive selling skills, *Journal of the Academy of Marketing Science*, 41: 91–110; J. R. Hough & M. A. White, 2004, Scanning actions and environmental dynamism: Gathering information for strategic decision making, *Management Decision*, 42: 781–793; V. K. Garg, B. A. Walters, & R. L. Priem, 2003, Chief executive scanning emphases, environmental dynamism, and manufacturing firm performance, *Strategic Management Journal*, 24: 725–744.

20. C.-H. Lee & T.-F. Chien, 2013, Leveraging microblogging big data with a modified density-based clustering approach for event awareness and topic ranking, *Journal of Information Science*, in press.

21. S. Garg, 2013, Venture boards: Distinctive monitoring and implications for firm performance, *Academy of Management Review*, 38: 90–108; Fahey, *Competitors*, 71–73.

22. K. Greene & V. Monga, 2013, Workers saving too little to retire, *Wall Street Journal*, www.wsj.com, March 19.

23. B. L. Connelly & E. J. Van Slyke, 2012, The power and peril of board interlocks, *Business Horizons*, 55: 403–408; C. Dellarocas, 2010, Online reputation systems: How to design one that does what you need, *MIT Sloan Management Review*, 51(3): 33–37.

24. K. L. Turner & M. V. Makhija, 2012, The role of individuals in the information processing perspective, *Strategic Management Journal*, 33: 661–680; X. Zhang, S. Majid, & S. Foo, 2010, Environmental scanning: An application of information literacy skills at the workplace, *Journal of Information Science*, 36(6): 719–732; M. J. Leiblein & T. L. Madsen, 2009, Unbundling competitive heterogeneity: Incentive structures and capability influences on technological innovation, *Strategic Management Journal*, 30: 711–735.

25. L. Sleuwaegen, 2013, Scanning for profitable (international) growth, *Journal of Strategy and Management*, 6: 96–110; J. Calof & J. Smith, 2010, The integrative domain of foresight and competitive intelligence and its impact on R&D management, *R & D Management*, 40(1): 31–39.

26. A. Chwolka & M. G. Raith, 2012, The value of business planning before start-up—A decision-theoretical perspective, *Journal of Business Venturing*, 27: 385–399; Fahey, *Competitors*.

27. S. D. Wu, K. G. Kempf, M. O. Atan, B. Aytac, S. A. Shirodkar, & A. Mishra, 2010, Improving new-product forecasting at Intel Corporation, *Interfaces*, 40: 385–396.

28. R. Klingebiel, 2012, Options in the implementation plan of entrepreneurial initiatives: Examining firms' attainment of flexibility benefit, *Strategic Entrepreneurship Journal*, 6: 307–334; T. Sueyoshi & M. Goto, 2011, Methodological comparison between two unified (operational and environmental) efficiency measurements for environmental assessment, *European Journal of Operational Research*, 210(3): 684–693; Fahey, *Competitors*, 75–77.

29. N. J. Foss, J. Lyngsie, & S. A. Zahra, 2013, The role of external knowledge sources and organizational design in the process of opportunity exploitation, *Strategic Management Journal*, 34: in press; M. Exu, V. Ong, Y. Duan, & B. Mathews, 2011, Intelligent agent systems for executive information scanning, filtering and interpretation: Perceptions and challenges, *Information Processing & Management*, 47(2): 186–201.

30. D. Grewal, A. Roggeveen, & R. C. Runyan, 2013, Retailing in a connected world, *Journal of Marketing Management*, 29: 263–270; R. King, 2010, Consumer demographics: Use demographic resources to target specific audiences, *Journal of Financial Planning*, 23(12): S4–S6.

31. 2013, U.S. Census Bureau, International Programs World Population, www.census. gov/population/international/data/ worldpop/, May 21.

32. 2013, The world population and the top ten countries with the highest population, *Internet World Stats*, www. internetworldstats.com, May 21.

33. T. Kambayashi, 2011, Brief: Aging Japan sees slowest population growth yet, *McClatchy-Tribune Business News*, www.mcclatchy.com,

February 25; S. Moffett, 2005, Fast-aging Japan keeps its elders on the job longer, *Wall Street Journal*, June 15, A1, A8.

34. D. Bloom & D. Canning, 2012, How companies must adapt for an aging workforce, *HBR Blog Network*, www.hbr.org, December 3.

35. 2012, Humanity's aging, *National Institute on Aging*, www.nia.nih.gov, March 27.

36. M. B. Dougherty, 2012, Stunning facts about Japan's demographic implosion, *Business Insider*, www.businessinsider.com, April 24.

37. 2013, The aging workforce: Finding the silver lining in the talent gap, *Deloitte*, www.deloitte.com, February.

38. 2013, 2013 Cal Facts, Legislative Analysts' Office, www.lao.ca.gov, January 2.

39. J. Goudreau, 2013, The states people are fleeing in 2013, *Forbes*, www.forbes.com, February 7.

40. R. Dobbs, S. Smit, J. Remes, J. Manyika, C. Roxburgh, & A. Restrepo, 2011, Urban world: Mapping the economic power of cities, Chicago: McKinsey Global Institute, March.

41. 2012, Population and population change statistics, *European Commission*, www.epp. eurostat.ec.europa.eu, October.

42. S. Reddy, 2011, U.S. News: Latinos fuel growth in decade, *Wall Street Journal*, March 25, A2.

43. M. Fisher, 2013, A revealing map of the world's most and least ethnically diverse countries, *The Washington Post*, www.washingtonpost.com, May 16.

44. A. Hain-Cole, 2010, Companies juggle cost cutting with competitive benefits for international assignments, *Benefits & Compensation International: A Magazine for Global Companies*, 40(5): 26.

45. J. Lee, 2010, Don't underestimate India's consumers, *Bloomberg Businessweek*, www.businessweek.com, January 21.

46. G. A. Shinkle & B. T. McCann, 2013, New product deployment: The moderating influence of economic institutional context, *Strategic Management Journal*, in press; L. Fahey & V. K. Narayanan, 1986, *Macroenvironmental Analysis for Strategic Management (The West Series in Strategic Management)*, St. Paul, Minnesota: West Publishing Company, 105.

47. N. Bloom, M. A. Kose, & M. E. Terrones, 2013, Held back by uncertainty, *Finance & Development*, 50: 38–41, March.

48. 2013, Global economy in 2013: Uncertainty weighing on growth, *Grant Thornton International Business Report*, www. internationalbusinessreport.com, March.

49. R. J. Sawant, 2012, Asset specificity and corporate political activity in regulated industries, *Academy of Management Review*, 37: 194–210; G. F. Holburne & B. A. Zelner, 2010, Political capabilities, policy risk, and international investment strategy: Evidence from the global electric power generation industry, *Strategic Management Journal*, 31(12): 1290–1315; C. Oliver & I. Holzinger, 2008, The effectiveness of strategic political

management: A dynamic capabilities framework, *Academy of Management Review*, 33: 496–520.

50. N. Jia, 2013, Are collective political actions and private political actions substitutes or complements? Empirical evidence from China's private sector, *Strategic Management Journal*, in press; R. K. Kozhikode & J. Li, 2012, Political pluralism, public schools, and organizational choices: Banking branch expansion in India, 1948–2003, *Academy of Management Journal*, 55: 339–359.

51. S. Zeidler, 2013, MGM assessing costs of operating online poker in Nevada, *Reuters*, www.mobile,reuters.com, May 2.

52. R. Ayadi, E. Arbak, W. P. de Goren, & D. T. Llewellyn, 2013, *Regulation of European Banks and Business Models: Towards a New Paradigm?* Brookings Institution Press, Washington, D.C.

53. K. J. O'Brien, 2013, Firms brace for new European data privacy law, *New York Times*, www.nytimes.com, May 13.

54. C. Jiang, S. Yao, & G. Feng, 2013, Bank ownership, privatization, and performance: Evidence from a transition country, *Journal of Banking & Finance*, 37: 3364–3372; N. Boubakri & L. Bouslimi, 2010, Analysts following of privatized firms around the world: The role of institutions and ownership structure, *International Journal of Accounting*, 45(4): 413–442.

55. L. Richards, 2013, The effects of socio-culture on business, *The Houston Chronicle*, www.chron.com, May 26.

56. 2013, Health strategy, *European Commission Public Health*, www.europa.eu, May 23.

57. C. Conover, 2013, Needed: A health system for adults, *Forbes*, www.forbes.com, April 30.

58. M. Toosi, 2012, Projections of the labor force to 2050: A visual essay, *Monthly Labor Review*, October.

59. Ibid., 13.

60. A. N. Smith, W. B. Morgan, E. B. King, M. R. Hebl, & C. I. Peddie, 2012, The ins and outs of diversity management: The effect of authenticity on outsider perceptions and insider behaviors, *Journal of Applied Psychology*, 42: E21–E55; M. DelCarmen Triana, M. F. Garcia, & A. Colella, 2010, Managing diversity: How organizational efforts to support diversity moderate the effects of perceived racial discrimination on affective commitment, *Personnel Psychology*, 63(4): 817–843.

61. R. Strack, J.-M. Caye, V. Bhalla, P. Tollman, C. von der Linden, P. Haen, & H. Quiros, 2012, Creating people advantage 2012, *bcg. perspectives*, www.bcgperspectives.com, October 18.

62. T. Grenness, 2011, The impact of national culture on CEO compensation and salary gaps between CEOs and manufacturing workers, *Compensation & Benefits Review*, 43(2): 100–108.

63. Y. Zeng, O. Shenkar, S.-H. Lee, & S. Song, 2013, Cultural differences, MNE learning

abilities, and the effect of experience on subsidiary mortality in a dissimilar culture: Evidence from Korean MNEs, *Journal of International Business Studies*, 44: 42–65; P. Dimitratos, A. Petrou, F. Plakoyiannaki, & J. E. Johnson, 2011, Strategic decision-making processes in internationalization: Does national culture of the focal firm matter?, *Journal of World Business*, 46(2): 194–204.

64. J. Liu, C. Hui, C. Lee, & Z. X. Chen, 2013, Why do I feel valued and why do I contribute? A relational approach to employee's organization-based self-esteem and job performance, *Journal of Management Studies*, in press; C. M. Chan, S. Makino, & T. Isobe, 2010, Does subnational region matter? Foreign affiliate performance in the United States and China, *Strategic Management Journal*, 31: 1226–1243; P. J. Buckley, J. Clegg, & H. Tan, 2006, Cultural awareness in knowledge transfer to China—The role of guanxi and mianzi, *Journal of World Business*, 41: 275–288.

65. N. Gil, M. Miozzo, & S. Massini, 2012, The innovation potential of new infrastructure development: An empirical study of Heathrow Airport's T5 project, *Research Policy*, 41: 452–466; J. Euchner, 2011, Managing disruption: An interview with Clayton Christensen, *Research Technology Management*, 54(1): 11–17; R. K. Sinha & C. H. Noble, 2008, The adoption of radical manufacturing technologies and firm survival, *Strategic Management Journal*, 29: 943–962.

66. B. I. Park & P. N. Ghauri, 2011, Key factors affecting acquisition of technological capabilities from foreign acquiring firms by small and medium-sized local firms, *Journal of World Business*, 46(1): 116–125; K. H. Tsai & J.-C. Wang, 2008, External technology acquisition and firm performance: A longitudinal study, *Journal of Business Venturing*, 23: 91–112.

67. D. Dean, S. DiGrande, D. Field, A. Lundmark, J. O'Day, J. Pineda, & P. Zwillenberg, 2012, The Internet economy in the G-20. *bcg. perspectives*, www.bcgperspectives.com, March 19.

68. 2013, Consumers (everywhere) know a good deal when they see it, *bcg. perspectives*, www.bcgperspectives.com, January 11.

69. E. R. Banalieva & C. Dhanaraj, 2013, Home-region orientation in international expansion strategies, *Journal of International Business Studies*, 44: 89–116.

70. K. Kyung-Tae, R. Seung-Kyu, & O. Joongsan, 2011, The strategic role evolution of foreign automotive parts subsidiaries in China, *International Journal of Operations & Production Management*, 31(1): 31–55.

71. 2013, Growth and globalization: Keeping a lid on capacity, KPMG, Automotive executive survey, www.kpmb.com, January 15.

72. K. E. Meyer, 2009, Uncommon commonsense, *Business Strategy Review*, 20: 38–43; K. E. Meyer, 2006, Globalfocusing: From

domestic conglomerates to global specialists, *Journal of Management Studies*, 43: 1110–1144.

73. R. G. Flores, R. V. Aguilera, A. Mahdian, & P. M. Vaaler, 2013, How well do supra-national regional grouping schemes fit international business research models? *Journal of International Business Studies*, 44: 451–474; R. E. Hoskisson, M. Wright, I. Filatotchev, & M. W. Peng, 2013, Emerging multinationals form mid-range economies: The influence of institutions and factor markets, *Journal of Management Studies*, in press.

74. F. J. Froese, 2013, Work values of the next generation of business leaders in Shanghai, Tokyo, and Seoul, *Asia Pacific Journal of Management*, 30: 297–315; M. Muethel & M. H. Bond, 2013, National context and individual employees' trust of the out-group: The role of societal trust, *Journal of International Business Studies*, 4: 312–333; M. A. Hitt, M. T. Dacin, B. B. Tyler, & D. Park, 1997, Understanding the differences in Korean and U.S. executives' strategic orientations, *Strategic Management Journal*, 18: 159–167.

75. X. Li, 2012, Behind the recent surge of Chinese patenting: An institutional view, *Research Policy*, 41: 236–249; M. A. Hitt, D. Ahlstrom, M. T. Dacin, E. Levitas, & L. Svobodina, 2004, The institutional effects on strategic alliance partner selection: China versus Russia, *Organization Science*, 15: 173–185.

76. T. Yu, M. Subramaniam, & A. A. Cannella, Jr., 2013, Competing globally, allying locally: Alliances between global rivals and host-country factors, *Journal of International Business Studies*, 44: 117–137; T. K. Das & R. Kumar, 2011, Regulatory focus and opportunism in the alliance development process, *Journal of Management*, 37(3): 682–708.

77. A. G. Scherer, G. Palazzo, & D. Seidl, 2013, Managing legitimacy in complex and heterogeneous environments: Sustainable development in a globalized world, *Journal of Management Studies*, 50: 259–284; J. Harris, 2011, Going green to stay in the black: Transnational capitalism and renewable energy, *Perspectives on Global Development & Technology*, 10(1): 41–59; L. Berchicci & A. King, 2008, Postcards from the edge: A review of the business and environment literature, in J. P. Walsh & A. P. Brief (eds.), *Academy of Management Annals*, New York: Lawrence Erlbaum Associates, 513–547.

78. P. Berrone, A. Fosfuri, L. Gelabert, & L. R. Gomez-Mejia, 2013, Necessity as the mother of 'green' inventions: Institutional pressures and environmental innovations, *Strategic Management Journal*, 34: 891–909; M. Delmas, V. H. Hoffmann, & M. Kuss, 2011, Under the tip of the iceberg: Absorptive capacity, environmental strategy, and competitive advantage, *Business & Society*, 50(1): 116–154.

79. 2013, What is sustainable development? International institute for sustainable development, www.iisd.org, May 5.

80. J. K. Hall, G. A. Daneke, & M. J. Lenox, 2010, Sustainable development and entrepreneurship: Past contributions and future directions, *Journal of Business Venturing*, 25(5): 439–448.

81. A. Schwartz, 2013, McDonald's now serves certifiably sustainable fish, but does it matter? *Fast Company*, www.fastcompany.com, January 25.

82. D. Ferris, 2012, Will economic growth destroy the environment—or save it? *Forbes*, www.forbes.com, October 17.

83. S. M. Ben-Menahern, Z. Kwee, H. W. Volberda, & F. A. J. Van Den Bosch, 2013, Strategic renewal over time: The enabling role of potential absorptive capacity in aligning internal and external rates of change, *Long Range Planning*, 46: 216–235; V. Souitaris & B. Maestro, 2010, Polychronicity in top management teams: The impact on strategic decision processes and performance of new technology ventures, *Strategic Management Journal*, 31(6): 652–678.

84. M. Schimmer & M. Brauer, 2012, Firm performance and aspiration levels as determinants of a firm's strategic repositioning within strategic group structures, *Strategic Organization*, 10: 406–435; J. Galbreath & P. Galvin, 2008, Firm factors, industry structure and performance variation: New empirical evidence to a classic debate, *Journal of Business Research*, 61: 109–117.

85. J. J. Tarzijan & C. C. Ramirez, 2011, Firm, industry and corporation effects revisited: A mixed multilevel analysis for Chilean companies, *Applied Economics Letters*, 18(1): 95–100; V. F. Misangyl, H. Elms, T. Greckhamer, & J. A. Lepine, 2006, A new perspective on a fundamental debate: A multilevel approach to industry, corporate, and business unit effects, *Strategic Management Journal*, 27: 571–590.

86. E. T. Fukui, A. B. Hammer, & L. Z. Jones, 2013, Are U.S. exports influenced by stronger IPR protection measures in recipient markets? *Business Horizons*, 56: 179-188; D. Sullivan & J. Yuening, 2010, Media convergence and the impact of the internet on the M&A activity of large media companies, *Journal of Media Business Studies*, 7(4): 21–40.

87. K. Muller, K. Huschelrath, & V. Bilotkach, 2012, The construction of a low-cost airline network—facing competition and exploring new markets, *Managerial and Decision Economics*, 33: 485–499; C. Lutz, R. Kemp, & S. Gerhard Dijkstra, 2010, Perceptions regarding strategic and structural entry barriers, *Small Business Economics*, 35(1): 19–33.

88. F. Karakaya & S. Parayitam, 2013, Barriers to entry and firm performance: A proposed model and curvilinear relationships, *Journal of Strategic Marketing*, 21: 25–47;

B. F. Schivardi & E. Viviano, 2011, Entry barriers in retail trade, *Economic Journal*, 121(551): 145–170; A. V. Mainkar, M. Lubatkin, & W. S. Schulze, 2006, Toward a product-proliferation theory of entry barriers, *Academy of Management Review*, 31: 1062–1075.

89. V. Niu, L. C. Dong, & R. Chen, 2012, Market entry barriers in China, *Journal of Business Research*, 65: 68–76.

90. V. K. Garg, R. L. Priem, & A. A. Rasheed, 2013, A theoretical explanation of the cost advantages of multi-unit franchising, *Journal of Marketing Channels*, 20(1–2): 52–72; S. S. Kien, C. Soh, & P. Weil, 2010, Global IT management: Structuring for scale, responsiveness, and innovation, *Communications of the ACM*, 53(3): 59–64; S. K. Ethiraj & D. H. Zhu, 2008, Performance effects of imitative entry, *Strategic Management Journal*, 29: 797–817.

91. P. Jackson & M. Iwata, 2012, Global deal: Mitsubishi Heavy, Hitachi to merge businesses, *Wall Street Journal*, www.wsj.com, November 30.

92. G. Yeung & V. Mok, 2013, Manufacturing and distribution strategies, distribution channels, and transaction costs: The case of parallel imported automobiles, *Managerial and Decision Economics*, 34: 44–58; X. Huang, M. Kristal, & R. G. Schroeder, 2010, The impact of organizational structure on mass customization capability: A contingency view, *Production & Operations Management*, 19(5): 515–530; M. J. Rungtusanatham & F. Salvador, 2008, From mass production to mass customization: Hindrance factors, structural inertia, and transition hazard, *Production and Operations Management*, 17: 385–396.

93. J. J. Ebbers & N. M. Wijnberg, 2013, Nascent ventures competing for start-up capital: Matching reputations and investors, *Journal of Business Venturing*, 27: 372–384; T. Rice & P. E. Strahan, 2010, Does credit competition affect small-firm finance? *Journal of Finance*, 65(3): 861–889.

94. 2013, Zara-owned Inditex's profits rise by 22%, *BBC News Business*, www.bbc.co.uk, March 13.

95. M. Hume, 2011, The secrets of Zara's success, *Telegraph.co.uk*, www.telegraph.co.uk, June 22.

96. S. Ansari & P. Krop, 2012, Incumbent performance in the face of radical innovation: Towards a framework for incumbent challenger dynamics, *Research Policy*, 41: 1357–1374; 2011, Airline deregulation, revisited, *Bloomberg Businessweek*, www.businessweek.com, January 21.

97. J. Jaeger, 2010, Anti-trust reviews: Suddenly, they're a worry, *Compliance Week*, 7(80): 48–59.

98. S. Bhattacharyya & A. Nain, 2011, Horizontal acquisitions and buying power: A product market analysis, *Journal of Financial Economics*, 99(1): 97–115.

99. I. Sherr & S. Ovide, 2013, Computer sales in free fall, *Wall Street Journal*, www.wsj.com, April 11.

100. S. Cernivec, 2013, Refreshing the carbonated soft drink category, *Beverage Industry*, www.bevindustry.com, April 11; C. Dieroff, 2011, Beverage trends: Consumers want it all, *Prepared Foods*, February: 49–55.

101. J. Cahill, 2012, How McDonald's is losing the burger brawl, *Chicago Business*, www.chicagobusiness.com, December 1.

102. P. Cohan, 2013, Samsung trouncing Apple, *Forbes*, http://www.forbes.com, April 26.

103. K. Bradsher, 2013, Chinese auto buyers grow hungry for larger cars, *New York Times*, www.nytimes.com, April 21.

104. C. Murphy, 2013, GM to build Cadillac plant in China, *Wall Street Journal*, www.wsj.com, May 7.

105. R. Wall, 2013, Airline profits to top $10 billion on improving sales outlook, *Bloomberg*, www.bloomberg.com, March 20; R. García-Castro & M. A. Ariño, 2011, The multidimensional nature of sustained competitive advantage: Test at a United States airline, *International Journal of Management*, 28(1): 230–248.

106. A. Goerzen, C. G. Asmussen & B. B. Nielsen, 2013, Global cities and multinational enterprise location strategy, *Journal of International Business Studies*, 44: 427–450; S. Nadkarni, P. Herrmann, & P. Perez, 2011, Domestic mindsets and early international performance: The moderating effect of global industry conditions, *Strategic Management Journal*, 32(5): 510–531.

107. M. E. Porter, 1980, *Competitive Strategy*, New York: Free Press.

108. F. J. Mas-Ruiz, F. Ruiz-Moreno, & A. L. de Guevara Martinez, 2013, Asymmetric rivalry within and between strategic groups, *Strategic Management Journal*, in press; M. S. Hunt, 1972, Competition in the major home appliance industry, 1960–1970 (doctoral dissertation, Harvard University); Porter, *Competitive Strategy*, 129.

109. D. Miller, I. Le Breton-Miller, & R. H. Lester, 2013, Family firm governance, strategic conformity, and performance: Institutional vs. strategic perspectives, *Organization Science*, 24: 189–209; S. Cheng & H. Chang, 2009, Performance implications of cognitive complexity: An empirical study of cognitive strategic groups in semiconductor industry, *Journal of Business Research*, 62(12): 1311–1320; G. McNamara, D. L. Deephouse, & R. A. Luce, 2003, Competitive positioning within and across a strategic group structure: The performance of core, secondary, and solitary firms, *Strategic Management Journal*, 24: 161–181.

110. N. Phillips, P. Tracey, & N. Karra, 2013, Building entrepreneurial tie portfolios through strategic homophily: The role of narrative identity work in venture creation and early growth, *Journal of Business Venturing*, 28: 134–150; D. Williams, C. Young, R. Shewchuk, & H. Qu, 2010, Strategic groupings of U.S. biotechnology initial public offerings and a measure of their market influence, *Technology Analysis & Strategic Management*, 22(4): 399–415.

111. M. Sytch & A. Tatarynowicz, 2013, Exploring the locus of invention: The dynamics of network communities and firms' invention productivity, *Academy of Management Journal*, in press; W. S. DeSarbo & R. Grewal, 2008, Hybrid strategic groups, *Strategic Management Journal*, 29: 293–317; M. Peteraf & M. Shanley, 1997, Getting to know you: A theory of strategic group identity, *Strategic Management Journal*, 18 (Special Issue): 165–186.

112. B. P. S. Murthi, A. A. Rasheed, & I. Goll, 2013, An empirical analysis of strategic groups in the airline industry using latent class regressions, *Managerial and Decision Economics*, 34(2): 59–73; J. Lee, K. Lee, & S. Rho, 2002, An evolutionary perspective on strategic group emergence: A genetic algorithm-based model, *Strategic Management Journal*, 23: 727–746.

113. T. Staake, F. Thiesse, & E. Fleisch, 2012, Business strategies in the counterfeit market, *Journal of Business Research*, 65: 658–665; P. Ebbes, R. Grewal, & W. S. DeSarbo, 2010, Modeling strategic group dynamics: A hidden Markov approach, *Quantitative Marketing and Economics*, 8: 241–274.

114. T. Keil, T. Laarmanen, & R. G. McGrath, 2013, Is a counterattack the best defense? Competitive dynamics through acquisitions, *Long Range Planning*, 46: 195–215; T. Yu, M. Subramaniam, & A. A. Cannella, Jr., 2009, Rivalry deterrence in international markets: Contingencies governing the mutual forbearance hypothesis, *Academy of Management Journal*, 52: 127–147.

115. Porter, *Competitive Strategy*, 49.

116. R. L. Priem, S. Li, & J. C. Carr, 2012, Insights and new directions from demand-side approaches to technology innovation, entrepreneurship, and strategic management research, *Journal of Management*, 38: 346–374; J. E. Prescott & R. Herko, 2010, TOWS: The role of competitive intelligence, *Competitive Intelligence Magazine*, 13(3): 8–17.

117. D. E. Hughes, J. Le Bon, & A. Rapp, 2013, Gaining and leveraging customer-based competitive intelligence: The pivotal role of social capital and salesperson adaptive selling skills, *Journal of the Academy of Marketing Science*, 41: 91–110; D. B. Montgomery, M. C. Moore, & J. E. Urbany, 2005, Reasoning about competitive reactions: Evidence from executives, *Marketing Science*, 24: 138–149.

118. H. Akbar & N. Tzokas, 2012, An exploration of new product development's front-end knowledge conceptualization process in discontinuous innovations, *British Journal of Management*, 24: 245–263; K. Xu, S. Liao, J. Li, & Y. Song, 2011, Mining comparative opinions from customer reviews for competitive intelligence, *Decision Support Systems*, 50(4): 743–754; S. Jain, 2008, Digital piracy: A competitive analysis, *Marketing Science*, 27: 610–626.

119. S. Wright, 2013, Converting input to insight: Organising for intelligence-based competitive advantage. In S. Wright (ed.), *Competitive Intelligence, Analysis and Strategy: Creating Organisational Agility*. Abingdon: Routledge, 1–35; J. G. York, 2009, Pragmatic sustainability: Translating environmental ethics into competitive advantage, *Journal of Business Ethics*, 85: 97–109.

120. X. Luo, J. Wieseke, & C. Homburg, 2012, Incentivizing CEOs to build customer- and employee-firm relations for higher customer satisfaction and firm value, *Journal of the Academy of Marketing Science*, 40: 745–758; R. Huggins, 2010, Regional competitive intelligence: Benchmarking and policy-making. *Regional Studies*, 44(5): 639–658.

121. L. T. Tuan, 2013, Leading to learning and competitive intelligence, *The Learning Organization*, 20: 216–239; K. A. Sawka, 2008, The ethics of competitive intelligence, *Kiplinger Business Resource Center Online*, www.kiplinger.com, March.

122. R. B. Bouncken & S. Kraus, 2013, Innovation in knowledge-intensive industries: The double-edged sword of coopetition, *Journal of Business Research*, 66: 2060–2070; T. Mazzarol & S. Reboud, 2008, The role of complementary actors in the development of innovation in small firms, *International Journal of Innovation Management*, 12: 223–253; A. Brandenburger & B. Nalebuff, 1996, *Co-opetition*, New York: Currency Doubleday.

123. 2013, SCIP Code of ethics for CI professionals, www.scip.org, May 22.

124. J. S. Harrison & D. A. Bosse, 2013, How much is too much? The limits to generous treatment of stakeholders, *Business Horizons*, 56: 313–322; L. T. Tuan, 2013, Corporate social responsibility, upward influence behavior, team processes and competitive intelligence, *Team Performance Management*, 19(1/2): 6–33; C. S. Fleisher & S. Wright, 2009, Examining differences in competitive intelligence practice: China, Japan, and the West, *Thunderbird International Business Review*, 51: 249–261.

3

The Internal Organization: Resources, Capabilities, Core Competencies, and Competitive Advantages

Studying this chapter should provide you with the strategic management knowledge needed to:

1 Explain why firms need to study and understand their internal organization.

2 Define value and discuss its importance.

3 Describe the differences between tangible and intangible resources.

4 Define capabilities and discuss their development.

5 Describe four criteria used to determine whether resources and capabilities are core competencies.

6 Explain how firms analyze their value chain for the purpose of determining where they are able to create value when using their resources, capabilities, and core competencies.

7 Define outsourcing and discuss reasons for its use.

8 Discuss the importance of identifying internal strengths and weaknesses.

9 Discuss the importance of avoiding core rigidities.

ZARA: THE CAPABILITIES BEHIND THE SPANISH "FAST FASHION" RETAIL GIANT

Amancio Ortega built the world's largest fashion empire through his Zara branded products and company-owned stores. Through his management approach, Ortega has become the third richest man in the world behind Microsoft's Bill Gates and Mexico's Carlos Slim Helú.

Headquartered in La Coruña in Spain's Galicia region, Ortega founded the Inditex Group with Zara as its flagship brand. Despite Spain's 24 percent unemployment rate and crippling debt, in 2012 Zara increased its revenue 17 percent. Also, in 2012 Zara averaged a new store opening every day, including its six thousandth store launched on London's Oxford Street. Although the influence of the economic environment (an influence from the external environment that we examined in Chapter 2) affects Zara's success, the way Zara uses its

resources and capabilities as the foundation for core competencies (defined in Chapter 1, core competencies are capabilities that serve as a potential source of competitive advantage for a firm over its rivals) demonstrates the value of understanding a firm's internal organization (this chapter's subject).

Ortega built this successful business based on two critical goals: Give customers what they want, and get it to them faster than anyone else. To do "fast fashion" as it is called, there are several critical capabilities that must be in place. The first critical capability is the ability to design quickly; the design pace at Zara has been described as "frantic". The designers create about three items of new clothing a day, and pattern makers cut one sample for each. Second are the commercial sales specialists from each region where Zara has stores. They provide input on customer tastes and buying habits which are reported through store man-

agers. Each specialist is trained to keep an eye on what people are wearing, which Ortega does personally as well since founding Zara. As such, Zara has a team approach to match quick and creative design to information coming in from the sales staff through regional specialists and sector specialists to operationalize new fashion ideas.

The supply chain is also managed much more efficiently than those of other companies. The logistics department is the essence of the company; rather than waiting for cloth to come in after designing, it already has much basic cloth and owns its own dyeing operation to maintain control and speed. Zara's objective is to deliver customized orders to every store in its empire with a 24-hour turnaround deadline for Europe, the Mideast, and much of the United States, and 48 hours for Asia and Latin America. The frequent shipments keep product inventories fresh but also scarce since they send out very few items in each shipment. This approach compels customers to visit stores frequently in search of what they want and, because of the scarcity, creates an incentive for them to buy on the spot because it will likely not be in stock tomorrow. Accordingly, Zara's global store average of 17 visits per customer per year is considerably higher than the average of three visits per year for its competitors.

Until 2010 Zara did not have an online strategy. Unlike most retailers it has used very little advertising because it has focused on a rather cheap but fashionable approach. The fashion draws the interest of customers, and thereby created a huge following on Facebook, with approximately 10 million followers. This compares favorably to other competitors such as Gap. The rarity of the individual pieces of clothing gives customers a sense of individuality. This gives Zara a stronger potential to pursue an online strategy relative to its competitors.

Most Zara stores are owned by the parent company, and many of its suppliers, although not owned by the company, are considered long-time, relationship-oriented partners. As such, these partners identify with the company and thereby are also loyal. This approach also sets it apart and makes its strategy difficult to duplicate because all of the various facets and capabilities of the company fit together through a unified culture. As noted above, Zara also operates its own dyeing plant for cloth, giving it significant control over its products. Likewise, it sews many of these garments in its own factories, and thus maintains a high level of quality control and an ability to make quick changes. Overall, the company has a unique set of capabilities which fit together well as it manages their activities to produce "fast fashion," which creates demand from their customers and loyalty from their partner suppliers.

Sources: E. Carlyle, 2013, The year's biggest winner: Zara billionaire Amancio Ortega, *Forbes*, www.forbes.com, March 4; R. Dudley, A. Devnath, & M. Townsend, 2013, The hidden cost of fast fashion, *Bloomberg Businessweek*, February 11, 15–17; V. Walt, 2013, Meet the third-richest man in the world, *Fortune*, January 14, 74–79; 2012, Inditex, Asos post double-digit sales gains, *Women's Wear Daily*, September 20, 6; B. Borzykowski, 2012, Zara eludes the pain in Spain, *Canadian Business*, September 17, 67; K. Willems, W. Janssens, G. Swinnen, M. Brengman, S. Streukens, & N. Vancauteren, 2012, From Armani to Zara: Impression formation based on fashion store patronage, *Journal of Business Research*, (65)10: 1487–1494.

Find out how fashion draws the interest of customers on Facebook.
www.cengagebrain.com

As discussed in the first two chapters, several factors in the global economy, including the rapid development of the Internet's capabilities[1] and globalization in general have made it increasingly difficult for firms to find ways to develop sustainable competitive advantages.[2] Increasingly, innovation appears to be a vital path to efforts to develop such advantages.[3] As the Opening Case indicates, Zara's ability to produce new clothing designs quickly is definitely an advantage for them; the continual appearance of fresh designs has led to 17 visits per customer per year in its stores compared to the average of three visits per year in competitor stores.

Innovation is key at most organizations, like Zara, to maintain their competitive advantage. For example, at General Motors, efforts are underway to reduce the "drag" the firm's bureaucracy creates on innovation. According to a company official, "GM still wastes millions of dollars developing engines and vehicle variants that interest few customers." To remedy this problem, GM is making changes with the intention of having the "right people and the right engineers on the right priorities and products, not just do the most vehicles possible."[4]

People are an especially critical resource for helping organizations learn how to continuously innovate as a means of achieving successful growth.[5] This is the case at 3M, where harnessing the innovative powers of the firm's employees is the means for rekindling growth; in 2012 3M was ranked third on Booz & Company's list of most innovative behind Apple and Google but did not spend the same proportion on R&D relative to its sales as many other companies.[6] At 3M and other companies, people who are able to facilitate their firm's efforts to innovate are themselves a valuable resource with the potential to be a competitive advantage.[7] A sign of the times is the fact that a global labor market now exists as firms seek talented individuals to add to their fold. As Richard Florida argues, "[W]herever talent goes, innovation, creativity, and economic growth are sure to follow."[8]

To identify and successfully use resources over time, those leading firms need to constantly think about how to manage resources for the purpose of increasing the value their goods or services create for customers as compared to the value rivals' products create. As this chapter shows, firms achieve strategic competitiveness and earn above-average returns by acquiring, bundling, and leveraging their resources for the purpose of taking advantage of opportunities in the external environment in ways that create value for customers.[9]

Even if the firm develops and manages resources in ways that create core competencies and competitive advantages, competitors will eventually learn how to duplicate the benefits of any firm's value-creating strategy; thus all competitive advantages have a limited life.[10] Because of this, the question of duplication of a competitive advantage is not if it will happen, but when. In general, a competitive advantage's sustainability is a function of three factors: (1) the rate of core competence obsolescence because of environmental changes, (2) the availability of substitutes for the core competence, and (3) the imitability of the core competence.[11] For all firms, the challenge is to effectively manage current core competencies while simultaneously developing new ones.[12] Only when firms are able to do this can they expect to achieve strategic competitiveness, earn above-average returns, and remain ahead of competitors (see Chapter 5).

We studied the general, industry, and competitor environments in Chapter 2. Armed with knowledge about the realities and conditions of their external environment, firms have a better understanding of marketplace opportunities and the characteristics of the competitive environment in which those opportunities exist. In this chapter, we focus on the firm itself. By analyzing its internal organization, a firm determines what it can do. Matching what a firm *can do* (a function of its resources, capabilities, and core competencies in the internal organization) with what it *might do* (a function of opportunities and threats in the external environment) is a process that yields insights the firm requires to select its strategies.

We begin this chapter by briefly describing conditions associated with analyzing the firm's internal organization. We then discuss the roles of resources and capabilities in developing core competencies, which are the sources of the firm's competitive advantages. Included in this discussion are the techniques firms use to identify and evaluate resources and capabilities and the criteria for identifying core competencies from among them. Resources by themselves typically are not competitive advantages; in fact, resources create value when the firm uses them to form capabilities, some of which become core competencies, and hopefully competitive advantages. Because of the relationship among resources, capabilities, and core competencies, we also discuss the value chain and examine four criteria firms use to determine if their capabilities are core competencies and, as such, sources of competitive advantage.[13] The chapter closes with cautionary comments about outsourcing and the need for firms to prevent their core competencies from becoming core rigidities. The existence of core rigidities indicates that the firm is too anchored to its past, which prevents it from continuously developing new capabilities and core competencies.

3-1 Analyzing the Internal Organization

3-1a The Context of Internal Analysis

One of the conditions associated with analyzing a firm's internal organization is the reality that in today's global economy, some of the resources that were traditionally critical to firms' efforts to produce, sell, and distribute their goods or services such as labor costs, access to financial resources and raw materials, and protected or regulated markets, although still important, are now less likely to become competitive advantages.[14] An important reason for this is that an increasing number of firms are using their resources to form core competencies through which they successfully implement an international strategy (discussed in Chapter 8) as a means of overcoming the advantages created by these more traditional resources.

The Volkswagen Group has established "Strategy 2018" as its international strategy. The firm, which sells its products in over 150 countries, employs 550,000 people to operate more than 100 production plants around the world. By using its resources to form technological and innovation capabilities, Volkswagen intends to create superior customer service and product quality as core competencies on which it will rely to implement its international strategy.[15]

Increasingly, those analyzing their firm's internal organization should use a global mind-set to do so. A **global mind-set** is the ability to analyze, understand, and manage an internal organization in ways that are not dependent on the assumptions of a single country, culture, or context.[16] Because they are able to span artificial boundaries, those with a global mind-set recognize that their firms must possess resources and capabilities that allow understanding of and appropriate responses to competitive situations that are influenced by country-specific factors and unique cultures. Using a global mind-set to analyze the internal organization has the potential to significantly help the firm in its efforts to outperform rivals.[17] A global mind-set was used to develop Volkswagen Group's "Strategy 2018."

Finally, analyzing the firm's internal organization requires that evaluators examine the firm's entire portfolio of resources and capabilities. This perspective suggests that individual firms possess at least some resources and capabilities that other companies do not—at least not in the same combination. Resources are the source of capabilities, some of which lead to the development of core competencies; in turn, some core competencies may lead to a competitive advantage for the firm.[18] Understanding how to leverage the firm's unique bundle of resources and capabilities is a key outcome decision makers seek when analyzing the internal organization.[19] Figure 3.1 illustrates the relationships among resources, capabilities, core competencies, and competitive advantages and shows how their integrated use can lead to strategic competitiveness. As we discuss next, firms use the assets in their internal organization to create value for customers.

A **global mind-set** is the ability to analyze, understand, and manage an internal organization in ways that are not dependent on the assumptions of a single country, culture, or context.

Figure 3.1 Components of an Internal Analysis

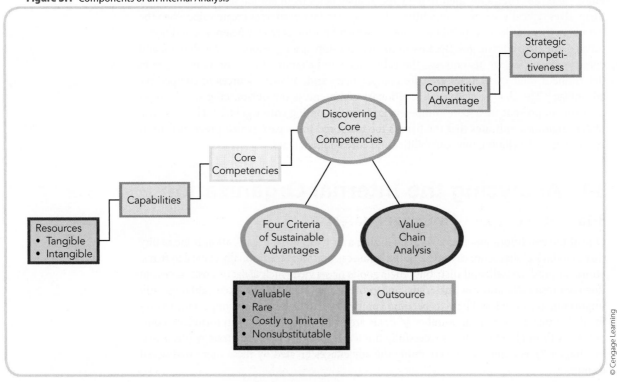

3-1b   Creating Value

Firms use their resources as the foundation for producing goods or services that will create value for customers.[20] **Value** is measured by a product's performance characteristics and by its attributes for which customers are willing to pay. Firms create value by innovatively bundling and leveraging their resources to form capabilities and core competencies.[21] Firms with a competitive advantage create more value for customers than do competitors.[22] Walmart uses its "every day low price" approach to doing business (an approach that is grounded in the firm's core competencies, such as information technology and distribution channels) to create value for those seeking to buy products at a low price compared to competitors' prices for those products.[23] The stronger these firms' core competencies, the greater the amount of value they're able to create for their customers.[24]

Ultimately, creating value for customers is the source of above-average returns for a firm. What the firm intends regarding value creation affects its choice of business-level strategy (see Chapter 4) and its organizational structure (see Chapter 11).[25] In Chapter 4's discussion of business-level strategies, we note that value is created by a product's low cost, by its highly differentiated features, or by a combination of low cost and high differentiation, compared with competitors' offerings. A business-level strategy is effective only when it is grounded in exploiting the firm's capabilities and core competencies. Thus, the successful firm continuously examines the effectiveness of current capabilities and core competencies while thinking about the capabilities and competencies it will require for future success.[26]

At one time, the firm's efforts to create value were largely oriented to understanding the characteristics of the industry in which it competed and, in light of those characteristics, determining how it should be positioned relative to competitors. This emphasis on industry characteristics and competitive strategy underestimated the role of the firm's resources and capabilities in developing core competencies as the source of competitive advantages. In fact, core competencies, in combination with product-market positions, are the firm's most important sources of competitive advantage.[27] A firm's core competencies, integrated with an understanding of the results of studying the conditions in the external environment, should drive the selection of strategies.[28] As Clayton Christensen noted, "Successful strategists need to cultivate a deep understanding of the processes of competition and progress and of the factors that undergird each advantage. Only thus will they be able to see when old advantages are poised to disappear and how new advantages can be built in their stead."[29] By emphasizing core competencies when selecting and implementing strategies, companies learn to compete primarily on the basis of firm-specific differences. However, while doing so they must be simultaneously aware of how things are changing in the external environment.[30]

3-1c   The Challenge of Analyzing the Internal Organization

The strategic decisions managers make about their firm's internal organization are non-routine,[31] have ethical implications,[32] and significantly influence the firm's ability to earn above-average returns.[33] These decisions involve choices about the resources the firm needs to collect and how to best manage them.

Making decisions involving the firm's assets—identifying, developing, deploying, and protecting resources, capabilities, and core competencies—may appear to be relatively easy. However, this task is as challenging and difficult as any other with which managers are involved; moreover, the task is increasingly internationalized.[34] Some believe that the pressure on managers to pursue only decisions that help the firm meet the quarterly earnings expected by market analysts makes it difficult to accurately examine the firm's internal organization.[35]

The challenge and difficulty of making effective decisions are implied by preliminary evidence suggesting that one-half of organizational decisions fail.[36] Sometimes, mistakes

Value is measured by a product's performance characteristics and by its attributes for which customers are willing to pay.

are made as the firm analyzes conditions in its internal organization.[37] Managers might, for example, think a capability is a core competence when it is not. This may have been the case at Polaroid Corporation as decision makers continued to believe that the capabilities it used to build its instant film cameras were highly relevant at the time its competitors were developing and using the capabilities required to introduce digital cameras. In this instance, Polaroid's decision makers may have concluded that superior manufacturing was a core competence, as was the firm's ability to innovate in terms of creating value-adding features for its instant cameras. If a mistake is made when analyzing and managing a firm's resources, such as appears to have been the case some years ago at Polaroid, decision makers must have the confidence to admit it and take corrective actions.[38]

A firm can improve by studying its mistakes; in fact, the learning generated by making and correcting mistakes can be important to efforts to create new capabilities and core competencies.[39] One capability that can be learned from failure is when to quit. Polaroid should have obviously changed its strategy earlier than it did, and by doing so it may have been able to avoid more serious failure. Another example is News Corp.'s acquisition of MySpace in 2006. It poured over $580 million of investment for several years as it lost market share to FaceBook, and the acquisition was eventually sold for only $34 million.[40]

As we discuss next, three conditions—uncertainty, complexity, and intraorganizational conflict—affect managers as they analyze the internal organization and make decisions about resources (see Figure 3.2).

Managers face uncertainty because of a number of issues, including those of new proprietary technologies, rapidly changing economic and political trends, transformations in societal values, and shifts in customers' demands.[41] Environmental uncertainty increases the complexity and range of issues to examine when studying the internal environment.[42] Consider how uncertainty affects how to use resources at coal companies such as Peabody Energy Corp and Arch Coal Corp.

Peabody is the world's largest private-sector coal company. The firm's coal products fuel approximately 11 percent of all U.S. electricity generation and 2 percent of worldwide electricity. But the firm faces a great deal of uncertainty with respect to how it might best use its resources today to prepare for its future. One reason for this is that at least for some, coal is thought of as a "dirty fuel." Partly to reduce the uncertainty the firm faces because of this, Peabody is using some of its resources to build a "clean" coal-fired plant and has signed agreements to develop clean coal in China. As a proponent of strong emissions standards, Peabody's leaders argue for more use of "clean coal." Besides having to deal with increasingly advanced technological improvements such as clean coal, demand situations around the world are also creating uncertainty. China, for instance, one of the U.S.'s largest coal

Figure 3.2 Conditions Affecting Managerial Decisions about Resources, Capabilities, and Core Competencies

Conditions	Uncertainty	Uncertainty exists about the characteristics of the firm's general and industry environments and customers' needs.
	Complexity	Complexity results from the interrelationships among conditions shaping a firm.
	Intraorganizational Conflicts	Intraorganizational conflicts may exist among managers making decisions as well as among those affected by the decisions.

© Cengage Learning

export markets, is increasing its own capacity in clean coal. Although India has continuingly increasing demand as it builds more coal-fired generating plants, pressure is growing to reduce their plants' CO_2 emissions. Tougher environmental regulations in Europe and a sluggish economy there have crippled coal demand in that region. Likewise, cheaper natural gas is continuing to displace coal in power generation in the United States.[43]

Also, biases about how to cope with uncertainty affect decisions made about how to manage the firm's resources and capabilities to form core competencies.[44] Additionally, intraorganizational conflict may surface when decisions are made about the core competencies a firm should develop and nurture. Conflict might surface in Peabody or Arch Coal about the degree to which resources and capabilities should be used to form new core competencies to support newer "clean technologies."

In making decisions affected by these three conditions, judgment is required. *Judgment* is the capability of making successful decisions when no obviously correct model or rule is available or when relevant data are unreliable or incomplete. In such situations, decision makers must be aware of possible cognitive biases, such as overconfidence. Individuals who are too confident in the decisions they make about how to use the firm's resources may fail to fully evaluate contingencies that could affect those decisions.[45]

When exercising judgment, decision makers often take intelligent risks. In the current competitive landscape, executive judgment can become a valuable capability. One reason is that, over time, effective judgment that decision makers demonstrate allows a firm to build a strong reputation and retain the loyalty of stakeholders whose support is linked to above-average returns.[46]

Finding individuals who can make the most successful decisions about using the organization's resources is challenging. Being able to do this is important because the quality of leaders' decisions regarding resources and their management affect a firm's ability to achieve strategic competitiveness. Individuals holding these key decision-making positions are called *strategic leaders*. Discussed fully in Chapter 12, for our purposes in this chapter we can think of strategic leaders as individuals with an ability to make effective decisions when examining the firm's resources, capabilities, and core competencies for the purpose of making choices about their use.

Next, we consider the relationships among a firm's resources, capabilities, and core competencies. While reading these sections, keep in mind that organizations have more resources than capabilities and more capabilities than core competencies.

3-2 Resources, Capabilities, and Core Competencies

Resources, capabilities, and core competencies are the foundation of competitive advantage. Resources are bundled to create organizational capabilities. In turn, capabilities are the source of a firm's core competencies, which are the basis of establishing competitive advantages.[47] We show these relationships in Figure 3.1. Here, we define and provide examples of these building blocks of competitive advantage.

3-2a Resources

Broad in scope, resources cover a spectrum of individual, social, and organizational phenomena. By themselves, resources do not allow firms to create value for customers as the foundation for earning above-average returns. Indeed, resources are combined to form capabilities.[48] Subway links its fresh ingredients with several other resources including the continuous training it provides to those running the firm's fast food restaurants as the foundation for customer service as a capability; customer service is also a core competence for Subway. As its sole distribution channel, the Internet is a resource for Amazon.com. The firm uses the Internet to sell goods at prices that typically are lower than those offered by competitors selling the same goods through what are more costly brick-and-mortar storefronts. By combining other resources (such as access to a wide product inventory), Amazon has developed a reputation for excellent customer service. Amazon's capability in terms of customer service is a core competence as well in that the firm creates unique value for customers through the services it provides to them. Amazon also uses its technological core competence to offer AWS (Amazon Web Services), services through which businesses can rent computing power from Amazon at a cost of pennies per hour. In the words of the leader of this effort, "AWS makes it possible for anyone with an Internet connection and a credit card to access the same kind of world-class computing systems that Amazon uses to run its $34 billion-a-year retail operation."[49]

Some of a firm's resources (defined in Chapter 1 as inputs to the firm's production process) are tangible while others are intangible. **Tangible resources** are assets that can be observed and quantified. Production equipment, manufacturing facilities, distribution centers, and formal reporting structures are examples of tangible resources. As indicated in the Strategic Focus, Kinder Morgan's pipelines are a tangible resource. **Intangible resources** are assets that are rooted deeply in the firm's history and have accumulated over time. Because they are embedded in unique patterns of routines, intangible resources are difficult for competitors to analyze and imitate. Knowledge, trust between managers and employees, managerial capabilities, organizational routines (the unique ways people work together), scientific capabilities, the capacity for innovation, brand name, the firm's reputation for its goods or services and how it interacts with people (such as employees, customers, and suppliers), and organizational culture are intangible resources.[50] As illustrated in the Strategic Focus, the marketing routines and brand Coca-Cola uses to facilitate consumer demand for its products are examples of intangible resources.

The four primary categories of tangible resources are financial, organizational, physical, and technological (see Table 3.1). The three primary categories of intangible resources are human, innovation, and reputational (see Table 3.2).

Tangible Resources

As tangible resources, a firm's borrowing capacity and the status of its physical facilities are visible. The value of many tangible resources can be established through financial statements, but these statements do not account for the value of all the firm's assets, because they disregard some intangible resources.[51] The value of tangible resources is also constrained

Tangible resources are assets that can be observed and quantified.

Intangible resources include assets that are rooted deeply in the firm's history, accumulate over time, and are relatively difficult for competitors to analyze and imitate.

Table 3.1 Tangible Resources

Financial Resources	• **The firm's capacity to borrow** • **The firm's ability to generate funds through internal operations**
Organizational Resources	• **Formal reporting structures**
Physical Resources	• **The sophistication of a firm's plant and equipment and the attractiveness of its location** • **Distribution facilities** • **Product inventory**
Technological Resources	• **Availability of technology-related resources such as copyrights, patents, trademarks, and trade secrets**

Sources: Adapted from J. B. Barney, 1991, Firm resources and sustained competitive advantage, *Journal of Management*, 17: 101; R. M. Grant, 1991, *Contemporary Strategy Analysis*, Cambridge: U.K.: Blackwell Business, 100-102.

Table 3.2 Intangible Resources

Human Resources	• Knowledge • Trust • Skills • Abilities to collaborate with others
Innovation Resources	• Ideas • Scientific capabilities • Capacity to innovate
Reputational Resources	• Brand name • Perceptions of product quality, durability, and reliability • Positive reputation with stakeholders such as suppliers and customers

Sources: Adapted from R. Hall, 1992, The strategic analysis of intangible resources, *Strategic Management Journal*, 13: 136-139: R. M. Grant, 1991, *Contemporary Strategy Analysis*, Cambridge: U.K.: Blackwell Business, 101-104.

Strategic Focus   SUCCESS

Emphasis on Value Creation through Tangible (Kinder Morgan) and Intangible (Coca-Cola Inc.) Resources

Some firms have valuable resources which allow them to ultimately create value as they manage these resources through their capabilities. As outlined in the chapter, tangible resources can be categorized into financial, organizational, physical, and technological, whereas intangible resources are human, innovation, and reputational.

Kinder Morgan is a company that has vast tangible resources through its system of oil and gas pipelines throughout the United States and into Canada. Richard Kinder, CEO of Kinder Morgan, manages the Kinder Morgan Corporation, which is the third largest energy firm headquartered in the United States in terms of overall valuation. In regard to specific physical tangible resources, Kinder Morgan has 75,000 miles of pipe and 180 storage terminals capable of handling 2.5 million barrels of oil and 55 billion cubic feet of gas per day. It has a number of publicly traded entities which total $100 billion in enterprise value (equity plus debt). Kinder Morgan also has assets in Canada to facilitate transporting gas liquids to Alberta to dilute thick tar sands, which are then carried to tankers on the Pacific Coast. Much of this natural gas comes from as far south as Texas. Furthermore, additional physical assets were picked up in an acquisition of El Paso, another pipeline company, which allows natural gas to be liquefied and transported to energy-starved markets such as Japan and Korea. The liquid natural gas is a nice play because gas prices in Japan and Korea can be $12 per thousand cubic feet, where the same gas in the United States may cost less than $4 per thousand cubic feet, creating a nice profit potential.

Interestingly, Kinder Morgan also has financial assets, as many firms do, but some of these assets come through creative tax

Bulk terminals in Tampa, Florida are some of Kinder Morgan's above-ground tangible resources.

approaches to earnings distribution. Most pipelines in the United States have the availability of a corporate structure known as a master limited partnership (MLP). MLPs have income-producing assets which are handled by the general partner and distributed to the limited partners. As such, all profits and tax liabilities are passed on to the unit holders such that the corporations involved pay no income tax. This has created an incentive to acquire assets where a corporate tax is paid and incorporating them into the MLP framework such that corporate taxes are no longer paid, although the unit limited partners do pay taxes. Although the resources noted above create the potential for value, the capabilities to choose the right resources and pipelines to buy as well as strong management capabilities and the foresight needed to manage the whole system is, of course, relevant to the ultimate profits that will be garnered. In this case, the U.S. shale drilling boom has created a significant increase in gas, propane, and oil liquid volumes on the market and has created a huge opportunity for MLPs such as Kinder Morgan because they can charge for every cubic foot of gas or barrel of oil passing through their pipelines, gas terminals, or storage tanks.

Coca-Cola Inc. likewise has many assets; however, many of the resources associated with Coca-Cola are of the intangible variety. In particular, Coca-Cola has its brand name and the ability to manage this brand in a way that creates continual value for its family of products. Coca-Cola has many ad agencies to help it manage its reputational message to its consumers. Although in the past TV spots were at the center of Coca-Cola's marketing strategy, more recently Coca-Cola's team has been able to create online viral approaches to support its image. It also created a musical single entitled "Anywhere in the World", which was heard throughout the 2012 Olympics. Furthermore, its online videos associated with the Super Bowl featuring its polar bears, which have been part of Coca-Cola advertising dating back to 1922, got 9.09 million live stream views. This shareable, online content was estimated to give soft drink earnings a 5 percent bump in global sales in 2012. Of course, a firm must be able to manage its reputational resources and brand through distinctive marketing capabilities as exampled here by Coca-Cola.

Coca-Cola also has resources that are focused on tangible financial abilities. Coke accounts for 17 percent of juice-related volume sold in the world's top 22 markets, compared with 9 percent for PepsiCo. It has massive storage tanks in Florida insulated and full of fresh-squeezed juice chilling at 30 °F to 34 °F. Coke and Cutrale (Coca-Cola's Brazilian juice partner) buy almost one-third of the 145 million boxes of oranges grown by more than 400 Florida growers. Coca-Cola markets its juice in the United States through the Minute Maid brand, which it bought in 1960. The "secret" formula in juices is the complex algorithm of business analytics to manage the flow from the farm to the distribution center, including the large tanks of frozen juice concentrate which is the base material used in the beverage. The financial analytics to manage this process are a distinct tangible resource that Coca-Cola uses to manage the flow of these products. Again, it takes distinct capabilities to manage both the intangible, reputational resources, as well as the tangible financial analytics that manage the flow of juices in Coke's worldwide operations.

Sources: 2013, Super Bowl: Classic vs. fresh, *Fast Company*, February, 22; J. Kirby, 2013, Creative that cracks the code, *Harvard Business Review*, (91)3: 86–89; Z. R. Mider, 2013, It pays to own a pipeline, *Bloomberg Businessweek*, January 28, 26–28; D. Stanford, 2013, Coke has a secret formula for orange juice, too, *Bloomberg Businessweek*, February 4, 19–21; N. Zmuda, 2013, Behind the scenes of Coca-Cola's Super Bowl in 2013 ad plans, *Advertising Age*, February 4, 24; C. Helman, 2012, Richard Kinder's energy kingdom, *Forbes*, December 10, 76–84; T. Shufelt, 2012, Why Kinder is winning the pipeline race, *Canadian Business*, October 1, 21; T. Stynes & A. Sider, 2012, Kinder Morgan sells assets as part of El Paso deal, *Wall Street Journal*, August 21, B3.

Strategy Right NOW

Find out more about Cutrale, Coca-Cola's Brazilian juice partner.
www.cengagebrain.com

because they are hard to leverage—it is difficult to derive additional business or value from a tangible resource. For example, an airplane is a tangible resource, but "You can't use the same airplane on five different routes at the same time. You can't put the same crew on five different routes at the same time. And the same goes for the financial investment you've made in the airplane."[52]

Although production assets are tangible, many of the processes necessary to use these assets are intangible. Thus, the learning and potential proprietary processes associated with a tangible resource, such as manufacturing facilities, can have unique intangible attributes, such as quality control processes, unique manufacturing processes, and technologies that develop over time.[53]

Intangible Resources

Compared to tangible resources, intangible resources are a superior source of capabilities and subsequently, core competencies.[54] In fact, in the global economy, "the success of a corporation lies more in its intellectual and systems capabilities than in its physical assets. [Moreover], the capacity to manage human intellect—and to convert it into useful products and services—is fast becoming the critical executive skill of the age."[55]

Because intangible resources are less visible and more difficult for competitors to understand, purchase, imitate, or substitute for, firms prefer to rely on them rather than on tangible

M. Stasy

resources as the foundation for their capabilities. In fact, the more unobservable (i.e., intangible) a resource is, the more valuable that resource is to create capabilities.[56] Another benefit of intangible resources is that, unlike most tangible resources, their use can be leveraged. For instance, sharing knowledge among employees does not diminish its value for any one person. To the contrary, two people sharing their individualized knowledge sets often can be leveraged to create additional knowledge that, although new to each individual, contributes potentially to performance improvements for the firm.

Reputational resources (see Table 3.2) are important sources of a firm's capabilities and core competencies. Indeed, some argue that a positive reputation can even be a source of competitive advantage.[57] Earned through the firm's actions as well as its words, a value-creating reputation is a product of years of superior marketplace competence as perceived by stakeholders.[58] A reputation indicates the level of awareness a firm has been able to develop among stakeholders and the degree to which they hold the firm in high esteem.[59]

Developing capabilities in specific functional areas can give companies a competitive edge. The effective use of social media to direct advertising to specific market segments has given some firms an advantage over their rivals.

A well-known and highly valued brand name is a specific reputational resource.[60] A continuing commitment to innovation and aggressive advertising facilitates firms' efforts to take advantage of the reputation associated with their brands.[61] Harley-Davidson has a reputation for producing and servicing high-quality motorcycles with unique designs. Because of the desirability of its reputation, the company also produces a wide range of accessory items that it sells on the basis of its reputation for offering unique products with high quality. Sunglasses, jewelry, belts, wallets, shirts, slacks, belts, and hats are just a few of the large variety of accessories customers can purchase from a Harley-Davidson dealer or from its online store.[62] However, reputation is also being facilitated more quickly now through social media. As one analyst wrote, "your brand is nothing more than the sum of conversations being had about it. That is why social media is so powerful."[63] One study showed that Hokey Pokey, a popular "super premium" ice cream retailer with a dozen outlets in India, improved its brand equity "by using social media platforms to connect with its target consumers and create an engaging brand experience."[64] As noted in the Strategic Focus, Coca-Cola is using social media effectively to build its reputational resources.

3-2b Capabilities

The firm combines individual tangible and intangible resources to create capabilities. In turn, capabilities are used to complete the organizational tasks required to produce, distribute, and service the goods or services the firm provides to customers for the purpose of creating value for them.[65] As a foundation for building core competencies and hopefully competitive advantages, capabilities are often based on developing, carrying, and exchanging information and knowledge through the firm's human capital.[66] Hence, the value of human capital in developing and using capabilities and, ultimately, core competencies cannot be overstated.[67] At IBM, for example, human capital is critical to forming and using the firm's capabilities for long-term customer relationships and deep scientific and research skills, and the breadth of the firm's technical skills in hardware, software, and services.[68]

As illustrated in Table 3.3, capabilities are often developed in specific functional areas (such as manufacturing, R&D, and marketing) or in a part of a functional area (e.g., advertising). Table 3.3 shows a grouping of organizational functions and the capabilities that some companies are thought to possess in terms of all or parts of those functions.

3-2c Core Competencies

Defined in Chapter 1, core competencies are capabilities that serve as a source of competitive advantage for a firm over its rivals. Core competencies distinguish a company competitively and reflect its personality. Core competencies emerge over time through an organizational process of accumulating and learning how to deploy different resources and capabilities.[69] As the capacity to take action, core competencies are "crown jewels of a company," the activities the company performs especially well compared to competitors and through which the firm adds unique value to the goods or services it sells to customers.[70]

Innovation is thought to be a core competence at Apple. As a capability, R&D activities are the source of this core competence. More specifically, the way Apple has combined some of its tangible (e.g., financial resources and research laboratories) and intangible (e.g., scientists and engineers and organizational routines) resources to complete research and development tasks creates a capability in R&D. By emphasizing its R&D capability, Apple is able to innovate in ways that create unique value for customers in the form of the products it sells, suggesting that innovation is a core competence for Apple.

Excellent customer service in its retail stores is another of Apple's core competencies. In this instance, unique and contemporary store designs (a tangible resource) are combined with knowledgeable and skilled employees (an intangible resource) to provide superior service to customers. A number of carefully developed training and development procedures are capabilities on which Apple's core competence of excellent customer service is based. The procedures that are capabilities include "… intensive control of how employees interact

Table 3.3 Example of Firms' Capabilities

Functional Areas	Capabilities	Examples of Firms
Distribution	• Effective use of logistics management techniques	• Walmart
Human Resources	• Motivating, empowering, and retaining employees	• Microsoft
Management Information Systems	• Effective and efficient control of inventories through point-of-purchase data collection methods	• Walmart
Marketing	• Effective promotion of brand-name products • Effective customer service • Innovative merchandising	• Procter & Gamble • Ralph Lauren Corp. • McKinsey & Co. • Nordstrom Inc. • Crate & Barrel
Management	• Ability to envision the future of clothing	• Hugo Boss • Zara
Manufacturing	• Design and production skills yielding reliable products • Product and design quality • Miniaturization of components and products	• Komatsu • Witt Gas Technology • Sony
Research & Development	• Innovative technology • Development of sophisticated elevator control solutions • Rapid transformation of technology into new products and processes • Digital technology	• Caterpillar • Otis Elevator Co. • Chaparral Steel • Thomson Consumer Electronics

Strategic Focus

TECHNOLOGY

Samsung Bests Apple in Smartphone Sales by Its Imitation Capability

Samsung is a large, diversified business group located in South Korea and accounts for 17 percent of South Korea's gross domestic product (GDP). The overall business group employs 370,000 people in more than 80 countries. Samsung's largest separate business is Samsung Electronics, which has grown to over $141 billion in sales in 2012. In particular, it has had strong strategic success in smartphones; in 2012 it overtook Apple, with 29 percent market share versus Apple's 22 percent. It realized a 7 percent gain in smartphone market share relative to other competitors compared to its position in 2011. Samsung got into the electronics business like other Korean conglomerates such as LG and Hyundai by starting small, making components for other firms in the industry.

Getting into the semiconductor industry requires a semiconductor fab (i.e., a silicon wafer fabrication plant) which costs $2 to $3 billion. Once you have the infrastructure in place, you can begin selling semiconductor components to other companies. The knowledge that comes from developing key components allows strong insight into how the industry works. "Indeed, part of Samsung's secret sauce is that it controls and manufactures many of the building blocks of its phones." The firm leverages this foothold to develop an advantage that other companies have little chance of matching. In 2012, Samsung Electronics devoted $21.5 billion to capital expenditures, more than twice the investment spent by Apple.

To get into smartphones, Samsung built upon an existing innovation, the iPhone. Over time, it built a more advanced product that sold better than the iPhone. Samsung has pursued a "copycat" strategy by innovating where it has an advantage and imitating every place else. The proof of the imitation strategy is found in a recent court ruling that went against Samsung in a case where Apple claimed patent infringement. Although Samsung has copied some design aspects of the iPhone, it has been in high technology screens for quite a long time, having been a maker of televisions and other LED screen technology applications. Product improvements in the smartphone came through Samsung's core competence, "producing big, beautiful screens." Furthermore, Samsung has cultivated an ability to quickly understand the functions and imitate—and where possible given its strengths, improve on—competitors' products. Because it has the ability to manufacture products quickly as a contract manufacturer, it has the skill to produce incremental product improvements quickly.

Interestingly, Samsung has risen with this strategic approach, which is focused on manufacturing its own components as well as other competitors' components, while others have failed in the smartphone market. Motorola split up its handset business and sold part of it to Google. Nokia's longstanding number one

Samsung has pursued a competitive strategy based on both innovation and imitation.

position in cell phones was eroded. Not only was it blindsided by smartphones earlier, but it was overtaken by Samsung on cell phones. Sony Ericsson's partnership dissolved, and Palm disappeared into Hewlett-Packard. BlackBerry is on the edge of failure as well. Samsung Electronics strives for manufacturing efficiency and excellence and stellar new product development across a range or product lines. It also has established a new institute in Silicon Valley to develop its own software, one area where it is behind. Samsung's Galaxy line of smartphones uses the Android operating system created by Google.

Although Samsung produces key components for other producers, including Apple, it suggests that it has a walled-off business where one side does not talk to the other to know what the other is doing. However, because they manufacture components for many other firms, "they can see three years ahead," one analyst commented. Of course, there are upstart Chinese firms that might become the next Samsung, just as Samsung has displaced Sony in consumer electronics. As such, Samsung's chairman, D. J. Lee, continues to suggest that, "We are in danger. We are in jeopardy." However, this perpetual crisis mentality has helped them to maintain their lead.

Source: M. Chafkin, 2013, Samsung: For elevating imitation to an art form, *Fast Company*, March, 108; S. Grobart, 2013, Think colossal: How Samsung became the world's no. 1 smartphone maker – and its plans to stay on top, *Bloomberg Businessweek*, April 1–April 7, 58–64; R. Hof, 2013, Report: Samsung gains in grab for Google's mobile ad revenues, *Forbes*, www.forbes.com, April 3; Y. Kim, F. Bellman, & S. Grundberg, 2013, Samsung covets low-end of smartphone market, too, *Wall Street Journal*, March 22, B5; M. Lev-Ram, 2013, Samsung's road to mobile domination, *Fortune*, February 4, 98–102; J. Osawa, M. Lee, & D. Wakabayashi, 2013, Samsung in talks to invest in Sharp, in deal that could lead to purchase of LCD panels, *Wall Street Journal*, March 6, B3; O. Shenkar, 2010, *Copycats: How Smart Companies Use Imitation to Gain a Strategic Edge*, Cambridge: Harvard Business School Press.

with customers, scripted training for on-site tech support and consideration of every store detail down to the pre-loaded photos and music on demo devices."[71]

Interestingly, even though Apple has excellent innovation capabilities, Samsung has overtaken Apple in smartphone sales, as illustrated in the Strategic Focus. It has done so largely through imitating Apple's products and by adding additional features such as larger screens, one of Samsung Electronics' core competencies. Samsung also has core competencies in manufacturing its own components and components for other competitors, which give it insight into future innovations and allow it to produce new products quickly. It also seems to retain these capabilities by continually maintaining a crisis mentality.[72]

Strategy Right NOW

Learn about Samsung, a competitor of Apple.
www.cengagebrain.com

3-3 Building Core Competencies

Two tools help firms identify their core competencies. The first consists of four specific criteria of sustainable competitive advantage that can be used to determine which capabilities are core competencies. Because the capabilities shown in Table 3.3 have satisfied these four criteria, they are core competencies. The second tool is the value chain analysis. Firms use this tool to select the value-creating competencies that should be maintained, upgraded, or developed and those that should be outsourced.

3-3a The Four Criteria of Sustainable Competitive Advantage

Capabilities that are valuable, rare, costly to imitate, and nonsubstitutable are core competencies (see Table 3.4). In turn, core competencies can lead to competitive advantages for the firm over its rivals. Capabilities failing to satisfy the four criteria are not core competencies, meaning that although every core competence is a capability, not every capability is a core competence. In slightly different words, for a capability to be a core competence, it must be valuable and unique from a customer's point of view. For a core competence to be a potential source of competitive advantage, it must be inimitable and nonsubstitutable by competitors.[73]

A sustainable competitive advantage exists only when competitors cannot duplicate the benefits of a firm's strategy or when they lack the resources to attempt imitation. For some period of time, the firm may have a core competence by using capabilities that are valuable and rare, but imitable. For example, some firms are trying to develop a core competence and potentially a competitive advantage by out-greening their competitors. (Interestingly, developing a "green" core competence can contribute to the firm's efforts to earn above-average returns while benefitting the broader society.) Since 2005, Walmart has used its

Table 3.4 The Four Criteria of Sustainable Competitive Advantage

Valuable Capabilities	• Help a firm neutralize threats or exploit opportunities
Rare Capabilities	• Are not possessed by many others
Costly-to-Imitate Capabilities	• Historical: A unique and a valuable organizational culture or brand name • Ambiguous cause: The causes and uses of a competence are unclear • Social complexity: Interpersonal relationships, trust, and friendship among managers, suppliers, and customers
Nonsubstitutable Capabilities	• No strategic equivalent

© Cengage Learning

M. Stasy

resources in ways that have allowed it to reduce its stores' carbon footprint by more than 10 percent and the carbon footprint of its trucking fleet by several times this percentage. It is also influencing its supply chain vendors to foster this same goal. For example, it has aligned with Patagonia, an outdoor apparel firm with a strong record in sustainability, "to launch the Sustainable Apparel Coalition, whose members now produce more than 30% of all clothing sold globally. The goal is to develop the tools to measure, monitor, and reduce the impact the apparel industry has on the environment."[74]

The length of time a firm can expect to create value by using its core competencies is a function of how quickly competitors can successfully imitate a good, service, or process. Value-creating core competencies may last for a relatively long period of time only when all four of the criteria we discuss next are satisfied. Thus, either Walmart or Patagonia would know that it has a core competence and possibly a competitive advantage in terms of green practices if the way the firm uses its resources to complete these practices satisfies the four criteria.

Valuable

Valuable capabilities allow the firm to exploit opportunities or neutralize threats in its external environment. By effectively using capabilities to exploit opportunities or neutralize threats, a firm creates value for customers.[75] For example, Groupon created the "daily deal" marketing space and reached $1 billion in revenue faster than any other company in history. However, many imitators appeared very quickly and often with lower fixed costs, which allowed them to survive in the space even though they were not the first mover. Groupon may succeed but shorter development cycles, especially for such online firms, makes it harder for successful startups to create enduring competitive advantage. "In other words, they are increasingly vulnerable to the same capital-market pressures that plague big companies—but before they've developed lasting corporate assets."[76]

Rare

Rare capabilities are capabilities that few, if any, competitors possess. A key question to be answered when evaluating this criterion is, "How many rival firms possess these valuable capabilities?" Capabilities possessed by many rivals are unlikely to become core competencies for any of the involved firms. Instead, valuable but common (i.e., not rare) capabilities are sources of competitive parity.[77] Competitive advantage results only when firms develop and exploit valuable capabilities that become core competencies and that differ from those shared with competitors. The central problem for Groupon is that its capabilities to produce the "daily deal" reached competitive parity quickly. Similarly, Walmart has developed capabilities to foster their sustainability/green initiatives which are valuable, but Target, another big-box retailer, may duplicate them and as such they may not be rare.

Costly to Imitate

Costly-to-imitate capabilities are capabilities that other firms cannot easily develop. Capabilities that are costly to imitate are created because of one reason or a combination of three reasons (see Table 3.4). First, a firm sometimes is able to develop capabilities because of *unique historical conditions*. As firms evolve, they often acquire or develop capabilities that are unique to them.[78]

A firm with a unique and valuable *organizational culture* that emerged in the early stages of the company's history "may have an imperfectly imitable advantage over firms founded in another historical period;"[79] one in which less valuable or less competitively useful values and beliefs strongly influenced the development of the firm's culture. Briefly discussed in Chapter 1, organizational culture is a set of values that are shared by members in the organization. We explain this in greater detail in Chapter 12. An organizational culture is a source of advantage when employees are held together tightly by their belief in it and the leaders

Valuable capabilities allow the firm to exploit opportunities or neutralize threats in its external environment.

Rare capabilities are capabilities that few, if any, competitors possess.

Costly-to-imitate capabilities are capabilities that other firms cannot easily develop.

ZUMA Press, Inc/Alamy

Even though it has well over 100 stores and 18,000 employees, CarMax has developed a small-company culture that is difficult for competitors to imitate.

who helped to create it.[80] With its emphasis on cleanliness, consistency, and service and the training that reinforces the value of these characteristics, McDonald's culture is thought by some to be a core competence and a competitive advantage. The same appears to be the case for CarMax, one of *Fortune* magazine's 100 Best Companies to Work For. CEO Tom Folliard visited 70 stores in 2012 and hosted grand openings, employee town hall meetings, and steak cookouts. CarMax epitomizes "the small-company culture" even as it "has grown to 119 stores and 18,000 employees."[81] Folliard states that "I've always believed the saying, 'if you take care of your associates, they'll take care of your customers, and the rest will take care of itself'."[82]

A second condition of being costly to imitate occurs when the link between the firm's core competencies and its competitive advantage is *causally ambiguous*.[83] In these instances, competitors can't clearly understand how a firm uses its capabilities that are core competencies as the foundation for competitive advantage. As a result, firms are uncertain about the capabilities they should develop to duplicate the benefits of a competitor's value-creating strategy. For years, firms tried to imitate Southwest Airlines' low-cost strategy but most have been unable to do so, primarily because they can't duplicate this firm's unique culture.

Social complexity is the third reason that capabilities can be costly to imitate. Social complexity means that at least some, and frequently many, of the firm's capabilities are the product of complex social phenomena. Interpersonal relationships, trust, friendships among managers and between managers and employees, and a firm's reputation with suppliers and customers are examples of socially complex capabilities. Southwest Airlines is careful to hire people who fit with its culture. This complex interrelationship between the culture and human capital adds value in ways that other airlines cannot, such as jokes on flights by the flight attendants or the cooperation between gate personnel and pilots.

Nonsubstitutable

Nonsubstitutable capabilities are capabilities that do not have strategic equivalents. This final criterion "is that there must be no strategically equivalent valuable resources that are themselves either not rare or imitable. Two valuable firm resources (or two bundles of firm resources) are strategically equivalent when they each can be separately exploited to implement the same strategies."[84] In general, the strategic value of capabilities increases as they become more difficult to substitute. The more intangible and hence invisible capabilities are, the more difficult it is for firms to find substitutes and the greater the challenge is to competitors trying to imitate a firm's value-creating strategy. Firm-specific knowledge and trust-based working relationships between managers and nonmanagerial personnel, such as existed for years at Southwest Airlines, are examples of capabilities that are difficult to identify and for which finding a substitute is challenging. However, causal ambiguity may make it difficult for the firm to learn as well and may stifle progress, because the firm may not know how to improve processes that are not easily codified and thus are ambiguous.[85]

In summary, only using valuable, rare, costly-to-imitate, and nonsubstitutable capabilities has the potential for the firm to create sustainable competitive advantages. Table 3.5 shows the competitive consequences and performance implications resulting from combinations of the four criteria of sustainability. The analysis suggested by the table helps managers determine the strategic value of a firm's capabilities. The firm should not emphasize

Nonsubstitutable capabilities are capabilities that do not have strategic equivalents.

Table 3.5 Outcomes from Combinations of the Criteria for Sustainable Competitive Advantage

Is the Capability Valuable?	Is the Capability Rare?	Is the Capability Costly to Imitate?	Is the Capability Nonsubstitutable?	Competitive Consequences	Performance Implications
No	No	No	No	• Competitive disadvantage	• Below-average returns
Yes	No	No	Yes/no	• Competitive parity	• Average returns
Yes	Yes	No	Yes/no	• Temporary competitive advantage	• Average returns to above-average returns
Yes	Yes	Yes	Yes/no	• Sustainable competitive advantage	• Above-average returns

© Cengage Learning

capabilities that fit the criteria described in the first row in the table (i.e., resources and capabilities that are neither valuable nor rare and that are imitable and for which strategic substitutes exist). Capabilities yielding competitive parity and either temporary or sustainable competitive advantage, however, will be supported. Some competitors such as Coca-Cola and PepsiCo and Boeing and Airbus may have capabilities that result in competitive parity. In such cases, the firms will nurture these capabilities while simultaneously trying to develop capabilities that can yield either a temporary or sustainable competitive advantage.

3-3b Value Chain Analysis

Value chain analysis allows the firm to understand the parts of its operations that create value and those that do not.[86] Understanding these issues is important because the firm earns above-average returns only when the value it creates is greater than the costs incurred to create that value.[87]

The value chain is a template that firms use to analyze their cost position and to identify the multiple means that can be used to facilitate implementation of a chosen strategy.[88] Today's competitive landscape demands that firms examine their value chains in a global rather than a domestic-only context.[89] In particular, activities associated with supply chains should be studied within a global context.[90]

We show a model of the value chain in Figure 3.3. As depicted in the model, a firm's value chain is segmented into value chain activities and support functions. **Value chain activities** are activities or tasks the firm completes in order to produce products and then sell, distribute, and service those products in ways that create value for customers. **Support functions** include the activities or tasks the firm completes in order to support the work being done to produce, sell, distribute, and service the products the firm is producing. A firm can develop a capability and/or a core competence in any of the value chain activities and in any of the support functions. When it does so, it has established an ability to create value for customers. In fact, as shown in Figure 3.3, customers are the ones firms seek to serve when using value chain analysis to identify their capabilities and core competencies. When using their unique core competencies to create unique value for customers that competitors cannot duplicate, firms have established one or more competitive advantages. This appears to be the case for Samsung as it relies on several core competencies, described earlier in a Strategic Focus, to quickly produce high-quality electronic products that are sold at lower prices than those of their competitors to customers throughout the world.

Value chain activities are activities or tasks the firm completes in order to produce products and then sell, distribute, and service those products in ways that create value for customers.

Support functions include the activities or tasks the firm completes in order to support the work being done to produce, sell, distribute, and service the products the firm is producing.

Figure 3.3 A Model of the Value Chain

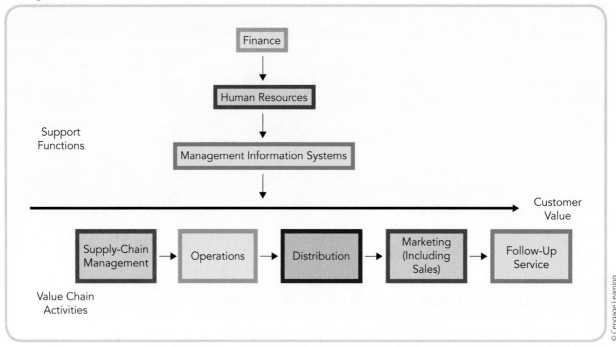

© Cengage Learning

The activities associated with each part of the value chain are shown in Figure 3.4, while the activities that are part of the tasks firms complete when dealing with support functions appear in Figure 3.5. All items in both figures should be evaluated relative to competitors' capabilities and core competencies. To become a core competence and a source of competitive advantage, a capability must allow the firm (1) to perform an activity in a manner that provides value superior to that provided by competitors, or (2) to perform a value-creating activity that competitors cannot perform. Only under these conditions does a firm create value for customers and have opportunities to capture that value.

Creating value for customers by completing activities that are part of the value chain often requires building effective alliances with suppliers (and sometimes others to which the firm outsources activities, as discussed in the next section) and developing strong positive relationships with customers. When firms have such strong positive relationships with suppliers and customers, they are said to have "social capital."[91] The relationships themselves have value because they produce knowledge transfer and access to resources that a firm may not hold internally.[92] To build social capital whereby resources such as knowledge are transferred across organizations requires trust between the parties. The partners must trust each other in order to allow their resources to be used in such a way that both parties will benefit over time and neither party will take advantage of the other.[93] Trust and social capital usually evolve over time with repeated interactions, but firms can also establish special means to jointly manage alliances that promote greater trust with the outcome of enhanced benefits for both partners.[94]

Evaluating a firm's capability to execute its value chain activities and support functions is challenging. Earlier in the chapter, we noted that identifying and assessing the value of a firm's resources and capabilities requires judgment. Judgment is equally necessary when using value chain analysis because no obviously correct model or rule is universally available to help in the process.

Figure 3.4 Creating Value through Value Chain Activities

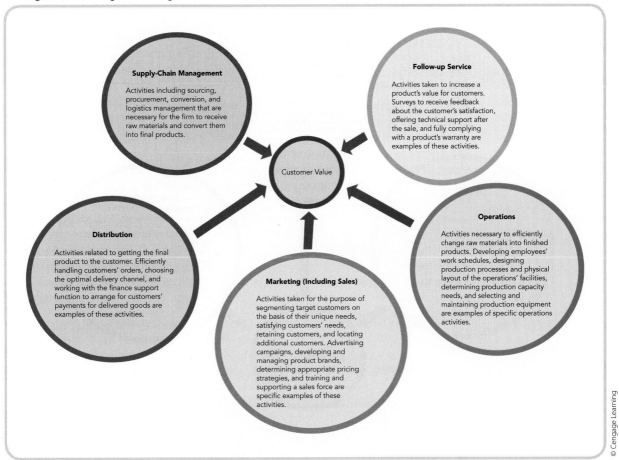

What should a firm do about value chain activities and support functions in which its resources and capabilities are not a source of core competence? Outsourcing is one solution to consider.

3-4 Outsourcing

Concerned with how components, finished goods, or services will be obtained, **outsourcing** is the purchase of a value-creating activity or a support function activity from an external supplier. Not-for-profit agencies as well as for-profit organizations actively engage in outsourcing. Firms engaging in effective outsourcing increase their flexibility, mitigate risks, and reduce their capital investments.[95] In multiple global industries, the trend toward outsourcing continues at a rapid pace.[96] Moreover, in some industries virtually all firms seek the value that can be captured through effective outsourcing. As with other strategic management process decisions, careful analysis is required before the firm decides to outsource.[97] And if outsourcing is to be used, firms must recognize that only activities where they cannot create value or where they are at a substantial disadvantage compared to competitors should be outsourced.[98]

outsourcing is the purchase of a value-creating activity or a support function activity from an external supplier.

Figure 3.5 Creating Value through Support Functions

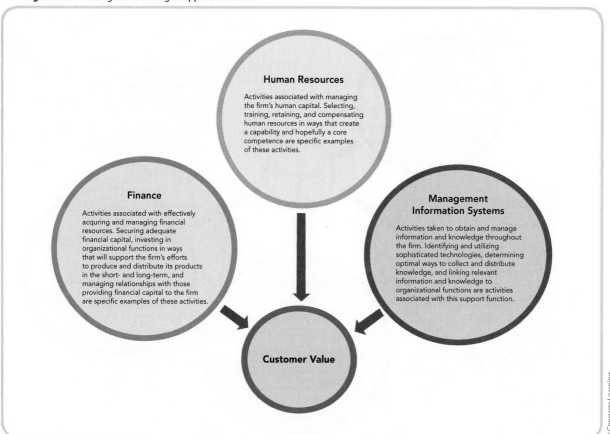

Outsourcing can be effective because few, if any, organizations possess the resources and capabilities required to achieve competitive superiority in all value chain activities and support functions. For example, research suggests that few companies can afford to develop internally all the technologies that might lead to competitive advantage.[99] By nurturing a smaller number of capabilities, a firm increases the probability of developing core competencies and achieving a competitive advantage because it does not become overextended. In addition, by outsourcing activities in which it lacks competence, the firm can fully concentrate on those areas in which it can create value. Many times firms establish cooperative relationships with outsourcing partners as illustrated in Chapter 9 on cooperative strategy.

The consequences of outsourcing cause additional concerns.[100] For the most part, these concerns revolve around the potential loss in firms' innovative ability and the loss of jobs within companies that decide to outsource some of their work activities to others. Thus, innovation and technological uncertainty are two important issues to consider when making outsourcing decisions. However, firms can also learn from outsource suppliers how to increase their own innovation capabilities.[101] Companies must be aware of these issues and be prepared to fully consider the concerns about opportunities from outsourcing suggested by different stakeholders (e.g., employees). The opportunities and concerns may be especially significant when firms outsource activities or functions to a foreign supply source (often referred to as offshoring).[102] Bangalore and Belfast are hotspots for technology

Strategy Right NOW

Learn more about new dimensions in outsourcing.
www.cengagebrain.com

outsourcing, competing with major operations in other nations such as China. Yet many firms, including Apple and General Electric, are moving activities back to the United States or keeping them home instead of moving them to a foreign location.[103] This is due in part to increasing wages in countries like China, but also because of abundant energy with low natural gas prices in the United States.

3-5 Competencies, Strengths, Weaknesses, and Strategic Decisions

David Silverman/Getty Images

This Belfast outsourcing center provides support for a U.S.-based telecom firm. Outsourcing can help firms lower costs and focus on those areas in which they can create value.

By analyzing the internal organization, firms are able to identify their strengths and weaknesses in resources, capabilities, and core competencies. For example, if a firm has weak capabilities or does not have core competencies in areas required to achieve a competitive advantage, it must acquire those resources and build the capabilities and competencies needed. Alternatively, the firm could decide to outsource a function or activity where it is weak in order to improve its ability to use its remaining resources to create value.[104]

In considering the results of examining the firm's internal organization, managers should understand that having a significant quantity of resources is not the same as having the "right" resources. The "right" resources are those with the potential to be formed into core competencies as the foundation for creating value for customers and developing competitive advantages as a result of doing so. Interestingly, decision makers sometimes become more focused and productive when seeking to find the right resources when the firm's total set of resources is constrained.[105]

Tools such as outsourcing help the firm focus on its core competencies as the source of its competitive advantages. However, evidence shows that the value-creating ability of core competencies should never be taken for granted. Moreover, the ability of a core competence to be a permanent competitive advantage can't be assumed. The reason for these cautions is that all core competencies have the potential to become *core rigidities*.[106] Typically, events occurring in the firm's external environment create conditions through which core competencies can become core rigidities, generate inertia, and stifle innovation. "Often the flip side, the dark side, of core capabilities is revealed due to external events when new competitors figure out a better way to serve the firm's customers, when new technologies emerge, or when political or social events shift the ground underneath."[107]

Historically, Borders Group Inc. relied on its large storefronts that were conveniently located for customers to visit and browse through books and magazines in a pleasant atmosphere as sources of its competitive success. Over the past decade or so, though, digital technologies (part of the firm's external environment) rapidly changed customers' shopping patterns for reading materials. Amazon.com's use of the Internet significantly changed the competitive landscape for Borders and similar competitors such as Barnes & Noble. It is possible that Borders' core competencies of store locations and a desirable physical environment for customers became core rigidities for this firm, eventually leading to its filing of bankruptcy in early 2011 and subsequent liquidation.[108] Managers studying the firm's internal organization are responsible for making certain that core competencies do not become core rigidities.

After studying its external environment to determine what it might choose to do (as explained in Chapter 2) and its internal organization to understand what it can do (as explained in this chapter), the firm has the information required to select a business-level strategy that it will use to compete against rivals. We describe different business-level strategies in the next chapter.

SUMMARY

- In the current competitive landscape, the most effective organizations recognize that strategic competitiveness and above-average returns result only when core competencies (identified by studying the firm's internal organization) are matched with opportunities (determined by studying the firm's external environment).

- No competitive advantage lasts forever. Over time, rivals use their own unique resources, capabilities, and core competencies to form different value-creating propositions that duplicate the focal firm's ability to create value for customers. Because competitive advantages are not permanently sustainable, firms must exploit their current advantages while simultaneously using their resources and capabilities to form new advantages that can lead to future competitive success.

- Effectively managing core competencies requires careful analysis of the firm's resources (inputs to the production process) and capabilities (resources that have been purposely integrated to achieve a specific task or set of tasks). The knowledge the firm's human capital possesses is among the most significant of an organization's capabilities and ultimately provides the base for most competitive advantages. The firm must create an organizational culture that allows people to integrate their individual knowledge with that held by others so that, collectively, the firm has a significant amount of value-creating organizational knowledge.

- Capabilities are a more likely source of core competence and subsequently of competitive advantages than are individual resources. How a firm nurtures and supports its capabilities

so they can become core competencies is less visible to rivals, making efforts to understand and imitate the focal firm's capabilities difficult.

- Only when a capability is valuable, rare, costly to imitate, and nonsubstitutable is it a core competence and a source of competitive advantage. Over time, core competencies must be supported, but they cannot be allowed to become core rigidities. Core competencies are a source of competitive advantage only when they allow the firm to create value by exploiting opportunities in its external environment. When this is no longer possible, the company shifts its attention to forming other capabilities that satisfy the four criteria of a sustainable competitive advantage.

- Value chain analysis is used to identify and evaluate the competitive potential of resources and capabilities. By studying their skills relative to those associated with value chain activities and support functions, firms can understand their cost structure and identify the activities through which they can create value.

- When the firm cannot create value in either a value chain activity or a support function, outsourcing is considered. Used commonly in the global economy, outsourcing is the purchase of a value-creating activity from an external supplier. The firm should outsource only to companies possessing a competitive advantage in terms of the particular primary or support activity under consideration. In addition, the firm must continuously verify that it is not outsourcing activities from which it could create value.

REVIEW QUESTIONS

1. Why is it important for a firm to study and understand its internal organization?

2. What is value? Why is it critical for the firm to create value? How does it do so?

3. What are the differences between tangible and intangible resources? Why is it important for decision makers to understand these differences? Are tangible resources more valuable for creating capabilities than are intangible resources, or is the reverse true? Why?

4. What are capabilities? How do firms create capabilities?

5. What four criteria must capabilities satisfy for them to become core competencies? Why is it important for firms to use these criteria to evaluate their capabilities' value-creating potential?

6. What is value chain analysis? What does the firm gain by successfully using this tool?

7. What is outsourcing? Why do firms outsource? Will outsourcing's importance grow in the future? If so, why?

8. How do firms identify internal strengths and weaknesses? Why is it vital that managers have a clear understanding of their firm's strengths and weaknesses?

9. What are core rigidities? What does it mean to say that each core competence could become a core rigidity?

EXPERIENTIAL EXERCISES

EXERCISE 1: WHAT MAKES A GREAT OUTSOURCING FIRM?

The focus of this chapter is on understanding how firm resources and capabilities serve as the cornerstone for competencies and, ultimately, a competitive advantage. However, when firms cannot create value in either a value chain or support activity, outsourcing becomes a potential strategy. According to the International Association of Outsourcing Professionals (IAOP) (http://www.iaop.org/) at their latest longitudinal survey the results suggested some interesting trends:

1. Outsourcing service providers are taking increased steps to diversify their services as offerings are becoming more globally commoditized.

2. Firms are offering more low-end and high-end services in search of improving margins.

3. There is a resurgent trend toward nearshoring, where service providers are relocating around the globe to be closer to their clients.

4. This is changing dramatically both the scale and scope of operations for outsourcing firms.

The IAOP annually announces its Global Outsourcing 100, which represents the world's best outsourcing service providers. The evaluation process mirrors that employed by many top customers and considers four key criteria: (1) size and growth in revenue, employees, centers, and countries served; (2) customer experience as demonstrated through the value being created at the company's top customers; (3) depth and breadth of competencies as demonstrated through industry recognition, relevant certifications, and investment in the development of people, processes, and technologies; and (4) management capabilities as reflected in the experience and accomplishments of the organization's top leaders and investment in management systems that ensure outsourcing success.

With a team, pick one of the Top 100 Global best outsourcing firms to analyze from the list on the IAOP Web site at (http://www. iaop.org/). Prepare a brief presentation formed around the contents of the chapter that addresses at a minimum the following questions:

▨ Why was this company chosen to be in the top 100? What has been the company's history as regards outsourcing as a source of revenue?

▨ How does the firm describe, or imply, its value proposition?

▨ What unique competitive advantage does the firm exhibit?

▨ Do you consider this to be a sustainable competitive advantage? Utilize the four criteria of sustainable competitive advantage as your guide.

EXERCISE 2: WHAT IS YOUR CORE COMPETENCY?

In this chapter, the concepts of resources, capabilities, and core competencies were introduced as the foundation for establishing a competitive advantage. Resources (tangible and intangible) alone do not create value for customers but are bundled to create organizational capabilities, which are the basis for a firm's core competencies.

According to Prahalad and Hamel (Harvard Business Review, May-June 1990) there are four guidelines to identifying core competencies:

1. They support the delivery and production of a variety of services and products (thereby giving access to a variety of markets).

2. They always make a significant contribution to perceptions of services and products (i.e., they impact something that your client cares about).

3. They are often difficult for competition to imitate (because they are generally developed with a significant investment of time and resources).

4. They tend to be relatively stable over time.

However, while we normally think of core competency as a concept to be applied to existing organizations, it can equally be effective in application to one personally. If done well the result can be a strategic advantage as you enter the hiring process in that you will be able to define your core competency on your resume and at interviews.

Some interesting research in this area is being done at the University of Victoria Co-Operative Education Program and Career Services. Their work highlights some areas that are the key to developing personal core competencies, as follows:

▨ Personal management
▨ Communication
▨ Managing information
▨ Research and analysis

- ■ Project and task management
- ■ Teamwork
- ■ Commitment to quality
- ■ Professional behavior
- ■ Social responsibility
- ■ Continuous learning

More information on this as well as worksheets to guide you through each area may be found at http://www.uvic.ca/coopandcareer/ studentsalumni/resources/competencykit/core.php. However numerous other avenues can provide you with a criteria map or create your own that best describes you.

This is an individual assignment. You are to create a personal core competency profile that assesses your individual assets (both tangible and intangible) as well as how those have or are developing into specific capabilities. Lastly identify 3-5 core competencies you currently possess. Your analysis will be due in a written report to your professor.

VIDEO CASE

ORGANIZATIONAL CULTURE CREATES STRATEGIC COMPETITIVENESS

Zappos.com, an online shoe retailer, has been listed in *Fortune* magazine's 100 best companies to work for over the past two years because employees feel empowered and respected. Recognized as a thriving company due to its unique organizational culture, from its untimed and unscripted call centers to "bald and blue" days, Zappos gives its employees the opportunity to shine in the workplace. Tony Shay, CEO, believes that Zappos is making the world a better place by allowing employees to be happy and to look at their job as a place to be for life. By receiving job security and benefits on par with competitors, Zappos employees remain dedicated to promoting branding opportunities with every customer. As a result, Amazon.com willingly purchased Zappos for $1.2 billion, and with both companies sharing such a strong passion for customer service, Zappos was excited to begin growing together. In 2010, Zappos experienced so much growth that it restructured the company into ten separate companies. The goal is to position Zappos as the online service leader.

Be prepared to discuss the following concepts and questions in class:

Concepts

- ■ Value
- ■ Resources, capabilities, and core competencies
- ■ Sustainable competitive advantage
- ■ Value chain
- ■ Outsourcing

Questions

1. How is Zappos' organizational culture creating value?

2. What resources and resulting capabilities and core competencies do you see within the Zappos organization that gives it strategic competitiveness?

3. Will Zappos' competitive advantage be sustainable?

4. What value chain activities performed by Zappos help to create value for its customers?

5. Why do you think Zappos is not outsourcing its call centers?

NOTES

1. E. Rueda-Sabater & D. Derosby, 2011, The evolving Internet in 2025: Four scenarios, *Strategy & Leadership*, 39(1): 32–38.
2. C. Gilbert, M. Eyring, & R. N. Foster, 2012, Two routes to resilience. *Harvard Business Review*, 90(12): 65–73; H. A. Ndofor, D. G. Sirmon, & X. He, 2011, Firm resources, competitive actions and performance: Investigating a mediated model with evidence from the in-vitro diagnostics industry, *Strategic Management Journal*, 32: 640–657.
3. K. Wilson & Y. L. Doz, 2012, 10 rules for managing global innovation, *Harvard Business Review*, 90(10): 84–90;

D. Dunlap-Hinkler, M. Kotabe, & R. Mudambi, 2010, A story of breakthrough versus incremental innovation: Corporate entrepreneurship in the global pharmaceutical industry, *Strategic Entrepreneurship Journal*, 4: 106–127.
4. S. Terlep, 2011, GM's latest change agent tackles designs, red tape, *Wall Street Journal*, www.wsj.com, June 15.
5. R. Bapna, N. Langer, A. Mehra, R. Gopal, & A. Gupta, 2013, Human capital investments and employee performance: An analysis of IT services industry, *Management Science*, 59(3): 641–658; R. E. Ployhart & T. P. Moliterno, 2011, Emergence of the

human capital resource: A multilevel model, *Academy of Management Review*, 36: 127–150; A. Leiponen, 2008, Control of intellectual assets in client relationships: Implications for innovation, *Strategic Management Journal*, 29: 1371–1394.
6. 2012, 3M ranks as one of the top innovators on Booz & Company list for third straight year, www.3m.com, press release, November 1.
7. M. A. Hitt, R. D. Ireland, D. G. Sirmon, & C. A. Trahms, 2011, Strategic entrepreneurship: Creating value for individuals, organizations, and society, *Academy of Management Perspective*, 25: 57–75;

C. D. Zatzick & R. D. Iverson, 2007, High-involvement management and work force reduction: Competitive advantage or disadvantage? *Academy of Management Journal*, 49: 999–1015.

8. R. Florida, 2005, *The Flight of the Creative Class*, New York: HarperBusiness.

9. L. Ngo & A. O'Cass, 2012, In search of innovation and customer-related performance superiority: The role of market orientation, marketing capability, and innovation capability interactions, *Journal of Product Innovation Management*, 29(5): 861–877; M. Gruber, F. Heinemann, M. Brettel, & S. Hunbeling, 2010, Configurations of resources and capabilities and their performance implications: An exploratory study on technology ventures, *Strategic Management Journal*, 31: 1337–1356; D. G. Sirmon, M. A. Hitt, & R. D. Ireland, 2007, Managing firm resources in dynamic markets to create value: Looking inside the black box, *Academy of Management Review*, 32: 273–292.

10. F. Polidoro, Jr. & P. K. Toh, 2011, Letting rivals come close or warding them off? The effects of substitution threat on imitation deterrence, *Academy of Management Journal*, 54: 369–392; A. W. King, 2007, Disentangling interfirm and intrafirm causal ambiguity: A conceptual model of causal ambiguity and sustainable competitive advantage, *Academy of Management Review*, 32: 156–178.

11. M. Semadeni & B. S. Anderson, 2010, The follower's dilemma: Innovation and imitation in the professional services industry, *Academy of Management Journal*, 53: 1175–1193; U. Ljungquist, 2007, Core competency beyond identification: Presentation of a model, *Management Decision*, 45: 393–402.

12. M. G. Jacobides, S. G. Winter, & S. M. Kassberger, 2012, The dynamics of wealth, profit, and sustainable advantage, *Strategic Management Journal*, 33(12): 1384–1410.

13. L. A. Costa, K. Cool, & I. Dierickx, 2013, The competitive implications of the deployment of unique resources, *Strategic Management Journal*, 34(4): 445–463; M. A. Peteraf & J. B. Barney, 2003, Unraveling the resource-based tangle, *Managerial and Decision Economics*, 24: 309–323; J. B. Barney, 2001, Is the resource-based "view" a useful perspective for strategic management research? Yes, *Academy of Management Review*, 26: 41–56.

14. T. N. Garavan, 2012, Global talent management in science-based firms: An exploratory investigation of the pharmaceutical industry during the global downturn, *International Journal of Human Resource Management*, 23(12): 2428–2449; P. Clements & J. McGregor, 2012, Better, faster, cheaper: Pick any three, *Business Horizons*, 55(2): 201–208; G. Zied & J. McGuire, 2011, Multimarket competition, mobility barriers, and firm performance, *Journal of Management Studies*, 48: 857–890.

15. Facebook, 2013, Volkswagen home page, www.volkswagen.com, March 20.

16. A. Arino, 2011, Building the global enterprise: Strategic assembly, *Global Strategy Journal*, 1: 47–49; M. Javidan, R. M. Steers, & M. A. Hitt (eds.), 2007, *The Global Mindset*: Amsterdam: Elsevier Ltd; T. M. Begley & D. P. Boyd, 2003, The need for a corporate global mindset, *MIT Sloan Management Review*, 44(2): 25–32.

17. A. Diaz, M. Magni, & F. Poh, 2012, From oxcart to Wal-Mart: Four keys to reaching emerging-market consumers, *McKinsey Quarterly*, October, 58–67; O. Levy, S. Taylor, & N. A. Boyacigiller, 2010, On the rocky road to strong global culture, *MIT Sloan Management Review*, 51: 20–22; O. Levy, S. Beechler, S. Taylor, & N. A. Boyacigiller, 2007, What we talk about when we talk about "global mindset": Managerial cognition in multinational corporations, *Journal of International Business Studies*, 38: 231–258.

18. R. A. D'Aveni, G. B. Dagnino, & K. G. Smith, 2010, The age of temporary advantage, *Strategic Management Journal*, 31: 1371–1385; E. Danneels, 2008, Organizational antecedents of second-order competences, *Strategic Management Journal*, 29: 519–543.

19. S. A. Zahra & S. Nambisan, 2012, Entrepreneurship and strategic thinking in business ecosystems, *Business Horizons*, 55(3): 219–229; H. Hoang & F. T. Rothaermel, 2010, Leveraging internal and external experience: Exploration, exploitation, and R&D project performance, *Strategic Management Journal*, 31: 734–758.

20. D. G. Sirmon, M. A. Hitt, R. D. Ireland, & B. A. Gilbert, 2011, Resource orchestration to create competitive advantage: Breadth, depth, and life cycle effects, *Journal of Management*, 37(5): 1390–1412; P. L. Drnevich & A. P. Kriauciunas, 2011, Clarifying the conditions and limits of the contributions of ordinary and dynamic capabilities to relative firm performance, *Strategic Management Journal*, 32: 254–279; R. Adner & R. Kapoor, 2010, Value creation in innovation ecosystems: How the structure of technological interdependence affects firm performance in new technology generations, *Strategic Management Journal*, 31: 306–333.

21. M. A. Hitt, R. D. Ireland, D. G. Sirmon, & C. A. Trahms, 2011, Strategic entrepreneurship: Creating value for individuals, organizations, and society, *Academy of Management Perspectives*, 25(2): 57–75; D. G. Sirmon, S. Gove, & M. A. Hitt, 2008, Resource management in dyadic competitive rivalry: The effects of resource bundling and deployment, *Academy of Management Journal*, 51: 919–935.

22. J. S. Harrison, D. A. Bosse, & R. A. Phillips, 2010, Managing for stakeholders, stakeholder utility functions, and competitive advantage, *Strategic Management Journal*, 31: 58–74; J. L. Morrow, Jr., D. G. Sirmon, M. A. Hitt, &

T. R. Holcomb, 2007, Creating value in the face of declining performance: Firm strategies and organizational recovery, *Strategic Management Journal*, 28: 271–283.

23. 2012, Why Walmart can pull off "everyday low prices" but everyone else keeps failing, www.businessinsider.com, September 3; K. Talley, 2011, Wal-Mart results to grab investor interest, *Wall Street Journal*, www.wsj.com, May 13.

24. V. Rindova, W. J. Ferrier, & R. Wiltbank, 2010, Value from gestalt: How sequences of competitive actions create advantage for firms in nascent markets, *Strategic Management Journal*, 31: 1474–1497.

25. A. O'Cass & P. Sok, 2012, Examining the role of within functional area resource-capability complementarity in achieving customer and product-based performance outcomes, *Journal of Strategic Marketing*, 20(4): 345–363; D. G. Sirmon, M. A. Hitt, J.-L. Arregle, & J. T. Campbell, 2010, The dynamic interplay of capability strengths and weaknesses: Investigating the bases of temporary competitive advantage, *Strategic Management Journal*, 31: 1386–1409.

26. F. Aime, S. Johnson, J. W. Ridge, & A. D. Hill, 2010, The routine may be stable but the advantage is not: Competitive implications of key employee mobility, *Strategic Management Journal*, 31: 75–87.

27. D. J. Teece, 2012, Dynamic capabilities: Routines versus entrepreneurial action, *Journal of Management Studies*, 49(8): 1395–1401; K. Z. Zhou & F. Wu, 2010, Technological capability, strategic flexibility, and product innovation, *Strategic Management Journal*, 31: 547–561.

28. M. H. Kunc & J. D. W. Morecroft, 2010, Managerial decision making and firm performance under a resource-based paradigm, *Strategic Management Journal*, 31: 1164–1182; J. Woiceshyn & L. Falkenberg, 2008, Value creation in knowledge-based firms: Aligning problems and resources, *Academy of Management Perspectives*, 22(2): 85–99; M. R. Haas & M. T. Hansen, 2005, When using knowledge can hurt performance: The value of organizational capabilities in a management consulting company, *Strategic Management Journal*, 26: 1–24.

29. C. M. Christensen, 2001, The past and future of competitive advantage, *Sloan Management Review*, 42(2): 105–109.

30. S. K. Parker & C. G. Collins, 2010, Taking stock: Integrating and differentiating multiple proactive behaviors, *Journal of Management*, 36: 633–662; O. Gottschalg & M. Zollo, 2007, Interest alignment and competitive advantage, *Academy of Management Review*, 32: 418–437.

31. Y. Y. Kor & A. Mesko, 2013, Dynamic managerial capabilities: Configuration and orchestration of top executives' capabilities and the firm's dominant logic, *Strategic Management Journal*, 34(2): 233–244; D. P. Forbes, 2007, Reconsidering

the strategic implications of decision comprehensiveness, *Academy of Management Review*, 32: 361–376.

32. J. Surroca, J. A. Tribo, & S. Waddock, 2010, Corporate responsibility and financial performance: The role of intangible resources, *Strategic Management Journal*, 31: 463–490; T. M. Jones, W. Felps, & G. A. Bigley, 2007, Ethical theory and stakeholder-related decisions: The role of stakeholder culture, *Academy of Management Review*, 32: 137–155.

33. M. S. Gary & R. E. Wood, 2011, Mental models, decision rules, and performance heterogeneity, *Strategic Management Journal*, 32: 569–594; Y. Deutsch, T. Keil, & T. Laamanen, 2007, Decision making in acquisitions: The effect of outside directors' compensation on acquisition patterns, *Journal of Management*, 33: 30–56.

34. C. B. Bingham & K. M. Eisenhardt, 2011, Rational heuristics: The 'simple rules' that strategists learn from process experience, *Strategic Management Journal*, 32(13): 1437–1464; S. W. Bradley, H. Aldrich, D. A. Shepherd, & J. Wiklund, 2011, Resources, environmental change and survival: Asymmetric paths of young independent and subsidiary organizations, *Strategic Management Journal*, 32: 486–509; A. Phene & P. Almeida, 2008, Innovation in multinational subsidiaries: The role of knowledge assimilation and subsidiary capabilities, *Journal of International Business Studies*, 39: 901–919.

35. Y. Zhang & J. Gimeno, 2010, Earnings pressure and competitive behavior: Evidence from the U.S. electricity industry, *Academy of Management Journal*, 53: 743–768; L. M. Lodish & C. F. Mela, 2007, If brands are built over years, why are they managed over quarters? *Harvard Business Review*, 85(7/8): 104–112.

36. P. M. Madsen & V. Desai, 2010, Failing to learn? The effects of failure and success on organizational learning in the global orbital launch vehicle industry, *Academy of Management Journal*, 53: 451–476; P. C. Nutt, 2002, *Why Decisions Fail*, San Francisco: Berrett-Koehler Publishers.

37. J. P. Eggers, 2012, All experience is not created equal: Learning, adapting and focusing in product portfolio management, *Strategic Management Journal*, 33(3): 315–335.

38. J. D. Ford & L. W. Ford, 2010, Stop blaming resistance to change and start using it, *Organizational Dynamics*, 39: 24–36.

39. K. Muehlfeld, P. Rao Sahib, & A. Van Witteloostuijn, 2012, A contextual theory of organizational learning from failures and successes: A study of acquisition completion in the global newspaper industry, 1981–2008, *Strategic Management Journal*, 33(8): 938–964; Y. Zhang, H. Li, Y. Li, & L.-A. Zhou, 2010, FDI spillovers in an emerging market: The role of foreign firms' country origin diversity and domestic firms'

absorptive capacity, *Strategic Management Journal*, 31: 969–989.

40. M. Nisen, 2012, You can learn more from failure than success, *Business Insider*, www.businessinsider.com, December 17.

41. 2013, Strategy in a world of "biblical change": Our era of uncertainty calls for business leaders with vision, foresight and a global perspective, *Strategic Direction*, 29(3): 19–22; G. S. Dowell, M. B. Shackell, & N. V. Stuart, 2011, Boards, CEOs, and surviving a financial crisis: Evidence from the internet shakeout, *Strategic Management Journal*, 32(10): 1025–1045; R. E. Hoskisson & L. W. Busenitz, 2001, Market uncertainty and learning distance in corporate entrepreneurship entry mode choice, in M. A. Hitt, R. D. Ireland, S. M. Camp, & D. L. Sexton (eds.), *Strategic Entrepreneurship: Creating a New Integrated Mindset*, Oxford, UK: Blackwell Publishers, 151–172.

42. A. Arora & A. Nandkumar, 2012, Insecure advantage? Markets for technology and the value of resources for entrepreneurial ventures, *Strategic Management Journal*, 33(3): 231–251; S. S. K. Lam & J. C. K. Young, 2010, Staff localization and environmental uncertainty on firm performance in China, *Asia Pacific Journal of Management*, 27: 677–695.

43. K. Harlin, 2012, Arch, Peabody down on slowing China coal imports, *Investor's Business Daily*, www.ibd.com, December 21.

44. A. Leiponen & C. E. Helfat, 2010, Innovation objectives, knowledge sources, and the benefits of breadth, *Strategic Management Journal*, 31: 224–236; G. P. West, III, 2007, Collective cognition: When entrepreneurial teams, not individuals, make decisions, *Entrepreneurship Theory and Practice*, 31: 77–102.

45. M. Gary, R. E. Wood, & T. Pillinger, 2012, Enhancing mental models, analogical transfer, and performance in strategic decision making, *Strategic Management Journal*, 33(11): 1229–1246; J. R. Mitchell, D. A. Shepherd, & M. P. Sharfman, 2011, Erratic strategic decisions: When and why managers are inconsistent in strategic decision making, *Strategic Management Journal*, 32(7): 683–704.

46. P. D. Windschitl, A. M. Scherer, A. R. Smith, & J. P. Rose, 2013, Why so confident? The influence of outcome desirability on selective exposure and likelihood judgment, *Organizational Behavior & Human Decision Processes*, 120(1): 73–86; G. Davies, R. Chum, & M. A. Kamins, 2010, Reputation gaps and the performance of service organizations, *Strategic Management Journal*, 31: 530–546.

47. C. Weigelt, 2013, Leveraging supplier capabilities: The role of locus of capability deployment, *Strategic Management Journal*, 34(1): 1–21; Ndofor, Sirmon, & He, Firm resources, competitive actions and performance; P. A. Geroski, J. Mata, & P. Portugal, 2010, Founding conditions

and the survival of new firms, *Strategic Management Journal*, 31: 510–529.

48. J. M. Shaver, 2011, The benefits of geographic sales diversification: How exporting facilitates capital investment, *Strategic Management Journal*, 32(10): 1046–1060; Sirmon, Hitt, Ireland, & Gilbert, Resource orchestration to create competitive advantage; K. Meyer, S. Estrin, S. K. Bhaumik, & M. W. Peng, 2009, Institutions, resources, and entry strategies in emerging economies, *Strategic Management Journal*, 30: 61–80.

49. A. Vance, 2011, The cloud: Battle of the tech titans, *Bloomberg Businessweek*, www.bloomberg.com, March 3.

50. B. S. Anderson & Y. Eshima, 2013, The influence of firm age and intangible resources on the relationship between entrepreneurial orientation and firm growth among Japanese SMEs, *Journal of Business Venturing*, 28(3): 413–429; D. Somaya, Y. Kim, & N. S. Vonortas, 2011, Exclusivity in licensing alliances: Using hostages to support technology commercialization, *Strategic Management Journal*, 32: 159–186.

51. J. Choi, G. W. Hecht, & W. B. Tayler, 2012, Lost in translation: The effects of incentive compensation on strategy surrogation, *Accounting Review*, 87(4): 1135–1163; A. M. Arikan & L. Capon, 2010, Do newly public acquirers benefit or suffer from their pre-IPO affiliations with underwriters and VCs? *Strategic Management Journal*, 31: 1257–1298; J. A. Dubin, 2007, Valuing intangible assets with a nested logit market share model, *Journal of Econometrics*, 139: 285–302.

52. A. M. Webber, 2000, New math for a new economy, *Fast Company*, January/February, 214–224.

53. F. Neffke & M. Henning, 2013, Skill relatedness and firm diversification, *Strategic Management Journal*, 34(3): 297–316; E. Danneels, 2011, Trying to become a different type of company: Dynamic capability at Smith Corona, *Strategic Management Journal*, 32: 1–31; M. Song, C. Droge, S. Hanvanich, & R. Calantone, 2005, Marketing and technology resource complementarity: An analysis of their interaction effect in two environmental contexts, *Strategic Management Journal*, 26: 259–276.

54. J. Gómez & P. Vargas, 2012, Intangible resources and technology adoption in manufacturing firms, *Research Policy*, 41(9): 1607–1619; K. E. Meyer, R. Mudambi, & R. Narula, 2011, Multinational enterprises and local contexts: The opportunities and challenges of multiple embeddedness, *Journal of Management Studies*, 48: 235–252.

55. J. B. Quinn, P. Anderson, & S. Finkelstein, 1996, Making the most of the best, *Harvard Business Review*, 74(2): 71–80.

56. R. E. Ployhart, C. H. Van Iddekinge, & W. I. MacKenzie, Jr., 2011, Acquiring and developing human capital in service

contexts: The interconnectedness of human capital resources, *Academy of Management Journal*, 54: 353–368; N. Stieglitz & K. Heine, 2007, Innovations and the role of complementarities in a strategic theory of the firm, *Strategic Management Journal*, 28: 1–15.

57. K. Kim, B. Jeon, H. Jung, W. Lu, & J. Jones, 2012, Effective employment brand equity through sustainable competitive advantage, marketing strategy, and corporate image, *Journal of Business Research*, 65(11): 1612–1617; L. Diestre & N. Rajagopalan, 2011, An environmental perspective on diversification: The effects of chemical relatedness and regulatory sanctions, *Academy of Management Journal*, 54: 97–115.

58. G. Dowling & P. Moran, 2012, Corporate reputations: Built in or bolted on? *California Management Review*, 54(2): 25–42; M. D. Pfarrer, T. G. Pollock, & V. P. Rindova, 2010, A tale of two assets: The effects of firm reputation and celebrity on earnings surprises and investors' reactions, *Academy of Management Journal*, 53: 1131–1152; T. G. Pollock, G. Chen, & E. M. Jackson, 2010, How much prestige is enough? Assessing the value of multiple types of high-status affiliates for young firms, *Journal of Business Venturing*, 25: 6–23.

59. Y. Wang, G. Berens, & C. van Riel, 2012, Competing in the capital market with a good reputation, *Corporate Reputation Review*, 15(3): 198–221; J. J. Ebbers & N. M. Wijnberg, 2012, Nascent ventures competing for start-up capital: Matching reputations and investors, *Journal of Business Venturing*, 27(3): 372–384; P. M. Lee, T. G. Pollock, & K. Jin, 2011, The contingent value of venture capitalist reputation, *Strategic Organization*, 9: 33–69.

60. J. D. Townsend, S. Cavusgil, & R. J. Calantone, 2012, Building market-based assets in a globally competitive market: A longitudinal study of automotive brands, *Advances in International Marketing*, 11(23): 3–37; K. T. Smith, M. Smith, & K. Wang, 2010, Does brand management of corporate reputation translate into higher market value? *Journal of Strategic Marketing*, 18: 201–221.

61. N. Rosenbusch & J. Brinckmann, 2011, Is innovation always beneficial? A meta-analysis of the relationship between innovation and performance in SMEs, *Journal of Business Venturing*, 26: 441–457; J. Blasberg & V. Vishwanath, 2003, Making cool brands hot, *Harvard Business Review*, 81(6): 20–22.

62. 2013, Harley-Davidson Motor Apparel, www.harley-davidson.com, April 5.

63. D. Sacks, 2013, Can you hear me now? *Fast Company*, February, 40.

64. V. V. Kumar, V. Bhaskaran, R. Mirchandani, & M. Shah, 2013, Creating a measurable social media marketing strategy: Increasing the value and ROI of intangibles and tangibles for Hokey Pokey, *Marketing Science*, 32(2): 194–212.

65. D. Lessard, R. Lucea, & L. Vives, 2013, Building your company's capabilities through global expansion, *MIT Sloan Management Review*, 54(2): 61–67; T. Isobe, S. Makino, & D. B. Montgomery, 2008, Technological capabilities and firm performance: The case of small manufacturing firms in Japan, *Asia Pacific Journal of Management*, 25: 413–425; S. Dutta, O. Narasimhan, & S. Rajiv, 2005, Conceptualizing and measuring capabilities: Methodology and empirical application, *Strategic Management Journal*, 26: 277–285.

66. R. W. Coff, 2010, The coevolution of rent appropriation and capability development, *Strategic Management Journal*, 31: 711–733; M. Kroll, B. A. Walters, & P. Wright, 2008, Board vigilance, director experience and corporate outcomes, *Strategic Management Journal*, 29(4): 363–382; J. Bitar & T. Hafsi, 2007, Strategizing through the capability lens: Sources and outcomes of integration, *Management Decision*, 45: 403–419.

67. A. M. Subramanian, 2012, A longitudinal study of the influence of intellectual human capital on firm exploratory innovation, *IEEE Transactions on Engineering Management*, 59(4): 540–550; T. Dalziel, R. J. Gentry, & M. Bowerman, 2011, An integrated agency-resource dependence view of the influence of directors' human and relational capital on firms' R&D spending, *Journal of Management Studies*, 48(6): 1217–1242; T. A. Stewart & A. P. Raman, 2007, Lessons from Toyota's long drive, *Harvard Business Review*, 85(7/8): 74–83.

68. G. Colvin, 2012, The economy is scary, but smart companies can still dominate, *Fortune*, September 24, 77; S. Lohr, 2011, Lessons in longevity, from IBM, *New York Times*, www.nytimes.com, June 18.

69. K. M. Heimeriks, M. Schijven, & S. Gates, 2012, Manifestations of higher-order routines: The underlying mechanisms of deliberate learning in the context of postacquisition integration, *Academy of Management Journal*, 55(3): 703–726; N. P. Tuan & T. Yoshi, 2010, Organisational capabilities, competitive advantage and performance in supporting industries in Vietnam, *Asian Academy of Management Journal*, 15: 1–21; C. Zott, 2003, Dynamic capabilities and the emergence of intraindustry differential firm performance: Insights from a simulation study, *Strategic Management Journal*, 24: 97–125.

70. H. R. Greve, 2009, Bigger and safer: The diffusion of competitive advantage, *Strategic Management Journal*, 30: 1–23; C. K. Prahalad & G. Hamel, 1990, The core competence of the corporation, *Harvard Business Review*, 68(3): 79–93.

71. Y. I. Kane & I. Sherr, 2011, Secrets from Apple's genius bar: Full loyalty, no negativity, *Wall Street Journal*, www.wsj.com, June 15.

72. S. Grobart, 2013, Think colossal: How Samsung became the world's no. 1 smartphone maker – and its plans to stay on top, *Bloomberg Businessweek*, April 1–April 7, 58–64.

73. C. Welter, D. A. Bosse, & S. A. Alvarez, 2013, The interaction between managerial and technological capabilities as a determinant of company performance: An empirical study of biotech firms, *International Journal of Management*, 30(2): 272–284; M. Makri, M. A. Hitt, & P. J. Lane, 2010, Complementary technologies, knowledge relatedness, and invention outcomes in high technology mergers and acquisitions, *Strategic Management Journal*, 31: 602–628; S. Newbert, 2008, Value, rareness, competitive advantage, and performance: A conceptual-level empirical investigation of the resource-based view of the firm, *Strategic Management Journal*, 29: 745–768.

74. B. Dumaine, 2012, Built to last, *Fortune*, August 13, 16; 2011, Wal-Mart's green initiatives shouldn't be ignored, *Los Angeles Times*, www.latimes.com, May 30.

75. D. S. K. Lim, N. Celly, E. A. Morse, & W. G. Rowe, 2013, Rethinking the effectiveness of asset and cost retrenchment: The contingency effects of a firm's rent creation mechanism, *Strategic Management Journal*, 34(1): 42–61.

76. S. D. Anthony, 2012, The new corporate garage, *Harvard Business Review*, 90(9): 44–53.

77. Q. Gu & J. W. Lu, 2011, Effects of inward investment on outward investment: The venture capital industry worldwide—1985–2007, *Journal of International Business Studies*, 42: 263–284; S. A. Zahra, 2008, The virtuous cycle of discovery and creation of entrepreneurial opportunities, *Strategic Entrepreneurship Journal*, 2: 243–257.

78. H. Rahmandad, 2012, Impact of growth opportunities and competition on firm-level capability development trade-offs, *Organization Science*, 23(1): 138–154; C. A. Coen & C. A. Maritan, 2011, Investing in capabilities: The dynamics of resource allocation, *Organization Science*, 22: 199–217.

79. J. B. Barney, 1991, Firm resources and sustained competitive advantage, *Journal of Management*, 17: 99–120.

80. C. M. Wilderom, P. T. van den Berg, & U. J. Wiersma, 2012, A longitudinal study of the effects of charismatic leadership and organizational culture on objective and perceived corporate performance, *Leadership Quarterly*, 23(5): 835–848; C. C. Maurer, P. Bansal, & M. M. Crossan, 2011, Creating economic value through social values: Introducing a culturally informed resource-based view, *Organization Science*, 22: 432–448.

81. E. Fry, 2013, How CarMax cares, *Fortune*, April 8, 21.

82. Ibid., 21.

83. L. Mulotte, P. Dussauge, & W. Mitchell, 2013, Does pre-entry licensing undermine the

performance of subsequent independent activities? Evidence from the global aerospace industry, 1944–2000, *Strategic Management Journal*, 34(3): 358–372; M. H. Kunc & J. D. W. Morecroft, 2010, Managerial decision making and firm performance under a resource-based paradigm, *Strategic Management Journal*, 31: 1164–1182; A. W. King & C. P. Zeithaml, 2001, Competencies and firm performance: Examining the causal ambiguity paradox, *Strategic Management Journal*, 22: 75–99.

84. Barney, Firm resources, 111.

85. E. Beleska-Spasova & K. W. Glaister, 2013, Intrafirm causal ambiguity in an international context, *International Business Review*, 22(1): 32–46; K. Srikanth & P. Puranam, 2011, Integrating distributed work: Comparing task design, communication, and tacit coordination mechanisms, *Strategic Management Journal*, 32: 849–875; A. K. Chatterji, 2009, Spawned with a silver spoon? Entrepreneurial performance and innovation in the medical device industry, *Strategic Management Journal*, 30: 185–206.

86. G. K. Acharyulu & B. Shekhar, 2012, Role of value chain strategy in healthcare supply chain management: An empirical study in India, *International Journal of Management*, 29(1): 91–97; R. Belderbos, W. van Olffen, & J. Zou, 2011, Generic and specific social learning mechanisms in foreign entry location choice, *Strategic Management Journal*, 32(12): 1309–1330; A. Leiponen & C. E. Helfat, 2010, Innovation objectives, knowledge sources, and the benefits of breadth, *Strategic Management Journal*, 31: 224–236.

87. M. E. Porter, 1985, *Competitive Advantage*, New York: Free Press, 33–61.

88. R. Amit & C. Zott, 2012, Creating value through business model innovation, *MIT Sloan Management Review*, 53(3): 41–49; Z. G. Zacharia, N. W. Nix, & R. F. Lusch, 2011, Capabilities that enhance outcomes of an episodic supply chain collaboration, *Journal of Operations Management*, 29: 591–603; J. Alcacer, 2006, Location choices across the value chain: How activity and capability influence co-location, *Management Science*, 52: 1457–1471.

89. N. Haworth, 2013, Compressed development: Global value chains, multinational enterprises and human resource development in 21st century Asia, *Journal of World Business*, 48(2): 251–259; A. Rugman, A. Verbeke, & W. Yuan, 2011, Re-conceptualizing Bartlett and Ghoshal's classification of national subsidiary roles in the multinational enterprise, *Journal of Management Studies*, 48: 253–277.

90. A. Jara & H. Escaith, 2012, Global value chains, international trade statistics and policymaking in a flattening world, *World Economics*, 13(4): 5–18; S. M. Mudambi & S. Tallman, 2010, Make, buy or ally? Theoretical perspectives on knowledge process outsourcing through alliances, *Journal*

of Management Studies, 47: 1434–1456; R. Locke & M. Romis, 2007, Improving world conditions in a global supply chain, *MIT Sloan Management Review*, 48(2): 54–62.

91. C. Galunic, G. Ertug, & M. Gargiulo, 2012, The positive externalities of social capital: Benefiting from senior brokers, *Academy of Management Journal*, 55(5): 1213–1231; U. Zander & L. Zander, 2010, Opening the grey box: Social communities, knowledge and culture in acquisitions, *Journal of International Business Studies*, 41: 27–37.

92. R. M. Wiseman, G. Cuevas-Rodriguez, & L. R. Gomez-Mejia, 2012, Towards a social theory of agency, *Journal of Management Studies*, 49(1): 202–222; L. F. Mesquita, J. An, & T. H. Brush, 2008, Comparing the resource-based and relational views: Knowledge transfer and spillover in vertical alliances, *Strategic Management Journal*, 29: 913–941.

93. S. E. Fawcett, S. L. Jones, & A. M. Fawcett, 2012, Supply chain trust: The catalyst for collaborative innovation, *Business Horizons*, 55(2): 163–178; A. A. Lado, R. R. Dant, & A. G. Tekleab, 2008, Trust-opportunism paradox, relationalism, and performance in interfirm relationships: Evidence from the retail industry, *Strategic Management Journal*, 29: 401–423; S. N. Wasti & S. A. Wasti, 2008, Trust in buyer-supplier relations: The case of the Turkish automotive industry, *Journal of International Business Studies*, 39: 118–131.

94. D. Lavie, P. R. Haunschild, & P. Khanna, 2012, Organizational differences, relational mechanisms, and alliance performance, *Strategic Management Journal*, 33(13): 1453–1479; D. Faems, M. Janssens, A. Madhok, & B. Van Looy, 2008, Toward an integrative perspective on alliance governance: Connecting contract design, trust dynamics and contract application, *Academy of Management Journal*, 51: 1053–1078.

95. S. Nadkami & P. Hermann, 2010, CEO personality, strategic flexibility, and firm performance: The case of the Indian business process outsourcing industry, *Academy of Management Journal*, 53: 1050–1073.

96. A. J. Mauri & J. Neiva de Figueiredo, 2012, Strategic patterns of internationalization and performance variability: Effects of US-based MNC cross-border dispersion, integration, and outsourcing, *Journal of International Management*, 18(1): 38–51; R. Liu, D. J. Feils, & B. Scholnick, 2011, Why are different services outsourced to different countries? *Journal of International Business Studies*, 42: 558–571.

97. C. Weigelt & M. B. Sarkar, 2012, Performance implications of outsourcing for technological innovations: Managing the efficiency and adaptability trade-off, *Strategic Management Journal*, 33(2): 189–216; F. Castellucci & G. Ertug, 2010, What's in it for them? Advantages of higher-status partners in exchange relationships, *Academy of Management Journal*, 53: 149–166; C. C. De Fontenay & J. S. Gans, 2008, A bargaining perspective on strategic

outsourcing and supply competition, *Strategic Management Journal*, 29: 819–839.

98. J. Li, 2012, The alignment between organizational control mechanisms and outsourcing strategies: A commentary essay, *Journal of Business Research*, 65(9): 1384–1386; M. H. Zack & S. Singh, 2010, A knowledge-based view of outsourcing, *International Journal of Strategic Change Management*, 2: 32–53.

99. N. Raassens, S. Wuyts, & I. Geyskens, 2012, The market valuation of outsourcing new product development, *Journal of Marketing Research*, 49(5): 682–695; M. Reitzig & S. Wagner, 2010, The hidden costs of outsourcing: Evidence from patent data, *Strategic Management Journal*, 31: 1183–1201; A. Tiwana, 2008, Does interfirm modularity complement ignorance? A field study of software outsourcing alliances, *Strategic Management Journal*, 29: 1241–1252.

100. A. Martinez-Noya, E. Garcia-Canal, & M. F. Guillen, 2013, R&D outsourcing and the effectiveness of intangible investments: Is proprietary core knowledge walking out of the door? *Journal of Management Studies*, 50(1): 67–91; C. S. Katsikeas, D. Skarmeas, & D. C. Bello, 2009, Developing successful trust-based international exchange relationships, *Journal of International Business Studies*, 40: 132–155.

101. S. Sonenshein, 2013, How organizations foster the creative use of resources, *Academy of Management Journal*, in press; C. Grimpe & U. Kaiser, 2010, Balancing internal and external knowledge acquisition: The gains and pains from R&D outsourcing, *Journal of Management Studies*, 47: 1483–1509; C. Weigelt & M. B. Sarkar, 2009, Learning from supply-side agents: The impact of technology solution providers' experiential diversity on clients' innovation adoption, *Academy of Management Journal*, 52: 37–60.

102. S. M. Handley, 2012, The perilous effects of capability loss on outsourcing management and performance, *Journal of Operations Management*, 30(1/2): 152–165; P. D. O. Jensen & T. Pederson, 2011, The economic geography of offshoring: The fit between activities and local context, *Journal of Management Studies*, 48: 352–372; F. J. Contractor, V. Kumar, S. K. Kundu, & T. Pedersen, 2010, Reconceptualizing the firm in a world of outsourcing and offshoring: The organizational and geographical relocation of high-value company functions, *Journal of Management Studies*, 47: 1417–1433.

103. A. Smith, 2013, Foreign factories come back home, *Kiplinger's Personal Finance*, March, 11–12.

104. M. Kang, X. Wu, P. Hong, & Y. Park, 2012, Aligning organizational control practices with competitive outsourcing performance, *Journal of Business Research*, 65(8): 1195–1201; Y. Li, Z. Wei, & Y. Liu, 2010, Strategic orientations, knowledge acquisition, and firm performance: The perspective of the

vendor in cross-border outsourcing, *Journal of Management Studies*, 47: 1457–1482.

105. D. M. Sullivan & M. R. Marvel, 2011, Knowledge acquisition, network reliance, and early-stage technology venture outcomes, *Journal of Management Studies*, 48(6): 1169–1193; M. Gibbert, M. Hoegl, &

L. Valikangas, 2007, In praise of resource constraints, *MIT Sloan Management Review*, 48(3): 15–17.

106. E. Rawley, 2010, Diversification, coordination costs, and organizational rigidity: Evidence from microdata, *Strategic Management Journal*, 31: 873–891.

107. D. L. Barton, 1995, *Wellsprings of Knowledge: Building and Sustaining the Sources of Innovation*, Boston: Harvard Business School Press, 30–31.

108. J. Milliot, 2013, As E-books grow, so does Amazon, *Publishers Weekly*, February 11, 4.

4

Business-Level Strategy

Studying this chapter should provide you with the strategic management knowledge needed to:

1 Define business-level strategy.

2 Discuss the relationship between customers and business-level strategies in terms of *who, what,* and *how*.

3 Explain the differences among business-level strategies.

4 Use the five forces of competition model to explain how above-average returns can be earned through each business-level strategy.

5 Describe the risks of using each of the business-level strategies.

IS J.C. PENNEY KILLING ITSELF WITH A FAILED STRATEGY?

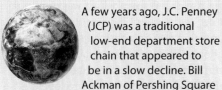

A few years ago, J.C. Penney (JCP) was a traditional low-end department store chain that appeared to be in a slow decline. Bill Ackman of Pershing Square Capital Management, a hedge fund investor, bought a large stake in the company and pushed to hire a new CEO, Ron Johnson. Johnson, who had successfully created the Apple retail store concept, was tasked with turning around the company's fortunes.

In January 2012, Johnson announced a new strategy for the company and the rebranding of JCP. This strategy entailed a remake of the JCP retail stores to create shops focused on specific brands, such as Levi's, IZOD, and Liz Claiborne, and types of goods, such as home goods featuring Martha Stewart products within each store. Simultaneously, Johnson announced a new pricing system. The old approach of offering special discounts throughout the year was eliminated in favor of

a new customer-value pricing approach that reduced prices on goods across the board by as much as 40 percent. The price listed was the price to be paid without further discounts. The intent was to offer customers a "better deal" on all products as opposed to providing special high discounts on selected products.

The intent of these changes was to build J.C. Penney into a higher-end (a little more upscale) retailer that provided good prices on branded merchandise (mostly clothes and home goods). However, these changes overlooked the firm's current customers; JCP began competing for customers who normally shopped at Target, Macy's, Nordstrom, and other similar stores. Unfortunately, the first year of this new strategy appeared to be a failure. Total sales in 2012 were $4.28 billion less than in 2011 and the firm's stock price declined by 55 percent. Interestingly, its Internet sales declined by 34 percent compared to an increase of 48 percent for its new

rival, Macy's. All of this translated into a net loss for the year of slightly less than $1 billion for JCP.

It seems that the new executive team at Penney's thought that they could retain their current customer base (perhaps with the value pricing across the board) while attracting new customers with the "store-within-a-store" concept. According to Roger Martin, a former executive, strategy expert, and current dean at the University of Toronto, "…the new J.C. Penney is competing against and absolutely slaughtering an important competitor, and it's called the old J.C. Penney." Only about one-third of the stores had been converted to the new approach when the company began to heavily promote the concept. Its new store sales produced increases in sales per square foot, but the old stores' sales per square foot markedly declined. It appears that Penney was not attracting customers from its rivals but rather cannibalizing customers from its old stores.

According to Martin, the new CEO likely understands a lot about capital markets but does not know how to satisfy customers and gain a competitive advantage. Additionally, the former CEO of J.C. Penney, Allen Questrom, described Johnson as having several capabilities (e.g., intelligent, strong communicator) but believes that he and his executive team made a major strategic error and were especially insensitive to the JCP customer base.

The question now is whether the company can survive such a major decline in sales and stock price. It recently announced the layoff of approximately 2,200 employees to reduce costs. CEO Johnson announced he was reinstituting selected discounts in pricing and offering comparative pricing on products (relative prices with rivals). The good news is that the transformed stores are obtaining sales of $269 per square foot whereas the older stores are producing $134 per square foot. Will Ron Johnson's strategy survive long enough for all of the stores to be converted and save the company? The answer is probably not, as Johnson was fired by the Penney board of directors on April 8, 2013, about a year and a half after he assumed the CEO position.

Sources: J. Reingold, A. Sloan, & D. Burke, 2013, When Wall Street wears the pants, *Fortune*, April 8, 74–81; Ron Johnson out as J.C. Penney chief, 2013, *New York Times*, www.nytimes.com, April 8; M. Nisen, 2013, Former JC Penney CEO says Ron Johnson is 'a very nice man' who will probably fail, *Yahoo! Finance*, http://finance.yahoo.com, accessed April 6; B. Byrnes, 2013, How J.C. Penney is killing itself, *The Motley Fool*, www.fool.com, March 31; B. Jopson, 2013, JC Penney cuts 2,200 jobs as retailer struggles, *Financial Times*, www.ft.com, March 8; J. Macke, 2013, J.C. Penney's last shot at survival, *Yahoo! Finance*, http://finance.yahoo.com, accessed March 1; S. Clifford, 2013, Chief talks of mistakes and big loss at J.C. Penney, *New York Times*, www.nytimes.com, February 27; M. Halkias, 2013, J.C. Penney CEO Ron Johnson says changes will return retailer to growth, *Dallas Morning news*, www.dallasnews.com, February 9; They're back: J.C. Penney adds sales, 2013, *USA Today*, www.usatoday.com, January 28; A. R. Sorkin, 2012, A dose of realism for the chief of J.C. Penney, *New York Times DealBook*, http://dealbook.nytimes.com, November 12.

Find out more about Martha Stewart products and which retailers feature them.
www.cengagebrain.com

A **business-level strategy** is an integrated and coordinated set of commitments and actions the firm uses to gain a competitive advantage by exploiting core competencies in specific product markets.

Increasingly important to firm success,[1] strategy is concerned with making choices among two or more alternatives.[2] As we noted in Chapter 1, when choosing a strategy, the firm decides to pursue one course of action instead of others. The choices are influenced by opportunities and threats in the firm's external environment[3] (see Chapter 2) as well as the nature and quality of the resources, capabilities, and core competencies in its internal organization[4] (see Chapter 3). As we see in the Opening Case, J.C. Penney, which was once a formidable retailer, has recently suffered a significant decline in sales (25 percent in 2012 alone) due to a poor strategy. It tried to develop more upscale stores and enrich its product offerings. However, doing so placed it in direct competition with other major retailers such as Macy's and Target. Thus, it lost most of its perceived differentiation and advantage. It also changed its pricing strategy. As a result, it appears that the "new" J.C. Penney has developed a competitive advantage—but only over the "old" J.C. Penney. So, it cannibalized its own sales and in the process suffered a severe decline. It lost many of its old customers and was unable to attract new ones. Therefore, it satisfied very few customers' needs.

In previous chapters, analysis of the external environment and of internal firm resources and capabilities, which is the first step in the strategic management process, was discussed. This chapter is the first on strategy, which is the second part of the strategic management process explained in Chapter 1. The fundamental objective of using any type of strategy (see Figure 1.1) is to gain strategic competitiveness and earn above-average returns.[5] Strategies are purposeful, precede the taking of actions to which they apply, and demonstrate a shared understanding of the firm's vision and mission.[6] An effectively formulated strategy marshals, integrates, and allocates the firm's resources, capabilities, and competencies so that it will be properly aligned with its external environment.[7] A properly developed strategy also rationalizes the firm's vision and mission along with the actions taken to achieve them.[8] Information about a host of variables including markets, customers, technology, worldwide finance, and the changing world economy must be collected and analyzed to properly form and use strategies. In the final analysis, sound strategic choices that reduce uncertainty regarding outcomes are the foundation for building successful strategies.[9]

Business-level strategy, this chapter's focus, is an integrated and coordinated set of commitments and actions the firm uses to gain a competitive advantage by exploiting core

M. Stasy

competencies in specific product markets.[10] Business-level strategy indicates the choices the firm has made about how it intends to compete in individual product markets. The choices are important because long-term performance is linked to a firm's strategies. Given the complexity of successfully competing in the global economy, the choices about how the firm will compete can be difficult.[11] For example, in 2006 Myspace, a social networking site, was the largest such site, with approximately 50 million users. But, within two years, it lost the lead to a fast-developing social networking site, Facebook. Facebook quickly enlarged its market share with more than 600 million users in 2011, while Myspace had only about 34 million users. Facebook has made several major competitive moves in recent years, challenging Myspace to further adjust its strategy as it engaged in various competitive battles. As a result, Myspace has steadily declined from 1600 employees in 2008 to around 200 in 2013. The company is now ranked 220th in amount of total traffic on the Internet.[12] Thus, it is now only a minor competitor trying to survive.

Every firm must develop and implement a business-level strategy. However, some firms may not use all the strategies—corporate-level, merger and acquisition, international, and cooperative—that we examine in Chapters 6 through 9. A firm competing in a single-product market in a single geographic location does not need a corporate-level strategy regarding product diversity or an international strategy to deal with geographic diversity. In contrast, a diversified firm will use one of the corporate-level strategies as well as a separate business-level strategy for each product market in which it competes. Every firm—ranging from the local dry cleaner to the multinational corporation—must develop and use at least one business-level strategy. Thus business-level strategy is the *core* strategy—the strategy that the firm forms to describe how it intends to compete in a product market.[13]

We discuss several topics to examine business-level strategies. Because customers are the foundation of successful business-level strategies and should never be taken for granted,[14] we present information about customers that is relevant to business-level strategies. In terms of customers, when selecting a business-level strategy the firm determines (1) *who* will be served, (2) *what* needs those target customers have that it will satisfy, and (3) *how* those needs will be satisfied. Selecting customers and deciding which of their needs the firm will try to satisfy, as well as how it will do so, are challenging tasks. Global competition has created many attractive options for customers, thus making it difficult to determine the strategy to best serve them.[15] Effective global competitors have become adept at identifying the needs of customers in different cultures and geographic regions as well as learning how to quickly and successfully adapt the functionality of a firm's good or service to meet those needs.

Descriptions of the purpose of business-level strategies—and of the five business-level strategies—follow the discussion of customers. The five strategies we examine are called *generic* because they can be used in any organization competing in any industry.[16] Our analysis describes how effective use of each strategy allows the firm to favorably position itself relative to the five competitive forces in the industry (see Chapter 2). In addition, we use the value chain (see Chapter 3) to show examples of the primary and support activities necessary to implement specific business-level strategies. Because no strategy is risk-free,[17] we also describe the different risks the firm may encounter when using these strategies. In Chapter 11, we explain the organizational structures and controls linked with the successful use of each business-level strategy.

4-1 Customers: Their Relationship with Business-Level Strategies

Strategic competitiveness results only when the firm satisfies a group of customers by using its competitive advantages as the basis for competing in individual product markets.[18] A key

Customers standing in a grocery store checkout line. Successful business strategies satisfy customers' needs.

Rubberball/Mike Kemp/Getty Images

reason firms must satisfy customers with their business-level strategy is that returns earned from relationships with customers are the lifeblood of all organizations.[19]

The most successful companies try to find new ways to satisfy current customers and/or to meet the needs of new customers. Being able to do this can be even more difficult when firms and consumers face challenging economic conditions. During such times, firms may decide to reduce their workforce to control costs. This can lead to problems, however, because having fewer employees makes it more difficult for companies to meet individual customers' needs and expectations. In these instances, firms can follow several possible courses of action, including paying extra attention to their best customers and developing a flexible workforce by cross-training employees so they can undertake a variety of responsibilities on their jobs.

4-1a Effectively Managing Relationships with Customers

The firm's relationships with its customers are strengthened when it delivers superior value to them. Strong interactive relationships with customers often provide the foundation for the firm's efforts to profitably serve customers' unique needs.

As the following statement shows, Caesars Entertainment (the world's largest provider of branded casino entertainment) is committed to providing superior value to customers: "At Caesars we believe that every guest should be treated as a Caesar…Caesars sets the standard of excellence…with employees who are devoted to delivering truly great service."[20] Importantly, as Caesars appears to anticipate, delivering superior value often results in increased customer satisfaction. In turn, customer satisfaction has a positive relationship with profitability because satisfied customers are most likely to be repeat customers. However, more choices and easily accessible information about the functionality of firms' products are creating increasingly sophisticated and knowledgeable customers, making it difficult to earn their loyalty.[21]

A number of companies have become skilled at the art of *managing* all aspects of their relationship with their customers.[22] For example, Amazon.com is widely recognized for the quality of information it maintains about its customers, the services it renders, and its ability to anticipate customers' needs. Using the information it has, Amazon tries to serve what it believes are the unique needs of each customer; and it has a strong reputation for being able to successfully do this.[23]

As we discuss next, firms' relationships with customers are characterized by three dimensions. Companies such as Acer and Amazon.com understand these dimensions and manage their relationships with customers in light of them.

4-1b Reach, Richness, and Affiliation

The *reach* dimension of relationships with customers is concerned with the firm's access and connection to customers. In general, firms seek to extend their reach, adding customers in the process of doing so.

Reach is an especially critical dimension for social networking sites such as Facebook and Myspace in that the value these firms create for users is to connect them with others.

As noted earlier, traffic to Myspace has been declining in recent years; at the same time, the number of Facebook users has been dramatically increasing in the United States and abroad. As a result, Facebook had more than 1 billion users in 2013—more than 1500 percent greater than the number of Myspace users.[24] Reach is also important to Netflix. Fortunately for this firm, recent results indicate that its reach continues to expand: Netflix ended 2012 with approximately 33 million total subscribers, representing a 43.5 percent increase from 2011.[25]

Richness, the second dimension of firms' relationships with customers, is concerned with the depth and detail of the two-way flow of information between the firm and the customer. The potential of the richness dimension to help the firm establish a competitive advantage in its relationship with customers leads many firms to offer online services in order to better manage information exchanges with their customers. Broader and deeper information-based exchanges allow firms to better understand their customers and their needs. Such exchanges also enable customers to become more knowledgeable about how the firm can satisfy them. Internet technology and e-commerce transactions have substantially reduced the costs of meaningful information exchanges with current and potential customers. As we have noted, Amazon is a leader in using the Internet to build relationships with customers. In fact, it bills itself as the most "customer-centric company" on earth. Amazon and other firms use rich information from customers to help them develop innovative new products that better satisfy customers' needs.[26]

Affiliation, the third dimension, is concerned with facilitating useful interactions with customers. Viewing the world through the customer's eyes and constantly seeking ways to create more value for the customer have positive effects in terms of affiliation. This approach enhances customer satisfaction and produces fewer customer complaints. In fact, for services, customers often do not complain when dissatisfied; instead they simply go to competitors for their service needs.[27] Internet navigators such as Microsoft's MSN Autos help online clients find and sort information. MSN Autos provides data and software to prospective car buyers that enable them to compare car models along multiple objective specifications. A prospective buyer who has selected a specific car based on comparisons of different models can then be linked to dealers that meet the customer's needs and purchasing requirements. Because its revenues come not from the final customer or end user but from other sources (such as advertisements on its Web site, hyperlinks, and associated products and services), MSN Autos represents the customer's interests, a service that fosters affiliation.[28]

As we discuss next, effectively managing customer relationships (along the dimensions of reach, richness, and affiliation) helps the firm answer questions related to the issues of *who, what,* and *how.*

4-1c Who: Determining the Customers to Serve

Deciding *who* the target customer is that the firm intends to serve with its business-level strategy is an important decision.[29] Companies divide customers into groups based on differences in the customers' needs (needs are discussed further in the next section) to make this decision. Dividing customers into groups based on their needs is called **market segmentation**, which is a process that clusters people with similar needs into individual and identifiable groups.[30] In the animal food products business, for example, the food-product needs of owners of companion pets (e.g., dogs and cats) differ from the needs for food and health-related products of those owning production animals (e.g., livestock). A subsidiary of Colgate-Palmolive, Hill's Pet Nutrition sells food products for pets. In fact, the company's mission is "to help enrich and lengthen the special relationship between people and their pets."[31] Thus, Hill's Pet Nutrition targets the needs of different segments of customers with the food products it sells for animals.

Market segmentation is a process used to cluster people with similar needs into individual and identifiable groups.

Table 4.1 Basis for Customer Segmentation

Consumer Markets
1. Demographic factors (age, income, sex, etc.)
2. Socioeconomic factors (social class, stage in the family life cycle)
3. Geographic factors (cultural, regional, and national differences)
4. Psychological factors (lifestyle, personality traits)
5. Consumption patterns (heavy, moderate, and light users)
6. Perceptual factors (benefit segmentation, perceptual mapping)

Industrial Markets
1. End-use segments (identified by SIC code)
2. Product segments (based on technological differences or production economics)
3. Geographic segments (defined by boundaries between countries or by regional differences within them)
4. Common buying factor segments (cut across product market and geographic segments)
5. Customer size segments

Source: Based on information in S. C. Jain, 2009, *Marketing Planning and Strategy*, Mason, OH: South-Western Cengage Custom Publishing.

Strategy Right NOW

Learn more about market segmentation.
www.cengagebrain.com

Almost any identifiable human or organizational characteristic can be used to subdivide a market into segments that differ from one another on a given characteristic. Common characteristics on which customers' needs vary are illustrated in Table 4.1.

4-1d   What: Determining Which Customer Needs to Satisfy

After the firm decides *who* it will serve, it must identify the targeted customer group's needs that its goods or services can satisfy. In a general sense, *needs (what)* are related to a product's benefits and features. Successful firms learn how to deliver to customers what they want, when they want it. Having close and frequent interactions with both current and potential customers helps the firm identify those individuals' and groups' current and future needs.[32]

From a strategic perspective, a basic need of all customers is to buy products that create value for them. The generalized forms of value that goods or services provide are either low cost with acceptable features or highly differentiated features with acceptable cost. The most effective firms continuously strive to anticipate changes in customers' needs. The firm that fails to anticipate and certainly to recognize changes in its customers' needs may lose its customers to competitors whose products can provide more value to the focal firm's customers. It is also recognized that consumer needs and desires have been changing in recent years. For example, more consumers desire to have an experience rather than to simply purchase a good or service. As a result, one of Starbucks' goals has been to provide an experience, not just a cup of coffee. Customers also prefer to receive customized goods and services. Again, Starbucks has been doing this for some time, allowing customers to design their own drinks, within their menus (which have become rather extensive over time).

They also demand fast service. Consumers in the United States have been known for their impatience, but rapid service is now expected by most consumers.[33] Unhappy consumers lead to lost sales—both theirs and those of others who learn of their dissatisfaction. Therefore, it is important to maintain customer satisfaction by meeting and satisfying their needs.[34]

4-1e   How: Determining Core Competencies Necessary to Satisfy Customer Needs

After deciding *who* the firm will serve and the specific *needs* of those customers, the firm is prepared to determine how to use its capabilities and competencies to develop products that can satisfy the needs of its target customers. As explained in Chapters 1 and 3, *core competencies* are resources and capabilities that serve as a source of competitive advantage for the firm over its rivals. Firms use core competencies (*how*) to implement value-creating strategies

M. Stasy

and thereby satisfy customers' needs. Only those firms with the capacity to continuously improve, innovate, and upgrade their competencies can expect to meet and hopefully exceed customers' expectations across time.[35] Firms must continuously upgrade their capabilities to ensure that they maintain the advantage over their rivals by providing customers with a superior product.[36] Often these capabilities are difficult for competitors to imitate partly because they are constantly being upgraded but also because they are integrated and used as configurations of capabilities to perform an important activity (e.g., R&D).[37]

Companies draw from a wide range of core competencies to produce goods or services that can satisfy customers' needs. For example, Merck is a large pharmaceutical firm well-known for its R&D capabilities. In recent times, Merck has been building on these capabilities by investing heavily in R&D. In 2012, Merck invested $7.9 billion to conduct research and identify major new drugs, which was almost 17 percent of its total sales revenue.[38] These new drugs are intended to meet the needs of consumers and to sustain Merck's competitive advantage in the industry.

SAS Institute is the world's largest privately owned software company and is the leader in business intelligence and analytics. Customers use SAS programs for data warehousing, data mining, and decision support purposes. SAS serves 60,000 sites in 135 countries and serves 90 percent of the top *Fortune* 100 firms. Allocating approximately 25 percent of revenues to research and development (R&D), a percentage that exceeds percentages allocated by its competitors, SAS relies on its core competence in R&D to satisfy the data-related needs of such customers as the U.S. Census Bureau and a host of consumer goods firms (e.g., hotels, banks, and catalog companies).[39]

Sometimes, firms may find it necessary to use their core competencies as the foundation for producing new goods or services for new customers. This may be the case for some small automobile parts suppliers in the United States. Given that U.S. auto production in recent years declined about one third from more typical levels, a number of these firms are seeking to diversify their operations, perhaps exiting the auto parts supplier industry as a result of doing so. Some analysts believe that the first rule for these small manufacturers is to determine how their current capabilities and competencies might be used to produce value-creating products for different customers. One analyst gave the following example of how this might work: "There may be no reason that a company making auto door handles couldn't make ball-and-socket joints for artificial shoulders."[40]

As explained in the Strategic Focus, many types of firms now emphasize innovation, not only those in high technology industries (e.g., Dell). This innovation appears to be driven by customers along with providing customers a product or service that satisfies their needs in a manner superior to that of rivals' products or services to gain or sustain a competitive advantage. In fact, the information in the Strategic Focus suggests that both Alaska Airlines and L'Oréal have gained competitive advantages due to their innovations.

Our discussion about customers shows that all organizations must use their capabilities and core competencies (the *how*) to satisfy the needs (the *what*) of the target group of customers (the *who*) the firm has chosen to serve. Next, we describe the different business-level strategies that are available to firms to use to satisfy customers as the foundation for earning above-average returns.

Find out more about innovations at Alaska Airlines.
www.cengagebrain.com

4-2 The Purpose of a Business-Level Strategy

The purpose of a business-level strategy is to create differences between the firm's position and those of its competitors.[41] To position itself differently from competitors, a firm must decide whether it intends to *perform activities differently* or to *perform different activities.*

M. Stasy

Strategic Focus   TECHNOLOGY

Continuously Innovating to Satisfy Customers' Needs

The competitive landscape has changed in recent years such that companies in many industries have to continue to innovate to maintain their competitive advantage by providing superior value to their customers. This requirement has existed in high technology industries for years but has now spread to consumer products industries such as cosmetics and airlines. Clayton Christiansen, a noted Harvard professor, suggested that many leading firms are afraid to change because of the fear of losing their current customers. He called this the "innovator's dilemma". In fact, these firms seemed to be captive to their current customers, which allows new entrants in the industry to introduce new technologies and innovative products that capture many of the customers served by the incumbent firms.

However, firms are learning from the mistakes of others. For example, L'Oréal has established a research center in Shanghai to develop new products and tailor existing products to the particular needs of Chinese customers. These products range from lipstick to shampoo. L'Oréal is using traditional herbal remedies in several of their products for the Chinese market. Its innovations have been successful, capturing some market share from the market leader, Procter & Gamble (P&G). The Chinese market is lucrative and growing, with the beauty and personal-care products market estimated at $34 billion in 2013. The growth in this market is demonstrated by the fact that although P&G has experienced a small decline in market share, its overall business has increased by approximately 50 percent in the last three years. P&G has also been innovative in this market.

Airlines have not been known for being innovative, but Alaska Airlines introduced a novel innovation that has contributed to its success in recent years—especially in providing better service to its customers. This innovation may revolutionize the air traffic control system in the United States. Alaska Airlines developed and implemented a satellite guidance system to help pilots land planes at Alaskan airports, which often have challenging weather conditions. It has greatly aided safe landings but also helped the airline to avoid costly delays and cancelled flights, thereby offering quality service to its customers. In fact, in 2012, Alaska Airlines had the best on-time performance in the industry, with 87 percent of its flights landing on time.

Of course, being innovative means that firms as well as their employees must take risks. Jeff Bezos, founder and CEO of Amazon.com, has propelled his company into a leadership

World Expo 2010 site opening ceremony in Shanghai, China. L'Oreal's Shanghai research center develops products to satisfy the needs of Chinese customers.

position through innovation. Bezos claims that one of the major reasons for his firm's innovation has been the promotion of experimentation. Bezos feels that one of his jobs as a leader is to encourage Amazon employees to experiment with new ideas.

Even Dell, which emphasized its highly efficient supply chain to maintain a competitive advantage in the past, is now investing significant resources in R&D to develop new products and services to satisfy customer needs. Dell executives claim that their company is selling solutions rather than specific products and focusing on the small and medium-sized business market. Dell is trying to quickly move its products and services to a cloud computing environment.

Many companies are trying to increase their innovation and in the process encourage employees to take more risks and experiment with new ideas. The new business landscape is now considerably different from the traditional one where employees were encouraged to "think inside the box".

Sources: L. Lin, 2013, L'Oréal tailors new cosmetics for China's beauty market, *Bloomberg Businessweek,* www.businessweek.com, March 28; H. Gregersen, 2013, Amazon's Jeff Bezos and Apollo 11. He's still innovating, *Bloomberg Businessweek,* www.businessweek.com, March 25; L. Kwoh, 2013, Memo to staff: Take more risks, *Wall Street Journal,* www.wsj.com, March 20; J. Mouawad, 2013, Alaska Airlines, flying above an industry's troubles, *New York Times,* www.nytimes.com, March 2; Q. Hardy, 2012, For Dell, consolidation is innovation, *New York Times—The Business of Technology,* http://bits.blogs.nytimes.com, October 18; N. Bilton, 2012, Disruptions: Innovation isn't easy, especially midstream, *New York Times—The Business of Technology,* http://bits.blogs.nytimes.com, April 15.

Strategy defines the path which provides the direction of actions to be taken by leaders of the organization.[42] In fact, "choosing to perform activities differently or to perform different activities than rivals" is the essence of business-level strategy.[43] Thus, the firm's business-level strategy is a deliberate choice about how it will perform the value chain's primary and support activities to create unique value. Indeed, in the current complex competitive landscape, successful use of a business-level strategy results from the firm learning how to integrate the activities it performs in ways that create superior value for customers.

Firms develop an activity map to show how they integrate the activities they perform. The manner in which Southwest Airlines has integrated its activities is the foundation for the successful use of its primary cost leadership strategy (this strategy is discussed later in the chapter) but also includes differentiation through the unique services provided to customers. The tight integration among Southwest's activities is a key source of the firm's ability to at least historically operate more profitably than its competitors.

Southwest Airlines has configured the activities it performs into six areas of strategic intent—limited passenger service; frequent, reliable departures; lean, highly productive ground and gate crews; high aircraft utilization; very low ticket prices; and short-haul, point-to-point routes between mid-sized cities and secondary airports. Individual clusters of tightly linked activities make it possible to achieve its strategic intent. For example, no meals, no seat assignments, and no baggage transfers form a cluster of individual activities that support the strategic intent to offer limited passenger service.

Southwest's tightly integrated activities make it difficult for competitors to imitate the firm's cost leadership strategy. The firm's unique culture and customer service are sources of competitive advantage that rivals have been unable to imitate, although some have tried and largely failed (e.g., US Airways' MetroJet subsidiary, United Airlines' United Shuttle, Delta's Song, and Continental Airlines' Continental Lite). Hindsight shows that these competitors offered low prices to customers, but weren't able to operate at costs close to those of Southwest or to provide customers with any notable sources of differentiation, such as a unique experience while in the air. The key to Southwest's success has been its ability to continuously maintain low costs while providing customers with *acceptable* levels of differentiation such as an engaging culture. Firms using the cost leadership strategy must understand that in terms of sources of differentiation accompanying the cost leader's product, the customer defines *acceptable*. Fit among activities is a key to the sustainability of competitive advantage for all firms, including Southwest Airlines. Strategic fit among the many activities is critical for competitive advantage. It is more difficult for a competitor to match a configuration of integrated activities than to imitate a particular activity such as sales promotion, or a process technology.[44]

4-3 Types of Business-Level Strategies

Firms choose between five business-level strategies to establish and defend their desired strategic position against competitors: *cost leadership, differentiation, focused cost leadership, focused differentiation,* and *integrated cost leadership/differentiation* (see Figure 4.1). Each business-level strategy can help the firm to establish and exploit a particular *competitive advantage* within a particular *competitive scope.* How firms integrate the activities they perform within each different business-level strategy demonstrates how they differ from one another.[45] For example, firms have different activity maps, and thus, a Southwest Airlines activity map differs from those of competitors JetBlue, Continental, American Airlines, and so forth. Superior integration of activities increases the likelihood of being able to gain an advantage over competitors and to earn above-average returns.

When selecting a business-level strategy, firms evaluate two types of potential competitive advantages: "lower cost than rivals, or the ability to differentiate and command a premium price that exceeds the extra cost of doing so."[46] Having lower cost derives from the firm's ability to perform activities differently than rivals; being able to differentiate indicates the firm's capacity to perform different (and valuable) activities. Thus, based on the nature and quality of its internal resources, capabilities, and core competencies, a firm seeks to form either a cost competitive advantage or a distinctiveness competitive advantage as the basis for implementing its business-level strategy.[47]

Two types of target markets are broad market and narrow market segment(s) (see Figure 4.1). Firms serving a broad market seek to use their capabilities to create value for customers on an industry-wide basis. A narrow market segment means that the firm intends to serve the needs of a narrow customer group. With focus strategies, the firm "selects a segment or group of segments in the industry and tailors its strategy to serving them to the exclusion of others."[48] Buyers with special needs and buyers located in specific geographic regions are examples of narrow customer groups.[49] As shown in Figure 4.1, a firm could also strive to develop a combined low cost/distinctiveness value creation approach as the foundation for serving a target customer group that is larger than a narrow market segment but not as comprehensive as a broad (or industry-wide) customer group. In this instance, the firm uses the integrated cost leadership/differentiation strategy.

None of the five business-level strategies shown in Figure 4.1 is inherently or universally superior to the others.[50] The effectiveness of each strategy is contingent both on the opportunities and threats in a firm's external environment and on the strengths and weaknesses derived from the firm's resource portfolio. It is critical, therefore, for the firm to select a

Figure 4.1 Five Business-Level Strategies

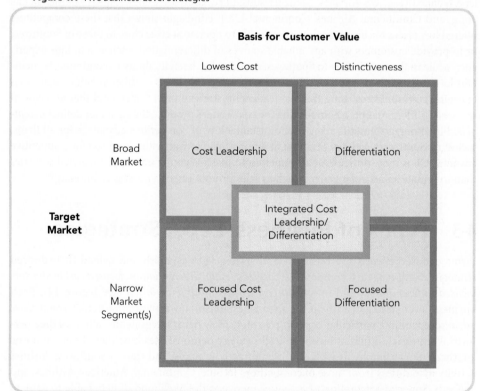

Source: Based on M. E. Porter, 1998, *Competitive Advantage: Creating and Sustaining Superior Performance*, New York: The Free Press; D. G. Sirmon, M. A. Hitt, & R. D. Ireland, 2007, Managing firm resources in dynamic environments to create value: Looking inside the black box, *Academy of Management Review*, 32: 273–292; D. G. Sirmon, M. A. Hitt, R. D. Ireland, & B. A. Gilbert, 2011, Resource orchestration to create competitive advantage: Breadth, depth and life cycles effects, *Journal of Management*, 37(5): 1390-1412.

business-level strategy that represents an effective match between the opportunities and threats in its external environment and the strengths of its internal organization based on its core competencies.[51] After the firm chooses its strategy, it should consistently emphasize actions that are required to successfully use it.

4-3a Cost Leadership Strategy

The **cost leadership strategy** is an integrated set of actions taken to produce goods or services with features that are acceptable to customers at the lowest cost, relative to those of competitors.[52] Firms using the cost leadership strategy commonly sell standardized goods or services (but with competitive levels of differentiation) to the industry's most typical customers. Process innovations, which are newly designed production and distribution methods and techniques that allow the firm to operate more efficiently, are critical to successful use of the cost leadership strategy. In recent years, firms have developed sourcing strategies to find low-cost suppliers to which they outsource various functions (e.g., manufacturing goods) in order to keep their costs very low.[53]

As noted, cost leaders' goods and services must have competitive levels of differentiation that create value for customers. For example, in recent years Kia Motors has emphasized the design of its cars in the U.S. market as a source of differentiation while implementing a cost leadership strategy.[54] Called "cheap chic," some analysts had a positive view of this decision, saying that "When they're done, Kia's cars will still be low-end (in price), but they won't necessarily look like it."[55] It is important for firms using the cost leadership strategy to ensure that they are concerned about the quality and attractiveness of the product for customers rather than solely concentrating on reducing costs because it could result in the firm efficiently producing products that no customer wants to purchase.[56] In fact, such extremes could limit the potential for important process innovations and lead to employment of lower-skilled workers, poor conditions on the production line, accidents, and a poor quality of work life for employees.[57]

As shown in Figure 4.1, the firm using the cost leadership strategy targets a broad customer segment or group. Cost leaders concentrate on finding ways to lower their costs relative to competitors by constantly rethinking how to complete their primary and support activities (such as highly efficient information systems) to reduce or maintain low costs while maintaining competitive levels of differentiation.[58]

For example, cost leader Greyhound Lines Inc. continuously seeks ways to reduce the costs it incurs to provide bus service while offering customers an acceptable level of differentiation. Greyhound offers additional services to customers trying to enhance the value of the experience customers have while they pay low prices for their service package. Interestingly, a number of customers now "insist on certain amenities that they receive on planes and trains—such as Internet access and comfortable seats, not to mention cleanliness." To maintain competitive levels of differentiation while using the cost leadership strategy, Greyhound has several "motor coaches" in its fleet that have leather seats, additional legroom, Wi-Fi access, and power outlets in every row.[59]

Greyhound enjoys economies of scale by serving more than 18 million passengers annually with about 3,800 destinations in North America, which produces 5.5 billion passenger miles. These scale economies allow the firm to keep its costs low while offering some of the differentiated services today's customers seek from the company. Demonstrating the firm's commitment to the physical environment segment of the general environment is the fact that "one Greyhound bus takes an average of 19 cars off the road for every 170 passengers."[60]

As primary activities, inbound logistics (e.g., materials handling, warehousing, and inventory control) and outbound logistics (e.g., collecting, storing, and distributing products to customers) often account for significant portions of the total cost to produce some goods and services. Research suggests that having a competitive advantage in logistics

The **cost leadership strategy** is an integrated set of actions taken to produce goods or services with features that are acceptable to customers at the lowest cost, relative to that of competitors.

creates more value with a cost leadership strategy than with a differentiation strategy.[61] Thus, cost leaders seeking competitively valuable ways to reduce costs may want to concentrate on the primary activities of inbound logistics and outbound logistics. In so doing many firms choose to outsource their manufacturing operations to low-cost firms with low-wage employees (e.g., China).[62] However, care must be taken because outsourcing also makes the firm more dependent on firms over which they have little control. Outsourcing creates interdependencies between the outsourcing firm and the suppliers. If dependencies become too great, it gives the supplier more power with which the supplier may increase prices of the goods and services provided. Such actions could harm the firm's ability to maintain a low-cost competitive advantage.[63]

Cost leaders also carefully examine all support activities to find additional potential cost reductions. Developing new systems for finding the optimal combination of low cost and acceptable levels of differentiation in the raw materials required to produce the firm's goods or services is an example of how the procurement support activity can facilitate successful use of the cost leadership strategy.

Big Lots Inc. uses the cost leadership strategy. With its vision of being "The World's Best Bargain Place," Big Lots is the largest closeout retailer in the United States with annual sales approaching $5 billion from more than 1,400 stores. For Big Lots, closeout goods are brand-name products from 3,000 manufacturers provided for sale at substantially lower prices than sold by other retailers.[64]

As described in Chapter 3, firms use value-chain analysis to identify the parts of the company's operations that create value and those that do not. Figure 4.2 demonstrates the value-chain activities and support functions that allow a firm to create value through the cost leadership strategy. Companies unable to effectively integrate the activities and functions shown in this figure typically lack the core competencies needed to successfully use the cost leadership strategy.

Effective use of the cost leadership strategy allows a firm to earn above-average returns in spite of the presence of strong competitive forces (see Chapter 2). The next sections (one for each of the five forces) explain how firms implement a cost leadership strategy.

Rivalry with Existing Competitors

Having the low-cost position is valuable when dealing with rivals. Because of the cost leader's advantageous position, rivals hesitate to compete on the basis of price, especially before evaluating the potential outcomes of such competition.[65] The changes Walmart made to attract upscale customers created vulnerability in its low-cost position to rivals. Dollar Store, Amazon.com, and others took advantage of the opportunity. Amazon appears to have become a low-cost leader, and the Dollar Stores provide low costs and easy access for customers. Both of these rivals have siphoned off some of Walmart's customers.

The degree of rivalry present is based on a number of different factors such as size and resources of rivals, their dependence on the particular market, and location and prior competitive interactions, among others.[66] Firms may also take actions to reduce the amount of rivalry that they face. For example, firms sometimes form joint ventures to reduce rivalry and increase the amount of profitability enjoyed by firms in the industry.[67] In China they build strong relationships, often referred to as guanxi, with key stakeholders such as important government officials and units, suppliers, and customers, thereby restraining rivalry.[68]

Bargaining Power of Buyers (Customers)

Powerful customers can force a cost leader to reduce its prices, but not below the level at which the cost leader's next-most-efficient industry competitor can earn average returns. Although powerful customers might be able to force the cost leader to reduce prices even below this level, they probably would choose not to do so. Prices that are low enough to

Figure 4.2 Examples of Value-Creating Activities Associated with the Cost Leadership Strategy

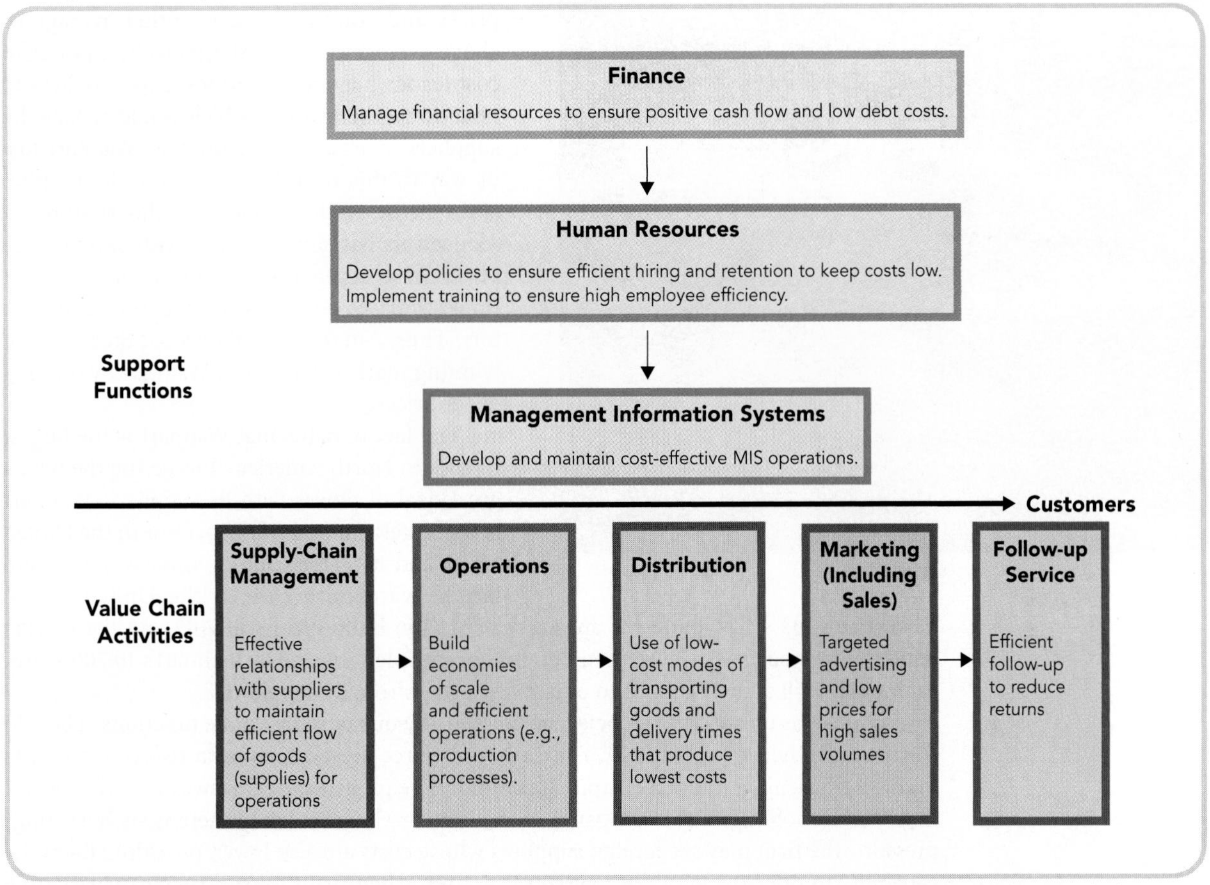

Source: Based on M. E. Porter, 1998, *Competitive Advantage: Creating and Sustaining Superior Performance,* New York: The Free Press; D. G. Sirmon, M. A. Hitt, & R. D. Ireland, 2007, Managing firm resources in dynamic environments to create value: Looking inside the black box, *Academy of Management Review,* 32: 273–292; D. G. Sirmon, M. A. Hitt, R. D. Ireland, & B. A. Gilbert, 2011, Resource orchestration to create competitive advantage: Breadth, depth and life cycles effects, *Journal of Management,* 37(5): 1390–1412.

prevent the next-most-efficient competitor from earning average returns would force that firm to exit the market, leaving the cost leader with less competition and in an even stronger position. Customers would thus lose their power and pay higher prices if they were forced to purchase from a single firm operating in an industry without rivals. In some cases, rather than forcing firms to reduce their prices, powerful customers may pressure firms to provide innovative products and services as explained in the earlier Strategic Focus.

Buyers can also develop a counterbalancing power to the customers' power by thoroughly analyzing and understanding each of their customers. To help in obtaining information and understanding the customers, buyers can participate in customers' networks. In so doing, they share information, build trust, and participate in joint problem solving with their customers.[69] In turn, they use the information obtained to provide a product that provides superior value to customers by most effectively satisfying their needs.

Bargaining Power of Suppliers

The cost leader generally operates with margins greater than those of competitors and often tries to increase its margins by driving costs lower. Among other benefits, higher gross margins relative to those of competitors make it possible for the cost leader to absorb its suppliers' price increases. When an industry faces substantial increases in the cost of its supplies,

Customers at a Sam's Club warehouse in Plano, Texas. The combined purchasing strength of Walmart and Sam's Club gives them a great deal of bargaining power with their suppliers.

only the cost leader may be able to pay the higher prices and continue to earn either average or above-average returns. Alternatively, a powerful cost leader may be able to force its suppliers to hold down their prices, which would reduce the suppliers' margins in the process. Walmart lost its way in this regard. By reducing the number and type of products sold in Walmart stores, it reduced its bargaining power with several suppliers. In so doing, it was unable to gain the best (lowest) prices on goods relative to its competitors. Thus, Amazon and the Dollar Stores began winning market share from Walmart by offering lower prices.

The fact remains that Walmart is the largest retailer in North America, thus giving the firm a great deal of power with its suppliers. Walmart is the largest supermarket operator in the United States and its Sam's Club division is the second largest warehouse club in the United States. Collectively, its sales volume of approximately $466 billion in fiscal 2013 and the market penetration it suggests (more than 200 million people visit one of Walmart's 10,700 stores each week) still allow Walmart to obtain low prices from its suppliers.[70]

Some firms create dependencies on suppliers by outsourcing whole functions. They do so to reduce their overall costs.[71] They may outsource these activities to reduce their costs because of earnings pressures from stakeholders (e.g., institutional investors who own a major stock holding in the company) in the industry.[72] Often when there is such earnings pressure, the firm may see foreign suppliers whose costs are also lower, providing them the capability to offer the goods at lower prices.[73] Yet, when firms outsource, particularly to a foreign supplier, they also need to invest time and effort into building a good relationship, hopefully developing trust between the firms. Such efforts facilitate the integration of the supplier into the firm's value chain.[74]

Potential Entrants

Through continuous efforts to reduce costs to levels that are lower than competitors, a cost leader becomes highly efficient. Because increasing levels of efficiency (e.g., economies of scale) enhance profit margins, they serve as a significant entry barrier to potential competitors.[75] New entrants must be willing to accept no-better-than-average returns until they gain the experience required to approach the cost leader's efficiency. To earn even average returns, new entrants must have the competencies required to match the cost levels of competitors other than the cost leader. The low profit margins (relative to margins earned by firms implementing the differentiation strategy) make it necessary for the cost leader to sell large volumes of its product to earn above-average returns. However, firms striving to be the cost leader must avoid pricing their products so low that they cannot operate profitably, even though volume increases.

Product Substitutes

Compared with its industry rivals, the cost leader also holds an attractive position relative to product substitutes. A product substitute becomes a concern for the cost leader when its features and characteristics, in terms of cost and differentiation, are potentially attractive to the firm's customers. When faced with possible substitutes, the cost leader has more flexibility than its competitors. To retain customers, it often can reduce the price of its good or service. With still lower prices and competitive levels of differentiation, the cost leader increases the probability that customers prefer its product rather than a substitute.

Competitive Risks of the Cost Leadership Strategy

The cost leadership strategy is not risk free. One risk is that the processes used by the cost leader to produce and distribute its good or service could become obsolete because of competitors' innovations.[76] These innovations may allow rivals to produce at costs lower than those of the original cost leader, or to provide additional differentiated features without increasing the product's price to customers.

A second risk is that too much focus by the cost leader on cost reductions may occur at the expense of trying to understand customers' perceptions of "competitive levels of differentiation." Walmart, for example, has been criticized for having too few salespeople available to help customers and too few individuals at checkout registers. These complaints suggest that there might be a discrepancy between how Walmart's customers define "minimal acceptable levels of service" and the firm's attempts to drive its costs increasingly lower.

Imitation is a final risk of the cost leadership strategy. Using their own core competencies, competitors sometimes learn how to successfully imitate the cost leader's strategy. When this happens, the cost leader must increase the value its good or service provides to customers. Commonly, value is increased by selling the current product at an even lower price or by adding differentiated features that create value for customers while maintaining price.

4-3b Differentiation Strategy

The **differentiation strategy** is an integrated set of actions taken to produce goods or services (at an acceptable cost) that customers perceive as being different in ways that are important to them.[77] While cost leaders serve a typical customer in an industry, differentiators target customers for whom value is created by the manner in which the firm's products differ from those produced and marketed by competitors. Product innovation, which is "the result of bringing to life a new way to solve the customer's problem—through a new product or service development—that benefits both the customer and the sponsoring company"[78] is critical to successful use of the differentiation strategy.[79]

Firms must be able to produce differentiated products at competitive costs to reduce upward pressure on the price that customers pay. When a product's differentiated features are produced at noncompetitive costs, the price for the product may exceed what the firm's target customers are willing to pay. If the firm has a thorough understanding of what its target customers value, the relative importance they attach to the satisfaction of different needs, and for what they are willing to pay a premium, the differentiation strategy can be effective in helping it earn above-average returns. Of course, to achieve these returns, the firm must apply its knowledge capital (knowledge held by its employees and managers) to provide customers with a differentiated product that provides them with superior value.[80]

Through the differentiation strategy, the firm produces nonstandardized (that is, distinctive) products for customers who value differentiated features more than they value low cost. For example, superior product reliability and durability and high-performance sound systems are among the differentiated features of Toyota Motor Corporation's Lexus products. However, Lexus offers its vehicles to customers at a competitive purchase price relative to other luxury automobiles. As with Lexus products, a product's unique attributes, rather than its purchase price, provide the value for which customers are willing to pay.

To maintain success with the differentiation strategy results, the firm must consistently upgrade differentiated features that customers value and/or create new valuable features (innovate) without significant cost increases.[81] This approach requires firms to constantly change their product lines.[82] These firms may also offer a portfolio of products

The **differentiation strategy** is an integrated set of actions taken to produce goods or services (at an acceptable cost) that customers perceive as being different in ways that are important to them.

that complement each other, thereby enriching the differentiation for the customer and perhaps satisfying a portfolio of consumer needs.[83] Because a differentiated product satisfies customers' unique needs, firms following the differentiation strategy are able to charge premium prices. The ability to sell a good or service at a price that substantially exceeds the cost of creating its differentiated features allows the firm to outperform rivals and earn above-average returns. Rather than costs, a firm using the differentiation strategy primarily concentrates on investing in and developing features that differentiate a product in ways that create value for customers.[84] Overall, a firm using the differentiation strategy seeks to be different from its competitors on as many dimensions as possible. The less similarity between a firm's goods or services and those of competitors, the more buffered it is from rivals' actions. Commonly recognized differentiated goods include Toyota's Lexus, Ralph Lauren's wide array of product lines, Caterpillar's heavy-duty earth-moving equipment, and McKinsey & Co.'s differentiated consulting services.

A good or service can be differentiated in many ways. Unusual features, responsive customer service, rapid product innovations and technological leadership, perceived prestige and status, different tastes, and engineering design and performance are examples of approaches to differentiation.[85] While the number of ways to reduce costs may be finite, virtually anything a firm can do to create real or perceived value is a basis for differentiation. Consider product design as a case in point. Because it can create a positive experience for customers, design is an important source of differentiation (even for cost leaders seeking to find ways to add functionalities to their low-cost products as a way of differentiating their products from competitors) and hopefully, for firms emphasizing it, of competitive advantage.[86] Apple is often cited as the firm that sets the standard in design, with the iPod, iPhone, and iPad demonstrating Apple's product design capabilities. Apple's extremely successful new product launches and market share captured with them has invited competition, the most significant of which is Samsung, as described in the Strategic Focus. As described in Chapter 3 Samsung has some strong capabilities and thus has become a formidable competitor. Although it largely imitates Apple's products, it also improves on them by adding features attractive to customers (imperfect imitation).[87] Therefore, Samsung is partially differentiating from Apple's unique (differentiated) products.

The value chain can be analyzed to determine if a firm is able to link the activities required to create value by using the differentiation strategy. Examples of value chain activities and support functions that are commonly used to differentiate a good or service are shown in Figure 4.3. Companies without the skills needed to link these activities cannot expect to successfully use the differentiation strategy. Next, we explain how firms using the differentiation strategy can successfully position themselves in terms of the five forces of competition (see Chapter 2) to earn above-average returns.

Rivalry with Existing Competitors

Customers tend to be loyal purchasers of products differentiated in ways that are meaningful to them. As their loyalty to a brand increases, customers' sensitivity to price increases is reduced. The relationship between brand loyalty and price sensitivity insulates a firm from competitive rivalry. Thus, reputations can sustain the competitive advantage of firms following a differentiation strategy.[88] Alternatively, when highly capable rivals such as Samsung practice imperfect imitation by imitating and improving on products, companies such as Apple must pay attention. Thus, Apple must try to incrementally improve its iPhone and iPad products to exploit its investments. However, it must also invest in exploring highly novel and valuable products to establish new markets to remain ahead of Samsung.[89]

Bargaining Power of Buyers (Customers)

The distinctiveness of differentiated goods or services reduces customers' sensitivity to price increases. Customers are willing to accept a price increase when a product still satisfies

Strategic Focus

TECHNOLOGY

Apple vs. Samsung: Apple Differentiates and Samsung Imperfectly Imitates

Apple is not only a product innovator; it creates new markets and then dominates them as a first mover. Apple has done this with the iPod, iPhone, and iPad. Almost none of its high-tech rivals, such as Dell, Hewlett-Packard, Nokia, and BlackBerry, have offered a serious challenge. However, in recent times Samsung has become a successful challenger of Apple. In fact, it has been so successful that Apple took Samsung to court with a lawsuit for patent infringement. Apple won the lawsuit and a $1 billion judgment against Samsung. Thus, Samsung appears to be a very good imitator—perhaps too good.

Actually, Samsung invests in R&D to design products for existing markets. As such, it is identified as a fast second mover in existing markets. In this regard, Samsung is effective at imitating but changing features. In fact, it improves on features that are attractive to customers. For example, it recently introduced the Galaxy 4 smartphone, which has a five-inch screen. This screen is larger than that of the iPhone 5S and supposedly produces sharper photos.

The rivalry between the two electronic product companies seems to focus on attempts to produce dominant designs. Samsung has acquired the services of one of the top designers in the world, Chris Bangle, who gained fame with his designs of autos for BMW. The design and product battles are now playing out in other product markets, such as tablets, and perhaps smart TVs and smart watches in the near future. During the 2012 Christmas holiday season, Apple sold 22.9 million iPads and Samsung sold 7.6 million tablets. Although Samsung appears to be an imitator, it spends far more money on R&D than does Apple. Samsung invests about three times as much money in R&D than Apple and, importantly, its R&D represents about 5.4 percent of its annual sales, whereas Apple invests about 2.2 percent of its annual sales in R&D.

Samsung Galaxy Tab 10.1. Even though Samsung trails Apple in several product categories, R&D spending suggests that it plans to keep pressure on the industry leader.

All of this suggests that Samsung is a formidable competitor. Knowledgeable sources predict that Apple will settle its suit against Samsung, as it cannot afford to invest heavily in the litigation and appeals and forgo investing the money in R&D if it wishes to remain ahead of Samsung.

Sources: M.-J. Lee, 2013, Samsung vs. Apple's next battleground: Watches? *Wall Street Journal*, http://blog.wsj.com, March 19; R. Pendola, 2013, Apple vs. Samsung explained with a burger and fries on Facebook, *The Street*, www.thestreet.com, March 18; H. Shaughnessy, 2013, Samsung vs. Apple, the battle for design dominance, *Forbes*, www.forbes.com, March 17; B. X. Chen, 2013, Samsung's new 8-inch tablet takes on the iPad Mini, *New York Times*, http://bits.blogs.nytimes.com, February 23; B. X. Chen, 2013, Samsung emerges as a potent rival to apple's cool, *New York Times*, February 10; M. Veverka, 2013, Unplugged: Apple-Samsung showdown has diaper whiff, *USA Today*, www.usatoday.com, January 22; K. Eaton, 2013, Apple rumor patrol: 2013 iPhone edition, *Fast company*, www.fastcompany.com, January 11.

their unique needs better than does a competitor's offering. Thus, the golfer whose needs are specifically satisfied by Callaway golf clubs will likely continue buying those products even if their cost increases. Purchasers of brand-name food items (e.g., Heinz ketchup and Kleenex tissues) accept price increases in those products as long as they continue to perceive that the product satisfies their distinctive needs at an acceptable cost. In all of these instances, the customers are relatively insensitive to price increases because they do not think that an acceptable product alternative exists.

Bargaining Power of Suppliers

Because the firm using the differentiation strategy charges a premium price for its products, suppliers must provide high-quality components, driving up the firm's costs. However, the

Figure 4.3 Examples of Value-Creating Activities Associated with the Differentiation Strategy

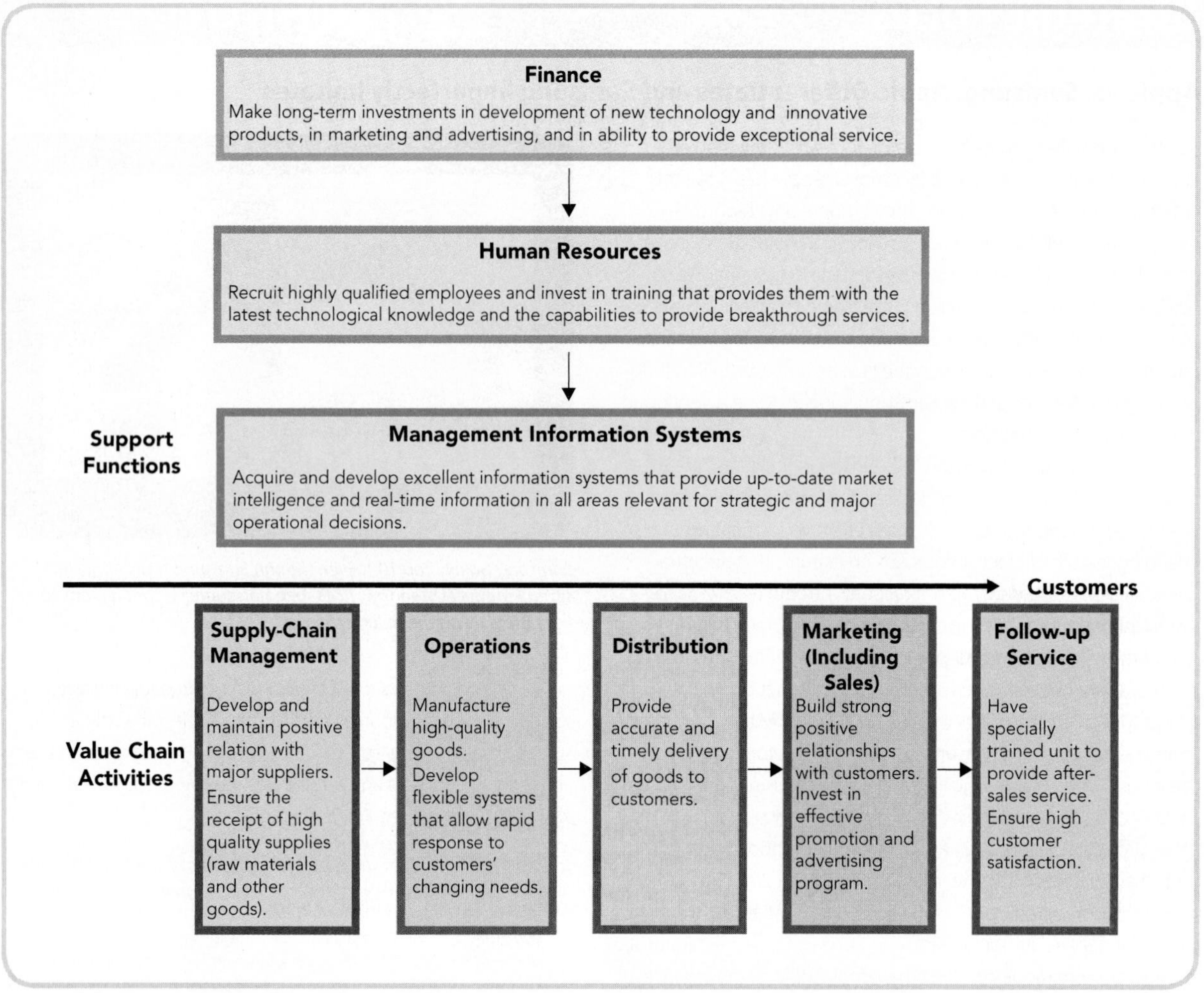

Source: Based on information from M. E. Porter, 1998, *Competitive Advantage: Creating and Sustaining Superior Performance*, New York: The Free Press; D. G. Sirmon, M. A. Hitt, & R. D. Ireland, 2007, Managing firm resources in dynamic environments to create value: Looking inside the black box, *Academy of Management Review*, 32: 273–292; D. G. Sirmon, M. A. Hitt, R. D. Ireland, & B. A. Gilbert, 2011, Resource orchestration to create competitive advantage: Breadth, depth and life cycles effects, *Journal of Management*, 37(5): 1390–1412.

high margins the firm earns in these cases partially insulate it from the influence of suppliers in that higher supplier costs can be paid through these margins.[90] Alternatively, because of buyers' relative insensitivity to price increases, the differentiated firm might choose to pass the additional cost of supplies on to the customer by increasing the price of its unique product. However, when buyers outsource the total function or large portions of it to a supplier, especially R&D for a firm following a differentiation strategy, they can become dependent on and thus vulnerable to that supplier.[91]

Potential Entrants

Customer loyalty and the need to overcome the uniqueness of a differentiated product create substantial barriers to potential entrants. Entering an industry under these conditions typically demands significant investments of resources and patience while seeking customers' loyalty. In these cases, some potential entrants decide to make smaller investments to see if they can gain a "foothold" in the market. If it does not work they will not lose major resources, but if it works they can then invest greater resources to enhance their competitive position.[92]

Product Substitutes

Firms selling brand-name goods and services to loyal customers are positioned effectively against product substitutes. In contrast, companies without brand loyalty face a higher probability of their customers switching either to products which offer differentiated features that serve the same function (particularly if the substitute has a lower price) or to products that offer more features and perform more attractive functions. As such, they may be vulnerable to innovations from outside the industry that better satisfy customers' needs (e.g., Apple's iPod in the music industry)[93]

Competitive Risks of the Differentiation Strategy

One risk of the differentiation strategy is that customers might decide that the price differential between the differentiator's product and the cost leader's product is too large. In this instance, a firm may be offering differentiated features that exceed target customers' needs. The firm then becomes vulnerable to competitors that are able to offer customers a combination of features and price that is more consistent with their needs.

This risk is generalized across a number of companies producing different types of products during an economic recession—a time when sales of luxury goods (e.g., jewelry and leather goods) often suffer. A decision made during the last economic recession by Coach Inc., a maker of high-quality, luxurious accessories and gifts for women and men, demonstrates one firm's reaction to the predicted decline in the sales of luxury goods. With an interest in providing products to increasingly cost-conscious customers without "cheapening" the firm's image, Coach introduced a new line of its products called "Poppy"; the average price of items in this line is approximately 20 percent lower than the average price of Coach's typical products.[94]

Richard Levine / Alamy

A woman carries a Coach Poppy handbag in New York's Times Square. Poppy was introduced during the recent economic recession to appeal to cost-conscious customers without cheapening Coach's image.

Another risk of the differentiation strategy is that a firm's means of differentiation may cease to provide value for which customers are willing to pay. A differentiated product becomes less valuable if imitation by rivals causes customers to perceive that competitors offer essentially the same good or service, but at a lower price.[95] A third risk of the differentiation strategy is that experience can narrow customers' perceptions of the value of a product's differentiated features. For example, customers having positive experiences with generic tissues may decide that the differentiated features of the Kleenex product are not worth the extra cost. To counter this risk, firms must continue to meaningfully differentiate their product (e.g., through innovation) for customers at a price they are willing to pay.[96]

Counterfeiting is the differentiation strategy's fourth risk. "Counterfeits are those products bearing a trademark that is identical to or indistinguishable from a trademark registered to another party, thus infringing the rights of the holder of the trademark."[97] Companies such as Hewlett-Packard must take actions to deal with the problems counterfeit goods create for them when their rights are infringed upon.

4-3c Focus Strategies

The **focus strategy** is an integrated set of actions taken to produce goods or services that serve the needs of a particular competitive segment. Thus, firms use a focus strategy when they utilize their core competencies to serve the needs of a particular industry segment or

The **focus strategy** is an integrated set of actions taken to produce goods or services that serve the needs of a particular competitive segment.

niche to the exclusion of others. Examples of specific market segments that can be targeted by a focus strategy include (1) a particular buyer group (e.g., youths or senior citizens), (2) a different segment of a product line (e.g., products for professional painters or the do-it-yourself group), or (3) a different geographic market (e.g., northern or southern Italy by using a foreign subsidiary).[98]

There are many specific customer needs firms can serve by using a focus strategy. For example, Goya Foods is the largest U.S.-based Hispanic-owned food company in the United States. Segmenting the Hispanic market into unique groups, Goya offers more than 1,500 products to consumers. The firm is a leading authority on Hispanic food and seeks "to be the premier source for authentic Latin cuisine."[99] By successfully using a focus strategy, firms such as Goya gain a competitive advantage in specific market niches or segments, even though they do not possess an industry-wide competitive advantage.

Although the breadth of a target is clearly a matter of degree, the essence of the focus strategy "is the exploitation of a narrow target's differences from the balance of the industry."[100] Firms using the focus strategy intend to serve a particular segment of an industry more effectively than can industry-wide competitors. In fact, entrepreneurial firms commonly serve a specific market niche or segment, partly because they do not have the knowledge or resources to serve the broader market. In fact, they generally prefer to operate "below the radar" of larger and more resource rich firms that serve the broader market.[101] They succeed when they effectively serve a segment whose unique needs are so specialized that broad-based competitors choose not to serve that segment or when they satisfy the needs of a segment being served poorly by industry-wide competitors.

Firms can create value for customers in specific and unique market segments by using the focused cost leadership strategy or the focused differentiation strategy.

Focused Cost Leadership Strategy

Based in Sweden, IKEA, a global furniture retailer with locations in 35 countries and territories and sales revenue of 27.5 billion euros in 2012, uses the focused cost leadership strategy. Young buyers desiring style at a low cost are IKEA's target customers.[102] For these customers, the firm offers home furnishings that combine good design, function, and acceptable quality with low prices. According to the firm, "Low cost is always in focus. This applies to every phase of our activities."[103]

IKEA emphasizes several activities to keep its costs low. For example, instead of relying primarily on third-party manufacturers, the firm's engineers design low-cost, modular furniture ready for assembly by customers. To eliminate the need for sales associates or decorators, IKEA positions the products in its stores so that customers can view different living combinations (complete with sofas, chairs, tables, etc.) in a single room-like setting, which helps the customer imagine how furniture will look in the home. A third practice that helps keep IKEA's costs low is requiring customers to transport their own purchases rather than providing delivery service.

Although it is a cost leader, IKEA also offers some differentiated features that appeal to its target customers, including its unique furniture designs, in-store playrooms for children, wheelchairs for customer use, and extended hours. Thus, IKEA's focused cost leadership strategy also includes some differentiated features with its low-cost products.

Focused Differentiation Strategy

Other firms implement the focused differentiation strategy. As noted earlier, there are many dimensions on which firms can differentiate their good or service. For example, the new generation of lunch trucks populating cities such as New York, San Francisco, Los Angeles, and even College Station, Texas, use the focused differentiation strategy. Serving "high-end fare such as grass-fed hamburgers, escargot and crème brulee," highly trained chefs and well-known restaurateurs own and operate many of these trucks. In fact, "the new breed of lunch truck is aggressively gourmet, tech-savvy and politically correct." Selling sustainably harvested fish tacos in a vehicle that is fueled by vegetable oil, the Green Truck, located in Los Angeles, demonstrates these characteristics. Moreover, the owners of these trucks often use Twitter and Facebook to inform customers of their locations as they move from point to point in their focal city.[104]

With a focus strategy, firms must be able to complete various primary value chain activities and support functions in a competitively superior manner to develop and sustain a competitive advantage and earn above-average returns. The activities required to use the focused cost leadership strategy are virtually identical to those of the industry-wide cost leadership strategy (see Figure 4.2), and activities required to use the focused differentiation strategy are largely identical to those of the industry-wide differentiation strategy (see Figure 4.3). Similarly, the manner in which each of the two focus strategies allows a firm to deal successfully with the five competitive forces parallels those of the two broad strategies. The only difference is in the firm's competitive scope; the firm focuses on a narrow industry segment. Thus, Figures 4.2 and 4.3 and the text describing the five competitive forces also explain the relationship between each of the two focus strategies and competitive advantage. However, the competitive forces in a given industry often favor either a cost leadership or a differentiation strategy.[105]

Competitive Risks of Focus Strategies

With either focus strategy, the firm faces the same general risks as does the company using the cost leadership or the differentiation strategy, respectively, on an industry-wide basis. However, focus strategies have three additional risks.

First, a competitor may be able to focus on a more narrowly defined competitive segment and thereby "out-focus" the focuser. This would happen to IKEA if another firm found a way to offer IKEA's customers (young buyers interested in stylish furniture at a low cost) additional sources of differentiation while charging the same price or to provide the same service with the same sources of differentiation at a lower price. Second, a company competing on an industry-wide basis may decide that the market segment served by the firm using a focus strategy is attractive and worthy of competitive pursuit.[106] For example, women's clothiers such as Chico's, Ann Taylor, and Liz Claiborne might conclude that the profit potential in the narrow segment being served by Anne Fontaine is attractive and decide to design and sell competitively similar clothing items. Initially, Anne Fontaine designed and sold only white shirts for women. However, the shirts were distinctive. They were quite differentiated on the basis of their design, craftsmanship, and high quality of raw materials.[107] The third risk involved with a focus strategy is that the needs of customers within a narrow competitive segment may become more similar to those of industry-wide customers as a whole over time. As a result, the advantages of a focus strategy are either reduced or eliminated. At some point, for example, the needs of Anne Fontaine's customers for high-quality, uniquely designed white shirts could dissipate. If this were to happen, Anne Fontaine's customers might choose to buy white shirts from chains such as Liz Claiborne that sell clothing items with some differentiation, but at a lower cost.

4-3d Integrated Cost Leadership/Differentiation Strategy

Most consumers have high expectations when purchasing a good or service. In general, it seems that most consumers want to pay a low price for products with somewhat highly differentiated features. Because of these customer expectations, a number of firms engage in primary value chain activities and support functions that allow them to simultaneously pursue low cost and differentiation. Firms seeking to do this use the **integrated cost leadership/ differentiation strategy**. The objective of using this strategy is to efficiently produce products with some differentiated features. Efficient production is the source of maintaining

The **integrated cost leadership/differentiation strategy** involves engaging in primary value chain activities and support functions that allow a firm to simultaneously pursue low cost and differentiation.

Preparing a Target store for opening in Quebec, Canada. Target successfully uses the integrated low cost/differentiation strategy.

low costs while differentiation is the source of creating unique value. Firms that successfully use the integrated cost leadership/differentiation strategy usually adapt quickly to new technologies and rapid changes in their external environments. Simultaneously concentrating on developing two sources of competitive advantage (cost and differentiation) increases the number of primary value chain activities and support functions in which the firm must become competent. Such firms often have strong networks with external parties that perform some of the value chain activities and/or support functions.[108] In turn, having skills in a larger number of activities and functions makes a firm more flexible.

Concentrating on the needs of its core customer group (higher-income, fashion-conscious discount shoppers), Target Stores uses an integrated cost leadership-differentiation strategy as shown by its "Expect More. Pay Less." brand promise. Target's annual report describes this strategy: "Our enduring 'Expect More. Pay Less.' brand promise helped us to deliver greater convenience, increased savings and a more personalized shopping experience." In 2012, Target celebrated its fiftieth anniversary and opened its first stores in Canada.[109]

The failed strategy implemented by J.C. Penney appeared to be an attempt to integrate low cost, reducing pricing on most goods in the store, with differentiation, creating specialized stores for name-brand goods within each store. It likely failed because this strategy is very difficult to implement effectively. Often firms are "caught in the middle" and do not differentiate effectively or provide lowest-cost goods. J. C. Penney is a prime example of this failure. It could not compete with the low-cost leaders such as Walmart and Dollar Stores, nor could it compete effectively with the more upscale and differentiated department stores, such as Target and Macy's.

Interestingly, most emerging market firms have competed using the cost leadership strategy. Their labor and other supply costs tend to be considerably lower than multinational firms based in developed countries. However, in recent years some of the emerging market firms are building their capabilities to produce innovation. Coupled with their capabilities to produce lower cost goods, they may be able to gain an advantage on large multinational firms. As such, some of the emerging market firms are beginning to use an integrated low cost-differentiation strategy.[110]

Flexibility is required for firms to complete primary value chain activities and support functions in ways that allow them to use the integrated cost leadership/differentiation strategy in order to produce somewhat differentiated products at relatively low costs. Chinese auto manufacturers have developed a means of product design that provides a flexible architecture that allows low-cost manufacturing but also car designs that are differentiated from competitors.[111] Flexible manufacturing systems, information networks, and total quality management systems are three sources of flexibility that are particularly useful for firms trying to balance the objectives of continuous cost reductions and continuous enhancements to sources of differentiation as called for by the integrated strategy.

Flexible Manufacturing Systems

Using a flexible manufacturing system (FMS), the firm integrates human, physical, and information resources to create relatively differentiated products at relatively low costs.

A significant technological advance, the FMS is a computer-controlled process used to produce a variety of products in moderate, flexible quantities with a minimum of manual intervention.[112] Often the flexibility is derived from modularization of the manufacturing process (and sometimes other value chain activities as well).[113]

The goal of an FMS is to eliminate the "low cost versus product variety" trade-off that is inherent in traditional manufacturing technologies. Firms use an FMS to change quickly and easily from making one product to making another. Used properly, an FMS allows the firm to respond more effectively to changes in its customers' needs, while retaining low-cost advantages and consistent product quality.[114] Because an FMS also enables the firm to reduce the lot size needed to manufacture a product efficiently, the firm's capacity to serve the unique needs of a narrow competitive scope is higher. In industries of all types, effective combinations of the firm's tangible assets (e.g., machines) and intangible assets (e.g., people's skills) facilitate implementation of complex competitive strategies, especially the integrated cost leadership/differentiation strategy.

Information Networks

By linking companies with their suppliers, distributors, and customers, information networks provide another source of flexibility. These networks, when used effectively, help the firm satisfy customer expectations in terms of product quality and delivery speed.[115]

Earlier, we discussed the importance of managing the firm's relationships with its customers in order to understand their needs. Customer relationship management (CRM) is one form of an information-based network process that firms use for this purpose.[116] An effective CRM system provides a 360-degree view of the company's relationship with customers, encompassing all contact points, business processes, and communication media and sales channels.[117] The firm can then use this information to determine the trade-offs its customers are willing to make between differentiated features and low cost—an assessment that is vital for companies using the integrated cost leadership/differentiation strategy. Such systems help firms to monitor their markets and stakeholders and allow them to better predict future scenarios. This capability helps firms to adjust their strategies to be better prepared for the future.[118] Thus, to make comprehensive strategic decisions with effective knowledge of the organization's context, good information flow is essential. Better quality managerial decisions require accurate information on the firm's environment.

Total Quality Management Systems

Total quality management (TQM) is a managerial process that emphasizes an organization's commitment to the customer and to continuous improvement of all processes through problem-solving approaches based on empowerment of employees.[119] Firms develop and use TQM systems to (1) increase customer satisfaction, (2) cut costs, and (3) reduce the amount of time required to introduce innovative products to the marketplace.[120]

Firms able to simultaneously reduce costs while enhancing their ability to develop innovative products increase their flexibility, an outcome that is particularly helpful to firms implementing the integrated cost leadership/differentiation strategy. Exceeding customers' expectations regarding quality is a differentiating feature, and eliminating process inefficiencies to cut costs allows the firm to offer that quality to customers at a relatively low price. Thus, an effective TQM system helps the firm develop the flexibility needed to identify opportunities to simultaneously increase differentiation and reduce costs. Research has found that TQM systems facilitate cost leadership strategies more effectively than they do differentiating strategies when the strategy is implemented alone.[121] However, it facilitates the potential synergy between the two strategies when they are integrated into one. TQM systems are available to all competitors so they may help firms maintain competitive parity, but rarely alone will they lead to a competitive advantage.[122]

Total quality management (TQM) is a managerial process that emphasizes an organization's commitment to the customer and to continuous improvement of all processes through problem-solving approaches based on empowerment of employees.

Competitive Risks of the Integrated Cost Leadership/Differentiation Strategy

The potential to earn above-average returns by successfully using the integrated cost leadership/differentiation strategy is appealing. However, it is a risky strategy, because firms find it difficult to perform primary value chain activities and support functions in ways that allow them to produce relatively inexpensive products with levels of differentiation that create value for the target customer. Moreover, to properly use this strategy across time, firms must be able to simultaneously reduce costs incurred to produce products (as required by the cost leadership strategy) while increasing product differentiation (as required by the differentiation strategy).

Firms that fail to perform the value chain activities and support functions in an optimum manner become "stuck in the middle."[123] Being stuck in the middle means that the firm's cost structure is not low enough to allow it to attractively price its products and that its products are not sufficiently differentiated to create value for the target customer. This appears to be the problem experienced by J.C. Penney. At least as perceived by the customers, its prices were not low enough and the differentiation not great enough to attract the customers needed. In fact, its declining sales suggest that it lost many of its current customers without attracting others to offset the loss. These firms will not earn above-average returns and will earn average returns only when the structure of the industry in which it competes is highly favorable.[124] Thus, companies implementing the integrated cost leadership/differentiation strategy must be able to produce (or offer) products that provide the target customer some differentiated features at a relatively low cost/price.

Firms can also become stuck in the middle when they fail to successfully implement *either* the cost leadership *or* the differentiation strategy. In other words, industry-wide competitors too can become stuck in the middle. Trying to use the integrated strategy is costly in that firms must pursue both low costs and differentiation.

Firms may need to form alliances with other companies to achieve differentiation, yet alliance partners may extract prices for the use of their resources that make it difficult to meaningfully reduce costs.[125] Firms may be motivated to make acquisitions to maintain their differentiation through innovation or to add products to their portfolio not offered by competitors.[126] Research suggests that firms using "pure strategies," either cost leadership or differentiation, often outperform firms attempting to use a "hybrid strategy" (i.e., integrated cost leadership/differentiation strategy). This research suggests the risky nature of using an integrated strategy.[127] However, the integrated strategy is becoming more common and perhaps necessary in many industries because of technological advances and global competition. This strategy often necessitates a long-term perspective to make it work effectively, and therefore requires dedicated owners that allow the implementation of a long-term strategy that can require several years to produce positive returns.[128]

SUMMARY

- A business-level strategy is an integrated and coordinated set of commitments and actions the firm uses to gain a competitive advantage by exploiting core competencies in specific product markets. Five business-level strategies (cost leadership, differentiation, focused cost leadership, focused differentiation, and integrated cost leadership/differentiation) are examined in the chapter.

- Customers are the foundation of successful business-level strategies. When considering customers, a firm simultaneously examines three issues: *who*, *what*, and *how*. These issues,

respectively, refer to the customer groups to be served, the needs those customers have that the firm seeks to satisfy, and the core competencies the firm will use to satisfy customers' needs. Increasing segmentation of markets throughout the global economy creates opportunities for firms to identify more distinctive customer needs they can serve with one of the business-level strategies.

- Firms seeking competitive advantage through the cost leadership strategy produce no-frills, standardized products for an industry's typical customer. However, these low-cost products must be offered with competitive levels of differentiation. Above-average returns are earned when firms continuously emphasize efficiency such that their costs are lower than those of their competitors, while providing customers with products that have acceptable levels of differentiated features.

■ Competitive risks associated with the cost leadership strategy include (1) a loss of competitive advantage to newer technologies, (2) a failure to detect changes in customers' needs, and (3) the ability of competitors to imitate the cost leader's competitive advantage through their own distinct strategic actions.

■ Through the differentiation strategy, firms provide customers with products that have different (and valued) features. Differentiated products must be sold at a cost that customers believe is competitive relative to the product's features as compared to the cost/feature combinations available from competitors' goods. Because of their distinctiveness, differentiated goods or services are sold at a premium price. Products can be differentiated on any dimension that some customer group values. Firms using this strategy seek to differentiate their products from competitors' goods or services on as many dimensions as possible. The less similarity to competitors' products, the more buffered a firm is from competition with its rivals.

■ Risks associated with the differentiation strategy include (1) a customer group's decision that the unique features provided by the differentiated product over the cost leader's goods or services are no longer worth a premium price, (2) the inability of a differentiated product to create the type of value for which customers are willing to pay a premium price,

(3) the ability of competitors to provide customers with products that have features similar to those of the differentiated product, but at a lower cost, and (4) the threat of counterfeiting, whereby firms produce a cheap imitation of a differentiated good or service.

■ Through the cost leadership and the differentiated focus strategies, firms serve the needs of a narrow market segment (e.g., a buyer group, product segment, or geographic area). This strategy is successful when firms have the core competencies required to provide value to a specialized market segment that exceeds the value available from firms serving customers across the total market (industry).

■ The competitive risks of focus strategies include (1) a competitor's ability to use its core competencies to "outfocus" the focuser by serving an even more narrowly defined market segment, (2) decisions by industry-wide competitors to focus on a customer group's specialized needs, and (3) a reduction in differences of the needs between customers in a narrow market segment and the industry-wide market.

■ Firms using the integrated cost leadership/differentiation strategy strive to provide customers with relatively low-cost products that also have valued differentiated features. Flexibility is required for firms to learn how to use primary value chain activities and support functions in ways that allow them to produce differentiated products at relatively low costs. The primary risk of this strategy is that a firm might produce products that do not offer sufficient value in terms of either low cost or differentiation. In such cases, the company becomes "stuck in the middle." Firms stuck in the middle compete at a disadvantage and are unable to earn more than average returns.

REVIEW QUESTIONS

1. What is a business-level strategy?

2. What is the relationship between a firm's customers and its business-level strategy in terms of *who*, *what*, and *how*? Why is this relationship important?

3. What are the differences among the cost leadership, differentiation, focused cost leadership, focused differentiation, and integrated cost leadership/differentiation business-level strategies?

4. How can each of the business-level strategies be used to position the firm relative to the five forces of competition in a way that helps the firm earn above-average returns?

5. What are the specific risks associated with using each business-level strategy?

EXPERIENTIAL EXERCISES

EXERCISE 1: MARKET SEGMENTATION THROUGH BRANDING

The "who" in a firm's target market is an extremely important decision. As discussed in the chapter, firms divide customers into groups

based upon differences in customer needs, which is the heart of market segmentation. For example, if you owned a restaurant and your target market was college-aged students, your strategy would be very different than if your target market was business professionals.

In this exercise, your team will be identifying market segmentation strategies used by various companies. Remember that market segmentation "is a process used to cluster people with similar needs into individual and identifiable groups."

Part One

Your team should select an advertised and prominent brand. You may choose a business or consumer product. However, you should choose a brand that is widely known and widely advertised. Once you have chosen the brand, find and collect at least four instances of this brand being advertised in print or digital media. Find your four or more instances from different publications, if possible.

Part Two

Assemble a poster with the images you collected from your research. Be prepared to present your findings to the class as regards:

1. Why did you choose this brand?

2. Review each of the criteria discussed in Table 4.1 for either your consumer market or industrial market.

EXERCISE 2: HOW INDUSTRIES DIFFER IN THEIR BUSINESS-LEVEL STRATEGY

This assignment brings together elements from the previous chapters. Accordingly, you and your team will create a business-level strategy for a firm in the hotel industry. The instructor will assign you a strategy (from the list below) and you will create a strategy for entering that industry using one of the five potential business-level strategies below:

- Cost leadership
- Differentiation
- Focused cost leadership
- Focused differentiation
- Integrated cost leadership/differentiation

Part One

Research the hotel industry and describe the general environment and the forces in the industry. Using the dimensions of the general environment, identify some factors for each dimension that are influential for your industry. Next, describe the industry environment using the Five Forces model. Database services like Mint Global, Datamonitor, or IBIS World can be helpful in this regard. If those are not available to you, consult your local librarian for assistance. You should be able to clearly articulate the opportunities and the threats that exist.

Part Two

Create on a poster the business-level strategy assigned to your team. Be prepared to describe the following in class:

- Mission statement
- Description of your target customer
- Picture of your business. Where is it located (downtown, suburb, rural, etc.)?
- Describe trends that provide opportunities and threats for your intended strategy.
- List the resources, both tangible and intangible, required to compete successfully in this market.
- How will you go about creating a sustainable competitive advantage?

You will find it interesting to note the difference in the hotel industry between the various business level strategies and the way in which firms compete essentially in the same industry. Remember that your text authors describe business level strategy as "an integrated and coordinated set of commitments and actions the firm uses to gain a competitive advantage by exploiting core competencies in specific product markets. Business-level strategy indicates the choices the firm has made about how it intends to compete in individual product markets."

VIDEO CASE

DIFFERENTIATION STRATEGY IN TOUGH ECONOMIC TIMES
Howard Schultz/CEO/Starbucks

Starbucks, 17,000 stores strong worldwide, offers 70,000 different ways to order coffee. Unfortunately, Starbucks has announced the closing of 900 underperforming stores in the United States and will cut more than 1,000 jobs. Howard Schultz, Starbucks CEO, admits that Starbucks may have grown too big too fast given today's economy, and a business plan was not in place to deal with the severity of the economic downturn. During this time, competitors like Dunkin Donuts are offering an upgraded coffee experience at a lower cost. However, Schultz maintains that

Starbucks will not cut corners but will reduce waste to save the company more than $400 million and continue to sell more than a cup of coffee.

The 2012 annual report shows a turnaround for Starbucks, with global revenues reaching $13.3 billion, a 14 percent increase. In the China and Asia Pacific region, through 2012 Starbucks posted 11 consecutive quarters of double-digit growth. With nearly 3,300 stores, plus hundreds more planned throughout Asia Pacific, Starbucks is transferring is core attributes and expertise, while respecting and reflecting regional customs.

Be prepared to discuss the following concepts and questions in class:

Concepts

- Business-level strategy
- Managing relationship with customers
- Market segmentation
- Differentiation strategy
- Five forces of competition

Questions

1. Describe Starbucks' business-level strategy.

2. How is Starbucks managing its relationship with customers?

3. How would you describe the market segment(s) that Starbucks serves?

4. Is the differentiation strategy appropriate for Starbucks, now or in the future? Why or why not?

5. Using the five forces model of competition, how should Starbucks plan to position itself in these economic times?

NOTES

1. R. D. Ireland, R. E. Hoskisson, & M. A. Hitt, 2012. *Understanding Business Strategy.* Mason, OH: Cengage Learning.

2. H. Greve, 2009, Bigger and safer: The diffusion of competitive advantage, *Strategic Management Journal*, 30: 1–23.

3. M. A. Delmas & M. W. Toffel, 2008, Organizational responses to environmental demands: Opening the black box, *Strategic Management Journal*, 29: 1027–1055; S. Elbanna & J. Child, 2007, The influence of decision, environmental and firm characteristics on the rationality of strategic decision-making, *Journal of Management Studies*, 44: 561–591.

4. M. G. Jacobides, S. G. Winter, & S. M. Kassberger, 2012, The dynamics of wealth, profit, and sustainable advantage, *Strategic Management Journal*, 33: 1384–1410; D. G. Sirmon, M. A. Hitt, R. D. Ireland, & B. A. Gilbert, 2011, Resource orchestration to create competitive advantage: Breadth, depth and life cycle effects, *Journal of Management*, 37: 1390–1412.

5. J. Schmidt & T. Keil, 2013, What makes a resource valuable? Identifying the drivers of firm-idiosyncratic resource value, *Academy of Management Review*, 38: 208–228; C. Zott & R. Amit, 2008, The fit between product market strategy and business model: Implications for firm performance, *Strategic Management Journal*, 29: 1–26.

6. S. Kaplan, 2008, Framing contests: Strategy making under uncertainty, *Organization Science*, 19: 729–752.

7. L. A. Costa, K. Cool, & I. Dierickx, 2013, The competitive implications of the deployment of unique resources, *Strategic Management Journal*, 34: 445–463; K. Shimizu & M. A. Hitt, 2004, Strategic flexibility: Organizational preparedness to reverse ineffective strategic decisions, *Academy of Management Executive*, 18(4): 44–59.

8. B. Chakravarthy & P. Lorange, 2008, Driving renewal: The entrepreneur-manager, *Journal of Business Strategy*, 29: 14–21.

9. J. A. Lamberg, H. Tikkanen, T. Nokelainen, & H. Suur-Inkeroinen, 2009, Competitive dynamics, strategic consistency, and organizational survival, *Strategic Management Journal*, 30: 45–60; R. D. Ireland & C. C. Miller, 2005, Decision-making and firm success, *Academy of Management Executive*, 18(4): 8–12.

10. I. Goll, N. B. Johnson, & A. A. Rasheed, 2008, Top management team demographic characteristics, business strategy, and firm performance in the U.S. airline industry: The role of managerial discretion, *Management Decision*, 46: 201–222; J. R. Hough, 2006, Business segment performance redux: A multilevel approach, *Strategic Management Journal*, 27: 45–61.

11. J. W. Spencer, 2008, The impact of multinational enterprise strategy on indigenous enterprises: Horizontal spillovers and crowding out in developing countries, *Academy of Management Review*, 33: 341–361.

12. Myspace, 2013, *Wikipedia*, http://en.wikipedia.org, April 8.

13. R. E. Hoskisson, M. A. Hitt, R. D. Ireland, & J. S. Harrison, 2013, *Competing for Advantage*, Mason, OH: Cengage Learning.

14. C. Senn, 2012, The booster zone: How to accelerate growth with strategic customers, *Journal of Business Strategy*, 33(6): 31–39; R. J. Harrington & A. K. Tjan, 2008, Transforming strategy one customer at a time, *Harvard Business Review*, 86(3): 62–72.

15. K. R. Fabrizio & L. G. Thomas, 2012, The impact of local demand on innovation in a global industry, *Strategic Management Journal*, 33: 42–64; M. Pynnonen, P. Ritala, & J. Hallikas, 2011, The new meaning of customer value: A systemic perspective, *Journal of Business Strategy*, 32(1): 51–57.

16. M. E. Porter, 1980, *Competitive Strategy*, New York: Free Press.

17. M. Baghai, S. Smit, & P. Viguerie, 2009, Is your growth strategy flying blind? *Harvard Business Review*, 87(5): 86–96.

18. D. G. Sirmon, S. Gove, & M. A. Hitt, 2008, Resource management in dyadic competitive rivalry: The effects of resource bundling and deployment, *Academy of Management Journal*, 51: 919–935; D. G. Sirmon, M. A. Hitt, & R. D. Ireland, 2007, Managing firm resources in dynamic environments to create value: Inside the black box, *Academy of Management Review*, 32: 273–292.

19. J. Singh, P. Lentz, & E. J. Nijssen, 2011, First- and second-order effects of institutional logics on firm-consumer relationships: A cross-market comparative analysis, *Journal of International Business Studies*, 42: 307–333.

20. 2013, Company information, Caesar's Entertainment, www.caesars.com, April 9.

21. Y. Liu & R. Yang, 2009, Competing loyalty programs: Impact of market saturation, market share, and category expandability, *Journal of Marketing*, 73: 93–108.

22. P. E. Frown & A. F. Payne, 2009, Customer relationship management: A strategic perspective, *Journal of Business Market Management*, 3: 7–27.

23. H. Green, 2009, How Amazon aims to keep you clicking, *BusinessWeek*, March 2: 34–35.

24. Myspace, 2013, *Wikipedia*, http://en.wikipedia.org, April 8; Facebook, 2013, *Wikipedia*, http://en.wikipedia.org, April 8.

25. 2013, Netflix Quarter 4 2012 Letter to Shareholders, Netflix, www.netflix.com, January 23.

26. S. E. Sampson & M. Spring, 2012, Customer roles in service supply chains and opportunities for innovation, *Journal of Supply Chain Management*, 48(4): 30–50; M. Bogers, A. Afuah, & B. Bastian, 2010, Users as innovators: A review, critique and future research directions, *Journal of Management*, 36: 857–875.

27. L-Y Jin, 2010, Determinants of customers' complaint intention, *Nankai Business Review International*, 1: 87–99.

28. 2013, MSN Autos, www.autos.msn.com, April 8.

29. S. F. Slater, E. M. Olson, & G. T. Hult, 2010, Worried about strategy implementation? Don't overlook marketing's role, *Business*

Horizons, 53: 469–479; I. C. MacMillan & L. Selden, 2008, The incumbent's advantage, *Harvard Business Review*, 86(10): 111–121.

30. P. Riefler, A. Diamantopoulos, & J. A. Siguaw, 2012, Cosmopolitan consumers as a target group for segmentation, *Journal of International Business Studies*, 43: 285–305.

31. 2013, About Hill's pet nutrition, Hill's Pet Nutrition, www.hillspet.com, April 8.

32. L. Tournois, 2013, Mass market leadership and shampoo wars: The L'Oréal strategy, *Journal of Business Strategy*, 34(1): 4–14.

33. R. Lewis & M. Dart, 2010, *The New Rules of Retail*, New York: Palgrave Macmillan.

34. S. E. Fawcett, A. M. Fawcett. B. J. Watdson, & G. M. Manan, 2012, Peeking inside the black box: Toward as understanding of supply chain collaboration dynamics, *Journal of Supply Chain Management*, 48(1): 44–72; C. A. Funk, J. D. Arthurs, L. J. Trevino, & J. Joireman, 2010, Consumer animosity in the global value chain: The effect of international shifts on willingness to purchase hybrid products. *Journal of International Business Studies*, 41: 639–651.

35. K. Z. Zhou & C. B. Li, 2012, How knowledge affects radical innovation: Knowledge base, market knowledge acquisition and internal knowledge sharing, *Strategic Management Journal*, 33: 1090–1102; T. Y. Eng & J. G. Spickett-Jones, 2009, An investigation of marketing capabilities and upgrading performance of manufacturers in Mainland China and Hong Kong, *Journal of World Business*, 44(4): 463–475.

36. D. J. Teece, 2012, Dynamic capabilities: Routines versus entrepreneurial action, *Journal of Management Studies*, 49: 1395–1401; P. L. Drnevich & A. P. Kriauciunas, 2011, Clarifying the conditions and limits of the contributions of ordinary and dynamic capabilities to relative firm performance, *Strategic Management Journal*, 32: 254–279.

37. M. Gruber, F. Heinimann, M. Brietel, & S. Hungeling, 2010, Configurations of resources and capabilities and their performance implications: An exploratory study on technology ventures, *Strategic Management Journal*, 31: 1337–1356.

38. Merck Company fact sheet, 2013, Merck, www.merck.com, accessed April 8.

39. 2013, About SAS, www.sas.com, April 8.

40. K. E. Klein, 2009, Survival advice for auto parts suppliers, *Wall Street Journal*, www.wsj.com, June 16.

41. M. E. Porter, 1985, *Competitive Advantage*, New York: Free Press, 26.

42. R. Rumelt, 2011, *Good Strategy/Bad Strategy*, New York: Crown Business.

43. M. E. Porter, 1996, What is strategy? *Harvard Business Review*, 74(6): 61–78.

44. Porter, What is strategy?

45. J. S. Srai & L. S. Alinaghian, 2013, Value chain reconfiguration in highly disaggregated industrial systems: Examining the emergence of health care diagnostics, *Global Strategy Journal*, 3: 88–108; M. Reitzig & P. Puranam, 2009, Value appropriation

as an organizational capability: The case of IP protection through patents, *Strategic Management Journal*, 30: 765–789.

46. M. E. Porter, 1994, Toward a dynamic theory of strategy, in R. P. Rumelt, D. E. Schendel, & D. J. Teece (Eds.), *Fundamental Issues in Strategy*, Boston: Harvard Business School Press: 423–461.

47. Porter, What is strategy?, 62.

48. Porter, *Competitive Advantage*, 15.

49. S. Sun, 2009, An analysis on the conditions and methods of market segmentation, *International Journal of Business and Management*, 4: 63–70.

50. J. Gonzales-Benito & I. Suarez-Gonzalez, 2010, A study of the role played by manufacturing strategic objectives and capabilities in understanding the relationship between Porter's generic strategies and business performance, *British Journal of Management*, 21(4): 1027–1043.

51. Ireland, Hoskisson, & Hitt, *Understanding Business Strategy*; G. B. Voss, D. Sirdeshmukh, & Z. G. Voss, 2008, The effects of slack resources and environmental threat on product exploration and exploitation, *Academy of Management Journal*, 51: 147–158.

52. Porter, *Competitive Strategy*, 35–40.

53. P. D. Orberg Jensen & B. Petersen, 2013, Global sourcing of services: Risk, process, and collaborative architecture, *Global Strategy Journal*, 3: 67–87; C. Weigelt, 2013, Leveraging supplier capabilities: The role of locus of capability deployment, *Strategic Management Journal*, 34: 1–21.

54. 2013, Explore Kia USA, Kia USA, www.kia.com, accessed April 10.

55. M. Ihlwan, 2009, Kia Motors: Still cheap, now chic, *BusinessWeek*, June 1, 58.

56. D. S. K. Lim, N. Celly, & E. A. Morse, 2013, Rethinking the effectiveness of asset and cost retrenchment: The contingency effects of a firm's rent creation mechanism, *Strategic Management Journal*, 34: 42–61.

57. D. Mehri, 2006, The dark side of lean: An insider's perspective on the realities of the Toyota production system, *Academy of Management Perspectives*, 20(2): 21–42.

58. C. Garcia-Olaverri & E. Huerta, 2012, Why do some companies adopt advanced management systems? The Spanish case, *Management Research*, 10: 99–124; N. T. Sheehan & G. Vaidyanathan, 2009, Using a value creation compass to discover "Blue Oceans," *Strategy & Leadership*, 37: 13–20.

59. A. M. Chaker, 2009, Planes, trains… and buses? *Wall Street Journal*, www.wsj.com, June 18.

60. 2013, Greyhound facts and figures, www.greyhound.com, accessed on April 10.

61. J.-K. Park & Y. K. Ro, 2013, Product architectures and sourcing decisions: Their impact on performance, *Journal of Management*, 39: 814–846; M. Kotabe & R. Mudambi, 2009, Global sourcing and value creation: Opportunities and challenges, *Journal of International Management*, 15: 121–125.

62. R. Liu, D. J. Feils, & B. Scholnick, 2011, Why are different services outsources to different countries? *Journal of International Business Studies*, 42: 558–571; J. Hatonen & T. Erikson, 2009, 30+ years of research and practice of outsourcing—exploring the past and anticipating the future, *Journal of International Management*, 15: 142–155.

63. M. J. Lennox, S. F. Rockart, & A. Y. Lewin, 2010, Does interdependency affect firm and industry profitability? An empirical test, *Strategic Management Journal*, 31: 121–139.

64. 2013, Corporate overview, Big Lots, www.biglots.com, April 10.

65. J. Morehouse, B. O'Mera, C. Hagen, & T. Huseby, 2008, Hitting back: Strategic responses to low-cost rivals, *Strategy & Leadership*, 36: 4–13; L. K. Johnson, 2003, Dueling pricing strategies, *The McKinsey Quarterly*, 44(3): 10–11.

66. G. J. Kilduff, H. A. Elfenbein, & B. W. Staw, 2010, The psychology of rivalry: A relationally dependent analysis of competition, *Academy of Management Journal*, 53: 943–969.

67. T. W. Tong & J. J. Reuer, 2010, Competitive consequences of interfirm collaboration: How joint ventures shape industry profitability, *Journal of International Business Studies*, 41: 1056–1073.

68. Y. Luo, Y. Huang, & S. L. Wang, 2011, Guanxi and organizational performance: A meta-analysis, *Management and Organization Review*, 8: 139–172.

69. O. D. Fjeldstad & A. Sasson, 2010, Membership matters: On the value of being embedded in customer networks, *Journal of Management Studies*, 47: 944–966.

70. 2013, Our story, http://corporate.walmart.com, accessed April 10.

71. F. J. Contractor, V. Kumar, S. K. Kundu, & T. Pedersen, 2010, Reconceptualizing the firm in a world of outsourcing and offshoring: The organizational and geographical relocation of high-value company functions. *Journal of Management Studies*, 47: 1417–1433.

72. Y. Zhang & J. Gimeno, 2010, Earnings pressure and competitive behavior: Evidence from the U.S. electricity industry, *Academy of Management Journal*, 53: 743–768.

73. B. Flynn, 2010, Introduction to the special topic forum on global supply chain management, *Journal of Supply Chain Management*, 46(2): 3–4.

74. T. J. Kull, S. C. Ellis, & R. Narasimhan, 2013, Reducing behavioral constraints to supplier integration: A socio-technical systems perspective, *Journal of Supply Chain Management*, 49(1): 64–86; J. Dyer & W. Chu, 2011, The determinants of trust in supplier-automaker relations in the U.S., Japan and Korea: A retrospective, *Journal of International Business Studies*, 42: 28–34; M-S. Cheung, M. B. Myers, & J. T. Mentzer, 2011, The value of relational learning in global buyer-supplier exchanges: A dyadic perspective and test of the pie-sharing

hypothesis, *Strategic Management Journal*, 32(10): 1061–1082.

75. O. Ormanidhi & O. Stringa, 2008, Porter's model of generic competitive strategies, *Business Economics*, 43: 55–64; J. Bercovitz & W. Mitchell, 2007, When is more better? The impact of business scale and scope on long-term business survival, while controlling for profitability, *Strategic Management Journal*, 28: 61–79.

76. A. Kaul, 2012, Technology and corporate scope: Firm and rival innovation as antecedents of corporate transactions, *Strategic Management Journal*, 33: 347–367; K. Z. Zhou & F. Wu, 2010, Technological capability, strategic flexibility and product innovation, *Strategic Management Journal*, 31: 547–561.

77. Porter, *Competitive Strategy*, 35–40.

78. 2009, Product innovation, www.1000ventures.com, June 19.

79. C. A. Siren, M. Kohtamaki, & A. Kuckertz, 2012, Exploration and exploitation strategies, profit performance and the mediating role of strategic learning: Escaping the exploitation trap, *Strategic Entrepreneurship Journal*, 6: 18–41; D. Dunlap-Hinkler, M. Kotabe, & R. Mudambi, 2010, A story of breakthrough versus incremental innovation: Corporate entrepreneurship in the global pharmaceutical industry, *Strategic Entrepreneurship Journal*, 4: 106–127.

80. U. Lichtenthaler & H. Ernst, 2012, Integrated knowledge exploitation: The complementarity of product development and technology licensing, *Strategic Management Journal*, 33: 513–534; Z. Simsek & C. Heavy, 2011, The mediating role of knowledge-based capital for corporate entrepreneurship effects on performance: A study of small-to medium sized firms, *Strategic Entrepreneurship Journal*, 5: 81–100.

81. R. Kotha, Y. Zheng, & G. George, 2011, Entry into new niches: The effects of firm age and the expansion of technological capabilities on innovative output and impact, *Strategic Management Journal*, 32(9): 1011–1024; D. Ashmos Plowman, L. T. Baker, T. E. Beck, M. Kulkarni, S. Thomas-Solansky, & D. V. Travis, 2007, Radical change accidentally: The emergence and amplification of small change, *Academy of Management Journal*, 50: 515–543.

82. J. T. Macher & C. Boerner, 2012, Technological development at the boundaries of the firm: A knowledge-based examination in drug development, *Strategic Management Journal*, 33: 1016–1036; R. Agarwal, D. Audretsch, & M. B. Sarkar, 2010, Knowledge spillovers and strategic entrepreneurship, *Strategic Entrepreneurship Journal*, 4: 271–283.

83. N. Kim & S. Min, 2012, Impact of industry incumbency and product newness on pioneer leadtime, *Journal of Management*, 38: 695–718; F. T. Rothaermel, M. A. Hitt, & L. A. Jobe, 2006, Balancing vertical integration and strategic outsourcing: Effects on product portfolio, product success and firm performance, *Strategic Management Journal*, 27: 1033–1056.

84. D. Somaya, 2012, Patent strategy and management: An integrative review and research agenda, *Journal of Management*, 38: 1084–1114; A. Cuervo-Cazurra & C. A. Un, 2010, Why some firms never invest in R&D, *Strategic Management Journal*, 31: 759–779.

85. N. E. Levitas & T. Chi, 2010, A look at the value creation effects of patenting and capital investment through a real-option lens: The moderation role of uncertainty, *Strategic Entrepreneurship Journal*, 4: 212–233; L. A. Bettencourt & A. W. Ulwick, 2008, The customer-centered innovation map, *Harvard Business Review*, 86(5): 109–114.

86. M. Abbott, R. Holland, J. Giacomin, & J. Shackleton, 2009, Changing affective content in brand and product attributes, *Journal of Product & Brand Management*, 18: 17–26.

87. H. E. Posen, J. Lee, & S. Yi, 2013, The power of imperfect imitation, *Strategic Management Journal*, 34: 149–164.

88. B. K. Boyd, D. D. Bergh, & D. J. Ketchen, 2010, Reconsidering the reputation-performance relationship: A resource-based view, *Journal of Management*, 36: 588–609; V. P. Rindova, I. O. Williamson, & A. P. Petkova, 2010, Reputation as an intangible asset: Reflections on theory and methods in two empirical studies of business school reputations, *Journal of Management*, 36: 610–619.

89. R. Mudambi & T. Swift, 2013, Knowing when to leap: Transitioning between exploitative and explorative R&R, *Strategic Management Journal*, in press.

90. O. Chatain, 2011, Value creation, competition and performance in buyer-supplier relationships, *Strategic Management Journal*, 32: 76–102.

91. A. Marinez-Noya, E. Garcia-Canal, & M. F. Guillen, 2013, R&D outsourcing and the effectiveness of intangible investments: Is proprietary core knowledge walking out the door? *Journal of Management Studies*, 5: 67–91.

92. J. W. Upson, S. J. Ketchen, B. L. Connelly, & A. L. Ranft, 2012, Competitor analysis and foothold moves, *Academy of Management Journal*, 55: 93–110.

93. S. Anokhin & J. Wincent, 2012, Start-up rates and innovation: A cross-country examination, *Journal of International Business Studies*, 43: 41–60.

94. S. Berfield, 2009, Coach's new bag, *BusinessWeek*, June 29: 41–43; S. Berfield, 2009, Coach's Poppy line is luxury for recessionary times, *BusinessWeek*, www.businessweek.com, June 18.

95. D. G. Sirmon, J.-L. Arregle, M. A. Hitt, & J. W. Webb, 2008, The role of family influence in firms' strategic responses to threat of imitation, *Entrepreneurship Theory and Practice*, 32: 979–998; F. K. Pil & S. K. Cohen, 2006, Modularity: Implications for imitation, innovation, and sustained advantage, *Academy of Management Review*, 31: 995–1011.

96. M. M. Crossan & M. Apaydin, 2010, A multi-dimensional framework of organizational innovation: A systematic review of the literature, *Journal of Management Studies*, 47: 1154–1180.

97. X. Bian & L. Moutinho, 2009, An investigation of determinants of counterfeit purchase consideration, *Journal of Business Research*, 62: 368–378.

98. Porter, *Competitive Strategy*; K. Blomkvist, P. Kappen, & I. Zander, 2010, Quo vadis? The entry into new technologies in advanced foreign subsidiaries of the multinational enterprise, *Journal of International Business Studies*, 41: 525–549.

99. 2013, About Goya foods, www.goyafoods. com, April 11.

100. Porter, *Competitive Advantage*, 15.

101. J. P. Eggers, 2012, All experience is not created equal: Learning, adapting, and focusing in product portfolio management, *Strategic Management Journal*, 33: 315–335; R. Katila, E. L. Chen, & H. Piezunka, 2012, All the right moves: How entrepreneurial firms compete effectively, *Strategic Entrepreneurship Journal*, 6: 116–132.

102. K. Kling & I. Goteman, 2003, IKEA CEO Andres Dahlvig on international growth and IKEA's unique corporate culture and brand identity, *Academy of Management Executive*, 17(1): 31–37.

103. 2013, About IKEA, IKEA, www.ikea.com, April 11.

104. K. McLaughlin, 2009, Food truck nation, *Wall Street Journal*, www.wsj.com, June 5.

105. A. Barroso & M. S. Giarratana, 2013, Product proliferation strategies and firm performance: The moderating role of product space complexity, *Strategic Management Journal*, in press.

106. C. E. Armstrong, 2012, Small retailer strategies for battling the big boxes: A "Goliath" victory?, *Journal of Strategy and Management*, 5: 41–56.

107. 2013, Ann Fontaine: History, www. annfontaine.com, accessed April 11; 2011, Anne Fontaine, www.factio-magazine.com, May 6.

108. H. A. Ndofor, D. G. Sirmon, & X. He, 2011, Firm resources, competitive actions and performance: Investigating a mediated model with evidence from the in-vitro diagnostics industry, *Strategic Management Journal*, 32: 640–657; R. A. D'Aveni, G. B. Dagnino, & K. G. Smith, 2010, The age of temporary advantage, *Strategic Management Journal*, 31: 1371–1385.

109. 2010, Letter to our shareholders, Target Annual Report, www.target.com, March 11.

110. G. A. Shinkle, A. P. Kriauciunas, & G. Hundley, 2013, Why pure strategies may be wrong for transition economy firms, *Strategic Management Journal*, in press; S. Awate, M. M. Larsen, & R. Mudambi, EMNE

catch-up strategies in the wind turbine industry: Is there a trade-off between output and innovation capabilities? *Global Strategy Journal*, 2: 205–223.

111. H. Wang & C. Kimble, 2010, Low-cost strategy through product architecture: Lessons from China, *Journal of Business Strategy*, 31(3): 12–20.

112. M. I. M. Wahab, D. Wu, and C.-G. Lee, 2008, A generic approach to measuring the machine flexibility of manufacturing systems, *European Journal of Operational Research*, 186: 137–149.

113. M. Kotabe, R. Parente, & J. Y. Murray, 2007, Antecedents and outcomes of modular production in the Brazilian automobile industry: A grounded theory approach, *Journal of International Business Studies*, 38: 84–106.

114. T. Raj, R. Shankar, & M. Sunhaib, 2009, An ISM approach to analyse interaction between barriers of transition to flexible manufacturing systems, *International Journal of Manufacturing Technology and Management*, 16: 417–438; E. K. Bish, A. Muriel, & S. Biller, 2005, Managing flexible capacity in a make-to-order environment, *Management Science*, 51: 167–180.

115. P. Theodorou & G. Florou, 2008, Manufacturing strategies and financial performance—the effect of advanced information technology: CAD/CAM systems, *Omega*, 36: 107–121.

116. N. A. Morgan & L. L. Rego, 2009, Brand portfolio strategy and firm performance, *Journal of Marketing*, 73: 59–74.

117. D. Elmuti, H. Jia, & D. Gray, 2009, Customer relationship management strategic application and organizational effectiveness: An empirical investigation, *Journal of Strategic Marketing*, 17: 75–96.

118. C. O. Scharmer & K. Kaeufer, 2010, In front of blank canvas: Sensing emerging futures, *Journal of Business Strategy*, 31(4): 21–29.

119. J. D. Westphal, R. Gulati, & S. M. Shortell, 1997, Customization or conformity: An institutional and network perspective on the content and consequences of TQM adoption, *Administrative Science Quarterly*, 42: 366–394.

120. S. Modell, 2009, Bundling management control innovations: A field study of organisational experimenting with total quality management and the balanced scorecard, *Accounting, Auditing & Accountability Journal*, 22: 59–90.

121. C. D. Zatzick, T. P. Moliterno, & T. Fang, 2012, Strategic (mis)fit: The implementation of TQM in manufacturing organizations, *Strategic Management Journal*, 33: 1321–1330.

122. A. Keramati & A. Albadvi, 2009, Exploring the relationship between use of information technology in total quality management and SMEs performance using canonical correlation analysis: A survey on Swedish car part supplier sector, *International Journal of Information Technology and Management*, 8: 442–462; R. J. David & S. Strang, 2006, When fashion is fleeting: Transitory collective beliefs and the dynamics of TQM consulting, *Academy of Management Journal*, 49: 215–233.

123. Porter, *Competitive Advantage*, 16.

124. Ibid., 17.

125. M. A. Hitt, L. Bierman, K. Uhlenbruck, & K. Shimizu, 2006, The importance of resources in the internationalization of professional service firms: The good, the bad, and the ugly, *Academy of Management Journal*, 49: 1137–1157.

126. P. Puranam, H. Singh, & M. Zollo, 2006, Organizing for innovation: Managing the coordination-autonomy dilemma in technology acquisitions, *Academy of Management Journal*, 49: 263–280.

127. S. Thornhill & R. E. White, 2007, Strategic purity: A multi-industry evaluation of pure vs. hybrid business strategies, *Strategic Management Journal*, 28: 553–561.

128. B. Connelly, L. Tihanyi, S. T. Certo, & M. A. Hitt, 2010, Marching to the beat of different drummers: The influence of institutional owners on competitive actions, *Academy of Management Journal*, 53: 723–742.

5

Competitive Rivalry and Competitive Dynamics

Studying this chapter should provide you with the strategic management knowledge needed to:

1. Define competitors, competitive rivalry, competitive behavior, and competitive dynamics.

2. Describe market commonality and resource similarity as the building blocks of a competitor analysis.

3. Explain awareness, motivation, and ability as drivers of competitive behavior.

4. Discuss factors affecting the likelihood a competitor will take competitive actions.

5. Describe factors affecting the likelihood a competitor will respond to actions taken by its competitors.

6. Explain competitive dynamics in slow-cycle, in fast-cycle, and in standard-cycle markets.

TESCO PLC: A CASE STUDY IN COMPETITIVE BEHAVIOR

Tesco PLC is the world's third-largest retailer, a fact that suggests its ability to compete successfully against companies both in the United Kingdom (its home market) and throughout the world. However, the firm's recent competitive struggles both domestically and globally appear to highlight the fact that, as noted in Chapter 1, no company's success at a point in time guarantees its future success.

So what are some descriptors of the situation Tesco is encountering? From a financial perspective, the firm reported a decline in profits in 2012 for the first time in approximately two decades. In 2013, Tesco closed its Fresh & Easy stores in the United States and also took a write-down of 804 million pounds to reflect the then-current value of its U.K. properties. In all, Tesco wrote down the value of its global operations by $3.5 billion in 2013. (The global write-down of $3.5 billion accounts for the firm's troubled operations in countries such as Turkey, China, and India as well as the closing of its U.S. operations.)

Another issue is that revenue is declining in Tesco's home market where the company still generates roughly two-thirds of its sales and profits. Part of the reason for the revenue decline is related to customer service, as suggested by the fact that the results from a recent survey of U.K. consumers "found that despite £1 billion of investment in the U.K. in FY2012/13 customer perceptions of Tesco's quality, prices, promotions and overall value for money had all deteriorated quarter on quarter and year on year." In light of these results, the firm is taking a number of actions, including adding more and better-trained staff members in its stores, refurbishing those stores, and revamping its product lines and the prices it charges for them.

Revamping product lines and changing the prices charged for items are tactical actions. In contrast, entering the U.S. market with the Fresh & Easy concept was a strategic action (strategic and tactical actions and responses are defined later in this chapter). On the surface, entering the large U.S. market seems to be a reasonable course of action for a successful global retailer to take. As is often the case though, execution of that strategic action appears to be where problems were encountered. Fresh & Easy stores were sized to be handy neighborhood stores such as those found in many European cities. This did not appeal to American consumers, as suggested by an analyst: "My sense is that what they tried to do was make a European model. Europeans tend to make more frequent trips to grocery stores, maybe every day or every other day, where Americans are used to going for bigger trips less frequently." Additionally, products carried in stores located in different parts of the United States were not customized to any degree, meaning that the potentially unique needs of any local consumers who might choose to shop daily were not being identified and satisfied.

Tesco is taking additional strategic actions as part of its current array of competitive behaviors. For example, it is taking positions in other companies for the purpose of being able to turn their stores into compelling retail destinations for customers. "Investments in the Harris & Hoole coffee chain, working with the Euphorium bakery brand in London and acquiring the Giraffe restaurant chain" are examples of the competitive behavior Tesco is displaying as a foundation for improving its performance and trying to outcompete its rivals in the process of doing so.

Sources: J. Davey & K. Holton, 2013, Tesco quits U.S. and takes $3.5 billion global writedown, *Reuters*, www.reuters.com, April 17; K. Gordon, 2013, No bonus for Tesco bosses until profit improves, *Wall Street Journal*, www.wsj.com, May 23; K. Gordon, 2013, Tesco leans on outside brands, *Wall Street Journal*, www.wsj.com, April 18; R. Head, 2013, Can Tesco outperform Wal-Mart stores? *Daily Finance*, www.dailyfinance.com, March 21; N. Pratley, 2013, Tesco's era of rolling out its aisles is over, for now, *The Guardian*, www.guardian.co.uk, April 17; A. Felsted, 2012, American dream that died for Tesco, *Financial Times*, www.ft.com, December 5.

Strategy Right NOW

Learn more about Giraffe, another company acquired by Tesco.
www.cengagebrain.com

Competitors are firms operating in the same market, offering similar products, and targeting similar customers.

Competitive rivalry is the ongoing set of competitive actions and competitive responses that occur among firms as they maneuver for an advantageous market position.

Competitive behavior is the set of competitive actions and responses a given firm takes to build or defend its competitive advantages and to improve its market position.

Firms operating in the same market, offering similar products, and targeting similar customers are **competitors**.[1] Southwest Airlines, Delta, United, and JetBlue are competitors as are Hulu, iTunes, and Netflix. J Sainsbury PLC and WM Morrison Supermarkets PLC are the primary domestic competitors for Tesco PLC, the focal firm of the Opening Case. However, Tesco also competes with global giants such as France's Carrefour SA, Germany's Metro, and the U.S.-based Wal-Mart Stores, Inc., meaning that the firm engages in a significant amount of competitive behavior (defined fully below, competitive behavior is essentially the set of actions and responses a firm takes as it competes against its rivals).

Firms interact with their competitors as part of the broad context within which they operate while attempting to earn above-average returns.[2] Another way to consider this is to note that no firm competes in a vacuum; rather, each firm's actions are part of a mosaic of competitive actions and responses taking place among a host of companies seeking the same objective—superior performance. And evidence shows that the decisions firms make about their interactions with competitors significantly affect their ability to earn above-average returns.[3] Because of this, firms seek to reach optimal decisions when considering how to compete against their rivals.[4]

Competitive rivalry is the ongoing set of competitive actions and competitive responses that occur among firms as they maneuver for an advantageous market position.[5] Especially in highly competitive industries, firms constantly jockey for advantage as they launch strategic actions and respond or react to rivals' moves.[6] It is important for those leading organizations to understand competitive rivalry, in that the reality is that some firms learn how to outperform their competitors, meaning that competitive rivalry influences an individual firm's ability to gain and sustain competitive advantages.[7] A sequence of firm-level moves, rivalry results from firms initiating their own competitive actions and then responding to actions taken by competitors.[8]

Zara, a clothing unit owned by Spanish retailer Inditex SA, which is the world's largest fashion retailer by sales, engages in competitive rivalry with a number of firms but especially Swedish-based Hennes & Mauritz AB (H&M). (Mango and Topshop are other important Zara competitors.) As explained in the Strategic Focus, Zara and H&M engage in a continuous stream of competitive actions and responses as they each seek the most advantageous positions in the many markets in which they are competitors. Zara uses its core competencies as the basis for competing against its rivals. Because the global retail clothing industry is highly competitive, the constant competitive jockeying between Zara and H&M is not surprising.

Competitive behavior is the set of competitive actions and responses a given firm takes to build or defend its competitive advantages and to improve its market position.[9] As explained in the Strategic Focus, Zara and H&M engage in competitive behavior to defend their advantages and to improve the attractiveness of their market positions.

M. Stasy

Strategic Focus

TECHNOLOGY

Competitive Rivalry in *Fast Fashion*: A Constant Stream of Actions and Responses

In our discussion of Zara in the Opening Case in Chapter 3, we noted that this company competing in the *fast fashion* segment of the retailing clothing industry "uses its resources and capabilities as the foundation for its core competencies." We also indicated that its core competencies allow Zara to "give customers what they want and get it to them faster than anyone else." Quick designs and its supply chain are two core competencies that remain critical to Zara's success.

In terms of design, analysts say that Zara gives customers decently made fashion items that are based on the latest looks from runways throughout the world yet are also sold at affordable prices—hence, the reason to ascribe the term "cheap chic" to the firm's clothes and to those produced by its major competitors as well. With respect to the supply chain competence, this is framed around the fact that parent-company Inditex owns a number of brands in addition to Zara, such as Massimo Dutti, Bershka, Pull & Bear, Stradivarius, and Oysho. In total, the clothing giant has over 6,000 stores located in close to 90 countries. Serving the product needs of all of its units, some say that "Inditex is something of a supply chain marvel: clothes move from concept to design to the Zara stores in a matter of days. And they move out of Zara stores within weeks."

With close to 3,000 stores located in almost 50 countries, H&M is another very large global clothing retailer. This firm also concentrates on the fast fashion market; and Zara and H&M compete on some of the same dimensions such as supply chain. But as discussed in Chapter 3, firms' resources are unique or idiosyncratic and as such do not yield identical capabilities and core competencies. This uniqueness is the foundation for how firms compete against one another. Relative to H&M, Zara's supply chain appears to be an advantage and a means of taking competitive actions. In the words of an analyst: "Zara has a lightning-fast supply chain with 50 percent of its clothes made in Western Europe. That allows it to capture catwalk and luxury trends and put product in its stores within weeks—something customers are willing to pay a premium for." While H&M's supply chain is impressive, it does not allow the firm to achieve competitive parity with Zara with respect to this competitive dimension. "H&M with its longer supply chain can't keep pace in terms of fashion, so it tries to compete on price instead: H&M's offerings are on average about 60 percent cheaper than Zara's. But the Stockholm-based chain is still more expensive than budget competitors such as Primark, owned by Associated British Foods PLC and U.S. chain Forever 21, leaving H&M struggling to position itself." Thus, in terms of competitive rivalry, Zara uses its supply chain advantage while H&M uses price as a competitive action to try to reduce the value Zara generates by emphasizing its supply chain.

There are additional examples of competitive rivalry between Zara and H&M. Recently H&M along with other retailers including

A window display from a Zara store. Zara's supply chain gives it a competitive advantage and underlies its ability to take competitive actions.

Gap, American Eagle Outfitters, and Forever 21 established units in Mexico. Steadily increasing incomes of Mexican citizens and the country's sizable and youthful population are reasons for these entries. However, Zara is a first mover in Mexico, having established its first unit there in 1992 and expanding that initial location to 246 stores currently. Thus, entry now by some additional clothing retailers is a competitive response to the competitive action Zara took long ago. On the other hand, H&M currently is seeking to expand more rapidly in India compared to Zara. In this instance, H&M is taking a competitive action to which Zara may have to respond.

The Internet is a growing source of competitive rivalry between Zara and H&M. More specifically, H&M announced that it would establish a significant online shopping presence in the United States. However, this intended action appears to be at least in part a response to Zara's increasing Internet-related success. In commenting about its Web site, a Zara official noted that the number of visitors to the site recently doubled and that the site is receiving over 2 million hits per day.

Overall, the never-ending string of competitive actions and responses occurring between Zara & H&M provide an interesting "picture" of competitive rivalry.

Sources: C. Bjork, 2013, Inditex profit rises as global expansion continues, *Wall Street Journal*, www.wsj.com, March 13; J. Cartner-Morley, 2013, How Zara took over the high street, *The Guardian*, www.guardian.co.uk, February 15; L. Dishman, 2013, H&M's competitive advantage: Expansion in India, *Forbes*, www.forbes.com, April 29; J. Hansegard, 2013, H&M plans U.S. online store in summer, *Wall Street Journal*, www.wsj.com, March 21; M. Moffett, 2013, Soul-searching in Spanish fashion after Bangladesh factory details, *Wall Street Journal*, www.wsj.com, May 23; M. Sanchantra & L. Burkitt, 2013, Asia gravitates to cheap chic, *Wall Street Journal*, www.wsj.com, April 23; M. J. Deschamps, 2012, Just-style management briefing: Fast fashion's competitive advantages, *Just-Style*, www.just-style.com, July 2; S. Hansen, 2012, How Zara grew into the world's largest fashion retailer, *New York Times*, www.nytimes.com, November 9.

Through competitive behavior, each of these firms seeks to successfully position itself relative to the five forces of competition (see Chapter 2) and to defend its current competitive advantages while building advantages for the future (see Chapter 3).

Increasingly, competitors engage in competitive actions and responses in more than one market.[10] Firms competing against each other in several product or geographic markets are engaged in **multimarket competition**.[11] All competitive behavior—that is, the total set of actions and responses taken by all firms competing within a market—is called **competitive dynamics**. The relationships among all of these key concepts are shown in Figure 5.1.

This chapter focuses on competitive rivalry and competitive dynamics. A firm's strategies are dynamic in nature because actions taken by one firm elicit responses from competitors that, in turn, typically result in responses from the firm that took the initial action.[12] For example, the strategies cigarette manufacturers are implementing today include actions related to electronic cigarettes as a relatively new product. Commonly called e-cigarettes and with their health benefits still unknown, this product is a battery-powered device that converts heated, nicotine-laced liquid into vapor. Altria Group and Reynolds American, Inc. (the two largest U.S. cigarette manufacturers) updated their "e-cigarette strategies" in mid-2013. Influencing these updates were the increasing size of the market for this product and the more prominent position Lorillard Inc., the third-largest U.S. tobacco firm, had already established in it. Additional competitive actions and responses among these firms and with international cigarette manufacturers as well are expected in the foreseeable future.[13]

Competitive rivalries affect a firm's strategies, as shown by the fact that a strategy's success is determined not only by the firm's initial competitive actions but also by how well it anticipates competitors' responses to them *and* by how well the firm anticipates and responds to its competitors' initial actions (also called attacks).[14] Although competitive

Multimarket competition occurs when firms compete against each other in several product or geographic markets.

Competitive dynamics refer to all competitive behaviors—that is, the total set of actions and responses taken by all firms competing within a market.

Figure 5.1 From Competition to Competitive Dynamics

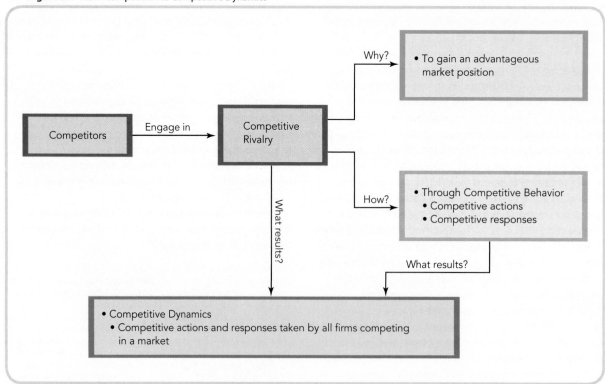

Source: Adapted from M. J. Chen, 1996, Competitor analysis and inferfirm rivalry: Toward a theoretical integration, *Academy of Management Review*, 21: 100-134.

M. Stasy

rivalry affects all types of strategies (e.g., corporate-level, merger and acquisition, and international), its dominant influence is on the firm's business-level strategy or strategies. Indeed, firms' actions and responses to those of their rivals are part of the basic building blocks of business-level strategies.[15]

Recall from Chapter 4 that business-level strategy is concerned with what the firm does to successfully use its core competencies in specific product markets. In the global economy, competitive rivalry is intensifying,[16] meaning that the significance of its effect on firms' strategies is increasing. However, firms that develop and use effective business-level strategies tend to outperform competitors in individual product markets, even when experiencing intense competitive rivalry.[17]

Learn more about **Competitive Behavior.** www.cengagebrain.com

5-1 A Model of Competitive Rivalry

Competitive rivalry evolves from the pattern of actions and responses as one firm's competitive actions have noticeable effects on competitors, eliciting competitive responses from them.[18] This pattern suggests that firms are mutually interdependent, that they are affected by each other's actions and responses, and that marketplace success is a function of both individual strategies and the consequences of their use.[19]

Increasingly, executives recognize that competitive rivalry can have a major effect on the firm's financial performance[20] and market position.[21] For example, research shows that intensified rivalry within an industry results in decreased average profitability for the competing firms.[22] Although Apple essentially created the smartphone market in 2007 by launching the iPhone, some believe that Google's Android has rapidly reshaped the market, as evidenced by the fact that nearly half of all smartphones shipped in 2012 ran on the Android platform. Another indicator of rivalry's effect on profitability is Symbian's virtual disappearance as a platform provider even though it was "the primary mobile operating system used by Nokia, Samsung, Motorola and Sony throughout the mid-2000s."[23]

Figure 5.2 presents a straightforward model of competitive rivalry at the firm level; this type of rivalry is usually dynamic and complex.[24] The competitive actions and responses the firm takes are the foundation for successfully building and using its capabilities and core competencies to gain an advantageous market position.[25]

Figure 5.2 A Model of Competitive Reality

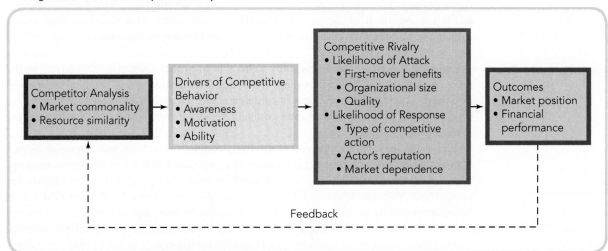

Source: Adapted from M. J. Chen, 1996, Competitor analysis and interfirm rivalry: Toward a theoretical integration, *Academy of Management Review*, 21: 100-134.

M. Stasy

The model in Figure 5.2 presents the sequence of activities commonly involved in competition between a firm and its competitors. Companies use this model to understand how to be able to predict a competitor's behavior and reduce the uncertainty associated with it.[26] Being able to predict competitors' actions and responses has a positive effect on the firm's market position and its subsequent financial performance.[27] The total of all the individual rivalries modeled in Figure 5.2 that occur in a particular market reflect the competitive dynamics in that market.

The remainder of the chapter explains components of the model shown in Figure 5.2. We first describe market commonality and resource similarity as the building blocks of a competitor analysis. Next, we discuss the effects of three organizational characteristics— awareness, motivation, and ability—on the firm's competitive behavior. We then examine competitive (interfirm) rivalry between firms. To do this, we explain the factors that affect the likelihood a firm will take a competitive action and the factors that affect the likelihood a firm will respond to a competitor's action. In the chapter's final section, we turn our attention to competitive dynamics to describe how market characteristics affect competitive rivalry in slow-cycle, fast-cycle, and standard-cycle markets.

5-2 Competitor Analysis

As previously noted, a competitor analysis is the first step the firm takes to be able to predict the extent and nature of its rivalry with each competitor. Competitor analyses are especially important when entering a foreign market in that firms doing so need to understand the local competition and foreign competitors currently operating in that market.[28] Without such analyses, they are less likely to be successful.

The number of markets in which firms compete against each other is called market commonality while the similarity in their resources is called resource similarity (both terms will be discussed later). These two dimensions of competition determine the extent to which firms are competitors. Firms with high market commonality and highly similar resources are direct and mutually acknowledged competitors.[29] The drivers of competitive behavior—as well as factors influencing the likelihood that a competitor will initiate competitive actions and will respond to its competitors' actions—influence the intensity of rivalry.[30]

In Chapter 2, we discussed competitor analysis as a technique firms use to understand their competitive environment. Together, the general, industry, and competitive environments comprise the firm's external environment. We also described how competitor analysis is used to help the firm *understand* its competitors. This understanding results from studying competitors' future objectives, current strategies, assumptions, and capabilities (see Figure 2.3 in Chapter 2). In this chapter, the discussion of competitor analysis is extended to describe what firms study to be able to *predict* competitors' behavior in the form of their competitive actions and responses. The discussions of competitor analysis in Chapter 2 and in this chapter are complementary in that firms must first *understand* competitors (Chapter 2) before their competitive actions and responses can be *predicted* (this chapter).

Being able to accurately predict rivals' likely competitive actions and responses helps a firm avoid situations in which it is unaware of competitors' objectives, strategies, assumptions, and capabilities. Lacking the information needed to predict these conditions for competitors creates *competitive blind spots*. Typically, competitive blind spots find a firm being surprised by a competitor's actions, potentially resulting in negative outcomes.[31] Increasingly, members of a firm's board of directors are expected to use their knowledge and expertise about other businesses and industry environments to help a firm avoid competitive blind spots.[32]

5-2a Market Commonality

Every industry is composed of various markets. The financial services industry has markets for insurance, brokerage services, banks, and so forth. To concentrate on the needs of different, unique customer groups, markets can be further subdivided. The insurance market could be broken into market segments (such as commercial and consumer), product segments (such as health insurance and life insurance), and geographic markets (such as Southeast Asia and Western Europe). In general, the capabilities the Internet's technologies generate help to shape the nature of industries' markets along with patterns of competition within those industries. For example, according to a Procter and Gamble (P&G) official: "Facebook is both a marketing and a distribution channel, as P&G has worked to develop 'f-commerce' capabilities on its fan pages, fulfilled by Amazon, which has become a top 10 retail account for Pampers," a disposable diaper product.[33]

Competitors tend to agree about the different characteristics of individual markets that form an industry. For example, in the transportation industry, the commercial air travel market differs from the ground transportation market, which is served by such firms as YRC Worldwide (one of the largest, most comprehensive less-than-truckload (LTL) carriers in North America) and major YRC competitors Arkansas Best, Con-way Inc., and FedEx Freight.[34] Although differences exist, many industries' markets are partially related in terms of technologies used or core competencies needed to develop a competitive advantage. For example, although railroads and truck ground transport compete in a different segment and can be substitutes, different types of transportation companies need to provide reliable and timely service. Commercial air carriers such as Southwest, United, and Jet Blue must therefore develop service competencies to satisfy their passengers while YRC, railroads, and their major competitors must develop such competencies to serve the needs of those using their services to ship goods.

Firms sometimes compete against each other in several markets, a condition called market commonality. More formally, **market commonality** is concerned with the number of markets with which the firm and a competitor are jointly involved and the degree of importance of the individual markets to each.[35] Firms competing against one another in several or many markets are said to be engaging in multimarket competition.[36] As we noted in Chapter 2's Opening Case, Coca-Cola and PepsiCo compete across a number of product markets (e.g., soft drinks, bottled water) as well as geographic markets (throughout North America and in many other countries throughout the world). Airlines, chemicals, pharmaceuticals, and consumer foods are examples of other industries with firms often competing against each other in multiple markets.

Firms competing in several of the same markets have the potential to respond to a competitor's actions not only within the market in which a given set of actions are taken, but also in other markets where they compete with the rival. This potential creates a complicated mosaic in which the competitive actions or responses a firm takes in one market may be designed to affect the outcome of its rivalry with a particular competitor in a second market.[37] This potential complicates the rivalry between competitors. In fact, research suggests that a firm with greater multimarket contact is less likely to initiate an attack, but more likely to move (respond) aggressively when attacked. For instance, research in the computer industry found that "firms respond to competitive attacks by introducing new products but do not use price as a retaliatory weapon."[38] Thus in general, multimarket competition reduces competitive rivalry, but some firms will still compete when the potential rewards (e.g., potential market share gain) are high.[39]

5-2b Resource Similarity

Resource similarity is the extent to which the firm's tangible and intangible resources are comparable to a competitor's in terms of both type and amount.[40] Firms with similar types

Market commonality is concerned with the number of markets with which the firm and a competitor are jointly involved and the degree of importance of the individual markets to each.

Resource similarity is the extent to which the firm's tangible and intangible resources are comparable to a competitor's in terms of both type and amount.

and amounts of resources are likely to have similar strengths and weaknesses and use similar strategies on the basis of their strengths to pursue what may be similar opportunities in the external environment.

As we discuss in the Strategic Focus, "resource similarity" describes part of the relationship between FedEx and United Parcel Service (UPS). In addition though, these companies compete in many of the same markets, and thus are also accurately described as having market commonality. In terms of resources, to mention only a few, the firms have similar types of truck and airplane fleets, similar levels of financial capital, and rely on equally talented reservoirs of human capital along with sophisticated information technology systems to complete their work. In addition to competing aggressively against each other in North America, the firms share many other markets in common, as FedEx delivers shipments in roughly 220 countries while UPS does so in approximately 200 countries. These comparisons between the two firms suggest why the rivalry between them is intense.

When performing a competitor analysis, a firm analyzes each of its competitors with respect to market commonality and resource similarity. The results of these analyses can be mapped for visual comparisons. In Figure 5.3, we show different hypothetical intersections between the firm and individual competitors in terms of market commonality and resource similarity. These intersections indicate the extent to which the firm and those with which it compares itself are competitors. For example, the firm and its competitor displayed in quadrant I have similar types and amounts of resources (i.e., the two firms have a similar portfolio of resources). The firm and its competitor in quadrant I would use their similar resource portfolios to compete against each other in many markets that are important to each. These conditions lead to the conclusion that the firms modeled in quadrant I are direct and mutually acknowledged competitors.

As discussed in the Strategic Focus, this is the case for FedEx and UPS, meaning that these firms would map each other as direct competitors and place themselves along with that competitor in quadrant I of Figure 5.3. In contrast, the firm and its competitor shown in quadrant III share few markets and have little similarity in their resources, indicating that they aren't direct and mutually acknowledged competitors. Thus a small, local,

Figure 5.3 A Framework of Competitor Analysis

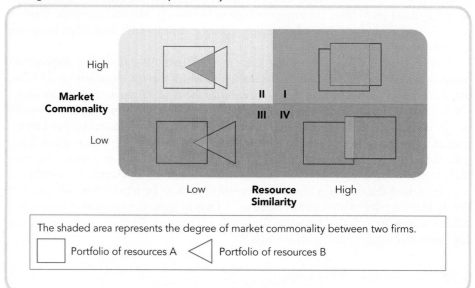

Source: Adapted from M. J. Chen, 1996, Competitor analysis and inferfirm rivalry: Toward a theoretical integration, *Academy of Management Review*, 21: 100-134.

M. Stasy

Strategic Focus

GLOBALIZATION

FedEx and United Parcel Service (UPS): Maintaining Success While Competing Aggressively

Identified recently as one of the 50 greatest or most intense competitive rivalries of all time, FedEx and UPS are similar in many ways, including their resources, the markets they serve, and the competitive dimensions they emphasize to implement similar strategies. These similarities mean that the firms are direct competitors and that they are keenly *aware* of each other and have the *motivation* and *ability* to respond to the competitive actions they take against each other. (Awareness, motivation, and ability and their importance in terms of competitive rivalry are discussed later.) The two firms are the largest global courier delivery companies in what is a highly competitive industry on a global basis.

FedEx and UPS compete in many of the same product markets including next day delivery, cheaper ground delivery, time-guaranteed delivery (both domestically and internationally), and freight services. However, the firms concentrate on different segments in attempting to create superior stakeholder value and avoid direct, head-to-head competition in a host of product segments and markets. In this regard, FedEx "intends to leverage and extend the FedEx brand and to provide customers with seamless access to its entire portfolio of integrated transportation services" while UPS "seeks to position itself as the primary coordinator of the flow of goods, information and funds throughout the entire supply chain (the movement from the raw materials and parts stage through final consumption of the finished product)."

Thus, while these firms are similar, they also seek to differentiate themselves in ways that enhance the possibility of being able to gain strategic competitiveness and earn above-average returns. In broad-stroke terms, FedEx concentrates more on transportation services and international markets (recently, FedEx was generating 48 percent of revenue internationally while UPS was earning 22 percent of its revenue from international markets) while UPS concentrates more on the entire value chain while competing domestically. FedEx is the world's largest international air shipping firm while UPS is the world's largest package delivery company.

There are many actions the firms have recently taken to sharpen their ability to outcompete their primary competitor. In mid-2013, FedEx learned that its contract to fly domestic mail for the U.S. Postal Service had been selected for renewal. UPS also bid on the contract, meaning that it lost this competitive battle to its rival. To support its strength in logistics as part of the

Back view of a UPS postal courier delivery van. UPS and FedEx share high degrees of both market commonality and resource similarity.

entire supply chain, UPS recently agreed to buy "Hungary-based pharmaceutical-logistics company Cemelog Zrt for an undisclosed amount in a deal to strengthen its health-care business in Europe, giving it access to the increasingly important markets of Central and Eastern Europe." UPS is also emphasizing trans-border European Union services as a growth engine for the foreseeable future. To enhance its ability to compete against UPS and other rivals as well, FedEx is restructuring some of its operations to increase efficiency. Similarly, the firm is increasing its emphasis on finding ways for its independent express, ground, and freight networks to work together more synergistically.

Although the rivalry between FedEx and UPS is intense and aggressive, it is also likely that it makes each firm stronger and more agile in that each has to be at its best in order to outperform the other. Thus in many ways, each of these firms is a "good competitor" for the other one.

Sources: 2013, FedEx Corp., *Standard & Poor's Stock Report*, www.standardandpoors. com, May 25; 2013, United Parcel Service, Inc., *Standard & Poor's Stock Report*, www. standardandpoors.com, May 25; L. Eaton, 2013, FedEx CEO: Truck fleets to shift to natural gas from diesel, *Wall Street Journal*, www.wsj.com, March 8; V. Mock, 2013, UPS to appeal EU's block of TNT merger, *Wall Street Journal*, www.wsj.com, April 7; B. Morris & B. Sechler, 2013, FedEx customers like slower and cheaper, *Wall Street Journal*, www. wsj.com, March 20; B. Sechler, 2013, Online shopping boosts profit for UPS, *Wall Street Journal*, www.wsj.com, April 25; B. Sechler, 2013, FedEx fends off rivals for U.S. Postal, *Wall Street Journal*, www.wsj.com, April 23.

family-owned restaurant concentrating on selling "gourmet" hamburgers does not compete directly against McDonald's. The mapping of competitive relationships is fluid as companies enter and exit markets and as rivals' resources change in type and amount, meaning that the companies with which a given firm is a direct competitor change over time.

5-3 Drivers of Competitive Behavior

Market commonality and resource similarity influence the drivers (awareness, motivation, and ability) of competitive behavior (see Figure 5.2). In turn, the drivers influence the firm's actual competitive behavior, as revealed by the actions and responses it takes while engaged in competitive rivalry.[41]

Awareness, which is a prerequisite to any competitive action or response taken by a firm, refers to the extent to which competitors recognize the degree of their mutual interdependence that results from market commonality and resource similarity.[42] (As suggested in the Strategic Focus, FedEx and UPS recognize the high degree of mutual dependence that exists between them.) Awareness affects the extent to which the firm understands the consequences of its competitive actions and responses. A lack of awareness can lead to excessive competition, resulting in a negative effect on all competitors' performance.[43]

Awareness tends to be greatest when firms have highly similar resources (in terms of types and amounts) to use while competing against each other in multiple markets. Komatsu Ltd., Japan's top construction machinery maker, and U.S.-based Caterpillar Inc. have similar resources and are aware of each other's actions given that they compete against each other in markets throughout the world. Founded in 1925, Caterpillar is the world's leading manufacturer of construction and mining equipment, diesel and natural gas engines, and industrial gas turbines, while Komatsu is the world's second largest seller of construction and mining machinery behind Caterpillar.[44] Over the years, these firms have competed aggressively against each other for market share in multiple countries and regions.

Motivation, which concerns the firm's incentive to take action or to respond to a competitor's attack, relates to perceived gains and losses. Thus, a firm may be aware of competitors but may not be motivated to engage in rivalry with them if it perceives that its position will not improve or that its market position won't be damaged if it doesn't respond.[45] A benefit of not having the motivation to engage in rivalry at a point in time with a competitor is that the unmotivated firm retains resources that can be used for other purposes including choosing to compete against a rival with whom there is more motivation to do so.

Market commonality affects the firm's perceptions and resulting motivation. For example, a firm is generally more likely to attack the rival with whom it has low market commonality than the one with whom it competes in multiple markets. The primary reason is the high stakes involved in trying to gain a more advantageous position over a rival with whom the firm shares many markets. As mentioned earlier, multimarket competition can result in a competitor responding to the firm's action in a market different from the one in which that action was taken. Actions and responses of this type can cause both firms to lose focus on core markets and to battle each other with resources that had been allocated for other purposes. Because of the high stakes of competition under the condition of market commonality, the probability is high that the attacked firm will respond to its competitor's action in an effort to protect its position in one or more markets.[46]

In some instances, the firm may be aware of the markets it shares with a competitor and be motivated to respond to an attack by that competitor, but lack the ability to do so. *Ability* relates to each firm's resources and the flexibility they provide. Without available resources (such as financial capital and people), the firm is not able to attack a competitor or respond to its actions. For example, smaller and newer firms tend to be more innovative but generally have fewer resources to attack larger and established competitors. Likewise, foreign firms often are at a disadvantage against local firms because of the local firms' social capital (relationships) with consumers, suppliers, and government officials.[47] However, similar resources suggest similar abilities to attack and respond. When a firm faces a competitor with similar resources, careful study of a possible attack before initiating it is essential because the similarly resourced competitor is likely to respond to that action.[48]

Resource *dissimilarity* also influences competitive actions and responses between firms, in that the more significant the difference between resources owned by the acting firm and those against whom it has taken action, the longer is the delay by the firm with a resource disadvantage.[49] For example, Walmart initially used a focused cost leadership strategy to compete only in small communities (those with a population of 25,000 or less). Using sophisticated logistics systems and

A Walmart store in Los Angeles, California. Walmart has developed resource dissimilarities that allow it to take actions to which competitors find it difficult to respond.

efficient purchasing practices, among other methods, to gain competitive advantages, Walmart created a new type of value (primarily in the form of wide selections of products at the lowest competitive prices) for customers in small retail markets. Local competitors lacked the ability to marshal needed resources at the pace required to respond to Walmart's actions quickly and effectively. However, even when facing competitors with greater resources (greater ability) or more attractive market positions, firms should eventually respond, no matter how daunting the task seems. Choosing not to respond can ultimately result in failure, as happened with at least some local retailers who didn't respond to Walmart's competitive actions. Today, with Walmart as the world's largest retailer, it is indeed difficult for smaller competitors to have the resources required to effectively respond to its competitive actions or competitive responses.

5-4   Competitive Rivalry

The ongoing competitive action/response sequence between a firm and a competitor affects the performance of both firms. Because of this, it is important for companies to carefully analyze and understand the competitive rivalry present in the markets in which they compete.[50]

As we described earlier, the predictions drawn from studying competitors in terms of awareness, motivation, and ability are grounded in market commonality and resource similarity. These predictions are fairly general. The value of the final set of predictions the firm develops about each of its competitors' competitive actions and responses is enhanced by studying the "Likelihood of Attack" factors (such as first-mover benefits and organizational size) and the "Likelihood of Response" factors (such as the actor's reputation) that are shown in Figure 5.2. Evaluating and understanding these factors allow the firm to refine the predictions it makes about its competitors' actions and responses.

5-4a   Strategic and Tactical Actions

Firms use both strategic and tactical actions when forming their competitive actions and competitive responses in the course of engaging in competitive rivalry.[51] A **competitive action** is a strategic or tactical action the firm takes to build or defend its competitive advantages or improve

A **competitive action** is a strategic or tactical action the firm takes to build or defend its competitive advantages or improve its market position.

its market position. A **competitive response** is a strategic or tactical action the firm takes to counter the effects of a competitor's competitive action. A **strategic action** or a **strategic response** is a market-based move that involves a significant commitment of organizational resources and is difficult to implement and reverse. A **tactical action** or a **tactical response** is a market-based move that is taken to fine-tune a strategy; it involves fewer resources and is relatively easy to implement and reverse. When engaging rivals in competition, firms must recognize the differences between strategic and tactical actions and responses and develop an effective balance between the two types of competitive actions and responses.

Nokia Corp. has completed a number of strategic actions in the past few years, none of which has more potentially significant possibilities than does its partnership with Microsoft. As part of this relationship, Nokia has adopted Windows Phone as its principal smartphone strategy. In announcing this collaboration, an official noted that "Nokia and Microsoft will combine our strengths to deliver an ecosystem with unrivalled global reach and scale."[52] This relationship may be at least in part a strategic response to Apple's success. An example of a recent strategic action taken relative to Nokia is Samsung's decision to locate its newest research and development center in Finland, Nokia's home market. Some analysts thought this action signaled even stiffer competition for Nokia, a firm that has now lost its market leadership position in the sales of smartphones to Samsung in its native country.[53]

Walmart prices aggressively as a means of increasing revenues and gaining market share at the expense of competitors. In this regard, the firm engages in a continuous stream of tactical actions to attack rivals by changing some of its products' prices and tactical responses to respond to price changes taken by competitors such as Costco and Target.

5-5   Likelihood of Attack

In addition to market commonality, resource similarity, and the drivers of awareness, motivation, and ability, other factors affect the likelihood a competitor will use strategic actions and tactical actions to attack its competitors. Three of these factors—first-mover benefits, organizational size, and quality—are discussed next. Second and late movers are considered as part of the discussion of first-mover benefits.

5-5a   First-Mover Benefits

A **first mover** is a firm that takes an initial competitive action in order to build or defend its competitive advantages or to improve its market position. The first-mover concept has been influenced by the work of the famous economist Joseph Schumpeter, who argued that firms achieve competitive advantage by taking innovative actions[54] (innovation is defined and discussed in Chapter 13). In general, first movers emphasize research and development (R&D) as a path to develop innovative goods and services that customers will value.[55]

The benefits of being a successful first mover can be substantial.[56] Especially in fast-cycle markets (discussed later in the chapter), where changes occur rapidly and where it is virtually impossible to sustain a competitive advantage for any length of time, a first mover can experience many times the valuation and revenue of a second mover.[57] This evidence suggests that although first-mover benefits are never absolute, they are often critical to a firm's success in industries experiencing rapid technological developments and relatively short product life cycles.[58] In addition to earning above-average returns until its competitors respond to its successful competitive action, the first mover can gain (1) the loyalty of customers who may become committed to the goods or services of the firm that first made them available, and (2) market share that can be difficult for competitors to take during future competitive rivalry.[59] The general evidence that first movers have greater survival rates than later market entrants is perhaps the culmination of first-mover benefits.[60]

A **competitive response** is a strategic or tactical action the firm takes to counter the effects of a competitor's competitive action.

A **strategic action** or a **strategic response** is a market-based move that involves a significant commitment of organizational resources and is difficult to implement and reverse.

A **tactical action** or a **tactical response** is a market-based move that is taken to fine-tune a strategy; it involves fewer resources and is relatively easy to implement and reverse.

A **first mover** is a firm that takes an initial competitive action in order to build or defend its competitive advantages or to improve its market position.

The firm trying to predict its rivals' competitive actions might conclude that they will take aggressive strategic actions to gain first movers' benefits. However, even though a firm's competitors might be motivated to be first movers, they may lack the ability to do so. First movers tend to be aggressive and willing to experiment with innovation and take higher yet reasonable levels of risk, and their long-term success depends on retaining the ability to do so.[61]

To be a first mover, the firm must have readily available the resources to significantly invest in R&D as well as to rapidly and successfully produce and market a stream of innovative products.[62] Organizational slack makes it possible for firms to have the ability (as measured by available resources) to be first movers. *Slack* is the buffer or cushion provided by actual or obtainable resources that aren't currently in use and are in excess of the minimum resources needed to produce a given level of organizational output.[63] As a liquid resource, slack can quickly be allocated to support competitive actions, such as R&D investments and aggressive marketing campaigns that lead to first-mover advantages. This relationship between slack and the ability to be a first mover allows the firm to predict that a first-mover competitor likely has available slack and will probably take aggressive competitive actions to continuously introduce innovative products. Furthermore, the firm can predict that as a first mover, a competitor will try to rapidly gain market share and customer loyalty in order to earn above-average returns until its competitors are able to effectively respond to its first move.

Firms evaluating their competitors should realize that being a first mover carries risk. For example, it is difficult to accurately estimate the returns that will be earned from introducing product innovations to the marketplace.[64] Additionally, the first mover's cost to develop a product innovation can be substantial, reducing the slack available to support further innovation. Thus, the firm should carefully study the results a competitor achieves as a first mover. Continuous success by the competitor suggests additional product innovations, while lack of product acceptance over the course of the competitor's innovations may indicate less willingness in the future to accept the risks of being a first mover.[65]

A **second mover** is a firm that responds to the first mover's competitive action, typically through imitation. More cautious than the first mover, the second mover studies customers' reactions to product innovations. In the course of doing so, the second mover also tries to find any mistakes the first mover made so that it can avoid them and the problems they created. Often, successful imitation of the first mover's innovations allows the second mover to avoid the mistakes and the major investments required of the pioneering first movers.[66]

Second movers have the time to develop processes and technologies that are more efficient than those used by the first mover or that create additional value for consumers.[67] The most successful second movers rarely act too fast (so they can fully analyze the first mover's actions) nor too slow (so they do not give the first mover time to correct its mistakes and "lock in" customer loyalty). Overall, the outcomes of the first mover's competitive actions may provide a blueprint for second and even late movers as they determine the nature and timing of their competitive responses.[68]

Determining whether a competitor is an effective second mover (based on its past actions) allows a first-mover firm to predict that the competitor will respond quickly to successful, innovation-based market entries. The first mover can expect a successful second-mover competitor to study its market entries and to respond with a new entry into the market within a short time period. As a second mover, the competitor will try to respond with a product that provides greater customer value than does the first mover's product. The most successful second movers are able to rapidly and meaningfully interpret market feedback to respond quickly yet successfully to the first mover's successful innovations.

Home-improvement rating site Angie's List was founded roughly two decades ago. More than two million U.S. households are using the service to gain information about the quality

A **second mover** is a firm that responds to the first mover's competitive action, typically through imitation.

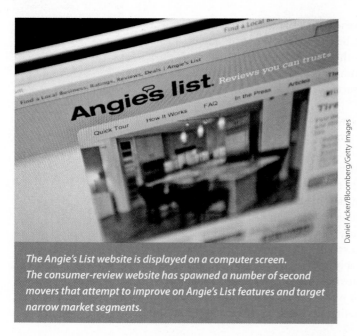

The Angie's List website is displayed on a computer screen. The consumer-review website has spawned a number of second movers that attempt to improve on Angie's List features and target narrow market segments.

of 700-plus services (plumbing, electrical work, and so forth) provided by local companies. Angie's List members submit reviews at the rate of over 60,000 per month. The firm's success is suggested by the fact that it generates roughly $220 million in annual revenue.

The fact that "a growing number of websites are taking aim at the giant home-improvement rating site" suggests that second movers are responding to Angie's List as a successful first mover.[69] Each of the second movers offers a slightly different service to customers, trying to improve on the quality, breath, and/or depth of what Angie's List offers. HomeAdvisor.com, for example, differs from the first mover through its exclusive focus on home projects. Houzz.com provides users with an archive of home improvement and design images as well as access to an extensive list of articles concerned with decorating and remodeling. Of course, Angie's List is responding to the challenge of second movers through several actions including an effort to improve the method through which members seek bids from professional providers.

A **late mover** is a firm that responds to a competitive action a significant amount of time after the first mover's action and the second mover's response. Typically, a late response is better than no response at all, although any success achieved from the late competitive response tends to be considerably less than that achieved by first and second movers. However, on occasion, late movers can be successful if they develop a unique way to enter the market and compete. For firms from emerging economies this often means a niche strategy with lower-cost production and manufacturing.[70]

The firm competing against a late mover can predict that the competitor will likely enter a particular market only after both the first and second movers have achieved success in that market. Moreover, on a relative basis, the firm can predict that the late mover's competitive action will allow it to earn average returns only after the considerable time required for it to understand how to create at least as much customer value as that offered by the first and second movers' products.

5-5b Organizational Size

An organization's size affects the likelihood it will take competitive actions as well as the types and timing of those actions.[71] In general, small firms are more likely than large companies to launch competitive actions and tend to do it more quickly. Smaller firms are thus perceived as nimble and flexible competitors who rely on speed and surprise to defend their competitive advantages or develop new ones while engaged in competitive rivalry, especially with large companies, to gain an advantageous market position.[72] Small firms' flexibility and nimbleness allow them to develop variety in their competitive actions; large firms tend to limit the types of competitive actions used.[73]

Large firms, however, are likely to initiate more competitive actions along with more strategic actions during a given period.[74] Thus, when studying its competitors in terms of organizational size, the firm should use a measurement such as total sales revenue or total number of employees. The competitive actions the firm likely will encounter from competitors larger than it is will be different from the competitive actions it will encounter from smaller competitors.

A **late mover** is a firm that responds to a competitive action a significant amount of time after the first mover's action and the second mover's response.

Daniel Acker/Bloomberg/Getty Images

The organizational size factor adds another layer of complexity. When engaging in competitive rivalry, firms prefer to be able to have the capabilities required to take a large number of unique competitive actions. For this to be the case, a firm needs to have the amount of slack resources that a large, successful company typically holds if it is to be able to launch a greater *number* of competitive actions. Simultaneously though, the firm needs to be flexible when considering competitive actions and responses it might take if it is to be able to launch a greater *variety* of competitive actions. Collectively then, firms are best served competitively when their size permits them to take an appropriate number of unique or diverse competitive actions and responses.

5-5c Quality

Quality has many definitions, including well-established ones relating it to the production of goods or services with zero defects[75] and as a cycle of continuous improvement.[76] From a strategic perspective, we consider quality to be the outcome of how a firm competes through its value chain activities and support functions (see Chapter 3). Thus, **quality** exists when the firm's goods or services meet or exceed customers' expectations. Some evidence suggests that quality may be the most critical component in satisfying the firm's customers.[77]

In the eyes of customers, quality is about doing the right things relative to performance measures that are important to them.[78] Customers may be interested in measuring the quality of a firm's goods and services against a broad range of dimensions. Sample quality dimensions in which customers commonly express an interest are shown in Table 5.1. Quality is possible only when top-level managers support it and when its importance is

Quality exists when the firm's goods or services meet or exceed customers' expectations.

Table 5.1 Quality Dimentions of Products and Services

Product Quality Dimensions
1. *Performance*—Operating characteristics
2. *Features*—Important special characteristics
3. *Flexibility*—Meeting operating specifications over some period of time
4. *Durability*—Amount of use before performance deteriorates
5. *Conformance*—Match with preestablished standards
6. *Serviceability*—Ease and speed of repair
7. *Aesthetics*—How a product looks and feels
8. *Perceived quality*—Subjective assessment of characteristics (Product image)

Service Quality Dimensions
1. *Timeliness*—Performed in the promised period of time
2. *Courtesy*—Performed cheerfully
3. *Consistency*—Giving all customers similar experiences each time
4. *Convenience*—Accessibility to customers
5. *Completeness*—Fully serviced, as required
6. *Accuracy*—Performed correctly each time

Source: Adapted from J. Evans, 2008, *Managing for Quality and Performance*, 7th Ed., Mason, OH: Thomson Publishing.

institutionalized throughout the entire organization and its value chain.[79] When quality is institutionalized and valued by all, employees and managers alike become vigilant about continuously finding ways to improve it.[80]

Quality is a universal theme in the global economy and is a necessary but insufficient condition for competitive success.[81] Without quality, a firm's products lack credibility, meaning that customers don't think of them as viable options. Indeed, customers won't consider buying a product or using a service until they believe that it can satisfy at least their base-level expectations in terms of quality dimensions that are important to them.[82]

This was the case recently with Boeing's new 787 aircraft. This plane's lithium-ion battery system proved to be of questionable quality when parts of it were found to sometimes catch fire. In response to this quality-related problem, the U.S. Federal Aviation Administration (FAA) grounded the airplane for what turned out to be 123 days while Boeing corrected the problem in a way that satisfied the FAA. An indication of the depth of the problem is the fact that Boeing invested "200,000 hours of engineering, design, analysis and testing in the ultimate package of fixes." After meeting the FAA's expectations, airlines around the world, including those in the China, Japan, and the United States, began ordering additional 787s and prepared to receive some of those already ordered. At the time of its "re-launch," some wondered if passengers would believe the plane is "safe enough" to fly. Thus, Boeing suffered in terms of sales revenue and reputation until it was able to correct the 787's quality-related deficiencies.[83] Moreover, during this time, major competitor Airbus benefitted as customers ordered larger quantities of its A330.[84]

Quality affects competitive rivalry. The firm evaluating a competitor whose products suffer from poor quality can predict declines in the competitor's sales revenue until the quality issues are resolved. In addition, the firm can predict that the competitor likely won't be aggressive in its competitive actions until the quality problems are corrected in order to gain credibility with customers.[85] However, after the problems are corrected, that competitor is likely to take more aggressive competitive actions.

5-6 Likelihood of Response

The success of a firm's competitive action is affected by the likelihood that a competitor will respond to it as well as by the type (strategic or tactical) and effectiveness of that response. As noted earlier, a competitive response is a strategic or tactical action the firm takes to counter the effects of a competitor's competitive action. In general, a firm is likely to respond to a competitor's action when (1) the action leads to better use of the competitor's capabilities to develop a stronger competitive advantage or an improvement in its market position, (2) the action damages the firm's ability to use its core competencies to create or maintain an advantage, or (3) the firm's market position becomes harder to defend.[86]

In addition to market commonality and resource similarity and awareness, motivation, and ability, firms evaluate three other factors—type of competitive action, actor's reputation, and market dependence—to predict how a competitor is likely to respond to competitive actions (see Figure 5.2).

5-6a Type of Competitive Action

Competitive responses to strategic actions differ from responses to tactical actions. These differences allow the firm to predict a competitor's likely response to a competitive action that has been launched against it. Strategic actions commonly receive strategic responses and tactical actions receive tactical responses. In general, strategic actions elicit fewer total competitive responses because strategic responses, such as market-based moves, involve a significant commitment of resources and are difficult to implement and reverse.[87]

Another reason that strategic actions elicit fewer responses than do tactical actions is that the time needed to implement a strategic action and to assess its effectiveness can delay the competitor's response to that action.[88] In contrast, a competitor likely will respond quickly to a tactical action, such as when an airline company almost immediately matches a competitor's tactical action of reducing prices in certain markets. Either strategic actions or tactical actions that target a large number of a rival's customers are likely to elicit strong responses.[89] In fact, if the effects of a competitor's strategic action on the focal firm are significant (e.g., loss of market share, loss of major resources such as critical employees), a response is likely to be swift and strong.[90]

5-6b Actor's Reputation

In the context of competitive rivalry, an *actor* is the firm taking an action or a response while *reputation* is "the positive or negative attribute ascribed by one rival to another based on past competitive behavior."[91] A positive reputation may be a source of above-average returns, especially for consumer goods producers.[92] Thus, a positive corporate reputation is of strategic value[93] and affects competitive rivalry. To predict the likelihood of a competitor's response to a current or planned action, firms evaluate the responses that the competitor has taken previously when attacked—past behavior is assumed to be a predictor of future behavior.

Competitors are more likely to respond to strategic or tactical actions when they are taken by a market leader.[94] In particular, evidence suggests that commonly successful actions, especially strategic actions, will be quickly imitated. For example, although a second mover, IBM committed significant resources to enter the information service market. Competitors such as Hewlett-Packard (HP), Dell Inc., and others responded with strategic actions to enter this market as well.[95]

In a never-ending cascade of competitive actions and responses, these competitors continue jockeying among themselves for the most favorable market positions. Dell still trails IBM and HP in the worldwide server market share. However, the firm "commands the market for hyperscale servers which (are) 'density optimized' machines that companies use to support large data centers."[96] Dell's position in this market is a result of a strategic decision it made in 2007 to develop and sell "efficient, bare-bones" servers to firms such as Microsoft Corp., Amazon.com, and Salesforce.com Inc. Hyperscale servers are not pre-loaded with costly redundancy and availability capabilities, a fact that appeals to a number of customers. Because of the attractiveness of the hyperscale server space and Dell's enhanced reputation in overall server sales, competitors such as IBM and HP may respond with their own strategic actions.

In contrast to a firm with a strong reputation, competitors are less likely to respond to actions taken by a company with a reputation for risky, complex, and unpredictable competitive behavior. For example, the firm with a reputation as a price predator (an actor that frequently reduces prices to gain or maintain market share) generates few responses to its pricing tactical actions because price predators, which typically increase prices once their market share objective is reached, lack credibility with their competitors.[97]

The Dell exhibit at the 2013 CeBIT Technology Trade Fair in Hannover, Germany. Through strategic actions it has taken, Dell has become the market leader in hyperscale servers.

Sean Gallup/Getty Imagesnews/Getty Images

5-6c Market Dependence

Market dependence denotes the extent to which a firm's revenues or profits are derived from a particular market.[98] In general, competitors with high market dependence are likely to respond strongly to attacks threatening their market position.[99] Interestingly, the threatened firm in these instances may not always respond quickly, even though an effective response to an attack on the firm's position in a critical market is important.

At an annual compound growth rate of 11 percent, recent predictions are that e-commerce sales will grow more than any other segment of the retail industry through at least 2017. Obviously, this growth rate is attractive to firms of all kinds including, as it turns out, Walmart. Established in 2000 as part of the world's largest firm by sales volume (with revenue of roughly $469 billion in 2012), Walmart.com is the giant retailer's attempt to become extremely successful in the e-commerce space. Today, over 1 million products are available through Walmart.com, with additional ones being regularly added to the site. Of course, competing in e-commerce pits Walmart.com squarely in competition with Amazon.com the largest online store on the planet.[100]

To date, Walmart's e-commerce business is generating roughly $9 billion per year in sales, which is just a bit over 2 percent of the firm's total revenue. Thus, Walmart currently has very little dependence for its success on the e-commerce market. Of course, Walmart is taking actions such as trying to better integrate its physical stores with its technological and logistics skills[101] and "considering a radical plan to have store customers deliver packages to online buyers, a new twist on speedier delivery services that the company hopes will enable it to better compete with Amazon.com, Inc."[102]

In contrast to Walmart, Amazon.com currently derives a strong majority of its sales volume from the e-commerce market, meaning that it has a high degree of market dependence. With $61 billion in revenue in 2012, the firm is substantially smaller than Walmart, although its total e-commerce sales revenue dwarfs that of Walmart.com's $9 billion. Given its dominant market position in e-commerce and in light of its dependence on the e-commerce market, it is virtually guaranteed that Amazon.com will continue responding to Walmart.com's competitive actions and responses.

5-7 Competitive Dynamics

Whereas competitive rivalry concerns the ongoing actions and responses between a firm and its direct competitors for an advantageous market position, *competitive dynamics* concerns the ongoing actions and responses among *all* firms competing within a market for advantageous positions.

To explain competitive dynamics, we explore the effects of varying rates of competitive speed in different markets (called slow-cycle, fast-cycle, and standard-cycle markets) on the behavior (actions and responses) of all competitors within a given market. Competitive behaviors as well as the reasons for taking them are similar within each market type, but differ across types of markets. Thus, competitive dynamics differ in slow-cycle, fast-cycle, and standard-cycle markets.

As noted in Chapter 1, firms want to sustain their competitive advantages for as long as possible, although no advantage is permanently sustainable. However, as we discuss next, the sustainability of the firm's competitive advantages differs by market type. In the main though, the degree of sustainability is affected by how quickly competitors can imitate a rival's competitive advantages and how costly it is to do so.

5-7a Slow-Cycle Markets

Slow-cycle markets are markets in which the firm's competitive advantages are shielded from imitation, commonly for long periods of time, and where imitation is costly.[103] Thus, competitive advantages are sustainable over longer periods of time in slow-cycle markets.

Slow-cycle markets are markets in which the firm's competitive advantages are shielded from imitation, commonly for long periods of time, and where imitation is costly.

Building a unique and proprietary capability produces a competitive advantage and success in a slow-cycle market. This type of advantage is difficult for competitors to under-stand. As discussed in Chapter 3, a difficult-to-understand and costly-to-imitate capability usually results from unique historical conditions, causal ambiguity, and/or social complex-ity. Copyrights and patents are examples of these types of capabilities. After a proprietary advantage is developed on the basis of using its capabilities, the competitive actions and responses a firm takes in a slow-cycle market are oriented to protecting, maintaining, and extending that advantage. Major strategic actions in these markets, such as acquisitions, usually carry less risk than in faster-cycle markets.[104]

Walt Disney Co. continues to extend its proprietary characters, such as Mickey Mouse, Minnie Mouse, and Goofy. These characters have a unique historical development as a result of Walt and Roy Disney's creativity and vision for entertaining people. Products based on the characters seen in Disney's animated films are sold through Disney's theme park shops as well as freestanding retail outlets called Disney Stores. Because copyrights shield it, the proprietary nature of Disney's advantage in terms of animated character trademarks protects the firm from imitation by competitors.

Consistent with another attribute of competition in a slow-cycle market, Disney protects its exclusive rights to its characters and their use. As with all firms competing in slow-cycle markets, Disney's competitive actions (such as building theme parks in France, Japan, and China) and responses (such as lawsuits to protect its right to fully control use of its animated characters) maintain and extend its proprietary competitive advantage while protecting it.

Patent laws and regulatory requirements such as those in the United States requiring FDA (Food and Drug Administration) approval to launch new products shield pharmaceutical com-panies' positions. Competitors in this market try to extend patents on their drugs to maintain advantageous positions that patents provide. However, after a patent expires, the firm is no longer shielded from competition, allowing generic imitations and usually leading to a loss of sales and profits. This was the case for Pfizer when Lipitor (which is the best-selling drug in his-tory) went off patent in the fall of 2011. The firm's profits declined 19 percent in the first quarter after that event. The loss of patents is an industry-level concern too, as suggested by the fact that roughly $38.5 billion in sales revenue was lost in 2012 as a result of drugs going off patent.[105]

The competitive dynamics generated by firms competing in slow-cycle markets are shown in Figure 5.4. In slow-cycle markets, firms launch a product (e.g., a new drug) that

Figure 5.4 Gradual Erosion of a Sustained Competitive Advantage

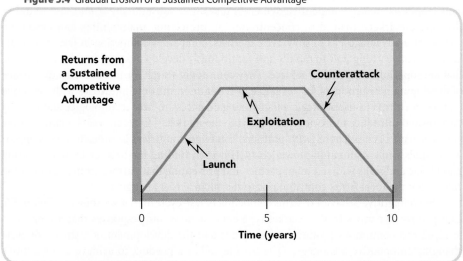

Source: Adapted from I. C. MacMillan, 1988, Controlling competitive dynamics by taking strategic initiative, *Academy of Management Executive*, II(2): 111–118.

has been developed through a proprietary advantage (e.g., R&D) and then exploit it for as long as possible while the product is shielded from competition. Eventually, competitors respond to the action with a counterattack. In markets for drugs, this counterattack commonly occurs as patents expire or are broken through legal means, creating the need for another product launch by the firm seeking a protected market position.

5-7b Fast-Cycle Markets

Fast-cycle markets are markets in which the firm's capabilities that contribute to competitive advantages aren't shielded from imitation and where imitation is often rapid and inexpensive.[106] Thus, competitive advantages aren't sustainable in fast-cycle markets. Firms competing in fast-cycle markets recognize the importance of speed; these companies appreciate that "time is as precious a business resource as money or head count—and that the costs of hesitation and delay are just as steep as going over budget or missing a financial forecast."[107] Such high-velocity environments place considerable pressures on top managers to quickly make strategic decisions that are also effective. The often substantial competition and technology-based strategic focus make the strategic decision complex, increasing the need for a comprehensive approach integrated with decision speed, two often-conflicting characteristics of the strategic decision process.[108]

Reverse engineering and the rate of technology diffusion facilitate the rapid imitation that takes place in fast-cycle markets. A competitor uses reverse engineering to quickly gain the knowledge required to imitate or improve the firm's products. Technology is diffused rapidly in fast-cycle markets, making it available to competitors in a short period. The technology often used by fast-cycle competitors isn't proprietary, nor is it protected by patents as is the technology used by firms competing in slow-cycle markets. For example, only a few hundred parts, which are readily available on the open market, are required to build a PC. Patents protect only a few of these parts, such as microprocessor chips. Interestingly, research also demonstrates that showing what an incumbent firm knows and its research capability can be a deterrent to other firms to enter a market, even a fast-cycle market.[109]

Fast-cycle markets are more volatile than slow-cycle and standard-cycle markets. Indeed, the pace of competition in fast-cycle markets is almost frenzied, as companies rely on innovations as the engines of their growth. Because prices often decline quickly in these markets, companies need to profit rapidly from their product innovations.

Recognizing this reality, firms avoid "loyalty" to any of their products, preferring to cannibalize their own before competitors learn how to do so through successful imitation. This emphasis creates competitive dynamics that differ substantially from those found in slow-cycle markets. Instead of concentrating on protecting, maintaining, and extending competitive advantages, as in slow-cycle markets, companies competing in fast-cycle markets focus on learning how to rapidly and continuously develop new competitive advantages that are superior to those they replace. They commonly search for fast and effective means of developing new products. For example, it is common in some industries with fast-cycle markets for firms to use strategic alliances to gain access to new technologies and thereby develop and introduce more new products into the market.[110] In recent years, many of these alliances have been offshore (with partners in foreign countries) in order to access appropriate skills while maintaining lower costs. However, finding the balance between sharing knowledge and skills with a foreign partner and preventing that partner from appropriating value from the focal firm's contributions to the alliance is challenging.[111]

The competitive behavior of firms competing in fast-cycle markets is shown in Figure 5.5. Competitive dynamics in this market type entail actions and responses that are oriented to rapid and continuous product introductions and the development of a stream of ever-changing competitive advantages. The firm launches a product to achieve a competitive advantage and then exploits the advantage for as long as possible. However, the firm also

Fast-cycle markets are markets in which the firm's capabilities that contribute to competitive advantages aren't shielded from imitation and where imitation is often rapid and inexpensive.

Figure 5.5 Developing Temporary Advantages to Create Sustained Advantage

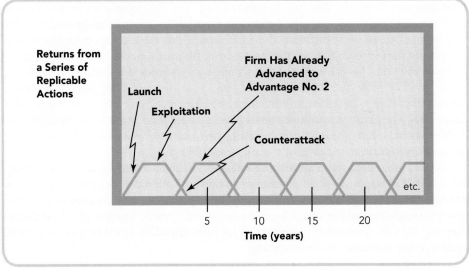

Source: Adapted from I. C. MacMillan, 1988, Controlling competitive dynamics by taking strategic initiative, *Academy of Management Executive*, II(2): 111–118.

tries to develop another temporary competitive advantage before competitors can respond to the first one. Thus, competitive dynamics in fast-cycle markets often result in rapid product upgrades as well as quick product innovations.[112]

As our discussion suggests, innovation plays a critical role in the competitive dynamics in fast-cycle markets. For individual firms then, innovation is a key source of competitive advantage. Through innovation, the firm can cannibalize its own products before competitors successfully imitate them and still maintain an advantage through next-generation products.

5-7c Standard-Cycle Markets

Standard-cycle markets are markets in which the firm's competitive advantages are partially shielded from imitation and imitation is moderately costly. Competitive advantages are partially sustainable in standard-cycle markets, but only when the firm is able to continuously upgrade the quality of its capabilities as a foundation for being able to stay ahead of competitors. The competitive actions and responses in standard-cycle markets are designed to seek large market shares, to gain customer loyalty through brand names, and to carefully control a firm's operations in order to consistently provide the same positive experience for customers.[113]

Companies competing in standard-cycle markets tend to serve many customers in what are typically highly competitive markets. Because the capabilities and core competencies on which their competitive advantages are based are less specialized, imitation is faster and less costly for standard-cycle firms than for those competing in slow-cycle markets. However, imitation is slower and more expensive in these markets than in fast-cycle markets. Thus, competitive dynamics in standard-cycle markets rest midway between the characteristics of dynamics in slow-cycle and fast-cycle markets. Imitation comes less quickly and is more expensive for standard-cycle competitors when a firm is able to develop economies of scale by combining coordinated and integrated design and manufacturing processes with a large sales volume for its products.

Because of large volumes, the size of mass markets, and the need to develop scale economies, the competition for market share is intense in standard-cycle markets. This form of competition is readily evident in the battles among consumer foods' producers, such as candy makers and major competitors Hershey Co.; Nestle, SA; Mondelez International, Inc.

Standard-cycle markets are markets in which the firm's competitive advantages are partially shielded from imitation and imitation is moderately costly.

(the new name for the former Kraft Foods Inc.); and Mars. (Of the firms, Hershey is far more dependent on candy sales than are the others.) Taste and the ingredients used to develop it, advertising campaigns, package designs, and availability through additional distribution channels are some of the many dimensions on which these competitors aggressively compete for the purpose of increasing their share of the candy market as broadly defined.[114]

Innovation can also drive competitive actions and responses in standard-cycle markets, especially when rivalry is intense. Some innovations in standard-cycle markets are incremental rather than radical in nature (incremental and radical innovations are discussed in Chapter 13). For example, consumer foods producers are innovating within their lines of healthy products. Today, many firms are relying on innovation as a means of competing in standard-cycle markets and earning above-average returns.

Overall, innovation has a substantial influence on competitive dynamics as it affects the actions and responses of all companies competing within a slow-cycle, fast-cycle, or standard-cycle market. We have emphasized the importance of innovation to the firm's strategic competitiveness in earlier chapters and do so again in Chapter 13. These discussions highlight the importance of innovation for firms regardless of the type of competitive dynamics they encounter while competing.

SUMMARY

■ Competitors are firms competing in the same market, offering similar products, and targeting similar customers. Competitive rivalry is the ongoing set of competitive actions and responses occurring between competitors as they compete against each other for an advantageous market position. The outcomes of competitive rivalry influence the firm's ability to sustain its competitive advantages as well as the level (average, below average, or above average) of its financial returns.

■ Competitive behavior is the set of competitive actions and responses an individual firm takes while engaged in competitive rivalry. Competitive dynamics is the set of actions and responses taken by all firms that are competitors within a particular market.

■ Firms study competitive rivalry in order to predict the competitive actions and responses each of their competitors are likely to take. Competitive actions are either strategic or tactical in nature. The firm takes competitive actions to defend or build its competitive advantages or to improve its market position. Competitive responses are taken to counter the effects of a competitor's competitive action. A strategic action or a strategic response requires a significant commitment of organizational resources, is difficult to successfully implement, and is difficult to reverse. In contrast, a tactical action or a tactical response requires fewer organizational resources and is easier to implement and reverse. For example, for an airline company, entering major new markets is an example of a strategic action or a strategic response; changing its prices in a particular market is an example of a tactical action or a tactical response.

■ A competitor analysis is the first step the firm takes to be able to predict its competitors' actions and responses. In Chapter 2, we discussed what firms do to *understand* competitors. This discussion was extended in this chapter to describe what the firm

does to *predict* competitors' market-based actions. Thus, understanding precedes prediction. Market commonality (the number of markets with which competitors are jointly involved and their importance to each) and resource similarity (how comparable competitors' resources are in terms of type and amount) are studied to complete a competitor analysis. In general, the greater the market commonality and resource similarity, the more firms acknowledge that they are direct competitors.

■ Market commonality and resource similarity shape the firm's awareness (the degree to which it and its competitors understand their mutual interdependence), motivation (the firm's incentive to attack or respond), and ability (the quality of the resources available to the firm to attack and respond). Having knowledge of these characteristics of a competitor increases the quality of the firm's predictions about that competitor's actions and responses.

■ In addition to market commonality and resource similarity and awareness, motivation, and ability, three more specific factors affect the likelihood a competitor will take competitive actions. The first of these concerns first-mover benefits. First movers, those taking an initial competitive action, often gain loyal customers and earn above-average returns until competitors can successfully respond to their action. Not all firms can be first movers in that they may lack the awareness, motivation, or ability required to engage in this type of competitive behavior. Moreover, some firms prefer to be a second mover (the firm responding to the first mover's action). One reason for this is that second movers, especially those acting quickly, can successfully compete against the first mover. By evaluating the first mover's product, customers' reactions to it, and the responses of other competitors to the first mover, the second mover may be able to avoid the early entrant's mistakes and find ways to improve upon the value created for customers by the first mover's good or service. Late movers (those that respond a long time after the original action was taken) commonly are lower performers and are much less competitive.

▦ Organizational size tends to reduce the variety of competitive actions that large firms launch while it increases the variety of actions undertaken by smaller competitors. Ideally, the firm would prefer to initiate a large number of diverse actions when engaged in competitive rivalry. The third factor, quality, is a base denominator to competing successfully in the global economy. It is a necessary prerequisite to achieving competitive parity. It is a necessary but insufficient condition for establishing an advantage.

▦ The type of action (strategic or tactical) the firm took, the competitor's reputation for the nature of its competitor behavior, and that competitor's dependence on the market in which the action was taken are studied to predict a competitor's response to the firm's action. In general, the number of tactical responses taken exceeds the number of strategic responses. Competitors respond more frequently to the actions taken by the firm with a reputation for predictable and understandable competitive behavior, especially if that firm is a market leader. In general, the firm can predict that when its competitor is highly dependent for its revenue and profitability in the

market in which the firm took a competitive action, that competitor is likely to launch a strong response. However, firms that are more diversified across markets are less likely to respond to a particular action that affects only one of the markets in which they compete.

▦ In slow-cycle markets, where competitive advantages can be maintained for at least a period of time, competitive dynamics often include firms taking actions and responses intended to protect, maintain, and extend their proprietary advantages. In fast-cycle markets, competition is substantial as firms concentrate on developing a series of temporary competitive advantages. This emphasis is necessary because firms' advantages in fast-cycle markets aren't proprietary and, as such, are subject to rapid and relatively inexpensive imitation. Standard-cycle markets have a level of competition between that in slow-cycle and fast-cycle markets; firms are moderately shielded from competition in these markets as they use capabilities that produce competitive advantages that are moderately sustainable. Competitors in standard-cycle markets serve mass markets and try to develop economies of scale to enhance their profitability. Innovation is vital to competitive success in each of the three types of markets. Companies should recognize that the set of competitive actions and responses taken by all firms differs by type of market.

REVIEW QUESTIONS

1. Who are competitors? How are competitive rivalry, competitive behavior, and competitive dynamics defined in the chapter?

2. What is market commonality? What is resource similarity? What does it mean to say that these concepts are the building blocks for a competitor analysis?

3. How do awareness, motivation, and ability affect the firm's competitive behavior?

4. What factors affect the likelihood a firm will take a competitive action?

5. What factors affect the likelihood a firm will initiate a competitive response to a competitor's action(s)?

6. What competitive dynamics can be expected among firms competing in slow-cycle markets? In fast-cycle markets? In standard-cycle markets?

EXPERIENTAL EXERCISES

EXERCISE 1: TRAGEDY OF THE COMMONS

The tragedy of the commons is a dilemma that encompasses elements from social psychology and competitive behavior, among other fields. The concept first appeared in 1968 in an article by Garrett Hardin in the journal *Science*. The dilemma arises from a situation in which individuals act in ways that may not necessarily be in everyone's long-term interests. In general, the tragedy of the commons occurs when individuals all have equal access to a shared resource and each individual seeks to maximize his or her own self-interest. For a contemporary example, think about global warming in general or localized pollution in particular as instances

of the dilemma: there is a distinct advantage for one country/state/business to pollute, which in turn imperils society as a whole.

As explained by R. De Young (1999, Tragedy of the commons, in D. E. Alexander and R. W. Fairbridge [Eds.] *Encyclopedia of Environmental Science*. Hingham, MA: Kluwer Academic Publishers), ecologist Garrett Hardin's parable involves a pasture "open to all." He asks us to imagine the grazing of animals on a common ground. Individuals are motivated to add to their flocks to increase personal wealth. Yet, every animal added to the total degrades the commons a small amount. Although the degradation for each additional animal is small relative to the gain in wealth for the owner, if all owners follow this pattern, the commons will ultimately be destroyed. And, being rational actors, all owners are motivated to add to their flock:

> *Therein is the tragedy. Each man is locked into a system that compels him to increase his herd without limit—in a world that is limited. Ruin is the destination toward which all men rush, each pursuing his own interest in a society that believes in the freedom of the commons (Hardin, 1968).*

In this exercise, the instructor needs four volunteers to participate. You will be asked to come to the front of the class and demonstrate the concept through a short exercise.

You should be familiar with the "Tragedy of the Commons". There are many good resources in the library, and you are encouraged to read Hardin's original 1968 article in *Science*, volume 162, pages 1243–1248, titled "The Tragedy of the Commons" before attending class.

EXERCISE 2: IS BEING THE FIRST MOVER USUALLY ADVANTAGEOUS?

Henry Ford is often credited with saying that he would rather be the first person to be second. This is strange coming from the innovator of the mass-produced automobile in the United States. So is the first-mover advantage really a myth, or is it something for which every firm should strive?

First movers are typically considered to be the ones that initially introduce an innovative product or service into a market segment (in other words, first to market in a new segment). The notion subscribed to first movers is that being one creates an almost impenetrable competitive advantage that later entrants find difficult to overcome. However, history is replete with situations where second or later movers find success. If the best way to succeed in the future is to understand the past, then an understanding of why certain

first movers succeeded and others failed should be instructive. Accordingly, this exercise requires you to investigate a first mover and identify specifically why, or why not, it was able to hold onto its first-mover advantage.

Part One

This assignment can be done individually or in a team. Select an industry that interests you or your team. Research that industry and identify one or two instances of a first mover; research the introduction of a new offering into new market segments. For example, you might pick consumer electronics and look for firms that initiated new products in new market segments. Your choice of industry must be approved in advance by your instructor as duplication of industries is to be avoided.

Part Two

Each individual or team is to present their findings with the discussion centering on the following at a minimum:

- Brief history and description of the industry chosen (e.g., was this a fast-, standard-, or slow-cycle market at the time the first mover initiated its strategic action)?

- How has innovation of new products traditionally been accomplished in this industry: through new firms entering the market or by existing firms launching new offerings?

- Identify one or two first movers and provide a review of what happened. If the product or offering is still considered successful, describe why. If not, why not?

- What did you learn as a result of this exercise? Do you consider trying to be the first mover a wise competitive action to take? Is your answer dependent upon industry, timing, or luck?

VIDEO CASE ▶

A FOCUS ON COMPETITIVE DYNAMICS: HYUNDAI SOUTH KOREA

With an objective "to sell more cars for less than the competition," consumers are flocking to Hyundai dealerships, causing the firm to recently experience an increase in its sales volume in the U.S. market. Auto executives both inside and outside the company recognize Hyundai's ability and desire to dominate the market through top-level quality. Durability, as evidenced by longer warranties and greater consumer awareness through major advertising, is foundational to Hyundai's strong rebound.

Be prepared to discuss the following concepts and questions in class:

Concepts

- Competitive behavior
- Competitive dynamics
- Multimarket competition
- Competitive response
- Strategic actions
- Late movers

Questions

1. How would you describe Hyundai's competitive behavior?

2. What kind of competitive dynamics might you expect from Hyundai and other automakers?

3. Is Hyundai involved in multimarket competition? Why or why not?

4. What impact will market commonality have on competitive responses in the auto industry?

5. What strategic actions and/or responses might occur as a result of your answer to question 4?

6. Can Hyundai be identified as a late mover? If so, why? If you determine that Hyundai is a late mover, what consequences should the company be aware of that result from being a late mover?

NOTES

1. S. Carnahan & D. Somaya, 2013, Alumni effects and relational advantage: The impact of outsourcing when your buyer hires employees from your competitors, *Academy of Management Journal*, in press; M.-J. Chen & D. Miller, 2012, Competitive dynamics: Themes, trends, and a prospective research platform, *Academy of Management Annals*, 6: 135–210; M.-J. Chen, 1996, Competitor analysis and interfirm rivalry: Toward a theoretical integration, *Academy of Management Review*, 21: 100–134.

2. P. C. Patel, S. A. Fernhaber, P. P. McDougall-Covin, & R. P. van der Have, 2013, Beating competitors to international markets: The value of geographically balanced networks for innovation, *Strategic Management Journal*, in press.

3. J. Bloodgood, 2013, Crowdsourcing: Useful for problem solving, but what about value capture? *Academy of Management Review*, 38: 455–457; T. Zahavi & D. Lavie, 2013, Intra-industry diversification and firm performance, *Strategic Management Journal*, 34: 978–998; M. Chen, H. Lin, & J. Michel, 2010, Navigating in a hypercompetitive environment: The roles of action aggressiveness and TMT integration, *Strategic Management Journal*, 31: 1410–1430.

4. P. T. M. Ingenbleek & I. A. van der Lans, 2013, Relating price strategies and price-setting practices, *European Journal of Marketing*, 47: 27–48; A. Eapen, 2012, Social structure and technology spillovers from foreign to domestic firms, *Journal of International Business Studies*, 43: 244–263.

5. F. J. Mas-Ruiz, F. Ruiz-Moreno, & A. L. de Guevara Martinez, 2013, Asymmetric rivalry within and between strategic groups, *Strategic Management Journal*, in press; P. J. Derfus, P. G. Maggitti, C. M. Grimm, & K. G. Smith, 2008, The red queen effect: Competitive actions and firm performance, *Academy of Management Journal*, 51: 61–80; C. M. Grimm, H. Lee, & K. G. Smith, 2006, *Strategy as Action: Competitive Dynamics and Competitive Advantage*, New York: Oxford University Press.

6. R. B. Mackay & R. Chia, 2012, Choice, chance, and unintended consequences in strategic change: A process understanding of the rise and fall of NorthCo Automotive, *Academy of Management Journal*, 56: 1–13; D. Di Gregorio, D. Thomas, & F. de Castilla, 2008, Competition between emerging market and multinational firms: Wal-Mart and Mexican retailers, *International Journal of Management*, 25: 532–545, 593.

7. M. Srivastava, A. Frankly, & L. Martinette, 2013, Building a sustainable competitive advantage, *Journal of Technology Management & Innovation*, 8: 47–60; G. J. Kilduff, H. A. Elfenbein, & B. M. Staw, 2010, The psychology of rivalry: A relationally dependent analysis of competition, *Academy of Management Journal*, 53: 943–969; D. G. Sirmon, S. Gove, & M. A. Hitt, 2008, Resource management in dyadic competitive rivalry: The effects of resource bundling and deployment, *Academy of Management Journal*, 51: 919–935.

8. S.-J. Chang & S. H. Park, 2012, Winning strategies in China: Competitive dynamics between MNCs and local firms, *Long Range Planning*, 45: 1–15; S. K. Ethitaj & D. H. Zhu, 2008, Performance effects of imitative entry, *Strategic Management Journal*, 29: 797–817.

9. A. Nair & D. D. Selover, 2012, A study of competitive dynamics, *Journal of Business Research*, 65: 355–361; Grimm, Lee, & Smith, *Strategy as Action*.

10. R. Chellappa, V. Sambamurthy, & N. Saraf, 2010, Competing in crowded markets: Multimarket contact and the nature of competition in the enterprise systems software industry, *Information Systems Research: Special Issue on Digital Systems and Competition*, 21: 614–630.

11. T. Yu, M. Subramaniam, & A. A. Cannella, 2009, Rivalry deterrence in international markets: Contingencies governing the mutual forbearance hypothesis, *Academy of Management Journal*, 52: 127–147; K. G. Smith, W. J. Ferrier, & H. Ndofor, 2001, Competitive dynamics research: Critique and future directions, in M. A. Hitt, R. E. Freeman, & J. S. Harrison (eds.), *Handbook of Strategic Management*, Oxford, UK: Blackwell Publishers, 326.

12. F. Bridoux, K. G. Smith, & C. M. Grimm, 2011, The management of resources: Temporal effects of different types of actions on performance, *Journal of Management*, 33: 1281–1310; G. Young, K. G. Smith, & C. M. Grimm, 1996, "Austrian" and industrial organization perspectives on firm-level competitive activity and performance, *Organization Science*, 73: 243–254.

13. M. Esteri, 2013, Big tobacco is about to dive into e-cigarettes, *Wall Street Journal*, www.wsj.com, May 29; C. Lobello, 2013, E-cigarettes: Could they change the tobacco industry forever? *The Week*, www.wsj.theweek.com, April 26.

14. R. Katila, E. L. Chen, & H. Piezunka, 2012, All the right moves: How entrepreneurial firms compete effectively, *Strategic Entrepreneurship Journal*, 6: 116–132; J. Marcel, P. Barr, & I. Duhaime, 2011, The influence of executive cognition on competitive dynamics, *Strategic Management Journal*, 32: 115–138.

15. R. Casadesus-Masanell & F. Zhu, 2013, Business model innovation and competitive imitation: The case of sponsor-based business models, *Strategic Management Journal*, 34: 464–482; M.-J. Chen & D. C. Hambrick, 1995, Speed, stealth, and selective attack: How small firms differ from large firms in competitive behavior, *Academy of Management Journal*, 38: 453–482.

16. J. M. Mol & N. M. Wijnberg, 2011, From resources to value and back: Competition between and within organizations, *British Journal of Management*, 22: 77–95.

17. V. K. Patel, T. M. Pieper, & J. F. Hair, Jr., 2012, The global family business: Challenges and drivers for cross-border growth, *Business Horizons*, 55: 231–239.

18. M. A. Abebe & A. Angriawan, 2013, Organizational and competitive influences of exploration and exploitation activities in small firms, *Journal of Business Research*, in press; V. Rindova, W. Ferrier, & R. Wiltbank, 2010, Value from gestalt: How sequences of competitive actions create advantage for firms in nascent markets, *Strategic Management Journal*, 31: 1474–1497; T. Yu & A. A. Cannella, Jr., Rivalry between multinational enterprises: An event history approach, *Academy of Management Journal*, 50: 665–686.

19. J. Villanueva, A. H. Van de Ven, & H. Sapienza, 2012, Resource mobilization in entrepreneurial firms, *Journal of Business Venturing*, 27: 19–30; Smith, Ferrier, & Ndofor, Competitive dynamics research, 319.

20. C. Boone, F. C. Wezel, & A. van Witteloostuijn, 2013, Joining the pack or going solo? A dynamic theory of new firm positioning, *Journal of Business Venturing*, 28: 511–527; H. Ndofor, D. G. Sirmon, & X. He, 2011, Firm resources, competitive actions and performance: Investigating a mediated model with evidence from the in-vitro diagnostics industry, *Strategic Management Journal*, 32: 640–657.

21. M. Gruber, I. C. MacMillan, & J. D. Thompson, 2013, Escaping the prior knowledge corridor: What shapes the number and variety of market opportunities identified before market entry of technology start-ups? *Organization Science*, 24: 280–300.

22. L. M. Ellram, W. L. Tate, & E. G. Feitzinger, 2013, Factor-market rivalry and competition for supply chain resources, *Journal of Supply Chain Management*, 49: 29–46; D. G. Sirmon, M. A. Hitt, J. Arregle, & J. Campbell, 2010, The dynamic interplay of capability strengths and weaknesses: Investigating the bases of temporary competitive advantage, *Strategic Management Journal*, 31: 1386–1409.

23. S. Crowly, 2013, The smartphone market's radical shakeup, *CNNMoney*, www.money.cnn.com, January 29.

24. W. Shi & J. E. Prescott, 2012, Rhythm and entrainment of acquisition and alliance initiatives and firm performance: A temporal perspective, *Organization Studies*, 33: 1281–1310.

25. H. Rahmandad, 2012, Impact of growth opportunities and competition on firm-level capability development trade-offs, *Organization Science*, 34: 138–154; Y. Y. Kor & J. T. Mahoney, 2005, How dynamics, management, and governance of resource deployments influence firm-level performance, *Strategic Management Journal*, 26: 489–496.

26. L. Mulotte, P. Dussauge, & W. Mitchell, 2013, Does pre-entry licensing undermine the performance of subsequent independent activities? Evidence from the global aerospace industry, 1944–2000, *Strategic Management Journal*, 34: 358–372; K. G. Fouskas & D. A. Drossos, 2010, The role of industry perceptions in competitive responses, *Industrial Management & Data Systems*, 110: 477–494.

27. L. K. S. Lim, 2013, Mapping competitive prediction capability: Construct conceptualization and performance payoffs, *Journal of Business Research*, 66: 1576–1586; J. C. Baum & A. Satorra, 2007, The persistence of abnormal returns at industry and firm levels: Evidence from Spain, *Strategic Management Journal*, 28: 707–722.

28. J.-L. Arregle, T. L. Miller, M. A. Hitt, & P. W. Beamish, 2013, Do regions matter? An integrated institutional and semiglobalization perspective on the internationalization of MNEs, *Strategic Management Journal*, 34: 910–934; B. I. Park & P. N. Ghauri, 2011, Key factors affecting acquisition of technological capabilities from foreign acquiring firms by small and medium sized local firms, *Journal of World Business*, 46: 116–125.

29. N. Zhou, S. H. Park, & G. R. Ungson, 2013, Profitable growth: Avoiding the 'growth fetish' in emerging markets, *Business Horizons*, 56: 473–481; Chen, Competitor analysis, 108.

30. O. Alexy, G. George, & A. Salter, 2013, Cui Bono? The selective revealing of knowledge and its implications for innovative activity, *Academy of Management Review*, in press; Chen, Competitor analysis, 109.

31. T. Lawton, T. Rajwani, & P. Reinmoeller, 2012, Do you have a survival instinct? Leveraging genetic codes to achieve fit in hostile business environments, *Business Horizons*, 55: 81–91; 2011, The power of blindspots. What companies don't know, surprises them. What they don't want to know, kills them, *Strategic Direction*, 27(4): 3–4; D. Ng, R. Westgren, & S. Sonka, 2009, Competitive blind spots in an institutional field, *Strategic Management Journal*, 30: 349–369.

32. E. Metayer, 2013, How intelligent is your company? *Competia*, www.competia.com, March.

33. J. Neff, 2011, P&G e-commerce chief sees blurring of sales, marketing, *Advertising Age*, April 11, 8.

34. 2013, About YRC, YRC homepage, www.yrc.com, May 29.

35. J. W. Upson, D. J. Ketchen, Jr., B. L. Connelly, & A. L. Ranft, 2012, Competitor analysis and foothold moves, *Academy of Management Journal*, 55: 93–110; Chen, Competitor analysis, 106.

36. T. Yu & A. A. Cannella, Jr., 2013, A comprehensive review of multimarket competition research, *Journal of Management*, 39: 76–109; J. Anand, L. F. Mesquita, & R. S. Vassolo, 2009, The dynamics of multimarket competition in exploration and exploitation activities, *Academy of Management Journal*, 52: 802–821.

37. A. Nair & D. D. Selover, 2012, A study of competitive dynamics, *Journal of Business Research*, 65: 355–361.

38. W. Kang, B. Bayus, & S. Balasubramanian, 2010, The strategic effects of multimarket contact: Mutual forbearance and competitive response in the personal computer industry, *Journal of Marketing Research*, 47: 415–427.

39. V. Bilotkach, 2011, Multimarket contact and intensity of competition: Evidence from an airline merger, *Review of Industrial Organization*, 38: 95–115; H. R. Greve, 2008, Multimarket contact and sales growth: Evidence from insurance, *Strategic Management Journal*, 29: 229–249; J. Gimeno, 1999, Reciprocal threats in multimarket rivalry: Staking out "spheres of influence" in the U.S. airline industry, *Strategic Management Journal*, 20: 101–128.

40. L. A. Costa, K. Cool, & I. Dierickx, 2013, The competitive implications of the deployment of unique resources, *Strategic Management Journal*, 34: 445–463; Chen, Competitor analysis, 107.

41. J. Haleblian, G. McNamara, K. Kolev, & B. J. Dykes, 2012, Exploring firm characteristics that differentiate leaders from followers in industry merger waves: A competitive dynamics perspective, *Strategic Management Journal*, 33: 1037–1052; Chen, Competitor analysis, 110.

42. C. Flammer, 2013, Corporate social responsibility and shareholder reaction: The environmental awareness of investors, *Academy of Management Journal*, in press.

43. J. Tang & B. S.-C. Liu, 2012, Strategic alignment and foreign entry performance: A holistic approach of the impact of entry timing, mode and location, *Business and Systems Research*, 6: 456–478; R. S. Livengood & R. K. Reger, 2010, That's our turf! Identity domains and competitive dynamics, *Academy of Management Review*, 35: 48–66.

44. B. Tita, 2013, Caterpillar expected to cut 2013 forecasts, *Wall Street Journal*, www.wsj.com, April 21.

45. Nair & Selover, *A study of competitive dynamics*; S. H. Park & D. Zhou, 2005,

Firm heterogeneity and competitive dynamics in alliance formation, *Academy of Management Review*, 30: 531–554.

46. T.-J. A. Peng, S. Pike, J. C.-H. Yang, & G. Roos, 2012, Is cooperation with competitors a good idea? An example in practice, *British Journal of Management*, 23: 532–560; Chen, Competitor analysis, 113.

47. C. Williams & S. Lee, 2011, Entrepreneurial contexts and knowledge coordination within the multinational corporation, *Journal of World Business*, 46: 253–264; M. Leiblein & T. Madsen, 2009, Unbundling competitive heterogeneity: Incentive structures and capability influences on technological innovation, *Strategic Management Journal*, 30: 711–735.

48. R. Makadok, 2010, The interaction effect of rivalry restraint and competitive advantage on profit: Why the whole is less than the sum of the parts, *Management Science*, 56: 356–372.

49. C. M. Grimm & K. G. Smith, 1997, *Strategy as Action: Industry Rivalry and Coordination*, Cincinnati: South-Western Publishing Co., 125.

50. J. Alcacer, C. L. Dezso, & M. Zhao, 2013, Firm rivalry, knowledge accumulation, and MNE location choices, *Journal of International Business Studies*, 44: 504–520; B. Markens, 2011, Be aware of your competition to increase market share, *Paperboard Packaging*, 96(1): 11.

51. G. Gavetti, 2012, Perspective—Toward a behavioral theory of strategy, *Organization Science*, 23: 267–285; B. L. Connelly, L. Tihanyi, S. T. Certo, & M. A. Hitt, 2010, Marching to the beat of different drummers: The influence of institutional owners on competitive actions, *Academy of Management Journal*, 53: 723–742.

52. 2011, Nokia and Microsoft announce plans for a broad strategic partnership to build a new global mobile ecosystem, Microsoft Home Page, www.microsoft.com, February 10.

53. M.-J. Lee, 2013, Samsung makes space on Nokia's turf, *Wall Street Journal*, www.wsj.com, May 30; J. D. Stoll, 2013, Nokia loses lead in home market, *Wall Street Journal*, www.wsj.com, May 28.

54. J. Schumpeter, 1934, *The Theory of Economic Development*, Cambridge, MA: Harvard University Press.

55. S. Bakker, H. van Lente, & M. T. H. Meeus, 2012, Dominance in the prototyping phase—The case of hydrogen passenger cars, *Research Policy*, 41: 871–883.

56. L. Sleuwaegen & J. Onkelinx, 2013, International commitment, post-entry growth and survival of international new ventures, *Journal of Business Venturing*, in press; F. F. Suarez & G. Lanzolla, 2007, The role of environmental dynamics in building a first mover advantage theory, *Academy of Management Review*, 32: 377–392.

57. G. M. McNamara, J. Haleblian, & B. J. Dykes, 2008, The performance implications of participating in an acquisition wave: Early mover advantages, bandwagon effects, and the moderating influence

of industry characteristics and acquirer tactics, *Academy of Management Journal*, 51, 113–130.

58. R. K. Sinha & C. H. Noble, 2008, The adoption of radical manufacturing technologies and firm survival, *Strategic Management Journal*, 29: 943–962; D. P. Forbes, 2005, Managerial determinants of decision speed in new ventures, *Strategic Management Journal*, 26: 355–366.

59. H. R. Greve, 2009, Bigger and safer: The diffusion of competitive advantage, *Strategic Management Journal*, 30: 1–23; W. T. Robinson & S. Min, 2002, Is the first to market the first to fail? Empirical evidence for industrial goods businesses, *Journal of Marketing Research*, 39: 120–128.

60. J. C. Short & G. T. Payne, 2008, First-movers and performance: Timing is everything, *Academy of Management Review*, 33: 267–270.

61. E. de Oliveira & W. B. Werther, Jr., 2013, Resilience: Continuous renewal of competitive advantages, *Business Horizons*, 56: 333–342.

62. N. M. Jakopin & A. Klein, 2012, First-mover and incumbency advantages in mobile telecommunications, *Journal of Business Research*, 65: 362–370.

63. H. Wang, J. Choi, G. Wan, & J. Q. Dong, 2013, Slack resources and the rent-generating potential of firm-specific knowledge, *Journal of Management*, in press; K. Mellahi & A. Wilkinson, 2010, A study of the association between level of slack reduction following downsizing and innovation output, *Journal of Management Studies*, 47: 483–508.

64. R. Mudambi & T. Swift, 2013, Knowing when to leap: Transitioning between exploitative and explorative R&D, *Strategic Management Journal*, 34: in press; M. B. Lieberman & D. B. Montgomery, 1988, First-mover advantages, *Strategic Management Journal*, 9: 41–58.

65. A. Hawk, G. Pacheco-De-Almeida, & B. Yeung, 2013, Fast-mover advantages: Speed capabilities and entry into the emerging submarket of Atlantic basin LNG, *Strategic Management Journal*, 34: in press; G. Pacheco-De- Almeida, 2010, Erosion, time compression, and self-displacement of leaders in hypercompetitive environments, *Strategic Management Journal*, 31: 1498–1526.

66. F. Zhu & M. Iansiti, 2012, Entry into platform-based markets, *Strategic Management Journal*, 33: 88–106; S. Jonsson & P. Regnér, 2009, Normative barriers to imitation: Social complexity of core competences in a mutual fund industry, *Strategic Management Journal*, 30: 517–536.

67. M. A. Stanko & J. D. Bohlmann, 2013, Demand-side inertia factors and their benefits for innovativeness, *Journal of the Academy of Marketing Science*, in press; M. Poletti, B. Engelland, & H. Ling, 2011, An empirical study of declining lead times: Potential ramifications on the performance

of early market entrants, *Journal of Marketing Theory and Practice*, 19(1): 27–38.

68. S. Bin, 2011, First-mover advantages: Flexible or not?, *Journal of Management & Marketing Research*, 7: 1–13; J. Gimeno, R. E. Hoskisson, B. B. Beal, & W. P. Wan, 2005, Explaining the clustering of international expansion moves: A critical test in the U.S. telecommunications industry, *Academy of Management Journal*, 48: 297–319; K. G. Smith, C. M. Grimm, & M. J. Gannon, 1992, *Dynamics of Competitive Strategy*, Newberry Park, CA: Sage Publications.

69. M. Weiker, 2013, Competitors challenge top rater Angie's List, *The Columbus Dispatch*, www.dispatch.com, May 19.

70. A. Yaprak, 2012, Market entry barriers in China: A commentary essay, *Journal of Business Research*, 65: 1216–1218; A. Fleury & M. Fleury, 2009, Understanding the strategies of late-movers in international manufacturing, *International Journal of Production Economics*, 122: 340–350; J. Li & R. K. Kozhikode, 2008, Knowledge management and innovation strategy: The challenge for latecomers in emerging economies, *Asia Pacific Journal of Management*, 25: 429–450.

71. F. Karakaya & P. Yannopoulos, 2011, Impact of market entrant characteristics on incumbent reactions to market entry, *Journal of Strategic Marketing*, 19(2): 171–185; S. D. Dobrev & G. R. Carroll, 2003, Size (and competition) among organizations: Modeling scale-based selection among automobile producers in four major countries, 1885–1981, *Strategic Management Journal*, 24: 541–558.

72. W. Stam, S. Arzianian, & T. Elfring, 2013, Social capital of entrepreneurs and small firm performance: A meta-analysis of contextual and methodological moderators, *Journal of Business Venturing*, in press; L. F. Mesquita & S. G. Lazzarini, 2008, Horizontal and vertical relationships in developing economies: Implications for SMEs access to global markets, *Academy of Management Journal*, 51: 359–380.

73. C. Zhou & A. Van Witteloostuijn, 2010, Institutional constraints and ecological processes: Evolution of foreign-invested enterprises in the Chinese construction industry, 1993–2006, *Journal of International Business Studies*, 41: 539–556; M. A. Hitt, L. Bierman, & J. D. Collins, 2007, The strategic evolution of U.S. law firms, *Business Horizons*, 50: 17–28; D. Miller & M. J. Chen, 1996, The simplicity of competitive repertoires: An empirical analysis, *Strategic Management Journal*, 17: 419–440.

74. Young, Smith, & Grimm, "Austrian" and industrial organization perspectives.

75. P. B. Crosby, 1980, *Quality Is Free*, New York: Penguin.

76. W. E. Deming, 1986, *Out of the Crisis*, Cambridge, MA: MIT Press.

77. R. C. Ford & D. R. Dickson, 2012, Enhancing customer self-efficacy in co-producing

service experiences, *Business Horizons*, 55: 179–188; G. C. Avery & H. Bergsteiner, 2011, Sustainable leadership practices for enhancing business resilience and performance, *Strategy & Leadership*, 39(3): 5–15.

78. L. A. Bettencourt & S. W. Brown, 2013, From goods to great: Service innovation in a product-dominated company, *Business Horizons*, 56: 277–283; X. Luo, 2010, Product competitiveness and beating analyst earnings target, *Journal of the Academy of Marketing Science*, 38: 253–264.

79. F. Pakdil, 2010, The effects of TQM on corporate performance. *The Business Review*, 15: 242–248; A. Azadegan, K. J. Dooley, P. L. Carter, & J. R. Carter, 2008, Supplier innovativeness and the role of interorganizational learning in enhancing manufacturing capabilities, *Journal of Supply Chain Management*, 44(4): 14–35.

80. M. Terziovski & P. Hermel, 2011, The role of quality management practice in the performance of integrated supply chains: A multiple cross-case analysis, *The Quality Management Journal*, 18(2): 10–25; K. E. Weick & K. M. Sutcliffe, 2001, *Managing the Unexpected*, San Francisco: Jossey-Bass, 81–82.

81. D. P. McIntyre, 2011, In a network industry, does product quality matter? *Journal of Product Innovation Management*, 28: 99–108; G. Macintosh, 2007, Customer orientation, relationship quality, and relational benefits to the firm, *Journal of Services Marketing*, 21: 150–159.

82. Q. Liu & D. Zhang, 2013, Dynamic pricing competition with strategic customers under vertical product differentiation, *Management Science*, 59: 84–101; S. Thirumalai & K. K. Sinha, 2011, Product recalls in the medical device industry: An empirical exploration of the sources and financial consequences, *Management Science*, 57: 376–392.

83. J. Chiu & D. Cameron, 2013, China clears Boeing 787 for commercial service, *Wall Street Journal*, www.wsj.com, May 23; P. LeBeau, 2013, Boeing dreamliners back in the air after lengthy grounding, *NBC News Business*, www.nbcnews.com, May 20; A. Pasztor, 2013, How Boeing rescued the 787, *Wall Street Journal*, www.wsj.com, April 20.

84. R. Aboulafia, 2013, 787 delays continue to boost Airbus, *Forbes*, www.forbes.com, May 24.

85. M. Su & V. R. Rao, 2011, Timing decisions of new product preannouncement and launch with competition, *International Journal of Production Economics*, 129(1): 51–64.

86. M. L. Sosa, 2013, Decoupling market incumbency from organizational prehistory: Locating the real sources of competitive advantage in R&D for radical innovation, *Strategic Management Journal*, 34: 245–255; T. R. Crook, D. J. Ketchen, J. G. Combs, & S. Y. Todd, 2008, Strategic resources and

performance: A meta-analysis, *Strategic Management Journal*, 29: 1141–1154.

87. R. K. Kozhikode & J. Li, 2012, Political pluralism, public policies, and organizational choices: Banking branch expansion in India, 1948–2003, *Academy of Management Journal*, 55: 339–359; C. Lutz, R. Kemp, & S. Gerhard Dijkstra, 2010, Perceptions regarding strategic and structural entry barriers, *Small Business Economics*, 35: 19–33; M. J. Chen & I. C. MacMillan, 1992, Nonresponse and delayed response to competitive moves, *Academy of Management Journal*, 35: 539–570.

88. S. M. Ben-Menahern, Z. Kwee, H. W. Volberda, & F. A. J. Van Den Bosch, 2013, Strategic renewal over time: The enabling role of potential absorptive capacity in aligning internal and external rates of change, *Long Range Planning*, 46: 216–235; M. J. Chen, K. G. Smith, & C. M. Grimm, 1992, Action characteristics as predictors of competitive responses, *Management Science*, 38: 439–455.

89. S. Ansari & P. Krop, 2012, Incumbent performance in the face of a radical innovation: Towards a framework for incumbent challenger dynamics, *Research Policy*, 41: 1357–1374; M. J. Chen & D. Miller, 1994, Competitive attack, retaliation and performance: An expectancy-valence framework, *Strategic Management Journal*, 15: 85–102.

90. K. Muller, K. Huschelrath, & V. Bilotkach, 2012, The construction of a low-cost airline network—facing competition and exploring new markets, *Managerial and Decision Economics*, 33: 485–499; N. Huyghebaert & L. M. van de Gucht, 2004, Incumbent strategic behavior in financial markets and the exit of entrepreneurial start-ups, *Strategic Management Journal*, 25: 669–688.

91. Smith, Ferrier, & Ndofor, Competitive dynamics research, 333.

92. V. Babic-Hodovic, M. Arlsanagic, & E. Mehic, 2013, Importance of internal marketing for service companies corporate reputation and customer satisfaction, *Journal of Business Administration Research*, 2: 49–57; T. Obloj & L. Capron, 2011, Role of resource gap and value appropriation: Effect of reputation gap on price premium in online auctions, *Strategic Management Journal*, 32: 447–456; V. P. Rindova, A. P. Petkova, & S. Kotha, 2007, Standing out: How firms in emerging markets build reputation, *Strategic Organization*, 5: 31–70.

93. Q. Gu & X. Lu, 2013, Unraveling the mechanisms of reputation and alliance formation: A study of venture capital syndication in China, *Strategic Management Journal*, 34: in press; D. D. Bergh &

P. Gibbons, 2011, The stock market reaction to the hiring of management consultants: A signalling theory approach, *Journal of Management Studies*, 48: 544–567; P. W. Roberts & G. R. Dowling, 2003, Corporate reputation and sustained superior financial performance, *Strategic Management Journal*, 24: 1077–1093.

94. B. Larraneta, S. A. Zahra, & J. L. G. Gonzalez, 2013, Strategic repertoire variety and new venture growth: The moderating effects of origin and industry dynamism, *Strategic Management Journal*, in press; W. J. Ferrier, K. G. Smith, & C. M. Grimm, 1999, The role of competitive actions in market share erosion and industry dethronement: A study of industry leaders and challengers, *Academy of Management Journal*, 42: 372–388.

95. R. Karlgaard, 2011, Transitions: Michael reinvents Dell, *Forbes*, www.forbes.com, May 9.

96. 2013, Dell floats clout with 'hyperscale' servers, *Wall Street Journal*, www.blogs.wsj.com, May 21.

97. M. Fassnacht & S. El Husseini, 2013, EDLP versus Hi-Lo pricing strategies in retailing—a state of the art article, *Journal of Business Economics*, 83: 259–289; Smith, Grimm, & Gannon, *Dynamics of Competitive Strategy*.

98. J. Xia & S. Li, 2013, The divestiture of acquired subunits: A resource dependence approach, *Strategic Management Journal*, 34: 131–148; A. Karnani & B. Wernerfelt, 1985, Multiple point competition, *Strategic Management Journal*, 6: 87–97.

99. L. Kwanghui, H. Chesbrough, & R. Yi, 2010, Open innovation and patterns of R&D competition, *International Journal of Technology Management*, 52: 295–321; Smith, Ferrier, & Ndofor, Competitive dynamics research, 330.

100. C. O'Connor, 2013, Wal-Mart vs. Amazon: World's biggest e-commerce battle could boil down to vegetables, *Forbes*, www.forbes.com, April 23.

101. J. Wohl & A. Barr, 2013, Wal-Mart steps up its online game with help from stores, *Reuters*, www.reuters.com, March 26.

102. A. Barr & J. Wohl, 2013, Exclusive: Wal-Mart may get customers to deliver packages to online buyers, *Reuters*, www.reuters.com, March 28.

103. C. Boone, F. C. Wezel, & A. van Witteloostuijn, 2013, Joining the pack or going solo? A dynamic theory of new firm positioning, *Journal of Business Venturing*, 28: 511–527; J. R. Williams, 1992, How sustainable is your competitive advantage? *California Management Review*, 34(3): 29–51.

104. R. A. D'Aveni, G. Dagnino, & K. G. Smith, 2010, The age of temporary advantage,

Strategic Management Journal, 31: 1371–1385; N. Pangarkar & J. R. Lie, 2004, The impact of market cycle on the performance of Singapore acquirers, *Strategic Management Journal*, 25: 1209–1216.

105. K. Thomas, 2012, Pfizer races to reinvent itself, *New York Times*, www.nytimes.com, May 1.

106. L.-C. Hsu & C.-H. Wang, 2012, Clarifying the effect of intellectual capital on performance: The mediating role of dynamic capability, *British Journal of Management*, 23: 179–205.

107. 2003, How fast is your company? *Fast Company*, June, 18.

108. R. Klingebiel & A. De Meyer, 2013, Becoming aware of the unknown: Decision making during the implementation of a strategic initiative, *Organization Science*, 24: 133–153; C. Hall & D. Lundberg, 2010, Competitive knowledge and strategy in high velocity environments, *IUP Journal of Knowledge Management*, 8(1/2): 7–17.

109. G. Clarkson & P. Toh, 2010, 'Keep out' signs: The role of deterrence in the competition for resources, *Strategic Management Journal*, 31: 1202–1225.

110. M. Kumar, 2011, Are joint ventures positive sum games? The relative effects of cooperative and noncooperative behavior, *Strategic Management Journal*, 32: 32–54; D. Li, L. Eden, M. A. Hitt, & R. D. Ireland, 2008, Friends, acquaintances or strangers? Partner selection in R&D alliances, *Academy of Management Journal*, 51: 315–334.

111. M. M. Larsen, S. Manning, & T. Pedersen, 2013, Uncovering the hidden costs of offshoring: The interplay of complexity, organizational design, and experience, *Strategic Management Journal*, 34: 533–552; F. Zirpoli & M. C. Becker, 2011, What happens when you outsource too much?, *MIT Sloan Management Review*, 52(2): 59–64.

112. D. Desai, 2013, The competitive advantage of adaptive networks: An extension of the dynamic capability view, *International Journal of Business Environment*, 5: 379–397; P. Carbonell & A. I. Rodriguez, 2006, The impact of market characteristics and innovation speed on perceptions of positional advantage and new product performance, *International Journal of Research in Marketing*, 23(1): 1–12.

113. S. P. Gudergan, T. Devinney, N. F. Richter, & R. S. Ellis, 2012, Strategic implications for (non-equity) alliance performance, *Long Range Planning*, 45: 451–476; V. Kumar, F. Jones, R. Venkatesan, & R. Leone, 2011, Is market orientation a source of sustainable competitive advantage or simply the cost of competing?, *Journal of Marketing*, 75: 16–30.

114. L. Josephs, 2011, Candy lovers face bitter Easter, *Wall Street Journal*, February 18, C10.

6

Corporate-level Strategy

Studying this chapter should provide you with the strategic management knowledge needed to:

1 Define corporate-level strategy and discuss its purpose.

2 Describe different levels of diversification achieved using different corporate-level strategies.

3 Explain three primary reasons firms diversify.

4 Describe how firms can create value by using a related diversification strategy.

5 Explain the two ways value can be created with an unrelated diversification strategy.

6 Discuss the incentives and resources that encourage diversification.

7 Describe motives that can encourage managers to overdiversify a firm.

GENERAL ELECTRIC: THE CLASSIC DIVERSIFIED FIRM

General Electric (GE) competes in many different industries ranging from appliances, aviation, and consumer electronics, to energy, financial services, health care, oil, and wind turbines. These industries are quite diverse, but there are similarities among several of them. In fact, GE's businesses are grouped in four divisions: GE Capital, GE Energy, GE Technology Infrastructure, and GE Home & Business Solutions. In recent years, more than 50 percent of GE's annual revenue has come from its financial services businesses. However, GE has reduced its assets in financial services—GE Capital provides approximately one-third of its total earnings. In 2012, much of GE's growth in revenues came from the manufacture and sale of jet engines for major airliners and from its increasing business in the oil and gas industry. In 2013 (based on 2012 data), GE was ranked the eighth

largest corporation in the *Fortune* 500. Additionally, in 2013 it was ranked eleventh in *Fortune* magazine's list of the 50 most admired companies. Thus, GE has been a highly successful company.

GE has an impressive history and is one of the few widely diversified firms to achieve such success. GE is a highly influential global corporation. Its CEO, Jeffrey Immelt, was selected by President Obama to chair an advisory group on economic and job creation concerns. However, GE has experienced some "bumps in the road" along the way. This is to be expected because it is difficult to manage a large, widely diversified set of businesses. For example, GE never achieved the desired success with its NBC assets and sold them in 2012. In addition, it experienced significant declines in revenues and profits from its financial services businesses with the substantial problems that occurred in that industry beginning in 2008. In 2012, GE Capital rebounded and added revenue

growth and profits but with a lower emphasis within the GE groups of businesses. Finally, partly because of these problems, it experienced reductions in stock value during the first decade of the twenty-first century.

GE has bounced back from these problems. Today, it is becoming a major player in the energy equipment industry, making several recent acquisitions. Additionally, GE is making large investments to be a major player in the new industrial Internet industry that is developing. GE has developed a new software R&D center in San Francisco with plans to have 400 computer scientists and software developers and invest $1 billion by 2015. The intent of GE is to develop and market Internet-connected machines that are designed to collect data and communicate it for a variety of purposes (e.g., servicing needs, quality control, etc.). GE is also beginning to experience strong growth from its investments in emerging economies such as China, India and Brazil.

A common strategy to achieve growth (and diversification) for GE over the years has been mergers and acquisitions. For example, in 2013, GE acquired Lufkin Industries for $3.3 billion. This company provides support equipment for oil and natural gas production industry. In addition, GE has at least $6 to $9 billion in cash to use for additional acquisitions in the near term from its sale of NBC Universal to Comcast. GE is also reversing its strategy of outsourcing to ensure it has the parts needed to fulfill its large amount of backorders of jet engines. For example, it acquired Avio, an Italian parts supplier, for $4.4 billion. It also plans to expand its new vertical integration strategy across its other businesses to provide it more control over the quality and timing of the output.

Sources: 2013, General Electric, 2012, Annual Report, www.ge.com/ar2012/, accessed on April 26; 2013, General Electric: The long game, *Financial Times*, www.ft.com, April 8; M. J. De La Merced, 2013, GE to buy Lufkin Industries for $3.3 billion, *New York Times DealBook*, http://dealbook.nytimes.com, April 8; 2013, The world's most admired companies, *Fortune*, March 18, 137, 142–147; S. Choudhury, 2013, GE expects India business to grow 15%–20%, *Wall Street Journal*, http://wsj. com, February 22; D. Benoit & B. Sechler, 2013, GE has cash for $6 billion to $9 billion in 2013 acquisitions, *Wall Street Journal*, http://wsj.com, February 13; K. Linebaugh, 2013, GE brings engine work back, *Wall Street Journal*, http://wsj.com, February 6; 2013, Jet engines and energy equipment lift profit at GE, *New York Times*, www.nytimes.com, January 18; S. Lohr, 2012, Looking to industry for the next digital disruption, *New York Times*, www.nytimes.com, November 23.

Learn more about Avio, another company acquired by GE.
www.cengagebrain.com

Our discussions of business-level strategies (Chapter 4) and the competitive rivalry and competitive dynamics associated with them (Chapter 5) have concentrated on firms competing in a single industry or product market.[1] In this chapter, we introduce you to corporate-level strategies, which are strategies firms use to *diversify* their operations from a single business competing in a single market into several product markets—most commonly, into several businesses. Thus, a **corporate-level strategy** specifies actions a firm takes to gain a competitive advantage by selecting and managing a group of different businesses competing in different product markets. Corporate-level strategies help companies to select new strategic positions—positions that are expected to increase the firm's value.[2] As explained in the Opening Case, General Electric competes in a number of widely diverse industries. In fact, as the title to the Opening Case suggests, some believe that GE is the classic diversified firm.[3]

As is the case with GE, firms use corporate-level strategies as a means to grow revenues and profits, but there can be additional strategic intents to growth. Firms can pursue defensive or offensive strategies that realize growth but have different strategic intents. Firms can also pursue market development by entering different geographic markets (this approach is discussed in Chapter 8). Firms can acquire competitors (horizontal integration) or buy a supplier or customer (vertical integration). As described in the Opening Case, GE has acquired a supplier of parts for the jet engines it manufactures, thereby increasing its vertical integration in this business. These strategies are discussed in Chapter 7. The basic corporate strategy, the topic of this chapter, focuses on diversification.

The decision to pursue growth is not a risk-free choice for firms. Indeed, as the Opening Case explored, GE experienced difficulty in its media businesses, especially with NBC, which it eventually sold. It also suffered significant revenue declines in its financial services businesses and thus reduced its assets in that area, choosing to seek growth in other businesses such as equipment for the oil industry and equipment for using the industrial Internet. Effective firms carefully evaluate their growth options (including the different corporate-level strategies) before committing firm resources to any of them.

Because the diversified firm operates in several different and unique product markets and likely in several businesses, it forms two types of strategies: corporate-level (or company-wide) and business-level (or competitive).[4] Corporate-level strategy is concerned with two key issues: in what product markets and businesses the firm should compete and how corporate headquarters should manage those businesses.[5] For the diversified company, a business-level strategy (see Chapter 4) must be selected for each of the businesses in which the firm has decided to compete. In this regard, each of GE's product divisions uses different business-level strategies; while most focus on differentiation, its consumer electronics

A **corporate-level strategy** specifies actions a firm takes to gain a competitive advantage by selecting and managing a group of different businesses competing in different product markets.

business has products that compete in market niches to include some that are intended to serve the average income consumer. Thus, cost must also be an issue along with some level of quality.

As is the case with a business-level strategy, a corporate-level strategy is expected to help the firm earn above-average returns by creating value.[6] Some suggest that few corporate-level strategies actually create value.[7] As the Opening Case indicates, realizing value through a corporate strategy can be achieved but it is challenging to do so. In fact, GE is one of the few large, widely diversified firms that has been successful over time.

Evidence suggests that a corporate-level strategy's value is ultimately determined by the degree to which "the businesses in the portfolio are worth more under the management of the company than they would be under any other ownership."[8] Thus, an effective corporate-level strategy creates, across all of a firm's businesses, aggregate returns that exceed what those returns would be without the strategy[9] and contributes to the firm's strategic competitiveness and its ability to earn above-average returns.[10]

Product diversification, a primary form of corporate-level strategies, concerns the scope of the markets and industries in which the firm competes as well as "how managers buy, create and sell different businesses to match skills and strengths with opportunities presented to the firm."[11] Successful diversification is expected to reduce variability in the firm's profitability as earnings are generated from different businesses.[12] Diversification can also provide firms with the flexibility to shift their investments to markets where the greatest returns are possible rather than being dependent on only one or a few markets.[13] Because firms incur development and monitoring costs when diversifying, the ideal portfolio of businesses balances diversification's costs and benefits. CEOs and their top-management teams are responsible for determining the best portfolio for their company.[14]

We begin this chapter by examining different levels of diversification (from low to high). After describing the different reasons firms diversify their operations, we focus on two types of related diversification (related diversification signifies a moderate to high level of diversification for the firm). When properly used, these strategies help create value in the diversified firm, either through the sharing of resources (the related constrained strategy) or the transferring of core competencies across the firm's different businesses (the related linked strategy). We then examine unrelated diversification, which is another corporate-level strategy that can create value. Thereafter, the chapter shifts to the incentives and resources that can stimulate diversification which is value neutral. However, managerial motives to diversify, the final topic in the chapter, can actually destroy some of the firm's value.

6-1   Levels of Diversification

Diversified firms vary according to their level of diversification and the connections between and among their businesses. Figure 6.1 lists and defines five categories of businesses according to increasing levels of diversification. The single and dominant business categories denote no or relatively low levels of diversification; more fully diversified firms are classified into related and unrelated categories. A firm is related through its diversification when its businesses share several links; for example, businesses may share product markets (goods or services), technologies, or distribution channels. The more links among businesses, the more "constrained" is the level of diversification. "Unrelated" refers to the absence of direct links between businesses.

6-1a   Low Levels of Diversification

A firm pursuing a low level of diversification uses either a single-or a dominant-business, corporate-level diversification strategy. A *single-business diversification strategy* is a

Figure 6.1 Levels and Types of Diversification

Low Levels of Diversification

Single business: 95% or more of revenue comes from a single business.

Dominant business: Between 70% and 95% of revenue comes from a single business.

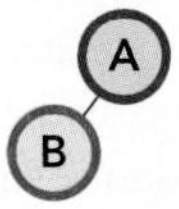

Moderate to High Levels of Diversification

Related constrained: Less than 70% of revenue comes from the dominant business, and all businesses share product, technological, and distribution linkages.

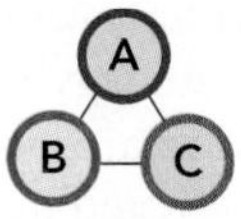

Related linked (mixed related and unrelated):   Less than 70% of revenue comes from the dominant business, and there are only limited links between businesses.

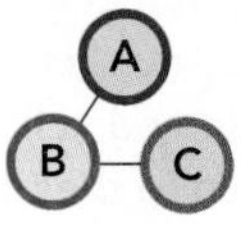

Very High Levels of Diversification

Unrelated: Less than 70% of revenue comes from the dominant business, and there are no common links between businesses.

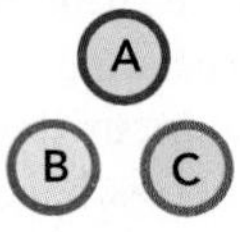

Source: Adapted from R. P. Rumelt, 1974, *Strategy, Structure and Economic Performance*, Boston: Harvard Business School.

corporate-level strategy wherein the firm generates 95 percent or more of its sales revenue from its core business area.[15] For example, Wm. Wrigley Jr. Company, the world's largest producer of chewing and bubble gums, historically used a single-business strategy while operating in relatively few product markets. Wrigley's trademark chewing gum brands include Spearmint, Doublemint, and Juicy Fruit, although the firm produces other products as well. Sugar-free Extra, which currently holds the largest share of the U.S. chewing gum market, was introduced in 1984.

In 2005, Wrigley shifted from its traditional focused strategy when it acquired the confectionary assets of Kraft Foods Inc., including the well-known brands Life Savers and Altoids. As Wrigley expanded, it may have intended to use the dominant-business strategy with the diversification of its product lines beyond gum; however, Wrigley was acquired in 2008 by Mars, a privately held global confection company (the maker of Snickers and M&Ms).[16]

With the *dominant-business diversification strategy*, the firm generates between 70 and 95 percent of its total revenue within a single business area. United Parcel Service (UPS) uses this strategy. Recently UPS generated 61 percent of its revenue from its U.S. package delivery business and 22 percent from its international package business, with the remaining 17 percent coming from the firm's non-package business.[17] Though the U.S. package delivery business currently generates the largest percentage of UPS's sales revenue, the firm anticipates that in the future its other two businesses will account for the majority of revenue growth. This expectation suggests that UPS may become more diversified, both in terms of its goods and services and in the number of countries in which those goods and services are offered.

Firms that focus on one or very few businesses and markets can earn positive returns, because they develop capabilities useful for these markets and can provide superior service to

Strategic Focus

GLOBALIZATION

Sany's Highly Related Core Businesses

A look inside one of Sany's manufacturing facilities. Sany is a global company in the construction machinery industry.

The Sany Heavy Industry Company, Limited is China's largest producer of heavy equipment. In fact, it is the fifth largest producer of this type of equipment globally. Sany's total sales revenue in 2012 was $12.9 billion, well behind industry leader Caterpillar at $65.9 billion. However, Sany has a goal of eventually unseating Caterpillar as the industry leader. Sany plans to achieve $47 billion in annual sales within 10 years. Sany has surpassed Caterpillar as a leader in its Chinese domestic markets.

Sany has four core businesses: (1) cranes, (2) road construction machinery, (3) port machinery, and (4) pumpover machinery. While each is distinct, some similar technologies are used in the production and equipment. Furthermore, similar technologies allow similarities in production processes and equipment for certain parts. Therefore, there is a transfer of knowledge across these businesses. In addition, customers and markets share some similarities because all relate to some form of construction. For this reason, in the United States Sany has become a major sponsor of a Chevrolet on the NASCAR auto racing circuit. Sany America's marketing director, Joe Hanneman, said that research showed NASCAR racing events to be the primary recreation event for people in the U.S. construction industry.

Sany invests 5 percent of its annual sales in R&D to continuously improve the quality of existing products, identify new technologies, and develop new products. Through the end of 2012, Sany held 3,303 patents as a result of its R&D efforts. Indicative of its intent to be a technological leader in its industry, Sany has developed new postdoctoral research centers to attract top research scientists. In 2013, the company was awarded China's National Technology Invention Prize for its "super-length-boom" technology.

Sany continues to grow organically and through acquisitions. For example, in 2012, it acquired Putzmeister, a well-known concrete machine manufacturer. In addition, it has established subsidiaries in many countries, including the United States and Brazil, to enhance its international equipment sales and broaden its market reach. Largely because of its major goal of internationalization, it is moving its corporate headquarters from Changsha to Beijing, for enriched international connections.

Sources: 2013, Sany Heavy industry C. Ltd. Web site, www.sanygroup.com, accessed on April 26; 2013, Yellow Table Survey: Sany ranks no. 5 among construction machinery manufacturers in 2013, China Construction Machinery Online, www.cmbol.com, April 15; M. Barris, 2013, Sany turns to NASCAR to fuel sales, *China Daily*, www.chinadaily.com, April 4; 2013, Awarded National Technology Invention Prize, *Get to Know Sany*, 15th issue, February 15; L. Hooks, P. J. Davis, & N. Munshi, 2013, Caterpillar digs into trouble in China, *Financial Times*, www.ft.com, February 12; J. R. Hagerty & C. Murphy, 2013, Sany tries to gain traction in the U.S., *Wall Street Journal*, http://wsj.com, January 28; 2013, Sany Heavy Industry Co. Ltd: Sany Group's top 10 events in 2012, *$-traders*, www.4-traders.com, January 22; Z. Yangpeng & F. Zhiwei, 2012, Sany to move HQ to Beijing from Changsha, *China Daily*, http://usa.chinadaily.com, November 11.

their customers. Additionally, there are fewer challenges in managing one or a very small set of businesses, allowing them to gain economies of scale and efficiently use their resources.[18] Family-owned and controlled businesses are commonly less diversified. They prefer the focus because the family's reputation is related closely to that of the business. Thus, family members prefer to provide quality goods and services which a focused strategy better allows.[19]

Sany, the company described in the Strategic Focus, might be evaluated by some to be using a single business corporate strategy because of its focus on heavy equipment manufacturing. If this is the case, it has a series of differentiated products and is likely following a product proliferation strategy. A product proliferation strategy represents a form of intra-industry diversification.[20] Yet, Sany also has four business divisions, one for each type of heavy equipment it manufactures. Thus, it might also be considered by some to engage in moderate diversification in the form of highly related constrained diversification.

6-1b Moderate and High Levels of Diversification

A firm generating more than 30 percent of its revenue outside a dominant business and whose businesses are related to each other in some manner uses a related diversification corporate-level strategy. When the links between the diversified firm's businesses are rather direct, it is a *related constrained diversification strategy*. Campbell Soup, Procter & Gamble, and Merck & Company all use a related constrained strategy. With a related constrained strategy, a firm shares resources and activities across its businesses.

For example, the Publicis Groupe uses a related constrained strategy, deriving value from the potential synergy across its various groups, especially the digital capabilities in its advertising business. Given its recent performance, the related constrained strategy has created value for Publicis customers and its shareholders.[21]

The diversified company with a portfolio of businesses that have only a few links between them is called a mixed related and unrelated firm and is using the *related linked diversification strategy* (see Figure 6.1). As displayed in the Opening Case, GE uses a related-linked corporate-level diversification strategy. Compared with related constrained firms, related linked firms share fewer resources and assets between their businesses, concentrating instead on transferring knowledge and core competencies between the businesses. GE has four strategic business units (see Chapter 11 for a definition of SBUs) it calls "divisions," each composed of related businesses. There are no relationships across the strategic business units, only within them. As with firms using each type of diversification strategy, companies implementing the related linked strategy constantly adjust the mix in their portfolio of businesses as well as make decisions about how to manage these businesses.[22] Managing a diversified firm such as GE is highly challenging, but GE appears to have been well managed over the years given its success.

A highly diversified firm that has no relationships between its businesses follows an *unrelated diversification strategy*. United Technologies, Textron, Samsung, and Hutchison Whampoa Limited (HWL) are examples of firms using this type of corporate-level strategy. Commonly, firms using this strategy are called *conglomerates*. HWL is a leading international corporation with five core businesses: ports and related services; property and hotels; retail; energy, infrastructure, investments and others; and telecommunications. These businesses are not related to each other, and the firm makes no efforts to share activities or to transfer core competencies between or among them. Each of these five businesses is quite large; for example, the retailing arm of the retail and manufacturing business has more than 9,300 stores in 33 countries. Groceries, cosmetics, electronics, wine, and airline tickets are some of the product categories featured in these stores. This firm's size and diversity suggest the challenge of successfully managing the unrelated diversification strategy. However, Hutchison's CEO Li Ka-shing has been successful at not only making smart acquisitions, but also at divesting businesses with good timing.[23]

6-2 Reasons for Diversification

A firm uses a corporate-level diversification strategy for a variety of reasons (see Table 6.1). Typically, a diversification strategy is used to increase the firm's value by improving its overall performance. Value is created either through related diversification or through unrelated diversification when the strategy allows a company's businesses to increase revenues or reduce costs while implementing their business-level strategies.[24]

Other reasons for using a diversification strategy may have nothing to do with increasing the firm's value; in fact, diversification can have neutral effects or even reduce a firm's value. Value-neutral reasons for diversification include a desire to match and thereby neutralize a competitor's market power (such as to neutralize another firm's advantage by acquiring a similar distribution outlet). Decisions to expand a firm's portfolio of businesses to reduce managerial risk can have a negative effect on the firm's value. Greater amounts of diversification reduce managerial risk in that if one of the businesses in a diversified firm fails, the top executive of that business does not risk total failure by the corporation. As such, this reduces the top executives' employment risk. In addition, because diversification can increase a firm's size and thus managerial compensation, managers have motives to diversify a firm to a level that reduces its value.[25] Diversification rationales that may have a neutral or negative effect on the firm's value are discussed later in the chapter.

Operational relatedness and corporate relatedness are two ways diversification strategies can create value (see Figure 6.2). Studies of these independent relatedness dimensions show the importance of resources and key competencies.[26] The figure's vertical dimension depicts opportunities to share operational activities between businesses (operational relatedness) while the horizontal dimension suggests opportunities for transferring corporate-level core competencies (corporate relatedness). The firm with a strong capability in managing

Table 6.1 Reasons for Diversification

Value-Creating Diversification
• Economies of scope (related diversification)
• Sharing activities
• Transferring core competencies
• Market power (related diversification)
• Blocking competitors through multipoint competition
• Vertical integration
• Financial economies (unrelated diversification)
• Efficient internal capital allocation
• Business restructuring
Value-Neutral Diversification
• Antitrust regulation
• Tax laws
• Low performance
• Uncertain future cash flows
• Risk reduction for firm
• Tangible resources
• Intangible resources
Value-Reducing Diversification
• Diversifying managerial employment risk
• Increasing managerial compensation

Figure 6.2 Value-Creating Diversification Strategies: Operational and Corporate Relatedness

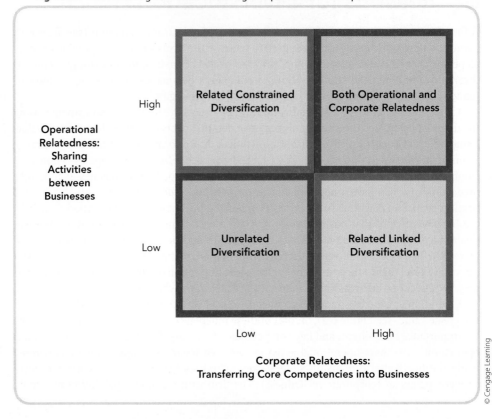

© Cengage Learning

operational synergy, especially in sharing assets between its businesses, falls in the upper left quadrant, which also represents vertical sharing of assets through vertical integration. The lower right quadrant represents a highly developed corporate capability for transferring one or more core competencies across businesses.

This capability is located primarily in the corporate headquarters office. Unrelated diversification is also illustrated in Figure 6.2 in the lower-left quadrant. Financial economies (discussed later), rather than either operational or corporate relatedness, are the source of value creation for firms using the unrelated diversification strategy.

6-3 Value-Creating Diversification: Related Constrained and Related Linked Diversification

Economies of scope are cost savings that the firm creates by successfully sharing some of its resources and capabilities or transferring one or more corporate-level core competencies that were developed in one of its businesses to another of its businesses.

With the related diversification corporate-level strategy, the firm builds upon or extends its resources and capabilities to build a competitive advantage by creating value for customers.[27] The company using the related diversification strategy wants to develop and exploit economies of scope between its businesses.[28] In fact, even nonprofit organizations have found that carefully planned and implemented related diversification can provide value to them.[29] Available to companies operating in multiple product markets or industries, **economies of scope** are cost savings that the firm creates by successfully sharing some of its resources and capabilities or transferring one or more corporate-level core competencies that were developed in one of its businesses to another of its businesses.[30]

As illustrated in Figure 6.2, firms seek to create value from economies of scope through two basic kinds of operational economies: sharing activities (operational relatedness) and transferring corporate-level core competencies (corporate relatedness). The difference between sharing activities and transferring competencies is based on how separate resources are jointly used to create economies of scope. To create economies of scope tangible resources, such as plant and equipment or other business-unit physical assets, often must be shared. Less tangible resources, such as manufacturing know-how and technological capabilities, can also be shared.[31] However, know-how transferred between separate activities with no physical or tangible resource involved is a transfer of a corporate-level core competence, not an operational sharing of activities.[32]

6-3a Operational Relatedness: Sharing Activities

Firms can create operational relatedness by sharing either a primary activity (such as inventory delivery systems) or a support activity (such as purchasing practices)—see Chapter 3's discussion of the value chain. Firms using the related constrained diversification strategy share activities in order to create value. Procter & Gamble uses this corporate-level strategy. Sany, described in the Strategic Focus, also shares activities. For example, its various businesses share marketing activities because all of their equipment is sold to firms in the construction industry. This is evidenced by the sponsorship of an auto in NASCAR in an attempt to reach executives in the construction industry.

Activity sharing is also risky because ties among a firm's businesses create links between outcomes. For instance, if demand for one business's product is reduced, it may not generate sufficient revenues to cover the fixed costs required to operate the shared facilities. These types of organizational difficulties can reduce activity-sharing success. Additionally, activity sharing requires careful coordination between the businesses involved. The coordination challenges must be managed effectively for the appropriate sharing of activities.[33]

Although activity sharing across businesses is not risk-free, research shows that it can create value. For example, studies of acquisitions of firms in the same industry (horizontal acquisitions), such as the banking industry and software, found that sharing resources and activities and thereby creating economies of scope contributed to post-acquisition increases in performance and higher returns to shareholders.[34] Additionally, firms that sold off related units in which resource sharing was a possible source of economies of scope have been found to produce lower returns than those that sold off businesses unrelated to the firm's core business.[35] Still other research discovered that firms with closely related businesses have lower risk.[36] These results suggest that gaining economies of scope by sharing activities across a firm's businesses may be important in reducing risk and in creating value. Further, more attractive results are obtained through activity sharing when a strong corporate headquarters office facilitates it.[37]

Corporate-level core competencies are complex sets of resources and capabilities that link different businesses, primarily through managerial and technological knowledge, experience, and expertise.

6-3b Corporate Relatedness: Transferring of Core Competencies

Over time, the firm's intangible resources, such as its know-how, become the foundation of core competencies. **Corporate-level core competencies** are complex sets of resources and capabilities that link different businesses, primarily through

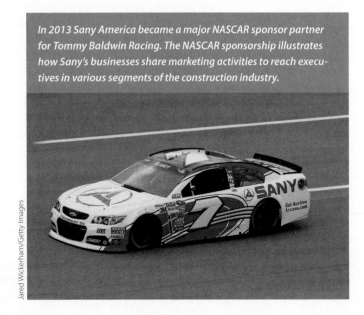

In 2013 Sany America became a major NASCAR sponsor partner for Tommy Baldwin Racing. The NASCAR sponsorship illustrates how Sany's businesses share marketing activities to reach executives in various segments of the construction industry.

Jared Wickerham/Getty Images

managerial and technological knowledge, experience, and expertise.[38] Firms seeking to create value through corporate relatedness use the related linked diversification strategy as exemplified by GE.

In at least two ways, the related linked diversification strategy helps firms to create value.[39] First, because the expense of developing a core competence has already been incurred in one of the firm's businesses, transferring this competence to a second business eliminates the need for that business to allocate resources to develop it. Resource intangibility is a second source of value creation through corporate relatedness. Intangible resources are difficult for competitors to understand and imitate. Because of this difficulty, the unit receiving a transferred corporate-level competence often gains an immediate competitive advantage over its rivals.[40]

A number of firms have successfully transferred one or more corporate-level core competencies across their businesses. Virgin Group Ltd. transfers its marketing core competence across airlines, cosmetics, music, drinks, mobile phones, health clubs, and a number of other businesses.[41] Honda has developed and transferred its competence in engine design and manufacturing among its businesses making products such as motorcycles, lawnmowers, and cars and trucks. Company officials state that Honda is a major manufacturer of engines and is focused on providing products for all forms of human mobility.[42]

One way managers facilitate the transfer of corporate-level core competencies is by moving key people into new management positions.[43] However, the manager of an older business may be reluctant to transfer key people who have accumulated knowledge and experience critical to the business's success. Thus, managers with the ability to facilitate the transfer of a core competence may come at a premium, or the key people involved may not want to transfer. Additionally, the top-level managers from the transferring business may not want the competencies transferred to a new business to fulfill the firm's diversification objectives.[44] Research also suggests too much dependence on outsourcing can lower the usefulness of core competencies and thereby reduce their useful transferability to other business units in the diversified firm.[45]

6-3c Market Power

Firms using a related diversification strategy may gain market power when successfully using a related constrained or related linked strategy. **Market power** exists when a firm is able to sell its products above the existing competitive level or to reduce the costs of its primary and support activities below the competitive level, or both.[46] Mars' acquisition of the Wrigley assets was part of its related constrained diversification strategy and added market share to the Mars/Wrigley integrated firm, as it realized 14.4 percent of the market share. This catapulted Mars/Wrigley above Cadbury and Nestle, which had 10.1 and 7.7 percent of the market share, respectively, at the time and left Hershey with only 5.5 percent of the market.[47]

As explained in the Strategic Focus, Ericsson has the largest share of the global market in telecommunications equipment, and for many years its leadership position has afforded the company considerable market power. That market power and its leadership position in research helped it garner major contracts in 2012 for telecommunications equipment from the four largest providers of mobile broadband networks in the United States (Verizon, AT&T, Sprint, and T-Mobile).[48]

In addition to efforts to gain scale as a means of increasing market power, firms can create market power through multipoint competition and vertical integration. **Multipoint competition** exists when two or more diversified firms simultaneously compete in the same product areas or geographic markets.[49] The actions taken by UPS and FedEx in two markets, overnight delivery and ground shipping, illustrate multipoint competition. UPS moved into overnight delivery, FedEx's stronghold; in turn, FedEx bought trucking and ground shipping assets to move into ground shipping, UPS's stronghold. Moreover, geographic

Market power exists when a firm is able to sell its products above the existing competitive level or to reduce the costs of its primary and support activities below the competitive level, or both.

Multipoint competition exists when two or more diversified firms simultaneously compete in the same product areas or geographical markets.

Strategic Focus

TECHNOLOGY

Ericsson's Substantial Market Power

Ericsson offices, Mississauga, Ontario, Canada. One of the ways Ericsson retains its market power is through significant investments in research and development.

Ericsson was founded in 1876 as a shop to repair telegraph equipment in Sweden. From that humble beginning, it has grown into the largest global manufacturer of equipment for mobile telecommunications networks. In 2012, it had a 38 percent share of the global market for telecommunications equipment. It has a presence in more than 180 countries and its business unit support systems provide charging and billing service for 1.6 billion people. Ericsson also holds the largest market share in global services.

Ericsson has three primary businesses: business unit networks, business unit support systems, and business unit global services. Until 2012, it also had a "devices" business unit, which was a joint venture with Sony to produce mobile phones, as well as accessories and PC cards. However, this is a highly competitive market with Apple's iPhones as well as strong-selling smartphones from Samsung, Nokia, and others. So, Ericsson sold its portion of this business to Sony. Although each of the other three business units represents a separate business market, they are complementary; because of this, Ericsson creates synergy across them. They are highly interrelated, so Ericsson uses the related-constrained diversification strategy to create synergy across the business units and thereby achieve greater market power.

Ericsson has several strong competitors, but the two primary ones are Huawei and Samsung. Huawei now holds the second largest market share in telecommunications equipment. Ericsson

and Huawei's total corporate sales revenues are very similar but they serve a few distinct markets. For example, Huawei has major sales in smartphones and corporate communications grids, while 43 percent of Ericsson's sales come from managing wireless networks. However, Huawei's sales in telecommunications equipment are growing.

One way Ericsson is fighting the competition is through major investments in research and development. This research is designed to develop new technologies and products to help Ericsson maintain its competitive advantage. For example, Ericsson's researchers predict that 5G wireless access will be needed by 2020. The R&D scientists are also targeting the development of a federated networked cloud to provide such services as computation, storage, and networking. Finally, they are working on the development of 3D visual communications. Therefore, the market leader intends to maintain its market power by sustaining its competitive advantage.

Sources: 2013, Ericsson Annual Report 2012, Ericsson, www.ericsson.com, accessed April 26; 2013, Ericsson, Wikipedia, http://en.wikipedia.org/wiki/ericsson, accessed April 26; 2013, What's next in Ericsson research, Ericsson Web site, www.ericsson. com, accessed April 26; K. J. O'Brien, 2013, Ericsson finds a Chinese rival hot on its wheels, *New York Times*, www.nytimes.com, February 24; B. McCarthy & D. Thomas, 2013, Ericsson shows signs of recovery, *Financial Times*, www.ft.com, January 31; 2012, Samsung hits back at Ericsson with its own request for U.S. import ban over wireless patents, Foss patents, www.fosspatents.com, December 24.

competition for markets increases. The strongest shipping company in Europe is DHL. All three competitors (UPS, FedEx, and DHL) entered large foreign markets to either gain a stake or to expand their existing share. If one of these firms successfully gains strong positions in several markets while competing against its rivals, its market power will increase. Interestingly, DHL had to exit the U.S. market because it was too difficult to compete against UPS and FedEx, which are dominant there.

Some firms using a related diversification strategy engage in vertical integration to gain market power. **Vertical integration** exists when a company produces its own inputs (backward integration) or owns its own source of output distribution (forward integration). In some instances, firms partially integrate their operations, producing and selling their products by using company businesses as well as outside sources.[50]

Vertical integration is commonly used in the firm's core business to gain market power over rivals. Market power is gained as the firm develops the ability to save on its operations, avoid market costs, improve product quality, possibly protect its technology from imitation by rivals, and potentially exploit underlying capabilities in the marketplace. Vertically integrated firms are better able to improve product quality and improve or create new technologies than specialized firms because they have access to more information and knowledge that are complementary.[51] Market power also is created when firms have strong ties between their assets for which no market prices exist. Establishing a market price would result in high search and transaction costs, so firms seek to vertically integrate rather than remain separate businesses.[52]

Vertical integration has its limitations. For example, an outside supplier may produce the product at a lower cost. As a result, internal transactions from vertical integration may be expensive and reduce profitability relative to competitors.[53] Also, bureaucratic costs can be present with vertical integration.[54] Because vertical integration can require substantial investments in specific technologies, it may reduce the firm's flexibility, especially when technology changes quickly. Finally, changes in demand create capacity balance and coordination problems. If one business is building a part for another internal business but achieving economies of scale requires the first division to manufacture quantities that are beyond the capacity of the internal buyer to absorb, it would be necessary to sell the parts outside the firm as well as to the internal business. Thus, although vertical integration can create value, especially through market power over competitors, it is not without risks and costs.[55]

Around the turn of the twenty-first century, de-integration became the focus of most manufacturing firms, such as Intel and Dell, and even some large auto companies, such as Ford and General Motors, as they developed independent supplier networks.[56] Flextronics, an electronics contract manufacturer, is a large contract manufacturer that helps to support this approach to supply-chain management.[57] Such firms often manage their customers' entire product lines and offer services ranging from inventory management to delivery and after-sales service. Interestingly, however, some firms are beginning to reintegrate in order to gain better control over the quality and timing of their supplies. The opening case described GE's actions to reintegrate some areas of their businesses (e.g., manufacture of jet engines) to ensure that they could meet their contractual obligations in the delivery of the goods.

6-3d Simultaneous Operational Relatedness and Corporate Relatedness

As Figure 6.2 suggests, some firms simultaneously seek operational and corporate relatedness to create economies of scope.[58] The ability to simultaneously create economies of scope by sharing activities (operational relatedness) and transferring core competencies (corporate relatedness) is difficult for competitors to understand and learn how to imitate. However, if the cost of realizing both types of relatedness is not offset by the benefits created, the result is diseconomies because the cost of organization and incentive structure is very expensive.[59]

Vertical integration
exists when a company produces its own inputs (backward integration) or owns its own source of output distribution (forward integration).

M. Stasy

Walt Disney Co. uses a related diversification strategy to simultaneously create economies of scope through operational and corporate relatedness. Disney has five separate but related businesses: Media Networks, Parks and Resorts, Studio Entertainment, Consumer Products, and Interactive Media. Within the firm's Studio Entertainment business, for example, Disney can gain economies of scope by sharing activities among its different movie distribution companies, such as Touchstone Pictures, Hollywood Pictures, and Dimension Films. Broad and deep knowledge about its customers is a capability on which Disney relies to develop corporate-level core competencies in terms of advertising and marketing. With these competencies, Disney is able to create economies of scope through corporate relatedness as it cross-sells products that are highlighted in its movies through the distribution channels that are part of its Parks and Resorts and Consumer Products businesses. Thus, characters created in movies become figures that are marketed through Disney's retail stores (which are part of the Consumer Products business). In addition, themes established in movies become the source of new rides in the firm's theme parks, which are part of the Parks and Resorts business, and provide themes for clothing and other retail business products.[60]

Thus, Walt Disney Co. has been able to successfully use related diversification as a corporate-level strategy through which it creates economies of scope by sharing some activities and by transferring core competencies. However, it can be difficult for investors to identify the value created by a firm (such as Walt Disney Co.) as it shares activities and transfers core competencies. For this reason, the value of the assets of a firm using a diversification strategy to create economies of scope often is discounted by investors.

Strategy Right NOW

Learn more about vertical integration.
www.cengagebrain.com

6-4 Unrelated Diversification

Firms do not seek either operational relatedness or corporate relatedness when using the unrelated diversification corporate-level strategy. An unrelated diversification strategy (see Figure 6.2) can create value through two types of financial economies. **Financial economies** are cost savings realized through improved allocations of financial resources based on investments inside or outside the firm.[61]

Financial economies are cost savings realized through improved allocations of financial resources based on investments inside or outside the firm.

Efficient internal capital allocations can lead to financial economies. Efficient internal capital allocations reduce risk among the firm's businesses—for example, by leading to the development of a portfolio of businesses with different risk profiles. The second type of financial economy concerns the restructuring of acquired assets. Here, the diversified firm buys another company, restructures that company's assets in ways that allow it to operate more profitably, and then sells the company for a profit in the external market.[62] Next, we discuss the two types of financial economies in greater detail.

The renowned Hollywood sign in Los Angeles, California. Walt Disney Co. uses a related diversification strategy to create economies of scope by sharing activities and transferring core competencies among its entertainment-focused businesses.

© Dan Breckwoldt/Shutterstock.com

6-4a Efficient Internal Capital Market Allocation

In a market economy, capital markets are believed to efficiently allocate capital. Efficiency results as investors take equity

M. Stasy

positions (ownership) with high expected future cash-flow values. Capital is also allocated through debt as shareholders and debt holders try to improve the value of their investments by taking stakes in businesses with high growth and profitability prospects.

In large diversified firms, the corporate headquarters office distributes capital to its businesses to create value for the overall corporation. The nature of these distributions can generate gains from internal capital market allocations that exceed the gains that would accrue to shareholders as a result of capital being allocated by the external capital market.[63] Because those in a firm's corporate headquarters generally have access to detailed and accurate information regarding the actual and potential future performance of the company's portfolio of businesses, they have the best information to make capital distribution decisions.

Compared with corporate office personnel, external investors have relatively limited access to internal information and can only estimate the performances of individual businesses as well as their future prospects. Moreover, although businesses seeking capital must provide information to potential suppliers (such as banks or insurance companies), firms with internal capital markets can have at least two informational advantages. First, information provided to capital markets through annual reports and other sources may not include negative information, instead emphasizing positive prospects and outcomes. External sources of capital have a limited ability to understand the operational dynamics within large organizations. Even external shareholders who have access to information are unlikely to receive full and complete disclosure.[64] Second, although a firm must disseminate information, that information also becomes simultaneously available to the firm's current and potential competitors. With insights gained by studying such information, competitors might attempt to duplicate a firm's value-creating strategy. Thus, an ability to efficiently allocate capital through an internal market helps the firm protect the competitive advantages it develops while using its corporate-level strategy as well as its various business-unit–level strategies.

If intervention from outside the firm is required to make corrections to capital allocations, only significant changes are possible because the power to make changes by outsiders is often indirect (e.g., through members of the board of directors). External parties can try to make changes by forcing the firm into bankruptcy or changing the top management team. Alternatively, in an internal capital market, the corporate headquarters office can fine-tune its corrections, such as choosing to adjust managerial incentives or encouraging strategic changes in one of the firm's businesses.[65] Thus, capital can be allocated according to more specific criteria than is possible with external market allocations. Because it has less accurate information, the external capital market may fail to allocate resources adequately to high-potential investments. The corporate headquarters office of a diversified company can more effectively perform such tasks as disciplining underperforming management teams through resource allocations.[66] GE (discussed in the Opening Case) has done an exceptionally good job of allocating capital across its many businesses. Although a related linked firm, it differentially allocates capital across its four major strategic business units. Although GE Capital produced the high returns for GE over the last few decades, it received a healthy amount of capital from internal allocations. However, as described in the case, its performance has suffered in recent years, and GE has reduced the resources provided to this business (increasing the resources for other businesses such as energy).

Large, highly diversified businesses often face what is known as the "conglomerate discount." This discount results from analysts not knowing how to value a vast array of large businesses with complex financial reports. To overcome this discount, many unrelated diversified or industrial conglomerates have sought to convince investors that the company is strong and will produce strong returns. For instance, United Technologies increased the dividend it paid to shareholders and divested some businesses that were not related closely to one of its five businesses. The CEO's letter to shareholders in the 2012 Annual Report suggested that these changes along with an acquisition of businesses complementary to its current portfolio and the new corporate structure implemented in 2011 would return the company to double-digit growth in the near term.[67] In spite of the challenges associated with it, a number of corporations continue to use the unrelated diversification strategy, especially in Europe and in emerging markets. As an example, Siemens is a large diversified German conglomerate that engages in substantial diversification in order to balance its economic risk. In economic downturns, diversification can help some companies improve future performance.[68]

The Achilles' heel for firms using the unrelated diversification strategy in a developed economy is that competitors can imitate financial economies more easily than they can replicate the value gained from the economies of scope developed through operational relatedness and corporate relatedness. This issue is less of a problem in emerging economies, in which the absence of a "soft infrastructure" (including effective financial intermediaries, sound regulations, and contract laws) supports and encourages use of the unrelated diversification strategy.[69] In fact, in emerging economies such as those in Korea, India, and Chile, research has shown that diversification increases the performance of firms affiliated with large diversified business groups.[70]

6-4b Restructuring of Assets

Financial economies can also be created when firms learn how to create value by buying, restructuring, and then selling the restructured companies' assets in the external market.[71] As in the real estate business, buying assets at low prices, restructuring them, and selling them at a price that exceeds their cost generates a positive return on the firm's invested capital.

Unrelated diversified companies that pursue this strategy try to create financial economies by acquiring and restructuring other companies' assets but it involves significant trade-offs. For example, Danaher's success requires a focus on mature manufacturing businesses because of the uncertainty of demand for high-technology products. It has acquired 400 businesses since 1984 and applied the Danaher Business System to reduce costs and create a lean organization.[72] In high-technology businesses, resource allocation decisions are highly complex, often creating information-processing overload on the small corporate headquarters offices that are common in unrelated diversified firms. High-technology businesses are often human-resource dependent; these people can leave or demand higher pay and thus appropriate or deplete the value of an acquired firm.[73]

Buying and then restructuring service-based assets so they can be profitably sold in the external market is also difficult. Thus, for both high-technology firms and service-based companies, relatively few tangible assets can be restructured to create value and sell profitably. It is difficult to restructure intangible assets such as human capital and effective relationships that have evolved over time between buyers (customers) and sellers (firm personnel). Ideally, executives will follow a strategy of buying businesses when prices are lower, such as in the midst of a recession, and selling them at late stages in an expansion.[74] Because of the increases in global economic activity, including more cross-border acquisitions, there is also a growing number of foreign divestitures and restructuring in internal markets (e.g., partial or full privatization of state-owned enterprises). Foreign divestitures are even more complex than domestic ones and must be managed carefully.[75]

6-5 Value-Neutral Diversification: Incentives and Resources

The objectives firms seek when using related diversification and unrelated diversification strategies all have the potential to help the firm create value through the corporate-level strategy. However, these strategies, as well as single-and dominant-business diversification strategies, are sometimes used with objectives that are value-neutral. Different incentives to diversify sometimes exist, and the quality of the firm's resources may permit only diversification that is value neutral rather than value creating.

6-5a Incentives to Diversify

Incentives to diversify come from both the external environment and a firm's internal environment. External incentives include antitrust regulations and tax laws. Internal incentives include low performance, uncertain future cash flows, and the pursuit of synergy and reduction of risk for the firm.

Antitrust Regulation and Tax Laws

Government antitrust policies and tax laws provided incentives for U.S. firms to diversify in the 1960s and 1970s.[76] Antitrust laws prohibiting mergers that created increased market power (via either vertical or horizontal integration) were stringently enforced during that period.[77] Merger activity that produced conglomerate diversification was encouraged primarily by the Celler-Kefauver Antimerger Act (1950), which discouraged horizontal and vertical mergers. As a result, many of the mergers during the 1960s and 1970s were "conglomerate" in character, involving companies pursuing different lines of business. Between 1973 and 1977, 79.1 percent of all mergers were conglomerate in nature.[78]

During the 1980s, antitrust enforcement lessened, resulting in more and larger horizontal mergers (acquisitions of target firms in the same line of business, such as a merger between two oil companies).[79] In addition, investment bankers became more open to the kinds of mergers facilitated by regulation changes; as a consequence, takeovers increased to unprecedented numbers.[80] The conglomerates, or highly diversified firms, of the 1960s and 1970s became more "focused" in the 1980s and early 1990s as merger constraints were relaxed and restructuring was implemented.[81]

In the 2000s, antitrust concerns emerged again with the large volume of mergers and acquisitions (see Chapter 7).[82] Mergers are now receiving more scrutiny than they did in the 1980s, 1990s, and the first decade of the 2000s.[83]

The tax effects of diversification stem not only from corporate tax changes, but also from individual tax rates. Some companies (especially mature ones) generate more cash from their operations than they can reinvest profitably. Some argue that *free cash flows* (liquid financial assets for which investments in current businesses are no longer economically viable) should be redistributed to shareholders as dividends.[84] However, in the 1960s and 1970s, dividends were taxed more heavily than were capital gains. As a result, before 1980, shareholders preferred that firms use free cash flows to buy and build companies in high-performance industries. If the firm's stock value appreciated over the long term, shareholders might receive a better return on those funds than if the funds had been redistributed as dividends, because returns from stock sales would be taxed more lightly than would dividends.

Google CEO Larry Page testifies at a U.S. Senate hearing on antitrust policy.

Bloomberg/Getty Images

Under the 1986 Tax Reform Act, however, the top individual ordinary income tax rate was reduced from 50 to 28 percent, and the special capital gains tax was changed to treat capital gains as ordinary income. These changes created an incentive for shareholders to stop encouraging firms to retain funds for purposes of diversification. These tax law changes also influenced an increase in divestitures of unrelated business units after 1984. Thus, while individual tax rates for capital gains and dividends created a shareholder incentive to increase diversification before 1986, they encouraged lower diversification after 1986, unless it was funded by tax-deductible debt. Yet, there have been changes in the maximum individual tax rates since the 1980s. The top individual tax rate has varied from 31 percent in 1992 to 39.6 percent in 2013. There have also been some changes in the capital gains tax rates.

Corporate tax laws also affect diversification. Acquisitions typically increase a firm's depreciable asset allowances. Increased depreciation (a non-cash-flow expense) produces lower taxable income, thereby providing an additional incentive for acquisitions. At one time, acquisitions were an attractive means for securing tax benefits, but changes recommended by the Financial Accounting Standards Board eliminated the "pooling of interests" method to account for the acquired firm's assets. It also eliminated the write-off for research and development in process, and thus reduced some of the incentives to make acquisitions, especially acquisitions in related high-technology industries (these changes are discussed further in Chapter 7).[85]

Thus, regulatory changes such as the ones we have described create incentives or disincentives for diversification. Interestingly, European antitrust laws have historically been stricter regarding horizontal mergers than those in the United States, but recently have become more similar.[86]

Low Performance

Some research shows that low returns are related to greater levels of diversification.[87] If high performance eliminates the need for greater diversification, then low performance may provide an incentive for diversification. In 2005, eBay acquired Skype for $3.1 billion in hopes that it would create synergies and improve communication between buyers and sellers. However, within three years, eBay decided to sell Skype because it has failed to increase cash flow for its core e-commerce business and the expected synergies were not realized. In 2011, eBay sold Skype to Microsoft for $8.5 billion. Although analysts thought the premium paid by Microsoft may have been too high, one review in the *Financial Times* suggested that Skype could play a prominent role in Microsoft's multimedia strategy. Thus, the potential synergies between Skype and Microsoft may be greater than those with eBay.[88] The poor performance may be because of errors made by top managers (such as eBay's original acquisition of Skype), and that lead to divestitures similar to eBay's action.[89]

Research evidence and the experience of a number of firms suggest that an overall curvilinear relationship, as illustrated in Figure 6.3, may exist between diversification and performance.[90] Although low performance can be an incentive to diversify, firms that are more broadly diversified compared to their competitors may have overall lower performance.

Uncertain Future Cash Flows

As a firm's product line matures or is threatened, diversification may be an important defensive strategy.[91] Small firms and companies in mature or maturing industries sometimes find it necessary to diversify for long-term survival.[92]

Diversifying into other product markets or into other businesses can reduce the uncertainty about a firm's future cash flows. Merck decided to expand into the biosimilars business (production of drugs that are similar to approved drugs) in hopes of stimulating its prescription drug business due to lower expected results as many of its drug patents expire.[93] Thus, in 2009 it purchased Insmed's portfolio of follow-on biologics for $130 million. It will

Figure 6.3 The Curvilinear Relationship between Diversification and Performance

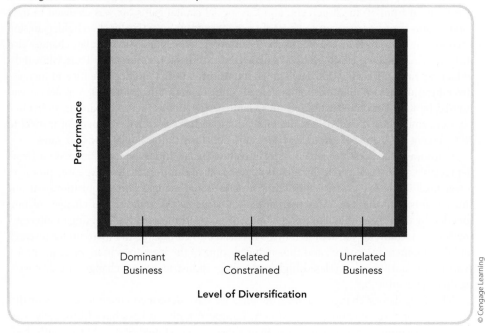

carry out the development of biologics that prevent infections in cancer patients receiving chemotherapy. One such drug, INS-19, is in late-stage trials, while INS-20 is in early-stage development.[94]

Synergy and Firm Risk Reduction

Diversified firms pursuing economies of scope often have investments that are too inflexible to realize synergy between business units. As a result, a number of problems may arise. **Synergy** exists when the value created by business units working together exceeds the value that those same units create working independently. However, as a firm increases its relatedness between business units, it also increases its risk of corporate failure because synergy produces joint interdependence between businesses that constrains the firm's flexibility to respond. This threat may force two basic decisions.

First, the firm may reduce its level of technological change by operating in environments that are more certain. This behavior may make the firm risk averse and thus uninterested in pursuing new product lines that have potential but are not proven. Alternatively, the firm may constrain its level of activity sharing and forgo potential benefits of synergy. Either or both decisions may lead to further diversification.[95] The former will likely lead to related diversification into industries in which more certainty exists[96] while the latter may produce additional, but unrelated, diversification. Research suggests that a firm using a related diversification strategy is more careful in bidding for new businesses, whereas a firm pursuing an unrelated diversification strategy may be more likely to overprice its bid because an unrelated bidder is less likely to have full information about the acquired firm.[97] However, firms using either a related or an unrelated diversification strategy must understand the consequences of paying large premiums.[98] These problems often cause managers to become more risk averse and focus on achieving short-term returns. When they do, they are less likely to be concerned about social problems and in making long-term investments (e.g., to develop innovation). Alternatively, diversified firms (related and unrelated) can be innovative.[99]

Synergy exists when the value created by business units working together exceeds the value that those same units create working independently.

© Cengage Learning

6-5b **Resources and Diversification**

As already discussed, firms may have several value-neutral incentives as well as value-creating incentives (such as the ability to create economies of scope) to diversify. However, even when incentives to diversify exist, a firm must have the types and levels of resources and capabilities needed to successfully use a corporate-level diversification strategy.[100] Although both tangible and intangible resources facilitate diversification, they vary in their ability to create value. Indeed, the degree to which resources are valuable, rare, difficult to imitate, and nonsubstitutable (see Chapter 3) influences a firm's ability to create value through diversification. For instance, free cash flows are a tangible financial resource that may be used to diversify the firm. However, compared with diversification that is grounded in intangible resources, diversification based on financial resources only is more visible to competitors and thus more imitable and less likely to create value on a long-term basis.[101] Tangible resources usually include the plant and equipment necessary to produce a product and tend to be less-flexible assets. Any excess capacity often can be used only for closely related products, especially those requiring highly similar manufacturing technologies. For example, large computer makers such as Dell and Hewlett-Packard have underestimated the demand for tablet computers, especially Apple's iPad. Apple developed the iPad and many expect it to eventually replace the personal computer (PC). In fact, HP's and Dell's sales of their PCs have been declining since the introduction of the iPad. Apple sold 42.4 million iPads in in the last quarter of 2012 and the first quarter of 2013. Samsung and competitors have developed rival pads and are selling a considerable number. Most analysts believe that the days of the personal computer are numbered, suggesting that Dell and HP must diversify into other product lines to make up for the loss of revenue from laptop sales.[102]

Excess capacity of other tangible resources, such as a sales force, can be used to diversify more easily. Again, excess capacity in a sales force is more effective with related diversification, because it may be utilized to sell products in similar markets (e.g., same customers). The sales force would be more knowledgeable about related product characteristics, customers, and distribution channels.[103] Tangible resources may create resource interrelationships in production, marketing, procurement, and technology, defined earlier as activity sharing. Intangible resources are more flexible than tangible physical assets in facilitating diversification. Although the sharing of tangible resources may induce diversification, intangible resources such as tacit knowledge could encourage even more diversification.[104]

Sometimes, however, the benefits expected from using resources to diversify the firm for either value-creating or value-neutral reasons are not gained.[105] For example, Sara Lee executives found that they could not realize synergy between elements of their company's diversified portfolio, and subsequently shed businesses accounting for 40 percent of company revenue to focus on food and food-related products and more readily achieve synergy.[106]

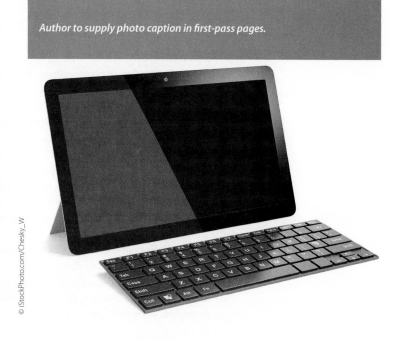

Author to supply photo caption in first-pass pages.

© iStockPhoto.com/Chesky_W

6-6 Value-Reducing Diversification: Managerial Motives to Diversify

Managerial motives to diversify can exist independent of value-neutral reasons (i.e., incentives and resources) and value-creating reasons (e.g., economies of scope). The desire for increased compensation and reduced managerial risk are two motives for top-level executives to diversify their firm beyond value-creating and value-neutral levels.[107] In slightly different words, top-level executives may diversify a firm in order to diversify their own employment risk, as long as profitability does not suffer excessively.[108]

Diversification provides additional benefits to top-level managers that shareholders do not enjoy. Research evidence shows that diversification and firm size are highly correlated, and as firm size increases, so does executive compensation.[109] Because large firms are complex, difficult-to-manage organizations, top-level managers commonly receive substantial levels of compensation to lead them, but the amounts vary across countries.[110] Greater levels of diversification can increase a firm's complexity, resulting in still more compensation for executives to lead an increasingly diversified organization. Governance mechanisms, such as the board of directors, monitoring by owners, executive compensation practices, and the market for corporate control, may limit managerial tendencies to overdiversify. These mechanisms are discussed in more detail in Chapter 10.

In some instances, though, a firm's governance mechanisms may not be strong, allowing executives to diversify the firm to the point that it fails to earn even average returns.[111] The loss of adequate internal governance may result in relatively poor performance, thereby triggering a threat of takeover. Although takeovers may improve efficiency by replacing ineffective managerial teams, managers may avoid takeovers through defensive tactics, such as "poison pills," or may reduce their own exposure with "golden parachute" agreements.[112] Therefore, an external governance threat, although restraining managers, does not flawlessly control managerial motives for diversification.[113]

Most large publicly held firms are profitable because the managers leading them are positive stewards of firm resources, and many of their strategic actions, including those related to selecting a corporate-level diversification strategy, contribute to the firm's success.[114] As mentioned, governance mechanisms should be designed to deal with exceptions to the managerial norms of making decisions and taking actions that increase the firm's ability to earn above-average returns. Thus, it is overly pessimistic to assume that managers usually act in their own self-interest as opposed to their firm's interest.[115]

Top-level executives' diversification decisions may also be held in check by concerns for their reputation. If a positive reputation facilitates development and use of managerial power, a poor reputation can reduce it. Likewise, a strong external market for managerial talent may deter managers from pursuing inappropriate diversification.[116] In addition, a diversified firm may acquire other firms that are poorly managed in order to restructure its own asset base. Knowing that their firms could be acquired if they are not managed successfully encourages executives to use value-creating diversification strategies.

As shown in Figure 6.4, the level of diversification with the greatest potential positive effect on performance is based partly on the effects of the interaction of resources, managerial motives, and incentives on the adoption of particular diversification strategies. As indicated earlier, the greater the incentives and the more flexible the resources, the higher the level of expected diversification. Financial resources (the most flexible) should have a stronger relationship to the extent of diversification than either tangible or intangible resources. Tangible resources (the most inflexible) are useful primarily for related diversification.

As discussed in this chapter, firms can create more value by effectively using diversification strategies. However, diversification must be kept in check by corporate governance

Figure 6.4 Summary Model of the Relationship between Diversification and Firm Performance

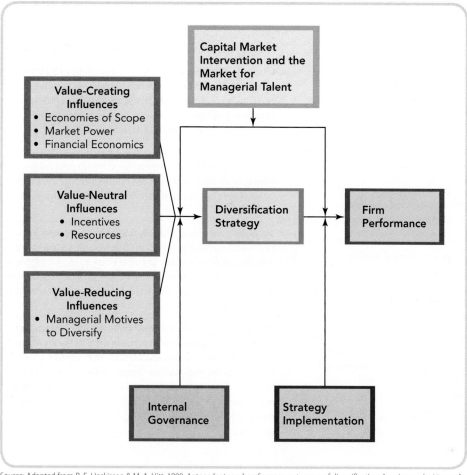

Source: Adapted from R. E. Hoskisson & M. A. Hitt, 1990, Antecedents and performace outcomes of diversification: A review and critique of theoretical perspectives, *Journal of Management*, 16: 498.

(see Chapter 10). Appropriate strategy implementation tools, such as organizational structures, are also important for the strategies to be successful (see Chapter 11).

We have described corporate-level strategies in this chapter. In the next chapter, we discuss mergers and acquisitions as prominent means for firms to diversify and to grow profitably. These trends toward more diversification through acquisitions, which have been partially reversed due to restructuring (see Chapter 7), indicate that learning has taken place regarding corporate-level diversification strategies.[117] Accordingly, firms that diversify should do so cautiously, choosing to focus on relatively few, rather than many, businesses. In fact, research suggests that although unrelated diversification has decreased, related diversification has increased, possibly due to the restructuring that continued into the 1990s and early twenty-first century. This sequence of diversification followed by restructuring has occurred in Europe and in countries such as Korea, following actions of firms in the United States and the United Kingdom.[118] Firms can improve their strategic competitiveness when they pursue a level of diversification that is appropriate for their resources (especially financial resources) and core competencies and the opportunities and threats in their country's institutional and competitive environments.[119]

SUMMARY

- The primary reason a firm uses a corporate-level strategy to become more diversified is to create additional value. Using a single-or dominant-business corporate-level strategy may be preferable to seeking a more diversified strategy, unless a corporation can develop economies of scope or financial economies between businesses, or unless it can obtain market power through additional levels of diversification. Economies of scope and market power are the main sources of value creation when the firm uses a corporate-level strategy to achieve moderate to high levels of diversification.

- The related diversification corporate-level strategy helps the firm create value by sharing activities or transferring competencies between different businesses in the company's portfolio.

- Sharing activities usually involves sharing tangible resources between businesses. Transferring core competencies involves transferring core competencies developed in one business to another business. It also may involve transferring competencies between the corporate headquarters office and a business unit.

- Sharing activities is usually associated with the related constrained diversification corporate-level strategy. Activity sharing is costly to implement and coordinate, may create unequal benefits for the divisions involved in the sharing, and can lead to fewer managerial risk-taking behaviors.

- Transferring core competencies is often associated with related linked (or mixed related and unrelated) diversification,

although firms pursuing both sharing activities and transferring core competencies can also use the related linked strategy.

- Efficiently allocating resources or restructuring a target firm's assets and placing them under rigorous financial controls are two ways to accomplish successful unrelated diversification. Firms using the unrelated diversification strategy focus on creating financial economies to generate value.

- Diversification is sometimes pursued for value-neutral reasons. Incentives from tax and antitrust government policies, low performance, or uncertainties about future cash flow are examples of value-neutral reasons that firms choose to become more diversified.

- Managerial motives to diversify (including to increase compensation) can lead to overdiversification and a subsequent reduction in a firm's ability to create value. Evidence suggests, however, that many top-level executives seek to be good stewards of the firm's assets and avoid diversifying the firm in ways that destroy value.

- Managers need to consider their firm's internal organization and its external environment when making decisions about the optimum level of diversification for their company. Of course, internal resources are important determinants of the direction that diversification should take. However, conditions in the firm's external environment may facilitate additional levels of diversification, as might unexpected threats from competitors.

REVIEW QUESTIONS

1. What is corporate-level strategy and why is it important?

2. What are the different levels of diversification firms can pursue by using different corporate-level strategies?

3. What are three reasons firms choose to diversify their operations?

4. How do firms create value when using a related diversification strategy?

5. What are the two ways to obtain financial economies when using an unrelated diversification strategy?

6. What incentives and resources encourage diversification?

7. What motives might encourage managers to overdiversify their firm?

EXPERIENTIAL EXERCISES

EXERCISE 1: WHAT'S MY CORPORATE-LEVEL STRATEGY AND HOW DID I GET THIS WAY?
Your text defines corporate-level strategy as "actions a firm takes to gain a competitive advantage by selecting and managing a group

of different businesses competing in different product markets." However, these actions are dynamic and longitudinal—they evolve over time. How did Ford Motor Company or IBM arrive at the corporate-level strategies they use today, and what are those strategies?

Part One

Form teams of four or five students and select a publicly traded firm, preferably one that has been in existence for a few decades. A comprehensive listing of all U.S. publicly traded firms may be found at the Investor Guide Web site (http://www.investorguide.com/stock-list.php) as well as links to each firm's homepage and other financial data. You will also want to access the firm's SEC filings, which could be available at your library or through the Securities and Exchange Commission's Web site at http://www.sec.gov/edgar.shtml.

Part Two

Complete a poster that can be displayed in class. Your poster should represent the firm and its evolution as far back in its history as you can get on one poster. The goal is to highlight the firm's beginnings, its acquisitions and divestiture activity, and its movement from one corporate-level strategy to another. You will need to do some extensive research on the firm to identify common linkages between operating units.

Be prepared to answer the following questions:

▪ How has the firm's corporate-level strategy evolved over time?

▪ What is the current corporate-level strategy and what links, if any, exist between operating units?

▪ Critique the current corporate-level strategy (e.g., too much diversification, too little, just right, and why).

EXERCISE 2: WHAT DOES THIS ANNOUNCEMENT MEAN?

Form 8K of the Securities and Exchange Commission is often called the current report due to the SEC requirement that companies must report or announce any major events that shareholders should know about. Many times the reporting is rather common such as the departure of an executive or changing of the firm's auditor. However, an important firm notification on their 8K filing is due to the announcement of a merger or acquisition which, as mentioned in the preceding chapter, has a significant impact on corporate level strategy.

This exercise requires teams of students to analyze 8K filings in the last 12 months. You can find many sources of this information but a good place to start is your university library. Contact your reference librarian for databases and financial analysis sites that will help you efficiently identify some good candidates. Teams are to pick one 8K filing that represents a firm's announced acquisition. It does not particularly matter if the acquisition was consummated, as the announcement in and of itself is sufficient. Once the team has identified the acquisition they must be prepared to at a minimum answer the following questions in the form of a presentation to the class:

1. Describe the acquiring firm in terms of its corporate level strategy.

2. Analyze the firm's press releases regarding the announced acquisition. How is the firm categorizing the event?

3. Describe the target in terms of its corporate level strategy.

4. Now analyze the announced acquisition in terms of its new corporate level strategy. How do you categorize the proposed entity? Does this match with press reports?

5. Rate the acquisition. Does this combination of two firms make sense in your team's opinion?

VIDEO CASE ▶

THE ROAD TO DIVERSIFICATION
Barry Diller/Senior Executive/IAC

Barry Diller, once the chairman and CEO of Paramount Pictures and Fox and intrigued by interactive commerce, purchased QVC only to lose it in other business acquisition attempts, particularly his bid to purchase Paramount. Losing the bid to own Paramount as well as other organizations, Barry Diller purchased QVC competitor HSN and began an interactive conglomerate from financial services to matchmaking services such as Match.com. Along the way, Diller discovered that his many businesses related to one another and united all his brands under one corporate headquarters. Barry Diller, driven by vision and the ability to grasp new and difficult concepts, insists that IAC/InterActiveCorp is a brand-by-brand endless multiproduct company similar to Procter & Gamble.

Be prepared to discuss the following concepts and questions in class:

Concepts

▪ Corporate-level strategy

▪ Levels of diversification

▪ Value-creating diversification

▪ Operational and corporate relatedness

▪ Related and unrelated diversification

▪ Motivations to overdiversify

Questions

1. Describe Diller's corporate-level strategy.

2. Describe IAC's level of diversification.

3. What do you think was Diller's reason to diversify?

4. Is Diller's approach value-creating diversification? Why or why not?

5. Explain how IAC businesses and brands are related. Do they have related diversification?

6. Is Diller in a position to overdiversify?

NOTES

1. M. E. Porter, 1980, *Competitive Strategy*, New York: The Free Press, xvi.

2. M. D. R. Chari, S. Devaraj, & P. David, 2008, The impact of information technology investments and diversification strategies on firm performance, *Management Science*, 54: 224–234; A. Pehrsson, 2006, Business relatedness and performance: A study of managerial perceptions, *Strategic Management Journal*, 27: 265–282.

3. J. Joseph & W. Ocasio, 2012, Architecture, attention and adaptation in the multibusiness firm: General Electric from 1951 to 2001, *Strategic Management Journal*, 33: 633–660.

4. M. E. Porter, 1987, From competitive advantage to corporate strategy, *Harvard Business Review*, 65(3): 43–59.

5. Ibid.; M. E. Raynor, 2007, What is corporate strategy, really? *Ivey Business Journal*, 71(8): 1–3.

6. W. P. Wan, R. E. Hoskisson, J. C. Short, & D. W. Yiu, 2011, Resource-based theory and corporate diversification: Accomplishments and opportunities, *Journal of Management*, 37(5): 1335–1368; A. A. Calart & J. E. Ricart, 2007, Corporate strategy: An agent-based approach, *European Management Review*, 4: 107–120.

7. K. Lee, M. W. Peng, & K. Lee, 2008, From diversification premium to diversification discount during institutional transitions, *Journal of World Business*, 43(1): 47–65; M. Ammann & M. Verhofen, 2006, The conglomerate discount: A new explanation based on credit risk, *International Journal of Theoretical & Applied Finance*, 9(8): 1201–1214; S. A. Mansi & D. M. Reeb, 2002, Corporate diversification: What gets discounted? *Journal of Finance*, 57: 2167–2183.

8. A. Campbell, M. Goold, & M. Alexander, 1995, Corporate strategy: The question for parenting advantage, *Harvard Business Review*, 73(2): 120–132.

9. K. Favaro, 2013, We're from corporate and we are here to help: Understanding the real value of corporate strategy and the head office, *Strategy+Business Online*, www.strategy-business.com, April 8; D. Collis, D. Young, & M. Goold, 2007, The size, structure, and performance of corporate headquarters, *Strategic Management Journal*, 28: 283–405.

10. G. Kenny, 2012, Diversification: Best practices of the leading companies, *Journal of Business Strategy*, 33: 12-20; D. Miller, 2006, Technological diversity, related diversification performance, *Strategic Management Journal*, 27: 601–619.

11. D. D. Bergh, 2001, Diversification strategy research at a crossroads: Established, emerging and anticipated paths, in M. A. Hitt, R. E. Freeman, & J. S. Harrison (eds.), *Handbook of Strategic Management*, Oxford, UK: Blackwell Publishers, 363–383.

12. S. F. Matusik & M. A. Fitza, 2012, Diversification in the venture capital industry: Leveraging knowledge under uncertainty, *Strategic Management Journal*, 33: 407–426; H. C. Wang & J. B. Barney, 2006, Employee incentives to make firm-specific investments: Implications for resource-based theories of corporate diversification, *Academy of Management Journal*, 31: 466–476.

13. A. Kaul, 2012, Technology and corporate scope: Firm and rival innovation as antecedents of corporate transactions, *Strategic Management Journal*, 33: 347–367; K. Z. Zhou & F. Wu, 2010, Technological capability, strategic flexibility and product innovation, *Strategic Management Journal*, 31: 547–561.

14. J. J. Marcel, 2009, Why top management team characteristics matter when employing a chief operating officer: A strategic contingency perspective, *Strategic Management Journal*, 30(6): 647–658; A. J. Ward, M. J. Lankau, A. C. Amason, J. A. Sonnenfeld, & B. R. Agle, 2007, Improving the performance of top management teams, *MIT Sloan Management Review*, 48(3): 85–90.

15. R. P. Rumelt, 1974, *Strategy, Structure, and Economic Performance*, Boston: Harvard Business School; L. Wrigley, 1970, *Divisional Autonomy and Diversification* (Ph.D. dissertation), Harvard Business School.

16. P. Gogoi, N. Arndt, & J. Crown, 2008, A bittersweet deal for Wrigley: Selling the family business wasn't William Wrigley Jr.'s plan, but the Mars offer was too good to refuse, *BusinessWeek*, May 12, 34.

17. 2013, United Parcel Service 2010 Annual Report, www.ups.com, May 7.

18. R. Rumelt, 2011, *Good Strategy/Bad Strategy: The Difference and Why it Matters*, New York: Crown Business Publishing.

19. M. Spriggs, A. Yu, D. Deeds, & R. L. Sorenson, 2012, Too many cooks in the kitchen: Innovative capacity, collaborative network orientation and performance in small family businesses, *Family Business Review*, 26: 32–50; L. R. Gomez-Mejia, M. Makri, & M. L. Kintana, 2010, Diversification decisions in family controlled firms, *Journal of Management Studies*, 47: 223–252.

20. A. Barroso & M. S. Giarratana, 2013, Product proliferation strategies and firm performance: The moderating role of product space complexity, *Strategic Management Journal*, in press.

21. 2013, Publicis Groupe, Wikipedia, http://en.wikipedia.org/wiki/Publicis, May 8.

22. J. L. Stimpert, I. M. Duhaime, & J. Chesney, 2010, Learning to manage a large diversified firm, *Journal of Leadership and Organizational Studies*, 17: 411–425.

23. 2013, Hutchison Whampoa Limited 2012 Annual Report, www.hutchison whampoa.com, accessed May 8; 2013, Hutchison Whampoa Limited, *Wikipedia*, http://en.wikipedia.org/wiki/Hutchison_Whampoa_Limited, accessed on May 8.

24. C.-N. Chen & W. Chu, 2012, Diversification, resource concentration and business group performance: Evidence from Taiwan, *Asia Pacific Journal of Management*, 29: 1045–1061.

25. D. H. Ming Chng, M. S. Rodgers, E. Shih, & X.-B. Song, 2012, When does incentive compensation motivate managerial behavior? An experimental investigation of the fit between incentive compensation, executive core self-evaluation and firm performance, *Strategic Management Journal*, 33: 1343–1362; J. E. Core & W. R. Guay, 2010, Is CEO pay too high and are incentives too low? A wealth-based contracting framework, *Academy of Management Perspectives*, 24(1): 5–19; I. Filatotchev & D. Allcock, 2010, Corporate governance and executive remuneration: A contingency framework, *Academy of Management Perspectives*, 24(1): 20–33.

26. D. G. Sirmon, M. A. Hitt, R. D. Ireland, & B. A. Gilbert, 2011, Resource orchestration to create competitive advantage: Breadth, depth and life cycle effects, *Journal of Management*, 37(5): 1390–1412; D. J. Miller, M. J. Fern, & L. B. Cardinal, 2007, The use of knowledge for technological innovation within diversified firms, *Academy of Management Journal*, 50: 308–326.

27. R. A. D'Aveni, G. B. Dagnino, & K. G. Smith, 2010. The age of temporary advantage, *Strategic Management Journal*, 31: 1371–1385; H. Tanriverdi & C.-H. Lee, 2008, Within-industry diversification and firm performance in the presence of network externalities: Evidence from the software industry, *Academy of Management Journal*, 51(2): 381–397.

28. M. E. Graebner, K. M. Eisenhardt, & P. T. Roundy, 2010, Success and failure of technology acquisitions: Lessons for buyers and sellers, *Academy of Management Perspectives*, 24(3): 73–92; M. D. R. Chari, S. Devaraj, & P. David, 2008, The impact of information technology investments and diversification strategies on firm performance, *Management Science*, 54(1): 224–234.

29. G. M. Kistruck, I. Qureshi, & P. W. Beamish, 2013, Geographic and product diversification in charitable organizations, *Journal of Management*, 39: 496–530.

30. F. Neffke & M. Henning, 2013, Skill relatedness and firm diversification, *Strategic Management Journal*, 34: 297–316.

31. M. Makri, M. A. Hitt, & P. J. Lane, 2010, Complementary technologies, knowledge relatedness and invention outcomes in high technology mergers and acquisitions, *Strategic Management Journal*, 31: 602–628.

32. N. Shin, 2009, Information technology and diversification: How their relationship

affects firm performance. *International Journal of E-Collaboration*, 5(1): 69–83; D. Miller, 2006, Technological diversity, related diversification, and firm performance, *Strategic Management Journal*, 27: 601–619.

33. M. V. S. Kumar, 2013, The costs of related diversification: The impact of core business on the productivity of related segments, *Organization Science*, in press; Y. M. Zhou, 2011, Synergy, coordination costs, and diversification choices, *Strategic Management Journal*, 32: 624–639.

34. M. A. Hitt, D. King, H. Krishnan, M. Makri, M. Schijven, K. Shimizu, & H. Zhu, 2012, Creating value through mergers and acquisitions: Challenges and opportunities, in D. Faulkner, S. Teerikangas, & R. Joseph (Eds.), *Oxford Handbook of Mergers and Acquisitions*, Oxford, UK: Oxford University Press, 2012, 71–113; P. Puranam & K. Srikanth, 2007, What they know vs. what they do: How acquirers leverage technology acquisitions, *Strategic Management Journal*, 28: 805–825.

35. L. B. Lien, 2013, Can the survivor principle survive diversification? *Organization Science*, in press; D. D. Bergh, 1995, Size and relatedness of units sold: An agency theory and resource-based perspective, *Strategic Management Journal*, 16: 221–239.

36. M. Lubatkin & S. Chatterjee, 1994, Extending modern portfolio theory into the domain of corporate diversification: Does it apply? *Academy of Management Journal*, 37: 109–136.

37. E. Dooms & A. A. Van Oijen, 2008, The balance between tailoring and standardizing control, *European Management Review*, 5(4): 245–252; T. Kono, 1999, A strong head office makes a strong company, *Long Range Planning*, 32(2): 225.

38. I.-C. Hsu & Y.-S. Wang, 2008, A model of intraorganizational knowledge sharing: Development and initial test. *Journal of Global Information Management*, 16(3): 45–73; Puranam & Srikanth, What they know vs. what they do; F. T. Rothaermel, M. A. Hitt, & L. A. Jobe, 2006, Balancing vertical integration and strategic outsourcing: Effects on product portfolio, product success, and firm performance, *Strategic Management Journal*, 27: 1033–1056.

39. A. Rodríguez-Duarte, F. D. Sandulli, B. Minguela-Rata, & J. I. López-Sánchez, 2007, The endogenous relationship between innovation and diversification, and the impact of technological resources on the form of diversification, *Research Policy*, 36: 652–664; L. Capron & N. Pistre, 2002, When do acquirers earn abnormal returns? *Strategic Management Journal*, 23: 781–794.

40. Miller, Fern, & Cardinal, The use of knowledge for technological innovation within diversified firms; J. W. Spencer, 2003, Firms' knowledge-sharing strategies in the global innovation system: Empirical evidence from the flat panel display industry, *Strategic Management Journal*, 24: 217–233.

41. J. Thottam, 2008, Branson's flight plan, *Time*, April 28, 40.

42. 2013, Operations overview, Honda Motor Company, www.honda.com, May 9.

43. L. C. Thang, C. Rowley, T. Quang, & M. Warner, 2007, To what extent can management practices be transferred between countries?: The case of human resource management in Vietnam, *Journal of World Business*, 42(1): 113–127; G. Stalk Jr., 2005, Rotate the core, *Harvard Business Review*, 83(3): 18–19.

44. J. A. Martin & K. M. Eisenhardt, 2010, Rewiring: Cross-business unit collaborations in multibusiness organizations, *Academy of Management Journal*, 53: 265–301.

45. S. Gupta, A. Woodside, C. Dubelaar, & D. Bradmore, 2009, Diffusing knowledge-based core competencies for leveraging innovation strategies: Modeling outsourcing to knowledge process organizations (KPOs) in pharmaceutical networks, *Industrial Marketing Management*, 38(2): 219–227.

46. A. Pehrsson, 2010, Business-relatedness and the strategy of moderations: Impacts on foreign subsidiary performance, *Journal of Strategy and Management*, 3: 110–133; S. Chatterjee & J. Singh, 1999, Are trade-offs inherent in diversification moves? A simultaneous model for type of diversification and mode of expansion decisions, *Management Science*, 45: 25–41.

47. J. Wiggins, 2008, Mars' move for Wrigley leaves rivals trailing, *Financial Times*, April 29, 24.

48. K. J. O'Brien, 2013, Despite sales growth, Ericsson profit plunges, *New York Times*, www.nytimes.com, April 24.

49. L. Fuentelsaz & J. Gomez, 2006, Multipoint competition, strategic similarity and entry into geographic markets, *Strategic Management Journal*, 27: 477–499; J. Gimeno & C. Y. Woo, 1999, Multimarket contact, economies of scope, and firm performance, *Academy of Management Journal*, 42: 239–259..

50. T. A. Shervani, G. Frazier, & G. Challagalla, 2007, The moderating influence of firm market power on the transaction cost economics model: An empirical test in a forward channel integration context, *Strategic Management Journal*, 28: 635–652; R. Gulati, P. R. Lawrence, & P. Puranam, 2005, Adaptation in vertical relationships: Beyond incentive conflict, *Strategic Management Journal*, 26: 415–440.

51. N. Lahiri & S. Narayanan, 2013, Vertical integration, innovation and alliance portfolio size: Implications for firm performance, *Strategic Management Journal*, 34: 1042–1064; D.J. Teece, 2012, *Strategy, Innovation and the Theory of the Firm*, Northampton, MA: Edward Elgar Publishing Ltd.

52. R. Carter & G. M. Hodgson, 2006, The impact of empirical tests of transaction cost economics on the debate on the nature of the firm, *Strategic Management Journal*, 27: 461–476; O. E. Williamson, 1996, Economics and organization: A primer, *California Management Review*, 38(2): 131–146.

53. R. Kapoor, 2013, Persistence of integration in the face of specialization: How firms navigated the winds of disintegration and shaped the architecture of the semiconductor industry, *Organization Science*, 24: 1195–1213; S. Novak & S. Stern, 2008, How does outsourcing affect performance dynamics? Evidence from the automobile industry, *Management Science*, 54: 1963–1979.

54. E. Rawley, 2010, Diversification, coordination costs and organizational rigidity: Evidence from microdata, *Strategic Management Journal*, 31: 873–891.

55. C. Wolter & F. M. Veloso, 2008, The effects of innovation on vertical structure: Perspectives on transaction costs and competences, *Academy of Management Review*, 33(3): 586–605; M. G. Jacobides, 2005, Industry change through vertical disintegration: How and why markets emerged in mortgage banking, *Academy of Management Journal*, 48: 465–498.

56. T. Hutzschenreuter & F. Grone, 2009, Changing vertical integration strategies under pressure from foreign competition: The case of U.S. and German multinationals, *Journal of Management Studies*, 46: 269–307.

57. 2011, Flextronics International Ltd., www.flextronics.com, May 31.

58. K. M. Eisenhardt & D. C. Galunic, 2000, Coevolving: At last, a way to make synergies work, *Harvard Business Review*, 78(1): 91–111.

59. P. David, J. P. O'Brien, T. Yoshikawa, & A. Delios, 2010, Do shareholders or stakeholders appropriate the rents from corporate diversification? The influence of ownership structure, *Academy of Management Journal*, 53: 636–654; J. A. Nickerson & T. R. Zenger, 2008, Envy, comparison costs, and the economic theory of the firm, *Strategic Management Journal*, 13: 1429–1449.

60. 2013, Corporate overview, Walt Disney company, http://corporate.disney.go.com, May 10; L Greene, 2009, Adult nostalgia for childhood brands, *Financial Times*, www.ft.com, February 14; M. Marr, 2007, The magic kingdom looks to hit the road, *Wall Street Journal*, www.wsj.com, February 8.

61. D. Lee & R. Madhaven, 2010, Divestiture and firm performance: A meta-analysis, *Journal of Management*, 36: 1345–1371; D. W. Ng, 2007, A modern resource-based approach to unrelated diversification. *Journal of Management Studies*, 44(8): 1481–1502; D. D. Bergh, 1997, Predicting divestiture of unrelated acquisitions: An integrative model of ex ante conditions, *Strategic Management Journal*, 18: 715–731.

62. Porter, *Competitive Advantage*.

63. S. Lee, K. Park, H. H. Shin, 2009, Disappearing internal capital markets:

Evidence from diversified business groups in Korea. *Journal of Banking & Finance*, 33(2): 326–334; D. Collis, D. Young, & M. Goold, 2007, The size, structure, and performance of corporate headquarters, *Strategic Management Journal*, 28: 283–405; O. E. Williamson, 1975, *Markets and Hierarchies: Analysis and Antitrust Implications*, New York: Macmillan Free Press.

64. R. Aggarwal & N. A. Kyaw, 2009, International variations in transparency and capital structure: Evidence from European firms. *Journal of International Financial Management & Accounting*, 20(1): 1–34; R. J. Indjejikian, 2007, Discussion of accounting information, disclosure, and the cost of capital, *Journal of Accounting Research*, 45(2): 421–426.

65. J. T. Campbell, T. C. Campbell, D. G. Sirmon, L. Bierman, & C. S. Tuggle, 2012, Shareholder influence over director nomination via proxy access: Implications for agency conflict and stakeholder value, *Strategic Management Journal*, 33: 1431–1451; A. Capezio, J. Shields, & M. O'Donnell, 2011, Too good to be true: Board structural independence as a moderator of CEO pay-for-performance, *Journal of Management Studies*, 48: 487–513.

66. A. Mackey, 2008, The effect of CEOs on firm performance, *Strategic Management Journal*, 29: 1357–1367; Dooms & Van Oijen, The balance between tailoring and standardizing control; D. Miller, R. Eisenstat, & N. Foote, 2002, Strategy from the inside out: Building capability-creating organizations, *California Management Review*, 44(3): 37–54; M. E. Raynor & J. L. Bower, 2001, Lead from the center: How to manage divisions dynamically, *Harvard Business Review*, 79(5): 92–100.

67. 2013, Shareowner letter, United Technologies 2012 Annual Report, http://2012ar.utc.com/letter, accessed May 10.

68. B. Quint. 2009, Companies deal with tough times through diversification, *Information Today*, 26(3): 7–8.

69. S. L. Sun, X. Zhoa, & H. Yang, 2010, Executive compensation in Asia: A critical review, *Asia Pacific Journal of Management*, 27: 775–802; A. Delios, D. Xu, & P. W. Beamish, 2008, Within-country product diversification and foreign subsidiary performance, *Journal of International Business Studies*, 39(4): 706–724.

70. Lee, Park, Shin, Disappearing internal capital markets: Evidence from diversified business groups in Korea; A. Chakrabarti, K. Singh, & I. Mahmood, 2006, Diversification and performance: Evidence from East Asian firms, *Strategic Management Journal*, 28: 101–120.

71. D. D. Bergh, R. A. Johnson, & R. L. Dewitt, 2008, Restructuring through spin-off or sell-off: Transforming information asymmetries into financial gain, *Strategic Management Journal*, 29(2): 133–148; C. Decker & M. Mellewigt, 2007, Thirty years after Michael E. Porter: What do we know about

business exit? *Academy of Management Perspectives*, 2: 41–55; S. J. Chang & H. Singh, 1999, The impact of entry and resource fit on modes of exit by multibusiness firms, *Strategic Management Journal*, 20: 1019–1035.

72. 2013, About us, Danaher, www.danaher. com, May 10.

73. R. Coff, 2003, Bidding wars over R&D-intensive firms: Knowledge, opportunism, and the market for corporate control, *Academy of Management Journal*, 46: 74–85.

74. J. Xia & S. Li, 2013, The divestiture of acquired subunits: A resource-dependence approach, *Strategic Management Journal*, 34: 131–148; C. Moschieri & J. Mair, 2012, Managing divestitures through time—Expanding current knowledge, *Academy of Management Perspectives*, 26(4): 35–50.

75. H. Berry, 2013, When do firms divest foreign operations? *Organization Science*, in press; D. Ma, 2012, A relational view of organizational restructuring: The case of transitional China, *Management and Organization Review*, 8: 51–75.

76. M. Lubatkin, H. Merchant, & M. Srinivasan, 1997, Merger strategies and shareholder value during times of relaxed antitrust enforcement: The case of large mergers during the 1980s, *Journal of Management*, 23: 61–81.

77. D. P. Champlin & J. T. Knoedler, 1999, Restructuring by design? Government's complicity in corporate restructuring, *Journal of Economic Issues*, 33(1): 41–57.

78. R. M. Scherer & D. Ross, 1990, *Industrial Market Structure and Economic Performance*, Boston: Houghton Mifflin.

79. A. Shleifer & R. W. Vishny, 1994, Takeovers in the 1960s and 1980s: Evidence and implications, in R. P. Rumelt, D. E. Schendel, & D. J. Teece (Eds.), *Fundamental Issues in Strategy*, Boston: Harvard Business School Press, 403–422.

80. S. Chatterjee, J. S. Harrison, & D. D. Bergh, 2003, Failed takeover attempts, corporate governance and refocusing, *Strategic Management Journal*, 24: 87–96; Lubatkin, Merchant, & Srinivasan, Merger strategies and shareholder value; D. J. Ravenscraft & R. M. Scherer, 1987, *Mergers, Sell-Offs and Economic Efficiency*, Washington, DC: Brookings Institution, 22.

81. D. A. Zalewski, 2001, Corporate takeovers, fairness, and public policy, *Journal of Economic Issues*, 35: 431–437; P. L. Zweig, J. P. Kline, S. A. Forest, & K. Gudridge, 1995, The case against mergers, *BusinessWeek*, October 30, 122–130.

82. E. J. Lopez, 2001, New anti-merger theories: A critique, *Cato Journal*, 20: 359–378; 1998, The trustbusters' new tools, *The Economist*, May 2, 62–64.

83. D. Bush & D. D. Gelb, 2012 Anti-trust enforcement: An inflection point? *Journal of Business Strategy*, 33(6): 15–21.

84. M. C. Jensen, 1986, Agency costs of free cash flow, corporate finance, and takeovers, *American Economic Review*, 76: 323–329.

85. M. A. Hitt, J. S. Harrison, & R. D. Ireland 2001, *Mergers and Acquisitions: A Guide to Creating Value for Stakeholders*, New York: Oxford University Press.

86. M. T. Brouwer, 2008, Horizontal mergers and efficiencies; theory and antitrust practice, *European Journal of Law and Economics*, 26(1): 11–26.

87. T. Afza, C. Slahudin, & M. S. Nazir, 2008, Diversification and corporate performance: An evaluation of Pakistani firms, *South Asian Journal of Management*, 15(3): 7–18; J. M. Shaver, 2006, A paradox of synergy: Contagion and capacity effects in mergers and acquisitions, *Academy of Management Journal*, 31: 962–976.

88. M. Palmer & T. Bradshaw, 2011, Skype can be the "glue" in Microsoft's multimedia strategy, *Financial Times*, http://blogs. ft.com, May 14.

89. K. Shimizu & M. A. Hitt, 2011, Errors at the top of the hierarchy, in D. A. Hofmann & M. Friese (Eds.), *Errors in Organizations*, New York: Routledge.

90. L. E. Palich, L. B. Cardinal, & C. C. Miller, 2000, Curvilinearity in the diversification-performance linkage: An examination of over three decades of research, *Strategic Management Journal*, 21: 155–174.

91. Sirmon, Hitt, Ireland, & Gilbert, Resource orchestration to create competitive advantage; A. E. Bernardo & B. Chowdhry, 2002, Resources, real options, and corporate strategy, *Journal of Financial Economics*, 63: 211–234.

92. W. H. Tsai, Y. C. Kuo, J.-H. Hung, 2009, Corporate diversification and CEO turnover in family businesses: Self-entrenchment or risk reduction? *Small Business Economics*, 32(1): 57–76; N. W. C. Harper & S. P. Viguerie, 2002, Are you too focused? *McKinsey Quarterly*, Mid-Summer, 29–38.

93. L. Jarvis, 2008, Pharma strategies: Merck launches into the bio-similars business, *Chemical & Engineering News*, December, 86(50): 7.

94. J. Carroll, 2009, Merck acquires bio-similars in \$130M pact, *Fierce Biotech*, www. fiercebiotech.com, February 12.

95. T. B. Folta & J. P. O'Brien, 2008, Determinants of firm-specific thresholds in acquisition decisions, *Managerial and Decision Economics*, 29(2/3): 209–225.

96. N. M. Kay & A. Diamantopoulos, 1987, Uncertainty and synergy: Towards a formal model of corporate strategy, *Managerial and Decision Economics*, 8: 121–130.

97. R. W. Coff, 1999, How buyers cope with uncertainty when acquiring firms in knowledge-intensive industries: Caveat emptor, *Organization Science*, 10: 144–161.

98. P. B. Carroll & C. Muim 2008, 7 ways to fail big, *Harvard Business Review*, 86(9): 82–91.

99. S. K. Kim, J. D. Arthurs, A. Sahaym, & J. B. Cullen, 2013, Search behavior of the diversified firm: The impact of fit on innovation, *Strategic Management Journal*, 34: 999–1009; J. Kang, 2013, The relationship

between corporate diversification and corporate social performance, *Strategic Management Journal*, 34: 94–109.

100. D. G. Sirmon, S. Gove, & M. A. Hitt, 2008, Resource management in dyadic competitive rivalry: The effects of resource bundling and deployment, *Academy of Management Journal*, 51(5): 919–935; S. J. Chatterjee & B. Wernerfelt, 1991, The link between resources and type of diversification: Theory and evidence, *Strategic Management Journal*, 12: 33–48.

101. E. N. K. Lim, S. S. Das, & A. Das, 2009, Diversification strategy, capital structure, and the Asian financial crisis (1997–1998): Evidence from Singapore firms, *Strategic Management Journal*, 30(6): 577–594; W. Keuslein, 2003, The Ebitda folly, *Forbes*, March 17, 165–167.

102. 2013, Apple's hot news, Apple Inc., www.apple.com, accessed May 10.

103. L. Capron & J. Hull 1999, Redeployment of brands, sales forces, and general marketing management expertise following horizontal acquisitions: A resource-based view, *Journal of Marketing*, 63(2): 41–54.

104. M. V. S. Kumar, 2009, The relationship between product and international diversification: The effects of short-run constraints and endogeneity. *Strategic Management Journal*, 30(1): 99–116; C. B. Malone & L. C. Rose, 2006. Intangible assets and firm diversification, *International Journal of Managerial Finance*, 2(2): 136–153.

105. C. Moschieri, 2011, The implementation and structuring of divestitures: The unit's perspective, *Strategic Management Journal*, 32: 368–401; K. Shimizu & M. A. Hitt, 2005, What constrains or facilitates divestitures of formerly acquired firms? The effects of organizational inertia, *Journal of Management*, 31: 50–72.

106. D. Cimilluca & J. Jargon, 2009, Corporate news: Sara Lee weighs sale of European business, *Wall Street Journal*, March 13, B3; J. Jargon & J. Vuocolo, 2007, Sara Lee CEO challenged on antitakeover defenses, *Wall Street Journal*, May 11, B4.

107. A. J. Nyberg, I. S. Fulmer, B. Gerhart, & M. A. Carpenter, 2010, Agency theory revisited: CEO return, and shareholder interest alignment, *Academy of Management*

Journal, 53: 1029–1049; J. G. Combs & M. S. Skill, 2003, Managerialist and human capital explanation for key executive pay premiums: A contingency perspective, *Academy of Management Journal*, 46: 63–73.

108. D. Souder, Z. Simsek, & S. G. Johnson, 2012, The differing effects of agent and founder CEOs on the firm's market expansion, *Strategic Management Journal*, 33: 23–41; L. L. Lan & L. Heracleous, 2010, Rethinking agency theory: The view from law, *Academy of Management Review*, 35: 294–314; R. E. Hoskisson, M. W. Castleton, & M. C. Withers, 2009, Complementarity in monitoring and bonding: More intense monitoring leads to higher executive compensation, *Academy of Management Perspectives*, 23(2): 57–74.

109. Geiger & Cashen, Organizational size and CEO compensation; J. J. Cordeiro & R. Veliyath, 2003, Beyond pay for performance: A panel study of the determinants of CEO compensation, *American Business Review*, 21(1): 56–66; Wright, Kroll, & Elenkov, Acquisition returns, increase in firm size, and chief executive officer compensation.

110. M. van Essen, P. P. Heugens, J. Otto, & J. van Oosterhout, 2012, An institution-based view of executive compensation: A multilevel meta-analytic test, *Journal of International Business Studies*, 43: 396–423; Y. Deutsch, T. Keil, & T. Laamanen, 2011, A dual agency view of board compensation: The joint effects of outside director and CEO options on firm risk, *Strategic Management Journal*, 32: 212–227.

111. A. J. Wowak & D. C. Hambrick, 2010, A model of person-pay interaction: How executives vary in their responses to compensation arrangements, *Strategic Management Journal*, 31: 803–821; J. Bogle, 2008, Reflections on CEO compensation, *Academy of Management Perspectives*, 22(2): 21–25.

112. M. Kahan & E. B. Rock, 2002, How I learned to stop worrying and love the pill: Adaptive responses to takeover law, *University of Chicago Law Review*, 69(3): 871–915.

113. R. C. Anderson, T. W. Bates, J. M. Bizjak, & M. L. Lemmon, 2000, Corporate governance and firm diversification, *Financial Management*, 29(1): 5–22; J. D. Westphal,

1998, Board games: How CEOs adapt to increases in structural board independence from management, *Administrative Science Quarterly*, 43: 511–537.

114. S. M. Campbell, A. J. Ward, J. A. Sonnenfeld, & B. R. Agle, 2008, Relational ties that bind: Leader-follower relationship dimensions and charismatic attribution, *Leadership Quarterly*, 19(5): 556–568; M. Wiersema, 2002, Holes at the top: Why CEO firings backfire, *Harvard Business Review*, 80(12): 70–77.

115. D. Allcock & I. Filatotchev, 2010, Executive incentive schemes in initial public offerings: The effects of multiple-agency conflicts and corporate governance, *Journal of Management*, 36: 663–686; J. M. Bizjak, M. L. Lemmon, & L. Naveen, 2008, Does the use of peer groups contribute to higher pay and less efficient compensation?, *Journal of Financial Economics*, 90(2): 152–168; N. Wasserman, 2006, Stewards, agents, and the founder discount: Executive compensation in new ventures, *Academy of Management Journal*, 49: 960–976.

116. E. F. Fama, 1980, Agency problems and the theory of the firm, *Journal of Political Economy*, 88: 288–307.

117. M. Y. Brannen & M. F. Peterson, 2009, Merging without alienating: Interventions promoting cross-cultural organizational integration and their limitations, *Journal of International Business Studies*, 40(3): 468–489; M. L. A. Hayward, 2002, When do firms learn from their acquisition experience? Evidence from 1990–1995, *Strategic Management Journal*, 23: 21–39.

118. R. E. Hoskisson, R. A. Johnson, L. Tihanyi, & R. E. White, 2005, Diversified business groups and corporate refocusing in emerging economies, *Journal of Management*, 31: 941–965.

119. C. N. Chung & X. Luo, 2008, Institutional logics or agency costs: The influence of corporate governance models on business group restructuring in emerging economies, *Organization Science*, 19(5): 766–784; W. P. Wan & R. E. Hoskisson, 2003, Home country environments, corporate diversification strategies, and firm performance, *Academy of Management Journal*, 46: 27–45.

7

Merger and Acquisition Strategies

Studying this chapter should provide you with the strategic management knowledge needed to:

1 Explain the popularity of merger and acquisition strategies in firms competing in the global economy.

2 Discuss reasons why firms use an acquisition strategy to achieve strategic competitiveness.

3 Describe seven problems that work against achieving success when using an acquisition strategy.

4 Name and describe the attributes of effective acquisitions.

5 Define the restructuring strategy and distinguish among its common forms.

6 Explain the short- and long-term outcomes of the different types of restructuring strategies.

STRATEGIC ACQUISITIONS AND ACCELERATED INTEGRATION OF THOSE ACQUISITIONS ARE A VITAL CAPABILITY OF CISCO SYSTEMS

Cisco Systems is in the business of building the infrastructure that allows the Internet to work. As the Internet evolved, however, Cisco's business was required to change with this evolution. As part of its advancement, Cisco Systems has used an acquisition strategy to build network products and extend their reach into new areas, both related and unrelated. In the beginning, digital connectivity was important through e-mail and Web browsing and searches. This evolved into a network economy facilitating ecommerce, digital supply chains, and digital collaboration. Subsequently, the digital interaction phase moved Cisco into developing infrastructure for social media, mobile and cloud computing, and digital video. The next stage seems to be "the Internet of everything" connecting people, processes, data, and things. This will require the basic core in routing, switching, and services, as well as large data centers to facilitate visualization through cloud computing. Video and collaboration as well as basic architecture of the business will be transforming to become the base strategic business blocks. Furthermore, the need to have strong digital security will be paramount.

Cisco has entered many aspects of this business through acquisitions. For instance, in 2012, Cisco acquired TV software developer NDS for $5 billion. NDS Group develops software for television networks. In particular, its solutions allow pay-TV providers to deliver digital content to TVs, DVRs, PCs, and other multimedia devices. It provides solutions that protect digital content so that only paid subscribers can access it. Because of Cisco's customer-driven focus, it has sought to help its customers capture these market transitions and meet their particular needs. Of course, Cisco also builds the routers that allow video data and e-mail communications to come together through their blade servers (individual and modular servers that cut down on cabling). These routers and servers support cloud computing for the mobile devices that deliver the video that NDS software enables on desktop and mobile devices.

Also in 2012, Cisco purchased Meraki for $1.2 billion. Meraki provides solutions that optimize services in the cloud. For instance, it offers mid-sized customers Wi-Fi, switching, security, and mobile device management centrally from a set of cloud servers. For instance, if you are a guest at a university or other company campus it supports, you can bring your own personal device into the network, which allows guest networking and facilitates application controls. It manages the firewall and other advanced networking services to protect security as well.

John Chambers, Cisco CEO, has helped the firm move through the many transitions noted earlier. In the IT sector, 90 percent of acquisitions fail. However, as Chambers notes, "although Cisco does better than anyone else, we know that a third of our acquisitions won't work." Chambers worked for companies that did not successfully make transitions. Wang Laboratories missed a transition, and after experiencing this as an executive, Chambers learned to have a "healthy paranoia." He adds: "More than anything, I've tried to make Cisco a company that can see big transitions and move." One way they do this is to "listen to the customers very closely" to understand the necessary changes.

As Cisco makes the transition into the all-everything network, not only must it manage the cloud, but it also must provide service to the mobile devices that work in cellular networks. Accordingly, Cisco also acquired Intucell, a self-optimizing network software developer, for $475 million. It likewise acquired Truviso, Inc., a provider of network data analysis and reporting software, for an undisclosed price (it was partly owned by venture capital firms and was headquartered in Israel). Most recently it acquired Ubiquisys, which cuts cellular carriers' costs "by shifting traffic from congested towers to more targeted locations inside an office, home or public space, which also boosts the service's reliability." This approach is especially efficient when seeking to improve "coverage in crowded areas such as stadiums, convention centers and subway stations." These acquisitions help cellular network customers manage their products in the network more efficiently in the delivery of data, e-mail, and video services. As you can see, for this series of acquisitions Cisco has used acquisitions strategically to move into new areas as its environment changes, to learn about new technologies, and to gain knowledge on new technologies as it experiences these transitions.

In the process of this rapid change, it has developed a distinct ability to integrate acquisitions. When Cisco contemplates an acquisition, along with financial due diligence to make sure that it is paying the right price, it also develops a detailed plan for possible post-merger integration. It begins communicating early with stakeholders about integration plans and conducts rigorous post-mortems to identify ways "to make subsequent integrations more efficient and effective." Once a deal is completed, this allows the company to hit the ground running when the deal becomes public. Cisco is ready "from Day 1 to explain how the two companies are going to come together and provide unique value and how the integration effort itself will be structured to realize value." The firm does not "want the [acquired] organization to go in limbo," which can happen if the integration process is not well thought out. Also, during the integration process, it is important to know how far the integration should go. Sometimes integration is too deep, and value is destroyed that was being sought in the acquisition. Sometimes it may even pay to keep the business separate from Cisco's other operations to allow the business to function without integration until the necessary learning is complete. "Cisco learned the hard way that complex deals require you to know at a high level of detail how you're going to drive value."

Sources: L. Capron, 2013, Cisco's corporate development portfolio: A blend of building, borrowing and buying, *Strategy & Leadership*, 41(2): 27–30; D. FitzGerald & S. Chaudhuri, 2013, Corporate news: Cisco doubles down on small-cell transmitters with Ubiquisys, *Wall Street Journal*, April 4, B7; T. Geron, 2012, Meraki-Cisco deal a boost for Sequoia, Google-connected VCs, *Forbes*, November 19, 18; R. Karlgaard, 2012, Cisco's Chambers: Driving change, *Forbes*, February 22, 68; A. Moscaritolo, 2012, Cisco to acquire TV software developer NDS for $5 billion, *PC Magazine*, March 1; B. Worthen, D. Cimilluca, & A. Das, 2012, Cisco hedges bet on video delivery, *Wall Street Journal*, March 16, B1; R. Myers, 2011, Integration acceleration, *CFO*, 27(1): 52–57.

Learn more about Meraki, another company acquired by Cisco.
www.cengagebrain.com

We examined corporate-level strategy in Chapter 6, focusing on types and levels of product diversification strategies that firms derive from their core competencies to create competitive advantages and value for stakeholders. As noted in that chapter, diversification allows a firm to create value by productively using excess resources to exploit new opportunities.[1] In this chapter, we explore merger and acquisition strategies. Firms throughout the world use these strategies, often in concert with diversification strategies, to become more diversified. As noted in the Opening Case, merger and acquisition strategies remain popular as a source of firm growth to meet new challenges and opportunities, and hopefully of above-average returns.

Most corporations are very familiar with merger and acquisition strategies. For example, as the opening case on Cisco Systems illustrates, the latter half of the twentieth century found major companies using these strategies to grow and to deal with the competitive challenges in their domestic markets as well as those emerging from global competitors. Today, smaller firms also use merger and acquisition strategies to grow in their existing markets and to enter new markets.[2]

Not unexpectedly, some mergers and acquisitions fail to reach their promise.[3] Accordingly, explaining how firms can successfully use merger and acquisition strategies to create stakeholder value[4] is a key purpose of this chapter. To do this, we first explain the continuing popularity of merger and acquisition strategies as a choice firms evaluate when seeking growth and strategic competitiveness. As part of this explanation, we describe the differences between mergers, acquisitions, and takeovers. We next discuss specific reasons firms choose to use acquisition strategies and some of the problems organizations may encounter when implementing them. We then describe the characteristics associated with effective acquisitions before closing the chapter with a discussion of different types of restructuring strategies. Restructuring strategies are commonly used to correct or deal with the results of ineffective mergers and acquisitions.

7-1 The Popularity of Merger and Acquisition Strategies

Merger and acquisition (M&A) strategies have been popular among U.S. firms for many years. Some believe that these strategies played a central role in the restructuring of U.S. businesses during the 1980s and 1990s and that they continue generating these types of benefits in the twenty-first century.[5]

Although popular, and appropriately so, as a means of growth with the potential to lead to strategic competitiveness, it is important to emphasize that changing conditions in the external environment influence the type of M&A activity firms pursue. During the recent financial crisis, tightening credit markets made it more difficult for firms to complete "megadeals" (those costing $10 billion or more). Although the flow of deals picked up in 2011 and 2012 in the United States, the global deal flow has not reached the number and overall total value realized in 2007. In the first quarter of 2013, deals valued at more than US$5 billion totaled US$542.8 billion, a 10 percent increase over 2012. However, "over 8,100 worldwide deals were announced during the first quarter of 2013, a 16 percent decline from 2012 and the slowest quarter for M&A, by number of deals, since the third quarter of 2004."[6] Worries over the U.S. budget deficit and the associated sequester and the overall health of government finances in the European region created uncertainty about the wisdom of pursuing deals. However, one analyst noted that "European companies have strong balance sheets and low economic growth in their markets, which means they have to acquire to grow."[7] For example, Heineken NV, a large beer producer headquartered in Europe, noted a revenue increase from 2012, but the increase "was entirely due to acquisitions, notably of Asia Pacific Breweries, maker of Tiger beer. Heineken acquired the bulk of the company for $6.4 billion" in late 2012.[8]

In the final analysis, firms use merger and acquisition strategies to improve their ability to create more value for all stakeholders, including shareholders. As suggested by Figure 1.1, this reasoning applies equally to all of the other strategies (e.g., business-level, corporate-level, international, and cooperative) a firm may formulate and then implement.

However, evidence suggests that using merger and acquisition strategies in ways that consistently create value is challenging. This is particularly true for acquiring firms in that some research results indicate that shareholders of acquired firms often earn above-average returns from acquisitions, while shareholders of acquiring firms typically earn returns that are close to zero.[9] Moreover, in approximately two-thirds of all acquisitions, the acquiring firm's stock price falls immediately after the intended transaction is announced. This negative response reflects investors' skepticism about the likelihood that the acquirer will be able to achieve the synergies required to justify the premium.[10] Premiums can sometimes appear to be excessive, as in the potential acquisition of Illumina (a biotech firm) by Roche (a Swiss pharmaceutical firm). One analyst suggested that "Roche was willing to pay 30.1 times Illumina's expected 2012 earnings and a 61 percent premium to its share price before takeover speculation gripped the stock, a much higher premium than in recent pharma deals."[11] Obviously, creating the amount of value required to account for this type of premium is not going to be easy. In fact, Roche ultimately dropped its offer because Illumina's board wanted an even larger premium. Franz Humer, chairman at Roche, noted: "Roche doesn't do acquisitions that don't create added value. We have self-discipline."[12] Overall then, those leading firms that are using merger and acquisition strategies must recognize that creating more value for their stakeholders by doing so is indeed difficult.[13]

7-1a   Mergers, Acquisitions, and Takeovers: What Are the Differences?

A **merger** is a strategy through which two firms agree to integrate their operations on a relatively coequal basis. Glencore and Xstrata announced their "merger of equals" in February 2012. Glencore was the larger coming in, headquartered in Switzerland, and is one of the world's largest commodity mining and trading companies in the world. Xstrata was an Anglo-Swiss company focused on mining commodities such as coal, nickel, and zinc. Together, they are an integrated mining and commodity trading power player.[14]

Even though the transaction between Glencore and Xstrata appears to be a merger, the reality is that few true mergers actually take place. The main reason for this is that one party to the transaction is usually dominant in regard to various characteristics such as market share, size, or value of assets. In this case the transaction is slanted more towards Glencore.[15]

An **acquisition** is a strategy through which one firm buys a controlling, or 100 percent, interest in another firm with the intent of making the acquired firm a subsidiary business within its portfolio. After completing the transaction, the management of the acquired firm reports to the management of the acquiring firm.

Although most of the mergers that are completed are friendly in nature, acquisitions can be friendly or unfriendly. A **takeover** is a special type of acquisition wherein the target firm does not solicit the acquiring firm's bid; thus, takeovers are unfriendly acquisitions. As explained in Chapter 10, firms have developed takeover defenses (mostly corporate governance devices) for preventing hostile takeovers when such a bid is undesired by the target's board of directors.[16] For example, the previously mentioned Illumina takeover attempt by Roche was a hostile bid.

Research evidence reveals that "preannouncement returns" of hostile takeovers "are largely anticipated and associated with a significant increase in the bidder's and target's

A merger is a strategy through which two firms agree to integrate their operations on a relatively coequal basis.

An **acquisition** is a strategy through which one firm buys a controlling, or 100 percent, interest in another firm with the intent of making the acquired firm a subsidiary business within its portfolio.

A **takeover** is a special type of acquisition wherein the target firm does not solicit the acquiring firm's bid; thus, takeovers are unfriendly acquisitions.

Glencore Company Headquarters in Zug/Baar, Switzerland.

© iStockphoto.com/eriktham

share prices."[17] This evidence provides a rationale why some firms are willing to pursue buying another company even when that firm is not interested in being bought. Often, determining the price the acquiring firm is willing to pay to "take over" the target firm is the core issue in these transactions. As noted above, the Roche bid failed because they could not agree on an appropriate price.

On a comparative basis, acquisitions are more common than mergers and takeovers. Accordingly, we focus the remainder of this chapter's discussion on acquisitions.

7-2 Reasons for Acquisitions

In this section, we discuss reasons firms decide to acquire another company. Although each reason can provide a legitimate rationale, acquisitions are not always as successful as the involved parties want them to be. Later in the chapter, we examine problems firms may encounter when seeking growth and strategic competitiveness through acquisitions.

7-2a Increased Market Power

Achieving greater market power is a primary reason for acquisitions.[18] Defined in Chapter 6, *market power* exists when a firm is able to sell its goods or services above competitive levels or when the costs of its primary or support activities are lower than those of its competitors. Market power usually is derived from the size of the firm and its resources and capabilities to compete in the marketplace;[19] it is also affected by the firm's share of the market. Therefore, most acquisitions that are designed to achieve greater market power entail buying a competitor, a supplier, a distributor, or a business in a highly related industry to allow the exercise of a core competence and to gain competitive advantage in the acquiring firm's primary market.

If a firm achieves enough market power, it can become a market leader, which is the goal of many firms. For example, in December 2012, Delta Airlines announced that it was purchasing a 49 percent stake in Virgin Atlantic Airways for $360 million as it seeks to boost its market share of transatlantic flights between Europe and the United States.[20]

Next, we discuss how firms use horizontal, vertical, and related types of acquisitions to increase their market power.

Horizontal Acquisitions

The acquisition of a company competing in the same industry as the acquiring firm is a *horizontal acquisition*. Horizontal acquisitions increase a firm's market power by exploiting cost-based and revenue-based synergies.[21] For instance, the combination of Delta and Virgin Atlantic noted above brings together two large players that increase the competitiveness of both carriers as they compete with other airlines.

Research suggests that horizontal acquisitions result in higher performance when the firms have similar characteristics,[22] such as strategy, managerial styles, and resource allocation patterns. Similarities in these characteristics, as well as previous alliance management experience, support efforts to integrate the acquiring and the acquired firm. Horizontal acquisitions are often most effective when the acquiring firm integrates the acquired firm's assets with its own assets, but only after evaluating and divesting excess capacity and assets that do not complement the newly combined firm's core competencies.[23] The Glencore and Xstrata deal noted above is a horizontal acquisition, and it also necessitates some asset divestiture to please antitrust authorities as well as layoffs of duplicate personnel performing the same function.

Vertical Acquisitions

A *vertical acquisition* refers to a firm acquiring a supplier or distributor of one or more of its goods or services. Through a vertical acquisition, the newly formed firm controls additional parts of the value chain (see Chapters 3 and 6),[24] which is how vertical acquisitions lead to increased market power.

Bob Evans Farms, Inc. is primarily known for its Bob Evans and Mimi's restaurants. It also produces meat and side items for sale in retail grocery stores in all 50 U.S. states. In 2012, it acquired Kettle Creations, which co-manufactured side dishes to Bob Evans' specifications. This represents a vertical acquisition as Kettle Creations is a supplier of prepared products for both restaurants and retail sales items under the Bob Evans label. In an environment where there can be disruptions in the supply chain, vertical acquisitions create better predictability and less disruption in the supply chain, especially when there is growth in the restaurant chain and in the food retail segment businesses to support the increased vertical capacity. Kettle Creations has been making mashed potatoes and macaroni and cheese for Bob Evans since 2009 and will be integrated with BEF Foods Inc., a subsidiary of Bob Evans Farms, Inc.[25]

Related Acquisitions

Acquiring a firm in a highly related industry is called a *related acquisition*. Through a related acquisition, firms seek to create value through the synergy that can be generated by integrating some of their resources and capabilities. For example, Oracle has been acquiring related acquisitions in telecommunications. Oracle, a dominant software provider, has focused on overall enterprise management software with a concentration on managing inventories, ledgers, and other business operations. It is now beginning to target facilitating networks that managers have to use external to the firm. For example, it recently acquired Tekelec from a private equity group led by Siris Capital Group LLC. This acquisition followed previous deals to buy Acme Packet Inc. and Xsigo Systems Inc., both telecom gear producers, to broaden its footprint to facilitate large corporate data centers in managing their external networks. Many of these deals are to compete with cloud offerings such as those from competitor Salesforce.com Inc. that provide Internet management software, which help firms manage and better target customers through Internet sales and distribution.[26]

Horizontal, vertical, and related acquisitions that firms complete to increase their market power are subject to regulatory review as well as to analysis by financial markets.[27] For example, UPS agreed to purchase Thomas Nationwide Transport (TNT) Express for over $6 billion. However, the European Commission questioned whether the merger would meet antitrust guidelines and lower the competitiveness of the package delivery business in Europe. After this ruling, in January 2013 the United Parcel Service (UPS) officially disbanded its attempt to purchase TNT Express.[28] Thus, firms seeking growth and market power through acquisitions must understand the political/legal segment of the general environment (see Chapter 2) in order to successfully use an acquisition strategy.

7-2b Overcoming Entry Barriers

Barriers to entry (introduced in Chapter 2) are factors associated with a market or with the firms currently operating in it that increase the expense and difficulty new firms encounter when trying to enter that particular market. For example, well-established competitors may have economies of scale in the manufacture or service of their products. In addition, enduring relationships with customers often create product loyalties that are difficult for new entrants to overcome. When facing differentiated products, new entrants typically must spend considerable resources to advertise their products and may find it necessary to sell below competitors' prices to entice new customers.

Facing the entry barriers that economies of scale and differentiated products create, a new entrant may find acquiring an established company to be more effective than entering the market as a competitor offering a product that is unfamiliar to current buyers. In fact, the higher the barriers to market entry, the greater the probability that a firm will acquire an existing firm to overcome them. For example, many video content consumers want to watch such content on mobile devices. However, DirecTV and Dish Network, two of the largest satellite television companies, do not have a way to readily produce and distribute content to mobile devices such as smartphones through their satellite networks. However, some firms can do this through software. Comcast, a cable TV firm, can use its Xfinity mobile app software to distribute televised content to their cable customers' mobile devices. As such, to overcome this barrier to entry, Dish Network has proposed an acquisition of Sprint Nextel, a mobile service provider. SoftBank is also bidding on Sprint Nextel as a way to enter into the U.S. market as a mobile service provider. As will be discussed later, SoftBank is the third largest mobile carrier in Japan.[29]

As this discussion suggests, a key advantage of using an acquisition strategy to overcome entry barriers is that the acquiring firm gains immediate access to a market. This advantage can be particularly attractive for firms seeking to overcome entry barriers associated with entering international markets.[30] Multinational corporations from developing economies seek to enter developed and other emerging economies because they are among the fastest-growing firms in the world.[31] As discussed next, completing a cross-border acquisition of a local target allows a firm to quickly enter fast-growing economies such as these.

Cross-Border Acquisitions

Acquisitions made between companies with headquarters in different countries are called *cross-border acquisitions*.[32] For example, as noted above, the third largest mobile operator in Japan in regard to market share, SoftBank, is seeking to buy a 70 percent stake in Sprint Nextel for $20.1 billion. SoftBank is seeking to extend its reach beyond its domestic market because Japan's growth is limited relative to other countries.[33]

There are other interesting changes taking place in terms of cross-border acquisition activity. Historically, North American and European companies were the most active acquirers of companies outside their domestic markets. However, the current global competitive landscape is one in which firms from other nations may use an acquisition strategy more frequently than do their counterparts in North America and Europe. In this regard, Chinese companies, in particular, are well positioned for cross-border acquisitions. Chinese corporations are well capitalized with strong balance sheets and cash reserves, and they have learned from their past failures, as indicated in the Strategic Focus.[34] In the Strategic Focus, we also describe recent cross-border acquisitions by emerging market companies and how their approaches differ. For example, Bimbo, a Mexican bakery operator, recently purchased bakery operations, Weston Foods, from Sara Lee in the U.S. As you will see, many of the deals cited are horizontal, vertical, or related acquisitions through which the acquiring companies seek to increase their market power.

As noted in the Strategic Focus, firms headquartered in mid-range developing economies such as China and Brazil are also completing more cross-border acquisitions than in the past. The weak U.S. dollar and more favorable government policies toward cross-border acquisitions are supporting such companies' desires to rapidly become more global.

Firms using an acquisition strategy to complete cross-border acquisitions should understand that these transactions are not risk free. For example, firms seeking to acquire companies in China must recognize that China remains a challenging environment for foreign investors. Political and legal obstacles make acquisitions in China risky and difficult.[35] Due diligence is problematic as well because corporate governance and transparency of financial statements are often obscure. For instance, Caterpillar, an earthmoving equipment company, acquired Chinese manufacturing company Siwei, but after the purchase discovered the company's accounting was fraudulent and as such the price it paid was misrepresented by management.[36] Thus, firms must carefully study the risks as well as the potential benefits when contemplating cross-border acquisitions.

Strategic Focus   GLOBALIZATION

Cross-Border Acquisitions by Firms from Emerging Economies: Leveraging Resources to Gain a Larger Global Footprint and Market Power

Historically, large multinational firms from North America and Europe have pursued international acquisitions in emerging and developing countries in order to establish stronger economies of scale for domestic brands as well as provide opportunities for sourcing of scarce resources. Although the Spanish economy is in the doldrums, Spanish firms have used this strategy relatively recently to expand, first into Latin America and then into other European countries. Telefónica and Banco Santander are Spanish companies that have extended their reach, especially through cross-border acquisitions. For instance, Telefónica is now the world's fifth largest telecommunication provider in terms of revenue, and Santander is the fourth largest bank on the same metric and has become Latin America's largest retail bank.

Like many Spanish firms, many emerging economy firms are seeking to build a global footprint through acquisitions. For example, after China was accepted into the World Trade Organization in 2000, many Chinese cross-border mergers and acquisitions were attempted. However, many Chinese companies who made cross-border acquisitions saw them end in failure in their first attempts. In 2003, there was $1.6 billion spent on acquisitions, which swelled to $18.2 billion by 2006. However, TLC Corporation's acquisition of France's Thomson Electronics, SAIC's takeover of South Korea's Ssangyong Motor Company, Ping An's investment in the Belgium-Dutch financial services group Fortis, and Ningbo Bird's strategic partnership with France's Sajan ended in stunning failures, where the Chinese either pulled out or had to sell off much of their acquired assets. The Chinese, however, have learned from their mistakes. Instead of buying global brands, sales networks, and goodwill in branded products, they are now mainly trying to acquire concrete assets such as mineral deposits, state of the art technologies, or R&D facilities. This strategy was encouraged by the government after pulling back from the failed acquisitions just mentioned. As the economy around the world depreciated assets and as the RMB (China's currency) appreciated relative to developed economies, the strategy focused on hard assets because it made better investing sense rather than seeking to buy established branded products in which they did not always have managerial capability to realize successful performance. Interestingly, research suggests that India's acquiring companies (comparative to Chinese companies) have focused on buying competitors (horizontal acquisitions) in less-developed nations to build global market power.

Bimbo is the world's largest bakery company, formed in 1945 by a Spanish immigrant to Mexico. Initially, Bimbo expanded its operations throughout Latin America from its Mexican base.

Spanish telecommunications company Telefonica has extended its market reach through cross-border acquisitions.

However, in 1996 it made its first acquisition in the United States. By 2012, it had acquired more than a dozen U.S. firms, including the bakery operations of Sara Lee, Weston Foods. Under Sara Lee, Weston Foods had declined because of a lack of focus on efficient execution in the low-margin bread and bakery business. Bimbo's leaders are continually on the road looking for ways to improve productivity. For instance, in China they used tricycle delivery bikes in urban areas where streets are too narrow for trucks, a practice first honed and implemented in Latin America. At the same time, their trucks are equipped with sophisticated computer systems that optimize delivery routes. In the process of developing better strategic execution, it has also created better ways of integrating new acquisitions into its operating procedures honed in emerging economies. As such, Bimbo is likely to increase the efficiency of the Weston baker operations.

Similarly, Orascom, a Cairo-based Egyptian conglomerate, has used the construction business as a base platform and has prospered by pursuing acquisitions in countries that others shun. Orascom Group has entered a set of turbulent countries, including Jordan, Yemen, Pakistan, Zimbabwe, Algeria, Tunisia, Iraq, Bangladesh, North Korea, Burundi, Central African Republic, Namibia, and Lebanon. For example, its entry into North Korea in 2007 was due to the desire to use North Korean labor on a project already underway in China. Orascom agreed to a $150 million modernization of a North Korean cement plant in exchange for a 50 percent equity in its operation and permission to use North Korean labor. Through this agreement, Orascom built trust with North Korean officials and, more importantly, gained insight into Korea's infrastructure plans. Since 2007, it has diversified into partial ownership of a North Korean bank and also helped build the Ryugyong Hotel, a 105-floor skyscraper in Pyongyang. Other diversifications have included a large mobile phone business in Egypt as well as other emerging countries' economies, mostly through acquisitions and subsequent internal development.

Brazil is another country with a large emerging economy whose companies have significant acquisition activity. In 2013, Natura Cosméticos, a Brazilian beauty products firm, acquired 65 percent ownership of Australian-based Emeis Holdings, owner of luxury beauty brand Aesop. Emeis sells Aesop branded products in more than 60 stores in 11 countries. In 2010, Marfrig, a Brazilian meat packer, acquired Keystone Foods for $1.25 billion. Keystone is a top supplier to American fast food chains such as Subway and McDonald's. JBS, now the world's largest meat packer, bought Pilgrim's Pride for $800 million as well as Swift for $1.4 billion. Both of these firms are meat packing operations, which gives JBS significant exposure in the United States. These acquisitions in large part were made possible by Brazil's national development bank (BNDES), which supports Brazilian firms in developing their international operations.

Although acquisitions allow emerging market firms to enter foreign developed country markets as well as industries outside their domestic market, such acquisitions come at a price. Research suggests that emerging economy firms pay a higher premium than other firms. Perhaps these firms feel they have to pay this premium in order to win the deal and persuade regulators that they are not a threat, especially in industries which domestic politics indicate are strategic. Much of the research suggests that government ownership leads firms to overpay and that the overpayment reduces value for minority shareholders (nongovernment shareholders). Many of these acquisitions are also becoming less focused on infrastructure development and more on consumer market acquisitions because the firms cannot only extend their power into developed companies, but they can help to improve technology in their own domestic market, where a large middle class is emerging with consumers having more buying power. It is expected that this trend of acquisitions from emerging economies to developed economies will continue.

Sources: F. Bonifacio, 2013, Natura acquires majority stake in Australian skin care company, *Global Cosmetic Industry*, March: 22–23; B. Grant & G. Stieglitz, 2013, Equipment maker crumbles as baking industry consolidates, *Journal of Corporate Renewal*, 26(3): 10–13; V. Chen, J. Li, & D. M. Shapiro, 2012, International reverse spillover effects on parent firms: Evidences from emerging-market MNEs in developed markets, *European Management Journal*, 30(3): 204–218; F. De Beule & J. Duanmu, 2012, Locational determinants of internationalization: A firm-level analysis of Chinese and Indian acquisitions, *European Management Journal*, 30(3): 264–277; M. F. Guillén & E. García-Canal, 2012, Execution as strategy, *Harvard Business Review*, 90(10): 103–107; G. Jones, 2012, The growth opportunity that lies next door, *Harvard Business Review*, 90(7/8): 141–145; B. Kedia, N. Gaffney, & J. Clampit, 2012, EMNEs and knowledge-seeking FDI, *Management International Review*, 52(2): 155–173; S. A. Nonis & C. Relyea, 2012, Business innovations from emerging market countries into developed countries: Implications for multinationals from developed countries, *Thunderbird International Business Review*, 54(3): 291–298; L. Rabbiosi, S. Elia, & F. Bertoni, 2012, Acquisitions by EMNCs in developed markets, *Management International Review*, 52(2): 193–212; P. J. Williamson & A. P. Raman, 2011, How China reset its global acquisition agenda, *Harvard Business Review*, 89(4): 109–114; J. Zhang, C. Zhou, & H. Ebbers, 2011, Completion of Chinese overseas acquisitions: Institutional perspectives and evidence, *International Business Review*, 20(2): 226–238.

7-2c Cost of New Product Development and Increased Speed to Market

Developing new products internally and successfully introducing them into the marketplace often requires significant investment of a firm's resources, including time, making it difficult to quickly earn a profitable return.[37] Because an estimated 88 percent of innovations fail to achieve adequate returns, firm managers are also concerned with achieving adequate returns from the capital invested to develop and commercialize new products. Potentially contributing to these less-than-desirable rates of return is the successful imitation of approximately 60 percent of innovations within four years after the patents are obtained. These types of outcomes may lead managers to perceive internal product development as a high-risk activity.[38]

Acquisitions are another means a firm can use to gain access to new products and to current products that are new to the firm. Compared with internal product development processes, acquisitions provide more predictable returns as well as faster market entry. Returns are more predictable because the performance of the acquired firm's products can be assessed prior to completing the acquisition.[39]

Medtronic is the world's largest medical device maker. While pharmaceutical firms invent many of their products internally, most of Medtronic's products are acquired from surgeons or other outside inventors.[40] Research confirms that it can be a good strategy to buy early stage products, especially if you have strong R&D capability, even though there is

Strategy Right NOW

Learn more about Bimbo.
www.cengagebrain.com

M. Stasy

risk and uncertainty in doing so.[41] Acquisitions can enable firms to enter markets quickly and to increase the predictability of returns on their investments.

7-2d Lower Risk Compared to Developing New Products

Because the outcomes of an acquisition can be estimated more easily and accurately than the outcomes of an internal product development process, managers may view acquisitions as being less risky.[42] However, firms should exercise caution when using acquisitions to reduce their risks relative to the risks the firm incurs when developing new products internally. Indeed, even though research suggests acquisition strategies are a common means of avoiding risky internal ventures (and therefore risky R&D investments), acquisitions may also become a substitute for innovation. Accordingly, acquisitions should always be strategic rather than defensive in nature. For example, the proposed Dish Network acquisition of Sprint Nextel, a mobile service provider, needs to be done with great care because Dish does not have experience operating a cellular service, given its operational experience as a satellite TV service provider.

7-2e Increased Diversification

Acquisitions are also used to diversify firms. Based on experience and the insights resulting from it, firms typically find it easier to develop and introduce new products in markets they are currently serving. In contrast, it is difficult for companies to develop products that differ from their current lines for markets in which they lack experience.[43] Thus, it is relatively uncommon for a firm to develop new products internally to diversify its product lines.[44]

For example, Xerox purchased Affiliated Computer Services, an outsourcing firm, to bolster its services business. Xerox is seen primarily as a hardware technology company, selling document management equipment. However, over time, Xerox has sought to diversify into helping firms to manage business processes and technology services. As such, through this acquisition it seeks to have more and more of its business in the technology service sector. In this way, Xerox seeks to take care of the document-intensive business processes behind the scenes.[45]

Acquisition strategies can be used to support use of both unrelated and related diversification strategies (see Chapter 6).[46] For example, United Technologies Corp. (UTC) uses acquisitions as the foundation for implementing its unrelated diversification strategy. Since the mid-1970s it has been building a portfolio of stable and noncyclical businesses, including Otis Elevator Co. (elevators, escalators, and moving walkways) and Carrier Corporation (heating and air conditioning systems) in order to reduce its dependence on the volatile aerospace industry. Pratt & Whitney (aircraft engines), Hamilton Sundstrand (aerospace and industrial systems), Sikorsky (helicopters), UTC Fire & Security (fire safety and security products and services), and UTC Power (fuel cells and power systems) are the other businesses in which UTC competes as a result of using its acquisition strategy. While each business UTC acquires manufactures industrial and/or commercial products, many have a relatively low focus on technology (e.g., elevators, air conditioners, and security systems). It has recently run into trouble, however, with its acquisition of Goodrich, a defense contractor, and a downturn in Europe and emerging economies.[47]

In contrast to UTC, Cisco Systems pursues mostly related acquisitions, as illustrated in the Opening Case. Cisco wants to make the transition into the "all-everything network"; as such, not only must it manage transfers between computing devices and the cloud, but it also must provide service to the mobile devices that work in cellular networks.[48] Historically, these acquisitions have helped the firm build its network components business, which is focused on producing network backbone hardware. These recent acquisitions have helped Cisco diversify its operations beyond its original expertise in network hardware and network management software into network connection software among a large variety of devices, including mobile devices and cellular networks and helping client firms manage cloud computing applications.[49]

Firms using acquisition strategies should be aware that, in general, the more related the acquired firm is to the acquiring firm, the greater is the probability the acquisition will be successful.[50] Thus, horizontal acquisitions and related acquisitions tend to contribute more to the firm's strategic competitiveness than do acquisitions of companies operating in product markets that are quite different from those in which the acquiring firm competes, although complementary acquisitions in different industries can help expand a firm's capabilities.

7-2f Reshaping the Firm's Competitive Scope

As discussed in Chapter 2, the intensity of competitive rivalry is an industry characteristic that affects the firm's profitability.[51] To reduce the negative effect of an intense rivalry on their financial performance, firms may use acquisitions to lessen their dependence on one or more products or markets. Reducing a company's dependence on specific markets shapes the firm's competitive scope.

Each time UTC pursues a new acquisition (Goodrich, its latest acquisition, focuses on the growing commercial aerospace market), it helps to reshape its competitive scope. In a more subtle manner, P&G's acquisition of Gillette reshaped its competitive scope by giving P&G a stronger presence in some products for whom men are the target market. Xerox's purchase of Affiliated Computer Services likewise has reshaped Xerox's competitive scope to focus more on services, and Cisco has become more focused on software to facilitate inter-network connections through its latest acquisitions. Thus, using an acquisition strategy reshaped the competitive scope of each of these firms.

7-2g Learning and Developing New Capabilities

Firms sometimes complete acquisitions to gain access to capabilities they lack. For example, acquisitions may be used to acquire a special technological capability. Research shows that firms can broaden their knowledge base and reduce inertia through acquisitions[52] and increase the potential of their capabilities when they acquire diverse talent through cross-border acquisitions.[53] Of course, firms are better able to learn these capabilities if they share some similar properties with the firm's current capabilities. Thus, firms should seek to acquire companies with different but related and complementary capabilities in order to build their own knowledge base.[54]

A number of large pharmaceutical firms are acquiring the ability to create "large molecule" drugs, also known as biological drugs, by buying biotechnology firms. Thus, these firms are seeking access to both the pipeline of possible drugs and the capabilities that these firms have to produce them. Such capabilities are important for large pharmaceutical firms because these biological drugs are more difficult to duplicate by chemistry alone (the historical basis on which most pharmaceutical firms have expertise).[55] For example, in 2012 Bristol-Myers Squibb acquired a bio-pharmaceutical firm, Amylin Pharmaceuticals, Inc., for $5.3 billion. Amylin focuses on diabetes drugs and will give Bristol-Myers more sales opportunities as many of its drugs have lost patent protection.[56] Biotech firms are focused on DNA research and have a biology base rather than a chemistry base. If the acquisition is successful, there is added capability and possibly new competitive advantage. Biological drugs must clear more regulatory barriers or hurdles which, when accomplished, add more to the advantage the acquiring firm develops through such acquisitions.

7-3 Problems in Achieving Acquisition Success

Acquisition strategies based on reasons described in this chapter can increase strategic competitiveness and help firms earn above-average returns. However, even when pursued for value-creating reasons, acquisition strategies are not problem-free. Reasons for the use of acquisition strategies and potential problems with such strategies are shown in Figure 7.1.

Figure 7.1 Reasons for Acquisitions and Problems in Achieving Success

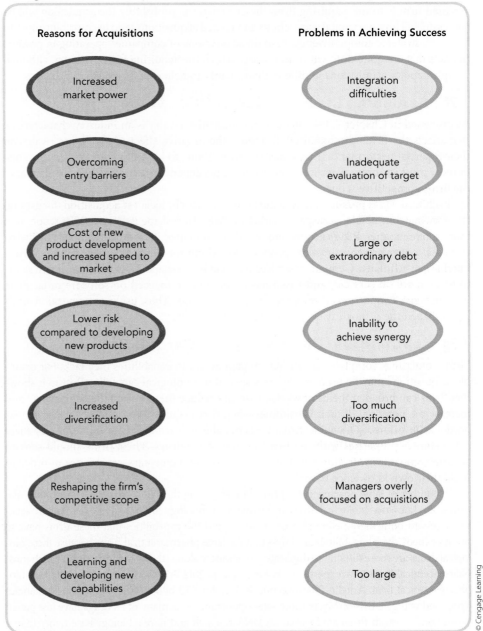

Research suggests that perhaps 20 percent of all mergers and acquisitions are successful, approximately 60 percent produce disappointing results, and the remaining 20 percent are clear failures; evidence on technology acquisitions reports even higher failure rates.[57] In general, though, companies appear to be increasing their ability to effectively use acquisition strategies. One analyst suggests that "Accenture research and subsequent work with clients show that half of large corporate mergers create at least marginal returns—an improvement from a decade ago, when many studies concluded that as many as three-quarters of all mergers destroyed shareholder value as measured two years after the merger announcement."[58] Greater acquisition success accrues to firms able to (1) select the "right" target,

(2) avoid paying too high a premium (doing appropriate due diligence), and (3) effectively integrate the operations of the acquiring and target firms.[59] In addition, retaining the target firm's human capital is foundational to efforts by employees of the acquiring firm to fully understand the target firm's operations and the capabilities on which those operations are based.[60] The Bristol-Myers acquisition of Amylin is an example of the importance of retaining the right employees because of Amylin's employees' expertise in biotechnology. As shown in Figure 7.1, several problems may prevent successful acquisitions.

7-3a Integration Difficulties

The importance of a successful integration should not be underestimated.[61] Post-merger integration is often a complex organizational process that is difficult and challenging to the managers involved. The processes tend to generate uncertainty and often resistance because of cultural clashes and organizational politics.[62] There is also a sense of fairness and unfairness as people get rewarded or laid off depending on how the employees involved experience a sense of fairness or distributive justice.[63] As suggested by a researcher studying the process, "Managerial practice and academic writings show that the post-acquisition integration phase is probably the single most important determinant of shareholder value creation (and equally of value destruction) in mergers and acquisitions."[64]

Although critical to acquisition success, firms should recognize that integrating two companies following an acquisition can be quite difficult. Melding two corporate cultures, linking different financial and control systems, building effective working relationships (particularly when management styles differ), and resolving problems regarding the status of the newly acquired firm's executives are examples of integration challenges firms often face.[65]

Integration is complex and involves a large number of activities, which if overlooked can lead to significant difficulties.[66] For example, when United Parcel Service (UPS) acquired Mail Boxes Etc., a large retail shipping chain, it appeared to be a merger that would generate benefits for both firms. The problem is that most of the Mail Boxes Etc. outlets were owned by franchisees. Following the merger, the franchisees lost the ability to deal with other shipping companies such as FedEx, which reduced their competitiveness. Furthermore, franchisees complained that UPS often built company-owned shipping stores close by franchisee outlets of Mail Boxes Etc. Additionally, a culture clash evolved between the free-wheeling entrepreneurs who owned the franchises of Mail Boxes Etc. and the efficiency-oriented corporate approach of the UPS operation, which focused on managing a large fleet of trucks and an information system to efficiently pick up and deliver packages. Also, Mail Boxes Etc. was focused on retail traffic, whereas UPS was focused more on the logistics of wholesale pickup and delivery. Although 87 percent of Mail Boxes Etc. franchisees decided to rebrand under the UPS name, many formed an owner's group and even filed suit against UPS in regard to the unfavorable nature of the franchisee contract.[67] In 2012, the Mail Boxes Etc. store brand has been dropped and the name changed to The UPS Store, Inc., and today UPS only franchises The UPS Store branded stores in the United States.[68]

Once an acquisition has been completed, the difficult task of integrating two companies begins.

© CoraMax/Shutterstock.com

7-3b   Inadequate Evaluation of Target

Due diligence is a process through which a potential acquirer evaluates a target firm for acquisition. In an effective due diligence process, hundreds of items are examined in areas as diverse as the financing for the intended transaction, differences in cultures between the acquiring and target firm, tax consequences of the transaction, and actions that would be necessary to successfully meld the two workforces. Due diligence is commonly performed by investment bankers such as Deutsche Bank, Goldman Sachs, and Morgan Stanley, as well as accountants, lawyers, and management consultants specializing in that activity, although firms actively pursuing acquisitions may form their own internal due diligence team. Firms almost always work with intermediaries like large investment banks to facilitate the due diligence of the transaction. Interestingly, research suggests that acquisition performance increases with the number of transactions facilitated by an investment bank but decreases when the relationship with a particular investment bank becomes exclusive.[69] As previously noted, Caterpillar's due diligence before its acquisition of Siwei in China was obviously inadequate.[70] Although due diligence often focuses on evaluating the accuracy of the financial position and accounting standards used (a financial audit), due diligence also needs to examine the quality of the strategic fit and the ability of the acquiring firm to effectively integrate the target to realize the potential gains from the deal.[71]

The failure to complete an effective due diligence process may easily result in the acquiring firm paying an excessive premium for the target company. Acquisition of Autonomy, which provides software to help customers analyze data, has burdened HP since it was acquired for $11 billion in 2011. There were claims of "serious accounting improprieties, disclosure failures and outright misrepresentations at Autonomy Corporation plc," which occurred prior to the acquisition.[72] Interestingly, research shows that in times of high or increasing stock prices due diligence is relaxed; firms often overpay during these periods, and long-run performance of the newly formed firm suffers.[73] The way boards pay CEOs indicates confidence or a lack of confidence in the value-creation potential of an announced acquisition. Often acquiring firms' CEOs' equity-based holdings (incentive compensation) "do not appear to anticipate long-term value creation from their acquisitions."[74] In other words, the incentive pay suggests that acquisitions may not be worth as much because CEOs have to be incented to make them pay off.

In addition, firms sometimes allow themselves to enter a "bidding war" for a target, even though they realize that their successive bids exceed the parameters identified through due diligence. Assumptions in financing deals suggest that investors are rational in regard to evaluating acquisition announcements. However, research in strategic management suggests that investors draw information from managers who have been shown to be biased; they often overpay, have escalation of commitment, experience hubris (feeling that they can manage a target firm better than the current management), and can be self-interest-seeking in such deals.[75] Earlier, we mentioned that Roche was willing to pay a 61 percent premium to acquire Illumina. We cannot be sure that Roche would have overpaid had the deal been consummated, but the point is that rather than enter a bidding war, firms should only extend bids that are consistent with the results of their due diligence process. It could be that Illumina would have provided Roche with a new platform for growth and over time this deal would look cheap, but the key is doing a strategic analysis along with rational due diligence so that both the strategic fit and financials make sense.

7-3c   Large or Extraordinary Debt

To finance a number of acquisitions completed during the 1980s and 1990s, some companies significantly increased their levels of debt. A financial innovation called junk bonds helped make this possible. *Junk bonds* are a financing option through which risky acquisitions are financed with money (debt) that provides a large potential return to lenders (bondholders). Because junk bonds are unsecured obligations that are not tied to specific assets for collateral, interest rates for these high-risk debt instruments sometimes reached between 18 and 20 percent during the 1980s.[76] Some prominent financial economists viewed debt as a means to discipline managers, causing them to act in the shareholders' best interests.[77] Managers holding this view are less concerned about the amount of debt their firm assumes when acquiring other companies.

Junk bonds are now used less frequently to finance acquisitions, and the conviction that debt disciplines managers is less strong.[78] Nonetheless, firms sometimes still take on what turns out to be too much debt when acquiring companies. As noted, both Dish Network and SoftBank have provided offers to buy Sprint Nextel. Interestingly, SoftBank brings a large cash infusion for Sprint, but does not provide synergy or possible additional spectrum for Sprint's cellular network. On the other hand, Dish provides better potential synergy but also would require a large load of debt. Dish needs to raise an additional $9.3 billion of debt to execute the deal. It is expected that the vast majority of this debt will be secured by Sprint assets. This could put Sprint at a disadvantage, especially considering that Sprint is a capital-intensive business that will require significant investment to keep up with its cellular competitors—AT&T and Verizon.[79] Thus, firms using an acquisition strategy must be certain that their purchases do not create a debt load that overpowers the company's ability to accomplish its strategic objectives while remaining solvent.

7-3d Inability to Achieve Synergy

Derived from *synergos*, a Greek word that means "working together," *synergy* exists when the value created by units working together exceeds the value those units could create working independently (see Chapter 6). That is, synergy exists when assets are worth more when used in conjunction with each other than when they are used separately. For shareholders, synergy generates gains in their wealth that they could not duplicate or exceed through their own portfolio diversification decisions.[80] Synergy is created by the efficiencies derived from economies of scale and economies of scope and by sharing resources (e.g., human capital and knowledge) across the businesses in the merged firm.[81]

A firm develops a competitive advantage through an acquisition strategy only when a transaction generates private synergy. *Private synergy* is created when combining and integrating the acquiring and acquired firms' assets, yield capabilities, and core competencies that could not be developed by combining and integrating either firm's assets with another company. Danone, a French diversified food producer and distributor, has made an acquisition of 92 percent of Happy Family, an organic food business launched in 2006. Happy Family has a 4 percent share of the U.S. baby foods market with such product labels as Amaranth Ratatouille, Orange Mango Coconut Smoothie, and Greek-Style Yogurt. This appears to be a good strategic acquisition for Danone because baby food is one of its fastest-growing portfolio areas.[82] However, it is not yet known what the private synergy might be. Private synergy is possible when firms' assets are complementary in unique ways; that is, the unique type of asset complementarity is not always possible simply by combining two companies' sets of assets with each other.[83] Because of its uniqueness, private synergy is difficult for competitors to understand and imitate, and it is also difficult to create.

A firm's ability to account for costs that are necessary to create anticipated revenue and cost-based synergies affects its efforts to create private synergy. Firms experience several expenses when trying to create private synergy through acquisitions. Called transaction costs, these expenses are incurred when firms use acquisition strategies to create synergy.[84] Transaction costs may be direct or indirect. Direct costs include legal fees and charges from investment bankers who complete due diligence for the acquiring firm. Indirect costs include managerial time to evaluate target firms and then to complete negotiations, as well as the loss of key managers and employees following an acquisition.[85] Firms tend to underestimate the sum of indirect costs when the value of the synergy that may be created by combining and integrating the acquired firm's assets with the acquiring firm's assets is calculated.

7-3e Too Much Diversification

As explained in Chapter 6, diversification strategies can lead to strategic competitiveness and above-average returns. In general, firms using related diversification strategies outperform those employing unrelated diversification strategies. However, conglomerates formed by using an unrelated diversification strategy also can be successful, as demonstrated by United Technologies Corp.

At some point, however, firms can become over-diversified. The level at which over-diversification occurs varies across companies because each firm has different capabilities to manage diversification. Recall from Chapter 6 that related diversification requires more information processing than does unrelated diversification. Because of this additional information processing, related diversified firms become over-diversified with a smaller number of business units than do firms using an unrelated diversification strategy.[86] Regardless of the type of diversification strategy implemented, however, over-diversification leads to a decline in performance, after which business units are often divested.[87] Commonly, such divestments, which tend to reshape a firm's competitive scope, are part of a firm's restructuring strategy. (We discuss the strategy in greater detail later in the chapter.)

Even when a firm is not over-diversified, a high level of diversification can have a negative effect on its long-term performance. For example, the scope created by additional amounts of diversification often causes managers to rely on financial rather than strategic controls to evaluate business units' performance (we define and explain financial and strategic controls in Chapters 11 and 12). Top-level executives often rely on financial controls to assess the performance of business units when they do not have a rich understanding of business units' objectives and strategies. Using financial controls, such as return on investment (ROI), causes individual business-unit managers to focus on short-term outcomes at the expense of long-term investments. When long-term investments are reduced to increase short-term profits, a firm's overall strategic competitiveness may be harmed.[88]

Another problem resulting from too much diversification is the tendency for acquisitions to become substitutes for innovation. As we noted earlier, pharmaceutical firms such as Roche must be aware of this tendency as they acquire other firms to gain access to their products and capabilities. Typically, managers have no interest in acquisitions substituting for internal R&D efforts and the innovative outcomes that they can produce. However, a reinforcing cycle evolves. Costs associated with acquisitions may result in fewer allocations to activities, such as R&D, that are linked to innovation. Without adequate support, a firm's innovation skills begin to atrophy. Without internal innovation skills, the only option available to a firm to gain access to innovation is to complete still more acquisitions. Evidence suggests that a firm using acquisitions as a substitute for internal innovations eventually encounters performance problems.[89]

7-3f Managers Overly Focused on Acquisitions

Typically, a considerable amount of managerial time and energy is required for acquisition strategies to be used successfully.

Over-diversification can have a negative effect on long-term firm performance. Well-conceived and effectively executed strategies only occur when leaders have a rich understanding of their businesses.

Larry Washburn/Getty Images

Activities with which managers become involved include (1) searching for viable acquisition candidates, (2) completing effective due diligence processes, (3) preparing for negotiations, and (4) managing the integration process after completing the acquisition.

Top-level managers do not personally gather all of the data and information required to make acquisitions. However, these executives do make critical decisions on the firms to be targeted, the nature of the negotiations, and so forth. Company experiences show that participating in and overseeing the activities required for making acquisitions can divert managerial attention from other matters that are necessary for long-term competitive success, such as identifying and taking advantage of other opportunities and interacting with important external stakeholders.[90]

Both theory and research suggest that managers can become overly involved in the process of making acquisitions.[91] One observer suggested, "Some executives can become preoccupied with making deals—and the thrill of selecting, chasing and seizing a target."[92] The over-involvement can be surmounted by learning from mistakes and by not having too much agreement in the boardroom. Dissent is helpful to make sure that all sides of a question are considered (see Chapter 10). For example, research suggests that there may be group bias in the decision making of boards of directors regarding acquisitions. The research suggests that possible group polarization leads to either higher premiums paid or lower premiums paid after group discussions about potential premiums for target firms paid.[93] When failure does occur, leaders may be tempted to blame the failure on others and on unforeseen circumstances rather than on their excessive involvement in the acquisition process.

The acquisitions strategy of Citigroup is a case in point. In 1998, Citigroup's CEO John Reed, in a merger between Citicorp and Travelers Group (CEO Sanford I. Weill), set out to cross-sell financial services to the same customer and thereby reduce sales costs (Weill ultimately became the CEO). To accomplish this goal, the merged firm focused on a set of acquisitions, including insurance and private equity investing beyond traditional banking services. However, as noted by one commentator, "More than once, ambitious executives, such as Sanford Weill of Citigroup fame, have assembled 'financial supermarkets,' and thinking that customers' needs for credit cards, checking accounts, wealth management services, insurance, and stock brokerage could be furnished most efficiently and effectively by the same company. Those efforts have failed, over and over again. Each function fulfills a different job that arises at a different point in a customer's life, so a single source for all of them holds no advantage."[94] Vikram Pandit, the CEO who took over after Charles Prince at Citigroup, was forced to sell off a lot of those peripheral financial service businesses during the financial crisis. However, most of the divestiture was handled by the subsequent CEO, Michael Corbat.[95]

7-3g Too Large

Most acquisitions create a larger firm, which should help increase its economies of scale. These economies can then lead to more efficient operations—for example, two sales organizations can be integrated using fewer sales representatives because such sales personnel can sell the products of both firms (particularly if the products of the acquiring and target firms are highly related).[96] However, size can also increase the complexity of the management challenge and create diseconomies of scope; that is, not enough economic benefit to outweigh the costs of managing the more complex organization created through acquisitions. This was also the case in the failed merger between DaimlerChrysler and Mitsubishi; it became too costly to integrate the operations of Mitsubishi to derive the necessary benefits of economies of scale in the merged firm.[97]

Many firms seek increases in size because of the potential economies of scale and enhanced market power (discussed earlier). At some level, the additional costs required to manage the larger firm will exceed the benefits of the economies of scale and additional market power. The complexities generated by the larger size often lead managers to implement more bureaucratic controls to manage the combined firm's operations. *Bureaucratic controls* are formalized supervisory and behavioral rules and policies designed to ensure consistency of decisions and actions across different units of a firm. However, through time, formalized controls often lead to relatively rigid and standardized managerial behavior.[98] Certainly, in the long run, the diminished flexibility that accompanies rigid and standardized managerial behavior may produce less innovation. Because of innovation's importance to competitive success, the bureaucratic controls resulting from a large organization (i.e., built by acquisitions) can have a detrimental effect on performance. For this reason, Cisco announced an internal restructuring to reduce bureaucracy after its numerous acquisitions; "it will dispense with most of a network of internal councils and associated boards that have been criticized for adding layers of bureaucracy and wasting managers' time."[99] As one analyst noted, "Striving for size per se is not necessarily going to make a company more successful. In fact, a strategy in which acquisitions are undertaken as a substitute for organic growth has a bad track record in terms of adding value."[100]

7-4 Effective Acquisitions

Earlier in the chapter, we noted that acquisition strategies do not always lead to above-average returns for the acquiring firm's shareholders.[101] Nonetheless, some companies are able to create value when using an acquisition strategy.[102] The probability of success increases when the firm's actions are consistent with the "attributes of successful acquisitions" shown in Table 7.1.

As illustrated in the Opening Case, Cisco Systems appears to pay close attention to Table 7.1's attributes when using its acquisition strategy. In fact, Cisco is admired for its ability to complete successful acquisitions and integrate them quickly, although as noted this has created a larger firm.[103] A number of other network companies pursued acquisitions to build up their ability to sell into the network equipment buying binge associated with the Internet's development, but only Cisco retained much of its value in the post-bubble era. Many firms, such as

Table 7.1 Attributes of Successful Acquisitions

Attributes	Results
1. Acquired firm has assets or resources that are complementary to the acquiring firm's core business	1. High probability of synergy and competitive advantage by maintaining strengths
2. Acquisition is friendly	2. Faster and more effective integration and possibly lower premiums
3. Acquiring firm conducts effective due diligence to select target firms and evaluate the target firm's health (financial, cultural, and human resources)	3. Firms with strongest complementarities are acquired and overpayment is avoided
4. Acquiring firm has financial slack (cash or a favorable debt position)	4. Financing (debt or equity) is easier and less costly to obtain
5. Merged firm maintains low to moderate debt position	5. Lower financing cost, lower risk (e.g., of bankruptcy), and avoidance of trade-offs that are associated with high debt
6. Acquiring firm has sustained and consistent emphasis on R&D and innovation	6. Maintain long-term competitive advantage in markets
7. Acquiring firm manages change well and is flexible and adaptable	7. Faster and more effective integration facilitates achievement of synergy

Lucent, Nortel, and Ericsson, teetered on the edge of bankruptcy after the dot-com bubble burst. When it makes an acquisition, "Cisco has gone much further in its thinking about integration. Not only is retention important, but Cisco also works to minimize the distractions caused by an acquisition. This is important, because the speed of change is so great that if the target firm's product development teams are distracted, they will be slowed, contributing to acquisition failure. So, integration must be rapid and reassuring."[104] For example, Cisco facilitates acquired employees' transitions to their new organization through a link on its Web site called "Cisco Acquisition Connection." This Web site has been specifically designed for newly acquired employees and provides up-to-date materials tailored to their new jobs.[105]

Results from a research study shed light on the differences between unsuccessful and successful acquisition strategies and suggest that a pattern of actions improves the probability of acquisition success.[106] The study shows that when the target firm's assets are complementary to the acquired firm's assets, an acquisition is more successful. With complementary assets, the integration of two firms' operations has a higher probability of creating synergy. In fact, integrating two firms with complementary assets frequently produces unique capabilities and core competencies. With complementary assets, the acquiring firm can maintain its focus on core businesses and leverage the complementary assets and capabilities from the acquired firm. In effective acquisitions, targets are often selected and "groomed" by establishing a working relationship prior to the acquisition.[107] As discussed in Chapter 9, strategic alliances are sometimes used to test the feasibility of a future merger or acquisition between the involved firms.[108]

The study's results also show that friendly acquisitions facilitate integration of the firms involved in an acquisition. The influence that target firms feel regarding their willingness to sell to an acquiring firm influences the likelihood of a friendly transaction taking place. For instance, the likelihood of a transaction in the Chinese beer industry has been the source for some research. The research showed that firms in the beer industry who established state-owned enterprises were more likely to be party to a transaction than firms that were able to attract more private investment.[109] Through friendly acquisitions, firms work together to find ways to integrate their operations to create synergy.[110] In hostile takeovers, animosity often results between the two top-management teams, a condition that in turn affects working relationships in the newly created firm. As a result, more key personnel in the acquired firm may be lost, and those who remain may resist the changes necessary to integrate the two firms.[111] With effort, cultural clashes can be overcome, and fewer key managers and employees will become discouraged and leave.[112]

Additionally, effective due diligence processes involving the deliberate and careful selection of target firms and an evaluation of the relative health of those firms (financial health, cultural fit, and the value of human resources) contribute to successful acquisitions.[113] Financial slack in the form of debt equity or cash, in both the acquiring and acquired firms, also frequently contributes to acquisition success. Even though financial slack provides access to financing for the acquisition, it is still important to maintain a low or moderate level of debt after the acquisition to keep debt costs low. When substantial debt was used to finance the acquisition, companies with successful acquisitions reduced the debt quickly, partly by selling off assets from the acquired firm, especially noncomplementary or poorly performing assets. For these firms, debt costs do not prevent long-term investments such as R&D, and managerial discretion in the use of cash flow is relatively flexible.

Another attribute of successful acquisition strategies is an emphasis on innovation, as demonstrated by continuing investments in R&D activities.[114] As noted earlier, Xerox purchased Affiliated Computer Services, which facilitated its transition from strictly a hardware producer focused on copiers to business services and processing. However, the company's research facility, Xerox PARC in Palo Alto, facilitated this transition.[115] This research facility helped to create the laser printer and ethernet cable, and early on developed the graphic user interface that Steve Jobs encountered in late 1979 and discerned to be the future of personal computing technology. This idea led to the founding of Apple Computer. Significant R&D investments show a strong managerial commitment to innovation, a characteristic that is increasingly important to overall competitiveness in the global economy as well as to acquisition success.

Flexibility and adaptability are the final two attributes of successful acquisitions. When executives of both the acquiring and the target firms have experience in managing change and learning from acquisitions, they will be more skilled at adapting their capabilities to new environments.[116] As a result, they will be more adept at integrating the two organizations, which is particularly important when firms have different organizational cultures.

As we have learned, firms use an acquisition strategy to grow and achieve strategic competitiveness. Sometimes, though, the actual results of an acquisition strategy fall short of the projected results. When this happens, firms consider using restructuring strategies.

7-5 Restructuring

Restructuring is a strategy through which a firm changes its set of businesses or its financial structure.[117] Restructuring is a global phenomenon.[118] From the 1970s into the 2000s, divesting businesses from company portfolios and downsizing accounted for a large percentage of firms' restructuring strategies. Commonly, firms focus on fewer products and markets following restructuring. The words of an executive describe this typical outcome: "Focus on your core business, but don't be distracted, let other people buy assets that aren't right for you."[119]

Although restructuring strategies are generally used to deal with acquisitions that are not reaching expectations, firms sometimes use these strategies because of changes they have detected in their external environment.[120] For example, opportunities sometimes surface in a firm's external environment that a diversified firm can pursue because of the capabilities it has formed by integrating firms' operations. In such cases, restructuring may be appropriate to position the firm to create more value for stakeholders given the environmental changes.[121]

As discussed next, firms use three types of restructuring strategies: downsizing, downscoping, and leveraged buyouts.

7-5a Downsizing

Downsizing is a reduction in the number of a firm's employees and, sometimes, in the number of its operating units, but it may or may not change the composition of businesses in the company's portfolio. Thus, downsizing is an intentional proactive management strategy whereas "decline is an environmental or organizational phenomenon that occurs involuntarily and results in erosion of an organization's resource base."[122] Downsizing is often a part of acquisitions that fail to create the value anticipated when the transaction was completed. Downsizing is often used when the acquiring firm paid too high of a premium to acquire the target firm.[123] Once thought to be an indicator of organizational decline, downsizing is now recognized as a legitimate restructuring strategy.

Reducing the number of employees and/or the firm's scope in terms of products produced and markets served occurs in firms to enhance the value being created as a result of completing an acquisition. When integrating the operations of the acquired firm and the acquiring firm, managers may not at first appropriately downsize. This is understandable in that "no one likes to lay people off or close facilities."[124] However, downsizing may be necessary because acquisitions often create a situation in which the newly formed firm has duplicate organizational functions such as sales, manufacturing, distribution, human

Restructuring is a strategy through which a firm changes its set of businesses or its financial structure.

resource management, and so forth. Failing to downsize appropriately may lead to too many employees doing the same work and prevent the new firm from realizing the cost synergies it anticipated.[125] Managers should remember that as a strategy, downsizing will be far more effective when they consistently use human resource practices that ensure procedural justice and fairness in downsizing decisions.[126]

7-5b Downscoping

Downscoping refers to divestiture, spin-off, or some other means of eliminating businesses that are unrelated to a firm's core businesses. Downscoping has a more positive effect on firm performance than does downsizing[127] because firms commonly find that downscoping causes them to refocus on their core business.[128] Managerial effectiveness increases because the firm has become less diversified, allowing the top management team to better understand and manage the remaining businesses.[129] Interestingly, sometimes the divested unit can also take advantage of unforeseen opportunities not recognized while under the leadership of the parent firm.[130] Interestingly, acquisitions of divested assets in the U.S. software industry performed better than acquisitions of privately held firms, and even better than acquisitions of publicly held firms. One can argue that when firms sell because of distress, this enhances the positive returns for the acquirers of these divested assets and the relative bargaining power of the acquiring firm over the price paid.[131] However, research also suggests that investors face considerable uncertainty in evaluating firms' divestiture decisions, and thus may look at social context to infer the quality of the decisions. That is, the divestitures take place in waves, as do acquisitions; if firms are leading the waves, the market will respond positively, but if they are following the waves (following other firms' leads in regard to divestiture activity), such later acquisitions generate the lowest stock market returns.[132]

Firms often use the downscoping and the downsizing strategies simultaneously. In Citigroup's restructuring (noted earlier) it used both downscoping and downsizing, as have many large financial institutions in the recession.[133] However, when doing this, firms need to avoid layoffs of key employees, as such layoffs might lead to a loss of one or more core competencies. Instead, a firm that is simultaneously downscoping and downsizing becomes smaller by reducing the diversity of businesses in its portfolio to focus on core areas.[134]

In general, U.S. firms use downscoping as a restructuring strategy more frequently than do European companies—in fact, the trend in Europe, Latin America, and Asia has been to build conglomerates. In Latin America, these conglomerates are called *grupos*. Many Asian and Latin American conglomerates have begun to adopt Western corporate strategies in recent years and have been refocusing on their core businesses. This downscoping has occurred simultaneously with increasing globalization and with more open markets that have greatly enhanced competition. By downscoping, these firms have been able to focus on their core businesses and improve their competitiveness.[135]

7-5c Leveraged Buyouts

A *leveraged buyout* (LBO) is a restructuring strategy whereby a party (typically a private equity firm) buys all of a firm's assets in order to take the firm private. The Strategic Focus on the strategic positioning of private equity firms' general partners expands on their overall approach to structuring their portfolio of firms. The Strategic Focus illustrates how private equity firms have been evolving into a number of different strategic types.

As explained in the Strategic Focus, once a PE firm completes the transaction of a new portfolio firm, the target firm's company stock is no longer traded publicly. Traditionally, leveraged buyouts were used as a restructuring strategy to correct for managerial mistakes or because the firm's managers were making decisions that primarily served their own interests rather than those of shareholders.[136] However, some firms use buyouts to build firm resources and expand rather than simply restructure distressed assets.

Learn more about
Downscoping.
www.cengagebrain.com

Strategic Focus

SUCCESS

Strategic Positioning of Private Equity Buyout Firms (General Partners)

Private equity (PE) is equity capital which is not traded on public equity exchanges such as the New York Stock Exchange. In general, PE firms can include investments in early stage by "angel investors" and venture capitalists but is more readily known for late-stage mature enterprise buyout, or acquisition, strategies. These late-stage PE buyout firms used to be called leveraged buyout associations (or LBO associations). General partners in PE firms manage funds contributed by PE investors (usually labeled limited partners and composed mostly of institutional investors). General partners orchestrate the acquisition of portfolio firms. Most firms use the capital provided by limited partners to leverage money from banks and debt markets to make the acquisitions. These acquired firms are often publicly traded firms that are taken private. Accordingly, PE firms have five general players: general partners who play the most important role as they solicit investor funds and choose target firms to acquire or invest in; limited partners, who provide equity capital; target portfolio firms purchased by general partners; and banks and other debt suppliers who provide additional finance for buyout deals. In this example, we will discuss four strategic positions that general partners use to establish their portfolio of acquired firms. Figure 7.2 depicts the strategic positions of PE firms (general partners).

As Figure 7.2 illustrates, there are two basic dimensions of the strategic positioning of these firms—the financial structure emphasis and the diversified scope of the portfolio firms acquired. The financial structure emphasis has two basic categories, one focused on debt provided by banks or other debt providers, and the other focused on equity providers such as limited partners (institutional investors). This vertical dimension (financial structure) emphasizes a long-term vs. short-term orientation. Usually debt providers have a shorter-term orientation and are more conservative, whereas limited partners/owners may have a longer-term partnership arrangement with the general partners, given the funding arrangement of targeted funds provided to the general partner by limited partners. The horizontal dimension focuses on the diversified scope of the portfolio firms. Some PE firms have a very focused scope—for example, in a particular industry; whereas others have a very diversified scope across a wide range of industries and sectors. Those firms with a narrow scope usually provide more professional guidance and nurture in-house cooperation between buyout firms and do many add-on acquisitions to bolster the viability of firms in the longer term.

The lower-left quadrant focuses on short-term efficiency players, where buyout firms seek to restructure operations of an acquired portfolio firm and, as quickly as possible through financial engineering, to put the firm back on the open market

Martin C. Halusa, CEO of Apax Partners Worldwide LLP, at the 38th Annual World Economic Forum in Davos, Switzerland. Apax Partners looks for long-term investments in growth companies with a strategy that is geared toward releasing potential of the firms in which it invests.

through an IPO or sale to another company. Many PE buyout firms seek to reduce the holding period for a portfolio firm. For example, in 2000, the average holding period was 3.57 years, whereas in 2011 it was 4.81 years. This is because the exit opportunities for buyout firms in the financial downturn were more limited. More recently, many of the buyouts have been secondary buyouts; that is, one PE firm buying a portfolio firm from another PE firm rather than through an IPO or sale to another firm.

The upper-left quadrant representing niche players has more investment from limited partners with longer-term equity positions, and the holding period is longer than the mean-reported years for a portfolio firm. SCF Partners is an example of such a niche player. SCF Partners has made $1.6 billion in investments in portfolio companies and has produced approximately 10 IPOs as exits. However, SCF Partners' investments are relatively small compared to KKR, which as of 2010 had managed more than $60 billion in investments in portfolio firms. SCF Partners has focused its portfolio in "energy services, manufacturing, and energy equipment industry segments." With its narrow focus, it can develop expertise, cultivate its networks, and build a solid reputation in its chosen industry. SCF Partners collaborates with entrepreneurial owners of buyout firms to implement reforms and pursue complementary acquisitions to build up both the size and breadth of services for portfolio firms. They also seek to keep the entrepreneurial owners in place in order to maintain the emphasis on business growth. They recently had an IPO of Form Energy Technologies, which provides technologies and products

Figure 7.2 Strategic Positioning of Private Equity Firm General Partner Portfolios

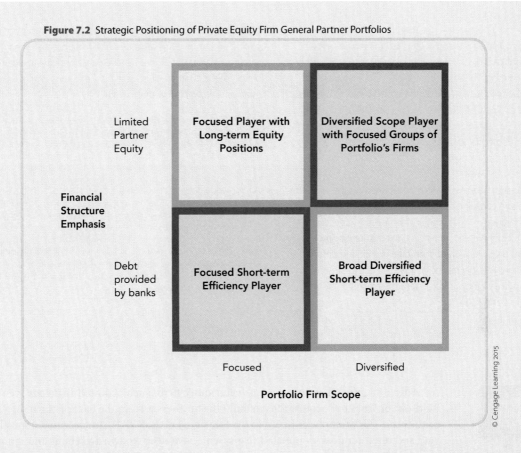

© Cengage Learning 2015

to undersea drilling and extraction operations, such as selling remote operating vehicles for inspection and survey of deep water well construction.

PE firms in the upper-right quadrant are diversified players with focused groups of portfolio firms and pursue more of a related diversification approach among portfolio firms (see Chapter 6). Furthermore, they have operational expertise that is provided to the firms, and usually the holding period for portfolio firms is longer than average. Apax Partners examples this type of portfolio firm. They invest in only five industries (financial services, health care, media, retailing, and telecom). Apax encourages the growth of its buyout firms to maximize value in its portfolio before pursuing an exit strategy.

PE firms in the lower-right quadrant focus on short-term efficiency but often have very large and diversified portfolios of firms. They might be represented by well-known firms such as KKR, Blackstone, and Carlyle. Interestingly, these particular general partner firms are publicly traded as well. As these large firms grow in size, they grow beyond the scope of particular industries and need to diversify to find new deals. Also, the size of the deal is increased because to have an impact on performance and overall value creation they generally have to do

large publicly traded firm buyouts. Although these firms have had to pay attention to operational improvement because holding times have grown longer, their focus on operational improvement is necessitated because they lack exit opportunities rather than from a desire to exchange better operational engineering for financial engineering. Also, as noted, this has also led to a major trend toward secondary buyouts of portfolio firms (one PE firm buying another PE firm's portfolio assets).

Finally, PE firms in the lower-left quadrant are focused on more short-term efficiency plays but in a more focused target market. Bain Capital is a good representative of this quadrant. Although the company is a typical short-term efficiency, it has historically focused on services industries (e.g., SunGard in business services, Toys"R"Us in retailing services, and Dunkin' Brands in the dining services industry). Because it has global reach, its focused strategy has enabled it to successfully implement corporate capital restructuring, operating earnings improvements, and acquisition development across countries.

Overall, PE firms provide advantages and disadvantages to portfolio firms. Some of the advantages are that there is stronger alignment between owners and managers because debt obligations constrain managerial discretion. Managers can take a longer-term perspective because they don't have to worry about quarterly earnings reports. Also, PE firms provide growth capital for firms unable to access public equity markets or other sources of financing. They also provide exit opportunities and enhance liquidity for small and medium-sized business owners, as illustrated in the SCF Partners example. However, PE firms have some drawbacks. Their high debt loads prevent portfolio firms from pursuing potentially valuable opportunities, especially long-term investment opportunities, and focus on high technology firms with R&D intensity.

There may also be some general advantages for the economy. PE firms facilitate consolidation and rationalizing of industries, and help to catalyze restructuring and removing excess capacity in mature industries when needed. Their investment approach also enhances diversification opportunities for limited partner institutional investors by creating a new class of investment. Finally, the approach they use broadens the market for corporate control, especially for distressed firms, leading to improved asset pricing and more efficient resource allocation in the economy at large. However, as Figure 7.2 illustrates, there are a wide range of approaches that are illustrated by the various examples in the quadrants associated with this figure.

Sources: 2013, PitchBook & Grant Thornton: Private equity exits report 2012 annual edition, www.grantthornton.com, Web site accessed May 7; N. Bacon, M. Wright, R. Ball, & M. Meuleman, 2013, Private equity, HRM, and employment, *Academy of Management Perspectives*, 27(1): 7–21; F. Cornelli, Z. Kominek, & A. Ljungqvist, 2013, Monitoring managers: Does it matter? *Journal of Finance*, 68(2): 431–481; R. Dezember, 2013, Carlyle Group lowers velvet rope – Offering allows some people to invest as little as $50,000 with the giant private-equity firm, *Wall Street Journal*, March 13, C1; R. E. Hoskisson, W. Shi, X. Yi, & J. Jin, 2013, The evolution and strategic positioning of private equity firms, *Academy of Management Perspectives*, 27(1): 22–38; P. G. Klein, J. L. Chapman, & M. P. Mondelli, 2013, Private equity and entrepreneurial governance: Time for a balanced view, *Academy of Management Perspectives*, 27(1): 39–51; H. Touryalai, 2013, A kinder, gentler KKR, *Forbes*, February 11, 82–87; J. Chang, 2012, Private equity revives in chemical M&A, *ICIS Chemical Business*, October 1, 16–17; R. Dezember & S. Terlep, 2012, Buyouts boom, but not like '07, *Wall Street Journal*, August 23, C1–C2; N. Vardi, 2012, The kings of capital, *Forbes*, October 22, 78–83.

Find out more about Apax Partners.
www.cengagebrain.com

After a firm is taken over by a private equity firm, such acquired firms are free to do "add-on" or "role-up" acquisitions to build the businesses from the base platform of a single acquisition. For example, as noted in the Strategic Focus, SCF Partners acquires mostly private and often founder-dominated firms, who have deep knowledge about and emotional connections with their ventures and are committed to growing their businesses. In other words, these entrepreneurial founder-owners are the key to buyout businesses' success by SCF Partners. As a result, in the post-buyout period, most top executives remain in the firm, and the role of SCF Partners is to assist these executives in improving firm performance. For example, the rapid growth of the tar sands industry in Canada requires increased investment in infrastructure (e.g., roads and metal buildings to accommodate workers), as most tar sands resources are located in the Canadian wilderness. Recognizing opportunities associated with this boom, SCF Partners established Site Energy Services Ltd. to acquire small energy services firms, consolidating local infrastructure services firms in Calgary by acquiring these local firms and getting them to partner with each other to increase scale and scope through joint operations.[137]

However, significant amounts of debt are commonly incurred to finance a buyout; hence the term *leveraged* buyout. To support debt payments and to downscope the company to concentrate on the firm's core businesses, the new owners may immediately sell a number of assets.[138] It is not uncommon for those buying a firm through an LBO to restructure the firm to the point that it can be sold at a profit within a five- to eight-year period.

Management buyouts (MBOs), employee buyouts (EBOs), and whole-firm buyouts, in which one company or partnership purchases an entire company instead of a part of it, are the three types of LBOs. In part because of managerial incentives, MBOs, more so than EBOs and whole-firm buyouts, have been found to lead to downscoping, increased strategic focus, and improved performance.[139] Research shows that management buyouts can lead to greater entrepreneurial activity and growth.[140] As such, buyouts can represent a form of firm rebirth to facilitate entrepreneurial efforts and stimulate strategic growth and productivity.[141]

7-5d Restructuring Outcomes

The short- and long-term outcomes associated with the three restructuring strategies are shown in Figure 7.3. As indicated, downsizing typically does not lead to higher firm performance.[142] In fact, some research results show that downsizing contributes to lower returns for both U.S. and Japanese firms. The stock markets in the firms' respective nations evaluated downsizing negatively, believing that it would have long-term negative effects on the firms' efforts to achieve strategic competitiveness. Investors also seem to conclude that downsizing occurs as a consequence of other problems in a company.[143] This assumption may be caused by a firm's diminished corporate reputation when a major downsizing is announced.[144]

The loss of human capital is another potential problem of downsizing (see Figure 7.3). Losing employees with many years of experience with the firm represents a major loss of knowledge. As noted in Chapter 3, knowledge is vital to competitive success in the global economy. Research also suggests that such loss of human capital can also spill over into dissatisfaction of customers.[145] Thus, in general, research evidence and corporate experience suggest that downsizing may be of more tactical (or short-term) value than strategic (or long-term) value,[146] meaning that firms should exercise caution when restructuring through downsizing.

Downscoping generally leads to more positive outcomes in both the short and long term than does downsizing or a leveraged buyout. Downscoping's desirable long-term outcome of higher performance is a product of reduced debt costs and the emphasis on strategic controls derived from concentrating on the firm's core businesses. In so doing, the refocused firm should be able to increase its ability to compete.[147]

Although whole-firm LBOs have been hailed as a significant innovation in the financial restructuring of firms, they can involve negative trade-offs.[148] First, the resulting large debt

Figure 7.3 Restructuring and Outcomes

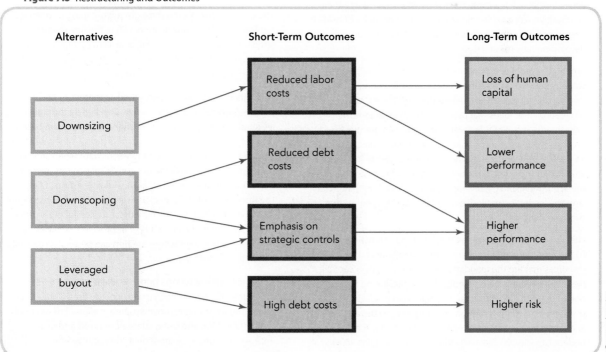

© Cengage Learning

increases the firm's financial risk, as is evidenced by the number of companies that filed for bankruptcy in the 1990s after executing a whole-firm LBO. Sometimes, the intent of the owners to increase the efficiency of the bought-out firm and then sell it within five to eight years creates a short-term and risk-averse managerial focus.[149] As a result, these firms may fail to invest adequately in R&D or take other major actions designed to maintain or improve the company's core competence.[150] Research also suggests that in firms with an entrepreneurial mindset, buyouts can lead to greater innovation, especially if the debt load is not too great.[151] However, because buyouts more often result in significant debt, most LBOs have been completed in mature industries where stable cash flows are normal, which can help the PE to meet the debt obligations.

SUMMARY

- Although the number of mergers and acquisitions completed declined in 2008 and 2009, largely because of the global financial crisis, merger and acquisition strategies became more frequent in 2010 and 2011 as a path to firm growth and earning strategic competitiveness. Globalization and deregulation of multiple industries in many economies are two of the factors making mergers and acquisitions attractive to large corporations and small firms.

- Firms use acquisition strategies to (1) increase market power, (2) overcome entry barriers to new markets or regions, (3) avoid the costs of developing new products and increase the speed of new market entries, (4) reduce the risk of entering a new business, (5) become more diversified, (6) reshape their competitive scope by developing a different portfolio of businesses, and (7) enhance their learning as the foundation for developing new capabilities.

- Among the problems associated with using an acquisition strategy are (1) the difficulty of effectively integrating the firms involved, (2) incorrectly evaluating the target firm's value, (3) creating debt loads that preclude adequate long-term investments (e.g., R&D), (4) overestimating the potential for synergy, (5) creating a firm that is too diversified, (6) creating an internal environment in which managers devote increasing amounts of their time and energy to analyzing and completing the acquisition, and (7) developing a combined firm that is too large, necessitating extensive use of bureaucratic, rather than strategic, controls.

- Effective acquisitions have the following characteristics: (1) the acquiring and target firms have complementary resources that are the foundation for developing new capabilities; (2) the acquisition is friendly, thereby facilitating integration of the firms' resources; (3) the target firm is selected and purchased based on thorough due diligence; (4) the acquiring and target firms have considerable slack in the form of cash or debt capacity; (5) the newly formed firm maintains a low or moderate level of debt by selling off portions of the acquired firm or some of the acquiring firm's poorly performing units; (6) the acquiring and acquired firms have experience in terms of adapting to change; and (7) R&D and innovation are emphasized in the new firm.

- Restructuring is used to improve a firm's performance by correcting for problems created by ineffective management. Restructuring by downsizing involves reducing the number of employees and hierarchical levels in the firm. Although it can lead to short-term cost reductions, they may be realized at the expense of long-term success, because of the loss of valuable human resources (and knowledge) and overall corporate reputation.

- The goal of restructuring through downscoping is to reduce the firm's level of diversification. Often, the firm divests unrelated businesses to achieve this goal. Eliminating unrelated businesses makes it easier for the firm and its top-level managers to refocus on the core businesses.

- Through an LBO, a firm is purchased so that it can become a private entity. LBOs usually are financed largely through debt, although limited partners (institutional investors) are becoming more prominent. General partners have a variety of strategies and some emphasize equity versus debt when limited partners have a longer time horizon. Management buyouts (MBOs), employee buyouts (EBOs), and whole-firm LBOs are the three types of LBOs. Because they provide clear managerial incentives, MBOs have been the most successful of the three. Often, the intent of a buyout is to improve efficiency and performance to the point where the firm can be sold successfully within five to eight years.

- Commonly, restructuring's primary goal is gaining or reestablishing effective strategic control of the firm. Of the three restructuring strategies, downscoping is aligned most closely with establishing and using strategic controls and usually improves performance more on a comparative basis.

REVIEW QUESTIONS

1. Why are merger and acquisition strategies popular in many firms competing in the global economy?

2. What reasons account for firms' decisions to use acquisition strategies as a means to achieving strategic competitiveness?

3. What are the seven primary problems that affect a firm's efforts to successfully use an acquisition strategy?

4. What are the attributes associated with a successful acquisition strategy?

5. What is the restructuring strategy, and what are its common forms?

6. What are the short- and long-term outcomes associated with the different restructuring strategies?

EXPERIENTIAL EXERCISES

EXERCISE 1: HOW DID THE DEAL WORK OUT?

The text argues that mergers and acquisitions are a popular strategy for businesses both in the United States and across borders. However, returns for acquiring firms do not always live up to expectations. This exercise seeks to address this notion by analyzing, pre- and post hoc, the results of actual acquisitions. By looking at the notifications of a deal beforehand, categorizing that deal, and then following it for a year, you will be able to learn about actual deals and their implications for strategists.

Working in teams, identify a merger or acquisition that was completed in the last few years. This may be a cross-border acquisition or a U.S.-centered one. A couple of possible sources for this information are Reuters' online M&A section or Yahoo! Finance's U.S. Mergers and Acquisitions Calendar. Each team must get their M&A choice approved in advance so as to avoid duplicates.

To complete this assignment, you should be prepared to answer the following questions:

1. Describe the environment for this arrangement at the time it was completed. Using concepts discussed in the text, focus on management's representation to shareholders, the industry environment, and the overall rationale for the deal.

2. Did the acquirer pay a premium for the target firm? If so, how much? In addition, search for investor comments regarding the wisdom of this agreement. Attempt to identify how the market reacted at the announcement of the deal (LexisNexis typically provides an article that will address this issue).

3. Describe the merger or acquisition going forward. Use the concepts from the text such as, but not limited to:
   a. The reason for the merger or acquisition (i.e., market power, overcoming entry barriers, etc.)
   b. Were there problems in achieving acquisition success?
   c. Would you categorize this deal as successful as of the time of your research? Give the reasons why or why not.

Plan on presenting your findings to the class in a 10- to 15-minute presentation. Organize the presentation as if you were updating the shareholders of the newly combined firm.

EXERCISE 2: WHAT REALLY GOES INTO A DUE DILIGENCE CHECKLIST?

Due diligence, according to your text, can potentially be a main determinant of whether or not an acquisition bucks the trend of unsatisfactory results. Since a significant number of acquisitions fail to live up to expectations, how is it that a due diligence process can provide such a benefit? An inadequate evaluation of the target seems hard to believe, noting that many times very sophisticated entities or individuals carry out this process like management consulting firms, investment banks, legal specialists, etc. Your assignment in this exercise is to research and produce a due diligence checklist that if implemented will provide to the extent possible a robust assessment of a target firm and attempt to prevent the aforementioned inadequate evaluation.

Working in teams, utilize library databases, trade associations, merger and acquisition clearing houses and the like to develop by category a due diligence checklist. This checklist is to be comprehensive in that it should cover the important topics as well as dive into the details underneath each one. Simply copying a checklist found on the internet will not suffice. You are to provide your checklist as a composite of the various readings, research, and examples you are able to find (make sure to provide references).

Be prepared to present to the class your findings and at a minimum explore:

1. What references went into your checklist?

2. Which areas do you feel would be the most difficult to quantify?

3. How long should this process take for an average acquisition?

4. How much will it cost?

5. Why do you think there are so many different varieties of due diligence checklists that are in use by various entities? Does this variety help or hurt accuracy? In other words, would a standard template across industries lead to a better process?

VIDEO CASE ▶

THE POWER OF A MERGER: SOUTHWEST

Southwest, long recognized for its discount airfares and its target-ing of the price-conscious consumer, has combined forces with another discount carrier—AirTran. AirTran asserts that with such a merger the potential exists for the expansion of discount airfares in the industry. In an industry where profit motive is high, consoli-dation is not uncommon even among major airlines, but the air traveler still sees fewer seats and higher prices. While major carri-ers seek profits, particularly in add-on fees, Southwest continues to press the competition by refraining from excessive fees.

Be prepared to discuss the following concepts and questions in class:

Concepts

▪ Mergers

▪ Acquisitions

▪ Restructuring

Questions

1. What would make the arrangement between Southwest and AirTran a merger and not an acquisition?

2. What were the reasons that Southwest and AirTran had for merging? What approach(es) did these companies use?

3. What would cause the Southwest/AirTran merger not to be successful?

4. What strategies would you recommend to Southwest should it need to restructure?

NOTES

1. M. Gruber, I. C. MacMillan, & J. D. Thompson, 2012, From minds to markets: How human capital endowments shape market opportunity identification of technology start-ups, *Journal of Management*, 38(5): 1421–1449; D. J. Teece, 2010, Alfred Chandler and "capabilities" theories of strategy and management, *Industrial and Corporate Change*, 19: 297–316.

2. H. R. Greve, 2011, Positional rigidity: Low performance and resource acquisition in large and small firms, *Strategic Management Journal*, 32(1): 103–114; R. Ragozzino & J. J. Reuer, 2010, The opportunities and challenges of entrepreneurial acquisitions, *European Management Review*, 7(2): 80–90.

3. K. Muehlfeld, P. Rao Sahib, & A. Van Witteloostuijn, 2012, A contextual theory of organizational learning from failures and successes: A study of acquisition completion in the global newspaper industry, 1981–2008, *Strategic Management Journal*, 33(8): 938–964; M. A. Hitt, D. King, H. Krishnan, M. Makri, M. Schijven, K. Shimizu, & H. Zhu, 2009, Mergers and acquisitions: Overcoming pitfalls, building synergy and creating value, *Business Horizons*, 52(6): 523–529.

4. A. S. Gaur, S. Malhotra, & P. Zhu, 2013, Acquisition announcements and stock market valuations of acquiring firms' rivals: A test of the growth probability hypothesis in China, *Strategic Management Journal*, 34(2): 215–232; C. M. Christensen, R. Alton, C. Rising, & A. Waldeck, 2011, The new M&A

playbook, *Harvard Business Review*, 89(3): 48–57; G. M. McNamara, J. Haleblian, & B. J. Dykes, 2008, The performance implications of participating in an acquisition wave: Early mover advantages, bandwagon effects, and the moderating influence of industry characteristics and acquirer tactics, *Academy of Management Journal*, 51: 113–130.

5. J. J. Reuer, T. W. Tong, & C. Wu, 2012, A signaling theory of acquisition premiums: Evidence from IPO targets, *Academy of Management Journal*, 55(3): 667–683; R. Dobbs & V. Tortorici, 2007, Cool heads will bring in the best deals; boardroom discipline is vital if the M&A boom is to benefit shareholders, *Financial Times*, February 28, 6.

6. 2013, Mergers & acquisitions review – financial advisors Q1 2013, www.thomsonreuters.com, April 4.

7. A. Kirchfeld & S. Saitto, 2012, Fourth-quarter M&A surge spurs optimism after 2012 deals decline, www.bloomberg.com, December 26.

8. 2013, Heineken reports rise in first quarter profits due to acquisitions; sees weaker 2013 growth, www.yahoofinance.com, April 24.

9. M. Cornett, B. Tanyeri, & H. Tehranian, 2011, The effect of merger anticipation on bidder and target firm announcement period returns, *Journal of Corporate Finance*, 17(3): 595–611; J. J. Reuer, 2005, Avoiding lemons in M&A deals, *MIT Sloan Management Review*, 46(3): 15–17.

10. C. Quinn Trank, J. E. Stambaugh, & H. Bemis, 2012, Capturing success, not taking the blame, *People & Strategy*, 35(3): 30–37; K. Cools & M. van de Laar, 2006, The performance of acquisitive companies in the U.S., in L. Renneboog (ed.), *Advances in Corporate Finance and Asset Pricing*, Amsterdam, Netherlands: Elsevier Science, 77–105.

11. A. Peaple, 2012, Roche is getting personal with Illumina, *Wall Street Journal*, January 26, C10.

12. N. Kresge & A. Edney, 2013, Illumina falls as Roche drops deal to buy U.S. company, www.bloomberg.com, January 13.

13. V. Ambrosini, C. Bowman, & R. Schoenberg, 2011, Should acquiring firms pursue more than one value creation strategy? An empirical test of acquisition performance, *British Journal of Management*, 22(1): 173–185; K. J. Martijn Cremers, V. B. Nair, & K. John, 2009, Takeovers and the cross-section of returns, *Review of Financial Studies*, 22: 1409–1445.

14. A. MacDonald, 2013, Glencore Xstrata unveils integration plan, *Wall Street Journal*, May 6, B3.

15. Ibid.

16. M. Humphery-Jenner, 2013, Takeover defenses as drivers of innovation and value-creation, *Strategic Management Journal*, in press.

17. M. Martynova & L. Renneboog, 2011, The performance of the European market for corporate control: Evidence from the

fifth takeover wave, *European Financial Management*, 17(2): 208–259; S. Sudarsanam & A. A. Mahate, 2006, Are friendly acquisitions too bad for shareholders and managers? Long-term value creation and top management turnover in hostile and friendly acquirers, *British Journal of Management: Supplement*, 17(1): S7–S30.

18. S. Bhattacharyya & A. Nain, 2011, Horizontal acquisitions and buying power: A product market analysis, *Journal of Financial Economics*, 99(1): 97–115; E. Akdogu, 2009, Gaining a competitive edge through acquisitions: Evidence from the telecommunications industry, *Journal of Corporate Finance*, 15: 99–112; E. Devos, P.-R. Kadapakkam, & S. Krishnamurthy, 2009, How do mergers create value? A comparison of taxes, market power, and efficiency improvements as explanations for synergies, *Review of Financial Studies*, 22: 1179–1211.

19. M. A. Hitt, D. King, H. Krishnan, M. Makri, M. Schijven, K. Shimizu, & H. Zhu, 2012, Creating value through mergers and acquisitions: Challenges and opportunities, in D. Faulkner, S. Teerikangas, & R. Joseph (Eds.), *Oxford Handbook of Mergers and Acquisitions*, Oxford, UK: Oxford University Press, 71–113; T. Hamza, 2011, Determinants of short-term value creation for the bidder: Evidence from France, *Journal of Management & Governance*, 15(2): 157–186; J. Haleblian, C. E. Devers, G. McNamara, M. A. Carpenter, & R. B. Davison, 2009, Taking stock of what we know about mergers and acquisitions: A review and research agenda, *Journal of Management*, 35: 469–502.

20. C. Winter, 2012, Bid & ask, *Bloomberg Businessweek*, December 17, 50.

21. Gaur, Malhotra, & Zhu, Acquisition announcements and stock market valuations of acquiring firms' rivals; K. E. Meyer, S. Estrin, S. K. Bhaumik, & M. W. Peng, 2009, Institutions, resources, and entry strategies in emerging economies, *Strategic Management Journal*, 30: 61–80; D. K. Oler, J. S. Harrison, & M. R. Allen, 2008, The danger of misinterpreting short-window event study findings in strategic management research: An empirical illustration using horizontal acquisitions, *Strategic Organization*, 6: 151–184.

22. M. Zollo & J. J. Reuer, 2010, Experience spillovers across corporate development activities, *Organization Science*, 21(6): 1195–1212; C. E. Fee & S. Thomas, 2004, Sources of gains in horizontal mergers: Evidence from customer, supplier, and rival firms, *Journal of Financial Economics*, 74: 423–460.

23. G. E. Halkos & N. G. Tzeremes, 2013, Estimating the degree of operational efficiency gains from a potential bank merger and acquisition: A DEA bootstrapped approach, *Journal of Banking & Finance*, 37(5): 1658–1668; L. Capron, W. Mitchell, & A. Swaminathan, 2001,

Asset divestiture following horizontal acquisitions: A dynamic view, *Strategic Management Journal*, 22: 817–844.

24. J. Shenoy, 2012, An examination of the efficiency, foreclosure, and collusion rationales for vertical takeovers, *Management Science*, 58(8): 1482–1501; M. F. Guillén & E. García-Canal, 2010, How to conquer new markets with old skills, *Harvard Business Review*, 88(11): 118–122; A. Parmigiani, 2007, Why do firms both make and buy? An investigation of concurrent sourcing, *Strategic Management Journal*, 28: 285–311.

25. D. Eaton, 2012, Bob Evans paying $50M for Kettle Creations, supplier of mashed potatoes and macaroni and cheese, *The Business Journal's Digital Network*, www.bizjournals.com, August 14.

26. D. FitzGerald, 2013, Oracle expands telecomm footprint with Tekelec buy, *Wall Street Journal*, www.wsj.com, March 25.

27. J. W. Brock & N. P. Obst, 2009, Market concentration, economic welfare, and antitrust policy, *Journal of Industry, Competition and Trade*, 9: 65–75; M. T. Brouwer, 2008, Horizontal mergers and efficiencies: Theory and antitrust practice, *European Journal of Law and Economics*, 26: 11–26.

28. J. Berman, 2013, UPS' planned acquisition of TNT Express officially withdrawn, *Logistics Management*, February, 14–15.

29. A. Sherman, 2013, Why DirecTV will take a pass on mobile, *Bloomberg Businessweek*, May 13–19, 44.

30. P. Zhu, V. Jog, & I. Otchere, 2011, Partial acquisitions in emerging markets: A test of the strategic market entry and corporate control hypotheses, *Journal of Corporate Finance*, 17(2): 288–305; K. E. Meyer, M. Wright, & S. Pruthi, 2009, Managing knowledge in foreign entry strategies: A resource-based analysis, *Strategic Management Journal*, 30: 557–574.

31. R. E. Hoskisson, M. Wright, I. Filatotchev, & M. W. Peng, 2013, Emerging multinationals from mid-range economies: The influence of institutions and factor markets, *Journal of Management Studies*, 50: in press; C. Y. Tseng, 2009, Technological innovation in the BRIC economies, *Research-Technology Management*, 52: 29–35; S. McGee, 2007, Seeking value in BRICs, *Barron's*, July 9, L10–L11.

32. I. Erel, R. C. Liao, & M. S. Weisbach, 2012, Determinants of cross-border mergers and acquisitions, *Journal of Finance*, 67(3): 1045–1082; K. Boeh, 2011, Contracting costs and information asymmetry reduction in cross-border M&A, *Journal of Management Studies*, 48(3): 568–590; R. Chakrabarti, N. Jayaraman, & S. Mukherjee, 2009, Mars-Venus marriages: Culture and cross-border M&A, *Journal of International Business Studies*, 40: 216–237.

33. I. Boudway, 2012, Bid & ask, *Bloomberg Businessweek*, October 22, 56.

34. F. De Beule & J. Duanmu, 2012, Locational determinants of internationalization: A firm-level analysis of Chinese and Indian acquisitions, *European Management Journal*, 30(3): 264–277; P. J. Williamson & A. P. Raman, 2011, How China reset its global acquisition agenda, *Harvard Business Review*, 89(4): 109–114; E. Zabinski, D. Freeman, & X. Jian, 2009, Navigating the challenges of cross-border M&A, *The Deal Magazine*, www.thedeal.com, May 29.

35. J. Lahart, 2012, Emerging risk for multinationals, *Wall Street Journal*, November 15, C12; Y. W. Chin, 2011, M&A under China's Anti-Monopoly Law, *Business Law Today*, 19(7): 1–5.

36. S. Montlake, 2013, Cat scammed, *Forbes*, March 4, 36–38.

37. L. Capron & W. Mitchell, 2012, *Build, Borrow or Buy: Solving the Growth Dilemma*, Cambridge: Harvard Business Review Press; G. K. Lee & M. B. Lieberman, 2010, Acquisition vs. internal development as modes of market entry, *Strategic Management Journal*, 31(2): 140–158; C. Homburg & M. Bucerius, 2006, Is speed of integration really a success factor of mergers and acquisitions? An analysis of the role of internal and external relatedness, *Strategic Management Journal*, 27: 347–367.

38. H. Evanschitzky, M. Eisend, R. J. Calantone, & Y. Jiang, 2012, Success factors of product innovation: An updated meta-analysis, *Journal of Product Innovation Management*, 29: 21–37; H. K. Ellonen, P. Wilstrom, & A. Jantunen, 2009, Linking dynamic-capability portfolios and innovation outcomes, *Technovation*, 29: 753–762; S. Karim, 2006, Modularity in organizational structure: The reconfiguration of internally developed and acquired business units, *Strategic Management Journal*, 27: 799–823.

39. M. Makri, M. A. Hitt, & P. J. Lane, 2010, Complementary technologies, knowledge relatedness, and invention outcomes in high technology M&As, *Strategic Management Journal*, 31: 602–628; R. E. Hoskisson & L. W. Busenitz, 2002, Market uncertainty and learning distance in corporate entrepreneurship entry mode choice, in M. A. Hitt, R. D. Ireland, S. M. Camp, & D. L. Sexton (eds.), *Strategic Entrepreneurship: Creating a New Mindset*, Oxford, U.K.: Blackwell Publishers, 151–172; M. A. Hitt, R. E. Hoskisson, R. A. Johnson, & D. D. Moesel, 1996, The market for corporate control and firm innovation, *Academy of Management Journal*, 39: 1084–1119.

40. A. DeRosa, 2012, Medtronic grows global reach, *Plastics News*, December 10, 11; M. Herper, 2010, Medtronic's bionic battle, *Forbes*, www.forbes.com, December 12.

41. S. Ransbotham & S. Mitra, 2010, Target age and the acquisition of innovation in high-technology industries, *Management Science*, 56(11): 2076–2093.

42. W. P. Wan & D. W. Yiu, 2009, From crisis to opportunity: Environmental jolt,

corporate acquisitions, and firm performance, *Strategic Management Journal*, 30: 791–801; G. Ahuja & R. Katila, 2001, Technological acquisitions and the innovation performance of acquiring firms: A longitudinal study, *Strategic Management Journal*, 22: 197–220.

43. J. R. Clark & R. S. Huckman, 2012, Broadening focus: Spillovers, complementarities, and specialization in the hospital industry, *Management Science*, 58(4): 708–722; X. Dean, Z. Changhui, & P. H. Phan, 2010, A real options perspective on sequential acquisitions in China, *Journal of International Business Studies*, 41(1): 166–174.

44. N. Zhou & A. Delios, 2012, Diversification and diffusion: A social networks and institutional perspective, *Asia Pacific Journal of Management*, 29(3): 773–798; U. Zander & L. Zander, 2010, Opening the grey box: Social communities, knowledge and culture in acquisitions, *Journal of International Business Studies*, 41(1): 27–37; F. Vermeulen, 2005, How acquisitions can revitalize companies, *MIT Sloan Management Review*, 46(4): 45–51; M. A. Hitt, R. E. Hoskisson, R. D. Ireland, & J. S. Harrison, 1991, Effects of acquisitions on R&D inputs and outputs, *Academy of Management Journal*, 34: 693–706.

45. S. Gamm, 2012, Xerox works to duplicate copier glory in digital services model, *Forbes*, July 19, 59; G. Colvin, 2010, Ursula Burns, *Fortune*, May 3, 161(6): 96–102.

46. H. Prechel, T. Morris, T. Woods, & R. Walden, 2008, Corporate diversification revisited: The political-legal environment, the multilayer-subsidiary form, and mergers and acquisitions, *The Sociological Quarterly*, 49: 849–878; C. E. Helfat & K. M. Eisenhardt, 2004, Inter-temporal economies of scope, organizational modularity, and the dynamics of diversification, *Strategic Management Journal*, 25: 1217–1232.

47. Z. Asher, 2012, X-ray: United Technologies, *Money*, September, 56; E. Crooks, 2011, United Technologies seeks emerging market expansion, *Financial Times*, April 28, 15.

48. B. Worthen, D. Cimilluca, & A. Das, 2012, Cisco hedges bet on video delivery, *Wall Street Journal*, March 16.

49. R. Kirkland, 2013, Connecting everything: A conversation with Cisco's Padmasree Warrior, *McKinsey Quarterly*, www.mckinseyquarterly.com, May.

50. Makri, Hitt, & Lane, Complementary technologies, knowledge relatedness, and invention outcomes in high technology M&As; T. Laamanen & T. Keil, 2008, Performance of serial acquirers: Toward an acquisition program perspective, *Strategic Management Journal*, 29: 663–672.

51. Bhattacharyya & Nain, Horizontal acquisitions and buying power; T. Yu, M. Subramaniam, & A. A. Cannella, Jr., 2009, Rivalry deterrence in international markets: Contingencies governing the mutual forbearance hypothesis, *Academy of Management Journal*, 52: 127–147; D. G. Sirmon, S. Gove, & M. A. Hitt, 2008, Resource management in dyadic competitive rivalry: The effects of resource bundling and deployment, *Academy of Management Journal*, 51: 919–933.

52. A. Kaul, 2012, Technology and corporate scope: Firm and rival innovation as antecedents of corporate transactions, *Strategic Management Journal*, 33(4): 347–367; M. Zollo & J. J. Reuer, 2010, Experience spillovers across corporate development activities, *Organization Science*, 21(6): 1195–1212; P. Puranam & K. Srikanth, 2007, What they know vs. what they do: How acquirers leverage technology acquisitions, *Strategic Management Journal*, 28: 805–825.

53. T. Gantumur & A. Stephan, 2012, Mergers & acquisitions and innovation performance in the telecommunications equipment industry, *Industrial & Corporate Change*, 21(2): 277–314; B. Park & P. N. Ghauri, 2011, Key factors affecting acquisition of technological capabilities from foreign acquiring firms by small and medium-sized local firms, *Journal of World Business*, 46(1): 116–125; S. A. Zahra & J. C. Hayton, 2008, The effect of international venturing on firm performance: The moderating influence of absorptive capacity, *Journal of Business Venturing*, 23: 195–220.

54. Makri, Hitt, & Lane, Complementary technologies, knowledge relatedness, and invention outcomes in high technology mergers and acquisitions; J. S. Harrison, M. A. Hitt, R. E. Hoskisson, & R. D. Ireland, 2001, Resource complementarity in business combinations: Extending the logic to organizational alliances, *Journal of Management*, 27: 679–690.

55. M. Friesl, 2012, Knowledge acquisition strategies and company performance in young high technology companies, *British Journal of Management*, 23(3): 325–343.

56. J. D. Rockoff, 2012, Bristol to buy Amylin in $5.3 billion deal, *Wall Street Journal*, www.wsj.com, July 1.

57. M. E. Graebner, K. M. Eisenhardt, & P. T. Roundy, 2010, Success and failure in technology acquisitions: Lessons for buyers and sellers, *Academy of Management Perspectives*, 24(3), 73–92; J. A. Schmidt, 2002, Business perspective on mergers and acquisitions, in J. A. Schmidt (ed.), *Making Mergers Work*, Alexandria, VA: Society for Human Resource Management, 23–46.

58. T. Herd, 2010, M&A success beating the odds, *Bloomberg Businessweek*, www.businessweek.com, June 23.

59. Muehlfeld, Rao Sahib, & Van Witteloostuijn, A contextual theory of organizational learning from failures and successes; M. Cording, P. Christmann, & D. R. King, 2008, Reducing causal ambiguity in acquisition integration: Intermediate goals as mediators of integration decisions and acquisition performance, *Academy of Management Journal*, 51: 744–767.

60. S. Teerikangas, 2012, Dynamics of acquired firm pre-acquisition employee reactions, *Journal of Management*, 38(2): 599–639; D. S. Siegel & K. L. Simons, 2010, Assessing the effects of mergers and acquisitions on firm performance, plant productivity, and workers: New evidence from matched employer-employee data, *Strategic Management Journal*, 31(8): 903–916; N. Kumar, 2009, How emerging giants are rewriting the rules of M&A, *Harvard Business Review*, 87(5): 115–121; M. C. Sturman, 2008, The value of human capital specificity versus transferability, *Journal of Management*, 34: 290–316.

61. A. Zaheer, X. Castañer, & D. Souder, 2013, Synergy sources, target autonomy, and integration in acquisitions, *Journal of Management*, 39(3): 604–632; K. M. Ellis, T. H. Reus, & B. T. Lamont, 2009, The effects of procedural and informational justice in the integration of related acquisitions, *Strategic Management Journal*, 30: 137–161.

62. T. H. Reus, 2012, Culture's consequences for emotional attending during cross-border acquisition implementation, *Journal of World Business*, 47(3): 342–351.

63. P. Monin, N. Noorderhaven, E. Vaara, & D. Kroon, 2013, Giving sense to and making sense of justice in postmerger integration, *Academy of Management Journal*, 56(1): 256–284.

64. M. Zollo, 1999, M&A—The challenge of learning to integrate: Mastering strategy (part eleven), *Financial Times*, December 6, 14–15.

65. J. Q. Barden, 2012, The influences of being acquired on subsidiary innovation adoption, *Strategic Management Journal*, 33(11): 1269–1285; E. Clark & M. Geppert, 2011, Subsidiary integration as identity construction and institution building: A political sensemaking approach, *Journal of Management Studies*, 48(2): 395–416; H. G. Barkema & M. Schijven, 2008, Toward unlocking the full potential of acquisitions: The role of organizational restructuring, *Academy of Management Journal*, 51: 696–722.

66. A. E. Rafferty & S. L. D. Restburg, 2010, The impact of change process and context on change reactions and turnover during a merger, *Journal of Management*, 36: 1309–1338.

67. R. Gibson, 2006, Package deal; UPS's purchase of Mail Boxes Etc. looked great on paper. Then came the culture clash, *Wall Street Journal*, May 8, R13.

68. 2013, Mail Boxes Etc., Wikipedia, www.wikipedia.org, accessed on May 17.

69. A. Sleptsov, J. Anand, & G. Vasudeva, 2013, Relationship configurations with information intermediaries: The effect of firm-investment bank ties on expected acquisition performance, *Strategic Management Journal*, 34(8): 957–977.

70. Montlake, Cat scammed.

71. R. Duchin & B. Schmidt, 2013, Riding the merger wave: Uncertainty, reduced

monitoring, and bad acquisitions, *Journal of Financial Economics*, 107(1): 69–88; J. DiPietro, 2010, Responsible acquisitions yield growth, *Financial Executive*, 26(10): 16–19.

72. A. Noto, 2013, HP assets conjure offers from tech buyers, *Mergers & Acquisitions Report*, January 21, 32.

73. T. B. Folta & J. P. O'Brien, 2008, Determinants of firm-specific thresholds in acquisition decisions, *Managerial and Decision Economics*, 29: 209–225; R. J. Rosen, 2006, Merger momentum and investor sentiment: The stock market reaction to merger announcements, *Journal of Business*, 79: 987–1017.

74. C. E. Devers, G. McNamara, J. Haleblian, & M. E. Yoder, 2013, Do they walk the talk or just talk the talk? Gauging acquiring CEO and director confidence in the value-creation potential of announced acquisitions, *Academy of Management Journal*, in press.

75. M. Schijven & M. A. Hitt, 2012, The vicarious wisdom of crowds: Toward a behavioral perspective on investor reactions to acquisition announcements, *Strategic Management Journal*, 33(11): 1247–1268.

76. G. Yago, 1991, *Junk Bonds: How High Yield Securities Restructured Corporate America*, New York: Oxford University Press, 146–148.

77. M. C. Jensen, 1986, Agency costs of free cash flow, corporate finance, and takeovers, *American Economic Review*, 76: 323–329.

78. S. Guo, E. S. Hotchkiss, & W. Song, 2011, Do buyouts (still) create value? *Journal of Finance*, 66(2): 479–517.

79. M. Gottfried, 2013, Debt Dish could give Sprint indigestion, *Wall Street Journal*, April 26, C8.

80. S. W. Bauguess, S. B. Moeller, F. P. Schlingemann, & C. J. Zutter, 2009, Ownership structure and target returns, *Journal of Corporate Finance*, 15: 48–65; H. Donker & S. Zahir, 2008, Takeovers, corporate control, and return to target shareholders, *International Journal of Corporate Governance*, 1: 106–134.

81. Zaheer, Castañer, & Souder, Synergy sources, target autonomy, and integration in acquisitions; Y. M. Zhou, 2011, Synergy, coordination costs, and diversification choices, *Strategic Management Journal*, 32: 624–639; A. B. Sorescu, R. K. Chandy, & J. C. Prabhu, 2007, Why some acquisitions do better than others: Product capital as a driver of long-term stock returns, *Journal of Marketing Research*, 44(1): 57–72.

82. S. Daneshkhu, 2013, Danone buys US organic baby food maker Happy Family, *Financial Times*, www.ft.com, May 13.

83. J. B. Barney, 1988, Returns to bidding firms in mergers and acquisitions: Reconsidering the relatedness hypothesis, *Strategic Management Journal*, 9 (Special Issue): 71–78.

84. O. E. Williamson, 1999, Strategy research: Governance and competence perspectives, *Strategic Management Journal*, 20: 1087–1108.

85. S. Snow, 2013, How to avoid a post-acquisition idea slump, *Fast Company*, February, 50; M. Cleary, K. Hartnett, & K. Dubuque, 2011, Road map to efficient merger integration, *American Banker*, March 22, 9; S. Chatterjee, 2007, Why is synergy so difficult in mergers of related businesses? *Strategy & Leadership*, 35(2): 46–52.

86. W. P. Wan, R. E. Hoskisson, J. C. Short, & D. W. Yiu, 2011, Resource-based theory and corporate diversification: Accomplishments and opportunities, *Journal of Management*, 37(5): 1335–1368; E. Rawley, 2010, Diversification, coordination costs and organizational rigidity: Evidence from microdata, *Strategic Management Journal*, 31: 873–891; C. W. L. Hill & R. E. Hoskisson, 1987, Strategy and structure in the multiproduct firm, *Academy of Management Review*, 12: 331–341.

87. S. Pathak, R. E. Hoskisson, & R. A. Johnson, 2013, Settling up in CEO compensation: The impact of divestiture intensity and contextual factors in refocusing firms, *Strategic Management Journal*, in press; M. L. A. Hayward & K. Shimizu, 2006, De-commitment to losing strategic action: Evidence from the divestiture of poorly performing acquisitions, *Strategic Management Journal*, 27: 541–557; R. A. Johnson, R. E. Hoskisson, & M. A. Hitt, 1993, Board of director involvement in restructuring: The effects of board versus managerial controls and characteristics, *Strategic Management Journal*, 14 (Special Issue): 33–50.

88. J. Hagedoorn & N. Wang, 2012, Is there complementarity or substitutability between internal and external R&D strategies? *Research Policy*, 41(6): 1072–1083; P. David, J. P. O'Brien, T. Yoshikawa, & A. Delios, 2010, Do shareholders or stakeholders appropriate the rents from corporate diversification? The influence of ownership structure, *Academy of Management Journal*, 53: 636–654; R. E. Hoskisson & R. A. Johnson, 1992, Corporate restructuring and strategic change: The effect on diversification strategy and R&D intensity, *Strategic Management Journal*, 13: 625–634.

89. R. D. Banker, S. Wattal, & J. M. Plehn-Dujowich, 2011, R&D versus acquisitions: Role of diversification in the choice of innovation strategy by information technology firms, *Journal of Management Information Systems*, 28(2): 109–144; J. L. Stimpert, I. M. Duhaime, & J. Chesney, 2010, Learning to manage a large diversified firm, *Journal of Leadership and Organizational Studies*, 17: 411–425; T. Keil, M. V. J. Maula, H. Schildt, & S. A. Zahra, 2008, The effect of governance modes and relatedness of external business development activities on innovative performance, *Strategic Management Journal*, 29: 895–907;

K. H. Tsai & J. C. Wang, 2008, External technology acquisition and firm performance: A longitudinal study, *Journal of Business Venturing*, 23: 91–112.

90. A. Kacperczyk, 2009, With greater power comes greater responsibility? Takeover protection and corporate attention to stakeholders, *Strategic Management Journal*, 30: 261–285; L. H. Lin, 2009, Mergers and acquisitions, alliances and technology development: An empirical study of the global auto industry, *International Journal of Technology Management*, 48: 295–307; M. L. Barnett, 2008, An attention-based view of real options reasoning, *Academy of Management Review*, 33: 606–628.

91. J. A. Martin & K. J. Davis, 2010, Learning or hubris? Why CEOs create less value in successive acquisitions, *Academy of Management Perspectives*, 24(1): 79–81; M. L. A. Hayward & D. C. Hambrick, 1997, Explaining the premiums paid for large acquisitions: Evidence of CEO hubris, *Administrative Science Quarterly*, 42: 103–127; R. Roll, 1986, The hubris hypothesis of corporate takeovers, *Journal of Business*, 59: 197–216.

92. F. Vermeulen, 2007, Business insight (a special report): Bad deals: Eight warning signs that an acquisition may not pay off, *Wall Street Journal*, April 28, R10.

93. D. H. Zhu, 2013, Group polarization on corporate boards: Theory and evidence on board decisions about acquisition premiums, *Strategic Management Journal*, 34(7): 800–822.

94. Christensen, Alton, Rising, & Waldeck, The new M&A playbook.

95. J. Reingold & D. Burke, 2013, Citigroup's new CEO is a banker. Imagine that, *Fortune*, May 20, 176–181.

96. V. Swaminathan, F. Murshed, & J. Hulland, 2008, Value creation following merger and acquisition announcements: The role of strategic emphasis alignment, *Journal of Marketing Research*, 45: 33–47.

97. J. Begley & T. Donnelly, 2011, The DaimlerChrysler Mitsubishi merger: A study in failure, *International Journal of Automotive Technology and Management*, 11(1): 36–48.

98. M. Wagner, 2011, To explore or to exploit? An empirical investigation of acquisitions by large incumbents, *Research Policy*, 40(9): 1217–1225; H. Greve, 2011, Positional rigidity: Low performance and resource acquisition in large and small firms, *Strategic Management Journal*, 32(1): 103–114.

99. D. Clark & S. Tibken, 2011, Corporate news: Cisco to reduce its bureaucracy, *Wall Street Journal*, May 6, B4.

100. Vermeulen, Business insight (a special report): Bad deals: Eight warning signs that an acquisition may not pay off.

101. E. Gomes, D. N. Angwin, Y. Weber, & S. Tarba, 2013, Critical success factors through the mergers and acquisitions process: Revealing pre- and post-M&A

connections for improved performance, *Thunderbird International Business Review*, 55(1): 13–35; M. Cording, P. Christmann, & C. Weigelt, 2010, Measuring theoretically complex constructs: The case of acquisition performance, *Strategic Organization*, 8(1): 11–41; H. G. Barkema & M. Schijven, 2008, How do firms learn to make acquisitions? A review of past research and an agenda for the future, *Journal of Management*, 34: 594–634.

102. A. Riviezzo, 2013, Acquisitions in knowledge-intensive industries: Exploring the distinctive characteristics of the effective acquirer, *Management Research Review*, 36(2): 183–212; S. Chatterjee, 2009, The keys to successful acquisition programmes, *Long Range Planning*, 42: 137–163.

103. R. Karlgaard, 2012, Driving change: Cisco's Chambers, *Forbes*, February 13, 32; R. Myers, 2011, Integration acceleration, *CFO*, 27(1): 52–57.

104. D. Mayer & M. Kenney, 2004, Economic action does not take place in a vacuum: Understanding Cisco's acquisition and development strategy, *Industry and Innovation*, 11(4): 299–325.

105. 2013, Business management case study: How Cisco applies companywide expertise for integrating acquired companies, www.cisco.com, accessed May 17.

106. M. A. Hitt, R. D. Ireland, J. S. Harrison, & A. Best, 1998, Attributes of successful and unsuccessful acquisitions of U.S. firms, *British Journal of Management*, 9: 91–114.

107. K. Uhlenbruck, M. A. Hitt, & M. Semadeni, 2006, Market value effects of acquisitions involving Internet firms: A resource-based analysis, *Strategic Management Journal*, 27: 899–913.

108. A. Zaheer, E. Hernandez, & S. Banerjee, 2010, Prior alliances with targets and acquisition performance in knowledge-intensive industries, *Organization Science*, 21: 1072–1094; P. Porrini, 2004, Can a previous alliance between an acquirer and a target affect acquisition performance? *Journal of Management*, 30: 545–562.

109. Y. Zeng, T. J. Douglas, & C. Wu, 2013, The seller's perspective on determinants of acquisition likelihood: Insights from China's beer industry, *Journal of Management Studies*, 50(4): 673–698.

110. A. Rouzies & H. L. Colman, 2012, Identification processes in post-acquisition integration: The role of social interactions, *Corporate Reputation Review*, 15(3): 143–157; D. K. Ellis, T. Reus, & B. Lamont, 2009, The effects of procedural and informational justice in the integration of related acquisitions, *Strategic Management Journal*, 30(2): 137–161; R. J. Aiello & M. D. Watkins, 2000, The fine art of friendly acquisition, *Harvard Business Review*, 78(6): 100–107.

111. J. Krug, P. Wright, & M. Kroll, 2013, Top management turnover following mergers and acquisitions: Solid research to date

but still much to be learned, *Academy of Management Perspectives*, in press; D. D. Bergh, 2001, Executive retention and acquisition outcomes: A test of opposing views on the influence of organizational tenure, *Journal of Management*, 27: 603–622; J. P. Walsh, 1989, Doing a deal: Merger and acquisition negotiations and their impact upon target company top management turnover, *Strategic Management Journal*, 10: 307–322.

112. D. A. Waldman & M. Javidan, 2009, Alternative forms of charismatic leadership in the integration of mergers and acquisitions, *The Leadership Quarterly*, 20: 130–142; F. J. Froese, Y. S. Pak, & L. C. Chong, 2008, Managing the human side of cross-border acquisitions in South Korea, *Journal of World Business*, 43: 97–108.

113. R. Agarwal, J. Anand, J. Bercovitz, & R. Croson, 2012, Spillovers across organizational architectures: The role of prior resource allocation and communication in post-acquisition coordination outcomes, *Strategic Management Journal*, 33(6): 710–733; K. Marmenout, 2010, Employee sensemaking in mergers: How deal characteristics shape employee attitudes, *Journal of Applied Behavioral Science*, 46(3): 329–359; M. E. Graebner, 2009, Caveat venditor: Trust asymmetries in acquisitions of entrepreneurial firms, *Academy of Management Journal*, 52: 435–472; N. J. Morrison, G. Kinley, & K. L. Ficery, 2008, Merger deal breakers: When operational due diligence exposes risk, *Journal of Business Strategy*, 29: 23–28.

114. Y. Suh, J. You, & P. Kim, 2013, The effect of innovation capabilities and experience on cross-border acquisition performance, *Global Journal of Business Research*, 7(3): 59–74; J. Jwu-Rong, H. Chen-Jui, & L. Hsieh-Lung, 2010, A matching approach to M&A, R&D, and patents: Evidence from Taiwan's listed companies, *International Journal of Electronic Business Management*, 8(3): 273–280.

115. E. McGirt, 2012, Fresh copy: How Ursala Burns reinvented Xerox, *Fast Company*, January, 132–138.

116. K. H. Heimeriks, M. Schijven, & S. Gates, 2013, Manifestations of higher-order routines: The underlying mechanisms of deliberate learning in the context of postacquisition integration, *Academy of Management Journal*, 55(3): 703–726; J. M. Shaver & J. M. Mezias, 2009, Diseconomies of managing in acquisitions: Evidence from civil lawsuits, *Organization Science*, 20: 206–222; M. L. McDonald, J. D. Westphal, & M. E. Graebner, 2008, What do they know? The effects of outside director acquisition experience on firm acquisition performance, *Strategic Management Journal*, 29: 1155–1177.

117. C. Moschieri & J. Mair, 2012, Managing divestitures through time—Expanding current knowledge, *Academy of*

Management Perspectives, 26(4): 35–50; D. Lee & R. Madhaven, 2010, Divestiture and firm performance: A meta-analysis, *Journal of Management*, 36: 1345–1371; D. D. Bergh & E. N.-K. Lim, 2008, Learning how to restructure: Absorptive capacity and improvisational views of restructuring actions and performance, *Strategic Management Journal*, 29: 593–616.

118. Y. Zhou, X. Li, & J. Svejnar, 2011, Subsidiary divestiture and acquisition in a financial crisis: Operational focus, financial constraints, and ownership, *Journal of Corporate Finance*, 17(2): 272–287; Y. G. Suh & E. Howard, 2009, Restructuring retailing in Korea: The case of Samsung-Tesco, *Asia Pacific Business Review*, 15: 29–40; Z. Wu & A. Delios, 2009, The emergence of portfolio restructuring in Japan, *Management International Review*, 49: 313–335.

119. S. Thurm, 2008, Who are the best CEOs of 2008? *Wall Street Journal*, www.wsj.com, December 15.

120. J. Xia & S. Li, 2013, The divestiture of acquired subunits: A resource-dependence approach, *Strategic Management Journal*, 34: 131–148; L. Diestre & N. Rajagopalan, 2011, An environmental perspective on diversification: The effects of chemical relatedness and regulatory sanctions, *Academy of Management Journal*, 54: 97–115.

121. A. Fortune & W. Mitchell, 2012, Unpacking firm exit at the firm and industry levels: The adaptation and selection of firm capabilities, *Strategic Management Journal*, 33(7): 794–819; J. L. Morrow, Jr., D. G. Sirmon, M. A. Hitt, & T. R. Holcomb, 2007, Creating value in the face of declining performance: Firm strategies and organizational recovery, *Strategic Management Journal*, 28: 271–283; J. L. Morrow, Jr., R. A. Johnson, & L. W. Busenitz, 2004, The effects of cost and asset retrenchment on firm performance: The overlooked role of a firm's competitive environment, *Journal of Management*, 30: 189–208.

122. G. J. Castrogiovanni & G. D. Bruton, 2000, Business turnaround processes following acquisitions: Reconsidering the role of retrenchment, *Journal of Business Research*, 48: 25–34; W. McKinley, J. Zhao, & K. G. Rust, 2000, A sociocognitive interpretation of organizational downsizing, *Academy of Management Review*, 25: 227–243.

123. J. D. Evans & F. Hefner, 2009, Business ethics and the decision to adopt golden parachute contracts: Empirical evidence of concern for all stakeholders, *Journal of Business Ethics*, 86: 65–79; H. A. Krishnan, M. A. Hitt, & D. Park, 2007, Acquisition premiums, subsequent workforce reductions and post-acquisition performance, *Journal of Management*, 44: 709–732.

124. K. McFarland, 2008, Four mistakes leaders make when downsizing, *BusinessWeek Online*, www.businessweek.com, October 24.

125. D. K. Lim, N. Celly, E. A. Morse, & W. Rowe, 2013, Rethinking the effectiveness of asset and cost retrenchment: The contingency effects of a firm's rent creation mechanism, *Strategic Management Journal*, 34(1): 42–61.

126. R. Iverson & C. Zatzick, 2011, The effects of downsizing on labor productivity: The value of showing consideration for employees' morale and welfare in high-performance work systems, *Human Resource Management*, 50(1): 29–43; C. O. Trevor & A. J. Nyberg, 2008, Keeping your headcount when all about you are losing theirs: Downsizing, voluntary turnover rates, and the moderating role of HR practices, *Academy of Management Journal*, 51: 259–276.

127. Bergh & Lim, Learning how to restructure; R. E. Hoskisson & M. A. Hitt, 1994, *Downscoping: How to Tame the Diversified Firm*, New York: Oxford University Press.

128. A. T. Nicolai, A. Schulz, & T. W. Thomas, 2010, What Wall Street wants – Exploring the role of security analysts in the evolution and spread of management concepts, *Journal of Management Studies*, 47(1): 162–189; L. Dranikoff, T. Koller, & A. Schneider, 2002, Divestiture: Strategy's missing link, *Harvard Business Review*, 80(5): 74–83.

129. R. E. Hoskisson & M. A. Hitt, 1990, Antecedents and performance outcomes of diversification: A review and critique of theoretical perspectives, *Journal of Management*, 16: 461–509.

130. C. Moschieri, 2011, The implementation and structuring of divestitures: The unit's perspective, *Strategic Management Journal*, 32: 368–401.

131. T. Laamanen, M. Brauer, & O. Junna, 2013, Performance of acquirers of divested assets: Evidence from the U.S. software industry, *Strategic Management Journal*, in press.

132. M. F. Brauer & M. F. Wiersema, 2012, Industry divestiture waves: How a firm's position influences investor returns, *Academy of Management Journal*, 55(6): 1472–1492.

133. Reingold & Burke, Citigroup's new CEO is a banker; 2010, Citi to shrink its consumer-lending unit, *American Banker*, June 2, 16.

134. Pathak, Hoskisson, & Johnson, Settling up in CEO compensation: The impact of divestiture intensity and contextual factors in refocusing firms; A. Kambil, 2008, What is your recession playbook? *Journal of Business Strategy*, 29: 50–52.

135. H. Berry, 2013, When do firms divest foreign operations? *Organization Science*, 24(1): 246–261; C. Chi-Nien & L. Xiaowei, 2008, Institutional logics or agency costs: The influence of corporate governance models on business group restructuring in emerging economies, *Organization Science*, 19(5): 766–784; R. E. Hoskisson, R. A. Johnson, L. Tihanyi, & R. E. White, 2005, Diversified business groups and corporate refocusing in emerging economies, *Journal of Management*, 31: 941–965.

136. S. N. Kaplan & P. Stromberg, 2009, Leveraged buyouts and private equity, *Journal of Economic Perspectives*, 23: 121–146; C. Moschieri & J. Mair, 2008, Research on corporate divestures: A synthesis, *Journal of Management & Organization*, 14: 399–422.

137. R. E. Hoskisson, W. Shi, X. Yi, & J. Jin, 2013, The evolution and strategic positioning of private equity firms, *Academy of Management Perspectives*, 27(1): 22–38.

138. K. H. Wruck, 2009, Private equity, corporate governance, and the reinvention of the market for corporate control, *Journal of Applied Corporate Finance*, 20: 8–21; M. F. Wiersema & J. P. Liebeskind, 1995, The effects of leveraged buyouts on corporate growth and diversification in large firms, *Strategic Management Journal*, 16: 447–460.

139. N. Wilson, M. Wright, D. S. Siegel, & L. Scholes, 2012, Private equity portfolio company performance during the global recession, *Journal of Corporate Finance*, 18(1): 193–205; R. Harris, D. S. Siegel, & M. Wright, 2005, Assessing the impact of management buyouts on economic efficiency: Plant-level evidence from the United Kingdom, *Review of Economics and Statistics*, 87: 148–153.

140. H. Bruining, E. Verwaal, & M. Wright, 2013, Private equity and entrepreneurial management in management buy-outs, *Small Business Economics*, 40(3): 591–605; M. Meuleman, K. Amess, M. Wright, & L. Scholes, 2009, Agency, strategic entrepreneurship, and the performance of private equity-backed buyouts, *Entrepreneurship Theory and Practice*, 33: 213–239.

141. Moschieri, The implementation and structuring of divestitures: The unit's perspective; Siegel & Simons, Assessing the effects of mergers and acquisitions on firm performance, plant productivity, and workers; W. Kiechel III, 2007, Private equity's long view, *Harvard Business Review*, 85(8): 18–20; M. Wright, R. E. Hoskisson, & L. W. Busenitz, 2001, Firm rebirth: Buyouts as facilitators of strategic growth and entrepreneurship, *Academy of Management Executive*, 15(1): 111–125.

142. E. G. Love & M. Kraatz, 2009, Character, conformity, or the bottom line? How and why downsizing affected corporate reputation, *Academy of Management Journal*, 52: 314–335; J. P. Guthrie & D. K. Datta, 2008, Dumb and dumber: The impact of downsizing on firm performance as moderated by industry conditions, *Organization Science*, 19: 108–123.

143. H. A. Krishnan & D. Park, 2002, The impact of work force reduction on subsequent performance in major mergers and acquisitions: An exploratory study, *Journal of Business Research*, 55(4): 285–292; P. M. Lee, 1997, A comparative analysis of layoff announcements and stock price reactions

in the United States and Japan, *Strategic Management Journal*, 18: 879–894.

144. D. J. Flanagan & K. C. O'Shaughnessy, 2005, The effect of layoffs on firm reputation, *Journal of Management*, 31: 445–463.

145. P. Williams, K. M. Sajid, & N. Earl, 2011, Customer dissatisfaction and defection: The hidden costs of downsizing, *Industrial Marketing Management*, 40(3): 405–413.

146. P. Galagan, 2010, The biggest losers: The perils of extreme downsizing, *T+D*, November, 27–29; D. S. DeRue, J. R. Hollenbeck, M. D. Johnson, D. R. Ilgen, & D. K. Jundt, 2008, How different team downsizing approaches influence team-level adaptation and performance, *Academy of Management Journal*, 51: 182–196; C. D. Zatzick & R. D. Iverson, 2006, High-involvement management and workforce reduction: Competitive advantage or disadvantage? *Academy of Management Journal*, 49: 999–1015.

147. C. Moschieri & J. Mair, 2011, Adapting for innovation: Including divestitures in the debate, *Long Range Planning*, 44(1): 4–25; K. Shimizu & M. A. Hitt, 2005, What constrains or facilitates divestitures of formerly acquired firms? The effects of organizational inertia, *Journal of Management*, 31: 50–72.

148. P. G. Klein, J. L. Chapman, & M. P. Mondelli, 2013, Private equity and entrepreneurial governance: Time for a balanced view, *Academy of Management Perspectives*, 27(1): 39–51; D. T. Brown, C. E. Fee, & S. E. Thomas, 2009, Financial leverage and bargaining power with suppliers: Evidence from leveraged buyouts, *Journal of Corporate Finance*, 15: 196–211.

149. S. B. Rodrigues & J. Child, 2010, Private equity, the minimalist organization and the quality of employment relations, *Human Relations*, 63(9): 1321–1342; G. Wood & M. Wright, 2009, Private equity: A review and synthesis, *International Journal of Management Reviews*, 11: 361–380; A.-L. Le Nadant & F. Perdreau, 2006, Financial profile of leveraged buy-out targets: Some French evidence, *Review of Accounting and Finance*, (4): 370–392.

150. M. Goergen, N. O'Sullivan, & G. Wood, 2011, Private equity takeovers and employment in the UK: Some empirical evidence, *Corporate Governance: An International Review*, 19(3): 259–275; G. D. Bruton, J. K. Keels, & E. L. Scifres, 2002, Corporate restructuring and performance: An agency perspective on the complete buyout cycle, *Journal of Business Research*, 55: 709–724; W. F. Long & D. J. Ravenscraft, 1993, LBOs, debt, and R&D intensity, *Strategic Management Journal*, 14 (Special Issue): 119–135.

151. S. A. Zahra, 1995, Corporate entrepreneurship and financial performance: The case of management leveraged buyouts, *Journal of Business Venturing*, 10: 225–248.

8

International Strategy

Studying this chapter should provide you with the strategic management knowledge needed to:

1 Explain incentives that can influence firms to use an international strategy.

2 Identify three basic benefits firms achieve by successfully implementing an international strategy.

3 Explore the determinants of national advantage as the basis for international business-level strategies.

4 Describe the three international corporate-level strategies.

5 Discuss environmental trends affecting the choice of international strategies, particularly international corporate-level strategies.

6 Explain the five modes firms use to enter international markets.

7 Discuss the two major risks of using international strategies.

8 Discuss the strategic competitiveness outcomes associated with international strategies, particularly with an international diversification strategy.

9 Explain two important issues firms should have knowledge about when using international strategies.

AN INTERNATIONAL STRATEGY POWERS ABB'S FUTURE

 ABB is a major competitor in the power and automation technologies industries across the major markets globally. It has 145,000 employees operating in almost 100 countries. In fact, it has five major businesses—power products, power systems, discrete automation, low voltage products, and process automation. It operates in eight major regions: (1) Northern Europe, (2) Central Europe, (3) the Mediterranean, (4) North America, (5) South America, (6) India, the Middle East, and Africa, (7) North Asia, and (8) South Asia. Over time, ABB has been a successful company using its geographic diversification across the globe to its advantage. However, it also exemplifies the difficulty of managing an international strategy and operations. For example, its power systems business has experienced performance problems in recent years due to poor performance in some countries.

As a result, it recently announced that it was going to reduce or eliminate operations in Lithuania, Nigeria, the Philippines, Slovakia, and six additional countries. The CEO stated that the returns from these operations had not justified the investments made.

In recent years, most of ABB's entries to new markets and expansions in existing markets have come from acquisitions of existing businesses in those markets. Recently, it acquired Siemens' solar energy business, Power-One, and U.S.-based Los Gatos Research, a manufacturer of gas analyzers used in environmental monitoring and research. The purchase of Power-One represents a major risk as the solar power industry is in a downturn, yet some analysts predict a brighter future for the industry over the long term. ABB also uses other modes of entry and expansion, exemplified by the 2013 joint venture with China's Jiangsu Jinke Smart Electric Company to design, manufacture, and

provide follow-up service on high voltage instrument transformers. It also recently procured major contracts for business in Brazil and South Africa.

Partly due to the global economic recession that began in 2008, recent weak economic performance, and some poor expansion decisions, ABB's performance has been weaker than expected. As a result, the CEO and chief technology officer announced their resignations in 2013. Despite these changes, ABB is a highly respected global brand and after its recent changes (e.g., closing some country operations), its revenues and earnings have started to rise. These positive changes have been largely attributed to the success of its North American businesses. Its acquisitions of Baldor (maker of industrial motors) in 2010 and Thomas & Betts in 2012 greatly enhanced its North American operations and revenues. Therefore, even in turbulent times, ABB's future looks bright.

Sources: 2013, ABB procures contract in Brazil, *Zacks Equity Research*, www.zacks.com, May 14; 2013, ABB's South African project, *Zacks Equity Research*, www.zacks.com, May 13; P. Winters, 2013, ABB loses Banerjee after Hogan's decision to step down, *Bloomberg Businessweek*, www.businessweek.com, May 13; J. Revill & A. Morse, 2013, ABB CEO to resign, *Wall Street Journal*, www.wsj.com, May 10; 2013, ABB strengthens footprints in China, *Zacks Equity Research*, www.zacks.com, May 10; J. Revill, 2013, ABB buys US gas analyzer company Los Gatos Research, *Wall Street Journal*, www.wsj.com, May 3; 2013, ABB/Power-One: Shining example, *Financial Times*, www.ft.com, April 22; W. Pentland, 2013, ABB gambles big on solar power, *Forbes*, www.forbes.com, April 22; M. Scott, 2013, ABB to buy Power-One for $1 billion, *New York Times Dealbook*, http://dealbook.nytimes.com, April 22; J. Shotter, 2013, ABB boosted by US ventures, *Financial Times*, www.ft.com, February 14; J. Shotter, 2012, ABB overhauls power systems division, *Financial Times*, www.ft.com, December 14.

Learn more about Baldor, another company acquired by ABB.
www.cengagebrain.com

Our description of ABB's competitive actions in this chapter's Opening Case (e.g., expansion in North American markets) highlights the importance of international markets for this firm. It is using its returns in the North American markets to overcome weaknesses in its European markets. Being able to effectively compete in countries and regions outside a firm's domestic market is increasingly important to firms of all types, as exemplified by ABB. One reason for this is that the effects of globalization continue to reduce the number of industrial and consumer markets in which only domestic firms can compete successfully. In place of what historically were relatively stable and predictable domestic markets, firms across the globe find they are now competing in globally oriented industries—industries in which firms must compete in all world markets where a consumer or commercial good or service is sold in order to be competitive.[1] Unlike domestic markets, global markets are relatively unstable and much less predictable.

The purpose of this chapter is to discuss how international strategies can be a source of strategic competitiveness for firms competing in global markets. To do this, we examine a number of topics (see Figure 8.1). After describing incentives that influence firms to identify international opportunities, we discuss three basic benefits that can accrue to firms that successfully use international strategies. We then turn our attention to the international strategies available to firms. Specifically, we examine both international business-level strategies

Figure 8.1 Opportunities and Outcomes of International Strategy

Identify International Opportunities	Explore Resources and Capabilities	Use Core Competence		Strategic Competitiveness Outcomes
Basic Benefits	International Strategies	Modes of Entry		
Increased market size	International business-level strategy	Exporting	Management problems and risk	Improved performance
Economies of scale and learning	International corporate-level strategy	Licensing		
	• Multidomestic strategy	Strategic alliances		
		Acquisitions		
Location advantages	• Global strategy	New wholly owned subsidiary	Management problems and risk	Enhanced Innovation
	• Transnational strategy			

© Cengage Learning

M. Stasy

and international corporate-level strategies. The five modes of entry firms can use to enter international markets for implementing their international strategies are then examined. Firms encounter economic and political risks when using international strategies. Some refer to these as economic and political institutions.[2] These risks must be effectively managed if the firm is to achieve the desired outcomes of higher performance and enhanced innovation. After discussing the outcomes firms seek when using international strategies, the chapter closes with mention of two cautions about international strategy that should be kept in mind.

8-1 Identifying International Opportunities

An **international strategy** is a strategy through which the firm sells its goods or services outside its domestic market.[3] In some instances, firms using an international strategy become quite diversified geographically as they compete in numerous countries or regions outside their domestic market. This is the case for ABB in that it competes in about 100 countries. In other cases, firms engage in less international diversification in that they only compete in a small number of markets outside their "home" market.

There are incentives for firms to use an international strategy and to diversify their operations geographically, and they can gain three basic benefits when they successfully do so.[4] We show international strategy's incentives and benefits in Figure 8.2.

8-1a Incentives to Use International Strategy

Raymond Vernon expressed the classic rationale for an international strategy.[5] He suggested that typically a firm discovers an innovation in its home-country market, especially in advanced economies such as those in Germany, France, Japan, Sweden, Canada, and the United States. Often demand for the product then develops in other countries, causing a firm to export products from its domestic operations to fulfil that demand. Continuing increases in demand can subsequently justify a firm's decision to establish operations outside of its domestic base. As Vernon noted, engaging in an international strategy has the potential to help a firm extend the life cycle of its product(s).

Gaining access to needed and potentially scarce resources is another reason firms use an international strategy. Key supplies of raw material—especially minerals and energy—are critical to firms' efforts in some industries to manufacture their products. Of course energy and mining companies have operations throughout the world to gain access to the raw materials they in turn sell to manufacturers requiring those resources. Rio Tinto is a leading international mining group. Operating as a global organization, the firm has 71,000 employees across six continents to include Australia, North America, Europe, South America, Asia and Africa. Rio Tinto uses its capabilities of technology and innovation (see first incentive noted above), exploration, marketing, and operational processes to identify, extract, and market mineral resources throughout the world.[6] In other industries where labor costs account for a significant portion of a company's expenses, firms may choose to establish facilities in other countries to gain access to less expensive labor. Clothing and electronics manufacturers are examples of firms pursuing an international strategy for this reason.

Increased pressure to integrate operations on a global scale is another factor influencing firms to pursue an international strategy. As nations industrialize, the demand for some products and commodities appears to become more similar. This borderless demand for globally branded products may be due to similarities in lifestyle in developed nations. Increases in global communications also facilitate the ability of people in different countries to visualize and model lifestyles in different cultures.[7] In an increasing number of industries,

An **international strategy** is a strategy through which the firm sells its goods or services outside its domestic market.

Figure 8.2 Incentives and Basic Benefits of International Strategy

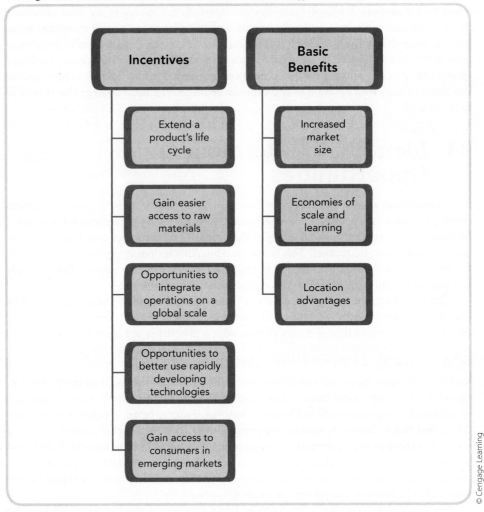

technology drives globalization because the economies of scale necessary to reduce costs to the lowest level often require an investment greater than that needed to meet domestic market demand. Moreover, in emerging markets the increasingly rapid adoption of technologies such as the Internet and mobile applications permits greater integration of trade, capital, culture, and labor. In this sense, technologies are the foundation for efforts to bind together disparate markets and operations across the world. International strategy makes it possible for firms to use technologies to organize their operations into a seamless whole.[8]

The potential of large demand for goods and services from people in emerging markets such as China and India is another strong incentive for firms to use an international strategy.[9] This is the case for French-based Carrefour Group. This firm is the world's second-largest retailer (behind only Walmart) and the largest in Europe. Carrefour operates five main grocery store formats—hypermarkets, supermarkets, cash & carry, hypercash stores, and convenience stores. The firm also sells products online.[10] In 2011, Carrefour acquired minority stakes in three mainland Chinese retailers to strengthen its presence there, as this market is critical to its growth plans.[11]

Even though India, another emerging market economy, differs from Western countries in many respects, including culture, politics, and the precepts of its economic system, it also offers a huge potential market and its government is becoming more supportive of foreign direct investment.[12] However, differences among Chinese, Indian, and Western-style economies and cultures make the successful use of an international strategy challenging. In particular, firms seeking to meet customer demands in emerging markets must learn how to manage an array of political and economic risks,[13] such as those we discuss later in the chapter.

We've now discussed incentives that influence firms to use international strategies. Firms derive three basic benefits by successfully using international strategies: (1) increased market size; (2) increased economies of scale and learning; and (3) development of a competitive advantage through location (e.g., access to low-cost labor, critical resources, or customers). These benefits will be examined here in terms of both their costs (such as higher coordination expenses and limited access to knowledge about host country political influences)[14] and their challenges.

Learn more about Globalization.
www.cengagebrain.com

8-1b Three Basic Benefits of International Strategy

As noted, effectively using one or more international strategies can result in three basic benefits for the firm. These benefits facilitate the firm's effort to achieve strategic competitiveness (see Figure 8.1) when using an international strategy.

Increased Market Size

Firms can expand the size of their potential market—sometimes dramatically—by using an international strategy to establish stronger positions in markets outside their domestic market. As noted, access to additional consumers is a key reason Carrefour sees China as a major source of growth.

Takeda, a large Japanese pharmaceutical company, acquired Swiss drug maker Nycomed in 2011, which exemplifies one form of its growth strategy. Buying Nycomed made Takeda a major player in European markets. More significantly, the acquisition broadened Takeda's distribution capability in emerging markets. The company is focusing on the development of its global business operations in emerging markets and developed economy countries, and organic growth through scientific and business process innovation.[15] Along with Starbucks, Carrefour and Takeda are two additional companies relying on international strategy as the path to increased market size in China and other regions of the world.

Firms such as Starbucks, Carrefour, and Takeda understand that effectively managing different consumer tastes and practices linked to cultural values or traditions in different markets is challenging. Nonetheless, they accept this challenge because of the potential to enhance the firm's performance. Other firms accept the challenge of successfully implementing an international strategy largely because of limited growth opportunities in their domestic market. This appears to be at least partly the case for major competitors Coca-Cola and PepsiCo, firms that have not been able to generate significant growth in their U.S. domestic (and North America) markets for some time. Indeed, most of these firms' growth is occurring in international markets. An international market's overall size also has the potential to affect the degree of benefit a firm can accrue as a result of using an international strategy. In general, larger international markets offer higher potential returns and thus pose less risk for the firm choosing to invest in those markets. Relatedly, the strength of the science base of the international markets in which a firm may compete is important in that scientific knowledge and the human capital needed to use that knowledge can facilitate efforts to more effectively sell and/or produce products that create value for customers.[16]

M. Stasy

An SAS Airbus A319. Airbus and Boeing achieve economies of scale by manufacturing in several regions of the world.

Economies of Scale and Learning

By expanding the number of markets in which they compete, firms may be able to enjoy economies of scale, particularly in their manufacturing operations. More broadly, firms able to standardize the processes used to produce, sell, distribute, and service their products across country borders enhance their ability to learn how to continuously reduce costs while hopefully increasing the value their products create for customers. For example, rivals Airbus SAS and Boeing have multiple manufacturing facilities and outsource some activities to firms located throughout the world, partly for the purpose of developing economies of scale as a source of being able to create value for customers.

Economies of scale are critical in a number of settings in addition to the airline manufacturing industry. Automobile manufacturers certainly seek economies of scale as a benefit of their international strategies. Ford employs 166,000 people worldwide and operates in six global regions: North America, Europe, Central and South America, Middle East, Africa, and Asia Pacific. Competing in these global markets, Ford Motor Company is planning on increasing sales in each region but especially in Asia.[17] Overall, Ford seeks to increase the annual number of products it sells outside of North America. For example, it increased its market share in Europe in 2013. Demonstrating the use of this international strategy is the fact that Ford is now run as a single global business developing cars and trucks that can be built and sold throughout the world.[18] Firms may also be able to exploit core competencies in international markets through resource and knowledge sharing between units and network partners across country borders.[19] By sharing resources and knowledge in this manner, firms can learn how to create synergy, which in turn can help each firm learn how to produce higher-quality products at a lower cost.

Working in multiple international markets also provides firms with new learning opportunities,[20] perhaps even in terms of research and development activities. Increasing the firm's R&D ability can contribute to its efforts to enhance innovation, which is critical to both short- and long-term success. However, research results suggest that to take advantage of international R&D investments, firms need to already have a strong R&D system in place to absorb knowledge resulting from effective R&D activities.[21]

Location Advantages

Locating facilities in markets outside their domestic market can sometimes help firms reduce costs. This benefit of an international strategy accrues to the firm when its facilities in international locations provide easier access to lower-cost labor, energy, and other natural resources. Other location advantages include access to critical supplies and to customers. Once positioned in an attractive location, firms must manage their facilities effectively to gain the full benefit of a location advantage.[22]

A firm's costs, particularly those dealing with manufacturing and distribution, as well as the nature of international customers' needs, affect the degree of benefit it can capture through a location advantage.[23] Cultural influences may also affect location advantages and disadvantages. International business transactions are less difficult for a firm to complete when there is a strong match among the cultures with which the firm is involved while implementing its international strategy.[24] Finally, physical distances influence firms' location choices as well as how to manage facilities in the chosen locations.[25]

8-2 International Strategies

Firms choose to use one or both basic types of international strategy: business-level international strategy and corporate-level international strategy. At the business level, firms select from among the generic strategies of cost leadership, differentiation, focused cost leadership, focused differentiation, and integrated cost leadership/differentiation. At the corporate level, multidomestic, global, and transnational international strategies (the transnational is a combination of the multidomestic and global strategies) are considered. To contribute to the firm's efforts to achieve strategic competitiveness in the form of improved performance and enhanced innovation (see Figure 8.1), each international strategy the firm uses must be based on one or more core competencies.[26]

8-2a International Business-Level Strategy

Firms considering the use of any international strategy first develop domestic-market strategies (at the business level and at the corporate level if the firm has diversified at the product level). One reason this is important is that the firm may be able to use some of the capabilities and core competencies it has developed in its domestic market as the foundation for competitive success in international markets.[27] However, research results indicate that the value created by relying on capabilities and core competencies developed in domestic markets as a source of success in international markets diminishes as a firm's geographic diversity increases.[28]

Figure 8.3 Determinants of National Advantage

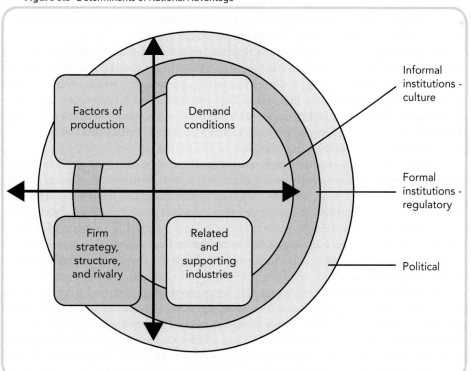

© Cengage Learning

As we know from our discussion of competitive dynamics in Chapter 5, firms do not select and then use strategies in isolation of market realities. In the case of international strategies, conditions in a firm's domestic market affect the degree to which the firm can build on capabilities and core competencies it established in that market to create capabilities and core competencies in international markets. The reason for this is grounded in Michael Porter's analysis of why some nations are more competitive than other nations and why and how some industries within nations are more competitive relative to those industries in other nations. Porter's core argument is that conditions or factors in a firm's home base—that is, in its domestic market—either hinder the firm's efforts to use an international business-level strategy for the purpose of establishing a competitive advantage in international markets or support those efforts. Porter identifies four factors as determinants of a national advantage that some countries possess (see Figure 8.3).[29] Interactions among these four factors influence a firm's choice of international business-level strategy.

The first determinant of national advantage is factors of production. This determinant refers to the inputs necessary for a firm to compete in any industry. Labor, land, natural resources, capital, and infrastructure (such as transportation, postal, and communication systems) represent such inputs. There are basic factors (for example, natural and labor resources) and advanced factors (such as digital communication systems and a highly educated workforce). Other factors of production are generalized (highway systems and the supply of debt capital) and specialized (skilled personnel in a specific industry, such as the workers in a port that specialize in handling bulk chemicals). If a country possesses advanced and specialized production factors, it is likely to serve an industry well by spawning strong home-country competitors that also can be successful global competitors.

Ironically, countries often develop advanced and specialized factors because they lack critical basic resources. For example, some Asian countries, such as South Korea, lack abundant natural resources but have a workforce with a strong work ethic, a large number of engineers, and systems of large firms to create an expertise in manufacturing. Similarly, Germany developed a strong chemical industry, partially because Hoechst and BASF spent years creating a synthetic indigo dye to reduce their dependence on imports, unlike Britain, whose colonies provided large supplies of natural indigo.[30]

The second factor or determinant of national advantage, demand conditions, is characterized by the nature and size of customers' needs in the home market for the products firms competing in an industry produce. Meeting the demand generated by a large number of customers creates conditions through which a firm can develop scale-efficient facilities and refine the capabilities, and perhaps core competencies, required to use those facilities. Once refined, the probability that the capabilities and core competencies will benefit the firm as it diversifies geographically increases.

This is the case for Chiquita Brands International, which spent years building its businesses and developing economies of scale and scale efficient facilities in the process of doing so. However, it diversified into too many different product lines and has refocused the firm in recent years on its bananas and packaged salads product lines. Now, it produces almost a third of the bananas it sells on its own farms in Latin America. It is the market leader in bananas in Europe and number two in the market in North America. So, it is using its capabilities and core competencies in growing and distributing Chiquita brand bananas in its international markets.[31]

The third factor in Porter's model of the determinants of national advantage is related and supporting industries. Italy has become the leader in the shoe industry because of related and supporting industries. For example, a well-established leather-processing industry provides the leather needed to construct shoes and related products. Also, many people travel to Italy to purchase leather goods, providing support in distribution. Supporting industries in leather-working machinery and design services also contribute to the success of the shoe

industry. In fact, the design services industry supports its own related industries,
such as ski boots, fashion apparel, and furniture. In Japan, cameras and copiers are
related industries. Similarly, Germany is
known for the quality of its machine tools,
and Eastern Belgium is known for skilled
manufacturing (supporting and related
industries are important in these two settings too).[32]

Firm strategy, structure, and rivalry
make up the final determinant of national
advantage and also foster the growth of
certain industries. The types of strategy,
structure, and rivalry among firms vary
greatly from nation to nation. The excellent technical training system in Germany
fosters a strong emphasis on continuous
product and process improvements. In
Italy, the national pride of the country's

High quality shoes on sale at a shop in Florence, Italy. Related and sup-
porting industries contribute to Italy's national advantage in the shoe
industry.

designers spawns strong industries not only in shoes but also sports cars, fashion apparel,
and furniture. In the United States, competition among computer manufacturers and software producers contributes to further development of these industries.

The four determinants of national advantage (see Figure 8.3) emphasize the structural
characteristics of a specific economy that contribute to some degree to national advantage
and influence the firm's selection of an international business-level strategy. Individual governments' policies also affect the nature of the determinants as well as how firms compete
within the boundaries governing bodies establish and enforce within a particular economy.[33] While studying their external environment (see Chapter 2), firms considering the
possibility of using an international strategy need to gather information and data that will
allow them to understand the effects of governmental policies and their enforcement on
their nation's ability to establish advantages relative to other nations as well as the relative
degree of competitiveness on a global basis of the industry in which firms might compete
on a global scale.

Those leading companies should recognize that a firm based in a country with a national
competitive advantage is not guaranteed success as it implements its chosen international
business-level strategy. The actual strategic choices managers make may be the most compelling reasons for success or failure as firms diversify geographically. Accordingly, the
factors illustrated in Figure 8.3 are likely to produce the foundation for a firm's competitive
advantages only when it develops and implements an appropriate international business-
level strategy that takes advantage of distinct country factors. Thus, these distinct country
factors should be thoroughly considered when making a decision about the international
business-level strategy to use. The firm will then make continuous adjustments to its international business-level strategy in light of the nature of competition it encounters in different international markets and in light of customers' needs. Lexus, for example, does not
have the share of the luxury car market in China that it desires. Accordingly, Toyota (Lexus'
manufacturer) is adjusting how it implements its international differentiation business-level
strategy in China to better serve customers. The firm is doing this by "turning to the feature
that cemented its early success in the United States: extreme customer service. Showroom
amenities such as cappuccino machines, Wi-Fi, Lego tables for the kids, and airport shuttles
for busy executives dropping off their cars for servicing are examples of the services now

being offered to customers in China."[34] Time will tell if this adjustment to Lexus' strategy in China will lead to the success the firm desires.

8-2b International Corporate-Level Strategy

A firm's international business-level strategy is also based at least partially on its international corporate-level strategy. Some international corporate-level strategies give individual country units the authority to develop their own business-level strategies, while others dictate the business-level strategies in order to standardize the firm's products and sharing of resources across countries.[35]

International corporate-level strategy focuses on the scope of a firm's operations through geographic diversification.[36] International corporate-level strategy is required when the firm operates in multiple industries that are located in multiple countries or regions (e.g., Southeast Asia or the European Union) and in which they sell multiple products. The headquarters unit guides the strategy, although as noted, business- or country-level managers can have substantial strategic input depending on the type of international corporate-level strategy the firm uses. The three international corporate-level strategies are shown in Figure 8.4; the international corporate-level strategies vary in terms of two dimensions—the need for global integration and the need for local responsiveness.

Multidomestic Strategy

A **multidomestic strategy** is an international strategy in which strategic and operating decisions are decentralized to the strategic business units in individual countries or regions for the purpose of allowing each unit the opportunity to tailor products to the local market.[37]

A **multidomestic strategy** is an international strategy in which strategic and operating decisions are decentralized to the strategic business units in individual countries or regions for the purpose of allowing each unit the opportunity to tailor products to the local market.

Figure 8.4 International Corporate-Level Strategies

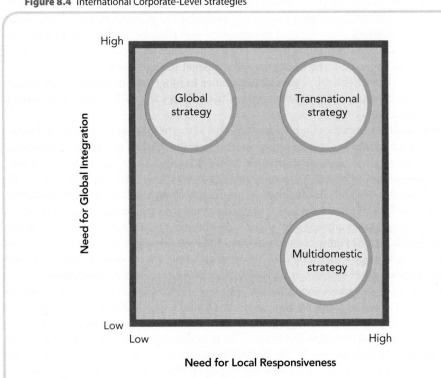

© Cengage Learning

With this strategy, the firm's need for local responsiveness is high while its need for global integration is low. Influencing these needs is the firm's belief that consumer needs and desires, industry conditions (e.g., the number and type of competitors), political and legal structures, and social norms vary by country. Thus, a multidomestic strategy focuses on competition within each country because market needs are thought to be segmented by country boundaries. To meet the specific needs and preferences of local customers, country or regional managers have the autonomy to customize the firm's products. Therefore, these strategies should maximize a firm's competitive response to the idiosyncratic requirements of each market.[38] The multidomestic strategy is most appropriate for use when the differences between the markets a firm serves and the customers in them are significant.

The use of multidomestic strategies usually expands the firm's local market share because the firm can pay attention to the local clientele's needs. However, using a multidomestic strategy results in less knowledge sharing for the corporation as a whole because of the differences across markets, decentralization, and the different international business-level strategies employed by local units.[39] Moreover, multidomestic strategies do not allow the development of economies of scale and thus can be more costly.

Unilever is a large European consumer products company selling products in over 180 countries. The firm has more than 400 global brands that are grouped into three business units—foods, home care, and personal care. Historically, Unilever has used a highly decentralized approach for the purpose of managing its global brands. This approach allows regional managers considerable autonomy to adapt the characteristics of specific products to satisfy the unique needs of customers in different markets. However, more recently, Unilever has sought to increase the coordination between its independent subsidiaries in order to establish an even stronger global brand presence. Part of the way it achieves some coordination is by having the presidents of each of the five global regions serve as members of the top management team.[40] As such, Unilever may be transitioning from a multidomestic strategy to a transnational strategy.

Global Strategy

A **global strategy** is an international strategy in which a firm's home office determines the strategies business units are to use in each country or region.[41] This strategy indicates that the firm has a high need for global integration and a low need for local responsiveness. These needs indicate that compared to a multidomestic strategy, a global strategy seeks greater levels of standardization of products across country markets. The firm using a global strategy seeks to develop economies of scale as it produces the same or virtually the same products for distribution to customers throughout the world who are assumed to have similar needs. The global strategy offers greater opportunities to take innovations developed at the corporate level or in one market and apply them in other markets.[42] Improvements in global accounting and financial reporting standards facilitate use of this strategy.[43] A global strategy is most effective when the differences between markets and the customers the firm is serving are insignificant.

Efficient operations are required to successfully implement a global strategy. Increasing the efficiency of a firm's international operations mandates resource sharing and greater coordination and cooperation across market boundaries. Centralized decision making as designed by headquarters details how resources are to be shared and coordinated across markets. Research results suggest that the outcomes a firm achieves by using a global strategy become more desirable when the strategy is used in areas in which regional integration among countries is occurring.[44]

CEMEX is a global building materials company that uses the global strategy. CEMEX is the world's leading supplier of ready-mix concrete and one of the world's largest producers of white Portland cement. CEMEX sells to customers in more than 50 countries in

A **global strategy** is an international strategy in which a firm's home office determines the strategies business units are to use in each country or region.

multiple regions, including North America, Latin America, Europe, the Mediterranean, and Asia. With annual sales of approximately $15 billion, the firm employs more than 44,000 people.[45]

To implement its global strategy, CEMEX has centralized a number of its activities. The Shared Services Model is a recent example of how this firm centralizes operations in order to gain scale economies, among other benefits. It uses its vertical integration to promote cooperation among the businesses to provide value-creating service for its customers[46] In essence, the Shared Services Model integrates and centralizes some support functions from the firm's value chain (see Chapter 3). This integration and centralization brings about the types of benefits sought by firms when using a global strategy. Significant cost savings, increases in the productivity of the involved support functions, the fostering of economies of scale, and the freeing up of resources all provide benefits to CEMEX.

Because of increasing global competition and the need to simultaneously be cost efficient and produce differentiated products, the number of firms using a transnational international corporate-level strategy is increasing.

Transnational Strategy

A **transnational strategy** is an international strategy through which the firm seeks to achieve both global efficiency and local responsiveness. With this strategy, the firm has strong needs for both global integration and local responsiveness. In the Opening Case, we discussed ABB's international strategy. It is known, however, for using the transnational strategy to pursue profitable growth in international markets. For example, ABB focuses on power and automation technologies that allow it to achieve some economies of scale through coordination of its technology development and application and by sharing resources to satisfy customer needs in different parts of the world. In doing so, it achieves a form of global integration. However, it also simultaneously decentralizes decisions to the country level to allow a local business to tailor products, and especially services, to local customers' needs (local responsiveness).

Realizing the twin goals of global integration and local responsiveness is difficult in that global integration requires close global coordination while local responsiveness requires local flexibility. "Flexible coordination"—building a shared vision and individual commitment through an integrated network—is required to implement the transnational strategy. Such integrated networks allow a firm to manage its connections with customers, suppliers, partners, and other parties more efficiently rather than using arm's-length transactions.[47] The transnational strategy is difficult to use because of its conflicting goals (see Chapter 11 for more on the implementation of this and other corporate-level international strategies). On the positive side, effectively implementing a transnational strategy often produces higher performance than does implementing either the multidomestic or global strategies.[48]

Transnational strategies are becoming increasingly necessary to successfully compete in international markets. Reasons for this include the fact that continuing increases in the number of viable global competitors challenge firms to reduce their costs. Simultaneously, the increasing sophistication of markets with greater information flows made possible largely by the diffusion of the Internet and the desire for specialized products to meet consumers' unique needs pressures firms to differentiate their products in local markets. Differences in culture and institutional environments also require firms to adapt their products and approaches to local environments. However, some argue that transnational strategies are not required to successfully compete in international markets. Those holding this view suggest that most multinational firms try to compete at the regional level (e.g., the European Union) rather than at the country level. To the degree this is the case, the need for the firm to simultaneously offer relatively unique products that are adapted to local markets and to produce those products at lower costs permitted by developing scale economies is reduced.[49]

A **transnational strategy** is an international strategy through which the firm seeks to achieve both global efficiency and local responsiveness.

The complexities of competing in global markets increase the need for the use of a transnational strategy, as shown in the discussion of Mondelez International in the Strategic Focus. In fact, Kraft Foods made a decision to spin off its domestic grocery products into a separate business in order to focus on its high-growth snack foods business, in which 80 percent of sales come from foreign markets. Mondelez is a $35 billion company that has power brands (brands that are globally known and respected) and local brands. So, it

Strategic Focus   GLOBALIZATION

Mondelez International: A Global Leader in Snack Foods Markets

In 2012, with 80 percent of its sales in faster-growing international markets, Kraft Foods decided that it needed to split into two separate companies—a North American grocery business and an international snack foods company. The business focused on North America will sell well-known, traditional Kraft brands such as Velveeta, Kraft Macaroni & Cheese, and Oscar Mayer. These goods are profitable despite being low growth. The snack food company will focus on such power brands as Oreo, Cadbury, and Ritz. It will also promote local brands tailored to the idiosyncratic needs of local markets.

The snack foods business was named Mondelez by combining two words: monde (meaning world) and delez (new word to mean delicious) to communicate the meaning of products that are "world delicious". The separation into different businesses allows each to use its own specialized strategy that best suits its products and markets, and the competitive landscape it faces. Mondelez International is the global market leader in biscuits, chocolate, candy, and powdered beverages and holds the number two position in the global markets for chewing gum and coffee. About 45 percent of its sales come from fast growing emerging markets. Some of the local brands designed for customers in the emerging markets include Barni (soft biscuits) sold in Russia, Bubbalo (bubble gum) sold in India, Mexico, Portugal, and Spain, and Corte Noire (coffee) sold in France, Ireland, Russia, Ukraine, and the U.K. Mondelez is reinvesting profits into emerging markets seeking more growth. In 2012, the combined net revenues for Asia-Pacific, Eastern Europe, Africa, Latin America, and the Middle East grew by 8 percent (excluding the effects of foreign currency valuation changes). Performance was especially strong in the BRIC countries (the large emerging markets of Brazil, Russia, India, and China), with double-digit growth.

Despite its success in the emerging markets, Mondelez's net income has declined recently due to lower coffee prices and a reduction in demand for gum and candy. The CEO and other top executives suggested that volatility in global markets also has affected the firm's results. These are problems experienced by most of the companies that enter and compete in global markets.

Juergen Leisse, head of the German Division of Kraft Foods, Inc., at the company's headquarters in Bremen, Germany. The name "Kraft Foods" will disappear from German supermarkets and be replaced with "Mondelez International."

Sources: 2013, Unleashing a global snacking powerhouse, Mondelez International, www.mondelezinternational.com, accessed on May 21; N. Munshi, 2013, Mondelez tergets emerging markets growth, *Financial Times*, www.ft.com, May 7; 2013, Mondelez International's CEO discusses Q1 2013 results – Earnings call transcript, Mondelez International, www.mondelezinternational.com, May 7; D. Gelles, D. McCrum & N. Munshi, Activists hope to profit when cookie crumbles, *Financial Times*, www.ft.com, April 14; 2013, Kraft and Mondelez: Snacks and snags, *Financial Times*, www.ft.com, April 8; S. Strom, 2012, For Oreo, Cadbury and Ritz, a new parent company, *New York Times*, www.nytimes.com, May 23; 2012, Kraft Foods proposes Mondelez International Inc. as new name for global snacks company, *PR Newswire*, www.printthis.clickability.com, March 21; M.J. de la Merced, 2012, Kraft, 'Mondelez' and the art of corporate rebranding, *New York Times Dealbook*, http://dealbook.nytimes.com, March 21.

globally integrates its operations to standardize and maintain its power brands while simultaneously developing and marketing local brands that are specialized to meet the needs of local customers. In Chapter 5, we referenced the significant competitive rivalry that Mondelez encounters in its consumer markets.

Next we discuss trends in the global environment that are affecting the choices firms make when deciding which international corporate-level strategies to use and in which international markets to compete.

8-3 Environmental Trends

Although the transnational strategy is difficult to implement, an emphasis on global efficiency is increasing as more industries and the companies competing within them encounter intensified global competition. Magnifying the scope of this issue is the fact that, simultaneously, firms are experiencing demands for local adaptations of their products. These demands can be from customers (for products to satisfy their tastes and preferences) and from governing bodies (for products to satisfy a country's regulations). In addition, most multinational firms desire coordination and sharing of resources across country markets to hold down costs, as illustrated by the CEMEX example.[50]

Because of these conditions, some large multinational firms with diverse products use a multidomestic strategy with certain product lines and a global strategy with others when diversifying geographically. Many multinational firms may require this type of flexibility if they are to be strategically competitive, in part due to trends that change over time.

Liability of foreignness and regionalization are two important trends influencing a firm's choice and use of international strategies, particularly international corporate-level strategies. We discuss these trends next.

8-3a Liability of Foreignness

The dramatic success of Japanese firms such as Toyota and Sony in the United States and other international markets in the 1980s was a powerful jolt to U.S. managers and awakened them to the importance of international competition and the fact that many markets were rapidly becoming globalized. In the twenty-first century, Brazil, Russia, India, and China (BRIC) represent major international market opportunities for firms from many countries, including the United States, Japan, Korea, and members of the European Union.[51] However, even if foreign markets seem attractive, as appears to be the case with the BRIC countries, there are legitimate concerns for firms considering entering these markets. This is the *liability of foreignness*,[52] a set of costs associated with various issues firms face when entering foreign markets, including unfamiliar operating environments; economic, administrative, and cultural differences; and the challenges of coordination over distances.[53] Four types of distances commonly associated with liability of foreignness are cultural, administrative, geographic, and economic.[54]

Walt Disney Company's experience while opening theme parks in foreign countries demonstrates the liability of foreignness. For example, Disney suffered "lawsuits in France, at Disneyland Paris, because of the lack of fit between its transferred personnel policies and the French employees charged to enact them."[55] Disney executives learned from this experience in building the firm's theme park in Hong Kong as the company "went out of its way to tailor the park to local tastes."[56] Thus, as with Walt Disney Company, firms thinking about using an international strategy to enter foreign markets must be aware of the four types of distances they'll encounter when doing so and determine actions to take to reduce the potentially negative effects associated with those distances.

M. Stasy

8-3b **Regionalization**

Regionalization is a second global environmental trend influencing a firm's choice and use of international strategies. This trend is becoming prominent largely because where a firm chooses to compete can affect its strategic competitiveness.[57] As a result, the firm considering using international strategies must decide if it should enter individual country markets or if it would be better served by competing in one or more regional markets rather than in individual country markets.

Currently, the global strategy is used less frequently. It remains difficult to successfully implement even when the firm uses Internet-based strategies.[58] In addition, the amount of competition vying for a limited amount of resources and customers can limit firms' focus to a specific region rather than on country-specific markets that are located in multiple parts of the world. A regional focus allows firms to marshal their resources to compete effectively rather than spreading their limited resources across multiple country-specific international markets.[59]

However, a firm that competes in industries where the international markets differ greatly (in which it must employ a multidomestic strategy) may wish to narrow its focus to a particular region of the world. In so doing, it can better understand the cultures, legal and social norms, and other factors that are important for effective competition in those markets. For example, a firm may focus on Far East markets only rather than competing simultaneously in the Middle East, Europe, and the Far East. Or the firm may choose a region of the world where the markets are more similar and some coordination and sharing of resources would be possible. In this way, the firm may be able not only to better understand the markets in which it competes, but also to achieve some economies, even though it may have to employ a multidomestic strategy. For instance, research suggests that most large retailers are better at focusing on a particular region rather than being truly global.[60] Firms commonly focus much of their international market entries on countries adjacent to their home country, which might be referred to as their home region.[61]

Countries that develop trade agreements to increase the economic power of their regions may promote regional strategies. The European Union (EU) and South America's Organization of American States (OAS) are country associations that developed trade agreements to promote the flow of trade across country boundaries within their respective regions.[62] Many European firms acquire and integrate their businesses in Europe to better coordinate pan-European brands as the EU tries to create unity across the European markets. With this process likely to continue as new countries are added to the agreement, some international firms may prefer to focus on regions rather than multiple country markets when entering international markets.

The North American Free Trade Agreement (NAFTA), signed by the United States, Canada, and Mexico, facilitates free trade across country borders in North America. NAFTA loosens restrictions on international strategies within this region and provides greater opportunity for regional international strategies.[63]

Most firms enter regional markets sequentially, beginning in markets with which they are more familiar. They also introduce their largest and strongest lines of business into these markets first, followed by other product lines once the initial efforts are deemed successful. The additional product lines typically are introduced in the original investment location.[64] However, research also suggests that the size of the market and industry characteristics can influence this decision.[65]

Regionalization is important to most multinational firms, even those competing in many regions across the globe. For example, most large multinational firms have organizational structures that group operations within the same region (across countries) for managing and coordination purposes. As explained in the Opening Case, ABB has eight regional managers to which country operations in each of the regions report. Managing businesses by regions helps multinational enterprises (MNEs) deal with the complexities and challenges of operating in multiple international markets.

After selecting its business- and corporate-level international strategies, the firm determines how it will enter the international markets in which it has chosen to compete. We turn to this topic next.

8-4 Choice of International Entry Mode

Five modes of entry into international markets are available to firms. We show these entry modes and their characteristics in Figure 8.5. Each means of market entry has its advantages and disadvantages, suggesting that the choice of entry mode can affect the degree of success

Figure 8.5 Modes of Entry and their Characteristics

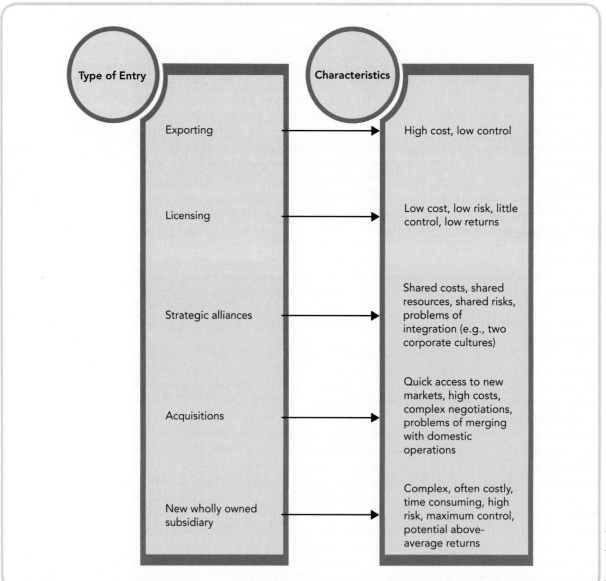

the firm achieves by implementing an international strategy.[66] Many firms competing in multiple markets commonly use more than one and may use all five entry modes.[67]

8-4a Exporting

For many firms, exporting is the initial mode of entry used.[68] *Exporting* is an entry mode through which the firm sends products it produces in its domestic market to international markets. Selection of exporting as the way of entering international markets is a popular entry mode choice for small businesses.[69]

The number of small U.S. firms using an international strategy is increasing, with some predicting that up to 50 percent of small U.S. firms will be involved in international trade by 2018, most of them through export.[70] By exporting, firms avoid the expense of establishing operations in host countries (that is, in countries outside their home country) in which they have chosen to compete. However, firms must establish some means of marketing and distributing their products when exporting. Usually, contracts are formed with host-country firms to handle these activities. Potentially high transportation costs to export products to international markets and the expense of tariffs placed on the firm's products as a result of host countries' policies are examples of exporting costs. The loss of some control when the firm contracts with local companies located in host countries for marketing and distribution purposes is another disadvantage of exporting. Moreover, contracting with local companies can be expensive, making it harder for the exporting firm to earn profits.[71] Evidence suggests that, in general, using an international cost leadership strategy when exporting to developed countries has the most positive effect on firm performance while using an international differentiation strategy with larger scale when exporting to emerging economies leads to the greatest amount of success. In either case, firms with strong market orientation capabilities are more successful.[72]

Firms export mostly to countries that are closest to their facilities because of the lower transportation costs and the usually greater similarity between geographic neighbors. For example, the United States' NAFTA partners Mexico and Canada account for more than half of the goods exported from Texas. The Internet has also made exporting easier. Firms of any size can use the Internet to access critical information about foreign markets, examine a target market, research the competition, and find lists of potential customers.[73] Governments also use the Internet to support the efforts of those applying for export and import licenses, facilitating international trade among countries while doing so.

8-4b Licensing

Licensing is an entry mode in which an agreement is formed that allows a foreign company to purchase the right to manufacture and sell a firm's products within a host country's market or a set of host countries' markets.[74] The licensor is normally paid a royalty on each unit produced and sold. The licensee takes the risks and makes the monetary investments in facilities for manufacturing, marketing, and distributing products. As a result, licensing is possibly the least costly form of international diversification. As with exporting, licensing is an attractive entry mode option for smaller firms, and potentially for newer firms as well.[75]

China, a country accounting for almost one-third of all cigarettes smoked worldwide, is obviously a huge market for this product. U.S. cigarette firms want to have a strong presence in China but have had trouble entering this market, largely because of successful lobbying by state-owned tobacco firms against such entry. Because of these conditions, cigarette manufacturer Philip Morris International (PMI) had an incentive to form a deal with these state-owned firms. Accordingly, PMI and the China National Tobacco Corporation (CNTC) completed a licensing agreement at the end of 2005. This agreement provides CNTC access to the most famous brand in the world, Marlboro.[76] Because it is a licensing agreement rather than a foreign direct investment by PMI, China maintains control of distribution. The Marlboro brand was launched at two Chinese manufacturing plants in 2008. The Chinese state-owned tobacco monopoly, as part of the agreement, also receives PMI's help through a joint venture in distributing its own brands in select foreign markets. To date, the Chinese cigarettes have been distributed in the Czech Republic and Poland.[77]

Another potential benefit of licensing as an entry mode is the possibility of earning greater returns from product innovations by selling the firm's innovations in international markets as well as in the domestic market.[78] Firms can obtain a larger market for their innovative new products, which helps them to pay off their R&D costs to develop them and to earn a return faster on the innovations than if they only sell them in domestic markets. And they do this with little risk without additional investment costs.

Licensing also has disadvantages. For example, after a firm licenses its product or brand to another party, it has little control over selling and distribution. Developing licensing agreements that protect the interests of both parties while supporting the relationship embedded within an agreement helps prevent this potential disadvantage.[79] In addition, licensing provides the least potential returns because returns must be shared between the licensor and the licensee. Another disadvantage is that the international firm may learn the technology of the party with whom it formed an agreement and then produce and sell a similar competitive product after the licensing agreement expires. In a classic example, Komatsu first licensed much of its technology from International Harvester, Bucyrus-Erie, and Cummins Engine to compete against Caterpillar in the earthmoving equipment business. Komatsu then dropped these licenses and developed its own products using the technology it had gained from the U.S. companies.[80] Because of potential disadvantages, the parties to a licensing arrangement should finalize an agreement only after they are convinced that both parties' best interests are protected.

8-4c   Strategic Alliances

Increasingly popular as an entry mode among firms using international strategies,[81] a *strategic alliance* finds a firm collaborating with another company in a different setting in order to enter one or more international markets.[82] Firms share the risks and the resources required to enter international markets when using strategic alliances.[83] Moreover, because partners bring their unique resources together for the purpose of working collaboratively, strategic alliances can facilitate developing new capabilities and possibly core competencies that may contribute to the firm's strategic competitiveness.[84] Indeed, developing and learning how to use new capabilities and/or competencies (particularly those related to technology) is often a key purpose for which firms use strategic alliances as an entry mode.[85] Firms should be aware that establishing trust between partners is critical for developing and managing technology-based capabilities while using strategic alliances.[86]

French-based Limagrain is the fourth largest seed company in the world through its subsidiary Vilmorin & Cie. An international agricultural cooperative group specializing in field seeds, vegetable seeds, and cereal products, part of Limagrain's strategy calls for it to continue to enter and compete in additional international markets. Limagrain is using strategic alliances as an entry mode. In 2011, the firm formed a strategic alliance with the Brazilian seed company Sementes Guerra in Brazil. The joint venture is named Limagrain Guerra do Brasil. Corn is the focus of the joint venture between these companies. Guerra is a family-owned company engaged in seed research, the production of corn, wheat, and soybeans, and the distribution of those products to farmers in Brazil and neighboring countries. Limagrain also had an earlier, successful joint venture with KWS in the United States. This venture, called AgReliant Genetics, focused primarily on corn and soybeans.[87]

Not all alliances formed for the purpose of entering international markets are successful.[88] Incompatible partners and conflict between the partners are primary reasons for failure when firms use strategic alliances as an entry mode. Another issue here is that international strategic alliances are especially difficult to manage. Trust is an important aspect of alliances and must be carefully managed. The degree of trust between partners strongly influences alliance success. The probability of alliance success increases as the amount of trust between partners expands. Efforts to build trust are affected by at least four fundamental issues: the initial condition of the relationship, the negotiation process to arrive at an agreement, partner interactions, and external events.[89] Trust is also influenced by the country cultures involved and the relationships between the countries' governments (e.g., degree of political differences) where the firms in the alliance are home based.[90] Firms should be aware of these issues when trying to appropriately manage trust.

Research has shown that equity-based alliances over which a firm has more control are more likely to produce positive returns.[91] (We discuss equity-based and other types of strategic alliances in Chapter 9.) However, if trust is required to develop new capabilities through an alliance, equity positions can serve as a barrier to the necessary relationship building. And trust can be an especially important issue when firms have multiple partners supplying raw materials and/or services in their value chain (often referred to as outsourcing).[92] If conflict in a strategic alliance formed as an entry mode is not manageable, using acquisitions to enter international markets may be a better option.[93]

8-4d Acquisitions

When a firm acquires another company to enter an international market, it has completed a cross-border acquisition. Specifically, a *cross-border acquisition* is an entry mode through which a firm from one country acquires a stake in or purchases all of a firm located in another country.

As free trade expands in global markets, firms throughout the world are completing a larger number of cross-border acquisitions. The ability of cross-border acquisitions to provide rapid access to new markets is a key reason for their growth. In fact, of the five entry modes, acquisitions often are the quickest means for firms to enter international markets.[94]

Today, there is a broad range of cross-border acquisitions being completed by a diverse set of companies. DJO Global is a market leader in providing orthopaedic rehabilitation services. It has achieved significant growth since its founding in the late 1970s through mergers. It was founded in the United States (California) but was acquired by a major British medical devices conglomerate, Smith & Nephew, in 1987. Thereafter, it made several acquisitions. In 2007, it was acquired by The Blackstone Group and another company involved in the same industry and was merged into DJO Global. Since that time, DJO has continued to grow through acquisitions in countries such as Canada, South Africa, and Tunisia. DJO now distributes its products in more than 36 countries and has approximately $1 billion in annual sales.[95] Interestingly, firms use cross-border acquisitions less frequently to enter markets where corruption affects business transactions and, hence, the use of international strategies. Firms' preference is to use joint ventures to enter markets in which corruption is an issue rather than using acquisitions. (Discussed fully in Chapter 9, a joint venture is a type of strategic alliance in which two or more firms create a legally independent company and share their resources and capabilities to operate it.) However, these ventures fail more often, although this is less frequently the case for firms experienced with entering "corrupt" markets. When acquisitions are made in such countries, acquirers commonly pay smaller premiums to buy firms in different markets.[96]

Although increasingly popular, acquisitions as an entry mode are not without costs, nor are they easy to successfully complete and operate. Cross-border acquisitions have some of the disadvantages of domestic acquisitions (see Chapter 7). In addition, they often require debt financing to complete, which carries an extra cost. Another issue for firms to consider is that negotiations for cross-border acquisitions can be exceedingly complex and are generally more complicated than are the negotiations associated with domestic

The CEOs of British Airways (Willie Walsh) and Iberia (Antonio Vazquez) merged their companies in 2011 to form the International Airlines Group (IAG). The multi-billion-euro merger created Europe's third largest airline.

acquisitions. Dealing with the legal and regulatory requirements in the target firm's country and obtaining appropriate information to negotiate an agreement are also frequent problems. Finally, the merging of the new firm into the acquiring firm is often more complex than is the case with domestic acquisitions. The firm completing the cross-border acquisition must deal not only with different corporate cultures, but also with potentially different social cultures and practices.[97] These differences make integrating the two firms after the acquisition more challenging; it is difficult to capture the potential synergy when integration is slowed or stymied because of cultural differences.[98] Therefore, while cross-border acquisitions are popular as an entry mode primarily because they provide rapid access to new markets, firms considering this option should be fully aware of the costs and risks associated with using it.

8-4e New Wholly Owned Subsidiary

A **greenfield venture** is an entry mode through which a firm invests directly in another country or market by establishing a new wholly owned subsidiary. The process of creating a greenfield venture is often complex and potentially costly, but this entry mode affords maximum control to the firm and has the greatest amount of potential to contribute to the firm's strategic competitiveness as it implements international strategies. This potential is especially true for firms with strong intangible capabilities that might be leveraged through a greenfield venture.[99] Moreover, having additional control over its operations in a foreign market is especially advantageous when the firm has proprietary technology.

Research also suggests that "wholly owned subsidiaries and expatriate staff are preferred" in service industries where "close contacts with end customers" and "high levels of professional skills, specialized know-how, and customization" are required.[100] Other research suggests that as investments, greenfield ventures are used more prominently when the firm's business relies significantly on the quality of its capital-intensive manufacturing facilities. In contrast, cross-border acquisitions are more likely to be used as an entry mode when a firm's operations are human capital intensive—for example, if a strong local union and high cultural distance would cause difficulty in transferring knowledge to a host nation through a greenfield venture.[101]

The risks associated with greenfield ventures are significant in that the costs of establishing a new business operation in a new country or market can be substantial. To support the operations of a newly established operation in a foreign country, the firm may have to acquire knowledge and expertise about the new market by hiring either host-country nationals, possibly from competitors, or through consultants, which can be costly. This new knowledge and expertise often is necessary to facilitate the building of new facilities, establishing distribution networks, and learning how to implement marketing strategies that can lead to competitive success in the new market.[102] Importantly, while taking these actions the firm maintains control over the technology, marketing, and distribution of its products. Research also suggests that when the country risk is high, firms prefer to enter

A **greenfield venture** is an entry mode through which a firm invests directly in another country or market by establishing a new wholly owned subsidiary.

with joint ventures instead of greenfield investments. However, if firms have previous experience in a country, they prefer to use a wholly owned greenfield venture rather than a joint venture.[103]

China has been an attractive market for foreign retailers (e.g., Walmart) because of its large population, the growing economic capabilities of Chinese citizens, and the opening of the Chinese market to foreign firms. For example, by 2005 more than 300 foreign retailers had entered China, many of them using greenfield ventures. Of course, China is a unique environment partly because of its culture but more so because of the government control and intervention. Good relationships with local and national government officials are quite important to foreign firms' success in China. Because of these complexities and the challenges they present, foreign retailers' success in this market has been mixed despite the substantial opportunities that exist there. Thus great care should be exercised when selecting the best mode for entering particular markets, as we discuss next.[104]

8-4f Dynamics of Mode of Entry

Several factors affect the firm's choice about how to enter international markets. Market entry is often achieved initially through exporting, which requires no foreign manufacturing expertise and investment only in distribution. Licensing can facilitate the product improvements necessary to enter foreign markets, as in the Komatsu example. Strategic alliances are a popular entry mode because they allow a firm to connect with an experienced partner already in the market. Partly because of this, geographically diversifying firms often use alliances in uncertain situations, such as an emerging economy where there is significant risk (e.g., Venezuela and Columbia).[105] However, if intellectual property rights in the emerging economy are not well protected, the number of firms in the industry is growing fast, and the need for global integration is high, other entry modes such as a joint venture (see Chapter 9) or a wholly owned subsidiary are preferred.[106] In the final analysis though, all three modes—export, licensing, and strategic alliance—can be effective means of initially entering new markets and for developing a presence in those markets.

Acquisitions, greenfield ventures, and sometimes joint ventures are used when firms want to establish a strong presence in an international market. Aerospace firms Airbus and Boeing have used joint ventures, especially in large markets, to facilitate entry, while military equipment firms such as Thales SA have used acquisitions to build a global presence. Japanese auto manufacturer Toyota has established a presence in the United States through both greenfield ventures and joint ventures. Because of Toyota's highly efficient manufacturing processes, the firm wants to maintain control over manufacturing when possible. To date, Toyota has established 52 manufacturing facilities in 27 countries. Demonstrating the importance of greenfield ventures and joint ventures to Toyota's international diversification strategy is the fact that in 2012 the firm opened its first new manufacturing plant in Japan in over 20 years.[107] Both acquisitions and greenfield ventures are likely to come at later stages in the development of a firm's international strategies.

Thus, to enter a global market, a firm selects the entry mode that is best suited to its situation. In some instances, the various options will be followed sequentially, beginning with exporting and eventually leading to greenfield ventures. In other cases, the firm may use several, but not all, of the different entry modes, each in different markets. The decision regarding which entry mode to use is primarily a result of the industry's competitive conditions, the country's situation and government policies, and the firm's unique set of resources, capabilities, and core competencies.

FEMSA, the large multibusiness Mexican firm, has been expanding its operations into multiple countries in recent years, as described in the Strategic Focus. Most of its expansion has been into other Latin American countries (where it better understands the culture and markets). But, it very recently expanded into the Philippines, a dramatic

Strategic Focus

Mexico's FEMSA: Building its International Prowess

Fomento Economico Mexicano SAB de CV has a market capitalization of $39.02 billion. It has more than 180,000 employees and is a major competitor in the beverage industry, convenience stores, and drugstores/pharmacies. In fact, Coca-Cola FEMSA SAB is the largest bottler of Coke not only in Latin America but in the entire world. In 2013, it continued to add to its strength in this business with a purchase of a regional bottler, Grupo Yoli, which was the largest soft-drink bottler in southern Mexico. In 2008, FEMSA decided to expand its convenience store chain, Oxxo, to other countries outside of Mexico. It now operates more than 10,600 stores in Mexico and Columbia. In 2012, it opened 1,040 new stores, which amounts to almost three per day. Oxxo is the largest and fastest-growing chain of convenience stores in Latin America.

Until 2010, FEMSA was a major beer producer in Mexico with operations in Brazil (which it entered through an acquisition of Kaiser Brewery) as well. However, Heineken acquired the FEMSA brewery business at that time. Yet, because the sale involved and exchange of equity, FEMSA now holds 20 percent of the equity in the Heineken Group (the second largest equity stake in this company).

Although FEMSA continues to promote organic growth, most of its major advances in size have come from acquisitions. For example, in 2013 FEMSA made its first foray outside of Latin America. It acquired a 51 percent stake (controlling interest) in Coca-Cola's bottling operations in the Philippines. It now has operations in nine countries, including eight in Latin America.

In 2013, it also expanded its drugstore/pharmacy chain with an acquisition by its retail subsidiary, FEMSA Comercio, of Farmacias FM Moderno. At the time of its acquisition, Farmacias FM Moderno operated more than 100 stores in Mexico's western state of Sinaloa.

Therefore, FEMSA is a multi-billion-dollar business that has used its stash of cash to build substantial growth through acquisitions. It has expanded its presence in Mexico but also in all of the most prominent economies in Latin America (e.g., Brazil, Argentina, Colombia, and Venezuela in addition to Mexico).

A Filipino worker collects empty Coca-Cola bottles in Manila. In 2013 FEMSA acquired the controlling interest in Coca-Cola Bottling Company's operations in the Philippines.

Sources: 2013, Strategic business, FEMSA Web site, http://femsa.com.en, Accessed on May 30; Sources:2013, Business units, FEMSA Web site, http://femsa.com.en, Accessed on May 30; 2013, Fomento Economico Mexicano SAB de CV, *DealBook, New York Times*, http://dealbook.on.nytimes.com, May 16; E. Garcis, 2013, Mexico's FEMSA: From convenience stores to pharmacies, *Financial Times*, http://blogs.ft.com, May 15; 2013, FEMSA expands drugstore chain, *Zacks Equity Research*, http://finance.yahoo.com, May 14; 2013, FEMSA announces acquisition of Farmacias FM Moderno, *Market Wire*, www.nbcnews.com, May 13; B. Case, 2013, Coca-Cola FEMSA expands with $700 million Yoli purchase, *Bloomberg Businessweek*, www.businessweek.com, January 18; A. Thomson, 2012, Mexico's FEMSA eyes Coca-Cola's Philippines unit, *Financial Times*, http://blogs.ft.com, February 21; M. J. de la Merced & C. V. Nicholson, 2010, Heineken in deal to buy a big Mexican Brewer, *New York Times*, www.nytimes.com, January 12; D. D. Stanford & T. Black, 2008, Mexico's Oxxo convenience stores to branch out, *Houston Chronicle*, www.chron.com, February 22.

entry into Asia. Its most common mode of entry has been acquisitions. It has considerable experience with acquisitions given that a large amount of its domestic growth has also come from acquisitions. Its latest acquisition in the Philippines will cause the executives to deal with unique institutions and new political and economic risks that they have not previously encountered.

8-5 Risks in an International Environment

International strategies are risky, particularly those that would cause a firm to become substantially more diversified in terms of geographic markets served. Firms entering markets in new countries encounter a number of complex institutional risks.[108] Political and economic risks cannot be ignored by firms using international strategies (see specific examples of political and economic risks in Figure 8.6).

Find out more about Oxxo.
www.cengagebrain.com

8-5a Political Risks

Political risks "denote the probability of disruption of the operations of multinational enterprises by political forces or events whether they occur in host countries, home country, or result from changes in the international environment."[109] Possible disruptions to a firm's operations when seeking to implement its international strategy create numerous problems, including uncertainty created by government regulation; the existence of many, possibly conflicting, legal authorities or corruption; and the potential nationalization of private assets.[110] Firms investing in other countries when implementing their international strategy may have concerns about the stability of the national government and the effects of unrest and government instability on their investments or assets.[111] To deal with these concerns, firms should conduct a political risk analysis of the countries or regions they may enter using one of the five entry modes. Through political risk analysis, the firm examines potential sources and factors of noncommercial disruptions of their foreign investments and the operations flowing from them.[112] However, occasionally firms might use political (institutional) weaknesses as an opportunity to transfer activities or practices that stakeholders see as undesirable for their operations in the home country to a new market so they can continue earning returns on these questionable practices.[113]

Figure 8.6 Risks in the International Environment

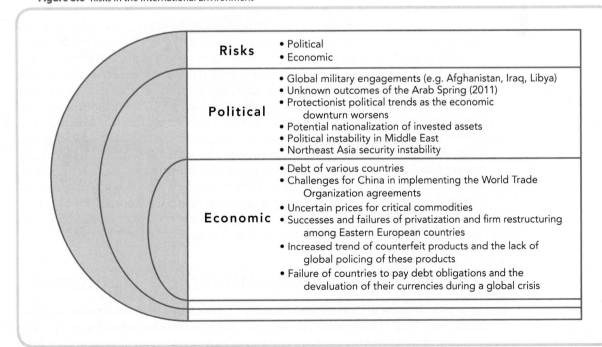

Risks	• Political • Economic
Political	• Global military engagements (e.g. Afghanistan, Iraq, Libya) • Unknown outcomes of the Arab Spring (2011) • Protectionist political trends as the economic downturn worsens • Potential nationalization of invested assets • Political instability in Middle East • Northeast Asia security instability
Economic	• Debt of various countries • Challenges for China in implementing the World Trade Organization agreements • Uncertain prices for critical commodities • Successes and failures of privatization and firm restructuring among Eastern European countries • Increased trend of counterfeit products and the lack of global policing of these products • Failure of countries to pay debt obligations and the devaluation of their currencies during a global crisis

M. Stasy

© Cengage Learning

Russia has experienced a relatively high level of institutional instability in the years following its revolutionary transition to a more democratic government. Decentralized political control and frequent changes in policies created chaos for many, but especially for those in the business landscape. In an effort to regain more central control and reduce the chaos, Russian leaders took actions such as prosecuting powerful private firm executives, seeking to gain state control of firm assets, and not approving some foreign acquisitions of Russian businesses. The initial institutional instability, followed by the actions of the central government, caused some firms to delay or avoid significant foreign direct investment in Russia. Although leaders in Russia have tried to reassure potential investors about their property rights, prior actions, the fact that other laws (e.g., environmental and employee laws) are weak, and commonplace government corruption make firms leery of investing in Russia. In fact, the *2013 World Economic Forum Competitiveness Report* suggested that the largest impediments to business in Russia are corruption, inefficient government bureaucracy, and weak access to financing.[114]

8-5b Economic Risks

Economic risks include fundamental weaknesses in a country or region's economy with the potential to cause adverse effects on firms' efforts to successfully implement their international strategies. As illustrated in the example of Russian institutional instability and property rights, political risks and economic risks are interdependent. If firms cannot protect their intellectual property, they are highly unlikely to use a means of entering a foreign market that involves significant and direct investments. Therefore, countries need to create, sustain, and enforce strong intellectual property rights in order to attract foreign direct investment.

Another economic risk is the perceived security risk of a foreign firm acquiring firms that have key natural resources or firms that may be considered strategic in regard to intellectual property. For instance, many Chinese firms have been buying natural resource firms in Australia and Latin America as well as manufacturing assets in the United States. This has made the governments of the key resource firms nervous about such strategic assets falling under the control of state-owned Chinese firms.[115] Terrorism has also been of concern. Indonesia has difficulty competing for investment against China and India, countries that are viewed as having fewer security risks.

As noted earlier, the differences and fluctuations in the value of currencies is among the foremost economic risks of using an international strategy.[116] This is especially true as the level of the firm's geographic diversification increases to the point where the firm is trading in a large number of currencies. The value of the dollar relative to other currencies determines the value of the international assets and earnings of U.S. firms; for example, an increase in the value of the U.S. dollar can reduce the value of U.S. multinational firms' international assets and earnings in other countries. Furthermore, the value of different currencies can at times dramatically affect a firm's competitiveness in global markets because of its effect on the prices of goods manufactured in different countries.[117] An increase in the value of the dollar can harm U.S. firms' exports to international markets because of the price differential of the products. Thus, government oversight and control of economic and financial capital in a country affect not only local economic activity, but also foreign investments in the country.[118] Certainly, the significant political and policy changes in Eastern Europe since the early 1990s have stimulated much more FDI there.[119]

8-6 Strategic Competitiveness Outcomes

As previously discussed, international strategies can result in three basic benefits (increased market size, economies of scale and learning, and location advantages) for firms. These basic benefits are gained when the firm successfully manages political, economic, and other institutional risks while implementing its international strategies; in turn, these benefits are critical to the firm's efforts to achieve strategic competitiveness (as measured by improved performance and enhanced innovation—see Figure 8.1).

Overall, the degree to which firms achieve strategic competitiveness through international strategies is expanded or increased when they successfully implement an international diversification strategy. As an extension or elaboration of international strategy, an **international diversification strategy** is a strategy through which a firm expands the sales of its goods or services across the borders of global regions and countries into a potentially large number of geographic locations or markets. Instead of entering one or just a few markets, the international diversification strategy finds firms using international business-level and international corporate-level strategies for the purpose of entering multiple regions and markets in order to sell their products.

8-6a International Diversification and Returns

Evidence suggests numerous reasons for firms to use an international diversification strategy,[120] meaning that international diversification should be related positively to firms' performance as measured by the returns it earns on its investments. Research has shown that as international diversification increases, a firm's returns decrease initially but then increase quickly as it learns how to manage the increased geographic diversification it has created.[121] In fact, the stock market is particularly sensitive to investments in international markets. Firms that are broadly diversified into multiple international markets usually achieve the most positive stock returns, especially when they diversify geographically into core business areas.[122]

Many factors contribute to the positive effects of international diversification, such as private versus government ownership, potential economies of scale and experience, location advantages, increased market size, and the opportunity to stabilize returns. The stabilization of returns helps reduce a firm's overall risk.[123] Large, well-established firms and entrepreneurial ventures can both achieve these positive outcomes by successfully implementing an international diversification strategy.

As described in the earlier Strategic focus, FEMSA was using an acquisition strategy to increase its international diversification. FEMSA's financial results suggest that it has achieved positive returns from this strategy. Of course, its recent entry into Asian markets with an acquisition of operations in the Philippines may pose greater challenges.

8-6b Enhanced Innovation

In Chapter 1, we indicated that developing new technology is at the heart of strategic competitiveness. As noted in our discussion of the determinants of national advantage (see Figure 8.3), a nation's competitiveness depends, in part, on the capacity of its industries to innovate. Eventually and inevitably, competitors outperform firms that fail to innovate. Therefore, the only way for individual nations and individual firms to sustain a competitive advantage is to upgrade it continually through innovation.[124]

An international diversification strategy and the geographic diversification it brings about create the potential for firms to achieve greater returns on their innovations (through larger or more numerous markets) while reducing the often substantial risks of R&D investments. Additionally, international diversification may be necessary to generate the resources required to sustain a large-scale R&D operation. An environment of rapid technological obsolescence makes it difficult to invest in new technology and the capital-intensive operations necessary to compete in such an environment. Firms operating solely in domestic markets may find such investments difficult because of the length of time required to recoup the original investment. However, diversifying into a number of international markets improves a firm's ability to appropriate additional returns from innovation before competitors can overcome the initial competitive advantage created by the innovation.[125] In addition, firms

An **international diversification strategy** is a strategy through which a firm expands the sales of its goods or services across the borders of global regions and countries into a potentially large number of geographic locations or markets.

moving into international markets are exposed to new products and processes. If they learn about those products and processes and integrate this knowledge into their operations, further innovation can be developed. To incorporate the learning into their own R&D processes, firms must manage those processes effectively in order to absorb and use the new knowledge to create further innovations.[126] For a number of reasons then, international strategies and certainly an international diversification strategy provide incentives for firms to innovate.[127]

The relationship among international geographic diversification, innovation, and returns is complex. Some level of performance is necessary to provide the resources the firm needs to diversify geographically; in turn, geographic diversification provides incentives and resources to invest in R&D. Effective R&D should enhance the firm's returns, which then provide more resources for continued geographic diversification and investment in R&D.[128] Of course, the returns generated from these relationships increase through effective managerial practices. Evidence suggests that more culturally diverse top management teams often have a greater knowledge of international markets and their idiosyncrasies, but their orientation to expand internationally can be affected by the nature of their incentives.[129] Moreover, managing the business units of a geographically diverse multinational firm requires skill, not only in managing a decentralized set of businesses, but also coordinating diverse points of view emerging from businesses located in different countries and regions. Firms able to do this increase the likelihood of outperforming their rivals.[130]

8-7 The Challenge of International Strategies

Effectively using international strategies creates basic benefits and contributes to the firm's strategic competitiveness. However, for several reasons, attaining these positive outcomes is difficult.

8-7a Complexity of Managing International Strategies

Pursuing international strategies, particularly an international diversification strategy, typically leads to growth in a firm's size and the complexity of its operations. In turn, larger size and greater operational complexity make a firm more difficult to manage. At some point, size and complexity either cause firms to become virtually unmanageable or increase the cost of their management beyond the value using international strategies creates. Different cultures and institutional practices (such as those associated with governmental agencies) that are part of the countries in which a firm competes when using an international strategy also can create difficulties.[131]

Toyota's experiences over the past few years appear to demonstrate the relationship between firm size and managerial complexity. Toyota became the world's largest car manufacturer at the end of 2008, surpassing General Motors (GM had been the largest auto manufacturer for 77 years). Volkswagen-Porsche briefly replaced Toyota as the world's largest car

Toyota's FT-86 on display at the 2010 Paris Motor Show.

© Maksim Toome/Shutterstock.com

and truck manufacturer, but in 2013 Toyota again became the largest. As always is the case though, larger size makes a firm harder to manage successfully. In spite of its legendary focus on and reputation for quality, over the past few years and after becoming the world's largest manufacturer, Toyota experienced product quality problems, particularly in the all-important U.S. market. Perhaps the increased difficulty of managing a larger firm contributed to Toyota's product quality problems. However, Toyota seems to have recovered from these difficulties and continues seeking additional growth through its international strategy. For example, its sales revenues in fiscal year 2013 increased by 18.7 percent over fiscal year 2012. Its net income increased by 239.3 percent for the same time period. And, international sales are quite important to Toyota, as they account for slightly more than 81 percent of its total vehicle sales.[132]

Firms have to build on their capabilities and other advantages to overcome the challenges encountered in international markets. For example, some firms from emerging economies that hold monopolies in their home markets can invest the resources gained there to enhance their competitiveness in international markets (because they don't have to be concerned about competitors in home markets).[133] The key is for firms to overcome the various liabilities of foreignness regardless of their source.[134]

8-7b Limits to International Expansion

Learning how to effectively manage an international strategy improves the likelihood of achieving positive outcomes such as enhanced performance. However, at some point the degree of geographic and (possibly) product diversification the firm's international strategies bring about causes the returns from using the strategies to level off and eventually become negative.[135]

There are several reasons for the limits to the positive effects of the diversification associated with international strategies. First, greater geographic dispersion across country borders increases the costs of coordination between units and the distribution of products. This is especially true when firms have multiple locations in countries that have diverse subnational institutions. Second, trade barriers, logistical costs, cultural diversity, and other differences by country (e.g., access to raw materials and different employee skill levels) greatly complicate the implementation of an international strategy.[136]

Institutional and cultural factors can be strong barriers to the transfer of a firm's core competencies from one market to another.[137] Marketing programs often have to be redesigned and new distribution networks established when firms expand into new markets. In addition, firms may encounter different labor costs and capital expenses. In general, it becomes increasingly difficult to effectively implement, manage, and control a firm's international operations with increases in geographic diversity.[138]

The amount of diversification in a firm's international operations that can be managed varies from company to company and is affected by managers' abilities to deal with ambiguity and complexity. The problems of central coordination and integration are mitigated if the firm's international operations compete in friendly countries that are geographically close and have cultures similar to its own country's culture. In that case, the firm is likely to encounter fewer trade barriers, the laws and customs are better understood, and the product is easier to adapt to local markets.[139] For example, U.S. firms may find it less difficult to expand their operations into Mexico, Canada, and Western European countries than into Asian countries.

The relationships between the firm using an international strategy and the governments in the countries in which the firm is competing can also be constraining.[140] The reason for this is that the differences in host countries' governmental policies and practices can be substantial, creating a need for the focal firm to learn how to manage what can be a large set of different enforcement policies and practices. At some point, the differences create too many problems for the firm to be successful. Using strategic alliances is another way firms can deal with this limiting factor. Partnering with companies in different countries allows the focal firm to rely on its partner to help deal with local laws, rules, regulations, and customs. But these partnerships are not risk free and managing them tends to be difficult.[141]

SUMMARY

■ The use of international strategies is increasing. Multiple factors and conditions are influencing the increasing use of these strategies, including opportunities to (1) extend a product's life cycle, (2) gain access to critical raw materials, sometimes including relatively inexpensive labor, (3) integrate a firm's operations on a global scale to better serve customers in different countries, (4) better serve customers whose needs appear to be more alike today as a result of global communications media and the Internet's capabilities to inform, and (5) meet increasing demand for goods and services that is surfacing in emerging markets.

■ When used effectively, international strategies yield three basic benefits: increased market size, economies of scale and learning, and location advantages. Firms use international business-level and international corporate-level strategies to geographically diversify their operations.

■ International business-level strategies are usually grounded in one or more home-country advantages. Research suggests that there are four determinants of national advantage: factors of production; demand conditions; related and supporting industries; and patterns of firm strategy, structure, and rivalry.

■ There are three types of international corporate-level strategies. A multidomestic strategy focuses on competition within each country in which the firm competes. Firms using a multidomestic strategy decentralize strategic and operating decisions to the business units operating in each country, so that each unit can tailor its products to local conditions. A global strategy assumes more standardization of products across country boundaries; therefore, a competitive strategy is centralized and controlled by the home office. Commonly, large multinational firms, particularly those with multiple diverse products being sold in many different markets, use a multidomestic strategy with some product lines and a global strategy with others.

■ A transnational strategy seeks to integrate characteristics of both multidomestic and global strategies for the purpose of being able to simultaneously emphasize local responsiveness and global integration.

■ Two global environmental trends—liability of foreignness and regionalization—are influencing firms' choices of international strategies as well as their implementation.

Liability of foreignness challenges firms to recognize that distance between their domestic market and international markets affects how they compete. Some firms choose to concentrate their international strategies on regions (e.g., the EU and NAFTA) rather than on individual country markets.

■ Firms can use one or more of five entry modes to enter international markets. Exporting, licensing, strategic alliances, acquisitions, and new wholly owned subsidiaries, often referred to as greenfield ventures, are the five entry modes. Most firms begin with exporting or licensing, because of their lower costs and risks, but later they often use strategic alliances and acquisitions as well. The most expensive and risky means of entering a new international market is establishing a new wholly owned subsidiary (greenfield venture). On the other hand, such subsidiaries provide the advantages of maximum control by the firm and, if successful, the greatest returns. Large, geographically diversified firms often use most or all five entry modes across different markets when implementing international strategies.

■ Firms encounter a number of risks when implementing international strategies. The two major categories of risks firms need to understand and address when diversifying geographically through international strategies are political risks (risks concerned with the probability a firm's operations will be disrupted by political forces or events, whether they occur in the firm's domestic market or in the markets the firm has entered to implement its international strategies) and economic risks (risks resulting from fundamental weaknesses in a country's or a region's economy with the potential to adversely affect a firm's ability to implement its international strategies).

■ Successful use of international strategies (especially an international diversification strategy) contributes to a firm's strategic competitiveness in the form of improved performance and enhanced innovation. International diversification facilitates innovation in a firm because it provides a larger market to gain greater and faster returns from investments in innovation. In addition, international diversification can generate the resources necessary to sustain a large-scale R&D program.

■ In general, international diversification helps to achieve above-average returns, but this assumes that the diversification is effectively implemented and that the firm's international operations are well managed. International diversification provides greater economies of scope and learning which, along with greater innovation, help produce above-average returns.

■ A firm using international strategies to pursue strategic competitiveness often experience complex challenges that must

be overcome. Some limits also constrain the ability to manage international expansion effectively. International diversification increases coordination and distribution costs, and management problems are exacerbated by trade barriers, logistical costs, and cultural diversity, among other factors.

REVIEW QUESTIONS

1. What incentives influence firms to use international strategies?

2. What are the three basic benefits firms can achieve by successfully using an international strategy?

3. What four factors are determinants of national advantage and serve as a basis for international business-level strategies?

4. What are the three international corporate-level strategies? What are the advantages and disadvantages associated with these individual strategies?

5. What are some global environmental trends affecting the choice of international strategies, particularly international corporate-level strategies?

6. What five entry modes do firms consider as paths to use to enter international markets? What is the typical sequence in which firms use these entry modes?

7. What are political risks and what are economic risks? How should firms approach dealing with these risks?

8. What are the strategic competitiveness outcomes firms can reach through international strategies, and particularly through an international diversification strategy?

9. What are two important issues that can potentially affect a firm's ability to successfully use international strategies?

EXPERIENTIAL EXERCISES

EXERCISE 1: CROSS-BORDER EXPANSION

Should Ronco Toys expand to Mexico? One of the important reasons for expanding internationally is location advantages through which placing facilities outside one's home country can provide cost advantages. Advantages don't necessarily always have to be about cost reduction; the international country might provide access to important raw materials, logistical support, and energy or other natural resources.

For purposes of this exercise you are to consider that your team has been hired to act as a consulting company for the purposes of analyzing a potential cross-border expansion of a U.S. firm. Your client, Ronco Toys Inc., has made the decision to expand internationally to Mexico under the Maquiladora Program. Under this program American companies (and other countries as well) can establish factories in Mexico close to the Texas border and thereby gain significant cost reductions in labor. This program began in the 1960s but expanded rapidly after NAFTA was approved in 1994. By some estimates today there are over one million Mexicans working in over 3,000 factories producing goods that will most likely be exported to the United States.

Your client makes toys that are rather labor intensive and has found that demand is outstripping supply from their U.S.-based factory. In addition, cost pressures from competitors are squeezing margins

uncomfortably. Therefore the CEO has decided to open up a new factory in a Mexican Maquiladora rather than expand domestically. Your challenge in this exercise is to critically examine this decision.

Provide both a list of pros and cons to help the CEO wade through the decision. Pay particular attention to the following:

1. Do you think this is the best solution possible given the limited data provided?

2. What other options should be considered?

3. What other items should go into this decision besides labor cost savings?

Be prepared to present your findings to the class.

EXERCISE 2: WHERE NEXT?

In this exercise, consider your team to be a consultant to a multinational fast food restaurant company that is trying to increase its international exposure in the coming years. As you recall from the chapter, an international strategy is one in which "the firm sells its goods or services outside its domestic market." The choices to do so are varied and include exporting, licensing, alliance, acquisition, or creating a new wholly owned subsidiary. The reasons are just as varied as the entry modes.

To identify a suitable candidate for analysis, consult research databases such as Datamonitor or Business Source Complete. For example, Jack in the Box operates more than 2,200 units but they are all in the United States, which provides advantages as well as disadvantages. Compare this with McDonald's, the world's largest food-service retailing chain, with 34,000 restaurants operating in 119 countries as of 2013. You will also find SWOT (strengths, weaknesses, opportunities, threats) analysis on companies through databases such as those mentioned above.

Your consulting firm has been retained by the fast-food retailer to investigate the feasibility of expanding internationally. You should be prepared to address the following questions:

1. Which international location(s) seem to fit best based on your research?

2. Which entry mode seems the most reasonable for the firms to use?

3. What macro environmental and industry trends support your recommendations? Economic characteristics include gross national product, wages, unemployment, and inflation. Trend analysis of these data (e.g., are wages rising or falling, rate of change in wages, etc.) is preferable to single point-in-time snapshots.

4. What country risks seem most problematic?

The following additional Internet resources may be useful in your research:

- The Library of Congress has a collection of country studies.

- *BBC News* offers country profiles.

- *The Economist Intelligence Unit* (http://www.eiu.com) offers country profiles.

- Both the United Nations and International Monetary Fund provide statistics and research reports.

- The *CIA World Factbook* has profiles of different regions.

- The *Global Entrepreneurship Monitor* provides reports with detailed information about economic conditions and social aspects for a number of countries.

- Links can be found at http://www.countryrisk.com to a number of resources that assess both political and economic risk for individual countries.

- For U.S. data, see http://www.census.gov.

- Be prepared to discuss and defend your recommendations in class.

VIDEO CASE ▶

THE LURE OF AN INTERNATIONAL STRATEGY: INDIA/INFOSYS

India, home to low-cost living and resources, has become a technology mecca that maintains the second-largest software industry in the world. The country has managed to amass the presence of big-name international companies and create a few of its own, such as InfoSys. The key to luring foreign investors and workers is to create companies on par with any in the West. InfoSys, which is similar to a resort spa, continues to offer more experience and opportunity for many young Americans from U.S. colleges than would be possible in the US. Infosys was ranked India's 'Most Admired Company' in Wall Street Journal Asia 200, a listing of Asia's leading companies in 2010, a distinction achieved for nine years in a row. Established in 1981 with capital of $250, Infosys has grown to a $6.4 billion IT services and consulting company.

Be prepared to discuss the following concepts and questions in class:

Concepts

- International strategy

- Business-level strategy

- Corporate-level strategy

- National advantage

Questions

1. What international strategy incentives does India offer to a foreign investor? What limitations exist in India for companies desiring international expansion?

2. What benefits does InfoSys receive from its international strategy?

3. How does India's national advantage(s) influence its business-level strategy?

4. What corporate-level strategy is used by InfoSys and why?

NOTES

1. C. N. Pitellis & D. J. Teece, 2012, Cross-border market co-creation, dynamic capabilities and the entrepreneurial theory of the multinational enterprise, in D. J. Teece (ed.), *Strategy, innovation and the theory of the firm*, Cheltenham, UK: Edward Elgar, 341–364; M. J. Nieto & A. Rodriguez, 2011, Offshoring of R&D: Looking abroad to improve innovation performance, *Journal of International Business Studies*, 42: 345–361.

2. R. M. Holmes, T. Miller, M. A. Hitt, & M. P. Salmador, 2013, The interrelationship among informal institutions, formal institutions and inward foreign direct investment, *Journal of Management*, 39: 531–566.

3. J.-L. Arregle, L. Naldi, M. Nordqvist & M. A. Hitt, 2012, Internationalization of family-controlled firms: A study of the effects of external involvement in governance, *Entrepreneurship Theory and Practice*, 36: 1115–1143; E. Golovko & G. Valentini, 2011, Exploring the complementarity between innovation and export for SMEs' growth, *Journal of International Business Studies*, 42: 362–380; M. A. Hitt, L. Tihanyi, T. Miller, & B. Connelly, 2006, International diversification: Antecedents, outcomes and moderators, *Journal of Management*, 32: 831–867.

4. M. F. Wiersema & H. P. Bowen, 2011, The relationship between international diversification and firm performance: Why it remains a puzzle, *Global Strategy Journal*, 1: 152–170.

5. R. Vernon, 1996, International investment and international trade in the product cycle, *Quarterly Journal of Economics*, 80: 190–207.

6. 2013, Our strategy, Rio Tinto homepage, www.riotinto.com, accessed on May 27.

7. E. Ko, C. R. Taylor, H. Sung, J. Lee, U. Wagner, D. Martin-Consuega Navarro, & F. Wang, 2012, Global marketing segmentation usefulness in the sportswear industry, *Journal of Business Research*, 65(11): 1565–1575.

8. J. Li, Y. Li, & D. Shapiro, 2012, Knowledge seeking and outward FDI of emerging market firms: The moderating effect of inward FDI, *Global Strategy Journal*, 2: 277–295; 2011, The globalization index 2010, Ernst & Young, http://www.ey.com, January.

9. B. Michael & S. H. Park, 2013, Who is your company? Where to locate to compete in emerging markets, *IEMS Market Brief*, Sklokovo Institute for Emerging Market Studies, vol. 13-03, February; K. E. Meyer, R. Mudambi, & R. Nanula, 2011, Multinational enterprises and local contexts: The opportunities and challenges of multiple embeddedness, *Journal of Management Studies*, 48: 235–252.

10. 2013, Our stores, Carrefour Group homepage, www.carrefour.com, May 28.

11. M. Colchester, 2011, Carrefour documents remain sealed, *Wall Street Journal*, www.wsj.com, June 24.

12. T. R. Annamalai & A. Deshmukh, 2011, Venture capital and private equity in India: An analysis of investments and exits, *Journal of Indian Business Research*, 3: 6–21; P. Zheng, 2009, A comparison of FDI determinants in China and India, *Thunderbird International Business Review*, 51: 263–279.

13. R. Ramamurti, 2012, What is really different about emerging market multinationals? *Global Strategy Journal*, 2: 41–47; S. Athreye & S. Kapur, 2009, Introduction: The internationalization of Chinese and Indian firms—trends, motivations and strategy, *Industrial and Corporate Change*, 18: 209–221.

14. M. Carney, E. R. Gedajlovic, P. M. A. R. Heugens, M. van Essen, & J. van Oosterhout, 2011, Business group affiliation, performance, context, and strategy: A meta-analysis, *Academy of Management Journal*, 54: 437–460; B. Elango, 2009, Minimizing effects of "liability of foreignness": Response strategies of foreign firm in the United States, *Journal of World Business*, 44: 51–62.

15. 2013, Midrange growth strategy starting from fiscal year 2013, News Release, www.takeda.com, May 9; K. Inagaki & J. Osawa, 2011, Takeda, Toshiba make $16 billion M&A push, *Wall Street Journal*, www.wsj.com, May 20; K. Iagaki, 2011, Takeda buys Nycomed for $14 billion, *Wall Street Journal*, www.wsj.com, May 20.

16. A. Verbeke & W. Yuan, 2013, The drivers of multinational enterprise subsidiary entrepreneurship in China: A resource-based view perspective, *Journal of Management Studies*, 50: 236–258; S. B. Choi, S. H. Lee, & C. Williams, 2011, Ownership and firm innovation in transition economy: Evidence from China, *Research Policy*, 40: 441–452.

17. 2013, Corporate, Ford Motor Company, www.ford.com, accessed May 28; N. E. Boudette, 2011, Ford forecasts sharp gains from Asian sales, *Wall Street Journal*, www.wsj.com, June 8.

18. 2013, Investor relations news, Ford Motor Company, www.ford.com, accessed May 28.

19. A. H. Kirka, G. T. Hult, S. Deligonul, M. Z. Perry, & S. T. Cavusgil, 2012, A multilevel examination of the drivers of firm multinationality: A meta-analysis, *Journal of Management*, 38: 502–530; L. Nachum & S. Song, 2011, The MNE as a portfolio: Interdependencies in MNE growth trajectory, *Journal of International Business Studies*, 42: 381–405.

20. G. Qian, T. A. Khoury, M. W. Peng, & Z. Qian, 2010, The performance implications of intra- and inter-regional geographic diversification, *Strategic Management Journal*, 31: 1018–1030; H. Zou & P. N. Ghauri, 2009, Learning through international acquisitions: The process of knowledge acquisition in China, *Management International Review*, 48: 207–226.

21. Y. Zhang, H. Li, Y. Li, & L.-A. Zhou, 2010, FDI spillovers in an emerging market: The role of foreign firms' country origin diversity and domestic firms' absorptive capacity, *Strategic Management Journal*, 31: 969–989; J. Song & J. Shin, 2008, The paradox of technological capabilities: A study of knowledge sourcing from host countries of overseas R&D operations, *Journal of International Business Studies*, 39: 291–303.

22. F. J. Froese, 2013, Work values of the next generation of business leaders in Shanghai, Tokyo and Seoul, *Asia Pacific Journal of Management*, 30: 297–315; H. Hoang & F. T. Rothaermel, 2010, Leveraging internal and external experience: Exploration, exploitation, and R&D project performance, *Strategic Management Journal*, 31: 734–758.

23. A. Gambardella & M. S. Giarratana, 2010, Localized knowledge spillovers and skill-based performance, *Strategic Entrepreneurship Journal*, 4: 323–339; A. M. Rugman & A. Verbeke, 2009, A new perspective on the regional and global strategies of multinational services firms, *Management International Review*, 48: 397–411.

24. O. Shenkar, 2012, Cultural distance revisited: Towards a more rigorous conceptualization and measurement of cultural differences, *Journal of International Business Studies*, 43: 1–11; R. Chakrabarti, Gupta-Mukherjee, & N. Jayaraman, 2009, Mars-Venus marriages: Culture and cross-border M&A, *Journal of International Business Studies*, 40: 216–236.

25. B. T. McCann & G. Vroom, 2010, Pricing response to entry and agglomeration effects, *Strategic Management Journal*, 31: 284–305; C. C. J. M. Millar & C. J. Choi, 2009, Worker identity, the liability of foreignness, the exclusion of local managers and unionism: A conceptual analysis, *Journal of Organizational Change Management*, 21: 460–470.

26. Y. Y. Chang, Y. Gong, & M. Peng, 2013, Expatriate knowledge transfer, subsidiary absorptive capacity and subsidiary performance, *Academy of Management Journal*, in press; P. Kappen, 2011, Competence-creating overlaps and subsidiary technological evolution in the multinational corporation, *Research Policy*, 40: 673–686.

27. A. Cuervo-Cazurra & M. Gene, 2008, Transforming disadvantages into advantages: Developing-country MNEs in the least developed countries, *Journal of International Business Studies*, 39: 957–979; M. A. Hitt, L. Bierman, K. Uhlenbruck, &

K. Shimizu, 2006, The importance of resources in the internationalization of professional service firms: The good, the bad and the ugly, *Academy of Management Journal*, 49: 1137–1157.

28. A. Arino, 2011, Building the global enterprise: Strategic assembly, *Global Strategy Journal*, 1: 47–49; P. Dastidar, 2009, International corporate diversification and performance: Does firm self-selection matter? *Journal of International Business Studies*, 40: 71–85.

29. M. E. Porter, 1990, *The Competitive Advantage of Nations*, New York: The Free Press.

30. Ibid., 84.

31. D. Englander, 2013, Chiquita Brands—Stocks with appeal, *Wall Street Journal*, www.wsj. com, April 28.

32. 2011, New building blocks for jobs and economic growth, Global competition and collaboration conference, Georgetown University, May 16 and 17.

33. C. Wang, J. Hong, M. Kafouros, & M. Wright, 2012, Exploring the role of government involvement in outward FDI from emerging economies, *Journal of International Business Studies*, 43: 655–676; J. Nishimura & H. Okamuro, 2011, Subsidy and networking: The effects of direct and indirect support programs of the cluster policy, *Research Policy*, 40: 714–727; S. Sheng, K. Z. Zhou, & J. J. Li, 2011, The effects of business and political ties on firm performance: Evidence from China, *Journal of Marketing*, 75: 1–15.

34. M. Kitamura, A. Ohnsman, & Y. Hagiwara, 2011, Why Lexus doesn't lead the pack in China, *Bloomberg Businessweek*, April 3, 32–33.

35. J. M. Shaver, 2011, The benefits of geographic sales diversification: How exporting facilitates capital investment, *Strategic Management Journal*, 32: 1046–1060.

36. L. Diestre & N. Rajagopalan, 2011, An environmental perspective on diversification: The effects of chemical relatedness and regulatory sanctions, *Academy of Management Journal*, 54: 97–115.

37. S. A. Appelbaum, M. Roy, & T. Gilliland, 2011, Globalization of performance appraisals: Theory and applications, *Management Decision*, 49: 570–585; D. A. Ralson, D. H. Holt, R. H. Terpstra, & Y. K. Cheng, 2008, The impact of national culture and economic ideology on managerial work values: A study of the United States, Russia, Japan, and China, *Journal of International Business Studies*, 39: 8–26.

38. S. Zaheer & L. Nachum, 2011, Sense of place: From location resources to MNE locational capital, *Global Strategy Journal*, 1: 96–108; N. Guimaraes-Costs & M. P. E. Cunha, 2009, Foreign locals: A liminal perspective of international managers, *Organizational Dynamics*, 38: 158–166.

39. J.-S. Chen & A. S. Lovvorn, 2011, The speed of knowledge transfer within multinational enterprises: The role of social capital,

International Journal of Commerce and Management, 21: 46–62; H. Kasper, M. Lehrer, J. Muhlbacher, & B. Muller, 2009, Integration-responsiveness and knowledge-management perspectives on the MNC: A typology and field study of cross-site knowledge-sharing practices, *Journal of Leadership & Organizational Studies*, 15: 287–303.

40. 2013, Introduction to Unilever global, Unilever homepage, www.unilever.com, accessed on May 28; J. Neff, 2008, Unilever's CMO finally gets down to business, *Advertising Age*, July 11.

41. M. P. Koza, S. Tallman, & A. Ataay, 2011, The strategic assembly of global firms: A microstructural analysis of local learning and global adaptation, *Global Strategy Journal*, 1: 27–46; P. J. Buckley, 2009, The impact of the global factory on economic development, *Journal of World Business*, 44: 131–143.

42. A. Zaheer & E. Hernandez, 2011, The geographic scope of the MNC and its alliance portfolio: Resolving the paradox of distance, *Global Strategy Journal*, 1: 109–126.

43. L. Hail, C. Leuz, & P. Wysocki, 2010, Global accounting convergence and the potential adoption of IFRS by the U.S. (part II): Political factors and future scenarios for U.S. accounting standards, *Accounting Horizons*, 24: 567–581; R. G. Barker, 2003, Trend: Global accounting is coming, *Harvard Business Review*, 81(4): 24–25.

44. J.-L. Arregle, T. Miller, M. A. Hitt, & P. W. Beamish, 2013, Do regions matter? An integrated institutional and semiglobalization perspective on the internationalization of MNEs, *Strategic Management Journal*, 34: 910–934; L. H. Shi, C. White, S. Zou, & S. T. Cavusgil, 2010, Global account management strategies: Drivers and outcomes, *Journal of International Business Studies*, 41: 620–638.

45. 2013, About us, CEMEX, www.cemex.com, accessed on May 28.

46. 2012, 2012 CEMEX Annual Report, www. cemex.com, accessed on May 28.

47. R. Greenwood, S. Fairclough, T. Morris, & M. Boussebaa, 2010, The organizational design of transnational professional service firms, *Organizational Dynamics*, 39: 173–183.

48. C. Stehr, 2010, Globalisation strategy for small and medium-sized enterprises, *International Journal of Entrepreneurship and Innovation Management*, 12: 375–391; A. M. Rugman & A. Verbeke, 2008, A regional solution to the strategy and structure of multinationals, *European Management Journal*, 26: 305–313.

49. 2010, Regional resilience: Theoretical and empirical perspectives, *Cambridge Journal of Regions, Economy and Society*, 3–10; Rugman & Verbeke, A regional solution to the strategy and structure of multinationals.

50. M. W. Peng & Y. Jiang, 2010, Institutions behind family ownership and control

in large firms, *Journal of Management Studies*, 47: 253–273; A. M. Rugman & A. Verbeke, 2003, Extending the theory of the multinational enterprise: Internationalization and strategic management perspectives, *Journal of International Business Studies*, 34: 125–137.

51. D. Klonowski, 2011, Private equity in emerging markets: Stacking up the BRICs, *Journal of Private Equity*, 14: 24–37.

52. J. Mata & E. Freitas, 2012, Foreignness and exit over the life cycle of firms, *Journal of International Business Studies*, 43: 615–630. R. G. Bell, I. Filatotchev & A. A. Rasheed, 2012, The liability of foreignness, in capital markets: Sources and remedies, *Journal of International Business Studies*, 43: 107–122.

53. R. Salomon & Z. Wu, 2012, Institutional distance and local isomorphism strategy, *Journal of International Business Studies*, 43: 347–367.

54. J. T. Campbell, L. Eden, & S. R. Miller, 2012, Multinationals and corporate social responsibility in host countries: Does distance matter? *Journal of International Business Studies*, 43: 84–106; P. Ghemawat, 2001, Distance still matters, *Harvard Business Review*, 79(8): 137–145.

55. N. Y. Brannen, 2004, When Mickey loses face: Recontextualization, semantic fit and semiotics of foreignness, *Academy of Management Review*, 29: 593–616.

56. M. Schuman, 2006, Disney's Hong Kong headache, *Time*, www.time.com, May 8.

57. Arregle, Miller, Hitt, & Beamish, Do regions matter?; J. Cantwell & Y. Zhang, 2011, Innovation and location in the multinational firm, *International Journal of Technology Management*, 54: 116–132.

58. K. Ito & E. L. Rose, 2010, The implicit return on domestic and international sales: An empirical analysis of U.S. and Japanese firms, *Journal of International Business Studies*, 41: 1074–1089; A. M. Rugman & A. Verbeke, 2007, Liabilities of foreignness and the use of firm-level versus country-level data: A response to Dunning et al. (2007), *Journal of International Business Studies*, 38: 200–205.

59. Arregle, Miller, Hitt, & Beamish, Do regions matter?; E. R. Banalieva, M. D. Santoro, & R. J. Jiang, 2012, Home region focus and technical efficiency of multinational enterprises: The moderating role of regional integration, *Management International Review*, 52(4): 493–518.

60. A. M. Rugman & S. Girod, 2003, Retail multinationals and globalization: The evidence is regional, *European Management Journal*, 21: 24–37.

61. D. E. Westney, 2006, Review of the regional multinationals: MNEs and global strategic management (book review), *Journal of International Business Studies*, 37: 445–449.

62. R. D. Ludema, 2002, Increasing returns, multinationals and geography of preferential trade agreements, *Journal of International Economics*, 56: 329–358.

63. M. Aspinwall, 2009, NAFTA-ization: Regionalization and domestic political adjustment in the North American economic area, *Journal of Common Market Studies*, 47: 1–24.

64. D. Zu & O. Shenar, 2002, Institutional distance and the multinational enterprise, *Academy of Management Review*, 27: 608–618.

65. A. Ojala, 2008, Entry in a psychically distant market: Finnish small and medium-sized software firms in Japan, *European Management Journal*, 26: 135–144.

66. K. D. Brouthers, 2013, Institutional, cultural and transaction cost influences on entry mode choice and performance, *Journal of International Business Studies*, 44: 1–13.

67. B. Maekelburger, C. Schwens, & R. Kabst, 2012, Asset specificity and foreign market entry mode choice of small and medium-sized enterprises: The moderating influence of knowledge safeguards and institutional safeguards, *Journal of International Business Studies*, 43: 458–476.

68. J. M. Shaver, The benefits of geographic sales diversification; C. A. Cinquetti, 2009, Multinationals and exports in a large and protected developing country, *Review of International Economics*, 16: 904–918.

69. P. Ganotakis & J. H. Love, 2012, Export propensity, export intensity and firm performance: The role of the entrepreneurial founding team, *Journal of International Business Studies*, 43: 693–718.

70. M. Bandyk, 2008, Now even small firms can go global, *U.S. News & World Report*, March 10, 52.

71. B. Cassiman & E. Golovko, 2010, Innovation and internationalization through exports, *Journal of International Business Studies*, 42: 56–75.

72. X. He, K. D. Brouthers, & I. Filatotchev, 2013, Resource-based and institutional perspectives on export channel selection and export performance, *Journal of Management*, 39: 27–47; M. Hughes, S. L. Martin, R. E. Morgan, & M. J. Robson, 2010, Realizing product-market advantage in high-technology international new ventures: The mediating role of ambidextrous innovation, *Journal of International Marketing*, 18: 1–21.

73. P. Ganotakis & J. H. Love, 2011, R&D, product innovation, and exporting: Evidence from UK new technology-based firms, *Oxford Economic Papers*, 63: 279–306; M. Gabrielsson & P. Gabrielsson, 2011, Internet-based sales channel strategies of born global firms, *International Business Review*, 20: 88–99.

74. P. S. Aulakh, M. Jiang, & Y. Pan, 2010, International technology licensing: Monopoly rents transaction costs and exclusive rights, *Journal of International Business Studies*, 41: 587–605; R. Bird & D. R. Cahoy, 2008, The impact of compulsory licensing on foreign direct investment: A collective bargaining approach, *American Business Law Journal*, 45: 283–330.

75. M. S. Giarratana & S. Torrisi, 2010, Foreign entry and survival in a knowledge-intensive market: Emerging economy countries' international linkages, technology competences, and firm experience, *Strategic Entrepreneurship Journal*, 4: 85–104; U. Lichtenthaler, 2008, Externally commercializing technology assets: An examination of different process stages, *Journal of Business Venturing*, 23: 445–464.

76. N. Byrnes & F. Balfour, 2009, Philip Morris unbound, *BusinessWeek*, May 4, 38–42.

77. 2013, PMI around the world, Philip Morris International homepage, www.pmi.com, accessed on May 29.

78. E. Dechenaux, J. Thursby, & M. Thursby, 2011, Inventor moral hazard in university licensing: The role of contracts, *Research Policy*, 40: 94–104; S. Hagaoka, 2009, Does strong patent protection facilitate international technology transfer? Some evidence from licensing contrasts of Japanese firms, *Journal of Technology Transfer*, 34: 128–144.

79. U. Lichtenthaler, 2011, The evolution of technology licensing management: Identifying five strategic approaches, *R&D Management*, 41: 173–189; M. Fiedler & I. M. Welpe, 2010, Antecedents of cooperative commercialization strategies of nanotechnology firms, *Research Policy*, 39: 400–410.

80. C. A. Barlett & S. Rangan, 1992, Komatsu Limited, in C. A. Bartlett & S. Ghoshal (eds.), *Transnational Management: Text, Cases and Readings in Cross-Border Management*, Homewood, IL: Irwin, 311–326.

81. S. Veilleux, N. Haskell, & F. Pons, 2012, Going global: How smaller enterprises benefit from strategic alliances, *Journal of Business Strategy*, 33(5): 22–31; C. Schwens, J. J. Eiche, & R. Kabst, 2011, The moderating impact of informal institutional distance and formal institutional risk on SME entry mode choice, *Journal of Management Business Studies*, 48: 330–351.

82. T. Barnes, S. Raynor, & J. Bacchus, 2012, A new typology of forms of international collaboration, *Journal of Business and Strategy*, 5: 81–102; S. Prashantham & S. Young, 2011, Post-entry speed of international new ventures, *Entrepreneurship Theory and Practice*, 35: 275–292.

83. Z. Bhanji & J. E. Oxley, 2013, Overcoming the dual liability of foreignness and privateness in international corporate citizenship partnerships, *Journal of International Business Studies*, 44: 290–311; J. S. Harrison, M. A. Hitt, R. E. Hoskisson, & R. D. Ireland, 2001, Resource complementarity in business combinations: Extending the logic to organization alliances, *Journal of Management*, 27: 679–690.

84. R. A. D'Aveni, G. B. Dagnino, & K. G. Smith, 2010, The age of temporary advantage, *Strategic Management Journal*, 31: 1371–1385; M. A. Hitt, D. Ahlstrom, M. T. Dacin, E. Levitas, & L. Svobodina, 2004,

The institutional effects on strategic alliance partner selection in transition economies: China versus Russia, *Organization Science*, 15: 173–185.

85. G. Vasudeva, J. W. Spencer, & H. J. Teegen, 2013, Bringing the institutional context back in: A cross-national comparison of alliance partner selection and knowledge acquisition, *Organization Science*, in press; R. A. Corredoira & L. Rosenkopf, 2010, Should auld acquaintance be forgot? The reverse transfer of knowledge through mobility ties, *Strategic Management Journal*, 31: 159–181.

86. J-P. Roy, 2012, IJV partner trustworthy behavior: The role of host country governance and partner selection criteria, *Journal of Management Studies*, 49: 332–355; M. J. Robson, C. S. Katsikeas, & D. C. Bello, 2008, Drivers and performance outcomes of trust in international strategic alliances: The role of organizational complexity, *Organization Science*, 19: 647–668.

87. 2013, Our activities: Partnerships, Limagrain, www.limagrain.com, accessed on May 30; 2011, Limagrain signs strategic alliance to enter Brazilian corn market, *Great Lakes Hybrids*, www.greatlakeshybrids.com, February 14.

88. S. Kotha & K. Srikanth, 2013, Managing a global partnership model: Lessons from the Boeing 787 'dreamliner' program, *Global Strategy Journal*, 3: 41–66; C. Schwens, J. Eiche, & R. Kabst, 2011, The moderating impact of informal institutional distance and formal institutional risk on SME entry mode choice, *Journal of Management Studies*, 48: 330–351.

89. Y. Luo, O. Shenkar, & H. Gurnani, 2008, Control-cooperation interfaces in global strategic alliances: A situational typology and strategic responses, *Journal of International Business Studies*, 39: 428–453.

90. I. Arikan & O. Shenkar, 2013, National animosity and cross-border alliances, *Academy of Management Journal*, in press; T. K. Das, 2010, Interpartner sensemaking in strategic alliances: Managing cultural differences and internal tensions, *Management Decision*, 48: 17–36.

91. B. B. Nielsen, 2010, Strategic fit, contractual, and procedural governance in alliances, *Journal of Business Research*, 63: 682–689; D. Li, L. Eden, M. A. Hitt, & R. D. Ireland, 2008, Friends, acquaintances and stranger? Partner selection in R&D alliances, *Academy of Management Journal*, 51: 315–334.

92. P. D. O. Jensen & B. Petersen, 2013, Global sourcing of services: Risk, process and collaborative architecture, *Global Strategy Journal*, 3: 67–87.

93. S.-F. S. Chen, 2010, A general TCE model of international business institutions; market failure and reciprocity, *Journal of International Business Studies*, 41: 935–959; J. Wiklund & D. A. Shepherd, 2009, The effectiveness of alliances and acquisitions: The role of resource combination activities,

Entrepreneurship Theory and Practice, 33: 193–212.

94. A. Guar, S. Malhotra, & P. Zhu, 2013, Acquisition announcements and stock market valuations of acquiring firms' rivals: A test of the growth probability hypothesis in China, *Strategic Management Journal*, 34: 215–232; M. A. Hitt & V. Pisano, 2003, The cross-border merger and acquisition strategy, *Management Research*, 1: 133–144.

95. 2013, Corporate information—Our company history, DJO Global, www.djoglobal.com accessed on May 15.

96. S. Malhotra, P.-C. Zhu, & W. Locander, 2010, Impact of host-country corruption on U.S. and Chinese cross-border acquisitions, *Thunderbird International Business Review*, 52: 491–507; P. X. Meschi, 2009, Government corruption and foreign stakes in international joint ventures in emerging economies, *Asia Pacific Journal of Management*, 26: 241–261.

97. J. Li & C. Qian, 2013, Principal-principal conflicts under weak institutions: A study of corporate takeovers in China, *Strategic Management Journal*, 34: 498–508; A. Madhok & M. Keyhani, 2012, Acquisitions as entrepreneurship: Asymmetries, opportunities, and the internationalization of multinationals from emerging economies, *Global Strategy Journal*, 2: 26–40.

98. E. Vaara, R. Sarala, G. K. Stahl, & I. Bjorkman, 2012, *Journal of Management Studies*, 49: 1–27; D. R. Denison, B. Adkins, & A. Guidroz, 2011, Managing cultural integration in cross-border mergers and acquisitions, in W. H. Mobley, 2011, M. Li, & Y. Wang (eds.), *Advances in Global Leadership*, vol. 6, Bingley, UK: Emerald Publishing Group, 95–115.

99. S.-J. Chang, J. Chung, & J. J. Moon, 2013, When do wholly owned subsidiaries perform better than joint ventures? *Strategic Management Journal*, 34: 317–337; Y. Fang, G.-L. F. Jiang, S. Makino, & P. W. Beamish, 2010, Multinational firm knowledge, use of expatriates, and foreign subsidiary performance, *Journal of Management Studies*, 47: 27–54.

100. C. Bouquet, L. Hebert, & A. Delios, 2004, Foreign expansion in service industries: Separability and human capital intensity, *Journal of Business Research*, 57: 35–46.

101. C. Schwens, J. Eiche, & R. Kabst, 2011, The moderating impact of informal institutional distance and formal institutional risk on SME entry mode choice, *Journal of Management Studies*, 48: 330–351; K. F. Meyer, S. Estrin, S., Bhaumik, & M. W. Peng, 2009, Institutions, resources, and entry strategies in emerging economics, *Strategic Management Journal*, 30: 61–80.

102. Chang, Chung, & Moon, When do wholly owned subsidiaries perform better than joint ventures?; K. D. Brouthers & D. Dikova, 2010, Acquisitions and real options: The greenfield alternative, *Journal of Management Studies*, 47: 1048–1071.

103. Y. Parke & B. Sternquist, 2008, The global retailer's strategic proposition and choice of entry mode, *International Journal of Retail & Distribution Management*; 36: 281–299.

104. L. Q. Siebers, 2012, Foreign retailers in China: The first ten years, *Journal of Business Strategy*, 33: 27–38.

105. J. Anand, R. Oriani, & R. S. Vassolo, 2010, Alliance activity as a dynamic capability in the face of a discontinuous technological change, *Organization Science*, 21: 1213–1232; R. Farzad, 2007, Extreme investing: Inside Colombia, *BusinessWeek*, May 28, 50–58.

106. A. M. Rugman, 2010, Reconciling internalization theory and the eclectic paradigm, *Multinational Business Review*, 18: 1–12; J. Che & G. Facchini, 2009, Cultural differences, insecure property rights and the mode of entry decision, *Economic Theory*, 38: 465–484.

107. 2013, Company profile-facilities, Toyota Motor Corporation, www.toyota-global.com, accessed on May 30.

108. B. Batjargal, M. Hitt, A. Tsui, J.-L. Arregle, J. Webb, & T. Miller, 2013, Institutional polycentrism, entrepreneurs' social networks and new venture growth, *Academy of Management Journal*, in press.

109. C. Giersch, 2011, Political risk and political due diligence, *Global Risk Affairs*, www.globalriskaffairs.com, March 4.

110. J. Li & Y. Tang, 2010, CEO hubris and firm risk taking in China: The moderating role of managerial discretion, *Academy of Management Journal*, 53: 45–68; I. Alon & T. T. Herbert, 2009, A stranger in a strange land: Micro political risk and the multinational firm, *Business Horizons*, 52: 127–137; P. Rodriguez, K. Uhlenbruck, & L. Eden, 2003, Government corruption and the entry strategies of multinationals, *Academy of Management Review*, 30: 383–396.

111. D. Quer, E. Claver, & L. Rienda, 2012, Political risk, cultural distance, and outward foreign direct investment: Empirical evidence from large Chinese firms, *Asia Pacific Journal of Management*, 29: 1089–1104; O. Branzei & S. Abdelnour, 2010, Another day, another dollar: Enterprise resilience under terrorism in developing countries, *Journal of International Business Studies*, 41: 804–825; F. Wu, 2009, Singapore's sovereign wealth funds: The political risk of overseas investment, *World Economics*, 9(3): 97–122.

112. Giersch, Political risk and political due diligence.

113. J. Surroca, J. A. Tribo, & S. A. Zahra, 2013, Stakeholder pressure on MNEs and the transfer of socially irresponsible practices to subsidiaries, *Academy of Management Journal*, 56: 549–572.

114. K. Schwab, 2012, *The global competitiveness report, 2012–2013*, World Economic Forum, Geneva, Switzerland; M. D. Hanous & A. Prazdnichnyky, 2011, The Russia

competitiveness report 2011, *World Economic Forum*, January.

115. G. Fornes & A. Butt-Philip, 2011, Chinese MNEs and Latin America: A review, *International Journal of Emerging Markets*, 6: 98–117; S. Globerman & D. Shapiro, 2009, Economic and strategic considerations surrounding Chinese FDI in the United States, *Asia Pacific Journal of Management*, 26: 163–183.

116. C. R. Goddard, 2011, Risky business: Financial-sector liberalization and China, *Thunderbird International Business Review*, 53: 469–482; I. G. Kawaller, 2009, Hedging currency exposures by multinationals: Things to consider, *Journal of Applied Finance*, 18: 92–98.

117. C. C. Chung, S.-H. Lee, P. W. Beamish, & T. Ksobe, 2010, Subsidiary expansion/contraction during times of economic crisis, *Journal of International Business Studies*, 41: 500–516.

118. R. G. Bell, I. Filatotchev, & R. V. Aguilera, 2013, Corporate governance and investors' perceptions of foreign IPO value: An institutional perspective, *Academy of Management Journal*, in press.

119. V. Monatiriotis & R. Alegria, 2011, Origin of FDI and intra-industry domestic spillovers: The case of Greek and European FDI in Bulgaria, *Review of Development Economics*, 15: 326–339; N. Bandelj, 2009, The global economy as instituted process: The case of Central and Eastern Europe, *American Sociological Review*, 74: 128–149; L. Tihanyi & W. H. Hegarty, 2007, Political interests and the emergence of commercial banking in transition economies, *Journal of Management Studies*, 44: 789–813.

120. F. J. Contractor, 2012, Why do multinational firms exist? A theory note about the effect of multinational expansion on performance and recent methodological critiques, *Global Strategy Journal*, 2: 318–331; P. David, J. P. O'Brien, T. Yoshikawa, & A. Delios, 2010, Do shareholders or stakeholders appropriate the rents from corporate diversification? The influence of ownership structure, *Academy of Management Journal*, 53: 636–654.

121. L. Li, 2007, Multinationality and performance: A synthetic review and research agenda, *International Journal of Management Reviews*, 9: 117–139; J. A. Doukas & O. B. Kan, 2006, Does global diversification destroy firm value? *Journal of International Business Studies*, 37: 352–371.

122. J. H. Fisch, 2012, Information costs and internationalization performance, *Global Strategy Journal*, 2: 296–312; S. E. Christophe & H. Lee, 2005, What matters about internationalization: A market-based assessment, *Journal of Business Research*, 58: 636–643.

123. H. Berry, 2013, When do firms divest foreign operations? *Organization Science*, in press; T. J. Andersen, 2011, The risk implications of multinational enterprise, *International Journal of Organizational Analysis*, 19: 49–70.

124. H. Berry, 2013, Global integration and innovation: Multi-country knowledge generation within MNCs, *Strategic Management Journal*, in press; A. Y. Lewin, S. Massini, & C. Peeters, 2011, Microfoundations of internal and external absorptive capacity routines, *Organization Science*, 22: 81-98.

125. P. C. Patel, S. A. Fernhaber, P. P. McDougal-Covin, & R. P. van der Have, 2013, Beating competitors to international markets: The value of geographically balanced networks for innovation, *Strategic Management Journal*, in press.

126. O. Bertrand & M. J. Mol, 2013, The antecedents and innovation effects of domestic and offshore R&D outsourcing: The contingent impact of cognitive distance and absorptive capacity, *Strategic Management Journal*, 34: 751–760; B. S. Reiche, 2012, Knowledge benefits of social capital upon repatriation: A longitudinal study of international assignees, *Journal of Management Studies*, 49: 1052–1072; H. A. Ndofor, D. G. Sirmon, & X. He, 2011, Firm resources, competitive actions and performance: Investigating a mediated model with evidence from the in-vitro diagnostics industry, *Strategic Management Journal*, 32: 81–98; 640–657.

127. G. R. G. Benito, R. Lunnan & S. Tomassen, 2011, Distant encounters of the third kind: Multinational companies locating divisional headquarters abroad, *Journal of Management Studies*, 48: 373–394; M. A. Hitt, L. Tihanyi, T. Miller, & B. Connelly, 2006, International diversification: Antecedents, outcomes, and moderators, *Journal of Management*, 32: 831–867.

128. I. Guler & A. Nerkar, 2012, The impact of global and local cohesion on innovation in the pharmaceutical industry, *Strategic Management Journal*, 33: 535–549.

129. X. Fu, 2012, Foreign direct investment and managerial knowledge spillovers through diffusion of management practices, *Journal of Management Studies*, 49: 970–999; D. Holtbrugge & A. T. Mohr, 2011, Subsidiary interdependencies and international human resource management practices in German MNCs, *Management International Review*, 51: 93–115.

130. M. Halme, S. Lindeman, & P. Linna, 2012, Innovation for inclusive business: Intrapreneurial bricolage in multinational corporations, *Journal of Management Studies*, 49: 743–784; I. Filatotchev & M. Wright, 2010, Agency perspectives on corporate governance of multinational enterprises, *Journal of Management Studies*, 47: 471–486.

131. J. I. Siegel & S. H. Schwartz, 2013, Egalitarianism, cultural distance and foreign direct investment: A new approach, *Organization Science*, in press; G. A. Shinkle & A. P. Kriauciunas, 2012, The impact of current and founding institutions on strength of competitive aspirations in transition economies, *Strategic Management Journal*, 33: 448–458; D. Dikova, P. R. Sahib, & A. van Witteloostuijn, 2010, Cross-border acquisition abandonment and completion: The effect of institutional differences and organizational learning in the international business service industry, 1981–2001, *Journal of International Business Studies*, 41: 223–245.

132. 2013, Earnings release presentation, Toyota Global Web site, www.toyotaglobal.com, May 8.

133. P. C. Nell & B. Ambos, 2013, Parenting advantage in the MNC: An embeddedness perspective on the value added by headquarters, *Strategic Management Journal*, in press; J.-F. Hennart, 2012, Emerging market multinationals and the theory of the multinational enterprise, *Global Strategy Journal*, 2: 168–187.

134. C. G. Asmussen & A. Goerzen, 2013, Unpacking dimensions of foreignness: Firm-specific capabilities and international dispersion in regional, cultural and institutional space, *Global Strategy Journal*, 3: 127–149.

135. Wiersema & Bowen, The relationship between international diversification and firm performance; C.-F. Wang, L.-Y. Chen, & S.-C. Change, 2011, International diversification and the market value of new product introduction, *Journal of International Management*, 17(4): 333–347.

136. R. Belderbos, T. W. Tong, & S. Wu, 2013, Multinationality and downside risk: The roles of option portfolio and organization, *Strategic Management Journal*, in press; W. Shi, S. L. Sun and M. W. Peng, 2012, Sub-national institutional contingencies, network positions and IJV partner selection, *Journal of Management Studies*, 49: 1221–1245.

137. B. Baik, J.-K. Kang, J.-M. Kim, & J. Lee, 2013, The liability of foreignness in international equity investments: Evidence from the U.S. stock market, *Journal of International Business Studies*, 44: 391–411.

138. S.-H. Lee & S. Song, 2012, Host country uncertainty, intra-MNC production shifts, and subsidiary performance, *Strategic Management Journal*, 33: 1331–1340.

139. L. Berchicci, A. King, & C. L. Tucci, 2011, Does the apple always fall close to the tree? The geographical proximity choice of spin-outs, *Strategic Entrepreneurship Journal*, 5: 120–136; A. Ojala, 2008, Entry in a psychically distant market: Finnish small and medium-sized software firms in Japan, *European Management Journal*, 26: 135–144.

140. B. L. Connelly, R. E. Hoskisson, L. Tihanyi, & S. T. Certo, 2010, Ownership as a form of corporate governance, *Journal of Management Studies*, 47: 1561–1589; M. L. L. Lam, 2009, Beyond credibility of doing business in China: Strategies for improving corporate citizenship of foreign multinational enterprises in China, *Journal of Business Ethics*, 87: 137–146.

141. E. Fang & S. Zou, 2010, The effects of absorptive capacity and joint learning on the instability of international joint ventures in emerging economies, *Journal of International Business Studies*, 41: 906–924; D. Lavie & S. Miller, 2009, Alliance portfolio internationalization and firm performance, *Organization Science*, 19: 623–646.

9

Cooperative Strategy

Studying this chapter should provide you with the strategic management knowledge needed to:

1. Define cooperative strategies and explain why firms use them.

2. Define and discuss the three major types of strategic alliances.

3. Name the business-level cooperative strategies and describe their use.

4. Discuss the use of corporate-level cooperative strategies in diversified firms.

5. Understand the importance of cross-border strategic alliances as an international cooperative strategy.

6. Explain cooperative strategies' risks.

7. Describe two approaches used to manage cooperative strategies.

ALLIANCE FORMATION, BOTH GLOBALLY AND LOCALLY, IN THE GLOBAL AUTOMOBILE INDUSTRY

The academic literature on alliances has some interesting recent findings. One of these findings is the rationale that because firms are often located in the same country, and often in the same region of the country, it is easier for them to collaborate on major projects. As such, they compete globally, but may cooperate locally. Historically, firms have learned to collaborate by establishing strategic alliances and forming cooperative strategies when there is intensive competition. This interesting paradox is due to several reasons. First, when there is intense rivalry, it is difficult to maintain market power. As such, cooperative strategy can reduce market power through better norms of competition; this pertains to the idea of *"mutual forbearance"* (this idea will be discussed later in this chapter). Another rationale which has emerged is based on the

resource-based view of the firm (see Chapter 3). To compete, firms often need resources that they don't have but may be found in other firms in or outside of the focal firm's home industry. As such, these "complementary resources" are another rationale for why large firms form joint ventures and strategic alliances within the same industry or in vertically related industries (this idea will be more clearly explained later in this chapter).

Because firms are co-located and have similar needs, it's easier for them to jointly work together, for example, to produce engines and transmissions as part of the powertrain. This is evident in the European alliance between Peugeot-Citroën and Opel-Vauxhall (owned by General Motors). It is also the reason for a recent U.S. alliance between Ford and General Motors in developing upgraded nine- and ten-speed transmissions. Furthermore, they are looking to develop together

eleven- and twelve-speed automatic transmissions to improve fuel efficiency and help them to meet new federal guidelines regarding such efficiency.

In regard to resource complementarity, a very successful alliance was formed in 1999 by French-based Renault and Japan-based Nissan. Each of these firms lacked the necessary size to develop economies of scale and economies of scope that were critical to succeed in the 1990s and beyond in the global automobile industry. When the alliance was formed, each firm took an ownership stake in the other. The larger of the two companies, Renault, holds a 43.3 percent stake in Nissan, while Nissan has a 15 percent stake in Renault. It is interesting to note that Carlos Ghosn serves as the CEO of both companies. Over time, this corporate-level synergistic alliance (we discuss this type of alliance later in the chapter) has developed three values to guide their relationship: (1) *trust* (work fairly, impartially, and professionally); (2) *respect* (honor commitments, liabilities, and responsibilities; and (3) *transparency* (be open, frank, and clear). Largely due to these established principles, the Renault-Nissan alliance is a recognized success. One could argue that the main reason for the success of this alliance is the complementary assets that both firms bring to the alliance; Nissan is strong in Asia while Renault is strong in Europe. Together they have been able to establish other production locations, such as those in Latin America, which they may not have obtained independently.

Some firms enter alliances because they are "squeezed in the middle;" that is, they have moderate volumes, mostly for the mass market, but need to collaborate to establish viable economies of scale. For example, Fiat-Chrysler needs to boost its annual sales from $4.3 billion to something like $6 billion, and likewise needs to strengthen its presence in the booming Asian market to have enough global market power. As such, it is entering joint ventures with two undersized Japanese carmakers, Mazda and Suzuki; however, the past history of Mazda and Suzuki with alliances may be a reason for their not being overly enthusiastic about the prospects of the current alliances. Fiat broke up with GM, Chrysler with Daimler, and Mazda with Ford.

This is also the situation in Europe locally for Peugeot-Citroën of France, which is struggling for survival along with the GM European subsidiary, Opel-Vauxhall. More specifically, Peugeot-Citroën and Opel-Vauxhall have struck a tentative agreement to share platforms and engines to get the capital necessary for investment in future models. As such, in all these examples, they need additional market share, but also enough capital to make the investment necessary to realize more market power to compete.

In summary, there are a number of rationales why competitors not only compete but also cooperate in establishing strategic alliances and joint ventures in order to meet strategic needs for increased market power, take advantage of complementary assets, and cooperate with close neighbors, often in the same region of the country.

Sources: 2013, Markets and makers: Running harder, *Economist*, April 20, ss4–ss7; J. Boxell, 2013, Peugeot reaffirms push into BRICs, *Financial Times*, www.ft.com, February 7; D. Pearson & J. Bennett, 2013, Corporate news: GM, Peugeot pledge to deepen car alliance – Tough market in Europe has slowed progress, but automakers now see opportunities to cooperate outside the region, *Wall Street Journal*, www.wsj.com, January 10; J. B. White, 2013, Mazda uses alliances to boost sales, *Wall Street Journal*, www.wsj.com, January 27; T. Yu, M. Subramaniam, & A. A. Cannella, Jr., 2013, Competing globally, allying locally: Alliances between global rivals and host-country factors, *Journal of International Business Studies*, 44: 117–137; W. Lim, 2012, The voyage of the Renault-Nissan Alliance: A successful venture, *Advances In Management*, 5(9): 25–29.

Learn more about Peugeot-Citroën, another strategic alliance.
www.cengagebrain.com

A **cooperative strategy** is a means by which firms collaborate for the purpose of working together to achieve a shared objective.

As explained in the Opening Case, Renault and Nissan have formed a cooperative strategy as a means of improving each firm's performance. Renault and Nissan, as is the case for all companies, are trying to use their resources and capabilities in ways that will create the greatest amount of value for stakeholders.[1]

Forming a cooperative strategy like the one between Renault and Nissan, or between other global automobile companies, has the potential to be a viable engine of firm growth. Specifically, a **cooperative strategy** is a means by which firms collaborate for the purpose of working together to achieve a shared objective.[2] Cooperating with other firms is a strategy firms use to create value for a customer that it likely could not create by itself. For example, Fiat and Chrysler are in an equity alliance where Fiat has a significant ownership position in Chrysler. In describing a Fiat-designed and developed compact car that Chrysler will build and sell in the United States under its own name, an auto industry analyst said that a product such as this is "why the two auto makers…have a relationship."[3]

Firms also try to create competitive advantages when using a cooperative strategy. A competitive advantage developed through a cooperative strategy often is called a *collaborative* or *relational* advantage,[4] denoting that the relationship that develops among collaborating partners is commonly the basis on which a competitive advantage is built. Importantly, successful use of cooperative strategies finds a firm outperforming its rivals in terms of strategic competitiveness and above-average returns,[5] often because they've been able to form a competitive advantage.

M. Stasy

We examine several topics in this chapter. First, we define and offer examples of different strategic alliances as primary types of cooperative strategies. We focus on strategic alliances because firms use them more frequently than other types of cooperative relationships. Next, we discuss the extensive use of cooperative strategies in the global economy and reasons for that use. In succession, we describe business-level, corporate-level, international, and network cooperative strategies. The chapter closes with a discussion of the risks of using cooperative strategies as well as how effectively managing the strategies can reduce those risks.

9-1 Strategic Alliances as a Primary Type of Cooperative Strategy

A **strategic alliance** is a cooperative strategy in which firms combine some of their resources and capabilities for the purpose of creating a competitive advantage. Strategic alliances involve firms with some degree of exchange and sharing of resources and capabilities to codevelop, sell, and service goods or services.[6] In addition, firms use strategic alliances to leverage their existing resources and capabilities while working with partners to develop additional resources and capabilities as the foundation for new competitive advantages.[7] To be certain, the reality today is that "strategic alliances have become a cornerstone of many firms' competitive strategy."[8] This means that for many firms, and particularly for large global competitors, strategic alliances are potentially many in number but are always important in efforts to outperform competitors.

Consider the strategic alliance between the Syfy Cable Network and Trion Worlds to jointly create a simultaneous TV show and associated video game. Both the show and video game are focused on Syfy's new TV series, "Defiance," "about aliens who came to Earth and their prickly relationship with the current inhabitants." Because of the newness and difficulty of coordinating strategies between the partners involved, there were many hurdles in forming the project. There was disagreement about how to finance and market the project as well as the timing to launch. Many cable channels now have their own popular and critically well-regarded TV programming, such as AMC's "Mad Men" and HBO's "Game of Thrones" (among many possible examples). Likewise, Amazon.com and Netflix are in the process of producing original shows. Syfy is owned by NBCUniversal, which is majority owned by Comcast, a large cable television service provider. Each week as fans watch the "Defiance" one-hour drama, they can participate in the video game and pursue elements of what happened in the plot. The video game has attracted one million registered users since it went live on April 2, 2012. The joint project has gained advertisers such as Fiat-Chrysler through its Dodge branded products. Many Dodge products are scattered throughout the Syfy and Trion show and game platforms. Although this is an interesting innovation, it is a risky gamble because the network has spent $40M on the show's first season and has agreed to cover half of the game's $70M production costs. One analyst suggested, however, that if it is successful, it could alter the way that Comcast and other media producers develop entertainment on multiple platforms.[9]

Before describing three types of major strategic alliances and reasons for their use, we need to note that for all cooperative strategies, success is more likely when partners behave cooperatively. Actively solving problems, being trustworthy, and consistently pursuing ways to combine partners' resources and capabilities to create value are examples of cooperative behavior known to contribute to alliance success.[10] Recall that *trust*, *respect*, and *transparency* are three core values on which the Renault-Nissan corporate-level cooperative strategy is based. Perhaps these values are instrumental to the success that is credited to this cooperative relationship.

A **strategic alliance** is a cooperative strategy in which firms combine some of their resources and capabilities for the purpose of creating a competitive advantage.

9-1a Types of Major Strategic Alliances

Joint ventures, equity strategic alliances, and nonequity strategic alliances are the three major types of strategic alliances firms use. The ownership arrangement is a key difference among these alliances.

A **joint venture** is a strategic alliance in which two or more firms create a legally independent company to share some of their resources and capabilities for the purpose of developing a competitive advantage. Typically, partners in a joint venture own equal percentages and contribute equally to the venture's operations. Some evidence suggests that recent global economic difficulties have increased the attractiveness of this type of strategic alliance. Often formed to improve a firm's ability to compete in uncertain competitive environments, such as those associated with economic downturns, joint ventures are effective in establishing long-term relationships and in transferring tacit knowledge. Interestingly, AIG's Chinese joint venture saved it in the 2008 financial meltdown. The large insurance giant was founded in Shanghai in 1919 by C. V. Starr, a California life insurance pioneer. In 1950, after Mau's Communist takeover, AIG left China and established itself in the United States. However, it maintained a joint venture relationship (with AIA) with large real estate and insurance holdings in some of Asia's most expensive districts. To repay AIG's debt to the U.S. government it received in the global financial crisis, it sold most of its AIA joint venture holdings. Recently, AIG announced an agreement with the People's Insurance Company of China, a state-owned insurer, to invest roughly $500M in a People's Insurance public offering in Hong Kong. As part of the deal, the two companies are expected to reinitiate a joint venture to sell life insurance in China.[11]

Because it can't be codified, tacit knowledge, which is increasingly critical to firms' efforts to develop core competencies, is learned through experiences such as those taking place when people from partner firms work together in a joint venture.[12] Overall, a joint venture may be the optimal type of cooperative arrangement when firms need to combine their resources and capabilities to create a competitive advantage that is substantially different from any they possess individually and when the partners intend to enter highly uncertain, hypercompetitive markets.

Because China has potentially significant shale gas reserves, multinational companies such as Shell, Chevron, and ConocoPhillips have been pursuing joint ventures with Chinese petroleum firms. They intend to conduct exploratory drilling using hydraulic fracturing techniques to extract the shale gas. The Chinese petroleum companies do not have the "fracking" technology needed and, as such, are seeking to benefit from joint ventures with foreign firms who have expertise in these techniques. For example, Chevron recently formed a joint venture with the China National Petroleum Corp. and has begun exploratory drilling in Sichuan province. Likewise, ConocoPhillips has announced a joint venture with Sinopec. China generates 80 percent of its electricity from coal and is building coal-fired electricity generating plants at the rate of about one a week. If it could use shale gas for these generating plants, they would emit approximately half the CO_2 of coal.[13] Joint ventures such as these in China are not necessarily permanent in nature. There are different reasons for the lack of permanence, including dissatisfaction from one or all parties with the partnership's outcomes or changes in the strategic direction one or more partners wish to pursue. If the exploratory drilling does not create a new opportunity, the partnership may be disbanded, or circumstances may change and one partner may want to buy out the other's investment.

An **equity strategic alliance** is an alliance in which two or more firms own different percentages of the company they have formed by combining some of their resources and capabilities for the purpose of creating a competitive advantage. Many foreign direct investments in China by multinational corporations are completed through equity strategic alliances. Likewise, many Chinese firms pursuing outward foreign direct investment are doing so through equity alliances, especially when the Chinese firm is a state-owned enterprise.[14]

Learn more about Equity Strategic Alliances.
www.cengagebrain.com

A **joint venture** is a strategic alliance in which two or more firms create a legally independent company to share some of their resources and capabilities for the purpose of developing a competitive advantage.

An **equity strategic alliance** is an alliance in which two or more firms own different percentages of the company they have formed by combining some of their resources and capabilities for the purpose of creating a competitive advantage.

M. Stasy

Equity alliances can be primarily for capital infusions alone, but also for changing one's strategy. For instance, recently Club Mediterranee SA (Club Med), a resort operator and one of France's best-known international brands, wanted to partner with a private equity firm, France's AXA Private Equity, as well as with a Chinese conglomerate, Fosun International Ltd. In essence, this is a private equity deal for the managers of Club Med to gain control and capital as it upgrades its European resorts, but also to partner with Fosun as it shifts emphasis to develop more Asian outlets because the Asian customer, especially the Chinese, are the most important growing segment of the global hospitality resort market. In recent years, Fosun also has looked to increase its overseas collaboration with other buyout firms such as Carlyle Group, which sought investment in Chinese companies.[15]

Katie Orlinsky/Getty Images

Fracking in Bradford County, Pennsylvania. Many Chinese petroleum companies are looking to form joint ventures with firms that possess fracking technology.

A **nonequity strategic alliance** is an alliance in which two or more firms develop a contractual relationship to share some of their resources and capabilities for the purpose of creating a competitive advantage.[16] In this type of alliance, firms do not establish a separate independent company and therefore do not take equity positions. For this reason, nonequity strategic alliances are less formal, demand fewer partner commitments than do joint ventures and equity strategic alliances, and generally do not foster an intimate relationship between partners; nonetheless, research evidence indicates that they can create value for the involved firms.[17] The relative informality and lower commitment levels characterizing nonequity strategic alliances make them unsuitable for complex projects where success requires effective transfers of tacit knowledge between partners.[18] Licensing agreements, distribution agreements, and supply contracts are examples of nonequity strategic alliances.

Commonly, outsourcing commitments are specified in the form of a nonequity strategic alliance. (Discussed in Chapter 3, *outsourcing* is the purchase of a value-chain activity, or a support-function activity from another firm.) Apple Inc. and most other computer, tablet, and smartphone firms outsource most or all of their production to nonequity strategic alliance partners. Apple has traditionally outsourced most of its manufacturing to one dominant partner, Foxconn Technology Group, a large Taiwanese contract manufacturer. More recently, however, under CEO Tim Cook, Pegatron Corp., also a Taiwanese firm, Apple has diversified its manufacturing suppliers by partnering with this smaller rival to Foxconn to produce the iPad mini. Pegatron has accepted lower margins given its smaller size; its margins are 0.8 percent compared to 1.7 percent for Foxconn.[19] Interestingly, many firms that outsource introduce modularity where the contract producer only generates a part of the whole product. This approach prevents the contracting partner or outsourcee from gaining too much knowledge or from sharing certain aspects of the business the outsourcing firm does not want revealed.[20]

9-1b Reasons Firms Develop Strategic Alliances

Cooperative strategies are an integral part of the competitive landscape and are quite important to many companies and even to educational institutions. In fact, many firms are

A **nonequity strategic alliance** is an alliance in which two or more firms develop a contractual relationship to share some of their resources and capabilities for the purpose of creating a competitive advantage.

cooperating with educational institutions to help commercialize ideas flowing from basic research projects completed at universities.[21] In for-profit organizations, many executives believe that strategic alliances are central to their firm's growth and success.[22] The fact that alliances can account for up to 25 percent or more of a typical firm's sales revenue demonstrates their importance. Also, highlighting alliances' importance is the fact that in some settings, such as the global airline industry, competition is increasingly between large alliances rather than between large companies.[23]

Among other benefits, strategic alliances allow partners to create value that they couldn't develop by acting independently and to enter markets more quickly and with greater market penetration possibilities.[24] For example, South America's largest retailer by market value, Chilean firm SACI Falabella, is seeking to establish a foothold in Brazil through its Sodimac home improvement unit by taking a 51 percent ownership position in Dicico, a chain of home improvement stores owned by Construdecor SA. Falabella owns department stores, supermarkets, shopping malls, and home improvement stores in Chile, Colombia, Peru, and Argentina. Falabella's chief executive, CEO Sandro Solari, said, "We see good value in having a [local] partner" in managing Dicico. Falabella purchased its ownership position from previous part-owner Markinvest Gestao de Participaceos Limitada. The Brazilian entry is important for Falabella because Brazil is home to half of South America's population and has a large and growing middle class.[25]

Another reason to form strategic alliances is that most (if not all) firms lack the full set of resources and capabilities needed to reach their objectives, which indicates that partnering with others will increase the probability of reaching firm-specific performance objectives. This may be especially true for small businesses—ones in which capital is scarce as well as larger ones. Given constrained resources, firms can collaborate for a number of purposes, including those of reaching new customers and broadening both the product offerings and the distribution of their products without adding significantly to their cost structures. The example noted earlier between Syfy Cable Network and Trion Worlds to create a simultaneous TV show and associated video game through a strategic alliance broadens both companies' offerings.

Unique competitive conditions characterize slow-cycle, fast-cycle, and standard-cycle markets.[26] We discussed these three market types in Chapter 5 while examining competitive rivalry and competitive dynamics. These unique conditions find firms using strategic alliances to reach objectives that differ slightly by market type (see Figure 9.1).

Slow-cycle markets are markets where the firm's competitive advantages are shielded from imitation for relatively long periods of time and where imitation is costly. These markets are close to monopolistic conditions. Railroads and, historically, telecommunications, utilities, and financial services are industries characterized as slow-cycle markets. In *fast-cycle markets*, the firm's competitive advantages are not shielded from imitation, preventing their long-term sustainability. Competitive advantages are moderately shielded from imitation in *standard-cycle markets*, typically allowing them to be sustained for a longer period of time than in fast-cycle market situations, but for a shorter period of time than in slow-cycle markets.

Slow-Cycle Markets

Firms in slow-cycle markets often use strategic alliances to enter restricted markets or to establish franchises in new markets. For example, in 2013, Choice Hotels International, a large franchised hotel operator with brands such as Comfort Suites, entered into a multi-year strategic alliance agreement with Bluegreen Vacations and Bluegreen Resorts Management, both subsidiaries of Bluegreen Corp. Choice Hotels set up its Ascend Hotel Collection of historic and boutique hotels as part of its independent hotel offerings in the United States, Canada, Scandinavia, and Latin America. Bluegreen Vacations will become

Figure 9.1 Reasons for Strategic Alliances by Market Type

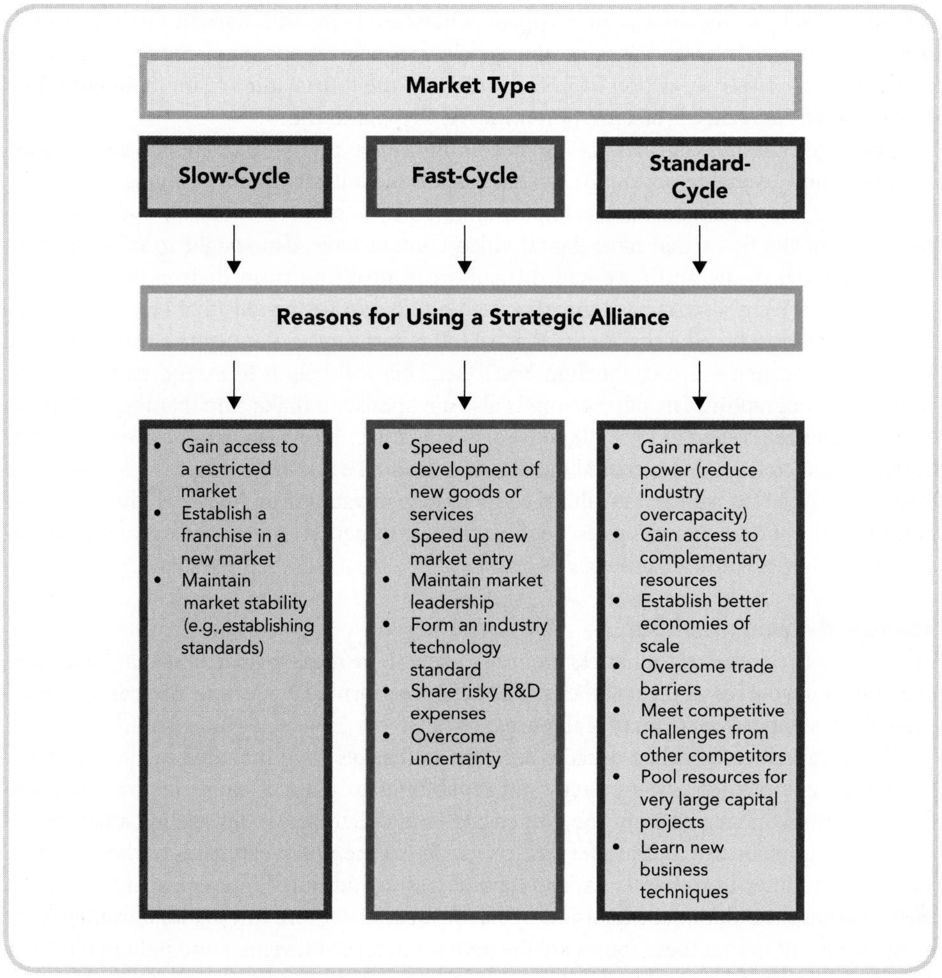

"the official vacation ownership provider of Choice Hotels." Choice Hotels' loyalty program, Choice Privileges, as well as Bluegreen's benefit program, TravelerPlus, are eligible to enroll each other's members through the alliance. For example, TravelerPlus participants will be upgraded to "Elite Gold status and receive special benefits," and will have access to all of Choice Hotels worldwide, including the 75 hotels in the Ascend Hotel Collection.[27]

Slow-cycle markets are becoming rare in the twenty-first century competitive landscape for several reasons, including the privatization of industries and economies, the rapid expansion of the Internet's capabilities for quick dissemination of information, and the speed with which advancing technologies make quickly imitating even complex products possible.[28] Firms competing in slow-cycle markets, including hotel chains, should recognize the future likelihood that they'll encounter situations in which their competitive advantages become partially sustainable (in the instance of a standard-cycle market) or unsustainable (in the case of a fast-cycle market). Cooperative strategies can help firms transition from relatively sheltered markets to more competitive ones.[29]

Fast-Cycle Markets

Fast-cycle markets are unstable, unpredictable, and complex; in a word, hypercompetitive.[30] Combined, these conditions virtually preclude establishing long-lasting competitive advantages, forcing firms to constantly seek sources of new competitive advantages while creating value by using current ones. Alliances between firms with current excess resources and capabilities and those with promising capabilities help companies compete in fast-cycle markets to effectively transition from the present to the future and to gain rapid entry into new markets. As such, a "collaboration mindset" is paramount.[31]

The entertainment business is fast becoming a new digital marketplace as television content is now available on the Web. This has led the entertainment business into a fast-cycle market where collaboration is important not only to succeed but to survive. For example, many of the firms that have digital video content have also sought to make a profit through digital music and have had difficulties in profiting from their earlier ventures. BuzzFeed is a Web-based news source focused on 18- to 34-year-olds that receives revenue from advertisers who advertise on its Web site. It is forming a joint venture with CNN and YouTube to create a video channel on YouTube. This will help it to extend its reach to its youthful demographic. The partnership is also a response to make sure that the content on CNN's Web site is relevant to the 18 to 34 age segment. Advertisers pay BuzzFeed to create hosted-brand content that is shared over Facebook and Twitter rather than solely relying on traditional Web site banner ads. BuzzFeed will take advantage of CNN's archives of news programming such as "amazing rescue moments for miners stranded underground" to create interest for its youthful audience.[32]

Standard-Cycle Markets

In standard-cycle markets, alliances are more likely to be made by partners that have complementary resources and capabilities. The alliances formed by airline companies are an example of standard-cycle market alliances.

When initially established decades ago, these alliances were intended to allow firms to share their complementary resources and capabilities to make it easier for passengers to fly between secondary cities in the United States and Europe. Today, airline alliances are mostly global in nature and are formed primarily so members can gain marketing clout, have opportunities to reduce costs, and have access to additional international routes.[33] Of these reasons, international expansion by having access to more international routes is the most important in that these routes are the path to increased revenues and potential profits. To support efforts to control costs, alliance members jointly purchase some items and share facilities such as passenger gates, customer service centers, and airport passenger lounges when possible. For passengers, airline alliances "offer simpler ticketing and smoother connections on intercontinental trips as well as the chance to earn and redeem frequent-flier miles on other member carriers."[34]

There are three major airline alliances operating today. Star Alliance is the largest with 28 members. With 12 members, Oneworld Alliance is the smallest while the 13-member SkyTeam Alliance has one more member. Given the geographic areas where markets are growing, these global alliances are adding partners from Asia. For example, in recent years, China Southern Airlines and China Eastern Airlines joined the SkyTeam Alliance, Air China and Shenzhen Airlines were added to the Star Alliance, and Malaysia Airlines joined OneWorld. In general, most airline alliances such as the ones we've described are formed to help firms gain economies of scale and meet competitive challenges (see Figure 9.1).

Within these large alliances and outside them as well, airlines are also forming dyadic or bilateral alliances between partners that have complementary opportunities. For example, Qantas Airways Ltd. has formed an alliance with Emirates Airline because it allows Qantas passengers to make only one stop on their way to the United States or Europe, whereas formerly, as part of its 17-year alliance with British Airlines (a Oneworld partner), they had to make two stops to get to distant continental European destinations (flying first to London Heathrow Airport). Now they can fly directly to 30 European destinations from Dubai, plus the flight time through the Mideast is two hours shorter than through Singapore, British Airways' hub. The size and the strategic positioning of the growing Mideast airlines such as Emirates, Qatar, and Etihad have been key in reframing these global travel routes and global alliances.[35]

9-2 Business-Level Cooperative Strategy

A **business-level cooperative strategy** is a strategy through which firms combine some of their resources and capabilities for the purpose of creating a competitive advantage by competing in one or more product markets. As discussed in Chapter 4, business-level strategy details what the firm intends to do to gain a competitive advantage in specific product markets. Thus, the firm forms a business-level cooperative strategy when it believes that combining some of its resources and capabilities with those of one or more partners will create competitive advantages that it can't create by itself and will lead to success in a specific product market. We list the four business-level cooperative strategies in Figure 9.2.

9-2a Complementary Strategic Alliances

Complementary strategic alliances are business-level alliances in which firms share some of their resources and capabilities in complementary ways for the purpose of creating a competitive advantage.[36] Vertical and horizontal are the two dominant types of complementary strategic alliances (see Figure 9.2).

Vertical Complementary Strategic Alliance

In a *vertical complementary strategic alliance*, firms share some of their resources and capabilities from different stages of the value chain for the purpose of creating a competitive advantage (see Figure 9.3).[37] Oftentimes, vertical complementary alliances are formed to adapt to environmental changes;[38] sometimes the changes represent an opportunity for partnering firms to innovate while adapting.[39]

China's Mengniu Dairy Company, a large state-owned enterprise, was implicated in 2008 during China's infamous food scandals, when six infants died and over 300,000 fell

Figure 9.2 Business-Level Cooperative Strategies

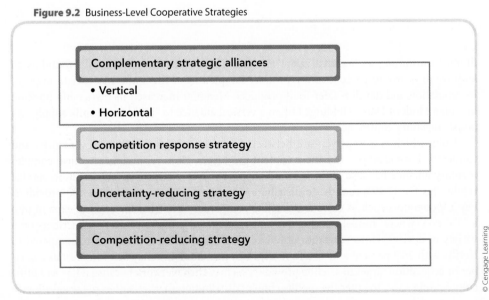

A **business-level cooperative strategy** is a strategy through which firms combine some of their resources and capabilities for the purpose of creating a competitive advantage by competing in one or more product markets.

Complementary strategic alliances are business-level alliances in which firms share some of their resources and capabilities in complementary ways for the purpose of creating a competitive advantage.

Figure 9.3 Vertical and Horizontal Complementary Strategic Alliances

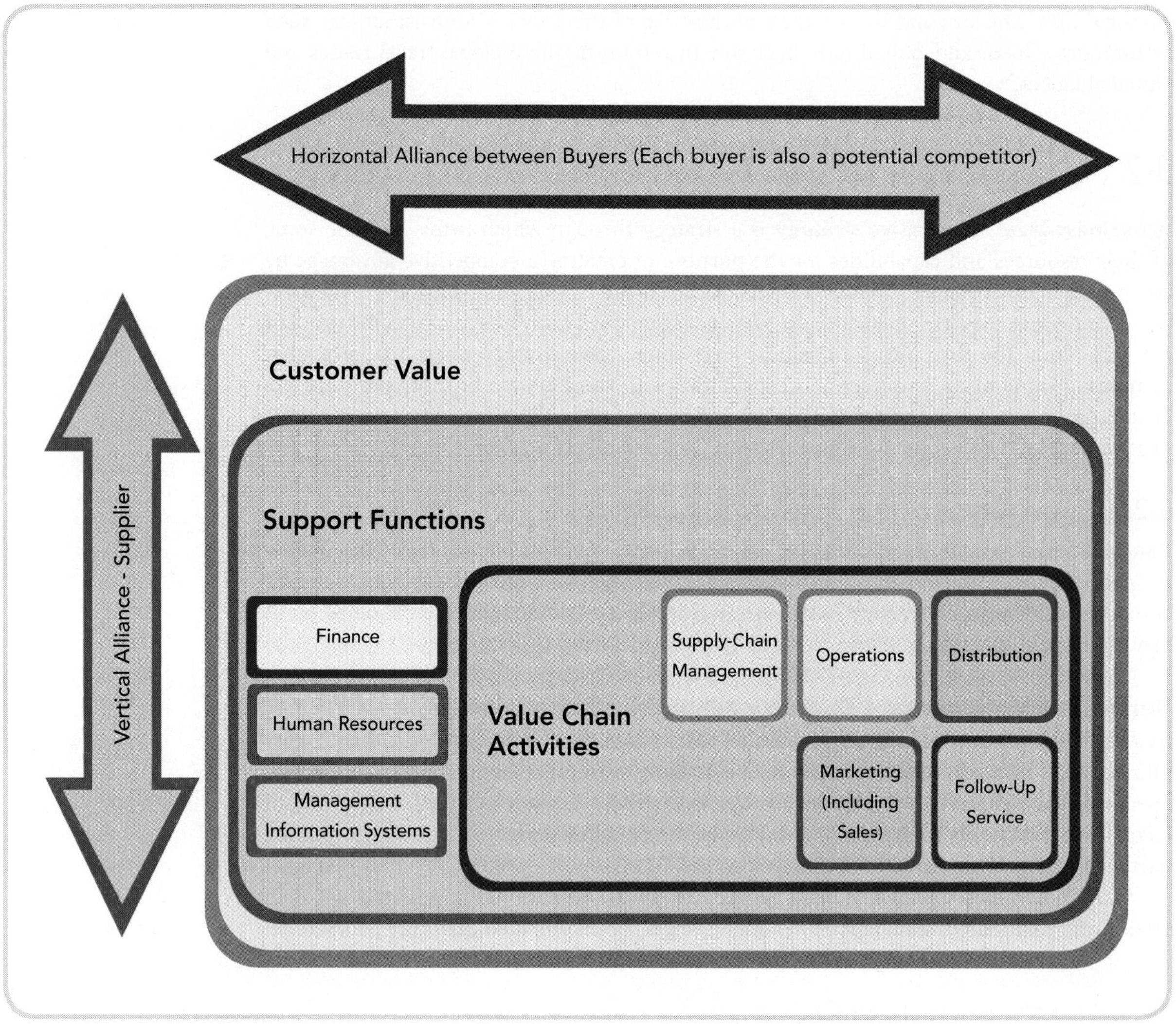

Horizontal Alliance between Buyers (Each buyer is also a potential competitor)

Vertical Alliance - Supplier

Customer Value

Support Functions

Finance

Human Resources

Management Information Systems

Value Chain Activities

Supply-Chain Management

Operations

Distribution

Marketing (Including Sales)

Follow-Up Service

ill after consuming its branded infant formula. The chemical melamine was found as an additive in nearly 10 percent of the product sampled from Mengniu. In order to improve its reputation and develop safer food products, Mengniu increased its ownership position in China Modern Dairy Holdings Ltd. in a vertical alliance to "build a safe milk supply and boost consumer confidence."[40]

Hulu, which is a joint venture between three companies—Disney, News Corp., and Comcast—is an example. For these content producers, Hulu represents a vertical complementary alliance because Hulu is an ad-supported free platform or subscription service (Hulu Plus for $7.99 a month) to distribute video content from more than 400 providers. Pay TV operators such as cable and satellite companies have tried for years to expand into a "TV everywhere" model offering live and on-demand programming to subscribers on a variety of devices. However, Hulu only has 2.2 percent of broadband traffic compared to Netflix with 28.9 percent and YouTube with 15.4 percent. Hulu may be of interest as a partner or acquisition target to satellite providers such as Dish Network because it has had difficulty finding a way to enter the mobile content distribution market. Other potential alliance targets might be firms like Yahoo! that are also seeking better mobile access. If a paid-TV provider (such as DISH) partners with or buys the firm, however, it would limit Hulu strategically because it would want to offer it only to its own subscribers and would thereby sacrifice much of Hulu's current revenue ($695M in 2012 split roughly evenly between advertising and subscriptions).[41]

Horizontal Complementary Strategic Alliance

A *horizontal complementary strategic alliance* is an alliance in which firms share some of their resources and capabilities from the same stage (or stages) of the value chain for the purpose of creating a competitive advantage. Commonly, firms use complementary strategic alliances to focus on joint long-term product development and distribution opportunities.[42] As noted previously, Hulu is a joint Web site that Comcast, News Corporation, and Walt Disney Company formed for the purpose of distributing video content. Through this horizontal equity strategic alliance, the alliance's partners provide content (one vertical stage of the value chain) to Hulu for distribution (another part of the value chain).

China's Mengniu Dairy Company is also forming a horizontal complementary strategic alliance with Danone SA, a large French food producer, to produce and distribute yogurt. Danone has strong brands such as Activia yogurt and Evian water. Danone is forming a joint venture with Mengniu to jointly produce and distribute yogurt branded products. Yogurt sales in China are up significantly, and Mengniu holds 17 percent while Danone holds 1.6 percent of the Chinese market share in yogurt. The joint venture will give Danone greater access to China's growing yogurt sales, and Mengniu will "gain a foreign partner in a market where foreign brands are seen as offering higher safety standards and quality."[43]

Pharmaceutical companies form a number of horizontal alliances. For example, as health care reform takes place in the United States, large pharmaceutical firms are seeking relationships with biotechnology drug producers.[44] Bristol-Myers Squibb and AstraZeneca have formed a horizontal alliance focused on diabetes. This alliance has been strengthened recently by Bristol-Myers's acquisition of Amylin Pharmaceuticals Inc. With Amylin's platform, the AstraZeneca and Bristol-Myers Squibb alliance will provide developmental strength and the ability to overcome regulatory and commercialization hurdles.[45]

As noted in the Opening Case, many horizontal complementary strategic alliances are formed in the automobile manufacturing industry. Around the world, rivals are joining forces to improve vehicle development and improve efficiency through alliances. Ford and General Motors, two of the largest auto manufacturers in the United States, have formed a partnership to "develop a new range of 9- and 10-speed automatic transmissions for cars, crossovers, and trucks." This strategic move is driven by more stringent federal efficiency standards. Interestingly, these companies previously collaborated on a 6-speed transmission, which is now used in Ford Fusion sedans, the Edge Crossover, and Escape and Explorer SUVs. GM uses them in the Chevrolet Malibu, Traverse Cruse, and other models as well. It also sounds like 11- and 12-speed transmissions may be in the near future. As competitive innovation occurs, firms often need to join together to keep up with competitive trends. Strategic alliances are a way to do this quickly and likewise share the development costs.[46] As such, cooperative strategies of all types are instrumental to automobile manufacturers' efforts to successfully compete globally.

9-2b Competition Response Strategy

As discussed in Chapter 5, competitors initiate competitive actions to attack rivals and launch competitive responses to their competitors' actions. Strategic alliances can be used at the business level to respond to competitors' attacks. Because they can be difficult to reverse and expensive to operate, strategic alliances are primarily formed to take strategic rather than tactical actions and to respond to competitors' actions in a like manner.

A woman rents a DVD at a Redbox kiosk located inside a Safeway store. Redbox and Verizon are partnering to launch a video streaming service.

KENNELL KRISTA/SIPA/Newscom

Coinstar is most broadly known for its Redbox subsidiary, which has kiosks at large retail outlets (such as Walmart) and drugstores (such as Walgreens) that offer dollar-a-day DVDs or video games for rent. However, the streaming video market has been threatening Redbox's business model through competitors such as Netflix, Amazon, and Hulu. Accordingly, in 2012, Redbox signed a strategic partnership agreement with Verizon to launch a streaming video service. Verizon offers broad consumer availability and service to the partnership, while Redbox offers strong relationships with media producers and has wide distribution. It seeks to be "an affordable service that will allow all consumers across the U.S. to enjoy the new and popular entertainment they want, whenever they choose, using the media and devices they prefer." It will be a subscription-based service. Customers will initially pay $8 per month and gain online access to a catalog of older films at no extra fee and have a set of newer movies available on demand for an additional fee. Additionally, patrons will get credits for four recent releases each month from Redbox's kiosks at supermarkets and drugstores around the country.[47]

9-2c   Uncertainty-Reducing Strategy

Firms sometimes use business-level strategic alliances to hedge against risk and uncertainty, especially in fast-cycle markets.[48] These strategies are also used where uncertainty exists, such as in entering new product markets and especially those of emerging economies.

As large global auto firms manufacture more hybrid vehicles, there is insufficient industry capacity to meet the demand for the type of batteries used in these vehicles. In turn, the lack of a sufficient supply of electric batteries creates uncertainty for automobile manufacturers. To reduce this uncertainty, auto firms are forming alliances. For example, Daimler AG of Germany buys Tesla batteries to insert into its "smart" minicar as well as its Freightliner trucks because it is confident that the batteries will be of sufficient quality.[49]

9-2d   Competition-Reducing Strategy

Used to reduce competition, collusive strategies differ from strategic alliances in that collusive strategies are often an illegal type of cooperative strategy. Explicit collusion and tacit collusion are the two types of collusive strategies.

Explicit collusion exists when two or more firms negotiate directly to jointly agree about the amount to produce as well as the prices for what is produced.[50] Explicit collusion strategies are illegal in the United States and most developed economies (except in regulated industries). Accordingly, companies choosing to use explicit collusion as a strategy should recognize that competitors and regulatory bodies might challenge the acceptability of their competitive actions.

Tacit collusion exists when several firms in an industry indirectly coordinate their production and pricing decisions by observing each other's competitive actions and responses.[51] Tacit collusion results in production output that is below fully competitive levels and above fully competitive prices. Unlike explicit collusion, firms engaging in tacit collusion do not directly negotiate output and pricing decisions. However, research suggests that joint ventures or cooperation between two firms can lead to less competition in other markets in which both firms operate.[52]

Tacit collusion tends to be used as a competition-reducing business-level strategy in industries with a high degree of concentration, such as the airline and breakfast cereal industries. Research in the airline industry suggests that tacit collusion reduces service quality and on-time performance.[53] Firms in these industries recognize their interdependence, which means that their competitive actions and responses significantly affect competitors' behavior toward them. Understanding this interdependence and carefully observing competitors can lead to tacit collusion.

Over time, four firms—Kellogg Company (producers of Kellogg's Corn Flakes, Fruit Loops, etc.), General Mills Inc. (Cheerios, Lucky Charms, etc.), Ralcorp Holdings, now owned by ConAgra Foods (producing mostly private store brands), and Quaker Foods North America, a part of PepsiCo (Quaker Oatmeal, Cap'n Crunch, etc.)—have accounted for as much as 80 percent of sales volume in the ready-to-eat segment of the U.S. cereal market.[54] Some believe that this high degree of concentration results in prices to consumers that substantially exceed the costs companies incur to produce and sell their products. If prices are above the competitive level in this industry, it may be a possibility that the dominant firms use a tacit collusion cooperative strategy.

Mutual forbearance is a form of tacit collusion in which firms do not take competitive actions against rivals they meet in multiple markets. Rivals learn a great deal about each other when engaging in multimarket competition, including how to deter the effects of their rivals' competitive attacks and responses. Given what they know about each other as competitors, firms choose not to engage in what could be destructive competition in multiple product markets.[55]

In general, governments in free-market economies seek to determine how rivals can form cooperative strategies for the purpose of increasing their competitiveness without violating established regulations about competition.[56] However, this task is challenging when evaluating collusive strategies, particularly tacit ones. For example, the regulation of securities analysts through Regulation Fair Disclosure (Reg-FD) promoted more potential competition through competitive parity by eliminating privileged access to proprietary firm information as a critical source of competitive advantage. In doing so, research suggests that it led to more mutual forbearance among competing firms because they had more awareness of information possessed by their competitors, thus leading to more tacit collusion.[57] However, individual companies must analyze the effect of a competition-reducing strategy on their performance and competitiveness and decide if pursuing such a strategy is an overall facilitator of their competitive success.

9-2e Assessing Business-Level Cooperative Strategies

Firms use business-level cooperative strategies to develop competitive advantages that can contribute to successful positions in individual product markets. Evidence suggests that complementary business-level strategic alliances, especially vertical ones, have the greatest probability of creating a competitive advantage and possibly even a sustainable one.[58] Horizontal complementary alliances are sometimes difficult to maintain because often they are formed between firms that compete against each other at the same time they are cooperating. Renault and Nissan still compete against each other with some of their products while collaborating to produce and sell other products. In a case such as this, partnering firms may feel a "push" toward and a "pull" from alliances. Airline firms, for example, want to compete aggressively against others serving their markets and target customers. However, the need to develop scale economies and to share resources and capabilities (such as scheduling systems) dictates that alliances be formed so the firms can compete by using cooperative actions and responses while they simultaneously compete against one another through competitive actions and responses. The challenge in these instances is for each firm to find ways to create the greatest amount of value from both their competitive and cooperative actions. It seems that Nissan and Renault may have learned how to achieve this balance.

Although strategic alliances designed to respond to competition and to reduce uncertainty can also create competitive advantages, these advantages often are more temporary than those developed through complementary (both vertical and horizontal) alliances. The primary reason for this is that complementary alliances have a stronger focus on creating value than do competition-reducing and uncertainty-reducing alliances, which are formed to respond to competitors' actions or reduce uncertainty rather than to attack competitors.

Of the four business-level cooperative strategies, the competition-reducing strategy has the lowest probability of creating a competitive advantage. For example, research suggests that firms following a foreign direct investment strategy using alliances as a follow-the-leader imitation approach may not have strong strategic or learning goals. Thus, such investment could be attributable to tacit collusion among the participating firms rather than trying to develop a competitive advantage (which should be the core objective).

9-3 Corporate-Level Cooperative Strategy

A **corporate-level cooperative strategy** is a strategy through which a firm collaborates with one or more companies for the purpose of expanding its operations. The alliance between Choice Hotels International and Bluegreen Corp. mentioned earlier is a corporate-level strategic alliance because it goes across the business-level hotel divisions of Choice and the subsidiaries of Bluegreen Corp. This alliance diversifies the lodging offering of both firms. Diversifying alliances, synergistic alliances, and franchising are the most commonly used corporate-level cooperative strategies (see Figure 9.4).

Firms use diversifying and synergistic alliances to improve their performance by diversifying their operations through a means other than or in addition to internal organic growth or a merger or acquisition.[59] When a firm seeks to diversify into markets in which the host nation's government prevents mergers and acquisitions, alliances become an especially appropriate option. Corporate-level strategic alliances are also attractive compared with mergers, and particularly acquisitions, because they require fewer resource commitments[60] and permit greater flexibility in terms of efforts to diversify partners' operations.[61] An alliance can be used as a way to determine whether the partners might benefit from a future merger or acquisition between them. This "testing" process often characterizes alliances formed to combine firms' unique technological resources and capabilities.[62]

9-3a Diversifying Strategic Alliance

A **diversifying strategic alliance** is a strategy in which firms share some of their resources and capabilities to engage in product and/or geographic diversification. The Strategic Focus on Samsung Electric discusses how Samsung uses diversifying alliances for a number of purposes, including reducing its dependence on Google's Android operating system for

A **corporate-level cooperative strategy** is a strategy through which a firm collaborates with one or more companies for the purpose of expanding its operations.

A **diversifying strategic alliance** is a strategy in which firms share some of their resources and capabilities to engage in product and/or geographic diversification.

Figure 9.4 Corporate-Level Cooperative Strategies

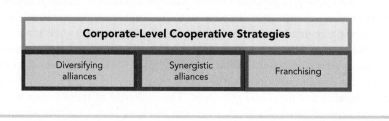

© Cengage Learning

Samsung Electric Is Using Diversifying Alliances to Reduce Its Dependence on Google's Android Operating System

Samsung signaled that it will start selling mobile phones featuring a new operating system called Tizen that is backed by Intel Corp. This appears to be a strategy to reduce its alliance on Google's Android operating system (OS), especially after the Internet search company acquired handset maker Motorola, who could potentially be a competitor for Samsung. The Tizen association (a strategic partnership) was formed in 2012 by executives from Intel, Samsung, NTT DOCOMO Inc., and Vodafone Group PLC to support an open-source software association, which has led to the Tizen operating system being available for mobile devices. Because Google is devoting more attention to producing mobile hardware devices as its rivalry with Apple accelerates, this has led to a reaction by Samsung, Intel, and others to make sure they are not too dependent upon any one operating system.

Samsung and Mozilla are also developing a strategic alliance to build a new mobile Web browser. It will be based on Android and ARM software architecture, and will be called Servo. It's interesting to know that Mozilla is hard at work on developing a mobile operating system. Again, it seems that Samsung is concerned about being overly dependent on Google's Android system even though it shipped 215.8 million handsets in 2012 using this operating system (OS). Furthermore, it has captured nearly 40 percent of the global market share in smartphones, so why would it be bothered with developing an alternative browser to Google Chrome as well as possibly pursuing a new mobile operating system? Additional evidence of this diversification is that Samsung intends to produce mobile devices managed by Microsoft's Windows phone OS. Again, it is seen by one analyst as a hedge against the company's overdependence on Android: "Samsung continues to have a strategic weakness in its reliance on an ecosystem that the company does not own."

Samsung also uses alliances to develop global industry standardization for products that provide reduced costs across the industry. For instance, in 2012 it established "an alliance for wireless power (A4WP) initialized between Qualcomm Inc. and Samsung Group to promote global standardization of a wireless power transfer technology, which could be utilized for cell phones, electric vehicles, and other devices." This is more of a technology alliance where the full use of technology is unknown at the start of the alliance. The partners hope that the commercialization of the technology that they jointly develop will create an industry-wide standard. Jointly developing technology suggests that it will more likely be adopted across the industry rather than if it is created by a single player.

A Google Nexus 7 digital tablet. Samsung is partnering with other firms to develop a new operating system that will reduce its reliance on Google's Android OS.

Samsung is also developing partnerships to help sell its hardware. For instance, Samsung has developed a strategic partnership with Houghton Mifflin Harcourt Publishing Co. (HMH) through its Samsung Electronics America Inc. subsidiary. It will partner with HMH to develop "educational content and solutions on the Android-powered tablet device of Samsung." This partnership will help power technology transformation in schools in the use of educational text material. Likewise, the partnership will help promote Samsung Android-powered tablets in schools and will provide schools with "special pricing, services, and support" besides helping them to implement their mobile education goals. The Samsung devices will use the "learning hub," an exclusive Samsung platform for educational content which is available worldwide.

As can be seen from these examples, Samsung is using alliances to diversify away from its dependence on the Android OS and also to have an edge in selling new devices based on new operating systems if they become popular. Likewise, it is using alliances to develop new sources of components, such as an alliance for wireless power, and new sources of distribution, such as its alliance with HMH. As such, it uses alliances as a form of corporate strategy to diversify among various operating systems to sell devices as well as for relationships with suppliers of parts and software (Mozilla) and distributors (HMH).

Sources: 2013, HMH partners with Samsung, *Educational Marketer*, February 11, 1–7; J. Lee, 2013, Samsung to sell Tizen-based handsets after Motorola deal, *Bloomberg*, www.bloomberg.com, January 3; J. Paczkowski, 2013, Samsung buddies up with Mozilla on new Android browser tech, *All Things D*, www.allthingsd.com, April 3; J. Paczkowski, 2013, Samsung plans multiple Tizen smartphones for 2013, *All Things D*, www.allthingsd.com, January 3; 2012, Samsung, Qualcomm establish wireless charging alliance, *Energy Daily*, May 14, 4.

mobile phones after Google purchased a potential competitor, Motorola. Also, Samsung is diversifying with the opportunity to get new hardware parts as well as major software inputs such as Mozilla browsers instead of being dependent on Google Chrome. Likewise, it is diversifying its ability to distribute its products to new customers such as schools through an alliance with a publisher, Houghton Mifflin Harcourt Publishing Co.[63]

9-3b Synergistic Strategic Alliance

A **synergistic strategic alliance** is a strategy in which firms share some of their resources and capabilities to create economies of scope. Similar to the business-level horizontal complementary strategic alliance, synergistic strategic alliances create synergy across multiple functions or multiple businesses between partner firms. The Renault-Nissan collaboration we discussed in the Opening Case is a synergistic strategic alliance in that among other outcomes, the firms seek to create economies of scope by sharing their resources and capabilities to develop manufacturing platforms that can be used to produce cars that will be either a Renault or a Nissan branded product. The cooperative arrangement between Fiat and Chrysler is also a synergistic alliance. It is interesting to note that corporate synergistic alliances can be carried out at the same time as their "twin", complementary alliances at the business-unit level. For instance, Fiat has also a signed a partnership deal with Mazda "to supply the Mazda Miata roadster as the foundation for a new Alfa Romeo sports car, taking a high-profile step forward in its fight to survive in a world of global giants."[64] Without economies of scope such as those between Fiat and Chrysler and between Fiat and Mazda at the business level, the probability of success for all companies involved is reduced.

9-3c Franchising

Franchising is a strategy in which a firm (the franchisor) uses a franchise as a contractual relationship to describe and control the sharing of its resources and capabilities with its partners (the franchisees).[65] A *franchise* is a "contractual agreement between two legally independent companies whereby the franchisor grants the right to the franchisee to sell the franchisor's product or do business under its trademarks in a given location for a specified period of time."[66] Often, success is determined in these strategic alliances by how well the franchisor can replicate its success across multiple partners in a cost-effective way.[67]

Franchising is a popular strategy. Recent estimates are that in the United States alone, the gross domestic product of all franchised businesses is approximately $1.2 trillion (this is about one-third of all sales generated in the United States) and that there are more than 828,000 individual franchise store locations employing a total of 18 million people.[68] Already frequently used in developed nations, franchising is also expected to account for significant portions of growth in emerging economies in the twenty-first century.[69] As with diversifying and synergistic strategic alliances, franchising is an alternative to pursuing growth through mergers and acquisitions. McDonald's, Choice Hotels International, Hilton International, Marriott International, Mrs. Fields Cookies, Subway, and Ace Hardware are well-known firms using the franchising corporate-level cooperative strategy.

Franchising is a particularly attractive strategy to use in fragmented industries, such as retailing, hotels and motels, and commercial printing. In fragmented industries, a large number of small and medium-sized firms compete as rivals; however, no firm or small set of firms has a dominant share, making it possible for a company to gain a large market share by consolidating independent companies through the contractual relationships that are a part of a franchise agreement.

In the most successful franchising strategy, the partners (the franchisor and the franchisees) work closely together.[70] A primary responsibility of the franchisor is to develop programs to transfer the knowledge and skills to the franchisees that are needed to successfully compete at the local level.[71] In return, franchisees should provide feedback to the franchisor

A **synergistic strategic alliance** is a strategy in which firms share some of their resources and capabilities to create economies of scope.

Franchising is a strategy in which a firm (the franchisor) uses a franchise as a contractual relationship to describe and control the sharing of its resources and capabilities with its partners (the franchisees).

regarding how their units could become more effective and efficient.[72] Working cooperatively, the franchisor and its franchisees find ways to strengthen the core company's brand name, which is often the most important competitive advantage for franchisees operating in their local markets.[73]

9-3d Assessing Corporate-Level Cooperative Strategies

Costs are incurred to implement each type of cooperative strategy.[74] Compared with their business-level counterparts, corporate-level cooperative strategies commonly are broader in scope and more complex, making them relatively more challenging and costly to use.

In spite of these costs, firms can create competitive advantages and value for customers by effectively using corporate-level cooperative strategies.[75] Internalizing successful alliance experiences makes it more likely that the strategy will attain the desired advantages. In other words, those involved with forming and using corporate-level cooperative strategies can also use them to develop useful knowledge about how to succeed in the future. To gain maximum value from this knowledge, firms should organize it and verify that it is always properly distributed to those involved with forming and using alliances.

We explain in Chapter 6 that firms answer two questions when dealing with corporate-level strategy—in which businesses and product markets will the firm choose to compete and how will those businesses be managed? These questions are also answered as firms form corporate-level cooperative strategies. Thus, firms able to develop corporate-level cooperative strategies and manage them in ways that are valuable, rare, imperfectly imitable, and nonsubstitutable (see Chapter 3) develop a competitive advantage that is in addition to advantages gained through the activities completed to implement business-level cooperative strategies. (Later in the chapter, we further describe alliance management as another potential competitive advantage.)

9-4 International Cooperative Strategy

The new competitive landscape finds firms using cross-border transactions for several purposes. In Chapter 7, we discussed cross-border acquisitions, actions through which a company located in one country acquires a firm located in a different country. In Chapter 8, we described how firms use cross-border acquisitions as a way of entering international markets. Here in Chapter 9, we examine cross-border strategic alliances as a type of international cooperative strategy. Thus, firms engage in cross-border activities to achieve several related objectives.

A **cross-border strategic alliance** is a strategy in which firms with headquarters in different countries decide to combine some of their resources and capabilities for the purpose of creating a competitive advantage. Taking place in virtually all industries, the number of cross-border alliances firms are completing continues to increase.[76] These alliances are sometimes formed instead of mergers and acquisitions, which can be riskier. Even though cross-border alliances can themselves be complex and hard to manage,[77] they have the potential to help firms use some of their resources and capabilities to create value in locations outside their home market.

Limited domestic growth opportunities and foreign government economic policies are key reasons firms use cross-border alliances. As discussed in Chapter 8, local ownership is an important national policy objective in some nations. In India and China, for example, governmental policies reflect a strong preference to license local companies. Thus, in some countries, the full range of entry mode choices we described in Chapter 8 may not be available to firms seeking to geographically diversify into a number of international markets. Indeed, investment by foreign firms in these instances may be allowed only through a partnership

A **cross-border strategic alliance** is a strategy in which firms with headquarters in different countries decide to combine some of their resources and capabilities for the purpose of creating a competitive advantage.

Playing Supercell's popular free game "Clash of Clans" on a 4th generation iPad. Through a cross-border strategic alliance with GungHo Online Entertainment, Inc., the game will be exposed to 14 million potential users in Japan.

with a local firm, such as in a cross-border alliance. Important too is the fact that strategic alliances with local partners can help firms overcome certain liabilities of moving into a foreign country, including those related to a lack of knowledge of the local culture or institutional norms.[78] A cross-border strategic alliance can also help foreign partners from an operational perspective, because the local partner has significantly more information about factors contributing to competitive success such as local markets, sources of capital, legal procedures, and politics.[79] Interestingly, research results suggest that firms with foreign operations have longer survival rates than domestic-only firms, although this is reduced if there are competition problems between foreign subsidiaries.[80]

A cross-border alliance has been struck between Japan's GungHo Online Entertainment, Inc. and Finland's Supercell Oy. Supercell's "Clash of Clans" ranked as one of the top grossing apps in Apple's App Store for iPhone and iPad apps in 112 countries. Likewise, "Puzzle & Dragons" surpassed Nintendo's "Super Mario Brothers" in number of players in Japan. Each company hopes to win new users through this strategic alliance for their respective products. In Japan, piggybacking on several firms' mobile games isn't unusual, but outside of Japan's game firms it is more unusual. The agreement will include a "Clash of Clans" dungeon theme in GungHo's game, while a banner illustrated by "Puzzle & Dragons" characters will appear in Supercell's game. For Supercell, which plans to open an office in Japan in 2013, the initial campaign of the alliance will allow it to be exposed to 14 million new possible users who currently play "Puzzle & Dragons" in Japan. The idea is to help each company market where the other is weak. Furthermore, they might work together on similar marketing efforts in the future. Both firms have a similar philosophy "to put fun and creativity first."[81]

In general, cross-border strategic alliances are more complex and risky than domestic strategic alliances, especially when used in emerging economies. However, the fact that firms competing internationally tend to outperform domestic-only competitors suggests the importance of learning how to geographically diversify into international markets. Compared with mergers and acquisitions, cross-border alliances may be a better way to learn this process, especially in the early stages of a firm's geographic diversification efforts.

9-5   Network Cooperative Strategy

In addition to forming their own alliances with individual companies, an increasing number of firms are collaborating in multiple alliances called networks.[82] A **network cooperative strategy** is a strategy wherein several firms agree to form multiple partnerships for the purpose of achieving shared objectives.

Through its Global Partner Network, Cisco has formed alliances with a host of individual companies including IBM, Microsoft, Infosys, Emerson, Fujitsu, Intel, and Nokia. According to Cisco, partnering allows a firm to "drive growth and differentiate (its) business

A **network cooperative strategy** is a strategy wherein several firms agree to form multiple partnerships for the purpose of achieving shared objectives.

by extending (its) capabilities to meet customer requirements."[83] Demonstrating the complexity of network cooperative strategies is the fact that Cisco also competes against a number of the firms with whom it has formed cooperative agreements. For example, Cisco is competing against IBM as it now sells and services servers. At the same time, Cisco and IBM's alliance is very active as the firms seek to help customers integrate "a broad range of industry-specific expertise and cutting-edge solutions, all based on respective core competencies in foundational technology architectures, software and services."[84] Overall, in spite of their complexity, the IBM/Cisco example shows how firms are using network cooperative strategies more extensively as a way of creating value for customers by offering many goods and services in many geographic (domestic and international) markets.

A network cooperative strategy is particularly effective when it is formed by geographically clustered firms,[85] as in California's Silicon Valley (where "the culture of Silicon Valley encourages collaborative webs"[86]). Effective social relationships and interactions among partners while sharing their resources and capabilities make it more likely that a network cooperative strategy will be successful,[87] as does having a productive *strategic center firm* (we discuss strategic center firms in detail in Chapter 11). Firms involved in networks gain information and knowledge from multiple sources. They can use these heterogeneous knowledge sets to produce more and better innovation. As a result, firms involved in networks of alliances tend to be more innovative.[88] However, there are disadvantages to participating in networks as a firm can be locked into its partnerships, precluding the development of alliances with others. In certain network configurations, such as Japanese *keiretsus*, firms in a network are expected to help other firms in that network whenever support is required. Such expectations can become a burden and negatively affect the focal firm's performance over time.[89] The Strategic Focus discusses industry clusters, with such geographic districts forming to focus on storage facilities for cloud computing and genomic research.

A new industrial district in China is focused on auto manufacturing. Volkswagen recently signed an $862 million deal to establish a gearbox production based in the Tianjin economic-technological development area (TEDA). This is a government-backed industrial park in Tianjin, a port city in China, about an hour away from Beijing by high-speed train. This is the initial investment, with a target of 450,000 units of production by 2014. Ultimately, they expect the total annual capacity to be 1.35 million units, with more than $4.8 billion invested. Other auto manufacturers in TEDA include Toyota, Great Wall Motors (which is China's top automotive exporter), and Xingma and Qingyuan (both of which make electric-powered vehicles). In 2010, 500,000 cars were manufactured in TEDA, a figure that TEDA hopes will increase to about 1.2 million by 2015. Furthermore, the park is setting up to increase suppliers who contribute parts to Toyota and Hyundai.[90] Within these districts, it is more likely that firms will become part of specific networks.

Find out more about the Human Genome Project.
www.cengagebrain.com

9-5a Alliance Network Types

An important advantage of a network cooperative strategy is that firms gain access to their partners' other partners. Having access to multiple collaborations increases the likelihood that additional competitive advantages will be formed as the set of shared resources and capabilities expands.[91] In turn, being able to develops new capabilities further stimulates product innovations that are critical to strategic competitiveness in the global economy.

The set of strategic alliance partnerships firms develop when using a network cooperative strategy is called an *alliance network*. Companies' alliance networks vary by industry characteristics. A *stable alliance network* is formed in mature industries where demand is relatively constant and predictable. Through a stable alliance network, firms try to extend their competitive advantages to other settings while continuing to profit from operations in their core, relatively mature industry. Thus, stable networks are built primarily to *exploit* the economies (scale and/or scope) that exist between the partners, such as in the airline and automobile industries.[92]

M. Stasy

Strategic Focus   GLOBALIZATION

Industrial Clusters: Geographic Centers for Collaborative Partnering

Clusters or *industrial districts* are geographic concentrations of a set of interconnected companies, often with specialized suppliers and service providers, and with education, government and trade association institutions focused on a particular industrial sector and agglomerated in a specific geographic region. Often these clusters begin because they increase company productivity, enabling them to lower costs and facilitate innovation. Developing such regions is important to government officials looking to increase economic development, as well as for companies seeking to co-locate with other reputable companies often with government tax incentives and institutions, such as universities to facilitate training of students with increased employment opportunities for graduates.

Research, in fact, shows that where there is cluster-driven agglomeration, there is also higher employment growth and higher wage growth, growth in the number of new establishments, and an increase in innovation and patenting. The strength of a dominant cluster, such as Silicon Valley, also strengthens related clusters in the region and adjacent regions. Often new industries emerge where there is a strong cluster environment. As such, there is good reason why governments are interested in incenting strong cluster growth in their geographic area.

For instance, African nations are increasingly seeking economic growth, and some have used innovation hubs to accelerate startup company growth. Kenya, for example, has over 40 percent of its population living on $2 a day, and political corruption, crippling droughts, and power outages have plagued the country. However, the Kenyan government revised its constitution in 2010 to create more transparency and better institutions supporting business. As such, a number of high-tech companies have sought to develop an iHub in downtown Nairobi, with supporting partners from Intel, Samsung, Google, Microsoft, and others in the cluster. It has also created mLab and NaiLab as incubators to foster growth-oriented startups focused on mobile software and hardware applications.

Research, however, suggests that such clusters or hubs have been implemented around the world, with varied results. Studies indicate that specializing in one area of R&D without added diversification often leads to eventual failure. As such, clusters with businesses, suppliers, think tanks, universities, multiple industries, and trade associations co-located in an industrial park or innovation cluster work best for stimulating economic growth and innovation. Accordingly, companies with a variety of purposes and specializations co-located with network suppliers, customers, and support services facilitate new and more innovative products and services and thus are more successful.

U.S. National Human Genome Research Institute Director Francis Collins at a press conference in Bethesda, Maryland, announcing that a six-country consortium has successfully mapped the human genome. Geographic clusters are now being developed around the world to create a database of genetic information.

Sometimes these clusters are driven by specific regional geographic strengths. For example, large data storage centers for high-tech companies using cloud resources have located such centers in Prineville, The Dalles, and other small towns in Oregon. Such locations in Oregon allow for more natural cooling of such large computer systems. Facebook executive Jay Park states that Prineville is "an ideal location for the crew and system Facebook uses for its data storage center." Other locations were chosen for more idiosyncratic reasons. Microsoft and the software cluster associated with it in Seattle was located there because Bill Gates, Microsoft's founder, was born in Seattle.

Research suggests that workers who began their career in industrial hub locations, such as people in the hedge fund industry who previously worked in New York and London, outperformed their peers once they leave these districts. As such, there is an individual effect on the human capital development in these industrial hubs. Furthermore, research also suggests that there is a collective impact on the firms that are in centralized positions (that is, have connections to more firms, suppliers, and customers in the industrial district); the more central firms have more and better innovation. Those who connect firms to each other (bridging ties) have a positive impact on innovation, but not as impactful as those that are more centralized in the hub.

Geographic clusters are being developed around the world focused on creating a vast database of genetic information. It took nearly 13 years and almost $14 million in government and private funding for the Human Genome Project to complete the first map of a person's genome. Now, for $1,000, a company in Iceland will chart your genetic propensities for 47 different diseases and traits. New preventative measures from this project "will save patients, insurers, and employers money, and studies project genomic medicine will generate $350 billion worth of economic activity and millions of jobs." But the industry is a long way from the ability to fully utilize the data encoded in our chromosomes. The question is, where will the various clusters be found around the world? There are a number in the United States and Canada—one in Vancouver, British Columbia, and one around La Jolla, California. The one at La Jolla includes the University of California-San Diego, the Salk Institute, the Scripps Research Institute, the Venter Institute, Synthetic Genomics, and 30 or 40 companies all within a few square miles and all using genomic methods and research. There is also a cluster growing in the Boston area, the Cambridge area in the United Kingdom, and the Genomics Institute in Beijing, China. Thus, the history of industrial districts is positive overall, and they are now being planned with more precision.

Sources: C. Casanueva, I. Castro, & J. L. Galán, 2013, Information networks and innovation in mature industrial clusters, *Journal of Business Research*, 66(5): 603–613; R. J. P. De Figueiredo, P. Meyer-Doyle, & E. Rawley, 2013, Inherited agglomeration effects in hedge fund spawns, *Strategic Management Journal*, 34(7): 843–862; L. Dobusch & E. Schübler, 2013, Theorizing path dependence: A review of positive feedback mechanisms in technology markets, regional clusters, and organizations, *Industrial & Corporate Change*, 22(3): 617–647; E. Francis, 2013, Building an auto industry hub through value creation, *Automotive Industries*, January, 111–112; G. Holden, 2013, Kenya's fertile ground for tech innovation, *Research Technology Management*, 56(3): 7–8; H. Milanov & D. A. Shepherd, 2013, The importance of the first relationship: The ongoing influence of initial network on future status, *Strategic Management Journal*, 34(6): 727–750; 2012, Not a cloud in sight, *Economist*, October 27, 19–20; F. Ghadar, J. Sviokla, & D. A. Stephan, 2012, Why life science needs its own Silicon Valley, *Harvard Business Review*, 90(7/8): 25–27.

Dynamic alliance networks are used in industries characterized by frequent product innovations and short product life cycles.[93] For instance, the pace of innovation in the information technology (IT) industry (as well as other fast-cycle market industries) is too fast for any one company to be successful across time if it only competes independently. Another example is the movie industry, an industry in which firms participate in a number of networks for the purpose of producing and distributing movies. Also, as the alliance between Syfy Cable Network and Trion Worlds to create a simultaneous TV show and associated video game based on a new TV series, "Defiance", suggests, such networks are becoming even larger and more dynamic.[94] In dynamic alliance networks, partners typically *explore* new ideas and possibilities with the potential to lead to product innovations, entries to new markets, and the development of new markets. Research suggests that firms that help to broker relationships between firms remain important network participants as these networks change.[95] Often, large firms in industries such as software and pharmaceuticals create networks of relationships with smaller entrepreneurial startup firms in their search for innovation-based outcomes.[96] An important outcome for small firms successfully partnering with larger firms in an alliance network is the credibility they build by being associated with their larger collaborators.[97]

Network strategies of multiple partners affect the overall success of many firms. For instance, a network set of alliances formed by Samsung and Sony with suppliers, sales channels, and R&D partners from 2008 to 2011 illustrates this point. Samsung is at the center of a network with a variety of diverse partners such as Dreamworks and KT, "which do interesting things with 3-D technologies but don't typically work together." Samsung is well-placed within its network of firms to look at the future because it provides many parts for many firms, such as for Apple's iPhone, even though it competes with Apple with its own Galaxy X4 phone. For instance, the Galaxy X4 has "cutting-edge gesture- and eye-tracking features."[98]

On the other hand, Sony, a large, diversified firm, also has a web of allies, including Sharp and Toshiba, that work together. Although its allies are highly integrated with Sony, the network is less likely to yield breakthrough innovations because it is less exposed to a diverse set of partners in new areas. In dynamic networks with high levels of strategic change, it provides an advantage if a firm is at the center of a hub and spoke network. In integrated stable networks, small firms can be helped when there are external shocks to the network because the relationships help them in a downturn. But such stable integrated networks are less likely to yield breakthrough product ideas.[99]

One of the reasons that Tesla, a manufacturer of plug-in electric vehicles, has been successful when others such as Fisker have failed is its efforts to partner with other firms as it developed its new models, facilitating not only its survival but its success. Of course, Tesla's new Model S sedan is a very impressive vehicle and has won *Motor Trend* and *Automobile* magazine awards as well as strong reviews from *Consumer Reports*. Tesla's founder and CEO, Elon Musk, has degrees in physics and business and has already started and sold a successful company, PayPal, and runs SpaceX, a maker of rockets and spacecraft. As such, he has the ability and connections to partner with other firms. This allowed him to get a strong bevy of investors who often are also partners. Daimler AG of Germany buys Tesla batteries to insert into its "smart" minicar as well as its Freightliner trucks. Likewise, it also invested $50 million in the company. Also, Toyota partnered with Tesla to develop its next-generation RAV4 plug-in electric vehicle offering, and likewise invested $50 million. Accordingly, one of the reasons for Tesla's survival when others have failed is the ability to get support from other partners, which has allowed it to survive and succeed.[100]

9-6 Competitive Risks with Cooperative Strategies

Stated simply, many cooperative strategies fail. In fact, evidence shows that two-thirds of cooperative strategies have serious problems in their first two years and that as many as 50 percent of them fail. This failure rate suggests that even when the partnership has potential complementarities and synergies, alliance success is elusive.[101] Although failure is undesirable, it can be a valuable learning experience, meaning that firms should carefully study a cooperative strategy's failure to gain insights with respect to how to form and manage future cooperative arrangements.[102] We show prominent cooperative strategy risks in Figure 9.5.

Figure 9.5 Managing Competitive Risks in Cooperative Strategies

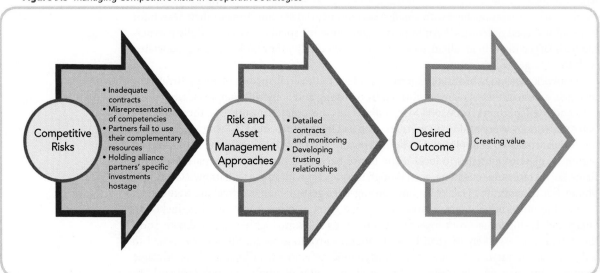

One cooperative strategy risk is that a firm may act in a way that its partner thinks is opportunistic. BP plc and OAO Rosneft developed a joint venture to explore Russia's Arctic Ocean in search of oil. However, the investment by minority partners of this joint venture was driven down in value at one point by 50 percent over concern that the Russian government, Rosneft's dominant owner, would expropriate value from the deal.[103] In general, opportunistic behaviors surface either when formal contracts fail to prevent them or when an alliance is based on a false perception of partner trustworthiness. Not infrequently, the opportunistic firm wants to acquire as much of its partner's tacit knowledge as it can.[104] Full awareness of what a partner wants in a cooperative strategy reduces the likelihood that a firm will suffer from another's opportunistic actions.[105]

Some cooperative strategies fail when it is discovered that a firm has misrepresented the competencies it can bring to the partnership. This risk is more common when the partner's contribution is grounded in some of its intangible assets. Superior knowledge of local conditions is an example of an intangible asset that partners often fail to deliver. An effective way to deal with this risk may be to ask the partner to provide evidence that it does possess the resources and capabilities (even when they are largely intangible) it will share in the cooperative strategy.[106]

A firm's failure to make available to its partners the resources and capabilities (such as the most sophisticated technologies) that it committed to the cooperative strategy is a third risk. For example, the effectiveness of a recently formed collaboration between BP plc and OAO Rosneft (the state-controlled Russian oil company) is dependent on each firm contributing some of its seismic and drilling-related resources and capabilities as the foundation for efforts to develop three areas in the Arctic Ocean.[107] A failure by either partner to contribute needed resources and capabilities to this alliance has the potential to diminish the likelihood of success. This particular risk surfaces most commonly when firms form an international cooperative strategy, especially in emerging economies.[108] In these instances, different cultures and languages can cause misinterpretations of contractual terms or trust-based expectations.

A final risk is that one firm may make investments that are specific to the alliance while its partner does not. For example, the firm might commit resources and capabilities to develop manufacturing equipment that can be used only to produce items coming from the alliance. If the partner isn't also making alliance-specific investments, the firm is at a relative disadvantage in terms of returns earned from the alliance compared with investments made to earn the returns.

9-7 Managing Cooperative Strategies

Cooperative strategies are an important means of firm growth and enhanced performance, but these strategies are difficult to effectively manage. Because the ability to effectively manage cooperative strategies is unevenly distributed across organizations in general, assigning managerial responsibility for a firm's cooperative strategies to a high-level executive or to a team improves the likelihood that the strategies will be well managed. In turn, being able to successfully manage cooperative strategies can itself be a competitive advantage.[109]

Those responsible for managing the firm's cooperative strategies should take the actions necessary to coordinate activities, categorize knowledge learned from previous experiences, and make certain that what the firm knows about how to effectively form and use cooperative strategies is in the hands of the right people at the right time. Firms must also learn how to manage both the tangible and intangible assets (such as knowledge) that are involved with a cooperative arrangement. Too often, partners concentrate on managing tangible assets at the expense of taking action to also manage a cooperative relationship's intangible assets.[110]

Cost minimization and opportunity maximization are the two primary approaches firms use to manage cooperative strategies[111] (see Figure 9.5). In the *cost-minimization* approach, the firm develops formal contracts with its partners. These contracts specify how the cooperative strategy is to be monitored and how partner behavior is to be controlled. The alliance mentioned earlier between Ford and General Motors to develop transmissions at a lower cost for each firm is based on such a contractual relationship. Thus it appears that at least at the outset, the cost-minimization approach is being used to manage this alliance. The goal of the cost-minimization approach is to minimize the cooperative strategy's cost and to prevent opportunistic behavior by a partner.

Maximizing a partnership's value-creating opportunities is the focus of the *opportunity-maximization* approach. In this case, partners are prepared to take advantage of unexpected opportunities to learn from each other and to explore additional marketplace possibilities. Less formal contracts, with fewer constraints on partners' behaviors, make it possible for partners to explore how their resources and capabilities can be shared in multiple value-creating ways. This is the approach Renault and Nissan use to manage their collaborative relationship. The values of *trust*, *respect*, and *transparency* on which this alliance is based facilitate use of the opportunity-maximization management approach.

Firms can successfully use both approaches to manage cooperative strategies. However, the costs to monitor the cooperative strategy are greater with cost minimization, in that writing detailed contracts and using extensive monitoring mechanisms is expensive, even though the approach is intended to reduce alliance costs. Although monitoring systems may prevent partners from acting in their own best interests, they also often preclude positive responses to new opportunities that surface to productively use alliance partners' resources and capabilities. Thus, formal contracts and extensive monitoring systems tend to stifle partners' efforts to gain maximum value from their participation in a cooperative strategy and require significant resources to be put into place and used.[112]

The relative lack of detail and formality that is a part of the contract developed when using the opportunity-maximization approach means that firms need to trust that each party will act in the partnership's best interests. The psychological state of *trust* in the context of cooperative arrangements is the belief that a firm will not do anything to exploit its partner's vulnerabilities even if it has an opportunity to do so. When partners trust each other, there is less need to write detailed formal contracts to specify each firm's alliance behaviors,[113] and the cooperative relationship tends to be more stable.[114]

On a relative basis, trust tends to be more difficult to establish in international cooperative strategies than domestic ones. Differences in trade policies, cultures, laws, and politics that are part of cross-border alliances account for the increased difficulty. When trust exists, monitoring costs are reduced and opportunities to create value are maximized. Essentially, in these cases the firms have built social capital.[115] Renault and Nissan have built social capital through their alliance by building their relationship on the mutual trust between the partners as well as their adherence to operating within the framework of agreed-upon confidentiality rules.[116]

Research showing that trust between partners increases the likelihood of success when using alliances highlights the benefits of the opportunity-maximization approach to managing cooperative strategies. Trust may also be the most efficient way to influence and control alliance partners' behaviors. Research indicates that trust can be a capability that is valuable, rare, imperfectly imitable, and often nonsubstitutable.[117] Thus, firms known to be trustworthy can have a competitive advantage in terms of how they develop and use cooperative strategies. Increasing the importance of trust in alliances is the fact that it is not possible to specify all operational details of a cooperative strategy in a formal contract. As such, being confident that its partner can be trusted reduces the firm's concern about its inability to contractually control all alliance details.

SUMMARY

- A cooperative strategy is one through which firms work together to achieve a shared objective. Strategic alliances, where firms combine some of their resources and capabilities for the purpose of creating a competitive advantage, are the primary form of cooperative strategies. Joint ventures (where firms create and own equal shares of a new venture), equity strategic alliances (where firms own different shares of a newly created venture), and nonequity strategic alliances (where firms cooperate through a contractual relationship) are the three major types of strategic alliances. Outsourcing, discussed in Chapter 3, commonly occurs as firms form nonequity strategic alliances.

- Collusive strategies are the second type of cooperative strategies (with strategic alliances being the other). In many economies, explicit collusive strategies are illegal unless sanctioned by government policies. Increasing globalization has led to fewer government-sanctioned situations of explicit collusion. Tacit collusion, also called mutual forbearance, is a cooperative strategy through which firms tacitly cooperate to reduce industry output below the potential competitive output level, thereby raising prices above the competitive level.

- The reasons firms use cooperative strategies vary by slow-cycle, fast-cycle, and standard-cycle market conditions. To enter restricted markets (slow cycle), to move quickly from one competitive advantage to another (fast cycle), and to gain market power (standard cycle) are among the reasons firms choose to use cooperative strategies.

- Four business-level cooperative strategies are used to help the firm improve its performance in individual product markets: (1) Through vertical and horizontal complementary alliances, companies combine some of their resources and capabilities to create value in different parts (vertical) or the same parts (horizontal) of the value chain. (2) Competition response strategies are formed to respond to competitors' actions, especially strategic actions. (3) Uncertainty-reducing strategies are used to hedge against the risks created by the conditions of uncertain competitive environments (such as new product markets). (4) Competition-reducing strategies are used to avoid excessive competition while the firm marshals its resources and capabilities to improve its strategic competitiveness. Complementary alliances have the highest probability of helping a firm form a competitive advantage; competition-reducing alliances have the lowest probability.

- Firms use corporate-level cooperative strategies to engage in product and/or geographic diversification. Through diversifying strategic alliances, firms agree to share some of their resources and capabilities to enter new markets or produce new products. Synergistic alliances are ones where firms share some of their resources and capabilities to develop economies of scope. Synergistic alliances are similar to business-level horizontal complementary alliances where firms try to develop operational synergy, except that synergistic alliances are used to develop synergy at the corporate level. Franchising is a corporate-level cooperative strategy where the franchisor uses a franchise as a contractual relationship to specify how resources and capabilities will be shared with franchisees.

- As an international cooperative strategy, a cross-border strategic alliance is used for several reasons, including the performance superiority of firms competing in markets outside their domestic market and governmental restrictions on a firm's efforts to grow through mergers and acquisitions. Commonly, cross-border strategic alliances are riskier than their domestic counterparts, particularly when partners aren't fully aware of each other's purpose for participating in the partnership.

- In a network cooperative strategy, several firms agree to form multiple partnerships to achieve shared objectives. A firm's opportunity to gain access "to its partner's other partnerships" is a primary benefit of a network cooperative strategy. Network cooperative strategies are used to form either a stable alliance network or a dynamic alliance network. Used in mature industries, stable networks are used to extend competitive advantages into new areas. In rapidly changing environments where frequent product innovations occur, dynamic networks are used primarily as a tool of innovation.

- Cooperative strategies aren't risk free. If a contract is not developed appropriately, or if a partner misrepresents its competencies or fails to make them available, failure is likely. Furthermore, a firm may be held hostage through asset-specific investments made in conjunction with a partner, which may be exploited.

- Trust is an increasingly important aspect of successful cooperative strategies. Firms place high value on opportunities to partner with companies known for their trustworthiness. When trust exists, a cooperative strategy is managed to maximize the pursuit of opportunities between partners. Without trust, formal contracts and extensive monitoring systems are used to manage cooperative strategies. In this case, the interest is "cost minimization" rather than "opportunity maximization."

REVIEW QUESTIONS

1. What is the definition of cooperative strategy, and why is this strategy important to firms competing in the twenty-first century competitive landscape?

2. What is a strategic alliance? What are the three major types of strategic alliances firms form for the purpose of developing a competitive advantage?

3. What are the four business-level cooperative strategies? What are the key differences among them?

4. What are the three corporate-level cooperative strategies? How do firms use each of these strategies for the purpose of creating a competitive advantage?

5. Why do firms use cross-border strategic alliances?

6. What risks are firms likely to experience as they use cooperative strategies?

7. What are the differences between the cost-minimization approach and the opportunity-maximization approach to managing cooperative strategies?

EXPERIENTIAL EXERCISES

EXERCISE 1: ALLIANCE MANAGEMENT AS A PROFESSION

According to your text, "a cooperative strategy is a means by which firms collaborate for the purpose of working together to achieve a shared objective. Cooperating with other firms is a strategy firms use to create value for a customer that it likely could not create by itself." This describes the end state and not the mechanics upon which firms rely to achieve a successful alliance partnership. So is there a career in alliance management?

This is an individual assignment and one in which you can learn more about strategic alliance as a career path to compliment your budding knowledge of the field. Begin by researching strategic alliance professionals in your library and on the Internet. You should also interview a strategic alliance management professional. You can find them through either firms that undertake alliances or consulting firms that assist them. Start your research by answering the following questions:

1. Find any trade associations of organizations or professionals that are aligned with the field.

2. Does the work get done mainly through in-company personnel or consulting firms?

3. What are the benefits, and downsides, to a career in strategic alliance management?

4. Are there entry level positions or is experience required to get into the field?

5. Put together, does this profession have an appeal to you personally? Why or why not?

EXERCISE 2: AIRLINES AND ALLIANCES

According to your text, a strategic alliance "is a partnership between firms whereby their resources and capabilities are combined to create a competitive advantage." So why is an alliance in the best interests for an airline company such as United, American, or British Airways? In this exercise, your instructor will assign one of the three main alliances (OneWorld, Star, or SkyTeam), and your teams will be asked to investigate the alliance and be prepared to discuss the following issues:

1. In general, why do airlines form an alliance with one another (particularly internationally) rather than expanding by acquisition?

2. What is the history of the alliance to which you were assigned?

3. Describe the main benefits that airlines hope to gain through membership. What is the competitive advantage of your particular alliance, if you find there is one?

4. Categorize the alliance in terms of the three types of strategic alliances. Also describe the cooperative strategy of a member firm in relation to its business-level and corporate-level strategy.

5. Think through issues of the future of airline alliances. If you were the CEO of a major U.S. airline, what might worry you about your particular alliance, if anything?

VIDEO CASE

A PARTNERSHIP WITH A COOPERATIVE TWIST: MICROSOFT AND YAHOO!

In its infancy, the Microsoft/Yahoo! partnership brought a cloud of layoff and market concerns, but the priority was to compete against Google for control of the Internet search market. Media and analysts predicted benefits to partners and consumers over the long term. Yahoo! remains an independent company with control of its user interface, while Microsoft added strength to its browser and gained a greater share of Internet advertising, which all provide an alternative to the Internet search market. Statistics show that Google has 66.5 percent of the Internet search market, with Yahoo! at 12 percent and Microsoft at 17.3 percent.

Be prepared to discuss the following concepts and questions in class:

Concepts

1. Cooperative strategy

2. Strategic alliance

3. Business-level cooperative strategies

4. Corporate-level cooperative strategies

Questions

1. What kind of competitive advantage is created through the Microsoft/Yahoo! cooperative strategy?

2. What kind of strategic alliance has occurred between Microsoft and Yahoo!? Explain your answer. For what reasons do you think they developed such an alliance?

3. Now that Microsoft and Yahoo! have partnered, what business-level cooperative strategies do you think we can expect? Why?

4. What corporate-level cooperative strategies do you think we can expect? Why?

NOTES

1. U. Wassmer & P. Dussauge, 2012, Network resource stocks and flows: How do alliance portfolios affect the value of new alliance formations? *Strategic Management Journal*, 33(7): 871–883; G. Schreyöegg & J. Sydow, 2011, Organizing for fluidity? Dilemmas of new organizational forms, *Organization Science*, 21: 1251–1262; D. Lavie, 2009, Capturing value from alliance portfolios, *Organizational Dynamics*, 38(1): 26–36.

2. D. Lavie, P. R. Haunschild, & P. Khanna, 2012, Organizational differences, relational mechanisms, and alliance performance, *Strategic Management Journal*, 33(13): 1453–1479; H. Yang, Z. Lin, & Y. Lin, 2010, A multilevel framework of firm boundaries: Firm characteristics, dyadic differences, and network attributes, *Strategic Management Journal*, 31: 237–261.

3. J. Bennett, 2011, Dodge will test Fiat alliance, *Wall Street Journal*, www.wsj.com, June 25.

4. J. H. Dyer & W. Chu, 2011, The determinants of trust in supplier–automaker relationships in the U.S., Japan, and Korea, *Journal of International Business Studies*, 31(2): 259–285; J. H. Dyer & H. Singh, 1998, The relational view: Cooperative strategy and sources of interorganizational competitive advantage, *Academy of Management Review*, 23: 660–679.

5. J. Walter, F. W. Kellermanns, & C. Lechner, 2012, Decision making within and between organizations: Rationality, politics, and alliance performance, *Journal of Management*, 38(5): 1582–1610; R. J. Jiang, Q. T. Tao, & M. D. Santoro, 2010, Alliance portfolio diversity and firm performance, *Strategic Management Journal*, 31: 1136–1144.

6. J. Charterina & J. Landeta, 2013, Effects of knowledge-sharing routines and dyad-based investments on company innovation and performance: An empirical study of Spanish manufacturing companies, *International Journal of Management*, 30(2): 197–216; F. Lumineau, M. Fréchet, & D. Puthod, 2011, An organizational learning perspective on the contracting process, *Strategic Organization*, 9: 8–32.

7. J. L. Cummings & S. R. Holmberg, 2012, Best-fit alliance partners: The use of critical success factors in a comprehensive partner selection process, *Long Range Planning*, 45(2/3): 136–159; S. Lahiri & B. L. Kedia, 2009, The effects of internal resources and partnership quality on firm performance: An examination of Indian BPO providers, *Journal of International Management*, 15: 209–222.

8. K. H. Heimeriks & G. Duysters, 2007, Alliance capability as a mediator between experience and alliance performance: An empirical investigation into the alliance capability development process, *Journal of Management Studies*, 44: 25–49.

9. D. Leonard, 2013, Syfy's ultimate transmedia adventure, *Bloomberg Businessweek*, May 20–May 26, 19–20.

10. J. Roy, 2012, IJV partner trustworthy behaviour: The role of host country governance and partner selection criteria, *Journal of Management Studies*, 49(2): 332–355; K. H. Heimeriks, E. Klijn, & J. J. Reuer, 2009, Building capabilities for alliance portfolios, *Long Range Planning*, 42: 96–114.

11. N. Chowdhury, 2013, AIG's Asian savior, *Fortune*, January 14, 17.

12. E. Chrysostome, R. Nigam, & C. Jarilowski, 2013, Revisiting strategic learning in international joint ventures: A knowledge creation perspective, *International Journal of Management*, 30(1): 88–98; D. Tan & K. E. Meyer, 2011, Country-of-origin and industry FDI agglomeration of foreign investors in an emerging economy, *Journal of International Business Studies*, 42: 504–520.

13. B. Dumaine, 2013, Fracking comes to China, *Fortune*, April 29, 102–107.

14. L. Cui & F. Jiang, 2012, State ownership effect on firms' FDI ownership decisions under institutional pressure: A study of Chinese outward-investing firms, *Journal of International Business Studies*, 43(3): 264–284; Z. Huang, X. Han, F. Roche, & J. Cassidy, 2011, The dilemma facing strategic choice of entry mode: Multinational hotels in China, *Global Business Review*, 12: 181–192; J. Xia, J. Tan, & D. Tan, 2008, Mimetic entry and bandwagon effect: The rise and decline of international equity joint venture in China, *Strategic Management Journal*, 29: 195–217.

15. T. Varela & L. Burkitt, 2013, Club Med gets a Chinese-backed bid: Conglomerate Fosun teams with private-equity firm for a proposed buyout of French resort operator, *Wall Street Journal*, May 28, B1.

16. A. Majocchi, U. Mayrhofer, & J. Camps, 2013, Joint ventures or non-equity alliances? Evidence from Italian firms, *Management Decision*, 51(2): 380–395; T. Das & N. Rahman, 2010, Determinants of partner opportunism in strategic alliances: A conceptual framework, *Journal of Business Psychology*, 25: 55–74; Y. Wang & S. Nicholas, 2007, The formation and evolution of non-equity strategic alliances in China, *Asia Pacific Journal of Management*, 24: 131–150.

17. S. P. Gudergan, T. Devinney, N. Richter, & R. Ellis, 2012, Strategic implications for (non-equity) alliance performance, *Long Range Planning*, 45(5/6): 451–476; J. J. Reuer, E. Klijn, F. A. J. van den Bosch, & H. W. Volberda, 2011, Bringing corporate governance to international joint ventures, *Global Strategy Journal*, 1: 54–66.

18. J. Schweitzer & S. P. Gudergan, 2011, Contractual complexity, governance and organisational form in alliances, *International Journal of Strategic Business Alliances*, 2: 26–40; C. Weigelt, 2009, The impact of outsourcing new technologies on integrative capabilities and performance, *Strategic Management Journal*, 30: 595–616.

19. E. Dou, 2013, Apple shifts from Foxconn to Pegatron, *Wall Street Journal*, May 30, B5.

20. A. Cabigiosu, F. Zirpoli, & A. Camuffo, 2013, Modularity, interfaces definition and the integration of external sources of innovation in the automotive industry, *Research Policy*, 42(3): 662–675; F. Zirpoli & M. C. Becker, 2011, The limits of design and

engineering outsourcing: Performance integration and the unfulfilled promise of modularity, *R&D Management*, 41: 21–43.

21. D. Mindruta, 2013, Value creation in university-firm research collaborations: A matching approach, *Strategic Management Journal*, 34(6): 644–665; A. L. Sherwood & J. G. Covin, 2008, Knowledge acquisition in university-industry alliances: An empirical investigation from a learning theory perspective, *Journal of Product Innovation Management*, 25: 162–179.

22. D. Faems, M. Janssens, & I. Neyens, 2012, Alliance portfolios and innovation performance: Connecting structural and managerial perspectives, *Group & Organization Management*, 37(2): 241–268; J. Kim, 2011, Alliance governance and technological performance: Some evidence from biotechnology alliances, *Industrial and Corporate Change*, 20: 969–990; P. Beamish & N. Lupton, 2009, Managing joint ventures, *Academy of Management Perspectives*, 23(2): 75–94.

23. X. Hu, R. Caldentey, & G. Vulcano, 2013, Revenue sharing in airline alliances, *Management Science*, 59(5): 1177–1195; U. Wassmer, 2010, Alliance portfolios: A review and research agenda, *Journal of Management*, 36: 141–171; S. G. Lazzarini, 2007, The impact of membership in competing alliance constellations: Evidence on the operational performance of global airlines, *Strategic Management Journal*, 28: 345–367.

24. Lavie, Haunschild, & Khanna, Organizational differences, relational mechanisms, and alliance performance; Yang, Lin, & Lin, A multilevel framework of firm boundaries: Firm characteristics, dyadic differences, and network attributes.

25. G. Ibanez, 2013, Chile's Falabella buys foothold in Brazil, *Wall Street Journal*, www.wsj.com, May 28.

26. J. R. Williams, 1998, *Renewable Advantage: Crafting Strategy Through Economic Time*, New York: Free Press.

27. 2013, BlueGreen, Choice form strategic partnership, *Hotel Management*, March, 48.

28. A. Tafti, S. Mithas, & M. S. Krishnan, 2013, The effect of information technology-enabled flexibility on formation and market value of alliances, *Management Science*, 59(1): 207–225; P. Savetpanuvong, U. Tanlamai, & C. Lursinsap, 2011, Sustaining innovation in information technology entrepreneurship with a sufficiency economy philosophy, *International Journal of Innovation Science*, 3(2): 69–82.

29. H. Ouyang, 2010, Imitator-to-innovator S curve and chasms, *Thunderbird International Business Review*, 52: 31–44; H. K. Steensma, J. Q. Barden, C. Dhanaraj, M. Lyles, & L. Tihanyi, 2008, The evolution and internalization of international joint ventures in a transitioning economy,

Journal of International Business Studies, 39: 491–507.

30. H. E. Posen & D. A. Levinthal, 2012, Chasing a moving target: Exploitation and exploration in dynamic environments, *Management Science*, 58(3): 587–601; K. M. Eisenhardt, 2002, Has strategy changed? *MIT Sloan Management Review*, 43(2): 88–91.

31. X. Yin, J. Wu, & W. Tsai, 2012, When unconnected others connect: Does degree of brokerage persist after the formation of a multipartner alliance? *Organization Science*, 23(6): 1682–1699; S. Lahiri, L. Pérez-Nordtvedt, & R. W. Renn, 2008, Will the new competitive landscape cause your firm's decline? It depends on your mindset, *Business Horizons*, 51: 311–320.

32. W. Launder, 2013, BuzzFeed, CNN and YouTube plan online-video channel, *Wall Street Journal*, May 28, B6.

33. Hu, Caldentey, & Vulcano, Revenue sharing in airline alliances; A.-P. de Man, N. Roijakkers, & H. de Graauw, 2010, Managing dynamics through robust alliance governance structures: The case of KLM and Northwest Airlines, *European Management Journal*, 28: 171–181; C. Czipura & D. R. Jolly, 2007, Global airline alliances: Sparking profitability for a troubled industry, *Journal of Business Strategy*, 28(2): 57–64.

34. S. Stellin, 2011, The clout of air alliances, *New York Times*, www.nytimes.com, May 2.

35. D. Cameron, J. Kell, D. Michaels, & D. Pearson, 2012, Airlines shuffle marketing alliances, *Wall Street Journal*, October 9, B3; J. Flottau, 2012, Alliance blues, *Aviation Week & Space Technology*, October 9, 24.

36. G. Vasudeva, J. W. Spencer, & H. J. Teegen, 2013, Bringing the institutional context back in: A cross-national comparison of alliance partner selection and knowledge acquisition, *Organization Science*, 24(2): 319–338; D. Elmuti, A. S. Abou-Zaid, & H. Jia, 2012, Role of strategic fit and resource complementarity in strategic alliance effectiveness, *Journal of Global Business & Technology*, 8(2): 16–28; W. Shi & J. E. Prescott, 2011, Sequence patterns of firms' acquisition and alliance behavior and their performance implications, *Journal of Management Studies*, 48: 1044–1070.

37. N. Lahiri & S. Narayanan, 2013, Vertical integration, innovation and alliance portfolio size: Implications for firm performance, *Strategic Management Journal*, 34(9): 1042–1064; S. M. Mudambi & S. Tallman, 2010, Make, buy or ally? Theoretical perspectives on knowledge process outsourcing through alliances, *Journal of Management Studies*, 47: 1434–1456.

38. J. Hagedoorn & N. Wang, 2012, Is there complementarity or substitutability between internal and external R&D strategies? *Research Policy*, 41(6): 1072–1083; M. Meuleman, A. Lockett, S. Manigart, & M. Wright, 2010, Partner selection decisions

in interfirm collaborations: The paradox of relational embeddedness, *Journal of Management Studies*, 47: 995–1019.

39. E. Revilla, M. Sáenz, & D. Knoppen, 2013, Towards an empirical typology of buyer–supplier relationships based on absorptive capacity, *International Journal of Production Research*, 51(10): 2935–2951; J. Zhang & C. Baden-Fuller, 2010, The influence of technological knowledge base and organizational structure on technology collaboration, *Journal of Management Studies*, 47: 679–704; J. Wiklund & D. A. Shepherd, 2009, The effectiveness of alliances and acquisitions: The role of resource combination activities, *Entrepreneurship Theory and Practice*, 33(1): 193–212.

40. L. Burkitt, 2013, Dairy giants join in China yogurt venture, *Wall Street Journal*, www.wsj.com, May 20.

41. M. Gottfried, 2013, Hulu dance partners should cut in, *Wall Street Journal*, May 24, C8.

42. C. Häeussler, H. Patzelt, & S. A. Zahra, 2012, Strategic alliances and product development in high technology new firms: The moderating effect of technological capabilities, *Journal of Business Venturing*, 27(2): 217–233; D. H. Hsu & S. Wakeman, 2011, Resource benefits and learning costs in strategic alliances, University of Pennsylvania, working paper: March; M. Makri, M. A. Hitt, & P. J. Lane, 2010, Complementary technologies, knowledge relatedness, and invention outcomes in high technology mergers and acquisitions, *Strategic Management Journal*, 31: 602–628.

43. Burkitt, Dairy giants join in China yogurt venture.

44. L. Diestre & N. Rajagopalan, 2012, Are all 'sharks' dangerous? New biotechnology ventures and partner selection in R&D alliances, *Strategic Management Journal*, 33(10): 1115–1134.

45. 2012, Two drug makers strengthen alliance, *Chain Drug Review*, 34(16): 103.

46. J. Welsh, 2013, Too many gears? GM and Ford join to build 10-speed transmissions, *Wall Street Journal*, http://blogs.wsj.com, April 15.

47. B. Stone, 2013, This theater is getting awfully crowded, *Bloomberg Businessweek*, January 21, 36–37; A. Carr, 2012, Redbox partners with Verizon to launch streaming video service, *Fast Company*, www.fastcompany.com, February 6.

48. N. Mouri, M. B. Sarkar, & M. Frye, 2012, Alliance portfolios and shareholder value in post-IPO firms: The moderating roles of portfolio structure and firm-level uncertainty, *Journal of Business Venturing*, 27(3): 355–371; C. López-Duarte & M. M. Vidal-Surez, 2010, External uncertainty and entry mode choice: Cultural distance, political risk and language diversity, *International Business Review*, 19: 575–588; J. J. Reuer & T. W. Tong, 2005, Real options

in international joint ventures, *Journal of Management*, 31: 403–423.

49. J. Mueller, 2013, The reason Tesla is still alive (and other green car companies aren't), *Forbes*, May 11, 7.

50. M. A. Fonseca & H. Normann, 2012, Explicit vs. tacit collusion—The impact of communication in oligopoly experiments, *European Economic Review*, 56(8): 1759–1772; M. Escrihuela-Villar & J. Guillén, 2011, On collusion and industry size, *Annals of Economics and Finance*, 12(1): 31–40; L. Tesfatsion, 2007, Agents come to bits: Toward a constructive comprehensive taxonomy of economic entities, *Journal of Economic Behavior & Organization*, 63: 333–346.

51. M. Van Essen & W. B. Hankins, 2013, Tacit collusion in price-setting oligopoly: A puzzle redux, *Southern Economic Journal*, 79(3): 703–726; Y. Lu & J. Wright, 2010, Tacit collusion with price-matching punishments, *International Journal of Industrial Organization*, 28: 298–306.

52. R. W. Cooper & T. W. Ross, 2009, Sustaining cooperation with joint ventures, *Journal of Law, Economics, and Organization*, 25(1): 31–54.

53. L. Zou, C. Yu, & M. Dresner, 2012, Multimarket contact, alliance membership, and prices in international airline markets, *Transportation Research Part E: Logistics and Transportation Review*, 48(2): 555–565; J. T. Prince & D. H. Simon, 2009, Multi-market contact and service quality: Evidence from on-time performance in the U.S. airline industry, *Academy of Management Journal*, 52: 336–354.

54. B. Chidmi, 2012, Vertical relationships in the ready-to-eat breakfast cereal industry in Boston, *Agribusiness*, 28(3): 241–259; N. Panteva, 2011, IBISWorld Industry Report 31123: Cereal production in the U.S., January.

55. Zou, Yu, & Dresner, Multimarket contact, alliance membership, and prices in international airline markets; Z. Guedri & J. McGuire, 2011, Multimarket competition, mobility barriers, and firm performance, *Journal of Management Studies*, 48: 857–890.

56. P. Massey & M. McDowell, 2010, Joint dominance and tacit collusion: Some implications for competition and regulatory policy, *European Competition Journal*, 6: 427–444.

57. A. H. Bowers, H. R. Greve, H. Mitsuhashi, & J. A. C. Baum, 2013, Competitive parity, status disparity, and mutual forbearance: Securities analysts' competition for investor attention, *INSEAD Working Papers Collection*, (43): 1–52

58. B. Nielsen, 2010, Strategic fit, contractual, and procedural governance in alliances, *Journal of Business Research*, 63: 682–689; P. Dussauge, B. Garrette, & W. Mitchell, 2004, Asymmetric performances: The market share impact of scale and link alliances in the global auto industry, *Strategic Management Journal*, 25: 701–711.

59. L. Capron & W. Mitchell, 2012, *Build, Borrow or Buy: Solving the Growth Dilemma*, Cambridge: Harvard Business Review Press; C. Häussler, 2011, The determinants of commercialization strategy: Idiosyncrasies in British and German biotechnology, *Entrepreneurship Theory and Practice*, 35: 653–681.

60. Y. Lew & R. R. Sinkovics, 2013, Crossing borders and industry sectors: Behavioral governance in strategic alliances and product innovation for competitive advantage, *Long Range Planning*, 46(1/2): 13–38; P. Ritala & H.-K. Ellonen, 2010, Competitive advantage in interfirm cooperation: Old and new explanations, *Competitiveness Review*, 20: 367–383.

61. H. Liu, X. Jiang, J. Zhang, & X. Zhao, 2013, Strategic flexibility and international venturing by emerging market firms: The moderating effects of institutional and relational factors, *Journal of International Marketing*, 21(2): 79–98; J. Anand, R. Oriani, & R. S. Vassolo, 2010, Alliance activity as a dynamic capability in the face of a discontinuous technological change, *Organization Science*, 21: 1213–1232; J. Li, C. Dhanaraj, & R. L. Shockley, 2008, Joint venture evolution: Extending the real options approach, *Managerial and Decision Economics*, 29: 317–336.

62. S. Chang & M. Tsai, 2013, The effect of prior alliance experience on acquisition performance, *Applied Economics*, 45(6): 765–773; A. Zaheer, E. Hernandez, & S. Banerjee, 2010, Prior alliances with targets and acquisition performance in knowledge-intensive industries, *Organization Science*, 21(5): 1072–1091.

63. J. Paczkowski, 2013, Samsung buddies up with Mozilla on new Android browser tech, *All Things D*, http://allthingsd.com, April 3; J. Paczkowski, 2013, Samsung plans multiple Tizen Smartphones for 2013, *All Things D*, http://allthingsd.com, January 3.

64. J. B. White, 2013, Mazda uses alliances to boost sales, *Wall Street Journal*, www.wsj.com, January 27.

65. V. K. Garg, R. L. Priem, & A. A. Rasheed, 2013, A theoretical explanation of the cost advantages of multi-unit franchising, *Journal of Marketing Channels*, 20(1/2): 52–72; J. G. Combs, D. J. Ketchen, Jr., C. L. Shook, & J. C. Short, 2011, Antecedents and consequences of franchising: Past accomplishments and future challenges, *Journal of Management*, 37: 99–126.

66. F. Lafontaine, 1999, Myths and strengths of franchising, "Mastering Strategy" (Part Nine), *Financial Times*, November 22, 8–10.

67. A. A. Perryman & J. G. Combs, 2012, Who should own it? An agency-based explanation for multi-outlet ownership and co-location in plural form franchising, *Strategic Management Journal*, 33(4): 368–386; D. Grewal, G. R. Iyer, R. G. Javalgi, & L. Radulovich, 2011, Franchise partnership and international expansion: A conceptual

framework and research propositions, *Entrepreneurship Theory and Practice*, 35: 533–557; A. M. Hayashi, 2008, How to replicate success, *MIT Sloan Management Review*, 49(3): 6–7.

68. 2013, Building local businesses one opportunity at a time, International Franchise Association, www.buildingopportunity.com, June 6.

69. G. M. Kistruck, J. W. Webb, C. J. Sutter, & R. D. Ireland, 2011, Microfranchising in base-of-the-pyramid markets: Institutional challenges and adaptations to the franchise model, *Entrepreneurship Theory and Practice*, 35: 503–531.

70. N. Mumdziev & J. Windsperger, 2013, An extended transaction cost model of decision rights allocation in franchising: The moderating role of trust, *Managerial and Decision Economics*, 34(3–5): 170–182; J. McDonnell, A. Beatson, & C.-H. Huang, 2011, Investigating relationships between relationship quality, customer loyalty and cooperation: An empirical study of convenience stores' franchise chain systems, *Asia Pacific Journal of Marketing and Logistics*, 23: 367–385.

71. B. Merrilees & L. Frazer, 2013, Internal branding: Franchisor leadership as a critical determinant, *Journal of Business Research*, 66(2): 158–164; T. M. Nisar, 2011, Intellectual property securitization and growth capital in retail franchising, *Journal of Retailing*, 87(3): 393–405; A. K. Paswan & C. M. Wittman, 2009, Knowledge management and franchise systems, *Industrial Marketing Management*, 38: 173–180.

72. D. Grace, S. Weaven, L. Frazer, & J. Giddings, 2013, Examining the role of franchisee normative expectations in relationship evaluation, *Journal of Retailing*, 89(2): 219–230; W. R. Meek, B. Davis-Sramek, M. S. Baucus, & R. N. Germain, 2011, Commitment in franchising: The role of collaborative communication and a franchisee's propensity to leave, *Entrepreneurship Theory and Practice*, 35: 559–581.

73. N. Gorovaia & J. Windsperger, 2013, Real options, intangible resources and performance of franchise networks, *Managerial and Decision Economics*, 34(3–5): 183–194; T. W. K. Leslie & L. S. McNeill, 2010, Towards a conceptual model for franchise perceptual equity, *Journal of Brand Management*, 18: 21–33.

74. M. Onal Vural, L. Dahlander, & G. George, 2013, Collaborative benefits and coordination costs: Learning and capability development in science, *Strategic Entrepreneurship Journal*, 7: 122–137; M. J. Nieto & A. Rodríguez, 2011, Offshoring of R&D: Looking abroad to improve innovation performance, *Journal of International Business Studies*, 42: 345–361.

75. G. Ahuja, C. Morris Lampert, & E. Novelli, 2013, The second face of appropriability: Generative appropriability and its determinants, *Academy of Management*

Review, 38(2): 248–269; C. Choi & P. Beamish, 2013, Resource complementarity and international joint venture performance in Korea, *Asia Pacific Journal of Management*, 30(2): 561–576.

76. S. Veilleux, N. Haskell, & F. Pons, 2012, Going global: How smaller enterprises benefit from strategic alliances, *Journal of Business Strategy*, 33(5): 22–31; L. D. Qiu, 2010, Cross-border mergers and strategic alliances, *European Economic Review*, 54: 818–831; H. Ren, B. Gray, & K. Kim, 2009, Performance of international joint ventures: What factors really make a difference and how? *Journal of Management*, 35: 805–832.

77. I. Arikan & O. Shenkar, 2013, National animosity and cross-border alliances, *Academy of Management Journal*, in press; Y. Yan, D. Ding, & S. Mak, 2009, The impact of business investment on capability exploitation and organizational control in international strategic alliances, *Journal of Change Management*, 9(1): 49–65.

78. Vasudeva, Spencer, & Teegen, Bringing the institutional context back in: A cross-national comparison of alliance partner selection and knowledge acquisition; L. Li, G. Qian, & Z. Qian, 2013, Do partners in international strategic alliances share resources, costs, and risks? *Journal of Business Research*, 66(4): 489–498; A. Zaheer & E. Hernandez, 2011, The geographic scope of the MNC and its alliance portfolio: Resolving the paradox of distance, *Global Strategy Journal*, 1: 109–126.

79. Roy, IJV partner trustworthy behaviour: The role of host country governance and partner selection criteria; M. Meuleman & M. Wright, 2011, Cross-border private equity syndication: Institutional context and learning, *Journal of Business Venturing*, 26: 35–48; T. J. Wilkinson, A. R. Thomas, & J. M. Hawes, 2009, Managing relationships with Chinese joint venture partners, *Journal of Global Marketing*, 22(2): 109–120.

80. B. B. Nielsen & S. Gudergan, 2012, Exploration and exploitation fit and performance in international strategic alliances, *International Business Review*, 21(4): 558–574; D. Kronborg & S. Thomsen, 2009, Foreign ownership and long-term survival, *Strategic Management Journal*, 30: 207–219.

81. N. Negishi & I. Sherr, 2013, East meets the west in mobile game, *Wall Street Journal*, June 7, B2.

82. Lavie, Capturing value from alliance portfolios; D. Lavie, C. Lechner, & H. Singh, 2007, The performance implications of timing of entry and involvement in multipartner alliances, *Academy of Management Journal*, 50(3): 578–604.

83. 2013, Partner with Cisco, Cisco homepage, www.cisco.com, June 6.

84. 2013, Strategic alliance—IBM, Cisco homepage, www.cisco.com, June 6.

85. W. Fu, J. Revilla Diez, & D. Schiller, 2013, Interactive learning, informal networks and innovation: Evidence from electronics firm survey in the Pearl River Delta, China, *Research Policy*, 42(3): 635–646; A. T. Ankan & M. A. Schilling, 2011, Structure and governance in industrial districts: Implications for competitive advantage, *Journal of Management Studies*, 48: 772–803.

86. F. Ghadar, J. Sviokla, & D. A. Stephan, 2012, Why life science needs its own silicon valley, *Harvard Business Review*, 90(7/8): 25–27.

87. C. Casanueva, I. Castro, & J. L. Galán, 2013, Informational networks and innovation in mature industrial clusters, *Journal of Business Research*, 66(5): 603–613; J. Wincent, S. Anokhin, D. Örtqvist, & E. Autio, 2010, Quality meets structure: Generalized reciprocity and firm-level advantage in strategic networks, *Journal of Management Studies*, 47: 597–624; D. Lavie, 2007, Alliance portfolios and firm performance: A study of value creation and appropriation in the U.S. software industry, *Strategic Management Journal*, 28: 1187–1212.

88. L. Dobusch & E. Schübler, 2013, Theorizing path dependence: A review of positive feedback mechanisms in technology markets, regional clusters, and organizations, *Industrial & Corporate Change*, 22(3): 617–647; A. M. Joshi & A. Nerkar, 2011, When do strategic alliances inhibit innovation by firms? Evidence from patent pools in the global optical disc industry, *Strategic Management Journal*, 32(11): 1139–1160.

89. J. P. MacDuffie, 2011, Inter-organizational trust and the dynamics of distrust, *Journal of International Business Studies*, 42: 35–47; H. Kim, R. E. Hoskisson, & W. P. Wan, 2004, Power, dependence, diversification strategy and performance in keiretsu member firms, *Strategic Management Journal*, 25: 613–636.

90. E. Francis, 2013, Building an auto industry hub through value creation, *Automotive Industries*, January, 111–112.

91. V. Van de Vrande, 2013, Balancing your technology-sourcing portfolio: How sourcing mode diversity enhances innovative performance, *Strategic Management Journal*, 34(5): 610–621; A. V. Shipilov, 2009, Firm scope experience, historic multimarket contact with partners, centrality, and the relationship between structural holes and performance, *Organization Science*, 20: 85–106.

92. A. Cui & G. O'Connor, 2012, Alliance portfolio resource diversity and firm innovation, *Journal of Marketing*, 76(4): 24–43; P.-H. Soh, 2010, Network patterns and competitive advantage before the emergence of a dominant design, *Strategic Management Journal*, 31: 438–461.

93. G. Soda, 2011, The management of firms' alliance network positioning: Implications for innovation, *European Management Journal*, 29(5): 377–388; T. Kiessling & M. Harvey, 2008, Globalisation of internal venture capital opportunities in developing small and medium enterprises' relationships, *International Journal of Entrepreneurship and Innovation Management*, 8: 233–253; V. Shankar & B. L. Bayus, 2003, Network effects and competition: An empirical analysis of the home video game industry, *Strategic Management Journal*, 24: 375–384.

94. Leonard, Syfy's ultimate transmedia adventure.

95. Yin, Wu & Tsai, When unconnected others connect: Does degree of brokerage persist after the formation of a multipartner alliance?

96. A. G. Karamanos, 2012, Leveraging micro- and macro-structures of embeddedness in alliance networks for exploratory innovation in biotechnology, *R&D Management*, 42(1): 71–89; D. Somaya, Y. Kim, & N. S. Vonortas, 2011, Exclusivity in licensing alliances: Using hostages to support technology commercialization, *Strategic Management Journal*, 32: 159–186.

97. Veilleux, Haskell, & Pons, Going global: How smaller enterprises benefit from strategic alliances; M. J. Nieto & L. Santamaría, 2010, Technological collaboration: Bridging the innovation gap between small and large firms, *Journal of Small Business Management*, 48: 44–69; P. Ozcan & K. M. Eisenhardt, 2009, Origin of alliance portfolios: Entrepreneurs, network strategies, and firm performance, *Academy of Management Journal*, 52: 246–279.

98. H. R. Greve, T. J. Rowley, & A. V. Shipilov, 2013, How partners shape strategy, *Harvard Business Review*, 91(6): 28.

99. Ibid.

100. Mueller, The reason Tesla is still alive (and other green car companies aren't).

101. H. R. Greve, H. Mitsuhashi, & J. A. C. Baum, 2013, Greener pastures: Outside options and strategic alliance withdrawal, *Organization Science*, 24(1): 79–98; H. R. Greve, J. A. C. Baum, H. Mitsuhashi, & T. J. Rowley, 2010, Built to last but falling apart: Cohesion, friction, and withdrawal from interfirm alliances, *Academy of Management Journal*, 53: 302–322; M. Rod, 2009, A model for the effective management of joint ventures: A case study approach, *International Journal of Management*, 26(1): 3–17.

102. G. Vasudeva & J. Anand, 2011, Unpacking absorptive capacity: A study of knowledge utilization from alliance portfolios, *Academy of Management Journal*, 54: 611–623; J.-Y. Kim & A. S. Miner, 2007, Vicarious learning from the failures and near-failures of others: Evidence from the U.S. commercial banking industry, *Academy of Management Journal*, 50(2): 687–714.

103. J. Marson, 2013, TNK-BP investors appeal to Rosneft's chief over shares, *Wall Street Journal*, www.wsj.com, April 17.

104. K. Zhou & D. Xu, 2012, How foreign firms curtail local supplier opportunism in China: Detailed contracts, centralized control, and relational governance,

Journal of International Business Studies, 43(7): 677–692; R. Agarwal, D. Audretsch, & M. B. Sarkar, 2010, Knowledge spillovers and strategic entrepreneurship, *Strategic Entrepreneurship Journal,* 4: 271–283; Y. Li, Y. Liu, M. Li, & H. Wu, 2008, Transformational offshore outsourcing: Empirical evidence from alliances in China, *Journal of Operations Management,* 26: 257–274.

105. Cummings & Holmberg, Best-fit alliance partners: The use of critical success factors in a comprehensive partner selection process; A. V. Werder, 2011, Corporate governance and stakeholder opportunism, *Organization Science,* 22(5): 1345–1358; T. K. Das & R. Kumar, 2011, Regulatory focus and opportunism in the alliance development process, *Journal of Management,* 37: 682–708.

106. A. S. Cui, 2013, Portfolio dynamics and alliance termination: The contingent role of resource dissimilarity, *Journal of Marketing,* 77(3): 15–32; M. S. Giarratana & S. Torrisi, 2010, Foreign entry and survival in a knowledge-intensive market: Emerging economy countries' international linkages, technology competencies, and firm experience, *Strategic Entrepreneurship Journal,* 4: 85–104; M. B. Sarkar, P. S. Aulakh, & A. Madhok, 2009, Process capabilities and value generation in alliance portfolios, *Organization Science,* 20: 583–600.

107. S. Williams & J. Marson, 2013, BP nears arctic deal with Rosneft, *Wall Street Journal,* www.wsj.com, March 23.

108. M. Nippa & S. Beechler, 2013, What do we know about the success and failure of international joint ventures? In search of relevance and holism, in T. M. Devinney, T. Pedersen, & L. Tihanyi (eds.), *Philosophy of Science and Meta-knowledge in International Business and Management,* 26: 363–396; Lumineau, Fréchet, & Puthod, An organizational learning

perspective on the contracting process; P.-X. Meschi, 2009, Government corruption and foreign stakes in international joint ventures in emerging economies, *Asia Pacific Journal of Management,* 26: 241–261.

109. I. Neyens & D. Faems, 2013, Exploring the impact of alliance portfolio management design on alliance portfolio performance, *Managerial & Decision Economics,* 34(3–5): 347–361; D. G. Sirmon, M. A. Hitt, R. D. Ireland, & B. A. Gilbert, 2011, Resource orchestration to create competitive advantage: Breadth, depth, and life cycle effects, *Journal of Management,* 37(5): 1390–1412; M. H. Hansen, R. E. Hoskisson, & J. B. Barney, 2008, Competitive advantage in alliance governance: Resolving the opportunism minimization-gain maximization paradox, *Managerial and Decision Economics,* 29: 191–208.

110. C. C. Chung & P. W. Beamish, 2010, The trap of continual ownership change in international equity joint ventures, *Organization Science,* 21: 995–1015.

111. Mudambi & Tallman, Make, buy or ally?; Hansen, Hoskisson, & Barney, Competitive advantage in alliance governance: Resolving the opportunism minimization-gain maximization paradox.

112. N. N. Arranz & J. C. F. de Arroyabe, 2012, Effect of formal contracts, relational norms and trust on performance of joint research and development projects, *British Journal of Management,* 23(4): 575–588; L. Poppo, K. Z. Zhou, & S. Ryu, 2008, Alternative origins to interorganizational trust: An interdependence perspective on the shadow of the past and the shadow of the future, *Organization Science,* 19: 39–55.

113. G. Ertug, I. Cuypers, N. Noorderhaven, & B. Bensaou, 2013, Trust between international joint venture partners: Effects of home countries, *Journal of International Business*

Studies, 44(3): 263–282; J. J. Li, L. Poppo, & K. Z. Zhou, 2010, Relational mechanisms, formal contracts, and local knowledge acquisition by international subsidiaries, *Strategic Management Journal,* 31: 349–370.

114. S. E. Fawcett, S. L. Jones, & A. M. Fawcett, 2012, Supply chain trust: The catalyst for collaborative innovation, *Business Horizons,* 55(2): 163–178; H. C. Dekker & A. Van den Abbeele, 2010, Organizational learning and interfirm control: The effects of partner search and prior exchange experience, *Organization Science,* 21: 1233–1250; T. K. Das & R. Kumar, 2009, Interpartner harmony in strategic alliances: Managing commitment and forbearance, *International Journal of Strategic Business Alliances,* 1(1): 24–52.

115. T. A. Khoury, M. Junkunc, & D. L. Deeds, 2013, The social construction of legitimacy through signaling social capital: Exploring the conditional value of alliances and underwriters at IPO, *Entrepreneurship Theory & Practice,* 37(3): 569–601; J. W. Rottman, 2008, Successful knowledge transfer within offshore supplier networks: A case study exploring social capital in strategic alliances, *Journal of Information Technology,* 23(10): 31–43.

116. 2013, The principles of the alliance, Renault homepage, www.renault.com, June 7.

117. R. Kumar & A. Nathwani, 2012, Business alliances: Why managerial thinking and biases determine success, *Journal of Business Strategy,* 33(5): 44–50; C. C. Phelps, 2010, A longitudinal study of the influence of alliance network structure and composition on firm exploratory innovation, *Academy of Management Journal,* 53: 890–913; C. E. Ybarra & T. A. Turk, 2009, The evolution of trust in information technology alliances, *Journal of High Technology Management Research,* 20(1): 62–74.

10

Corporate Governance

Studying this chapter should provide you with the strategic management knowledge needed to:

1 Define corporate governance and explain why it is used to monitor and control top-level managers' decisions.

2 Explain why ownership is largely separated from managerial control in organizations.

3 Define an agency relationship and managerial opportunism and describe their strategic implications.

4 Explain the use of three internal governance mechanisms to monitor and control managers' decisions.

5 Discuss the types of compensation top-level managers receive and their effects on managerial decisions.

6 Describe how the external corporate governance mechanism—the market for corporate control—restrains top-level managers' decisions.

7 Discuss the nature and use of corporate governance in international settings, especially in Germany, Japan, and China.

8 Describe how corporate governance fosters ethical decisions by a firm's top-level managers.

MR. JAMES DIMON

THE IMPERIAL CEO, JPMORGAN CHASE'S JAMIE DIMON: IS IT THE END OF CORPORATE GOVERNANCE?

Jamie Dimon, CEO of JPMorgan Chase, is one of the very few top executives at large banks or major financial services firms who was unscathed by the substantial economic recession which began in 2008—a recession largely caused by those firms taking inappropriate risks. He is described as charismatic and an excellent leader. Yet, in 2012, JPMorgan Chase experienced its own scandal caused by exceptional risk taking. Traders in its London operations were allowed to build a huge exposure in credit derivatives that breached the acceptable risk limits of most analytical models. As a result, the bank suffered losses of more than $6 billion. It is referred to as the London Whale trading debacle.

Because of the huge loss and concerns about the lack of oversight that led to this debacle, there was a move by shareholder activists to separate the CEO and chair of the board positions, requiring Dimon to hold only the CEO title. Playing key roles were the American Federation of State, County and Municipal Employees (AFSCME) and the Institutional Shareholder Services (ISS). The AFSCME was pushing to separate the holders of the CEO and chair positions at JPMorgan Chase. The ISS was pushing for shareholders to withhold the votes for three directors currently on the Morgan's board policy committee.

Dimon described the London Whale debacle as an anomaly caused by the inappropriate behavior of a few bad employees. However, it seems to suggest serious weaknesses in the bank's oversight of activities involving significant risk.

Executives and board members of JPMorgan Chase worked hard to thwart these efforts. Lee Raymond, the former CEO of Exxon Mobil who has been on the Morgan board for

25 years, played a key role in these efforts to support Dimon and avoid a negative vote. They lobbied major institutional shareholders, and even asked former U.S. president Bill Clinton to help work out a compromise with the AFSCME (though he declined). They even suggested that Dimon would quit if he had to give up one of the roles and it would harm the stock price. In the end, Dimon and the bank won the vote with a two-thirds majority for Dimon to retain both positions.

Several analysts decried the vote and suggested that having a third of the shareholders vote against Dimon is not a major vote of confidence. One even suggested that the vote is not surprising because of the 10 largest institutional owners of the bank's stock, 7 have CEOs who also hold the chair position. So, how could they openly argue that this is bad for JPMorgan when they do it in their organizations? Furthermore, these major institutional investors want the banks to engage in high-risk activities with the potential to produce high returns. This is especially true because the downside risk of losses is low as the government cannot afford to allow the big banks to fail.

One analyst suggested that the shareholders voted out of fear (potential loss of Dimon) and for personality instead of good corporate governance. Analysts for the *Financial Times* argued that the outcome of this vote demonstrates how weak shareholder rights are in the United States. Finally, another analyst noted that while splitting the CEO and chair positions does not guarantee good governance, it is a prerequisite for it. Lee Raymond suggested that the board would take action. Several speculate that such actions will not relate to Dimon but rather to a reconfiguration of the board members on the risk and audit committees. Some have argued that certain members of these committees have little knowledge of their function and/or have financial ties to the bank thereby creating a potential conflict of interest.

Sources: J. Eisinger, 2013, Flawed system suits the shareholders just fine, *New York Times DealBook*, http://dealbook. nytimes.com, May 29; J. Plender, 2013, The divine right of the imperial CEO, *Financial Times*, www.ft.com, May 26; J. Sommer, 2013, The CEO triumphant (at least at Apple and Chase), *New York Times*, www.nytimes.com, May 25; H. Moore, 2013, JP Morgan CEO Jamie Dimon remains the Indiana Jones of corporate America, *The Guardian*, www.guardian.com, May 21; J. Silver-Greenberg & S. Craig, 2013, Strong lobbying helps Dimon thwart a shareholder challenge, *New York Times DealBook*, http://dealbook.nytimes.com, May 21; D. Fitzpatrick, J. S. Lublin, & J. Steinberg, 2013, Vote strengthens Dimon's grip, *Wall Street Journal*, www.wsj.com, May 21; A.T. Crane & A. Currie, 2013, Dimon's Pyrrhic victory, *New York Times DealBook*, http://dealbook.nytimes.com, May 21; D. Benoit, 2013, J.P. Morgan's powerful board members, *Wall Street Journal*, www.wsj.com, May 20; M. Egan, 2013, Top J.P. Morgan directors back Dimon as CEO, Chair, *Fox Business*, www.foxbusiness.com, May 10.

Strategy Right NOW

Learn more about the American Federation of State, County and Municipal Employees.

www.cengagebrain.com

As the Opening Case suggests, corporate governance is complex and designed to provide oversight of how firms operate. At a broader level, reflects the type of infrastructure provided by individual nations as the framework within which companies compete. Given that we are concerned with the strategic management process firms use, our focus in this chapter is on corporate governance in companies (although we do also address governance at the level of nations). The complexity and the potential problems with corporate governance, such as having true checks and balances in the system of governance, are shown by the JPMorgan Chase example in the Opening Case. In fact, it appears that there were very few checks and balances in the corporate governance of JPMorgan Chase. Company CEO Jamie Dimon appears to more like a "king" than an officer under the watchful eye of the board of directors.

Comprehensive in scope and complex in nature, corporate governance is a responsibility that challenges firms and their leaders. Successfully dealing with this challenge is important, as evidence suggests that corporate governance is critical to firms' success; because of this, governance is an increasingly important part of the strategic management process.[1] For example, if the board makes the wrong decisions in selecting, governing, and compensating the firm's CEO as its strategic leader, the shareholders and the firm suffer. When CEOs are motivated to act in the best interests of the firm—in particular, the shareholders—the company's value is more likely to increase. Additionally, effective succession plans and appropriate monitoring and direction-setting efforts by the board of directors contribute positively to a firm's performance.

Corporate governance is the set of mechanisms used to manage relationships among stakeholders and to determine and control the strategic direction and performance of organizations.[2] At its core, corporate governance is concerned with identifying ways to ensure that decisions (especially strategic decisions) are made effectively and that they facilitate a firm's efforts to achieve strategic competitiveness.[3] Governance can also be thought of as a means to establish and maintain harmony between parties (the firm's owners and its top-level managers) whose interests may conflict.

In modern corporations—especially those in nations with "Westernized" infrastructures and business practices such as the United States and the United Kingdom—ensuring that top-level managers' interests are aligned with other stakeholders' interests, particularly those of shareholders, is a primary objective of corporate governance. Thus, corporate governance involves oversight in areas where owners, managers, and members of boards of directors

Corporate governance is the set of mechanisms used to manage the relationships among stakeholders and to determine and control the strategic direction and performance of organizations.

M. Stasy

may have conflicts of interest. Processes used to elect members of the firm's board of directors, the general management of CEO pay and more focused supervision of director pay, and the corporation's overall strategic direction are examples of areas in which oversight is sought.[4] Because corporate governance is an ongoing process concerned with how a firm is to be managed, its nature evolves in light of the types of never-ending changes in a firm's external environment that we discussed in Chapter 2.

The recent global emphasis on corporate governance stems mainly from the apparent failure of corporate governance mechanisms to adequately monitor and control top-level managers' decisions (as exemplified by the Opening Case on JPMorgan Chase). In turn, undesired or unacceptable consequences resulting from using corporate governance mechanisms cause changes such as electing new members to the board of directors with the hope of providing more effective governance. A second and more positive reason for this interest comes from evidence that a well-functioning corporate governance system can create a competitive advantage for an individual firm.[5]

As noted earlier, corporate governance is of concern to nations as well as to individual firms.[6] Although corporate governance reflects company standards, it also collectively reflects the societal standards of nations.[7] Commenting about governance-related changes being made in Singapore, an official noted that, "Good corporate governance plays an important role in ensuring the effective functioning of Singapore's capital markets."[8] Ensuring the independence of board members and practices a board should follow to exercise effective oversight of a firm's internal control efforts are examples of recent changes to governance standards being applied in Singapore. Efforts such as these are important in that research shows that how nations govern their corporations affects firms' investment decisions. In other words, firms seek to invest in nations with national governance standards that are acceptable to them.[9] This is particularly the case when firms consider the possibility of geographically expanding into emerging markets.

In the chapter's first section, we describe the relationship on which the modern corporation is built—namely, the relationship between owners and managers. We use the majority of the chapter to explain various mechanisms owners use to govern managers and to ensure that they comply with their responsibility to satisfy stakeholders' needs, especially those of shareholders.

Three internal governance mechanisms and a single external one are used in the modern corporation. The three internal governance mechanisms we describe in this chapter are (1) ownership concentration, represented by types of shareholders and their different incentives to monitor managers; (2) the board of directors; and (3) executive compensation. We then consider the market for corporate control, an external corporate governance mechanism. Essentially, this market is a set of potential owners seeking to acquire undervalued firms and earn above-average returns on their investments by replacing ineffective top-level management teams.[10] The chapter's focus then shifts to the issue of international corporate governance. We briefly describe governance approaches used in several countries outside of the United States and United Kingdom. In part, this discussion suggests that the structures used to govern global companies competing in both developed and emerging economies are becoming more, rather than less, similar. Closing our analysis of corporate governance is a consideration of the need for these control mechanisms to encourage and support ethical behavior in organizations.

10-1 Separation of Ownership and Managerial Control

Historically, U.S. firms were managed by founder-owners and their descendants. In these cases, corporate ownership and control resided in the same people. As firms grew larger, "the managerial revolution led to a separation of ownership and control in most large corporations, where control of the firm shifted from entrepreneurs to professional managers while ownership became dispersed among thousands of unorganized stockholders who were removed from the day-to-day management of the firm."[11] These changes created the modern public corporation, which is based on the efficient separation of ownership and managerial control. Supporting the separation is a basic legal premise suggesting that the primary objective of a firm's activities is to increase the corporation's profit and, thereby, the owners' (shareholders') financial gains.[12]

The separation of ownership and managerial control allows shareholders to purchase stock, which entitles them to income (residual returns) from the firm's operations after paying expenses. This right, however, requires that shareholders take a risk that the firm's expenses may exceed its revenues. To manage this investment risk, shareholders maintain a diversified portfolio by investing in several companies to reduce their overall risk.[13] The poor performance or failure of any one firm in which they invest has less overall effect on the value of the entire portfolio of investments. Thus, shareholders specialize in managing their investment risk.

Commonly, those managing small firms also own a significant percentage of the firm. In such instances, there is less separation between ownership and managerial control. Moreover, in a large number of family-owned firms, ownership and managerial control are not separated at all. Research shows that family-owned firms perform better when a member of the family is the CEO than when the CEO is an outsider.[14]

In many regions outside the United States, such as in Latin America, Asia, and some European countries, family-owned firms dominate the competitive landscape.[15] The primary purpose of most of these firms is to increase the family's wealth, which explains why a family CEO often is better than an outside CEO. Family ownership is also significant in U.S. companies in that at least one-third of the S&P 500 firms have substantial family ownership, holding on average about 18 percent of a firm's equity.[16]

In family-owned firms there is little, if any, separation between ownership and control.

EIGHTFISH/The Image Bank/Getty Images

Family-controlled firms face at least two critical issues related to corporate governance. First, as they grow, they may not have access to all of the skills needed to effectively manage the firm and maximize returns for the family. Thus, outsiders may be required to facilitate growth. Also, as they grow, they may need to seek outside capital and thus give up some of the ownership. In these cases, protecting the minority owners' rights becomes important.[17] To avoid these potential problems, when family firms grow and become more complex, their owner-managers may contract with managerial specialists. These managers make major decisions in the owners' firm and are compensated on the basis of their decision-making skills. Research suggests that firms in which families own enough equity to have influence without major control tend to make the best strategic decisions.[18]

Without owner (shareholder) specialization in risk bearing and management specialization in decision making, a firm may be limited by its owners' abilities to simultaneously manage it and make effective strategic decisions relative to risk. Thus, the separation and specialization of ownership (risk bearing) and managerial control (decision making) should produce the highest returns for the firm's owners.

10-1a Agency Relationships

The separation between owners and managers creates an agency relationship. An agency relationship exists when one or more persons (the principal or principals) hire another person or persons (the agent or agents) as decision-making specialists to perform a service.[19] Thus, an **agency relationship** exists when one party delegates decision-making responsibility to a second party for compensation (see Figure 10.1).

In addition to shareholders and top-level managers, other examples of agency relationships are consultants and clients and insured and insurer. Moreover, within organizations, an agency relationship exists between managers and their employees, as well as between top-level managers and the firm's owners.[20] However, in this chapter we focus on the agency relationship between the firm's owners (the principals) and top-level managers (the principals' agents) because these managers are responsible for formulating and implementing the firm's strategies, which have major effects on firm performance.[21]

The separation between ownership and managerial control can be problematic. Research evidence documents a variety of agency problems in the modern corporation.[22] Problems can surface because the principal and the agent have different interests and goals or because shareholders lack direct control of large publicly traded corporations. Problems also surface when an agent makes decisions that result in pursuing goals that conflict with those of

An **agency relationship** exists when one party delegates decision-making responsibility to a second party for compensation.

Figure 10.1 An Agency Relationship

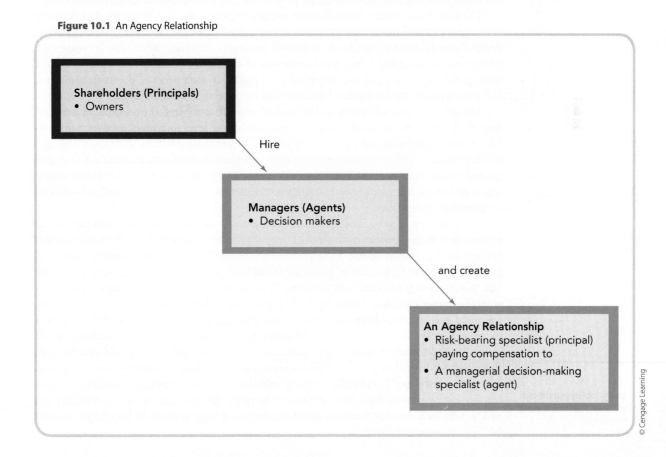

the principals. Thus, the separation of ownership and control potentially allows divergent interests (between principals and agents) to occur, which can lead to managerial opportunism.

Managerial opportunism is the seeking of self-interest with guile (i.e., cunning or deceit).[23] Opportunism is both an attitude (e.g., an inclination) and a set of behaviors (i.e., specific acts of self-interest).[24] Principals do not know beforehand which agents will or will not act opportunistically. A top-level manager's reputation is an imperfect predictor; moreover, opportunistic behavior cannot be observed until it has occurred. Thus, principals establish governance and control mechanisms to prevent agents from acting opportunistically, even though only a few are likely to do so. Interestingly, research suggests that when CEOs feel constrained by governance mechanisms, they are more likely to seek external advice that in turn helps them make better strategic decisions.[25]

The agency relationship suggests that any time principals delegate decision-making responsibilities to agents, the opportunity for conflicts of interest exists. Top-level managers, for example, may make strategic decisions that maximize their personal welfare and minimize their personal risk.[26] Decisions such as these prevent maximizing shareholder wealth. Decisions regarding product diversification demonstrate this situation.

10-1b Product Diversification as an Example of an Agency Problem

As explained in Chapter 6, a corporate-level strategy to diversify the firm's product lines can enhance a firm's strategic competitiveness and increase its returns, both of which serve the interests of all stakeholders and certainly shareholders and top-level managers. However, product diversification can create two benefits for top-level managers that shareholders do not enjoy, meaning that they may prefer product diversification more than shareholders do.[27]

The fact that product diversification usually increases the size of a firm and that size is positively related to executive compensation is the first of the two benefits of additional diversification that may accrue to top-level managers. Diversification also increases the complexity of managing a firm and its network of businesses, possibly requiring additional managerial pay because of this complexity.[28] Thus, increased product diversification provides an opportunity for top-level managers to increase their compensation.[29]

The second potential benefit is that product diversification and the resulting diversification of the firm's portfolio of businesses can reduce top-level managers' employment risk. *Managerial employment risk* is the risk of job loss, loss of compensation, and loss of managerial reputation.[30] These risks are reduced with increased diversification, because a firm and its upper-level managers are less vulnerable to the reduction in demand associated with a single or limited number of product lines or businesses. Events that occurred at Lockheed demonstrate these issues.

For a number of years, Lockheed has been a major defense contractor with the federal government as its primary customer. Although it provides a variety of products and services (processes U.S. census forms, handles $600 billion of Social Security benefits each year, and manages over 50 percent of global air traffic), 82 percent of its revenue came from the U.S. government (61 percent was from the Department of Defense). This dependence on a single customer is risky, as shown by the U.S. government's recent attempts to reduce overall spending and to wind down the wars in Iraq and Afghanistan. Therefore, there are high incentives for Lockheed to diversify. Earlier attempts to diversify into products that targeted other customer markets were largely unsuccessful. For example, it acquired Comcast with the intent of diversifying into the telecommunications industry. However, the acquisition was unsuccessful and Lockheed eventually sold the business. Essentially, Lockheed's organization and operations have been structured to serve the government, and specifically the military. Indeed, existing weapons systems compose a large portion of Lockheed's current $47 billion in annual revenue.

Managerial opportunism is the seeking of self-interest with guile (i.e., cunning or deceit).

Lockheed's new CEO, Marillyn Hewson, is charged with charting a future for the company that likely includes diversification. The firm's Center for Innovation is working on several potential products and services in health care and cybersecurity. So, it appears that it will try to diversify organically by developing innovations internally (using its current capabilities) rather than acquiring other firms as it did in the past. In fact, Hewson describes Lockheed as a global security enterprise, suggesting its new focus and vision. So, while previous diversification efforts were unsuccessful, Lockheed is trying again with a new CEO and emphasis on internal innovation.[31]

Free cash flow is the source of another potential agency problem. Calculated as operating cash flow minus capital expenditures, free cash flow represents the cash remaining after the firm has invested in all projects that have positive net present value within its current businesses.[32] Top-level managers may decide to invest free cash flow in product lines that are not associated with the firm's current lines of business to increase the firm's degree of diversification (as is currently being done at Lockheed). However, when managers use free cash flow to diversify the firm in ways that do not have a strong possibility of creating additional value for stakeholders and certainly for shareholders, the firm is overdiversified. Overdiversification is an example of self-serving and opportunistic managerial behavior. In contrast to managers, shareholders may prefer that free cash flow be distributed to them as dividends, so they can control how the cash is invested.[33]

In Figure 10.2, Curve *S* shows shareholders' optimal level of diversification. As the firm's owners, shareholders seek the level of diversification that reduces the risk of the firm's total failure while simultaneously increasing its value by developing economies of scale and scope (see Chapter 6). Of the four corporate-level diversification strategies shown in Figure 10.2, shareholders likely prefer the diversified position noted by point *A* on Curve *S*—a position that is located between the dominant business and related-constrained diversification strategies. Of course, the optimum level of diversification owners seek varies from firm to firm.[34] Factors that affect shareholders' preferences include the firm's primary industry, the intensity

Figure 10.2 Manager and Shareholder Risk and Diversification

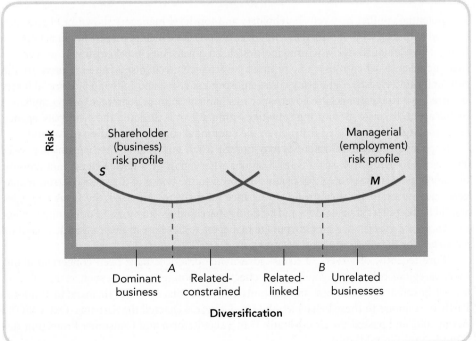

© Cengage Learning

of rivalry among competitors in that industry, the top management team's experience with implementing diversification strategies, and the firm's perceived expertise in the new business and its effects on other firm strategies, such as its entry into international markets.[35]

As is the case for principals, top-level managers—as agents—also seek an optimal level of diversification. Declining performance resulting from too much diversification increases the probability that external investors (representing the market for corporate control) will purchase a substantial percentage of or the entire firm for the purpose of controlling it. If a firm is acquired, the employment risk for its top-level managers increases significantly. Furthermore, these managers' employment opportunities in the external managerial labor market (discussed in Chapter 12) are affected negatively by a firm's poor performance. Therefore, top-level managers prefer that the firms they lead be diversified. However, their preference is that the firm's diversification falls short of the point at which it increases their employment risk and reduces their employment opportunities.[36] Curve M in Figure 10.2 shows that top-level managers prefer higher levels of product diversification than do shareholders. Top-level managers might find the optimal level of diversification as shown by point B on Curve M.

In general, shareholders prefer riskier strategies and more focused diversification. Shareholders reduce their risk by holding a diversified portfolio of investments. Alternatively, managers cannot balance their employment risk by working for a diverse portfolio of firms; therefore, managers may prefer a level of diversification that maximizes firm size and their compensation while also reducing their employment risk. Finding the appropriate level of diversification is difficult for managers. Research has shown that too much diversification can have negative effects on the firm's ability to create innovation (managers' unwillingness to take on higher risks). Alternatively, diversification that strategically fits the firm's capabilities can enhance its innovation output.[37] However, too much or inappropriate diversification can also divert managerial attention from other important firm activities such as corporate social responsibility.[38] Product diversification, therefore, is a potential agency problem that could result in principals incurring costs to control their agents' behaviors.

10-1c Agency Costs and Governance Mechanisms

The potential conflict between shareholders and top-level managers shown in Figure 10.2, coupled with the fact that principals cannot easily predict which managers might act opportunistically, demonstrates why principals establish governance mechanisms. However, the firm incurs costs when it uses one or more governance mechanisms. **Agency costs** are the sum of incentive costs, monitoring costs, enforcement costs, and individual financial losses incurred by principals because governance mechanisms cannot guarantee total compliance by the agent. Because monitoring activities within a firm is difficult, the principals' agency costs are larger in diversified firms given the additional complexity of diversification.[39]

In general, managerial interests may prevail when governance mechanisms are weak and therefore ineffective, such as in situations where managers have a significant amount of autonomy to make strategic decisions. If, however, the board of directors controls managerial autonomy, or if other strong governance mechanisms are used, the firm's strategies should better reflect stakeholders and certainly shareholders' interests.[40] For example, effective corporate governance may encourage managers to develop strategies that demonstrate a concern for the environment (i.e., "green strategies").[41]

More recently, observers of firms' governance practices have been concerned about more egregious behavior beyond mere ineffective corporate strategies, such as that discovered at Enron and WorldCom, and the more recent actions by major financial institutions. Partly in response to these behaviors, the U.S. Congress enacted the Sarbanes-Oxley (SOX) Act in 2002 and passed the Dodd-Frank Wall Street Reform and Consumer Protection Act (Dodd-Frank) in mid-2010.

Agency costs are the sum of incentive costs, monitoring costs, enforcement costs, and individual financial losses incurred by principals because governance mechanisms cannot guarantee total compliance by the agent.

Because of these two acts, corporate governance mechanisms should receive greater scrutiny.[42] While the implementation of SOX has been controversial to some, most believe that its use has led to generally positive outcomes in terms of protecting stakeholders and certainly shareholders' interests. For example, Section 404 of SOX, which prescribes significant transparency improvement on internal controls associated with accounting and auditing, has arguably improved the internal auditing scrutiny (and thereby trust) in firms' financial reporting. Moreover, research suggests that internal controls associated with Section 404 increase shareholder value.[43] Nonetheless, some argue that the Act, especially Section 404, creates excessive costs for firms. In addition, a decrease in foreign firms listing on U.S. stock exchanges occurred at the same time as listing on foreign exchanges increased. In part, this shift may be because of the costs SOX generates for firms seeking to list on U.S. exchanges.

President Barack Obama signing the Dodd-Frank Wall Street Reform and Consumer Protection Act. The full impact of this controversial governance mechanism has yet to be determined.

Dodd-Frank is recognized as the most sweeping set of financial regulatory reforms in the United States since the Great Depression. The Act is intended to align financial institutions' actions with society's interests. Dodd-Frank includes provisions related to the categories of consumer protection, systemic risk oversight, executive compensation, and capital requirements for banks. Some legal analysts offer the following description of the Act's provisions: "(Dodd-Frank) creates a Financial Stability Oversight Council headed by the Treasury Secretary, establishes a new system for liquidation of certain financial companies, provides for a new framework to regulate derivatives, establishes new corporate governance requirements, and regulates credit rating agencies and securitizations. The Act also establishes a new consumer protection bureau and provides for extensive consumer protection in financial services."[44]

More intensive application of governance mechanisms as mandated by legislation such as Sarbanes-Oxley and Dodd-Frank affects firms' choice of strategies. For example, more intense governance might find firms choosing to pursue fewer risky projects, possibly decreasing shareholder wealth as a result. In considering how some provisions associated with Dodd-Frank that deal with banks might be put into practice, a U.S. federal regulator said, "To put it plainly, my view is that we are in danger of trying to squeeze too much risk and complexity out of banking."[45] As this comment suggests, determining governance practices that strike an appropriate balance between protecting stakeholders' interests and allowing firms to implement strategies with some degree of risk is difficult.

Next, we explain the effects of the three internal governance mechanisms on managerial decisions regarding the firm's strategies.

10-2 Ownership Concentration

Ownership concentration is defined by the number of large-block shareholders and the total percentage of the firm's shares they own. **Large-block shareholders** typically own

Ownership concentration is defined by the number of large-block shareholders and the total percentage of the firm's shares they own.

Large-block shareholders typically own at least 5 percent of a company's issued shares.

at least 5 percent of a company's issued shares. Ownership concentration as a governance mechanism has received considerable interest because large-block shareholders are increasingly active in their demands that firms adopt effective governance mechanisms to control managerial decisions so that they will best represent owners' interests.[46] In recent years, the number of individuals who are large-block shareholders has declined. Institutional owners have replaced individuals as large-block shareholders.

In general, diffuse ownership (a large number of shareholders with small holdings and few, if any, large-block shareholders) produces weak monitoring of managers' decisions. One reason for this is that diffuse ownership makes it difficult for owners to effectively coordinate their actions. As noted earlier, diversification beyond the shareholders' optimum level can result from ineffective monitoring of managers' decisions. Higher levels of monitoring could encourage managers to avoid strategic decisions that harm shareholder value, such as too much diversification. Research evidence suggests that ownership concentration is associated with lower levels of firm product diversification.[47] Thus, with high degrees of ownership concentration, the probability is greater that managers' decisions will be designed to maximize shareholder value.[48] However, the influence of large-block shareholders is mitigated to a degree in Europe by strong labor representation on boards of directors.[49]

As noted, ownership concentration influences decisions made about the strategies a firm will use and the value created by their use. In general, but not in every case, ownership concentration's influence on strategies and firm performance is positive. For example, when large-block shareholders have a high degree of wealth, they have power relative to minority shareholders to appropriate the firm's wealth; this is particularly the case when they are in managerial positions. Excessive appropriation at the expense of minority shareholders is somewhat common in emerging economy countries where minority shareholder rights often are not as protected as they are in the United States. In fact, in some of these countries state ownership of an equity stake (even minority ownership) can be used to control these potential problems.[50] The importance of boards of directors to mitigate excessive appropriation of minority shareholder value has been found in firms with strong family ownership where family members have incentives to appropriate shareholder wealth, especially in the second generation after the founder has departed.[51] In general, family-controlled businesses will outperform nonfamily businesses, especially smaller and nonpublic firms because of the importance of enhancing the family's wealth and maintaining the family business.[52] However, families often try to balance the pursuit of economic and noneconomic objectives such that they sometimes may be moderately risk averse (thereby influencing their innovative output).[53]

10-2a The Increasing Influence of Institutional Owners

A classic work published in the 1930s argued that a separation of ownership and control had come to characterize the "modern" corporation.[54] This change occurred primarily because growth prevented founders-owners from maintaining their dual positions in what were increasingly complex companies. More recently, another shift has occurred: Ownership of many modern corporations is now concentrated in the hands of institutional investors rather than individual shareholders.[55]

Institutional owners are financial institutions such as mutual funds and pension funds that control large-block shareholder positions. Because of their prominent ownership positions, institutional owners, as large-block shareholders, have the potential to be a powerful governance mechanism. Estimates of the amount of equity in U.S. firms held by institutional owners held range from 60 to 75 percent. Recent commentary suggests the importance of pension funds to an entire economy: "Pension funds are critical drivers of growth and economic activity in the United States because they are one of the only significant sources of long-term, patient capital."[56]

Institutional owners are financial institutions such as mutual funds and pension funds that control large-block shareholder positions.

These percentages suggest that as investors, institutional owners have both the size and the incentive to discipline ineffective top-level managers and that they can significantly influence a firm's choice of strategies and strategic decisions.[57] Research evidence indicates that institutional and other large-block shareholders are becoming more active in their efforts to influence a corporation's strategic decisions, unless they have a business relationship with the firm. Initially, these shareholder activists and institutional investors concentrated on the performance and accountability of CEOs and contributed to the dismissal of a number of them. Activists often target the actions of boards more directly via proxy vote proposals that are intended to give shareholders more decision rights because they believe board processes have been ineffective.[58] A rule approved by the U.S. Securities and Exchange Commission allowing large shareholders (owning 1 to 5 percent of a company's stock) to nominate up to 25 percent of a company's board of directors enhances shareholders' decision rights.[59]

The institutional investor BlackRock is the largest manager of financial assets in the world, with just under $4 trillion invested and holdings in most of the largest global corporations. Interestingly, it was once described as a "silent giant" because it did not engage in activism. However, recently the silent giant has been awakened, as it has begun asking more questions of the firms in which it holds significant investments. Most of its actions are "behind the scenes," only voting against a director or a company proposal when its unobtrusive actions have failed to change the firm's behavior. BlackRock has become more "confrontational" in order to ensure the value of its investments, and some wish that it would become even more active because of the power of its large equity holdings.[60] To date, research suggests that institutional activism may not have a strong direct effect on firm performance but may indirectly influence a targeted firm's strategic decisions, including those concerned with international diversification and innovation. Thus, to some degree at least, institutional activism has the potential to discipline managers and to enhance the likelihood of a firm taking future actions that are in shareholders' best interests.[61] However, the Opening Case suggests that large institutional owners often go along with the desires of powerful CEOs and boards such as at JPMorgan Chase.

10-3 Board of Directors

Shareholders elect the members of a firm's board of directors. The **board of directors** is a group of elected individuals whose primary responsibility is to act in the owners' best interests by formally monitoring and controlling the firm's top-level managers.[62] Those elected to a firm's board of directors are expected to oversee managers and to ensure that the corporation operates in ways that will best serve stakeholders' interests, and particularly the owners' interests. Helping board members reach their expected objectives are their powers to direct the affairs of the organization and reward and discipline top-level managers.

Though important to all shareholders, a firm's individual shareholders with small ownership percentages are very dependent on the board of directors to represent their interests. Unfortunately, evidence suggests that boards have not been highly effective in monitoring and controlling top-level managers' decisions and subsequent actions.[63] Because of their relatively ineffective performance and in light of the recent financial crisis, boards are experiencing increasing pressure from shareholders, lawmakers, and regulators to become more forceful in their oversight role to prevent top-level managers from acting in their own best interests. Moreover, in addition to their monitoring role, board members increasingly are expected to provide resources to the firms they serve. These resources include their personal knowledge and expertise and their relationships with a wide variety of organizations.[64]

board of directors is a group of elected individuals whose primary responsibility is to act in the owners' best interests by formally monitoring and controlling the firm's top-level managers.

Generally, board members (often called directors) are classified into one of three groups (see Table 10.1). *Insiders* are active top-level managers in the company who are elected to the board because they are a source of information about the firm's day-to-day operations.[65] *Related outsiders* have some relationship with the firm, contractual or otherwise, that may create questions about their independence, but these individuals are not involved with the corporation's day-to-day activities. *Outsiders* provide independent counsel to the firm and may hold top-level managerial positions in other companies or may have been elected to the board prior to the beginning of the current CEO's tenure.[66]

Historically, inside managers dominated a firm's board of directors. A widely accepted view is that a board with a significant percentage of its membership from the firm's top-level managers provides relatively weak monitoring and control of managerial decisions.[67] With weak board monitoring, managers sometimes use their power to select and compensate directors and exploit their personal ties with them. In response to the SEC's proposal to require audit committees to be composed of outside directors, in 1984 the New York Stock Exchange implemented a rule requiring outside directors to head the audit committee. Subsequently, other rules required that independent outsider directors lead important committees such as the compensation committee and the nomination committee.[68] These other requirements were instituted after the Sarbanes-Oxley Act was passed, and policies of the New York Stock Exchange now require companies to maintain boards of directors that are composed of a majority of outside independent directors and to maintain full independent audit committees. Thus, additional scrutiny of corporate governance practices is resulting in a significant amount of attention being devoted to finding ways to recruit quality independent directors and to encourage boards to take actions that fully represent shareholders' best interests.[69]

Critics advocate reforms to ensure that independent outside directors are a significant majority of a board's total membership; research suggests this has been accomplished.[70] However, others argue that having outside directors is not enough to resolve the problems in that CEO power can strongly influence a board's decision. One proposal to reduce the power of the CEO is to separate the chair's role and the CEO's role on the board so that the same person does not hold both positions.[71] A situation in which an individual holds both the CEO and chair of the board title is called *CEO duality*. As is shown with the Opening Case about CEO duality at JPMorgan Chase, it is often very difficult to separate the CEO and chair positions after they have been given to one person. Unfortunately, having a board that actively monitors top-level managers' decisions and actions does not ensure high performance. The value that the directors bring to the company also influences the outcomes. For example, boards with members having significant relevant experience and knowledge are the most likely to help the firm formulate and implement effective strategies.[72]

Table 10.1 Classification of Board of Directors' Members

Insiders
• **The firm's CEO and other top-level managers**
Related outsiders
• **Individuals not involved with the firm's day-to-day operations, but who have a relationship with the company**
Outsiders
• **Individuals who are independent of the firm in terms of day-to-day operations and other relationships**

© Cengage Learning

Alternatively, having a large number of outside board members can also create some problems. For example, because outsiders typically do not have contact with the firm's day-to-day operations and do not have ready access to detailed information about managers and their skills, they lack the insights required to fully and effectively evaluate their decisions and initiatives.[73] Outsiders can, however, obtain valuable information through frequent interactions with inside board members and during board meetings to enhance their understanding of managers and their decisions.

Because they work with and lead the firm daily, insiders have access to information that facilitates forming and implementing appropriate strategies. Accordingly, some evidence suggests that boards with a critical mass of insiders typically are better informed about intended strategic initiatives, the reasons for the initiatives, and the outcomes expected from pursuing them.[74] Without this type of information, outsider-dominated boards may emphasize financial, as opposed to strategic, controls to gather performance information to evaluate managers' and business units' performances. A virtually exclusive reliance on financial evaluations shifts risk to top-level managers who, in turn, may make decisions to maximize their interests and reduce their employment risk. Reducing investments in R&D, further diversifying the firm, and pursuing higher levels of compensation are some of the results of managers' actions to reach the financial goals set by outsider-dominated boards.[75] Additionally, boards can make mistakes in strategic decisions because of poor decision processes, and in CEO succession decisions because of the lack of important information about candidates as well as the firm's specific needs. Overall, knowledgeable and balanced boards are likely to be the most effective over time.[76]

10-3a Enhancing the Effectiveness of the Board of Directors

Because of the importance of boards of directors in corporate governance and as a result of increased scrutiny from shareholders—in particular, large institutional investors—the performances of individual board members and of entire boards are being evaluated more formally and with greater intensity.[77] The demand for greater accountability and improved performance is stimulating many boards to voluntarily make changes. Among these changes are (1) increases in the diversity of the backgrounds of board members (e.g., a greater number of directors from public service, academic, and scientific settings; a greater percentage of ethnic minorities and women; and members from different countries on boards of U.S. firms); (2) the strengthening of internal management and accounting control systems; (3) establishing and consistently using formal processes to evaluate the board's performance; (4) modifying the compensation of directors, especially reducing or eliminating stock options as a part of their package; and (5) creating the "lead director" role[78] that has strong powers with regard to the board agenda and oversight of non-management board member activities.

An increase in the board's involvement with a firm's strategic decision-making processes creates the need for effective collaboration between board members and top-level managers. Some argue that improving the processes used by boards to make decisions and monitor managers and firm outcomes is important for board effectiveness.[79] Moreover, because of the increased pressure from owners and the potential conflict among board members, procedures are necessary to help boards function effectively while seeking to discharge their responsibilities.

Increasingly, outside directors are being required to own significant equity stakes as a prerequisite to holding a board seat. In fact, some research suggests that firms perform better if outside directors have such a stake; the trend is toward higher pay for directors with more stock ownership, but with fewer stock options.[80] However, other research suggests that too much ownership can lead to lower independence for board members.[81] In addition, other research suggests that diverse boards help firms make more effective strategic

The Board of Directors is an important internal governance mechanism. It is widely believed that increased director independence and board member diversity lead to more effective governance.

decisions and perform better over time.[82] Although questions remain about whether more independent and diverse boards enhance board effectiveness, the trends for greater independence and increasing diversity among board members are likely to continue.

10-3b Executive Compensation

The compensation of top-level managers, and especially of CEOs, generates a great deal of interest and strongly held opinions. Some believe that top-management team members and certainly CEOs have a great deal of responsibility for a firm's perform- ance and that they should be rewarded accordingly.[83] Others conclude that these individuals (and again, especially CEOs) are greatly overpaid and that their com- pensation is not as strongly related to firm performance as should be the case.[84] One of the three internal governance mechanisms attempts to deal with these issues. Specifically, **executive compensation** is a governance mechanism that seeks to align the interests of managers and owners through salaries, bonuses, and long-term incentives, such as stock awards and options.[85]

Long-term incentive plans (typically involving stock options and stock awards) are an increasingly important part of compensation packages for top-level managers, especially those leading U.S. firms. Theoretically, using long-term incentives facilitates the firm's efforts (through the board of directors' pay-related decisions) to avoid potential agency problems by linking managerial compensation to the wealth of common shareholders.[86] Effectively designed long-term incentive plans have the potential to prevent large-block stockholders (e.g., institutional investors) from pressing for changes in the composition of the board of directors and the top-management team in that they assume that when exercised, the plans will ensure that top-level managers will act in shareholders' best inter- ests. Additionally, shareholders typically assume that top-level managers' pay and the firm's performance are more properly aligned when outsiders are the dominant block of a board's membership. Research results suggesting that fraudulent behavior can be associated with stock option incentives, such as earnings manipulation,[87] demonstrate the importance of the firm's board of directors (as a governance mechanism) actively monitoring the use of executive compensation as a governance mechanism.

Effectively using executive compensation as a governance mechanism is particularly challenging for firms implementing international strategies. For example, the interests of the owners of multinational corporations may be best served by less uniformity in the firm's foreign subsidiaries' compensation plans.[88] Developing an array of unique compensa- tion plans requires additional monitoring, potentially increasing the firm's agency costs. Importantly, pay levels vary by regions of the world. For example, managerial pay is highest in the United States and much lower in Asia. Historically, compensation for top-level man- agers has been lower in India partly because many of the largest firms have strong family ownership and control.[89] Also, acquiring firms in other countries increases the complexity associated with a board of directors' efforts to use executive compensation as an effective internal corporate governance mechanism.[90]

Executive compensation is a governance mechanism that seeks to align the interests of managers and owners through salaries, bonuses, and long-term incentives such as stock awards and options.

10-3c The Effectiveness of Executive Compensation

As an internal governance mechanism, executive compensation—especially long-term incentive compensation—is complicated, for several reasons. First, the strategic decisions top-level managers make are complex and nonroutine, meaning that direct supervision (even by the firm's board of directors) is likely to be ineffective as a means of judging the quality of their decisions. The result is a tendency to link top-level managers' compensation to outcomes the board can easily evaluate, such as the firm's financial performance. This leads to a second issue in that, typically, the effects of top-level managers' decisions are stronger on the firm's long-term performance than its short-term performance. This reality makes it difficult to assess the effects of their decisions on a regular basis (e.g., annually). Third, a number of other factors affect a firm's performance besides top-level managerial decisions and behavior. Unpredictable changes in segments (economic, demographic, political/legal, etc.) in the firm's general environment (see Chapter 2) make it difficult to separate out the effects of top-level managers' decisions and the effects (both positive and negative) of changes in the firm's external environment on the firm's performance.

Properly designed and used incentive compensation plans for top-level managers may increase the value of a firm in line with shareholder expectations, but such plans are subject to managerial manipulation.[91] Additionally, annual bonuses may provide incentives to pursue short-run objectives at the expense of the firm's long-term interests. Although long-term, performance-based incentives may reduce the temptation to underinvest in the short run, they increase executive exposure to risks associated with uncontrollable events, such as market fluctuations and industry decline. The longer term the focus of incentive compensation, the greater are the long-term risks top-level managers bear. Also, because long-term incentives tie a manager's overall wealth to the firm in a way that is inflexible, such incentives and ownership may not be valued as highly by a manager as by outside investors who have the opportunity to diversify their wealth in a number of other financial investments.[92] Thus, firms may have to overcompensate for managers using long-term incentives.[93]

Even though some stock option-based compensation plans are well designed with option strike prices substantially higher than current stock prices, some have been developed for the primary purpose of giving executives more compensation. Research of stock option repricing where the strike price value of the option has been lowered from its original position suggests that action is taken more frequently in high-risk situations.[94] However, repricing also happens when firm performance is poor, to restore the incentive effect for the option. Evidence also suggests that politics are often involved, which has resulted in "option backdating."[95] While this evidence shows that no internal governance mechanism is perfect, some compensation plans accomplish their purpose. For example, recent research suggests that long-term pay designed to encourage managers to be environmentally friendly has been linked to higher success in preventing pollution.[96]

The Strategic Focus summarizes some issues regarding executive compensation and the Board's ouster of one CEO and appointment of a new one at Citigroup. Vikram Pandit was awarded compensation of $14.9 million for 2011 but this action was placed before the shareholders, 55 percent of whom voted against it. A new chair of the board was appointed who clashed with the CEO over major strategic actions he took. This CEO was forced to resign in October of 2012 and was given $6.7 million in pay for his work in 2012. The newly appointed CEO was awarded a pay package of $11.5 million in compensation for 2012. The new compensation system for Citigroup executives will more closely link pay with the performance of the bank, with shareholder value relative to peer banks and return on assets as the primary factors. As the discussion suggests, this internal governance mechanism is likely to continue receiving a great deal of scrutiny in the years to come. When designed properly and used effectively, each of the three internal governance mechanisms can contribute positively to the firm operating in ways that best serve stakeholders and

Strategic Focus

FAILURE

CEO Pay and Performance: Board Revolution at Citigroup

Vikram Pundit was appointed as CEO of Citigroup in 2007. He had to try to correct the major problems from the financial disaster that struck Citigroup and most major banking organizations in the United States. In fact, because of the poor risk management at Citigroup that resulted in major losses from collateralized debt obligations related to bad mortgages, Citigroup received the largest federal bailout to stay afloat.

Pandit brought in a new management team and set about restructuring the bank. Approximately 11,000 jobs were eliminated and some units were sold off. These actions finally produced a small profit in 2010 and a net profit of $11 billion in 2011. Although the turnaround seemed to be successful, some analysts felt that more assets should have been sold off and the bank should become smaller and more focused. Perhaps most critical is that shareholder value decreased by 89 percent during Pandit's tenure.

A new chair of the board, Michael O'Neill, was appointed in April 2012. Shareholders and the board were displeased by two major actions taken by Pandit. First, he requested approval from the Federal Reserve to return capital to shareholders through a stock buyback (such actions commonly increase the stock price) or by issuing dividends. When the Fed did not approve this request, shareholders blamed Pandit. The second action that concerned shareholders and the board was the selloff of Citigroup's stake in Morgan Stanley at a loss.

In 2012, shareholders were given a vote on the proposed compensation package for Pandit of $14.9 million and 55 percent voted against it. Additionally, Pandit clashed with new board chair O'Neill on the executive team pay packages (presumably his own as well) and for the failure of recent strategic actions.

In October 2012, Pandit was forced to resign and awarded $6.7 million for his work as CEO during 2012. Michael Corbat, a long-time employee of Citigroup, was immediately named the new CEO. Interestingly, he was given a pay package of $11.5 million in 2012, which included a $4.2 million cash bonus. The board's compensation committee consulted the major shareholders (institutional investors) who collectively own about 30 percent of the equity in the bank to determine the compensation package for Corbat. They changed the way in which Citigroup's top executives would be paid. Instead of deferred cash compensation,

Michael L. Corbat, CEO of Citigroup, arrives at the Planalto Palace before a meeting with Brazil's President, Dilma Rousseff, in Brasilia on April 9, 2013. Corbat is restructuring Citi in the wake of the forced resignation of his predecessor, Vikram Pandit.

the performance portion was composed of stock grants that vested three years in the future. The amount of stock award will be based on the bank's shareholder value relative to peer banks and to return on assets.

Although Corbat suggested that the bank was on the right path, he is expected to engage in additional restructuring. He also appointed a new top management team. After Corbat was on the job for slightly more than half a year, Citigroup's stock price was already up about 30 percent. So, he has had a strong start. Of course, he will have to perform well if he wishes to receive higher compensation and, indeed, keep his job as CEO.

Sources: M. Farrel, 2013, Citi's stock surges 30% under Corbat, *CNNMoney*, http://money.cnn.com, March 13; S. S. Patel, 2013, Citi on the right strategic path: CEO Corbat-restructuring mainly in the past, but more on tap if needed, *MarketWatch*, www.marketwatch.com, March 5; C. Isidore, 2013, Citigroup CEO Corbat's pay: $11.5 million, *CNNMoney*, http://money.cnn.com, February 22; D. Enrich, S. Kapner, & D. Fitzpatrick, 2012, Pandit is forced out at Citi, *Wall Steet Journal*, www.wsj.com, October 17; S. Schaefer, 2012, Meet the new boss: Citi taps Michael Corbat for CEO job after Pandit resigns, *Forbes*, www.forbes.com, October 16; R. Cox, M. Goldstein, & J. Horowitz, 2012, Citi's Pandit exits abruptly after board clash, *Reuters*, www.reuters.com, October 16; B. Protess, 2012, Adept moves in financial crisis clear Citigroup Chief's path to top job, *New York Times DealBook*, http://dealbook.nytimes.com, October 16; J. E. David, 2012, Meet Michael Corbat, Citigroup's new boss, CNBC.com, www.cnbc.com, October 16.

especially shareholders' interests. By the same token, because none of the three mechanisms are perfect in design or execution, the market for corporate control, an external governance mechanism, is sometimes needed.

10-4 Market for Corporate Control

The **market for corporate control** is an external governance mechanism that is active when a firm's internal governance mechanisms fail.[97] The market for corporate control is composed of individuals and firms that buy ownership positions in or purchase all of potentially undervalued corporations typically for the purpose of forming new divisions in established companies or merging two previously separate firms. Because the top-level managers are assumed to be responsible for the undervalued firm's poor performance, they are usually replaced. An effective market for corporate control ensures that ineffective and/or opportunistic top-level managers are disciplined.[98]

Commonly, target firm managers and board members are sensitive about takeover bids emanating from the market for corporate control in that being a target suggests that they have been ineffective in fulfilling their responsibilities. For top-level managers, a board's decision to accept an acquiring firm's offer typically finds them losing their jobs in that the acquirer usually wants different people to lead the firm. At the same time, rejection of an offer also increases the risk of job loss for top-level managers because the pressure from the board and shareholders for them to improve the firm's performance becomes substantial.[99]

A hedge fund is an investment fund that can pursue many different investment strategies, such as taking long and short positions, using arbitrage, and buying and selling undervalued securities for the purpose of maximizing investors' returns. Growing rapidly, in 2012 the top 100 hedge funds invested about $1.35 trillion in the United States alone.[100] Given investors' increasing desire to hold underperforming funds and their managers accountable, hedge funds have become increasingly active in the market for corporate control.[101]

In general, activist pension funds (as institutional investors and as an internal governance mechanism) are reactive in nature, taking actions when they conclude that a firm is underperforming. In contrast, activist hedge funds (as part of the market for corporate control) are proactive, "identifying a firm whose performance could be improved and then investing in it."[102] This means that "hedge funds are better at identifying undervalued companies, locating potential acquirers for them, and removing opposition to a takeover."[103]

In March 2013, investor Carl Icahn made a bid to purchase Dell. In January 2013, it was announced that Michael Dell was leading a group of investors to complete a management buyout of his company. Because of poor performance it had been the target of acquisition rumors, and the buyout is intended to avoid Dell losing control (although the stated purpose is to make the company stronger and more competitive). In announcing his bid, Icahn criticized Dell for what he believed was the firm's underperformance relative to its potential. Importantly, he criticized Dell's offer for being too low. Dell's buyout offer was for $13.65 per share. Icahn originally offered $15 per share for up to 58.1 percent of the shares. In May, Icahn teamed with Southwestern to offer $12 per share or additional Dell stock. Michael Dell's buyout team claims that Icahn is short of having the required money to complete the deal. Interestingly, in June 2013, Dell Inc. announced a 14 percent reduction in pay for its CEO, Michael Dell, because of its poor performance (declining sales, profits, and stock price). Regardless of who wins this battle, it seems that Dell's strategy failed and so did its governance system because performance continues to decline.[104]

The situation between Icahn and Dell demonstrates the possibility that the firm may have been underperforming and, as such, that the market for corporate control should be active to discipline managers and to represent shareholders' best interests. However, another

The **market for corporate control** is an external governance mechanism that is active when a firm's internal governance mechanisms fail.

M. Stasy

possibility is suggested by research results—namely, that as a governance mechanism, investors sometimes use the market for corporate control to take an ownership position in firms that are performing well.[105] A study of active corporate raiders in the 1980s showed that takeover attempts often were focused on above-average performance firms in an industry.[106] This work and other recent research suggest that the market for corporate control is an imperfect governance mechanism.[107] Actually, mergers and acquisitions are highly complex strategic actions with many purposes and potential outcomes. Some are successful and many are not—even when they have potential to do well—because implementation challenges when integrating two diverse firms can limit their ability to realize their potential.[108]

In summary, the market for corporate control is a blunt instrument for corporate governance; nonetheless, this governance mechanism does have the potential to represent shareholders' best interests. Accordingly, top-level managers want to lead their firms in ways that make disciplining by activists outside the company unnecessary and/or inappropriate.

There are a number of defense tactics top-level managers can use to fend off a takeover attempt. Managers leading a target firm that is performing well are almost certain to try to thwart the takeover attempt. Even in instances when the target firm is underperforming its peers, managers might use defense tactics to protect their own interests. In general, managers' use of defense tactics is considered to be self-serving in nature.

10-4a Managerial Defense Tactics

In the majority of cases, hostile takeovers are the principal means by which the market for corporate control is activated. A *hostile takeover* is an acquisition of a target company by an acquiring firm that is accomplished "not by coming to an agreement with the target company's management but by going directly to the company's shareholders or fighting to replace management in order to get the acquisition approved."[109] Dell's potential management buyout by Michael Dell and a team of investors is not a hostile bid because it has been initiated by management (namely Michael Dell). However, it can be considered as a defense tactic against potential hostile bids. Alternatively, Carl Icahn's offer represents a hostile takeover bid.

Firms targeted for a hostile takeover may use multiple defense tactics to fend off the takeover attempt. Increased use of the market for corporate control has enhanced the sophistication and variety of managerial defense tactics that are used in takeovers.

Because the market for corporate control tends to increase risk for managers, managerial pay may be augmented indirectly through golden parachutes (wherein a CEO can receive up to three years' salary if his or her firm is taken over). Golden parachutes, similar to most other defense tactics, are controversial. Another takeover defense strategy is traditionally known as a "poison pill." This strategy usually allows shareholders (other than the acquirer) to convert "shareholders' rights" into a large number of common shares if an individual or company acquires more than a set amount of the target firm's stock (typically 10 to 20 percent). Increasing the total number of outstanding shares dilutes the potential acquirer's existing stake, meaning that to maintain or expand its ownership position the potential acquirer must buy additional shares at premium prices. The additional purchases increase the potential acquirer's costs. Some firms amend the corporate charter so board member elections are staggered, resulting in only one third of members being up for reelection each year. Research shows that this results in managerial entrenchment and reduced vulnerability to hostile takeovers.[110] Additional takeover defense strategies are presented in Table 10.2.

Most institutional investors oppose the use of defense tactics. TIAA-CREF and CalPERS have taken actions to have several firms' poison pills eliminated. Many institutional investors also oppose severance packages (golden parachutes), and the opposition is increasing significantly in Europe as well.[111] However, an advantage to severance packages is that they may encourage top-level managers to accept takeover bids with the potential to best serve

Table 10.2 Hostile Takeover Defense Strategies

Defense strategy	Success as a strategy	Effects on shareholder wealth
Capital structure change Dilution of the target firm's stock, making it more costly for an acquiring firm to continue purchasing the target's shares. Employee stock option plans (ESOPs), recapitalization, issuance of additional debt, and share buybacks are actions associated with this strategy.	Medium	Inconclusive
Corporate charter amendment An amendment to the target firm's charter for the purpose of staggering the elections of members to its board of directors so that all are not elected during the same year. This change to the firm's charter prevents a potential acquirer from installing a completely new board in a single year.	Very low	Negative
Golden parachute A lump-sum payment of cash that is given to one or more top-level managers when the firm is acquired in a takeover bid.	Low	Negligible
Greenmail The repurchase of the target firm's shares of stock that were obtained by the acquiring firm at a premium in exchange for an agreement that the acquirer will no longer target the company for takeover.	Medium	Negative
Litigation Lawsuits that help the target firm stall hostile takeover attempts. Antitrust charges and inadequate disclosure are examples of the grounds on which the target firm could file.	Low	Positive
Poison pill An action the target firm takes to make its stock less attractive to a potential acquirer.	High	Positive
Standstill agreement A contract between the target firm and the potential acquirer specifying that the acquirer will not purchase additional shares of the target firm for a specified period of time in exchange for a fee paid by the target firm.	Low	Negative

Source: R. Campbell, C. Ghosh, M. Petrova, & C. F. Sirmans, 2011, Corporate governance and performance in the market for corporate control: The case of REITS, *Journal of Real Estate Finance & Economics*, 42: 451-480; M. Ryngaert & R. Schlten, 2010, Have changing takeover defense rules and strategies entrenched management and damaged shareholders? The case of defeated takeover bids, *Journal of Corporate Finance*, 16: 16-37; N, Ruiz-Mallorqui & D. J. Santana-Martin, 2009, Ultimate institutional owner and takeover defenses in the controlling versus minority shareholders context, *Corporate Governance: An International Review*, 17: 238-254; J. A. Pearce II & R. B. Robinson, Jr., 2004, Hostile takeover defenses that maximize shareholder wealth, *Business Horizons*, 47(5): 15-24.

shareholders' interest.[112] Alternatively, research results show that using takeover defenses reduces the amount of pressure managers feel to seek short-term performance gains, resulting in them concentrating on developing strategies with a longer time horizon and a high probability of serving stakeholders' interests. Such firms are more likely to invest in and develop innovation; when they do so, the firm's market value increases, thereby rewarding shareholders.[113]

An awareness on the part of top-level managers about the existence of external investors in the form of individuals (e.g., Carl Icahn) and groups (e.g., hedge funds) often positively influences them to align their interests with those of the firm's stakeholders, especially the shareholders. Moreover, when active as an external governance mechanism, the market for corporate control has brought about significant changes in many firms' strategies and, when used appropriately, has served shareholders' interests. Of course, the goal is to have the managers develop the psychological ownership of principals.[114]

As described in the Strategic Focus, the top-level executives at Smithfield stand to profit handsomely from the sale of the company to a Chinese firm, Shuanghui International. Their personal fortunes will increase by more than $85 million with the completion of the acquisition. They will benefit even though Smithfield has been the second worst-performing food company in the United States. It has achieved negative returns and paid shareholders no dividends for five years. Their benefits come from defense tactics that immediately vest their holdings of stock options and other stock granted for future performance increases.

Strategic Focus   GLOBALIZATION

Rewarding Top Executives of One of the Worst-Performing Food Companies in the World: The Chinese Takeover of Smithfield Foods

The proxy filing by Smithfield Foods in 2012 described how top executives of the company would profit from a change of control in the company. Specifically, if Smithfield is acquired by an external party, the senior executives of the company would have their stock options, restricted stock, and performance-based shares vest immediately. In addition, they would retain their jobs (very unusual as immediate vesting is normally allowed only when the executives lose their jobs due to the acquisition). If they lose their jobs, the benefits are even greater.

In 2012, Smithfield had $13.1 billion in annual revenues. Smithfield is vertically integrated and the largest U.S. pork producer (11 percent of its revenues are from international sales). However, the company has achieved a negative return of 18 percent over the five years ending in March 2013. It also paid no dividends to shareholders during this time. During this time, Smithfield is the second-worst performer of all U.S. food producers, with sales of more than $10 billion.

In March, one of Smithfield's largest owners, Continental Grain (it holds 6.8 percent of the company's stock), sent a letter encouraging the top executives and board to focus on creating value. The shareholders have gained little benefit in recent years with negative returns and no dividends. Competitors Tyson and Hormel have paid $429 million and $728 million in dividends, respectively, during the five years when Smithfield paid none.

A Chinese company has come to the rescue, as Shuanghui International has made an offer to acquire Smithfield and pay a 31 percent premium. Because of the "change of control" provisions, the senior executives are scheduled to receive $85.4 million if the acquisition is completed, and the executives will all be retained in their current positions. If by chance the executives' employment is terminated within two years of the acquisition, they will collectively receive a minimum of $126.4 million.

Some have expressed concerns that a Chinese company will control Smithfield. The acquisition will have to be approved by the Committee on Foreign Investment in the United States, a government group that evaluates national security risks. Others have expressed concern because of the lack of controls and scandals in the food industry in China. However, industry analysts note that pork consumption is on the decline in the United

In one of the largest-ever purchases of a U.S. firm, China's Shuanghui International entered into a deal to buy Smithfield Foods for $4.7 billion. Through this acquisition, Shuanghui International will secure a strong supply of U.S. pork for the Chinese market.

States and on the increase in China. So, Smithfield is most likely to produce pork for the Chinese market rather than import meat from China for the U.S. market. In fact, the acquisition will provide Smithfield an opportunity to sell its goods in the lucrative pork food market in China.

Unless Continental balks at the acquisition or another suitor makes a better offer, it is expected that Smithfield will be acquired by Shuanghui. And, although the senior executives have not created value for shareholders in some time, they stand to profit handsomely from the sale of their company.

Sources: T. Biesheuvel & S. Casey, 2013, Smithfield bosses to pocket $85.4 million from Chinese deal, *Charlotte Observer*, www.charlotteobserver.com, May 31; D. Kesmodel & S. Thurm, 2013, Smithfield CEO in line for big stock payout, *Wall Street Journal*, www.wsj.com, May 30; D. Thomas & O. Oran, 2013, China's appetite for pork spurs $4.7 billion Smithfield buy, *Yahoo! Finance*, http://finance.yahoo.com, May 30; K.B. Grant, 2013, Bacon backlash unlikely over Smithfield deal, *Yahoo! Finance*, http://finance.yahoo.com, May 30; S. Montlake, 2013, Why Chinese purchase of Smithfield could be game changer for pork trade, *Forbes*, www.forbes.com, May 30; P. Kavilanz, 2013, China's expensive love affair with pork, *CNNMoney*, http://money.cnn.com, May 29; S. Strom, 2013, China's food deal extends its reach, already mighty, *New York Times*, www.nytimes.com, May 29.

And their compensation will be more than 48 percent higher if they are terminated within two years after the acquisition. So, it largely ensures they will keep their jobs as well.

Next, we describe international governance practices to explain how they differ across regions and countries.

10-5 International Corporate Governance

Find out more about Tyson.
www.cengagebrain.com

Corporate governance is an increasingly important issue in economies around the world, including emerging economies. Globalization in trade, investments, and equity markets increases the potential value of firms throughout the world using similar mechanisms to govern corporate activities. Moreover, because of globalization, major companies want to attract foreign investment. For this to happen, foreign investors must be confident that adequate corporate governance mechanisms are in place to protect their investments.

Although globalization is stimulating an increase in the intensity of efforts to improve corporate governance and potentially to reduce the variation in regions and nations' governance systems,[115] the reality remains that different nations do have different governance systems in place. Recognizing and understanding differences in various countries' governance systems as well as changes taking place within those systems improves the likelihood a firm will be able to compete successfully in the international markets it chooses to enter. Next, to highlight the general issues of differences and changes taking place in governance systems, we discuss corporate governance practices in two developed economies—Germany and Japan—and in China, an emerging economy.

10-5a Corporate Governance in Germany and Japan

In many private German firms, the owner and manager may be the same individual. In these instances, agency problems are not present.[116] Even in publicly traded German corporations, a single shareholder is often dominant. Thus, the concentration of ownership is an important means of corporate governance in Germany, as it is in the United States.[117]

Historically, banks occupied the center of the German corporate governance system. This is the case in other European countries as well, such as Italy and France. As lenders, banks become major shareholders when companies they financed seek funding on the stock market or default on loans. Although the stakes are usually less than 10 percent, banks can hold a single ownership position up to but not exceeding 15 percent of the bank's capital. Although shareholders can tell banks how to vote their ownership position, they generally do not do so. The banks monitor and control managers, both as lenders and as shareholders, by electing representatives to supervisory boards.

German firms with more than 2,000 employees are required to have a two-tiered board structure that places the responsibility for monitoring and controlling managerial (or supervisory) decisions and actions in the hands of a separate group.[118] All the functions of strategy and management are the responsibility of the management board (the Vorstand); however, appointment to the Vorstand is the responsibility of the supervisory tier (the Aufsichtsrat). Employees, union members, and shareholders appoint members to the Aufsichtsrat. Proponents of the German structure suggest that it helps prevent corporate wrongdoing and rash decisions by "dictatorial CEOs." However, critics maintain that it slows decision making and often ties a CEO's hands. The corporate governance practices in Germany make it difficult to restructure companies as quickly as can be done in the United States. Because of the role of local government (through the board structure) and the power of banks in Germany's corporate governance structure, private shareholders rarely have major ownership positions in German firms. Additionally, there is a significant amount of cross-shareholdings among firms.[119] However, large institutional investors, such as pension funds (outside of banks and insurance companies), are also relatively insignificant owners of corporate stock. Thus, at least historically, German executives generally have not been dedicated to maximizing shareholder wealth to the degree that is the case for top-level managers in the United Kingdom and the United States.[120]

However, corporate governance practices used in Germany have been changing in recent years. A manifestation of these changes is that a number of German firms are gravitating toward U.S. governance mechanisms. Recent research suggests that the traditional system in Germany produced some agency costs because of a lack of external ownership power. Interestingly, German firms with listings on U.S. stock exchanges have increasingly adopted executive stock option compensation as a long-term incentive pay policy.[121]

The concepts of obligation, family, and consensus affect attitudes toward corporate governance in Japan. As part of a company family, individuals are members of a unit that envelops their lives; families command the attention and allegiance of parties throughout corporations. In addition, Japanese firms are concerned with a broader set of stakeholders than are firms in the United States, including employees, suppliers, and customers.[122] Moreover, a *keiretsu* (a group of firms tied together by cross-shareholdings) is more than an economic concept—it, too, is a family. Some believe, though, that extensive cross-shareholdings impede the type of structural change that is needed to improve the nation's corporate governance practices.[123] Consensus, another important influence in Japanese corporate governance, calls for the expenditure of significant amounts of energy to win the hearts and minds of people whenever possible, as opposed to top-level managers issuing edicts.[124] Consensus is highly valued, even when it results in a slow and cumbersome decision-making process.

As in Germany, banks in Japan have an important role in financing and monitoring large public firms.[125] Because the main bank in the keiretsu owns the largest share of stocks and holds the largest amount of debt, it has the closest relationship with a firm's top-level managers. The main bank provides financial advice to the firm and also closely monitors managers. Thus, Japan has a bank-based financial and corporate governance structure, whereas the United States has a market-based financial and governance structure.[126]

Aside from lending money, a Japanese bank can hold up to 5 percent of a firm's total stock; a group of related financial institutions can hold up to 40 percent. In many cases, main-bank relationships are part of a horizontal keiretsu. A keiretsu firm usually owns less than 2 percent of any other member firm; however, each company typically has a stake of that size in every firm in the keiretsu. As a result, 30 to 90 percent of a firm is owned by other members of the keiretsu. Thus, a keiretsu is a system of relationship investments.

Japan's corporate governance practices have been changing in recent years. For example, because of Japanese banks' continuing development as economic organizations, their role in the monitoring and control of managerial behavior and firm outcomes is less significant than in the past.[127] Also, deregulation in the financial sector has reduced the cost of mounting hostile takeovers.[128] As such, deregulation facilitated additional activity in Japan's market for corporate control, which was nonexistent in past years. And there are pressures for more changes because of weak performance by many Japanese companies. In fact, there has been significant criticism of the corporate governance practices of the Tokyo Electric Power Company after the severe problems at the Fukushima Daiichi nuclear power plant following the earthquake and tsunami in 2011. Most Japanese firms have boards that are largely composed of internal management so they reflect the upper echelon of management. As a result, these boards exercise little monitoring of the top-level managers in Japanese firms. Independent nonexecutive board members are rare but the practice is beginning to increase in Japanese firms. A recent study showed that outside directors composed about 13.5 percent of the Japanese firm boards that are listed on the Nikkei 500.[129]

10-5b Corporate Governance in China

"China has a unique and large, socialist, market-oriented economy. The government has done much to improve the corporate governance of listed companies."[130] These comments suggest that corporate governance practices in China have been changing with increasing privatization of businesses and the development of equity markets. However, the stock markets in China remain young and are continuing to develop. In their early years, these markets were weak because of significant insider trading, but with stronger governance these markets have improved.[131]

There has been a gradual decline in China in the equity held in state-owned enterprises and the number and percentage of private firms have grown, but the state still relies on direct and/or indirect controls to influence the strategies firms use. Even private firms try to develop political ties with the government because of their role in providing access to resources and to the economy.[132] In terms of long-term success, these conditions may affect firms' performance in that research shows that firms with higher state ownership tend to have lower market value and more volatility in that value across time. This is because of agency conflicts in the firms and because the executives do not seek to maximize shareholder returns given that they must also seek to satisfy social goals placed on them by the government.[133] This suggests a potential conflict between the principals, particularly the state owner and the private equity owners of the state-owned enterprises.[134]

Some evidence suggests that corporate governance in China may be tilting toward the Western model. For example, recent research shows that with increasing frequency, the compensation of top-level executives in Chinese companies is closely related to prior and current financial performance of their firm.[135] Research also shows that due to the weaker institutions, firms with family CEOs experience more positive financial performance than others without the family influence.[136]

Changing a nation's governance systems is a complicated task that will encounter problems as well as successes while seeking progress. Thus, corporate governance in Chinese companies continues to evolve and likely will for some time to come as parties (e.g., the Chinese government and those seeking further movement toward free-market economies) interact to form governance mechanisms that are best for their nation, business firms, and citizens. However, along with changes in the governance systems of specific countries, multinational companies' boards and managers are also evolving. For example, firms that have entered more international markets are likely to have more top executives with greater international experience and to have a larger proportion of foreign directors on theory boards.[137]

10-6 Governance Mechanisms and Ethical Behavior

The three internal and one external governance mechanisms are designed to ensure that the agents of the firm's owners—the corporation's top-level managers—make strategic decisions that best serve the interests of all stakeholders. In the United States, shareholders are commonly recognized as the company's most significant stakeholders. Increasingly though, top-level managers are expected to lead their firms in ways that will also serve the needs of product market stakeholders (e.g., customers, suppliers, and host communities) and organizational stakeholders (e.g., managerial and nonmanagerial employees).[138] Therefore, the firm's actions and the outcomes flowing from them should result in at least minimal satisfaction of the interests of all stakeholders. Without at least minimal satisfaction of its interests, a dissatisfied stakeholder will withdraw its support from the firm and provide it to another (e.g., customers will purchase products from a supplier offering an acceptable substitute).

Some believe that the internal corporate governance mechanisms designed and used by ethically responsible companies increase the likelihood the firm will be able to at least minimally satisfy all stakeholders' interests.[139] Scandals at companies such as Enron, WorldCom, HealthSouth, and Satyam (a large information technology company based in India), among others, illustrate the negative effects of poor ethical behavior on a firm's efforts to satisfy stakeholders. The issue of ethical behavior by top-level managers as a foundation for best serving stakeholders' interests is being taken seriously in countries throughout the word.[140]

The decisions and actions of the board of directors can be an effective deterrent to unethical behaviors by top-level managers. Indeed, evidence suggests that the most effective boards set boundaries for their firms' business ethics and values.[141] After the boundaries for ethical behavior are determined and likely formalized in a code of ethics, the board's ethics-based expectations must be clearly communicated to the firm's top-level managers and to other stakeholders (e.g., customers and suppliers) with whom interactions are necessary for the firm to produce and sell its products. Moreover, as agents of the firm's owners, top-level managers must understand that the board, acting as an internal governance mechanism, will hold them fully accountable for developing and supporting an organizational culture in which only ethical behaviors are permitted. As explained in Chapter 12, CEOs can be positive role models for improved ethical behavior.

Learn more about ethical behavior.
www.cengagebrain.com

A major issue confronted by multinational companies operating in international markets is that of bribery.[142] As a whole, countries with weak institutions that have greater bribery activity tend to have fewer exports as a result. In addition, small and medium-sized firms are the most harmed by bribery. Thus, bribery tends to limit entrepreneurial activity that can help a country's economy grow. While larger multinational firms tend to experience fewer negative outcomes, their power to exercise more ethical leadership allows them greater flexibility in selecting which markets they will enter and how they will do so.[143]

Through effective governance that results from well-designed governance mechanisms and the appropriate country institutions, top-level managers, working with others, are able to select and use strategies that result in strategic competitiveness and earning above-average returns. While some firms' governance mechanisms are ineffective, other companies are recognized for the quality of their governance activities.

World Finance evaluates the corporate governance practices of companies throughout the world. For 2013, this group's "Best Corporate Governance Awards" by country were given to Royal Bank of Canada (Canada), COSCO (China), Continental AG (Germany), Royal Philips Electronics (Netherlands), GlaxoSmithKline (United Kingdom), and AECOM (United States). These awards are determined by analyzing a number of issues concerned with corporate governance, such as board accountability and financial disclosure, executive compensation, shareholder rights, ownership base, takeover provisions, corporate behavior, and overall responsibility exhibited by the company.[144]

SUMMARY

- Corporate governance is a relationship among stakeholders that is used to determine a firm's direction and control its performance. How firms monitor and control top-level managers' decisions and actions affects the implementation of strategies. Effective governance that aligns managers' decisions with shareholders' interests can help produce a competitive advantage for the firm.

- Three internal governance mechanisms are used in the modern corporation: (1) ownership concentration, (2) the board of directors,

and (3) executive compensation. The market for corporate control is an external governance mechanism influencing managers' decisions and the outcomes resulting from them.

- Ownership is separated from control in the modern corporation. Owners (principals) hire managers (agents) to make decisions that maximize the firm's value. As risk-bearing specialists, owners diversify their risk by investing in multiple corporations with different risk profiles. Owners expect their agents (the firm's top-level managers, who are decision-making specialists) to make decisions that will help to maximize the value of their firm. Thus, modern corporations are characterized by an agency relationship that is created when one party (the firm's owners) hires and pays another party (top-level managers) to use its decision-making skills.

◼ Separation of ownership and control creates an agency problem when an agent pursues goals that conflict with the principals' goals. Principals establish and use governance mechanisms to control this problem.

◼ Ownership concentration is based on the number of large-block shareholders and the percentage of shares they own. With significant ownership percentages, such as those held by large mutual funds and pension funds, institutional investors often are able to influence top-level managers' strategic decisions and actions. Thus, unlike diffuse ownership, which tends to result in relatively weak monitoring and control of managerial decisions, concentrated ownership produces more active and effective monitoring. Institutional investors are a powerful force in corporate America and actively use their positions of concentrated ownership to force managers and boards of directors to make decisions that best serve shareholders' interests.

◼ In the United States and the United Kingdom, a firm's board of directors, composed of insiders, related outsiders, and outsiders, is a governance mechanism expected to represent shareholders' interests. The percentage of outside directors on many boards now exceeds the percentage of inside directors. Through implementation of the SOX Act, outsiders are expected to be more independent of a firm's top-level managers compared with directors selected from inside the firm. Relatively recent rules formulated and implemented by the U.S. Securities and Exchange Commission to allow owners with large stakes to propose new directors are beginning to change the balance even more in favor of outside and independent directors. Additional governance-related regulations have resulted from the Dodd-Frank Act.

◼ Executive compensation is a highly visible and often criticized governance mechanism. Salary, bonuses, and long-term

incentives are used for the purpose of aligning managers' and shareholders' interests. A firm's board of directors is responsible for determining the effectiveness of the firm's executive compensation system. An effective system results in managerial decisions that are in shareholders' best interests.

◼ In general, evidence suggests that shareholders and boards of directors have become more vigilant in controlling managerial decisions. Nonetheless, these mechanisms are imperfect and sometimes insufficient. When the internal mechanisms fail, the market for corporate control—as an external governance mechanism—becomes relevant. Although it too is imperfect, the market for corporate control has been effective resulting in corporations reducing inefficient diversification and implementing more effective strategic decisions.

◼ Corporate governance structures used in Germany, Japan, and China differ from each other and from the structure used in the United States. Historically, the U.S. governance structure focused on maximizing shareholder value. In Germany, employees, as a stakeholder group, take a more prominent role in governance. By contrast, until recently, Japanese shareholders played virtually no role in monitoring and controlling top-level managers. However, Japanese firms are now being challenged by "activist" shareholders. In China, the central government still plays a major role in corporate governance practices. Internationally, all these systems are becoming increasingly similar, as are many governance systems both in developed countries, such as France and Spain, and in transitional economies, such as Russia and India.

◼ Effective governance mechanisms ensure that the interests of all stakeholders are served. Thus, strategic competitiveness results when firms are governed in ways that permit at least minimal satisfaction of capital market stakeholders (e.g., shareholders), product market stakeholders (e.g., customers and suppliers), and organizational stakeholders (managerial and nonmanagerial employees; see Chapter 2). Moreover, effective governance produces ethical behavior in the formulation and implementation of strategies.

REVIEW QUESTIONS

1. What is corporate governance? What factors account for the considerable amount of attention corporate governance receives from several parties, including shareholder activists, business press writers, and academic scholars? Why is governance necessary to control managers' decisions?

2. What is meant by the statement that ownership is separated from managerial control in the corporation? Why does this separation exist?

3. What is an agency relationship? What is managerial opportunism? What assumptions do owners of corporations make about managers as agents?

4. How is each of the three internal governance mechanisms—ownership concentration, boards of directors, and executive compensation—used to align the interests of managerial agents with those of the firm's owners?

5. What trends exist regarding executive compensation? What is the effect of the increased use of long-term incentives on top-level managers' strategic decisions?

6. What is the market for corporate control? What conditions generally cause this external governance mechanism to become active? How does this mechanism constrain top-level managers' decisions and actions?

7. What is the nature of corporate governance in Germany, Japan, and China?

8. How can corporate governance foster ethical decisions and behaviors on the part of managers as agents?

EXPERIENTIAL EXERCISES

EXERCISE 1: WHAT IS HAPPENING TO EXECUTIVE PAY?

Your text describes executive compensation as "a governance mechanism that seeks to align the interests of managers and owners through salaries, bonuses, and long-term incentives such as stock awards and options." There is a great deal of interest in setting executive compensation for public corporations. There are those with strongly held beliefs that the system is broken and pay is out of control. Those in this camp feel that Dodd-Frank finally puts some controls in place, particularly for those whose pay increases while firm performance lags. They also argue that shareholders are not well protected. Additionally those who feel Dodd-Frank is an overreach of regulation argue that free market mechanisms should allow the proper setting of executive compensation.

The Dodd-Frank Wall Street Reform and Consumer Protection Act of 2010 contained some important regulations regarding executive compensation, in particular "say-on-pay" shareholder voting requirements and provisions that companies must disclose the relationship between executive compensation and firm performance. There also is a move to link these measures to Total Shareholder Return (TSR) as a way to align executive compensation.

Many pundits on both sides predicted significant changes to executive compensation as a result of the passage of this bill. Since a few years have passed, what has been the impact? Individually, research trends in executive compensation since the passage of the law in 2010.

Be prepared to answer the following questions:

1. What has happened to executive pay packages since passage of the act?

2. What is total shareholder return and how is it calculated? Provide an example.

3. Has there been any impact on long term incentive pay for executives?

4. Do you feel that passage of Dodd-Frank as regards executive compensation has been effective?

EXERCISE 2: GOVERNANCE: DOES IT MATTER COMPETITIVELY?

Governance mechanisms are effective when they meet the needs of all stakeholders. Governance mechanisms are also a key way in which to ensure that strategic decisions are made effectively. As a potential employee, how would you go about investigating a firm's governance structure, and would that investigation weigh in your decision to become an employee? Identify a firm that you currently

would like to join or one that you just find interesting. Working individually, research the following aspects of your target firm.

■ Find a copy of the firm's most recent proxy statement and 10-K. Proxy statements are sent to shareholders prior to each year's annual meeting and contain detailed information about the company's governance and issues on which a shareholder vote might be held. Proxy statements are typically available from a firm's Web site (look for an "Investors" submenu). You can also access proxy statements and other government filings such as the 10-K from the SEC's EDGAR database (http://www.sec.gov/edgar.shtml). Alongside the proxy you should also be able to access the firm's annual report. Here you will find information concerning performance, governance, and the firm's outlook, among other matters.

■ Identify one of the firm's main competitors for comparison. You can find one of the firm's main competitors by using company analysis tools such as Datamonitor.

Some of the topics that you should examine include:

■ Compensation plans (for both the CEO and board members–be sure to look for differences between fixed and incentive compensation)

■ Board composition (e.g., board size, insiders and outsiders, interlocking directorates, functional experience, how many active CEOs, how many retired CEOs, what is the demographic makeup, and age diversity)

■ Committees (e.g., number, composition, compensation)

■ Stock ownership by officers and directors—identify beneficial ownership from stock owned (you will need to look through the notes of the ownership tables to comprehend this)

■ Ownership concentration—how much of the firm's outstanding stock is owned by institutions, individuals, insiders? How many large-block shareholders are there (owners of 5 percent or more)?

■ Does the firm utilize a dual structure for the CEO and chair of the board?

■ Is there a lead director who is not an officer of the company?

■ Activities by activist shareholders regarding corporate governance issues of concern

■ Are there any managerial defense tactics employed by the firm? For example, what does it take for a shareholder proposal to come to a vote and be adopted?

- Does the firm have a code of ethical conduct? If so, what does it contain?

Prepare a report summarizing the results of your findings that compares your target firm and its competitor side by side. Your memo should include the following topics:

- Summarize the key aspects of the firms' governance mechanisms.

- Create a single graph covering the last 10-year historical stock performance for both companies. If applicable, find a representative index to compare both with, such as S&P or NASDAQ.

- Highlight key differences between your target firm and its competitor.

- Based on your review of the firm's governance, did you change your opinion of the firm's desirability as an employer? Why or why not? How does the target firm compare to the main competitor you identified?

VIDEO CASE

KNOWLEDGE BRINGS CORPORATE GOVERNANCE: WHISTLEBLOWING AT STAFFORD GENERAL HOSPITAL

Emphasizing targets rather than proper care, Stafford General Hospital created a culture that discouraged complaints and resulted in high mortality rates. The public campaigns of family members and relatives to vocalize their knowledge of Stafford's failures in basic nursing care stimulated government investigations, which revealed that doctors and nurses knew of the hospital's poor care and that their concerns were ignored. While whistleblower provisions were already in place, this investigation and new leadership has made quality of care a primary concern along with monetary commitments to staff, facilities, and training, and a "no blame whistleblowing policy" to bring poor practices out in the open. A 2011 Care Quality Commission inspection found a lack of suitably trained nurses in the emergency room, so the ER was closed at night for three months for staff development. In 2013 the hospital trust was almost insolvent following a 67 percent drop in the number of patients, due to a loss of confidence after the scandal. However, Stafford Hospital's mortality rate is now amongst the best within the West Midlands.

Be prepared to discuss the following concepts and questions in class:

Concepts

1. Corporate governance

2. Agency relationship

3. Market for corporate control

4. International corporate governance

Questions

1. What corporate governance mechanisms failed at Stafford General Hospital?

2. Were there possibilities of agency problems within Stafford? Why or why not? Could managerial opportunism be an issue?

3. Can the Trust Foundation for Stafford be effective as a market for corporate control?

4. What role do you think the corporate governance structure of the United Kingdom played in the problems at Stafford?

5. How do you think the situation at Stafford will impact international corporate governance?

NOTES

1. X. Castaner & N. Kavadis, 2013, Does good governance prevent bad strategy? A study of corporate governance, financial diversification, and value creation by French corporations, 2000–2006, *Strategic Management Journal*, in press; D. R. Dalton & C. M. Dalton, 2011, Integration of micro and macro studies in governance research: CEO duality, board composition, and financial performance, *Journal of Management*, 37: 404–411.

2. A. P. Cowen & J. J. Marcel, 2011, Damaged goods: Board decisions to dismiss reputationally compromised directors, *Academy of Management Journal*, 54: 509–527; I. Okhmatovskiy & R. J. David, 2012, Setting your own standards: Internal corporate governance codes as a response to institutional pressure, *Organization Science*, 23: 155–176.

3. P. J. Davis, 2013, Senior executives and their boards: Toward a more involved director, *Journal of Business Strategy*, 34(1): 3–40; G. D. Bruton, I. Filatotchev, S. Chahine, & M. Wright, 2010, Governance, ownership structure, and performance of IPO firms: The impact of different types of private equity investors and institutional environments, *Strategic Management Journal*, 31: 491–509.

4. A. T. Arikan & M. A. Schilling, 2011, Structure and governance in industrial districts: Implications for competitive advantage, *Journal of Management Studies*, 48: 772–803; D. R. Dalton, M. A. Hitt, S. T. Certo, & C. M. Dalton, 2008, The fundamental agency problem and its mitigation: Independence, equity and the market for corporate control, in J. P. Walsh and A. P. Brief (eds.),

The Academy of Management Annals, New York: Lawrence Erlbaum Associates, 1–64; E. F. Fama & M. C. Jensen, 1983, Separation of ownership and control, *Journal of Law and Economics*, 26: 301–325.

5. R. V. Aguilera, 2011, Interorganizational governance and global strategy, *Global Strategy Journal*, 1: 90–95; J. S. Harrison, D. A. Bosse, & R. A. Phillips, 2010, Managing for stakeholders, stakeholder utility functions, and competitive advantage, *Strategic Management Journal*, 31: 58–74.

6. Y. Huang, A. Chen & L. Kao, 2012, *Asia Pacific Journal of Management*, 29: 39–58; T. J. Boulton, S. B. Smart, & C. J. Zutter, 2010, IPO underpricing and international corporate governance, *Journal of International Business Studies*, 41: 206–222.

7. E. Vaara, R. Sarala, G. K. Stahl, & I. Bjorkman, 2012, The impact of organizational and national cultural differences on social conflict and knowledge transfer in international acquisitions, *Journal of Management Studies*, 49: 1–27; W. Judge, 2010, Corporate governance mechanisms throughout the world, *Corporate Governance: An International Review*, 18: 159–160.

8. A. Tan, 2011, Singapore proposes corporate governance changes to shield image, *Bloomberg Businessweek*, www.businessweek.com, June 14.

9. G. Bell, I. Filatotchev, & R. Aguilera, 2013, Corporate governance and investors' perceptions of foreign IPO value: An institutional perspective, *Academy of Management Journal*, in press; W. Kim, T. Sung, & S.-J. Wei, 2011, Does corporate governance risk at home affect investment choice abroad? *Journal of International Economics*, 85: 25–41.

10. J. Lee, 2013, Dancing with the enemy? Relational hazards and the contingent value of repeat exchanges in M&A markets, *Organization Science*, 24: 1237–1256; S. Boivie, D. Lange, M. L. McDonald, & J. D. Westphal, 2011, Me or we: The effects of CEO organizational identification on agency costs, *Academy of Management Journal*, 54: 551–576; M. A. Hitt, R. E. Hoskisson, R. A. Johnson, & D. D. Moesel, 1996, The market for corporate control and firm innovation, *Academy of Management Journal*, 45: 697–716.

11. G. E. Davis & T. A. Thompson, 1994, A social movement perspective on corporate control, *Administrative Science Quarterly*, 39: 141–173.

12. V. V. Acharya, S. C. Myers, & R. G. Rajan, 2011, The internal governance of firms, *Journal of Finance*, 66: 689–720; R. Bricker & N. Chandar, 2000, Where Berle and Means went wrong: A reassessment of capital market agency and financial reporting, *Accounting, Organizations, and Society*, 25: 529–554.

13. A. M. Colpan, T. Yoshikawa, T. Hikino, & E. G. Del Brio, 2011, Shareholder heterogeneity

and conflicting goals: Strategic investments in the Japanese electronics industry, *Journal of Management Studies*, 48: 591–618; R. M. Wiseman & L. R. Gomez-Mejia, 1999, A behavioral agency model of managerial risk taking, *Academy of Management Review*, 23: 133–153.

14. D. L. Deephouse & P. Jaskiewicz, 2013, Do family firms have better reputations than non-family firms? An integration of socioecomotional wealth and social identity theory, *Journal of Management Studies*, 50: 337–360; A. Minichilli, G. Corbetta, & I. C. MacMillan, 2010, Top management teams in family-controlled companies: 'Familiness', 'faultlines', and their impact on financial performance, *Journal of Management Studies*, 47: 205–222.

15. D. Miller, I. Le Breton-Miller, & R. Lester, 2013, Family firm governance, strategic conformity and performance: Institutional vs. strategic perspectives, *Organization Science*, in press; M. W. Peng & Y. Jiang, 2010, Institutions behind family ownership and control in large firms, *Journal of Management Studies*, 47: 253–273.

16. E. Gedajlovic, M. Carney, J. J. Chrisman, & F. W. Kellermans, 2012, The adolescence of family firm research: Taking stock and planning for the future, *Journal of Management*, 38: 1010–1037; R. C. Anderson & D. M. Reeb, 2004, Board composition: Balancing family influence in S&P 500 firms, *Administrative Science Quarterly*, 49: 209–237.

17. E. Lutz & S. Schrami, 2012, Family firms: Should they hire an outside CFO? *Journal of Business Strategy*, 33(1): 39–44; E.-T. Chen & J. Nowland, 2010, Optimal board monitoring in family-owned companies: Evidence from Asia, *Corporate Governance: An International Review*, 18: 3–17; M. Santiago-Castro & C. J. Brown, 2007, Ownership structure and minority rights: A Latin American view, *Journal of Economics and Business*, 59: 430–442.

18. J. L. Arregle, L. Naldi, M. Nordquvist, & M. A. Hitt, 2012, Internationalization of family controlled firm: A study of the effects of external involvement in governance, *Entrepreneurship Theory and Practice*, 36: 1115–1143; D. G. Sirmon, J.-L. Arregle, M. A. Hitt, & J. W. Webb, 2008, Strategic responses to the threat of imitation, *Entrepreneurship Theory and Practice*, 32: 979–998.

19. R. M. Wiseman, G. Cuevas-Rodriguez, & L. R. Gomez-Mejia, 2012, Towards a social theory of agency, *Journal of Management Studies*, 49: 202–222; G. Dushnitsky & Z. Shapira, 2010, Entrepreneurial finance meets organizational reality: Comparing investment practices and performance of corporate and independent venture capitalists, *Strategic Management Journal*, 31: 990–1017.

20. T. J. Quigley & D. C. Hambrick, 2012, When the former CEO stays on as board chair: Effects on successor discretion, strategic

change and performance, *Strategic Management Journal*, 33: 834–859; S. Machold, M. Huse, A. Minichilli, & M. Nordqvist, 2011, Board leadership and strategy involvement in small firms: A team production approach, *Corporate Governance: An International Review*, 19: 368–383.

21. T. Yoshikawa, A. A. Rasheed, & E. B. Del Brio, 2010, The impact of firm strategy and foreign ownership on executive bonus compensation in Japanese firms, *Journal of Business Research*, 63: 1254–1260; A. Mackey, 2008, The effects of CEOs on firm performance, *Strategic Management Journal*, 29: 1357–1367.

22. W. Li & Y. Lu, 2012, CEO dismissal, institutional development and environmental dynamism, *Asia Pacific Journal of Management*, 29: 1007–1026; L. L. Lan & L. Heracleous, 2010, Rethinking agency theory: The view from law, *Academy of Management Review*, 35: 294–314; Dalton, Hitt, Certo, & Dalton, 2008, The fundamental agency problem and its mitigation: Independence, equity and the market for corporate control.

23. K. Vafai, 2010, Opportunism in organizations, *Journal of Law, Economics, and Organization*, 26: 158–181; O. E. Williamson, 1996, *The Mechanisms of Governance*, New York: Oxford University Press, 6.

24. F. Lumineau & D. Malhotra, 2011, Shadow of the contract: How contract structure shapes interfirm dispute resolution, *Strategic Management Journal*, 32: 532–555; B. E. Ashforth, D. A. Gioia, S. L. Robinsson, & L. K. Trevino, 2008, Reviewing organizational corruption, *Academy of Management Review*, 33: 670–684.

25. M. L. McDonald, P. Khanna, & J. D. Westphal, 2008, Getting them to think outside the circle: Corporate governance CEOs' external advice networks, and firm performance, *Academy of Management Journal*, 51: 453–475.

26. J. Harris, S. Johnson, & D. Souder, 2013, Model theoretic knowledge accumulation: The case of agency theory and incentive alignment, *Academy of Management Review*, 38: 442–454; L. Weber & K. J. Mayer, 2011, Designing effective contracts: Exploring the influence of framing and expectations, *Academy of Management Review*, 36: 53–75.

27. T. Hutzschenreuter & J. Horstkotte, 2013, Performance effects of top management team demographic faultlines in the process of product diversification, *Strategic Management Journal*, 34: 704–726; E. Levitas, V. L. Barker, III, & M. Ahsan, 2011, Top manager ownership levels and incentive alignment in inventively active firms, *Journal of Strategy and Management*, 4: 116–135.

28. I. K. El Medi & S. Seboui, 2011, Corporate diversification and earnings management, *Review of Accounting and Finance*, 10: 176–196; P. David, J. P. O'Brien, T. Yoshikawa, &

A. Delios, 2010, Do shareholders or stakeholders appropriate the rents from corporate diversification? The influence of ownership structure, *Academy of Management Journal*, 53: 636–654; G. P. Baker & B. J. Hall, 2004, CEO incentives and firm size, *Journal of Labor Economics*, 22: 767–798.

29. S. W. Geiger & L. H. Cashen, 2007, Organizational size and CEO compensation: The moderating effect of diversification in downscoping organizations, *Journal of Managerial Issues*, 9: 233–252.

30. M. Larraza-Kintana, L. R. Gomez-Mejia, & R. M. Wiseman, 2011, Compensation framing and the risk-taking behavior of the CEO: Testing the influence of alternative reference points, *Management Research: The Journal of the Iberoamerican Academy of Management*, 9: 32–55; S. Rajgopal, T. Shevlin, & V. Zamaora, 2006, CEOs' outside employment opportunities and the lack of relative performance evaluation in compensation contracts, *Journal of Finance*, 61: 1813–1844.

31. B. Kowitt, 2013, Lockheed's secret weapon, *Fortune*, May 20, 196–204.

32. M. S. Jensen, 1986, Agency costs of free cash flow, corporate finance, and takeovers, *American Economic Review*, 76: 323–329.

33. R. E. Meyer & M. A. Hollerer, 2010, Meaning structures in a contested issue field: A topographic map of shareholder value in Austria, *Academy of Management Journal*, 53: 1241–1262; A. V. Douglas, 2007, Managerial opportunism and proportional corporate payout policies, *Managerial Finance*, 33(1): 26–42; M. Jensen & E. Zajac, 2004, Corporate elites and corporate strategy: How demographic preferences and structural position shape the scope of the firm, *Strategic Management Journal*, 25: 507–524.

34. S. F. Matusik & M. A. Fitza, 2012, Diversification in the venture capital industry: Leveraging knowledge under uncertainty, *Strategic Management Journal*, 33: 407–426; G. Kenny, 2012, Diversification: Best practices of the leading companies, *Journal of Business Strategy*, 33: (1): 12-20.

35. M. V. Shyam Kumar, 2013, The costs of related diversification: The impact of the core business on the productivity of related segments, *Organization Science*, in press; F. Neffke & M. Henning, Skill relatedness and firm diversification, *Strategic Management Journal*, 34: 297–316; M. V. S. Kumar, 2009, The relationship between product and international diversification: The effects of short-run constraints and endogeneity, *Strategic Management Journal*, 30: 99–116.

36. A. Milidonis & K. Stathopoulos, 2011, Managerial incentives, conservatism, and debt, Working paper, http://ssrn.com/abstract=1879186, July 5; D. D. Bergh, R. A. Johnson, & R.-L. Dewitt, 2008, Restructuring through spin-off or sell-off: Transforming information asymmetries into financial gain, *Strategic Management Journal*, 29: 133–148.

37. S. K. Kim, J. D. Arthurs, A. Sahaym, & J. B. Cullen, 2013, Search behavior of the diversified firm: The impact of fit on innovation, *Strategic Management Journal*, 34: 999–1009.

38. J. Kang, 2013, The relationship between corporate diversification and corporate social performance, *Strategic Management Journal*, 34: 94–109.

39. R. Duchin, 2010, Cash holdings and corporate diversification, *Journal of Finance*, 65: 955–992; E. Rawley, 2010, Diversification, coordination costs, and organizational rigidity: Evidence from microdata, *Strategic Management Journal*, 31: 873–891; T. K. Berry, J. M. Bizjak, M. L. Lemmon, & L. Naveen, 2006, Organizational complexity and CEO labor markets: Evidence from diversified firms, *Journal of Corporate Finance*, 12: 797–817.

40. R. Krause & M. Semadeni, 2013, Apprentice, departure and demotion: An examination of the three types of CEO-board chair separation, *Academy of Management Journal*, 56: 805–826.

41. J. L. Walls, P. Berrone, & P. H. Phan, 2012, Corporate governance and environmental performance: Is there really a link? *Strategic Management Journal*, 33: 885–913; C. J. Kock, J. Santalo, & L. Diestre, 2012, Corporate governance and the environment: What type of governance creates greener companies? *Journal of Management Studies*, 49: 492–514.

42. M. Hossain, S. Mitra, Z. Rezaee, & B. Sarath, 2011, Corporate governance and earnings management in the pre- and post-Sarbanes-Oxley act regimes: Evidence from implicated option backdating firms, *Journal of Accounting Auditing & Finance*, 28: 279–315; V. Chhaochharia & Y. Grinstein, 2007, Corporate governance and firm value: The impact of the 2002 governance rules, *Journal of Finance*, 62: 1789–1825.

43. Z. Singer & H. You, 2011, The effect of Section 404 of the Sarbanes-Oxley Act on earnings quality, *Journal of Accounting and Finance*, 26: 556–589; D. Reilly, 2006, Checks on internal controls pay off, *Wall Street Journal*, August 10, C3.

44. 2010, The Dodd-Frank Act: Financial reform update index, Faegre & Benson, www.faegre.com, September 7.

45. B. Appelmaum, 2011, Dodd-Frank supporters clash with currency chief, *New York Times*, www.nytimes.com, July 23.

46. M. Goranova, R. Dhanwadkar, & P. Brandes, 2010, Owners on both sides of the deal: Mergers and acquisitions and overlapping institutional ownership, *Strategic Management Journal*, 31: 1114–1135; F. Navissi & V. Naiker, 2006, Institutional ownership and corporate value, *Managerial Finance*, 32: 247–256.

47. B. L. Connelly, R. E. Hoskisson, L. Tihanyi, & S. T. Certo, 2010, Ownership as a form of corporate governance, *Journal of Management Studies*, 47: 1561–1589; M. Singh, I. Mathur, & K. C. Gleason, 2004, Governance and performance implications of diversification strategies: Evidence from large U.S. firms, *Financial Review*, 39: 489–526.

48. K. A. Desender, R. A. Aguilera, R. Crespi, & M. Garcia-Cestona, 2013, When does ownership matter? Board characteristics and behavior, *Strategic Management Journal*, 34: 823–842; J. Wu, D. Xu, & P. H. Phan, 2011, The effects of ownership concentration and corporate debt on corporate divestitures in Chinese listed firms, *Asia Pacific Journal of Management*, 28: 95–114.

49. M. van Essen, J. van Oosterhout, & P. Heugens, 2013, Competition and cooperation in corporate governance: The effects of labor institutions on blockholder effectiveness in 23 European countries, *Organization Science*, in press.

50. C. Inoue, S. Lazzarni, & A. Musacchio, 2013, Leviathan as a minority shareholder: Firm-level implications of equity purchases by the state, *Academy of Management Journal*, in press.

51. C. Singla, R. Veliyath, & R. George, 2013, Family firms and internationalization-governance relationships: Evidence of secondary agency issues, *Strategic Management Journal*, in press; S.-Y. Collin & J. Ahlberg, 2012, Blood in the boardroom: Family relationships influencing the functions of the board, *Journal of Family Business Strategy*, 3: 207–219.

52. D. Miller, A. Minichilli, & G. Corbetta, 2013, Is family leadership always beneficial? *Strategic Management Journal*, 34: 553–571; J. J. Chrisman, J. H. Chua, A. W. Pearson, & T. Barnett, 2012, Family involvement, family influence and family-centered non-economic goals in small firms, *Entrepreneurship Theory and Practice*, 36: 1103–1113.

53. A. Konig, N. Kammerlander, & A Enders, 2013, The family innovator's dilemma: How family influence affects the adoption of discontinuous technologies by incumbent firms, *Academy of Management Review*, 38: 418–441; J. J. Chrisman & P. C. Patel, 2012, Variations in R&D investments of family and nonfamily firms: Behavioral agency and myopic loss aversion perspectives, *Academy of Management Journal*, 55: 976–997; A. Stewart & M. A. Hitt, 2012, Why can't a family business be more like a nonfamily business? Modes of professionalization in family firms, *Family Business Review*, 25: 58–86.

54. A. Berle & G. Means, 1932, *The Modern Corporation and Private Property*, New York: Macmillan.

55. R. A. Johnson, K. Schnatterly, S. G. Johnson, & S.-C. Chiu, 2010, Institutional investors and institutional environment: A comparative analysis and review, *Journal*

of Management Studies, 47: 1590–1613; M. Gietzmann, 2006, Disclosure of timely and forward-looking statements and strategic management of major institutional ownership, *Long Range Planning*, 39: 409–427.

56. D. Marchick, 2011, Testimony of David Marchick—The power of pensions: Building a strong middle class and a strong economy, The Carlyle Group homepage, www.carlyle.com, July 12.

57. J. Chou, L. Ng, V. Sibilkov, & Q. Wang, 2011, Product market competition and corporate governance, *Review of Development Finance*, 1: 114–130; S. D. Chowdhury & E. Z. Wang, 2009, Institutional activism types and CEO compensation: A time-series analysis of large Canadian corporations, *Journal of Management*, 35: 5–36.

58. Y. Ertimur, F. Ferri, & S. R. Stubben, 2010, Board of directors' responsiveness to shareholders: Evidence from shareholder proposals, *Journal of Corporate Finance*, 16: 53–72; T. W. Briggs, 2007, Corporate governance and the new hedge fund activism: An empirical analysis, *Journal of Corporation Law*, 32: 681–723.

59. D. Brewster, 2009, U.S. investors get to nominate boards, *Financial Times*, www.ft.com, May 20.

60. P. Barnett, 2013, Are BlackRock's actions a sign that short-termism can be defeated? *Strategy Snack*, Strategic Management Bureau, May 23; S. Craig, 2013, The giant of shareholders, quietly stirring, *New York Times*, www.nytimes.com, May 18; 2013, About us, BlackRock, www.blackrock.com, accessed on June 6.

61. M. Hadani, M. Goranova, & R. Khan, 2011, Institutional investors, shareholder activism, and earnings management, *Journal of Business Research*, 64: 1352–1360; S. M. Jacoby, 2007, Principles and agents: CalPERS and corporate governance in Japan, *Corporate Governance*, 15: 5–15; L. Tihanyi, R. A. Johnson, R. E. Hoskisson, & M. A. Hitt, 2003, Institutional ownership differences and international diversification: The effects of boards of directors and technological opportunity, *Academy of Management Journal*, 46: 195–211.

62. S. Garg, 2013, Venture boards: Differences with public boards and implications for monitoring and firm performance, *Academy of Management Review*, in press; O. Faleye, R. Hoitash, & U. Hoitash, 2011, The costs of intense board monitoring, *Journal of Financial Economics*, 101: 160–181.

63. J. T. Campbell, T. C. Campbell, D. G. Sirmon, L. Bierman, & C. S. Tuggle, 2012, Shareholder influence over director nomination via proxy access: Implications for agency conflict and stakeholder value, *Strategic Management Journal*, 33: 1431–1451; C. M. Dalton & D. R. Dalton 2006, Corporate governance best practices: The proof is in the process, *Journal of Business Strategy*, 27(4): 5–7.

64. A. Tushke, W. G. Sanders, & E. Hernandez, 2013, Whose experience matters in the boardroom? The effects of experiential and vicarious learning on emerging market entry, *Strategic Management Journal*, in press; T. Dalziel, R. J. Gentry, & M. Bowerman, 2011, An integrated agency-resource dependence view of the influence of directors' human and relational capital on firms' R&D spending, *Journal of Management Studies*, 48: 1217–1242.

65. O. Faleye, 2011, CEO directors, executive incentives, and corporate strategic initiatives, *Journal of Financial Research*, 34: 241–277; C. S. Tuggle, D. G. Sirmon, C. R. Reutzel, & L. Bierman, 2010, Commanding board of director attention: Investigating how organizational performance and CEO duality affect board members' attention to monitoring, *Strategic Management Journal*, 31: 946–968.

66. S. Chahine, I. Filatotchev, & S. A. Zahra, 2011, Building perceived quality of founder-involved IPO firms: Founders' effects on board selection and stock market performance, *Entrepreneurship Theory and Practice*, 35: 319–335; Y. Ertimur, F. Ferri, & S. R. Stubben, 2010, Board of directors' responsiveness to shareholders: Evidence from shareholder proposals, *Journal of Corporate Finance*, 16: 53–72.

67. M. A. Valenti, R. Luce, & C. Mayfield, 2011, The effects of firm performance on corporate governance, *Management Research Review*, 34: 266–283; D. Reeb & A. Upadhyay, 2010, Subordinate board structures, *Journal of Corporate Finance*, 16: 469–486.

68. A. K. Gore, S. Matsunaga, & P. C Yeung, 2011, The role of technical expertise in firm governance structure: Evidence from chief financial officer contractual incentives, *Strategic Management Journal*, 32: 771–786; R. Duchin, J. G. Matsusaka, & O. Ozbas, 2010, *Journal of Financial Economics*, 96: 195–214.

69. A. Holehonnur & T. Pollock, 2013, Shoot for the stars? Predicting the recruitment of prestigious directors at newly public firms, *Academy of Management Journal*, in press; M. McDonald & J. Westphal, 2013, Not let in on the secret to success: How low levels of mentoring from incumbent directors negatively affect women and racial minority first-time director appointment to additional corporate boards, *Academy of Management Journal*, in press.

70. R. C. Anderson, D. M. Reeb, A. Upadhyay, & W. Zhao, 2011, The economics of director heterogeneity, *Financial Management*, 40: 5–38; S. K. Lee & L. R. Carlson, 2007, The changing board of directors: Board independence in S&P 500 firms, *Journal of Organizational Culture, Communication and Conflict*, 11(1): 31–41.

71. S. Crainer, 2011, Changing direction: One person can make a difference, *Business Strategy Review*, 22: 10–16; M. Z. Islam, 2011, Board-CEO-chair relationship, Working

paper, http://ssrn.com/abstract=1861386; R. C. Pozen, 2006, Before you split that CEO/chair, *Harvard Business Review* 84(4): 26–28.

72. M. Huse, R. E. Hoskisson, A. Zattoni, & R. Vigano, 2011, New perspectives on board research: Changing the research agenda, *Journal of Management and Governance*, 15(1): 5–28; M. Kroll, B. A. Walters, & P. Wright, 2008, Board vigilance, director experience and corporate outcomes, *Strategic Management Journal*, 29: 363–382.

73. S. Boivie, S. D. Graffin, & T. G. Pollock, 2012, Time for me to fly: Predicting director exit at large firms, *Academy of Management Journal*, 55: 1334–1359; A. Agrawal & M. A. Chen, 2011, Boardroom brawls: An empirical analysis of disputes involving directors, http://ssrn.com/abstracts=1362143.

74. S. Muthusamy, P. A. Bobinski, & D. Jawahar, 2011, Toward a strategic role for employees in corporate governance, *Strategic Change*, 20: 127–138; Y. Zhang & N. Rajagopalan, 2010, Once an outsider, always an outsider? CEO origin, strategic change, and firm performance *Strategic Management Journal*, 31: 334–346.

75. B. Baysinger & R. E. Hoskisson, 1990, The composition of boards of directors and strategic control: Effects on corporate strategy, *Academy of Management Review*, 15: 72–87.

76. D. H. Zhu, 2013, Group polarization on corporate boards: Theory and evidence on board decisions about acquisition premiums, *Strategic Management Journal*, 800–822; G. A. Ballinger & J. J. Marcel, 2010, The use of an interim CEO during succession episodes and firm performance, *Strategic Management Journal*, 31: 262–283.

77. Boivie, Graffin, & Pollock, Time for me to fly; C. Shropshire, 2010, The role of the interlocking director and board receptivity in the diffusion of practices, *Academy of Management Review*, 35: 246–264.

78. D. Carey, J. J. Keller, & M. Patsalos-Fox, 2010, How to choose the right nonexecutive board leader, *McKinsey Quarterly*, May.

79. M. K. Bednar, 2012, Watchdog or lapdog? A behavioral role view of the media as a corporate governance mechanism, *Academy of Management Journal*, 55: 131–150; D. Northcott & J. Smith, 2011, Managing performance at the top: A balanced scorecard for boards of directors, *Journal of Accounting & Organizational Change*, 7: 33–56; L. Erakovic & J. Overall, 2010, Opening the 'black box': Challenging traditional governance theorems, *Journal of Management & Organization*, 16: 250–265.

80. I. Okhmatovskiy & R. J. David, 2011, Setting your own standards: Internal corporate governance codes as a response to institutional pressure, *Organization Science*, 1–22; J. L. Koors, 2006, Director pay: A work in progress, *The Corporate Governance Advisor*, 14(5): 14–31.

81. Y. Deutsch, T. Keil, & T. Laamanen, 2007, Decision making in acquisitions: The

effect of outside directors' compensation on acquisition patterns, *Journal of Management*, 33: 30–56.

82. F. A. Gul, B. Srinidhi, & A. C. Ng, 2011, Does board gender diversity improve the informativeness of stock prices? *Journal of Accounting and Economics*, 51: 314–338; D. A. Matsa & A. R. Miller, 2011, Chipping at the glass ceiling: Gender spillovers in corporate leadership, http:// ssrn.com/abstract=1709462; A. J. Hillman, C. Shropshire, & A. A. Cannella, Jr., 2007, Organizational predictors of women on corporate boards, *Academy of Management Journal*, 50: 941–952.

83. M. van Essen, P. Heugens, J. Otten, & J. van Oosterhout, 2012, An institution-based view of executive compensation: A multilevel meta-analytic test, *Journal of International Business Studies*, 43: 396–423; M. J. Conyon, J. E. Core, & W. R. Guay, 2011, Are U.S. CEOs paid more than U.K. CEOs? Inferences from risk-adjusted pay, *Review of Financial Studies*, 24: 402–438.

84. C. Mangen & M. Magnan, 2012, "Say on pay": A wolf in sheep's clothing? *Academy of Management Perspectives*, 26 (1): 86–104; E. A. Fong, V. F. Misangyi, Jr., & H. L. Tosi, 2010, The effect of CEO pay deviations on CEO withdrawal, firm size, and firm profits, *Strategic Management Journal*, 31: 629–651; J. P. Walsh, 2009, Are U.S. CEOs overpaid? A partial response to Kaplan, *Academy of Management Perspectives*, 23(1): 73–75.

85. G. P. Martin, L. R. Gomez-Mejia, & R. M. Wiseman, 2013, Executive stock options as mixed gambles: Revisiting the behavioral agency model, *Academy of Management Journal*, 56: 451–472; K. Rehbein, 2007, Explaining CEO compensation: How do talent, governance, and markets fit in? *Academy of Management Perspectives*, 21(1): 75–77.

86. T. M. Alessandri, T. W. Tong, & J. J. Reuer, 2012, Firm heterogeneity in growth option value: The role of managerial incentives, *Strategic Management Journal*, 33: 1557–1566; D. H. M. Chng, M. S. Rodgers, E. Shih, & X.-B. Song, 2012, When does incentive compensation motivate managerial behaviors? An experimental investigation of the fit between compensation, executive core self-evaluation, and firm performance, *Strategic Management Journal*, 33: 1343–1362; D. Souder & J. M. Shaver, 2010, Constraints and incentives for making long horizon corporate investments, *Strategic Management Journal*, 31: 1316–1336.

87. E. A. Fong, 2010, Relative CEO underpayment and CEO behavior towards R&D spending, *Journal of Management Studies*, 47: 1095–1122; X. Zhang, K. M. Bartol, K. G. Smith, M. D. Pfarrer, & D. M. Khanin, 2008, CEOs on the edge: Earnings manipulations and stock-based incentive misalignment, *Academy of Management Journal*, 51: 241–258; J. P. O'Connor, R. L. Priem, J. E. Coombs, & K. M. Gilley, 2006,

Do CEO stock options prevent or promote fraudulent financial reporting? *Academy of Management Journal*, 49: 483–500.

88. Y. Du, M. Deloof, & A Jorissen, 2011, Active boards of directors in foreign subsidiaries, *Corporate Governance: An International Review*, 19: 153–168; J. J. Reuer, E. Klijn, F. A. J. van den Bosch, & H. W. Volberda, 2011, Bringing corporate governance to international joint ventures, *Global Strategy Journal*, 1: 54–66; K. Roth & S. O'Donnell, 1996, Foreign subsidiary compensation: An agency theory perspective, *Academy of Management Journal*, 39: 678–703.

89. B. Balasubramanian, B. S. Black, & V. Khanna, 2010, The relation between firm-level corporate governance and market value: A study of India, University of Michigan working paper series; A. Ghosh, 2006, Determination of executive compensation in an emerging economy: Evidence from India, *Emerging Markets, Finance & Trade*, 42(3): 66–90.

90. M. Ederhof, 2011, Incentive compensation and promotion-based incentives of mid-level managers: Evidence from a multinational corporation, *The Accounting Review*, 86: 131–154; C. L. Staples, 2007, Board globalization in the world's largest TNCs 1993–2005, *Corporate Governance*, 15: 311–332.

91. G. Pandher & R. Currie, 2013, CEO compensation: A resource advantage and stakeholder-bargaining perspective, *Strategic Management Journal*, 34: 22–41; Y. Deutsch, T. Keil, & T. Laamanen, 2011, A dual agency view of board compensation: The joint effects of outside director and CEO stock options on firm risk, *Strategic Management Journal*, 32: 212–227; P. Kalyta, 2009, Compensation transparency and managerial opportunism: A study of supplemental retirement plans, *Strategic Management Journal*, 30: 405–423.

92. R. Krause, K. Whitler, & M. Semadeni, 2013, Power to the principals! An experimental look at shareholder say-on-pay voting, *Academy of Management Journal*, in press; L. K. Meulbroek, 2001, The efficiency of equity-linked compensation: Understanding the full cost of awarding executive stock options, *Financial Management*, 30(2): 5–44.

93. 2013, The experts: Do companies spend too much on 'superstar' CEOs? *Wall Street Journal*, www.wsj.com, March 14.

94. Z. Dong, C. Wang, & F. Xie, 2010, Do executive stock options induce excessive risk taking? *Journal of Banking & Finance*, 34: 2518–2529; C. E. Devers, R. M. Wiseman, & R. M. Holmes, Jr., 2007, The effects of endowment and loss aversion in managerial stock option valuation, *Academy of Management Journal*, 50: 191–208.

95. D. Anginer, M. P. Narayanan, C. A. Schipani, & H. N. Seyhun, 2011, Should size matter when regulating firms? Implications from

backdating of executive options, Ross School of Business working paper; T. G. Pollock, H. M. Fischer, & J. B. Wade, 2002, The role of politics in reprising executive options, *Academy of Management Journal*, 45: 1172–1182.

96. P. Berrone & L. R. Gomez-Mejia, 2009, Environmental performance and executive compensation: An integrated agency-institutional perspective, *Academy of Management Journal*, 52: 103–126.

97. V. V. Acharya, S. C. Myers, & R. G. Rajan, 2011, The internal governance of firms, *Journal of Finance*, 66: 689–720; R. Sinha, 2006, Regulation: The market for corporate control and corporate governance, *Global Finance Journal*, 16: 264–282.

98. T. Laamanen, M. Brauer, & O. Junna, 2013, Performance of divested assets: Evidence from the U.S. software industry, *Strategic Management Journal*, in press; T. Yoshikawa & A. A. Rasheed, 2010, Family control and ownership monitoring in family-controlled firms in Japan, *Journal of Management Studies*, 47: 274–295; R. W. Masulis, C. Wang, & F. Xie, 2007, Corporate governance and acquirer returns, *Journal of Finance*, 62: 1851–1889.

99. C. Devers, G. McNamara, J. Haleblian & M. Yoder, 2013, Do they walk the talk or just talk the talk? Gauging acquiring CEO and director confidence in the value-creation potential of announced acquisitions, *Academy of Management Journal*, in press; P.-X. Meschi & E. Metais, 2013, Do firms forget about their past acquisitions? Evidence from French acquisitions in the United States (1988–2006), *Journal of Management*, 39: 469–495; J. A. Krug & W. Shill, 2008, The big exit: Executive churn in the wake of M&As, *Journal of Business Strategy*, 29(4): 15–21.

100. 2013, Hedge fund 100 ranking, Institutional Investors Alpha, www. institutionalinvestorsalpha.com, accessed on June 7.

101. N. M. Boyson & R. M. Mooradian, 2011, Corporate governance and hedge fund activism, *Review of Derivatives Research*, 169–204; L. A. Bebchuk & M. S. Weisbach, 2010, The state of corporate governance research, *Review of Financial Studies*, 23: 939–961; T. W. Briggs, 2007, Corporate governance and a new hedge fund activism, *Empirical Analysis*, 32: 681–723.

102. S. Bainbridge, 2011, Hedge funds as activist investors, *ProfessorBainbridge.com*, www. professorbainbridge.com, March 21.

103. R. Greenwood, 2007, The hedge fund as activist, HBR Working knowledge, www. hbrworkingknowledge.com, August 22.

104. S. Saitto, 2013, Dell projects Icahn buyout has a $3.9 funding gap, *Bloomberg*, www. bloomberg.com, June 5; A. Ricadela, 2013, Dell trims CEO's pay by 14% as performance slips ahead of buyout, *Bloomberg*, www. bloomberg.com, June 4.

105. M. L. Humphery-Jenner & R. G. Powell, 2011, Firm size, takeover profitability, and the

effectiveness of the market for corporate control: Does the absence of anti-takeover provisions make a difference? *Journal of Corporate Finance*, 17: 418–437; K. Ruckman, 2009, Technology sourcing acquisitions: What they mean for innovation potential, *Journal of Strategy and Management*, 2: 56–75.

106. J. P. Walsh & R. Kosnik, 1993, Corporate raiders and their disciplinary role in the market for corporate control, *Academy of Management Journal*, 36: 671–700.

107. M. Schijven & M. A. Hitt, 2012, The vicarious wisdom of crowds: Toward a behavioral perspective on investor reactions to acquisition announcements, *Strategic Management Journal*, 33: 1247–1268; J. Haleblian, C. E. Devers, G. McNamara, M. A. Carpenter, & R. B. Davison, 2009, Taking stock of what we know about mergers and acquisitions: A review and research agenda, *Journal of Management*, 35: 469–502.

108. F. Bauer & K. Matzler, 2013, Antecedents of M&A success: The role of strategic complementarity, cultural fit and degree and speed of integration, *Strategic Management Journal*, in press; S. Mingo, 2013, The impact of acquisitions on the performance of existing organizational units In the acquiring firm: The case of the agribusiness company, *Management Science*, in press; A. Sleptsov, J. Anand, & G. Vasudeva, 2013, Relational configurations with information intermediaries: The effect of firm-investment bank ties on expected acquisition performance, *Strategic Management Journal*, in press.

109. 2013, Hostile takeover, *Investopedia*, www. investopedia.com, accessed on June 7.

110. P. Jiraporn & Y. Liu, 2011, Staggered boards, accounting discretion and firm value, *Applied Financial Economics*, 21: 271–285; O. Faleye, 2007, Classified boards, firm value, and managerial entrenchment, *Journal of Financial Economics*, 83: 501–529.

111. T. Sokoly, 2011, The effects of antitakeover provisions on acquisition targets, *Journal of Corporate Finance*, 17: 612–627; M. Martynova & L. Renneboog, 2010, A corporate governance index: Convergence and diversity of national corporate governance regulations, http://ssrn.com/ abstract=1557627; 2007, Leaders: Pay slips; management in Europe, *Economist*, June 23, 14.

112. J. A. Pearce II & R. B. Robinson, Jr., 2004, Hostile takeover defenses that maximize shareholder wealth, *Business Horizons* 47(5): 15–24.

113. M. Humphery-Jenner, 2013, Takeover defenses, innovation and value creation: Evidence from acquisition decisions, *Strategic Management Journal*, in press; A. Kacperzyk, 2009, With greater power comes greater responsibility? Takeover protection and corporate attention to stakeholders, *Strategic Management Journal*, 30: 261–285.

114. P. Sieger, T. Zellweger, & K. Aquino, 2013, Turning agents into psychological principals: Aligning interests of non-owners through psychological ownership, *Journal of Management Studies*, 50: 361–388.

115. I. Haxhi & H. Ees, 2010, Explaining diversity in the worldwide diffusion of codes of good governance, *Journal of International Business Studies*, 41: 710–726; P. Witt, 2004, The competition of international corporate governance systems—a German perspective, *Management International Review*, 44: 309–333.

116. J. Block & F. Spiegel, 2011, Family firms and regional innovation activity: Evidence from the German Mittelstand, http://ssrn.com/ abstract=1745362.

117. S. K. Bhaumik & A. Gregoriou, 2010, 'Family' ownership, tunneling and earnings management: A review of the literature, *Journal of Economic Surveys*, 24: 705–730; A. Tuschke & W. G. Sanders, 2003, Antecedents and consequences of corporate governance reform: The case of Germany, *Strategic Management Journal*, 24: 631–649; J. Edwards & M. Nibler, 2000, Corporate governance in Germany: The role of banks and ownership concentration, *Economic Policy*, 31: 237–268.

118. Tuschke, Sanders, & Hernandez, Whose experience matters in the boardroom?; D. Hillier, J. Pinadado, V. de Queiroz, & C. de la Torre, 2010, The impact of country-level corporate governance on research and development, *Journal of International Business Studies*, 42: 76–98.

119. Tuschke, Sanders, & Hernandez, Whose experience matters in the boardroom?

120. J. T. Addison & C. Schnabel, 2011, Worker directors: A German product that did not export? *Industrial Relations: A Journal of Economy and Society*, 50: 354–374; P. C. Fiss & E. J. Zajac, 2004, The diffusion of ideas over contested terrain: The (non)adoption of a shareholder value orientation among German firms, *Administrative Science Quarterly*, 49: 501–534.

121. A. Chizema, 2010, Early and late adoption of American-style executive pay in Germany: Governance and institutions, *Journal of World Business*, 45: 9–18; W. G. Sanders & A. C. Tuschke, 2007, The adoption of the institutionally contested organizational practices: The emergence of stock option pay in Germany, *Academy of Management Journal*, 50: 33–56.

122. F. Allen & M. Zhao, 2007, The corporate governance model of Japan: Shareholders are not rulers, working paper, University of Pennsylvania, www.finance.wharton. upenn.edu (a version also appears in *Peking University Business Review*, 2007).

123. 2010, Japan: Principles of corporate governance, *eStandards Forum*, www. estandardsforum.org, May.

124. D. R. Adhikari & K. Hirasawa, 2010, Emerging scenarios of Japanese corporate management, *Asia-Pacific Journal of Business Administration*, 2: 114–132; M. A. Hitt, H. Lee, & E. Yucel, 2002, The importance of social capital to the management of multinational enterprises: Relational networks among Asian and Western firms, *Asia Pacific Journal of Management*, 19: 353–372.

125. W. P. Wan, D. W. Yiu, R. E. Hoskisson, & H. Kim, 2008, The performance implications of relationship banking during macroeconomic expansion and contraction: A study of Japanese banks' social relationships and overseas expansion, *Journal of International Business Studies*, 39: 406–427.

126. P. M. Lee & H. M. O'Neill, 2003, Ownership structures and R&D investments of U.S. and Japanese firms: Agency and stewardship perspectives, *Academy of Management Journal*, 46: 212–225.

127. X. Wu & J. Yao, 2012, Understanding the rise and decline of the Japanese main bank system: The changing effects of bank rent extraction, *Journal of Banking & Finance*, 36: 36–50; I. S. Dinc, 2006, Monitoring the monitors: The corporate governance in Japanese banks and their real estate lending in the 1980s, *Journal of Business*, 79: 3057–3081.

128. K. Kubo & T. Saito, 2012, The effect of mergers on employment and wages: Evidence from Japan, *Journal of the Japanese and International Economics*, 26: 263–284; N. Isagawa, 2007, A theory of unwinding of cross-shareholding under managerial entrenchment, *Journal of Financial Research*, 30: 163–179.

129. B. Tricker, 2011, Tokyo Electric Power and the disaster at Fukushima Daiichi, Corporate Governance Blog, Oxford University Press, http://corporategovernanceoup.wordpress. com, April 20.

130. J. Yang, J. Chi, & M. Young, 2011, A review of corporate governance in China, *Asian-Pacific Economic Literature*, 25: 15–28.

131. H. Berkman, R. A. Cole, & L. J. Fu, 2010, Political connections and minority-shareholder protection: Evidence from securities-market regulation in China, *Journal of Financial and Quantitative Analysis*, 45: 1391–1417; S. R. Miller, D. Li, E. Eden, & M. A. Hitt, 2008, Insider trading and the valuation of international strategic alliances in emerging stock markets, *Journal of International Business Studies*, 39: 102–117.

132. W.A. Li & D.T. Yan, 2013, Transition from administrative to economic model of corporate governance, *Nankai Business Review International*, 4: 4–8.

133. J. Chi, Q. Sun, & M. Young, 2011, Performance and characteristics of acquiring firms in the Chinese stock markets, *Emerging Markets Review*, 12: 152–170; Y.-L. Cheung, P. Jiang, P. Limpaphayom, & T. Lu, 2010, Corporate governance in China: A step forward, *European Financial Management*, 16: 94–123; H. Zou & M. B. Adams, 2008, Corporate

ownership, equity risk and returns in the People's Republic in China, *Journal of International Business Studies*, 39: 1149–1168.

134. J. Li & C. Qian, 2013, Principal-principal conflicts under weak institutions: a study of corporate takeovers in China, *Strategic Management Journal*, 34: 498–508; S. Globerman, M. W. Peng, & D. M. Shapiro, 2011, Corporate governance and Asian companies, *Asia Pacific Journal of Management*, 28: 1–14.

135. P. Adithipyangkul, I. Alon, & T. Zhang, 2011, Executive perks: Compensation and corporate performance in China, *Asia Pacific Journal of Management*, 28: 401–425; T. Buck, X. Lui, & R. Skovoroda, 2008, Top executives' pay and firm performance in China, *Journal of International Business Studies*, 39: 833–850.

136. A. Cai, J.-H. Luo, & D.-F. Wan, 2012, Family CEOs: Do they benefit firm governance In China? *Asia Pacific Journal of Management*, 29: 923–947.

137. I. Oxelheim, A. Gregoric, T. Randoy, & S. Thomsen, 2013, On the internationalization of corporate boards: The case of Nordic firms, *Journal of International Business Studies*, 44: 173–194.

138. S. Muthusamy, P. A. Bobinski, & D. Jawahar, 2011, Toward a strategic role for employees in corporate governance, *Strategic Change*, 20: 127–138; T. Tse, 2011, Shareholder and stakeholder theory: After the financial crisis, *Qualitative Research in Financial Markets*, 3(1): 51–63; C. Shropshire & A. J. Hillman, 2007, A longitudinal study of significant change in stakeholder management, *Business & Society*, 46(1): 63–87.

139. J. M. Schaubroeck, S. T. Hannah, B. J. Avolio, S. W. J. Kozlowski, R. G. Lord, L. K. Trevino, N. Dimotakis, & A. C. Peng, 2012, Embedding ethical leadership within and across organizational levels, *Academy of Management Journal*, 55: 1053–1078; R. A. G. Monks & N. Minow, 2011, *Corporate governance*, 5th ed., New York: John Wiley & Sons.

140. J. S. Chun, Y. Shin, J. N. Choi, & M. S. Kim, 2013, How does corporate ethics contribute to firm financial performance? The mediating role of collective organizational commitment and organizational citizenship behavior, *Journal of Management*, 39: 853–877; S. P. Deshpande, J. Joseph, & X. Shu, 2011, Ethical climate and managerial success in China, *Journal of Business Ethics*, 99: 527–534.

141. A. P. Cowan & J. J. Marcel, 2011, Damaged goods: Board decisions to dismiss reputationally compromised directors, *Academy of Management Journal*, 54: 509–527; J. R. Knapp, T. Dalziel, & M. W. Lewis, 2011, Governing top managers: Board control, social categorization, and their unintended influence on discretionary behaviors, *Corporate Governance: An International Review* 19: 295–310.

142. Y. Jeong & R. J. Weiner, 2012, Who bribes? Evidence from the United Nations' oil-for-food program, *Strategic Management Journal*, 33: 1363–1383.

143. S.-H. Lee & D. H. Weng, 2013, Does bribery in the home country promote or dampen firm exports? *Strategic Management Journal*, in press; J. O. Zhou & M. W. Peng, 2012, Does bribery help or hurt firm growth around the world? *Asia Pacific Journal of Management*, 29: 907–921.

144. 2013, Corporate governance awards 2013, *World Finance*, www.worldfinance.com/awards, March 13.

11

Organizational Structure and Controls

Studying this chapter should provide you with the strategic management knowledge needed to:

1 Define organizational structure and controls and discuss the difference between strategic and financial controls.

2 Describe the relationship between strategy and structure.

3 Discuss the functional structures used to implement business-level strategies.

4 Explain the use of three versions of the multidivisional (M-form) structure to implement different diversification strategies.

5 Discuss the organizational structures used to implement three international strategies.

6 Define strategic networks and discuss how strategic center firms implement such networks at the business, corporate, and international levels.

BIG-BOX RETAILERS STRUGGLE TO CHANGE THEIR STRATEGIES AND STRUCTURES IN THE FACE OF ONLINE COMPETITION

A string of big-box retailers in consumer electronics and books have suffered bankruptcies due to the changing nature of competition in the retail sector. CompUSA closed through bankruptcy in 2008. This was followed by Circuit City's bankruptcy in November 2008, and its final door closings in March 2009. Borders, one of the original big-box booksellers, declared bankruptcy in 2011.

Early in its history, Borders had a well-developed inventory system and was popular, and the company began to take market share from independent book retailers. However, Borders began to make mistakes when Amazon.com's success at selling books on the Internet led it to diversification growth initiatives, such as its push into international markets. Borders seemed unable to structure its operations in a way that would allow different businesses in each country to market

effectively. Borders seemed to have an insular and centralized management structure that was impervious to changes in the market. For example, when Barnes & Noble developed the capability to sell online, Borders signed an agreement with Amazon to handle its Internet sales. This was great for Amazon but a disaster for Borders because it sent customers and business to a major competitor. Not only does a company need to change its strategy appropriately, but it must also facilitate the management structure in a way that improves the implementation of the strategy. Although Barnes & Noble has done better than Borders, primarily because of its online strategy and through its NOOK reader and eBook store, its sales decreased in 2012, although its net income was still positive. Getting the strategy and structural emphases right between retail sales, NOOK sales, and Web site sales is a continuing challenge.

Getting the strategy and management structure emphases right is also a challenge for consumer electronics retailer Best Buy. Relative to Amazon, Best Buy has a number of disadvantages to which it is trying to adjust its management structure to get an appropriate mix. Amazon began as an online bookseller and had an earlier impact on Borders and Barnes & Noble because of its approach and its successful Kindle and Kindle Fire devices. Amazon eventually expanded its offerings into consumer electronics and many other department store products such as toys and furniture. Amazon played a large role in popularizing online shopping. Relative to big-box retailers, it has a number of advantages. Its virtual stores are much less costly than the brick and mortar buildings used by big-box retailers such as Best Buy. With no physical stores, Amazon incurs lower costs in leasing relative to long-term leases, labor costs, insurance, utilities, and other expenses associated with negotiating real estate and build-ings for brick and mortar stores. It also has an efficient logistics network and distribution system with efficient warehousing. Interestingly, because Amazon does not operate physical stores with a location, it has traditionally been exempt from charging state sales taxes. As such, these cost differentials have allowed the company to offer lower prices and thus undercut sales available to brick and mortar stores such as Best Buy. Furthermore, Amazon has built its customer service to improve the shopping experience for its customers. It follows up to make sure that customers are satisfied with their purchases and offers hassle-free return policies. Best Buy, on the other hand, has frustrated customers through restocking fees if a return is sought. Amazon also has encouraged buyers to submit reviews on products purchased. This approach has been able to substitute somewhat for in-store customer sales representatives that provide advice to custom-ers about which products to purchase.

Because consumer electronic products are visible in stores like Best Buy and Walmart, a new term has developed called "showrooming." This is where shoppers go to a brick and mortar store such as Best Buy and look at products and handle them, and then buy them online. In fact, there was a "price check mobile phone app" that appeared in 2011 which allowed in-store shoppers to scan and search a product and then immediately price-compare with Amazon.com or other online merchants. Best Buy and others responded with "price match guarantee" approaches. Also, brick and mortar stores are fighting back through customized technology and store-within-a-store concepts. Reebok, for instance, installed a build-your-own-sneakers kiosk in many brick and mortar shoe stores. Best Buy has recently signed a deal with Samsung to have a store-within-a-store approach to peddle Samsung consumer electronic products. Overall, the shopping public is turning to more digital experiences, especially for the age 40 and under shopper, and this approach may need to be developed by brick and mortar stores to update and improve in-store experiences.

Best Buy has tried an experiment internationally as well. In 2008, it formed a joint venture dubbed Best Buy Europe with Carphone Warehouse Europe, an independent mobile phone seller in Europe, where they initially planned to build American-style big-box electronic stores. However, this plan was aborted in 2011. As such, it has retreated from Europe, selling its 50 percent interest in this joint venture for $755 million and reporting a $200 million charge in 2013. This sale was spurred by its new CEO, Hubert Joly. However, Best Buy announced that it is not going to pull back from other international ventures such as those in Mexico, Canada, and China.

Best Buy is also seeking to increase revenue through better store space optimization and introducing a better Web-based platform to increase traffic and conversion rates through Inter-net sales. The change in strategy seems to be working, with the first quarter of 2013 showing the company's same-store U.S. sales increased for the first time in over a year. This change has also taken place because of a new leader, senior vice president Shawn Score, who has helped to improve the in-store shopping experience. This is very important because the retailer still drives more than 90 percent of its $50 billion in annual revenue from stores.

Although Best Buy wants to make changes through leadership and adjusting its strategy, it also needs to make structural changes as it implements this strategy through better control systems. It needs to monitor the number of sales it makes in each brick and mortar store, and those that it loses to online sales. Hopefully, its online sales will pick up after a customer comes to its online store. Best Buy estimates that roughly 20 percent of all consumer electron-ics are now bought online. As such, it needs to improve its online product descriptions and selections and reduce its high operating cost. Although its recent sales closure rate hasn't improved, customer satisfaction scores have ticked up. However, it confronts a high staff turnover rate. Staff turnover was around 60 percent in 2012, although it has eased a bit more recently. The historical average is 35 percent. As such, it needs to do a better job of struc-turally managing its human capital. Otherwise, consumers will go to online sources to get product information rather than from their sales staff. It remains to be seen whether Best Buy will be able to survive the online competition; however, recently it won a battle over legisla-tion reducing the sales tax cost differential that Amazon has enjoyed versus brick and mortar stores. Best Buy's turnaround, so far, has been effective, but it remains to be seen whether it will make the right adjustments to survive and avoid bankruptcy such as those of CompUSA, Circuit City, and Borders.

Sources: G. Colvin, 2013, Your business model doesn't work anymore, *Fortune*, February 25, 42; S. Jakab, 2013, Best Buy's comeback story worth a read, *Wall Street Journal*, www.wsj.com, May 20; J. Lahart, 2013, You needn't be best to be a buy, *Wall Street Journal*, May 1, C16; J. Milliot, 2013, Barnes & Noble at the crossroads, *Publishers Weekly*, March 4, 6; C. O'Connor, 2013, Game on, Amazon! eBay rolls out one-hour delivery, targeting the Web and Wal-Mart, *Forbes*, May 7, 16; E. Savitz, 2013, Best Buy: Barclays, Stifel see turnaround, boost ratings, *Forbes*, www.forbes.com, February 19; D. Wolfe, 2013, Citi to buy $7 billion Best Buy card portfolio from Capital One, *American Banker*, February 20, 3; A. Zimmerman, 2013, Best Buy sells Europe business back to Carphone Warehouse, *Wall Street Journal*, www.wsj.com, April 30; A. Zimmerman, 2013, Can this former clerk save Best Buy? – Executive hopes to address 'pain points' that drive customers away, and reduce staff turnover, *Wall Street Journal*, April 26, B1; H. E. Combs, 2012, Best Buy's decline shows need to evaluate online strategies, *Furniture/Today*, September 19, 40.

As we explained in Chapter 4, all firms use one or more business-level strategies. In Chapters 6 through 9, we discuss other strategies firms may choose to use (corporate-level, international, and cooperative). After they are selected, strategies must be implemented effectively to make them work. Organizational structure and controls, this chapter's topic, provide the framework within which strategies are implemented and used in both for-profit organizations and not-for-profit agencies.[1] However, as we explain, separate structures and controls are required to successfully implement different strategies. In all organizations, top-level managers have the final responsibility for ensuring that the firm has matched each of its strategies with the appropriate organizational structure and that both change when necessary. Thus, the CEO of Best Buy, as illustrated in the Opening Case, is responsible for changing its organizational structure to effectively implement its business or corporate-level strategies to adjust to its competitive challenges. The match or degree of fit between strategy and structure influences the firm's attempts to earn above-average returns.[2] Thus, the ability to select an appropriate strategy and match it with the appropriate structure is an important characteristic of effective strategic leadership.[3]

Learn more about **Barnes & Noble.** www.cengagebrain.com

Best Buy, eBay, and Staples have different challenges and have employed different strategies and different implementation approaches given the strategies selected. For example, eBay is in a different strategic position relative to Amazon. While Amazon competes directly with brick and mortar retail stores such as Best Buy, eBay has chosen to be an outlet of choice to support the Internet selling strategies of traditional brick and mortar retailers. Such stores can partner with eBay to develop an improved online strategy. This approach has helped eBay to improve its business model from its decline in consumer online auctions. Also, Staples has been protected somewhat from the retailing competition with Amazon because its main focus is on business customers rather than consumers. They are not as likely to use all the online information available the way consumers do and would rather have a high assortment of products and delivery convenience, which Staples provides for them. Also, Staples has been developing its online product base and has over 100,000 items available online as additional protection.[4]

Given their bankruptcies, it is clear that CompUSA, Circuit City, and Borders failed in their implementation approaches. As illustrated in the opening case, the jury is still out on Best Buy; in 2006 Best Buy was known as a well-run company, but now it is fighting for competitive parity with Amazon—if not survival. First, its decision to enter international markets likely failed because of poor implementation and management of international operations. Perhaps the fine tuning of its new leadership practices will help, but regional and even individual store adjustments will be needed. If it becomes overly centralized in its approach as did Borders, this may cause problems. If it is too decentralized, then the changes made may create disunity in the sales experience. Strategic management scholar Richard Rumelt sums up the problems challenging organizations such as Best Buy in his statement that "… weakly managed organizations tend to become less organized and focused."[5]

General Electric's Chairman and CEO, Jeffrey Immelt, delivers opening remarks during the company's four-day event, "American Competitiveness: What Works." As part of its "Hire Our Heroes" program, GE says it will hire 5,000 veterans over the next five years and invest $580 million to expand its aviation business.

This chapter opens with an introduction to organizational structure and controls. We then provide more details about the need for the firm's strategy and structure to be properly matched. Affecting firms' efforts to match strategy and structure is their influence on each other.[6] As we discuss, strategy has a more important influence on structure, although once in place, structure influences strategy.[7] Next, we describe the relationship between growth and structural change successful firms experience. We then discuss the different organizational structures firms use to implement separate business-level, corporate-level, international, and cooperative strategies. A series of figures highlights the different structures firms match with strategies. Across time and based on their experiences, organizations, especially large and complex ones, customize these general structures to meet their unique needs.[8] Typically, the firm tries to form a structure that is complex enough to facilitate use of its strategies but simple enough for all parties to understand and implement.[9] When strategies become more diversified, a firm must adjust its structure to deal with the increased complexity.

11-1 Organizational Structure and Controls

Research shows that organizational structure and the controls that are a part of the structure affect firm performance.[10] In particular, evidence suggests that performance declines when the firm's strategy is not matched with the most appropriate structure and controls.[11] Even though mismatches between strategy and structure do occur, research indicates that managers try to act rationally when forming or changing their firm's structure.[12] His record of success at General Electric (GE) suggests that CEO Jeffrey Immelt pays close attention to the need to make certain that strategy and structure remain matched, as evidenced by restructuring alignments in GE Capital, GE's financial services group, during the economic downturn. Since the downturn, GE Capital has shrunk by over a third; it previously accounted for 46 percent of GE's earnings. Immelt wants to reduce that to 30 percent while increasing the focus on the industrial businesses.[13]

11-1a Organizational Structure

Organizational structure specifies the firm's formal reporting relationships, procedures, controls, and authority and decision-making processes.[14] Developing an organizational structure that effectively supports the firm's strategy is difficult, especially because of the uncertainty (or unpredictable variation) about cause-effect relationships in the global economy's rapidly changing competitive environments.[15] When a structure's elements (e.g., reporting relationships, procedures, etc.) are properly aligned with one another, the structure facilitates effective use of the firm's strategies. Thus, organizational structure is a critical component of effective strategy implementation processes.[16]

A firm's structure specifies the work to be done and how to do it, given the firm's strategy or strategies. Thus, organizational structure influences how managers work and the decisions resulting from that work. Supporting the implementation of strategies, structure

Organizational structure specifies the firm's formal reporting relationships, procedures, controls, and authority and decision-making processes.

is concerned with processes used to complete organizational tasks.[17] Having the right structure and process is important. For example, many product-oriented firms have been moving to develop service businesses associated with those products. As we learned in Chapter 6, GE is a successful diversified firm. The service extension strategy has been used by GE, for example, in financial services and oil and gas equipment services. However, research suggests that developing a separate division for such services in product-oriented companies, rather than managing the service business within the product divisions, leads to additional growth and profitability in the service business. GE developed a separate division for its financial services businesses. This helped facilitate GE's growth over the last two decades, although this business has been shrinking given the financial downturn.[18]

Effective structures provide the stability a firm needs to successfully implement its strategies and maintain its current competitive advantages while simultaneously providing the flexibility to develop advantages it will need in the future.[19] *Structural stability* provides the capacity the firm requires to consistently and predictably manage its daily work routines[20] while *structural flexibility* provides the opportunity to explore competitive possibilities and then allocate resources to activities that will shape the competitive advantages the firm will need to be successful in the future.[21] An effectively flexible organizational structure allows the firm to *exploit* current competitive advantages while *developing* new ones that can potentially be used in the future.[22] Alternatively, an ineffective structure that is inflexible may drive good employees away because of frustration and an inability to complete their work in the best way possible. As such, it can lead to a loss of knowledge by the firm, sometimes referred to as a knowledge spillover, which benefits competitors.[23]

Modifications to the firm's current strategy or selection of a new strategy call for changes to its organizational structure. However, research shows that once in place, organizational inertia often inhibits efforts to change structure, even when the firm's performance suggests that it is time to do so.[24] In his pioneering work, Alfred Chandler found that organizations change their structures when inefficiencies force them to.[25] Chandler's contributions to our understanding of organizational structure and its relationship to strategies and performance are quite significant. Indeed, some believe that Chandler's emphasis on "organizational structure so transformed the field of business history that some call the period before Chandler's work was published 'B.C.,' meaning 'before Chandler.'"[26]

Firms seem to prefer the structural status quo and its familiar working relationships until the firm's performance declines to the point where change is absolutely necessary.[27] For example, necessity is obviously the case for General Motors given that it went into bankruptcy to force the required restructuring.[28] As noted in the Opening Case, many firms are adjusting to a digital world, such as the competition between Best Buy and Amazon. It is unclear how Best Buy and other big-box retailers will survive given their cost structure relative to online competitors as they make the adjustment to have their own online approach to selling their products.

Top-level managers often hesitate to conclude that the firm's structure (or its strategy, for that matter) is the problem, because doing so suggests that their previous choices were not the best ones. Because of these inertial tendencies, structural change is often induced instead by actions from stakeholders (e.g., those from the capital market and customers— see Chapter 2 and Chapter 7) who are no longer willing to tolerate the firm's performance. For example, this happened at large department store operator J.C. Penney, as the former CEO, Myron Ullman, replaced a relatively new CEO, Ron Johnson, whose turnaround was not working.[29] Evidence shows that appropriate timing of structural change happens when top-level managers recognize that a current organizational structure no longer provides the coordination and direction needed for the firm to successfully implement its strategies.[30] Interestingly, many organizational changes take place in economic downturns because poor performance reveals organizational weaknesses. As we discuss next, effective organizational controls help managers recognize when it is time to adjust the firm's structure.

11-1b **Organizational Controls**

Organizational controls are an important aspect of structure.[31] **Organizational controls** guide the use of strategy, indicate how to compare actual results with expected results, and suggest corrective actions to take when the difference is unacceptable. It is difficult for the company to successfully exploit its competitive advantages without effective organizational controls. Properly designed organizational controls provide clear insights regarding behaviors that enhance firm performance.[32] Firms use both strategic controls and financial controls to support the implementation and use of their strategies.

Strategic controls are largely subjective criteria intended to verify that the firm is using appropriate strategies for the conditions in the external environment and the company's competitive advantages. Thus, strategic controls are concerned with examining the fit between what the firm *might do* (as suggested by opportunities in its external environment) and what it *can do* (as indicated by its competitive advantages). Effective strategic controls help the firm understand what it takes to be successful, especially where significant strategic change is needed.[33] Strategic controls demand rich communications between managers responsible for using them to judge the firm's performance and those with primary responsibility for implementing the firm's strategies (such as middle and first-level managers). These frequent exchanges are both formal and informal in nature.[34]

Strategic controls are also used to evaluate the degree to which the firm focuses on the requirements to implement its strategies. For a business-level strategy, for example, the strategic controls are used to study value chain activities and support functions (see Figures 3.3, 3.4, and 3.5, in Chapter 3) to verify that the critical value chain activities and support functions are being emphasized and properly executed. In fact, Nokia failed to employ effective strategic controls and is now fighting for survival due to its late response after the emergence of the smartphone.[35] With related corporate-level strategies, strategic controls are used by corporate strategic leaders to verify the sharing of appropriate strategic factors such as knowledge, markets, and technologies across businesses. To effectively use strategic controls when evaluating related diversification strategies, headquarter executives must have a deep understanding of each unit's business-level strategy.[36] As we described in the Opening Case, Borders' significant strategic problems likely stemmed at least partly from the ineffective use of strategic controls.

Financial controls are largely objective criteria used to measure the firm's performance against previously established quantitative standards. Accounting-based measures such as return on investment (ROI) and return on assets (ROA) as well as market-based measures such as economic value added are examples of financial controls. Partly because strategic controls are difficult to use with extensive diversification,[37] financial controls are emphasized to evaluate the performance of the firm using the unrelated diversification strategy. The unrelated diversification strategy's focus on financial outcomes (see Chapter 6) requires using standardized financial controls to compare performances between business units and associated managers.[38]

When using financial controls, firms evaluate their current performance against previous outcomes as well as against competitors' performance and industry averages. In the global economy, technological advances are being used to develop highly sophisticated financial controls, making it possible for firms to more thoroughly analyze their performance results and to assure compliance with regulations. Companies such as Oracle and SAP sell software tools that automate processes firms use to meet the financial reporting requirements specified by the Sarbanes-Oxley Act in the United States. As noted in Chapter 10, this act requires a firm's principal executive and financial officers to certify corporate financial and related information in quarterly and annual reports submitted to the Securities and Exchange Commission. These companies will likely develop software to help the financial services industry deal with the newest federal regulations on banking.

Organizational controls guide the use of strategy, indicate how to compare actual results with expected results, and suggest corrective actions to take when the difference is unacceptable.

Strategic controls are largely subjective criteria intended to verify that the firm is using appropriate strategies for the conditions in the external environment and the company's competitive advantages.

Financial controls are largely objective criteria used to measure the firm's performance against previously established quantitative standards.

Both strategic and financial controls are important aspects of each organizational structure, and as noted previously, any structure's effectiveness is determined using a combination of strategic and financial controls. However, the relative use of controls varies by type of strategy. For example, companies and business units of large diversified firms using the cost leadership strategy emphasize financial controls (such as quantitative cost goals), while companies and business units using the differentiation strategy emphasize strategic controls (such as subjective measures of the effectiveness of product development teams).[39] As previously explained, a corporation-wide emphasis on sharing among business units (as called for by related diversification strategies) results in an emphasis on strategic controls, while financial controls are emphasized for strategies in which activities or capabilities are not shared (e.g., in an unrelated diversification strategy).

As firms consider controls, it is important they properly balance the use of strategic and financial controls.[40] Indeed, overemphasizing one at the expense of the other can lead to performance declines. According to Michael Dell, an overemphasis on financial controls to produce attractive short-term results contributed to performance difficulties at Dell Inc. In addressing this issue, Dell said the following: "The company was too focused on the short term, and the balance of priorities was way too leaning toward things that deliver short-term results."[41] However, although there later was some improvement, there are continuing problems as Dell has not improved its competitive position and is now seeking a takeover by a private equity company to facilitate its restructuring effort.[42]

11-2 Relationships between Strategy and Structure

Strategy and structure have a reciprocal relationship, and if aligned properly, performance improves.[43] This relationship highlights the interconnectedness between strategy formulation (Chapters 4, 6–9) and strategy implementation (Chapters 10–13). In general, this reciprocal relationship finds structure flowing from or following selection of the firm's strategy. Once in place though, structure can influence current strategic actions as well as choices about future strategies. Consider, for example, the possible influences of Borders' structure and control system in influencing its strategy, as illustrated in the Opening Case. The overly centralized approach that it pursued led to a lack of adaptability in its businesses as it sought to meet the challenge of a change to digital books and online distribution. The centralized structure did not provide information from local stores that might have been useful in changing its technology strategy much sooner than it did. The general nature of the strategy/structure relationship means that changes to the firm's strategy create the need to change how the organization completes its work.

Alternatively, because structure likely influences strategy by constraining the potential alternatives considered, firms must be vigilant in their efforts to verify how their structure not only affects implementation of chosen strategies, but also the limits the structure places on possible future strategies. Research shows, however, that "strategy has a much more important influence on structure than the reverse."[44]

Regardless of the strength of the reciprocal relationships between strategy and structure, those choosing the firm's strategy and structure should be committed to matching each strategy with a structure that provides the stability needed to use current competitive advantages as well as the flexibility required to develop future advantages. Therefore, when changing strategies, the firm should simultaneously consider the structure that will be needed to support use of the new strategy; properly matching strategy and structure can create a competitive advantage. This process can be influenced by outside forces such as significant media attention, which may either hinder the change or foster it.[45]

11-3 Evolutionary Patterns of Strategy and Organizational Structure

Research suggests that most firms experience a certain pattern of relationships between strategy and structure. Chandler[46] found that firms tend to grow in somewhat predictable patterns: "first by volume, then by geography, then integration (vertical, horizontal), and finally through product/business diversification"[47] (see Figure 11.1). Chandler interpreted his findings as an indication that firms' growth patterns determine their structural form.

As shown in Figure 11.1, sales growth creates coordination and control problems the existing organizational structure cannot efficiently handle. Organizational growth creates the opportunity for the firm to change its strategy to try to become even more successful. However, the existing structure's formal reporting relationships, procedures, controls, and

Figure 11.1 Strategy and Structure Growth Pattern

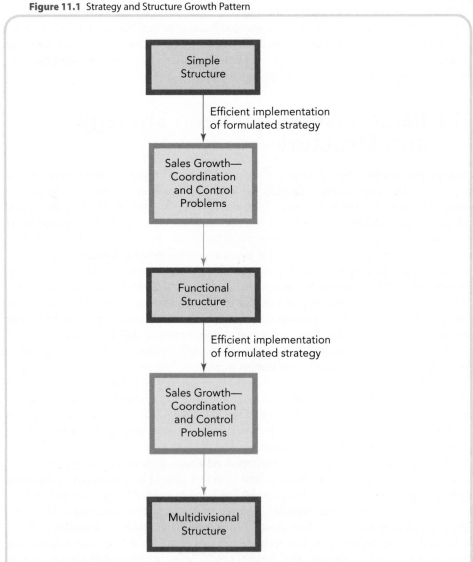

authority and decision-making processes lack the sophistication required to support using the new strategy.[48] A new structure is needed to help decision makers gain access to the knowledge and understanding required to effectively integrate and coordinate actions to implement the new strategy.[49]

Firms choose from among three major types of organizational structures—simple, functional, and multidivisional—to implement strategies. Across time, successful firms move from the simple to the functional to the multidivisional structure to support changes in their growth strategies.[50]

11-3a Simple Structure

The **simple structure** is a structure in which the owner-manager makes all major decisions and monitors all activities while the staff serves as an extension of the manager's supervisory authority.[51] Typically, the owner-manager actively works in the business on a daily basis. Informal relationships, few rules, limited task specialization, and unsophisticated information systems characterize this structure. Frequent and informal communications between the owner-manager and employees make coordinating the work to be done relatively easy. The simple structure is matched with focus strategies and business-level strategies, as firms implementing these strategies commonly compete by offering a single product line in a single geographic market. Local restaurants, repair businesses, and other specialized enterprises are examples of firms using the simple structure.

As the small firm grows larger and becomes more complex, managerial and structural challenges emerge. For example, the amount of competitively relevant information requiring analysis substantially increases, placing significant pressure on the owner-manager. Additional growth and success may cause the firm to change its strategy. Even if the strategy remains the same, the firm's larger size dictates the need for more sophisticated workflows and integrating mechanisms. At this evolutionary point, firms tend to move from the simple structure to a functional organizational structure.[52]

11-3b Functional Structure

The **functional structure** consists of a chief executive officer and a limited corporate staff, with functional line managers in dominant organizational areas such as production, accounting, marketing, R&D, engineering, and human resources.[53] This structure allows for functional specialization,[54] thereby facilitating active sharing of knowledge within each functional area. Knowledge sharing facilitates career paths as well as professional development of functional specialists. However, a functional orientation can negatively affect communication and coordination among those representing different organizational functions. For this reason, the CEO must verify that the decisions and actions of individual business functions promote the entire firm rather than a single function. The functional structure supports implementing business-level strategies and some corporate-level strategies (e.g., single or dominant business) with low levels of diversification. When changing from a simple to a functional structure, firms want to avoid introducing value-destroying bureaucratic procedures such as failing to promote innovation and creativity. As noted by Gary Hamel, "top-down control and bureaucracy are the fundamental principles of modern business management which are poisonous to innovation."[55]

11-3c Multidivisional Structure

With continuing growth and success, firms often consider greater levels of diversification. Successfully using a diversification strategy requires analyzing substantially greater amounts of data and information when the firm offers the same products in different markets (market or geographic diversification) or offers different products in several markets (product diversification). In addition, trying to manage high levels of diversification through functional

The **simple structure** is a structure in which the owner-manager makes all major decisions and monitors all activities while the staff serves as an extension of the manager's supervisory authority.

The **functional structure** consists of a chief executive officer and a limited corporate staff, with functional line managers in dominant organizational areas such as production, accounting, marketing, R&D, engineering, and human resources.

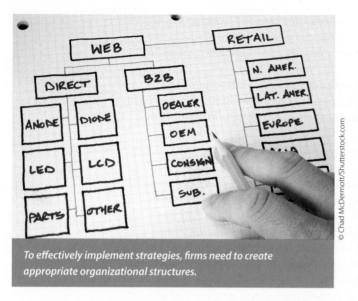

To effectively implement strategies, firms need to create appropriate organizational structures.

structures creates serious coordination and control problems,[56] a fact that commonly leads to a new structural form.[57]

The **multidivisional (M-form) structure** consists of a corporate office and operating divisions, each operating division representing a separate business or profit center in which the top corporate officer delegates responsibilities for day-to-day operations and business-unit strategy to division managers. Each division represents a distinct, self-contained business with its own functional hierarchy.[58] As initially designed, the M-form was thought to have three major benefits: "(1) it enabled corporate officers to more accurately monitor the performance of each business, which simplified the problem of control; (2) it facilitated comparisons between divisions, which improved the resource allocation process; and (3) it stimulated managers of poorly performing divisions to look for ways of improving performance."[59] Active monitoring of performance through the M-form increases the likelihood that decisions made by managers heading individual units will be in stakeholders' best interests. Because diversification is a dominant corporate-level strategy used in the global economy, the M-form is a widely adopted organizational structure.[60]

Used to support implementation of related and unrelated diversification strategies, the M-form helps firms successfully manage diversification's many demands.[61] Chandler viewed the M-form as an innovative response to coordination and control problems that surfaced during the 1920s in the functional structures then used by large firms such as DuPont and General Motors.[62] Research shows that the M-form is appropriate when the firm grows through diversification.[63] Partly because of its value to diversified corporations, some consider the multidivisional structure to be one of the twentieth century's most significant organizational innovations.[64]

No single organizational structure (simple, functional, or multidivisional) is inherently superior to the others.[65] Peter Drucker says the following about this matter: "There is no one right organization.... Rather the task … is to select the organization for the particular task and mission at hand."[66] This statement suggests that the firm must select a structure that is "right" for successfully using the chosen strategy. Because no single structure is optimal in all instances, managers concentrate on developing proper matches between strategies and organizational structures rather than searching for an "optimal" structure. We now describe the strategy/structure matches that evidence shows positively contribute to firm performance.

The **multidivisional (M-form) structure** consists of a corporate office and operating divisions, each operating division representing a separate business or profit center in which the top corporate officer delegates responsibilities for day-to-day operations and business-unit strategy to division managers.

11-3d Matches between Business-Level Strategies and the Functional Structure

Firms use different forms of the functional organizational structure to support implementing the cost leadership, differentiation, and integrated cost leadership/differentiation strategies. The differences in these forms are accounted for primarily by different uses of three important structural characteristics: *specialization* (concerned with the type and number of jobs required to complete work[67]), *centralization* (the degree to which decision-making authority is retained at higher managerial levels[68]), and *formalization* (the degree to which formal rules and procedures govern work[69]).

Using the Functional Structure to Implement the Cost Leadership Strategy

Firms using the cost leadership strategy sell large quantities of standardized products to an industry's typical customer. Firms using this strategy need a structure and capabilities that allow them to achieve efficiencies and produce their goods at costs lower than those of competitors.[70] Simple reporting relationships, a few layers in the decision-making and authority structure, a centralized corporate staff, and a strong focus on process improvements through the manufacturing function rather than the development of new products by emphasizing product R&D help to achieve the efficiencies and thus characterize the cost leadership form of the functional structure[71] (see Figure 11.2). This structure contributes to the emergence of a low-cost culture—a culture in which employees constantly try to find ways to reduce the costs incurred to complete their work.[72] They can do this through the development of a product design that is simple and easy to manufacture, as well as through the development of efficient processes to produce the goods.[73]

In terms of centralization, decision-making authority is centralized in a staff function to maintain a cost-reducing emphasis within each organizational function (engineering, marketing, etc.). While encouraging continuous cost reductions, the centralized staff also verifies that further cuts in costs in one function won't adversely affect the productivity levels of other functions.[74]

Jobs are highly specialized in the cost leadership functional structure; work is divided into homogeneous subgroups. Organizational functions are the most common subgroup, although work is sometimes batched on the basis of products produced or clients served.

Figure 11.2 Functional Structure for Implementing a Cost Leadership Strategy

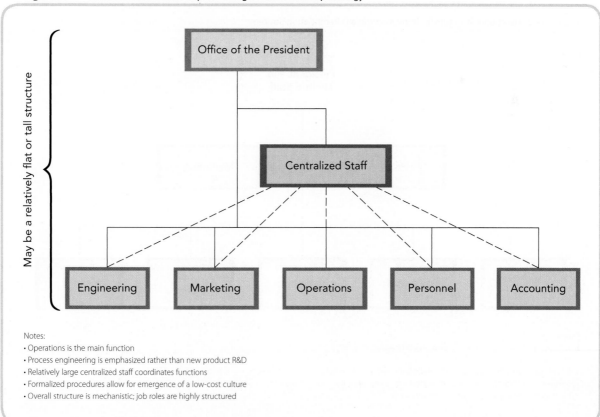

May be a relatively flat or tall structure

Office of the President

Centralized Staff

Engineering Marketing Operations Personnel Accounting

Notes:
- Operations is the main function
- Process engineering is emphasized rather than new product R&D
- Relatively large centralized staff coordinates functions
- Formalized procedures allow for emergence of a low-cost culture
- Overall structure is mechanistic; job roles are highly structured

© Cengage Learning

Specializing in their work allows employees to increase their efficiency, resulting in reduced costs. Guiding individuals' work in this structure are highly formalized rules and procedures, which often emanate from the centralized staff.

Walmart Stores Inc. uses the functional structure to implement cost leadership strategies in each of its three segments (Walmart Stores, Sam's Clubs, and International Division). In the Walmart Stores segment (which generates the largest share of the firm's total sales), the cost leadership strategy is used in the firm's Supercenter, Discount, and Neighborhood Market retailing formats.[75] The stated purpose of Walmart from the beginning has been "saving people money to help them live better."[76] Although the slogan is relatively new, Walmart continues using the functional organizational structure in its divisions to drive costs lower. As discussed in Chapter 4, competitors' efforts to duplicate the success of Walmart's cost leadership strategies have generally failed, partly because of the effective strategy/structure matches in each of the firm's segments.

Using the Functional Structure to Implement the Differentiation Strategy

Firms using the differentiation strategy produce products that customers hopefully perceive as being different in ways that create value for them. With this strategy, the firm wants to sell nonstandardized products to customers with unique needs. Relatively complex and flexible reporting relationships, frequent use of cross-functional product development teams, and a strong focus on marketing and product R&D rather than manufacturing and process R&D (as with the cost leadership form of the functional structure) characterize the differentiation form of the functional structure (see Figure 11.3). From this structure emerges a

Figure 11.3 Functional Structure for Implementing a Differentiation Strategy

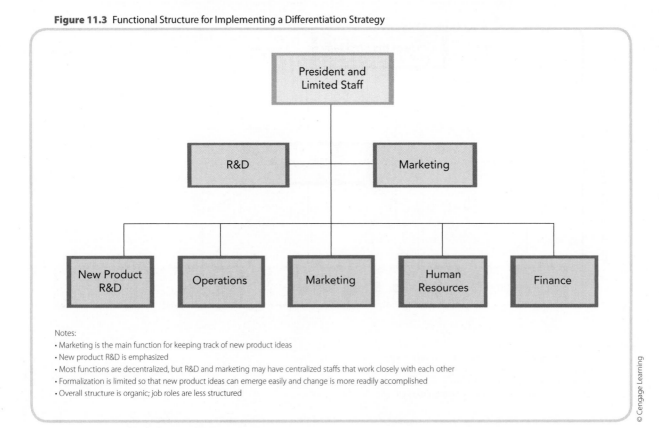

Notes:
• Marketing is the main function for keeping track of new product ideas
• New product R&D is emphasized
• Most functions are decentralized, but R&D and marketing may have centralized staffs that work closely with each other
• Formalization is limited so that new product ideas can emerge easily and change is more readily accomplished
• Overall structure is organic; job roles are less structured

© Cengage Learning

development-oriented culture in which employees try to find ways to further differentiate current products and to develop new, highly differentiated products.[77]

Continuous product innovation demands that people throughout the firm interpret and take action based on information that is often ambiguous, incomplete, and uncertain. Following a strong focus on the external environment to identify new opportunities, employees often gather this information from people outside the firm (e.g., customers and suppliers). Commonly, rapid responses to the possibilities indicated by the collected information are necessary, suggesting the need for decentralized decision-making responsibility and authority. It also requires building a strong technological capability and strategic flexibility, which allow the organization to take advantage of opportunities created by changes in the market.[78] To support the creativity needed and the continuous pursuit of new sources of differentiation and new products, jobs in this structure are not highly specialized. This lack of specialization means that workers have a relatively large number of tasks in their job descriptions. Few formal rules and procedures also characterize this structure. Low formalization, decentralization of decision-making authority and responsibility, and low specialization of work tasks combine to create a structure in which people interact frequently to exchange ideas about how to further differentiate current products while developing ideas for new products that can be crisply differentiated.

Under Armour has used a differentiation strategy and matching structure to create success in the sports apparel market. Under Armour's objective is to create improved athletic performance through innovative design, testing, and marketing, especially to professional athletes and teams, and translate that perception to the broader market. With a strong match between strategy and structure, it has successfully created innovative sports performance products and challenged Nike and other sports apparel competitors.[79]

Using the Functional Structure to Implement the Integrated Cost Leadership/Differentiation Strategy

Firms using the integrated cost leadership/differentiation strategy sell products that create value because of their relatively low cost and reasonable sources of differentiation. The cost of these products is low "relative" to the cost leader's prices while their differentiation is "reasonable" when compared with the clearly unique features of the differentiator's products.

Although challenging to implement, the integrated cost leadership/differentiation strategy is used frequently in the global economy. The challenge of using this strategy is due largely to the fact that different value chain and support activities (see Chapter 3) are emphasized when using the cost leadership and differentiation strategies. To achieve the cost leadership position, production and process engineering need to be emphasized, with infrequent product changes. To achieve a differentiated position, marketing and new product R&D need to be emphasized while production and process engineering are not. Thus, effective use of the integrated strategy depends on the firm's successful combination of activities intended to reduce costs with activities intended to create additional differentiation features. As a result, the integrated form of the functional structure must have decision-making patterns that are partially centralized and partially decentralized. Additionally, jobs are semi-specialized, and rules and procedures call for some formal and some informal job behavior. All of this requires a measure of flexibility to emphasize one or the other set of functions at any given time.[80]

11-3e Matches between Corporate-Level Strategies and the Multidivisional Structure

As explained earlier, Chandler's research shows that the firm's continuing success leads to product or market diversification or both.[81] The firm's level of diversification is a function of decisions about the number and type of businesses in which it will compete as well as how it will manage the businesses (see Chapter 6). Geared to managing individual organizational functions, increasing diversification eventually creates information processing, coordination, and control problems that the functional structure cannot handle. Thus, using a diversification strategy requires the firm to change from the functional structure to the multidivisional structure to develop an appropriate strategy/structure match.

As defined in Figure 6.1, corporate-level strategies have different degrees of product and market diversification. The demands created by different levels of diversification highlight the need for a unique organizational structure to effectively implement each strategy (see Figure 11.4).

Cisco must use a differentiation strategy in order to compete in its several high technology product market segments. However, given the presence of major competitors in those markets, such as Hewlett-Packard and Huawei, and its loss of market share in its core market of routers, Cisco must also be sensitive to costs. Thus, cross-function cooperative structures and processes can be useful to integrate the two disparate dimensions of structure needed to implement Cisco's integrated cost leadership–differentiation strategy. In addition, Cisco needs to coordinate several related product units, and a parallel cooperative structure and processes should facilitate this cooperation at the corporate level. Therefore, Cisco's approach is similar to the cooperative M-form structure, discussed next.

Using the Cooperative Form of the Multidivisional Structure to Implement the Related Constrained Strategy

The **cooperative form** is an M-form structure in which horizontal integration is used to bring about interdivisional cooperation. Divisions in a firm using the related constrained diversification strategy commonly are formed around products, markets, or both. In Figure 11.5, we use product divisions as part of the representation of the cooperative form of the multidivisional structure, although market divisions could be used instead of or in addition to product divisions to develop the figure.

Using this structure, News Corporation, as explained in the Strategic Focus, is moving to two separate businesses, one in print (News Corporation) and one in TV cable broadcast and movie production (21st Century Fox). Each of these separate businesses will be related constrained diversifiers implementing the cooperative structure. Cisco has implemented the related constrained strategy by acquiring a number of related businesses (see

The **cooperative form** is an M-form structure in which horizontal integration is used to bring about interdivisional cooperation.

Figure 11.4 Three Variations of the Multidivisional Structure

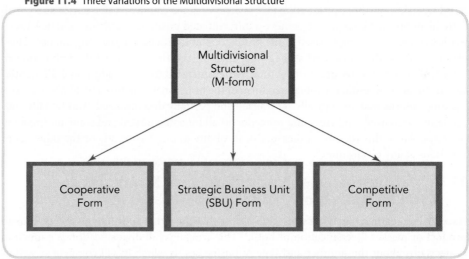

© Cengage Learning

Figure 11.5 Cooperative Form of the Multidivisional Structure for Implementing a Related Constrained Strategy

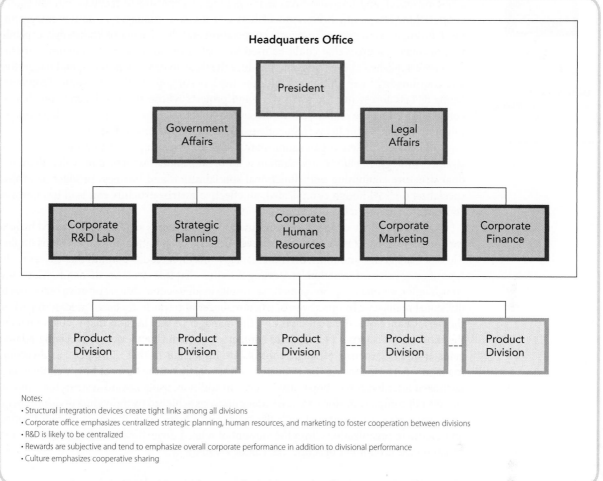

Headquarters Office

President

Government Affairs

Legal Affairs

Corporate R&D Lab

Strategic Planning

Corporate Human Resources

Corporate Marketing

Corporate Finance

Product Division — Product Division — Product Division — Product Division — Product Division

Notes:
- Structural integration devices create tight links among all divisions
- Corporate office emphasizes centralized strategic planning, human resources, and marketing to foster cooperation between divisions
- R&D is likely to be centralized
- Rewards are subjective and tend to emphasize overall corporate performance in addition to divisional performance
- Culture emphasizes cooperative sharing

© Cengage Learning

the Opening Case in Chapter 7). Cisco tried to enter 30 consumer markets related to its core businesses in routers. This required implementation of the cooperative M-form, and Cisco tried to manage it with significant decentralization among the various business units to foster cooperation and synergy. However, there were too many markets, and the horizontal teams designed to foster collaboration and coordination across related businesses created significant challenges. In the end, there was not enough vertical structure to provide oversight and avoid the chaos created by the multiple cross-functional teams and management boards. Thus, Cisco has streamlined its set of businesses and balanced its vertical and horizontal structure to mirror the more common form of the cooperative structure. Interestingly, research suggests that informal ties may be even more important than formal coordination devices in achieving cooperation.[82]

Sharing divisional competencies facilitates the corporation's efforts to develop economies of scope. As explained in Chapter 6, economies of scope (cost savings resulting from the sharing of competencies developed in one division with another division) are linked with successful use of the related constrained strategy. Interdivisional sharing of competencies depends on cooperation, suggesting the use of the cooperative form of the multidivisional structure.[83] Cisco's new structure and processes hopefully will accomplish this.

Learn more about
Organizational Structure.
www.cengagebrain.com

The cooperative structure uses different characteristics of structure (centralization, standardization, and formalization) as integrating mechanisms to facilitate interdivisional cooperation. Frequent, direct contact between division managers, another integrating mechanism, encourages and supports cooperation and the sharing of knowledge, capabilities, or other resources that could be used to create new advantages.[84] Sometimes, liaison roles are established in each division to reduce the time division managers spend integrating and coordinating their unit's work with the work occurring in other divisions. Temporary teams or task forces may be formed around projects whose success depends on sharing competencies that are embedded within several divisions. Formal integration departments might be established in firms frequently using temporary teams or task forces.

Ultimately, a matrix organization may evolve in firms implementing the related constrained strategy. A *matrix organization* is an organizational structure in which there is a dual structure combining both functional specialization and business product or project specialization.[85] Although complicated, an effective matrix structure can lead to improved coordination among a firm's divisions.[86]

The success of the cooperative multidivisional structure is significantly affected by how well divisions process information. However, because cooperation among divisions implies a loss of managerial autonomy, division managers may not readily commit themselves to the type of integrative information-processing activities that this structure demands. Moreover, coordination among divisions sometimes results in an unequal flow of positive outcomes to divisional managers. In other words, when managerial rewards are based at least in part on the performance of individual divisions, the manager of the division that is able to benefit the most by the sharing of corporate competencies might be viewed as receiving relative gains at others' expense. Strategic controls are important in these instances, as divisional managers' performance can be evaluated at least partly on the basis of how well they have facilitated interdivisional cooperative efforts. In addition, using reward systems that emphasize overall company performance, besides outcomes achieved by individual divisions, helps overcome problems associated with the cooperative form. Still, the costs of coordination and inertia in organizations limit the amount of related diversification attempted (i.e., they constrain the economies of scope that can be created).[87]

Using the Strategic Business Unit Form of the Multidivisional Structure to Implement the Related Linked Strategy

Firms with fewer links or less constrained links among their divisions use the related linked diversification strategy. The strategic business unit form of the multidivisional structure supports implementation of this strategy. The **strategic business unit (SBU) form** is an M-form structure consisting of three levels: corporate headquarters, SBUs, and SBU divisions (see Figure 11.6). The SBU structure is used by large firms and can be complex, given associated organization size and product and market diversity.

The divisions within each SBU are related in terms of shared products or markets or both, but the divisions of one SBU have little in common with the divisions of the other SBUs. Divisions within each SBU share product or market competencies to develop economies of scope and possibly economies of scale. The integrating mechanisms used by the divisions in this structure can be equally well used by the divisions within the individual strategic business units that are part of the SBU form of the multidivisional structure. In this structure, each SBU is a profit center that is controlled and evaluated by the headquarters office. Although both financial and strategic controls are important, on a relative basis, financial controls are vital to headquarters' evaluation of each SBU; strategic controls are critical when the heads of SBUs evaluate their divisions' performances. Strategic controls are also critical to the headquarters' efforts to determine whether the company has formed an effective portfolio of businesses and whether those businesses are being successfully

Learn more about
Constellation Brands.
www.cengagebrain.com

The **strategic business unit (SBU) form** is an M-form consisting of three levels: corporate headquarters, strategic business units (SBUs), and SBU divisions.

Strategic Focus   GLOBALIZATION

A Change in Corporate Strategy Requires a Change in the Corporate Organizational Structure

In 2013, Constellation Brands Inc. became the third largest beer producer in the United States behind Anheuser-Busch InBev and MillerCoors. The opportunity appeared for Constellation through a merger between Anheuser-Busch InBev and Mexico's Grupo Modelo. The Justice Department would not allow the merger to take place unless Grupo Modelo's top import brand, Corona, was divested. This is the asset that Constellation acquired with the associated brewery over the Texas border in Mexico with distribution rights in the United States. Constellation had already signed a 50/50 joint venture with Modelo in 2007 to distribute the Mexican company's beer in the United States. As such, Constellation got to continue its distribution rights but also became a producer with the acquisition of the large brewery. Through this acquisition, Constellation will control nearly 50 percent of U.S. beer imports. Even though beer distribution is shrinking relative to other segments of overall alcohol sales, imported beers are a growing segment. In part, this is due to the growth of the Hispanic population in the United States.

With the acquisition of Corona from Anheuser-Busch InBev, Constellation Brands became the third largest beer producer in the United States.

Constellation started out as a small family wine producer in upstate New York. Through acquisitions, Constellation Brands has become the largest wine producer in the world. In particular, it has the largest share of premium wine distribution in the United States, the United Kingdom, Australia, and Canada, and the second largest in New Zealand. It also has a large set of brands in the spirits category. For instance, it owns Svedka Vodka and competes with Grey Goose, owned by Bacardi Limited, and Smirnoff owned by Diageo. It also owns other spirit brands including Black Velvet Canadian Whisky and Paul Masson Grande Amber Brandy.

Because it has three different types of producing technologies in wine, spirits, and beer, it must understand each of these processes and be able to have strategic control of these separate operations. Accordingly, the appropriate structure for these three types of operations requires the SBU structure such that you combine the wine, spirits, and beer operations into three different business groups with divisional structures for each brand within the group. As it has moved from being the producer of only wines to being a producer of spirits and beer, it has had to change its operating structure because it moved from being a related constrained diversifier to a related linked diversifier (mixed-related-unrelated). With this change, the better fit between strategy and structure would be the installation

of the SBU structure and a move away from the cooperative structure. It may be possible to run the premium wine and spirits in the same group because they have similar distribution outlets. However, because there is not much production or operational relatedness in these business units, it may be better to keep them separate. Beer is both distributed differently (more of a consumer product) and produced differently than wine and spirits. Robert Sands, CEO of Constellation, acknowledges, "Constellation has a lot to learn about mixing barley and hops, but he notes the brewery is highly automated." He also sees some cost benefits across the whole corporation in being able to strike cheaper procurement deals for "glass bottles, cardboard, and freight, three big input costs, and improve its negotiation position with retailers by offering a full menu of alcohol." Although Constellation Brands has to change its structure due to its diversification strategy, News Corporation is reducing its diversification by splitting up its business into two separate firms.

In 2013, News Corporation approved a split of its media businesses. Over a number of years, it has acquired a number of media businesses both in television and print. It has been organized into an SBU-type of organization given its focus in different areas. In the split-up, the print media company will be called News Corp. and will have newspaper assets including the *Wall Street Journal, New York Post*, and *Times of London*. It will also have the book publisher HarperCollins. The other business will be called 21st Century Fox and will include the Fox broadcast and cable networks and 20th Century Fox studio, which produces movies and television programming. Rupert Murdock will continue as the CEO of 21st Century Fox and will remain the executive chairman of the board of News Corp.

The organization of these two businesses will likely have to change. The television and movie businesses will have more tightly related divisions and will likely move to the cooperative structure. Similarly, the print media business (News Corp.) will also have to move to the cooperative structure because it will be pursuing the related constrained strategy with all its business units

interrelated. As such, it will likely change into two separate organizations using the cooperative structure where businesses are more related as a unitary firm that formerly used the SBU structure.

Sources: A. Collins, 2013, Strategic buyer AB InBev sells U.S. rights and other Modelo brands to Constellation, *Mergers & Acquisitions Report*, February 25, 5; A. Deckert, 2013, Constellation Brands gears up for changes, *Rochester Business Journal*, April 12, 3; M. Esterl, 2013, New U.S. brewing giant is crowned, *Wall Street Journal*, June 7, B6; B. Kindle, 2013, Constellation wants legal role in beer merger battle, *Wall Street Journal*, February 11, B5; A. Sharma, 2013, News Corp. shareholders approve split, *Wall Street Journal*, June 12, B5.

managed. Therefore, there is need for strategic structures that promote exploration to identify new products and markets, but also for actions that exploit the current product lines and markets.[88]

As illustrated in the Strategic Focus, Constellation Brands is likely to implement the SBU structure as it has different operational needs among its wine, spirits, and beer business

Figure 11.6 SBU Form of the Multidivisional Structure for Implementing a Related Link Strategy

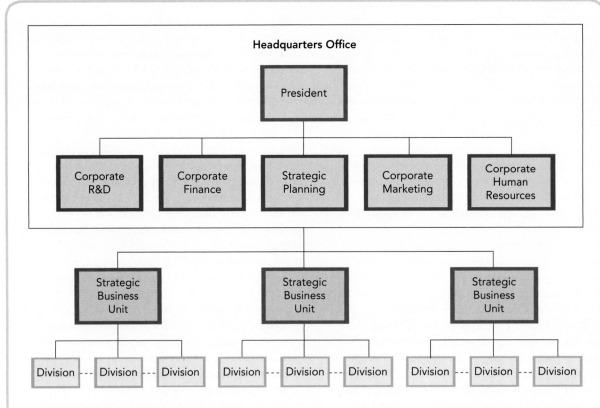

Notes:
• Structural integration among divisions within SBUs, but independence across SBUs
• Strategic planning may be the most prominent function in headquarters for managing the strategic planning approval process of SBUs for the president
• Each SBU may have its own budget for staff to foster integration
• Corporate headquarters staff members serve as consultants to SBUs and divisions, rather than having direct input to product strategy, as in the cooperative form

© Cengage Learning

units. Sharing competencies among units within an SBU is an important characteristic of the SBU form of the multidivisional structure (see the notes to Figure 11.6). A drawback to the SBU structure is that multifaceted businesses often have difficulties in communicating this complex business model to stockholders.[89] Furthermore, if coordination between SBUs is needed, as is the case with Constellation Brands, problems can arise because the SBU structure, similar to the competitive form discussed next, does not readily foster cooperation across SBUs.

Using the Competitive Form of the Multidivisional Structure to Implement the Unrelated Diversification Strategy

Firms using the unrelated diversification strategy want to create value through efficient internal capital allocations or by restructuring, buying, and selling businesses.[90] The competitive form of the multidivisional structure supports implementation of this strategy.

The **competitive form** is an M-form structure characterized by complete independence among the firm's divisions, which compete for corporate resources (see Figure 11.7). Unlike the divisions included in the cooperative structure, divisions that are part of the competitive structure do not share common corporate strengths. Because strengths are not shared, integrating devices are not developed for use by the divisions included in the competitive structure.

The efficient internal capital market that is the foundation for using the unrelated diversification strategy requires organizational arrangements emphasizing divisional competition

The **competitive form** is an M-form structure characterized by complete independence among the firm's divisions which compete for corporate resources.

Figure 11.7 Competitive Form of the Multidivisional Structure for Implementing an Unrelated Strategy

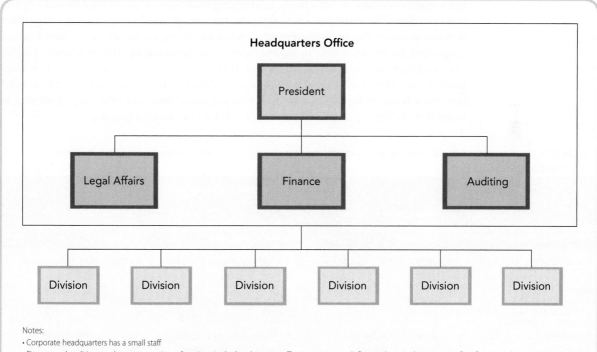

Notes:
- Corporate headquarters has a small staff
- Finance and auditing are the most prominent functions in the headquarters office to manage cash flow and assure the accuracy of performance data coming from divisions
- The legal affairs function becomes important when the firm acquires or divests assets
- Divisions are independent and separate for financial evaluation purposes
- Divisions retain strategic control, but cash is managed by the corporate office
- Divisions compete for corporate resources

© Cengage Learning

rather than cooperation.[91] Three benefits are expected from the internal competition. First, internal competition creates flexibility (e.g., corporate headquarters can have divisions working on different technologies and projects to identify those with the greatest potential). Resources can then be allocated to the division appearing to have the most potential to fuel the entire firm's success. Second, internal competition challenges the status quo and inertia, because division heads know that future resource allocations are a product of excellent current performance as well as superior positioning in terms of future performance. Last, internal competition motivates effort in that the challenge of competing against internal peers can be as great as the challenge of competing against external rivals.[92] In this structure, organizational controls (primarily financial controls) are used to emphasize and support internal competition among separate divisions and as the basis for allocating corporate capital based on divisions' performances.

Textron Inc., a large "multi-industry" company, seeks to identify, research, select, acquire, and integrate companies and has developed a set of rigorous criteria to guide decision making. Textron continuously looks to enhance and reshape its portfolio by divesting non-core assets and acquiring branded businesses in attractive industries with substantial long-term growth potential. Textron operates five independent businesses—Bell Helicopter, Cessna Aircraft, Textron Systems and Industrial (all manufacturing businesses), and Finance, "which are responsible for the day-to-day operation of their businesses." The "segment profit is an important measure used for evaluating performance and for decision-making purposes."[93] Many such firms use return on invested capital (ROIC) as a way to evaluate the contribution of its diversified set of businesses as they compete internally for resources.

To emphasize competitiveness among divisions, the headquarters office maintains an arm's-length relationship with them, intervening in divisional affairs only to audit operations and discipline managers whose divisions perform poorly. In emphasizing competition between divisions, the headquarters office relies on strategic controls to set rate-of-return targets and financial controls to monitor divisional performance relative to those targets. The headquarters office then allocates cash flow on a competitive basis, rather than automatically returning cash to the division that produced it. Thus, the focus of the headquarters' work is on performance appraisal, resource allocation, and long-range planning to verify that the firm's portfolio of businesses will lead to financial success.

Table 11.1 Characteristics of the Structures Necessary to Implement the Related Constrained, Related Linked, and Unrelated Diversification Strategies

Structural Characteristics	Overall Structural Form		
	Cooperative M-Form (Related Constrained Strategy)	**SBU M-Form (Related Linked Strategy)**	**Competitive M-Form (Unrelated Diversification Strategy)**
Centralization of operations	Centralized at corporate office	Partially centralized (in SBUs)	Decentralized to divisions
Use of integration mechanisms	Extensive	Moderate	Nonexistent
Divisional performance evaluation	Emphasizes subjective (strategic) criteria	Uses a mixture of subjective (strategic) and objective (financial) criteria	Emphasizes objective (financial) criteria
Divisional incentive compensation	Linked to overall corporate performance	Mixed linkage to corporate, SBU, and divisional performance	Linked to divisional performance

The three major forms of the multidivisional structure should each be paired with a particular corporate-level strategy. Table 11.1 shows these structures' characteristics. Differences exist in the degree of centralization, the focus of the performance evaluation, the horizontal structures (integrating mechanisms), and the incentive compensation schemes. The most centralized and most costly structural form is the cooperative structure. The least centralized, with the lowest bureaucratic costs, is the competitive structure. The SBU structure requires partial centralization and involves some of the mechanisms necessary to implement the relatedness between divisions. Also, the divisional incentive compensation awards are allocated according to both SBUs and corporate performance.

11-3f Matches between International Strategies and Worldwide Structure

As explained in Chapter 8, international strategies are becoming increasingly important for long-term competitive success in what continues to become an increasingly borderless global economy.[94] Among other benefits, international strategies allow the firm to search for new markets, resources, core competencies, and technologies as part of its efforts to outperform competitors.[95]

As with business-level and corporate-level strategies, unique organizational structures are necessary to successfully implement the different international strategies given the different cultural, institutional, and legal environments around the world.[96] Forming proper matches between international strategies and organizational structures facilitates the firm's efforts to effectively coordinate and control its global operations. More importantly, research findings confirm the validity of the international strategy/structure matches we discuss here.[97]

Using the Worldwide Geographic Area Structure to Implement the Multidomestic Strategy

The *multidomestic strategy* decentralizes the firm's strategic and operating decisions to business units in each country so that product characteristics can be tailored to local preferences. Firms using this strategy try to isolate themselves from global competitive forces by establishing protected market positions or by competing in industry segments that are most affected by differences among local countries. The worldwide geographic area structure is used to implement this strategy. The **worldwide geographic area structure** emphasizes national interests and facilitates the firm's efforts to satisfy local differences (see Figure 11.8).

Since the 2008 economic crisis, the world has become more fragmented and there is more of a local or regional focus. For example, Caterpillar, a globally oriented company, is trying to localize better than in the past. One analyst noted the following: "Caterpillar thinks less about a single world market than many regional ones. The company is global, but where it can, it sources and produces locally, which is a natural hedge against everything from oil prices to currency risk to changing customer tastes."[98] Although Caterpillar is not necessarily a multidomestic firm per se, it is becoming more multidomestic in that it is emphasizing more localization. Many consumer product companies such as Procter and Gamble and Unilever have employed the multidomestic strategy because consumer products often need to be more locally responsive.[99] Using the multidomestic strategy requires little coordination between different country markets, meaning that integrating mechanisms among divisions around the world are not needed. Coordination among units in a firm's worldwide geographic area structure is often informal. As mentioned earlier, this may be the most effective form of cooperation.

The multidomestic strategy/worldwide geographic area structure match evolved as a natural outgrowth of the multicultural European marketplace. Friends and family members of the main business who were sent as expatriates into foreign countries

The **worldwide geographic area structure** emphasizes national interests and facilitates the firm's efforts to satisfy local differences.

Figure 11.8 Worldwide Geographic Area Structure for Implementing a Multidomestic Strategy

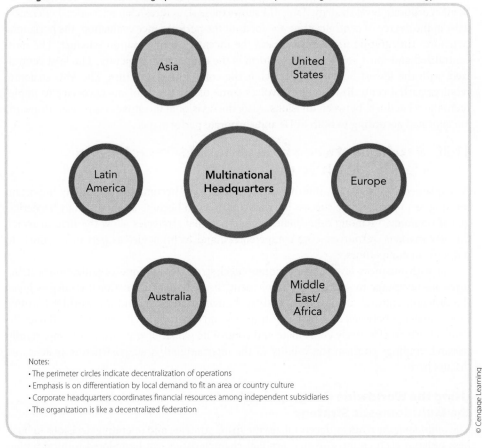

Notes:
• The perimeter circles indicate decentralization of operations
• Emphasis is on differentiation by local demand to fit an area or country culture
• Corporate headquarters coordinates financial resources among independent subsidiaries
• The organization is like a decentralized federation

© Cengage Learning

to develop the independent country subsidiary often used this structure for the main business. The relationship to corporate headquarters by divisions took place through informal communication.

A key disadvantage of the multidomestic strategy/worldwide geographic area structure match is the inability to create strong global efficiency. With an increasing emphasis on lower-cost products in international markets, the need to pursue worldwide economies of scale has also increased. These changes foster use of the global strategy and its structural match, the worldwide product divisional structure.

Using the Worldwide Product Divisional Structure to Implement the Global Strategy

With the corporation's home office dictating competitive strategy, the *global strategy* is one through which the firm offers standardized products across country markets. The firm's success depends on its ability to develop economies of scope and economies of scale on a global level. Decisions to outsource or maintain integrated subsidiaries may in part depend on the country risk and institutional environment into which the firm is entering.[100]

In the **worldwide product divisional structure,** decision-making authority is centralized in the worldwide division headquarters to coordinate and integrate decisions and actions among divisional business units.

The worldwide product divisional structure supports use of the global strategy. In the **worldwide product divisional structure**, decision-making authority is centralized in the worldwide division headquarters to coordinate and integrate decisions and actions among divisional business units (see Figure 11.9). This structure is often used in rapidly growing firms that want to effectively manage their diversified product lines. Avon Products, Inc. is an example of a firm using the worldwide product divisional structure.

Figure 11.9 Worldwide Product Divisional Structure for Implementing a Global Strategy

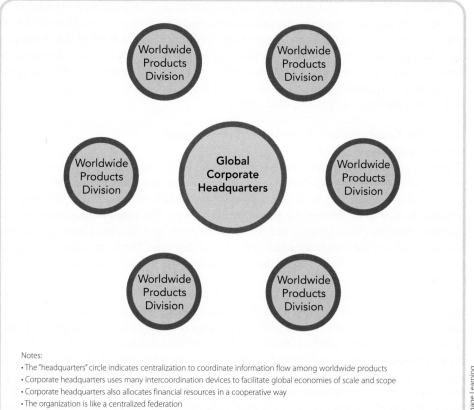

Notes:
- The "headquarters" circle indicates centralization to coordinate information flow among worldwide products
- Corporate headquarters uses many intercoordination devices to facilitate global economies of scale and scope
- Corporate headquarters also allocates financial resources in a cooperative way
- The organization is like a centralized federation

© Cengage Learning

Avon is a global brand leader in products for women such as lipsticks, fragrances, and anti-aging skin care. Committed to "empowering women all over the world since 1886," Avon relies on product innovation to be a first mover in its markets. For years, Avon used the multidomestic strategy. However, the firm's growth came to a screeching halt in 2006. Contributing to this decline were simultaneous stumbles in sales revenues in emerging markets (e.g., Russia and Central Europe), the United States, and Mexico. To cope with its problems, the firm moved to implement aspects of the global strategy and to the worldwide product divisional structure to support its use. Today, Avon is organized around product divisions including Avon Color, the firm's "flagship global color cosmetics brand, which offers a variety of color cosmetics products, including foundations, powders, lip, eye, and nail products," Skincare, Bath & Body, Hair Care, Wellness, and Fragrance. The analysis of these product divisions' performances is conducted by individuals in the firm's New York headquarters. One of the purposes of changing strategy and structure is for Avon to control its costs and gain additional scale economies as paths to performance improvements. In 2012, a new CEO, Sheri McCoy, replaced Andrea Jung with the goal of continuing to foster integration and cost saving. She has signaled that Avon will exit Korea, Ireland, and Vietnam and continue to emphasize its brands. Direct selling online has become more important, but this can all be driven by Avon's 100,000 direct representatives, for example, through their Facebook contacts.[101]

Integrating mechanisms are important in the effective use of the worldwide product divisional structure. Direct contact between managers, liaison roles between departments, and both temporary task forces and permanent teams are examples of these mechanisms. The disadvantages of the global strategy/worldwide structure combination are the difficulty involved with coordinating decisions and actions across country borders and the inability to quickly respond to local needs and preferences. To deal with these types of disadvantages, Avon has approximately 6 million local salespeople in 100 countries who are committed to the organization and who help the company to become locally responsive. Another solution is to develop a regional approach in addition to the product focus, which might be similar to the combination structure discussed next.

Using the Combination Structure to Implement the Transnational Strategy

The *transnational strategy* calls for the firm to combine the multidomestic strategy's local responsiveness with the global strategy's efficiency. Firms using this strategy are trying to gain the advantages of both local responsiveness and global efficiency.[102] The combination structure is used to implement the transnational strategy. The **combination structure** is a structure drawing characteristics and mechanisms from both the worldwide geographic area structure and the worldwide product divisional structure. The transnational strategy is often implemented through two possible combination structures: a global matrix structure and a hybrid global design.[103]

The global matrix design brings together both local market and product expertise into teams that develop and respond to the global marketplace. The global matrix design (the basic matrix structure was defined earlier) promotes flexibility in designing products and responding to customer needs. However, it has severe limitations in that it places employees in a position of being accountable to more than one manager. At any given time, an employee may be a member of several functional or product group teams. Relationships that evolve from multiple memberships can make it difficult for employees to be simultaneously loyal to all of them. Although the matrix places authority in the hands of the managers who are most able to use it, it creates problems in regard to corporate reporting relationships that are so complex and vague that it is difficult and time-consuming to receive approval for major decisions.

We illustrate the hybrid structure in Figure 11.10. In this design, some divisions are oriented toward products while others are oriented toward market areas. Thus, in cases when

> The **combination structure** is a structure drawing characteristics and mechanisms from both the worldwide geographic area structure and the worldwide product divisional structure.

Figure 11.10 Hybrid Form of the Combination Structure for Implementing a Transnational Strategy

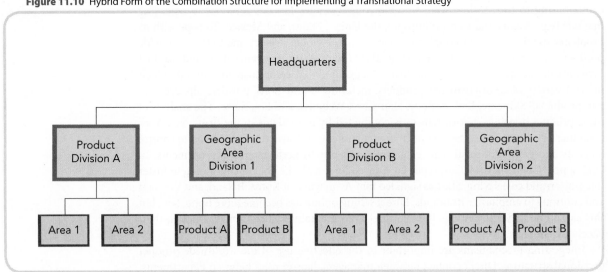

© Cengage Learning

the geographic area is more important, the division managers are area-oriented. In other divisions where worldwide product coordination and efficiencies are more important, the division manager is more product-oriented.

The fit between the multidomestic strategy and the worldwide geographic area structure and between the global strategy and the worldwide product divisional structure is apparent. However, when a firm wants to implement the multidomestic and global strategies simultaneously through a combination structure, the appropriate integrating mechanisms are less obvious. The structure used to implement the transnational strategy must be simultaneously centralized and decentralized; integrated and nonintegrated; formalized and nonformalized. Sometimes the structure becomes too complex. P&G has been said to have a costly organization structure using the hybrid form: "P&G has a complex organizational structure that includes global business units that manage its brands and develop products in different categories, and geographical 'market development organizations' that work with retailers to sell products."[104]

When Panasonic Corporation (a Japanese company formally named Matsushita) started selling home appliances in the Chinese market several decades ago, its only attempt at localization was to offer less expensive versions of its developed market standard offerings. Japanese firms often sold standard products across the world, implementing the global strategy using the worldwide product divisional structure. However, they found that local competitors such as Haier were quickly outpacing their appliance sales in China, Haier's home market. Through this experience, Panasonic learned to engage more deeply within a country or regional market to adapt their appliances more closely to the demands of the local consumer. This led to Panasonic rethinking its company using the global strategy, and it has since sought to develop both the integrated global strategy as well as place emphasis on the local adaptations necessary to improve sales.[105]

IKEA has done a good job of balancing these organization aspects in implementing the transnational strategy.[106] IKEA is a global furniture retailer with more than 300 outlets in 39 countries and regions. IKEA focuses on lowering its costs and understanding its customers' needs, especially the needs of younger customers. It has been able to manage these seemingly opposite characteristics through its structure and management process. It has also been able to encourage its employees to understand the effects of cultural and geographic diversity on firm operations. The positive results from this are evident in the more than 600 million visitors to IKEA stores per year. It is also planning a large expansion in China and will need to adjust to the local market.[107] IKEA's system also has internal network attributes,[108] which are discussed next in regard to external interorganizational networks.

11-3g Matches between Cooperative Strategies and Network Structures

As discussed in Chapter 9, a network strategy exists when partners form several alliances in order to improve the performance of the alliance network itself through cooperative endeavors.[109] The greater levels of environmental complexity and uncertainty facing companies in today's competitive environment are causing more firms to use cooperative strategies such as strategic alliances and joint ventures.[110] The strategic focus on Unilever illustrates how it implements many cooperative strategies to accomplish both its growth objectives and environmental sustainability strategies (a topic introduced in Chapter 2 that relates to the physical environment).

As described in the Strategic Focus on Unilever, the breadth and scope of firms' operations in the global economy create many opportunities for them to cooperate.[111] In fact, a firm can develop cooperative relationships with many of its stakeholders, including customers, suppliers, and competitors, as well as NGOs. When a firm becomes involved with combinations of cooperative relationships, it is part of a strategic network, or what others call an alliance constellation or portfolio.[112]

Find out more about Jacobs Engineering Group.
www.cengagebrain.com

M. Stasy

Strategic Focus   SUCCESS

Unilever Cooperates with Many Firms and Nonprofit Organizations to Implement Its Strategy While Creating a More Sustainable Environment

Unilever, a European-headquartered (in both the Netherlands and the United Kingdom) consumer products company focused on producing and distributing many food and beverage products, has sought to lead in making their products using a sustainable environment strategy. Historically consumer products companies, especially those from Europe, have pursued the multidomestic strategy, needing to adapt their products to each country or region market. Accordingly, most have implemented their strategy using the worldwide geographic area structure. Many consumer product companies, such as Avon, have begun to use aspects of the worldwide product structure to become more efficient. This is also the case with Unilever. However, Unilever has continued to emphasize the geographic areas but has done so using the transnational strategy while implementing the combination structure to meet local market responsiveness as well as better global efficiency objectives. Moreover, its CEO, Paul Pullman, who took the job in 2009, has also suggested, "Our purpose is to have a sustainable business model that is put at the service of the greater good."

Accordingly, it created a manifesto in 2010 called the Sustainable Living Plan where Unilever promised to double its sales at the same time as it cuts its environmental footprint in half by 2020. For example, one goal is to source all of its agricultural products in ways that "don't degrade the Earth." It also has a campaign promising to improve the well-being of one billion people by "persuading them to wash their hands or brush their teeth, or by selling them food with less salt or fat." It seeks to realize many of these goals through cooperative strategies with other profit-seeking organizations as well as nonprofit entities.

In 2011, for instance, Unilever signed a contract with Jacobs Engineering Group Inc. forming a global (overall corporate) alliance to facilitate the efficiency of Unilever's capital improvement projects around the world. Unilever has 250 manufacturing sites and is expanding aggressively, especially in developing and emerging economies, to support its ambitious growth goals. For example, it expects emerging economies to drive 75 percent of its growth in the long term. The alliance with Jacobs Engineering will be managed out of Singapore and will provide engineering services for Unilever's manufacturing facilities around the world. Both companies will "work as a team to insure their sustainable growth model," implement cost reductions, and "drive co-innovation and implement the harmonization and cross-category standardization of designs." The alliance will also work with supply

Unilever North America head Kees Kruythoff discusses how the global company sustainably sourced 100% of the palm oil it uses in products like shampoo, margarine, and soap by the end of 2012, achieving its goal three years ahead of schedule. This achievement is a direct result of its Sustainable Living Plan, launched in November 2010.

chain team members to increase speed to market with designs that "reduce carbon, water, and waste footprints across its manufacturing sites."

In alignment with marketing growth goals, Unilever has initiated the Unilever Nutrition Network. This organization has divided the world into six regions focused on providing world-class nutrition and health innovation. Its goal is to generate ideas to facilitate sustainable product launches and improve existing products while strengthening their brand value. As part of this overall strategy, Unilever has used Salesforce's Chatter technology in the implementation of its new social marketing platform. This technology allows local markets and distributors of Unilever products to share insights and best practices with the marketing team from Unilever to help drive its "crafting brands for life" strategy.

The recent Unilever Sustainable Living Plan report (2012) described how the company is working with a number of non-profit, nongovernment organizations (NGOs) to help address real issues, facilitate solutions for suppliers for improving sustainable living, and reach customers in society at large who need information to improve their sustainability approaches to life with better food security and poverty alleviation. Initiatives include partnering with the following NGOs: the Consumer Goods Forum; the World Business Council for Sustainable Development; the World Economic Forum; the Tropical Forest Alliance 2020; Refrigerants, Naturally; the Global Green Foundation Forum; and Zero Hunger Challenge and Scale-Up Nutrition initiatives supported by the United Nations.

Interestingly, Unilever no longer gives quarterly earnings guidance reports and suggests that this has allowed it to focus shareholders on its longer-term goals. Furthermore, since Pullman took over in 2009 it has sustained its positive growth trajectory with better income performance and associated stock market performance. As can be seen, it is accomplishing these things through better organizational design, lofty objectives, but also by using a number of cooperative strategies with many organizations outside the organization such as Jacobs Engineering and many NGOs.

Sources: 2013, In the green corner: How IBM, Unilever and P&G started winning again: Why big business is wising up to sustainability, *Strategic Direction*, 29(5): 19–22; 2013, Our nutrition network, www.unilever.com, accessed June 17; 2013, Unilever drives efficiency in capital investment program, www.unilever.com, accessed June 17; 2013, Unilever Sustainable Living Plan, www.unilever.com, accessed June 17; 2013, Unilever Annual Report 2012, www.unilever.com, accessed June 17; S. Anand & N. Gopalan, 2013, Consumers in India are an M&A target, *Wall Street Journal*, www.wsj.com, May 1; M. Gunther, 2013, Unilever's CEO has a green thumb, *Fortune*, June 10, 124–128; R. Shields, 2013, Unilever boosts international collaboration with social rollout, *Marketing Week*, www.marketingweek.com, May 2; A. Ignatius, 2012, Captain planet, *Harvard Business Review*, 90(6): 112–118.

A *strategic network* is a group of firms that has been formed to create value by participating in multiple cooperative arrangements. An effective strategic network facilitates discovering opportunities beyond those identified by individual network participants. A strategic network can be a source of competitive advantage for its members when its operations create value that is difficult for competitors to duplicate and that network members can't create by themselves.[113] Strategic networks are used to implement business-level, corporate-level, and international cooperative strategies.

Commonly, a strategic network is a loose federation of partners participating in the network's operations on a flexible basis. At the core or center of the strategic network, the *strategic center firm* is the one around which the network's cooperative relationships revolve (see Figure 11.11).

Because of its central position, the strategic center firm is the foundation for the strategic network's structure. Concerned with various aspects of organizational structure, such as formally reporting relationships and procedures, the strategic center firm manages what are often complex, cooperative interactions among network partners. To perform the tasks discussed next, the strategic center firm must make sure that incentives for participating in the network are aligned so that network firms continue to have a reason to remain connected.[114] The strategic center firm is engaged in four primary tasks as it manages the strategic network and controls its operations:[115]

Strategic outsourcing. The strategic center firm outsources and partners with more firms than other network members. At the same time, the strategic center firm requires network partners to be more than contractors. Members are expected to find opportunities for the network to create value through its cooperative work.[116]

Competencies. To increase network effectiveness, the strategic center firm seeks ways to support each member's efforts to develop core competencies with the potential of benefiting the network.

Technology. The strategic center firm is responsible for managing the development and sharing of technology-based ideas among network members. The structural requirement that members submit formal reports detailing the technology-oriented outcomes of their efforts to the strategic center firm facilitates this activity.[117]

Race to learn. The strategic center firm emphasizes that the principal dimensions of competition are between value chains and between networks of value chains. Because of

Figure 11.11 A Strategic Network

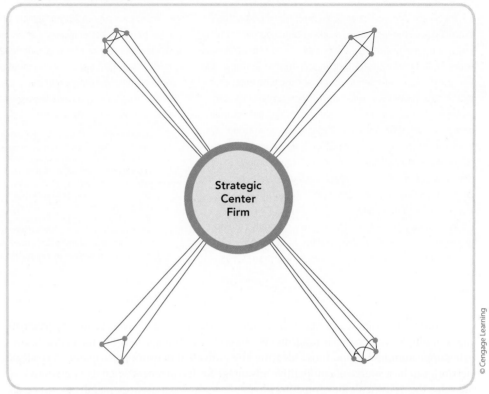

© Cengage Learning

this interconnection, the strategic network is only as strong as its weakest value-chain link. With its centralized decision-making authority and responsibility, the strategic center firm guides participants in efforts to form network-specific competitive advantages. The need for each participant to have capabilities that can be the foundation for the network's competitive advantages encourages friendly rivalry among participants seeking to develop the skills needed to quickly form new capabilities that create value for the network.[118]

Interestingly, strategic networks are being used more frequently, partly because of the ability of a strategic center firm to execute a strategy that effectively and efficiently links partner firms. Improved information systems and communication capabilities (e.g., the Internet) make such networks possible.

11-4 Implementing Business-Level Cooperative Strategies

As noted in Chapter 9, the two types of business-level complementary alliances are vertical and horizontal. Firms with competencies in different stages of the value chain form a vertical alliance to cooperatively integrate their different, but complementary, skills. Firms combining their competencies to create value in the same stage of the value chain are using a horizontal alliance. Vertical complementary strategic alliances such as those developed by Toyota Motor Company are formed more frequently than horizontal alliances.[119]

A strategic network of vertical relationships such as the network in Japan between Toyota and its suppliers often involves a number of implementation issues.[120] First, the strategic center firm encourages subcontractors to modernize their facilities and provides them with technical and financial assistance to do so, if necessary. Second, the strategic center firm reduces its transaction costs by promoting longer-term contracts with subcontractors, so that supplier-partners increase their long-term productivity. This approach is diametrically opposed to that of continually negotiating short-term contracts based on unit pricing. Third, the strategic center firm enables engineers in upstream companies (suppliers) to have better communication with those companies with whom it has contracts for services. As a result, suppliers and the strategic center firm become more interdependent and less independent.

The lean production system (a vertical complementary strategic alliance) pioneered by Toyota and others has been diffused throughout many industries.[121] In vertical complementary strategic alliances, such as the one between Toyota and its suppliers, the strategic center firm is obvious, as is the structure that firm establishes. However, the same is not always true with horizontal complementary strate-

Five jets form a star at Frankfurt Airport to mark the launch of the Star Alliance among Thai Airways, United Airlines, Lufthansa, Air Canada, and Scandinavian Airlines Systems. Horizontal complementary alliances are common in the airline industry.

gic alliances where firms try to create value in the same part of the value chain. For example, airline alliances are commonly formed to create value in the marketing and sales primary activity segment of the value chain (see Table 3.6). Because air carriers commonly participate in multiple horizontal complementary alliances such as the Star Alliance between Lufthansa, United (and originally Continental before its merger with United), US Airways, Thai, Air Canada, SAS, and others, it is difficult to determine the strategic center firm. Moreover, participating in several alliances can cause firms to question partners' true loyalties and intentions. Also, if rivals band together in too many collaborative activities, one or more governments may suspect the possibility of illegal collusive activities. For these reasons, horizontal complementary alliances are used less often and less successfully than their vertical counterpart, although there are examples of success, for instance, among auto and aircraft manufacturers.

11-5 Implementing Corporate-Level Cooperative Strategies

Some corporate-level strategies are used to facilitate cost improvement. The Strategic Focus illustrates this through the global alliances between Unilever and Jacobs Engineering Group Inc. to facilitate the efficiency of Unilever's manufacturing sites around the world, while also emphasizing innovation to accomplish Unilever's sustainability objectives. Corporate-level cooperative strategies (such as franchising) are used to facilitate product and market diversification. As a cooperative strategy, franchising allows the firm to use its competencies to extend or diversify its product or market reach, but without completing a merger or acquisition.[122] Research suggests that knowledge embedded in corporate-level cooperative strategies facilitates synergy.[123] For example, McDonald's Corporation pursues a franchising strategy, emphasizing a limited value-priced menu in more than 100 countries. The McDonald's franchising system is a strategic network. McDonald's headquarters serves as the strategic center firm for the network's franchisees. The headquarters office uses strategic and financial controls to verify that the franchisees' operations create the greatest value for the entire network.

An important strategic control issue for McDonald's is the location of its franchisee units. Because it believes that its greatest expansion opportunities are outside the United States, the firm has decided to continue expanding in countries such as China and India, where it often needs to adjust its menu according to the local culture. For example, "McDonald's adapts its restaurants in India to local tastes; in a nation that is predominantly Hindu and reveres the cow, beef isn't on the menu, for instance, replaced by chicken burgers and vegetable patties."[124] As the strategic center firm around the globe for its restaurants, McDonald's is devoting the majority of its capital expenditures to develop units in non–U.S. markets.

11-6 Implementing International Cooperative Strategies

Strategic networks formed to implement international cooperative strategies result in firms competing in several countries.[125] Differences among countries' regulatory environments increase the challenge of managing international networks and verifying that, at a minimum, the network's operations comply with all legal requirements.[126]

Distributed strategic networks are the organizational structure used to manage international cooperative strategies. As shown in Figure 11.12, several regional strategic center firms are included in the distributed network to manage partner firms' multiple cooperative arrangements.[127] The structure used to implement the international cooperative strategy is complex and demands careful attention to be used successfully. This structure is illustrated in the Strategic Focus by the network of NGOs through which Unilever manages its various sustainability strategies as it seeks to realize its objective of improving the lives of one billion people around the world.

Figure 11.12 A Distributed Strategic Network

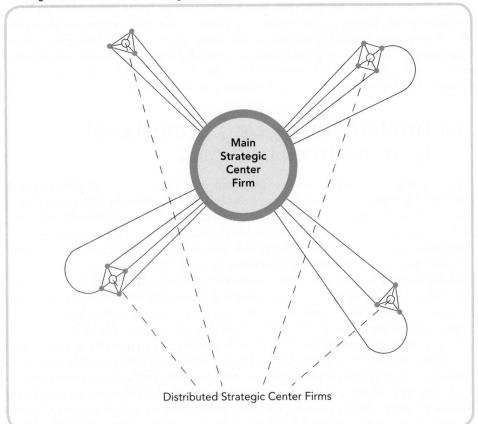

Distributed Strategic Center Firms

© Cengage Learning

SUMMARY

- Organizational structure specifies the firm's formal reporting relationships, procedures, controls, and authority and decision-making processes. Essentially, organizational structure details the work to be done in a firm and how that work is to be accomplished. Organizational controls guide the use of strategy, indicate how to compare actual and expected results, and suggest actions to take to improve performance when it falls below expectations. A proper match between strategy and structure can lead to a competitive advantage.

- Strategic controls (largely subjective criteria) and financial controls (largely objective criteria) are the two types of organizational controls used to implement a strategy. Both controls are critical, although their degree of emphasis varies based on individual matches between strategy and structure.

- Strategy and structure influence each other; overall though, strategy has a stronger influence on structure. Research indicates that firms tend to change structure when declining performance forces them to do so. Effective managers anticipate the need for structural change and quickly modify structure to better accommodate the firm's strategy when evidence calls for that action.

- The functional structure is used to implement business-level strategies. The cost leadership strategy requires a centralized functional structure—one in which manufacturing efficiency and process engineering are emphasized. The differentiation strategy's functional structure decentralizes implementation-related decisions, especially those concerned with marketing, to those involved with individual organizational functions. Focus strategies, often used in small firms, require a simple structure until such time that the firm diversifies in terms of products and/or markets.

- Unique combinations of different forms of the multidivisional structure are matched with different corporate-level diversification strategies to properly implement these strategies. The cooperative M-form, used to implement the related constrained corporate-level strategy, has a centralized corporate office and extensive integrating mechanisms. Divisional

incentives are linked to overall corporate performance to foster cooperation among divisions. The related linked SBU M-form structure establishes separate profit centers within the diversified firm. Each profit center or SBU may have divisions offering similar products, but the SBUs are often unrelated to each other. The competitive M-form structure, used to implement the unrelated diversification strategy, is highly decentralized, lacks integrating mechanisms, and utilizes objective financial criteria to evaluate each unit's performance.

- The multidomestic strategy, implemented through the worldwide geographic area structure, emphasizes decentralization and locates all functional activities in the host country or geographic area. The worldwide product divisional structure is used to implement the global strategy. This structure is centralized in order to coordinate and integrate different functions' activities so as to gain global economies of scope and economies of scale. Decision-making authority is centralized in the firm's worldwide division headquarters.

- The transnational strategy—a strategy through which the firm seeks the local responsiveness of the multidomestic strategy and the global efficiency of the global strategy—is implemented through the combination structure. Because it must be simultaneously centralized and decentralized, integrated and nonintegrated, and formalized and nonformalized, the combination structure is difficult to organize and successfully manage. However, two structural designs are suggested: the matrix and the hybrid structure with both geographic and product-oriented divisions.

- Increasingly important to competitive success, cooperative strategies are implemented through organizational structures framed around strategic networks. Strategic center firms play a critical role in managing strategic networks. Business-level strategies are often employed in vertical and horizontal alliance networks. Corporate-level cooperative strategies are used to pursue product and market diversification. Franchising is one type of corporate strategy that uses a strategic network to implement this strategy. This is also true for international cooperative strategies, where distributed networks are often used.

REVIEW QUESTIONS

1. What is organizational structure and what are organizational controls? What are the differences between strategic controls and financial controls? What is the importance of these differences?

2. What does it mean to say that strategy and structure have a reciprocal relationship?

3. What are the characteristics of the functional structures used to implement the cost leadership, differentiation, integrated cost leadership/differentiation, and focused business-level strategies?

4. What are the differences among the three versions of the multidivisional (M-form) organizational structures that are used to implement the related constrained, the related linked, and the unrelated corporate-level diversification strategies?

5. What organizational structures are used to implement the multidomestic, global, and transnational international strategies?

6. What is a strategic network? What is a strategic center firm? How is a strategic center used in business-level, corporate-level, and international cooperative strategies?

EXPERIENTIAL EXERCISES

EXERCISE 1: STRATEGY AND STRUCTURE RESPONSES TO "SHOWROOMING"

As highlighted in the opening case of this chapter, showrooming is the practice of shoppers examining merchandise in a traditional bricks and mortar store, then searching and buying online--often at a reduced price. A store in Australia went so far last year as to charge its customers $5 just to get inside the premises in an effort to forestall the practice. Further, a 2013 study by Anderson Robbins Research found that 67% of shoppers utilize their smartphones to see if there is a better price to be had elsewhere. Their work also found that a solid majority (62%) would leave the store and buy elsewhere for a 20% differential; 13 percent would buy elsewhere for any price differential. Companies can expect those numbers to climb unless steps are taken to mitigate the impact.

So what can organizations do to thwart the threat of this practice? Thanks to free shipping and easy returns (and, until recently, no taxes) the practice has flourished. It has been argued that Best Buy (some have dubbed them the Amazon showroom) and Walmart are the two stores most targeted by showrooming. However, the concept is not just aimed at large big box retailers as small businesses are at risk as well. So what is a company to do? The ability to select an appropriate strategy and match it with the appropriate structure is an important characteristic of effective strategic leadership,[128] according to your text. Your challenge in this assignment is to research the strategy and structure efforts underway at a firm level of analysis. Be prepared to identify in class how your firm is impacted negatively (do not pick a company favorably affected by showrooming for this assignment [i.e., Amazon]). In particular the assignment requires you to:

1. Identify a firm that you suspect is a target of showrooming. Get the instructor's approval ahead of time to avoid duplicates. You may identify a top retailer or other firm you think influential in this arena. You do not have to pick a large publicly held corporation; a small business you are familiar with that is impacted is a good choice as well.

2. Showrooming has really become influential in the last few years. Describe how your firm has changed during this time in terms of structure and strategy.

3. Summarize how these efforts are, or are not, paying off.

Complete this assignment using your teams.

EXERCISE 2: IS STRUCTURE CONTAGIOUS?

Form two teams to analyze and recommend changes (if any) regarding pairs of competitors. Are these competitors, such as Walgreens and CVS, structured similarly or differently? How do their strategies and organization structures compare?

PART ONE

Select a pair of competitors. You have wide latitude in this choice, such as large publicly held companies (i.e., Walgreens/CVS; Whole Foods/Kroger; American Airlines/Delta Airlines; Loews/Home Depot). Another option is to select two competitors that operate in your town that may be small to medium-sized firms. The important thing is that the firms should be competitors and roughly comparable in size.

PART TWO

Research the firms and be prepared to address the following issues:

■ Describe the strategies of the two firms—differences and similarities.

■ Present the two firms' organizational structures and note differences and similarities.

■ Does structure follow strategy as Chandler argues?

■ Are the boards of directors structured similarly between the pair with regard to committees, meetings, and titles?

■ Which one of these companies would you most likely desire to work for, all else being equal?

Be prepared to discuss your findings in a PowerPoint presentation to the class.

VIDEO CASE ▶

A MATCH FOR ORGANIZATIONAL STRUCTURE AND CONTROL—GM BANKRUPTCY

Emerging from bankruptcy, GM's commitment to smaller, more fuel-efficient cars has resulted in a move from a GM corporation to a smaller GM company. Selling off and phasing out brands along with changing logos are steps toward a new GM. With the Obama administration's desire for a complete overhaul of GM's structure, the U.S. Treasury became the company's biggest stockholder while American taxpayers had greater than 60 percent ownership in the new company. New management teams representing stability and design appear to set the stage for a match point. On November 18, 2010, GM completed its initial public offering, emerging with a solid financial foundation that has enabled the company to produce great vehicles and build a bright future for employees, partners, and shareholders. A seasoned leadership team is committed to delivering vehicles with compelling designs, flawless quality and reliability, and leading safety, fuel economy and infotainment features.

Be prepared to discuss the following concepts and questions in class:

Concepts

1. Organizational structure

2. Organizational controls

3. Strategic controls

4. Strategy and structure relationships

Questions

1. Is GM's organizational structure aligned with its strategies? If so, why? If not, what is needed?

2. What organizational controls do you think were lacking in the old GM? What organizational controls are needed in the new GM?

3. What specific strategic controls do you believe are key to GM's future success? Should GM's value chain change?

4. Recognizing GM's current state, how do you see the new GM strategy and structure relationship? How do you see it evolving?

NOTES

1. T. Felin, N. J. Foss, K. H. Heimeriks, & T. L. Madsen, 2012, Microfoundations of routines and capabilities: Individuals, processes, and structure, *Journal of Management Studies*, 49(8): 1351–1374; K. M. Eisenhardt, N. R. Furr, & C. B. Bingham, 2010, Microfoundations of performance: Balancing efficiency and flexibility in dynamic environments, *Organization Science*, 21: 1263–1273; P. Jarzabkowski, 2008, Shaping strategy as a structuration process, *Academy of Management Journal*, 51(4): 621–650.

2. R. Wilden, S. P. Gudergan, B. Nielsen, & I. Lings, 2013, Dynamic capabilities and performance: Strategy, structure and environment, *Long Range Planning*, 46(1/2): 72-96; R. Gulati & P. Puranam, 2009, Renewal through reorganization: The value of inconsistencies between formal and informal organization, *Organization Science*, 20(2): 422–440; R. E. Miles & C. C. Snow, 1978, *Organizational Strategy, Structure and Process*, New York: McGraw-Hill.

3. Y. Y. Kor & A. Mesko, 2013, Dynamic managerial capabilities: Configuration and orchestration of top executives' capabilities and the firm's dominant logic, *Strategic Management Journal*, 34(2): 233–244; S. T. Hannah & P. B. Lester, 2009, A multilevel approach to building and leading learning organizations, *Leadership Quarterly*, 20(1):

34–48; E. M. Olson, S. F. Slater, & G. T. M. Hult, 2007, The importance of structure and process to strategy implementation, *Business Horizons*, 48(1): 47–54; D. N. Sull & C. Spinosa, 2007, Promise-based management, *Harvard Business Review*, 85(4): 79–86.

4. J. P. Mangalindan, 2013, eBay is back!, *Fortune*, February 25, 58.

5. R. Rumelt, 2011, *Good Strategy/Bad Strategy: The Difference and Why It Matters*, New York: Crown Publishing Company.

6. P. Boumgarden, J. Nickerson, & T. R. Zenger, 2012, Sailing into the wind: Exploring the relationships among ambidexterity, vacillation, and organizational performance, *Strategic Management Journal*, 33(6): 587–610; R. D. Ireland, J. Covin, & D. Kuratko, 2009, Conceptualizing corporate entrepreneurship strategy, *Entrepreneurship Theory and Practice*, 33(1): 19–46; T. Amburgey & T. Dacin, 1994, As the left foot follows the right? The dynamics of strategic and structural change, *Academy of Management Journal*, 37: 1427–1452.

7. C. Gilbert, M. Eyring, & R. N. Foster, 2012, Two routes to resilience, *Harvard Business Review*, 90(12): 65–73; L. F. Monteiro, N. Arvidsson, & J. Birkinshaw, 2008, Knowledge flows within multinational corporations: Explaining subsidiary

isolation and its performance implications, *Organization Science*, 19(1): 90–107; B. Keats & H. O'Neill, 2001, Organizational structure: Looking through a strategy lens, in M. A. Hitt, R. E. Freeman, & J. S. Harrison (eds.), *Handbook of Strategic Management*, Oxford, UK: Blackwell Publishers, 520–542.

8. R. E. Hoskisson, C. W. L. Hill, & H. Kim, 1993, The multidivisional structure: Organizational fossil or source of value? *Journal of Management*, 19: 269–298.

9. B. Grøgaard, 2012, Alignment of strategy and structure in international firms: An empirical examination, *International Business Review*, 21(3): 397–407; E. M. Olson, S. F. Slater, & G. T. M. Hult, 2005, The performance implications of fit among business strategy, marketing organization structure, and strategic behavior, *Journal of Marketing*, 69(3): 49–65.

10. F. A. Csaszar, 2012, Organizational structure as a determinant of performance: Evidence from mutual funds, *Strategic Management Journal*, 33(6): 611–632; T. Burns & G. M. Stalker, 1961, *The Management of Innovation*, London: Tavistok; P. R. Lawrence & J. W. Lorsch, 1967, *Organization and Environment*, Homewood, IL: Richard D. Irwin; J. Woodward, 1965, *Industrial Organization: Theory and Practice*, London: Oxford University Press.

11. A. Verbeke & L. Kano, 2012, An internalization theory rationale for MNE regional strategy, *Multinational Business Review*, 20(2): 135–152; A. M. Rugman & A. Verbeke, 2008, A regional solution to the strategy and structure of multinationals, *European Management Journal*, 26(5): 305–313; H. Kim, R. E. Hoskisson, L. Tihanyi, & J. Hong, 2004, Evolution and restructuring of diversified business groups in emerging markets: The lessons from chaebols in Korea, *Asia Pacific Journal of Management*, 21: 25–48.

12. M. Reilly, P. Scott, & V. Mangematin, 2012, Alignment or independence? Multinational subsidiaries and parent relations, *Journal of Business Strategy*, 33(2): 4–11; R. Kathuria, M. P. Joshi, & S. J. Porth, 2007, Organizational alignment and performance: Past, present and future, *Management Decision*, 45: 503–517.

13. K. Linebaugh, 2013, GE Capital chief expected to leave, *Wall Street Journal*, May 30, B1.

14. J. Qiu, L. Donaldson, & B. Luo, 2012, The benefits of persisting with paradigms in organizational research, *Academy of Management Perspectives*, 26(1): 93–104; R. Greenwood & D. Miller, 2010, Tackling design anew: Getting back to the heart of organization theory, *Academy of Management Perspectives*, 24(4): 78–88.

15. C. Cella, A. Ellul, & M. Giannetti, 2013, Investors' horizons and the amplification of market shocks, *Review of Financial Studies*, 26(7): 1607–1648; T. Yu, M. Sengul, & R. H. Lester, 2008, Misery loves company: The spread of negative impacts resulting from an organizational crisis, *Academy of Management Review*, 33(2): 452–472; R. L. Priem, L. G. Love, & M. A. Shaffer, 2002, Executives' perceptions of uncertainty sources: A numerical taxonomy and underlying dimensions, *Journal of Management*, 28: 725–746.

16. E. Claver-Cortés, E. M. Pertusa-Ortega, & J. F. Molina-Azorín, 2012, Characteristics of organizational structure relating to hybrid competitive strategy: Implications for performance, *Journal of Business Research*, 65(7): 993–1002; J. R. Maxwell, 2008, Work system design to improve the economic performance of the firm, *Business Process Management Journal*, 14(3): 432–446; Olson, Slater, & Hult, The importance of structure and process to strategy implementation.

17. B. Gong & R. A. Greenwood, 2012, Organizational memory, downsizing, and information technology: A theoretical inquiry, *International Journal of Management*, 29: 99–109; P. Legerer, T. Pfeiffer, G. Schneider, & J. Wagner, 2009, Organizational structure and managerial decisions, *International Journal of the Economics of Business*, 16(2): 147–159.

18. 2013, General Electric: The long game, *Financial Times*, www.ft.com, April 8; H. Gebauer & F. Putz, 2009, Organisational structures for the service business in product-oriented companies, *International Journal of Services Technology and Management*, 11(1): 64–81.

19. R. Kapoor & J. Lee, 2013, Coordinating and competing in ecosystems: How organizational forms shape new technology investments, *Strategic Management Journal*, 34(3): 274–296; R. D. Ireland & J. W. Webb, 2007, Strategic entrepreneurship: Creating competitive advantage through streams of innovation, *Business Horizons*, 50: 49–59; T. J. Andersen, 2004, Integrating decentralized strategy making and strategic planning processes in dynamic environments, *Journal of Management Studies*, 41: 1271–1299.

20. M. S. Feldman & W. J. Orlikowski, 2011, Theorizing practice and practicing theory, *Organization Science*, 22(5): 1240–1253; J. Rivkin & N. Siggelkow, 2003, Balancing search and stability: Interdependencies among elements of organizational design, *Management Science*, 49: 290–311; G. A. Bigley & K. H. Roberts, 2001, The incident command system: High-reliability organizing for complex and volatile task environments, *Academy of Management Journal*, 44: 1281–1299.

21. A. J. Bock, T. Opsahl, G. George, & D. M. Gann, 2012, The effects of culture and structure on strategic flexibility during business model innovation, *Journal of Management Studies*, 49(2): 279–305; S. Nadkarni & V. K. Narayanan, 2007, Strategic schemas, strategic flexibility, and firm performance: The moderating role of industry clockspeed, *Strategic Management Journal*, 28: 243–270; K. D. Miller & A. T. Arikan, 2004, Technology search investments: Evolutionary, option reasoning, and option pricing approaches, *Strategic Management Journal*, 25: 473–485.

22. S. A. Fernhaber & P. C. Patel, 2012, How do young firms manage product portfolio complexity? The role of absorptive capacity and ambidexterity, *Strategic Management Journal*, 33(13): 1516–1539; S. Raisch & J. Birkinshaw, 2008, Organizational ambidexterity: Antecedents, outcomes, and moderators, *Journal of Management*, 34: 375–409.

23. C. Camisón & A. Villar-López, 2012, On how firms located in an industrial district profit from knowledge spillovers: Adoption of an organic structure and innovation capabilities, *British Journal of Management*, 23(3): 361–382; R. Agarwal, D. Audretsch, & M. B. Sarkar, 2010, Knowledge spillovers and strategic entrepreneurship, *Strategic Entrepreneurship Journal*, 4: 271–283.

24. Rumelt, *Good Strategy/Bad Strategy*; B. W. Keats & M. A. Hitt, 1988, A causal model of linkages among environmental dimensions, macroorganizational characteristics, and performance, *Academy of Management Journal*, 31: 570–598.

25. A. Chandler, 1962, *Strategy and Structure*, Cambridge, MA: MIT Press.

26. D. Martin, 2007, Alfred D. Chandler, Jr., a business historian, dies at 88, *New York Times*, www.nytimes.com, May 12.

27. B. T. Pentland, M. S. Feldman, M. C. Becker, & P. Liu, 2012, Dynamics of organizational routines: A generative model, *Journal of Management Studies*, 49(8): 1484–1508; R. E. Hoskisson, R. A. Johnson, L. Tihanyi, & R. E. White, 2005, Diversified business groups and corporate refocusing in emerging economies, *Journal of Management*, 31: 941–965; J. D. Day, E. Lawson, & K. Leslie, 2003, When reorganization works, *The McKinsey Quarterly*, (2): 20–29.

28. B. Simon, 2009, Restructuring chief sees benefits in GM's maligned culture, *Financial Times*, July 4, 16.

29. D. Moin & E. Clark, 2013, Ullman returns as Johnson exits, *WWD: Women's Wear Daily*, April 9, 1.

30. S. Sonenshein, 2013, How organizations foster the creative use of resources, *Academy of Management Journal*, in press; S. K. Ethiraj, 2007, Allocation of inventive effort in complex product systems, *Strategic Management Journal*, 28: 563–584.

31. L. Marengo & C. Pasquali, 2012, How to get what you want when you do not know what you want: A model of incentives, organizational structure, and learning, *Organization Science*, 23(5): 1298–1310; A. M. Kleinbaum & M. L. Tushman, 2008, Managing corporate social networks, *Harvard Business Review*, 86(7/8): 26–27; P. K. Mills & G. R. Ungson, 2003, Reassessing the limits of structural empowerment: Organizational constitution and trust as controls, *Academy of Management Review*, 28: 143–153.

32. D. W. Lehman & J. Hahn, 2013, Momentum and organizational risk taking: Evidence from the National Football League, *Management Science*, 59(4): 852–868; M. A. Hitt, K. T. Haynes, & R. Serpa, 2010, Strategic leadership for the 21st century, *Business Horizons*, 53: 437–444; M. A. Desai, 2008, The finance function in a global corporation, *Harvard Business Review*, 86(7/8): 108–112.

33. R. MacKay & R. Chia, 2013, Choice, chance, and unintended consequences in strategic change: A process understanding of the rise and fall of Northco Automotive, *Academy of Management Journal*, 56(1): 208–230; I. Filatotchev, J. Stephan, & B. Jindra, 2008, Ownership structure, strategic controls and export intensity of foreign-invested firms in transition economies, *Journal of International Business Studies*, 39(7): 1133–1148; G. J. M. Braam & E. J. Nijssen, 2004, Performance effects of using the balanced scorecard: A note on the Dutch experience, *Long Range Planning*, 37: 335–349.

34. D. M. Cable, F. Gino, & B. R. Staats, 2013, Breaking them in or eliciting their best? Reframing socialization around newcomers' authentic self-expression, *Administrative*

Science Quarterly, 58(1): 1–36; J. Kratzer, H. G. Gemünden, & C. Lettl, 2008, Balancing creativity and time efficiency in multi-team R&D projects: The alignment of formal and informal networks, *R&D Management*, 38(5): 538–549; D. F. Kuratko, R. D. Ireland, & J. S. Hornsby, 2004, Corporate entrepreneurship behavior among managers: A review of theory, research, and practice, in J. A. Katz & D. A. Shepherd (eds.), *Advances in Entrepreneurship: Firm Emergence and Growth: Corporate Entrepreneurship*, Oxford, UK: Elsevier Publishing, 7–45.

35. M. Lev-Ram, 2013, Samsung's road to mobile domination, *Fortune*, February 04, 98–102; P. Burrows, 2011, Elop's fable, *Bloomberg Businessweek*, June 6, 56–61; Y. Doz & M. Kosonen, 2008, The dynamics of strategic agility: Nokia's rollercoaster experience, *California Management Review*, 50(3): 95–118.

36. K. Favaro, 2013, We're from corporate and we are here to help: Understanding the real value of corporate strategy and the head office, *Strategy+Business Online*, www.strategy+business.com, April 8; K. L. Turner & M. V. Makhija, 2006, The role of organizational controls in managing knowledge, *Academy of Management Review*, 31: 197–217; M. A. Hitt, R. E. Hoskisson, R. A. Johnson, & D. D. Moesel, 1996, The market for corporate control and firm innovation, *Academy of Management Journal*, 39: 1084–1119.

37. W. P. Wan, R. E. Hoskisson, J. C. Short, & D. W. Yiu, 2011, Resource-based theory and corporate diversification: Accomplishments and opportunities, *Journal of Management*, 37(5): 1335–1368; M. A. Hitt, L. Tihanyi, T. Miller, & B. Connelly, 2006, International diversification: Antecedents, outcomes, and moderators, *Journal of Management*, 32: 831–867; R. E. Hoskisson & M. A. Hitt, 1988, Strategic control and relative R&D investment in multiproduct firms, *Strategic Management Journal*, 9: 605–621.

38. I. Clark, 2013, Templates for financial control? Management and employees under the private equity business model, *Human Resource Management Journal*, 23(2): 144–159; S. Lee, K. Park, & H.-H. Shin, 2009, Disappearing internal capital markets: Evidence from diversified business groups in Korea, *Journal of Banking & Finance*, 33(2): 326–334; D. Collis, D. Young, & M. Goold, 2007, The size, structure, and performance of corporate headquarters, *Strategic Management Journal*, 28: 383–405.

39. S. S. Alsoboa & J. Aldehayyat, 2013, The impact of competitive business strategies on managerial accounting techniques: A study of Jordanian public industrial companies, *International Journal of Management*, 31(1): 545–555; X. S. Y. Spencer, T. A. Joiner, & S. Salmon, 2009, Differentiation strategy, performance measurement systems and organizational performance: Evidence from Australia,

International Journal of Business, 14(1): 83–103; K. Chaharbaghi, 2007, The problematic of strategy: A way of seeing is also a way of not seeing, *Management Decision*, 45: 327–339.

40. S. K. Kim, J. D. Arthurs, A. Sahaym, & J. B. Cullen, 2013, Search behavior of the diversified firm: The impact of fit on innovation, *Strategic Management Journal*, 34(8): 999-1009.

41. S. Lohr, 2007, Can Michael Dell refocus his namesake? *New York Times*, www.nytimes.com, September 9.

42. S. Ovide, 2013, Dell: Icahn, Southeastern are $4 billion short, *Wall Street Journal*, www.wsj.com, June 3.

43. R. G. Eccles & G. Serafeim, 2013, The performance frontier, *Harvard Business Review*, 91(5): 50–60; Gebauer & Putz, Organisational structures for the service business in product-oriented companies; X. Yin & E. J. Zajac, 2004, The strategy/governance structure fit relationship: Theory and evidence in franchising arrangements, *Strategic Management Journal*, 25: 365–383.

44. Keats & O'Neill, Organizational structure, 531.

45. M. K. Bednar, S. Boivie, & N. R. Prince, 2013, Burr under the saddle: How media coverage influences strategic change, *Organization Science*, 24(3): 910–925; K. M. Green, J. G. Covin, & D. P. Slevin, 2008, Exploring the relationship between strategic reactiveness and entrepreneurial orientation: The role of structure-style fit, *Journal of Business Venturing*, 23(3): 356–383; Olson, Slater, & Hult, The importance of structure and process to strategy implementation; D. Miller & J. O. Whitney, 1999, Beyond strategy: Configuration as a pillar of competitive advantage, *Business Horizons*, 42(3): 5–17.

46. D. C. Mowery, 2010, Alfred Chandler and knowledge management within the firm, *Industrial & Corporate Change*, 19(2): 483–507; Chandler, *Strategy and Structure*.

47. Keats & O'Neill, Organizational structure, 524.

48. Wan, Hoskisson, Short & Yiu, 2011, Resource-based theory and corporate diversification: Accomplishments and opportunities; E. Rawley, 2010, Diversification, coordination costs and organizational rigidity: Evidence from microdata, *Strategic Management Journal*, 31: 873–891.

49. A. Campbell & H. Strikwerda, 2013, The power of one: Towards the new integrated organization, *Journal of Business Strategy*, 34(2): 4–12.

50. J. J. Strikwerda & J. W. Stoelhorst, 2009, The emergence and evolution of the multidimensional organization, *California Management Review*, 51(4): 11–31; I. Daizadeh, 2006, Using intellectual property to map the organisational evolution of firms: Tracing a biotechnology company from startup to bureaucracy to a multidivisional firm, *Journal of Commercial Biotechnology*, 13: 28–36.

51. C. Levicki, 1999, *The Interactive Strategy Workout*, 2nd ed., London: Prentice Hall.

52. P. L. Drnevich & D. C. Croson, 2013, Information technology and business-level strategy: Toward an integrated theoretical perspective, *MIS Quarterly*, 37(2): 483–509; E. E. Entin, F. J. Diedrich, & B. Rubineau, 2003, Adaptive communication patterns in different organizational structures, *Human Factors and Ergonomics Society Annual Meeting Proceedings*, 405–409; H. M. O'Neill, R. W. Pouder, & A. K. Buchholtz, 1998, Patterns in the diffusion of strategies across organizations: Insights from the innovation diffusion literature, *Academy of Management Review*, 23: 98–114.

53. 2013, Organizational structure, *Wikipedia*, en.wikipedia.org; Spencer, Joiner, & Salmon, Differentiation strategy, performance measurement systems and organizational performance.

54. P. Leinwand & C. Mainardi, 2013, Beyond functions, *Strategy+Business*, www.strategy-business.com, Spring, 1-5; Keats & O'Neill, Organizational structure, 539.

55. J. Cable, 2012, For innovation to flourish, "Bureaucracy must die", *Industry Week/IW*, 261(6): 54; C. M. Christensen, S. P. Kaufman, & W. C. Shih, 2008, Innovation killers, *Harvard Business Review*: Special HBS Centennial Issue, 86(1): 98–105; J. Welch & S. Welch, 2006, Growing up but staying young, *BusinessWeek*, December 11, 112.

56. O. E. Williamson, 1975, *Markets and Hierarchies: Analysis and Anti-Trust Implications*, New York: The Free Press.

57. T. Hutzschenreuter & J. Horstkotte, 2013, Performance effects of top management team demographic faultlines in the process of product diversification, *Strategic Management Journal*, 34: 704–726; S. H. Mialon, 2008, Efficient horizontal mergers: The effects of internal capital reallocation and organizational form, *International Journal of Industrial Organization*, 26(4): 861–877; Chandler, *Strategy and Structure*.

58. J. Joseph & W. Ocasio, 2012, Architecture, attention, and adaptation in the multibusiness firm: General Electric from 1951 to 2001, *Strategic Management Journal*, 33(6): 633–660; R. Inderst, H. M. Müller, & K. Wärneryd, 2007, Distributional conflict in organizations, *European Economic Review*, 51: 385–402; J. Greco, 1999, Alfred P. Sloan, Jr. (1875–1966): The original "organization" man, *Journal of Business Strategy*, 20(5): 30–31.

59. Hoskisson, Hill, & Kim, The multidivisional structure, 269–298.

60. V. Binda, 2012, Strategy and structure in large Italian and Spanish firms, 1950–2002, *Business History Review*, 86(3): 503–525; W. G. Rowe & P. M. Wright, 1997, Related and unrelated diversification and their effect on human resource management controls, *Strategic Management Journal*, 18: 329–338.

61. C. E. Helfat & K. M. Eisenhardt, 2004, Inter-temporal economies of scope,

organizational modularity, and the dynamics of diversification, *Strategic Management Journal*, 25: 1217–1232; A. D. Chandler, 1994, The functions of the HQ unit in the multibusiness firm, in R. P. Rumelt, D. E. Schendel, & D. J. Teece (eds.), *Fundamental Issues in Strategy*, Cambridge, MA: Harvard Business School Press, 327.

62. O. E. Williamson, 1994, Strategizing, economizing, and economic organization, in R. P. Rumelt, D. E. Schendel, & D. J. Teece (eds.), *Fundamental Issues in Strategy*, Cambridge, MA: Harvard Business School Press, 361–401.

63. Hoskisson, Hill, & Kim, The multidivisional structure: Organizational fossil or source of value?

64. R. Duchin & D. Sosyura, 2013, Divisional managers and internal capital markets, *Journal of Finance*, 68(2): 387–429; O. E. Williamson, 1985, *The Economic Institutions of Capitalism: Firms, Markets, and Relational Contracting*, New York: Macmillan.

65. Keats & O'Neill, Organizational structure, 532.

66. M. F. Wolff, 1999, In the organization of the future, competitive advantage will lie with inspired employees, *Research Technology Management*, 42(4): 2–4.

67. E. Schulz, S. Chowdhury, & D. Van de Voort, 2013, Firm productivity moderated link between human capital and compensation: The significance of task-specific human capital, *Human Resource Management*, 52(3): 423–439; R. H. Hall, 1996, *Organizations: Structures, Processes, and Outcomes*, 6th ed., Englewood Cliffs, NJ: Prentice Hall, 13; S. Baiman, D. F. Larcker, & M. V. Rajan, 1995, Organizational design for business units, *Journal of Accounting Research*, 33: 205–229.

68. L. G. Love, R. L. Priem, & G. T. Lumpkin, 2002, Explicitly articulated strategy and firm performance under alternative levels of centralization, *Journal of Management*, 28: 611–627.

69. T. F. Gonzalez-Cruz, A. Huguet-Roig, & S. Cruz-Ros, 2012, Organizational technology as a mediating variable in centralization-formalization fit, *Management Decision*, 50(9): 1527–1548; Hall, *Organizations*, 64–75.

70. D. G. Sirmon, M. A. Hitt, R. D. Ireland, & B. A. Gilbert, 2011, Resource orchestration to create competitive advantage: Breadth, depth and life cycle effects, *Journal of Management*, 37(5): 1390–1412.

71. J. B. Barney, 2001, *Gaining and Sustaining Competitive Advantage*, 2nd ed., Upper Saddle River, NJ: Prentice Hall, 257.

72. H. Karandikar & S. Nidamarthi, 2007, Implementing a platform strategy for a systems business via standardization, *Journal of Manufacturing Technology Management*, 18: 267–280.

73. V. K. Garg, R. L. Priem, & A. A. Rasheed, 2013, A theoretical explanation of the cost advantages of multi-unit franchising, *Journal of Marketing Channels*, 20(1/2): 52–72; H. Wang & C. Kimble, 2010, Low-cost strategy through product architecture:

Lessons from China, *Journal of Business Strategy*, 31(3): 12–20.

74. Olson, Slater, & Hult, The performance implications of fit.

75. M. Troy, 2012, Supplier expectations offer insight at Walmart, *Drug Store News*, November 19, 20–22; 2007, Wal-Mart Stores, Inc., *New York Times*, www.nytimes.com, July 21.

76. 2013, Our story, Walmart Corporate, www.walmartstores.com, June 14.

77. N. Takagoshi & N. Matsubayashi, 2013, Customization competition between branded firms: Continuous extension of product line from core product, *European Journal of Operational Research*, 225(2): 337–352; Sirmon, Hitt, Ireland, & Gilbert, Resource orchestration to create competitive advantage; Olson, Slater, & Hult, The performance implications of fit.

78. Bock, Opsahl, George, & Gann, The effects of culture and structure on strategic flexibility during business model innovation; K. Z. Zhou & F. Wu, 2010, Technological capability, strategic flexibility and product innovation, *Strategic Management Journal*, 31: 547–561.

79. 2013, Mission of Under Armour, www.underarmour.com, June 14; T. Heath, 2008, In pursuit of innovation at Under Armour: Founder Kevin Plank says Super Bowl commercial has generated "buzz," *Washington Post*, February 25, D03.

80. Claver-Cortés, Pertusa-Ortega, & Molina-Azorín, Characteristics of organizational structure relating to hybrid competitive strategy.

81. Chandler, *Strategy and Structure*.

82. L. Capron, 2013, Cisco's corporate development portfolio: A blend of building, borrowing and buying, *Strategy & Leadership*, 41(2): 27–30; R. M. Kanter, 2011, Cisco and a cautionary tale about teams, *Harvard Business Review*, blogs.hbr.org, May 9.

83. Y. M. Zhou, 2011, Synergy, coordination costs, and diversification choices, *Strategic Management Journal*, 32: 624–639; C. C. Markides & P. J. Williamson, 1996, Corporate diversification and organizational structure: A resource-based view, *Academy of Management Journal*, 39: 340–367; C. W. L. Hill, M. A. Hitt, & R. E. Hoskisson, 1992, Cooperative versus competitive structures in related and unrelated diversified firms, *Organization Science*, 3: 501–521.

84. Sirmon, Hitt, Ireland, & Gilbert, Resource orchestration to create competitive advantage; M. Makri, M. A. Hitt, & P. J. Lane, 2010, Complementary technologies, knowledge relatedness and invention outcomes in high technology mergers and acquisitions, *Strategic Management Journal*, 31: 602–628.

85. J. Wolf & W. G. Egelhoff, 2013, An empirical evaluation of conflict in MNC matrix structure firms, *International Business Review*, 22(3): 591–601; S. H. Appelbaum,

D. Nadeau, & M. Cyr, 2008, Performance evaluation in a matrix organization: A case study (part two), *Industrial and Commercial Training*, 40(6): 295–299.

86. S. H. Appelbaum, D. Nadeau, & M. Cyr, 2009, Performance evaluation in a matrix organization: A case study (part three), *Industrial and Commercial Training*, 41(1): 9–14; M. Goold & A. Campbell, 2003, Structured networks: Towards the well-designed matrix, *Long Range Planning*, 36(5): 427–439.

87. O. Alexy, G. George, & A. J. Salter, 2013, Cui bono? The selective revealing of knowledge and its implications for innovative activity, *Academy of Management Review*, 38(2): 270–291; Rawley, Diversification, coordination costs, and organizational rigidity.

88. J. Huang & H. Kim, 2013, Conceptualizing structural ambidexterity into the innovation of human resource management architecture: The case of LG Electronics, *International Journal of Human Resource Management*, 24(5): 922–943; C. Fang, J. Lee, & M. A. Schilling, 2010, Balancing exploration and exploitation through structural design: The isolation of subgroups and organizational learning, *Organization Science*, 21: 625–642.

89. M. Kruehler, U. Pidun, & H. Rubner, 2012, How to assess the corporate parenting strategy? A conceptual answer, *Journal of Business Strategy*, 33(4): 4–17; M. M. Schmid & I. Walter, 2009, Do financial conglomerates create or destroy economic value? *Journal of Financial Intermediation*, 18(2): 193–216; P. A. Argenti, R. A. Howell, & K. A. Beck, 2005, The strategic communication imperative, *MIT Sloan Management Review*, 46(3): 84–89.

90. N. T. Dorata, 2012, Determinants of the strengths and weaknesses of acquiring firms in mergers and acquisitions: A stakeholder perspective, *International Journal of Management*, 29(2): 578–590; M. F. Wiersema & H. P. Bowen, 2008, Corporate diversification: The impact of foreign competition, industry globalization, and product diversification, *Strategic Management Journal*, 29: 115–132; R. E. Hoskisson & M. A. Hitt, 1990, Antecedents and performance outcomes of diversification: A review and critique of theoretical perspectives, *Journal of Management*, 16: 461–509.

91. A. Varmaz, A. Varwig, & T. Poddig, 2013, Centralized resource planning and yardstick competition, *Omega*, 41(1): 112–118; Hill, Hitt, & Hoskisson, Cooperative versus competitive structures, 512.

92. D. Holod, 2012, Agency and internal capital market inefficiency: Evidence from banking organizations, *Financial Management*, 41(1): 35–53; Lee, Park, & Shin, Disappearing internal capital markets: Evidence from diversified business groups in Korea; J. Birkinshaw, 2001, Strategies for

managing internal competition, *California Management Review*, 44(1): 21–38.

93. 2013, Our company, www.textron.com, June 14; Textron 2012 Annual Report.

94. R. M. Holmes, Jr., T. Miller, M. A. Hitt, & M. P. Salmador, 2013, The interrelationships among informal institutions, formal institutions and inward foreign direct investment, *Journal of Management*, in press; T. Yu & A. A. Cannella, Jr., 2007, Rivalry between multinational enterprises: An event history approach, *Academy of Management Journal*, 50: 665–686; S. E. Christophe & H. Lee, 2005, What matters about internationalization: A market-based assessment, *Journal of Business Research*, 58: 636–643.

95. A. H. Kirca, G. T. M. Hult, S. Deligonul, M. Z. Perryy, & S. T. Cavusgil, 2012, A multilevel examination of the drivers of firm multinationality: A meta-analysis, *Journal of Management*, 38: 502–530.

96. J.-L. Arregle, T. Miller, M. A. Hitt, & P. W. Beamish, 2013, Do regions matter? An integrated institutional and semiglobalization perspective on the internationalization of MNEs, *Strategic Management Journal*, 34(8): 910-934; T. M. Begley & D. P. Boyd, 2003, The need for a corporate global mind-set, *MIT Sloan Management Review*, 44(2): 25–32.

97. P. Almodóvar, 2012, The international performance of standardizing and customizing Spanish firms: The M curve relationships, *Multinational Business Review*, 20(4): 306–330; G. R. G. Benito, R. Lunnan, & S. Tomassen, 2011, Distant encounters of the third kind: Multinational companies locating divisional headquarters abroad, *Journal of Management Studies*, 48: 373–394; T. Kostova & K. Roth, 2003, Social capital in multinational corporations and a micro-macro model of its formation, *Academy of Management Review*, 28: 297–317.

98. R. Foroohar, 2012, The economy's new rules: Go glocal, *Time*, August 20, 26–32.

99. P. Punyatoya, 2013, Consumer evaluation of brand extension for global and local brands: The moderating role of product similarity, *Journal of International Consumer Marketing*, 25(3): 198–215; A. I. Mockaitis, L. Salciuviene, & P. N. Ghauri, 2013, On what do consumer product preferences depend? Determining domestic versus foreign product preferences in an emerging economy market, *Journal of International Consumer Marketing*, 25(3): 166–180.

100. J. H. Johnson, Jr., B. Arya, & D. A. Mirchandani, 2013, Global integration strategies of small and medium multinationals: Evidence from Taiwan, *Journal of World Business*, 48(1): 47–57; C. A. Bartlett & S. Ghoshal, 1989, *Managing Across Borders: The Transnational Solution*, Boston: Harvard Business School Press.

101. J. Goudreau, 2013, New Avon CEO vows to restore the 126-year-old beauty company to former glory, *Forbes*, www.forbes.com, February 27.

102. B. Brenner & B. Ambos, 2013, A question of legitimacy? A dynamic perspective on multinational firm control, *Organization Science*, 24(3): 773–795; M. P. Koza, S. Tallman, & A. Ataay, 2011, The strategic assembly of global firms: A microstructural analysis of local learning and global adaptation, *Global Strategy Journal*, 1: 27–46.

103. J. Qiu & L. Donaldson, 2012, Stopford and Wells were right! MNC matrix structures do fit a "high-high" strategy, *Management International Review*, 52(5): 671–689; B. Connelly, M. A. Hitt, A. DeNisi, & R. D. Ireland, 2007, Expatriates and corporate-level international strategy: Governing with the knowledge contract, *Management Decision*, 45: 564–581.

104. J. S. Lublin & S. Ng, 2013, P&G lines up executives in race for CEO Lafley's successor, *Wall Street Journal*, www.wsj.com, May 30.

105. T. Wakayama, J. Shintaku, & A. Tomofumi, 2012, What Panasonic learned in China, *Harvard Business Review*, 90(12): 109–113.

106. A. Ringstrom, 2013, One size doesn't fit all: IKEA goes local for India, China, www.reuters.com, March 7.

107. L. Lin, 2013, Ikea's Ohlsson targets fourfold increase in China stores by 2020, www.bloomberg.com, April 2.

108. J. Hultman, T. Johnsen, R. Johnsen, & S. Hertz, 2012, An interaction approach to global sourcing: A case study of IKEA, *Journal of Purchasing & Supply Management*, 18(1): 9–21.

109. I. Neyens & D. Faems, 2013, Exploring the impact of alliance portfolio management design on alliance portfolio performance, *Managerial & Decision Economics*, 34(3-5): 347–361.

110. J.-P. Roy, 2012, IJV partner trustworthy behaviour: The role of host country governance and partner selection criteria, *Journal of Management Studies*, 49: 332–355; V. A. Aggarwal, N. Siggelkow, & H. Singh, 2011, Governing collaborative activity: Interdependence and the impact of coordination and exploration, *Strategic Management Journal*, 32: 705–730; J. Li, C. Zhou, & E. J. Zajac, 2009, Control, collaboration, and productivity in international joint ventures: Theory and evidence, *Strategic Management Journal*, 30: 865–884.

111. L. Li, G. Qian, & Z. Qian, 2013, Do partners in international strategic alliances share resources, costs, and risks? *Journal of Business Research*, 66(4): 489–498; D. Li, L. E. Eden, M. A. Hitt, & R. D. Ireland, 2008, Friends, acquaintances, or strangers? Partner selection in R&D alliances, *Academy of Management Journal*, 51(2): 315–334.

112. R. Gulati, P. Puranam, & M. Tushman, 2012, Meta-organization design: Rethinking design in interorganizational and community context, *Strategic Management Journal*, 33: 571–586; J. Wincent, S. Anokhin, D. Örtqvist, & E. Autio, 2010, Quality meets

structure: Generalized reciprocity and firm-level advantage in strategic networks, *Journal of Management Studies*, 47: 597–624.

113. V. Van de Vrande, 2013, Balancing your technology-sourcing portfolio: How sourcing mode diversity enhances innovative performance, *Strategic Management Journal*, 34(5): 610–621; T. P. Moliterno & D. M. Mahony, 2011, Network theory of organization: A multilevel approach, *Journal of Management*, 37: 443–467.

114. L. Dooley, D. Kirk, & K. Philpott, 2013, Nurturing life-science knowledge discovery: Managing multi-organisation networks, *Production Planning & Control*, 24(2/3): 195-207; A. T. Arikan & M. A. Schilling, 2011, Structure and governance of industrial districts: Implications for competitive advantage, *Journal of Management Studies*, 48: 772–803; R. D. Ireland & J. W. Webb, 2007, A multi-theoretic perspective on trust and power in strategic supply chains, *Journal of Operations Management*, 25: 482–497.

115. S. Albers, F. Wohlgezogen, & E. J. Zajac, 2013, Strategic alliance structures: An organization design perspective, *Journal of Management*, in press.

116. B. Baudry & V. Chassagnon, 2012, The vertical network organization as a specific governance structure: What are the challenges for incomplete contracts theories and what are the theoretical implications for the boundaries of the (hub-) firm? *Journal of Management & Governance*, 16(2): 285–303.

117. K. Zhou & D. Xu, 2012, How foreign firms curtail local supplier opportunism in China: Detailed contracts, centralized control, and relational governance, *Journal of International Business Studies*, 43(7): 677–692; J. Bae, F. C. Wezel, & J. Koo, 2011, Cross-cutting ties, organizational density and new firm formation in the U.S. biotech industry, 1994–98, *Academy of Management Journal*, 54: 295–311; J. Zhang & C. Baden-Fuller, 2010, The influence of technological knowledge base and organizational structure on technological collaboration, *Journal of Management Studies*, 47: 679–704.

118. R. Gulati, F. Wohlgezogen, & P. Zhelyazkov, 2012, The two facets of collaboration: Cooperation and coordination in strategic alliances, *Academy of Management Annals*, 6: 531–583; M. H. Hansen, R. E. Hoskisson, & J. B. Barney, 2008, Competitive advantage in alliance governance: Resolving the opportunism minimization-gain maximization paradox, *Managerial and Decision Economics*, 29: 191–208; G. Lorenzoni & C. Baden-Fuller, 1995, Creating a strategic center to manage a web of partners, *California Management Review*, 37(3): 146–163.

119. E. Revilla, M. Sáenz, & D. Knoppen, 2013, Towards an empirical typology of buyer–supplier relationships based on

absorptive capacity, *International Journal of Production Research*, 51(10): 2935–2951; A. C. Inkpen, 2008, Knowledge transfer and international joint ventures: The case of NUMMI and General Motors, *Strategic Management Journal*, 29(4): 447–453; J. H. Dyer & K. Nobeoka, 2000, Creating and managing a high-performance knowledge-sharing network: The Toyota case, *Strategic Management Journal*, 21: 345–367.

120. N. Lahiri & S. Narayanan, 2013, Vertical integration, innovation and alliance portfolio size: Implications for firm performance, *Strategic Management Journal*, 34(9): 1042–1064; L. F. Mesquita, J. Anand, & J. H. Brush, 2008, Comparing the resource-based and relational views: Knowledge transfer and spillover in vertical alliances, *Strategic Management Journal*, 29: 913–941; M. Kotabe, X. Martin, & H. Domoto, 2003, Gaining from vertical partnerships: Knowledge transfer, relationship duration and supplier performance improvement in the U.S. and Japanese automotive industries, *Strategic Management Journal*, 24: 293–316.

121. A. Alblas & H. Wortmann, 2012, Impact of product platforms on lean production systems: Evidence from industrial machinery manufacturing, *International Journal of Technology Management*, 57(1/2/3): 110–131; S. G. Lazzarini, D. P. Claro, & L. F. Mesquita, 2008, Buyer-supplier and supplier-supplier alliances: Do they reinforce or undermine one another? *Journal of Management Studies*, 45(3): 561–584; P. Dussauge, B. Garrette, & W. Mitchell, 2004, Asymmetric performance: The market share impact of scale and link alliances

in the global auto industry, *Strategic Management Journal*, 25: 701–711.

122. Garg, Priem, & Rasheed, A theoretical explanation of the cost advantages of multi-unit franchising; A. M. Hayashi, 2008, How to replicate success, *MIT Sloan Management Review*, 49(3): 6–7; M. Tuunanen & F. Hoy, 2007, Franchising: Multifaceted form of entrepreneurship, *International Journal of Entrepreneurship and Small Business*, 4: 52–67.

123. W. Vanhaverbeke, V. Gilsing, & G. Duysters, 2012, Competence and governance in strategic collaboration: The differential effect of network structure on the creation of core and noncore technology, *Journal of Product Innovation Management*, 29(5): 784–802; A. Zaheer, R. Gözübüyük, & H. Milanov, 2010, It's the connections: The network perspective in interorganizational research, *Academy of Management Perspectives*, 24(1): 62–77.

124. J. DeTar, 2012, McDonald's shares rise amid India expansion move, *Investor's Business Daily*, www.news.investor.com, December 7; E. Bellman, 2009, Corporate news: McDonald's plans expansion in India, *Wall Street Journal*, June 30, B4.

125. Y. Lew & R. R. Sinkovics, 2013, Crossing borders and industry sectors: Behavioral governance in strategic alliances and product innovation for competitive advantage, *Long Range Planning*, 46(1/2): 13–38; T. W. Tong, J. J. Reuer, & M. W. Peng, 2008, International joint ventures and the value of growth options, *Academy of Management Journal*, 51: 1014–1029; C. Jones, W. S. Hesterly, & S. P. Borgatti, 1997, A general theory of network governance: Exchange conditions and social

mechanisms, *Academy of Management Review*, 22: 911–945.

126. H. Liu, X. Jiang, J. Zhang, & X. Zhao, 2013, Strategic flexibility and international venturing by emerging market firms: The moderating effects of institutional and relational factors, *Journal of International Marketing*, 21(2): 79–98; M. W. Hansen, T. Pedersen, & B. Petersen, 2009, MNC strategies and linkage effects in developing countries, *Journal of World Business*, 44(2): 121–130; A. Goerzen, 2005, Managing alliance networks: Emerging practices of multinational corporations, *Academy of Management Executive*, 19(2): 94–107.

127. C. C. Phelps, 2010, A longitudinal study of the influence of alliance network structure and composition on firm exploratory innovation, *Academy of Management Journal*, 53: 890–913; L. H. Lin, 2009, Mergers and acquisitions, alliances and technology development: An empirical study of the global auto industry, *International Journal of Technology Management*, 48(3): 295–307.

128. Y. Y. Kor & A. Mesko, 2013, Dynamic managerial capabilities: Configuration and orchestration of top executives' capabilities and the firm's dominant logic, *Strategic Management Journal*, 34(2): 233–244; S. T. Hannah & P. B. Lester, 2009, A multilevel approach to building and leading learning organizations, *Leadership Quarterly*, 20(1): 34–48; E. M. Olson, S. F. Slater, & G. T. M. Hult, 2007, The importance of structure and process to strategy implementation, *Business Horizons*, 48(1): 47–54; D. N. Sull & C. Spinosa, 2007, Promise-based management, *Harvard Business Review*, 85(4):79–86.

12

Strategic Leadership

Studying this chapter should provide you with the strategic management knowledge needed to:

1 Define strategic leadership and describe top-level managers' importance.

2 Explain what top management teams are and how they affect firm performance.

3 Describe the managerial succession process using internal and external managerial labor markets.

4 Discuss the value of strategic leadership in determining the firm's strategic direction.

5 Describe the importance of strategic leaders in managing the firm's resources.

6 Explain what must be done for a firm to sustain an effective culture.

7 Describe what strategic leaders can do to establish and emphasize ethical practices.

8 Discuss the importance and use of organizational controls.

A CHANGE AT THE TOP AT PROCTER & GAMBLE (P&G): AN INDICATION OF HOW MUCH THE CEO MATTERS?

A. G. Lafley joined Procter & Gamble (P&G) in 1977 as brand assistant for Joy dishwashing liquid. From this beginning, he worked his way through the firm's laundry division, becoming highly visible as a result of number of successes including the launching of liquid Tide. A string of continuing accomplishments throughout the firm resulted in Lafley's appointment as P&G's CEO in June 2000, a post he held until retiring in mid-2009. Bob McDonald, who joined P&G in 1980, was Lafley's handpicked successor. McDonald took the top position at P&G in July 2009, but resigned under pressure in May 2013. Lafley, revered by many, was asked to come out of retirement and return to P&G as president, CEO and chairman of the board of directors. Lafley said that when contacted to return to P&G, he agreed immediately to do so, committing to remain "as long as needed to improve the company's performance." However, speculation is that Lafley likely would not remain beyond three years.

What went wrong for McDonald, a long-time P&G employee who seemed to know the firm well and who received Lafley's support? Not surprisingly, a number of possibilities have been mentioned in response to this question. Some concluded that under McDonald's leadership, P&G suffered from "poor execution globally," an outcome created in part by P&G's seemingly ineffective responses to aggressive competition in emerging markets. Other apparent problems were a failure to control the firm's costs and employees' loss of confidence in McDonald's leadership. Still others argued that McDonald did not fully understand the effects on U.S. consumers of the recession in place when he took over and that during that time period, P&G "was selling BMWs when cash-tight consumers were looking for Kias." The net result of these types of problems included P&G "losing a step to rivals like Unilever." In turn, this caused investors to become frustrated by "P&G's inability to consistently keep up with its rivals' sales growth and share price gains."

But why bring Lafley back? In a few words, because of his previous success. Among other achievements during his first stint as P&G's main strategic leader were building up the firm's beauty business, acquiring Gillette, expanding the firm's presence in emerging markets, and launching hit products such as Swiffer and Febreze. An overall measure of P&G's success during Lafley's initial tenure as CEO is the fact that the firm's shares increased 63 percent in value while the S&P fell 37 percent in value. Thus, multiple stakeholders including investors and employees may believe that Lafley can return the firm to the "glory days" it experienced from 2000 to 2009.

What are some actions Lafley is considering as he returns to P&G? Product innovations are a core concern and an area receiving a significant amount of attention. Analysts suggest that P&G needs to move beyond incremental innovations, seeking to again create entirely new product categories as it did with Swiffer and Febreze. This will be challenging at least in the short run given recent declines in allocations to the firm's research and development (R&D) programs. These reductions have resulted in a product pipeline focused mainly on "reformulating rather than inventing." Additionally, efforts are underway to continue McDonald's strong, recent commitments to reduce the firm's "bloated" cost structure and reenergize the competitive actions it will take in global markets.

Restructuring P&G's multiple brands and products into four sectors, each of which will be headed by a president, is a major change Lafley is initiating. Currently, the firm has two global business divisions—beauty and grooming and household care. Final decisions about the precise compositions of the four sectors were not announced by mid-2013. Speculation, though, was that each sector would be formed "to reflect synergies between various businesses." For example, one expectation was that paper-based products such as "Bounty paper towels, Charmin toilet paper, Pampers diapers and Always feminine care products" would be combined to form a sector. Moreover, Lafley's replacement was expected to be selected from among the four presidents who would be chosen to lead the new sectors.

Sources: D. Benoit, 2013, Critical P&G analysts still waiting on results, *Wall Street Journal*, www.wsj.com, May 24; D. Benoit, 2013, Procter & Gamble gets an upgrade, *Wall Street Journal*, www.wsj.com, May 24; J. Bogaisky, 2013, Congrats, Bill Ackman: Bob McDonald out at P&G; A. G. Lafley returning as CEO, *Forbes*, www.forbes.com, May 23; E. Byron & J. S. Lublin, 2013, Embattled P&G chief replaced by old boss, *Wall Street Journal*, www.wsj.com, May 23; L. Coleman-Lochner & C. Hymowitz, 2013, Lafley's CEO encore at P&G puts rock star legacy at risk: Retail, *Bloomberg*, www.bloomberg.com, May 28; J. S. Lublin & S. Ng, 2013, P&G lines up executives in race for CEO Lafley's successor, *Wall Street Journal*, www.wsj.com, May 30; J. Ritchie, 2013, P&G's hiring of Lafley may buy time for innovation, *Business Courier*, www.bizjournals.com, May 31.

Strategy Right NOW

Learn more about Procter & Gamble.
www.cengagebrain.com

As the Opening Case suggests, strategic leaders' work is demanding, challenging, and requires balancing short-term performance outcomes with long-term performance goals. Regardless of how long (or short) they remain in their positions, strategic leaders (and most prominently CEOs) affect a firm's performance.[1] A. G. Lafley affected Procter & Gamble's (P&G) performance during his initial service as CEO as did Bob McDonald during his slightly less than four-year term. Moreover, as described in the Opening Case, analysts, employees, and perhaps even customers are hopeful that Lafley's second stint as P&G's CEO will be as successful—and hopefully even more successful—than the first one.

A major message in this chapter is that effective strategic leadership is the foundation for successfully using the strategic management process. As implied in Figure 1.1 in Chapter 1 and through the Analysis-Strategy-Performance model, strategic leaders guide the firm in ways that result in forming a vision and mission. Often, this guidance finds leaders thinking of ways to create goals that stretch everyone in the organization as a foundation for enhancing firm performance. A positive outcome of stretch goals is their ability to provoke breakthrough thinking—thinking that often leads to innovation.[2] Additionally, strategic leaders work with others to verify that the analysis and strategy parts of the A-S-P model are completed in order to increase the likelihood the firm will achieve strategic competitiveness and earn above-average returns. We show how effective strategic leadership makes all of this possible in Figure 12.1.[3]

To begin this chapter, we define strategic leadership and discuss its importance and the possibility of strategic leaders being a source of competitive advantage for a firm. These introductory comments include a brief consideration of different styles strategic leaders may use. We then examine the role of top-level managers and top management teams and their effects on innovation, strategic change, and firm performance. Following this discussion is an analysis of managerial succession, particularly in the context of the internal and external managerial labor markets from which strategic leaders are selected. Closing the chapter are descriptions of five key leadership actions that contribute to effective strategic

M. Stasy

Figure 12.1 Strategic Leadership and the Strategic Management Process

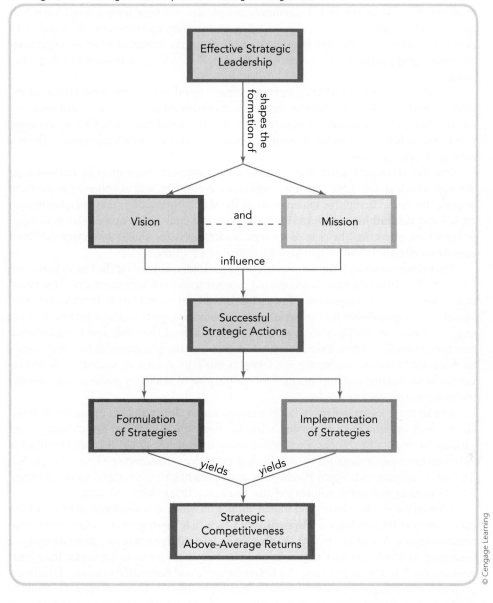

© Cengage Learning

leadership—determining strategic direction, effectively managing the firm's resource portfolio, sustaining an effective organizational culture, emphasizing ethical practices, and establishing balanced organizational controls.

12-1 Strategic Leadership and Style

Strategic leadership is the ability to anticipate, envision, maintain flexibility, and empower others to create strategic change as necessary. **Strategic change** is change brought about as a result of selecting and implementing a firm's strategies. Multifunctional in nature, strategic leadership involves managing through others, managing an entire organization rather

Strategic leadership is the ability to anticipate, envision, maintain flexibility, and empower others to create strategic change as necessary.

Strategic change is change brought about as a result of selecting and implementing a firm's strategies.

372 Part 3: Strategic Actions: Strategy Implementation

than a functional subunit, and coping with change that continues to increase in the global economy. Because of the global economy's complexity, strategic leaders must learn how to effectively influence human behavior, often in uncertain environments. By word or by personal example, and through their ability to envision the future, effective strategic leaders meaningfully influence the behaviors, thoughts, and feelings of those with whom they work.[4]

The ability to attract and then manage human capital may be the most critical of the strategic leader's skills,[5] especially because the lack of talented human capital constrains firm growth. Indeed, in the twenty-first century, intellectual capital that the firm's human capital possesses, including the ability to manage knowledge and produce innovations, affects a strategic leader's success.[6]

Effective strategic leaders also create and then support the context or environment through which stakeholders (such as employees, customers, and suppliers) can perform at peak efficiency.[7] Being able to demonstrate the skills of attracting and managing human capital and establishing and nurturing an appropriate context for that capital to flourish is important, given that the crux of strategic leadership is the ability to manage the firm's operations effectively and sustain high performance over time.[8]

The primary responsibility for effective strategic leadership rests at the top, in particular with the CEO. Other commonly recognized strategic leaders include members of the board of directors, the top management team, and divisional general managers. In truth, any individual with responsibility for the performance of human capital and/or a part of the firm (e.g., a production unit) is a strategic leader. Regardless of their title and organizational function, strategic leaders have substantial decision-making responsibilities that cannot be delegated.[9] Strategic leadership is a complex but critical form of leadership. Strategies cannot be formulated and implemented for the purpose of achieving above-average returns without effective strategic leaders.

As a strategic leader, a firm's CEO is involved with a large number and variety of tasks, all of which in some form or fashion relate to effective use of the strategic management process. In the Strategic Focus, we describe many issues with which Heinrich Hiesinger is currently involved through his service as chief executive of Germany's ThyssenKrupp AG. The range of issues with which Hiesinger is dealing highlights the complexity of a strategic leader's work as well as the influence of that work on a firm's shape and scope.

A leader's style and the organizational culture in which it is displayed often affect the productivity of those being led. ThyssenKrupp's Heinrich Hiesinger has spoken about these realities, saying that in the past at the firm he is leading there was an "understanding of leadership in which 'old boys' networks' and blind loyalty were more important than business success."[10] In Hiesinger's view, this leadership style and culture led to many of the firm's problems and resulted in a loss of trust in and credibility for ThyssenKrupp. He believes the firm must now do everything possible to again earn both trust and credibility with stakeholders.

Transformational leadership is the most effective strategic leadership style. This style entails motivating followers to exceed the expectations others have of them, to continuously enrich their capabilities, and to place the interests of the organization above their own.[11] Transformational leaders develop and communicate a vision for the organization and formulate a strategy to achieve that vision. They make followers aware of the need to achieve valued organizational outcomes and encourage them to continuously strive for higher levels of achievement.

Transformational leaders have a high degree of integrity (Ray Kroc, founder of McDonald's, was a strategic leader valued for his high degree of integrity)[12] and character. Speaking about character, one CEO said the following: "Leaders are shaped and defined by character. Leaders inspire and enable others to do excellent work and realize their potential.

Learn more about Strategic Leadership.
www.cengagebrain.com

Learn more about Strategic Change.
www.cengagebrain.com

M. Stasy

Strategic Focus

FAILURE

The Life of a CEO as a Firm's Primary Strategic Leader: Breadth, Depth, and Complexity

Based in Germany and known historically as a steel manufacturer, ThyssenKrupp AG is a diversified firm organized into six business areas—components technology, elevator technology, industrial solutions, materials services, steel Europe, and steel Americas (as of September 30, 2012, this business area is formally classified as a discontinued operation according to International Financial Reporting Standards). Globally, ThyssenKrupp has over 150,000 employees working in approximately 80 countries. The company, recognized today as a steel and engineering firm, is Germany's largest steelmaker by output.

The recent past has been unkind to ThyssenKrupp in terms of financial performance and relative to issues warranting attention. Accepting responsibility for reshaping the firm and handling the controversies facing it as a foundation for turning around its performance is Dr.-Ing. Heinrich Hiesinger. Formerly affiliated with another large German firm—Siemens—Hiesinger became chairman of the executive board of ThyssenKrupp in January 2011. To hopefully begin to ease stakeholders' concerns, Hiesinger has pledged a "fresh start" and indicated that he seeks to "put things right and implement a new corporate culture."

What are some of the issues Hiesinger is facing? One is financial in that the firm reported heavy losses during 2011 and 2012; the quality of 2013's financial performance was uncertain at mid-year. Contributing to these difficulties were ThyssenKrupp's steel operations in Brazil and the United States. With hindsight, deciding to expand into these markets was a mistake as indicated by the fact that both of them were unprofitable, largely because of "waning demand from the auto and construction industries and competition from China," conditions that weakened prices for the firm's products and negatively affected its profit margins. Brazil's third largest steelmaker, Cia. Siderurgica nacional SA (SID) was the leading bidder for ThyssenKrupp's plants in both Brazil and the United States.

The resignation in March 2013 of ThyssenKrupp's supervisory chairman and various scandals that emerged during the chairman's service were additional problems requiring Hiesinger's attention. Allegations of "price-fixing at the firm's railway-track-construction unit and charges of inappropriate business trips with union representatives and journalists" were issues that demanded Hiesinger's time and energy. As a result

ThyssenKrupp AG's headquarters in Essen, Germany. A change in strategic leadership at the heavy industry giant has resulted in a change in strategy.

of the price-fixing charge, the firm was fined by the German competition authority. Another action taken to deal with the quality of ThyssenKrupp's corporate governance that the scandals suggest was the establishment of a whistleblower program for employees.

Hiesinger is also involved in reshaping the focus of ThyssenKrupp's competitive efforts. With a goal of converting the firm into an integrated technology provider, Hiesinger's decisions are causing the firm to concentrate on "making components for cars and heavy vehicles, building naval ships and submarines, and its elevator business." Once implemented, the firm's new emphases in terms of the business areas in which it competes will find it generating only about 30 percent of its revenue from steelmaking. Additionally, Hiesinger believes that China and Asia are growth markets for the firm, particularly for the elevator division. Accordingly, plans are underway for ThyssenKrupp to more than double its workforce in China by mid-2017.

Sources: T. Andresen, 2013, Thyssen woes tarnish 99-year-old steel baron's legacy, *Bloomberg*, www.bloomberg.com, May 21; J. Hromadko, 2013, Thyssen earnings: Loss widens on write-down of Brazil, U.S. plants, *Wall Street Journal*, www.wsj.com, May 15; J. Hromadko, 2013, ThyssenKrupp offers workers amnesty to resolve corruption case, *Wall Street Journal*, www.wsj.com, April 16; J. Hromadko, 2013, ThyssenKrupp chairman to step down, *Wall Street Journal*, www.wsj.com, March 8; A. Kirchfeld, J. P. Spinetto & C. Lucchesi, 2013, CSN said to be leading bidder for ThyssenKrupp Americas plants, *Bloomberg*, www.bloomberg.com, May 2; J. Ng, 2013, ThyssenKrupp looks to China, Asia for growth, *Wall Street Journal*, www.wsj.com, June 3.

As a result, they build successful, enduring organizations."[13] Additionally, transformational leaders have emotional intelligence. Emotionally intelligent leaders understand themselves well, have strong motivation, are empathetic with others, and have effective interpersonal skills.[14] As a result of these characteristics, transformational leaders are especially effective in promoting and nurturing innovation in firms.[15]

12-2 The Role of Top-Level Managers

As strategic leaders, top-level managers are critical to a firm's efforts to effectively use the strategic management process. To exercise the duties of this role, top-level managers make many decisions, such as the strategic actions and responses that are part of the competitive rivalry with which the firm is involved at a point in time (see Chapter 5). More broadly, they are involved with making many decisions associated with first selecting and then implementing the firm's strategies.

When making decisions related to using the strategic management process, managers (certainly top-level ones) often use their discretion (or latitude for action).[16] Managerial discretion differs significantly across industries. The primary factors that determine the amount of decision-making discretion held by a manager (especially a top-level manager) are (1) external environmental sources such as the industry structure, the rate of market growth in the firm's primary industry, and the degree to which products can be differentiated; (2) characteristics of the organization, including its size, age, resources, and culture; and (3) characteristics of the manager, including commitment to the firm and its strategic outcomes, tolerance for ambiguity, skills in working with different people, and aspiration levels (see Figure 12.2). Because strategic leaders' decisions are intended to help the firm outperform competitors, how managers exercise discretion when making decisions is critical to the firm's success[17] and affects or shapes the firm's culture.

Top-level managers' roles in verifying that their firm effectively uses the strategic management process are complex and challenging. Because of this, top management teams rather than a single top-level manager typically make the decisions relative to this important task.

12-2a Top Management Teams

The **top management team** is composed of the individuals who are responsible for making certain the firm uses the strategic management process, especially for the purpose of selecting and implementing strategies. Typically, the top management team includes the officers of the corporation, defined by the title of vice president and above or by service as a member of the board of directors.[18] Among other outcomes, the quality of a top management team's decisions affects the firm's ability to innovate and change in ways that contribute to its efforts to earn above-average returns.[19]

As previously noted, the complex challenges facing most organizations require the exercise of strategic leadership by a team of executives rather than by a single individual. Using a team to make decisions about how the firm will compete also helps to avoid another potential problem when these decisions are made by the CEO alone: managerial hubris. Research shows that when CEOs begin to believe glowing press accounts and to feel that they are unlikely to make errors, the quality of their decisions suffers.[20] Top-level managers need to have self-confidence but must guard against allowing it to become arrogance and a false belief in their own invincibility.[21] To guard against CEO overconfidence and the making of poor decisions, firms often use the top management team to make decisions required by the strategic management process.

The **top management team** is composed of the individuals who are responsible for making certain the firm uses the strategic management process, especially for the purpose of selecting and implementing strategies.

Figure 12.2 Factors Affecting Managerial Discretion

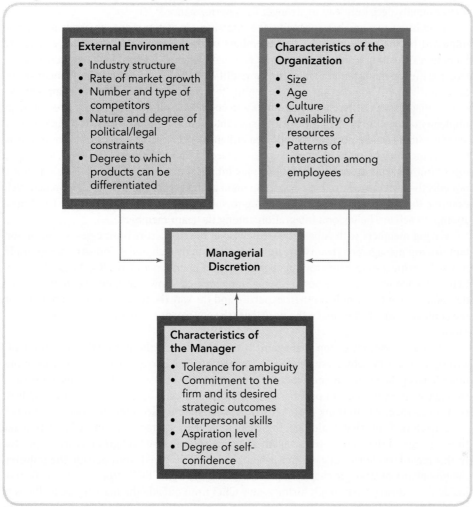

Source: Adapted from S. Finkelstein & D C. Hambrick, 1996, *Strategic Leadership: Top Executives and Their Effects on Organizations,* St. Paul, MN: West Publishing Company.

Top Management Teams, Firm Performance, and Strategic Change

The job of top-level managers is complex and requires a broad knowledge of the firm's internal organization (see Chapter 3) as well as the three key parts of its external environment—the general, industry, and competitor environments (see Chapter 2). Therefore, firms try to form a top management team with knowledge and expertise needed to operate the internal organization, yet that also can deal with the firm's stakeholders as well as its competitors.[22] To have these characteristics normally requires a heterogeneous top management team. A **heterogeneous top management team** is composed of individuals with different functional backgrounds, experience, and education. Increasingly, having international experience is a critical aspect of the heterogeneity that is desirable in top management teams, given the globalized nature of the markets in which most firms now compete.

Research evidence indicates that members of a heterogeneous top management team benefit from discussing their different perspectives.[23] In many cases, these discussions and the debates they often engender increase the quality of the team's decisions, especially

A **heterogeneous top management team** is composed of individuals with different functional backgrounds, experience, and education.

when a synthesis emerges within the team after evaluating different perspectives.[24] In turn, higher-quality decisions lead to stronger firm performance.[25]

In addition to their heterogeneity, the effectiveness of top management teams is also impacted by the value gained when members of these teams work together cohesively. Sometimes affecting team cohesion is the fact that, in general, the more heterogeneous and larger is the top management team, the more difficult it is for the team to implement strategies effectively.[26] Also noteworthy is the finding that communication difficulties among top-level managers with different backgrounds and cognitive skills can negatively affect strategy implementation efforts.[27] On the positive side, interactions among diverse top management team members can be positively supported and influenced through electronic communications, sometimes reducing the barriers before face-to-face meetings.[28] However, a group of top executives with diverse backgrounds may inhibit the process of decision making if it is not effectively managed. In these cases, top management teams may fail to comprehensively examine threats and opportunities, leading to suboptimal decisions. Thus, the CEO must attempt to achieve behavioral integration among the team members.[29]

Having members with substantive expertise in the firm's core businesses is also important to a top management team's effectiveness.[30] In a high-technology industry, for example, it may be critical for a firm's top management team members to have R&D expertise, particularly when growth strategies are being implemented. However, their eventual effect on decisions depends not only on their expertise and the way the team is managed but also on the context in which they make the decisions (the governance structure, incentive compensation, etc.).[31]

The characteristics of top management teams and even the personalities of the CEO and other team members are related to innovation and strategic change.[32] For example, more heterogeneous top management teams are positively associated with innovation and strategic change, perhaps in part because heterogeneity may influence the team or at least some of its members to think more creatively when making decisions and taking actions.[33]

Therefore, firms that could benefit by changing their strategies are more likely to make those changes if they have top management teams with diverse backgrounds and expertise. In this regard, evidence suggests that when a new CEO is hired from outside the industry, the probability of strategic change is greater than if the new CEO is from inside the firm or inside the industry.[34] Although hiring a new CEO from outside the industry adds diversity to the team, the top management team must be managed effectively to gain the benefits associated with that diversity. Consistent with earlier comments, we highlight here the value of transformational leadership to strategic change as the CEO helps the firm match environmental opportunities with its strengths, as indicated by its capabilities and core competencies, as a foundation for selecting and/or implementing new strategies.[35]

The CEO and Top Management Team Power

We noted in Chapter 10 that the board of directors is an important governance mechanism for monitoring a firm's strategic direction and for representing stakeholders' interests, especially shareholders. In fact, higher performance normally is achieved when the board of directors is more directly involved in helping to shape the firm's strategic direction.[36]

Boards of directors, however, may find it difficult to direct the decisions and resulting actions of powerful CEOs and top management teams.[37] Often, a powerful CEO appoints a number of sympathetic outside members to the board or may have inside board members who are also on the top management team and report to her or him.[38] In either case, the CEO may significantly influence actions such as appointments to the board. Thus, the amount of discretion a CEO has in making decisions is related to the board of directors and the decision latitude it provides to the CEO and the remainder of the top management team.[39]

CEOs and top management team members can also achieve power in other ways. For example, a CEO who also holds the position of chairperson of the board usually has more power than the CEO who does not.[40] Some analysts and corporate "watchdogs" criticize the practice of *CEO duality* (which is when the CEO and the chairperson of the board are the same) because it can lead to poor performance and slow responses to change, partly because the tendency is for the board to reduce its efforts to monitor the CEO and other top management team members when CEO duality exists.[41]

Although it varies across industries, CEO duality occurs most commonly in larger firms. Increased shareholder activism has brought CEO duality under scrutiny and attack in both U.S. and European firms. In this regard, we noted in Chapter 10 that a number of analysts, regulators, and corporate directors believe that an independent board leadership structure without CEO duality has a net positive effect on the board's efforts to monitor top-level managers' decisions and actions, particularly with respect to financial performance. However, CEO duality's actual effects on firm performance (and particularly financial performance) remain inconclusive.[42] Moreover, recent evidence suggests that at least in a sample of firms in European countries, CEO duality positively affects performance when a firm encounters a crisis.[43] Thus, it seems that nuances or situational conditions must be considered when analyzing the outcomes of CEO duality on firm performance.

The power of the CEO and top management team relative to the board of directors is influenced by a number of factors.

Top management team members and CEOs who have long tenure—on the team and in the organization—have a greater influence on board decisions. In general, long tenure may constrain the breadth of an executive's knowledge base. Some evidence suggests that with the limited perspectives associated with a restricted knowledge base, long-tenured top executives typically develop fewer alternatives to evaluate when making strategic decisions.[44] However, long-tenured managers also may be able to exercise more effective strategic control, thereby obviating the need for board members' involvement because effective strategic control generally leads to higher performance.[45] Intriguingly, it may be that "the liabilities of short tenure ... appear to exceed the advantages, while the advantages of long tenure—firm-specific human and social capital, knowledge, and power—seem to outweigh the disadvantages of rigidity and maintaining the status quo."[46] Overall then the relationship between CEO tenure and firm performance is complex and nuanced,[47] indicating that a board of directors should develop an effective working relationship with the top management team as part of its efforts to enhance firm performance.

Another nuance or situational condition to consider is the case in which a CEO acts as a *steward* of the firm's assets. In this instance, holding the dual roles of CEO and board chair facilitates the making of decisions and the taking of actions that benefit stakeholders. The logic here is that the CEO desiring to be the best possible steward of the firm's assets gains efficiency through CEO duality.[48] Additionally, because of this person's positive orientation and actions, extra governance and the coordination costs resulting from an independent board leadership structure become unnecessary.[49]

In summary, the relative degrees of power held by the board and top management team members should be examined in light of an individual firm's situation. For example, the abundance of resources in a firm's external environment and the volatility of that environment may affect the ideal balance of power between the board and the top management team. Moreover, a volatile and uncertain environment may create a situation where a powerful CEO is needed to move quickly. In such an instance, a diverse top management team may create less cohesion among team members, perhaps stalling or even preventing appropriate decisions from being made in a timely manner as a result. In the final analysis, an effective working relationship between the board and the CEO and other top management team members is the foundation through which decisions are made that have the highest probability of best serving stakeholders' interests.[50]

12-3 Managerial Succession

The choice of top-level managers—particularly CEOs—is a critical decision with important implications for the firm's performance.[51] As discussed in Chapter 10, selecting the CEO is one of the board of directors' most important responsibilities as it seeks to represent the best interests of a firm's stakeholders. Many companies use leadership screening systems to identify individuals with strategic leadership potential as well as to determine the criteria individuals should satisfy to be a candidate for the CEO position.

The most effective of these screening systems assesses people within the firm and gains valuable information about the capabilities of other companies' strategic leaders.[52] Based on the results of these assessments, training and development programs are provided to various individuals in an attempt to preselect and shape the skills of people with strategic leadership potential.

A number of firms have high-quality leadership programs in place, including Procter & Gamble (P&G), GE, IBM, and Dow Chemical. For example, P&G is thought to have talent throughout the organization that is trained to accept the next level of leadership responsibility when the time comes. Managing talent on a global basis, P&G seeks to consistently provide leaders at all levels in the firm with meaningful work and significant responsibilities as a means of simultaneously challenging and developing them. The value created by GE's leadership training programs is suggested by the fact that many companies recruit leadership talent from this firm.[53]

In spite of the value high-quality leadership training programs can create, there are many companies that have not established training and succession plans for their top-level managers or for others holding key leadership positions (e.g., department heads, sections heads). With respect to family-owned firms operating in the United States, a recent survey found that only 41 percent of those surveyed have established leadership contingency plans while 49 percent indicated that they "review succession plans (only) when a change in management requires it."[54] On a global scale, recent evidence suggests that "Only 45 percent of executives from 34 countries around the world say their companies have a process for conducting CEO succession planning."[55] Those leading firms throughout the world should recognize that the need for continuity in the use of their strategic management process is difficult to attain without an effective succession plan and process in place.

Organizations select managers and strategic leaders from two types of managerial labor markets—internal and external.[56] An **internal managerial labor market** consists of a firm's opportunities for managerial positions and the qualified employees within that firm. An **external managerial labor market** is the collection of managerial career opportunities and the qualified people who are external to the organization in which the opportunities exist.

Employees commonly prefer that the internal managerial labor market be used for selection purposes, particularly when the firm is choosing members for its top management team and a new CEO. Evidence suggests that these preferences are often fulfilled. For example, almost 70 percent of new CEOs selected in S&P 500 companies in the first quarter of 2013 were promoted from within.[57] In the same set of firms, roughly 75 percent of CEO appointments between 2007 and 2009 were from the internal managerial labor market, indicating that the primary source of CEO appointments in S&P 500 companies from 2007

An **internal managerial labor market** consists of a firm's opportunities for managerial positions and the qualified employees within that firm.

An **external managerial labor market** is the collection of managerial career opportunities and the qualified people who are external to the organization in which the opportunities exist.

until 2013 remained the same.[58] And in all probability, A. G. Lafley's replacement as CEO of Procter & Gamble (P&G), as discussed in the Opening Case, will be an internal candidate. Although some analysts anticipated that investors might champion the perceived need to hire from the external market to replace Lafley when he retires a second time, the general thinking was that such a hire was highly unlikely given the firm's "historically strong commitment to select new CEOs from within the company."[59]

With respect to the CEO position, several benefits are thought to accrue to a firm using the internal labor market to select a new CEO, one of which is the continuing commitment such a selection creates with respect to the existing vision, mission, and strategies. Also, because of their experience with the firm and the industry in which it competes, inside CEOs are familiar with company products, markets, technologies, and operating procedures. Another benefit is that choosing to hire a new CEO from within usually results in lower turnover among existing personnel, many of whom possess valuable firm-specific knowledge and skills. In summary, CEOs selected from inside the firm tend to benefit from their (1) clear understanding of the firm's personnel and their capabilities, (2) appreciation of the company's culture and its associated core values, (3) deep knowledge of the firm's core competencies as well as abilities to develop new ones as appropriate, and (4) "feel" for what will and will not "work" in the firm.[60]

In spite of the understandable and legitimate reasons to select CEOs from inside the firm, boards of directors sometimes prefer to choose a new CEO from the external managerial labor market. Conditions suggesting a potentially appropriate preference to hire from outside include (1) the firm's need to enhance its ability to innovate, (2) the firm's need to reverse its recent poor performance, and (3) the fact that the industry in which the firm competes is experiencing rapid growth.

Overall, the decision to use either the internal or the external managerial labor market to select a firm's new CEO is one that should be based on expectations; in other words, what does the board of directors want the new CEO and top management team to accomplish? We address this issue in Figure 12.3 by showing how the composition of the top management team and the CEO succession source (managerial labor market) interact to affect strategy. For example, when the top management team is homogeneous (its members have

Figure 12.3 Effects of CEO Succession and Top Management Team Composition on Strategy

© Cengage Learning

similar functional experiences and educational backgrounds) and a new CEO is selected from inside the firm, the firm's current strategy is unlikely to change. If the firm is performing well absolutely and relative to peers, continuing to implement the current strategy may be precisely what the board of directors wants to happen. Alternatively, when a new CEO is selected from outside the firm and the top management team is heterogeneous, the probability is high that strategy will change. This of course would be a board's preference when the firm's performance is declining, both in absolute terms and relative to rivals. When the new CEO is from inside the firm and a heterogeneous top management team is in place, the strategy may not change, but innovation is likely to continue. An external CEO succession with a homogeneous team creates a more ambiguous situation. Furthermore, outside CEOs who lead moderate change often achieve increases in performance, but high strategic change by outsiders frequently leads to declines in performance.[61] In summary, a firm's board of directors should use the insights shown in Figure 12.3 to inform its decision about which of the two managerial labor markets to use when selecting a new CEO.

An interim CEO is commonly appointed when a firm lacks a succession plan or when an emergency occurs requiring an immediate appointment of a new CEO. Companies throughout the world use this approach.[62] Interim CEOs are almost always from inside the firm; their familiarity with the company's operations supports their efforts to "maintain order" for a period of time. Indeed, a primary advantage of appointing an interim CEO is that doing so can generate the amount of time the board of directors requires to conduct a thorough search to find the best candidate from the external and internal markets. Legg Mason, one of the largest asset management firms in the world with eight affiliates serving individual and institutional clients on six continents, recently chose to promote its then-current interim CEO to the CEO position. This selection was made after the firm spent five months to evaluate over a dozen candidates in total from the external and internal managerial labor markets combined. Although supportive of the selected insider, an analyst also said that turnarounds of asset management firms (which is what many thought needed to happen at Legg Mason) are difficult, perhaps especially so for someone intimately familiar with the firm and its current structure.[63]

As we have discussed, managerial succession especially with respect to the CEO position is an important organizational event. In the Strategic Focus we further describe the importance of these plans and how some firms use them. Increasingly, because of their importance, all of a firm's stakeholders are expressing their strong desire that the board of directors has an effective succession plan in place.

Next, we discuss key actions that effective strategic leaders demonstrate while helping their firm use the strategic management process.

12-4 Key Strategic Leadership Actions

Certain actions characterize effective strategic leadership; we present the most important ones in Figure 12.4. Many of the actions interact with each other. For example, managing the firm's resources effectively includes developing human capital and contributes to establishing a strategic direction, fostering an effective culture, exploiting core competencies, using effective and balanced organizational control systems, and establishing ethical practices. The most effective strategic leaders create viable options in making decisions regarding each of the key strategic leadership actions.[64]

12-4a Determining Strategic Direction

Determining strategic direction involves specifying the vision and the strategy or strategies to achieve this vision over time.[65] The strategic direction is framed within the context of

Strategy Right NOW

Find out more about Ford.
www.cengagebrain.com

Determining strategic direction involves specifying the vision and the strategy or strategies to achieve this vision over time

M. Stasy

Strategic Focus

Keeping Quality People at the Top of The Firm's Leadership Structure: The Importance of Planning for Managerial Succession

As noted in Chapter 10 and as emphasized in this chapter as well, the board of directors is responsible for the firm having "an effective and sustainable CEO succession plan." Interestingly, surveys continue to reveal that boards note that succession planning is the top or second-most significant challenge they face in exercising their responsibilities. Moreover, only 16 percent of recently surveyed directors indicated that their board is effective at succession planning. This is potentially an issue in that the CEO succession process is being used more frequently in many nations and regions. In North America, for example, the average tenure for a CEO has declined from 10-plus years in the mid-1990s to under 5 years today.

Once in place, a CEO succession plan is the foundation for the CEO and the top management team to establish and operationalize effective succession plans for use throughout the organization regarding leadership positions and the management of the human capital that will fill those positions. Certainly with respect to the CEO, a fully developed and effective succession plan deals with actions to take for the purpose of selecting, developing, evaluating, and compensating the CEO. Obvious benefits from an effective CEO succession plan include those of supporting the firm's corporate governance procedures and increasing stakeholders' confidence that the board is acting in their best interests. In this regard, some analysts believe that "when a robust plan provides for a smooth CEO transition—whether a company is faced with a planned or an emergency succession—it will yield returns for stakeholders." Indeed, effective succession planning and execution are "absolutely vital to a company's sustainability."

In spite of the statistics reported here, a number of firms do have active succession plans in place. For example, Ford Motor Company's vice president of communications says that the firm "takes succession planning very seriously" and that the company has "succession plans in place for each of (its) key leadership positions." As is true with many companies though, Ford does not discuss its *specific* succession plans externally for competitive reasons. Many are interested to learn about Berkshire Hathaway's CEO succession plans. Warren Buffett, the firm's long-term CEO, has noted for several years in the firm's annual report that plans are in place and that in all likelihood, his job will be split into two (with one person becoming CEO of Berkshire's operating company and a second one assuming the leadership of Berkshire's investment portfolio).

In addition to selecting a new CEO from the formally defined internal and external managerial labor markets, a

Gilt Groupe CEO Michelle Peluso assumed the position of CEO after previously serving on the firm's board of directors.

trend of selecting a CEO from the firm's board of directors may be emerging. For example, board member Michelle Peluso was selected as Gilt Group's CEO to replace founder and then-current CEO Kevin Ryan. (Founded in 2007, Gilt Group offers "flash sales" opportunities to customers to buy luxury items at substantially reduced prices. Firms are willing to sell at steep discounts in order to reduce overstocked inventories.) As is the case with Peluso, a key advantage is that as a board member, an individual is deeply familiar with the firm's operations and the opportunities and threats facing it. Thus, "the director-turned-CEO succession model provides companies with a chief executive who is familiar with corporate strategy and key stakeholders, thereby reducing leadership transition risk."

Sometimes a firm "selects" a former CEO to return to the firm he or she previously led. This is the situation with A. G. Lafley at Procter & Gamble as described in this chapter's Opening Case. It is also the situation with India's Infosys Ltd., where founder and former CEO N. R. Narayana Murthy was brought back as the firm's CEO "in response to shareholder demands to revive the struggling technology company." Regardless of the approach used, the critical issue is for a firm's board of directors to intentionally form and then effectively use managerial succession plans that will best represent stakeholders' interests.

Sources: 2013, CEO succession planning and talent considerations, *Risk & Compliance Journal*, www.deloitte.wsj.com, May 28; 2013, CFO change at Time Warner Cable may underscore CEO succession, *CFO Journal*, www.blogs.wsj.com, May 1; 2013, Succession planning, *SpencerStuart*, www.stuartspencer.com, February; 2013, The experts: Do companies spend too much on 'superstar' CEOs? *Wall Street Journal*, www.wsj.com, March 14; 2013, More companies looking outside for their next CEO, *The Conference Board*, www.conference-board.org, May 1; V. Fuhrmans, 2013, GM names new Opel chief, *Wall Street Journal*, www.wsj.com, January 31; D. A. Thoppil, 2013, Infosys brings back founder, *Wall Street Journal*, www.wsj.com, June 1.

Figure 12.4 Exercise of Effective Strategic Leadership

© Cengage Learning

the conditions (i.e., opportunities and threats) strategic leaders expect their firm to face in roughly the next three to five years.

The ideal long-term strategic direction has two parts: a core ideology and an envisioned future. The core ideology motivates employees through the company's heritage while the envisioned future encourages them to stretch beyond their expectations of accomplishment and requires significant change and progress to be realized.[66] The envisioned future serves as a guide to many aspects of a firm's strategy implementation process, including motivation, leadership, employee empowerment, and organizational design. The strategic direction could include a host of actions such as entering new international markets and developing a set of new suppliers to add to the firm's value chain.[67]

Sometimes though, the work of strategic leaders does not result in selecting a strategy that helps a firm reach the vision that is part of its strategic direction. This can happen when top management team members and certainly the CEO are too committed to the status quo. While the firm's strategic direction remains rather stable across time, actions taken to implement strategies to reach that direction should be somewhat fluid, largely so the firm can deal with unexpected opportunities and threats that surface in the external environment.

An inability to adjust strategies as appropriate is often caused by an aversion to what decision makers conclude are risky actions. An aversion to perceived risk is common in firms that have performed well in the past and for CEOs who have been in their jobs for extended periods of time.[68] Research also suggests that some CEOs are erratic or even ambivalent in their choices of strategic direction, especially when their competitive environment is turbulent and it is difficult to identify the best strategy.[69] Of course, these behaviors are unlikely to produce high performance and may lead to CEO turnover. Interestingly, research has found that incentive compensation in the form of stock options encourages talented executives to select the best strategies and thus achieve the highest performance. However, the same incentives used with less talented executives produce lower performance.[70]

In contrast to risk-averse CEOs, charismatic ones may foster stakeholders' commitment to a new vision and strategic direction. Nonetheless, even when being guided by a charismatic CEO, it is important for the firm not to lose sight of its strengths and weaknesses when making changes required by a new strategic direction. The most effective charismatic CEO leads a firm in ways that are consistent with its culture and with the actions permitted by its capabilities and core competencies.[71]

Finally, being ambicultural can facilitate efforts to determine the firm's strategic direction and select and use strategies to reach it. Being ambicultural means that strategic leaders are committed to identifying the best organizational activities to take particularly when implementing strategies, regardless of their cultural origin.[72] Ambicultural actions help the firm succeed in the short term as a foundation for reaching its vision in the longer term.[73]

12-4b Effectively Managing the Firm's Resource Portfolio

Effectively managing the firm's portfolio of resources is another critical strategic leadership action. The firm's resources are categorized as financial capital, human capital, social capital, and organizational capital (including organizational culture).[74]

Clearly, financial capital is critical to organizational success; strategic leaders understand this reality.[75] However, the most effective strategic leaders recognize the equivalent importance of managing each remaining type of resource as well as managing the integration of resources (e.g., using financial capital to provide training opportunities to the firm's human capital). Most importantly, effective strategic leaders manage the firm's resource portfolio by organizing the resources into capabilities, structuring the firm to facilitate using those capabilities, and choosing strategies through which the capabilities can be successfully leveraged to create value for customers.[76] Exploiting and maintaining core competencies and developing and retaining the firm's human and social capital are actions taken to reach these important objectives.

Exploiting and Maintaining Core Competencies

Examined in Chapters 1 and 3, *core competencies* are capabilities that serve as a source of competitive advantage for a firm over its rivals. Typically, core competencies relate to skills within organizational functions such as manufacturing, finance, marketing, and research and development. Strategic leaders must verify that the firm's core competencies are understood when selecting strategies and then emphasized when implementing those strategies. This suggests, for example, that with respect to their strategies, Apple understands and emphasizes its design competence while Netflix recognizes and concentrates on its competence of being able to deliver physical, digital, and original content.[77]

Core competencies are developed over time as firms learn from the results of the competitive actions and responses taken during the course of competing with rivals. On the basis of what they learn, firms continuously reshape their capabilities for the purpose of verifying that they are indeed the path through which core competencies are being developed and used to establish one or more competitive advantages.

Dan Akerson became CEO of GM in July, 2009, a time when the firm required a transformation in order to survive as the foundation for then being able to compete successfully against its global rivals. One of the first decisions Akerson made was to allocate resources for the purpose of building new capabilities in technology development and in marketing, especially in customer service. In turn, he wants the firm to find ways to develop these capabilities into core competencies.[78]

Efforts to reach these goals remain in place. With respect to customer service for example, GM now offers "two years of free oil changes, tire rotations and vehicle inspections on most new vehicle sales…"[79] The firm hopes that these services will increase customer loyalty and create "buzz" around its efforts to "upgrade" its Chevrolet portfolio. To further enhance its technological capabilities, GM hired 4,000 high technology workers who are to develop proprietary software for the firm's use and increased its total capital expenditures from $6.2 billion in 2011 to $8.1 billion in 2012.[80]

As we discuss next, human capital and social capital are critical to a firm's success. This is the case for GM as the firm strives to continuously improve its performance. One reason for human capital's importance is that it is the resource through which core competencies are developed and used.

Developing Human Capital and Social Capital

Human capital refers to the knowledge and skills of a firm's entire workforce. From the perspective of human capital, employees are viewed as a capital resource requiring continuous investment.[81]

Bringing talented human capital into the firm and then developing that capital has the potential to yield positive outcomes. A key reason for this is that individuals' knowledge and skills are proving to be critical to the success of many global industries (e.g., automobile manufacturing) as well as industries within countries (e.g., leather and shoe manufacturing in Italy). This fact suggests that "as the dynamics of competition accelerate, people are perhaps the only truly sustainable source of competitive advantage."[82] In all types of organizations—large and small, new and established, and so forth—human capital's increasing importance suggests a significant role for the firm's human resource management function.[83] As one of a firm's support functions on which firms rely to create value (see Chapter 3), human resource management practices facilitate selecting and especially implementing the firm's strategies.[84]

Human capital refers to the knowledge and skills of a firm's entire workforce.

A firm's human capital is critical to its success. One of strategic leaders most important responsibilities is developing human capital.

© Goodluz/Shutterstock.com

Effective training and development programs increase the probability that some of the firm's human capital will become effective strategic leaders. Increasingly, the link between effective programs and firm success is becoming stronger in that the knowledge gained by participating in these programs is integral to forming and then sustaining a firm's competitive advantage.[85] In addition to building human capital's knowledge and skills, these programs inculcate a common set of core values and present a systematic view of the organization, thus promoting its vision and helping form an effective organizational culture.

Effective training and development programs also contribute positively to the firm's efforts to form core competencies.[86] Furthermore, the programs help strategic leaders improve skills that are critical to completing other tasks associated with effective strategic leadership, such as determining the firm's strategic direction, exploiting and maintaining the firm's core competencies, and developing an organizational culture that supports ethical practices. Thus, building human capital is vital to the effective execution of strategic leadership.

When investments in human capital (such as providing high-quality training and development programs) are successful, the outcome is a workforce capable of learning continuously. This is an important outcome in that continuous learning and leveraging the firm's expanding knowledge base are linked with strategic success.[87]

Learning also can preclude errors. Strategic leaders may learn more from failure than success because they sometimes make the wrong attributions for the successes.[88] For example, the effectiveness of certain approaches and knowledge can be context specific. Thus, some "best practices" may not work well in all situations. We know that using teams to make decisions can be effective, but sometimes it is better for leaders to make decisions alone, especially when the decisions must be made and implemented quickly (e.g., in crisis situations).[89] As such, effective strategic leaders recognize the importance of learning from success *and* from failure when helping their firm use the strategic management process.

When facing challenging conditions, firms may decide to lay off some of their human capital, a decision that can result in a significant loss of knowledge. Research shows that moderate-sized layoffs may improve firm performance primarily in the short run, but large layoffs produce stronger performance downturns in firms because of the loss of human capital.[90] Although it is also not uncommon for restructuring firms to reduce their investments in training and development programs, restructuring may actually be an important time to increase investments in these programs. The reason for this is that restructuring firms have less slack and cannot absorb as many errors; moreover, the employees who remain after layoffs may find themselves in positions without all the skills or knowledge they need to create value through their work.

Viewing employees as a resource to be maximized rather than as a cost to be minimized facilitates successful implementation of a firm's strategies, as does the strategic leader's ability to approach layoffs in a manner that employees believe is fair and equitable. A critical issue for employees is the fairness in the layoffs and how they are treated in their jobs, especially relative to their peers.[91]

Social capital involves relationships inside and outside the firm that help in efforts to accomplish tasks and create value for stakeholders.[92] Social capital is a critical asset given that employees must cooperate with one another and others, including suppliers and customers, in order to complete their work. In multinational organizations, employees often must cooperate across country boundaries on activities such as R&D to achieve performance objectives (e.g., developing new products).[93]

External social capital is increasingly critical to firm success in that few if any companies possess all of the resources needed to successfully compete against their rivals. Firms can use cooperative strategies such as strategic alliances (see Chapter 9) to develop social capital. Social capital can be built in strategic alliances as firms share complementary resources. Resource sharing must be effectively managed to ensure that the partner trusts the firm and is willing to share its resources.[94] Social capital created this way yields many benefits. For example, firms with strong social capital are able to be more ambidextrous; that is, they can develop or have access to multiple capabilities providing them with the flexibility to take advantage of opportunities and to respond to threats.[95]

Research evidence suggests that the success of many types of firms may partially depend on social capital. Large multinational firms often must establish alliances in order to enter new foreign markets; entrepreneurial firms often must establish alliances to gain access to resources, venture capital, or other types of resources (e.g., special expertise that the entrepreneurial firm cannot afford to maintain in-house).[96] However, a firm's culture affects its ability to retain quality human capital and maintain strong internal social capital.

Social capital involves relationships inside and outside the firm that help in efforts to accomplish tasks and create value for stakeholders.

12-4c Sustaining an Effective Organizational Culture

In Chapter 1, we defined *organizational culture* as the complex set of ideologies, symbols, and core values that are shared throughout the firm and influence how the firm conducts business. Because organizational culture influences how the firm conducts its business and helps regulate and control employees' behavior, it can be a source of competitive advantage.[97] Given that each firm's culture is unique, it is possible that a vibrant organizational culture is an increasingly important source of differentiation for firms to emphasize when pursuing strategic competitiveness and above-average returns. Thus, shaping the context within which the firm formulates and implements its strategies—that is, shaping the organizational culture—is another key strategic leadership action.[98]

Entrepreneurial Mind-Set

Especially in large organizations, an organizational culture often encourages (or discourages) strategic leaders and those with whom they work from pursuing (or not pursuing) entrepreneurial opportunities. (We define and discuss entrepreneurial opportunities in some detail in Chapter 13.) This is the case in both for-profit and not-for-profit organizations.[99] This issue is important because entrepreneurial opportunities are a vital source of growth and innovation.[100] Therefore, a key action for strategic leaders to take is to encourage and promote innovation by pursuing entrepreneurial opportunities.[101]

One way to encourage innovation is to invest in opportunities as real options—that is, invest in an opportunity in order to provide the potential option of taking advantage of the opportunity at some point in the future.[102] For example, a firm might buy a piece of land to have the option to build on it at some time in the future should the company need more space and should that location increase in value to the company. Oil companies take out land leases with an option to drill for oil. Firms might enter strategic alliances for similar reasons. In this instance, a firm might form an alliance to have the option of acquiring the partner later or of building a stronger relationship with it (e.g., developing a new joint venture).[103]

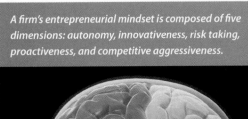

A firm's entrepreneurial mindset is composed of five dimensions: autonomy, innovativeness, risk taking, proactiveness, and competitive aggressiveness.

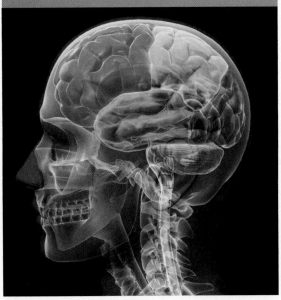

© Digital Storm/Shutterstock.com

In Chapter 13, we describe how firms of all sizes use strategic entrepreneurship to pursue entrepreneurial opportunities as a means of earning above-average returns. Companies are more likely to achieve the success they desire by using strategic entrepreneurship when their employees have an entrepreneurial mind-set.[104]

Five dimensions characterize a firm's entrepreneurial mind-set: autonomy, innovativeness, risk taking, proactiveness, and competitive aggressiveness.[105] In combination, these dimensions influence the actions a firm takes to be innovative when using the strategic management process.

Autonomy, the first of an entrepreneurial orientation's five dimensions, allows employees to take actions that are free of organizational constraints and encourages them to do so. The second dimension, *innovativeness,* "reflects a firm's tendency to engage in and support new ideas, novelty, experimentation, and creative processes that may result in new products, services, or technological processes."[106] Cultures with a tendency toward innovativeness encourage employees to think beyond existing knowledge, technologies, and parameters to find creative ways to add value. *Risk taking* reflects a willingness by employees and their firm to accept measured levels of risks when pursuing entrepreneurial opportunities. The fourth dimension of an entrepreneurial orientation, *proactiveness,* describes a firm's ability to be a market leader rather than a follower. Proactive organizational cultures constantly use processes to anticipate future market needs and to satisfy them before competitors learn how to do so. Finally, *competitive aggressiveness* is a firm's propensity to take actions that allow it to consistently and substantially outperform its rivals.[107]

Changing the Organizational Culture and Restructuring

Changing a firm's organizational culture is more difficult than maintaining it; however, effective strategic leaders recognize when change is needed. Incremental changes to the firm's culture typically are used to implement strategies.[108] More significant and sometimes even radical changes to organizational culture support selecting strategies that differ from those the firm has implemented historically. Regardless of the reasons for change, shaping and reinforcing a new culture requires effective communication and problem solving, along with selecting the right people (those who have the values desired for the organization), engaging in effective performance appraisals (establishing goals that support the new core values and measuring individuals' progress toward reaching them), and using appropriate reward systems (rewarding the desired behaviors that reflect the new core values).[109]

Evidence suggests that cultural changes succeed only when the firm's CEO, other key top management team members, and middle-level managers actively support them.[110] To effect change, middle-level managers in particular need to be highly disciplined to energize the culture and foster alignment with the firm's vision and mission.[111] In addition, managers must be sensitive to the effects of other changes on organizational culture. For example, downsizings can negatively affect an organization's culture, especially if they are not implemented in accordance with the dominant organizational values.[112]

12-4d Emphasizing Ethical Practices

The effectiveness of processes used to implement the firm's strategies increases when they are based on ethical practices. Ethical companies encourage and enable people at all levels to act ethically when doing what is necessary to implement strategies. In turn, ethical practices and the judgment on which they are based create "social capital" in the organization, increasing the "goodwill available to individuals and groups" in the organization.[113] Alternatively, when unethical practices evolve in an organization, they may become acceptable to many managers and employees.[114] Once deemed acceptable, individuals are more likely to engage in unethical practices to meet their goals when current efforts to meet them are insufficient.[115]

To properly influence employees' judgment and behavior, ethical practices must shape the firm's decision-making process and be an integral part of organizational culture. In fact, a values-based culture is the most effective means of ensuring that employees comply with the firm's ethical standards. However, developing such a culture requires constant nurturing and support in corporations located in countries throughout the world.[116]

As explained in Chapter 10, some strategic leaders and managers may occasionally act opportunistically, making decisions that are in their own best interests. This tends to happen when firms have lax expectations in place for individuals to follow regarding ethical behavior. In other words, individuals acting opportunistically take advantage of their positions, making decisions that benefit themselves to the detriment of the firm's stakeholders.[117] Strategic leaders as well as others in the organization are most likely to integrate ethical values into their decisions when the company has explicit ethics codes, the code is integrated into the business through extensive ethics training, and shareholders expect ethical behavior.[118] Thus, establishing and enforcing a meaningful code of ethics is an important action to take to encourage ethical decision making as a foundation for using the strategic management process.

Strategic leaders can take several actions to develop and support an ethical organizational culture. Examples of these actions include (1) establishing and communicating specific goals to describe the firm's ethical standards (e.g., developing and disseminating a code of conduct); (2) continuously revising and updating the code of conduct, based on inputs from people throughout the firm and from other stakeholders; (3) disseminating the code of conduct to all stakeholders to inform them of the firm's ethical standards and practices; (4) developing and implementing methods and procedures to use in achieving the firm's ethical standards (e.g., using internal auditing practices that are consistent with the standards); (5) creating and using explicit reward systems that recognize acts of courage (e.g., rewarding those who use proper channels and procedures to report observed wrongdoings); and (6) creating a work environment in which all people are treated with dignity.[119] The effectiveness of these actions increases when they are taken simultaneously and thereby are mutually supportive. When strategic leaders and others throughout the firm fail to take actions such as these—perhaps because an ethical culture has not been created—problems are likely to occur.

12-4e Establishing Balanced Organizational Controls

Organizational controls (discussed in Chapter 11) have long been viewed as an important part of the strategic management process particularly the parts related to implementation (see Figure 1.1). Controls are necessary to help ensure that firms achieve their desired outcomes. Defined as the "formal, information-based … procedures used by managers to maintain or alter patterns in organizational activities," controls help strategic leaders build credibility, demonstrate the value of strategies to the firm's stakeholders, and promote and support strategic change.[120] Most critically, controls provide the parameters for implementing strategies as well as the corrective actions to be taken when implementation-related adjustments are required. For example, in light of an insider-trading scandal, KPMG LLP recently announced that it intends to consider the possibility of enhancing its training and monitoring programs. The firm's existing safeguards "include training for employees, a whistleblower system and monitoring of the personal investments of partners and managers."[121]

In this chapter, we focus on two organizational controls—strategic and financial—that were introduced in Chapter 11. Strategic leaders are responsible for helping the firm develop and properly use these two types of controls.

As we explained in Chapter 11, financial control focuses on short-term financial outcomes. In contrast, strategic control focuses on the *content* of strategic actions rather than their *outcomes*. Some strategic actions can be correct but still result in poor financial outcomes because of external conditions such as an economic recession, unexpected domestic or foreign government actions, or natural disasters. Therefore, emphasizing financial controls often produces more short-term and risk-averse decisions, because financial outcomes may be caused by events beyond leaders and managers' direct control. Alternatively, strategic control encourages lower-level managers to make decisions that incorporate moderate and acceptable levels of risk because leaders and managers throughout the firm share the responsibility for the outcomes of those decisions and actions resulting from them.

The challenge for strategic leaders is to balance the use of strategic and financial controls for the purpose of supporting efforts to improve the firm's performance. The Balanced Scorecard is a tool strategic leaders use to achieve the sought after balance.

The Balanced Scorecard

The **balanced scorecard** is a tool firms use to determine if they are achieving an appropriate balance when using strategic and financial controls as a means of positively influencing performance.[122] This tool is most appropriate to use when evaluating business-level strategies; however, it can also be used with the other strategies firms implement (e.g., corporate, international, and cooperative).

The underlying premise of the balanced scorecard is that firms jeopardize their future performance when financial controls are emphasized at the expense of strategic controls.[123]

The **balanced scorecard** is a tool firms use to determine if they are achieving an appropriate balance when using strategic and financial controls as a means of positively influencing performance.

This occurs because financial controls provide feedback about outcomes achieved from past actions but do not communicate the drivers of future performance. Thus, an over-emphasis on financial controls may promote behavior that sacrifices the firm's long-term, value-creating potential for short-term performance gains.[124] An appropriate balance of strategic controls and financial controls, rather than an overemphasis on either, allows firms to achieve higher levels of performance.

Four perspectives are integrated to form the balanced scorecard: *financial* (concerned with growth, profitability, and risk from the shareholders' perspective), *customer* (concerned with the amount of value customers perceive was created by the firm's products), *internal business processes* (with a focus on the priorities for various business processes that create customer and shareholder satisfaction), and *learning and growth* (concerned with the firm's effort to create a climate that supports change, innovation, and growth). Thus, using the balanced scorecard finds the firm seeking to understand how it responds to shareholders (financial perspective), how customers view it (customer perspective), the processes to emphasize to successfully use its competitive advantage (internal perspective), and what it can do to improve its performance in order to grow (learning and growth perspective).[125] Generally speaking, firms tend to emphasize strategic controls when assessing their performance relative to the learning and growth perspective, whereas the tendency is to emphasize financial controls when assessing performance in terms of the financial perspective.

Firms use different criteria to measure their standing relative to the scorecard's four perspectives. We show sample criteria in Figure 12.5. The firm should select the number of

Figure 12.5 Strategic Controls and Financial Controls in a Balanced Scorecard Framework

Perspectives	Criteria
Financial	• Cash flow • Return on equity • Return on assets
Customer	• Assessment of ability to anticipate customers' needs • Effectiveness of customer service practices • Percentage of repeat business • Quality of communications with customers
Internal Business Processes	• Asset utilization improvements • Improvements in employee morale • Changes in turnover rates
Learning and Growth	• Improvements in innovation ability • Number of new products compared to competitors • Increases in employees' skills

© Cengage Learning

criteria that will allow it to have both a strategic and financial understanding of its performance without becoming immersed in too many details.[126]

Strategic leaders play an important role in determining a proper balance between strategic and financial controls, whether they are in single-business firms or large diversified firms. A proper balance between controls is important, in that "wealth creation for organizations where strategic leadership is exercised is possible because these leaders make appropriate investments for future viability [through strategic control], while maintaining an appropriate level of financial stability in the present [through financial control]."[127] In fact, most corporate restructuring is designed to refocus the firm on its core businesses, thereby allowing top executives to reestablish strategic control of their separate business units.[128]

Successfully using strategic control frequently is integrated with appropriate autonomy for the various subunits so that they can gain a competitive advantage in their respective markets.[129] Strategic control can be used to promote the sharing of both tangible and intangible resources among interdependent businesses within a firm's portfolio. In addition, the autonomy provided allows the flexibility necessary to take advantage of specific marketplace opportunities. As a result, strategic leadership promotes simultaneous use of strategic control and autonomy.

As we have explained in this chapter, strategic leaders are critical to a firm's ability to successfully use all parts of the strategic management process, including strategic entrepreneurship, which is the final topic included in the "strategy" part of this book's Analysis-Strategy-Performance model. We turn our attention to this topic in the final chapter.

SUMMARY

- Effective strategic leadership is a prerequisite to successfully using the strategic management process. Strategic leadership entails the ability to anticipate events, envision possibilities, maintain flexibility, and empower others to create strategic change.

- Top-level managers are an important resource for firms to develop and exploit competitive advantages. In addition, when they and their work are valuable, rare, imperfectly imitable, and nonsubstitutable, strategic leaders are also a source of competitive advantage.

- The top management team is composed of key managers who play a critical role in selecting and implementing the firm's strategies. Generally, they are officers of the corporation and/or members of the board of directors.

- The top management team's characteristics, a firm's strategies, and its performance are all interrelated. For example, a top management team with significant marketing and research and development (R&D) knowledge positively contributes to the firm's use of a growth strategy. Overall, having diverse skills increases the effectiveness of most top management teams.

- Typically, performance improves when the board of directors and the CEO are involved in shaping a firm's strategic direction. However, when the CEO has a great deal of power, the board may be less involved in decisions about strategy formulation and implementation. By appointing people to the board and

simultaneously serving as CEO and chair of the board, CEOs increase their power.

- In managerial succession, strategic leaders are selected from either the internal or the external managerial labor market. Because of their effect on firm performance, the selection of strategic leaders has implications for a firm's effectiveness. There are a variety of reasons that companies select the firm's strategic leaders from either internal or external sources. In most instances, the internal market is used to select the CEO, but the number of outsiders chosen is increasing. Outsiders often are selected to initiate major changes in strategy.

- Effective strategic leadership has five key leadership actions: determining the firm's strategic direction, effectively managing the firm's resource portfolio (including exploiting and maintaining core competencies and managing human capital and social capital), sustaining an effective organizational culture, emphasizing ethical practices, and establishing balanced organizational controls.

- Strategic leaders must develop the firm's strategic direction, typically working with the board of directors to do so. The strategic direction specifies the image and character the firm wants to develop over time. To form the strategic direction, strategic leaders evaluate the conditions (e.g., opportunities and threats in the external environment) they expect their firm to face over the next three to five years.

- Strategic leaders must ensure that their firm exploits its core competencies, which are used to produce and deliver products that create value for customers, when implementing its strategies. In related diversified and large firms in particular, core competencies are exploited by sharing them across units and products.

- The ability to manage the firm's resource portfolio and the processes used to effectively implement its strategy are critical elements of strategic leadership. Managing the resource portfolio includes integrating resources to create capabilities and leveraging those capabilities through strategies to build competitive advantages. Human capital and social capital are perhaps the most important resources.

- As a part of managing resources, strategic leaders must develop a firm's human capital. Effective strategic leaders view human capital as a resource to be maximized—not as a cost to be minimized. Such leaders develop and use programs designed to train current and future strategic leaders to build the skills needed to nurture the rest of the firm's human capital.

- Effective strategic leaders build and maintain internal and external social capital. Internal social capital promotes cooperation and coordination within and across units in the firm. External social capital provides access to resources the firm needs to compete effectively.

- Shaping the firm's culture is a central task of effective strategic leadership. An appropriate organizational culture encourages the development of an entrepreneurial mind-set among employees and an ability to change the culture as necessary.

- In ethical organizations, employees are encouraged to exercise ethical judgment and to always act ethically. Improved ethical practices foster social capital. Setting specific goals to meet the firm's ethical standards, using a code of conduct, rewarding ethical behaviors, and creating a work environment where all people are treated with dignity are actions that facilitate and support ethical behavior.

- Developing and using balanced organizational controls is the final key leadership action associated with effective strategic leadership. The balanced scorecard is a tool that measures the effectiveness of the firm's strategic and financial controls. An effective balance between these two controls allows for flexible use of core competencies, but within the parameters of the firm's financial position.

REVIEW QUESTIONS

1. What is strategic leadership? Why are top-level managers considered to be important resources for an organization?

2. What is a top management team, and how does it affect a firm's performance and its abilities to innovate and design and bring about effective strategic change?

3. What is the managerial succession process? How important are the internal and external managerial labor markets to this process?

4. What is the effect of strategic leadership on determining the firm's strategic direction?

5. How do strategic leaders effectively manage their firm's resource portfolio to exploit its core competencies and leverage the human capital and social capital to achieve a competitive advantage?

6. What must strategic leaders do to develop and sustain an effective organizational culture?

7. As a strategic leader, what actions could you take to establish and emphasize ethical practices in your firm?

8. Why are strategic controls and financial controls important aspects of strategic leadership and the firm's strategic management process?

EXPERIENTIAL EXERCISES

EXERCISE 1: THE CEO AND THE TOP MANAGEMENT TEAM

Corporate governance and the fiduciary role the board of directors plays as it oversees the company's operations were examined in Chapter 10. The composition of the top management team is critical in assessing the strategic direction of a firm. It is not uncommon for a powerful CEO and top management team to thwart the desires of the board. There are various ways in which a CEO may become powerful; it may be the result of equity ownership, tenure, expertise, or by appointing sympathetic board members. This exercise will allow you to assess the power of a CEO and his or her team and develop your thoughts regarding their relationship to the board.

Part One

Identify with your team the firm you would like to study. Pick a company that is publicly traded so that you have adequate information about the executives.

Part Two

Explore the power relationship between the CEO and his/her top management team (TMT) and the board. You should at a minimum be able to address the following points:

1. CEO tenure

2. TMT tenure

3. TMT relationships to the CEO (i.e., were they hired during the tenure of the current CEO or his/her predecessor?)

4. Board member tenure and structure (i.e., does the board structure possess a lead independent director? Is CEO duality present?)

5. Describe the CEO and his/her TMT in terms of experience and networks. For example, do members of the TMT sit on other firms' boards of directors? Are there any overlaps with their employer's board?

6. What conclusions do you reach regarding the power relationship between the CEO and the board?

Be prepared to discuss this utilizing a PowerPoint presentation of your findings and conclusions.

EXERCISE 2: HOW COME THEY HIRED THAT PERSON?

According to a study by Booz & Co., 15% of CEOs left their large public corporations in 2012, the second highest turnover percentage since the consulting firm started keeping records over a decade ago. There is some thinking that this 15% or so is the new normal and that firms' boards are becoming less willing to allow an incumbent CEO to remain when performance or other issues arise. Of course many of these turnover events are scheduled as a result of the board undertaking its fiduciary role in planning for the succession of an incumbent.

ABC News ran a report on the most recent top 7 CEO disasters. They named, in no particular order:

- Ron Johnson, J.C. Penney

- John Riccitiello, Electronic Arts Inc

- Andrew Mason, Groupon

- Brian Dunn, Best Buy

- Andrea Jung, Avon

- Leo Apotheker, HP

- Christopher Kubasik, Lockheed Martin

In your teams, analyze one of the above CEO dismissals with the approval of your instructor. During your analysis, answer at a minimum the following questions:

1. Characterize the dismissal. Why was the CEO fired?

2. Examine the replacement in terms of either the external or internal labor market. Why did the company choose one over the other?

3. Does it appear that a succession plan was in place?

4. Describe the impact of the CEO dismissal upon the top management team.

Be prepared to present your results in class.

VIDEO CASE ▶

AN EXAMPLE OF STRATEGIC LEADERSHIP: MEG WHITMAN, FORMER CEO OF EBAY

Meg Whitman, former CEO of eBay and current CEO of Hewlett-Packard (HP), is a pioneer at creating a global marketplace and contributing to the development of an e-commerce revolution. However, Whitman has encountered challenges and difficulties while achieving the significant levels of success she has recorded. The long hours she has worked sacrifices time with her family, a reality for which she occasionally feels somewhat guilty. To some degree though, Whitman's love of working with others within corporations and helping individuals reach their potential as they contribute to their firm's success allows her to feel that she is facilitating the growth and development of an entire corporation such as eBay. Despite having trade-offs between home and work, Whitman contends that she would do it all over again. Whitman resigned as CEO of eBay in November 2007, but remained on the board and served as an advisor to the current CEO, John Donahoe, until late 2008. Whitman left a very positive legacy as a result of her effectiveness as eBay's CEO. Of course, she seeks to make positive, value-creating contributions during her current work as HP's CEO.

After watching the video, be prepared to discuss the following concepts and questions in class:

Concepts

- Strategic leadership

- Top management team

- Human capital

- Social capital

- Organizational culture

Questions

1. In what ways did Meg Whitman's characteristics and the orientations resulting from them contribute to her effectiveness as CEO at eBay?

2. How is Meg Whitman appropriate for a top management team?

3. What do you think would be Whitman's approach to human capital?

4. How important is social capital to eBay's success?

5. What was the organizational culture like at eBay during Whitman's time as the firm's CEO? Is there evidence that an entrepreneurial mind-set was a part of that culture? If so, what is that evidence?

NOTES

1. C.-N. Chung & X. R. Luo, 2013, Leadership succession and firm performance in an emerging economy: Successor origin, relational embeddedness, and legitimacy, *Strategic Management Journal*, 34: 338–357; A. Mackey, 2008, The effect of CEOs on firm performance, *Strategic Management Journal*, 29: 1357–1367.

2. V. Govindarajan, 2012, The timeless strategic value of unrealistic goals, *HBR Blog Network*, www.hbr.org, October 22.

3. B.-J. Moon, 2013, Antecedents and outcomes of strategic thinking, *Journal of Business Research*, 66: 1698–1708; M. A. Hitt, K. T. Haynes, & R. Serpa, 2010, Strategic leadership for the 21st century, *Business Horizons*, 53: 437–444; R. D. Ireland & M. A. Hitt, 2005, Achieving and maintaining strategic competitiveness in the 21st century: The role of strategic leadership, *Academy of Management Executive*, 19: 63–77.

4. M. T. Hansen, H. Ibarra, & U. Peyer, 2013, The best-performing CEOs in the world, *Harvard Business Review*, 91(1): 81–95; M. D. Watkins, 2012, How managers become leaders, *Harvard Business Review*, 90(6): 65–72.

5. B. A. Campbell, R. Coff, & D. Kryscynski, 2012, Rethinking sustained competitive advantage from human capital, *Academy of Management Review*, 37: 376–395; M. A. Hitt, C. Miller, & A. Colella, 2011, *Organizational Behavior*, 3rd ed., Hoboken, NJ: John Wiley & Sons.

6. M. A. Axtle-Ortiz, 2013, Perceiving the value of intangible assets in context, *Journal of Business Research*, 56: 417–424.

7. P. J. H. Schoemaker, S. Krupp, & S. Howland, 2013, Strategic leadership: The essential skills, *Harvard Business Review*, 91(1/2): 131–134.

8. J. J. Sosik, W. A. Gentry, & J. U. Chun, 2012, The value of virtue in the upper echelons: A multisource examination of executive character strengths and performance, *Leadership Quarterly*, 23: 367–382.

9. D. M. Cable, F. Gino, & B. R. Staats, 2013, Breaking them in or eliciting their best? Reframing socialization and newcomers' authentic self-expression,

Administrative Science Quarterly, 58: 1–36; T. Hulzschenreuter, I. Kleindienst, & C. Greger, 2012, How new leaders affect strategic change following a succession event: A critical review of the literature, *The Leadership Quarterly*, 23: 729–755.

10. J. Ewing, 2012, Embattled German steel maker reports a huge loss, *New York Times*, www.nytimes.com, December 11.

11. J. C. Ryan & S. A. A. Tipu, 2013, Leadership effects on innovation propensity: A two-factor full range of leadership model, *Journal of Business Research*, 66: 2116–2129; A. E. Colbert, A. L. Kristof-Brown, B. H. Bradley, & M. R. Barrick, 2008, CEO transformational leadership: The role of goal importance congruence in top management teams, *Academy of Management Journal*, 51: 81–96.

12. T. G. Buchholz, 2007, The Kroc legacy at McDonald's, *The Conference Review Board*, July/August, 14–15.

13. H. S. Givray, 2007, When CEOs aren't leaders, *BusinessWeek*, September 3, 102.

14. Y. Dong, M.-G. Seo, & K. Bartol, 2013, No pain, no gain: An affect-based model of developmental job experience and the buffering effects of emotional intelligence, *Academy of Management Journal*, in press; D. Goleman, 2004, What makes a leader? *Harvard Business Review*, 82(1): 82–91.

15. C. M. Leitch, C. McMullan, & R. T. Harrison, 2013, The development of entrepreneurial leadership: The role of human, social and institutional capital, *British Journal of Management*, 24: 347–366; Y. Ling, Z. Simsek, M. H. Lubatkin, & J. F. Veiga, 2008, Transformational leadership's role in promoting corporate entrepreneurship: Examining the CEO-TMT interface, *Academy of Management Journal*, 51: 557–576.

16. T. Hutzschenreuter & I. Kleindienst, 2013, (How) does discretion change over time? A contribution toward a dynamic view of managerial discretion, *Scandinavian Journal of Management*, in press; T. L. Waldron, S. D. Graffin, J. F. Porac, & J. B. Wade, 2013, Third-party endorsements of CEO quality, managerial discretion, and stakeholder reactions, *Journal of Business Research*, in press.

17. R. Klingebiel, 2012, Options in the implementation plan of entrepreneurial initiatives: Examining firms' attainment of flexibility benefit, *Strategic Entrepreneurship Journal*, 6: 307–334; D. G. Sirmon, J.-L. Arregle, M. A. Hitt, & J. W. Webb, 2008, The role of family influence in firms' strategic responses to threat of imitation, *Entrepreneurship Theory and Practice*, 32: 979–998.

18. M. Menz, 2012, Functional top management team members: A review, synthesis, and research agenda, *Journal of Management*, 38: 45–80; A. M. L. Raes, U. Glunk, M. G. Heijltjes, & R. A. Roe, 2007, Top management team and middle managers, *Small Group Research*, 38: 360–386.

19. A. Ganter & A. Hecker, 2013, Configurational paths to organizational innovation: Qualitative comparative analyses of antecedents and contingencies, *Journal of Business Research*, in press; O. R. Mihalach, J. J. P. Jansen, F. A. J. Van Den Bosch, & H. W. Volberda, 2012, Offshoring and firm innovation: The moderating role of top management team attributes, *Strategic Management Journal*, 33: 1480–1498.

20. J. Li & Y. Tang, 2010, CEO hubris and firm risk taking in China: The moderating role of managerial discretion, *Academy of Management Journal*, 53: 45–68; M. L. A. Hayward, V. P. Rindova, & T. G. Pollock, 2004, Believing one's own press: The causes and consequences of CEO celebrity, *Strategic Management Journal*, 25: 637–653.

21. J. J. Reuer, T. W. Tong, & C.-W. Wu, 2012, A signaling theory of acquisition premiums: Evidence from IPO targets, *Academy of Management Journal*, 55: 667–683.

22. A. Carmeli, A. Tishler, & A. C. Edmondson, 2012, CEO relational leadership and strategic decision quality in top management teams: The role of team trust and learning from failure, *Strategic Organization*, 10: 31–54; V. Souitaris & B. M. M. Maestro, 2010, Polychronicity in top management teams: The impact on strategic decision processes and performance in new technology ventures, *Strategic Management Journal*, 31: 652–678.

23. R. Olie, A. van Iteraon, & Z. Simsek, 2012–13, When do CEOs versus top management

teams matter in explaining strategic decision-making processes? Toward an institutional view of strategic leadership effects, *International Studies of Management and Organization*, 42(4): 86–105; Y. Ling & F. W. Kellermans, 2010, The effects of family firm specific sources of TMT diversity: The moderating role of information exchange frequency, *Journal of Management Studies*, 47: 322–344.

24. R. Klingebiel & A. De Meyer, 2013, Becoming aware of the unknown: Decision making during the implementation of a strategic initiative, *Organization Science*, 24: 133–153; A. Srivastava, K. M. Bartol, & E. A. Locke, 2006, Empowering leadership in management teams: Effects on knowledge sharing, efficacy, and performance, *Academy of Management Journal*, 49: 1239–1251; D. Knight, C. L. Pearce, K. G. Smith, J. D. Olian, H. P. Sims, K. A. Smith, & P. Flood, 1999, Top management team diversity, group process, and strategic consensus, *Strategic Management Journal*, 20: 446–465.

25. T. Buyl, C. Boone, W. Hendricks, & P. Matthyssens, 2011, Top management team functional diversity and firm performance: The moderating role of CEO characteristics, *Journal of Management Studies*, 48: 151–177; B. J. Olson, S. Parayitam, & Y. Bao, 2007, Strategic decision making: The effects of cognitive diversity, conflict, and trust on decision outcomes, *Journal of Management*, 33: 196–222.

26. S. Finkelstein, D. C. Hambrick, & A. A. Cannella, Jr., 2008, *Strategic Leadership: Top Executives and Their Effects on Organizations*, New York: Oxford University Press.

27. A. Minichilli, G. Corbetta, & I. C. Macmillan, 2010, Top management teams in family-controlled companies: 'Familiness', 'faultlines', and their impact on financial performance, *Journal of Management Studies*, 47: 205–222; J. J. Marcel, 2009, Why top management team characteristics matter when employing a chief operating officer: A strategic contingency perspective, *Strategic Management Journal*, 30: 647–658.

28. J. I. Canales, 2013, Constructing interlocking rationales in top-driven strategic renewal, *British Journal of Management*, in press; B. J. Avolio & S. S. Kahai, 2002, Adding the "e" to e-leadership: How it may impact your leadership, *Organizational Dynamics*, 31: 325–338.

29. T. Buyl, C. Boone, & W. Hendriks, 2013, Top management team members' decision influence and cooperative behavior: An empirical study in the information technology industry, *British Journal of Management*, in press; Z. Simsek, J. F. Veiga, M. L. Lubatkin, & R. H. Dino, 2005, Modeling the multilevel determinants of top management team behavioral integration, *Academy of Management Journal*, 48: 69–84.

30. A. A. Cannella, J. H. Park, & H. U. Lee, 2008, Top management team functional background diversity and firm performance: Examining the roles of team member collocation and environmental uncertainty, *Academy of Management Journal*, 51: 768–784.

31. A. S. Cui, R. J. Calantone, & D. A. Griffith, 2011, Strategic change and termination of interfirm partnerships, *Strategic Management Journal*, 32: 402–423; M. Jensen & E. J. Zajac, 2004, Corporate elites and corporate strategy: How demographic preferences and structural position shape the scope of the firm, *Strategic Management Journal*, 25: 507–524.

32. A. E. Colbert, M. R. Barrick, & B. H. Bradley, 2013, Personality and leadership composition in top management teams: Implications for organizational effectiveness, *Personnel Psychology*, in press; S. Nadkarni & P. Hermann, 2010, CEO personality, strategic flexibility and firm performance: The case of the Indian business process outsourcing industry, *Academy of Management Journal*, 53: 1050–1073.

33. K. Liu, J. Li, W. Hesterly, & A. A. Cannella, Jr., 2012, Top management team tenure and technological inventions at post-IPO biotechnology firms, *Journal of Business Research*, 65: 1349–1356; H. Li & J. Li, 2009, Top management team conflict and entrepreneurial strategy making in China, *Asia Pacific Journal of Management*, 26: 263–283; S. C. Parker, 2009, Can cognitive biases explain venture team homophily? *Strategic Entrepreneurship Journal*, 3: 67–83.

34. J. Tian, J. Haleblian, & N. Rajagopalan, 2011, The effects of board human and social capital on investor reactions to new CEO selection, *Strategic Management Journal*, 32: 731–747; Y. Zhang & N. Rajagopalan, 2003, Explaining the new CEO origin: Firm versus industry antecedents, *Academy of Management Journal*, 46: 327–338.

35. P. Y. T. Sun & M. H. Anderson, 2012, Civic capacity: Building on transformational leadership to explain successful integrative public leadership, *The Leadership Quarterly*, 23: 309–323; I. Barreto, 2010, Dynamic capabilities: A review of the past research and an agenda for the future, *Journal of Management*, 36: 256–280.

36. M. L. McDonald & J. D. Westphal, 2010, A little help here? Board control, CEO identification with the corporate elite, and strategic help provided to CEOs at other firms, *Academy of Management Journal*, 53: 343–370; L. Tihanyi, R. A. Johnson, R. E. Hoskisson, & M. A. Hitt, 2003, Institutional ownership and international diversification: The effects of boards of directors and technological opportunity, *Academy of Management Journal*, 46: 195–211.

37. K. B. Lewellyn & M. I. Muller-Kahle, 2012, CEO power and risk taking: Evidence from the subprime lending industry, *Corporate Governance: An International Review*, 20: 289–307; S. Wu, X. Quan, & L. Xu, 2011, CEO power, disclosure quality and the variability in firm performance, *Nankai Business Review International*, 2: 79–97; B. R. Golden & E. J. Zajac, 2001, When will boards influence strategy? Inclination times power equals strategic change, *Strategic Management Journal*, 22: 1087–1111.

38. S. Kaczmarek, S. Kimino, & A. Pye, 2012, Antecedents of board composition: The role of nomination committees, *Corporate Governance: An International Review*, 20: 474–489; M. Carpenter & J. Westphal, 2001, Strategic context of external network ties: Examining the impact of director appointments on board involvement in strategic decision making, *Academy of Management Journal*, 44: 639–660.

39. M. van Essen, P.-J. Engelen, & M. Carney, 2013, Does 'good' corporate governance help in a crisis? The impact of country- and firm-level governance mechanisms in the European financial crisis, *Corporate Governance: An International Review*, 21: 201–224; M. A. Abebe, A. Angriawan, & Y. Lui, 2011, CEO power and organizational turnaround in declining firms: Does environment play a role? *Journal of Leadership and Organizational Studies*, 18: 260–273.

40. C.-H. Liao & A. W.-H. Hsu, 2013, Common membership and effective corporate governance: Evidence from audit and compensation committees, *Corporate Governance: An International Review*, 21: 79-92.

41. C. P. Cullinan, P. B. Roush, & X. Zheng, 2012, CEO/Chair duality in the Sarbanes-Oxley era; board independence versus unity of command, *Research on Professional Responsibility and Ethics in Accounting*, 16: 167–183; C. S. Tuggle, D. G. Sirmon, C. R. Reutzel, & L. Bierman, 2010, Commanding board of director attention: Investigating how organizational performance and CEO duality affect board members' attention to monitoring, *Strategic Management Journal*, 32: 640–657; J. Coles & W. Hesterly, 2000, Independence of the chairman and board composition: Firm choices and shareholder value, *Journal of Management*, 26: 195–214.

42. R. Krause & M. Semadeni, 2013, Apprentice, departure, and demotion: An examination of the three types of CEO-board chair separation, *Academy of Management Journal*, 56: 805–826.

43. M. van Essen, P.-J. Engelen, & M. Carney, 2013, Does "good" corporate governance help in a crisis? The impact of country- and firm-level governance mechanisms in the European financial crisis, *Corporate Governance: An International Review*, 21: 201–224.

44. E. Matta & P. W. Beamish, 2008, The accentuated CEO career horizon problem: Evidence from international acquisitions, *Strategic Management Journal*, 29: 683–700; N. Rajagopalan & D. Datta, 1996, CEO characteristics: Does industry matter? *Academy of Management Journal*, 39: 197–215.

45. B. W. Lewis, J. L. Walls, & G. W. S. Dowell, 2013, Difference in degrees: CEO

characteristics and firm environmental disclosure, *Strategic Management Journal*, 34: in press; R. A. Johnson, R. E. Hoskisson, & M. A. Hitt, 1993, Board involvement in restructuring: The effect of board versus managerial controls and characteristics, *Strategic Management Journal*, 14 (Special Issue): 33–50.

46. Z. Simsek, 2007, CEO tenure and organizational performance: An intervening model, *Strategic Management Journal*, 28: 653–662.

47. X. Luo, V. K. Kanuri, & M. Andrews, 2013, How does CEO tenure matter? The mediating role of firm-employee and firm-customer relationships, *Strategic Management Journal*, 34: in press.

48. M. Hernandez, 2012, Toward an understanding of the psychology of stewardship, *Academy of Management Review*, 37: 172–193.

49. B. K. Boyd, M. F. Santos, & W. Shen, 2012, International developments in executive compensation, *Corporate Governance: An International Review*, 20: 511–518; D. Miller, I. LeBreton-Miller, & B. Scholnick, 2008, Stewardship vs. stagnation: An empirical comparison of small family and non-family businesses, *Journal of Management Studies*, 51: 51–78; J. H. Davis, F. D. Schoorman, & L. Donaldson, 1997, Toward a stewardship theory of management, *Academy of Management Review*, 22: 20–47.

50. A. Holehonnur & T. Pollock, 2013, Shoot for the stars? Predicting the recruitment of prestigious directors at newly public firms, *Academy of Management Journal*, in press; B. Espedal, O. Kvitastein, & K. Gronhaug, 2012, When cooperation is the norm of appropriateness: How does CEO cooperative behavior affect organizational performance? *British Journal of Management*, 23: 257–271.

51. X. Zhang, N. Li, J. Ullrich, & R. van Dick, 2013, Getting everyone on board: The effect of differentiated transformational leadership by CEOs on top management team effectiveness and leader-related firm performance, *Journal of Management*, in press.

52. S. D. Graffin, S. Boivie, & M. A. Carpenter, 2013, Examining CEO succession and the role of heuristics in early-stage CEO evaluation, *Strategic Management Journal*, 34: 383–403; W. Shen & A. A. Cannella, 2002, Revisiting the performance consequences of CEO succession: The impacts of successor type, postsuccession senior executive turnover, and departing CEO tenure, *Academy of Management Journal*, 45: 717–734.

53. J. P. Donlon, 2013, 40 best companies for leaders 2013, *Chief Executive*, www.chiefexecutive.net, January 12.

54. 2013, Deloitte, Perspectives on family-owned businesses: Governance and succession planning, www.deloitte.com, January.

55. 2013, Intersearch survey reveals status of CEO succession plans in companies around the world, Intersearch, www.pendlpiswanger.at/images/content/file/Artikel/CEO succession, February.

56. S. Mobbs & C. G. Raheja, 2012, Internal managerial promotions: Insider incentives and CEO succession, *Journal of Corporate Finance*, 18: 1337–1353; S. Rajgopal, D. Taylor, & M. Venkatachalam, 2012, Frictions in the CEO labor market: The role of talent agents in CEO compensation, *Contemporary Accounting Research*, 29: 119–151.

57. 2013, 2013 Q1 S&P CEO transitions, SpencerStuart, www.spencerstuart.com, May.

58. A. Guarino & D. X. Martin, 2013, The $40 trillion succession risk: Most boards think it's hedged, but it isn't, Korn/Ferry Institute, www.kornferry.com, March.

59. B. Jopson, 2013, P&G reshuffle to help line up Lafley successor, *Financial Times*, www.ft.com, May 31.

60. C. M. Elson & C. K. Ferrere, 2012, When searching for a CEO, there's no place like home, *Wall Street Journal*, www.wsj.com, October 29.

61. Y. Zhang & N. Rajagopalan, 2010, Once an outsider, always an outsider? CEO origin, strategic change and firm performance, *Strategic Management Journal*, 31: 334–346.

62. V. Mehrotra, R. Morck, J. Shim, & Y. Wiwattanakantang, 2013, Adoptive expectations: Rising sons in Japanese family firms, *Journal of Financial Economics*, 108: 840–854; G. A. Ballinger & J. J. Marcel, 2010, The use of an interim CEO during succession episodes and firm performance, *Strategic Management Journal*, 31: 262–283.

63. K. Grind, J. S. Lublin, & M. Lamar, 2013, Daunting challenges at Legg Mason, *Wall Street Journal*, www.wsj.com, February 13.

64. T. Hutzschenreuter, I. Kleindienst, & C. Greger, 2012, How new leaders affect strategic change following a succession event: A critical review of the literature, *The Leadership Quarterly*, 23: 729–755; J. Kotter, 2012, Accelerate! *Harvard Business Review*, 90(11): 45–58.

65. L. Mirabeau & S. Maguire, 2013, From autonomous strategic behavior to emergent strategy, *Strategic Management Journal*, 34: in press; G. A. Shinkle, A. P. Kriauciunas, & G. Hundley, 2013, Why pure strategies may be wrong for transition economy firms, *Strategic Management Journal*, 34: in press.

66. P. Herrmann & S. Nadkarni, 2013, Managing strategic change: The duality of CEO personality, *Strategic Management Journal*, 34: in press; T. Barnett, R. G. Long, & L. E. Marler, 2012, Vision and exchange in intra-family succession: Effects on procedural justice climate among nonfamily managers, *Entrepreneurship Theory and Practice*, 36: 1207–1225.

67. S. Mantere, H. A. Schildt, & J. A. A. Sillince, 2012, Reversal of strategic change, *Academy of Management Journal*, 55: 172–196; S. Sonenshein, 2012, Explaining employee engagement with strategic change implementation: A meaning-making approach, *Organization Science*, 23: 1–23.

68. P. Chaigneau, 2013, Explaining the structure of CEO incentive pay with decreasing relative risk aversion, *Journal of Economics and Business*, 67(May/June): 4–23; G. Chen & D. C. Hambrick, 2012, CEO replacement in turnaround situations: Executive (mis) fit and its performance implications, *Organization Science*, 23: 225–243; P. L. McClelland, X. Ling, & V. L. Barker, 2010, CEO commitment to the status quo: Replication and extension using content analysis, *Journal of Management*, 36: 1251–1277.

69. J. R. Mitchell, D. A. Shepherd, & M. P. Sharfman, 2011, Erratic strategic decisions: When and why managers are inconsistent in strategic decision making, *Strategic Management Journal*, 32: 683–704; N. Plambeck & K. Weber, 2010, When the glass is half full and half empty: CEOs' ambivalent interpretations of strategic issues, *Strategic Management Journal*, 31: 689–710.

70. A. J. Wowak & D. C. Hambrick, 2010, A model of person-pay interaction: How executives vary in their response to compensation arrangements, *Strategic Management Journal*, 31: 803–821.

71. C. P. M. Wilderom, P. T. van den Berg, & U. J. Wiersma, 2012, A longitudinal study of the effects of charismatic leadership and organizational culture on objective and perceived corporate performance, *The Leadership Quarterly*, 23: 835–848.

72. M.-J. Chen & D. Miller, 2012, West meets east: Toward an ambicultural approach to management, *Academy of Management Perspectives*, 24: 17–24; M.-J. Chen & D. Miller, 2011, The relational perspective as a business mindset: Managerial implications for East and West, *Academy of Management Perspectives*, 25: 6–18.

73. M. Y. C. Chen, C. Y. Y. Lin, H.-E. Lin, & E. F. McDonough, III, 2012, Does transformational leadership facilitate technological innovation? The moderating roles of innovative culture and incentive compensation, *Asia Pacific Journal of Management*, 29: 239–264.

74. M. D. Huesch, 2013, Are there always synergies between productive resources and resource deployment capabilities? *Strategic Management Journal*, 34: in press; J. Kraaijenbrink, J.-C. Spender, & A. J. Groen, 2010, The resource-based view: A review and assessment of its critiques, *Journal of Management*, 36: 349–372; J. Barney & A. M. Arikan, 2001, The resource-based view: Origins and implications, in M. A. Hitt, R. E. Freeman, & J. S. Harrison (eds.), *Handbook of Strategic Management*, Oxford, UK: Blackwell Publishers, 124–188.

75. S. D. Julian & J. C. Ofori-dankwa, 2013, Financial resource availability and corporate social responsibility expenditures in a sub-Saharan economy: The institutional difference hypothesis, *Strategic Management Journal*, 34: in press;

T. Vanacker, V. Collewaert, & I. Pacleman, 2013, The relationship between slack resources and the performance of entrepreneurial firms: The role of venture capital and angel investors, *Journal of Management Studies*, in press.

76. E. A. Clinton, S. Sciascia, R. Yadav, & F. Roche, 2013, Resource acquisition in family firms: The role of family-influenced human and social capital, *Entrepreneurship Research Journal*, 3: 44–61; H. A. Ndofor, D. G. Sirmon & X. He, 2011, Firm resources, competitive actions and performance: Investigating a mediated model with evidence from the in-vitro diagnostics industry, *Strategic Management Journal*, 32: 640–657.

77. A. Carr, 2013, Death to core competency: Lessons from Nike, Apple, Netflix, *Fast Company*, www.fastcompany.com, February 14.

78. B. Simon, 2011, GM's new chief executive in reshuffle, *Financial Times*, www..ft.com, January 20.

79. J. Bennett, 2013, GM offers free car-care to bolster U.S. sales, *Wall Street Journal*, www.wsj.com, June 6.

80. M. Wayland, 2013, GM CEO and chairman Dan Akerson's remarks at 2013 annual shareholders meeting, *MLive*, http://blog.mlive.com, June 6.

81. A. J. Nyberg & R. E. Ployhart, 2013, Context-emergent turnover (CET) theory: A theory of collective turnover, *Academy of Management Review*, 38: 109–131; R. E. Ployhart, C. H. Van Idderkinge, & W. J. MacKenzie, 2011, Acquiring and developing human capital in service contexts: The interconnectedness of human capital resources, *Academy of Management Journal*, 54: 353–368; N. W. Hatch & J. H. Dyer, 2004, Human capital and learning as a source of sustainable competitive advantage, *Strategic Management Journal*, 25: 1155–1178.

82. M. A. Hitt, L. Bierman, K. Uhlenbruck, & K. Shimizu, 2006, The importance of resources in the internationalization of professional service firms: The good, the bad and the ugly, *Academy of Management Journal*, 49: 1137–1157; M. A. Hitt, L. Bierman, K. Shimizu, & R. Kochhar, 2001, Direct and moderating effects of human capital on strategy and performance in professional service firms: A resource-based perspective, *Academy of Management Journal*, 44: 13–28.

83. H. Aquinis, H. Joo, & R. K. Gottfredson, 2013, What monetary rewards can and cannot do: How to show employees the money, *Business Horizons*, 56: 241–249; M. F. Correia, R. Campose Cunha, & M. Scholten, 2013, Impact of M&A on organizational performance: The moderating role of HRM centrality, *European Management Journal*, 31: 323–332.

84. R. R. Kehoe & P. M. Wright, 2013, The impact of high-performance human resource practices on employees' attitudes and behaviors, *Journal of Management*, 39: 366–391.

85. Z. J. Zhao & J. Anand, 2013, Beyond boundary spanners: The 'collective bridge' as an efficient interunit structure for transferring collective knowledge, *Strategic Management Journal*, 34: in press; J. Pfeffer, 2010, Building sustainable organizations: The human factor, *Academy of Management Perspectives*, 24(1): 34–45.

86. K. Z. Zhou & C. B. Li, 2012, How knowledge affects radical innovation: Knowledge base, market knowledge acquisition, and internal knowledge sharing, *Strategic Management Journal*, 33: 1090–1102.

87. J. R. Lecuona & M. Reitzig, 2013, Knowledge worth having in 'excess': The value of tacit and firm-specific human resource slack, *Strategic Management Journal*, 34: in press; T. R. Holcomb, R. D. Ireland, R. M. Holmes, & M. A. Hitt, 2009, Architecture of entrepreneurial learning: Exploring the link among heuristics, knowledge, and action, *Entrepreneurship, Theory & Practice*, 33: 173–198.

88. Y. Zheng, A. S. Miner, & G. George, 2013, Does the learning value of individual failure experience depend on group-level success? Insights from a university technology transfer office, *Industrial and Corporate Change*, in press; R. Hirak, A. C. Peng, A. Carneli, & J. M. Schaubroeck, 2012, Linking leader inclusiveness to work unit performance: The importance of psychological safety and learning from failure, *The Leadership Quarterly*, 23: 107–117.

89. Hitt, Miller, & Colella, *Organizational Behavior*.

90. R. Hoskisson, W. Shi, H. Yi, & J. Jin, 2013, The evolution and strategic positioning of private equity firms, *Academy of Management Perspectives*, 27: 22–38; P. M. Norman, F. C. Butler, & A. L. Ranft, 2013, Resources matter: Examining the effects of resources on the state of firms following downsizing, *Journal of Management*, in press; R. D. Nixon, M. A. Hitt, H. Lee, & E. Jeong, 2004, Market reactions to corporate announcements of downsizing actions and implementation strategies, *Strategic Management Journal*, 25: 1121–1129.

91. R. J. Bies, 2013, The delivery of bad news in organizations: A framework for analysis, *Journal of Management*, 39: 136–162; B. C. Holtz, 2013, Trust primacy: A model of the reciprocal relations between trust and perceived justice, *Journal of Management*, 37: in press.

92. C. Galunic, G. Krtug, & M. Gargiulo, 2012, The positive externalities of social capital: Benefiting from senior brokers, *Academy of Management Journal*, 55: 1213–1231; P. S. Adler & S. W. Kwon, 2002, Social capital: Prospects for a new concept, *Academy of Management Review*, 27: 17–40.

93. Y.-Y. Chang, Y. Gong, & M. W. Peng, 2012, Expatriate knowledge transfer, subsidiary absorptive capacity, and subsidiary performance, *Academy of Management Journal*, 55: 927–948; S. Gao, K. Xu, & J. Yang, 2008, Managerial ties, Absorptive capacity & innovation, *Asia Pacific Journal of Management*, 25: 395–412.

94. K. H. Heimeriks, M. Schijven, & S. Gates, 2012, Manifestations of higher-order routines: The underlying mechanisms of deliberate learning in the context of postacquisition integration, *Academy of Management Journal*, 55: 703–726; P. Ozcan & K. M. Eisenhardt, 2009, Origin of alliance portfolios: Entrepreneurs, network strategies, and firm performance, *Academy of Management Journal*, 52: 246–279; W. H. Hoffmann, 2007, Strategies for managing a portfolio of alliances, *Strategic Management Journal*, 28: 827–856.

95. Q. Cao, Z. Simsek, & H. Zhang, 2010, Modelling the joint impact of the CEO and the TMT on organizational ambidexterity, *Journal of Management Studies*, 47: 1272–1296; A. S. Alexiev, J. J. P. Jansen, F. A. J. Van den Bosch. & H. W. Volberda, 2010, Top management team advice seeking and exploratory innovation: The moderating role of TMT heterogeneity, *Journal of Management Studies*, 47: 1343–1364.

96. G. Cuevas-Rodriguez, C. Cabello-Medina, & A. Carmona-Lavado, 2013, Internal and external social capital for radical product innovation: Do they always work well together? *British Journal of Management*, in press; B. J. Hallen & K. M. Eisenhardt, 2012, Catalyzing strategies and efficient tie formation: How entrepreneurial firms obtain investment ties, *Academy of Management Journal*, 55: 35–70.

97. A. Klein, 2011, Corporate culture: Its value as a resource for competitive advantage, *Journal of Business Strategy*, 32(2): 21–28; J. B. Barney, 1986, Organizational culture: Can it be a source of sustained competitive advantage? *Academy of Management Review*, 11: 656–665.

98. B. Schneider, M. G. Ehrhart, & W. H. Macey, 2013, Organizational climate and culture, *Annual Review of Psychology*, 64: 361–388; E. F. Goldman & A. Casey, 2010, Building a culture that encourages strategic thinking, *Journal of Leadership and Organizational Studies*, 17: 119–128.

99. P. G. Klein, J. T. Mahoney, A. M. McGahan, & C. N. Pitelis, 2013, Capabilities and strategic entrepreneurship in public organizations, *Strategic Entrepreneurship Journal*, 7: 70–91; R. D. Ireland, J. G. Covin, & D. F. Kuratko, 2009, Conceptualizing corporate entrepreneurship strategy, *Entrepreneurship Theory and Practice*, 33(1): 19–46.

100. M. S. Wood, A. McKelvie, & J. M. Haynie, 2013, Making it personal: Opportunity individuation and the shaping of opportunity beliefs, *Journal of Business Venturing*, in press; R. D. Ireland & J. W. Webb, 2007, Strategic entrepreneurship: Creating competitive advantage through streams of innovation, *Business Horizons*, 50: 49–59.

101. P. L. Schultz, A. Marin, & K. B. Boal, 2013, The impact of media on the legitimacy

of new market categories: The case of broadband internet, *Journal of Business Venturing,* in press; S. A. Alvarez & J. B. Barney, 2008, Opportunities, organizations and entrepreneurship, *Strategic Entrepreneurship Journal,* 2: 171–174.

102. R. E. Hoskisson, M. A. Hitt, R. D. Ireland, & J. S. Harrison, 2013, *Competing for Advantage,* 3rd ed., Thomson Publishing, Mason, OH. Y. Li & T. Chi, 2013, Venture capitalists' decision to withdraw: The role of portfolio configuration from a real options lens, *Strategic Management Journal,* 34: in press.

103. T. W. Tong & S. Li, 2013, The assignment of call option rights between partners in international joint ventures, *Strategic Management Journal,* 34: in press.

104. C. Bjornskov & N. Foss, 2013, How strategic entrepreneurship and the institutional context drive economic growth, *Strategic Entrepreneurship Journal,* 7: 50–69; M. A. Hitt, R. D. Ireland, D. G. Sirmon, & C. A. Trahms, 2011, Strategic entrepreneurship: Creating value for individuals, organizations and society, *Academy of Management Perspectives,* 25(2): 57–75; P. G. Kein, 2008, Opportunity discovery, entrepreneurial action and economic organization, *Strategic Entrepreneurship Journal,* 2: 175–190.

105. G. T. Lumpkin & G. G. Dess, 1996, Clarifying the entrepreneurial orientation construct and linking it to performance, *Academy of Management Review,* 21: 135–172.

106. Lumpkin & Dess, Clarifying the entrepreneurial orientation construct, 142.

107. Ibid., 137.

108. C. L. Wang & M. Rafiq, 2013, Ambidextrous organizational culture, contextual ambidexterity and new product innovation: A comparative study of UK and Chinese high-tech firms, *British Journal of Management,* in press; P. Pyoria, 2007, Informal organizational culture: The foundation of knowledge workers' performance, *Journal of Knowledge Management,* 11(3): 16–30.

109. A. W. Langvardt, 2012, Ethical leadership and the dual roles of examples, *Business Horizons,* 55: 373–384; M. Kuenzi & M. Schminke, 2009, Assembling fragments into a lens: A review, critique, and proposed research agenda for the organizational work climate literature, *Journal of Management,* 35: 634–717.

110. M. N. Kastanakis & B. G. Voyer, 2013, The effect of culture on perception and cognition: A conceptual framework, *Journal of Business Research,* in press; J. Kotter, 2011, Corporate culture: Whose job is it? *Forbes,* http://blog.forbes.com/johnkotter, February 17.

111. M. I. Garces & P. Morcillo, 2012, The role of organizational culture in the resource-based view: An empirical study of the Spanish nuclear industry, *International Journal of Strategic Change Management,*

4: 356–378; E. Mollick, 2012, People and process, suits and innovators: the role of individuals in firm performance, *Strategic Management Journal,* 33: 1001–1015.

112. W. McKinley, S. Latham, & M. Braun, 2013, Organizational decline and innovation: Turnarounds and downward spirals, *Academy of Management Review,* in press; R. Fehr & M. J. Gelfand, 2012, The forgiving organization: A multilevel model of forgiveness at work, *Academy of Management Review,* 37: 664–688; E. G. Love & M. Kraatz, 2009, Character, conformity, or the bottom line? How and why downsizing affected corporate reputation, *Academy of Management Journal,* 52: 314–335.

113. Adler & Kwon, Social capital.

114. J. L. Campbell & A. S. Goritz, 2013, Culture corrupts! A qualitative study of organizational culture in corrupt organizations, *Journal of Business Ethics,* in press; J. Pinto, C. R. Leana, & F. K. Pil, 2008, Corrupt organizations or organizations of corrupt individuals? Two types of organization-level corruption, *Academy of Management Review,* 33: 685–709.

115. A. Arnaud & M. Schminke, 2012, The ethical climate and context of organizations: A comprehensive model, *Organization Science,* 23: 1767–1780; M. E. Scheitzer, L. Ordonez, & M. Hoegl, 2004, Goal setting as a motivator of unethical behavior, *Academy of Management Journal,* 47: 422–432.

116. J. A. Pearce, 2013, Using social identity theory to predict managers' emphases on ethical and legal values in judging business issues, *Journal of Business Ethics,* 112: 497–514; M. Zhao, 2013, Beyond cops and robbers: The contextual challenge driving the multinational corporation public crisis in China and Russia, *Business Horizons,* 56: 491–501.

117. I. Okhmaztovksiy & R. J. David, 2012, Setting your own standards: Internal corporate governance codes as a response to institutional pressure, *Organization Science,* 23: 155–176; X. Zhang, K. M. Bartol, K. G. Smith, M. D. Pfaffer, & D. M. Khanin, 2008, CEOs on the edge: Earnings manipulation and stock-based incentive misalignment, *Academy of Management Journal,* 51: 241–258; M. A. Hitt & J. D. Collins, 2007, Business ethics, strategic decision making, and firm performance, *Business Horizons,* 50: 353–357.

118. M. S. Schwartz, 2013, Developing and sustaining an ethical corporate culture: The core elements, *Business Horizons,* 56: 39–50; J. M. Stevens, H. K. Steensma, D. A. Harrison, & P. L. Cochran, 2005, Symbolic or substantive document? Influence of ethics codes on financial executives' decisions, *Strategic Management Journal,* 26: 181–195.

119. W. H. Bishop, 2013, The role of ethics in 21st century organizations, *Journal of Business Ethics,* in press; B. E. Ashforth, D. A. Gioia, S. L. Robinson, & L. K. Trevino, 2008, Re-viewing organizational corruption,

Academy of Management Review, 33: 670–684.

120. Control (management), 2013, *Wikipedia,* http://en.wikipedia.org/wiki/control, June 6; M. D. Shields, F. J. Deng, & Y. Kato, 2000, The design and effects of control systems: Tests of direct- and indirect-effects models, *Accounting, Organizations and Society,* 25: 185–202.

121. M. Rapoport, 2013, KPMG finds its safeguards 'sound and effective,' *Wall Street Journal,* www.wsj.com, June 4.

122. M. Friesl & R. Silberzahn, 2012, Challenges in establishing global collaboration: Temporal, strategic and operational decoupling, *Long Range Planning,* 45: 160–181; R. S. Kaplan & D. P. Norton, 2009, The balanced scorecard: Measures that drive performance (HBR OnPoint Enhanced Edition), *Harvard Business Review,* Boston, MA, March; R. S. Kaplan & D. P. Norton, 2001, The strategy-focused organization, *Strategy & Leadership,* 29(3): 41–42.

123. B. E. Becker, M. A. Huselid, & D. Ulrich, 2001, *The HR Scorecard: Linking People, Strategy, and Performance,* Boston: Harvard Business School Press, 21.

124. R. S. Kaplan & D. P. Norton, 2001, Transforming the balanced scorecard from performance measurement to strategic management: Part I, *Accounting Horizons,* 15(1): 87–104.

125. R. S. Kaplan, 2012, The balanced scorecard: Comments on balanced scorecard commentaries, *Journal of Accounting and Organizational Change,* 8: 539–545; R. S. Kaplan & D. P. Norton, 1992, The balanced scorecard—measures that drive performance, *Harvard Business Review,* 70(1): 71–79.

126. A. Danaei & A. Hosseini, 2013, Performance measurement using balanced scorecard: A case study of pipe industry, *Management Science Letters,* 3: 1433–1438; M. A. Mische, 2001, *Strategic Renewal: Becoming a High-Performance Organization,* Upper Saddle River, NJ: Prentice Hall, 181.

127. G. Rowe, 2001, Creating wealth in organizations: The role of strategic leadership, *Academy of Management Executive,* 15(1): 81–94.

128. J. Xia & S. Li, 2013, The divestiture of acquired subunits: A resource dependence approach, *Strategic Management Journal,* 34: 131–148; R. E. Hoskisson, R. A. Johnson, D. Yiu, & W. P. Wan, 2001, Restructuring strategies of diversified business groups: Differences associated with country institutional environments, in M. A. Hitt, R. E. Freeman, & J. S. Harrison (eds.), *Handbook of Strategic Management,* Oxford, UK: Blackwell Publishers, 433–463.

129. J. Wincent, S. Thorgren, & S. Anokhin, 2013, Managing maturing government-supported networks: The shift from monitoring to embeddedness controls, *British Journal of Management,* in press.

13

Strategic Entrepreneurship

Studying this chapter should provide you with the strategic management knowledge needed to:

1 Define strategic entrepreneurship and corporate entrepreneurship.

2 Define entrepreneurship and entrepreneurial opportunities and explain their importance.

3 Define invention, innovation, and imitation, and describe the relationship among them.

4 Describe entrepreneurs and the entrepreneurial mind-set.

5 Explain international entrepreneurship and its importance.

6 Describe how firms internally develop innovations.

7 Explain how firms use cooperative strategies to innovate.

8 Describe how firms use acquisitions as a means of innovation.

9 Explain how strategic entrepreneurship helps firms create value.

INNOVATION'S IMPORTANCE TO COMPETITIVE SUCCESS

In survey after survey, chief executive officers (CEOs) say that innovation (defined in this chapter as a process firms use to create a commercial product from an invention) is critically important to their firm's success, and there is evidence supporting this assessment. For example, research results show that particularly for firms competing in turbulent global business environments and with respect to their efforts to develop innovations internally, "innovation is an important driver of the organic growth necessary to generate sustained, above-average returns." Simultaneously though, a large percentage of CEOs say that they are relatively dissatisfied with the number of innovations their firm is producing. Thus, while CEOs place high value on innovation, they are dissatisfied with the output flowing from their firm's efforts to innovate. In this chapter, we suggest that engaging in strategic entrepreneurship (defined later) is an approach firms can use to deal with this issue in that through strategic entrepreneurship firms learn how to produce a larger quantity of successful innovations.

Successful innovations satisfy needs that are important to customers. For this reason, innovative companies develop and nurture strong ties or relationships with current and potential customers. Identifying product functionalities or features for which companies are willing to pay is a key outcome firms seek when interacting with customers. Increasingly, firms are discovering that a larger number of customers are interested in understanding "a product's sustainability credentials and (are) willing to pay a premium for environmentally sound products and services." Knowing this, firms are then able to pursue innovations that will satisfy customers' needs or interests.

Thus, with a focus on customers, the number of ways companies can innovate is virtually unlimited. For example, some argue that a number of Chinese companies are targeting "middle-market" consumers, defined as individuals who desire to purchase "good enough" products. Broadly speaking, these are products "that emphasize price competitiveness and sufficient functionalities, rather than customization and the most advanced technologies." By focusing on cost innovation, these firms demonstrate their belief that for middle-market customers, firms should orient their innovation efforts to learning how to be highly competitive on price while delivering value with which customers are satisfied in light of the price they pay for a product. Several factors facilitate the efforts of Chinese cost innovators, including a relentless focus on finding "unconventional ways to economize through product design, production processes, or choice of materials" and the intention of producing products with a balance among price, quality, and functions that appeal to middle-market consumers. The important point here is that firms should seek to innovate within the context of a customer's group's needs.

In terms of competitive rivalry (see Chapter 5), successful innovations have competitive implications. This is the case with respect to premeasured pod detergents, a recent innovation in the laundry-soap business. A number of firms now produce this product but Procter & Gamble (P&G) is dominant, with roughly 75 percent of total pod sales. A competitive issue is that some in the industry argue that "Pod is killing the laundry detergent category." How is this possible? At issue here is the fact that an attribute of the innovative pod is that it "ushered in the area of 'unit dose' products." In this sense, consumers use the exact amount of detergent needed each time clothes are washed. The disadvantage for laundry-soap manufacturers is that historically, they could count on extra sales from customers who used too much detergent virtually every time they used a washing machine. With pods, product waste is eliminated, resulting in a reduction in the overall laundry detergent market. The situation with pods highlights the complexity that can be associated with successful innovations!

Sources: D. Boyd & J. Goldenberg, 2013, Think inside the box, *Wall Street Journal*, www.wsj.com, June 14; D. Kiron, N. Kruschwitz, K. Haanaes, M. Reeves, & E. Goh, 2013, The innovation bottom line, *bcg.perspectives*, www.bcgperspectives.com, February 5; M. Krigsman, 2013, The new CIO: Chief innovation officer, *Wall Street Journal*, www.wsj.com, June 10; M. Reeves, K. Haanaes, J. Hollingsworth, & F. L. S. Pasini, Ambidexterity: The art of thriving in complex environments, *bcg.perspectives*, www.bcgperspectives.com, February 19; H. Zablit & B. Chui, 2013, The next wave of Chinese cost innovators, *bcg.perspectives*, bcgperspectives.com, January 23.

Strategy Right NOW

Learn more about strategic entrepreneurship.
www.cengagebrain.com

Strategic entrepreneurship is the taking of entrepreneurial actions using a strategic perspective.

In previous chapters, we noted that *organizational culture* refers to the complex set of ideologies, symbols, and core values that are shared throughout the firm and that influence how the firm conducts business. Thus, as the social energy that drives or fails to drive an organization's actions, culture influences firms' efforts to innovate.[1]

As noted in the Opening Case, establishing effective relationships with various stakeholders and particularly with customers is critical to firms' efforts to innovate. One reason for this is that through these relationships, firms gain access to knowledge that typically has the potential to meaningfully inform the innovations they seek to produce.[2] This association between networks of relationships and innovation exists as firms compete both domestically and internationally.[3] Moreover, this set of relationships helps firms identify opportunities to pursue and strategies to implement to exploit today's opportunities while simultaneously trying to find opportunities to exploit in the future.

The focus of this chapter is on strategic entrepreneurship, which is a framework firms use to effectively integrate their entrepreneurial and strategic actions. More formally, **strategic entrepreneurship** is the taking of entrepreneurial actions using a strategic perspective. In this process, the firm tries to find opportunities in its external environment that it can exploit through innovations. Identifying opportunities to exploit through innovations is the *entrepreneurship* dimension of strategic entrepreneurship; determining the best way to competitively manage the firm's innovation efforts is the *strategic* dimension.[4] Thus, firms using strategic entrepreneurship integrate their actions to find opportunities, innovate, and then implement strategies for the purpose of appropriating value from the innovations they have developed to pursue identified opportunities.[5]

We consider several topics to explain strategic entrepreneurship. First, we examine entrepreneurship and innovation in a strategic context. Definitions of entrepreneurship, entrepreneurial opportunities, and entrepreneurs as those who engage in entrepreneurship to pursue entrepreneurial opportunities are presented. We then describe international entrepreneurship, a process through which firms take entrepreneurial actions outside of their home market. After this discussion, the chapter shifts to descriptions of the three ways firms innovate—internally, through cooperative strategies, and by acquiring other companies.[6] We discuss these methods separately. Not surprisingly, most large firms use all three methods to innovate. The chapter closes with summary comments about how firms use strategic entrepreneurship to create value.

M. Stasy

Before turning to the chapter's topics, we note that a major portion of the material in this chapter deals with entrepreneurship and innovation that takes place in established organizations. This phenomenon is called **corporate entrepreneurship**, which is the use or application of entrepreneurship within an established firm.[7] Corporate entrepreneurship is critical to the survival and success of for-profit organizations[8] as well as public agencies.[9] Of course, innovation and entrepreneurship play a critical role in the degree of success achieved by startup entrepreneurial ventures as well. Because of this, a significant portion of the content examined in this chapter is equally important in both entrepreneurial ventures and established organizations.

13-1 Entrepreneurship and Entrepreneurial Opportunities

Entrepreneurship is the process by which individuals, teams, or organizations identify and pursue entrepreneurial opportunities without being immediately constrained by the resources they currently control.[10] **Entrepreneurial opportunities** are conditions in which new goods or services can satisfy a need in the market. These opportunities exist because of competitive imperfections in markets and among the factors of production used to produce them or because they were independently developed by entrepreneurs.[11] Entrepreneurial opportunities come in many forms, such as the chance to develop and sell a new product and the chance to sell an existing product in a new market.[12] Firms should be receptive to pursuing entrepreneurial opportunities whenever and wherever they may surface.

As these two definitions suggest, the essence of entrepreneurship is to identify and exploit entrepreneurial opportunities—that is, opportunities others do not see or for which they do not recognize the commercial potential—and manage risks appropriately as they arise.[13] As a process, entrepreneurship results in the "creative destruction" of existing products (goods or services) or methods of producing them and replaces them with new products and production methods.[14] Thus, firms committed to entrepreneurship place high value on individual innovations as well as the ability to continuously innovate across time.[15]

We study entrepreneurship at the level of the individual firm. However, evidence suggests that entrepreneurship is the economic engine driving many nations' economies in the global competitive landscape.[16] Thus, entrepreneurship and the innovation it spawns are important for companies competing in the global economy and for countries seeking to stimulate economic climates with the potential to enhance the living standard of their citizens.

13-2 Innovation

In his classic work, Schumpeter argued that firms engage in three types of innovative activities.[17] **Invention** is the act of creating or developing a new product or process. **Innovation** is a process used to create a commercial product from an invention. Thus, innovation follows invention[18] in that invention brings something new into being while innovation brings something new into use. Accordingly, technical criteria are used to determine the success of an invention whereas commercial criteria are used to determine the success of an innovation.[19] Finally, **imitation** is the adoption of a similar innovation by different firms. Imitation usually leads to product standardization, and imitative products often are offered at lower prices but without as many features. Entrepreneurship is critical to innovative activity in that it acts as the linchpin between invention and innovation.[20]

For most companies, innovation is the most critical of the three types of innovative activities. The reason for this is that while many companies are able to create ideas that lead

Corporate entrepreneurship is the use or application of entrepreneurship within an established firm.

Entrepreneurship is the process by which individuals, teams, or organizations identify and pursue entrepreneurial opportunities without being immediately constrained by the resources they currently control.

Entrepreneurial opportunities are conditions in which new goods or services can satisfy a need in the market.

Invention is the act of creating or developing a new product or process.

Innovation is a process used to create a commercial product from an invention.

Imitation is the adoption of a similar innovation by different firms.

Learn more about
innovation.
www.cengagebrain.com

to inventions, commercializing those inventions sometimes proves to be difficult.[21] Patents are a strategic asset and the ability to regularly produce them can be an important source of competitive advantage, especially when a firm intends to commercialize an invention and when it competes in a knowledge-intensive industry (e.g., pharmaceuticals).[22] In a competitive sense, patents create entry barriers for a firm's potential competitors.[23]

Peter Drucker argued that "innovation is the specific function of entrepreneurship, whether in an existing business, a public service institution, or a new venture started by a lone individual."[24] Moreover, Drucker suggested that innovation is "the means by which the entrepreneur either creates new wealth-producing resources or endows existing resources with enhanced potential for creating wealth."[25] Thus, entrepreneurship and the innovation resulting from it are critically important for all firms seeking strategic competitiveness and above-average returns.

The realities of global competition suggest that to be market leaders, companies must regularly innovate. This means that innovation should be an intrinsic part of virtually all of a firm's activities.[26] Moreover, firms should recognize the importance of their human capital to efforts to innovate.[27] Thus, as this discussion suggests, innovation is a key outcome firms seek through entrepreneurship and is often the source of competitive success, especially for companies competing in highly competitive and turbulent environments.[28]

13-3 Entrepreneurs

Entrepreneurs are individuals, acting independently or as part of an organization, who perceive an entrepreneurial opportunity and then take risks to develop an innovation to exploit it.

The person with an **entrepreneurial mind-set** values uncertainty in markets and seeks to continuously identify opportunities in those markets that can be pursued through innovation.

Entrepreneurs are individuals, acting independently or as part of an organization, who perceive an entrepreneurial opportunity and then take risks to develop an innovation to exploit it. Entrepreneurs can be found throughout different parts of organizations—from top-level managers to those working to produce a firm's products.

Entrepreneurs tend to demonstrate several characteristics: they are highly motivated, willing to take responsibility for their projects, self-confident, and often optimistic.[29] In addition, entrepreneurs tend to be passionate and emotional about the value and importance of their innovation-based ideas.[30] They are able to deal with uncertainty and are more alert to opportunities than others.[31] To be successful, entrepreneurs often need to have good social skills and to plan exceptionally well (e.g., to obtain venture capital).[32] Entrepreneurship entails much hard work if it is to be successful, but it can also be highly satisfying—particularly when entrepreneurs recognize and follow their passions. According to Jeff Bezos, Amazon.com's founder: "One of the huge mistakes people make is that they try to force an interest on themselves. You don't choose your passions; your passions choose you."[33]

Evidence suggests that successful entrepreneurs have an entrepreneurial mind-set that includes recognition of the importance of competing internationally as well as domestically.[34] The person with an **entrepreneurial mind-set** values uncertainty in markets and seeks to continuously identify opportunities in those markets that can be pursued through innovation.[35] Those without an entrepreneurial mind-set tend to view opportunities to innovate as threats.[36]

Because it has the potential to lead to continuous innovations, an individual's entrepreneurial mind-set can be a source of competitive

Jeff Bezos, CEO of Amazon.com, at the Kindle launch in Santa Monica, California. Bezos has demonstrated an entrepreneurial mind-set throughout his tenure at Amazon.com.

Ted Soqui/Ted Soqui Photography/Corbis

M. Stasy

advantage for a firm. Entrepreneurial mind-sets are fostered and supported when knowledge is readily available throughout a firm. Indeed, research shows that units within firms are more innovative when people have access to new knowledge.[37] Transferring knowledge, however, can be difficult, often because the receiving party must have adequate absorptive capacity (or the ability) to understand the knowledge and how to productively use it.[38] Learning requires that the new knowledge be linked to the existing knowledge. Thus, managers need to develop the capabilities of their human capital to build on their current knowledge base while incrementally expanding it.

Some companies are known to be highly committed to entrepreneurship, suggesting that many working within them have an entrepreneurial mind-set. In 2012, *Fast Company* identified Nike as the most innovative company with Amazon.com, Square, Splunk, Fab, Uber, Sprovil, Pinterest, Safaricom, and Target also among the top 10 most innovative firms.[39] Nike was chosen as the most innovative company for 2012 largely because the firm launched two successful innovations—FuelBand and Flyknit Racer—during that year. FuelBand is an electronic bracelet that measures an individual's movement throughout the day whether playing tennis, jogging, or simply walking. The Flyknit Racer is a featherlight shoe that to the person wearing it, feels like a sock sitting on top of a sole. The shoe is thought to be more environmentally friendly and, over the long term, is expected to be less expensive to manufacture.

13-4 International Entrepreneurship

International entrepreneurship is a process in which firms creatively discover and exploit opportunities that are outside their domestic markets.[40] Thus, entrepreneurship is a process that many firms exercise at both the domestic and international levels.[41] This is true for entrepreneurial ventures as suggested by the fact that approximately one-third of them move into international markets early in their life cycle. Large, established companies commonly have significant foreign operations and often start new ventures in international markets, too. For example, Microsoft and Huawei recently formed a partnership to launch "a new full-functionality Windows Phone specifically designed for Africa—Huawei 4Afrika."[42]

A key reason that firms choose to engage in international entrepreneurship is that in general, doing so enhances their performance.[43] Nonetheless, those leading firms should also understand that taking entrepreneurial actions in markets outside the firm's home setting is challenging and not without risks, including those of unstable foreign currencies, problems with market efficiencies, insufficient infrastructures to support businesses, and limitations on market size.[44] Thus, the decision to engage in international entrepreneurship should be a product of careful analysis.

Even though entrepreneurship is a global phenomenon, meaning that it is practiced across the world, its rate of use differs within individual countries. For example, the results of a well-known study that is completed annually (called the Global Entrepreneurship Monitor) showed that the 10 most entrepreneurial countries in 2012 were (from the most to the least entrepreneurial): the United States, Sweden, Australia, Iceland, Denmark, Canada, Switzerland, Belgium, Norway, Netherlands, and Taiwan (the Netherlands and Taiwan tied for the tenth position).[45] The 2012 analysis of entrepreneurship throughout the world also showed that for the first time in the report's 13-year history, "the rate of business formation among women eclipsed the rate among men in three nations (Ghana, Nigeria, and Thailand)" and was nearly equal in four other nations.[46] As usual, the report also found a strong positive relationship between the rate of entrepreneurship and economic development within a country.

International entrepreneurship is a process in which firms creatively discover and exploit opportunities that are outside their domestic markets.

Culture is one reason for the different rates of entrepreneurship among countries across the globe. Research suggests that a balance between individual initiative and a spirit of cooperation and group ownership of innovation is needed to encourage entrepreneurial behavior. This means that for firms to be entrepreneurial, they must provide appropriate autonomy and incentives for individual initiative to surface while simultaneously promoting cooperation and group ownership of an innovation as a foundation for successfully exploiting it. Thus, international entrepreneurship often requires teams of people with unique skills and resources, especially in cultures that place high value on either individualism or collectivism. In addition to a balance of values for individual initiative and cooperative behaviors, firms engaging in international entrepreneurship must concentrate more so than companies engaging in domestic entrepreneurship only on building the capabilities needed to innovate and on acquiring the resources needed to make strategic decisions through which innovations can be successfully exploited.[47]

The level of investment outside of the home country made by young ventures is also an important dimension of international entrepreneurship. In fact, with increasing globalization, a larger number of new ventures have been "born global."[48] One reason for this is likely related to the fact that new ventures that enter international markets increase their learning of new technological knowledge and thereby enhance their performance.[49]

The probability of entering and successfully competing in international markets increases when the firm's strategic leaders, and especially its top-level managers, have international experience.[50] Because of the learning and economies of scale and scope afforded by operating in international markets, both young and established internationally diversified firms often are stronger competitors in their domestic market as well. Additionally, as research has shown, internationally diversified firms are generally more innovative.[51]

The ability of a firm to develop and sustain a competitive advantage may be based partly or largely on its ability to innovate. This is true for firms engaging in international entrepreneurship as well as those that have yet to do so. As we discuss next, firms can follow different paths to innovate internally. Internal innovation is the first of three approaches firms use to innovate.

13-5 Internal Innovation

Efforts in firms' research and development (R&D) function are the source of internal innovations. Through effective R&D, firms are able to generate patentable processes and goods that are innovative in nature. Increasingly, successful R&D results from integrating the skills available in the global workforce. Thus, the ability to have a competitive advantage based on innovation is more likely to accrue to firms capable of integrating the talent of human capital from countries around the world.[52]

R&D and the new products and processes it can spawn affect a firm's efforts to earn above-average returns while competing in today's global environment. Because of this, firms try to use their R&D labs to create disruptive technologies and products. This is the case for China's Huawei Technologies Co. a firm that is increasing its allocations to R&D. Currently, the amount Huawei allocates to R&D is second among firms competing in the telecom equipment industry. Huawei is increasing its emphasis on R&D to become more innovative as a foundation for surviving in a highly competitive and rapidly consolidating industry structure.[53] Being able to continuously and successfully innovate such as Huawei is trying to do can create a competitive advantage for firms in many industries.[54] Although critical to long-term competitive success, the outcomes of R&D investments are uncertain and often not achieved in the short term, meaning that patience is required as firms evaluate the outcomes of their R&D efforts.[55]

13-5a Incremental and Radical Innovation

Firms invest in R&D to produce two types of innovations—incremental and radical. Most innovations are *incremental*—that is, they build on existing knowledge bases and provide small improvements in current products. Incremental innovations are evolutionary and linear in nature.[56] In general, incremental innovations tend to be introduced into established markets where customers understand and accept a product's characteristics. From the firm's perspective, incremental innovations tend to yield lower profit margins compared to those associated with the outcomes of radical innovations, largely because competition among firms offering products to customers that have incremental innovations is primarily on the price variable.[57] Adding a different kind of whitening agent to a soap detergent is an example of an incremental innovation, as are minor improvements in the functionality in televisions (e.g., slightly better picture quality). Companies introduce more incremental than radical innovations to markets, largely because they are cheaper, easier, and faster to produce, and involve less risk. However, incremental innovation can be risky for firms if its frequency of introduction creates more change than can be appropriately absorbed.[58]

In contrast to incremental innovations, *radical innovations* usually provide significant technological breakthroughs and create new knowledge. Revolutionary and nonlinear in nature, radical innovations typically use new technologies to serve newly created markets. The development of the original personal computer was a radical innovation.

Second Sight Medical Products has requested approval from the U.S. Food and Drug Administration (FDA) for its bionic eye, called Argus II. Technically, this product is "a retinal prosthesis, which appears to help some blind or nearly blind individuals see again."[59] The Argus II is a radical innovation, as would be the development of painkilling drugs that are difficult to abuse. With encouragement from the FDA, more than a dozen pharmaceutical companies from Pfizer Inc. to startups are trying to develop these products. The FDA's interest is for companies to find ways to manufacture legitimate drugs in ways that would make it very difficult for abusers to tamper with them to obtain benefits the federal agency deems undesirable and counterproductive—both for individuals and society.[60]

Because they establish new functionalities for users, radical innovations have strong potential to lead to significant growth in revenue and profits. For example, Toyota's innovation, embodied in the Prius, "the first mass-produced hybrid-electric car," changed this segment of the automobile industry.[61] Developing new processes is a critical part of producing radical innovations. Both types of innovations can create value, meaning that firms should determine when it is appropriate to emphasize either incremental or radical innovation. However, radical innovations have the potential to contribute more significantly to a firm's efforts to earn above-average returns, although they may be more risky.

Radical innovations are rare because of the difficulty and risk involved in their development. The value of the technology and the market opportunities are highly uncertain.[62] Because radical innovation creates new knowledge and uses only some or little of a firm's current product or technological knowledge, creativity is required; and creativity is as important to efforts to innovate in not-for-profit organizations as it is in for-profit

Second Sight Medical Products' implantable device takes the place of damaged cells inside the eye. The device may help patients to perform daily tasks by allowing them to detect light and dark in the environment.

AP Photo/ Second Sight Medical Products

firms.[63] Creativity is an outcome of using one's imagination. In the words of Jay Walker, founder of Priceline.com, "Imagination is the fuel. You're not going to get innovation if you don't have imagination." Imagination finds firms thinking about what customers will want in a changing world. For example, Walker says, those seeking to innovate within a firm could try to imagine "what the customer is going to want in a world where for instance, their cellphone is in their glasses."[64] Imagination is more critical to radical than incremental innovations.

Creativity itself does not directly lead to innovation. Rather, creativity as generated through imagination discovers, combines, or synthesizes current knowledge, often from diverse areas.[65] Increasingly, when trying to innovate, firms seek knowledge from current users to understand their perspective about what could be beneficial innovations to the firm's products.[66] Collectively, the gathered knowledge is then applied to develop new products that can be used in an entrepreneurial manner to move into new markets, capture new customers, and gain access to new resources.[67] Such innovations are often developed in separate business units that start internal ventures.[68]

Strong, supportive leadership is required for the type of creativity and imagination needed to develop radical innovations. The fact that creativity is "messy, chaotic, sometimes even disgusting, and reeks of failure, experimentation and disorganization"[69] is one set of reasons leadership is so critical to its success.

This discussion highlights the fact that internally developed incremental and radical innovations result from deliberate efforts. These deliberate efforts are called *internal corporate venturing*, which is the set of activities firms use to develop internal inventions and especially innovations.[70]

As shown in Figure 13.1, autonomous and induced strategic behaviors are the two types of internal corporate venturing. Each venturing type facilitates development of both incremental and radical innovations. However, a larger number of radical innovations spring from autonomous strategic behavior while a larger number of incremental innovations come from induced strategic behavior.

In essence, autonomous strategic behavior results in influences to change aspects of the firm's strategy and the structure in place to support its implementation. In contrast, induced strategic behavior results from the influences of the strategy and structure the firm currently

Figure 13.1 Model of Internal Corporate Venturing

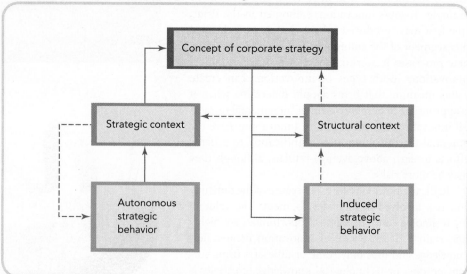

Source: Adapted from R. A. Burgelman, 1983, A model of the interactions of strategic behavior, corporate context, and the concept of strategy, *Academy of Management Review*, 8:65.

has in place to support efforts to innovate (see Figure 13.1). These points are emphasized in the discussions below of the two types of internal corporate venturing.

13-5b Autonomous Strategic Behavior

Autonomous strategic behavior is a bottom-up process in which product champions pursue new ideas, often through a political process, by means of which they develop and coordinate the actions required to innovate and to bring the innovation to the market.[71] A *product champion* is an individual with an entrepreneurial mind-set who seeks to create support for developing an innovation. Product champions play critical roles in moving innovations forward.[72] Commonly, product champions use their social capital to develop informal networks within the firm. As progress is made, these networks become more formal as a means of pushing an innovation to marketplace success.[73] Internal innovations springing from autonomous strategic behavior differ from the firm's current strategy and structure, taking it into new markets and perhaps new ways of creating value.

As a means of innovating, autonomous strategic behavior is more effective when new knowledge, especially tacit knowledge, is diffused continuously throughout the firm.[74] Interestingly, some of the processes important to promote innovation through autonomous strategic behavior vary by the environment and country in which a firm operates. For example, the Japanese culture is high on uncertainty avoidance. As such, research has found that Japanese firms are more likely to engage in autonomous strategic behavior under conditions of low uncertainty because they prefer stability.[75]

13-5c Induced Strategic Behavior

Induced strategic behavior, the second form of corporate venturing through which innovations are developed internally, is a top-down process whereby the firm's current strategy and structure foster innovations that are closely associated with that strategy and structure.[76] In this form of venturing, the strategy in place is filtered through a matching structural hierarchy. In essence, induced strategic behavior results in internal innovations that are consistent with the firm's current strategy. Thus, the firm's CEO and its top management team play an active and key role in induced strategic behavior.[77] This is the case at IBM, where CEO Virginia Rometty recently challenged the firm's employees "to move faster and respond more quickly to customers" as a foundation for developing innovations that will facilitate the firm's efforts to "shift to new computing models."[78]

Other companies are also interested in stimulating induced strategic behavior. Playing catchup to Amazon.com in the e-commerce space, Walmart is relying on its existing strategy and structure to develop "a vast new logistics system that includes building new warehouses for Web orders, but also uses workers in stores to pack and mail items to customers." In describing these enhancements to the firm's strategy, CEO Mike Duke said that after a rough start, the firm is beginning to gain traction in its efforts to innovatively find ways to successfully compete against Amazon.com.[79] Given its interest in expanding its hardware offerings, Microsoft is using its current strategy and structure to innovate for the purpose of developing new products such as "a smaller, 7-inch version of a tablet to compete with popular gadgets like Apple's iPad Mini."[80]

Apple's iPad Mini is another in a long line of successful internal innovations.

Max Herman/Alamy

13-6 Implementing Internal Innovations

An entrepreneurial mind-set is critical to firms' efforts to innovate internally, partly because such a mind-set helps them deal with the environmental and market uncertainty that are associated with efforts taken to commercialize inventions. When facing uncertainty, firms try to continuously identify the most attractive opportunities to pursue strategically. This means that using an entrepreneurial mind-set finds firms being simultaneously oriented to identifying opportunities, developing innovations that are appropriate to those opportunities, and to executing strategies to successfully exploit opportunities in the marketplace. Often, firms provide incentives to individuals to be more entrepreneurial as a foundation for successfully developing internal innovations, sometimes encouraging work teams to specify what they believe are the most appropriate incentives for the firm to use.[81]

Having processes and structures in place through which a firm can successfully exploit developed innovations is critical. In the context of internal corporate ventures, managers must allocate resources, coordinate activities, communicate with many different parties in the organization, and make a series of decisions to convert the innovations resulting from either autonomous or induced strategic behaviors into successful market entries.[82] As we describe in Chapter 11, organizational structures are the sets of formal relationships that support processes managers use to exploit the firm's innovations.

Effective integration of the functions involved in internal innovation efforts—from engineering to manufacturing and distribution—is required to implement the incremental and radical innovations resulting from internal corporate ventures.[83] Increasingly, product development teams are being used to achieve the desired integration across organizational functions. Such integration involves coordinating and applying the knowledge and skills of different functional areas to maximize innovation.[84] Teams must help to make decisions as to the projects to continue supporting as well as those to terminate. Emotional commitments sometimes increase the difficulty of deciding to terminate an innovation-based project.

13-6a Cross-Functional Product Development Teams

Cross-functional product development teams facilitate efforts to integrate activities associated with different organizational functions, such as design, manufacturing, and marketing. These teams may also include people from major suppliers because they have knowledge that can meaningfully inform a firm's innovation processes.[85] In addition, new product development processes can be completed more quickly and the products more easily commercialized when cross-functional teams work collaboratively.[86] Using cross-functional teams, product development stages are grouped into parallel processes so the firm can tailor its product development efforts to its unique core competencies and to the needs of the market.

Horizontal organizational structures support cross-functional teams in their efforts to integrate innovation-based activities across organizational functions.[87] Therefore, instead of being designed around vertical hierarchical functions or departments, the organization is built around core horizontal processes that are used to produce and manage innovations. Some of the horizontal processes that are critical to innovation efforts are formal and are defined and documented as procedures and practices. More commonly, however, these important processes are informal and are supported properly through horizontal organizational structures—structures that typically find individuals communicating frequently on a face-to-face basis.

Team members' independent frames of reference and organizational politics are two barriers with the potential to prevent effective use of cross-functional teams to integrate the activities of different organizational functions.[88] Team members working within a distinct specialization (e.g., a particular organizational function) may have an independent frame of reference typically based on common backgrounds and experiences. They are likely to use the same decision criteria to evaluate issues such as product development efforts when making decisions within their functional units.

Research suggests that functional departments vary along four dimensions: time orientation, interpersonal orientation, goal orientation, and formality of structure.[89] Thus, individuals from different functional departments having different orientations in terms of these dimensions can be expected to perceive innovation-related activities differently. For example, a design engineer may consider the characteristics that make a product functional and workable to be the most important of its characteristics. Alternatively, a person from the marketing function may judge characteristics that satisfy customer needs to be most important. These different orientations can create barriers to effective communication across functions and may even generate intra-team conflict as different parts of the firm try to work together to innovate.[90]

Some organizations experience a considerable amount of political activity (called organizational politics). How resources will be allocated to different functions is a key source of such activity. This means that inter-unit conflict may result from aggressive competition for resources among those representing different organizational functions. This type of conflict between functions creates a barrier to cross-functional integration efforts. Those trying to form effective cross-functional product development teams seek ways to mitigate the damaging effects of organizational politics. Emphasizing the critical role each function plays in the firm's overall efforts to innovate is a method used in many firms to help individuals see the value of inter-unit collaborations.

13-6b Facilitating Integration and Innovation

Shared values and effective leadership are important for achieving cross-functional integration and implementing internal innovations.[91] As part of culture, shared values are framed around the firm's vision and mission and become the glue that promotes integration between functional units.

Strategic leadership is also important to efforts to achieve cross-functional integration and promote internal innovation. Working with others, leaders are responsible for setting goals and allocating resources needed to achieve them. The goals include integrated development and commercialization of new products. Effective strategic leaders also ensure a high-quality communication system to facilitate cross-functional integration. A critical benefit of effective communication is the sharing of knowledge among team members who in turn are then able to communicate an innovation's existence and importance to others in the organization. Shared values and leadership practices shape the communication routines that make it possible to share innovation-related knowledge throughout the firm.[92]

13-6c Creating Value from Internal Innovation

The model in Figure 13.2 shows how firms seek to create value through internal innovation processes (autonomous strategic behavior and induced strategic behavior). As shown, an entrepreneurial mind-set is foundational to the firm's efforts to consistently identify entrepreneurial opportunities that it can pursue strategically with and through innovations. Cross-functional teams are important for promoting integrated new product design ideas and commitment to their subsequent implementation. Effective leadership and shared values promote integration and vision for innovation and commitment to it. The end result of successful innovations is the creation of value for stakeholders such as customers and shareholders.[93] However, competitive rivalry (see Chapter 5) affects the degree of success a firm achieves through its innovations. Thus, firms must carefully study competitors' responses to their innovations to have the knowledge required to know how to adjust their innovation-based efforts and even when to abandon them if market conditions indicate the need to do so.[94]

Figure 13.2 Creating Value through Internal Innovation Processes

```
┌─────────────────────────────────────────────────────────────────────┐
│                    ┌──────────────────────┐                          │
│                    │   Cross-functional   │                          │
│                    │ product development  │                          │
│                    │        teams         │                          │
│                    └──────────────────────┘                          │
│                                                                       │
│  ┌──────────────────┐                      ┌──────────────────┐      │
│  │  Entrepreneurial │                      │  Creating value  │      │
│  │     mind-set     │                      │ through innovation│     │
│  └──────────────────┘                      └──────────────────┘      │
│                                                                       │
│                    ┌──────────────────────┐                          │
│                    │Facilitating integration                         │
│                    │    and innovation    │                          │
│                    │  • Shared values     │                          │
│                    │  • Entrepreneurial   │                          │
│                    │    leadership        │                          │
│                    └──────────────────────┘                          │
└─────────────────────────────────────────────────────────────────────┘
```

© Cengage Learning

But as we discuss in the Strategic Focus, some efforts to create value through internal innovation fail. This appears to be J.C. Penney's experience during Ron Johnson's short tenure as the firm's CEO. We discussed some of Johnson's innovations and the strategy through which they were to be exploited in Chapter 4's Opening Case. Overall, the innovations Johnson developed were more radical than incremental. However, it seems that these internal innovations did not create value for JCP's stakeholders because the efforts undertaken to implement the strategy through which these innovations were to be exploited resulted in significant declines in sales revenue and the price of the firm's stock, as well as Johnson's ouster as CEO.

In the next two sections, we discuss the other approaches firms use to innovate—cooperative strategies and acquisitions.

Learn more about Disney.
www.cengagebrain.com

13-7 Innovation through Cooperative Strategies

Alliances with other firms can contribute to innovations in several ways. First, they provide information on new business opportunities and the innovations that might be developed to exploit them.[95] In other instances, firms use cooperative strategies to align what they believe are complementary assets with the potential to lead to future innovations. Compared to other approaches to innovation, combining complementary assets through alliances has the potential to more frequently result in "breakthrough" innovations.[96]

Rapidly changing technologies, globalization, and the need to innovate at world-class levels are primary influences on firms' decisions to innovate by cooperating with other companies. Indeed, some believe that because of these conditions, firms are becoming increasingly dependent on cooperative strategies as a path to innovation and, ultimately, to competitive success in the global economy.[97]

M. Stasy

An Innovation Failure at JC Penney: Its Causes and Consequences

In Chapter 4's Opening Case, we described the strategy that now former CEO Ron Johnson designed and tried to implement at JC Penney (JCP). As it turns out, part of the trouble was that the firm's target "middle market" customers did not respond well to the new strategy and the innovations associated with it. In fact, some say that Johnson's innovations and strategy alienated what had historically been the firm's target customers.

Johnson came to JCP after successful stints at Target and Apple. At Apple, he was admired for the major role he played in developing that firm's wildly successful Apple Stores, which a number of analysts say brought about "a new world order in retailing." It was Johnson's ability to establish what some viewed as path-breaking visions and to develop innovations to reach them that appealed to JCP's board when he was hired.

Likening JCP to the Titanic, Johnson came to the CEO position believing that innovation was the key to shaking up the firm. Moreover, he reminded analysts, employees, and the like that he came to JCP to "transform" the firm, not to marginally improve its performance. Describing what he intended to do at JCP, Johnson said that "In the U.S., the department store has a chance to regain its status as the leader in style, the leader in excitement. It will be a period of true innovation for this company."

The essence of Johnson's vision for JCP was twofold. First, he eliminated the firm's practice of marking up prices on goods and then offering discounts, heavy promotions, and coupons to entice its bargain-hunting target customers. Instead, Johnson introduced a three-tiered pricing structure that focused on what were labelled "everyday low prices." To customers though, the pricing structure was confusing and failed to convince them that the "everyday low prices" were actually "low enough" compared to competitors' prices.

Innovation was at the core of the second part of the new CEO's vision, with one objective being to give JCP a younger, hipper image. The innovations Johnson put into place to create this image included establishing branded boutiques within JCP's stores. To do this, JCP set up branded boutiques "along a wide aisle, or 'street' dotted with places to sit, grab a cup of coffee or play with Lego blocks." With an initial intention of having 100 branded shops within JCP stores by 2015, Johnson asked people "to envision an entire store of shops with a street and square in the middle representing a new way to interface with the customer." Disney was one of the brands to be included as a shopping destination, as were Caribou Coffee, Dallas-based Paciugo Gelato & Café, and Giggle, a store dedicated to making "it a whole lot easier to become a parent" by offering innovative and stylish "must-have baby items." In addition, and as noted in Chapter 4's Opening Case, Levi's, IZOD, Liz Claiborne, and Martha

Merchandise by Jonathan Adler is on display in a remodeled portion of JC Penney at Citrus Park Mall in Tampa, Florida.

Stewart branded items were to be included as part of the boutiques.

But as noted, these innovations and the strategy used to exploit them did not work. So what went wrong? Considering the components of the model shown in Figure 13.2 yields a framework to answer this question. While it is true that Johnson had an entrepreneurial mind-set, cross-functional teams were not used to facilitate implementation of the desired innovations such as the boutique stores. In essence, it seems that Johnson himself, without the involvement of others throughout the firm, was instrumental in deciding that the boutiques were to be used as well as how they were to be established and operated within selected JCP's stores. In addition, the values associated with efforts to change JCP from its historic roots of being a general merchant in the space between department stores and discounters to becoming a firm with a young, hip image were not shared among the firm's stakeholders. Finally, Johnson's work as an entrepreneurial leader was seemingly not as effective as should have been the case. Among mistakes made in this regard were trying to implement too many changes too quickly without adequately testing customers' reactions to those changes, and more broadly, a failure to fully understand customers and their needs. Because of mistakes such as these, the level of success desired at JCP through internally developed innovations was not attained.

Sources: 2013, J.C. Penney ousts CEO Ron Johnson, *Wall Street Journal*, www.wsj.com, April 8; D. Benoit, 2013, J.C. Penney asks customers for second chance, *Wall Street Journal*, www.wsj.com, May 1; D. Benoit, 2013, Ackman thought Johnson could turn around 'titanic' JCPenney, *Wall Street Journal*, www.wsj.com, April 8; S. Gerfield, 2013, J.C. Penney rehires Myron Ullman to clean up Ron Johnson's mess, *Bloomberg Businessweek*, www.businessweek.com, April 11; S. Clifford, 2013, J.C. Penney's new plan is to reuse its old plans, *New York Times*, www.nytimes.com, May 16; S. Denning, 2013, J.C. Penney: Was Ron Johnson's strategy wrong? *Forbes*, www.forbes.com, April 9; M. Halkias, 2012, J.C. Penney's Ron Johnson shows off his vision of future to 300 analysts, *Dallas News*, www.dallasnews.com, September 19.

Both entrepreneurial ventures and established firms use cooperative strategies to innovate. An entrepreneurial venture, for example, may seek investment capital as well as established firms' distribution capabilities to successfully introduce one of its innovative products to the market.[98] Alternatively, more-established companies may need new technological knowledge and can gain access to it by forming a cooperative strategy with entrepreneurial ventures.[99] Alliances between large pharmaceutical firms and biotechnology companies increasingly have been formed to integrate the knowledge and resources of both to develop new products and bring them to market.

In some instances, large established firms form an alliance to innovate. This is the case for Inter IKEA Group, the parent company of the IKEA furniture brand, and Marriott International Inc. These firms have formed an alliance to develop Moxy, a new hotel brand that the companies believe is innovative in its design and the value it will create for customers. Novel construction techniques that will keep manufacturing costs down is IKEA's innovation for the alliance while unique design for the "value-oriented" segment is Marriott's innovation. Thus, the Moxy brand is being developed to innovatively combine value with style. In the words of Marriott's CEO: "This is a fresh new take on the economy segment. I think it will benefit from being new and combining value with style. Too much of the value product you see in Europe is devoid of style." Initially, 50 units of the budget hotels with style will open in Europe.[100]

However, alliances formed to foster innovation are not without risks. In addition to conflict that is natural when firms try to work together to reach a mutual goal, the members of an alliance also take a risk that a partner will appropriate their technology or knowledge and use it for its own benefit.[101] Carefully selecting partner firms mitigates this risk. The ideal partnership is one in which the firms have complementary skills as well as compatible strategic goals.[102] When this is the case, firms encounter fewer challenges and risks as they try to effectively manage the partnership they formed to develop innovations. Companies also want to constrain the number of cooperative arrangements they form to innovate in that becoming involved in too many alliances puts them at risk of losing the ability to successfully manage each of them.[103]

13-8 Innovation through Acquisitions

Firms sometimes acquire companies to gain access to their innovations and to their innovative capabilities.[104] One reason companies do this is that capital markets value growth; acquisitions provide a means to rapidly extend one or more product lines and increase the firm's revenues.[105] In spite of this fact, a firm should have a strategic rationale for a decision to acquire a company. Typically, the rationale is to gain ownership of an acquired company's innovations and access to its innovative capabilities. A number of large pharmaceutical companies have acquired firms, largely for these purposes. For example, Pfizer Inc. recently acquired NextWave Pharmaceuticals, Inc., a company with a focus on developing and commercializing products to treat attention deficit hyperactivity disorder (ADHD). Through this acquisition, Pfizer gained ownership of NextWave's innovative Quillivant XR drug that treats ADHD as well as access to the firm's efforts to develop an extended-release chewable tablet version of the drug.[106]

Similar to internal corporate venturing and strategic alliances, acquisitions are not a risk free approach to innovation. A key risk of acquisitions is that a firm may substitute an ability to buy innovations for an ability to develop them internally. This may result when a firm concentrates on financial controls to identify, evaluate, and then manage acquisitions. Of course, strategic controls are the ones through which a firm identifies a strategic rationale to acquire another company as a means of developing innovations. Thus, the likelihood a firm will be successful in its efforts to innovate increases by developing an appropriate balance between financial and strategic controls. In spite of the risks though, choosing to acquire companies with complementary capabilities and knowledge sets can support a firm's efforts to innovate successfully when the acquisitions are made for strategic purposes and are then properly integrated into the acquired firm's strategies.[107]

The ability to learn new capabilities that can facilitate innovation-related activities from acquired companies is an important benefit that can accrue to an acquiring firm. Additionally, firms that emphasize innovation and carefully select companies to acquire that also emphasize innovation and the technological capabilities on which innovations are often based are likely to remain innovative.[108] To gain this benefit though, the operations of the companies with this emphasis must be effectively integrated.[109]

To close this chapter, we describe how strategic entrepreneurship helps firms create value for stakeholders.

13-9 Creating Value through Strategic Entrepreneurship

Entrepreneurial ventures and younger firms often are more effective at identifying opportunities than are larger established companies.[110] As a consequence, entrepreneurial ventures often produce more radical innovations than do larger, more established organizations. Entrepreneurial ventures' strategic flexibility and willingness to take risks at least partially account for their ability to identify opportunities and then develop radical innovations as a foundation for exploiting them. Alternatively, larger, well-established firms often have more resources and capabilities to manage their resources for the purpose of exploiting identified opportunities, but these efforts by large firms generally result in more incremental than radical innovations.

Thus, younger, entrepreneurial ventures generally excel in the *taking of entrepreneurial actions* part of strategic entrepreneurship while larger, more established firms generally excel at the *using a strategic perspective* part of strategic entrepreneurship. Another way of thinking about this is to say that entrepreneurial ventures excel at opportunity-seeking (that is, entrepreneurial) behavior while larger firms excel at advantage-seeking (that is, strategic) behavior. However, competitive success and superior performance relative to competitors accrues to firms that are able to identify and exploit opportunities and establish a competitive advantage as a result of doing so.[111] On a relative basis then, entrepreneurial ventures are challenged to become more strategic while older, more established firms are challenged to become more entrepreneurial.

Firms trying to learn how to simultaneously be more entrepreneurial and strategic (that is, firms trying to use strategic entrepreneurship) recognize that after identifying opportunities, entrepreneurs within entrepreneurial ventures and established organizations must develop capabilities that will become the basis of their firm's core competencies and competitive advantages. The process of identifying opportunities is entrepreneurial, but this activity alone is not sufficient to create maximum wealth or even to survive over time. As we learned in Chapter 3, to successfully exploit opportunities, a firm must develop capabilities that are valuable, rare, difficult to imitate, and nonsubstitutable. When capabilities satisfy these four criteria, the firm has one or more competitive advantages to use in efforts to exploit the identified opportunities. Without a competitive advantage, the firm's success will be only temporary (as explained in Chapter 1). An innovation may be valuable and rare early in its life, if a market perspective is used in its development. However, competitive actions must be taken to introduce the new product to the market and protect its position in the market against competitors to gain a competitive advantage.[112] In combination, these actions constitute strategic entrepreneurship.

Strategic Focus   SUCCESS

Pursuing Competitive Success by Using Strategic Entrepreneurship

Over the years, both Boeing and Airbus have shown an ability to identify and pursue entrepreneurial opportunities. For these firms, this means that they are able to produce innovative airplanes that satisfy a need in the markets they serve.

Fuel to operate airplanes is a major cost borne by airline companies, Boeing and Airbus's customers. For some time, these two firms have recognized that an opportunity exists to manufacture highly fuel-efficient products as a way of helping customers reduce their costs. The two companies also knew that innovation and a strategic perspective would be critical to their efforts to profitably produce, sell, and maintain highly fuel-efficient medium- and long-range jets. Indeed, with respect to the long-range market, some analysts suggest for example, that a "war of the wide-bodies" now exists between Boeing and Airbus. Given the expenses incurred to produce these innovative products, "investors are focusing more on how profitably the companies produce planes than on how many more contracts they land."

These firms have developed similar innovations as the foundation for producing their new fuel-efficient products. The 350 is the core new product for Airbus while the 787 Dreamliner serves this role for Boeing. Initially, Boeing committed to innovations with respect to a number of dimensions (cabin pressure, a smoother ride, less maintenance, larger windows, changes to pilot training to enhance the efficiency and effectiveness of these efforts, and engine swapping—an innovation that makes it possible to easily convert from one manufacturer's engine to another's if a plane is sold to another customer) when producing the 787.

Demonstrating the competitive rivalry between these companies (firms that have resource similarity and market commonality—see Chapter 5) is the opinion among some analysts that "The A350 has the same innovations more or less as the Dreamliner, the 787." In this regard, the belief is that the A350 "is pretty equivalent, the same amount or proportion of carbon for the lightness of the material, just as many electrical devices" and so forth. Thus, both firms are using carbon-fiber composites for the skin of the planes. Additionally, the underneath of the 787 includes "highly engineered" titanium as well as an assortment of cutting-edge aluminum alloys. Overall, the A350 "is 53% composites by weight compared to 50% for the Dreamliner."

For the most part, Airbus and Boeing have pursued radical innovations to develop the A350 and 787, respectively. As discussed in this chapter, radical innovation can lead to significant increases in sales and profitability for firms. These outcomes are achieved when

A New Boeing 787 Dreamliner rolls out of the hangar. The 787 incorporates several radical innovations designed to help Boeing capture a larger share of the airliner market and improve its profitability.

innovation and the entrepreneurial actions associated with it are taken through a strategic perspective. Boeing's decision to offer three versions of the 787 to serve different customer groups is an example of a strategic action the firm is taking to gain maximum benefit from the 787. Not surprisingly, Airbus has developed or is developing products that compete against these versions of the 787. Thus, the two firms are using a strategic perspective as a foundation to the entrepreneurial actions they are taking.

Risk is another issue associated with radical innovations. In the words of an airline company official: "You can't introduce an airplane so radically different without there being issues." Boeing has indeed encountered issues with its radically innovative 787 such as those concerning the use of lithium-ion batteries (see the discussion of this issue in Chapter 5). This is not unexpected though. In fact, some believe that "Boeing's experience (with the 787) offers a reminder that innovation—for all its value—doesn't come as easily as a catchphrase. It can get messy." In this regard, a key challenge both Airbus and Boeing face going forward is to execute strategies that will allow them to benefit fully from their innovative products.

Sources: M. Cauchi, 2013, Carriers buy more fuel-efficient jets, *Wall Street Journal*, www.wsj.com, April 22; M. Dunlop, 2013, Innovations that make the 787 different, *HeraldNet*, www.heraldnet.com, January 24; D. Michaels, 2103, Airbus A350 completes maiden flight, *Wall Street Journal*, www.wsj.com, June 14; D. Michaels, 2013, Innovation is messy business, *Wall Street Journal*, www.wsj.com, January 24; D. Michaels, 2013, Their new materials, *Wall Street Journal*, www.wsj.com, June 16; D. Terdiman, 2013, It's Airbus' A350 vs. Boeing's Dreamliner in the 'war of the wide-bodies', *CNET*, www.cnet.com, March 20.

Some large organizations are trying to become more capable of effectively using strategic entrepreneurship. For example, an increasing number of large, widely known firms, including Wendy's International, Gucci Group, Starbucks, and Perry Ellis International have established a top-level managerial position commonly called president or executive vice president of emerging brands. Other companies such as Coca-Cola, GE, Whirlpool, and Humana have established a position within their top management teams to focus on innovation.[113] These individuals are often known as chief innovation officers.

The essential responsibility of top-level managers focusing on emerging brands or innovation is to verify that their firm is consistently finding entrepreneurial opportunities. Those holding these positions work collaboratively with the firm's chief strategy officer. In this sense, those responsible for identifying opportunities the firm might want to pursue and those responsible for selecting and implementing the strategies the company would use to pursue those opportunities share responsibility for verifying that the firm is taking entrepreneurial actions using a strategic perspective. Through their work, these individuals also help the firm determine the innovations necessary to pursue an opportunity and if those innovations should be developed internally, through a cooperative strategy, or by completing an acquisition. In the final analysis, the objective of these top-level managers is to help firms identify opportunities and then develop successful incremental and radical innovations and strategies to exploit them.

In the Strategic Focus, we describe how Boeing and Airbus (a part of European Aeronautic Defence & Space Co.) have both pursued opportunities to create innovative new airplanes (the A350 for Airbus and the 787 for Boeing). As you will see by reading the Strategic Focus, the firms are using strategic entrepreneurship as a foundation for efforts to achieve success with their new products.

Find out more about Airbus.
www.cengagebrain.com

SUMMARY

- Strategic entrepreneurship is the taking of entrepreneurial actions using a strategic perspective. Firms using strategic entrepreneurship simultaneously engage in opportunity-seeking and advantage-seeking behaviors. The purpose is to continuously find new opportunities and quickly develop innovations to exploit them.

- Entrepreneurship is a process used by individuals, teams, and organizations to identify entrepreneurial opportunities without being immediately constrained by the resources they control. Corporate entrepreneurship is the application of entrepreneurship (including the identification of entrepreneurial opportunities) within ongoing, established organizations. Entrepreneurial opportunities are conditions in which new goods or services can satisfy a need in the market. Increasingly, entrepreneurship positively contributes to individual firms' performance and stimulates growth in countries' economies.

- Firms engage in three types of innovative activities: (1) invention, which is the act of creating a new good or process, (2) innovation, or the process of creating a commercial product from an invention, and (3) imitation, which is the adoption of similar innovations by different firms. Invention brings

something new into being while innovation brings something new into use.

- Entrepreneurs see or envision entrepreneurial opportunities and then take actions to develop innovations to exploit them. The most successful entrepreneurs (whether they are establishing their own venture or are working in an ongoing organization) have an entrepreneurial mind-set, which is an orientation that values the potential opportunities available because of marketplace uncertainties.

- International entrepreneurship, or the process of identifying and exploiting entrepreneurial opportunities outside the firm's domestic markets, is important to firms around the globe. Evidence suggests that firms capable of effectively engaging in international entrepreneurship outperform those competing only in their domestic markets.

- Three basic approaches are used to produce innovation: (1) internal innovation, which involves R&D and forming internal corporate ventures, (2) cooperative strategies such as strategic alliances, and (3) acquisitions. Autonomous strategic behavior and induced strategic behavior are the two forms of internal

M. Stasy

corporate venturing. Autonomous strategic behavior is a bottom-up process through which a product champion facilitates the commercialization of an innovation. Induced strategic behavior is a top-down process in which a firm's current strategy and structure facilitate the development and implementation of product or process innovations. Thus, induced strategic behavior is driven by the organization's current corporate strategy and structure while autonomous strategic behavior can result in a change to the firm's current strategy and structure arrangements.

■ Firms create two types of innovations—incremental and radical—through internal innovation that takes place in the form of autonomous strategic behavior or induced strategic behavior. Overall, firms produce more incremental innovations, but radical innovations have a higher probability of significantly increasing sales revenue and profits. Cross-functional integration is often vital to a firm's efforts to develop and implement internal corporate venturing activities and to commercialize the resulting innovation. Cross-functional

teams now commonly include representatives from external organizations such as suppliers. Additionally, integration and innovation can be facilitated by developing shared values and effectively using strategic leadership.

■ To gain access to the specialized knowledge required to innovate in the global economy, firms may form a cooperative relationship such as a strategic alliance with other companies, some of which may be competitors.

■ Acquisitions are another means firms use to obtain innovation. Innovation can be acquired through direct acquisition, or firms can learn new capabilities from an acquisition, thereby enriching their internal innovation abilities.

■ The practice of strategic entrepreneurship by all types of firms, large and small, new and more established, creates value for all stakeholders, especially for shareholders and customers. Strategic entrepreneurship also contributes to the economic development of countries.

REVIEW QUESTIONS

1. What is strategic entrepreneurship? What is corporate entrepreneurship?

2. What is entrepreneurship and what are entrepreneurial opportunities? Why are they important aspects of the strategic management process?

3. What are invention, innovation, and imitation? How are these concepts interrelated?

4. What is an entrepreneur and what is an entrepreneurial mind-set?

5. What is international entrepreneurship? Why is it important?

6. How do firms develop innovations internally?

7. How do firms use cooperative strategies to innovate and to have access to innovative capabilities?

8. How does a firm acquire other companies to increase the number of innovations it produces and improve its capability to innovate?

9. How does strategic entrepreneurship help firms create value?

EXPERIENTIAL EXERCISES

EXERCISE 1: CAN CORPORATIONS REALLY INNOVATE?

According to an article in the Harvard Business Review titled "The New Corporate Garage" by Scott Anthony (2012), big companies are unshackling innovation in ways that resemble their more nimble and smaller counterparts. Anthony suggests there are three trends behind this shift. "First, the increasing ease and decreasing cost of innovation mean that start-ups now face the same short-term pressures that have constrained innovation at large companies; as soon as a young company gets a whiff of success, it has to race against dozens of copycats. Second, large companies, taking a page from start-up strategy, are embracing open innovation and less hierarchical management and are integrating entrepreneurial behaviors with their existing capabilities. And third, although innovation has

historically been product- and service-oriented, it increasingly involves creating business models that tap big companies' unique strengths."

While the press is replete with innovation stories for startups, many large corporations are taking significant steps to instill an entrepreneurial culture within their bureaucracy. Your challenge in this exercise is to identify some ways that corporations are igniting innovation capabilities at their organizations. You can complete this assignment in one of two ways. First, you may choose a particular company and research it for the purpose of identifying steps the firm is taking to improve its innovation capabilities. A second approach is to utilize any one of a number of websites that are designed to assist companies help to foster and improve their innovative capabilities. These sites can be studied to identify a number of activities firms complete to enhance their innovation skills. A few websites that can be examined for this purpose are listed below, but you should feel free to uncover and use a site that you find.

- Rocket Space (http://rocket-space.com/)
- Corporate Innovation Lab (http://corporateinnovationlab.com/)
- Nine Sigma (http://www.ninesigma.com/)
- InnoCentive (http://www.innocentive.com/)
- YourEncore (http://www.yourencore.com/)
- Yet2.com (http://www.yet2.com/)

Working in teams, your assignment is to research a company or a web enabler for companies interested in improving their innovation or entrepreneurial capabilities. You should be prepared to describe:

1. The mission of your web or company.

2. What you find interesting or unusual about the approach to innovation specified by the web provider or the company you selected.

3. How the organization goes about improving innovative capabilities.

4. Your overall impression of the approach and its usefulness.

EXERCISE 2: THE SOCIAL NATURE OF ENTREPRENEURSHIP

Entrepreneurship is said to be as much about social connections and networks as it is about the fundamentals of running a new venture. The relationships that an entrepreneur can count on are also key resources of financial capital, human capital, mentoring, and legal advice.

Various popular blogs covering social media and Web 2.0 identify some of the top social networks for entrepreneurs. Some of the more popular ones are:

- LinkedIn
- The Funded
- PartnerUp
- Young Entrepreneur
- Startup Nation
- Go BIG Network
- Biznik
- Perfect Business
- Cofounder
- Entrepreneur Connection

In teams, pick one social network from the list or another you might favor (your instructor will ensure that there is a unique choice for each team). Spend some time on the selected network's website reading the posts to get a feel for the types of information presented. Prepare a 10-minute presentation to the class on your network site and be sure to address the following, at a minimum:

1. Provide an overview of the site—what it is used for, how popular it is, features, types of conversations, etc.

2. What is unique about this site and why does it attract followers? What technologies are enabled here—RSS, Twitter, etc.?

3. Describe the target audience for this website. Who would use it and what types of information are available to entrepreneurs?

4. How do you think this site maintains its presence? Does it support itself with ad revenue, corporate sponsors, not-for-profit sponsors, or by some other means?

5. Would this site be useful for corporate entrepreneurs as well as startup entrepreneurs? If so, how?

VIDEO CASE

A NEW ENTREPRENEUR ON THE BLOCK: SARA BLAKELY, FOUNDER AND ENTREPRENEUR/SPANX

SPANX, creating a slimming/invisible underlayer garment, surfaced about 10 years ago. Sara Blakely, founder and entrepreneur, confronted with the male-dominated manufacturing of women's shapewear, was able to offer a female-oriented solution. With shapewear an expanding segment in a newly competitive market, Blakely designs a wide range of SPANX products by placing herself in the position of a customer. Currently, SPANX generates around $250 million in annual sales.

Be prepared to discuss the following concepts and questions in class as they apply to SPANX and Sara Blakely:

Concepts

- Strategic entrepreneurship
- Corporate entrepreneurship
- Entrepreneurial opportunities
- Innovation
- Entrepreneurial mind-set
- International entrepreneurship

Questions

1. Is there evidence of strategic entrepreneurship in the account of Sara Blakely?

2. Does Sara Blakely set the stage for corporate entrepreneurship?

3. What entrepreneurial opportunities do you see ahead for Sara Blakely?

4. How would you classify the SPANX innovation? What advantages and risks are associated with the SPANX innovation?

5. Does Sara Blakely have an entrepreneurial mind-set?

6. Should Sara Blakely pursue international entrepreneurship? Why or why not? What concerns might she have?

NOTES

1. T. Buschgens, A. Bausch, & D. B. Balkin, 2013, Organizational culture and innovation: A meta-analytic review, *Journal of Product Innovation Management*, 30: 763–781.

2. A. Lipparini, G. Lorenzoni, & S. Ferriani, 2013, From core to periphery and back: A study on the deliberate shaping of knowledge flows in interfirm dyads and networks, *Strategic Management Journal*, in press.

3. P. C. Patel, S. A. Fernhaber, P. P. McDougall-Covin, & R. P. van der Have, 2013, Beating competitors to international markets: The value of geographically balanced networks for innovation, *Strategic Management Journal*, in press.

4. M. Wright, B. Clarysse, & S. Mosey, 2012, Strategic entrepreneurship, resource orchestration and growing spin-offs from universities, *Technology Analysis & Strategic Management*, 24: 911–927.

5. P. G. Klein, J. T. Mahoney, A. M. McGahan, & C. N. Pitelis, 2013, Capabilities and strategic entrepreneurship in public organizations, *Strategic Entrepreneurship Journal*, 7: 70–91; M. A. Hitt, R. D. Ireland, D. G. Sirmon, & C. A. Trahms, 2011, Strategic entrepreneurship: Creating value for individuals, organizations, and society. *Academy of Management Perspectives*, 25: 57–75.

6. H. Yang, Y. Zheng, & X. Zhao, 2013, Exploration or exploitation? Small firms' alliance strategies with large firms, *Strategic Management Journal*, in press; J. Q. Barden, 2012, The influences of being acquired on subsidiary innovation adoption, *Strategic Management Journal*, 33: 1269–1285.

7. D. F. Kuratko & D. B. Audretsch, 2013, Clarifying the domains of corporate entrepreneurship, *International Entrepreneurship and Management Journal*, in press; K. Shimizu, 2012, Risks of corporate entrepreneurship: Autonomy and agency issues, *Organization Science*, 23: 194–206.

8. D. Urbano & A. Turro, 2013, Conditioning factors for corporate entrepreneurship: An in(ex)ternal approach, *International Entrepreneurship and Management Journal*, in press; A. J. Kacperczyk, 2012, Opportunity structures in established firms: Entrepreneurship versus intrapreneurship

in mutual funds, *Administrative Science Quarterly*, 57: 484–521.

9. V. Hinz & S. Ingerfurth, 2013, Does ownership matter under challenging conditions? *Public Management Review*, in press.

10. M. Griffiths, J. Kickul, S. Bacq, & S. Terjesen, 2012, A dialogue with William J. Baumol: Insights on entrepreneurship theory and education, *Entrepreneurship Theory and Practice*, 36: 611–625; P. M. Moroz & K. Hindle, 2012, Entrepreneurship as a process: Toward harmonizing multiple perspectives, *Entrepreneurship Theory and Practice*, 36: 781–818.

11. J. T. Perry, G. N. Chandler, & G. Markova, 2012, Entrepreneurial effectuation: A review and suggestions for future research, *Entrepreneurship Theory and Practice*, 36: 837–861; S. A. Alvarez & J. B. Barney, 2008, Opportunities, organizations and entrepreneurship, *Strategic Entrepreneurship Journal*, 2: 265–267.

12. N. J. Foss, J. Lyngsie, & S. A. Zahra, 2013, The role of external knowledge sources and organizational design in the process of opportunity exploitation, *Strategic Management Journal*, in press; P. G. Klein, 2008, Opportunity discovery, entrepreneurial action and economic organization, *Strategic Entrepreneurship Journal*, 2: 175–190.

13. J. Tang, K. M. Kacmar, & L. Busenitz, 2012, Entrepreneurial alertness in the pursuit of new opportunities, *Journal of Business Venturing*, 27: 77–94; S. A. Zahra, 2008, The virtuous cycle of discovery and creation of entrepreneurial opportunities, *Strategic Entrepreneurship Journal*, 2: 243–257.

14. J. Schumpeter, 1934, *The Theory of Economic Development*, Cambridge, MA: Harvard University Press.

15. C. A. Siren, M. Kohtamaki, & A. Kuckertz, 2012, Exploration and exploitation strategies, profit performance, and the mediating role of strategic learning: Escaping the exploitation trap, *Strategic Entrepreneurship Journal*, 6: 18–41; M. Hughes, S. Martin, R. Morgan, & M. Robson, 2010, Realizing product-market advantage

in high-technology international new ventures: The mediating role of ambidextrous innovation, *Journal of International Marketing*, 18: 1–21; J. H. Dyer, H. B. Gregersen, & C. Christensen, 2008, Entrepreneur behaviors and the origins of innovative ventures, *Strategic Entrepreneurship Journal*, 2: 317–338.

16. C. Bjornskov & N. Foss, 2013, How strategic entrepreneurship and the institutional context drive economic growth, *Strategic Entrepreneurship Journal*, 7: 50–69; W. J. Baumol, R. E. Litan, & C. J. Schramm, 2007, *Good Capitalism, Bad Capitalism, and the Economics of Growth and Prosperity,* New Haven: Yale University Press.

17. Schumpeter, *The Theory of Economic Development.*

18. L. Aarikka-Stenroos & B. Sandberg, 2012, From new-product development to commercialization through networks, *Journal of Business Research*, 65: 198–206.

19. M. I. Leone & T. Reichstein, 2012, Licensing-in fosters rapid invention! The effect of the grant-back clause and technological unfamiliarity, *Strategic Management Journal*, 33: 965–985; R. A. Burgelman & L. R. Sayles, 1986, *Inside Corporate Innovation: Strategy, Structure, and Managerial Skills,* New York: Free Press.

20. K. R. Fabrizio & L. G. Thomas, 2012, The impact of local demand on innovation in a global industry, *Strategic Management Journal*, 33: 42–64; M. W. Johnson, 2011, Making innovation matter. *Bloomberg Businessweek,* www.businessweek.com, March 3.

21. H. Scarbrough, J. Swan, K. Amaeshi, & T. Briggs, 2013, Exploring the role of trust in the deal-making process for early-stage technology ventures, *Entrepreneurship Theory and Practice*, in press; S. F. Latham & M. Braun, 2009, Managerial risk, innovation and organizational decline, *Journal of Management*, 35: 258–281.

22. L. Marengo, C. Pasquali, M. Valente, & G. Dosi, 2012, Appropriability, patents, and rates of innovation in complex products industries, *Economics of Innovation and New Technology*, 21: 753–773; S. Moon, 2011, How does the management of research impact

the disclosure of knowledge? Evidence from scientific publications and patenting behavior, *Economics of Innovation & New Technology*, 20: 1–32.

23. M. Ridley, 2013, A welcome turn away from patents, *Wall Street Journal*, www.wsj.com, June 21.

24. P. F. Drucker, 1998, The discipline of innovation, *Harvard Business Review*, 76(6): 149–157.

25. Ibid.

26. B. R. Bhardwaj, Sushil, & K. Momaya, 2011, Drivers and enablers of corporate entrepreneurship: Case of a software giant from India, *Journal of Management Development*, 30: 187–205.

27. Y. Yanadori & V. Cui, 2013, Creating incentives for innovation? The relationship between pay dispersion in R&D groups and firm innovation performance, *Strategic Management Journal*, in press.

28. J. Lampel, P. P. Jha, & A. Bhalla, 2012, Test-driving the future: How design competitions are changing innovation, *Academy of Management Perspectives*, 26: 71–85; G. F. Alberti, S. Sciascia, C. Tripodi, & F. Visconti, 2011, The entrepreneurial growth of firms located in clusters: A cross-case study, *International Journal of Technology Management*, 54: 53–79.

29. C. J. Sutter, J. W. Webb, G. M. Kistruck, & A. V. G. Bailey, 2013, Entrepreneurs' responses to semi-formal illegitimate institutional arrangements, *Journal of Business Venturing*, in press; D. Ucbasaran, P. Westhead, M. Wright, & M. Flores, 2010, The nature of entrepreneurial experience, business failure and comparative optimism, *Journal of Business Venturing*, 25: 541–555; K. M. Hmieleski & R. A. Baron, 2009, Entrepreneurs' optimism and new venture performance: A social cognitive perspective, *Academy of Management Journal*, 52: 473–488.

30. J.-L. Arregle, B. Batjargal, M. A. Hitt, J. W. Webb, T. Miller, & A. S. Tsui, 2013, Family ties in entrepreneurs' social networks and new venture growth, *Entrepreneurship Theory and Practice*, in press; M.-D. Foo, 2011, Emotions and entrepreneurial opportunity evaluation, *Entrepreneurship: Theory & Practice*, 35: 375–393; M. S. Cardon, J. Wincent, J. Singh, & M. Drovsek, 2009, The nature and experience of entrepreneurial passion, *Academy of Management Review*, 34: 511–532.

31. M. McCaffrey, 2013, On the theory of entrepreneurial incentives and alertness, *Entrepreneurship Theory and Practice*, in press; M. S. Wood, A. McKelvie, & J. M. Haynie, 2013, Making it personal: Opportunity individuation and the shaping of opportunity beliefs, *Journal of Business Venturing*, in press.

32. S. W. Smith & S. K. Shah, 2013, Do innovative users generate more useful insights? An analysis of corporate venture capital investments in the medical device industry, *Strategic Entrepreneurship Journal*, 7: 151–167;

W. Stam, S. Arzlanian, & T. Elfring, 2013, Social capital of entrepreneurs and small firm performance: A meta-analysis of contextual and methodological moderators, *Journal of Business Venturing*, in press.

33. T. Prive, 2013, Top 32 quotes every entrepreneur should live by, *Forbes*, www.forbes.com, May 2.

34. J. G. Covin & D. Miller, 2013, International entrepreneurial orientation: Conceptual considerations, research themes, measurement issues, and future research directions, *Entrepreneurship Theory and Practice*, in press.

35. J. York, S. Sarasvathy, & A. Wicks, 2013, An entrepreneurial perspective on value creation in public-private ventures, *Academy of Management Review*, 28: 307–309; A. Chwolka & M. G. Raith, 2012, The value of business planning before start-up— A decision-theoretical perspective, *Journal of Business Venturing*, 27: 385–399.

36. P. C. Ross, 2013, Encouraging innovation in the corporate environment, *Wall Street Journal*, www.wsj.com, May 30.

37. W. Drechsler & M. Natter, 2012, Understanding a firm's openness decisions in innovation, *Journal of Business Research*, 65: 438–445; W. Tsai, 2001, Knowledge transfer in intraorganizational networks: Effects of network position and absorptive capacity on business unit innovation and performance, *Academy of Management Journal*, 44: 996–1004.

38. M. Spraggon & V. Bodolica, 2012, A multidimensional taxonomy of intra-firm knowledge transfer processes, *Journal of Business Research*, 65: 1273–1282; S. A. Zahra & G. George, 2002, Absorptive capacity: A review, reconceptualization, and extension, *Academy of Management Review*, 27:185–203.

39. A. Carr, 2013, Nike: The No. 1 most innovative company of 2013, *Fast Company*, www.fastcompany.com, February 11.

40. S. Terjesen, J. Hessels, & D. Li, 2013, Comparative international entrepreneurship: A review and research agenda, *Journal of Management*, in press; P. Ellis, 2011, Social ties and international entrepreneurship: Opportunities and constraints affecting firm internationalization, *Journal of International Business Studies*, 42: 99–127.

41. A. N. Kiss, W. M. Davis, & S. T. Cavusgil, 2012, International entrepreneurship research in emerging economies: A critical review and research agenda, *Journal of Business Venturing*, 27: 266–290; C. Williams & S. H. Lee, 2011, Political heterarchy and dispersed entrepreneurship in the MNC, *Journal of Management Studies*, 48: 1243–1268.

42. 2013, Microsoft, Huawei partner to launch affordable Windows smartphones for Africa, *Ventures*, www.ventures-africa.com, February 5.

43. P. Almodovar & A. M. Rugman, 2013, The M curve and the performance of

Spanish international new ventures, *British Journal of Management*, in press; S. A. Fernhaber, B. A. Gilbert, & P. P. McDougal, 2008, International entrepreneurship and geographic location: An empirical examination of new venture internationalization, *Journal of International Business Studies*, 39: 267–290.

44. P. Stenholm, Z. J. Acs, & R. Wuebker, 2013, Exploring country-level institutional arrangements on the rate and type of entrepreneurial activity, *Journal of Business Venturing*, 28: 176–193; H. Ren, B. Gray, & K. Kim, 2009, Performance of international joint ventures: What factors really make a difference and how? *Journal of Management*, 35: 805–832.

45. 2013, Switzerland ranks in the top ten most entrepreneurial countries, *Startupticker.ch*, http://startupticker.ch, May 6.

46. J. D. Harrison, 2013, New rankings: The world's top nations for female entrepreneurs, *On Small Business*, www.washingtonpost.com, June 17.

47. E. Autio, S. Pathak, & K. Wennberg, 2013, Consequences of cultural practices for entrepreneurial behaviors, *Journal of International Business Studies*, 44: 334–362; U. Stephan & L. M. Uhlaner, 2010, Performance-based vs. socially supportive culture: A cross-cultural study of descriptive norms and entrepreneurship, *Journal of International Business Studies*, 41: 1347–1364; R. A. Baron & J. Tang, 2009, Entrepreneurs' social skills and new venture performance: Mediating mechanisms and cultural generality, *Journal of Management*, 35: 282–306.

48. T. K. Madsen, 2013, Early and rapidly internationalizing ventures: Similarities and differences between classifications based on the original international new venture and born global literatures, *Journal of International Entrepreneurship*, 11: 65–79; D. Kim, C. Basu, G. M. Naidu, & E. Cavusgil, 2011, The innovativeness of born-globals and customer orientation: Learning from Indian Born-Globals, *Journal of Business Research*, 64: 879–886.

49. S. A. Fernhaber & D. Li, 2013, International exposure through network relationships: Implications for new venture internationalization, *Journal of Business Venturing*, 28: 316–334; L. Sleuwaegen & J. Onkelinx, 2013, International commitment, post-entry growth and survival of international new ventures, *Journal of Business Venturing*, 28: in press; S. A. Zahra, R. D. Ireland, & M. A. Hitt, 2000, International expansion by new venture firms: International diversity, mode of market entry, technological learning and performance, *Academy of Management Journal*, 43: 925–950.

50. D. J. McCarthy, S. M. Puffer, & S. V. Darda, 2010, Convergence in entrepreneurial leadership style: Evidence from Russia, *California Management Review*, 52(4): 48–72; H. U. Lee & J. H. Park, 2008, The influence

of top management team international exposure on international alliance formation, *Journal of Management Studies,* 45: 961–981; H. G. Barkema & O. Chvyrkov, 2007, Does top management team diversity promote or hamper foreign expansion? *Strategic Management Journal,* 28: 663–680.

51. C. B. Bingham & J. P. Davis, 2012, Learning sequences: Their existence, effect, and evolution, *Academy of Management Journal,* 55: 611–641; M. Mors, 2010, Innovation in a global consulting firm: When the problem is too much diversity, *Strategic Management Journal,* 31: 841–872.

52. A. Pe'er & T. Keil, 2013, Are all startups affected similarly by clusters? Agglomeration, competition, firm heterogeneity, and survival, *Journal of Business Venturing,* 28: 354–372; A. Teixeira & N. Fortuna, 2010, Human capital, R&D, trade, and long-run productivity: Testing the technological absorption hypothesis for the Portuguese economy, 1960–2001, *Research Policy,* 39: 335–350.

53. S. Schechner, S. E. Ante, & S. Grundberg, 2013, Huawei builds clout through R&D, *Wall Street Journal,* www.wsj.com, February 24.

54. R. Kapoor & R. Adner, 2012, What firms make vs. what they know: How firms' production and knowledge boundaries affect competitive advantage in the face of technological change, *Organization Science,* 23: 1227–1248; R. Reed, S. Storrud-Barnes, & L. Jessup, 2012, How open innovation affects the drivers of competitive advantage: Trading the benefits of IP creation and ownership for free invention, *Management Decision,* 50: 58–73.

55. R. J. Genry & W. Shen, 2013, The impacts of performance relative to analyst forecasts and analyst coverage on firm R&D intensity, *Strategic Management Journal,* 34: 121–130; L. A. Bettencourt & S. L. Bettencourt, 2011, Innovating on the cheap, *Harvard Business Review,* 89(6): 88–94.

56. P. Ritala & P. Hurmelinna-Laukkanen, 2013, Incremental and radical innovation in coopetition—The role of absorptive capacity and appropriability, *Journal of Product Innovation Management,* 30: 154–169; C. B. Bingham & J. P. Davis, 2012, Learning sequences: Their existence, effect, and evolution, *Academy of Management Journal,* 55: 611–641.

57. S. Roy & K. Sivakumar, 2012, Global outsourcing relationships and innovation: A conceptual framework and research propositions, *Journal of Product and Innovation Management,* 29: 513–530.

58. D. McKendrick & J. Wade, 2010, Frequent incremental change, organizational size, and mortality in high-technology competition, *Industrial and Corporate Change,* 19(3): 613–639.

59. S. Wang, 2013, Why a startup, not big pharma, leads development of a bionic eye, *Wall Street Journal,* www.wsj.com, January 30.

60. T. W. Martin & J. D. Rockoff, 2013, Unmeltable, uncrushable: The holy grail in painkillers, *Wall Street Journal,* www.wsj.com, May 5.

61. T. Magnusson & C. Berggren, 2011, Entering an era of ferment—radical vs incrementalist strategies in automotive power train development, *Technology Analysis & Strategic Management,* 23: 313–330; 2005, Getting an edge on innovation, *BusinessWeek,* March 21, 124.

62. B. Buisson & P. Silberzahn, 2010, Blue Ocean or fast-second innovation? A four-breakthrough model to explain successful market domination, *International Journal of Innovation Management,* 14: 359–378; A. J. Chatterji, 2009, Spawned with a silver spoon? Entrepreneurial performance and innovation in the medical device industry, *Strategic Management Journal,* 30: 185–206.

63. Z. Lindgardt & B. Shaffer, 2012, Business model innovation in social-sector organizations, *bcg.perspectives,* bcgperspectives.com, November 7.

64. 2013, The power of imagination, *Wall Street Journal,* www.wsj.com, February 25.

65. D. Lavie & I. Drori, 2012, Collaborating for knowledge creation and application: The case of nanotechnology research programs, *Organization Science,* 23: 704–724.

66. A. K. Chatterji & K. Fabrizio, 2012, How do product users influence corporate invention? *Organization Science,* 23: 971–987.

67. N. R. Furr, F. Cavarretta, & S. Garg, 2012, Who changes course? The role of domain knowledge and novel framing in making technology changes, *Strategic Entrepreneurship Journal,* 6: 236–256; J. M. Oldroyd & R. Gulati, 2010, A learning perspective on intraorganizational knowledge spill-ins, *Strategic Entrepreneurship Journal,* 4: 356–372.

68. M. L. Sosa, 2013, Decoupling market incumbency from organizational prehistory: Locating the real sources of competitive advantage in R&D for radical innovation, *Strategic Management Journal,* 34: 245–255; S. A. Hill, M. V. J. Maula, J. M. Birkinshaw, & G. C. Murray, 2009, Transferability of the venture capital model to the corporate context: Implications for the performance of corporate venture units, *Strategic Entrepreneurship Journal,* 3: 3–27.

69. J. Brady, 2013, Some companies foster creativity, others fake it, *Wall Street Journal,* www.wsj.com, May 21.

70. A. Sahaym, H. K. Steensma, & J. Q. Barden, 2010, The influence of R&D investment on the use of corporate venture capital: An industry-level analysis, *Journal of Business Venturing,* 25(4): 376–388; R. A. Burgelman, 1995, *Strategic Management of Technology and Innovation,* Boston: Irwin.

71. D. Kandemir & N. Acur, 2012, Examining proactive strategic decision-making flexibility in new product development, *Journal of Product Innovation Management,* 29: 608–622.

72. K. B. Kahn, G. Barczak, J. Nicholas, A. Ledwith, & H. Perks, 2012, An examination of new product development best practice, *Journal of Product Innovation Management,* 29: 180–192.

73. S. S. Durmusoglu, 2013, Merits of task advice during new product development: Network centrality antecedents and new product outcomes of knowledge richness and knowledge quality, *Journal of Product Innovation Management,* 30: 487–499; D. Kelley & H. Lee, 2010, Managing innovation champions: The impact of project characteristics on the direct manager role, *Journal of Product Innovation Management,* 27: 1007–1019.

74. N. Kim, S. Im, & S. F. Slater, 2013, Impact of knowledge type and strategic orientation on new product creativity and advantage in high-technology firms, *Journal of Product Innovation Management,* 30: 136–153; U. de Brentani & S. E. Reid, 2012, The fuzzy front-end of discontinuous innovation: Insights for research and management, *Journal of Product Innovation Management,* 29: 70–87.

75. C. Webster & A. White, 2010, Exploring the national and organizational cultural mix in service firms, *Journal of the Academy of Marketing Science,* 38: 691–703; M. Song & M. M. Montoya-Weiss, 2001, The effect of perceived technological uncertainty on Japanese new product development, *Academy of Management Journal,* 44: 61–80.

76. L. Mirabeau & S. Maguire, 2013, From autonomous strategic behavior to emergent strategy, *Strategic Management Journal,* in press.

77. S. Im, M. M. Montoya, & J. P. Workman, Jr., 2013, Antecedents and consequences of creativity in product innovation teams, *Journal of Product Innovation Management,* 30: 170–185; S. Borjesson & M. Elmquist, 2012, Aiming at innovation: A case study of innovation capabilities in the Swedish defence industry, *International Journal of Business Innovation and Research,* 6: 188–201.

78. S. E. Ante, 2013, IBM's chief to employees: Think fast, move faster, *Wall Street Journal,* www.wsj.com, April 24.

79. S. Banjo, 2013, Wal-Mart's e-stumble, *Wall Street Journal,* www.wsj.com, June 18.

80. L. Luk & S. Ovide, 2013, Microsoft working with suppliers on designs for touch-enabled watch device, *Wall Street Journal,* www.wsj.com, April 15.

81. P. Patanakul, J. Chen, & G. S. Lynn, 2012, Autonomous teams and new product development, *Journal of Product Innovation Management,* 29: 734–750.

82. S. Kuester, C. Homburg, & S. C. Hess, 2012, Externally directed and internally directed market launch management: The role of organizational factors in influencing new product success, *Journal of Product Innovation Management,* 29: 38–52.

83. G. Barcjak & K. B. Kah, 2012, Identifying new product development best practice, *Business Horizons*, 56: 291–305; C. Nakata & S. Im, 2010, Spurring cross-functional integration for higher new product performance: A group effectiveness perspective, *Journal of Product Innovation Management*, 27: 554–571.

84. J. P. Eggers, 2012, All experience is not created equal: Learning, adapting, and focusing in product portfolio management, *Strategic Management Journal*, 33: 315-335; R. Slotegraaf & K. Atuahene-Gima, 2011, Product development team stability and new product advantage: The role of decision-making processes, *Journal of Marketing*, 75: 96–108; R. Cowan & N. Jonard, 2009, Knowledge portfolios and the organization of innovation networks, *Academy of Management Review*, 34: 320–342.

85. M. Brettel, F. Heinemann, A. Engelen, & S. Neubauer, 2011, Cross-functional integration of R&D, marketing, and manufacturing in radical and incremental product innovations and its effects on project effectiveness and efficiency, *Journal of Product Innovation Management*, 28: 251–269.

86. D. De Clercq, N. Thongpapanl, & d. Dimov, 2013, Getting more from cross-functional fairness and product innovativeness: Contingency effects of internal resource and conflict management, *Journal of Product Innovation Management*, 30: 56–69; G. Gemser & M. M. Leenders, 2011, Managing cross-functional cooperation for new product development success, *Long Range Planning*, 44: 26–41.

87. F. Aime, S. Humphrey, D. DeRue, & J. Paul, 2013, The riddle of heterarchy: Power transitions in cross-functional teams, *Academy of Management Journal*, 56: in press.

88. E. L. Anthony, S. G. Green, & S. A. McComb, 2013, Crossing functions above the cross-functional project team: The value of lateral coordination among functional department heads, *Journal of Engineering and Technology Management*, in press; V. V. Baunsgaard & S. Clegg, 2013, 'Walls or boxes': The effects of professional identity, power and rationality on strategies for cross-functional integration, *Organization Studies*, in press.

89. M. Baer, K. T. Dirks, & J. A. Nickerson, 2013, Microfoundations of strategic problem formulation, *Strategic Management Journal*, 34: 197–214; R. Oliva & N. Watson, 2011, Cross-functional alignment in supply chain planning: A case study of sales and operations planning, *Journal of Operations Management*, 29: 434–448; A. C. Amason, 1996, Distinguishing the effects of functional and dysfunctional conflict on strategic decision making: Resolving a paradox for top management teams, *Academy of Management Journal*, 39: 123–148.

90. H. K. Gardner, 2012, Performance pressure as a double-edged sword: Enhancing team motivation while undermining the use of team knowledge, *Administrative Science Quarterly*, 57: 1–46; D. Clercq, B. Menguc, & S. Auh, 2009, Unpacking the relationship between an innovation strategy and firm performance: The role of task conflict and political activity, *Journal of Business Research*, 62: 1046–1053; M. A. Cronin & L. R. Weingart, 2007, Representational gaps, information processing, and conflict in functionally heterogeneous teams, *Academy of Management Review*, 32: 761–773.

91. Y. Chung & S. E. Jackson, 2013, The internal and external networks of knowledge-intensive teams: The role of task routineness, *Journal of Management*, 39: 442–468; J. Daspit, C. J. Tillman, N. G. Boyd, & V. McKee, 2013, Cross-functional team effectiveness: An examination of internal team environment, shared leadership, and cohesion influences, *Team Performance Management*, 19: 34–56.

92. H. K. Gardner, F. Gino, & B. R. Staats, 2012, Dynamically integrating knowledge in teams: Transforming resources into performance, *Academy of Management Journal*, 55: 998–1022; A. Grant, 2012, Leading with meaning: Beneficiary contact, prosocial impact, and the performance effects of transformational leadership, *Academy of Management Journal*, 55: 458–476.

93. Q. Li, P. Maggitti, K. Smith, P. Tesluk, & R, Katila, 2013, Top management attention to innovation: The role of search selection and intensity in new product introductions, *Academy of Management Journal*, 55: in press; N. Stieglitz & L. Heine, 2007, Innovations and the role of complementarities in a strategic theory of the firm, *Strategic Management Journal*, 28: 1–15.

94. V. Gaba & S. Bhattacharya, 2012, Aspirations, innovation, and corporate venture capital: A behavioral perspective, *Strategic Entrepreneurship Journal*, 6: 178–199; K. Wennberg, J. Wiklund, D. R. DeTienne, & M. S. Cardon, 2010, Reconceptualizing entrepreneurial exit: Divergent exit routes and their drivers, *Journal of Business Venturing*, 25: 361–375.

95. H. Milanov & S. A. Fernhaber, 2013, When do domestic alliances help ventures abroad? Direct and moderating effects from a learning experience, *Journal of Business Venturing*, in press; S. Terjesen, P. C. Patel, & J. G. Covin, 2011, Alliance diversity, environmental context and the value of manufacturing capabilities among new high technology ventures, *Journal of Operations Management*, 29: 105–115; P. Ozcan & K. M. Eisenhardt, 2009, Origin of alliance portfolios: Entrepreneurs, network strategies, and firm performance, *Academy of Management Journal*, 52: 246–279.

96. S. Zu, F. Wu, & E. Cavusgil, 2013, Complements or substitutes? Internal technological strength, competitors alliance participation, and innovation development, *Journal of Product Innovation Management*, 30: 750–762; D. Dunlap-Hinkler, M. Kotabe, & R. Mudambi, 2010, A story of breakthrough versus incremental innovation: Corporate entrepreneurship in the global pharmaceutical industry, *Strategic Entrepreneurship Journal*, 4: 106–127.

97. J. West & M. Bogers, 2013, Leveraging external sources of innovation: A review of research on open innovation, *Journal of Product Innovation Management*, in press; D. Li, L. Eden, M. A. Hitt, & R. D. Ireland, 2008, Friends, acquaintances, or strangers? Partner selection in R&D alliances, *Academy of Management Journal*, 51: 315–334.

98. C. Beckman, K. Eisenhardt, S. Kotha, A. Meyer, & N. Rajagopalan, 2012, Technology entrepreneurship, *Strategic Entrepreneurship Journal*, 6: 89-93; J. T. Eckhardt & S. A. Shane, 2011, Industry changes in technology and complementary assets and the creation of high-growth firms, *Journal of Business Venturing*, 26: 412–430.

99. D. Li, 2013, Multilateral R&D alliances by new ventures, *Journal of Business Venturing*, 28: 241–260; G. Dushnitsky & D. Lavie, 2010, How alliance formation shapes corporate venture capital investment in the software industry: A resource-based perspective, *Strategic Entrepreneurship Journal*, 4: 22–48 S. A. Alvarez & J. B. Barney, 2001, How entrepreneurial firms can benefit from alliances with large partners, *Academy of Management Executive*, 15(1): 139–148.

100. A. Berzon & K. Hudson, 2013, IKEA's parent plans a hotel brand, *Wall Street Journal*, www.wsj.com, March 5.

101. X. Jiang, M. Li, S. Gao, Y. Bao, & F. Jiang, 2013, Managing knowledge leakage in strategic alliances: The effects of trust and formal contracts, *Industrial Marketing Management*, in press; A. Kaul, 2013, Entrepreneurial action, unique assets, and appropriation risk: Firms as a means of appropriating profit from capability creation, *Organization Science*, in press; B. Lokshin, J. Hagedoorn, & W. Letterie, 2011, The bumpy road of technology partnerships: Understanding causes and consequences of partnership and mal-functioning, *Research Policy*, 40: 297–308.

102. G. Cuevas-Rodriguez, C. Cabello-Medina, & A. Carmona-Lavado, 2013, Internal and external social capital for radical product innovation: Do they always work well together? *British Journal of Management*, in press; M. A. Hitt, M. T. Dacin, E. Levitas, J. L. Arregle, & A. Borza, 2000, Partner selection in emerging and developed market contexts: Resource-based and organizational learning perspectives, *Academy of Management Journal*, 43: 449–467.

103. R. Vandaie & A. Zaheer, 2013, Surviving bear hugs: Firm capability, large partner alliances, and growth, *Strategic Management Journal*, in press; G. Duysters & B. Lokshin, 2011, Determinants of alliance portfolio complexity and its effect on innovative performance of companies, *Journal of Product Innovation Management,* 28: 570–585.

104. A. Madhok & M. Keyhani, 2012, Acquisitions as entrepreneurship: Asymmetries, opportunities, and the internationalization of multinationals from emerging economies, *Global Strategy Journal*, 2: 26–40;

105. M. A. Hitt, D. King, H. Krishnan, M. Makri, M. Schijven, K. Shimizu, & H. Zhu, 2009, Mergers and acquisitions: Overcoming pitfalls, building synergy and creating value, *Business Horizons,* 52: 523–529; H. G. Barkema & M. Schijven, 2008, Toward unlocking the full potential of acquisitions: The role of organizational restructuring, *Academy of Management Journal,* 51: 696–722.

106. 2012, Pfizer acquires NextWave Pharmaceuticals, Inc., *Pfizer News & Media,* www.pfizer.com, November 28.

107. M. Humphrey-Jenner, 2013, Takeover defenses, innovation, and value creation: Evidence from acquisition decisions, *Strategic Management Journal*, 34: in press;

M. Makri, M. A. Hitt, & P. J. Lane, 2010, Complementary technologies, knowledge relatedness, and invention outcomes in high technology M&As, *Strategic Management Journal,* 31: 602–628.

108. M. Wagner, 2013, Determinants of acquisition value: The role of target and acquirer characteristics, *International Journal of Technology Management*, 62: 56–74; M. E. Graebner, K. M. Eisenhardt, & P. T. Roundy, 2010, Success and failure in technology acquisitions: Lessons for buyers and sellers, *Academy of Management Perspectives*, 24: 73–92; M. A. Hitt, J. S. Harrison, & R. D. Ireland, 2001, *Mergers and Acquisitions: A Guide to Creating Value for Stakeholders,* New York: Oxford University Press.

109. F. Bauer & K. Matzler, 2013, Antecedents of M&A success: The role of strategic complementarity, cultural fit, and degree and speed of integration, *Strategic Management Journal*, in press; S. Mingo, 2013, The impact of acquisitions on the performance of existing organizational units in the acquiring firm: The case of an agribusiness company, *Management Science*, in press.

110. R. Fini, R. Grimaldi, G. L. Marzocchi, & M. Sobrero, 2012, The determinants of corporate entrepreneurial intention within small and newly established firms, *Entrepreneurship Theory and Practice*,

36: 387–414; D. Elfenbein & B. Hamilton, 2010, The small firm effect and the entrepreneurial spawning of scientists and engineers, *Management Science,* 56: 659–681.

111. B. Larraneta, S. A. Zahra, & J. L. G. Gonzalez, 2012, Enriching strategic variety in new ventures through external knowledge, *Journal of Business Venturing,* 27: 401–413; H. Greve, 2011, Positional rigidity: Low performance and resource acquisition in large and small firms, *Strategic Management Journal*, 32: 103–114.

112. S. M. Lee, D. L. Olson, & S. Trimi, 2012, Co-innovation: Convergenomics, collaboration, and co-creation for organizational values, *Management Decision*, 50: 817–831;G. Wu, 2012, The effect of going public on innovative productivity and exploratory search, *Organization Science*, 23: 928–950; D. G. Sirmon & M. A. Hitt, 2009, Contingencies within dynamic managerial capabilities: Interdependent effects of resource investment and deployment on firm performance, *Strategic Management Journal,* 30: 1375–1394.

113. R. B. Tucker, 2013, Are chief innovation officers delivering results? *Innovation Excellence,* www.innovationexcellence.com, March 22.

CASE STUDIES

Case Title	Manu-facturing	Service	Consumer Goods	Food/Retail	High Technology	Internet	Transportation/Communication	International Perspective	Social/Ethical Issues	Industry Perspecti
Ally Bank		●				●				●
AstraZeneca										
Avon			●	●				●	●	
Black Canyon				●				●		
Blue Nile			●	●		●		●		●
Campbell		●		●						
Chick-fil-A		●		●					●	
Chipotle				●						●
Columbia Sportswear	●		●						●	●
Common Ground	●								●	
Equal Exchange		●		●				●	●	●
Facebook					●	●				
Glencore, Xstrata	●							●		●
Harley-Davidson	●		●				●	●		
Herman Miller	●		●	●					●	
Itaipu Binacional	●							●	●	
J.C. Penney			●	●				●		
Kipp Schools		●								
Krispy Kreme	●			●					●	●
Lockheed Martin	●							●	●	●
Logitech	●				●			●		●
lululemon		●		●				●	●	
Movie Exhibition Industry		●								●
Phase Separation	●				●			●	●	●
RIM					●	●		●		
Sirius		●			●	●	●	●		●
Tata Motors	●						●	●		
TEOCO		●			●	●		●	●	
Tesla	●						●			
Yahoo!					●	●				

Case Title	Chapters												
	1	2	3	4	5	6	7	8	9	10	11	12	13
Ally Bank		●			●	●					●		●
AstraZeneca	●	●			●								●
Avon	●			●				●		●			
Black Canyon		●	●	●	●								
Blue Nile		●	●	●	●			●					
Campbell				●	●	●					●	●	
Chick-fil-A	●			●	●								
Chipotle			●	●	●								
Columbia Sportswear		●	●	●	●							●	
Common Ground	●	●										●	●
Equal Exchange	●		●							●		●	●
Facebook	●		●						●			●	●
Glencore, Xstrata	●	●				●	●	●					
Harley-Davidson		●	●	●	●	●	●						
Herman Miller		●	●	●								●	●
Itaipu Binacional							●	●	●			●	●
J.C. Penney		●	●	●	●						●		
Kipp Schools		●	●										●
Krispy Kreme		●	●	●								●	●
Lockheed Martin	●	●				●	●	●				●	
Logitech		●		●		●	●	●					●
lululemon	●	●	●	●				●					●
Movie Exhibition Industry		●		●	●								
Phase Separation		●				●	●	●			●		
RIM					●				●			●	●
Sirius						●	●	●			●		●
Tata Motors						●	●	●					
TEOCO								●	●		●	●	●
Tesla		●		●							●		●
Yahoo!	●									●		●	

Preparing an
Effective Case Analysis

What to Expect from In-Class Case Discussions

As you will learn, classroom discussions of cases differ significantly from lectures. The case method calls for your instructor to guide the discussion and to solicit alternative views as a way of encouraging your active participation when analyzing a case. When alternative views are not forthcoming, your instructor might take a position just to challenge you and your peers to respond thoughtfully as a way of generating still additional alternatives. Often, instructors will evaluate your work in terms of both the quantity and the quality of your contributions to in-class case discussions. The in-class discussions are important in that you can derive significant benefit by having your ideas and recommendations examined against those of your peers and by responding to thoughtful challenges by other class members and/or the instructor.

During case discussions, your instructor will likely listen, question, and probe to extend the analysis of case issues. In the course of these actions, your peers and/or your instructor may challenge an individual's views and the validity of alternative perspectives that have been expressed. These challenges are offered in a constructive manner; their intent is to help all parties involved with analyzing a case develop their analytical and communication skills. Developing these skills is important in that they will serve you well when working for all types of organizations. Commonly, instructors will encourage you and your peers to be innovative and original when developing and presenting ideas. Over the course of an individual discussion, you are likely to form a more complex view of the case as a result of listening to and thinking about the diverse inputs offered by your peers

and instructor. Among other benefits, experience with multiple case discussions will increase your knowledge of the advantages and disadvantages of group decision-making processes.

Both your peers and instructor will value comments that contribute to identifying problems as well as solutions to them. To offer relevant contributions, you are encouraged to think independently and, through discussions with your peers outside of class, to refine your thinking. We also encourage you to avoid using "I think," "I believe," and "I feel" to discuss your inputs to a case analysis process. Instead, consider using a less emotion laden phrase, such as "My analysis shows…." This highlights the logical nature of the approach you have taken to analyze a case. When preparing for an in-class case discussion, you should plan to use the case data to explain your assessment of the situation. Assume that your peers and instructor are familiar with the basic facts included in the case. In addition, it is good practice to prepare notes regarding your analysis of case facts before class discussions and use them when explaining your perspectives. Effective notes signal to classmates and the instructor that you are prepared to engage in a thorough discussion of a case. Moreover, comprehensive and detailed notes eliminate the need for you to memorize the facts and figures needed to successfully discuss a case.

The case analysis process described above will help prepare you effectively to discuss a case during class meetings. Using this process results in consideration of the issues required to identify a focal firm's problems and to propose strategic actions through which the firm can increase the probability it will outperform its rivals. In some instances, your instructor may ask you to prepare either an oral or a written analysis of a particular case. Typically, such an assignment demands even more thorough study and analysis of the case contents. At your instructor's discretion, oral and written analyses may be completed by individuals or by groups of three or more people. The information and insights gained by completing the six steps shown in Table 1 often are of value when developing an oral or a written analysis. However, when preparing an oral or written presentation, you must consider the overall framework in which your information and inputs will be presented. Such a framework is the focus of the next section.

Preparing an Oral/Written Case Presentation

Experience shows that two types of thinking (analysis and synthesis) are necessary to develop an effective oral or written presentation (see Exhibit 1). In the analysis stage, you should first analyze the general external environmental issues affecting the firm. Next, your environmental analysis should focus on the particular industry (or industries, in the case of a diversified company) in which a firm operates. Finally, you should examine companies against which the focal firm competes. By studying the three levels of the external environment (general, industry, and competitor), you will be able to identify a firm's opportunities and threats. Following the external environmental analysis is the analysis of the firm's internal organization. This analysis provides the insights needed to identify the firm's strengths and weaknesses.

As noted in Exhibit 1, you must then change the focus from analysis to synthesis. Specifically, you must synthesize information gained from your analysis of the firm's external environment and internal organization. Synthesizing information allows you to generate alternatives that can resolve the significant problems or challenges facing the focal firm. Once you identify a best alternative, from an evaluation based on predetermined criteria and goals, you must explore implementation actions.

In Table 2, we outline the sections that should be included in either an oral or a written presentation: strategic profile and case analysis purpose, situation analysis, statements of strengths/weaknesses and opportunities/threats, strategy formulation, and strategy implementation. These sections are described in the following discussion. Familiarity with the contents of your book's thirteen chapters is helpful because the general outline for an oral or a written presentation shown in Table 2 is based on an understanding of the strategic management process detailed in those chapters. We follow the discussions of the parts of Table 2 with a few comments about the "process" to use to present the results of your case analysis in either a written or oral format.

Table 1 An Effective Case Analysis Process

Step 1: Gaining Familiarity	a. In general—determine who, what, how, where, and when (the critical facts of the case).
	b. In detail—identify the places, persons, activities, and contexts of the situation.
	c. Recognize the degree of certainty/uncertainty of acquired information.
Step 2: Recognizing Symptoms	a. List all indicators (including stated "problems") that something is not as expected or as desired.
	b. Ensure that symptoms are not assumed to be the problem (symptoms should lead to identification of the problem).
Step 3: Identifying Goals	a. Identify critical statements by major parties (for example, people, groups, the work unit, and so on).
	b. List all goals of the major parties that exist or can be reasonably inferred.
Step 4: Conducting the Analysis	a. Decide which ideas, models, and theories seem useful.
	b. Apply these conceptual tools to the situation.
	c. As new information is revealed, cycle back to substeps a and b.
Step 5: Making the Diagnosis	a. Identify predicaments (goal inconsistencies).
	b. Identify problems (discrepancies between goals and performance).
	c. Prioritize predicaments/problems regarding timing, importance, and so on.
Step 6: Doing the Action Planning	a. Specify and prioritize the criteria used to choose action alternatives.
	b. Discover or invent feasible action alternatives.
	c. Examine the probable consequences of action alternatives.
	d. Select a course of action.
	e. Design an implementation plan/schedule.
	f. Create a plan for assessing the action to be implemented.

Source: C. C. Lundberg and C. Enz, 1993, A framework for student case preparation, *Case Research Journal*, 13 (Summer): 144, NACRA, North American Case Research Association.

Exhibit 1 Types of Thinking in Case Preparation: Analysis and Synthesis

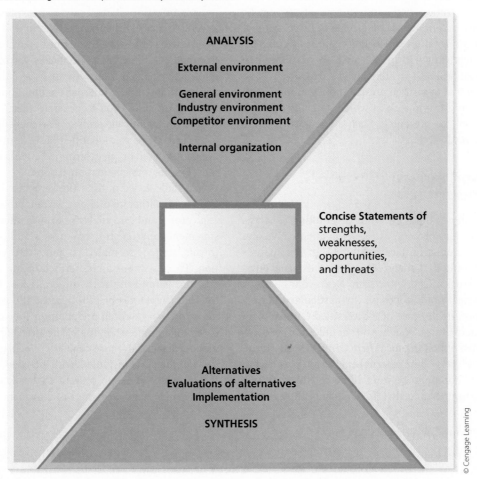

© Cengage Learning

Strategic Profile and Case Analysis Purpose

You will use the strategic profile to briefly present the critical facts from the case that have affected the focal firm's historical strategic direction and performance. The case facts should not be restated in the profile; rather, these comments should show how the critical facts lead to a particular focus for your analysis. This primary focus should be emphasized in this section's conclusion. In addition, this section should state important assumptions about case facts on which your analyses are based.

Situation Analysis

As shown in Table 2, a general starting place for completing a situation analysis is the general environment.

General Environmental Analysis. Your analysis of the general environment should focus on trends in the seven segments of the general environment (see Table 3).

Table 2 General Outline for an Oral or Written Presentation

I. Strategic Profile and Case Analysis Purpose
II. Situation Analysis
A. General environmental analysis
B. Industry analysis
C. Competitor analysis
D. Internal analysis
III. Identification of Environmental Opportunities and Threats and Firm Strengths and Weaknesses (SWOT Analysis)
IV. Strategy Formulation
A. Strategic alternatives
B. Alternative evaluation
C. Alternative choice
v. Strategic Alternative Implementation
A. Action items
B. Action plan

Many of the segment issues shown in Table 3 for the seven segments are explained more fully in Chapter 2 of your book. The objective you should have in evaluating these trends is to be able to *predict* the segments that

Table 3 Sample General Environmental Categories

Technological Trends
- Information technology continues to become cheaper with more practical applications
- Database technology enables organization of complex data and distribution of information
- Telecommunications technology and networks increasingly provide fast transmission of all sources of data, including voice, written communications, and video information
- Computerized design and manufacturing technologies continue to facilitate quality and flexibility

Demographic Trends
- Regional changes in population due to migration
- Changing ethnic composition of the population
- Aging of the population
- Aging of the "baby boom" generation

Economic Trends
- Interest rates
- Inflation rates
- Savings rates
- Exchange rates
- Trade deficits
- Budget deficits

Political/Legal Trends
- Antitrust enforcement
- Tax policy changes
- Environmental protection laws
- Extent of regulation/deregulation
- Privatizing state monopolies
- State-owned industries

Sociocultural Trends
- Women in the workforce
- Awareness of health and fitness issues
- Concern for overcoming poverty
- Concern for customers

Global Trends
- Currency exchange rates
- Free-trade agreements
- Trade deficits

Physical Environment Trends
- Environmental sustainability
- Corporate social responsibility
- Renewable energy
- Goals of zero waste
- Ecosystem impact of food and energy production

you expect to have the most significant influence on your focal firm over the next several years (say three to five years) and to explain your reasoning for your predictions.

Industry Analysis. Porter's five force model is a useful tool for analyzing the industry (or industries) in which your firm competes. We explain how to use this tool in Chapter 2. In this part of your analysis, you want to determine the attractiveness of an industry (or a segment of an industry) in which your firm is competing. As attractiveness increases, so does the possibility your firm will be able to earn profits by using its chosen strategies. After evaluating the power of the five forces relative to your firm, you should make a judgment as to *how* attractive the industry is in which your firm is competing.

Competitor Analysis. Firms also need to *analyze* each of their primary competitors. This analysis should identify competitors' current strategies, strategic intent, strategic mission, capabilities, core competencies, and a competitive response profile (see Chapter 2). This information is useful to the focal firm in formulating an appropriate strategy and in predicting competitors' probable responses. Sources that can be used to gather information about an industry and companies with whom the focal firm competes are listed in Appendix I. Included in this list is a wide range of publications, such as periodicals, newspapers, bibliographies, directories of companies, industry ratios, forecasts, rankings/ratings, and other valuable statistics.

Internal Analysis. Assessing a firm's strengths and weaknesses through a value chain analysis facilitates moving from the external environment to the internal organization. Analysis of the value chain activities and the support functions of the value chain provides opportunities to understand how external environmental trends affect the specific activities of a firm. Such analysis helps highlight strengths and weaknesses (see Chapter 3 for an explanation and use of the value chain).

For purposes of preparing an oral or a written presentation, it is important to note that strengths are internal resources and capabilities that have the potential to be core competencies. Weaknesses, on the other hand, are internal resources and capabilities that have the potential to place a firm at a competitive disadvantage relative to its rivals. Thus, some of a firm's resources and capabilities are strengths; others are weaknesses.

When evaluating the internal characteristics of the firm, your analysis of the functional activities emphasized is critical. For instance, if the strategy of the firm is primarily technology driven, it is important to evaluate the firm's R&D activities. If the strategy is market driven, marketing functional activities are of paramount importance. If a firm has financial difficulties, critical financial ratios would require careful evaluation. In fact, because of the importance of financial health, most cases require financial analyses. Appendix II lists and operationally defines several common financial ratios. Included are tables describing profitability, liquidity, leverage, activity, and shareholders' return ratios. Leadership, organizational culture, structure, and control systems are other characteristics of firms you should examine to fully understand the "internal" part of your firm.

Identification of Environmental Opportunities and Threats and Firm Strengths and Weaknesses (SWOT Analysis). The outcome of the situation analysis is the identification of a firm's strengths and weaknesses and its environmental threats and opportunities. The next step requires that you *analyze* the strengths and weaknesses and the opportunities and threats for configurations that benefit or do not benefit your firm's efforts to perform well. Case analysts and organizational strategists as well seek to match a firm's strengths with its opportunities. In addition, strengths are chosen to prevent any serious environmental threat from negatively affecting the firm's performance. The key objective of conducting a SWOT analysis is to determine how to position the firm so it can take advantage of opportunities, while simultaneously avoiding or minimizing environmental threats. Results from a SWOT analysis yield valuable insights into the selection of a firm's strategies. The analysis of a case should not be overemphasized relative to the synthesis of results gained from your analytical efforts. There may be a temptation to spend most of your oral or written case analysis on results from the analysis. It is important, however, that you make an equal effort to develop and evaluate alternatives and to design implementation of the chosen strategy.

Strategy Formulation—Strategic Alternatives, Alternative Evaluation, and Alternative Choice. Developing alternatives is often one of the most difficult steps in preparing an oral or a written presentation. Developing three to four alternative strategies is common (see Chapter 4 for business-level strategy alternatives and Chapter 6 for corporate-level strategy alternatives). Each alternative should be feasible (i.e., it should match the firm's strengths, capabilities, and especially core competencies), and feasibility should be demonstrated. In addition, you should show how each alternative takes advantage of the environmental opportunity or avoids/buffers against environmental threats. Developing carefully thought out alternatives requires synthesis of your analyses' results and creates greater credibility in oral and written case presentations.

Once you develop strong alternatives, you must evaluate the set to choose the best one. Your choice should be defensible and provide benefits over the other alternatives. Thus, it is important that both alternative development and evaluation of alternatives be thorough. The choice of the best alternative should be explained and defended.

Strategic Alternative Implementation-Action Items and Action Plan. After selecting the most appropriate strategy (that is, the strategy with the highest probability of helping your firm in its efforts to earn profits), implementation issues require attention. Effective synthesis is important to ensure that you have considered and evaluated all critical implementation issues. Issues you might consider include the structural changes necessary to implement the new strategy. In addition, leadership changes and new controls or incentives may be necessary to implement strategic actions. The implementation actions you recommend should be explicit and thoroughly explained. Occasionally, careful evaluation of implementation actions may show the strategy to be less favorable than you thought originally. A strategy is only as good as the firm's ability to implement it.

Process Issues. You should ensure that your presentation (either oral or written) has logical consistency throughout. For example, if your presentation identifies one purpose, but your analysis focuses on issues that differ from the stated purpose, the logical inconsistency will be apparent. Likewise, your alternatives should flow from the configuration of strengths, weaknesses, opportunities, and threats you identified by analyzing your firm's external environment and internal organization.

Thoroughness and clarity also are critical to an effective presentation. Thoroughness is represented by the comprehensiveness of the analysis and alternative generation. Furthermore, clarity in the results of the analyses, selection of the best alternative strategy, and design of implementation actions are important. For example, your statement of the strengths and weaknesses should flow clearly and logically from your analysis of your firm's internal organization.

Presentations (oral or written) that show logical consistency, thoroughness, and clarity of purpose, effective analyses, and feasible recommendations (strategy and implementation) are more effective and are likely to be more positively received by your instructor and peers. Furthermore, developing the skills necessary to make such presentations will enhance your future job performance and career success.

Appendix I Sources for Industry and Competitor Analyses

Abstracts and Indexes	
Periodicals	ABI/*Inform*
	Business Periodicals Index
	InfoTrac Custom Journals
	InfoTrac Custom Newspapers
	InfoTrac OneFile
	EBSCO Business Source Premiere
	Lexis/Nexis Academic
	Public Affairs Information Service Bulletin (PAIS)
	Reader's Guide to Periodical Literature
Newspapers	*NewsBank—Foreign Broadcast Information*
	NewsBank-Global NewsBank
	New York Times Index
	Wall Street Journal Index
	Wall Street Journal/Barron's Index
	Washington Post Index
Bibliographies	*Encyclopedia of Business Information Sources*
Directories	
Companies—General	*America's Corporate Families and International Affiliates*
	Hoover's Online: The Business Network www.hoovers.com/free
	D&B Million Dollar Directory (databases: http://www.dnbmdd.com)
	Standard & Poor's Corporation Records
	Standard & Poor's Register of Corporations, Directors, and Executives (http://www.netadvantage.standardandpoors.com for all of *Standard & Poor's*)
	Ward's Business Directory of Largest U.S. Companies
Companies—International	*America's Corporate Families and International Affiliates*
	Business Asia
	Business China
	Business Eastern Europe
	Business Europe
	Business International
	Business International Money Report
	Business Latin America

(Continued)

Appendix I (Continued) Sources for Industry and Competitor Analyses

Abstracts and Indexes	
	Directory of American Firms Operating in Foreign Countries *Directory of Foreign Firms Operating in the United States* *Hoover's Handbook of World Business* *International Directory of Company Histories* *Mergent's International Manual* Mergent Online (http://www.fisonline.com—for "Business and Financial Information Connection to the World") *Who Owns Whom*
Companies—Manufacturers	*Thomas Register of American Manufacturers* U.S. Office of Management and Budget, Executive Office of the President, *Standard* *Industrial Classification Manual* *U.S. Manufacturer's Directory, Manufacturing & Distribution, USA*
Companies—Private	*D&B Million Dollar Directory* *Ward's Business Directory of Largest U.S. Companies*
Companies—Public	Annual Reports and 10-K Reports *Disclosure* (corporate reports) *Q-File* Securities and Exchange Commission Filings & Forms (EDGAR) http://www.sec.gov/edgar.shtml *Mergent's Manuals:* ■ *Mergent's Bank and Finance Manual* ■ *Mergent's Industrial Manual* ■ *Mergent's International Manual* ■ *Mergent's Municipal and Government Manual* ■ *Mergent's OTC Industrial Manual* ■ *Mergent's OTC Unlisted Manual* ■ *Mergent's Public Utility Manual* ■ *Mergent's Transportation Manual* Standard & Poor's Corporation, *Standard Corporation Descriptions:* http://www.netadvantage.standardandpoors.com ■ *Standard & Poor's Analyst Handbook* ■ *Standard & Poor's Industry Surveys* ■ *Standard & Poor's Statistical Service*
Companies—Subsidiaries and Affiliates	*America's Corporate Families and International Affiliates* *Ward's Directory* *Who Owns Whom* *Mergent's Industry Review* *Standard & Poor's Analyst's Handbook* *Standard & Poor's Industry Surveys* (2 volumes) U.S. Department of Commerce, *U.S. Industrial Outlook*
Industry Ratios	Dun & Bradstreet, *Industry Norms and Key Business Ratios* *RMA's Annual Statement Studies* *Troy Almanac of Business and Industrial Financial Ratios*
Industry Forecasts	International Trade Administration, *U.S. Industry & Trade Outlook*
Rankings & Ratings	Annual Report on American Industry in *Forbes Business Rankings Annual* *Mergent's Industry Review* http://www.worldcatlibraries.org *Standard & Poor's Industry Report Service* http://www.netadvantage.standardandpoors.com *Value Line Investment Survey* *Ward's Business Directory of Largest U.S. Companies*

Statistics	*American Statistics Index (ASI)* Bureau of the Census, U.S. Department of Commerce,
	    Economic Census Publications
	Bureau of the Census, U.S. Department of Commerce, *Statistical Abstract of the United States*
	Bureau of Economic Analysis, U.S. Department of Commerce, *Survey of Current Business*
	Internal Revenue Service, U.S. Treasury Department, *Statistics of Income: Corporation Income*
	    Tax Returns
	Statistical Reference Index (SRI)

Appendix II Financial Analysis in Case Studies

Table A-1 Profitability Ratios

Ratio	Formula	What It Shows
1. Return on total assets	$\dfrac{\text{Profits after taxes}}{\text{Total assets}}$ or $\dfrac{\text{Profits after taxes} + \text{Interest}}{\text{Total assets}}$	The net return on total investments of the firm or The return on both creditors' and shareholders' investments
2. Return on stockholders' equity (or return on net worth)	$\dfrac{\text{Profits after taxes}}{\text{Total stockholders' equity}}$	How profitably the company is utilizing shareholders' funds
3. Return on common equity	$\dfrac{\text{Profits after taxes} - \text{Preferred stock dividends}}{\text{Total stockholders' equity} - \text{Par value of preferred stock}}$	The net return to common stockholders
4. Operating profit margin (or return on sales)	$\dfrac{\text{Profits before taxes and before interest}}{\text{Sales}}$	The firm's profitability from regular operations
5. Net profit margin (or net return on sales)	$\dfrac{\text{Profits after taxes}}{\text{Sales}}$	The firm's net profit as a percentage of total sales

© Cengage Learning

Table A-2 Liquidity Ratios

Ratio	Formula	What It Shows
1. Current ratio	$\dfrac{\text{Current assets}}{\text{Current liabilities}}$	The firm's ability to meet its current financial liabilities
2. Quick ratio (or acid-test ratio)	$\dfrac{\text{Current assets} - \text{Inventory}}{\text{Current liabilities}}$	The firm's ability to pay off short-term obligations without relying on sales of inventory
3. Inventory to net working capital	$\dfrac{\text{Inventory}}{\text{Current assets} - \text{Current liabilities}}$	The extent to which the firm's working capital is tied up in inventory

© Cengage Learning

Table A-3 Leverage Ratios

Ratio	Formula	What It Shows
1. Debt-to-assets	$\dfrac{\text{Total debt}}{\text{Total assets}}$	Total borrowed funds as a percentage of total assets
2. Debt-to-equity	$\dfrac{\text{Total debt}}{\text{Total shareholders' equity}}$	Borrowed funds versus the funds provided by shareholders
3. Long-term debt-to-equity	$\dfrac{\text{Long-term debt}}{\text{Total shareholders' equity}}$	Leverage used by the firm
4. Times-interest-earned (or coverage ratio)	$\dfrac{\text{Profits before interest and taxes}}{\text{Total interest charges}}$	The firm's ability to meet all interest payments
5. Fixed charge coverage	$\dfrac{\text{Profits before taxes and interest} + \text{Lease obligations}}{\text{Total interest charges} + \text{Lease obligations}}$	The firm's ability to meet all fixed-charge obligations including lease payments

© Cengage Learning

Table A-4 Activity Ratios

Ratio	Formula	What It Shows
1. Inventory turnover	$\dfrac{\text{Sales}}{\text{Inventory of finished goods}}$	The effectiveness of the firm in employing inventory
2. Fixed-assets turnover	$\dfrac{\text{Sales}}{\text{Fixed assets}}$	The effectiveness of the firm in utilizing plant and equipment
3. Total assets turnover	$\dfrac{\text{Sales}}{\text{Total assets}}$	The effectiveness of the firm in utilizing total assets
4. Accounts receivable turnover	$\dfrac{\text{Annual credit sales}}{\text{Accounts receivable}}$	How many times the total receivables have been collected during the accounting period
5. Average collecting period	$\dfrac{\text{Accounts receivable}}{\text{Average daily sales}}$	The average length of time the firm waits to collect payment after sales

© Cengage Learning

Table A-5 Shareholders' Return Ratios

Ratio	Formula	What It Shows
1. Dividend yield on common stock	$\dfrac{\text{Annual dividend per share}}{\text{Current market price per share}}$	A measure of return to common stockholders in the form of dividends
2. Price-earnings ratio	$\dfrac{\text{Current market price per share}}{\text{After-tax earnings per share}}$	An indication of market perception of the firm; usually, the faster-growing or less risky firms tend to have higher PE ratios than the slower-growing or more risky firms
3. Dividend payout ratio	$\dfrac{\text{Annual dividends per share}}{\text{After-tax earnings per share}}$	An indication of dividends paid out as a percentage of profits
4. Cash flow per share	$\dfrac{\text{After-tax profits + Depreciation}}{\text{Number of common shares outstanding}}$	A measure of total cash per share available for use by the firm

© Cengage Learning

Eli Erickson, Sarah Hassan, Amey Karnik, Jason Shin, Brian Turnley

Texas A&M University

Introduction and History

Ally Bank, a subsidiary of Ally Financial Inc., offers customers a different type of bank and a different type of banking experience. Unlike traditional banks with hundreds of branches and thousands of ATMs, Ally Bank has only two offices and no ATMs. What the company lacks in physical presence, it makes up for with a 24/7 call center and instant online banking. What it saves by not paying to rent a large number of locations, it returns to the customer in the form of competitive interest rates on certificates of deposit (CDs), as well as savings, money market, and checking accounts. And instead of maintaining its own ATMs, it piggybacks on existing ATM networks and compensates its customers for any fees incurred.

Although Ally Bank is a new name, it is not a new company. Ally Bank and its parent company—Ally Financial Inc.—originally stemmed from General Motors Acceptance Corporation (GMAC), which was formed in 1919. GMAC was the main provider of automotive financing to General Motors dealerships. As the demand for cars grew, so did GMAC. Its success in auto financing provided it with the capital to expand into other product areas, such as insurance, direct banking, mortgage, and commercial finance.

In 2006, General Motors spun GMAC off as a separate entity. Although it was still the primary source of funding for General Motor vehicle purchases, the bank had grown its portfolio and exposure in a number of markets. Because of its diversification into the subprime mortgage market, the 2008 financial meltdown caused a liquidity crisis at GMAC and set the stage for the creation of Ally Bank.

The banking division of GMAC was formed in the final days of 2008 as part of a year-end deal with the Federal Reserve. On December 24, 2008, GMAC officially became a bank holding company. Five days later on December 29, 2008, the US Treasury announced it would invest $5 billion of its Troubled Asset Relief Program (TARP) funds in GMAC and receive preferred shares in return.[1] In May 2009, GMAC officially changed its name to Ally Bank.[2] The rationale for the name change stemmed from the impending bankruptcy of General Motors and a desire to distance the bank from the automobile manufacturing company and its relationship with that firm.

Ally Bank is classified as a direct bank,[3] which means it has no bricks-and-mortar locations. This form of banking has cost-saving benefits for the bank as well as investment opportunities for customers. The bank is able to save on overhead costs and transfer those savings to its customers in the form of higher interest rates if it chooses to do so. With increasing consumer comfort in web-based technology and the Internet, online banking may be the heir apparent of the industry. By offering only online services, Ally Bank has enjoyed these costs savings since its inception.

Ally Bank returns its savings to customers in three ways. First, Ally Bank offers superior customer service. Where most banks have automated systems to save money, Ally Bank has focused on providing 24/7 customer service. As a courtesy, an estimated call wait time is posted on its website, thus helping alleviate frustrations associated with phone banking services.

Second, where most banks charge fees for certain options, Ally Bank offers 'free stuff.' These items include: "no minimum balance to open an account, free online banking with online bill pay, free account alerts and notifications, and free 'sleeping money' alerts" (alerts advising customers of opportunities for their inactive accounts—or 'sleeping money'—to earn more interest from a CD).[4]

A general complaint from customers about the banking industry concerns their perception that firms try to nickel and dime them as depositors through hidden costs, fees, and charges. Because of its exclusively online presence, Ally Bank is able to minimize those costs and provide many services at no charge for which similar banks charge a premium. For the services for which it *does* charge, the bank clearly states the type, amount, and rationale for each charge. Regarding the checking sector of Ally's business, the cost savings the bank offers include services such as unlimited check writing, no monthly maintenance fees, no ATM fees, and free balance alerts.[5] This transparency is thought to contribute to creating customer trust, satisfaction, and loyalty.

The third way Ally Bank returns its savings to customers is by paying higher interest rates on interest bearing accounts. The company offers many services such as checking, savings, and individual retirement accounts (IRAs). Regarding the savings and CD division of the company, Ally Bank is able to offer competitive rates for its CDs, no penalty CDs, and 'raise your rate' CDs.[6] For bank depository customers, getting the most return for their money has become a primary concern since the policies of the US Federal Reserve have resulted in the offering of extremely low interest rates on checking account, savings, and CD-related deposits. To address these concerns, Ally Bank seeks to ensure that it offers competitive rates for savings alternatives and offers options for individuals who are unable to let their savings accumulate until the maturity date. This flexibility attracts clients of all economic backgrounds and goals. By offering competitive rates and comparisons to other banks' savings rates on its website, Ally Bank once again creates a level of transparency that is uncommon in the banking industry. Regarding IRAs, Ally Bank offers its customers many perks such as the ability to raise their rates for particular CDs, daily interest compounding, and the 'Ally Ten-Day Best Rate Guarantee,' which gives customers the right to choose the highest rate within 10 days of the CD renewal date.[7] These investment vehicles attract customers who value every penny of their investments.

Ally Bank's quality customer service, competitive rates, free perks, and transparent business model are the foundation for its stellar reputation—an asset the bank hopes to use as a foundation for achieving and maintaining a strong competitive position.

Uncertainty in Banking

The year 2012 presented an uncertain future: the presidential election, the constitutionality and possible repeal of the Patient Protection and Affordable Care Act, the expiration of the Bush tax cuts, high unemployment, the impact of the growing federal debt, and even the Mayan prophecy of apocalypse in December all contributed to the uncertainty for US citizens and perhaps for some citizens in other nations throughout the world as well. Perhaps with the exception of the Mayan apocalypse prophecy, these issues affected how business leaders made decisions and ran their firms. Business leaders were especially unclear about future government regulations and tax policies,[8] which may explain why companies delayed investments and hoarded cash[9] until they could confidently assess the future impact of their investments. In addition, unemployment remained high at around or above 8 percent[10] and household income fell 6.7 percent from June 2009 to June 2011.[11] Along with these grim statistics, the European debt crisis, fierce global competition, and increasing oversight and regulations contributed to a tough business environment—especially in the financial industry.

Conditions in the Banking Industry

The great recession of 2008 shook US financial foundations. From September 2008[12] through April 2012, 420 banks failed and the recession continues to have a lasting impact on the housing and financial industries. This was especially true for Ally Bank as its parent company, Ally Financial (then GMAC), received $16 billion from the federal government under the TARP and has yet to pay it back. In contrast, its competitors such as Bank of America, Citigroup, and Wells Fargo have all paid back their bailout loans.[13]

To understand the industry in which Ally Bank competes requires an appreciation for and understanding of the differences between online banking and traditional banking operations. Although most traditional banks maintain an online presence and offer various services through Internet and mobile banking, strictly online banks are notable because of their lack of a physical presence—they do not operate bricks-and-mortar branches and use the Internet as their single distribution channel to provide their products and services to customers.

According to the American Bankers Association, online banking is experiencing explosive popularity and growth. In 2007, only 23 percent of bank customers indicated that their preferred banking method was through the Internet with 35 percent preferring to go to their local branch for banking needs. However, by 2011, 62 percent of customers preferred banking via the Internet while only 20 percent preferred banking at a branch office.[14]

The growth of online banks is perhaps not surprising given their advantages over traditional banking. Online banking provides a level of convenience that bricks-and-mortar banks cannot match. Online banks—where customers can check balances, pay bills, and transfer funds—are open 24 hours a day. The only requirement is access to a computer or mobile device and an Internet connection. In addition, because online banks do not incur overhead costs associated with bricks-and-mortar branches, they can offer customers better rates on various financial products including CDs as well as checking and savings accounts.

Despite the rapid growth of online banking, the industry is not without challenges. At a traditional bank, tellers, loan officers, and bank managers make a deliberate effort to get to know their customers and to develop personal relationships with them. By doing so, a bank tries to establish a relationship with its customers through personal contact and by providing excellent customer service and understanding customer needs. Online banking is much less personal with customers only speaking to a bank representative if they call the bank's call center. A customer who expects a close relationship with their bank may be disappointed with the lack of personal service from an online bank. In addition, most online banks do not offer financial services that are as comprehensive as those offered by a traditional bank. For example, online banks typically do not offer business loans or allow complex international financial transactions that require close coordination with customers.[15]

Because banks are in the business of buying and selling money, suppliers in the banking industry are those who supply capital to banks. They include depositors, other banks, and the Federal Reserve.[16] It is critical for banks to raise capital when needed to meet the reserve requirement ratio and to honor withdrawals. However, the suppliers of capital are not dominated by a few large entities; in fact, there are many options for a bank to consider when it seeks to raise capital. For example, there are 6,259 commercial banks operating in the United States[17] and millions of individual depositors. In addition, the current federal funds rate during the latter part of 2012—"the interest rate at which banks and other depository institutions lend money to each other"—was incredibly low at 0.25 percent as a result of the US Federal Reserve's policies that were then in place.[18] Also, other banks may compete for customers but, in terms of being suppliers, they do not pose a credible threat. In other words, banks would not withhold capital from Ally Bank to use as leverage or a bargaining tool. As long as Ally Bank agrees to borrow at the federal funds rate, it can have access to the capital it needs.

It is interesting to note that customers in this industry can be considered both suppliers and buyers. Customers provide money to the banks as suppliers, but they also buy financial services such as checking services, savings accounts, and IRAs. Deposits lead to the majority of Ally Bank's revenues and provide a funding source for the auto loans and mortgages offered by its parent company, Ally Financial.[19] Customers' dual roles raise interesting questions and issues regarding how much power than have—individually as well as collectively. Given this, Ally is challenged to devote time to determining the degree of power it has relative to customers—both as customers and as suppliers. Customer loyalty is also of interest to a bank such as Ally; but as an online banking institution, what can it do to generate customer loyalty[20] and influence the degree to which customers switch their accounts from one provider to another?[21]

Banks come and go in the banking industry. In 2010, however, only three new banks were established in the United States while none were established in 2011—a first since 1984. Two factors appear to have influenced this matter during these two years. First, the conditions facing banks increase the difficulty of earning profits. In turn of course this difficulty places greater weight on individual strategic leaders to select and then effectively implement a strategy that is appropriate for the bank they are leading. Also, because of the large number of failed banks, it has been easier for investors wishing to own a bank to purchase one that was in financial distress rather than establish a new one.[22] A question however revolves around what will happen in the banking industry with improving economic conditions. Would improving conditions make the industry more attractive to additional entrants? If so, what conditions might result in a more attractive industry? Ally's strategic leaders give thought to these matters on a continuous basis and seek to keep their analyses up to date.

As previously mentioned, Ally Bank offers three main financial products: checking, savings and CDs, and IRAs,[23] meaning that the bank was dependent on a relatively small number of products to generate revenues and profits. Ally's leaders wondered if there were substitute products that could affect the degree of attractiveness of their product offerings to customers. If substitute products did exist for checking and savings accounts as well as for CDs, what might they be and how should Ally deal with any potential threat generated by those substitutes?

Ally Bank and Its Competitors

There are over 6,000 commercial banks in the United States; and of course, each bank is interested in out-performing its rivals. During the recent and difficult economic times, evidence suggests that "The weak econ-omy's impact on consumer finances combined with the banking crisis have made it increasingly challenging for banks to attract new customers and to cross-sell to exist-ing clients." In addition, the level of consolidation occur-ring in the industry has allowed larger banks to launch aggressive marketing campaigns to attract customers.[24] Also affecting the nature of competition among banks is the meager 1.2 percent projected annual revenue growth in US retail banking until 2014.[25] Ally wondered about the exact meaning of a prediction on competitive practices and patterns in its industry and on the bank itself as well. And of course, Ally's strategic leaders were concerned about its major competitors in terms of how to best compete against them and about the actions its competitors might take to compete against Ally.

ING Direct. "ING Direct exists to help you save your money. We do business online, over the phone, and by mail. The direct way. We're available to our customers 24/7."[26] Originally part of ING Group N.V.—a financial services firm based in the Netherlands—ING Direct was sold to Capital One in February 2012.[27] ING Direct is an online bank with deposits of $83 billion;[28] it provides checking and savings accounts, home loans, IRAs, and business accounts to its customers. Known for its com-petitive interest rates and low fees, consumersearch.com rated ING's Orange Savings Account as the "Best Online Savings Account" in 2010.[29] Unlike most online banks that reimburse ATM fees, ING Direct only provides free ATM use on Allpoint Network ATMs.[30] Although ING Direct does not maintain any bricks-and-mortar branches, it recently opened ING Direct Cafés in select markets where customers can enjoy coffee and snacks and learn about ING Direct's financial products.[31] While ING Direct customers love the customer service and competi-tive rates, they do not see Capital One in the same posi-tive light. The future challenge for ING Direct appears to be that of retaining if not expanding its customer base while maintaining the competitive advantages it enjoyed prior to being acquired by Capital One.[32] Those leading Ally Bank wonder what actions ING Direct might take to retain its positive image with customers.

United Services Automobile Association (USAA). The stated mission of USAA is "to facilitate the financial security of its members, associates, and

their families through provision of a full range of highly competitive financial products and services; in so doing, USAA seeks to be the provider of choice for the mili-tary community."[33] Based in San Antonio, Texas, USAA is a *Fortune* 500 financial services company that offers banking, investing, and insurance to members. Auto and property insurance is available to members only and affiliation with the military is a requirement of member-ship. However, investment and banking services are open to non-members.[34] Known for its exceptional customer service and strong and supportive culture for employ-ees, USAA has garnered multiple honors and awards including the J.D. Power and Associates 2011 "Customer Service Champion" and *Fortune's* "100 Best Companies to Work For" (2010-2012). In addition, Forrester Research included USAA in its 2011 list of top-ranked companies in bank servicing.[35]

The USAA Federal Savings Bank handles deposits of over $46.6 billion[36] and offers no-fee checking, reim-bursement of ATM fees, and check deposits through online and mobile applications. As a banking technology leader, USAA launched a popular feature called Deposit@ Mobile in 2009 that allows customers to make deposits by transmitting a photo of a check taken by a smartphone or tablet. Deposits made through this method are imme-diately available for use.[37] USAA has very successfully targeted a niche market of military-affiliated customers. USAA has slowly opened its membership criteria over the years to include children, spouses, and widows/wid-owers of military members while thus far resisting offer-ing membership to the general public.

Charles Schwab Bank. Opened in 2003, Charles Schwab Bank is a subsidiary of The Charles Schwab Corporation and is headquartered in Reno, Nevada.[38] The bank has $60.8 billion[39] in deposits and offers checking, savings, money market, CDs, and home loans. The bank provides free checks, free online bill pay, and unlimited ATM fee reimbursements.[40] However, cus-tomers interested in a high-yield checking account must open a linked brokerage account with the bank's parent company, Charles Schwab.[41] The challenge for Charles Schwab Bank is thought to be that of learning how to attract new, young customers who know little about investing and those who only wish to use its banking services.

Bank of Internet USA. Established in July 2000 and based in San Diego, California, Bank of Internet calls itself "American's oldest and most trusted Internet bank."[42] With over $1.5 billion[43] in deposits, Bank of

Internet offers checking, savings, CDs, mortgages, and business banking. Although its stop payment and return deposit fees are the highest among those compared, the bank offers many extra services such as Popmoney (a money transfer service via email or text message), free bill pay, its FinanceWorks budgeting tool, and debit card rewards.[44] Although the bank is relatively unknown, it has carved out a niche market in the "multifamily-lending and jumbo home loan market."[45] In fact, the bank was able to achieve an impressive 18 percent increase in profit in the fourth quarter of 2011 over the previous year.[46] The challenge for Bank of Internet is to become a recognizable brand and take market share from the bigger players (see Exhibit 1 for additional information about Ally's competitors).

The Birth of Ally Bank

Spinning from the peak of the financial crisis in 2008, the banking industry needed a major overhaul—assets had to be revalued, heavy losses curtailed, the image of the banking industry had to be changed and most importantly, investor confidence needed to be restored. As highlighted previously, for GMAC Bank, this meant a rebranding of GMAC Bank into Ally Bank. The rebranding involved not only a name change, but also the creation of a fresh mission to achieve the bank's goals.

Exhibit 1 Bank Fee Comparison

Fee Type	Ally Bank	ING Direct	USAA	Charles Schwab	Bank of Internet
Monthly Inactivity	–	–	–	–	–
Non-Sufficient Funds	9.00	–	29.00	25.00	35.00
Stop Payment Item	15.00	25.00	29.00	–	35.00
Return Deposit	7.50	9.00	5.00	5.00	10.00
Domestic Wire Transfer (Outbound)	20.00	–	20.00	25.00	35.00
Domestic Wire Transfer (Inbound)	–	–	–	–	–
Non-Bank ATM	–	–	2.00*	–	–

* no fees on first 10 transactions
Sources: www.mybanktracker.com; www.ingdirect.com; www.bankofinternet.com.

The Role of Ally Financial

The pie chart in Exhibit 2 indicates the primary business interests of Ally Financial Inc. and the share of revenues earned by each in 2011.[47] As seen, 65.7 percent of Ally Financial Inc.'s revenues came from global automotive services, indicating that automotive financing was its dominant business. However, because less than 70 percent of the revenues came from this sector, Ally Financial could also be said to be strongly interested in being able to generate revenues from other sources in addition to Global Automotive Services.

Overall though, Ally Financial continues to concentrate on providing retail financial services for purchases and insurance to the automotive sector. This focus allows Ally Financial to innovate within the automotive financing sector and compete as the best in its industry. In fact, Ally Financial won a number of awards in recognition of its innovative financial services for automotive purchases including *Auto Dealers* "Dealer's Choice Award."[48]

The Role of Ally Bank

In terms of the nature of its business operations, Ally Bank is committed to provide its customers with the highest level of customer service at the lowest possible cost. To fulfill this commitment, Ally Bank ensures that its customers are provided with a great degree of personalized service above and beyond what they would be able to receive from another Internet bank or even a traditional bank.

Ally Bank tries to identify and fully understand customers' preferences as a means of determining actions it will take when competing against its rivals. To do this, the firm studies a number of sources. An example of these sources is a 2010 survey by the American Banking Association which indicated that 36 percent of retail banking customers prefer performing online transactions rather than going to a branch location.[49] By establishing

Exhibit 2 Ally Financial Inc. Revenues by Source

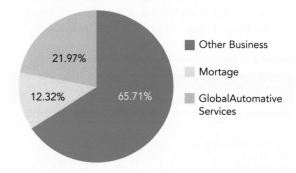

Source: Ally Financial Inc. Form 10-K for fiscal year ended December 31, 2011.

itself as a direct service bank, Ally Bank allows customers to do their banking online, as and when required. This is different from the traditional banking model where customers have to perform their transactions during the operating hours of the bank. With direct banks, customers can not only check their account balances but deposit and withdraw money at their convenience. Customers are also freed from the hassle of traveling to and from their bank. Ally Bank makes this process easy by providing an intuitive website for its customers. But "how unique is this service compared to competitors' offerings" is a question for Ally's strategic leaders to consider.

Ally Bank's Product Offerings

Exceptional customer service is only an advantage when backed by an acceptable product. Ally Bank attempts to offer financial products at rates superior to those of its bricks-and-mortar rivals. Eliminating physical locations helps Ally Bank reduce the cost of servicing customers, thus allowing it to offer higher rates on its financial products. At times, it may even offer the highest interest rates on products. However, since Ally Financial accepted funds from the US government, its rates are closely scrutinized by competitors who cry foul when Ally Bank offers above-market rates. In response, the US Treasury has asked it to remove these rates from the market to maintain fairness.[50]

Ally Bank also eliminates banking fees where possible. Customers seem satisfied with Ally Bank because of its less expensive services and reduced fees on transactions. These lower fees are seen across its entire product offering.

Checking Accounts.[51] Unlike most other banks, Ally Bank does not require its customers to maintain a minimum balance and does not charge monthly maintenance fees. There are also no fees for withdrawing money from any ATM. Ally Bank allows unlimited check writing, incentivizing customers to open and retain an account with it. Exhibit 3 provides a comparison of checking account interest rates at a point in time in 2012.[52]

Savings Accounts.[53] In addition to a free savings account, Ally Bank obtains a great amount of deposits because of its highly competitive interest rates. Interest rates are compounded daily and deposits are FDIC insured. Exhibit 4 compares Ally Bank's savings account interest rates at a point in time in 2012 to its competitors.[54]

Other Services and Benefits.[55] Other services Ally offers in efforts to meet customers' needs include high yield CDs, IRAs, money market accounts, 24/7 customer care, free online bill payments, as well as free account alerts and notifications. The Ally Bank website has an ATM locator application that locates the ATMs of all banks in the vicinity and whether Ally Bank reimburses fees at each particular location.

The Ally Bank Brand

"…if your bank doesn't let you talk to a real person 24/7, you need an ally…Ally Bank: No Nonsense, just People Sense." These statements are part of a TV advertisement developed by Ally Bank for the purpose of demonstrating what the firm believes is a strong commitment to serve its customers.[56] Another statement, which appears on the Ally Bank website, captures the bank's philosophy: "Our customers are at the heart of everything we do, including the three principles our company is built on: We talk straight. We do right by our customers. We strive to be obviously better."[57] But what do these principles mean?

Talking Straight. Many banks have costs hidden within the fine print of their contracts. Ally Bank decided to distinguish itself from other banks by clearly indicating to its customers that the bank will not hide any transaction behind confusing jargon or fine print on its contracts. An article dealing with Ally Bank featured the following quote that the bank uses to describe itself:

We're a bank that values integrity as much as deposits. A bank that will always be open, accountable, and honest. Yes, honest. We won't deal in half-truths, kinda-truths, or truths only buried in fine print. That's because we don't have anything to hide. We're always going to give it to you straight.[58]

Exhibit 3 Checking Account Interest Rate Comparison

Bank	Ally Bank	ING Direct	Bank of America	ETRADE
Annual % Yield	0.40%*	0.20%†	0.05%†	0.05%†

APY displayed as for California.
* As of 4/13/2012.
† As of 4/16/2012.
Source: www.mybanktracker.com.

Exhibit 4 Savings Account Interest Rate Comparison

Bank	Ally Bank	HSBC Advance	ING Direct	Bank of America	Chase	Wells Fargo
Annual % Yield	0.84%	0.80%	0.80%	0.05%	0.01%	0.01%

APY displayed as for California.
Competitor APY accurate as of 4/16/2012.
Source: www.mybanktracker.com.

Doing Right. Ally Bank claims to 'do right' for the benefit of its customers. This means advising customers about optimum investment options. This also involves customized financial plans for individual customers. Ally Bank believes that customer loyalty should be earned; hence, it strives to dispel the concerns of its customers by satisfying their needs.

Striving to be Better. Ally Bank strives to add value to the accounts of its customers by designing innovative products and services. This includes providing customized and direct retail financial services. Additionally, Ally Bank guarantees that a customer calling the helpline will hear a real person on the other end and not the usual automated routine that other banks provide to customers. This attitude is aligned with Ally Financial's strength of better services in automotive financing. This indicates that the importance of innovation is shared across the Ally brand.

In Summary, the Ally Bank Brand. Ally Bank has leveraged the expertise and innovation gathered in the past 92 years by Ally Financial. Ally Financial believes that the design of pioneering services for financial products that add value to customer investments is a core competence. But is there sufficient evidence to support

this belief? A key reason for concluding that this competence is transferred to Ally Bank is the bank's focus on a high standard of customer service and the possibility that its type of customer service is truly different from competitors in both the online banking industry as well as bricks-and-mortar banks. The sharing of cost savings with its customers emphasizes Ally's focus on being a customer-friendly bank. Ally Bank's competitive approaches have helped it build a strong brand reputation and gain customer satisfaction and loyalty. To illustrate its good reputation further, CNN Money named Ally Bank one of the 'eight least evil banks.'[59] But, is such a standing sufficient as a foundation for long-term success? And, how imitable are Ally's apparent sources of advantage?

Leadership at Ally Bank

The executives and key managers at Ally Bank have a cumulative total of over 183 years of banking experience. When the bank holding company was created in December 2008, it was initially comprised of GMAC executives and managers. Since that time, the company has both expanded and diversified its executives and managers, hiring particularly from Bank of America (see Exhibit 5).

Exhibit 5   Executives and Managers

Title	Name	Previous Company	Years of Banking Experience	Start Date with Ally Bank
Chief Executive Officer of Ally, President Ally Financial Inc.	Michael A. Carpenter	CitiGroup	25	2009
President, Ally Financial Inc.	William F. Muir	General Motors	20	2008
Chief Financial Executive	James N. Young	KPMG LLP	30	2008
Deposits and Line of Business Integration Executive	Diane Morais	Bank of America	25	2008
Chief Privacy Officer	Jana Laney	American Express	10	2011
Director of Finance	Aaron Blankenstein	Advanta Bank	14	2011
Director, Home Lending Marketing - Consumer Value Proposition And Brand Manage	Jessica Pate	Bank of America	6	2009
Business Integration Manager	Ryan Pagan	Bank of America	10	2008
Director Enerprise Risk Operations Strategy	Craig Houston	Capital One	13	2008
Customer Experience Manager	Cindy Clear	Bank of America	12	2009
Home Lending Marketing Director	Shelley Riley	Bank of America	9	2009
Director of Marketing	Jason Moskal	Bank of America	9	2009

Source: "Ally Bank," Hoovers.com, accessed April 20, 2012; LinkedIn.com, accessed April 2012; "Leadership," Ally Bank, accessed April 20, 2012, http://media.ally.com/index.php?s=20.

The dependency of Ally Financial Inc. on the deposits and government recognition of Ally Bank has caused cross fertilization amongst leadership. The corporate management team works closely with the bank management team to ensure the alignment of goals. Since 2008, the bank has been under the direction of four key leaders:

Michael A. Carpenter, CEO of Ally Financial Inc.

Although Carpenter is not a direct bank employee, he is the CEO of Ally Financial and ultimately responsible for the results at Ally Bank. Carpenter has over 25 years of executive banking experience, beginning in 1986 as an executive vice president at GE Capital Corporation where he eventually became chairman and CEO of Kidder, Peabody Group.[60] He was forced out of this position due to the fraud associated with a bond trading scandal[61] and later became CEO of Citigroup's Global Corporate & Investment Bank and chairman and CEO of Citigroup Alternative Investments.[62] He joined the board of Ally Financial Inc. in May 2009 and was named CEO in November of the same year.[63] For his first month and a half of service as CEO, the executive compensation committee awarded him nearly $1.2 million in salary and restricted stock.[64] Annualized, this would have been a salary of $9.5 million, which is comparable to other bank executives. However, because Ally Financial had received $17.3 billion in US TARP money in December 2008 and had not paid the government back, this salary caused some controversy.[65]

William F. Muir, President, Ally Financial Inc.

Like Carpenter, Muir operates at Ally Financial Inc. and is responsible for the company's auto financing and servicing operations. He also sits on the board of directors of Ally Bank.[66] Muir is a natural leader for the auto group, having been with General Motors since 1983 and with GMAC since 1992.[67] After 27 years in the auto industry, he announced his retirement plans in 2010, stating that he would not leave until a suitable replacement was found.[68] Because replacements are difficult to find, he is still at his post.

James N. Young, Chief Financial Executive, Ally Bank.

Young has over 30 years of banking industry experience. This includes 23 years with KPMG LLP where he eventually became the partner responsible for the Chicago banking practice and Midwest area banking practice development.[69] In 2005, he was hired by Residential Capital, LLC (ResCap) to oversee its mortgage operation. At the time, ResCap was a subsidiary of GMAC Bank, responsible for mortgage and home loans.

He became part of GMAC Bank in 2008 when the company was spun off from General Motors.

Diane Morais, Deposits and Line of Business Integration Executive.

With over 25 years of banking experience and stints at CitiGroup and Bank of America, Morais became part of the top management team with the creation of Ally Bank.[70] She took responsibility for her current position in June 2011.[71] Her primary responsibilities include obtaining new depositors and keeping existing ones. Her main tools for doing this include product mix, pricing optimization, and customer feedback.[72]

In April 2012, Ally Bank lost a key leader when Vinoo Vijay, formerly Global Brand and Product Marketing Executive, accepted a similar position at TD Bank.[73] Vijay had been the driving force behind Ally Bank's rebranding effort and marketing campaign since 2008. He focused the company on the motto of "building a better bank" and positioned the company as an alternative to conventional banking.[74]

A bank that claims to be your "ally" needs employees that provide above average service. Ally Bank believes that proof that the company has developed an above average staff is shown by the customer service awards it has received. For example, Ally Bank's customer focus has won it awards for customer service such as the Forrester "Groundswell Award"[75] for its innovative use of social media to connect with customers as well as the Netbanker[76] "2011 Best of the Web" award for customer service experience. However, the results are mixed if commentary and feedback from the user community on customer satisfaction is included from sites such as MyBankTracker.com where Ally Bank received only 3 out of 5 stars for customer service.[77] What do these mixed results say about the actual level of quality and innovation associated with Ally Bank's customer service?

Financials Statements

Financial Results—Ally Financial Inc.

Although the history of GMAC can be traced to 1919, the financial results of Ally Financial Inc. can only be traced to 2008 (see Exhibit 6). The company has shown mixed results over the past few years (2009–2011), with a net loss of $10,298 million in 2009, a net gain of $1,057 million in 2010, and another net loss of $157 million in 2011. In general, the company's financial performance has been negatively affected by ResCap's exposure to the subprime market. Indeed, its total exposure to the subprime market has forced it to consider either selling the troubled subsidiary or allowing it to declare bankruptcy.[78]

Exhibit 6 Financial Statements for Ally Financial Inc.

Standardized Annual Balance Sheet			
Report Date	12/31/2011	12/31/2010	12/31/2009
Currency	USD	USD	USD
Audit Status	Not Qualified	Not Qualified	Not Qualified
Consolidated	Yes	Yes	Yes
Scale	Millions	Millions	Millions
Cash & Equivalents	13,035	11,670	14,788
Cash & Equivs & ST Investments	13,035	11,670	14,788
Receivables (ST)	663	882	1,172
Other Current Assets	5,905	4,215	3,000
Total Current Assets	19,603	16,767	18,960
Gross Property Plant & Equip	1,152	1,315	1,416
Accumulated Depreciation	787	939	1,080
Net Property Plant & Equip	365	376	336
Receivables (LT)	1,342	879	899
Assets Held for Sale (LT)	1,070	690	6,584
Long Term Investments	16,637	16,256	14,474
Intangible Assets	3,037	4,263	4,080
Deferred LT Assets	972	1,050	1,202
Other Assets	141,033	131,727	125,771
Total Assets	184,059	172,008	172,306
Accounts Payable & Accrued Exps	3,414	3,687	3,315
Accounts Payable	1,178	1,267	1,275
Accrued Expenses	2,236	2,420	2,040
Current Debt	7,680	7,508	10,292
Other Current Liabilities	51,193	43,465	34,657
Total Current Liabilities	62,287	54,660	48,264
LT Debt & Leases	92,794	86,612	88,021
Deferred LT Liabilities	2,687	3,501	4,250
Other Liabilities	6,920	6,746	10,932
Total Liabilities	164,688	151,519	151,467
Preferred Share Capital	6,940	6,972	12,180
Retained Earnings	(7,324)	(6,410)	(5,630)
Accum Other Comprehensive Income	87	259	460
Other Equity	19,668	19,668	13,829
Total Equity	19,371	20,489	20,839
Total Liabilities & Equity	184,059	172,008	172,306

Exhibit 6 Financial Statements for Ally Financial Inc.

Standardized Annual Income Statement			
Report Date	12/31/2011	12/31/2010	12/31/2009
Currency	USD	USD	USD
Audit Status	Not Qualified	Not Qualified	Not Qualified
Consolidated	Yes	Yes	Yes
Scale	Millions	Millions	Millions
Sales Revenue	2,251	3,035	2,140
Affiliates Revenue	86	56	17
Other Revenue	10,436	13,090	14,915
Total Revenue	13,332	16,768	17,517
Direct Costs	7,480	9,308	16,626
Gross Profit	5,852	7,460	891
Selling General & Admin	4,090	4,381	4,956
Depreciation & Amortization	97	92	85
Restruct Remediation & Impair	51	80	63
Other Operating Expense	1,547	1,728	2,746
Total Indirect Operating Costs	5,785	6,281	7,850
Operating Income	67	1,179	(6,959)
Earnings Before Tax	67	1,179	(6,959)
Taxation	179	153	74
Discontinued Operations	(45)	49	(3,265)
Net Income	(157)	1,075	(10,298)

As the majority stakeholder in the bank, the US government is concerned that Ally Financial is undercapitalized. In February 2012, the US Central Bank conducted a stress test of the 19 largest banks in the Unites States to determine whether they could withstand another economic downturn. Ally Bank was one of four banks that failed the test. The test claimed that the company needed to raise an additional $11.5 billion in capital to withstand any future shocks to the economy.[79]

Ally Bank Results

Taken alone, Ally Bank does not face the same problems and potentially the same strategic challenges as its parent company. In 2011, total assets at the bank increased from $70 billion to $85 billion, an increase of 21 percent while net income rose from $900 million to $1.2 billion, an increase of 35 percent (see Exhibit 7). Since the rebranding effort of 2009, Ally Bank has managed to increase total deposits

Exhibit 6   Financial Statements for Ally Financial Inc.

Standardized Annual Cash Flows			
Report Date	12/31/2011	12/31/2010	12/31/2009
Currency	USD	USD	USD
Audit Status	Not Qualified	Not Qualified	Not Qualified
Consolidated	Yes	Yes	Yes
Scale	Millions	Millions	Millions
Net Income	(157)	1,075	(10,298)
Adjustments from Inc to Cash	4,804	10,470	3,927
Change in Working Capital	300	602	2,653
Other Operating Cash Flows	546	(540)	(1,414)
Cash Flow from Operations	5,493	11,607	(5,132)
Purchase of Investments	(19,377)	(24,116)	(21,148)
Disposal of Investments	19,197	22,399	14,680
Change in Business Activities	50	161	296
Other Investing Cash Flows	(13,998)	(6,011)	23,300
Cash Flow from Investing	(14,128)	(7,567)	17,128
Change in ST Debt	514	(3,629)	(338)
Change in LT Debt	4,281	(10,528)	(30,814)
Change in Equity	–	–	9,997
Payment of Dividends	(819)	(1,253)	(1,592)
Other Financing Cash Flows	6,074	7,425	11,767
Cash Flow from Financing	10,050	(7,985)	(10,980)
Effect of Exchange Rate	49	102	(602)
Change in Cash	1,464	(3,843)	414
Opening Cash	11,670	14,788	15,151
Closing Cash	13,035	11,670	14,788
Depn & Amortn (CF)	2,713	4,972	6,100

Source: Mergent (2012). *Ally Financial Inc. Company Report*. Retrieved from Mergent Online database

each year. In 2011 alone, it grew deposits by $5.9 billion, representing a 27 percent increase for the year.[80]

   In comparison to competitors, its results are impressive. Recall that Ally Bank only has two offices. If total deposits are compared by number of branches, then Ally Bank has

Exhibit 7   Ally Bank Balance Sheet and Income Statement

Ally Bank 6985 Union Park Ctr Suite 43 Midvale, UT 84047 FDIC Ceritificate #: 57803 Bank Charter Class: NM			
Defi-nition	Dollar figures in thousands	Ally Bank Midvale, UT 31-Dec-11	Ally Bank Midvale, UT 31-Dec-10
All Summary Information			
Assets and Liabilities			
1	Total employees (full-time equivalent)	1,033	718
2	**Total Assets**	**85,331,885**	**70,284,088**
3	Cash and due from depository institutions	3,647,173	3,065,704
4	Interest-bearing balances	3,594,957	3,003,140
5	Securities	9,443,480	7,668,076
6	Federal funds sold & reverse repurchase agreements	0	0
7	Net loans & leases	65,288,616	54,419,637
8	Loan loss allowance	722,389	786,438
9	Trading account assets	0	0
10	Bank premises and fixed assets	17	39
11	Other real estate owned	8,269	7,212
12	Goodwill and other intangibles	1,286,061	1,746,222
13	All other assets	5,658,269	3,377,198
14	**Total Liabilities and Capital**	85,331,886	70,284,087
15	**Total Liabilities**	**72,270,458**	**59,397,907**
16	Total deposits	41,264,280	34,652,206
17	Interest-bearing deposits	39,206,078	32,522,081
18	Deposits held in domestic offices	41,264,280	34,652,206
19	% insured	93.01%	95.21%
20	Federal funds purchased & repurchase agreements	0	0
21	Trading liabilities	0	0
22	Other borrowed funds	30,454,692	23,850,518
23	Subordinated debt	0	0
24	All other liabilities	551,486	895,183
25	**Total Equity Capital**	**13,061,428**	**10,886,180**

Source: www2.fdic.gov

Exhibit 7 Ally Bank Balance Sheet and Income Statement

	Ally Bank 6985 Union Park Ctr Suite 43 Midvale, UT 84047 FDIC Ceritificate #: 57803 Bank Charter Class: NM			
Defi-nition	Dollar figures in thousands	Ally Bank	Ally Bank
		Midvale, UT	Midvale, UT
		31-Dec-11	31-Dec-10
Income and Expense		(year-to-date)	(year-to-date)
1	Number of institutions reporting	1	1
2	Total interest income	3,148,994	2,572,966
3	Total interest expense	1,049,489	951,166
4	Net interest income	2,099,505	1,621,800
5	Provision for loan and lease losses	182,007	336,002
6	Total noninterest income	676,836	441,042
7	Fiduciary activities	0	0
8	Service charges on deposit accounts	168	223
9	Trading account gains & fees	0	0
10	Additional noninterest income	676,668	440,819
11	Total noninterest expense	1,357,349	906,381
12	Salaries and employee benefits	114,023	74,638
13	Premises and equipment expense	599	673
14	Additional noninterest expense	1,242,727	831,070
15	Pre-tax net operating income	1,236,985	820,459
16	Securities gains (losses)	40,989	109,319
17	Applicable income taxes	56,019	27,401
18	Income before extraordinary items	1,221,955	902,377
19	Extraordinary gains - net	0	0
20	**Net income attributable to bank**	1,221,955	902,377

Source: www2.fdic.gov

$19 billion in assets for each branch. In comparison, Bank of America has almost 6,000 branches and a trillion in deposits, but only $182 million per branch (see Exhibit 8).[81]

In addition, deposits have been growing at Ally Bank each year for the past three years (2009-2011), from $25 billion in 2009 to $38 billion in 2011. In comparison to its competitors, Ally Bank is showing 20 percent growth each year while ING averages only 4.5 percent and USAA is steady (see Exhibit 9).

The increase in bank deposits may be for a number of reasons. First, it could reflect that people trust Ally Bank and believe it is providing above average banking service. Or, it could indicate that it is providing above average rates on deposit accounts such as savings, CDs, and money market funds. Last, it could represent that people are becoming increasingly comfortable with trusting their money in cyberspace.

Current Investors

With the freezing of the global credit markets, GMAC Bank was in trouble. It was severely exposed to the sub-prime meltdown through its subsidiary, ResCap and needed to convert into a bank holding company to be eligible to receive Federal bailout funds.[82] In turn, GMAC's financial position was causing problems for the auto industry. In late 2008, the company "raised the credit requirements for car loans so high at the time as virtually eliminating leasing, that they have been responsible for a sizable chunk of lost sales at GM due to customers' inability to secure financing."[83] This result saw the US government become involved and, in an end-of-the-year deal, the government accepted GMAC's petition to become a holding company and provided $5 billion in capital.[84] Since that time, the US government has had to increase its stake in the company to 73.8 percent.

Having the government as a majority shareholder has been difficult. In 2009, Ally Bank was offering the highest interest rate in the nation on depository accounts. This attracted depositors and the bank received over $20 billion in new money assets. However, competitors complained, stating that Ally Bank was using free government funds to pass savings to its depositors.[85] After receiving a large number of complaints, the government stepped in and disallowed Ally Bank's above average rates.[86] Other government intervention included salary freezes for top managers.[87]

Challenges—What to Do Next?

Ally Bank and its leaders are facing a difficult and challenging road. Even though Ally Bank has experienced remarkable increases in its retail deposits,[88] it must still work to shed its image of being the product of a government bailout. The barrage of advertising through commercials, print, and other distribution channels has helped Ally Bank establish its brand name

Exhibit 8 Deposits/Branch Offices

Bank Holding Company	# Offices	# Employees	Total Deposits	$ per Branch	$ per Employee
Bank of America Corp.	5,856	179,598	$1,066,655,151.00	$182,147.00	$5,939.
Wells Fargo & Co.	6,386	224,477	793,617,901.00	124,275.00	3,535.
JPMorgan Chase & Co.	5,437	205,849	768,955,618.00	141,430.00	3,736.
Citigroup Inc.	1,064	193,044	320,158,438.00	300,901.00	1,658.
US Bancorp	3,139	62,529	198,455,053.00	63,222.00	3,173.
Ally Bank	2	1,751	38,461,259.00	19,230,630.00	21,965.

Source: Top 50 Bank Holding Companies by Total Domestic Deposits. *FDIC Summary of Deposits*. Accessed 24 Apr 2012 at http://www2.fdic.gov/sod/sodSumReport.asp?barItem=3&sInfoAsOf=2011.

Exhibit 9 Percentage Change in Total Deposits

Bank Name	Total Deposits, in Thousands			Percentage Change	
	2011	2010	2009	2011	2010
Ally Bank	$38,461,259.00	$31,887,653.00	$25,422,496.00	20.6%	25.4%
ING Direct	82,106,986.00	77,431,828.00	74,837,532.00	6.0%	3.5%
USAA	43,839,346.00	37,296,300.00	31,820,600.00	17.5%	17.2%
Charles Schwab	50,239,169.00	43,875,975.00	31,172,608.00	14.5%	40.8%

Source: Top 50 Bank Holding Companies by Total Domestic Deposits. *FDIC Summary of Deposits*. Accessed 24 Apr 2012 at http://www2.fdic.gov/sod/sodSumReport.asp?barItem=3&sInfoAsOf=2011.

effectively. Indeed, eighteen months after unveiling the new brand, Ally Bank reported that "40 percent of the financial institution's target audience is familiar with the brand, 29 percent say they know something about the brand, while another 27 percent report having a fair—to significant amount of knowledge about the bank."[89] Subsequently, Ally's Chief Marketing Officer added, "We've been thrilled not only with the way the brand has taken traction but also the attributes that the brand stands for."[90]

However, despite the positive reactions to the new brand, there are still those who complain about the US government's involvement with Ally Bank; additionally, because of the government's involvement, some believe that the bank is truly operating on borrowed funds. Extending the nature of this viewpoint and complaint a bit farther, there are those who suggest that all U.S. taxpayers are "involuntary investors" in the company and that as a result, Ally Bank's advertising messages are ripe with hypocrisy.[91] These realities seem to highlight the importance of Ally Bank finding effective ways to continue focusing on building its brand and giving

customers a reason to look beyond its origins and focus instead on the great customer service. But how does the bank do this? What resources and capabilities are needed to form core competencies that will result in Ally Bank being able to better serve customers as a foundation for outperforming rivals?

Ally Bank must also be prepared to deal with the uncertainty surrounding its struggling parent company, Ally Financial. The company still owes the US Treasury Department money and in turn, the Treasury is starting to put on the pressure. An IPO was suggested, but too many factors are working against Ally. For example, the Federal Reserve stress test discussed earlier "found Ally had some of the smallest capital cushions against losses among 19 of the largest US lenders."[92] In addition, ResCap, Ally's mortgage subsidiary, is nearing bankruptcy and just recently missed a $20 million bond payment.[93]

Since an IPO appears to be out of the picture, the two other alternatives suggested by the Treasury are to split Ally Financial into its two major operations; auto finance and online deposits (Ally Bank) or sell the whole company outright.[94] Going forward, Ally Bank's leaders must remain flexible and adaptive to whatever changes await the company. With little turnover at the top level, Ally Bank will be better prepared to deal with any adversity; however, it will be difficult to keep its top leaders on board and, should it become necessary, attract new talent, with its parent company struggling. In the interim, Ally Bank must keep its customers satisfied and instill confidence lest customers begin to lose faith in the company and take their deposits elsewhere. And all of these actions must be taken during a time period when uncertainty in the external environment remains the reality. What effects can Ally Bank anticipate from conditions in its external environment? And what about competitors? What actions might competitors take in efforts to strengthen their position relative to Ally Bank's position in the competitive arenas in which it has chosen to compete?

NOTES

1. Henery, J. (2 Jan 2009) GMAC Didn't Need Bank Status, After All. *CBSNews/CBS Interactive*. Accessed 22 Apr 2012 at http://www.cbsnews.com/8301-505123_162-42940334/gmac-didnt-need-bank-status-after-all/.

2. Our History. *Ally.com*. Accessed 20 Apr 2012 at http://www.ally.com/about/company-structure/history/index.html.

3. Interest Checking Account: Overview. *Ally.com*. Accessed 20 Apr 2012 at http://www.ally.com/bank/interest-checking-account/.

4. Banking with Ally: Overview. *Ally.com*. Accessed 20 Apr 2012 at http://www.ally.com/bank/online-banking/.

5. Interest Checking Account: Overview. *op. cit.*

6. Savings & CDs. *Ally.com*. Accessed 20 Apr 2012 at http://www.ally.com/bank/savings/.

7. IRA Raise Your Rate Certificate of Deposit (CD): Overview. *Ally.com*. Accessed 20 Apr 2012 at http://www.ally.com/bank/ira/raise-your-rate-cd/?INTCMPID=iraMenuPage_RYRCD_Nav.

8. Sahadi, J. (19 Dec 2011). Business Tax Breaks: Fate Uncertain. *CNNMoney*. Accessed 17 Apr 2012 at http://money.cnn.com/2011/12/19/news/economy/business_tax_breaks/index.htm.

9. Casselman, B and Lahart, J. (17 Sept 2011). Companies Shun Investment, Hoard Cash. *WSJ.com*. Accessed 17 Apr 2012 at http://online.wsj.com/article/SB10001424053111903927204576574720017009568.html.

10. Bureau of Labor Statistics: Databases, Tables & Calculators by Subject. *Bureau of Labor Statistics Data*. Accessed 17 Apr 2012 at http://data.bls.gov/timeseries/LNS14000000.

11. Pear, R. (9 Oct 2011) Recession Officially Over, U.S. Incomes Kept Falling. *Nytimes.com*. Accessed 17 Apr 2012 at http://www.nytimes.com/2011/10/10/us/recession-officially-over-us-incomes-kept-falling.html.

12. FDIC: Failed Bank List. *FDIC: Failed Bank List*. Accessed 17 Apr 2012 at http://www.fdic.gov/bank/individual/failed/banklist.html.

13. Bailout Recipients. (3 Apr 2012) *Propulica.org*. Accessed 17 Apr 2012 at http://projects.propublica.org/bailout/list.

14. Press Room: ABA Survey: Popularity of Online Banking Explodes. (8 Sep 2011) *Aba.com*. Accessed 15 Apr 2012 at http://www.aba.com/Press+Room/090811ConsumerPreferencesSurvey.htm.

15. Sanibel, M. (14 Apr 2011). The Pros and Cons of Internet Banks. *Investopedia*. Accessed 15 Apr 2012 at http://www.investopedia.com/articles/pf/11/benefits-and-drawbacks-of-internet-banks.asp.

16. Marquit, M. How Banks Make Money. *Depositaccounts.com*. Accessed 18 Apr 2012 at http://www.depositaccounts.com/blog/how-banks-make-money.html.

17. FDIC Key Statistics. (12 Apr 2012). *FDIC.gov*. Accessed 18 Apr 2012 at http://www2.fdic.gov/IDASP/KeyStatistics.asp?tdate=4/12/2012&pDate=4/11/2012.

18. Fed Funds Rate. *Bankrate.com*. Accessed 18 Apr 2012 at http://www.bankrate.com/rates/interest-rates/federal-funds-rate.aspx.

19. Ally Financial Inc. Form 10-K for fiscal year ended December 31, 2011. *sec.gov*. Accessed 18 Apr 2012 at http://www.sec.gov/Archives/edgar/data/40729/000004072912000011/gjm2011123110k.htm.

20. Block, S. (18 Oct 2011). Some Things to Consider before Switching Your Bank. *USA Today*. Accessed 19 Apr 2012 at http://www.usatoday.com/money/perfi/columnist/block/story/2011-10-17/switching-banks/50806568/1.

21. Lieber, R. (24 Mar 2010). Switch Banks? You Might Find There's a Perk in It for You. *Nytimes.com*. Accessed 18 Apr 2012 at http://www.nytimes.com/2010/03/25/your-money/brokerage-and-bank-accounts/25BANK.html.

22. Alloway, T. (4 Mar 2012). First Year in Decades without New US Bank. *FT.com*. Accessed 17 Apr 2012 at http://www.ft.com/intl/cms/s/0/df4c2dd8-63af-11e1-b85b-00144feabdc0.html#axzz1sM0SXKO6.

23. Products & Services. *Ally.com*. Accessed 18 Apr 2012 at http://www.ally.com/about/products-services/.

24. Competition for Banking Customers Intensifies Among Top U.S. Online Banks. (22 Jan 2009). *ComScore, Inc*. Accessed 19 Apr 2012 at http://www.comscore.com/Press_Events/Press_Releases/2009/1/Online_Banking_Competition.

25. Hyde, P., Jain, A., Girolami, S. and Landau, B. (2010). Capturing Growth in U.S. Retail Banking Building a Sustainable Right to Win. *Booz.com*. Accessed 19 Apr 2012 at http://www.booz.com/media/uploads/Capturing_Growth_in_US_Retail_Banking.pdf.

26. Who We Are—ING DIRECT Overview. *ING DIRECT.com*. Accessed 19 Apr 2012 at https://home.ingdirect.com/about-us.

27. Campbell, D. (15 Feb 2012). Capital One's $9 Billion Acquisition of ING Direct USA Wins Fed's Approval. *Bloomberg*. Accessed 19 Apr 2012 at http://www.bloomberg.com/news/2012-02-14/capital-one-s-9-billion-acquisition-of-ing-direct-usa-wins-fed-s-approval.html.

28. ING DIRECT. *FDIC.gov*. Accessed 19 Apr 2012 at fdic.gov.

29. Online Banking: Reviews. (Aug 2010). *Consumersearch*. Accessed 19 Apr 2012 at http://www.consumersearch.com/online-banking.

30. Find a FREE Allpoint ATM Near You. *ING DIRECT.com*. Accessed 19 Apr 2012 at https://secure.ingdirect.com/myaccount/INGDirect/atm_locate.vm.

31. ING DIRECT Cafe. *ING DIRECT.com*. Accessed 19 Apr 2012 at http://cafes.ingdirect.com/.

32. Cole, M. (24 Feb 2012). Capital One's Next Challenge: Persuade ING Direct Customers to Stay. *Adage.com*. Accessed 19 Apr 2012 at http://adage.com/article/news/capital-s-challenge-retain-ing-direct-customers/232961/.

33. Corporate Overview. *USAA.com*. Accessed 19 Apr 2012 https://www.usaa.com/inet/pages/about_usaa_corporate_overview_main.

34. Why Join USAA. *USAA.com*. Accessed 19 Apr 2012 at https://www.usaa.com/inet/pages/why_choose_usaa_main?showtab=legacyPassDown.

35. Awards and Rankings. *USAA.com*. Accessed 19 Apr 2012 at https://www.usaa.com/inet/pages/about_usaa_corporate_overview_awards_and_rankings.

36. USAA. *FDIC.gov*. Accessed 19 Apr 2012 at fdic.gov.

37. Deposit@Mobile. *USAA.com*. Accessed 19 Apr 2012 at https://www.usaa.com/inet/pages/mobile_banking_dm.

38. Charles Schwab Bank. *About Schwab*. Accessed 19 Apr 2012 at http://www.aboutschwab.com/about/overview/schwab_bank/.

39. Charles Schwab. *FDIC.gov*. Accessed 19 Apr 2012 at fdic.gov.

40. Schwab Bank High Yield Investor Checking. *Consumersearch.com*. Accessed 19 Apr 2012 at http://www.consumersearch.com/online-banking/schwab-bank-high-yield-investor-checking.

41. Checking Account FAQs. *Charles Schwab Bank*. Accessed 19 Apr 2012 at http://www.schwab.com/public/schwab/banking_lending/checking_account/checking_account_FAQs.

42. Why Bank of Internet USA. *BankofInternet.com*. Accessed 20 Apr 2012 at https://www.bankofinternet.com/bofi/about/why_bank_of_internet.aspx.

43. Bank of Internet. *FDIC.gov*. Accessed 20 Apr 2012 at fdic.gov.

44. Griffith, E. (8 Nov 2011). Five Great Internet Banks. *PCMAG*. Accessed 21 Apr 2012 at http://www.pcmag.com/article2/0,2817,2396006,00.asp.

45. Maio, P. (1 Nov 2010). BANKING: Bank of Internet finds growth in borrowers with mansions and apartments. *North County Times*. Accessed 21 Apr 2012 at http://www.nctimes.com/business/6c1c9b68-76a6-5a30-820a-a01a40e6c7a1.html.

46. Maio, P. (12 Aug 2011). BANKING: Bank of Internet USA sees profit rise 18 percent in 4Q. *North County Times*. Accessed 21 Apr 2012 at http://www.nctimes.com/news/local/del-mar/article_3342c61d-5633-5ad1-b91e-fee096c751ea.html.

47. Ally Financial Inc. Form 10-K for fiscal year ended December 31, 2011. *op. cit.*

48. Awards & Recognitions. *Ally.com*. Accessed 23 Apr 2012 at http://media.ally.com/index.php?s=59.

49. Ally Bank Asks: Why Has Branchless Banking Become So Popular? (29 May 2011). *Ally.com*. Accessed 23 Apr 2012 at http://community.ally.com/straight-talk/2011/05/ally-bank-asks-why-has-branchless-banking-become-so-popular/.

50. FDIC Steps In to Keep Ally Bank's Interest Rates Lower. (16 Jun 2009). *Consumerism Commentary*. 25 Apr 2012 at http://www.consumerismcommentary.com/fdic-steps-in-to-keep-ally-banks-interest-rates-lower/.

51. Interest Checking Account: Overview. *op. cit.*

52. *Ibid.*

53. Online Savings Account - Overview. *Ally.com*. Accessed 23 Apr 2012 at http://www.ally.com/bank/online-savings-account?INTCMPID=344694089.

54. *Ibid.*

55. Banking with Ally - Overview. *op. cit.*

56. Ally Story - Our Commercials. *Ally.com*. Accessed 23 Apr 2012 at http://www.ally.com/about/ally-story/commercials.html.

57. Ally Story - Who We Are. *Ally.com*. Accessed 23 Apr 2012 at http://www.ally.com/about/ally-story/our-difference.html.

58. Bye Bye, GMAC: Will Ally Bank Work or Not? (15 May 2009). *WSJ.com*. Accessed 23 Apr 2012 at http://blogs.wsj.com/deals/2009/05/15/bye-bye-gmac-will-ally-bank-work-or-not/.

59. The 8 Least Evil Banks. *CNNMoney*. Accessed 23 Apr 2012 at http://money.cnn.com/galleries/2011/pf/1101/gallery.least_evil_banks/index.html.

60. Leadership. Media Center: *Ally Financial Inc*. Accessed 18 Apr 2012 at http://media.ally.com/index.php?s=20.

61. Fitzpatrick, D. and Enrich, D. (18 Nov 2009). GMAC Chief Ousted by Board. *WSJ.com*. Accessed 20 Apr 2012 at http://online.wsj.com/article/SB10001424052748704538404574540032497128084.html.

62. Corkery, M. (16 Nov 2009). The Nine Lives of GMACs New CEO Michael Carpenter. *WSJ.com*. Accessed 20 Apr 2012 at http://blogs.wsj.com/deals/2009/11/16/the-nine-lives-of-gmacs-new-ceo-michael-carpenter/.

63. GMAC Names Michael A. Carpenter Chief Executive Officer; Will Lead Next Phase Of Renewal. (16 Nov 2009). *PR Newswire*. Accessed 20 Apr 2012 at http://www.prnewswire.com/news-releases/gmac-names-michael-a-carpenter-chief-executive-officer--will-lead-next-phase-of-renewal-70219362.html.

64. GMAC's Chief Gets Payout Comparable to Blankfein's. (2 Mar 2010). DealBook - *New York Times*. Accessed 17 Apr 2012 at http://dealbook.nytimes.com/2010/03/02/gmacs-chief-gets-payout-comparable-to-blankfeins/.

65. Campbell, D. (2 Mar 2010). GMAC's Carpenter Gets Pay Package Rivaling Blankfein. *Bloomberg*. Accessed 20 Apr 2012 at http://www.bloomberg.com/apps/news?pid=newsarchive.

66. Leadership. *op. cit.*

67. GMAC Financial Services Statement on the Retirement of William Muir. (12 Apr 2010). *Ally - Media Center*. Accessed 20 Apr 2012 at http://media.ally.com/index.php?s=43.

68. William Muir to Retire from GMAC Next Year. *Autoevolution News*. Accessed 20 Apr 2012 at http://www.autoevolution.com/news/william-muir-to-retire-from-gmac-next-year-19166.htm.

69. Leadership. *op. cit.*

70. Morais, D. *Linkedin*. Accessed 18 Apr 2012 at http://www.linkedin.com/pub/diane-morais/a/768/957.

71. Leadership. *op. cit.*

72. *Ibid.*

73. TD Bank Names Vinoo Vijay Chief Marketing Officer. (12 Apr 2012). *TD Bank News Releases*. Accessed 20 Apr 2012 at https://mediaroom.tdbank.com/index.php?s=30379&item=126854.

74. Ally Executive Takes Marketing Post At TD Bank. (16 Apr 2012). *CMO.com*. Accessed 20 Apr 2012 at http://www.cmo.com/people/ally-executive-takes-marketing-post-td-bank.

75. Ally Bank Wins Award for Online Consumer Engagement. (10 Oct 2011). *PRNewswire*. Accessed 20 Apr 2012 at http://photos.prnewswire.com/prnh/20110609/DE17177LOGO-c.

76. Ally Bank Wins Best of the Web for Customer Service Innovation. (28 Apr 2011). *Ally Straight Talk*. Accessed 20 Apr 2012 at http://community.ally.com/straight-talk/2011/04/ally-bank-wins-best-of-the-web-for-customer-service-innovation/.

77. Ally Bank Review. *MyBankTracker*. Accessed 20 Apr 2012 at http://www.mybanktracker.com/Ally-Bank/Reviews.

78. Campbell, D. (13 Apr 2012) Ally's ResCap Loan May Precede Bankruptcy, Fitch Says. *BloombergBusinessweek*. Accessed 20 Apr 2012 at http://www.businessweek.com/news/2012-04-13/ally-s-rescap-loan-may-precede-bankruptcy-fitch-says.

79. GMAC (now Ally Financial). *ProPublica*. Accessed 21 Apr 2012 at http://projects.propublica.org/bailout/entities/236-gmac.

80. Staley, W. (2 Apr 2012). Ally Q4 Earnings: Deposits Grow Amid Mortgage Woes. *MyBankTracker.com*. Accessed 20 Apr 2012 at http://www.mybanktracker.com/bank-news/2012/02/03/ally-q4-earnings-strong-deposit-grow-amid-mortgage-woes/.

81. Top 50 Bank Holding Companies by Total Domestic Deposits. *FDIC Summary of Deposits*. Accessed 24 Apr 2012 at http://www2.fdic.gov/sod/sodSumReport.asp?barItem=3&sInfoAsOf=2011.

82. Snow, D. (17 Dec 2008). Cerberus Indirectly Linked to Madoff Scandal. *Private Equity International*. Accessed 20 Apr 2012 at http://www.privateequityonline.com/Article.aspx?article=33204.

83. Smith, T. (10 Dec 2008). Cerberus Capital Management: CHRYSLER LLC & GMAC BANKRUPTCY! *Zimbio*. Accessed 20 Apr 2012 http://www.zimbio.com/Cerberus+Capital+Management/articles/52/Cerberus+Capital+Management+CHRYSLER+LLC+GMAC.

84. GMAC Gets $5 Billion in TARP Funds. (30 Dec 2008). *Atlanta Business Chronicle*. Accessed 20 Apr 2012 http://www.bizjournals.com/atlanta/stories/2008/12/29/daily20.html.

85. Yingling, E. (27 May 2009). GMAC letter 52709. *Scribd*. Accessed 21 Apr 2012 at http://www.scribd.com/doc/16024825/GMACLetter52709.

86. Fitzpatrick, D. (2 Nov 2009). U.S. Turns Screws on Bailed-Out GMAC. *The Wall Street Journal*. Accessed 21 Apr 2012 at http://online.wsj.com/article/SB125712736353621959.html.

87. Treasury Freezes Pay for CEOs at Ally Financial, GM, AIG. (6 Apr 2012). *Yahoo! Finance*. Accessed 21 Apr 2012 at http://finance.yahoo.com/news/treasury-freezes-pay-ceos-ally-172309205.html.

88. Ally Financial Inc. Form 10-K for fiscal year ended December 31, 2011. *op. cit.*

89. If Advertising Doesn't Work, Then Why Is 'Ally' a Household Word? (12 Nov 2010). *The Financial Brand*: Marketing Insights for Banks & Credit Unions. Accessed 19 Apr 2012

at http://thefinancialbrand.com/15653/ally-bank-proves-advertising-works/.

90. Ally Bank's CMO Ignites Rebranding. (1 Jan 2011). *Direct Marketing News*. Accessed 19 Apr 2012 at http://www.dmnews.com/ally-banks-cmo-ignites-rebranding/article/193145/.

91. Ally Bank's Straight Talk Is Crooked. (17 Mar 2011). *SmartMoney*. Accessed 19 Apr 2012 at http://www.smartmoney.com/ invest/stocks/ally-banks-straight-talk-is-crooked-1300374728021/.

92. Treasury Said to Want Ally Sale With IPO Seen Unlikely. (26 Mar 2012). *Bloomberg*. Accessed 19 Apr 2012 at http://www.bloomberg.com/news/2012-03-26/treasury-said-to-want-ally-sale-with-ipo-seen-unlikely.html.

93. Ally's ResCap Misses $20M Bond Payment Due Today. (17 Apr 2012). *WSJ*. Accessed 19 Apr 2012 at http://blogs.wsj.com/deals/2012/04/17/allys-rescap-misses-20m-bond-payment-due-today/?KEYWORDS=ally+bank.

94. U.S. Treasury Said to Want Ally Financial Sale, Not IPO. (26 Mar 2012). *InvestorPlace*. Accessed 19 Apr 2012 at http://www.investorplace.com/2012/03/u-s-treasury-said-to-want-ally-financial-sale-not-ipo/.

AstraZeneca: Transforming How New Medicines Flow to Patients[1]

David Brennan had started in sales. By 2006, he was CEO of AstraZeneca UK Limited (AZN), an international biopharmaceutical firm headquartered in London. Having been on the front line with doctors, Brennan was passionate about bringing new medicines to patients. He would need that experience, because the industry was transforming to one that featured less patent protection, more competition from generic drugs, stiffer government regulations, and decreased productivity in R&D. So, from the beginning, he addressed all areas of AZN's value chain—from drug discovery to development, manufacturing, and commercial. The strategy? Build a pipeline with new prescription drugs that were unique enough to provide a differentiated benefit to patients, grow the business globally, streamline the organization and increase efficiency, and build a culture of courage, creativity, and collaboration.

This was a challenging prescription to fill but the good news was that Brennan's strategy delivered some key successes by 2012, with six new products launched, a growing business in emerging markets, an organizational restructure that had realized $1.6 billion in annual savings, and an annual employee survey (FOCUS) that showed improved employee engagement and leadership. The bad news, however, was that challenges remained with a number of key products failing to reach the market, patents expiring on a number of important medicines, and the economic environment continuing to falter. All that placed downward pressures on revenues and jeopardized the firm's ability to replenish the pipeline. The strategy meant going head to head with competitors and

beating them to market, particularly in the relatively new frontier of biopharmaceutical medicines, dealing with generic brands, and attracting and retaining the brightest in the field—at a time when sales growth was near a 25-year low.[2] And the real kicker was that even if AZN developed an average of two new products each year, less than one third of marketed drugs made it to blockbuster status.

To realize its strategic goals, the bull's-eye was squarely on AZN's R&D function to deliver. Indeed Brennan told an interviewer that the firm's R&D teams had lagged behind and he wanted "to see sustainable delivery on a consistent basis from our research and development organization, and that's why they have been set a goal."

In shareholder conferences and meetings with analysts, Brennan used phrases such as *world-class* R&D performance and *innovative-driven* biopharmaceutical business. Would the firm be able to provide a sustainable and consistent pipeline of new products—at lower cost, likely with fewer people? How might the firm average two new products to market each year? What areas of R&D should the company invest in, and what would the R&D transformation look like?

The Pharmaceutical Industry

The world pharmaceutical market in 2010 was valued at $754 billion, with established markets averaging a 3.2% growth and emerging markets 13.8% growth.[3] But after 40 years of being steady and predictable, the industry had begun a radical transformation. Heightened competition, slower pipelines, patent expirations, and loss of business to generics were just some of the threats to revenues. Drug safety issues led to bad press, which diminished consumer confidence. High prescription costs further fueled consumer resentment, along with HMOs' inclination to cover generic drugs over brand names—and patients' acceptance of substitutions. Regulators required more safety data, which meant higher costs because additional resources were needed to conduct more safety studies. And the U.S. Food and Drug Administration (FDA) and other regulatory organizations were approving fewer products (see Figure 1), which meant slower time to market.

Traditionally, the lifeblood of the pharmaceutical industry had been R&D—the most successful firms had been those that delivered the most effective medicines. Doing so required a deeply sophisticated level of knowledge about human biology and chemistry as well as an instinctive curiosity and an ability to develop hypotheses about what the causes of disease were. Bringing one medicine to market required 10 to 15 years, a multidisciplinary team of talented scientists and clinicians, and an investment of more than $1.3 billion.[4]

It was estimated that the industry spent a combined $45.7 billion on drug development in 2009.[5] Indeed, the odds against success were high, but when a newly launched compound made every pharmacy or doctor's shelf, profit margins could be significant. Companies worked on several medicines at once, using profits from existing products to fund R&D of other drugs and drug components, with no guarantee of success. "There's not necessarily been a lack of productivity from their own pipelines, but Big Pharma is lacking breakthrough drugs that can generate big margins," said biotech stock analyst Bryan Rye.[6] AstraZeneca, like its competitors, had to find ways to discover, develop, produce, and market drugs faster, for less money, while maintaining quality.

Industry Pressure

Research and Development

Essentially, developing new drugs involved identifying molecular compounds (small- or large-molecule), studying them for effectiveness (often on animals or in test tubes), observing the length of time they took to be absorbed into the human system, and detecting any side effects. This process eliminated most candidates for development. But if all went well and one candidate looked promising enough to move forward, it advanced to the human clinical trial stage. Before it could be tested on humans, however, it had to be submitted to the FDA as an investigational new drug.

A critical area of strategic interest was the cycle time for drug discovery and development: reducing the time it took to shepherd a promising new compound from exploration and discovery through clinical trails—with animal, then human trials—to determine optimal dosage and delivery method.(See Figure 2 for value chain.)

Successfully bringing a drug to market was challenging. Approximately 5% of experimental medicines that entered the development phase would actually be approved as new medicines.[7] "Increasing the success rates and reducing the time it takes to develop a medicine are critical challenges facing the entire industry," Anders Ekblom, EVP for Global Medicines Development at AZN, said.

Figure 1 Global sales, R&D expenditure, development times, and new medical entities (NME) output, 1998–2008. (in percent, indexed to 1998)

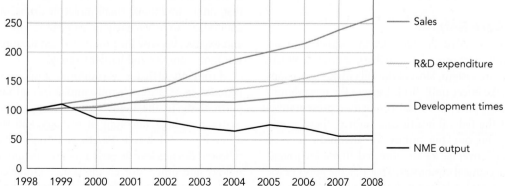

Data source: AstraZeneca.

Figure 2 Simplified Big Pharma value chain.

Discovery	Development	Commercial
Identify target	Pre-clinical	Manufacture
Identify lead compounnd	Phase I (safety)	Sales and marketing
Optimize lead	Phase II (efficacy)	Distribution
Develop track	Phase III (scale)	
	Submission and apprroval	

Data sources: AstraZeneca Q4 media presentation annual results, 2008 (used with permission); Stine Jessen Haakonsson, "The Changing Governance Structures of the Global Pharmaceutial Value Chain," Competition & Change, 13, no. 1 (2009): 85.

Patents and Generics

Typically, a company would apply for a patent on a potential medicine during the research phase. Under World Trade Organization rules, patent life for a pharmaceutical product was 20 years from the time of application. About half of the 20 years would be spent testing and developing the medicines, leaving the remaining years for the company to exclusively market the product. When the patent expired, market exclusivity ended, and any company could apply to the FDA to manufacture and sell a generic version of that product, provided it had the same ingredients, strength, and use and was manufactured to FDA standards.

The inevitability of patent expiration led drug companies to devise ways to limit competition from generics. Some attempted to "evergreen" their products by suing to preserve or extend patent life or seeking new patents on different forms of the drug compounds. In turn, generic manufacturers might then seek to invalidate them. Industry-wide, billions of dollars in sales were lost every year through patent expiration. Between 2010 and 2014, researchers estimated a cumulative loss of $142 billion in sales.[8] (AZN's Seroquel IR schizophrenia drug, set to expire in 2012, sold $4.9 billion in 2009.)

Health Care Reform

In the spring of 2010, President Obama signed into law the Patient Protection and Affordable Care Act to reform the health care system. Most of the bill's major provisions wouldn't take effect until 2014. Despite the reservations and concerns pharmaceutical company representatives had about the federal health care reform, there would eventually be one big bonus for the industry—an expansion of coverage for an estimated 30 million potential pharmaceutical customers. That was the good news.

The less attractive feature was the set of cost control measures in the federal health care plan that would likely present longer-term pricing issues for the industry. The fear was that generic drug makers' lower cost products would be preferred over brand names in any health care reform plan. Industry insiders predicted that the Act would require Big Pharma sales forces to change their direct sales focus away from detailing[9] to include more diverse customers, such as government payers, who would likely influence policymakers about prescription drugs.[10]

Shift to Biopharmaceuticals

For years, Big Pharma had focused primarily on chemical compounds, or small-molecule pharmaceuticals, as a foundation for new drug discovery. Roche Laboratories was the first to move in the biotech direction, becoming a majority stakeholder in Genentech in 1990. Biologically manufactured, or large-molecule pharmaceuticals, were derived from living cells, and therefore were more expensive to develop and manufacture than small-molecule pharmaceuticals. More significantly, they represented a different scientific field: biologics were medicines made from sugars, proteins, nucleic acids, and even cells and tissues—all extracted from natural sources, usually via recombinant DNA technology. A distinct advantage of biologics was that, unlike traditional small-molecule drugs, *monoclonal antibodies*[11] were less likely to "go generic" once their patents expired, because the process to manufacture biologics was more complex and harder to copy.

From an efficacy standpoint, biologics showed promise in treating chronic and terminal conditions, particularly in the fields of cardiology, dermatology, gastroenterology, oncology, neurology, and rheumatology. Johnson & Johnson, Wyeth, and Abbott Laboratories followed Roche's lead as early investors in antibody technology and other biotech interests.[12] Other companies created partnerships with biotech firms, but acquisition efforts were a new development.

The U.S. health care reform law granted new biotech drugs 12 years of patent-protected market exclusivity.[13] Industry-wide, the pharmaceutical industry derived close to 20% of revenues from biologics.[14] One analyst estimated that, by 2014, nearly half of the top 100 sellers, commonly referred to as "blockbuster" drugs, would be biotech products.[15] Indeed, researchers at S&P estimated that, in 2010, biologics made up about one third of new compounds in the pipeline.[16]

Competition

Global competition made rivalry within the industry intense and never far from anyone's radar screen at the firm. Among AZN's key competitors were GlaxoSmithKline (GSK), Merck & Co (MRK), and Novartis (NVS). (See Exhibit 1 for gross margin, ratio, and SWOT analysis.) Each firm competed in a number of countries and across select therapeutic areas simultaneously with AZN. (See Exhibit 2 for R&D spending and pipeline reports.) Data showed that some firms were responding to the pressures through diversifying, pursuing scale, or innovating. (See Figure 3 for AZN's review of its strategic groups.)

Given the challenges facing the industry, AZN instituted an in-depth strategic review to examine key drivers in the present and in the future. The key health care trends were reviewed together with the opportunities for the industry out to 2020.

AstraZeneca: From A to Z

With 2010 sales of more than $33 billion and income before taxes of almost $11 billion, AZN ranked among the world's leading Big Pharmaceutical companies. (See Exhibit 3 for financials.) The firm specialized in the areas of cardiovascular, gastrointestinal, inflammation and respiratory, oncology, neuroscience and infection medicine. "In the mid 90s AZN had many new blockbuster drugs," Simon King, VP for R&D human resources, said. Its best known products were Arimidex (cancer), Crestor (cardiovascular), Nexium (gastrointestinal disease), Seroquel (schizophrenia and bipolar disorder), and Symbicort (asthma and chronic obstructive pulmonary disease). In 2010, the company had 10 blockbuster medicines with sales of more than $1 billion each and operated in over 100 countries. AZN had worldwide R&D capacity, with centres in the United States, Canada, United kingdom, Sweden, France, Japan, China, and India, representing more than 12,500 employees (see Figure 4).

Exhibit 1 Gross Margin 2010, DuPont Financial Ratio Analysis, and SWOT Analysis

Gross Margin Percentage 2010			DuPont Financial Ratio Analysis			
Company	Percent	ROS %	Asset Turnover	ROA %	Financial Leverage %	ROE %
Astra-Zeneca	82.68	22.7	0.65	14.8	27.5	41.1
Glaxo-SmithKline	74.91	19	0.73	14.1	56.5	64.4
Merck	76.50	47	0.39	16.2	18.6	33.2
Novartis	72.85	19	0.52	9.7	12.3	15.6
Industry	73.57					

Data sources: Yahoo! Finance, Standard & Poor's, and Fool.com.

SWOT Analysis			
AZN		MRK	
Strengths	Weaknesses	Strengths	Weaknesses
Widespread geographic presence	Limited investor confidence	Widespread geographic presence	Vioxx-product liability lawsuits
Diversified product portfolio	Legal proceedings	Diversified product portfolio	Limited investor confidence
Opportunities	Threats	Opportunities	Threats
Strategic agreements and collaboration	Stringent government regulations	Agreements and collaborations	Loss of patent protection
Robust product pipeline	Uncertain R&D outcomes	Strategic acquisitions	Competitive environment
GSK		NVS	
Strengths	Weaknesses	Strengths	Weaknesses
Global manufacturing and supply network	Limited investor confidence	Strong financial performance	Limited liquidity position
Focused R&D capabilities	Patient infringement claims	Expanding operating margin	Legal proceedings
Opportunities	Threats	Opportunities	Threats
Target indications-market potential	Uncertain R&D outcomes	Changing demographics	Interruptions in raw material supply
Market potential-oncology	Increase in prevalence of counterfeit drugs	Emerging markets	Consolidation among US distributors

Data sources: Global Data Financial and Strategic Analysis Reviews, August–September 2010.

Exhibit 2 R&D Spending 2010 (in millions of dollars) (AstraZeneca, GlaxoSmithKline, Merck, Novartis)

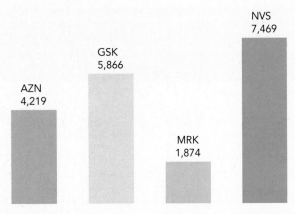

Data source: MedTrack Industry Statistics, http://www.medtrack.com/research/Istats.asp.

Pipeline Report 2010 (Number of Products)				
	AZN	**GSK**	**MRK**	**NVS**
Unknown/Research	25	26	19	16
Pre-Clinical	23	32	28	14
CT Phase I	61	77	71	33
CT Phase II	100	148	100	125
CT Phase III	18	67	37	60
Pending Approval	8	10	19	14
Approved	2	7	–	5
On the Market	110	604	318	411
Discontinued	353	536	334	319
Failed	4	18	6	11

Data sources: Life Science Analytics Pipeline Reports, May thru September 2010.

Formulating Strategy

While AZN executives considered different strategic options that included diversifying into consumer health, medical products and the like, in the end, their decisions came back to few industry facts. There were unmet medical needs and a healthy Big pharma market—they concluded that staying in it was best. "Our corporate strategy is to be an innovation-driven biopharmaceutical business," Brennan said, "that delivers on our purpose of making the most meaningful difference to patient health through great medicines." (See Figure 6). The conclusion reached from the in-depth strategic review was that there continued to be a demand for differentiated medicines to address unmet

Exhibit 3 Income Statement (in millions of dollars)

	2007	**2008**	**2009**	**2010**
Net Sales	29,559	31,601	32,804	33,269
Cost of Goods Sold	6,419	6,598	5,775	6,389
Gross Profits	23,140	25,003	27,029	26,880
Selling, General and Admin	10,134	10,894	11,227	10,376
Research & Development	5,089	5,013	4,341	4,219
Depreciation/Amortization	0	84	79	59
Interest Expense (Income) Net Operating	–	–	–	–
Unusual Expense (Income)	543	578	557	1,561
Other Operating Expenses, Total	(528)	(592)	(502)	(829)
Operating Expenses	21,465	22,457	21,261	21,775
Net Income from Operations	8,094	9,144	11,543	11,494
Interest Expense	–	–	–	–
Income Before Taxes	7,983	8,681	10,807	10,977
Income Taxes	2,388	2,580	3,286	2,924
Net Income	5,595	6,101	7,521	8,053

Data source: Google Finance.

medical needs and that AZN should continue to be a globally integrated, innovation–driven biopharmaceutical company rather than to diversify.

In its decision to focus on R&D innovation, the leadership team fit the corporate strategy to the firm capabilities. They recognized the risks of concentration and fully acknowledged that some competitors were taking a more diversified tack but decided that risks could be mitigated through external partnerships and acquisitions. AZN embraced three strategies: partner with others to co-develop compounds, acquire the compound during exploration phase through an acquisition, or buy the whole company.

To that end AstraZeneca had already spent $1.1 billion to purchase Cambridge Antibody Technology (CAT), a company in which it had previously held a 19.2% interest, in 2006. One year later, AstraZeneca

Exhibit 3 Continued Shareholder's Equity; Long-Term
(in millions of dollars)

	2007	2008	2009	2010
Assets				
Cash	5,867	4,286	9,918	11,068
Net Receivables	8,224	9,161	1 0,584	9,961
Inventory	2,119	1,636	1,750	1,682
Other Current Assets	786	786	1,508	2,420
Current Assets	16,996	15,869	23,760	25,131
Property, Plant & Equipment, net	16,835	14,614	15,168	15,583
Accumulated Depreciation	(8,537)	(7,571)	(7,861)	(8,626)
Goodwill	9,884	9,874	9,889	9,871
Long Term Investments	182	156	184	211
Intangible Assets	11,467	12,323	12,226	12,158
Deferred Long Term Asset Charges	1,161	1,685	1,554	1,799
Total Assets	47,988	46,950	54,920	56,127
Total Liabilities				
Accounts Payable	1,983	1,940	2,316	2,257
Accrued Expenses	2,606	2,249	2,715	2,620
Note Payable/ Short Term Debt	4,280	993	1,926	125
Other Current Liabilities	6,349	8,233	10,683	11,785
Current Liabilities	15,218	13,415	17,640	16,787
Long Term Debt	10,876	10,855	9,137	9,097
Total Debt	15,156	11,848	11,063	9,222
Deferred Income Tax	4,119	3,126	3,247	3,145
Minority Interest	137	148	161	197
Other Liabilities	2,860	3,494	4,075	3,688
Total Liabilities	33,210	31,038	3 4,260	32,914
Shareholder's Equity				
Common Stock	364	362	363	352
Retained Earnings	12,526	13,504	18,117	20,189
Additional Paid-In Capital	1,888	2,046	2,180	2,672
Shareholder's Equity	14,778	15,912	20,660	23,213

Exhibit 3 Continued AstraZeneca Cash Flows
(in millions of dollars)

	2007	2008	2009	2010
Net Income	7,983	8,681	10,807	10,977
Operating Activities, Cash Flows Provided By or Used In Depreciation	1,856	2,620	2,087	2,741
Non-Cash Items	1,012	550	536	54
Changes in Working Capital	(3,341)	(3,109)	(1,691)	(3,092)
Total Cash Flow From Operating Activities	7,510	8,742	11,739	10,680
Investing Activities, Cash Flows Provided By or Used In Capital Expenditures	(1,679)	(4,039)	(1,586)	(2,181)
Other Cash Flows From Investing Activities	(13,208)	(143)	(890)	(159)
Total Cash Flow From Investing Activities	(14,887)	(3,896)	(2,476)	(2,340)
Financing Activities, Cash Flows Provided By or Used In Dividends Paid	(2,641)	(2,739)	(2,977)	(3,361)
Issuance (Retirement) of Stock	(3,952)	(451)	135	(2,110)
Issuance (Retirement) of Debt	12,644	(3,172)	(787)	(1,749)
Total Cash Flows From Financing Activities	6,051	(6,362)	(3,629)	(7,220)
Effect of Exchange Rate Changes	64	(88)	71	33
Change in Cash and Cash Equivalents	(1,262)	(1,604)	5,705	1,153

Data source: Google Finance.

Figure 3 AZN straregy amoung competitors.

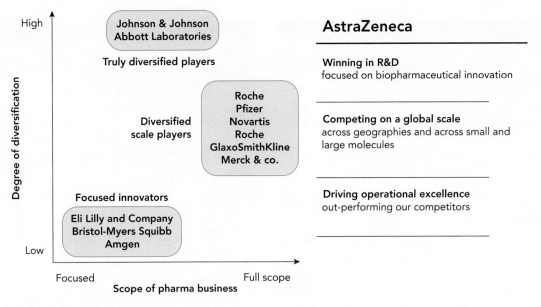

Source: Adapted from AstraZeneca. Used with permission.

Figure 4 AZN employees by geographical area.

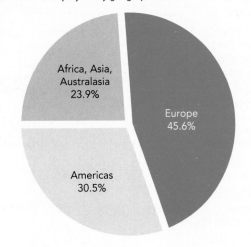

Data source: AstraZeneca 20–F, April 28, 2011.

Figure 6 Corporate strategy.

AstraZeneca

is an **innovation-driven**, integrated biopharmaceutical business that delivers on our purpose of "making the most **meaningful difference** to patient health through **great medicines**"

Source: AstraZeneca. Used with permission.

bought MedImmune, among the largest fully integrated biotech companies in the world, for $15.6 billion. The two subsidiaries were united under the MedImmune name. With those purchases, AstraZeneca staked a significant portion of its future growth on biologics, anticipating that they would constitute 25% of product development in the future. That goal was in keeping with predictions that, industry-wide, large molecule pharmaceutical products would comprise the bulk of sales growth by the end of the decade. "We now have one of the world's largest biologics pipelines," Brennan said in

January 2008, "and we have established AstraZeneca as a leader in biotechnology among our Big Pharmaceutical peers. The feedback we received is that [people have been] impressed by the quality of the people, the depth and breadth of the technology platforms, and the pipeline of more than 100 projects."[17]

Implementing the Strategy: Transforming R&D

When asked what it would take to serve AZN shareholders effectively, Brennan replied:

I would say research and development…We have to discover and develop drugs and figure out a way to get them to market effectively and appropriately. Everything else is

just hanging on for dear life…Winning will require a steep change in our R&D performance.[18]

He challenged his organization to deliver, on average, two new valuable medicines per year to the market. Doing so would require that the firm transform its R&D organization to deliver world class performance.

In 2010, a new R&D strategy was launched with four key pillars. First, the company had to invest in building industry-leading capabilities in emerging science. Second, it had to embed a culture of courageous leadership, innovation, and collaboration. Third, it had to establish a more effective, efficient, and flexible operating model for R&D. And fourth, it had to rationalize the product line to create a more focused portfolio where AZN could "play to win" in the most attractive disease areas.

Industry-Leading Capabilities

The executive team began by looking externally for a model or framework that other companies had used to benchmark capabilities needed in R&D. "What we found was it didn't exist," King said. "So we did a piece of work where we identified 21 capabilities that we believe you need to run a successful R&D function." Among that list of 21, the group identified four key capabilities that needed to improve—and really needed to be world-class—to differentiate AZN in the industry (Figure 7).

The first was *predictive science*, examining how data and knowledge from previous research might help

scientists design and run the next stage, throughout the whole R&D process. Seven different groups of scientists and experts had looked at different capabilities such as DMPK (drug metabolism and pharmacokinetics) to model what might happen to a compound or drug when a trial reached the human testing phase. Groups of experts were brought together to build tools (statistical models) to share very complex information, which was then shared upstream and downstream and *across* different phase groups.

The second capability was *personalized health care*, the use of diagnostic tests such as blood tests to indicate whether a product would work for a given patient. There were diseases, such as lung cancer, for which a particular drug will work in some patients but not others. Understanding biomarkers in patients indicating particular diseases allows identification of those who would respond to specific medicines more effectively (i.e., this medicine would benefit patients with this specific protein in their blood). World-renowned experts in diagnostics were recruited, and a team of 100 people was formed to drill deeper into patient subsets, refine the process, and develop systems to enable information sharing throughout.

The third capability was *clinical trial design*, running clinical trials to test as effectively as possible whether the compound worked and was safe. If a candidate drug progressed through pre-clinical and Phase I testing, it could move to Phase II (about 10 to 200 patients), and if

Figure 7 Example of grid used to analyze the key R&D capabilities.

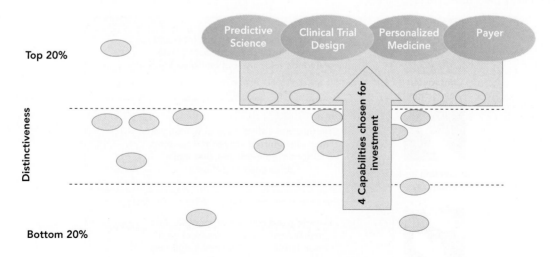

Source: Adapted from AstraZeneca. Used with permission.

it worked there, it moved through to late-stage development, which meant Phase III clinical trials involving perhaps thousands of patients. "We were not differentiated here, and there was clearly room for improvement," said King. AZN established a disciplined standard approach to clinical trials and created a single database called *Design Workbench*, which gave clinicians access to previous clinical trials, as well as best practices and protocols for the design of clinical trials. Every doctor and statistician was trained to enter information in the same way so it could be cataloged and extracted with ease.

The fourth capability was *gaining patient and payer insight at an earlier point in time*. If AZN knew what treatments payers would be willing to fund in the future and what regulatory authorities would need to understand about the drug, it would know what to expect when the drug hit the market. Bringing that information back to the front end of R&D to decide which diseases and science to work on would tie it all together. To accomplish this, AZN built a group of over 30 specialists who collaborated with internal and external experts to share and examine *real-world* data (medical records about length of hospital stay, re-admissions, cost of care; claims information; and patient surveys) to assess cost and determine who might be willing to pay for it. The team built a database to house its findings and share information across AZN.

The idea behind the four capabilities was that smarter clinical design, better understanding the disease and

potential drug, making it personal and getting customer and patient insights right from the start, would help AZN R&D achieve world-class status. The R&D team planned to invest from $200 million to $300 million over three to five years to enhance these capabilities. The goal was to deliver more valuable, cutting-edge medicines to patients while decreasing cycle time, improving the probability of success, and decreasing costs.

Culture of Courageous Leadership, Innovation, and Collaboration

Although Brennan's leadership team had never considered culture change a strategic priority, that soon changed (Figure 8). According to King:

Our number-one priority is a culture of courageous leadership, innovation, and collaboration. It didn't start off on that point, but when we looked at it, breakthroughs in science, a rapidly changing world in terms of politics, demographics and economics, a changing industry, changing regulatory process. What that said to us is the companies that are going to be successful are those that get the smartest leaders, who have got the best judgment, who can look to the future and make key decisions and inspire others to follow them. Hence, instead of it being our people strategy, it's our number-one priority in our R&D strategy.

To act on this, the company conducted a culture survey of 1,000 employees followed by 130 interviews. Employee

Figure 8 Three areas of culture change

Courageous Leadership

Leaders who foster an inspiring and compelling vision, and spend time involving, developing and empowering their people

Innovation and creativity

Creating innovative ways of working and new ideasm to discover and develop diffentiated mesicines that make a difference to patients.

Collaboration

Inspiring and connecting people, who actively collaborate, irrespective of boundaries, to share knowledge and expertise to the benefit of our customers

Source: Adapted from AstraZeneca. Used with permission.

feedback was very clear: they wanted more inspiring leadership, less of a focus on detailed metrics, and a culture that supported individuals being courageous.

To address these concerns, a new cadre of R&D leaders were appointed with Martin Mackay from Pfizer as president of R&D and Mene Pangalos, also from Pfizer, as head of the new Innovative Medicines function. Mackay, Pangalos, and King, together with Anders Ekblom, (head of Global Medicines Development) and Bahija Jallal (head of Medimmune R&D), reviewed all current internal leaders and the best leaders externally. As a result, 50 new executives were recruited externally, and the best internal talent was appointed to senior R&D leadership roles. Mackay explained, "We want leaders who have excellent strategic vision and can inspire others to follow, have strong technical judgment and a track record of successfully bringing drugs to the market, and who have a deep and authentic interest in developing people." King added:

Every leader appointed to the these roles has undergone a rigorous assessment involving an external four-hour assessment of their leadership capabilities, a three-hour external assessment of their professional capabilities, and an internal assessment of their strategic vision, technical judgment, and passion to develop people. Each candidate

also met with the key stakeholders, up to and including David Brennan.

This clearly signaled that a transformed R&D function required a transformed R&D leadership team. Kick-off events were held for each of senior R&D leadership teams, and collectively, the new teams visited companies outside the industry (93 companies in 2010–11, ranging from key hospitals to Apple, Google, 3**M**, and Pixar), returning to share what they learned about customers and employees.

Finally, to build the culture, an investment was made to develop all R&D employees in *learner* (openness to new ideas) and *player* (active acceptance of personal responsibility in contrast to *victim* where it is believed that events happen) behaviors, together with creative events on each site to stimulate innovation and ensure the strategic direction was fully embedded

The R&D Operating Model

In addition to changing the culture, the R&D team also had to change its operating model—the structure, process, and ways of working to enhance effectiveness and flexibility (Figure 9). "We were saying, let's get back to good science, collaborate, and share, " Mackay said.

Figure 9 New operating model.

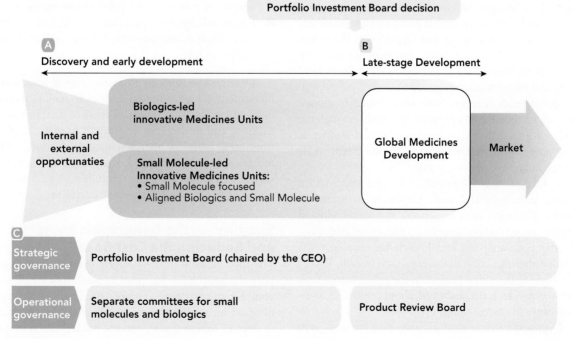

Source: Adapted from AstraZeneca. Used with permission.

Governance of R&D was a staying point. A Portfolio Investment Board (PIB) was established to assess and provide oversight of investment opportunities across disease areas and modalities. Chaired by Brennan, the PIB also included CFO Simon Lowth and Mackay. The team would take a three-year strategic investment view of internal and external project opportunities that competed with each other for development funding.

In addition to the PIB, the Product Review Board was established to provide clear progression of late-stage drug products. Separate operational committees were established for the early phase to bring forward products earlier in the pipeline. To ensure that compounds with the greatest chance of becoming a medicine were chosen and progressed, the 200 projects in the portfolio over the previous five years were reviewed according to a set of rigorous and consistent criteria:

- Was this the right disease target?
- Did it achieve the right exposure in the right tissue?
- Was this the right patient population?
- Was the drug safe?
- Did it bring value to a patient?

The organizational structure was also redesigned around *Innovative Medicines Units* (iMeds), whose goal was to discover new drugs and deliver potential medicines. The eight iMeds delivered new potential medicines to a single *Global Medicines Development* group whose job it was to develop them for approval and launch. This organization design combined innovative, fast-moving research and early development groups on one hand and a single, highly efficient global function on the other, that was charged with developing the medicine for every market in the world. The goal was to achieve both local agility and global efficiency.

Global product teams were also created to ensure that each medicine could progress smoothly through the pipeline with a dedicated team designing and leading its development while retaining access to others with skills that might be needed at each stage.

To further improve productivity and information sharing, databases and tools important to scientists across the business were integrated, and teams adopted the practice, on completion of a project, to set aside time for reflection, analysis, and knowledge sharing. This included sharing across discovery teams as well. Rather than rushing from one project to the other, teams took time to examine, learn, and think about creative or alternative ways to change things up.

To provide a clear strategic direction, metrics were simplified from several based on the volume of the pipeline to two: developmental track (DT) compounds that looked promising and the approval of new medical entities (NMEs) for patients.

A Focused Portfolio

The R&D transformation focused on what the firm would do differently, but it also needed to focus on what it would not do at all. According to many AZN executives, Pharma had grown beyond what it could produce. To develop a more focused portfolio, the leadership team conducted a thorough portfolio review to determine the attractiveness level of each disease area. Ekblom said:

We have to make some tough choices, though, around those diseases where we believe we've got the best opportunity of succeeding. My analogy is a bit like a freeway. When you have a freeway which is in a traffic jam, if you add more cars into it, it just slows down even more. If you take a number of the cars away, suddenly the traffic flows freely. In Pharma, it was about ensuring the portfolio consisted of the right projects at a size that allowed them to be progressed rapidly.

Four criteria were used to determine the attractiveness rating of each therapeutic area in the portfolio:

- Prevalence: Population afflicted with disease
- Discoverability: Risks associated with target identification and scientific capabilities
- Developability: Level of risk associated with trial design, number of patients, and regulatory environment
- Future willingness to pay: Based on the level of unmet need, competitive intensity, pricing, and anticipated market access

Decisions were made to increase or at least sustain investment in highly attractive areas, to maintain investment to key decision points in areas of medium attractiveness, and to decrease investment or exit completely from areas with low attractiveness. As a result, 25% of the disease areas were exited. Following this disease area review, each project was also carefully reviewed, and 30% of them were stopped in the early portfolio.

Simplifying the Geographic Footprint and Reducing the Cost Base

The final element of the strategic overhaul was to simplify the geographic footprint to move to a smaller, less complex organization (Figure 10). This simpler organization meant the closure of five sites, cost avoidance of over $1 billion a year, and the net reduction of 1,800 R&D staff.

Figure 10 Geographic footprint

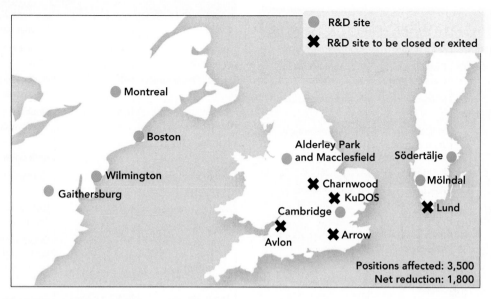

Source: Adapted from AstraZeneca. Used with permission.

Looking Ahead at AstraZeneca

AstraZeneca's blockbuster-driven growth had worked well, delivering robust sales over the period from 1999 to 2011, with revenues increasing from $15 billion to $33 billion and a compound annual growth rate of 15%. The portfolio had begun to deliver an average of two new medicines a year since 2008 (Exhibit 5). In addition, key deals had been made to strengthen the portfolio:

- Olaparib (a novel treatment for cancer)
- Ceftaroline (a next generation cephalosporin for bacterial infections)
- Avibactum (a beta lactamase inhibitor that enables antibiotics to work in resistant strains of bacteria)
- NKTR-118 (a novel treatment of opioid constipation)
- TC-5214 (a treatment for depression)
- Fostamatinib (a treatment for Rheumatoid arthritis)
- Tremelimumab (a novel treatment for cancer)

These successes were counterbalanced with five late-stage product failures: Zactima (for cancer), Recentin (for cancer), Zibotentan (for cancer), Certriad (to lower cholesterol), and Motavizumab (for respiratory diseases). In addition, the in-licensed products Olaparib and TC- 5214 failed to meet their primary end points in Phase III trials.

Even with the disappointments, the strategy implementation met or exceeded all the original objectives. New leadership was in place; there were 52 new executives from 22 different companies, and the culture was evolving toward greater accountability and learning, with a "people engagement" score of 83% on company surveys. The R&D function had been completely re-organized, with iMeds focused on discovering new drugs and managing their progression to the end of Phase II and Global Medicines Development managing the progression of the late stage portfolio to be approved and then launched to markets across the world.

Simple metrics and governance have been put in place to measure the key outputs of R&D, and the performance management system and rewards had been aligned to support their achievement. Capabilities were built with over 60% (post candidate drug selection) of the portfolio employing a personalized health care approach and 90% of projects using real-world evidence. More than 40 projects were employing predictive science approaches and were using new tools (e.g., Design Workbench system) to design and interpret clinical trials. These methods had been rolled out to more than 80% of the clinical project teams. The portfolio was reduced by 17% to ensure that only those projects that were competitive and felt to have the greatest chance of success were progressed. In addition, 200 projects had been reviewed and five key success criteria (The 5 R's) used to review each and every project. Finally, the footprint of R&D had been greatly simplified with nine site closures and over 40% reduction of facility square footage. R&D headcount was reduced by over 3,000 full time employees, and annual savings targets were achieved.

Exhibit 4 AZN Partners 2010

Name	Partnership Type	Hierarchy Focused Sector Path
Astellas Pharma	Distribution	Biopharmaceuticals
Par Pharmaceutical	Distribution, Out-licensing	Biopharmaceuticals
Rigel Pharmaceuticals	In-licensing	Biopharmaceuticals
Merck	In-licensing, Joint Venture, Marketing, Out-licensing	Biopharmaceuticals
Bristol Myers Squibb	Research Collaboration, Supplier	Biopharmaceuticals
Targacept	In-licensing, Marketing, Research Collaboration, Supplier	Biopharmaceuticals-Neurology
Array BioPharma	In-licensing, Research Collaboration, Supplier	Biopharmaceuticals Oncology
Dynavax Technologies	In-licensing, Research Collaboration, Supplier	Biopharmaceuticals
Pozen	In-licensing, Research Collaboration, Supplier	Biopharmaceuticals-Neurology
Cubist Pharmaceuticals	In-licensing, Supplier	Biopharmaceuticals-Infectious Disease
Takeda Pharmaceutical	In-licensing, Supplier	Biopharmaceuticals
Forest Laboratories	Integrated product Offering, Research Collaboration	Biopharmaceuticals-Neurology
Salix Pharmaceuticals	Marketing	Biopharmaceuticals-Digestive
Abbott	Marketing, Out-licensing, Research Collaboration	Biopharmaceuticals
GlaxoSmithKline	Out-licensing, Research Collaboration	Biopharmaceuticals
Cephalon	N/A	Biopharmaceuticals
Crucell N.V.	N/A	Biopharmaceuticals-Infectious Diseases

Name	Partnership Type	Hierarchy Focused Sector Path
Dyax	N/A	Biopharmaceuticals
Infinity Pharmaceuticals	N/A	Biopharmaceuticals-Oncology
Nektar Therapeutics	N/A	Outsourced Biomedical Services
Palatin Technologies	N/A	Biopharmaceuticals-Cardiovascular
PDL BioPharma	N/A	Discovery Services, Antibodies
Regeneron Pharmaceuticals	N/A	Biopharmaceuticals
Seattle Genetics	N/A	Biopharmaceuticals-Oncology
SkyePharma	N/A	Outsourced Biomedical Services, Drug Delivery, Technology
The Medicines Company	N/A	Biopharmaceuticals, Surgery, Cardiovascular
Theravance	N/A	Biopharmaceuticals
Xoma	N/A	Biopharmaceuticals
Ranbaxy	Distribution	N/A
BTG	In-Licensing, Supplier	N/A
Dainippon Sumitomo Pharma	In-Licensing, Supplier	N/A
Shionogi	In-Licensing, Supplier	N/A
Dako	Integrated Product Offering	N/A
Silence Therapeutics	Marketing, Research Collaboration	N/A
Argenta Discovery	Research Collaboration	N/A
CrystalGenomics	Research Collaboration	N/A
Jubilant Organosys	Research Collaboration	N/A
NIAID	Research Collaboration	N/A
Psychogenics	Research Collaboration	N/A
University of Virginia	Research Collaboration	N/A
Avalon Pharmaceuticals	Research Collaboration	N/A

(Continued)

Data source: Mergent Horizon.

Exhibit 5 New Medicines, 2008–2011

Product	Function
Onglyza	For the treatment of diabetes
H1N1 flu vaccine	To protect against a new strain of the flu virus
Kombiglyze	A combination of Metformin and Onglyza for the treatment of diabetes
Vimovo	For the treatment of osteoarthritis pain
Brilinta	A new standard of care for acute coronary syndrome
Caprelsa	For the treatment of medullary thyroid cancer

Data source: AstraZeneca.

Still, many questions remained. Would the portfolio continue to deliver? How much would the new products begin to off-set patent expirations? Would the improved performance of the pipeline be sustainable? Were the changes enough?

NOTES

1. This is a field-based case. All information and quotations, unless otherwise noted, derive from case writer interviews with company representatives.
2. Herman Saftlas, "Industry Surveys, Healthcare: Pharmaceuticals," *Standard & Poor's Industry Surveys*. (New York: McGraw-Hill, 2009), 12.
3. AstraZeneca annual report, 2010, 10.
4. Matthew Herper, "The Truly Staggering Cost of Inventing New Drugs," *Forbes*, http://www.forbes.com/sites/matthewherper/2012/02/10/the-truly-staggering-cost-of-inventing-new-drugs/ (accessed April 13, 2012).
5. Saftlas, 21.

6. Lisa M. Jarvis, "The Lure of Biologics," *Chemical and Engineering News*, June 12, 2006, 22.
7. Saftals, 22.
8. Saftlas, 5.
9. Visits to doctor offices were called *details*.
10. Andrew Tolve, "US Healthcare Reform Has Arrived. Now What?" Eye for Pharma website, March 22, 2010, http://social.eyeforpharma.com/uncategorised/us-healthcare-reform-has-arrived-now-what (accessed October 14, 2010).
11. Antibodies produced by a single clone of cells.
12. Jarvis.
13. 111th Congress of the United States, "The Patient Protection and Affordable Care Act," H.R. 3590, 689.

14. Saftlas, 4.
15. EP Vantage, "Biotech Set to Dominate Drug Industry Growth," http://www.evaluatepharma.com/Universal/View.aspx?type=Story&id=188700&isEPVantage=yes (accessed September 30, 2010).
16. Saftlas, 4.
17. AstraZeneca Q4 2007 earnings call transcript, January 31, 2008, http://goliath.ecnext.com/coms2/gi_0199-9758004/Q4-2007-AstraZeneca-PLC-Earnings.html (accessed September 19, 2011).
18. Matthew Gwyther, "How to Survive Complexity," *Management Today*, April 2008: 37.

Kristen Arndt, Danny Baum, Arunkishore Ramgopal, Prosper Nwokocha

Texas A&M University

Introduction

Avon Products, Inc. is the world's largest direct seller; it markets beauty, fashion, and home products to women in more than 100 countries through approximately 6.4 million active independent sales representatives.[1] Having previously enjoyed great success as a leading global beauty company, the company is now facing an array of issues. In response, in December 2011, Avon Products, Inc. announced that its CEO and Executive Chairman – Andrea Jung – would step down from her position as soon as her replacement was found. Over the two years prior to the announcement, Avon's share price had decreased by more than 50 percent. The company was also facing bribery charges in some of its overseas operations as well as an SEC investigation into whether an Avon official made confidential comments to an analyst.[2] Clearly, Andrea Jung's replacement would face many challenges.

History

While working as a traveling book salesman David H. McConnell discovered that women were much more interested in the free perfume samples he offered than the books he sought to sell to them. This prompted him to create The California Perfume Company in 1886, later to be renamed Avon Products, Inc. Aware of the fact that many women were at home while their husbands were at work and with the belief that they could relate to other women and help network, market, and sell his products, McConnell decided to offer these women a commission for selling his products. In essence, he offered women the opportunity to create and manage their own direct-selling businesses. And with that simple brainstorm, "The

company for women" was on its way to selling beauty products and empowering women throughout the world.[3]

According to Avoncompany.com, direct selling at Avon "connected women, who were otherwise isolated and immersed in domestic life, in what the company calls 'the original social network.'" Through Avon, women could sample and purchase beauty products without having to travel miles to the nearest department or drug store. By focusing on personal relationships, Avon's sales exceeded $1 million by 1920, $1 billion by 1972, and $10 billion by 2008.[4]

As an increasing number of women entered the more traditional workplace, Avon made adjustments. In the 1970s, the firm developed a brochure with samples that could be left on the doorknob of an unoccupied home. In 1986, Avon began selling within the workplace in addition to homes. Beginning in the 1990s, representatives could earn money not only by selling, but by recruiting and training representatives as well. Shortly thereafter, Avon integrated Internet access into the arsenal of representative's tools.[5]

Avon has a history of working with celebrities to market the brand. Beginning in the 1940s, Avon's products were endorsed by Rosalind Russell, Loretta Young, Claudette Colbert, Joe DiMaggio, and Jimmy Stewart. More recent celebrity endorsers include Fergie, Salma Hayek, Zoe Saldana, Ashley Greene, and Patrick Dempsey. Cher, Billy Dee Williams, and Catherine Deneuve market fragrances through Avon and Reese Witherspoon serves as the firm's Global Ambassador.[6]

Products and Brands

Avon's products include cosmetics, skincare, fragrance, personal care, hair care, and jewelry. Additionally, Avon carries various brands. "mark." is a brand that includes fashion, accessories, scents, and color pallets geared toward the younger generation. "Liz Earle" is a skincare line that uses natural active ingredients. Since 2010, Avon has owned "Silpada," which is the largest and fastest-growing sterling silver jewelry home party company. Avon also offers products for mothers and their babies including toys, bath, and clothing products for babies as well as beauty "must-haves" and accessories for mom.[7] Though Avon directs most products toward women, it offers men's products as well including a body wash and fragrance endorsed by Derek Jeter.

Vision, Mission, and Values

Vision: "To be the company that best understands and satisfies the product, service and self-fulfillment needs of women—globally."

Mission: Avon has a six-point list of aspirations that the company strives to achieve:

- To be a leader in global beauty
- To be women's choice for buying
- To be a premier direct-selling company
- To be a "most admired" company
- To be a "best place to work"
- To have the largest foundation dedicated to women's causes.[8]

Values: Founder David McConnell felt it was beneficial to provide a supportive and "family-like" environment, even naming the company newsletter the "Family Album."[9]

Avon continues to focus on the five values and seven guiding principles he implemented. The values include trust, respect, belief, humility, and integrity, while the principles include the opportunity to earn [money], serve families by providing high quality products, render outstanding service, fully recognize employees and representatives, share rewards with others, meet obligations of corporate citizenship, and maintain and cherish the friendly spirit of Avon.[10]

Outside the Company

Avon Products, Inc. is a global firm. According to the firm, its "International operations are conducted primarily through subsidiaries in 64 countries and territories outside of the U.S. In addition to these countries and territories, [Avon's] products are distributed in 42 other countries and territories."[11] Avon generates 83 percent of its consolidated revenue from outside the United States (see Exhibit 1). The 2008 financial crisis resulted in increased unemployment, tightening of credit markets, and the failures of financial institutions, all of which negatively impacted the global economy. As a result, consumers had less income to spend on "discretionary items, such as beauty and related products," which negatively affected Avon's product sales. Avon faced continued economic challenges in fiscal 2012 because consumers continued to struggle with increased "job losses, foreclosures, bankruptcies, reduced access to credit, and sharply falling home prices, among other things."[12]

Because 83 percent of consolidated sales are of international origin, fluctuations in exchange rates pose a

Exhibit 1 Sales Distribution - Geography

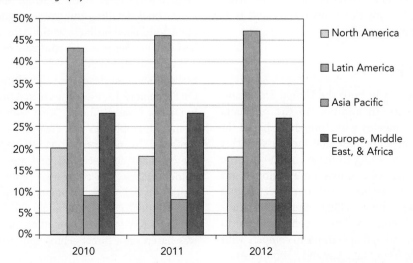

Source: Applicable AVP 10-K SEC filings retrieved from http://www.sec.gov/cgi-bin/browse-edgar?action=getcompany&CIK=0000008868&owner=exclude&count=40&hidefilings=0

critical risk for Avon. For the majority of Avon's international operations, the local currency is used as the functional currency. As a result, exchange rates have a significant impact on Avon's earnings, assets, cash flow, and financial position. To mitigate the risk of exchange rate fluctuations, Avon "implements foreign currency hedging and risk management strategies to reduce exposure to fluctuations in earnings and cash flows."[13]

In addition to currency fluctuations, Avon is vulnerable to the policies of foreign governments in the countries in which it operates. Notably, Avon faces currency transfer restrictions in Venezuela as the Venezuelan government has been implementing and intensifying currency restrictions since 2003. At present, Avon's subsidiary in Venezuela is unable to exchange local currency for USD through the government. As a result, Avon is forced to use a third party to exchange the currency, which burdens it with an increased cost to obtain all imported products necessary for production.

Lastly, Avon initiated an internal audit in 2008 to investigate its compliance with the Foreign Corrupt Practices Act (FCPA) and related U.S. and foreign laws, specifically with China. In October 2011, the U.S. Securities and Exchange Commission (SEC) subpoenaed financial documents from Avon and officially ordered an investigation of any violations to the FCPA.[14] According to the *New York Times*, "the legal fees and costs for outside counsel conducting the internal investigation totaled $59 million in 2009 and $95 million in 2010."[15] It is estimated that Avon will spend $250 million total for the internal investigation, not including any fines the company may incur. The Justice Department and SEC will rely on the findings from Avon's internal investigation to determine a resolution.[16] Avon has already incurred a serious financial loss for this investigation and is at future risk if found in violation.

Competitive Fronts

Avon faces competition in both the United States and international markets. In addition to the products themselves, Avon competes with companies based on direct-selling strategies, Internet, and the mass-market channels of retail. According to the firm, "Within the direct-selling channel, we compete on a regional and often country-by-country basis, with our direct-selling competitors."[17] Several direct-selling companies including Mary Kay and Arbonne sell product lines similar to Avon and have international operations to compete with Avon globally. Aside from Mary Kay and Arbonne, Avon competes with other beauty companies using a distinct

business model that relies heavily on the success of its representatives. To ensure it can continue to hire quality representatives, Avon competes with other direct-selling companies to provide the best earning opportunities. Avon believes its representatives are just as essential as the development of innovative products. In essence, Avon competes on two fronts: recruiting quality representatives first and the sales of beauty products second.

"Within the broader Consumer Product Goods (CPG) industry, Avon competes against large and well-known cosmetics and fragrances companies such as L'Oréal and P&G that manufacture and sell broad product lines through various types of retail establishment."[18] The beauty industry is highly competitive. Companies such as L'Oréal and P&G generate higher sales volume and have larger resource portfolios compared to their competitors, including Avon.

The beauty segment of Avon's business generates the majority of its revenue. In 2012, the beauty business generated 73 percent of Avon's total revenue.[19] In addition to competing against strong competitors within the industry, Avon competes in the fashion and home business as well. According to Avon, it competes "in the gift and decorative products and apparel industries globally."[20] Typical competitors in the fashion and home industries establish themselves in "retail establishments, principally department stores, gift shops, and specialty retailers, and direct-mail companies specializing in these products."[21]

Direct-Selling Competitors

Mary Kay

Mary Kay Ash retired from her 25-year career in direct sales in early 1963. Upon retiring, Mary Kay wanted to write a book detailing how women could be successful in a male dominated business world. After compiling her two lists of what her previous company did well versus what she concluded would benefit from improvement, Ash realized she had developed the ultimate business plan. On September 13, 1963, she created Mary Kay Cosmetics in Dallas, Texas. Its motto, "One Woman Can," continues to inspire employees and customers alike. It was Mary Kay's goal to "make everyone feel important."[22] The way the company achieved this goal was by establishing the golden rule[i] as the company's philosophy. Mary Kay's vision was to empower women, providing them with the opportunity to achieve personal and financial success.

Mary Kay achieved immediate success. The company was based on a direct-selling model, with independent

---

i. "Do unto others as you would have them do unto you."

consultants marketing and selling her products. This became the main source of revenue for the firm. In 1969, Mary Kay awarded the first (of over 19,000 to date[23]) pink Cadillacs to the top five Independent Sales Directors.[24] By 1973, the total sales force exceeded 20,000 representatives.[25] In 1976, Mary Kay was listed on the NYSE. Through a leveraged buyout, the company returned as a privately owned family firm in 1985. Today, the company generates more than $2.5 billion in sales and maintains a sales force of more than two million people with 1.7 million of them located in the United States.[26] Mary Kay is the sixth Top Selling Direct firm worldwide and has almost five percent market share of the $53.7 billion dollar beauty and skincare industry.[27]

Arbonne

Arbonne was founded in 1975 by Petter Morck in Switzerland. Morck worked with a team of biochemists, biologists, and herbalists to develop pure, safe, and beneficial skincare and personal wellness products. Arbonne expanded its sales to the Unites States in 1980. Arbonne only sells its products through independent consultants.[28] There are currently 365,600 consultants in the United States.[29] Today, the company carries over 200 products including cosmetics, nutrition and weight loss goods, and aromatherapy items. Currently these products are sold in the United States, Canada, Australia, and the United Kingdom.[30]

Arbonne is privately owned; as a result, its available financial data is limited. However, Arbonne's parent company, Natural Products Group, filed Chapter 11 bankruptcy in January 2010. As of November 30, 2009, Natural Products Group's consolidated balance sheet reflected assets of approximately $286 million and liabilities of approximately $804 million. Arbonne had $378 million in revenue at the end of this same period, resulting in 0.704 percent of the total market share.[31] Despite the financial struggles faced by Natural Products Group, it was named "Top Corporate Turnaround of the Year" in the upper middle market category by *M&A Advisor Magazine*. According to *Investment Weekly News*, Natural Products Group developed a restructuring plan that resulted in 80 percent less debt, a stronger balance sheet, and financial flexibility that will allow it to invest in and develop future products for Arbonne.[32]

Leaders in the Beauty Industry

L'Oréal

L'Oréal is the leader in the beauty and cosmetics industry. Eugene Schueller founded what would become The L'Oréal Group in 1909. Mr. Schueller graduated with a chemistry degree from France's national chemical engineering school – Ecole Nationale Supérieure de Chimie de Paris – in 1904. The company originated from one of the first hair dyes he formulated, produced, and sold to hairdressers in Paris. The company grew as Mr. Schueller invested in the hair coloring school on Rue du Louvre in Paris and closely linked the success of his products to the stylists. Despite the external conditions of the war, L'Oréal's success spread beyond France to Italy, Austria, and the United States.[33]

Today, the company holds 39 percent of the total market share of the beauty industry. L'Oréal operates in more than 130 countries and produces more than 35 brands of products in four segments. L'Oréal has earned more than € 22.5 billion in revenue. Its ambition is to "win over another one billion consumers around the world by creating cosmetic products that meet the diversity of their beauty needs."[34] L'Oréal differs from Avon in that it sells its products through traditional retail vendors. However, as is the case for Avon, L'Oréal has a wide range of suppliers that must comply with the company's quality standards. Because it creates products that meet the demands of local markets, L'Oréal's worldwide market share is increasing. To meet its goal of acquiring another billion consumers, L'Oréal is investing in new distribution and manufacturing centers, increasing its edge over all other firms within the beauty industry.

Procter & Gamble Co. (P&G)

P&G had a serendipitous beginning when two immigrants met. William Procter was born in 1801 and along with his family, immigrated to the United States from England where he had worked as a general store apprentice learning to "dip candles." After arriving in Cincinnati, Procter began working at a bank, but decided to make and sell candles to earn extra income. James Gamble, born in 1803, emigrated with his family from Ireland in 1819. During their journey, Gamble became very ill and his parents decided to take him ashore in Cincinnati. Upon turning 18, Gamble began working as an apprentice to a soap maker. The two men would have never met had they not married sisters Olivia and Elizabeth Norris. Because they were often competing for the same raw materials, their father-in-law encouraged the two to create a joint venture. P&G was created on October 31, 1837.[35]

After 172 years of business, P&G remains a global leader in its industry. P&G operates in more than 180 countries and serves about 4.6 billion of the 7 billion people on the planet with its products. In 2012, its gross revenue totaled more than $83 billion with nearly $13 billion in net income. The beauty segment includes the iconic Cover Girl, Max Factor, and Olay brands as well as DDF and SK-II – two complete skincare systems – and a Dolce & Gabbana line of makeup. This segment generated $20.3 billion in revenue in 2012, placing P&G a close second behind L'Oréal with a market share of 37.8 percent. P&G's success is the result of the company's commitment to its core values and purpose. P&G's purpose is to "provide branded products and services of superior quality and value that improves the lives of the world's consumers, now and for generations to come."[36] In 2013, former CEO A. G. Lafley returned to lead P&G at the request of the board of directors. A change to the firm's organizational structure was expected. More specifically, an initial expectation was that the firm's two Global Business Units (Beauty & Grooming and Household Care) would be restructured into four sectors.

Doing Business with Suppliers

Suppliers can directly affect a company's profit potential. If Avon's suppliers decreased the quality or increased the cost of their products, its profitability might suffer. While Avon relies on numerous suppliers for the raw materials of its products – specifically essential oils, chemicals, containers, and packaging components – it manufactures and packages almost all of its beauty products in house. Most of its fashion and home segment products are purchased from a variety of third-party suppliers. According to Avon's annual report, "The loss of any one supplier would not have a material impact on ability to source raw materials for Beauty products or source products for Fashion and Home categories."[37]

In 2006, Avon began its Strategic Sourcing Initiative. "Under this initiative, the company will shift its purchasing strategy toward a global supplier orientation from one that today is more local and component oriented."[38] In addition, Avon began implementing an Enterprise Resource Planning (ERP) system on a worldwide basis in 2009. The goal of the ERP system is to increase the efficiency of Avon's supply chain and reduce costs.[39] Initiatives such as these provide Avon with the ability to absorb increasing costs from its suppliers without passing the cost on to consumers.

Selling Products to Customers

Firms seek to find the most appropriate and potentially unique approach to use to sell their products to customers.[40] This is certainly the case for Avon. In fact, the firm employs approximately 6.4 million active independent representatives worldwide for the purpose of being able to provide customers with access to a personalized one-on-one purchasing experience that differentiates Avon's products in a highly competitive market. Aware of how it is portrayed in the popular media as a dowdy firm represented by middle age women in rural America and with a decrease of active representatives in the United States (see Exhibit 2), Avon began attempting to convert

Exhibit 2 Avon Representatives

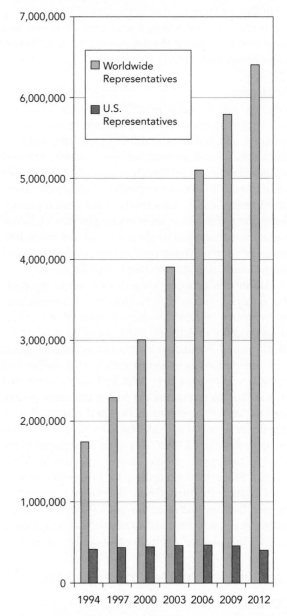

Source: Applicable AVP 10-K SEC filings retrieved from http://www. sec.gov/cgi-bin/browse-edgar?action=getcompany&CIK=00000088 68&owner=exclude&count=40&hidefilings=0

"what it calls the 'smarter woman' to its products from more expensive brands." Avon believes these women read labels and, looking to save money where and when possible, will conclude that Avon's products are of comparable quality to those of competitors but are available to them at a lower price.[41]

Deciding How to Compete

Competing on a Day-to-Day Basis

As mentioned previously, Avon aspires to offer, in a unique way, quality products that meet women's needs. Avon distinguishes its products through their innovativeness and the distribution channel used to sell the firm's products. The increased personalization that goes hand-in-hand with direct selling creates customer loyalty.

Without question, Avon's success depends upon its sales representatives. The foundation Avon was built on depends on the company's ability to provide financial and personal success to its representatives. As a result, the firm is involved with several investments for the purpose of recruiting and retaining high-quality personnel. The "Representative Value Proposition," or RVP, is an example of these investments. RVP is an extensive web-based project that Avon developed that provides "cutting-edge online training opportunities" with the intent to allow representatives to expand their businesses online. RVP provides an incentive to potential representatives and has the potential to serve as a competitive advantage for Avon relative to its rivals who also use the direct-selling model.

In addition to the direct-selling model, Avon strives to increase its brand competitiveness by maintaining "sustained focus on new technology and product innovation to deliver first-to-market products that provide visible consumer benefits."[42] In fact, Avon has directed an increasing amount of revenue to research and development (R&D) in the recent past. In 2011 for example, the firm allocated $77.7 million to R&D compared to the allocation of $72.6 million in 2010 and $65.4 million in 2009.[43]

Additional Approaches to Competing

Avon's approach to competing on a day-to-day basis makes it possible for the firm to focus on a few specific tasks. In turn, this focus creates opportunities for the firm to gain valuable experience as it seeks to identify how to provide maximum satisfaction for its customers relative to their needs. In addition, how the firm competes allows Avon to gain economies of scale and use its resources more efficiently. Avon achieves economies of scale through the organization of its manufacturing, distribution, and administrative facilities. As previously

mentioned, beginning in 2005, Avon initiated a multi-year, multi-phase, global rollout of an ERP system.[44] The ERP system was designed to improve the efficiency of the supply chain and financial transaction processes. Avon first implemented the ERP system in its European manufacturing facilities, Avon's larger European direct-selling operations, and in the United States. These locations were part of a pilot initiative; Avon will eventually incorporate the ERP system in all regions. Avon intends to study the strengths and weaknesses of the ERP system and then implement any changes when initiated in other countries. Avon expanded the ERP supply chain module to Brazil in 2011. As with any new initiative, there is a learning curve, the effects of which were seen in Brazil's less profitable second half of 2011. In spite of the initial setbacks, Avon believes the ERP system will provide long-term benefits to it as well as to those it serves.[45]

Competing on a Global Basis

Avon sells standardized products to countries and regions throughout the world. This orientation to product standardization and sales facilitates the firm's efforts to develop economies of scales throughout its operations. However, because of this approach, local cultures and trends have little influence on the product lines Avon develops and sells. In the future, Avon may devote attention to determining if identifying and serving any unique needs that may exist for the firm's products across cultures, countries, and regions could create more value for customers.

Mergers and Acquisitions

According to Avon's 2010 10-K, the firm spent $828 million on the acquisitions of Silpada – a seller of hand-crafted sterling silver jewelry – and Liz Earle – a skincare products firm. Silpada followed the same direct-selling model and valued similar core values as Avon.[46] In the terms of the acquisition, Silpada would remain a stand-alone business and the co-founders and management team would continue to lead the company.[47] Unlike Avon and Silpada, Liz Earle, a U.K. based firm, did not follow the direct-selling model[48] with sales generated in stores or by phone instead. As with Silpada, Liz Earle would remain a stand-alone business unit and would continue to be run by its founders.[49]

Avon believed that these acquisitions would result in several benefits. Both companies have well-established clientele, Avon has increased diversification, and both businesses allow Avon to learn new capabilities. The most important advantage, however, comes from the increased diversification. Most often firms do not diversify due to the risk associated with the development of new product lines. Because it would be difficult for Avon to develop products for unfamiliar markets, the acquisition of firms such as Silpada and Liz Earle helps mitigate this risk and positions Avon for increased future profits. However, it shifts Avon's focus from its core competency of direct selling and further increases the product line, a key complaint of many sales representatives.

Strategic Leaders

"The vision is to restore Avon to an iconic beauty brand and to our leadership position in global direct selling, as well as continuing to ensure that we live up to our mission of empowering women. In terms of the plan, it's really about driving growth–getting the right growth platforms–simplifying and getting our business much more efficient, and in doing that driving costs out, and ultimately to build organizational capabilities and strengths for the future. It's really those three areas."—Sheri McCoy, CEO, Avon Products[50]

Sherilyn McCoy left her position as Vice Chairman of Johnson & Johnson and joined Avon in April 2012 as its new CEO. The Avon board decided that at least initially, former CEO Andrea Jung would be available to support as she began her service as Avon's key strategic leader. Other firms have established this type of arrangement between a new and a former CEO. However, the degree to which this arrangement would generate benefits for McCoy and create value for Avon was unknown. However, it is clear that Jung supports McCoy, as she stated that McCoy has a "…track record of successfully achieving results and driving change across highly diverse operating units with widely varying product lines, customers, distribution channels, and business models."[51]

Sherilyn S. McCoy, CEO and Director

Sheri S. McCoy is the CEO and a director of Avon Products, Inc. McCoy received a B.S. degree from Dartmouth, a master's degree from Princeton, and an MBA from Rutgers University.

Before moving to Avon, McCoy served 30 years at Johnson & Johnson. She was the Vice Chairman of the Executive Committee for pharmaceuticals and consumer business. She has the experience of handling and leading a significant business, as the pharmaceuticals and consumer business contributes 60 percent of Johnson & Johnson's revenue. She also has the experience of reinventing an organization through restructuring and integration, having done so within her segment at Johnson & Johnson.

Andrea Jung, Senior Advisor

Andrea Jung has been a Senior Advisor to Avon Products, Inc. since January 1, 2013. Jung graduated magna cum laude from Princeton University and served as the CEO of Avon from November 1999 to May 2012. She developed and executed all of Avon's long-term growth strategies, developed earnings opportunities for women worldwide, and defined Avon as the premier direct seller of beauty products. She served as President of Avon from January 1998 to January 2001 and its COO from July 1998 to November 1999. She served as an Executive VP of Avon since March 1997 and its President of Global Marketing from July 1996 to 1997.[52]

Patricia Perez-Ayala, Senior VP and Chief Marketing Officer

Patricia Perez-Ayala is Senior VP and Chief Marketing Officer for Avon and a member of the company's Executive Committee. Perez-Ayala graduated in 1983 with a B.S. in Business Administration from the School of Management at Boston College.

Perez-Ayala joined P&G and has served the firm in various roles for more than two decades. Most recently, she served as GM and VP of Eastern Europe at P&G, handling one of the company's biggest regions. Prior to that, she was VP of FemCare North America. Her industry and marketing experience in North America and Latin America has been a perfect fit for Avon. At Avon, she is responsible for global management of the Avon brand and marketing, including consumer insights and analytics, commercial and digital marketing, product category strategy, and execution. She also oversees Avon's R&D and the integration of Liz Earle.[53]

Financials

In 2011, Avon's comprehensive income had dropped 60 percent and cash flow was poor (see Exhibits 3 and 4).[54] In fact, in 2010, the cash flows were negative, primarily because of the acquisition of Silpada.[55] The corruption charges in Asia, distribution problems in Brazil, and declining sales in North America further affected the firm's financial performance. Nevertheless, ten months into the job, CEO McCoy certainly had an idea of the vision, mission, and strategic direction for the company. After visiting with representatives on a worldwide tour to become familiar with all aspects of the firm and its direct selling model, McCoy rolled up her sleeves and put together a major restructuring plan that included eliminating 1,500 jobs, withdrawing from Vietnam and South Korea, and tightening belts to the

Exhibit 3 Consolidated Statements of Income

(USD $) In Millions, except Per Share data, unless otherwise specified						
	12 Months Ended					
	Dec. 31, 2012		**Dec. 31, 2011**		**Dec. 31, 2010**	
Net sales	$10,546.10		$11,112		$10,731.30	
Other revenue	171	[1]	179.6	[1]	131.5	[1]
Total revenue	10,717.10		11,291.60		10,862.80	
Costs, expenses and other:						
Cost of sales	4,169.30		4,148.60		4,041.30	
Selling, general and administrative expenses	5,980		6,025.40		5,748.40	
Impairment of goodwill and intangible asset	253		263		0	
Operating profit	314.8		854.6		1,073.10	
Interest expense	104.3		92.9		87.1	
Interest income	−15.1		−16.5		−14	
Other expense, net	7		35.6		54.6	
Total other expenses	96.2		112		127.7	
Income from continuing operations, before taxes	218.6	[2]	742.6		945.4	
Income taxes	256.8		216.2		350.2	
(Loss) income from continuing operations, net of tax	−38.2	[2] [3]	526.4		595.2	
Discontinued operations, net of tax	0		−8.6		14.1	
Net (loss) income	−38.2		517.8		609.3	
Net income attributable to noncontrolling interests	−4.3	[2] [3]	−4.2		−3	
Net (loss) income attributable to Avon	($42.50)	[2] [3]	$513.60		$606.30	
(Loss) earnings per share:						
Basic from continuing operations	($0.10)	[2] [3] [4]	$1.20	[4]	$1.37	
Basic from discontinued operations	$0		($0.02)		$0.04	
Basic attributable to Avon	($0.10)		$1.18		$1.40	
Diluted from continuing operations	($0.10)	[2] [3] [4]	$1.20	[4]	$1.36	
Diluted from discontinued operations	$0		($0.02)		$0.03	
Diluted attributable to Avon	($0.10)		$1.18		$1.39	
Weighted-average shares outstanding:						
Basic	431.9		430.5		428.8	
Diluted	431.9		432.1		431.4	

[1] Other revenue primarily includes shipping and handling and order processing fees billed to Representatives.

[2] In addition to the items impacting operating profit above, income (loss) from continuing operations during 2012 was impacted by a benefit of $23.8 to other expense, net in 2012 due to the release of a provision in the fourth quarter associated with the excess cost of acquiring U.S. dollars in Venezuela at the regulated market rate as compared to the official exchange rate. This provision was released as the Company capitalized the associated intercompany liabilities.

[3] Income (loss) from continuing operations, net of tax during 2012 was impacted by an additional provision for income taxes of $168.3. During the fourth quarter of 2012, we determined that the Company may repatriate offshore cash to meet certain domestic funding needs. Accordingly, we are no longer asserting that the undistributed earnings of foreign subsidiaries are indefinitely reinvested.

[4] The sum of per share amounts for the quarters does not necessarily equal that for the year because the computations were made independently.

Source: Avon Products Inc. Sec.gov. http://www.sec.gov/cgi-bin/viewer?action=view&cik=8868&accession_number=0000008868-13-000016&xbrl_type=v#

Exhibit 4 Consolidated Balance Sheets

(USD $) In Millions, unless otherwise specified	Dec. 31, 2012	Dec. 31, 2011
Current Assets		
Cash, including cash equivalents of $762.9 and $623.7	$1,209.60	$1,245.10
Accounts receivable (less allowances of $161.4 and $174.5)	751.9	761.5
Inventories	1,135.40	1,161.30
Prepaid expenses and other	832	930.9
Total current assets	3,928.90	4,098.80
Property, plant and equipment, at cost		
Land	66.6	65.4
Buildings and improvements	1,165.90	1,150.40
Equipment	1,479.30	1,493
Property, plant and equipment, at cost	2,711.80	2,708.80
Less accumulated depreciation	−1,161.60	−1,137.30
Property, plant and equipment, net, total	1,550.20	1,571.50
Goodwill	374.9	473.1
Other intangible assets, net	120.3	279.9
Other assets	1,408.20	1,311.70
Total assets	7,382.50	7,735
Current Liabilities		
Debt maturing within one year	572	849.3
Accounts payable	920	850.2
Accrued compensation	266.6	217.1
Other accrued liabilities	661	663.6
Sales and taxes other than income	211.4	212.4
Income taxes	73.6	98.4
Total current liabilities	2,704.60	2,891
Long-term debt	2,623.90	2,459.10
Employee benefit plans	637.6	603
Accrued Income Taxes, Noncurrent	52	67
Other liabilities	131.1	129.7
Total liabilities	6,149.20	6,149.80
Commitments and contingencies (Notes 14 and 16)		
Shareholders' equity		
Common stock, par value $.25 - authorized 1,500 shares; Issued 746.7 and 744.9 shares	188.3	187.3
Additional paid-in capital	2,119.60	2,077.70
Retained earnings	4,357.80	4,726.10
Accumulated other comprehensive loss	−876.7	−854.4
Treasury stock, at cost (314.5 and 314.1 shares)	−4,571.90	−4,566.30
Total Avon shareholders' equity	1,217.10	1,570.40
Noncontrolling interest	16.2	14.8
Total shareholders' equity	1,233.30	1,585.20
Total liabilities and shareholders' equity	$7,382.50	$7,735

Source: Avon Products Inc. Sec.gov. http://www.sec.gov/cgi-bin/viewer?action=view&cik=8868&accession_number=0000008868-13-000016&xbrl_type=v#

tune of $400 million. The plan also included a commitment to invest $200 million "to update its information systems, embrace digital and social media as contemporary selling tools, stop the bleeding in hard-hit markets like the U.S. and the U.K., and push premium brands like anti-aging line Anew."[56]

Challenges

Missing the Target

As the competitive environment becomes more complex and rivalries intensify, Avon faces pressure to outperform new players in the market while maintaining its leadership among existing competitors. With large diversified companies expanding their portfolios and entering the market as direct competitors, Avon chose to focus on its tried and true products – beauty and skincare. The problem occurred when Avon began concentrating too much on *what* it was selling instead of *how* it was sold. This set Avon adrift from its core competencies of entrepreneurship, personal marketing, and direct selling – the elements that make Avon what it is. Avon tried to innovate almost exclusively with the products it offered instead of trying to innovate both with the products themselves and how they were sold, and customers were supported after buying the products. Avon was compromising its competitive advantage by deviating from its strengths and uniqueness as it took on companies with the scale and scope for more efficient, diverse, and innovative production.

Additionally, rather than understanding and building on Avon's traditional style and focus, Andrea Jung, who typically dons designer suits and accessories, wanted Avon to adapt to her style and vision for the company. With experience working for Neiman Marcus, I. Magnin, and Bloomingdale's, Jung was drawn to the allure of trying to make Avon something it is not – a high-end retail beauty company. Jung wanted to bring additional sophistication to the brand. As Avon began targeting new demographics among women, such as trendy college-aged women as well as high-end clientele, the company impaired the efforts and positioning of its representatives who were usually working women earning on average less than $50,000 a year. These women typically sold Avon products on a part-time basis to a customer base that flowed from their extended network of friends, family, and associates. Because of their limited reach, representatives' clientele typically consist of women of similar status and demographics. Thus, when Avon set its sights on new segments, it did not have representatives with the experience or contacts to reach this new customer base. Instead, Avon had to depend on increased media advertising, retail chains, and a pull marketing strategy to achieve success. Avon was trying to pull customers, rather than employing its proven push strategy. Implementing this new pull strategy was very costly for Avon, as "advertising spending climbed from $63.4 million in 1999 to its peak of $400 million in 2010."[57] While many firms in multiple industries consider push marketing outdated, it is very effective in emerging markets where Avon saw immense growth and profit potential.

Alan Kennedy, a longtime executive in the industry who worked at Avon in the 1970s and 1980s, said: "The fundamental challenge in direct selling is getting people to sell your stuff, not so much getting people to buy your stuff."[58] This idea suggests that Avon should have remained fully committed to its grassroots beginnings and maintained the direct door-to-door model that lifted the company to prominence. Rick Goings, CEO of direct-seller Tupperware Brands, worked for Avon from 1985 to 1992 and stated, "effective direct-selling companies are 25 percent about the brand and 75 percent about the sales channel."[59]

Revitalizing the Sales Force

As Avon tried to innovate and upgrade its products, customers started having difficulty finding products that they considered staples. Some of these items were discontinued and some were just hard to locate in a steadily growing catalog. Consumers and representatives alike were complaining that products were changing too often and that Avon was no longer the company that they had loved. Keeping up with the ever-changing and expanding product line affected the product knowledge, customer service and, ultimately, the confidence of representatives. In a model where customers depend on the expertise and recommendation of the seller, Avon's website was an inadequate substitute for a knowledgeable representative. With women's growing presence in corporate America and Avon's weakening corporate strategy and leadership, the opportunity and incentive that the company once offered entrepreneurial women was fading. The number of active Avon representatives in North America fell 8 percent in 2011, leaving an estimated 420,000 representatives in the United States.[60]

Those at the heart of Avon's business model and past success – direct sales representatives – were experiencing a growing discontent with the company's policies, objectives, and initiatives. They felt that the company was putting too much emphasis on recruiting new representatives instead of focusing on expanding relationships with current and prospective customers. In addition, representatives were not happy with the increasing cost of sales materials and felt that sales commissions should be increased. These grievances made the opportunity to be an Avon sales representative less and less appealing, as evidenced by the decline of representatives.[61]

Improving Corporate Governance and Management

Despite an impressive background and resume, many shareholders and experts felt that Jung's profile did not align with the company's core values and vision and that she was not the right person to lead the company. In spite of some major successes under Jung's leadership, the company experienced inconsistent growth and execution. The board, likely because of Jung's occasional home run, did not establish a proper succession plan in the event of continued performance lags. A takeover bid by fragrance company Coty provided further evidence of the firm's questionable internal corporate governance.

Adding to its already crippling legal woes, Avon is now under investigation to determine if the board of directors failed in its fiduciary duty to act in the best interest of shareholders when it rejected Coty's $10.7 billion takeover bid. While rejecting the offer may have been at least partially tied to socioeconomic wealth,[ii] Avon stated that it believed the offer undervalued the company. In addition to the costs associated with the rejection of the Coty offer, total legal fees attributed to the internal investigation of possible violations of the FCPA with its China operations are estimated at $250 million.[62]

When Andrea Jung stepped down as CEO, Avon decided to separate the role of board chairman and CEO. With Jung possessing great intellect, experience, and the ability to innovate, Avon kept her as chairman in the hopes that it can exploit these qualities. Effective collaboration between Jung and McCoy could bring great value to the company and may be the foundation for turning the company around in ways that will meet stakeholders' expectations.

Getting Back on Track

Former CEO Jung is not, of course, solely responsible for Avon's underperformance, particularly over the last few years of her tenure. Years before she took the helm, the company was struggling to meet earnings expectations amidst a growing industry with new entrants vying for

market share. Many competitors were able to leverage technology and economies of scale and scope to challenge Avon. Diversified companies such as P&G achieve economies of scope across their different businesses and products to save costs. In addition, the firms' large size contributes to economies of scale, helping to keep costs down. These cost-cutting advantages allow companies to offer their products at competitive prices. This leaves Avon with the challenge of matching the price premium with innovation and differentiation or maintaining value by lowering prices.

"Yes, Avon has plenty of proprietary products, but we live in a copycat world where online retailers with lean overhead can undersell Avon when it comes to mainstream beauty-care products."[63] Products are easily imitable, but intangibles, such as 125 years of direct-selling experience, are much harder to match. This style of product offering and delivery brings value to customers in ways that online and bricks-and-mortar stores cannot. Avon's door-to-door, direct selling model allows customers to sample and buy cosmetics from the convenience of their homes. Unfortunately, the Internet has reduced the amount of value this model creates for today's customers. Moreover, online warehouses and drugstores that can keep their costs and prices low by reducing overhead are offering lower-priced beauty products, forcing Avon to reevaluate its own costs and price structures.[64] "We have to continue to look at how we make direct selling more modern in some ways," including using technology to amplify the social connections forged by the representatives.[65]

Avon does not have the size or capital to match retail giants and consumer goods competitors such as P&G when it comes to media advertising and marketing. Its strength is in relationship advertising and marketing. Making marketing a line function with its customer-facing representatives reduces Avon's dependency on media marketing and thus, reduces costs.

Taking Action

As mentioned, in December 2012, McCoy announced plans to downsize by cutting 1,500 jobs and exiting from the South Korea and Vietnam markets. On April 8, 2013, Avon announced plans to downsize further by cutting 400 additional jobs and restructuring or abandoning operations in Africa, the Middle East, and Europe, including exiting from Ireland, as it aims to save $400 million by the end of 2016.[66]

While abandoning some foreign markets will cut costs, 83 percent of the company's revenue comes from outside of North America.[67] Therefore, Avon's future success depends on its ability to efficiently meet demand

---

ii. An emotional tie to a firm, usually within a family-owned or dominated company, in which the family members or owners try to maintain the identity or existence of the firm even when it may not be in the best interest of shareholders.

in the high-priority foreign markets, such as Brazil and Russia, where profits started declining in 2010 and 2006, respectively. Cultural needs and preferences pose challenges for the company as it competes with local competitors for market share. While Avon products are generally standardized, different cultures and ethnicities have different needs and wants from its products. Because of the high growth potential in these emerging markets, Avon cannot afford to abandon them or reduce its reps as suggested by its cost-cutting initiatives. When Avon moved to a global strategy under Andrea Jung in order to standardize and improve controls and coordination, the company suffered in its ability to optimize local responsiveness. Remote management coupled with increased competition and changing needs, have led to Avon's stalled sales in Brazil and Russia.[68] Recently, Avon took steps to better meet the needs of its local markets by introducing products that match the preferences of the customers there. First quarter 2013 results show a 10 percent and 3 percent sales increase in Brazil and Russia, respectively, proving this response was effective.[69]

Conclusion

Avon's long history is attributed to its unique approach to meeting the needs of women. Today, "Avon markets leading beauty, fashion, and home products to women in more than 100 countries through more than 6 million active independent Avon Sales Representatives."[70] This vast market requires the company to be in tune with what women all around the world want. Avon's continued success depends on its ability to effectively identify and meet the ever-changing needs and preferences of the women it serves both internally and externally – as representatives and consumers. As time constantly welcomes change in the external environment and competitive landscape, Avon must find a way to sustain its unique approach and core competencies. With looming pressures to innovate, outperform competitors, yield expected earnings, and ensure future profitability, Avon should not stray from the foundation of direct selling that brought it success. However, it must modernize the direct selling model to enhance its ability to create value for customers not only today, but "tomorrow" as well. Different markets must be matched with local responsiveness and cultural understanding and adaptability. Ethical concerns and moral hazards must be matched with corporate governance and value alignment. Competitive rivalry must be matched with innovation, effective leverage, and execution of core competencies. Developing and then using strategies that blend appropriately with the firm's vision and mission is critical to the firm's success. Risks must be matched with calculated and controlled growth and diversification. The combination of each individual challenge makes up the daunting task of returning Avon to its previous greatness, a responsibility falling on the new CEO's shoulders. Is CEO Sheri McCoy the right match for the challenge?" More specifically, is she the strategic leader who can work with others to find ways to facilitate Avon's efforts to create value for all stakeholders and perhaps especially for shareholders? Is the plan she is putting into place going to lead to the turnaround at Avon that many believe is necessary?

NOTES

1. Avon. About Avon. http://www.avoncompany.com/aboutavon/index.html
2. McIntyre, D. A. (14 Dec 2011). *How did Andrea Jung stay so long as Avon CEO?* 24/7 Wall St. http://247wallst.com/2011/12/14/how-did-andrea-jung-stay-so-long-as-avon-ceo/
3. Ibid
4. Ibid
5. Ibid
6. Ibid
7. Ibid
8. Avon / Corporate Citizenship / Corporate Responsibility Report / Vision & Mission. AvonCompany.com. http://www.avoncompany.com/corporatecitizenship/corporateresponsibility/vmvp/index.html#mission
9. Avon / About Avon. AvonCompany.com. http://www.avoncompany.com/aboutavon/index.html
10. Ibid
11. Form 10-K for the fiscal year ended December 31, 2011. Avon Products, Inc. http://www.sec.gov/Archives/edgar/data/8868/000000886812000010/d10k.htm
12. Ibid
13. Ibid
14. Ibid
15. Henning, P.J. (6 May 2011). *The high price of internal inquiries.* New York Times / DealB%k. http://dealbook.nytimes.com/2011/05/06/the-high-price-of-internal-investigations/
16. Ibid
17. Avon Annual Report, 2010. op cit.
18. Avon Annual Report, 2011. op cit.
19. Avon Annual Report, 2012. op cit.
20. Ibid
21. Ibid
22. About Mary Kay / Company and Founder. http://www.marykay.com/en-US/About-Mary-Kay/CompanyFounder
23. About Mary Kay / Press Room / Press Releases / Happy Birthday, Pink Cadillac. (3 Aug 2012).
24. Ibid
25. Staff. (14 Apr 2013). *Top Direct Selling Firms Worldwide, 2010.* Market Share Reporter. Detroit: Gale, 2012. Business Insights: Global. Web.
26. About Mary Kay / Company and Founder. op cit.
27. Staff. (14 Apr 2013). *Personal Care Industry, 2011.* Market Share Reporter. Detroit: Gale, 2012. Business Insights: Global. Web.
28. Arbonne: https://www.arbonne.com/company/info/iccs.asp
29. *Direct Sales Companies with the Most U.S. Salespeople, 2008.* Business Rankings

Annual. Deborah J. Draper. 2010 ed. Detroit: Gale, 2010. Business Insights: Global. Web. 14 Apr. 2013.

30. Arbonne: op cit.

31. Abbott, L. (1 Feb 2010). *Arbonne bankrupt.* MLM the whole truth.com. http://www.mlm-thewholetruth.com/network-marketing-news/arbonne-bankrupt/

32. *Parent Company of Arbonne International Recognized for Successful Corporate Turnaround in 2010.* Investment Weekly News 7 May 2011: 673. Business Insights: Global. Web. 14 Apr. 2013.

33. L'Oréal / Commitments / Sustainable Development / Our Vision. L'Oréal.com. http://www.loreal.com/DD/loreal/Article.aspx?topcode=CorpTopic_Group_ID_Vision

34. Ibid

35. Procter & Gamble / Our History – How it Began. pg.com. http://www.pg.com/en_US/downloads/media/Fact_Sheets_CompanyHistory.pdf

36. Procter & Gamble / Company / Purpose & People / The Power of Purpose. pg.com. http://www.pg.com/en_US/company/purpose_people/index.shtml

37. Avon Annual Report, 2012. http://investor.avoncompany.com/phoenix.zhtml?c=90402&p=irol-reportsAnnualArchive

38. Avon Annual Report, 2006. http://investor.avoncompany.com/phoenix.zhtml?c=90402&p=irol-reportsAnnualArchive

39. Avon Annual Report, 2009. http://investor.avoncompany.com/phoenix.zhtml?c=90402&p=irol-reportsAnnualArchive

40. Ireland, R.D., Hoskisson, R.E., Hitt, M.A. The Management of Strategy: Concepts and Cases. 10th ed. Cengage South-Western, 2012. Print.

41. Mortimer, R. (21 May 2009). *Avon calling for a new generation.* Marketing Week. http://www.marketingweek.co.uk/avon-calling-for-a-new-generation/2065550.article

42. Avon Annual Report, 2011. op cit.

43. Ibid

44. Avon Annual Report, 2005. http://investor.avoncompany.com/phoenix.zhtml?c=90402&p=irol-reportsAnnualArchive

45. Ibid

46. Silpada. About Us. Silpada.com. https://www.silpada.com/public/aboutUs/index.jsf

47. Staff. (12 Jul 2010). *Avon enters agreement to acquire Silpada Designs, Inc.* PR Newswire. http://www.prnewswire.com/news-releases/avon-enters-agreement-to-acquire-silpada-designs-inc-98231104.html

48. Liz Earle / Our Story / Where to Buy. us.lizearle.com. http://us.lizearle.com/where-to-buy

49. Nichol, K. (25 Mar 2010). *Avon acquires British skincare company Liz Earle.* Cosmetics design.com. http://www.cosmeticsdesign.com/Business-Financial/Avon-acquires-British-skincare-company-Liz-Earle

50. Goudreau, J. (27 Feb 2013). op cit.

51. Goudreau, J. (9 Apr 2012). *Avon names Sherilyn McCoy as new CEO.* Forbes. http://www.forbes.com/sites/jennagoudreau/2012/04/09/avon-names-sherilyn-mccoy-as-new-ceo/

52. Staff. (Aug 2011). *Andrea Jung.* Forbes / World's Most Powerful Women. http://www.forbes.com/profile/andrea-jung/

53. Avon / About Avon / Executive Leadership / Patricia Perez-Ayala. AvonCompany.com. http://www.avoncompany.com/aboutavon/executiveleadership/Patricia_Perez_Ayala.html

54. Avon Annual Report, 2011. op cit.

55. Cheng, A. (12 Jul 2010). *Avon to buy Silpada in biggest acquisition in at least 10 years.* WSJ / Market Watch. http://articles.marketwatch.com/2010-07-12/industries/30766710_1_avon-products-new-york-based-avon-independent-sales-representatives

56. Goudreau, J. (27 Feb 2013). *New Avon CEO vows to restore the 126-year-old*

beauty company to former glory. Forbes. http://www.forbes.com/sites/jennagoudreau/2013/02/27/new-avon-ceo-vows-to-restore-126-year-old-beauty-company-to-former-glory/

57. Kowitt, B. (30 Apr 2012). *Avon: the Rise and Fall of a Beauty Icon.* CNN Money. http://management.fortune.cnn.com/2012/04/11/avon-adrea-jung-downfall/

58. Ibid

59. Ibid

60. Wahba, P. (16 Mar 2012). *Avon Ladies See Need for Complete Company Makeover.* Thomson Reuters. http://www.reuters.com/article/2012/03/16/us-avon-idUSBRE82F0VN20120316

61. Munarriz, R.A. (2 May 2012). *Why Avon Will Never Be Great Again.* Daily Finance. AOL, Inc. http://www.dailyfinance.com/2012/05/02/why-avon-will-never-be-great-again/

62. Henning, P.J. (6 May 2011). op cit.

63. Munarriz, R.A. (2 May 2012). op cit.

64. Seghetti, N. (9 Jul 2012). *3 Reasons to Worry About Avon.* Daily Finance. AOL, Inc. http://www.dailyfinance.com/2012/07/09/3-reasons-to-worry-about-avon/

65. Coleman-Lochner, L. (22 Feb 2013). *Avon CEO Embraces Technology to Reverse Profit Slump.* Bloomberg. http://www.bloomberg.com/news/2013-02-22/avon-ceo-mccoy-embraces-technology-to-reverse-profit-slump.html

66. Chaudhuri, S. (8 Apr 2013). *Avon to Cut Headcount by 400, Exit Ireland Among Other Cost Cutting Moes.* Wall Street Journal. http://online.wsj.com/article/BT-CO-20130408-703486.html

67. Seghetti, N. (9 Jul 2012). op cit.

68. Wahba, Phil. (12 Feb 2013). *Avon Shares Climb as Long-Awaited Improvements Start Kicking In.* Thomson Reuters. http://www.reuters.com/article/2013/02/12/us-avon-results-idUSBRE91B0NX20130212

69. Coleman-Lochner, L. (22 Feb 2013). op cit.

70. Avon / About Avon / Avon Markets. op cit.

IVEY | Publishing

Background

Black Canyon Coffee (BCC) celebrated its 10th year of business operations in 2002. Starting with a single Bangkok location in 1993, the company eventually operated the largest chain of coffee shops in Thailand. Revenues were THB318 million[1] in 2002, with a profit margin of 10 per cent. BCC had been experiencing 15 to 20 per cent annual growth and had little debt. The chain employed 1,000 staff — 500 as direct employees and the remainder working for joint venture partners or franchisees. The founder and managing director,[2] Pravit C. Pong, had recently begun to pursue international expansion. Concurrently, Starbucks and other international chains had recently begun to focus on Thailand and other Asian markets. Experts predicted a consolidation phase in the industry that would leave five or six global competitors. What steps should Pravit consider to help ensure the survival of his company?

History

While the bases for many startups are prior experience or a personal interest, BCC's founders had no restaurant expertise and were not even coffee drinkers. In the early 1990s, relatively few Asian consumers drank coffee, and Thailand was no exception. For many Thais, Nescafé instant was the only coffee product with which they were familiar. How did a group of computer consultants end up building Thailand's coffee house market leader? Pravit explained:[3]

Ten years ago, we were actively involved in the IT [information technology] business. We found that it was a very tough business. We did not own any intellectual property, but just represented someone else, such as IBM or HP. We wanted to own something that belonged to us. The IT business was up and down, up and down, very fast. The change in the new technology came every two or three months, and the margin was less and less. Many people would go into the same market, and the competition was very high. So, I [thought] that we [could] build our own brand name. Secondly, the things that we thought about would be the basic needs of human beings such as clothes, food, medicine and household necessities. I cannot do the house, I cannot do medicine, I cannot do clothes, so coffee and food are the easiest to do.

We had no experience at all, but we were young and had the energy to do these things. I went and looked at the food business and thought that I would like to sell American food. But, [Thailand] already had McDonald's, Pizza Hut and Kentucky Fried Chicken. If I do anything [to] compete with them, there would be no way to grow. So, I looked at the coffee business.

Coffee, at that time, was just becoming a popular drink. In other countries, the number of coffee drinkers was growing every year. But in Thailand we just depended on Nescafé — instant coffee. In other countries, people did not drink [only] instant coffee, but all styles of specialty coffee. So, we decided to do that, and go into business without any background at all.

Pravit believed that given the success of fast food in the United States, an American theme would help to attract customers. Cowboy movies were popular among Thai people, so an Old West theme was chosen for the business. The company logo depicted a coffee-drinking cowboy, complete with a 10-gallon hat and a sheriff's star. The first restaurant was decorated as an 1800s saloon, including a bar, clapboard siding and a saddle mounted on the wall. Pravit explained how the name was selected:

Thai people like the cowboy, and the native American. There [were]a lot of movies playing at that time about the Indians and cowboys, and people were fascinated with that. When we were children, we would like to play at being a cowboy. Because the culture — the Western culture — went all over the world, we wanted to do something that made the Thai people feel they [were] part of the American, Indian or cowboy culture. We opened some books and tried to search out places that were [typical] of cowboy[s] — where they lived. We found Black Canyon on a map of Arizona, and thought it was great. It sounded like it fit in a John Wayne movie.

Given the name and the décor, many customers assumed that BCC was yet another American chain that was expanding into Thailand; in fact, in the 1990s, the U.S. embassy in Bangkok sponsored a trade fair for American firms that were doing business in Thailand. BCC was invited on the basis of its name, and event coordinators were surprised when a group of Thai managers attended the fair! The initial learning curve for BCC managers was steep. Pravit commented:

We found it very difficult to start the business, because we did not have any background at all. We knew nothing — not even how to make coffee, make the food, supervise or take care of the customer. I knew that I could not do everything myself, so I recruited people to help me. There was no expert in coffee in Thailand at that time, so our IT people had to work very hard to try and find information from books [and] magazines, or travel to Italy and other countries to see how to make coffee and how people drink coffee. We also called some of the expresso machine companies to teach us how to make coffee. If I had to go back to that time, I do not know if I would do it again; the first two years were a very difficult time.

The initial capital for BCC was self-funded. The computer consultancy firm had recently purchased an office building, which management leveraged to generate cash for the initial investment. One of the partners invested additional funds. Based on the success

of the initial location, BCC took out short-term loans to finance infrastructure costs of new locations. Two shops opened in 1994, and the fourth store opened in 1996; the first franchised location also opened in 1996 (see Exhibit 1).

An Asian economic crisis struck in 1997. The crisis was precipitated by solvency issues with Thai banks and a subsequent decision by the Thai government to de-peg the baht from the U.S. dollar. After decoupling the two currencies there were significant contractions in Thailand's gross domestic product (GDP) and per capita income. Despite the economic circumstances, the crisis was associated with a faster growth rate for BCC. Pravit described the firm's reaction to the crisis:

We did not know anything until the government announced the flotation of the baht — it was a shock. We were lucky that we did not borrow any foreign money: both of our loans were in Thai baht. The good thing about the crisis is that there were many businesses that could not continue. So, many shopping malls had empty space and the rent went down. We could afford to pay for good locations at a very reasonable price. I believe that people, [whether] they suffer or have happiness, still eat or drink. So, business still continued.

Founder Background

Pravit started his career as a programmer for Chase Manhattan Bank. He became a systems analyst and spent five years at Chase before taking an electronic data processing supervisory position with Warner-Lambert. He spent another five years at Warner-Lambert and

Exhibit 1 Black Canyon Expansion History

Year	Owned	Joint Venture	Franchise	Total
1993	1	0	0	1
1994	2	0	0	2
1995	0	0	0	0
1996	1	0	2	3
1997	0	3	3	6
1998	3	4	6	13
1999	1	2	4	7
2000	5	4	0	9
2001	1	9	4	14
2002	8	5	10	23
Total	**22**	**27**	**29**	**78**

Source: Company documents.

then accepted a position as IT manager for a Dutch multinational. Pravit noted that many Thai people were not entrepreneurially oriented, but rather preferred to work for the government or large firms; however, the Chinese Thai people had a much stronger interest in working for themselves. Pravit's father was also a businessman, and Pravit decided that there was a good opportunity to start a technology consulting business in Thailand. He founded Pro-Line in 1987. He served as managing director of Pro-Line, and took the same role when Black Canyon was founded in 1993. Pravit described the job of a managing director (MD) in the following interview:

Q: What are the greatest challenges of the MD job?

A: You have to support everything by yourself — managing problem[s], marketing problem[s], staff problem[s] — everything! So, there are many things you have to learn by yourself, that no one can teach you. You have to use your experience, talent and knowledge.

Q: What experiences did you have that best prepared you for being an MD?

A: Having good partners — shareholders, managers, staff are all our partners. Having good partners can release you from much of the burden of being an MD. Many of our people have an entrepreneurial spirit and have helped with the challenge of growing this business. They have contributed a lot to our success.

Market Conditions

Country Setting

In 2002, Thailand had a population of approximately 62 million. Of these, roughly 12 million lived in urban areas — six million in Bangkok and the remainder in a number of smaller cities. Thailand was politically stable, with a democratic government and a popular king who provided moral and social leadership. Per capita gross national product was THB84,246 in 2002 (see Exhibit 2); in U.S. dollars, this was $1,959 per year, or $5.36 per person per day. The literacy rate was 94 per cent, and life expectancy was 69 years. In 2000, there were roughly 2.4 computers per 100 people, and 23 million Internet users in the country. The country was overwhelmingly Buddhist, with a small Muslim population in the south. The Thai government was a strong advocate of building relationships with other southeast Asian countries; however, ties with some of its immediate neighbors — particularly Cambodia and Myanmar — had been uneven.[4]

Beverage Consumption Patterns

Brewed tea had been the dominant hot beverage served in Asia. The consumption of tea became popular in China during the Tang dynasty, around AD 800 to 900. Tea became popular in neighboring Asian countries but spread more slowly to other parts of the world. While tea remained a popular beverage in Thailand, per capita consumption was significantly higher in British and Middle Eastern countries. In recent years, prepackaged and iced tea products had become more popular alternatives to freshly brewed tea.

Levels of coffee consumption in Thailand were low in comparison to other nations, but growing at a substantial rate: 8,000 tons of coffee were consumed annually in Thailand in the mid-1980s — one-tenth of a per cent of worldwide consumption. Annual coffee demand in Thailand nearly tripled between 1990 to 2000, growing from 10,000 tons to 28,000 tons. By 2010, annual demand was forecast to reach 42,000 tons.[5] Per capita statistics revealed a similar pattern. In 1976, average coffee consumption was 0.1 kilograms per person in Thailand. By 2003, per capita consumption in Thailand had grown to 0.5 kilos per year. In comparison, Americans consumed 4.1 kilos per person, while Australians consumed 2.6 and Italians 5.7 (see Exhibit 3)[6]. Scandinavians had the highest levels of coffee consumption, with a typical Finnish person consuming 11.3 kilos per year. Japan was often viewed as a leading indicator of trends in southeast Asia; both gourmet coffee shops and ready-to-drink coffees had seen wide adoption in that country. In 2003, Japanese coffee consumption was 3.2 kilos per person.

Anecdotal evidence suggested that in addition to drinking more coffee, Thai consumers were also changing the types of coffee they drank. Joe Thawilvejjakul, an importer, noted that growing sophistication of consumers — in conjunction with the entry of chains such as Starbucks — had led to the creation of an upscale Thai coffee culture. As evidence of this trend, Thai imports of Lavazza, a premium European brand, had grown from 3.5 tons in 2001 to 14 tons in 2003.[7] As a comparison, the growth of specialty coffee in the United States had come almost entirely from switching, versus increased consumption. While the amount of coffee drank by Americans had remained relatively flat, the number of daily consumers of specialty coffee had grown from three per cent of the population in 1997 (seven million drinkers), to 14 percent in 2001 (29 million drinkers). Similarly, the number of occasional specialty coffee drinkers had grown from 35 per cent in 1997 (80 million drinkers), to 62 per cent in 2001 (127 million drinkers).[8]

Exhibit 2 Thailand Economic Statistics

	1990	1997	1998	1999	2000	2001	2002
Population and employment							
Population (millions)	56.3	60.82	61.47	61.66	61.88	62.31	62.8
Unemployment rate	3.9	1.5	4.4	4.2	3.6	3.2	2.2
Gross domestic product (1988 prices)							
(Billions of baht)	1,945	3,073	2,750	2,872	3,005	3,064	3,224
Real GDP growth % Consumption expenditure (1988=100)	11.2	−1.4	−10.5	4.4	4.6	1.9	5.2
– Private (+,– %)	12.9	−1.4	−11.5	4.3	4.9	3.7	4.7
– Public (+,–%)	6.9	−2.8	3.9	3.1	2.6	2.9	0.5
Manufacturing production index							
(1995=100 : sa)	66.2	107.2	96.5	108.6	112.1	113.6	123.3
(+,– %)	9.6	−0.6	−10	12.5	3.2	1.3	8.5
Private consumption index							
(1995=100)	na.	101.4	95.4	96.9	100.2	102.9	106.7
(+, %).	na.	−0.9	−5.9	1.6	3.4	2.6	3.8
External position (billions of baht)							
Exports	583	1,790	2,18	2,15	2,731	2,808	2,872
% annual change	14.4	29.8	21.9	−1.4	27	2.8	2.3
(% growth in US$)	14.9	3.8	−6.8	7.4	19.5	−6.9	5.8
Imports	838	1,875	1,678	1,800	2,514	2,696	2,723
% annual change	29	4.3	−10.5	7.3	39.6	7.2	1
(% growth in US$)	−29.5	−13.3	−33.8	16.9	31.3	−2.8	4.6
Inflation Rate							
Headline CPI (+,– %)	6	5.6	8.1	0.3	1.6	1.6	0.7
Core CPI (+,– %)	6.2	4.7	7.2	1.8	0.7	1.3	0.4
Exchange Rate							
Baht/US$	25.64	31.48	41.59	37.96	40.27	44.58	43.11

Source: "Thailand's Key Economic Indicators," *Bangkok Bank*, www.bangkokbank.com/download/02_glance.xls, accessed September 1, 2003.

In addition to coffee and tea, there were a number of other beverages that competed for 'share of throat.' The main alternatives included:

■ Soy beverages
■ Energy drinks
■ Bottled water
■ Juice and nectars
■ Ready-to-drink tea
■ Beer
■ Jellied beverages.

With the exception of beer, these beverages were usually marketed as nutraceuticals, or health-enhancing drinks. Demand for bottled water had grown tremendously in Thailand, and consumption of juice and nectars was expected to grow by 30 per cent between 2001 and 2004.[9] Across Asia, bottled water had seen the greatest growth in demand.[10] The following trends were expected to affect beverage demand patterns in the following years:

■ Changes in distribution points: these included a growing presence of western-style fast food outlets, western-style supermarkets and continued growth of Asian convenience stores;
■ Gradual westernization of Asian diets;
■ Growing visibility of global and regional brands.[11]

Exhibit 3 Per Capita Coffee Consumption (Kilos Per Person)

	2003	2000	1997	1994	1991	1988	1985	1982	1979	1975
World	1.1	1.1	1	1	1	1	1	1.1	1.1	1.1
Australia	2.6	2.6	2.6	2.6	2.3	2.4	2.2	2.5	2.3	1.8
Austria	5.2	6.4	8	7.8	10	8.2	7.3	8.2	5.9	4.8
Brazil	4.7	4.6	4.1	3.5	3.4	3.3	3.1	3.7	3.3	3.8
Brunei	4.1	3.3	5.6	1.8	2.3	1.7	1.7	1.4	1.2	0.9
Cambodia	0	0	0	0	0	0	0	0	0	0
Canada	4.1	4.6	4.5	5	4.4	4	4.3	4.2	4.3	4.5
China	0	0	0	0	0	0	0	0	0	0
Finland	11.3	10.4	11.5	13.5	12.1	10.7	10.7	12.9	13.5	12.7
France	5.3	5.5	5.7	5.4	5.8	5.7	5.6	5.9	5.9	5.6
Germany	6.7	6.8	7.2	7.5	7.5	7.2	6.1	6.6	6	5.1
Hong Kong	0.8	0	0	0	0	0	0	0	0	0
India	0.1	0.1	0.1	0.1	0.1	0.1	0	0.1	0.1	0.1
Indonesia	0.5	0.5	0.5	0.7	0.4	0.4	0.4	0.5	0.5	0.5
Italy	5.7	5.4	5.1	5	4.5	4.5	5	4.3	4	3.6
Japan	3.2	3.2	2.8	3	2.4	2.4	2.1	1.8	1.7	1.1
Jordan	1.6	2	1	0.6	1	1.3	0.5	0	0.4	0.9
Korea, Rep	1.6	1.6	1.4	1.5	1.1	0.7	0.5	0.3	0.2	0.1
Kuwait	1.6	1.3	1.2	1.1	0.5	1.2	0.9	2	0.7	1.2
Lao	1.1	0	0	0	0	0	0	0	0	0
Malaysia	0	0	6.7	0.6	0.6	1.1	0.4	0.4	0.1	0.3
Mexico	0.9	0.8	0.8	0.7	0.8	1.3	1.5	1.4	1.2	1.7
Norway	9	8.8	9.2	11.1	10.7	9.4	10.3	10.5	10.2	9.7
Oman	1.5	1.7	1.2	1.1	1.6	2.3	1.8	2.1	3.7	1.4
Philippines	0.7	0.6	0.7	0.7	0.7	0.6	0.5	0.6	0.8	0.8
Poland	3.5	2.8	3.4	2.9	0.4	1	1.2	0.6	1	0.9
Qatar	2	1.4	1.2	0.8	1.3	1	0.8	2.5	2.9	2.8
Russian Federation	1.5	0.7	0.7	0.7	0	0	0	0	0	0
Saudi Arabia	1.2	1.2	1.4	0.3	1.2	1.2	1.5	2.6	1.6	1.1
Singapore	0	0	0	0	0	0	0	0	0	0
Sweden	7.9	8	8.5	11.4	11.2	11.1	11.3	11.9	12.3	13.6
Switzerland	7.3	7.1	5.8	7.6	8.5	7.1	6.6	5.4	5.5	7.3
Thailand	0.5	0.5	0.4	0.3	0.2	0.2	0.2	0.2	0.1	–
Turkey	0.4	0.3	0.2	0.1	0.2	0.1	0.1	0.1	0	0.1
United Kingdom	2.3	2.4	2.5	2.7	2.4	2.5	2.5	2.4	2.7	1.9
United States	4.1	4.5	3.9	3.1	4.4	3.7	4.7	4.5	5.2	5.6
Viet Nam	0.4	0.4	0.2	0.1	0.1	0.1	0.1	0.1	–	–

Source: http://earthtrends.wru.org/text/energy-resources/variable-294.html, accessed August 10, 2011.

Competition

Precise statements of market size and competition in the Thai premium coffee market were lacking. Estimates of the total market for premium coffee varied widely: Thai Farmers Research Center had characterized this as a THB3.5 billion annual business, while other sources placed annual revenues as low as THB500 to 700 million. Additionally, market share estimates from various sources disagreed as to whether Starbucks or local firms held the dominant market share. Sources also differed regarding their expectations for industry growth: both Thai Farmers and the MD of Starbucks Thailand had predicted continued high levels of growth. In contrast, Oliver Janssens, the MD of Coffee World, had anticipated a significant decline in market growth, resulting in a much greater prevalence of head-to-head battles for market share. Janssens had characterized this market as a "low margin" business.[12] Pravit had a more negative assessment, stating his belief that most Thai coffee shops are not profitable. In neighboring Korea, Starbucks reported a positive profit margin in 2003, while their Japanese operations were operating at a loss during this period.[13]

Generally, there were three types of competitors in the Thai premium coffee market: foreign chains, local chains and independent shops. If the number of locations was used as a proxy for market share, then Black Canyon Coffee would have been the clear leader: they had 78 locations in 2002, and nearly 100 locations in mid-2003.

Of the top coffee chains worldwide (see Exhibit 4), Starbucks was the only firm that had entered the Thailand market, having 34 Thailand locations in mid-2003. Of those locations, 28 were in Bangkok, with two more stores each in Chiang Mai and Pattaya and one store each in Phuket and Koh Samui. Michael Holland, a business consultant to Black Canyon, commented on Starbucks' location strategy:

What we've seen in Thailand, and in other developing countries, [is that] they go after the very top end of the market. If you look at Siam Square, the main shopping area, you can throw a rock in any direction and there's a Starbucks. But, come out to this part of town, and there's nothing. They're only at A-class locations, while we will go in a much wider range.

Starbucks had roughly 6,400 outlets worldwide by mid-2003, and had stated a goal of having 10,000 locations worldwide by 2005, with a 50-50 split between domestic and overseas operations. When Starbucks entered Korea, it captured 40 per cent of the market shortly after entry.[14] Despite Starbucks' success, it only controlled a small portion of the overall premium coffee market — its worldwide market share had been estimated at four per cent.[15]

Many of the other leading chains had expressed comparable expansion goals; for instance, both Coffee Bean and Segafredo Zanetti had stated plans to open several hundred new locations. Industry analysts suggested that these trends would lead to industry consolidation. Melvin Elias of Coffee Bean commented: What we've seen in the burger industry will happen to coffee. After consolidation, there will be five or maybe seven global players.[16]

Other foreign chains active in Thailand included Au Bon Pain and Gloria Jeans. Au Bon Pain served baked goods and coffee, and had 26 locations in Thailand in

Exhibit 4 Top Coffee Chains Worldwide

Rank	Name	Country of Ownership	Main Market	Founded	Public/ Private	Outlets
1	Starbucks	United States	United States	1971	public	6,444
2	Doutor	Japan	Japan	1962	public	1,218
3	Tchibo	Germany	Germany	1949	private	455
4	Diedrich	United States	United States	1983	public	406
5	Second Cup	Canada	Canada	1975	public	388
6	Segafredo Zanetti	Italy	Italy	1962	private	350
7	Costa	United Kingdom	United Kingdom	1978	public	306
8	McCafe (by McDonald's)	United States	Australia	1993	public	300
9	Coffee Bean	Singapore/U.S.	United States	1963	private	222
10	Caribou	Bahrain	United States	1992	private	216

Source: Justin Doebele, "The Brew to Be No. 2," *Forbes Global*, May 12, 2003, p. 23.

2003. Gloria Jeans had three Thailand locations in 2003, all in Bangkok. There were a number of regional chains headquartered in Asia — Coffee Bean in Singapore, Pacific Coffee in Hong Kong — but none had entered the Thailand market.

Coffee World was the second-largest domestic chain, with 36 locations in mid-2003. Baan Rai was a second local chain that started with roadside locations. PTT (a

Thai oil company) announced plans to imitate the Baan Rai strategy and opened two Café Amazon concept stores in 2003. If successful, PPT executives stated that as many as 200 to 250 franchises could be opened at petrol stations across Thailand.[17] Much of the Thai coffee market was fragmented, with a large number of single-location outlets.

Prices and food offerings varied across competitors (see Exhibit 5). Starbucks and Coffee World were located

Exhibit 5 Price and Menu Comparison for Selected Shops, Chiang Mai

Starbucks	Location: In Night Bazaar Tourist District				
Selected Beverages	**short**	**medium**	**tall**	**Food**	
Latte	65	75	90	Brownie	45
Cappuccino	65	75	90	Blueberry cheese pie	80
Coffee, plain	50	70	80	Mango cheesecake	90
Hot chocolate	45	55	65	Banana muffin	55
Extra shot of espresso		15		Cinnamon roll	30
				Oreo cheesecake cookie	40
Additional products				Green tea cake	75
Whole coffee beans — 9 types					
Coffee products and logo merchandise					
Coffee World	**Location: In Night Bazaar Tourist District**				
Selected Beverages	**short**	**medium**	**tall**	**Food**	
Latte	50	65	75	Waffle	40
Cappuccino	50	65	75	Blueberry waffle	45
Coffee, plain	45	65	75	Strawberry waffle	45
Hot chocolate	30	50	n/a	Ham & cheese waffle	65
Extra shot of espresso		10		Ham & cheese sandwich	70
Additional products					
Coffee products and logo merchandise					
Black Canyon Coffee	**Location: In Residential Shopping Center**				
Selected Beverages	**(all medium size)**			**Food**	
Latte	55			Cashew chicken	70
Cappuccino	55			Spicy seafood tom yum soup	80
Coffee, plain	45			Pad thai	75
Irish coffee	70			Spicy grilled beef	65
Samui Romance smoothie	55			Pepper beef steak	125
Iced mocha	50			Caesar salad	65
Additional products				Spaghetti with beef	60
Coffee products and logo merchandise				Vegetarian macaroni	60
				Chicken green curry	70

Note: All prices given in Thai baht. Exchange rate is approximately THB43 per U.S. dollar, as of May, 2003.
Food listing for Starbucks and Coffee World is a complete list of available items. Food listing for Black Canyon is a subset of available items.

Source: collected by the case author during site visits, May 2003.

in the tourist Night Bazaar district, while Black Canyon was located in a residential shopping mall. A medium cappuccino was priced at THB75 at Starbucks, 65 at Coffee World and 55 at Black Canyon.

Black Canyon Strategy and Operations

Strategy

Pravit summarized the firm's elevator pitch to potential investors as "[the] best of the largest coffee house chains at good locations, which can provide good food and fine coffee at a reasonable price. To achieve that objective, we have good people" (see Exhibit 6). The MD noted that the mission statement was written in the early 1990s, and could benefit from revision.

Many of the Thai coffee shops had adopted a store layout and menu similar to Starbucks; in contrast, Black Canyon had tried to make itself as different from Starbucks as possible. Pravit explained:

A few years ago, I had a chance to talk to some students about 'Are you afraid of Starbucks?' [Note: excerpts from this presentation are shown in Exhibit 7]. Before they came to Thailand, we had the feeling that they [were] the giant, [had] been successful in many markets and [had] taught the world how to drink coffee — but not good coffee. So, what can a small company do when they encounter a big company like this?

At BCC, we like breaking the rules. We do not want to be the same as Starbucks, because we know that we can't compete with them directly. So, we want to differentiate from them. We think that drinking ice coffee while eating Thai food is a very enjoyable experience. We try to offer better service and products. The autonomy of operations means that local owners can be creative and flexible. We run the business with our heart and soul.

The full-service Black Canyon outlets offered nearly 100 food items, in addition to hot and cold beverages,

Exhibit 6 Vision, Mission and Goals

(a) Vision
TO BE THE BEST COFFEE HOUSE AND INTERNATIONAL CUISINE RESTAURANT IN THAILAND
By the best, we mean a Company that excels in pride and profitability in the relationships between the Company and our Customers, Franchisees, Employees, Investors and Suppliers. We believe the following are fundamental to our success:

- Pride in our products and properties
- Opportunities
- Customer acceptance
- Quality in relationships

(b) Mission Statement
To be the leading coffee house and international cuisine restaurant with the highest quality of products, services and all levels of personnel, and to develop the franchise system which meets the standards by utilizing suitable technology and adapting to achieve the efficiency in administration and services. All Black Canyon's consumers should always be satisfied with both the products, services, and personnel of Black Canyon.

(c) The five main objectives supporting the company's mission

- To satisfy the consumers and franchisees
- To create a good image of the organization
- To be the leading coffee house chain of Thailand
- To develop the knowledge and abilities of the team as professionals
- To manage the financials and balance the budget properly and profitably

Source: Company documents.

Exhibit 7 Excerpts From 'Breaking the Chains' Presentation by Pravit C. Pong

Breaking the Chains
Strengths of Local Stores

- Offering better service and better product
- Autonomy in operations
- The style of local outlets can be creative
- Local stores can develop their uniqueness
- Coffeehouses operated by owners
- Knowledge of the community

Breaking the Chains
Weaknesses of Local Stores

- Local stores do not have sufficient resources
- They do not have a good training program
- They do not have effective marketing and promotion
- Less brand awareness
- Limited R&D budget

Breaking the Chains
Strengths of Big Chains

- Their employees are well trained
- They have considerable financial resources
- They have effective public relations
- Global image
- Sell at higher price/make more profit

Breaking the Chains
Weaknesses of Big Chains

- They do not have local community knowledge
- Their identification looks alike, boring
- Lack of personal contact with customers
- Their product quality can be different from one another
- Their outlets operated by a manager
- Coffee and products are not as fresh and fine as local supplies

Source: Pravit C. Pong, undated document.

including beer. Food offerings included Western items (e.g., spaghetti, caesar salad), Thai specialties and other Asian fare (e.g., cashew chicken, curry). Holland emphasized the role of food to Black Canyon's strategy:

Most people perceive us as a coffee house, so they categorize us with a Starbucks, Gloria Jeans or Coffee Bean. But, we're really unique in our food offering. Starbucks has snacks and sandwiches, and that's it. Most of our competitors are clones of Starbucks. Our niche overseas is the food. Particularly when we go to the more first-world markets — Australia and the United States — a lot of people love Thai food. Thai food, and not in a fine-dining atmosphere, is going to be very attractive. Pad Thai and Som Tam become very strategic: they're the difference overseas.

In comparison, a typical Starbucks offered a much more limited food and drink menu. The Starbucks in Chiang Mai, for instance, offered only dessert. Coffee World also offered limited food choices, consisting of four types of waffles and a ham and cheese sandwich. There were also significant differences in pricing across these three outlets. Beverages were more expensive at Starbucks than Coffee World or BCC. A medium latte or cappuccino, for example, cost one-third more at Starbucks than at BCC. Prices at Coffee World were slightly higher than BCC, on average.

Operations

BCC operated three distinct types of outlets: kiosks, mini-restaurants and full restaurants. As of mid-2003, the chain operated 80 full restaurants, five mini-restaurants and 10 kiosks; however, because most restaurants were located in malls or shopping centers, future growth was constrained by levels of commercial development. Consequently, management expected a growing emphasis on kiosks in locations such as gas stations or bookstores. The economics of these outlets varied substantially; for instance, cost of goods sold for a kiosk was double that of a full restaurant. Productivity (sales per square meter) was double for a kiosk versus a restaurant, while rent was typically four times higher (per square foot) for a kiosk.

Roughly two-thirds of coffee used was grown locally in Thailand, with the remainder coming from South America. Local coffee was considered to be of much higher quality than neighboring Vietnam, and the industry was supported by the Thai government. BCC worked with a local university to design their coffee processing system. Its roasting equipment had the capacity to handle significant increases in demand.

A headquarters staff of 50 provided support to both corporate management and individual restaurants. Key tasks included procurement of raw materials, menu design, restaurant design and support, employee development and other back-office duties. Pravit noted that improvement of systems, policies and documentation was a critical task for BCC, particularly as the firm began to expand abroad.

Product and Geographic Expansion

BCC had not ventured beyond its core business of coffee and food; however, at least two new market opportunities had been considered. The first option was to sell branded Black Canyon coffee beans in supermarkets and other retail outlets. A second option was to draw on the firm's expertise in food service and franchising to develop a separate restaurant concept. According to Holland, the main impediment to such diversification was not the attractiveness of the options but rather the time constraints associated with managing growth in core products.

In 2002, BCC began its push to internationalize. Their first overseas location was in Singapore, which was also the headquarters of the Coffee Bean multinational chain. Later in the year, a second BCC outlet opened in Malaysia. A second Malaysian location was opened in 2003, as well as two new shops in Indonesia. Holland described other possible targets for expansion:

The Middle East is where we have seen the most activity. We have some agreements in development to go to the Middle East by the end of the year. We have also been talking to Australia and even North America, for the next year or two. We're really worried about North America — our ability to process orders needs to be a lot better.

In the spring of 2003, the United States invaded Iraq. Holland addressed the potential problems associated with marketing an American-themed restaurant in the Middle East:

It's curious about the logo, particularly as we start to go international. When I meet people in Saudi Arabia and ask them, 'Is this logo going to be a problem?' I get an answer that it is a macho image, not necessarily an American image. I think that Americans think of it as [an] iconic American image, but globally it is Wild West versus an American icon.

The Singaporean location was structured as a joint venture, with BCC taking a small equity stake. Other foreign outlets had been franchises, partly because BCC did not have the capital to fund investments in multiple countries.

Fees to franchisees varied depending on the type of outlet (see Exhibit 8). When asked how much menu customization was done in different countries, Holland stated:

A little. One thing we recognized, that took McDonald's and other companies years [to recognize], is that Asia is not one monolithic culture or taste. You have to adapt to each country, and be flexible. One reason for going the franchise route is the need for a local partner who understands that market.

When opening an overseas location, BCC sent experienced Thai staff abroad for three months to facilitate the start-up. While this was a popular assignment — due to the extra pay and opportunity to travel — the company was limited by a scarcity of English-speaking employees. Holland commented:

One of the biggest problems when we talk about international [expansion] is the internal skills. It's the infrastructure itself, and a big part of that is the people. There's not a lot of people who speak English — there's one restaurant manager who speaks English. So, we can only have him in one place at a time. If he has to be in Jakarta for three months, we can't open anywhere else during that time.

A separate challenge for overseas expansion was the increased complexity of the supply chain. All of the coffee and Thai-based food ingredients were sourced in Bangkok, then shipped to Singapore, Kuala Lumpur, etc. Inefficiencies in procurement and delivery had minimal effect on local outlets; however, having foreign outlets scattered across a number of countries created greater potential for problems such as stale inventory or stock shortages.

Financing[18]

Much of BCC's capital had come from internal sources. Pravit indicated that the use of internal capital stemmed more from necessity than desire, citing an initial reluctance of financial institutions to support a new business concept. To maintain growth, Pravit expected that BCC would have to start spending more on advertising and public relations, and that the firm "will need a lot more cash in the pocket" to support global expansion. Consequently, the firm became more active in soliciting external capital. Pravit retained Ernst & Young to serve as auditors, and recruited a 'farang' (a foreigner, referring to Holland) to increase credibility with investors.

Exhibit 8 Outlet Configuration and Franchise Fees (in US$)

	Restaurant Type		
	Coffee Corner or Kiosk	**Mini-restaurant**	**Full Restaurant**
Range of services	Coffee, beverages, and snacks	Coffee, beverages, snacks, fast food, spicy salad cooked without using a stove	Coffee, beverages, and food
Size	Maximum of 50 square meters	Maximum of 70 square meters	Minimum of 80 square meters
Franchise fee	$15,000	$20,000	$25,000
Damage and debt insurance	$4,000	$5,000	$25,000
Royalty fee (three per cent of monthly total sales, or a minimum of)	$5,000 Note: No royalty fee for first three years of operation	$12,000	$12,000
Marketing promotion fee	2% of monthly total sales		
Location survey fee	Charged on a cost-incurred basis. These fees are deducted from the franchise fee if the contract is approved.		
Design fee	Design is according to company policy, and typically runs 8-15% of decoration budget.		
Decoration expense	$15,000 – 25,000	$25,000 – 50,000	
Kitchenware	$6,000 – $10,000	$6,000 – $10,000	
Cash register	$4,000 – $5,000		
Trademark and related fees	Trademark fee is $25, plus fees for property taxes, signboards, custom duty, etc.		
Other expenses	Franchisees must have sufficient cash reserve available for salary, raw material, tax, payroll and related expenses.		

Source: Company documents.

In 2002, the company traded a 15 per cent stake in the firm for THB18 million. Half of this money was allocated for development (research and development, international expansion and infrastructure needs), with the remainder used to refinance existing loans.[19] The investment was made by a government sponsored venture capital fund targeted at small and medium businesses. Management had also considered taking the company public as another way to raise capital.

Summary

Worldwide, the coffee beverage market had been estimated as a US$100 billion per year business, with a consistent upward trend in demand. Additionally, demand for premium coffee in Asia was likely to grow at a faster rate than that of Western countries. While the coffee market continued to grow in size, it was still a challenging business: Diedrich in the United States had solvency problems and investors shied away whenever Coffee Bean mentioned the prospect of an initial public offering.[20] Many coffee shops in Thailand were not profitable, and it was rumoured that one of BCC's local competitors was pursuing an exit strategy.

Black Canyon had been opening 10 to 20 new locations per year, and believed that one new location per month was a sustainable target. By the end of their second decade of business, Pravit hoped to have upwards of 200 locations and to be operating in 10 countries. In contrast, Holland had a much more optimistic view of the firm's growth potential:

I would actually say that in 10 years, we could be at 1,000 branches. Once the countries get up and running — having three or four branches — they should be self-sufficient. If each one of them is opening 10 branches a year, and we have 10 countries, it doesn't take long to get to a 1,000.

What goals should the company set, and what steps are needed to achieve these goals?

Case development was supported by a grant from the Hong Kong University of Science and Technology.

NOTES

1. As of May 2003, there were approximately 43 Thai baht (THB) per US dollar.
2. This title is equivalent to chief executive officer.
3. Except where otherwise noted, all direct quotations from Pravit C. Pong or Michael Holland are taken from an interview with the case author, May 2003.
4. For additional background on Thailand, consult the CIA World Factbook, www.cia.gov/library/publications/the-worldfactbook/geos/th.html or the Library of Congress Country Studies, http://lcweb2.loc.gov/frd/cs/thtoc.html, both websites accessed June 1, 2003.
5. "Medium-term prospects for agricultural commodities: Projections to the Year 2010," Food and Agricultural Organization of the United Nations, Self-published, Rome, 2003, ftp://ftp.fao.org/docrep/fao/006/y5143e/y5143e00.pdf, accessed September 8, 2011.

6. http://earthtrends.wri.org/text/energy-resources/variable-294.html, accessed 8/10/2011.
7. Laurie Rosenthal, "Trader sniffs a mature market," *The Nation*, May 27, 2003, pp. 1B, 4B.
8. Data reported in a speech by Robert Nelson at the ICO World Coffee Conference, May 17, 2001. http://dev.ico.org/event_pdfs/nelson.pdf, accessed September 8, 2011.
9. Thailand Beverage Forecasts, Canadean Ltd, self-published, 2003.
10. Brisk sales for Asia's beverage industries, A.C. Nielson press release, June 7, 2002.
11. Ibid.
12. "Premium coffee: Stellar trend for Thai cafes," Business brief issued by the Thai Farmers Research Center, January 24, 2003; Natalie Suwanprakorn, "Thai Coffee Shops Start to Lose Their 'Cream,' As Market Nears

Saturation," *Bangkok Post*, December 8, 2002.
13. Starbucks Annual Report, 2003. http://library.corporate-ir.net/library/99/995/99518/items/178281/Annual_Report_2003_part2.pdf, accessed September 8, 2011.
14. Ibid.
15. Justin Doebele, "The Brew to Be No. 2," *Forbes Global*, May 12, 2003, pp. 22-25.
16. Ibid.
17. "Oil giant comes up with new brew for success," *Bangkok Post*, January 14, 2003.
18. Detailed financial data was not available as the firm was privately held.
19. "Venture capital fund helps Thailand coffee house-restaurant," *Bangkok Post*, March 22, 2002.
20. Justin Doebele, "The Brew to Be No. 2," *Forbes Global*, May 12, 2003, pp. 22-25.

CASE 5

Blue Nile, Inc.: "Stuck in the Middle" of the Diamond Engagement Ring Market

Alan N. Hoffman

Bentley University and Rotterdam School of Management, Erasmus University

Built on the premise of making engagement rings selection simpler, Blue Nile, Inc. (formerly known as Internet Diamonds, Inc.) has developed into the largest online retailer of diamond engagement rings. Unlike traditional jewelry retailers, Blue Nile operates completely storefront-free, without in-person consultation services. The business conducts all sales online or by phone and sales include both engagement (70%) and non-engagement (30%) categories.[1] Therefore, the company focuses on perfecting its online shopping experience and "providing extraordinary jewelry, useful guidance, and easy-to-understand jewelry education to help you find the jewelry that's perfect for your occasion."

Blue Nile's vision is to educate its customer base so that customers can make an informed, confident decision no matter what event they are celebrating.[2] It wants to make the entire diamond-buying-process easy and hassle-free.[3] In addition, an important part of Blue Nile's vision, as CEO Diane Irvine said in a recent webinar with Kaihan Krippendorf, is for the company to be seen as the "smart" way to buy diamonds, while saving 20-40% more than one would in the typical jewelry store. Blue Nile is working to become "the Tiffany for the next generation."[4]

Company Background

Blue Nile started in Seattle Washington in 1999, when Mark Vadon, the founder of the company, decided to act upon his and his friends' dissatisfaction with their experience in searching for an engagement ring. As a result, to battle their concerns, he created a company that offered customers education, guidance, quality and value, allowing customers to shop with confidence.[5]

Blue Nile operates its business through its three websites: www.bluenile.com, www.bluenile.co.uk and www.bluenile.ca. Customers from the UK and all the member states of the European Union are served by Blue Nile's subsidiary, Blue Nile Worldwide, through the UK website. Canadian customers are served through the Canadian website, and the US customers along with 14 additional countries worldwide are directed to the primary website. In addition, Blue Nile owns another subsidiary in Dublin, Ireland named Blue Nile Jewelry, Ltd, which acts as a customer service and fulfillment center.

Furthermore, in order to enhance and facilitate the purchasing process to serve both local and foreign demand, Blue Nile has given customers the choice to purchase their products in 22 foreign currencies, as well as in the U.S. Dollar.[6] As of the beginning of 2010, the company has offered sales to customers in over 40 countries worldwide.[7]

Not being built as a traditional brick-and-mortar jewelry company, Blue Nile uses its websites to exhibit its fine jewelry offerings, which include diamond, gold, gemstone, platinum and sterling silver as well as rings, earrings, pendants, wedding bands, bracelets, necklaces,

The author would like to thank Abdullah Al-Hadlaq, Rashid Alhamer, Chris Harbert, Sarah Martin, Adnan Rawji and Will Hoffman for their research. Please address all correspondence to Dr. Alan N. Hoffman, Dept. of Management, Bentley University, 175 Forest Street, Waltham, MA 02452; ahoffman@bentley.edu. Printed by permission of Dr. Alan N. Hoffman.

RSM Case Development Centre prepared this teaching case to provide material for class discussion rather than to illustrate either effective or ineffective handling of a management situation. The author has disguised identifying information to protect confidentiality.

and watches. Blue Nile's revolutionary and innovative ways of restructuring industry standards did not just stop with its lack of a physical presence. The company offers a "Diamond Search" tool that lets customers examine their entire directory of diamonds to choose the right one in seconds. It also offers the popular "Build Your Own" tool that helps customers customize their own diamond jewelry and then view it on the computer before executing the order. Moreover, Blue Nile offers customers financing options, insurance for the jewelry, a 30-day return policy and free shipping.[8]

Diamond sales represent the majority of Blue Nile's business and revenues. Diamonds, which are certified for high quality by an "independent diamond grading lab,"[9] are differentiated based on "shape, cut, color, clarity and carat weight."[10] Blue Nile uses a just-in-time ordering system from its suppliers, which is initiated once a diamond purchase is made on the website, eliminating the burden and the costs of keeping high-ticket items in inventory. However, the company does keep in inventory rings, earrings, and pendants that it uses as a base to attach the diamond to, in order to be able to customize diamond jewelry to customer requirements. In order to succeed in this industry, Blue Nile maintains a strong relationship with over 40 suppliers.

After its IPO in 2004, Blue Nile shares traded on the NASDAQ (ticker NILE). The company has been awarded the Circle of Excellence Platinum Award, which customers use to rank the best online company in customer service, by Bizrate.com since 2002. Being the only jeweler to be recognized for this excellence is a true testament to Blue Nile's solid business[11].

Strategic Direction

Blue Nile is in the business of offering "high-quality diamonds and fine jewelry at outstanding prices."[12] It is a publicly traded company, making its ultimate business objective to achieve the highest return possible for its shareholders. In order to do this, Blue Nile focuses on the following:

1. Cause disruption in the diamond industry by creating a "two-horned dilemma". According to Kaihan Krippendorff, Blue Nile has been able to effectively put its competitors in a position where if they try to compete with Blue Nile directly, they compromise an area of their own business (one edge of the horn), and if they do not choose to compete with Blue Nile, they slowly lose market share and competitive positioning

(the other edge of the horn). Blue Nile's decision to offer the highest quality diamonds in spite of it operating in an online environment where it could easily position itself purely as a "discounter" has been key to creating this dilemma. Competitors with brick and mortar locations are then left to decide whether they should sell their product online at a lower cost than a customer would find in-store in order to compete (knowing that this could negatively impact the brick-and-mortar location) or not go head-to-head with Blue Nile online.[13] This dilemma helps Blue Nile keep its stronghold as the largest online jewelry retailer.

2. Keep the consumer in mind and establish relationships with customers during a very important time in their lives. The idea for Blue Nile was born during an unpleasant shopping experience. The company remains focused on perfecting its user experience by investing in online education tools and resources within its website to help customers make educated decisions.[14] Blue Nile is not able to show its customers diamonds in person before a purchase is made so it must reassure customers by providing a comprehensive website, a 30-day return policy and providing grading reports on their diamonds from two independent diamond grading laboratories—GIA or AGSL.[15]

3. Capture market share and emerge after the recession in a strong competitive position. Some competitors have pulled back during the recession by closing locations, while others have closed their doors all together.[16] Blue Nile has been investing in its website and is working to aggressively grow its market share.[17]

The Jewelry Industry

It is estimated that 2010 U.S. jewelry sales finished at $49.3 billion for the year, a 2.6% growth over 2009.[18] According to First Research.com, the U.S. retail jewelry industry is considered to be fragmented as "the top 50 jewelry chains generate less than half of (total) revenue" and there are 28,800 specialty stores that generate around $30 billion in revenue. Diamond jewelry and loose diamonds account for approximately 45% of total jewelry store sales.[19]

A closer look at this industry reveals that 17.2% of total U.S. jewelry sales took place in non-store retailers. Still though, retail locations continue to be the primary source of jewelry sales, accounting for 50% of total U.S. jewelry sales in 2009 in spite of these sales decreasing by 7.8% between 2007 and 2009.[20]

According to Compete.com, Blue Nile controls 4.3%[21] of Internet jewelry sales, and as of 2009 Blue Nile had about 4% of the engagement ring business in the U.S.,[22] which is 50% of the American online engagement jewelry market.[23]

Blue Nile's Competitors

Blue Nile's many competitors include various different retail outlets like department stores, major jewelry store chains, independently owned jewelry stores, online retailers, catalogue retailers, television shopping retailers, discount superstores and lastly wholesale clubs. Many local jewelers have great relations with their clientele in smaller communities, which poses a challenge for Blue Nile to achieve greater market share. Online retailers include Amazon, Overstock.com and Bidz.com, which are well-known for their discounting, creating tremendous competition for Blue Nile. Most major firms who specialize in jewelry have their own online presence as well, such as Zales, Signet, Tiffany and Helzberg.

DeBeers

DeBeers, which owns 40% of the world's diamond supply,[24] is establishing its presence online as a trusted advisor as Blue Nile has done. Upon visiting DeBeers' website, it is clear that Blue Nile's consultative approach online has made an impression on DeBeers, as the website has an "Advice" section under Bridal rings and an "Art of Diamond Jewelry" section that both educates and serves as a source of confidence of quality.

Tiffany & Co.

Tiffany & Co., one of the best known luxury brand names, had revenues in 2010 of $2.9 billion, compared to Blue Nile's $302 million.[25] Tiffany & Co. continues to stand out in the jewelry sector by opening stores in urban America and has shown to be a success as there are many consumers who are willing to pay extra for a well-known brand name. Tiffany also offers great service at its stores through product information. Lastly, owning a piece of jewelry from Tiffany's—and receiving the iconic blue box—has an air of prestige all its own that Blue Nile cannot replicate.[26] In spite of the value associated with the Tiffany name, due to its lean business model, Blue Nile's return on capital is three to four times better than Tiffany's.[27]

Blue Nile's many powerful competitors require the business to compete through differentiation, and Blue Nile gains an advantage over its competition through its unique operating structure. Its strategy, distribution channel, and supply chain help to keep Blue Nile in the market as it also creates barriers to entry. Some competitive advantages include its partnership with Bill Me Later® and its direct contracts with major diamond suppliers. Blue Nile partners with Bill Me Later®[28] in order to offer financing for fine jewelry and diamond purchases. Blue Nile also has direct contracts with major diamond suppliers, which in turn allow the company to sell stones online at lower prices than brick-and-mortar locations because it has lower overhead costs and fewer distribution interceptions.

Guild Jewelers

It is difficult to find a competitor that can be compared directly to Blue Nile because of the unique way in which the business operates. While Guild Jewelers are not necessarily a united force that Blue Nile must respond to, Blue Nile CEO Diane Irvine considers Guild Jewelers to be the company's major competitor because Guild has the local relationships with potential customers that are difficult for Blue Nile to establish online.[29]

Barriers to Entry/Imitation

Barriers to entry in the jewelry industry are high as the following are needed: capital, strong supplier relationships and reputation. With regards to capital, traditional jewelry stores must fund their brick-and-mortar locations, on-site inventory and store labor. Supplier relationships with diamond cutters and distributors are also key and as seen with Blue Nile can greatly impact the profitability of a given retailer. Finally, due to the expense associated with jewelry purchases, Blue Nile's "average ticket" is 2,000 dollars;[30] customers are looking for a trusted source with a strong reputation.

In regards to imitation, Blue Nile leverages a few unique systems and services that are hard for the competition to imitate. First, Blue Nile's "build your own" functionality online differentiates it from competitors by allowing the customer to personally create their ideal diamond ring, earrings, pendant, multiple stone rings, and/or multiple stone pendants. The consumer also has access to an interactive search function, which references an inventory of 50,000 diamonds, including signature diamonds that are hand-selected and cut with extreme precision.[31]

Second, Blue Nile has its own customer service team of diamond and jewelry consultants that offer suggestions and assist customers with their purchases. This online interactive customer service approach creates a barrier to entry as the information technology platform for these functions is complex.

Lastly, Blue Nile also offers exclusive colored diamonds, which include rare diamonds that are red and pink.[32] It has a more diversified product range than its competitors because it does not have to hold inventory in stock.

The threat of new entrants is always a concern, but Blue Nile has been successful thus far at staying ahead of new entrants and has established a reputation as a quality, reputable online service.

One of the most significant resources for jewelers is diamonds and with DeBeers owning 40% of the world's jewelry supply, diamonds are considered scarce and unique. Large diamond suppliers like DeBeers are not as powerful as they once were—DeBeers at one time sold 80% of the world's diamonds[33]—but their presence is still felt. In addition, diamonds are generally obtained in politically unstable regions of the world, like Africa, and companies must be aware of the risk of obtaining conflict diamonds. The diamond trade is complex with regards to politics and legal issues, as the majority of diamond mines exist in underdeveloped countries, where corruption is prevalent and the rule of law is not easily enforced. Many of the diamond mines are located in African countries such as Botswana, which currently produces 27% of the global diamond supply.[34] However, recent global initiatives including the Clean Diamond Trade Act of 2003, and the Kimberly Process Certification Scheme of 2002 have made significant impacts on violence and illegal trade in the last decade.[35]

The lack of legal and political stability in many of the diamond source countries represents a threat to Blue Nile, and the industry as a whole. With unstable changes in leadership and power, threats to the global supply chain of a valuable commodity are possible, and perhaps even likely to occur. Takeover of diamond mines by militia groups, government claims of eminent domain, diamond smuggling, and obsolescing contract negotiations with foreign governments all have potential deleterious impact on the jewelry industry.

Finally, given the increased valuation of gold in recent years, this jewelry material has become harder to obtain. In just April, 2011, *The Times (London)* reported, "Gold prices hit a record $1,500 an ounce as investors continued to seek a safe haven."[36]

Social and Demographic Trends

There are a number of social and demographic trends that offer opportunities for Blue Nile. First, the average age of first-time newlyweds is increasing in the United States, currently 28[37] for men and 26[38] for women.

A *USA TODAY* analysis of the Census figures shows that just 23.5% of men and 31.5% of women ages 20–29 were married in 2006 (The analysis excludes those who are married but separated.) Both the number and percentage of those in their 20s fell from 2000, when 31.5% of men and 39.5% of women were married.[39]

Higher marrying ages tend to translate into greater spending power for marriage-related items, such as engagement rings.

Next, people nowadays are more receptive to handheld technologies and apps. These on-the-go technologies are an opportunity for Blue Nile to reach busy customers who do not have time to drop by a jewelry store to research their product choices and make a purchase. Mobile sites and apps allow a customer with a smart phone to make purchases on his/her own schedule, without adhering to a brick-and-mortar schedule. As this generation ages and people become comfortable with technology, Blue Nile will have more segments to cater to and a broader reach. With online purchases becoming more of a cultural norm, with less associated negative stigma, and as higher percentages of the global population gains reliable access to the internet, Blue Nile is poised to capitalize on its web-only strategy.

Finally, with historical events like the marriage of Prince William and Kate Middleton dominating the media, Blue Nile and other jewelry retailers reap the benefits of Kate's sapphire ring being displayed and/or mentioned in countless media venues throughout the world. Jewelers could not have planned that great of a publicity stunt for making jewelry top of mind, and have the opportunity to ride the wave for a while.

One social threat Blue Nile faces is tied to issues of internet fraud and online security in today's environment. The relatively high purchase price for quality jewelry increases the perceived risk for consumers making online purchases.

Another threat is that with each new generation, traditions (such as the purchase and gifting of engagement rings) risk becoming outdated or out of fashion. While the gifting of jewelry is highly entrenched in many cultures around the world, it is possible that potential customers in Generation Y or later may perceive lower value in this gifting tradition.

Global Opportunities

Blue Nile wants to expand internationally as it sees great potential in the global marketplace. Currently non-US sales represent 13% of the total sales at Blue Nile.[40]

Blue Nile's international sales have continuously been growing. Recent numbers show that in 2010 the sales figure grew by 30.4% compared to the previous year.[41] It is a high priority to grow internationally at Blue Nile. It is important for Blue Nile to monitor online purchasing rates globally, and expand to those countries accordingly.

One major global threat for Blue Nile is the lack of adoption of online purchasing. Many countries have not yet advanced to the American consumer habits. Developed countries are continuing to adopt this as they have realized the efficiency, effectiveness and overall convenience. Lack of consumer confidence for high-value online purchases may continue to follow Blue Nile as it expands internationally until it has built a reputation in each foreign country of operations, which may delay return on investment for international expansion programs.

Many consumers in developing nations do not have reliable access to the internet. Blue Nile currently has no way to tap the buying power of these would-be customers. Sending huge sums of money and receiving valuable goods when they clear customs is a risk many people are not willing to take, knowing its ramifications. Many countries around the world are corrupt, and thus one cannot be sure that the product has reached the customer safely.

Blue Nile's Finances

Net sales have been strong each year for Blue Nile since 2006, except in 2008 when the financial crisis impacted the company's performance, as seen in Exhibit 1. Sales have grown by $81.3 million since 2006, a 32% increase. Growth was most substantial in 2007 (26.9%) due to the huge increase in demand for diamond and fine jewelry products ordered through the website. International sales contributed significantly to the surge in demand in 2007, with an increase of 104.8%, due mainly to the new product offerings and the ability of U.K. and Canadian customers to purchase in their local currency[42]. Sales decreased by 7.5% in 2008, primarily due to the sluggish economy, which negatively impacted the popularity of luxury goods, and due to the increase in diamond prices worldwide[43]. In 2009, sales rebounded slightly with an increase of 2.3%, due mostly to an increase of 20% in Q4 year-over-year. The increase in Q4 is attributed to the boost in international sales, which represented 1.9% of the 2.3% total growth, as a result of the new website enhancements and the ability to purchase in 22 other foreign currencies[44].

In 2010, sales returned to double digit growth with an increase of 10.2%. Both US sales and International sales grew considerably with 7.7% and 30.4%, respectively, due mainly to a better economy, which led to increased

Exhibit 1 Blue Nile Net Sales 2006-2010 (In Thousands)

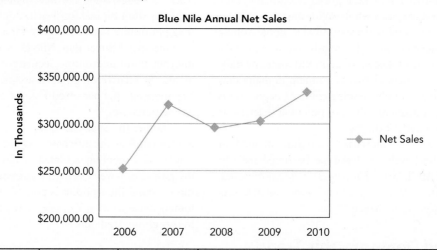

Year	2006	2007	2008	2009	2010
Net Sales	$ 251,587.00	$ 319,264.00	$ 295,329.00	$ 302,134.00	$ 332,889.00
Growth		26.90%	–7.50%	2.30%	10.18%

Source: All data in Exhibits 1-8 come from the 2010 Blue Nile Annual Report.

consumer spending. Marketing spending, better brand recognition, and the favorable exchange rate of foreign currencies against the US dollar contributed to the strong sales in Q4, which reached an all-time record of $114.8 million[45]. However, although Q1, Q2, Q4 numbers are growing annually due to events such as Valentine's Day, Mother's Day, Christmas and New Year, Q3 continues to present a challenge due to the lack of a special holiday or event.

Net income levels from 2006 to 2010 tracked the performance of net sales, but were more severe as seen in Exhibits 2 and 3. Net income increased by 33.64% in 2007, 10.06% in 2009, and 10.48% in 2010, but decreased by -33.39% in 2008. Not including the decrease in earnings during the financial meltdown, the net income numbers are considered healthy for a company that was started 12 years ago.

Gross profit has grown similar to net sales from 2006-2010 as can be seen in Exhibit 4. However, the most telling difference is in year 2009, where it outpaced net sales growth with an increase of 8.91%. The growth was a result of cost savings achieved with regards to sourcing and selling products, which increased the gross profit margin from 20.2% to 21.6% as can be seen in Exhibit 4. Blue Nile's increasing gross profit margin is a good sign for the company since it shows strict financial management, and an emphasis on the bottom line.

Blue Nile has no long-term debt. The company only has lease obligations that it needs to pay every year.

The lease obligations decreased from $880,000 in 2007 to $748,000 in 2010[46]. Long-term debt to equity ratio is effectively zero as a result, and even if we include lease obligations then it is minimal with a value of 0.01, meaning that equity can cover the remaining debt obligations.

Cash at the company is generated mostly through ongoing operations. The increase in cash from 2009 is a result of an increase in accounts payable and the tax benefits received from the execution of stock options. Investing activities also increased the cash amount with the expiration of short-term investment maturity dates. In addition, a slight increase can be attributed to the financing activities coming from the profits of the stock option execution.[47]

In 2011, Blue Nile had only $79 million in cash. In 2008 the company purchased back 1.6 million shares of stock ($66.5 million) in order to increase consumer confidence in the stock and because Blue Nile's management team believed the stock was being undervalued.

Blue Nile acquires the majority of its inventory on a just-in-time basis. Moreover, the company is successful in growing cash because its uses for it are minimal such as improving the website and maintaining facilities and warehouses.[48]

Marketing

Blue Nile's marketing strengths include: its use of technology to enhance customer experience, its dedication to

Exhibit 2 Blue Nile Net Income 2006-2010 (In Thousands)

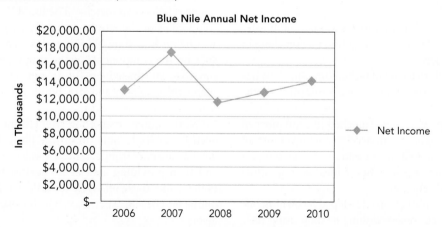

Year	2006	2007	2008	2009	2010
Net Income	$ 13,064.00	$ 17,459.00	$ 11,630.00	$ 12,800.00	$ 14,142.00
Growth		33.64%	–33.39%	10.06%	10.48%

Source: All data in Exhibits 1-8 come from the 2010 Blue Nile Annual Report.

Exhibit 3 Blue Nile Net Sales vs. Net Income (Percentage change)

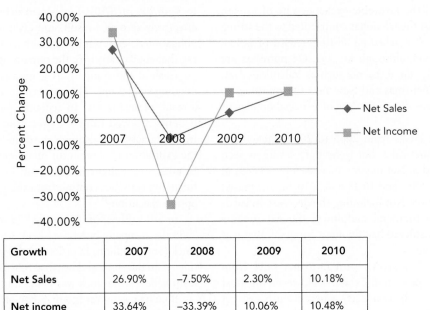

Growth	2007	2008	2009	2010
Net Sales	26.90%	−7.50%	2.30%	10.18%
Net income	33.64%	−33.39%	10.06%	10.48%

Source: All data in Exhibits 1-8 come from the 2010 Blue Nile Annual Report.

Exhibit 4 Gross Profit Margin and Operating Margin

Year	2006	2007	2008	2009	2010
Gross Profit Margin	20.2%	20.4%	20.3%	21.6%	21.6%
Operating Margin	6.600%	7.00%	5.400%	6.400%	6.400%

making the diamond-buying-process as easy and hassle-free as possible, and its ability to capture market share in spite of the recession.

First, in regards to its use of technology, Blue Nile has been investing in introducing and perfecting online technology that enhances customer experience. For example, the Blue Nile App, which was launched in September of 2010, gives customers instant access to its inventory of 70,000 diamonds and allows a customer to customize a particular diamond or gem with the ideal setting "while standing at a rival's counter."[49]

Likewise, Blue Nile has also developed its own mobile site that caters to customers wishing to shop using their iPhone, iPod touch, and Android mobile devices. "The mobile version, launched in spring 2010, is smaller than the PC site in scope, with quick tabs to find diamonds, engagement rings, and other gift ideas. The company reports that more than 20% of its shoppers are using the mobile site."[50]

Finally, Blue Nile has done an excellent job of making its website educational, easy to navigate and a trusted advisor for potential diamond buyers. The company completely revamped its website in 2009 in order to include larger images, better zoom functionality and enhanced product filtering features.[51] The site also utilizes interactive search tools that few other online retailers can match.[52] The Build Your Own Ring® component of the site is extremely easy to use, while also being fun. Blue Nile provides step-by-step guidance on the components of the ring a person can personalize, and based on filling out specifications on shape, color, quality and size, builds the ideal ring right before its customers' eyes.

Next, another marketing strength for Blue Nile has been its ability to hone in on the obstacles that might deter a customer from making a jewelry purchase online, and then providing assurances against those barriers. Policies like these all work to build confidence in the online purchasing experience, which works in Blue Nile's favor:

1. Offering a 30-day money-back guarantee;[53]
2. Orders being shipped fully insured to the customer;
3. Providing grading reports for all certified diamonds and professional appraisals for diamond, gemstone, and pearl jewelry over $1,000.[54]

Finally, in spite of the trying economic environment, Blue Nile has been able to capture market share while many other jewelry sellers have had to close their doors. According to CEO Diane Irvine, the company saw U.S. sales growth of 23% year over year in November and December of 2009, while its competitors ranged from 12% growth to a 12% decline in the same timeframe.[55] In trying economic times, customers have valued the 20–40% reduced price found at Blue Nile in comparison to brick-and-mortar retailers.

Although Blue Nile has done a good job of anticipating and catering to the barriers that exist in purchasing an expensive piece of jewelry online, the fact still remains that Blue Nile operates with no storefront locations. This means that customers cannot physically touch and inspect their piece of jewelry before making purchase. There are traditionally minded members of the jewelry market that are not comfortable with this limitation and will not consider Blue Nile a viable alternative. It is also more difficult to develop a lasting, long-term relationship with the customer when the transaction lacks the face-to-face experience found at brick-and-mortar stores. Blue Nile's business is completely dependent on online or phone transactions, making it subject to the adjustment period consumers must go through in order to be comfortable with this purchasing experience.

Building on this weakness is the fact that Blue Nile's online traffic and site visits has been in decline. According to 2010 data from Compete.com, "Blue Nile saw its number of unique site visitors decrease year over year in the majority of months, while one of its main competitors, Tiffany's, saw its online traffic increase. Similarly, Compete.com reports that when viewing Blue Nile's unique visitor trend between 2007 and 2009, the company has seen a 36% decrease in unique visitors."[56]

Operations and Logistics

Blue Nile aims to offer a wide range of finished and partially customizable jewelry products to online shoppers, made from ethically sourced materials, via a convenient, hassle-free experience. The company looks to leverage its sourcing power to offer exclusive jewels to exclude competition and retain high selling prices, while maximizing profitability through implementation of just-in-time manufacturing tactics to minimize inventory costs.

Blue Nile employs a flexible manufacturing strategy in its operations. The company heavily advertises the ability to customize your desired product – "Build Your Own Ring®" is an example of how Blue Nile allows a customer to pick a diamond and an engagement ring setting, and get a unique product.[57] Blue Nile also offers a similar type of customization for earrings, pendants, and other jewelry items.

On the one hand, it seems as though the company would be utilizing an "intermittent job shop" approach. However, while the company does offer full customization, through a special order service, the "customization" service is basically allowing online shoppers to pick from a pre-determined list of jewels and settings. The jewels are listed from a Blue Nile database (maintained in partnership with its source providers), and the materials are pre-fabricated in mass production style to minimize cost.[58]

Using the same methods, Blue Nile makes both finished goods (non-customizable products for direct sale over the web) and customer-directed finished goods. By using the same supply chain and methods, Blue Nile is able to achieve rapid turnaround of "customized" products, adding value to the service offering.[59]

Blue Nile partners with FedEx for both shipping and returns of all of its products. By maintaining one carrier partnership, the company is able to reach economies of scale in shipping expenditures, and also take advantage of FedEx's international shipping capabilities (other carriers, such as UPS, or USPS, are more limited in their international shipping offers). Also, by partnering with FedEx, Blue Nile is able to take advantage of FedEx's best-in-class shipment tracking functions, which alleviates potential customer concerns about expensive online purchases being "lost in the mail."[60]

Although the majority of revenues for Blue Nile come from the sale of diamonds, it typically does not receive diamonds into inventory until an order is placed, following a just-in-time manufacturing strategy. Instead, Blue Nile partners with its diamond sources, many of them in an exclusive agreement, to provide up-to-date records of available diamond inventory. When a customer places an order for a particular diamond, Blue Nile in turn orders the specified diamond from its supplier, receives the stone, finishes the good, enters the product into inventory and ships to the customer.[61]

Financially, this puts the company in a strong position, since it does not have to maintain high inventory carrying costs for the diamonds, which can be valued at several hundred to several thousand dollars each. The company actually produces a positive cash flow of approximately 30-45 days, depending on its contract with a particular supplier.[62]

While partnering with a single distribution partner does provide economic and logistical benefits to the company, it also puts Blue Nile at some degree of risk. Although FedEx has yet to experience a strike by its employees, its rival UPS faced this situation some years ago.[63] If the same situation should occur with FedEx, Blue Nile may be hard-pressed to quickly develop new distribution channels, both domestically and abroad.

In addition, there are also risks associated with Blue Nile's just-in-time inventory approach. First, this approach requires that Blue Nile establish and maintain a direct and accurate path of visibility to its suppliers' diamond inventory. Since many of its diamond suppliers are in less developed regions of the world, this is not an insignificant feat.[64]

Second, since the diamonds are not actually in the possession of Blue Nile at the time the customer places the order, it is possible that any type of geo-political disruption (natural disaster, governmental turmoil, etc.) could interrupt the flow of the customer's product, and require subsequent customer service follow-up and potential product replacement.

Despite these risks, Blue Nile's success in establishing exclusive sourcing agreements with diamond suppliers and cutters has yielded significant benefits, and is one source of competitive advantage for the organization. By negotiating directly with diamond suppliers and cutters, rather than operating through wholesalers, Blue Nile is able to reduce its diamond procurement costs by more than 20%, compared to other diamond retailers.[65] It is therefore able to offer lower prices than its competition, while simultaneously achieving higher profit margins on its products. Blue Nile's exclusive contracts do offer the company opportunities to be a "sole source" for particular diamond cuts or rare colors, although many diamond retailers have also followed this trend, and each major retailer appears to have its own "exclusive" diamonds.[66]

Human Resources and Ethics

Blue Nile employs 193 full-time workers, with 26 of these full-time positions listed at the executive level.[67] The company maintains employee testimonials on its website as part of its career section, with several comments from employees who have been with the organization for 10 years or more.[68] However, when looking for examples of Blue Nile employee satisfaction outside of the company's own website, the picture is not as rosy. The most common complaints pertain to employee development and retention. Unverified reports of hyper-control by senior

management, instead of empowerment and distribution of responsibility to managerial staff, if true, may have a significant impact on Blue Nile's ability to attract and retain high-performance employees, and as a result, grow its business.[69] While the company has made a significant leap forward compared to other jewelry retailers, both brick-and-mortar and internet-based, if the company focuses exclusively on technology, and not on human talent development, it has little chance to continue its recent growth trends.

While Blue Nile has a significant section of its website devoted to its policies around the ethical sourcing of its diamonds and other materials, the company does not detail any of its policies regarding the handling of its own employees. There are no statements regarding employee diversity, the cultural environment, or employee training/advancement programs. Despite listing nine senior managers listed in the company's investor relations section of its website, not one of the nine is involved in Human Resource Management.[70] This absence, taken with the company's wordage from its corporate reports, paints a picture that suggests attention to human assets is limiting at Blue Nile, Inc.

Stuck in the Middle

Operating in a niche segment, Blue Nile is "stuck in the middle" of the diamond engagement ring market. It is not at the top end of the jewelry retail market, with the likes of Tiffany & Co. or DeBeers. It is neither at the low end of the market, with the likes of Amazon or Overstock.com. Blue Nile has found a strong growth market by providing high quality jewelry at discounted prices. Unfortunately, as the company increasingly grows its market share, competitors at the high end and the low end will look to squeeze into the middle niche that Blue Nile currently dominates. Tiffany & Co. and DeBeers have already begun to infuse their online presence with aspects of Blue Nile's approach. Amazon and Overstock.com are likely to look to add higher-priced jewels to their offerings, as broad market acceptance of purchasing jewelry online increases. Michael Porter states that the middle is the worst place to be. The challenge for Blue Nile is how to move up the ladder and become a "high end" diamond retailer—not an easy task for an "online only" retailer.

NOTES

1. Blue Nile, Inc. Datamonitor. www. datamonitor.com. September 10, 2010.
2. http://www.bluenile.com/blue-nile-advantage
3. http://www.bluenile.com/about-blue-nile
4. http://www.kaihan.net/vpw_login. php?img=blue-nile
5. http://www.bluenile.com/blue-nile-history
6. http://www.reuters.com/finance/stocks/ companyProfile?symbol=NILE.O
7. http://www.reuters.com/finance/stocks/ companyProfile?symbol=NILE.O
8. http://www.bluenile.com/blue-nile-history
9. http://www.bluenile.com/about-blue-nile
10. http://www.reuters.com/finance/stocks/ companyProfile?symbol=NILE.O
11. http://www.bluenile.com/about-blue-nile
12. http://www.bluenile.com/blue-nile-advantage
13. Krippendorff, Kaihan. "Creating a Two-Horned Dilemma." Fast Company.com. September 8, 2010.
14. http://www.kaihan.net/vpw_login. php?img=blue-nile
15. http://www.bluenile.com/why-choose-blue-nile
16. Blue Nile, Inc. Datamonitor. www. datamonitor.com. September 10, 2010.
17. MacMillan, Douglas. "How Four Rookie CEO's Handled the Great Recession." *Bloomberg Businessweek*. February 18, 2010.
18. Mintel. Accessed May 8, 2011. http:// academic.mintel.com/sinatra/oxygen_ academic/search_results/show&/display/ id=482738/display/id=540585#hit1
19. Jewelry Retail Industry Profile. First Research.com. February 14, 2011.
20. Mintel. Accessed May 8, 2011. http:// academic.mintel.com/sinatra/oxygen_ academic/search_results/show&/display/ id=482738/display/id=540590#hit1
21. DeFotis, Dimitra. "No Diamond in the Rough." Barron's. February 15, 2010.
22. Plourd, Kate. "I Like Innovative, Disruptive Businesses." CFO Magazine. February 1, 2009.
23. Blue Nile, Inc. Datamonitor. www. datamonitor.com. September 10, 2010.
24. Jewelry Retail Industry Profile. First Research.com. February 14, 2011.
25. DeFotis, Dimitra. "No Diamond in the Rough." *Barron's*. February 15, 2010.
26. https://collab.itc.virginia.edu/access/ content/group/dff17973-f012-465d-9e73-a05fa4456644/Research/Memos/MII%20 Memos/Archive/Short/S%20-NILE_2.pdf
27. http://www.kaihan.net/vpw_login. php?img=blue-nile
28. http://www.bluenile.com/services_channel. jsp
29. http://www.kaihan.net/vpw_login. php?img=blue-nile
30. "Blue Nile- CEO interview." CEO Wire. November 29, 2010. http://ezp.bentley. edu/login?url=http://search.proquest. com/?url=http://search.proquest.com/docv iew/814841480?accountid=8576
31. http://www.bluenile.com/why-choose-blue-nile
32. http://www.bluenile.com/diamonds/ fancy-colordiamonds?keyword_search_ value=colored+diamonds
33. Levine, Joshua. "A Beautiful Mine." *New York Times*. April 17, 2011.
34. (2008), DIAMONDS: Kimberley Process Effective. Africa Research Bulletin: Economic, Financial and Technical Series, 44: 17640A–17641A.
35. http://www.kimberleyprocess.com/ background/index_en.html
36. "Gold at $1,500." *The Times (London)*. April 20, 2011.
37. http://factfinder.census.gov/servlet/ GRTTable?_bm=y&-geo_id=01000US&-_ box_head_nbr=R1204&-ds_ name=ACS_2009_1YR_G00_&-redoLog=false&-mt_name=ACS_2005_EST_ G00_R1204_US30&-format=US-30
38. http://factfinder.census.gov/ servlet/GRTTable?_bm=y&-geo_ id=D&_box_head_nbr=R1205&ds_ name=ACS_2009_1YR_G00_&-_lang=en&-redoLog=false&format=D&mt_ name=ACS_2009_1YR_G00_R1204_US30
39. DeBarros, Anthony and Jayson, Sharon. "Young Adults Delaying Marriage; Data Show 'Dramatic' Surge in Single Twentysomethings." *USA Today*. September 12, 2007.
40. 2010 Blue Nile Annual Report. Page 27.
41. 2010 Blue Nile Annual Report. Page 27.
42. Annual report 2008. Pg 31.
43. Annual report 2008. Pg 30.
44. Annual report 2010. Pg 31.
45. Annual report 2010. Pg 30.
46. Annual report 2010. Pg 30.
47. Annual report 2010. Pg 32.
48. Annual report 2010. Pg 33.
49. Birchall, Jonathan. "Smartphone Apps: Competition Set to Intensify for Online Retailers." FT.com. Nov 13, 2010.
50. Blue Nile, Inc. Overview. Hoovers. http:// cobrands.hoovers.com/global/cobrands/ proquest/overview.xhtml?ID=100858
51. Byron Acohido and Edward C. Baig. "Blue Nile Gets a New Look." *USA Today*. September 2, 2009.
52. Blue Nile, Inc. Datamonitor. www. datamonitor.com. September 10, 2010.
53. Blue Nile, Inc. Datamonitor. www. datamonitor.com. September 10, 2010.
54. "Blue Nile Unwraps Cyber Monday Promotions." *Information Technology Newsweekly*. December 8, 2009.
55. DeFotis, Dimitra. "No Diamond in the Rough." *Barron's*. February 15, 2010.
56. DeFotis, Dimitra. "No Diamond in the Rough." *Barron's*. February 15, 2010.
57. http://www.bluenile.com/build-your-own-diamond-ring?track=head
58. http://www.glassdoor.com/Reviews/ Blue-Nile-Reviews-E11944.htm
59. http://www.glassdoor.com/Reviews/ Blue-Nile-Reviews-E11944.htm
60. http://www.fedex.com/us/track/index.html
61. http://www.reuters.com/finance/stocks/ companyProfile?symbol=NILE.O
62. http://seekingalpha.com/article/11593-the-bull-and-bear-cases-for-blue-nile-nile
63. http://www.businessweek.com/smallbiz/ news/date/9811/e981119.htm
64. http://seekingalpha.com/article/11593-the-bull-and-bear-cases-for-blue-nile-nile
65. http://seekingalpha.com/article/11593-the-bull-and-bear-cases-for-blue-nile-nile
66. http://www.diamondsnews.com/hearts_ on_fire.htm
67. http://www.hoovers.com/company/Blue_ Nile_Inc/rffxhxi-1.html
68. http://www.bluenile.com/employee_ testimonials.jsp
69. http://www.glassdoor.com/Reviews/Blue-Nile-Reviews-E11944.htm
70. http://investor.bluenile.com/management.cfm

Campbell: Is the Soup Still Simmering?

Alan B. Eisner

Pace University

Dan Baugher

Pace University

Helaine J. Korn

Baruch College, CUNY

Introduction

Change is stirring at Campbell Soup. Douglas R. Conant is stepping down as the chief executive of Campbell Soup on July 31, 2011 closing the book on a stint that began in January 2001. On deck to take his position is Denise Morrison, who currently heads the company's North American soup business, whose sales fell 5 percent in the last quarter of 2010, as consumers opted for frozen pizza and microwave dinners instead of the comfort of soup. The change at the top for the company received a lukewarm response from investors, who are left wondering what meaningful change will come from this new CEO (Gutierrez, 2010). The company may have missed an opportunity by picking insider Denise Morrison to eventually lead the world's largest soupmaker, instead of bringing in outside talent to revive sales, analysts said. "It is not a surprise to us that Campbell is making a change, given how it has struggled recently," said one analyst. "What is surprising is that Conant will be replaced by the executive who currently heads the business unit that has struggled the most. Putting the head of the soup business in charge of the company doesn't seem to be the way to go when you consider this is the business that appears to have most of the problems" (Boyle, 2010).

In November 2010, Campbell Soup Co. said it will begin moving attention away from reducing salt in its products to focusing more on "taste adventure" as its U.S. soup business has turned cold. Campbell Soup was one of the first large U.S. packaged-food makers to focus heavily on decreasing sodium across its product line. The salt-reduction push was one of the company's biggest initiatives of the past decade. "The company had pursued reducing sodium levels and other nutritional health initiatives partly to prepare for expected nutritional labeling changes in the U.S. But amid the attention on salt-cutting, management focused less on other consumer needs, such as better tastes and exciting varieties," said Mr. Conant. "I think we've addressed the sodium issue in a very satisfactory way. The challenge for us now is to create some taste adventure" (Brat & Ziobro, 2010). This change comes as heavy supermarket promotions of simple meals such as boxed macaroni and cheese have battered Campbell earnings in recent quarters of 2010 (Brat & Ziobro, 2010).

Company Background

Probably known best for its red and white soup cans, The Campbell Soup Company was founded in 1869 by Abram Anderson and Joseph Campbell as a canning and preserving business. Almost 140 years later, Campbell offers a whole lot more than just soup in a can. Today the company, headquartered in Camden, NJ, competitively operates in four segments: U.S. Soup, Sauces, and Beverages; Baking and Snacking; International Soup and Sauces; and Other ("Campbell Soup Co. Profile") (see Figure 1).

In 2010 Campbell's products were sold in 120 countries around the world, and the company had operations in the United States, Canada, Mexico, and Latin America (campbellsoupcompany.com, 2010) (see Figure 2).

The company was pursuing strategies designed to expand the availability of its products in existing markets and to capitalize on opportunities in emerging channels and markets around the globe. As a first step, Campbell Soup Company, synonymous with the all-American kitchen for 125 years, acquired in 1994 Pace Foods Ltd., the world's largest producer of Mexican sauces. Mr. Weise, CFO at that time, said that a major motivation for the purchase was to diversify Campbell, and to extend the Pace brand to other products. In addition, he said, the company saw a strong potential for Pace products internationally. Campbell also saw an overlap with its raw-materials purchasing operations, since peppers, onion and tomatoes were already used in the company's soups, V-8, barbecue sauce and pasta sauces (Collins, 1994). To help reduce some of the price volatility for ingredients, the company used various commodity risk management tools for a number of its ingredients and commodities, such as natural gas, heating oil, wheat, soybean oil, cocoa, aluminum and corn (Annual Report, 2009).

Campbell Soup, a leading food producer in the United States, had a presence in approximately 85 percent of U.S. households ("Investor News (a)"). However, in recent years, the company faced a slowdown in its soups sales as consumers were seeking out more convenient meal options, such as ready meals and dining out. In order to compete more effectively, especially against

Figure 2 Campbell's Principal Manufacturing Facilities

Inside the U.S.		Outside the U.S.	
California • Dixon (SSB) • Sacramento (SSB) • Stockton (SSB) **Connecticut** • Bloomfield (BS) **Florida** • Lakeland (BS) **Illinois** • Downers Grove (BS) **Michigan** • Marshall (SSB) **New Jersey** • South Plainfield (SSB) • East Brunswick (BS) **North Carolina** • Maxton (SSB)	**Ohio** • Napoleon (SSB/NAFS/ISSB) • Willard (BS) **Pennsylvania** • Denver (BS) • Downingtown (BS/NAFS) **South Carolina** • Aiken (BS) **Texas** • Paris (SSB/ISSB) **Utah** • Richmond (BS) **Washington** • Everett (NAFS) **Wisconsin** • Milwaukee (SSB)	**Australia** • Huntingwood (BS) • Marleston (BS) • Shepparton (ISSB) • Virginia (BS) **Belgium** • Purus (ISSB) **Canada** • Toronto (ISSB/NAFS) **France** • LePontet (ISSB) **Germany** • Luebeck (ISSB)	**Indonesia** • Jawa Barat (BS) **Malaysia** • Selangor Darul Ehsan (ISSB) **Mexico** • Villagran (ISSB) **Netherlands** • Utrecht (ISSB) **Sweden** • Kristianstad (ISSB)

SSB – U.S. Soup, Sauces and Beverages

BS – Baking and Snacking

ISSB – International Soup, Sauces and Beverages

NAFS – North America Foodservice

Source: Annual Report, 2010.

Figure 1 Sales by Segment

	(Millions)			% Change	
	2010	2009	2008	2010/ 2009	2009/ 2008
U.S. Soup, Sauces and Beverages	$3,700	$3,784	$3674	(2)	3
Baking and Snacking	1,975	1,846	2,058	7	(10)
International Soup, Sauces and Beverages	1,423	1,357	1,610	5	(16)
North America Foodservice	578	599	656	(4)	(9)
	$7,676	$7,586	$7,998	1	(5)

Source: Annual Report, 2010.

General Mills' Progresso brand, Campbell had undertaken various efforts to improve the quality and convenience of its products.

In 2006, in just under six years since he came on board as CEO, Conant, 55, had transformed Campbell from a beleaguered old brand rumored to be on the auction block to one of the food industry's best performers. The stock was up 100% since March, 2003, more than double other comparable food companies. The turnaround had been catalyzed by cost-cutting, smart innovations, and a concerted effort to reinvigorate the workforce. "We're hitting our stride a little bit more [than our peers]," said Conant, in his usual understated style ("Lighting a fire under Campbell", 2006).

China and Russia

In addition to improving and expanding its product offerings within the U.S., in September 2007, Campbell launched new products in the emerging markets of China and Russia. Consumption of soup in Russia and

China far exceeded that of the U.S., but in both countries, nearly all of the soup was homemade. With the launch of products tailored to the local tastes, trends, and eating habits, Campbell had the potential of leading the soup commercialization activity in Russia and China. "We have an unrivaled understanding of consumers' soup consumption behavior and innovative technology capabilities within the Simple Meals category. The products we developed are designed to serve as a base for the soups and other meals Russian and Chinese consumers prepare at home" (Annual Report, 2007).

In July 2008, Campbell was planning to increase its overseas product offerings, as well as the number of Russian and Chinese markets their products would be available in. If the company could capture at least 3% of the at-home consumption, said Larry S. McWilliams, president of Campbell's international group, the size of the business would equal that of the U.S. "The numbers blow your hair back," he said (Boyle, 2009). In 2009 Campbell was offering three broth-like products that Russians could use as a base for soups. Campbell was preparing for expansion in Russia based on the recent distribution agreement with Coca-Cola Hellenic. Campbell planned to increase points of distribution and the variety of its "Domashnaya Klassika" line in fiscal 2010. The Russian portfolio would increase from three varieties in 1,500 stores in Moscow in 2009 to 14 varieties in more than 32,000 stores in 100 cities in fiscal 2010 ("Investor News (b)").

For about three years, in both Russia and China, Campbell sent its marketing teams to study the local markets. The main focus was on how Russians and Chinese eat soup, and how can Campbell offer something new. Larry McWilliams, President of Campbell International, said how surprised he was by Russians' love for soup while doing the research. "In Moscow, one lady was telling me very enthusiastically for a half an hour what soups she loves and how she prepares them," said McWilliams in an interview with Vedomosti newspaper. "It felt like I have asked her about her children." As a result Campbell came up with a production line specifically created for the local market, called "Domashnaya Klassika." It is a stock base for soups that contains pieces of mushrooms, beef or chicken. Based on this broth, the main traditional Russian soup recipes can be prepared. Maksim Klyagin, a financial analyst and Finam, stated that Campbell Soup successfully launched its business in Russia. In his opinion, an important contribution to it had a large marketing campaign, successful adaptation of the product line to the traditional Russian kitchen, and the aggressive price policies: Campbell's offer was cheaper than that of its competitors. During its 10 months of operation in Moscow, Russia, Campbell's market share rose to 5-8%. The Company, in the Finam's opinion, was still far from its local producers, such as Mars (Gurmania brand), Unilever (Knorr brand) and DHV-S (Rollton brand), that controlled about 80% of the soup market in Russia (www.rb.ru). While not yet in the ready-to-serve soup category, these soup stocks were a natural entry point into the Russian soup culture.

U.S. Soup Revitalization

In July 2009, Campbell announced additional plans for revitalizing the U.S. soup business ("Investor News (c)"):

- "Campbell's Chunky" soups will undergo the most comprehensive series of enhancements in its 40-year history. The soups will feature "better for you" credentials now with 24 varieties made with lean meat and 30 items containing a full serving of vegetables.
- In the wellness arena, Campbell's iconic tomato soup, which is enjoyed by 25 million Americans at least once a week, will feature the same great taste with a major sodium reduction of 32 percent to 480 mg per serving. Campbell will reposition "Healthy Request" soups in the heart-health space by further reducing the sodium levels to 410 mg per serving and featuring the American Heart Association certification on a redesigned label. Both products will be available in September.
- Building on the successful launch of the "Select Harvest" line, Campbell will add five new Mediterranean-style varieties this fall, including Greek-style Minestrone and Zesty Tomato Bisque.
- Campbell will introduce five new condensed light soups to tap into this fast-growing segment of the category.
- As consumers continue to eat more meals at home, Campbell will increase its emphasis on value with a focus on money-saving meals and in-store merchandising. Campbell plans to enhance its Campbell's Kitchen web site [www.campbellskitchen.com] to help people find and prepare affordable, tasty and easy meals using Campbell's products.

In September 2010, Campbell launched its first-ever umbrella advertising campaign to support all of its U.S. soup brands with the slogan "It's amazing what soup can do," highlighting the convenience and health benefits of canned soup. The new campaign supported Campbell's condensed soup, Campbell's Chunky soup, Campbell's Healthy Request soups, Campbell's Select Harvest soup, as well as soups sold in microwaveable bowls and cups under these brands (News Release, 2010(a)).

Firm Structure and Management

Campbell Soup was controlled by the descendants of John T. Dorrance, the chemist who invented condensed soup more than a century ago. In struggling times, the Dorrance family faced agonizing decisions: Should they sell the Campbell Soup Company, which had been in the family's hands for three generations? Or should they hire new management to revive flagging sales of its chicken noodle and tomato soups and Pepperidge Farm cookies and perhaps become an acquirer itself? The company went public in 1954 when William Murphy was the president and CEO. Campbell is family held as well as publicly held. After CEO David W. Johnson left Campbell in 1998, the company started to weaken and lose customers (Aberson, 2000), until Douglas R. Conant became CEO and transformed Campbell into one of the food industry's best performers.

Douglas R. Conant became CEO and Director of Campbell Soup Co. in January 2001. Mr. Conant entered the Campbell's team with an extensive background in the processed and packaged food industry. He spent ten years with General Mills, Inc., filled top management positions in marketing and strategy at Kraft Foods, and served as President of Nabisco Foods Company. Mr. Conant had worked toward a goal of implementing the Campbell's mission of "building the world's most extraordinary food company by nourishing people's lives everywhere, every day" (Annual Report, 2007). He was confident that the company possessed the people, the products, the capabilities, and the plans in place to actualize that mission.

Under Mr. Conant's direction, Campbell made many reforms through investments in improving product quality, packaging, marketing, and creating a company characterized by innovation. During his tenure the company improved its financial profile, upgraded its supply chain system, developed a more positive relationship with its customers, and enhanced employee engagement. Starting in 2005, Mr. Conant focused on winning in both the marketplace and the workplace. His efforts produced an increase in net sales of $7.1 billion in fiscal 2005 to $7.67 billion in fiscal 2010 (Annual Report, 2010).

The main targets for investment for Mr. Conant, following the divestiture of many other brands, included: Simple Meals, Baked Snacks, and Vegetable-Based Beverages. In 2010, Baking and Snacking sales increased 7% primarily due to currency. Pepperidge Farm sales were comparable to a year ago, as the additional sales from the acquisition of Ecce Panis, Inc. and volume gains were offset by increased promotional spending. Some of the reasons for this growth were the brand's positioning, advertising investments, and some improvements and additions in the distribution system. Mr. Conant also secured an agreement with Coca-Cola North America and Coca-Cola Enterprises Inc. for distribution of the refrigerated single-serve beverages in the U.S. and Canada through the Coca-Cola bottler network (Press Release, 2007). In fiscal 2010, the company continued its focus on delivering superior long-term total shareowner returns by executing against the following seven key strategies (Annual Report, 2010):

- Grow its icon brands within simple meals, baked snacks and healthy beverages;
- Deliver higher levels of consumer satisfaction through superior innovation focused on wellness while providing good value, quality and convenience;
- Make its products more broadly available and relevant in existing and new markets, consumer segments and eating occasions;
- Strengthen its business through outside partnerships and acquisitions;
- Increase margins by improving price realization and company-wide total cost management;
- Improve overall organizational excellence, diversity and engagement; and
- Advance a powerful commitment to sustainability and corporate social responsibility.

Consistent with these strategies, the company had undertaken several portfolio adjustments, including: the divestiture of its luxury chocolate business Godiva for US$850 million to Turkish diversified food company Yildiz; divestiture of its United Kingdom and Ireland businesses to Premier Foods in 2006; and the sale of its ownership interest in Papua New Guinea operations. All these portfolio adjustments intend to better focus Campbell on its competitive advantages of simple meal, baked snack, and vegetable-based beverage businesses in markets with the greatest potential for growth (Annual Report, 2007).

Another major focus for Mr. Conant and the Campbell company was care for the customers' wellness needs, overall product quality, and product convenience. Some of the main considerations regarding wellness with the U.S. market were obesity and high-blood pressure. For example, in fiscal 2011, building on the success of the V8 V-Fusion juice offerings, the company plans to introduce a number of new V8 V-Fusion Plus Tea products.

In the baked snacks category, the company plans to continue upgrading the health credentials of its cracker (or savory biscuit) offerings. Responding to the consumer's value-oriented focus, Campbell's condensed soups will be re-launched with a new contemporary packaging design and an upgrade to the company's gravity-fed shelving system (Annual Report, 2010).

In order to build employee engagement, Campbell provides manager training across the organization. It is just one part of the curriculum at Campbell University, the company's internal employee learning and development program. Exemplary managers have also built strong engagement among their teams through consistent action planning. The company emphasizes employee innovation capabilities, leadership behavior, workplace flexibility and employee wellness.

Challenges Ahead

Conant made many reforms, yet the core soup business is still on a low simmer with slow sales growth overall. In July 2011, Conant is stepping down as the CEO and Denise Morrison will take over his place with the task of trying to reinvigorate sluggish sales in the company's soup category. Morrison joined Campbell in 2003 and served as president of the company's North America soup, sauce and beverages division before taking over as COO in September 2010. In her new role, Morrison says she plans to "accelerate the rate of innovation" at the company. The current executive vice president and COO says that Campbell plans to grow its brands through a combination of more healthy food and beverage offerings, global expansion and the use of technology to woo younger consumers. While "innovation" isn't a term typically associated with the food-processing industry, Morrison says it is key to the company's future success. As an example, she cites Campbell's development of an iPhone application that provides consumers with its Campbell Kitchen recipes. The company's marketing team devised the plan as a way to appeal to technologically savvy, millennial-generation consumers, Morrison says (Katz, 2011).

But analysts have a lukewarm response about Morrison taking over. They are skeptical about a CEO replacement who currently heads the business unit that has struggled the most. They have expressed doubt about whether Morrison is the right choice over some new blood as a CEO replacement.

Industry Overview

In 2010, the U.S. packaged food market experienced moderate value growth, similar to that of the previous year. However, the value growth rate for 2010 was lower than the average for the five-year review period as a whole, which had been driven up by price increases in previous years. Growth in 2010 was driven by consumers preparing more meals at home rather than going out to restaurants in response to a weak economy. Products offering convenience and health benefits such as frozen pizzas, fresh cut fruits, and nuts performed well in 2010 (Euromonitor, 2011).

The providers and consumers of food and nonalcoholic beverages were adapting to a conflicting confluence of economic, sociological, and demographic change. Overall, in a weak economic environment, the underlying demand for food and beverages was holding up relatively well: consumers were less likely to sharply reduce or defer such spending than they were for other products. However, in an effort to cut costs, there had been a shift toward consumers trading down to less expensive products, and toward more eating and cooking at home (Graves & Kwon, 2009).

The U.S. packaged foods market would continue to grow in the future, particularly in the areas of premium, wellness and convenient products. Manufacturers would introduce more restaurant-quality foods in the areas of ready meals and frozen pizzas as well as gourmet varieties of chocolate in the premium sector. In the wellness products sector, functional yogurt, wholegrain breads, and reduced-salt products will be the main focus. Convenient products would continue to expand, following the demand for quick, on-the-go meals ("Global Market Information Database Reports").

With considerable competition in the relatively mature U.S. food market, and limited population growth expected, major food manufacturers were turning to the emerging markets of Eastern Europe and Asia. As countries in these regions increasingly participated in world trade, economies of both regions were growing quickly and consumer incomes had been rising. In addition, the pervasiveness of electronic media, especially Western media, had been making overseas consumers more aware of Western tastes and products. It is expected that the market for processed foods will grow, especially in urban areas, where busy consumers are seeking some of the same features (e.g., convenience, healthier choices, variety, and quality) that were valued in the U.S. The increasing availability of refrigeration and other kinds of storage space in homes would also influence demand for packaged goods in emerging markets. However, for consumers that lack the ability to preserve and keep larger quantities, U.S. companies could look to sell smaller packages, with portions that could be consumed more quickly (Graves & Kwon, 2009) (see Figure 3).

Competition

Campbell operates in the highly competitive food industry and experiences worldwide competition in all of its principal products. The principal areas of competition are brand recognition, quality, price, advertising, promotion, convenience and service (see Figure 4).

Nestlé

Nestlé is the world's #1 food company in terms of sales, the world leader in coffee (Nescafé), one of the world's largest bottled water (Perrier) makers, and a top player in the pet food business (Ralston Purina). Its most well-known global brands include Buitoni, Friskies, Maggi, Nescafé, Nestea, and Nestlé. The company owns Gerber Products, Jenny Craig, about 75% of Alcon Inc. (ophthalmic drugs, contact-lens solutions, and equipment for ocular surgery), and almost 28% of L'Oréal (hoovers.com). In July 2007 it purchased Novartis Medical Nutrition, and in August 2007 it purchased the Gerber business from Sandoz Ltd., with the goal of becoming a nutritional powerhouse. Furthermore, by adding Gerber baby foods to its baby formula business,

Nestlé now becomes a major player in the U.S. baby food sector ("Global Market Information Database Reports").

General Mills

General Mills is the U.S. #2 cereal maker behind Kellogg. Its brands include Cheerios, Chex, Total, Kix, and Wheaties. General Mills is also a brand leader in flour (Gold Medal), baking mixes (Betty Crocker, Bisquick), dinner mixes (Hamburger Helper), fruit snacks (Fruit Roll-Ups), grain snacks (Chex Mix, Pop Secret), and yogurt (Colombo, Go-Gurt, and Yoplait). In 2001 it acquired Pillsbury from Diageo and doubled the company's size, making General Mills one of the world's largest food companies (hoovers.com).

Kraft Foods

Kraft Foods is the U.S. #1 food company and #2 in the world behind Nestlé. Its North America unit makes the world's largest cheese brand (Kraft), owns a large share of the cookie and cracker business (Nabisco) and makes the all-American favorite Oreos. Its international business unit offers most of its U.S. brands, plus national favorites, including the Oscar Mayer, Kraft, Philadelphia, Maxwell House, Nabisco, Oreo, Jacobs, Milka, and LU brands that have revenues of at least $1 billion.

Figure 3 World Total and Top 15 U.S. Agricultural Export Destinations, $U.S. (in billions)

Country	FY 2010	Country	FY 2009	Country	FY 2008
World Total	108	World Total	96	World Total	114.9
Canada	16.5	Canada	15.5	Canada	16.2
China	15	Mexico	13.3	Japan	15.1
Mexico	13.9	Japan	11.1	China	13
Japan	11.2	China	11	Mexico	11.1
European Union-27	8.5	European Union-27	7.6	European Union-27	10.6
South Korea	4.9	South Korea	3.8	South Korea	5.5
Taiwan	3.1	Taiwan	2.8	Taiwan	3.5
Hong Kong	2.4	Hong Kong	1.7	Indonesia	2.2
Indonesia	2.1	Indonesia	1.6	Turkey	2.1
Turkey	2	Egypt	1.4	Dominican Republic	1.8
Philippines	1.6	Russia	1.4	Egypt	1.7
Egypt	1.5	Turkey	1.3	Russia	1.7
Vietnam	1.2	Philippines	1.2	Hong Kong	1.5
Thailand	1	Venezuela	1	Thailand	1.4
Venezuela	1	Thailand	0.9	Venezuela	1.1

Source: US Economic Research Service, United States Department of Agriculture, 2010

Figure 4 Campbell's Competitors by Market Capitalization and Summary Financial Ratios

Direct Competitor Comparison					
	CPB	**GIS**	**HNZ**	**KFT**	**Industry**
Market Cap:	10.63B	24.58B	16.43B	58.62B	596.93M
Employees:	18,400	33,000	29,600	127,000	1.50K
Qtrly Rev Growth (yoy):	−1.20%	1.60%	1.50%	N/A	10.50%
Revenue (ttm):	7.62B	14.94B	10.54B	49.21B	625.14M
Gross Margin (ttm):	40.53%	39.73%	36.84%	36.38%	30.54%
EBITDA (ttm):	1.56B	3.17B	1.91B	7.99B	67.84M
Operating Margin (ttm):	17.09%	18.08%	15.31%	13.34%	7.35%
Net Income (ttm):	787.00M	1.69B	956.34M	2.47B	N/A
EPS (ttm):	2.33	2.51	2.97	2.40	0.65
P/E (ttm):	14.26	15.33	17.19	13.99	17.54
PEG (5 yr expected):	2.45	2.02	2.45	1.63	1.73
P/S (ttm):	1.39	1.65	1.56	1.19	1.06

CPB = Campbell Soup Co.
GIS = General Mills, Inc.
HNZ = HJ Heinz Co.
KFT = Kraft Foods Inc.
Industry = Processed & Packaged Goods

Source: Yahoo Finance.

Kraft removed itself from the tobacco business and Altria in 2007, and later the same year announced the sale of its Post Cereals business to Ralcorp (hoovers.com).

Heinz Company

H. J. Heinz has thousands of products. Heinz products enjoy #1 or #2 market share in more than 50 countries. One of the world's largest food producers, Heinz produces ketchup, condiments, sauces, frozen foods, beans, pasta meals, infant food and other processed food products. Its flagship product is ketchup, and the company dominates the U.S. ketchup market. Its leading brands include Heinz ketchup, Lea & Perrins sauces, Ore-Ida frozen potatoes, Boston Market, T.G.I. Friday's, and Weight Watchers foods (hoovers.com).

Financials

For fiscal 2010, adjusted net earnings were $767 million compared with $758 million in the prior fiscal year. Adjusted net earnings per share were $2.42 for the current fiscal year compared with $2.05 for the prior fiscal year. Marketing and selling expenses decreased by 2 percent in 2010 from previous year, primarily due to lower advertising and consumer promotion costs and lower marketing expenses (Annual Report, 2010).

While advertising increased in the U.S. Soup business, the company reduced marketing expenses in other businesses to fund increased promotional activity (see Figures 5 and 6).

Earnings from U.S. Soup, Sauces and Beverages increased 2% in 2010, primarily due to an improvement in gross margin percentage and lower advertising expenses, partially offset by lower sales. For fiscal 2010, sales in Baking and Snacking increased by 23 percent to $3.22 billion. In regard to International Soup, Sauces and Beverages, sales increased to $1.6 billion from $69 million (Annual Report, 2010).

The company's capital stock is listed and principally traded on the New York Stock Exchange. The company's capital stock is also listed on the SWX Swiss Exchange. On September 15, 2010, there were 26,190 holders of record of the company's capital stock (Annual Report, 2010). Since its lowest dip to US$25 in April 2009, the stock prices have been on a steady pattern of growth over the past two years as of April 2011 (see Figure 8 for stock prices as of April 25, 2011 and stock prices over the previous two years).

With regard to financials, Douglas R. Conant, Campbell's President and Chief Executive Officer, said,

In a challenging year, we delivered strong earnings growth, overcoming softer-than-expected sales, particularly in our

Figure 5　Campbell Balance Sheet

Period Ending	Aug 1, 2010	Aug 2, 2009	Aug 3, 2008
Assets			
Current Assets			
Cash and Cash Equivalents	254,000	51,000	81,000
Net Receivables	512,000	528,000	666,000
Inventory	724,000	824,000	870,000
Other Current Assets	197,000	148,000	76,000
Total Current Assets	**1,687,000**	**1,551,000**	**1,693,000**
Long Term Investments	-	7,000	8,000
Property Plant and Equipment	2,051,000	1,977,000	1,967,000
Goodwill	1,919,000	1,901,000	1,998,000
Intangible Assets	509,000	522,000	605,000
Other Assets	110,000	105,000	183,000
Deferred Long Term Asset Charges	–	24,000	20,000
Total Assets	**6,276,000**	**6,056,000**	**6,474,000**
Liabilities			
Current Liabilities			
Accounts Payable	1,230,000	1,250,000	2,382,000
Short/Current Long Term Debt	835,000	378,000	–
Other Current Liabilities	–	–	21,000
Total Current Liabilities	**2,065,000**	**1,628,000**	**2,403,000**
Long Term Debt	1,945,000	2,246,000	1,713,000
Other Liabilities	1,079,000	1,214,000	536,000
Deferred Long Term Liability Charges	258,000	237,000	504,000
Minority Interest	3,000	3,000	–
Total Liabilities	**5,350,000**	**5,328,000**	**5,156,000**
Stockholders' Equity			
Common Stock	20,000	20,000	20,000
Retained Earnings	8,760,000	8,288,000	7,909,000
Treasury Stock	(7,459,000)	(7,194,000)	(6,812,000)
Capital Surplus	341,000	332,000	337,000
Other Stockholder Equity	(736,000)	(718,000)	(136,000)
Total Stockholder Equity	**926,000**	**728,000**	**1,318,000**
Net Tangible Assets	**(1,502,000)**	**(1,695,000)**	**(1,285,000)**

Source: Yahoo Finance.

U.S. soup business. We had another year of strong cash flow performance, generating more than $1 billion in cash flow from operations. For the year, we expanded gross margins through supply chain productivity improvements and previously announced cost-savings initiatives. By effectively managing our margins in a tough economic environment, we have set the stage for next year and positioned the company for growth through continued innovation, category leading marketing spending and competitive pricing. I am confident that we have the right strategies to drive growth across our strong portfolio of healthy beverages, baked snacks and simple meals. In healthy beverages, we will build on our track record of innovation and continue our effective marketing efforts. In baked snacks, we have a

Figure 6 Campbell Income Statement

Period Ending	Aug 1, 2010	Aug 2, 2009	Aug 3, 2008
Total Revenue	7,676,000	7,586,000	7,998,000
Cost of Revenue	4,526,000	4,558,000	4,827,000
Gross Profit	3,150,000	3,028,000	3,171,000
Operating Expenses			
Research Development	123,000	114,000	115,000
Selling General and Administrative	1,667,000	1,729,000	1,770,000
Non-recurring	12,000	–	175,000
Operating Income or Loss	1,348,000	1,185,000	1,111,000
Income from Continuing Operations			
Total Other Income/ Expenses Net	6,000	4,000	(5,000)
Earnings Before Interest and Taxes	1,354,000	1,189,000	1,106,000
Interest Expense	112,000	110,000	167,000
Income Before Tax	1,242,000	1,079,000	939,000
Income Tax Expense	398,000	347,000	268,000
Net Income From Continuing Ops	844,000	732,000	671,000
Discontinued Operations	–	4,000	494,000
Net Income	844,000	736,000	1,165,000

Source: Yahoo Finance.

Figure 7 Campbell's Key Ratios

Valuation Ratio: CPB		Per Share Ratio: CPB	
P/E (TTM)	14.60	Dividend Per Share (TTM)	1.12
Price to CashFlow	7.59	Book Value Per Share	4.45
Price to Sales (TTM)	1.55	EPS Fully Diluted	2.38
Price to Book	13.03	Revenue Per Share	22.38
5 Year Annual Growth: CPB		**Dividends: CPB**	
Net Income	3.26%	Dividend Yield	3.38%
Revenue	0.34%	Dividend Yield - 5 Yr. Avg.	2.64%
Dividend Per Share (TTM)	9.78%	Dividend Per Share (TTM)	1.12
EPS	5.28%	Dividend Payout Ratio	48.29
Profit Margins: CPB		**Financial Strength: CPB**	
Operation Margin	17.86%	Quick Ratio (MRQ)	0.38
Net Profit Margin	10.81%	Current Ratio (MRQ)	0.79
Gross Profit Margin	41.04%	LT Debt to Equity (MRQ)	217.89
		Total Debt to Equity (MRQ)	351.07
Assets: CPB		Return on Equity (ROE) Per Share	76.74
Asset Turnover	1.23	Return on Assets (ROA)	13.60
Inventory Turnover	5.52	Return on Invested Capital (ROIC)	25.54

Source: Retrieved from http://www.dailyfinance.com/financials/campbell-soup-company/cpb/nys/key-ratios

full slate of innovation across our portfolio with exciting new products for Pepperidge Farm and Arnott's. In U.S. soup, we have significant plans to enhance our condensed soups, strengthen our competitiveness in ready-to-serve soups and introduce a new advertising campaign to support the entire U.S. portfolio of 'Campbell's' soup brands and to help drive category growth. (Annual Report, 2010).

Sustainability

Campbell Soup Company had been named to the Dow Jones Sustainability Indexes (DJSI) for the second year in a row in 2010 and to the DJSI World Index for the first time. This independent ranking recognizes the company's strategic and management approach to delivering economic, environmental, and social performance. Launched in 1999, the DJSI tracks the financial performance of leading sustainability-driven companies worldwide. In selecting the top performers in each

business sector, DJSI reviews companies on several general and industry-specific topics related to economic, environmental, and social dimensions. These include corporate governance, environmental policy, climate strategy, human capital development, and labor practices. Campbell includes sustainability and corporate social responsibility as one of its seven core business strategies (News Release, 2010(b)).

In 2010, Campbell Soup placed second on *Corporate Responsibility Magazine's* 12th annual 100 Best Corporate Citizens List, regarded as the top corporate responsibility ranking based on publicly available information. Campbell moved up ten places from its ranking from previous year.

CEO Douglas Conant said,

Campbell is committed to advancing our commitment to corporate social responsibility and sustainability. It is gratifying to have Campbell's corporate responsibility practices

Figure 8 Campbell's 2-Year Period Stock Prices – As of April 27, 2011

Source: Yahoo Finance.

and performance be recognized. This honor reflects the effort of thousands of dedicated Campbell people around the world who are absolutely committed to winning in the workplace, marketplace and community. (News Release, 2011).

What's Next?

A new food rating system, the Affordable Nutrition Index (ANI), that analyzes both nutrition and cost value of food, might make it easier for people to find budget-friendly, nutritious foods in today's tough economy. Dark colored vegetables, certain fruits, and vegetable soups were among the most affordable, nutritious foods. "In today's economy, more people are making food choices based solely on cost, so it's important to guide them on ways to get nutritious options without hurting their wallets," said Adam Drewnowski, PhD, professor at University of Washington, "It is important to identify a wide range of affordable, nutritious choices that can help

people build a balanced diet that fits their lifestyle and budget" (Anonymous, 2009). Twenty-five Campbell's soups followed closely on the ANI scale, particularly condensed vegetable soup varieties that were lower in sodium, like Campbell's® Healthy Request® condensed vegetable soup, which was certified as heart-healthy by the American Heart Association, and Campbell's® Tomato soup, which underwent a 32 percent reduction in sodium and was one of the top-selling soups in the United States (Investor News(d)).

Even though Campbell's Baking and Snacking and International Soup, Sauces and Beverages segments grew during 2010, the Soup, Sauces and Beverages sales dropped by 2 percent and North American Foodservice sales dropped by almost 4 percent. But when the economic recession ends and the economy improves, will Campbell's name still resonate with American consumers? Will consumers venture back to restaurants or continue to take comfort in soup at home?

REFERENCES

Abelson, R. (2000, July). The first family of soup, feeling the squeeze; Should it sell or try to go it alone? *The New York Times*. Section 3. p1.

Anonymous (2009, October). New affordable nutrition index is first measurement tool to evaluate affordable nutrition. *Supermarket News*. Retrieved from http://supermarketnews.com/company/campbell/archives/1009-nutrition-index/

Boyle, M. (2009, September). Campbell's: Not about to let the soup cool. *BusinessWeek*.

Boyle, M. (2010, September). Campbell CEO pick may be lost chance, analysts say. Retrieved April 18, 2011, from http://www.businessweek.com/news/2010-09-29/campbell-ceo-pick-may-be-lost-chance-analysts-say.html

Brat, I. & Ziobro, P. (2010, November). Campbell to put new focus on taste. Retrieved April 20, 2011 from http://online.wsj.com/article/0,,SB10001424052748704369304575632342839464532,00.html

Campbell Soup Co. (2007). Annual Report

Campbell Soup Co. (2009). Annual Report

Campbell Soup Co. (2010). Annual Report

Campbell Soup Co. Retrieved from http://www.campbellsoupcompany.com/around_the_world.asp

Campbell Soup Co. Profile. Retrieved from http://finance.yahoo.com/q/pr?s=CPB

Collins, G. (1994, November 29). Campbell Soup takes the big plunge into salsa. *The New York Times*, Section D, p1.

Euromonitor International (2011, February). Packaged food in the US. Retrieved April 25, 2011 from http://www.euromonitor.com/packaged-food-in-the-us/report

Global Market Information Database Reports

Graves, T. & Kwon, E.Y. (2009, July). Standard and Poor's Foods and Nonalcoholic Beverages Industry Report

Gutierrez, C. (2010, November). CEO exit no surprise at Campbell Soup, but replacement is. Retrieved April 16, 2011, from http://www.forbes.com/2010/09/29/campbell-soup-conant-markets-equities-morrison.html

Investor News (a). Retrieved from http://investor.shareholder.com/campbell/releasedetail.cfm?ReleaseID=319256

Investor News (b). Retrieved from http://investor.shareholder.com/campbell/releasedetail.cfm?ReleaseID=396590

Investor News (c). Retrieved from http://investor.shareholder.com/campbell/releasedetail.cfm?ReleaseID=396590

Investor News (d). Retrieved from http://investor.shareholder.com/campbell/releasedetail.cfm?ReleaseID=416429

Katz, J. (2011, January). Campbell Soup cooking up a new recipe? Retrieved April 18, 2011 from www.industryweek.com

Lighting a Fire under Campbell (2006, December 4). *BusinessWeek*

News Release (2010(a), September). Campbell launches "It's Amazing What Soup Can Do"

Ad campaign to promote Campbell's U.S. soup brands. Retrieved April 22, 2011, from http://investor.campbellsoupcompany.com/phoenix.zhtml?c=88650&p=irolnewsArticle&ID=1467644&highlight=

News Release (2010(b), September). Campbell Soup company named to Dow Jones Sustainability Indexes. Retrieved April 18, 2011 from http://investor.campbellsoupcompany.com/phoenix.zhtml?c=88650&p=irolnewsArticle&ID=1471159&highlight=

News Release (2011, March). Campbell Soup company rises to second on list of 100 best corporate citizens. Retrieved April 18, 2011 from http://investor.campbellsoupcompany.com/phoenix.zhtml?c=88650&p=irolnewsArticle&ID=1535750&highlight=

Press Release (2007, June). The Coca-Cola Company, Campbell Soup Company and Coca-Cola Enterprises sign agreement for distribution of Campbell's beverage portfolio. Retrieved from http://investor.shareholder.com/campbell/releasedetail.cfm?ReleaseID=247903

Retrieved from http://www.hoovers.com

Retrieved from http://www.rb.ru/topstory/business/2008/05/30/203525.html - Translated from Russian

Chick-fil-A: Bird of a Different Feather

In 2011, sales at Chick-fil-A (CFA), a southern U.S. restaurant chain, surpassed $4 billion, an increase of 13% over 2010. The privately held, family-run business headquartered in Atlanta, Georgia, was ranked 13th among U.S. quick-serve restaurant franchises, second only to KFC in the fried-chicken category.[1]

CFA's business model varied significantly from that of most other fast-food chains. Advertising budgets and debt loads were lower than average, and operating hours were reduced. Franchisee recruitment, financial commitment, and management expectations also deviated from industry norms. Due to ownership's aversion to debt, the pace of expansion was significantly slower than the fast-food-segment average. But perhaps the most significant differences between CFA and other fast-food chains were its private, family-controlled ownership structure and its management philosophy, which was based on biblical principles.[2]

In 2012, CFA came under fire for statements made by its COO, Dan Truett, in favor of the "biblical definition of marriage."[3] These statements were perceived to be critical of gay marriage, a pending legal issue in a number of states that had been gaining popular support. Gay rights groups called for a CFA boycott; CFA supporters, meanwhile, flocked to local restaurants for Appreciation Day, for which CFA reported record sales. Nevertheless, the controversy raised questions about the extent to which an ownership's views could affect or even compromise an enterprise's long-term viability.

Southern Roots: Samuel Truett Cathy and Chick-fil-A

The CFA story began with the humble roots of its founder, Samuel Truett Cathy. Cathy was born in 1921 in Eatonton, Georgia, approximately 75 miles southeast of Atlanta. He was named Samuel after a respected family friend and Truett in honor of Baptist evangelist George W. Truett. It was the name Truett that stuck.

He was born into a family of cotton farmers, although just prior to his birth, when the family farm failed in the wake of a boll weevil attack, his father turned to selling insurance. To help make ends meet, the family took boarders into their small home, as many did during the Great Depression. The family served each guest two square meals a day, and the entrepreneurial Cathy, who had delivered newspapers and sold Coca-Cola door to door, helped with meal preparation. This laid the foundation for his entry into the restaurant industry.

At the age of 25, in the Atlanta suburb of Hapeville, Cathy and his brother Ben opened his first restaurant, which featured only four tables and 10 counter seats, aptly named The Dwarf Grill (later renamed Dwarf House). Customers had a choice of a hamburger (15 cents), bacon and tomato sandwich (25 cents), steak sandwich (30 cents), bacon and eggs (30 cents), fried ham (25 cents), and pie (10 cents per slice). Over the next 15 years, Cathy tested various menu items, including fried chicken, although that item was soon removed because

This case was prepared by Virginia Weiler, Instructor of Marketing, College of Business, University of Southern Indiana, and Peter Gerardo under the supervision of Paul W. Farris, Landmark Communications Professor of Business Administration, and Paul J. Simko, Associate Professor of Business Administration and Associate Dean, MBA for Executives. It was written as a basis for class discussion rather than to illustrate effective or ineffective handling of an administrative situation. Copyright 2013 by the University of Virginia Darden School Foundation, Charlottesville, VA. All rights reserved. *To order copies, send an e-mail to sales@dardenbusinesspublishing.com. No part of this publication may be reproduced, stored in a retrieval system, used in a spreadsheet, or transmitted in any form or by any means—electronic, mechanical, photocopying, recording, or otherwise—without the permission of the Darden School Foundation.*

it took too long to cook and presented quality assurance problems. In 1961, however, Cathy's big breakthrough was realized:

Jim and Hall Goode, owners of Goode Brothers Poultry, came to me in a quandary. They had been asked by an airline to provide a boneless, skinless chicken breast that would fit the plastic trays they used to serve meals on planes. The Goodes met the request, but their process left boneless breast pieces that didn't meet the airline's size requirements. They were trying to develop a market for these excess pieces… I knew immediately that they had provided the answer to the chicken problem. After the bone was removed, the chicken would cook evenly and thoroughly…Then I discovered the recently introduced Henny Penny cooker, a pressure cooker that used oil and could cook a boneless chicken breast in four minutes, start to finish. Cooking so quickly meant we wouldn't have to cook our products ahead and hold them in a warming cabinet or under a heating lamp. All our chicken would be served fresh.[4]

Cathy devised a seasoning formula of 20 ingredients, put the chicken breasts between two buttered buns, and trademarked the name *Chick-fil-A* for the new sandwich. The name was intended to draw comparisons with already popular steak fillets. The Chick-fil-A sandwich was soon licensed to other restaurants and food service operations. At the time, Cathy had no interest in establishing a restaurant chain; his earlier expansion attempt ended badly when a second Dwarf House restaurant burned to the ground.

Over the next six years, however, Cathy became increasingly disturbed with the chicken sandwich licensing model, given his inability to control the quality of a product in which he took so much pride:

We began to realize…that licensing our product might not be such a good idea, for while it was one of the easiest ways to sell, it was almost impossible to maintain consistent quality. Some restaurants, for example, would cook all their Chick-fil-A breasts in the morning for the lunch crowd, then leave them sitting around for a couple of hours. Hours before Braves baseball games at Atlanta Stadium, they cooked the chicken downstairs, then put it in a refrigerator until just before game time, then sent it upstairs to be reheated and sold as Chick-fil-A. The result, as described by Major League Baseball umpire Ron Luciano, was a lousy chicken sandwich. Luciano disliked the sandwich so much he wrote about it in a book years later. I needed to control the quality, and the only solution I could think of was to open my own restaurants—a prospect that didn't appeal to me.[5]

In 1967, Cathy opened his first chain restaurant in a 384 sq. ft. space at Atlanta's Greenbriar Mall, the same mall where his sister Gladys operated a gift shop. The initial upfront investment was a modest $17,000, allowing him to reserve funds to develop other mall locations. The first freestanding restaurant did not open until 1986, nearly two decades later. Over the years, CFA's menu expanded to include a number of variations on the original Chick-fil-A sandwich. By 2012, the menu included chicken nuggets, sandwich wraps, numerous sides, kids' meals, desserts, and a breakfast menu.

Corporate Strategy: A Focus on People

From the start, Cathy was zealous about controlling not just the quality of the products, but the quality of the people who operated the restaurants. CFA's mission was stated flatly as "to glorify God by being a faithful steward of all that is entrusted to us and to have a positive influence on all who come in contact with Chick-fil-A," and to be "America's best quick-serve restaurant." To achieve these goals, Cathy repeatedly stressed the importance of focusing on personal relationships, often sacrificing short-term growth and profits for the sake of building enduring loyalty among employees and customers. The strategy was premised on his Golden Rule philosophy, which prized people over profits. All restaurants closed on Sundays, in keeping with the tradition of reserving that day for worship and for operators and employees to spend time with their families. Regarding restaurant operators, Cathy stated:

We would be loyal to them, treating them as we wished to be treated, and they would reciprocate. They did. Fewer than 5% of our operators leave the chain in any given year. Other chains tout their "knowledge management" systems; we manage knowledge by keeping people—and their knowledge—in the organization. The food tastes better with that kind of long-term operator stability.[6]

Chick-fil-A as a company had developed a customer base that was almost fanatical in its support, along the way receiving numerous awards for customer service. Operators were carefully screened, often enduring a year-long interview process, and chosen based on demonstrated management skills and talents. Of course their past business track records were important, as well as their affiliations with church, civic, and other organizations that could help them promote their restaurants in the communities. In short, each operator was expected to spearhead an extensive, ongoing networking campaign in his or her community, one designed to build awareness of the brand, enhance its reputation, and encourage as many people as possible to visit CFA.

An operator's (i.e., franchisee's) upfront investment in a CFA restaurant was minuscule: an initial $5,000 franchise fee; there were no minimum net worth or other personal financial requirements, and the operator was guaranteed a base income of $30,000. CFA purchased the land, constructed the restaurant, purchased equipment, and took a hefty sum from the operator's revenue and profit base: 15% of annual sales revenue and 50% of net profits.[7] In contrast, KFC requires, among other things, a franchise fee of $45,000 and a mimimum net worth of $1.5 million (Exhibit 1).

Franchisees at CFA were required to be managers. As an operator, franchisees had to be free from all other business commitments to fully concentrate on managing the location. Operators were responsible for setting up business plans for the restaurant, overseeing hiring and firing, setting wages, and managing equipment and day-to-day operations. With few exceptions, CFA operators were allowed to own only one restaurant, and all were strongly encouraged to be consistently present, personally managing employees and the processes they were tasked to oversee:

Another key to operator loyalty lies in our decision to allow each operator to have only one restaurant. At first, this policy may seem counterintuitive. Many companies reward success by enlarging territories or bringing them into the company to oversee operations of other franchisees. I want our best people right there full-time in the restaurant they've built, serving the customers and team members who have become loyal to them.[8]

The belief was that, once people visited the restaurants, they would be so impressed with the cleanliness, the friendliness of employees, and the quality of the food served that they would become customers for life. The strategy proved extraordinarily successful, and CFA consistently met its promises regarding superior customer service, quality products, and competitive prices.

The income earned by the operators depended on their performance. In 2002, more than half of the operators earned more than $100,000, and a few even topped $300,000.[9]

Corporate Culture

CFA's Mission Statement reads, "Be America's Best Quick-Service Restaurant." The company was known for playing "involved parent" when it came to screening franchise applicants and spelling out how the restaurants must be run, as well as how franchisees "operated" their personal lives:

Loyalty to the company isn't the only thing that matters to Cathy, who wants married workers, believing they are more industrious and productive. One in three company operators have attended Christian-based relationship-building retreats through WinShape at Berry College in Mount Berry, GA. The programs include classes on conflict resolution and communication. Family members of prospective operators—children, even—are frequently interviewed so Cathy and his family can learn more about job candidates and their relationships at home. "If a man can't manage his own life, he can't manage a business," says Cathy, who says he would probably fire an employee or terminate an operator who "has been sinful or done something harmful to their family members."

The parent company asks people who apply for an operator license to disclose marital status, number of dependents, and involvement in "community, civic, social, church and/or professional organizations."

Danielle Alderson, 30, a Baltimore operator, says some fellow franchisees find that Chick-fil-A butts into its workers' personal lives a bit much. She says she can't hire a good manager who, say, moonlights at a strip club because it would irk the company. "We are watched very closely by Chick-fil-A," she says. "It's very weird."[10]

Cathy sees this through a different business prism: that significant business relationships with people should be made with the same care and caution

Exhibit 1 Chick-fil-A: Bird of a Different Feather: Comparison of Franchisee Capital Investment for KFC, Chick-fil-A

Company	Established	Franchising Since	Minimum Liquid Capital	Minimum Net Worth	Total Investment	Franchise Fee
KFC	1930	1950	$750,000	$1.5 million	$1.3 million–$2.47 million	$45,000
CFA	1946	1967	None	None	$281,000–$815,000	$5,000

Data source: KFC website, http://www.kfcfranchise.com/requirements-investment-fast-food-franchise.php (accessed March 5, 2013) and Franchise Direct website, http://www.franchisedirect.com/foodfranchises/chickfil-a-franchise-07431/ufoc/ (accessed March 5, 2013).

with which one might approach one's personal relationships.

In my first meeting with a potential operator, I explain that our commitment is going to be like a marriage, with no consideration given to divorce. We're much more careful about selecting operators when we know we can't easily get rid of them.[11]

Despite this level of perceived intrusion, CFA received thousands of applications from would-be franchisees every year. Out of more than 10,000 applicants per year, fewer than 50, or 0.05%, became new operators. For the few who received the call, extensive training classes into the basics of how to run a Chick-fil-A franchise and assimilation into the company's management culture soon followed. The end result was that operators at Chick-fil-A tended to be a tightly knit group who shared a common commitment to the corporate mission.[12]

The WinShape Foundation, founded in 1982 by Cathy and his wife Jeannette, was a cornerstone of CFA's charitable activities and a direct reflection of the CFA culture. The foundation originally provided tuition assistance to students attending Berry College, a small nondenominational Christian college in Georgia. Later it sponsored other programs, including WinShape Camps, a Christian-themed camp for young people through high school, and WinShape Homes, which operated foster homes throughout Tennessee, Georgia, and Alabama that served children who had been abused or neglected. As stated on its website, the goal of this program was to provide children with "a place they will grow physically, spiritually, and emotionally, surrounded by tenderness, wisdom, and structure. A place where they will be loved for life."[13] Additional WinShape initiatives include marriage retreats and international natural disaster relief support.

Marketing and CSR Approach: Send in the Cows

In addition to operating only six days a week, a perceived financial handicap—estimated to cost approximately $500 million annually—was CFA's relatively tiny advertising budget. In 2009, the chain spent just $27 million on advertising media, compared with the nearly $1 billion McDonald's spent. But there was a bright side: On average, despite the smaller budget, CFA generated an annual volume per restaurant of $3 million, compared to McDonald's $2.3 million. Faced with such competition, Chuck Bradford, CFA's manager of media integration, said his company took on a "David and Goliath" mindset to doing business: "We're going out to try to slay some giants," he said.[14]

A particular success, developed by the Dallas-based Richards Group, took advantage of the media presence in Atlanta during the 1996 Summer Olympics. A billboard campaign depicted Holstein cows as underground revolutionaries avoiding a hamburger fate by encouraging the public to "Eat Mor Chikin." The strategy was obvious and very effective: to position chicken—memorably—as an alternative to hamburgers. In addition, a marketing program was developed that integrated point of purchase, merchandise promotion, direct mail, and public relations efforts.

In the immediate aftermath of the campaign's roll-out, same-store sales rose four times above the industry average, and three times greater than the rate CFA stores had experienced before the campaign. This growth in same-store sales was all the more impressive given that CFA, unlike most quick-serve competitors, hadn't made any major shifts, additions, or changes to its menu or marketing campaign since 1996. It devoted the lion's share of the advertising budget to outdoor media, with radio, television, and print advertising distant seconds. Rated among America's most popular advertising icons in an *Advertising Week* poll, the "Eat Mor Chikin" cows were enshrined in the Madison Avenue Advertising Walk of Fame in New York, inducted into The Outdoor Advertising Association of America's (OAAA) OBIE Hall of Fame, and given a Silver Lion at the Cannes Advertising Festival.

CFA did not offer any kind of frequent-buyer card to develop relationships with customers, but it utilized creative sales promotions quite effectively. CFA developed its customer community electronically, particularly through its website. When opening a new store, CFA generated excitement through its First 100 promotional event. Customers could register on the company website to receive a free meal every week for a year at the new location, with 100 names drawn at random to receive the prize. Additionally, customers were encouraged to upload videos and pictures that told their Chick-fil-A stories, how they connected with CFA in a special way. For example, one grandmother posted a picture with her grandson, who was suffering from cancer, and wrote that whenever he left the hospital, he wanted to go straight to Chick-fil-A. Another described how a couple visited Chick-fil-A on their wedding day.

Another highly successful CFA event was Cow Appreciation Day. Customers who went to a CFA dressed in full cow regalia received a free meal, and awards were given out for "best herd" and "best calf." CFA solicited customer experiences on Cow Appreciation Day, also to be posted to the website.

The company also purchased rights to the former Peach Bowl, a college football bowl game played each December on national television, and changed the name to the Chick-fil-A Bowl.

Compared to quick-serve burger restaurants McDonald's, Burger King, and Wendy's, CFA's customers were more affluent, more active, and more educated. Visitors to the Chick-fil-A website were slightly more likely to be female, between the ages of 25 and 44, and have a college education (Exhibit 2).

Company Outlook and Finance

Forecasts called for quick-service restaurants to achieve stronger growth in 2011 after three years of declining sales. As a whole, the quick-service segment was expected to achieve sales of more than $167 billion, a gain of 3.3% over 2010.[15] CFA posted record sales of $4 billion in 2011, an increase of 13% over 2010. This followed a sales increase in 2010 of more than 11% overall sales and close to a 6% increase in same-store sales over 2009. By this point, CFA had enjoyed uninterrupted strong year-over-year sales growth since its founding.[16]

Ranked second among U.S. quick-serve chicken restaurants, CFA's 2010 sales revenue dwarfed that of Popeye's and was gaining on KFC, which had struggled in recent years. "KFC continues to cede a lot of market share to privately held Chick-fil-A," wrote Mark Kalinowski of Janney Capital Markets. "Lapping an easy −7% comparison from the second quarter of last year did not help KFC U.S."[17] Between 2010 and 2012, KFC shuttered more than 400 U.S. outlets. In 2010, CFA surpassed Popeye's, McDonald's, and Burger King in total sales growth and same-store sales growth despite having far fewer locations and closing its stores 52 days of the year. (See Exhibit 3 for summary revenue statistics in the quick-serve restaurant industry and Exhibit 4 for summary financial characteristics of publicly traded competitors.)

In 2012, most of CFA's 1,600+ restaurants, which employed approximately 6,100 people, were located in the southeastern United States; approximately 1,100—more than two-thirds—were below the Mason–Dixon line (Figure 1). The West Coast had fewer than 50, all in California, while New England and New York had 3. The company's growth focus was on the Midwest and Southern California.

CFA was also one of the world's largest privately owned restaurant companies. By all accounts, Cathy and his sons intended to keep the business in the family, a goal stemming from their desire to maintain very tight control over the business.

Many others have achieved our size by offering ownership in their companies to the public. We have resisted and will continue to resist that status. In the early days, we did not offer stock for sale because I could not predict how fast the company might grow or what dividends we might pay to anyone who might invest. Additionally, I'm afraid the directors, if we had a bad year, might tell me I'm old-fashioned and fire me.

Many people who are creating and running companies couldn't care less about anything but their personal bottom lines. If the stock goes down the tubes after they've sold their options, they say that's just the risk an investor takes… If I had a widow invest her savings in Chick-fil-A and the company didn't pay the return she expected,

Exhibit 2 Chick-fil-A: Bird of a Different Feather: Chick-fil-A Website Visitor Demographics

Demographic	Percentage of Customers
Age	
18 and under	18%
18–24	11%
25–34	22%
35–44	24%
55–64	7%
65+	3%
Gender	
Male	43%
Female	57%
Household Income	
$0–$50,000	13%
$50,000–$100,000	26%
$100,000–$150,000	31%
$150,000+	30%
Education	
No College	38%
College	47%
Grad School	15%
Ethnicity	
Caucasian	74%
African American	16%
Asian	4%
Hispanic	5%
Other	1%

Data source: Adapted from Quantcast data display, http://www.quantcast.com/chick-fil-a.com (accessed March 5, 2013).

Exhibit 3 Chick-fil-A: Bird of a Different Feather:
Select Competitor Revenue Summary, 2010

	U.S. Sales 2010 (in Millions)	Percent Change from 2009	Percent Change from 2009 (same-store sales)	Number of Stores
CFA	$3,582	11.37	5.92	1,606
Popeye's	$1,635	2.5	2.6	1,977
McDonald's	$24,075	4.4	5.0	32,737
Burger King	$9,070	(2.5)	(2.3)	2,376
KFC	4,710	(3.9)	(3.0)	5,200

Data source: Company annual reports and 10-K filings; "Fastest Growing Limited-Service Chains > $200 Million," Technomic Information Services, http://www.technomic.com/Resources/Industry_Facts/dyn_10_limited_sales.php (accessed February 18, 2013).

Exhibit 4 Chick-fil-A: Bird of a Different Feather:
Select 2011 and 2010 Quick-Serve Restaurant Financial Data Summary (in millions of dollars)

	McDonald's		Wendy's		Yum!Brands	
	MCD		WEN		YUM	
	2011	2010	2011	2010	2011	2010
Sales	18,293	16,233	2,127	2,079	10,893	9,783
Franchise Revenues	8,713	7,841	305	296	1,733	1,560
Total Sales	27,006	24,075	2,431	2,375	12,626	11,343
Cost of Sales	14,838	13,060	1,816	1,757	9,140	8,120
Gross Profits	12,168	11,015	615	618	3,486	3,223
Gross Profit %	45.1%	45.8%	25.3%	26.0%	27.6%	28.4%
Financing Costs	493	451	114	118	156	175
Net Income from Cont. Ops.	5,503	4,946	18	18	1,319	1,158
Profit Margin	20.4%	20.5%	0.7%	0.8%	10.4%	10.2%
Operating Cash Flow	7,150	6,342	247	226	2,170	1,968
Investing Cash Flow	(2,571)	(2,056)	(58)	(113)	(1,006)	(579)
Financing Cash Flow	(4,533)	(3,729)	(225)	(194)	(1,413)	(337)
Assets	32,990	31,975	4,301	4,733	8,834	8,316
Stockholders' Equity	14,390	14,634	1,996	2,163	1,916	1,669
Long-Term Debt	12,500	11,505	1,357	1,572	2,997	2,915
Store Count						
Company-Operated	6,435	6,399	1,417	1,394	8,024	7,796
Franchised	27,075	26,338	5,177	5,182	29,097	30,039
Total	33,510	32,737	6,594	6,576	37,121	37,835
Dividends	2,610	2,408	32,366	27,621	481	412
Shares Outstanding	1,021	1,054	390	418	460	469
Price per Share	101.33	77.10	5.42	4.64	59.61	49.30
Market Cap (billions)	103.5	81.2	2.1	1.9	27.4	23.1
Market-to-Book	7.2	5.6	1.1	0.9	14.3	13.9
Price-to-Earnings	18.8	16.4	117.9	107.2	20.8	20.0

Data source: Company 10-K filings and case writer calculations.

Figure 1 Chick-fil-A Store Locations in the United States by County, 2012. (Darker Areas Denote More Stores)

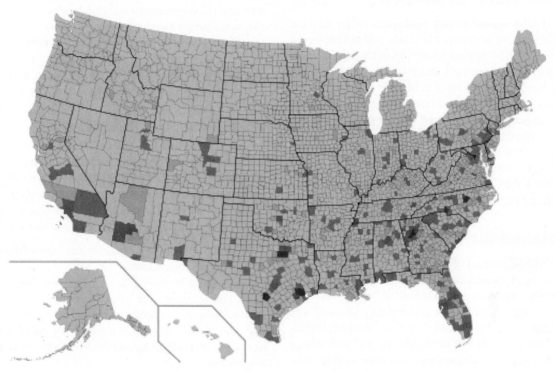

Source: Wikimedia Commons.

I would feel obligated to make up the difference to her… The value of the stock would always be determined by the profits of the corporation, and if I cut into those profits by giving away a bunch of the company's money, employees and stockholders might resent my charity… Our system puts the cash in the hands of the operator today, instead of sometime down the road with a lump sum, and encourages them to earn all they can, save all they can, and give all they can right now. Their focus is on today's customer.[18]

Though Cathy, now 92, was less involved in day-to-day operations than in years past, sons Dan (COO) and Donald (senior VP) inherited their father's aversion to financing expansion through debt, preferring to reinvest CFA's profits. Cathy made no secret that low (or no) debt was, in part, a reaction to his childhood: "In the Great Depression, you bought something if you had the cash to buy it. We are just about debt-free right now [2010], stretching that dollar as far as it will go. If you have debt, you have to worry about it."[19]

For these reasons, and because Cathy was fearful of expanding too rapidly, CFA pursued a slow, steady increase in the number of locations:

I have never tried to overextend. I'm satisfied stepping from one plateau to the next, making sure we're doing everything right before moving on. Financial experts tell me our strength would allow us to open restaurants at a much more aggressive pace than our current 70 per year. But I'd rather have 70 restaurants operating efficiently and professionally than 500 restaurants where half are run well and the other half not.[20]

CFA's location strategy included a significant presence in malls (320 locations as of January 2013) in addition to its more than 1,000 stand-alone locations.

Awards

CFA had a devoted customer base and had accumulated numerous consumer and industry awards. In 2011, CFA won the *Consumer Reports* "Nation's Top Chicken Chain" award, based on a survey of 36,000 readers. Other awards CFA accumulated include Zagat's 2011 "Top Large Chain" in the fast-food category and "Best Value" and "Best Milkshakes" in Zagat's 2010 fast-food survey.

International Expansion

In 2011, CFA opened 92 new restaurants rather than the "traditional" 70 or fewer. The chain still maintained a "slow and steady" attitude toward domestic expansion, as that pace could have been much quicker. The company had a handful of restaurants in Mexico, Puerto Rico, and Canada, but showed little interest in overseas expansion. The company had announced neither plans nor intention to capitalize on the slow growth of Popeye's or negative growth of KFC. It also had shown no inclination to blunt KFC's extremely successful expansion into China, with more than 3,000 restaurants in 650 Chinese cities—in 2011, a new restaurant every day.

Sustainability

As "a faithful steward of all that is entrusted to us," CFA had a stated commitment to being a good steward of the environment, though it admitted "we are still very early in our environmental sustainability journey." The company boasted a number of green initiatives, including plans to retrofit 900 restaurants in 2012 with energy efficient lighting, refrigeration, and water-saving technologies. The company continued to use Styrofoam cups because of the insulating properties, but stated that its current cups were recyclable where facilities existed. This included all 58 of its California locations as well as restaurants in Denver, Salt Lake City, and Philadelphia. The company's goals included adding 400 more stores to its foam cup recycling initiative in 2012 as well as chain-wide implementation slated for 2014. Additionally, as of January, 2013, in 90 of its stores, all napkins, tray liners, and kids'-meal bags were recycled.

Succession Planning

Family business ownership has a 30% chance of retention by the second generation, 12% by the third, and 3% by the fourth. Yet data from the Family Business Institute relates that a full 88% of family business owners believe that the family will still own the business in five years:

The statistics reveal a disconnect between the optimistic belief of today's family business owners and the reality of the massive failure of family companies to survive through the generations. Research indicates that family business failures can essentially be traced to one factor: an unfortunate lack of family business succession planning.[21]

The Cathy family was an exception. To prevent CFA from being sold or carved up by succeeding generations,

second-generation stakeholders gathered four times a year, and third-generation stakeholders met twice annually. Some family members worked directly for CFA, and each third-generation family member oversaw a significant foundation. Every family member had to graduate from college and work outside the company for at least two years before employment with CFA. Once employed by the company, family members underwent the same employment channels as other applicants.

Despite high divorce rates and the changing mores of society, the family sees no need for prenuptial agreements, according to Dan Cathy. "There have been no divorces, and we are quite proud of the fact that we have stayed the course with our values," he added. "We don't worry about future generations changing that. They are rock-solid."

John White, the son of Truett Cathy's daughter Trudy, sees no trouble with perpetuating his grandfather's values. "I think it would be unwise to seek out something else in hopes that it would work when it already works the way it does," he said. "Typically what happens in families this size is they break into segments, but we are still meeting all as one group. I talk to my cousins frequently. We've made it a priority."[22]

Controversy

Relations between CFA and gay and lesbian advocacy groups had been strained in recent years. In 2011, CFA donations (almost $2 million in 2009 alone) to organizations such as Focus on the Family and the Family Research Council prompted protests and boycotts among college students and others supporting gay rights. Dan Cathy, COO of CFA, protested that the company was "not anti-anybody."[23]

The conflict erupted into a firestorm after a Dan Cathy interview in July 2012:

We are very much supportive of the family—the biblical definition of the family unit. We are a family-owned business, a family-led business, and we are married to our first wives. We give God thanks for that.[24]

The article ran under the headline, "'Guilty as Charged,' Dan Cathy Says of Chick-fil-A's Stand on Faith, Family Values." The reaction from gay rights supporters was swift and loud. Boston mayor Thomas Merino told the *Boston Herald* that Chick-fil-A "doesn't belong in Boston."[25] Chicago alderman Joe Moreno vowed to block the construction of CFA restaurants in Chicago until the company drafted an anti-discrimination policy.

In response to the criticism Chick-fil-A was receiving, former Arkansas governor Mike Huckabee called for a CFA "Appreciation Day" to be held on August 1, 2012. Customers were encouraged to show their support for CFA by patronizing CFA on that day. Huckabee created a dedicated Facebook page, which received more than 670,000 RSVPs to promote the awareness of the event. Appreciation Day was an enormous success. Customers flocked to CFA locations, with many patrons waiting hours in line to be served. Although CFA refused to release specific sales numbers, Steve Robinson, executive vice president of marketing for CFA stated that Appreciation Day sales were "record-setting."[26]

A counter-protest organized by gay rights activists, National Same-Sex Kiss Day, was held on August 3, 2012. It called for same-sex couples to go to a CFA and engage in public displays of affection. The event did not achieve anywhere near the same degree of participation as Appreciation Day. In the short run, CFA appeared to benefit from the controversy, with quarterly consumer use up 2.2% compared to prior year, market share up 0.6%, and awareness up 6.5%.[27]

NOTES

1. Sam Oches, "The Nation's Top Chicken Concepts," in *The QSR 50, QSR* Special Report, *QSR*, August 2012.
2. K. Allan Blume, "'Guilty as Charged,' Dan Cathy Says of Chick-fil-A's Stand on Faith, Family Values," *Biblical Recorder*, July 7, 2012.
3. Blume.
4. S. Truett Cathy, *Eat Mor Chikin: Inspire More People* (Decatur, GA: Looking Glass Books, 2002), 75–76.
5. Cathy, 79–80.
6. Cathy, 96.
7. Yale Center for Faith & Culture, Yale School of Management, "Chick-fil-A: Adding Value by Closing on Sunday?," http://nexus.som.yale.edu/chick-fil-a/ (accessed February 6, 2013).
8. Cathy, 100.
9. Cathy, 99.
10. Emily Schmal, "The Cult of Chick-fil-A," *Forbes*, March 23, 2007.
11. Cathy, 97.

12. Yale Center for Faith & Culture.
13. WinShape Foundation website.
14. Mary Sue Penn, "Media Manager Outlines Brand Strategy for Students," *Chicago Booth News*, October 13, 2010.
15. "NRA Forecasts Return to Industry Sales Growth." *Nation's Restaurant News*. February 1, 2011.
16. "Chick-fil-A Continues Sales Growth Momentum in 2010," company press release, February 21, 2011.
17. Mark Brandau, "Yum! Marketing: KFC," *Nation's Restaurant News*, July 19, 2011.
18. Cathy, 88–89.
19. Jeremiah McWilliams, "Chick-fil-A Founder Truett Cathy Dishes on Wealth, Debt, Longevity." *The Atlanta Journal-Constitution*, June 23, 2011.
20. Cathy, 87.
21. "Succession Planning," Family Business Institute website.

22. Catherine Cobb, "Successful succession in family-owned-and-operated businesses can be a complex affair," *Nation's Restaurant News*, February 3, 2008.
23. Jeremiah McWilliams, "Chick-fil-A Counters Criticism from Gay Rights Groups: 'We're not anti-anybody,'" *Atlanta Journal-Constitution*, January 31, 2011.
24. K. Allan Blume, "'Guilty as Charged,' Dan Cathy Says of Chick-fil-A's Stand on Faith, Family Values," *Biblical Recorder*, July 7, 2012.
25. Greg Turner, "Mayor Menino on Chick-fil-A: Stuff It," *Boston Herald*, July 20, 2012.
26. Rene Lunch, "Chick-fil-A 'Appreciation Day': Frenzied Sales Set Record," *Los Angeles Times*, August 2, 2012.
27. Bruce Horovitz, "Chick-fil-A Thrives Despite Gay Rights Issue," *USA Today* online, October 24, 2012.

CASE 8

Chipotle: Mexican Grill, Inc.: Food with Integrity[i]

IVEY | Publishing

On October 18, 2012, Steven Ells, the founder, chairman of the board, and co-chief executive officer (CEO) of the Denver, Colorado-based restaurant chain, Chipotle Mexican Grill (CMG), completed the conference call following the release of the company's third quarter 2012 results. While the reported results were positive, analysts picked on the slowing down of same-stores sales (a key metric for restaurant chains), the competition from Yum Brands' Taco Bell and their recent launch of the Cantina Bell menu and CMG's announcement that food costs were expected to increase in the near future. Following the announcement of third quarter results, CMG's stock went down by nearly 12 percent in intra-day trading to finally stabilize at a 4 percent drop over the previous day's price. At the end of trading on October 18, CMG's stock price was at $285.93, a significant decline from a 52-week high of $442.40.[1] CMG had been the darling of both Wall Street and its customer base ever since the company's founding in 1993 and its 2006 initial public offering (IPO). Investors were attracted to CMG for its fast growth and sizeable profit margins, while customers responded favorably to its "Food with Integrity" mission of serving good quality food with inputs sourced using sustainable farming practices. Both Ells and his co-CEO, Montgomery F. Moran, had to respond to the challenges confronting the company.

The U.S. Restaurant Industry[2]

Profile

For the year 2012, the National Restaurant Association projected total U.S. restaurant sales of $631.8 billion (compared to $379 billion in 2000 and $239.3 in 1990), which represented nearly 4 percent of the gross domestic product. There were 970,000 restaurant locations, and the industry employed 12.9 million people (10 percent of the total workforce). The restaurant industry's share of the food dollar was 48 percent in 2012 compared to 25 percent in 1955.[3]

The restaurant industry consisted of a number of segments such as eating places, bars and taverns and lodging place restaurants. The three largest segments were full service, quick service and fast casual. Full service restaurants offered table ordering, and the average check (revenue per customer) was the highest of the three segments. While national chains such as Darden Restaurants (operator of Red Lobster, Olive Garden and Longhorn Steakhouse) and Dine Equity (IHOP and Applebee's) existed in this segment, the majority of operators were individuals, families or limited partnerships. This segment accounted for 31.7 percent of industry revenues in 2011.

The quick service segment (previously referred to as "fast food") consisted of restaurants that offered fast

i. This case has been written on the basis of published sources only. Consequently, the interpretation and perspectives presented in this case are not necessarily those of Chipotle Mexican Grill or any of its employees.

Ram Subramanian wrote this case solely to provide material for class discussion. The author does not intend to illustrate either effective or ineffective handling of a managerial situation. The author may have disguised certain names and other identifying information to protect confidentiality.

Version: 2013-06-11

counter service and meals to eat in or take out. This segment was further broken down into outlets that specialized in selected menu items such as hamburgers, pizza, sandwiches and chicken. Because of this segment's focus on quick service and price (the average check was the lowest of the three segments), large chains tended to dominate. Accounting for about $168.5 billion in revenues in 2011, this segment held a 28 percent share of the restaurant market.

The fast casual segment was the smallest of the three, accounting for about 4 percent in market share and $24 billion in 2011 revenues. Operators in this segment offered portable convenient food and focused on fresh healthful ingredients and customizable made-to-order dishes. The average check in this segment ranged between $7 and $10, price points typically lower than the full service segment and higher than the quick service segment. Fast casual was the fastest growing of the three segments, with an 11 percent growth rate between 2007 and 2011. The NPD Group, an industry research firm, indicated that as this segment was in its growth phase, it faced intense competition from both the quick service and the full service segments. Buoyed by the growth in fast casual restaurants, several full service operators had recently entered this segment. For example, P.F. Chang's opened its Pei Wei locations, and Ruby Tuesday planned to increase the number of its Lime Fresh eateries to 200 locations by the end of 2012. Panera Bread, CMG, Five Guys Burgers and Qdoba (owned by Jack in the Box) were the leading fast casual players.

Industry Economics

Restaurant running costs varied by segment. In addition, costs were a function of size and location. Upscale formats (typically full service restaurants and some fast casual chains) made higher investments in interior design and also incurred higher input costs. Many chain restaurants typically chose locations with high population density or a large geographic draw. Food and beverage, labor and real estate costs were the three largest expense categories for restaurants. Typically, both food and beverage and labor costs accounted for around 30 percent each of revenues, while real estate costs were around 5 percent. Marketing and general administrative overhead were the significant non-operating expense categories. The National Restaurant Association reported that in 2010 the average income before income taxes of a restaurant operator ranged between 3 and 6 percent of revenues.

To control the cost of inputs, many large national and regional chains negotiated directly with their suppliers (to benefit both company-owned and franchisee-owned

restaurants) to ensure competitive prices. Many chains also engaged in forward pricing to ensure stability in input costs. The National Restaurant Association reported that beef prices hit record levels in 2011 and were expected to be even higher when the prices for 2012 were finally tallied. Beef prices rose 53 percent in 2012 above 2009 levels as the three largest exporters of beef to the United States — Australia, Canada and New Zealand — all reduced their shipments due to a variety of global factors. While the price of various dairy items (milk, butter, cheese) had remained fairly stable over the last few years, the price of grains such as wheat and corn had fluctuated due to changes in supply and demand as well as weather-related factors. The price of a bushel of wheat went up from $6.48 in 2007 to $7.30 in 2011, after falling to $4.87 in 2009. Similarly, while the average price of a bushel of corn was $4.20 in 2007, it rose to $6.20 in 2011 after falling to $3.55 in 2009.[4]

Key Competitors

A former CEO of Taco Bell, the Mexican food chain owned by Yum Brands, captured the competition in the restaurant industry in the following observation: "We are all competing for a share of the customer's stomach."[5]

Players in the restaurant industry competed not only with their segment's players but also with those of other segments. In addition, they competed with meals prepared at home as well as frozen or packaged food items available in supermarkets. While restaurants accounted for about 48 percent of the dollar amount spent on food in 2012, the economy played a major role in this. In a 2011 National Household Survey reported in Standard & Poor's Industry Surveys, 21 percent of those surveyed indicated that they would increase their eating out spending in 2012, while 42 percent would decrease it slightly and 37 percent would reduce it significantly.

CMG faced two major competitors in the Mexican food category of the restaurant industry. While Taco Bell was a player in the quick service segment, Qdoba competed, like CMG, in the fast casual segment.

Qdoba[6]. Qdoba was a wholly owned subsidiary of the San Diego, California-based Jack in the Box chain and in 2012 had 600 restaurants in 42 U.S. states and the District of Columbia. Qdoba was founded in Boulder, Colorado in 1995 and grew nationally by featuring Mission-style burritos (made famous first in San Francisco). After Jack in the Box acquired Qdoba in 2003, it expanded the brand rapidly. Of the 600 restaurants in the chain in 2012, around 350 were franchisee-owned and the rest were company-owned. A franchisee spoke about his rationale for launching a Qdoba restaurant:

What attracted us to the chain was quality. What brought us to this is that everything is handcrafted and made daily. We consider ourselves to be an artisan fast food chain. We come in every morning about three hours prior to opening and start cooking our meals. We start our slowroasted pork and shredded beef that cooks for 6 to 8 hours. Our chicken is marinated in adobo spices for 24 hours before we serve it. We have an artisan table where we make our pico de gallo salsa, mix our cilantro with rice and prepare our guacamole as customers watch. What makes us stand out is the quality of the ingredients we use and our signature flavors. I believe being fast, friendly and fresh is what makes us successful in business.[7]

The company reported an average check of $9.74 in fiscal 2011 for company-operated restaurants. The average yearly revenue per restaurant was $961,000 in 2011, an increase of 5.3 percent over 2010. Jack in the Box had revenues of $2.17 billion and net income of $67.83 million in 2011. The company stated that there was long-term potential to open 1,600 to 2,000 units across the United States.[8]

Taco Bell. Taco Bell was part of Yum Brands, Inc., which also owned the KFC and Pizza Hut chains. Yum Brands was the world's largest restaurant company in terms of units, with nearly 38,000 restaurants in 120 countries. In fiscal 2011, Yum Brands reported revenues of $12.626 billion and a net income of $1.319 billion. At the end of fiscal 2011, there were 5,670 Taco Bell restaurants in the United States, of which 27 percent were company-owned. Taco Bell reported a 50 percent market share in the U.S. Mexican quick service segment. For fiscal 2011, the average annual revenues per restaurant were $1.284 million.[9]

In March 2012, Taco Bell began testing a new menu called "Cantina Bell" in 75 U.S. restaurants. It worked with a Miami-based chef and television personality, Lorena Garcia, to create a new line of upscale menu items including CMG staples such as black beans, cilantro rice and corn salsa. Greg Creed, Taco Bell's president, talked about the motivation behind Cantina Bell:

Chipotle is an opportunity because what it's done has expanded the trial and usage of Mexican food. It's got people to believe they can pay $8 for a bowl or a burrito. Taco Bell can make food every bit as good as Chipotle and instead charge less than $5.[10]

Exhibit 1 Zagat Comparison of Cantina Bell and CMG in New York City

Item	Price	
	Cantina Bell	**CMG**
Burrito bowl with chicken	$5.99	$ 9.88
Steak burrito	$5.99	$10.34
Overall assessment: For practically half the price, the Cantina Bell menu is a definite value, but you get what you pay for, and the overall quality and taste of Chipotle still has an edge over Taco Bell.		

Source: http://blog.zagat.com/2012/07/taco-bell-vs-chipotle-taste-testing.html., accessed October 19, 2012

Taco Bell's target market was an 18- to 24-year-old value-conscious male. Creed saw Cantina Bell as helping Taco Bell appeal to an older and less value-conscious group of customers. The Cantina Bell launch (and subsequent expansion nationwide in July 2012) was cited as one of the reasons for Taco Bell's same-store sales growth of 7 percent for third quarter 2012 (compared to the similar period in 2011).[11] Exhibit 1 presents the summary of a Zagat comparison survey of Cantina Bell and CMG in New York City.

Chipotle Mexican Grill's History and Profile

Origin and Early Growth

In 1990, after graduating from the Culinary Institute of America in New York City, Colorado-born Steven Ells moved to San Francisco to work as a sous chef at a restaurant. In 1993, he opened a *taqueria* (a Spanish word meaning "taco shop") in Denver, Colorado, using $85,000 as capital obtained from his father. His goal was to reinvent Mexican food. He reflected on the origins of his first restaurant:

I wanted layers of bold flavors that had nuance and depth, not just hot, not just spicy: cumin, cilantro, cloves, fresh oregano, lemon, and lime. It looked, smelled, and tasted different from traditional fast food. And it didn't take long before there was a line of people waiting to get in. So I thought, maybe I'll open one more. I was always quite rebellious and did things my own way. Friends said Mexican food is cheap — you can't charge $5 for a burrito. But I said this is real food, the highest-quality food. Friends said you can't have an open kitchen, but I wanted the restaurant to be like a dinner party, where everyone's in the kitchen watching what's going on. They said people have to order their meal by number. But I said no, you *have to go through the line and select your ingredients. And everyone gave me grief over the name: Nobody will be able to pronounce it.*[12]

Ells opened a second restaurant using the profits from the first and a third (all in Denver, Colorado) with a loan from the Small Business Administration. When he had opened 16 restaurants by 1998, McDonald's Corporation (the global leader in fast food in terms of revenue) made an initial investment to help fund the company's growth. The company quickly grew to more than 500 units in 2005 (primarily using McDonald's $360 million capital infusion) and on January 26, 2006 made its IPO. In October 2006, McDonald's fully divested its holdings in CMG for a value of $1.5 billion. Ells talked about CMG and McDonald's: "They funded our growth which allowed us to open 535 restaurants. We learned from each other, but we use different kinds of food, and we aim for a different kind of experience and culture altogether. So we ended up going our separate ways."[13]

The Push to Sustainable Sourcing

Ells happened to read an article by Edward Behr that told the story of an Iowa farmer who raised pigs without using antibiotics or confining them. Behr went on to add that the meat tasted much better than the mass market meat that was served in most restaurants. The Behr article led Ells to learn about concentrated animal feeding operations (CAFOs).[14] In many developed countries, the dominant method of raising livestock for commercial purposes was through CAFOs, starting with poultry in the 1950s and extending to cattle and pork by the 1970s. A CAFO enabled raising livestock by using limited space. The U.S. Environmental Protection Agency (EPA) defined a CAFO as "an animal feeding operation that confines animals for more than 45 days during the growing season in an area that does not produce vegetation and meets certain size thresholds."[15]

CAFO confined large number of animals in a limited space and substituted man-made structures (for feeding, temperature and manure control) for natural ones. A study[16] reported that while it took one million farms in 1966 to house 57 million pigs, through CAFO it took only 80,000 farms in 2001 to house the same number of pigs. CAFOs had a negative impact on water and air quality and hence were regulated by the EPA. In addition, many commercial CAFOs established agricultural water treatment plants to control manure, which had a negative impact on the environment.[17] After Ells visited several CAFOs, he decided to source from open-range pork suppliers starting in 2000, naturally raised chicken

from 2002 and naturally raised beef soon after. The company formalized its sourcing policy in 2001 when it launched its "Food with Integrity" mission statement:

Food with integrity is our commitment to finding the very best ingredients raised with respect for the animals, the environment and the farmers. It means serving the very best sustainably raised food possible with an eye to great taste, great nutrition and great value.[18]

CMG owned and operated 1,316 restaurants in June 2012, of which four were in Canada, three in the United Kingdom, one in France, and the rest in the United States. It reported revenues of $2.270 billion and a net income of $215 million in fiscal 2011. It employed 28,370 hourly workers and 2,570 salaried employees. Ells was CMG's CEO till January 1, 2009, when Montgomery F. Moran (who had been the company's chief operating officer since March 2005) was appointed co-CEO along with Ells. Ells, however, retained his title as chairman of the board.[19]

Business Operations

Restaurant Operations

All of CMG's restaurants were company-owned. They were either end-caps (at the end of a line of retail outlets), in-lines (in a line of retail outlets) or free-standing. A typical restaurant ranged in size between 1,000 and 2,800 square feet depending on the market and cost $850,000 to open. The smaller restaurants were called "A Model" restaurants, the first of which was opened in 2010 to serve less densely trafficked areas. Restaurants served a limited menu of burritos, tacos, burrito bowls (a burrito without the tortilla) and salads, all prepared with fresh ingredients. Customers placed their order (burrito or taco) at the beginning of a line and added ingredients of their choice as they moved along the line. None of the restaurants had freezers, microwave ovens or can openers.[20]

Given their higher than average food costs, CMG focused on operational efficiency at the restaurant level. The restaurant size was typically smaller than those of its peers, and it economized on labor by keeping its menu options limited and by using an assembly line system for food preparation. Chris Arnold, CMG's communication director, spoke about the company's efficiency focus:

We are big believers in what author Jim Collins calls 'the genius of and.'[21] *You can serve great food made with ingredients from more sustainable sources and do it at a reasonable price. You can have higher food costs than your peers and still have strong margins. It just takes the discipline to figure it out.*[22]

In 2009, the company entered into a partnership with a company to install solar panels in its restaurants. CMG aimed to be the largest direct producer of solar energy in the restaurant industry in the next five years. Ells talked about this:

Our effort to change the way people think about and eat fast food began with our commitment to serving food made with ingredients from more sustainable sources, and that same kind of thinking now influences all areas of our business. Today, we're following a similar path in the way we design and build restaurants, looking for more environmentally friendly building materials and systems that make our restaurants more efficient.[23]

CMG's rationale for using solar panels was to reduce the restaurant's traditional energy consumption during the peak period of 11:00 a.m. to 7:00 p.m. Solar panels also reduced the company's carbon footprint. Starting with a restaurant in Illinois, CMG began to obtain LEED certification (Leadership in Energy and Environmental Design, a certification program of different levels) by using on-site wind turbines and cisterns for rainwater harvesting. It was the first restaurant to obtain the highest level (platinum) of LEED certification.[24] By 2012, three of its restaurants were LEED certified.

Supply Chain

CMG's supply chain was closely tied to the company's "Food with Integrity" mission. The company's 22 independently owned and operated distribution centers served restaurants in a specific geographic area. These centers sourced inputs from suppliers who were evaluated on quality and understanding of the company's mission. Key ingredients included various meats; vegetables such as lettuce, cilantro and tomatoes; and dairy items such as sour cream and cheese.

In 2008, the company embarked on a program to increase local (grown within 350 miles of the restaurant) sourcing to 35 percent of at least one bulk produce item. The seasonal produce program was meant to cut down on fossil fuels used to transport produce, give local family farms a boost, and improve the taste of the food served to customers by using ingredients during their peak season. CMG created a network of 25 local farms to supply some of its romaine lettuce, green bell peppers, jalapeno peppers, red onions, and oregano to area restaurants.[25] The local sourcing program resulted

in five million pounds of produce in 2009 and 10 million pounds by 2012.[26]

In 2012, 100 percent of CMG's pork, 80 percent of its chicken and 50 percent of its beef were classified as "naturally raised" meat — defined as open-range, antibiotic free and fed with a vegetarian diet. Forty percent of CMG's beans were organically grown, while all of its sour cream and cheese were made from milk that came from cows that were not given rBGH (recombinant bovine growth hormone). In addition, a substantial percentage of the milk for sour cream and cheese was sourced from dairies that provided pasture access for their cows.[27]

Organic agriculture[28] was still in its infancy in the United States in 2012. Less than 1 percent of the total agricultural area was managed organically. Of that, the percentage was highest for produce, followed by livestock and then poultry. Starting in the 1990s, the demand for organic food drove the conversion of traditional farms to organic at a rapid rate (for example, 14 percent in 2007–2008). The U.S. Department of Agriculture (USDA) reported that the average annual profitability of organic farms in 2011 was $45,697 versus $25,448 for traditional farms. However, the downturn in the economy that started in 2008 slowed down the conversion to organic farming to 6 percent between 2009 and 2011.[29] Retail chains such as Whole Foods and Trader Joe's competed with full service restaurants and other restaurant chains for organic inputs, often driving up the prices well above those for conventional inputs. Ells commented on the pricing challenges and continuing availability of organic inputs: "The supply chain has yet to catch up, organic ingredients are still pricey, and supply is limited. What we are doing is an 'incremental revolution.' If we went all-organic and natural now, a burrito would be like $17 or $18."[30]

Marketing

CMG's marketing budget was $32 million in 2011 versus $26 million in 2010 and $21 million in 2009. The company had reduced its advertising spending more than three years from $7.9 million in 2009 to $7.5 million in 2010 and $5.8 million in 2011.[31] It stated its policy on advertising in its annual report: "Our marketing has always been based on the belief that the best and most recognizable brands aren't built through advertising or promotional campaigns alone, but rather through all of the ways people experience the brand. Our main method of promotion is word-of-mouth publicity."[32]

When CMG hired Mark Crumpacker as its first chief marketing officer in 2009, the first decision that he made was to bring the company's advertising in-house rather than use the services of an outside agency. He also made the decision not to advertise in traditional media such as TV and instead rely on various loyalty programs. He gave his rationale for it:

The alternative is to switch to the type of marketing that every other fast-food company uses with these new menu items and big ad campaigns to promote them. I think once you get on that model, I think it's very, very hard to get off. I want to try to do this [loyalty programs] as long as I can.[33]

One loyalty program was called "Farm Team." This was an invitation-only online program that quizzed users on sustainability, organic farming and humane food sourcing and rewarded them when they shared the knowledge with others via social media. Arnold talked about the program: "This is a passion program. Through Farm Team, we are looking to identify our most loyal and passionate customers, and giving them tools to share their passion for Chipotle. It's much more about building evangelism than it is about rewarding frequency."[34]

In August 2011, CMG released an online commercial titled "Back to the Start," that featured Willie Nelson singing a reworded version of Coldplay's "The Scientist." The commercial told the story (in animated form) of a farmer who moved from inhumane industrial farming that used confined spaces to a more humane sustainable farming method. The popularity of this commercial led to CMG releasing it first in 5,700 movie theatres in September 2011 and running it once on television during the 2012 Grammy Awards show.[35]

A one-day festival called "Cultivate" held in Chicago in October 2011 brought together farmers, chefs and music bands. The goal of the festival was to promote sustainable family farms. Other promotional items included iPhone games and local print advertising to accompany store openings.[36] A marketing expert assessed CMG's non-traditional marketing strategy:

Chipotle has found a "sweet spot" with millennials by solidifying its reputation for freshness and offering a healthier fare than its competitors. The brand also gains reputation by shying away from traditional media, because younger audiences feel like it's more authentic, down-to-earth and easy to connect with. Millennials view the lack of TV as more authentic. Millennials are likely to dismiss a lot of claims. They are responding to everything the brand does and says.[37]

Finances

Exhibit 2 gives a cost comparison of key expenses for CMG and its competitors, Exhibit 3 presents CMG's

Exhibit 2 Selected Cost Comparison — Key Competitors (Costs as Percentage of Revenues)

	2011	2010	2009
YUM Brands[1]			
Food & packaging	30.57	29.09	28.62
Labor	30.40	29.63	29.99
Occupancy & other restaurant operating costs	26.97	27.06	27.50
Qdoba			
Food & packaging	29.00	28.30	29.80
Labor	28.00	27.70	28.30
Occupancy & other restaurant operating costs	29.40	30.00	28.90
CMG			
Food & packaging	32.55	30.56	30.69
Labor	23.93	24.71	25.36
Occupancy & other restaurant operating costs	17.56	18.10	19.20

[1] YUM Brands does not break down data for each of its three chains (KFC, Pizza Hut, and Taco Bell).

Source: Company 10-K's.

Exhibit 3 CMG Consolidated Statement of Income (for Year Ending December 31 in $ Thousands)

	2011	2010	2009
Revenue	2,269,548	1,835,922	1,518,417
Restaurant operating costs			
Food, beverage and packaging	738,720	561,107	466,027
Labor	543,119	453,573	385,072
Occupancy	147,274	128,933	114,218
Other operating costs (marketing, credit card, etc.)	251,208	202,904	174,581
General and administrative expenses	149,426	118,590	99,149
Depreciation and amortization	74,938	68,921	61,308
Pre-opening costs	8,495	7,767	8,401
Loss on disposal of assets	5,806	6,296	5,956
Income from operations	**350,562**	**287,831**	**203,705**
Net income (after interest and taxes)	**214, 945**	**178,981**	**126,845**

(Continued)

Exhibit 3 (Continued) Consolidated Balance Sheet (condensed for December 31 in $ thousands)

	2011	2010
Assets:		
Current assets:		
Cash and cash equivalents	401,243	224,838
Accounts receivable (net)	8,389	5,658
Inventory	8,913	7,098
Current deferred tax asset	6,238	4,317
Prepaid expenses and other current assets	21,404	16,016
Income tax receivable		23,528
Investments	55,005	124,766
Leasehold improvements, property and equipment, net	751,951	676,881
Long-term investments	128,241	
Other assets	21,985	16,564
Goodwill	21,939	21,939
Total assets	**1,425,308**	**1,121,605**
Liabilities and shareholders' equity		
Current liabilities:		
Accounts payable	46,382	33,705
Accrued payroll and benefits	60,241	50,336
Accrued liabilities	46,456	38,892
Current portion of deemed landlord financing	133	121
Income tax payable	4,241	
Deferred rent	143,284	123,667
Deemed landlord financing	3,529	3,661
Deferred income tax liability	64,381	50,525
Other liabilities	12,435	9,825
Total liabilities	**381,082**	**310,732**
Total shareholders' equity	**1,044,226**	**810,873**
Total liabilities and shareholders' equity	**1,425,308**	**1,121,605**

Summary Consolidated Statement of Cash Flows[1] (for year ended December 31, in $ thousands)			
	2011	2010	2009
Net cash provided by operating activities	411,096	289,191	260,673
Net cash used in investing activities	(210,208)	(189,881)	(67,208)
Net cash used in financing activities	(24,268)	(94,522)	(61,943)

[1] The company made an adjustment for exchange rates to reconcile opening and closing cash balances.

Source: Chipotle Mexican Grill, Inc. 2011 10-K.

Exhibit 4 CMG Selected Stock Price Data (in $ At Close of Day)

Date	Stock Price
January 26, 2006 **(IPO)**	45.00
January 3, 2007	59.42
January 2, 2008	120.38
January 2, 2009	47.76
January 4, 2010	96.46
January 3, 2011	218.92
January 3, 2012	367.29
April 2, 2012	414.15
April 13, 2012	442.40
May 1, 2012	413.07
June 1, 2012	379.95
July 2, 2012	292.33
August 1, 2012	288.64
October 1, 2012	316.33
October 2, 2012 **(Einhorn)**	302.96

Source: Compiled from Yahoo Finance, www.finance.yahoo.come/charts?s=CMG+Interactive#symbol=cmg;range=5y;compare=;indicator=volume;charttype=area;crosshair=on;ohlcvalues=0;logscale=off;source=undefined;, accessed October 19, 2012.

financial statements, while Exhibit 4 gives a list of the company's stock on specific dates. Third quarter 2012 results showed a revenue increase of 18.4 percent over the same period in 2011 and a net income increase of 19.6 percent. Same-store sales increased by 4.8 percent in the quarter compared to 11.3 percent in third quarter 2011. Revenue growth was attributed to both new restaurant openings and menu price increases. The company launched a system-wide menu price increase in 2011 whose implementation was completed in third quarter 2012.[38]

The "Einhorn Effect"

On October 2, 2012, Jeff Einhorn, who headed a hedge fund, made a presentation at the Value Investors Conference in New York City. In his presentation, Einhorn said that CMG was an attractive stock for short sellers because the company faced significant competition, principally from Taco Bell's Cantina Bell menu, and increased food costs, both due to its sustainable sourcing practices and a global increase in food commodity prices. He said that a survey conducted by his firm found that 75 percent of self-identified Chipotle customers also frequented Taco Bell and that Taco

Bell came out on top on both price and convenience. Einhorn stated:

Twenty three percent of Chipotle customers had already tried Taco Bell's Cantina Bell menu — which features burritos and burrito bowls made with fresh ingredients — and two-thirds of those customers indicated they would return. What's more, the customers most likely to return to Taco Bell were also those most likely to eat at Chipotle, a dynamic that indicates to me that Chipotle is most at risk of losing its frequent customers.[39]

Within hours of Einhorn's presentation, CMG's stock began to fall. It fell by more than 4 percent by the end of the day, and stock analysts stated that CMG had been "Einhorned."[40]

CMG's Challenges

In his conference call with analysts on October 18, 2012, Ells indirectly compared Cantina Bell with CMG (without actually naming his competitor):

The way Chipotle does its business is not an easy thing to copy, and though a competitor could offer a similar item, it's probably only on the surface. Take a company that sells grilled chicken, for instance. Yet that company does not have a grill, nor do they have knives or cutting boards. So how do they make real chicken and cut it up? And in the end the customers realize the difference. Be careful of those who have a lower cost opportunity. The customer's not easily fooled. Our interactive format — the burrito assembly line that every customer runs through — is an important part of what Chipotle does.[41]

He also indicated that CMG would consider raising its menu prices in 2013 to make up for expected higher food costs. As he conferred with co-CEO Moran following the call, both men listened in on Chief Financial Officer Jack Hartung talking to a reporter:

The company will be patient with its pricing decisions, so as not to deter customers. We could move quickly, but we're going to choose not to be in too much of a hurry. We don't want to be the first ones out of the box with price increases. We'd rather see what happens with the economy, see what happens with consumer spending, see what other competitors do and how consumers respond.[42]

CMG faced a host of challenges. While the depressed economy favored quick service and fast casual restaurants over full service restaurants because of lower check prices, consumer sentiment indicated that the majority of them would either curtail their spending on eating or at best maintain it at current levels. In addition, Taco Bell was proving to be a formidable competitor with its 5,670 U.S. restaurants pushing the higher margin Cantina Bell menu through aggressive and large-scale advertising. Finally, the expected increase in food costs was bound to affect CMG both in its margins and in its quest to increase its usage of sustainable inputs. Both men recalled a statement made by Arnold to an interviewer a few years ago:

Chipotle is a good example of what can happen when you buck conventional wisdom. We've built a chain of fast food restaurants shirking many of the things the industry was built on — we spend more on food, not less; we own our restaurants rather than franchising; and we don't market using lots of price promotions and other gimmicks. Going that route, we've built one of the most successful restaurant companies in years.[43]

Were sustainability and the "Food with Integrity" campaign luxuries that CMG could ill afford in these difficult economic times? Could CMG continue to use quality and sustainably sourced inputs as differentiators to justify a higher priced menu?

NOTES

1. Yahoo Finance, accessed October 18, 2012.
2. Unless otherwise indicated, the information in this section is based on Standard & Poor's Industry Surveys: Restaurants, June 7, 2012.
3. National Restaurant Association, "Restaurants by the Numbers," www.restaurant.org, accessed October 10, 2012.
4. John T. Barone, "Commodity Outlook 2012," National Restaurant Association, www.restaurant.org, accessed October 10, 2012.
5. Thomas O. Jones and W. Earl Sasser, Jr., "Why Satisfied Customers Defect," *Harvard Business Review*, November–December 1995, pp. 88–99.
6. Jack in the Box, 2011 10-K.
7. Paul Sebert, "Good Eats: San Francisco Style Hits Huntington with Qdoba," www.herald-dispatch.com/entertainment/x1543286410/San-Francisco-style-hits-Huntington-with-Qdoba?i=0, accessed October 11, 2012.
8. Jack in the Box, 2011 10-K.
9. Yum Brands, Inc. 2011 10-K.
10. "Taco Bell Takes on Chipotle with New Menu," www.brandchannel.com/home/post/2012/01/24/Taco-Bell-vs-Chipotle-012412.aspx, accessed October 11, 2012.
11. Yum Brands, Inc. Press Release., October 9, 2012
12. Margaret Heffernan, "Dreamers: Chipotle Founder Steve Ells," www.rd.com/advice/work-career/dreamers-chipotlefounder-steve-ells/, accessed October 12, 2012.
13. Ibid.
14. Chipotle website, "About Us," www.chipotle.com/en-us/company/about_us.aspx, accessed October 11, 2012.

15. www.epa.gov/region7/water/cafo/, accessed October 11, 2012.

16. Polly Walker, Pamela Rhubart-Berg, Shawn McKenzie, Kristin Kelling, and Robert S. Lawrence, "Public Health Implications of Meat Production and Consumption," Public Health Nutrition, 8(4): 348-356, 2005, www.jhsph.edu/sebin/y/h/PHN_meat_consumption.pdf, accessed October 11, 2012.

17. Ibid.

18. Chipotle 2011 10-K

19. Ibid.

20. Thomson Reuters, Chipotle Mexican Grill, Inc. Stock Report, research.scottrade.com/qnr/Stocks/GetPDF?docKey=1581-AB585-6CJHB2E4R1H0C6R0PI1L9MO8A6, accessed October 9, 2012.

21. Jim Collins was the author of two popular business books: Good to Great (Harper Business, New York, 2001) and Great by Choice (Harper Business, New York, 2011). In the former book, Collins introduced the notion that most companies are ruled by the tyranny of "or" where they choose between options rather than attempting to do both, the "and."

22. "Chipotle's Unique Take on Sustainable Sourcing," www.cokesolutions.com/BusinessSolutions/Pages/Site%20Pages/DetailedPage.aspx?ArticleURL=/BusinessSolutions/Pages/Articles/ChipotlesUniqueTakeonSustainableSourcing.aspx&smallImage=yes&LeftNav=Customer+Spotlight+, accessed October 12, 2012.

23. "Chipotle Plans Major Solar Power Initiative," Business Wire, October 20, 2009, www.thefreelibrary.com/Chipotle+Plans+Major+Solar+Power+Initiative.-a0210101557, accessed October 12, 2012.

24. Ibid.

25. "Chipotle Expands Locally Grown Produce Program," Food Business Week, June 4, 2007.

26. Chipotle Press Release, July 30, 2012.

27. Chipotle, 2012 Third Quarter 10-Q.

28. While the terms "organic" and "sustainable" are used interchangeably, the two are different. Organic products can be unsustainably produced on large industrial farms, and farms that are not certified organic can produce food using methods that can sustain the farm's productivity for a long time. The term "organic" is used to mean products produced or grown at a facility that is certified as such, while "sustainable" is more a philosophy or way of life. Since organic farming generally falls within the accepted definition of sustainable agriculture and since data is collected on organic rather than sustainable agriculture, most observers believed that organic was a good proxy for sustainable.

29. United States Department of Agriculture, Alternative Farming Systems Information Center, afsic.nal.usda.gov/organic-production, accessed October 19, 2012.

30. Sarah Rose, "A Fast Organic Nation?" Plenty, October/November 2005, pp. 70—75.

31. Jim Edwards, "How Chipotle's Business Model Depends on Never Running TV Ads," Business Insider, March 16, 2012, http://articles.businessinsider.com/2012-03-16/news/31199897_1_chipotle-advertising-marketing, accessed October 19, 2012.

32. Chipotle 2011 10-K.

33. Edwards, "How Chipotle's Business Model Depends on Never Running TV Ads."

34. "Building Evangelism: Chipotle's Farm Team," www.reasonedpr.com/blog/building-evangelism-chipotles-farm-team/, accessed October 20, 2012.

35. Chipotle Press Release, February 10, 2012.

36. "Chipotle's Bold New Marketing Plan," www.monkeydish.com/ideas/articles/chipotle%E2%80%99s-bold-new-marketingplan, accessed October 20, 2012.

37. Edwards, "How Chipotle's Business Model Depends on Never Running TV Ads."

38. Chipotle Press Release, October 18, 2012.

39. Chris Barth, "Hold the Guacamole, Einhorn's Shorting Chipotle," Forbes, http://www.forbes.com/sites/chrisbarth/2012/10/02/hold-the-guacamole-einhorns-shorting-chipotle/?partner=yahootix, accessed October 19, 2012.

40. Kate Kelly, "GM, Chipotle Get "Einhorned" by Comments," http://finance.yahoo.com/news/gm-chipotle-einhornedcomments-201207168.html, accessed October 19, 2012.

41. Kim Bhasin, "Chipotle CEO Shreds Unnamed Competitor for Not Having Grills, Knives or Cutting Boards," Business Insider, www.businessinsider.com/chipotle-ceo-taco-bell-2012-10, accessed October 20, 2012.

42. Annie Gasparro, "Chipotle Shares Sink on Outlook," http://online.wsj.com/article/SB10000872396390443684104578066484037301320.html, accessed October 21, 2012.

43. "Chipotle's Unique Take on Sustainable Sourcing," www.cokesolutions.com/BusinessSolutions/Pages/Site%20Pages/DetailedPage.aspx?ArticleURL=/BusinessSolutions/Pages/Articles/ChipotlesUniqueTakeonSustainableSourcing.aspx&smallImage=yes&LeftNav=Customer+Spotlight+, accessed October 21, 2012.

Nathan DeLano, Craig Hooker, James Mendiola, and Alisha Sanford

Texas A&M University

Early to bed, early to rise, work like hell and advertise.

Gert Boyle
Chairperson of Columbia Sportswear

Columbia Sportswear Company (Columbia) is a leader in the highly competitive industry of active outdoor apparel. The firm's success is a result of its ability to effectively design, manufacture, and distribute outdoor apparel. Making these outcomes possible are Columbia's innovation skills, the equity of its brand, and strong marketing. Columbia's broad product lines include everything from outerwear and footwear to camping equipment and skiwear. The firm has grown from a small hat company founded in the 1930s into a company with a global strategy and a physical and online presence spanning Asia, Latin America, Africa, and Europe.

To appreciate fully the evolution of Columbia from "a corporation that was a niche manufacturer of outdoor clothing aimed at fishermen…into an international brand and publicly traded powerhouse,"[1] one must understand the level of perseverance, work ethic, dedication, and attitude of Gertrude Boyle: now in her late eighties, but still "One Bad Mother."[2] Gert Boyle took over the family business in the early 70s after the sudden death of her husband. A candid and straightforward person, Boyle has often admitted that, having never worked a day in her life, she had no idea what to do when she first began running the company.[3] Despite her lack of experience, Boyle helped turn Columbia from near bankruptcy and collapse into a billion dollar publicly traded organization. Along the way, she relied on her natural business savvy and perseverance, overcoming family tragedy and even an attempted kidnapping.

Columbia's corporate culture and business personality reflect a great number of the ideals that Gert Boyle's leadership had imbued into the company. Her sharp wit, dedication, and love for the company are legendary, as proven in November 2010 when an armed assailant forced Boyle at gunpoint from her garage and into her home. Thinking on her feet, Boyle activated a silent alarm to contact police and escaped shaken, but largely unharmed.[4] After the incident, the local police chief stopped by Boyle's home but "made the mistake of wearing a North Face jacket," … "The police chief asked if she was all right. True to her personality Boyle said, 'I was OK until that jacket walked in here.'"[5] As evidenced, even in the most unimaginable and frightening situations Boyle stays true to herself. Her relentless commitment has been a driving force behind Columbia's growth and profitability, proving that "the buck still stops with Ma."[6]

History of Columbia Sportswear

The story of Columbia Sportswear began in 1937 when the Lanfrom family escaped Nazi-controlled Germany and settled in Portland, Oregon. There, Paul Lanfrom bought a small hat distributorship named Rosenfeld Hat Company and, fearing the name could hurt sales, renamed it The Columbia Hat Company.[7]

The Columbia Hat Company became relatively successful but like many small companies, Paul started to butt heads with the firm's suppliers. In Paul's opinion, the best solution for The Columbia Hat Company was to begin manufacturing its own hats. This decision would greatly affect the direction Columbia would take, ultimately becoming the juggernaut that it is today. In the late 40s, Paul's daughter, Gertrude, married Neal Boyle and he began working alongside his father-in-law learning the ins and outs of the business. In 1963, Neal Bole assumed control of the Lafrom family business. With the help of Gert, who designed and created the first Columbia fishing vest, Neal turned The Columbia Hat Company into Columbia Sportswear. Columbia Sportswear manufactured and sold high quality hunting and fishing apparel. In 1970, tragedy struck when Neal died suddenly of a heart attack, leaving Gert in sole control of Columbia.

When she took control of the company, Columbia was "teetering on the brink of insolvency," causing Gert to look for someone to buy the business.[8] After a long search, Gert was only able to find one potential buyer who offered her a paltry $1,400 to buy Columbia. True to her feisty personality, she laughed at and then declined the offer.

A few years later Gert's son, Tim, came on board to help run Columbia. In 1976, Tim led Columbia in a new direction, dropping the wholesale unit of the business to focus on building Columbia's brand name and presence. Tim also placed Don Santorufoin in charge of Columbia's purchasing and manufacturing divisions. Tim's choice paid off as Don was integral in moving the majority of Columbia's manufacturing operations to Korea. The decision allowed Columbia to produce outdoor apparel at the exceptional quality that its customers had come to expect, but at a fraction of the cost. Once this happened, Columbia was able to lower its prices and sell its apparel to the more cost-conscious outdoorsman.

During the 80s, Columbia's designers created a jacket that propelled Columbia to a leadership position in the outdoor apparel market. Known as the Interchange System, the product's design was made up of a "lightweight shell jacket and a warm liner that zipped together, giving the wearer three jackets for different weather conditions."[9] Columbia used its Interchange System to create its first ski jacket – the Bugaboo. Columbia introduced the Bugaboo to the market in 1986 and sold the millionth Bugaboo jacket in 1992, making it "the best-selling parka in ski apparel history."[10]

Over the next two decades, Columbia continued expanding its presence in the outdoor apparel market by introducing new apparel lines. These lines included the Convert snowboarding line in 1994, the Omni-Shade sun protection line in 2008, and the Titanium golf apparel line in 2009. Columbia also grew by acquiring some of its competitors. It acquired Sorel in 2000, Mountain Hardwear in 2004, both Montrail and Pacific Trail in 2006, and OutDry Technologies in 2010.[11] During this time, Columbia also expanded into the retail business both domestically and internationally. In 1995, the firm

opened its first store in Portland and two years later it opened its first international retail store in Seoul, South Korea.[12] These business decisions allowed Columbia to record sales of $1 billion in 2004.[13]

Today, Columbia has net sales of nearly $1.69 billion, and its products are available for purchase in over 100 different countries. Columbia reports that its products are "distributed through a mix of wholesale distribution channels, direct-to-customer channels (retail stores and e-commerce), independent distributors, and licensees."[14] Columbia's retail stores include 63 outlet retail stores and 51 brand retail stores around the world.[15] Exhibit 1 shows that Columbia's operations are broken into four distinct geographic regions: the U.S. (56.0 percent of net sales), Latin America and Asia Pacific (LAAP–20.1 percent of net sales), Europe, Middle East and Africa (EMEA–16.3 percent of net sales), and Canada (7.6 percent of net sales). Exhibit 2 shows the firm's two business units (or divisions): Apparel, Accessories, and Equipment (78.8 percent of net sales) and Footwear (21.2 percent of net sales).[16] Exhibits 3a and 3b provide consolidated financial data.

Exhibit 1 Columbia Regions

	Year Ended December 31,		
	2011	2010	% Change
	(In millions, except for percentage changes)		
United States	$948.0	$881.0	8%
LAAP	341.0	263.4	29%
EMEA	275.4	222.4	24%
Canada	129.6	116.7	11%
	$1,694.0	$1,483.5	14%

Source: Shareholder Information. *Columbia*. Accessed 20 Apr 2012 at http://investor.columbia.com/annuals.cfm.

Exhibit 2 Columbia Divisions

	Year Ended December 31,		
	2011	2010	% Change
	(In millions, except for percentage changes)		
Apparel, Accessories and Equipment	$1,334.9	$1,213.3	10%
Footwear	359.1	270.2	33%
	$1,694.0	$1,483.5	14%

Source: Shareholder Information. *Columbia*. Accessed 20 Apr 2012 at http://investor.columbia.com/annuals.cfm.

Exhibit 3a Columbia Sportswear Company Consolidated Statements of Operations

(In thousands, except per share amounts)	2011	2011 (% of net sales)	2010	2010 (% of net sales)	2009	2009 (% of net sales)
			Year Ended December 31,			
Net sales	$1,693,985		$1,483,524		$1,244,023	
Cost of sales	958,677	56.6%	854,120	57.6%	719,945	57.9%
Gross profit	735,308	43.4%	629,404	42.4%	524,078	42.1%
SG&A	614,658	36.3%	534,068	36.0%	444,715	35.7%
Net licensing income	15,756	0.9%	7,991	0.5%	8,399	0.7%
Income from operations	136,406	8.1%	103,327	7.0%	87,762	7.1%
Interest income, net	1,274	0.1%	1,564	0.1%	2,088	0.2%
Income before income tax	137,680	8.1%	104,891	7.1%	89,850	7.2%
Income tax expense	(34,201)	−2.0%	(27,854)	−1.9%	(22,829)	−1.8%
Net Income	$103,479	6.1%	$77,037	5.2%	67,021	5.4%
Earning per share:						
Basic	$3.06		$2.28		$1.98	
Diluted	3.03		2.26		1.97	
Cash dividends per share:	$0.86		$2.24		$0.66	
Weighted average shares outstanding:						
Basic	33,808		33,725		33,846	
Diluted	34,204		34,092		33,981	

Source: Shareholder Information. *Columbia.* Accessed 20 Apr 2012 at http://investor.columbia.com/annuals.cfm.

The Apparel Industry and Commodity Prices

Columbia specializes in designing, sourcing, and distributing outdoor apparel products. Because of the nature of the raw materials required to produce its products for sale to customers, commodity prices significantly affect Columbia and its operations. The price of crude oil provides a clear example of these effects. After falling to a cost of $35 a barrel in December 2008, Brent Crude spot prices increased steadily to $120 a barrel by mid-2011.[17] This 243 percent increase in oil prices dramatically affected Columbia's cost of doing business. Specifically, oil prices directly affect the price of the petrochemicals used in the textiles incorporated into Columbia's garments. It had pushed up the price of the purified terephthalic acid used in the production of polyester fiber by 60 percent during the time between roughly September 2010 and the late spring of 2011, translating into a higher cost of goods.[18]

Oil prices also affect the cost of transporting and distributing Columbia's products. Being dependent on products manufactured outside the United States and having a global distribution footprint, the effect of oil prices on freight costs are a large concern for the company. In fact, in the United States, the average cost to import a 20-foot container increased 5.6 percent from 2008 to 2011.[19] With crude oil prices expected to increase 3.2 percent each year from 2011 through 2016, the price of oil is an especially important issue for Columbia Sportswear to monitor and to incorporate into its cost structures.[20]

The Apparel Industry and Weather Phenomena

In February 2012, Columbia reported record-setting revenues of $1.69 billion – a 14 percent increase from the previous year.[21] Yet, despite a financially successful year, in March 2012, Columbia announced a 2 percent reduction in its worldwide workforce of 4,100. Part of the reason given by CEO, Tim Boyle, was Columbia's historic trend of weak growth in years following unseasonably warm winters. According to Boyle, "orders for the following winter are lower if the previous winter was mild." Company sources state that unseasonably warm weather slows winter gear turnover and negatively affects orders for the following year.[22]

Exhibit 3b Columbia Sportswear Company Consolidated Balance Sheets

(In thousands)	December 31,			
	2011	Vertical Analysis 2011	2010	Vertical Analysis 2010
ASSETS				
Current Assets:				
Cash and cash equivalents	$ 241,034	17.4%	$234,257	18.1%
Short-term investments	2,878	0.2%	68,812	5.3%
Accounts receivable, net	351,538	25.4%	300,181	23.2%
Investories, net	365,199	26.4%	314,298	24.3%
Deferred income taxes	52,485	3.8%	45,091	3.5%
Prepaid expenses and other current assets	36,392	2.6%	28,241	2.2%
Total current assets	1,049,526	75.9%	990,880	76.5%
Property, plant, and equipment, net	250,910	18.1%	221,813	17.1%
Intangible assets, net	39,020	2.8%	40,423	3.1%
Goodwill	14,438	1.0%	14,470	1.1%
Other non-current assets	28,648	2.1%	27,168	2.1%
Total assets	$1,382,542	100.0%	$1,294,754	100.0%
LIABILITIES AND SHAREHOLDERS' EQUITY				
Current Liabilities:				
Accounts payable	$148,973	10.8%	$130,626	10.1%
Accrued liabilities	104,496	7.6%	102,810	7.9%
Income taxed payable	12,579	0.9%	16,037	1.2%
Deferred income taxes	954	0.1%	2,153	0.2%
Total current liabilities	267,002	19.3%	251,626	19.4%
Other long-term liabilities	23,853	1.7%	21,456	1.7%
Income taxes payable	15,389	1.1%	19,698	1.5%
Deferred income taxes	1,753	0.1%	–	0.0%
Total liabilities	307,997	22.3%	292,780	22.6%
Shareholders' Equity				
Preferred stock, 10,000 shares authorized; none issued and outstanding	–	0.0%	–	0.0%
Common stock (no par value); 125,000 shares authorized; 33,638 and 33,683 issued and outstanding	3,037	0.2%	5,052	0.4%
Retained earnings	1,024,611	74.1%	950,207	73.4%
Accumulated other comprehensive income	46,897	3.4%	46,715	3.6%
Total shareholders' equity	1,074,545	77.7%	1,001,974	77.4%
Total liabilities and shareholders' equity	$1,382,542	100.0%	$1,294,754	100.0%

Source: Shareholder Information. *Columbia*. Accessed 20 Apr 2012 at http://investor.columbia.com/annuals.cfm.

According to the National Oceanic and Atmospheric Administration, the winter of 2011-2012 was the fourth warmest winter recorded in the last 117 years.[23] While on a global scale the general society continues to debate climate change and global warming, the fact that climate and temperature affect companies with products that are heavily skewed toward a particular season is a given and is a reality with which Columbia must cope.

The Apparel Industry and Shifting Demographics of Participation in Outdoor Activities

As a company dedicated to outfitting outdoor activities such as skiing, mountaineering, climbing, and trail activities, one of the primary issues that affects the firm is the changing demographics related to outdoor activities. According to the 2011 Outdoor Participation Report published by the Outdoor Foundation, there were strong growth trends in participation in some of Columbia's key outfitting sports such as climbing, trail running, and backpacking at 19.8, 5.8, and 9.2 percent respectively.[24] These growth percentages (that occurred despite economic recession that was occurring at the time) help bolster a relatively strong counter-cyclical trend for outdoor activities.

In terms of future growth, specific figures important to Columbia include youth participation rates and key growth demographics. For example, male youth participation in outdoor activities declined from 57 percent to 53 percent from 2009 to 2010 while female participation increased from 43 percent to 47 percent.[25] If this trend continues, it may create some long-term effects on the design and marketing of Columbia's product line. Additionally, recent data suggests increasing participation of non-Caucasian groups in outdoor activities, which may also affect the nature of the products Columbia chooses to manufacture for different customer groups.[26]

Columbia's Omni-Heat Electric Products and Legal Issues

In March 2012, Innovative Sports Design filed a lawsuit against Columbia, claiming that the company pilfered technology that led to the creation of Columbia's electrically heated clothing line, Omni-Heat Electric. According to the lawsuit, Innovative Sports met with Columbia from 2004 to 2007 to pursue a partnership to develop battery-powered clothing. The partnership never materialized and meetings ended in 2008. The lawsuit claims that Columbia later developed a product with elements similar to Innovative Sports' technology.[27] Perhaps as a direct response to intellectual property based lawsuits, Columbia stated the following in its year-ended 2011 10-K, "As we strive to achieve technical innovations, we face a greater risk of inadvertent infringements of third party rights or compliance issues with regulations applicable to products with technical innovations such as electrical components."[28] The electric products are part of the general Omni-Heat line, which has grown to 40 percent of Columbia's total SKU and is believed to be a primary source of growth.[29]

Columbia's Competitive Rivals

Nike Inc.

With over $20.86 billion in revenues in 2011 and 38,000 employees, the small company created by Bill Bowerman and Phil Knight in 1972 is the undeniable king of sportswear. Nike has a strong global presence as indicated by the fact that the firm has a sales presence in 170 countries as it sells apparel, footwear, sports equipment, and accessories.[30] With the scope of its product line, Nike is a heavyweight in the highly competitive apparel industry. Anchored by its innovative product R&D and world-class marketing, Nike seeks to satisfy the needs of its loyal customers. It also benefits from an array of subsidiaries such as Converse, Hurley, and Umbro.

While both Columbia and Nike compete in the sports apparel and footwear industry, Columbia's focus on outdoor apparel and footwear narrows the competitive space within which the firms compete against each other. Key products, such as Nike's winter athletic jackets, and accessories, such as backpacks, are common ground for competition between the two companies. However, Nike's All Conditions Gear footwear – with its line of outdoor boots and trail running products – pits Columbia and Nike products head to head. Exhibits 4a and 4b provide financial data for Nike.

VF Corporation – Timberland and The North Face

One of the largest apparel companies in the world with $9.3 billion in annual revenues and 58,000 full-time employees, VF Corporation (VF) designs, sources, manufactures, and distributes a wide variety of apparel and accessories through its basket of brands.[31] Brands owned by VF include Wrangler, Vans, and Nautica, with its primary form of competition with Columbia coming from its Timberland footwear and The North Face outerwear brands. As evidenced by its diversification, VF's businesses focus on different market segments. Accordingly, Columbia's challenge is to understand the degree to which VF will emphasize its businesses (such as The North Face) that compete directly with one or more of Columbia's product lines.

Established in 1968, The North Face brand specializes in outfitting outdoor enthusiasts and athletes with products that target specific activities such as climbing,

Exhibit 4a Nike Consolidated Statements of Income

(In thousands, except per share amounts)	Year Ended May 31,					
	2011	2011 (% of net sales)	2010	2010 (% of net sales)	2009	2009 (% of net sales)
Revenues	$20,862,000		$19,014,000		$19,176,000	
Cost of sales	11,354,000	54.4%	10,214,000	53.7%	10,572,000	55.1%
Gross Margin	9,508,000	45.6%	8,800,000	46.3%	8,604,000	44.9%
Demand creation expense	2,448,000	11.7%	2,356,000	12.4%	2,352,000	12.3%
Operating overhead expense	4,245,000	20.3%	3,970,000	20.9%	3,798,000	19.8%
Total selling and administrative expense	6,693,000	32.1%	6,326,000	33.3%	6,150,000	32.1%
Restructuring charges	–	0.0%	–	0.0%	195,000	1.0%
Goodwill impairment	–	0.0%	–	0.0%	199,000	1.0%
Intangible and other asset impairment	–	0.0%	–	0.0%	202,000	1.1%
Interest expense (income), net	4,000	0.0%	6,000	0.0%	(10,000)	−0.1%
Other (income), net	(33,000)	−0.2%	(49,000)	−0.3%	(89,000)	−0.5%
Income before income taxes	2,844,000	13.6%	2,517,000	13.2%	1,957,000	10.2%
Income taxes	711,000	3.4%	610,000	3.2%	470,000	2.5%
Net Income	$2,133,000	10.2%	$1,907,000	10.0%	$1,487,000	7.8%
Earnings per share:						
Basic	$4.48		$3.93		$3.07	
Diluted	4.39		3.86		3.03	
Dividends declared per common share	$1.20		$1.06		$0.98	

Source: Annual Reports. *Nike*. Accessed 20 Apr 2012 at http://investors.nikeinc.com/Investors/Financial-Reports-and-Filings/Annual-Reports/default.aspx.

hiking, and trail running.[32] Its popular brand of jackets using third-party waterproof technology (such as Gore-Tex fabrics) directly competes against Columbia's Omni products. Established in 1978, Timberland is an outdoor apparel and footwear company acquired in September 2011 by VF. The combination of The North Face and Timberland brands creates formidable competition in almost every category in which Columbia produces products.

At the corporate level, it seems that VF has the skill needed to form and then manage the roughly 30 unique brands that constitute its overall portfolio of product offerings. Its ability to handle everything from design to distribution and remain competitive in diverse segments of the apparel market is a testament to its understanding of its customers. Exhibits 5a and 5b provide VF's financial data.

L.L. Bean

Leon Leonwood Bean launched his firm, called L. L. Bean, in 1912. At the time of its founding, this company was a mail-order firm selling a single product: the waterproof boot. In operation now for over 100 years,

L.L. Bean has grown from its humble beginnings into a global company specializing in outdoor apparel and gear. With revenues of $1.44 billion in 2011 and 4,600 worldwide employees, L.L. Bean is Columbia's most similar competitor in terms of size and target market.[33] Even so, the company is significantly different in terms of how it competes.

Started as a mail-order business, L.L. Bean continues to exploit its established reputation and brand equity by circulating over 200 million catalogues each year, worldwide. As a mail order firm, L.L. Bean was an early adopter of the online retail model, launching its online shopping service in 1996.[34] The firm remains a strong competitor in the outdoor apparel and gear business by leveraging its historic brand name and well-developed distribution capabilities. Additionally, L.L. Bean has a strong reputation for the quality of its customer service standards. These standards were the foundation for the firm's earning of Customer Choice awards for best retail customer service in 2008, 2009, and 2010 from the National Retail Federation Foundation and American Express.[35] The ongoing outdoor learning classes L.L. Bean offers in its retail outlets are a prime example of

Exhibit 4b Nike Consolidated Balance Sheets

(In thousands)	May 31,			
	2011	Vertical Analysis 2011	2010	Vertical Analysis 2010
ASSETS				
Current Assets:				
Cash and equivalent	$1,955,000	13.0%	$3,079,000	21.4%
Short-term investments	2,583,000	17.2%	2,067,000	14.3%
Accounts receivable, net	3,138,000	20.9%	2,650,000	18.4%
Inventories	2,715,000	18.1%	2,041,000	14.2%
Deferred income taxes	312,000	2.1%	249,000	1.7%
Prepaid expenses and other current assets	594,000	4.0%	873,000	6.1%
Total	11,297,000	75.3%	10,959,000	76.0%
Property, plant, and equipment, net	2,115,000	14.1%	1,932,000	13.4%
Identifiable intangible assets, net	487,000	3.2%	467,000	3.2%
Goodwill	205,000	1.4%	188,000	1.3%
Deferred income taxes and other assets	894,000	6.0%	873,000	6.1%
Total Assets	$14,998,000	100.0%	$14,419,000	100.0%
LIABILITIES AND SHAREHOLDERS' EQUITY				
Current Liabilities:				
Current portion of long-term debt	$200,000	1.3%	$7,000	0.0%
Notes payable	187,000	1.2%	139,000	1.0%
Accounts payable	1,469,000	9.8%	1,255,000	8.7%
Accrued liabilities	1,985,000	13.2%	1,904,000	13.2%
Income taxes payable	117,000	0.8%	59,000	0.4%
Total	3,958,000	26.4%	3,364,000	23.3%
Long-term debt	276,000	1.8%	446,000	3.1%
Deferred income taxes and other liabilities	921,000	6.1%	855,000	5.9%
Commitments and contingencies	–	0.0%	–	0.0%
Reedeemable preferred stock	–	0.0%	–	0.0%
Total Liabilities	5,155,000	34.4%	4,665,000	32.4%
Shareholders Equity:				
Common stock at started at value				
Class A convertible – 90 and 90 shares outstanding	–	0.0%	–	0.0%
Class B – 378 and 394 shares outstanding	3,000	0.0%	3,000	0.0%
Captical in excess of stated value	3,944,000	26.3%	3,441,000	23.9%
Accumulated other comprehensive income	95,000	0.6%	215,000	1.5%
Retained earnings	5,801,000	38.7%	6,095,000	42.3%
Total shareholders' equity	9,843,000	65.6%	9,754,000	67.6%
Total liabilities and shareholder' equity	$14,998,000	100.0%	$14,419,000	100.0%

Source: Annual Reports. *Nike.* Accessed 20 Apr 2012 at http://investors.nikeinc.com/Investors/Financial-Reports-and-Filings/Annual-Reports/default.aspx.

Exhibit 5a VF Corp Income Statement

(In thousands, except per share amounts)	2011	2011 (% of net sales)	2010	2010 (% of net sales)	2009	2009 (% of net sales)
Net Sales	$9,365,477		$7,624,599		$7,143,074	
Royalty Income	93,755	1.0%	77,990	1.0%	77,212	1.1%
Total Revenues	9,459,232	101.0%	7,702,589	101.0%	7,220,286	101.1%
Costs and Operating Expenses:						
Cost of goods sold	5,128,602	54.8%	4,105,201	53.8%	4,025,122	56.3%
Marketing, administrative and general expenses	3,085,839	32.9%	2,574,790	33.8%	2,336,394	32.7%
Impairment of goodwill and intangible assets	0	0.0%	201,738	2.6%	121,953	1.7%
Total	8,214,441	87.7%	6,881,729	90.3%	6,483,469	90.8%
Operating Income	1,244,791	13.3%	820,860	10.8%	736,817	10.3%
Other Income (Expense):						
Interest income	4,778	0.1%	2,336	0.0%	2,230	0.0%
Interest expense	(77,578)	−0.8%	(77,738)	−1.0%	(85,902)	−1.2%
Miscellaneous. Net	(7,248)	−0.1%	4,754	0.1%	1,528	0.0%
Total	(80,048)	−0.9%	(70,648)	−0.9%	(82,144)	−1.1%
Income Before Income Taxes	1,164,743	12.4%	750,212	9.8%	654,673	9.2%
Income Taxes	274,350	2.9%	176,700	2.3%	196,215	2.7%
Net Income	$890,393	9.5%	$573,512	7.5%	$458,458	6.4%
Net (Income) Loss Attributable to Noncontrolling Interests	(2,304)		(2,150)		2,813	
Net Income Attributable to VF Corporation	$888,089		$571,362		$461,271	
Earnings per share:						
Basic	$8.13		$5.25		$4.18	
Diluted	7.98		5.18		4.13	
Cash Dividends Per Common Share	$2.61		$2.43		$2.37	

Source: Investor Relations, Annual Reports. *VF.* Accessed 20 Apr 2012 at http://phx.corporate-ir.net/phoenix.zhtml?c=61559&p=irol-reportsAnnual.

the company's strong focus on customer service. In recent years, the company has expanded by increasing its number of bricks-and-mortar stores worldwide to 40 stores domestically, 20 stores in Japan, and 63 stores in China.[36] Because L.L. Bean is a privately held corporation, detailed financial data are not available.

Recreational Equipment Incorporated (REI)

Better known by its acronym, REI focuses on high-end outdoor gear and clothing and operates as the largest consumer cooperative in the United States with 4 million members. From its modest beginning as a 23-member cooperative located at a gas station in Seattle, REI has not only opened 110 retail outlets but has developed

a strong online presence as well. REI carries well-known brands such as Columbia as well as its own REI branded products.[37]

With revenues of $1.79 billion and 10,000 employees, the company is similar in size and target customers to Columbia. As a cooperative, the company enjoys some unique privileges. For example, REI's strong brand equity – as an environmentally responsible company committed to cooperative activism based on a common love for nature – define the company's personality and image.

REI perhaps best represents a unique element associated with the competitive arena that Columbia faces; while REI carries Columbia brand outdoor clothing and accessories, the company also competes with Columbia with its own product lines. Major retailers that order, stock, and

Exhibit 5b VF Corp Balance Sheet

(In thousands)	December			
	2011	Vertical Analysis 2011	2010	Vertical Analysis 2010
ASSETS				
Current Assets:				
Cash and equivalents	$341,228	3.7%	$792,239	12.3%
Accounts receivable, less allowance for doubtful accounts of $54,010 in 2011 and $44,599 in 2010	1,120,246	12.0%	773,083	12.0%
Inventories	1,453,645	15.6%	1,070,694	16.6%
Deferred income taxes	106,717	1.1%	68,220	1.1%
Other current assets	166,108	1.8%	121,824	1.9%
Total current assets	3,187,944	34.2%	2,826,060	43.8%
Property, Plant and Equipment	737,451	7.9%	602,908	9.3%
Intangible Assets	2,958,463	31.8%	1,490,925	23.1%
Goodwill	2,023,460	21.7%	1,166,638	18.1%
Other Assets	405,808	4.4%	371,025	5.7%
Total assets	$9,313,126	100.0%	$6,457,556	100.0%
LIABILITIES AND STOCKHOLDERS EQUITY				
Current Liabilities:				
Short-term borrowings	$281,686	3.0%	$36,576	0.6%
Current portion of long-term debt	2,744	0.0%	2,737	0.0%
Accounts payable	637,116	6.8%	510,998	7.9%
Accrued liabilities	744,486	8.0%	559,164	8.7%
Total current liabilities	1,666,032	17.9%	1,109,475	17.2%
Long-term Debt	1,831,781	19.7%	935,882	14.5%
Other Liabilities	1,290,138	13.9%	550,880	8.5%
Total Liabilities	4,787,951	51.4%	2,596,237	40.2%
Stockholders Equity:				
Preferred Stock, par value $1; shares authorized, 25,000,000; no shares outstanding in 2011 and 2010	0	0.0%	0	0.0%
Common stock, stated value $1; shares authorized, 300,000,000; 110,556,981 shares outstanding in 2011 amd 107,938,105 outstanding in 2010	110,557	1.2%	107,938	1.7%
Additional paid-in capital	2,316,107	24.9%	2,081,367	32.2%
Accumulated other comprehensive income (loss)	(421,477)	−4.5%	(268,594)	−4.2%
Retained earnings	2,520,804	27.1%	1,940,508	30.1%
Total equity attributable to VF Corporation	4,525,991	48.6%	3,861,219	59.8%
Noncontrolling interests	(816)	0.0%	100	0.0%
Total stockholders equity	4,525,175	48.6%	3,861,319	59.8%
Total liabilities and stockholders equity	$9,313,126	100.0%	$6,457,556	100.0%

Source: Investor Relations, Annual Reports. *VF.* Accessed 20 Apr 2012 at http://phx.corporate-ir.net/phoenix.zhtml?c=61559&p=irol-reportsAnnual

sell Columbia products have begun to manufacture and promote their own private label brands. This phenomenon represents a complex yet increasingly common element Columbia faces while competing with other firms. See Exhibits 6a and 6b for REI's financial data and Exhibit 7 for a comparison of Columbia and its competitors.

Starting and Finish Lines

Columbia sources all of its products from independent manufacturers based in Asia. According to Columbia, the company sources from independent factories in 15 countries with 72 percent of its apparel, accessories, and equipment manufactured in China and Vietnam. While Columbia maintains that using independent manufacturers allows it to increase or decrease production capacity, maximize flexibility and, ultimately, improve product pricing, the fact remains that it deals with large suppliers that also manufacture apparel, accessories, and equipment for Columbia's competitors. In fact, five of the top factory groups that Columbia contracts supply 25 percent of the global production of apparel and accessories.[38] However, because Columbia lacks the ability to produce apparel internally it has no choice currently but to rely on outsourced production for marketplace success. Because of this situation, Columbia's performance in the volatile and seasonal apparel market depends on the ability of its suppliers to deliver products in an efficient and timely manner.

Columbia relies on sales through wholesale, direct-to-consumer, and independent distributors. While Columbia's brand and ability to innovate are strong, it is not unique. Aside from the competitors discussed previously, major retailers served through the wholesale channel are increasingly competing against Columbia products through private label merchandise.[39]

Potential New Competitors

Columbia primarily competes in an industry that is driven by consumer demand and highly susceptible to seasonal volatility. Successful entry into the apparel industry is challenging due to the economies of scale and operational efficiencies needed to compete successfully. The saturated nature of the apparel industry, even within the smaller sportswear segment in which Columbia competes, and the fact that it appears to be a standard-cycle industry forces firms to compete for market share and brand equity – a situation that usually requires significant resources.[40] In addition to resources, the nurturing of relationships for many years is the foundation for forming efficient distribution channels within wholesale channels in the apparel industry. Because of this, new entrants may find the forming of efficient distribution

Exhibit 6a REI Consolidated Statements of Income

(In thousands)	Year Ended December,			
	2011	2011 (% of net sales)	2010	2010 (% of net sales)
Net sales	$1,798,009		$1,658,751	
Cost of sales	1,034,924	57.6%	929,787	56.1%
Gross profit	763,085	42.4%	728,964	43.9%
Operating expenses:				
Payroll-related expenses	336,175	18.7%	331,159	20.0%
Occupancy, general and administrative	310,674	17.3%	281,233	17.0%
Total	646,849	36.0%	612,392	36.9%
Operating income	116,236	6.5%	116,572	7.0%
Other income, net	12,190	0.7%	13,055	0.8%
Income before patronage refunds and in come taxes	128,426	7.1%	129,627	7.8%
Patronage refunds, net	81,871	4.6%	79,848	4.8%
Income before income taxes	46,555	2.6%	49,779	3.0%
Provision for income taxes	16,387	0.9%	19,549	1.2%
Net Income	$30,168	1.7%	$30,230	1.8%

Source: Financial Statements and Report of Independent Certified Public Accountants. *REI.* Accessed 20 Apr 2012 at http://www.rei.com/content/dam/documents/pdf/2011%20REI%20Financial%20Statements.pdf

Exhibit 6b REI Consolidated Balance Sheets

(In thousands)	December 31,			
	2011	Vertical Analysis 2011	2010	Vertical Analysis 2010
ASSETS				
Current assets:				
Cash and cash equivalents	$140,813	12%	$177,454	17%
Short-term investments	197,443	17%	174,993	16%
Accounts receivable, net	17,048	2%	16,153	2%
Inventories	316,088	28%	259,961	24%
Current deffered income taxes, net	34,439	3%	41,196	4%
Prepaid expenses and other	12,457	1%	11,504	1%
Total current assets	718,288	63%	681,261	64%
		0%		0%
Property and equipment, net	399,282	35%	366,609	35%
Deferred income taxes, net	5,967	1%	6,747	1%
Other	7,934	1%	7,757	1%
Total assets	$1,131,471	100%	$1,062,374	100%
LIABILITIES AND MEMBERS' EQUITY				
Current Liabilities:				
Accounts payable	$146,610	13.0%	$117,019	11.0%
Customer-related obligations	115,200	10.2%	100,438	9.5%
Patronage refunds payable	94,704	8.4%	90,942	8.6%
REI Visa rebate payable	40,799	3.6%	37,738	3.6%
Accrued payroll and related benefits	45,369	4.0%	59,514	5.6%
Retirement and profit-sharing liabilities	13,753	1.2%	26,528	2.5%
Business taxes and other accrued liabilities	30,335	2.7%	26,074	2.5%
Income taxes payable	5,923	0.5%	16,178	1.5%
Total	492,693	43.5%	474,431	44.7%
Deferred rent and other long-term liabilities	57,667	5.1%	54,098	5.1%
Total Liabilities	550,360	48.6%	528,529	49.7%
Members Equity:				
Memberships	160,054	14.1%	143,217	13.5%
Accumulated other comprehensive income	392	0.0%	131	0.0%
Retained earnings	420,665	37.2%	390,497	36.8%
Total	581,111	51.4%	533,845	50.3%
Total liabilities and members equity	$1,131,471	100.0%	$1,062,374	100.0%

Source: Financial Statements and Report of Independent Certified Public Accountants. *REI.* Accessed 20 Apr 2012 at http://www.rei.com/content/dam/documents/pdf/2011%20REI%20Financial%20Statements.pdf

channels quite difficult even if they have the resources to organize and use them.

In spite of these challenges, opportunities may exist for new competitors to enter the markets in which Columbia and its competitors compete. This may be especially true in emerging markets. For example, some domestic firms that are located in the emerging markets in which Columbia competes may have an easier time

Exhibit 7 Competitor Comparison

(Dollar value in thousands)	Columbia	VF Corp	NIKE	REI	LL BEAN
General Comparison:					
Sales Volume	$1,693,985.00	$ 9,365,477.00	$20,862,000.00	$1,798,009.00	$1,440,000.00
Number of physical stores	114	1053	689	110	93
Ownership	Public	Public	Public	Co-operative	Private
Valuation Measures:					
Market Capitalization	$1,640,000.00	$16,480,000.00	$49,870,000.00	N/A	N/A
Forward P/E Ratio	13.61	13.80	18.79	N/A	N/A
Enterprise Value/EBIT DA	7.49	12.65	13.60	N/A	N/A
Liability Ratios:					
Liquidity					
Current Ratio (Current Assets/Current Liabilities)	3.93	1.91	3.21	1.46	N/A
Quick Ratio (Cash and Equivalents/Current Liabilities)	0.90	0.20	0.49	0.29	N/A
Solvency (Total Debt/Equity for most recent quarter)	0	46.77	3.63	0.10	N/A
Common Size (Total Liabilities/Total Assets)	0.22	0.51	0.34	0.49	N/A
Turnover (A/P Turnover: COGS/AP)	6.44	8.05	7.73	7.06	N/A
Asset Ratios:					
Accounts Receivable					
Common Size (AR/Total Assets)	25.43%	12.03%	20.92%	1.51%	N/A
Turnover (Sales/AR Average)	2.60	4.95	3.60	54.16	N/A
Inventory					
Common Size (Gross Profit/Sales)	43.41%	46.24%	45.58%	42.44%	N/A
(Inventory/Total Assets)	26.42%	15.61%	18.10%	27.94%	N/A
Growth ([2011 Inv – 2010 Inv]/2010 Inv)	16.20%	35.77%	33.02%	21.59%	N/A
Turnover (COGS/Average Inventory)	1.41	2.03	2.39	1.80	N/A
Fixed Assets					
Common Size (PPE/Total Assets)	18.15%	7.92%	14.10%	35.29%	N/A
Turnover (Sales/Average PPE)	3.58	7.06	5.15	2.35	N/A
Management Effectiveness:					
ROA (Trailing 12 Months)[*]	6.66%	9.87%	12.99%	2.67%	N/A
ROE (Trailing 12 Months)[*]	9.97%	21.23%	22.59%	N/A	N/A
Profit Margin (Trailing 12 Months)[*]	6.11%	9.39%	9.68%	1.68%	N/A
Stock Information:					
Beta[*]	1.34	0.90	1.01	N/A	N/A
Dividend Payout Ratio (Dividends/Net Income)[*]	28.00%	33.00%	27.00%	N/A	N/A

[*] Source: finance.yahoo.com accessed 14 Apr 2012. Yahoo Finance retrieves Forward P/E Ratio from Thomson Reuters and Dividend Payout Ratio from Morningstar, Inc.

Other Sources: Columbia 10-K year ended December 31, 2011 at http://investor.columbia.com/annuals.cfm; VF Corp 10-K year ended December 31, 2011 at http://phx. corporate-ir.net/phoenix.zhtml?c=61559&p=irol-reportsAnnual; Nike 10-K year ended December 31, 2011 at http://investors.nikeinc.com/Investors/Financial-Reports-and-Filings/Annual-Reports/default.aspx; REI Audited Financial Statements at http://www.rei.com/content/dam/documents/pdf/2011%20REI%20Financial%20Statements.pdf; L.L. Bean Company Fact Sheet at http://llbean.com/customerService/aboutLLBean/images/110531_LLB-Fact-Sheet.pdf.

negotiating lower costs with suppliers with headquarters in the same nation or region. Additionally, cultural knowledge may expose opportunities to yield greater sales – for example, perhaps through more culturally attuned marketing or design as executed by domestic firms. Overall then, Columbia's executives must constantly study its industry environment to assess the likelihood of facing new competitors at different points in time and in different markets.

Faster, Higher, Better

Columbia has made a name for itself by providing exceptional apparel and footwear at a reasonable price. For example, an average Interchange jacket costs approximately $200, whereas the same style jacket made by The North Face costs around $300. Columbia incorporates an equal or greater amount of technology into each product it sells, and does so at a lower price.

Throughout the majority of its existence, Columbia Sportswear has focused on technology and innovation. This mindset has allowed the firm to create different technologies that ultimately create value for its customers. These technologies (listed below) are the foundation for developing different products with the ability to satisfy different customer needs.

- Omni-Tech and Omni-Dry: these technologies help apparel repel outside elements while still allowing the product to be breathable.
- Insect Blocker: a chemical built into the apparel that repels different types of insects and lasts for over 70 machine washes.
- Techlite: a technology used in Columbia's footwear lines to reduce the symptoms of impact as well as increase the overall support and foot comfort of the wearer.
- Omni-Wick: a new development that removes excess perspiration by absorbing it and allowing it to evaporate quickly.
- Omni-Shield: an innovation that resists stains from almost all liquids (such as drinks, mud, tree sap, and/or animal blood) that one might encounter in the outdoors.
- Omni-Grip: a technology used to increase the traction and stability of its footwear lines.[41]

At the end of the day, Columbia Sportswear does not seek recognition as just another innovative company; instead, the firm is striving for recognition as the leader of innovation in its market. A great example of this mindset occurred in October 2010 when Columbia announced the creation of its Omni-Heat Thermal Electric technology. The new line of products using this technology incorporates an electric heating system in all of the product line's jackets, gloves, and boots. This move not only proved its commitment to innovation to its consumers; it also allowed Columbia the opportunity to capture the high-price market segment on which competitors tend to focus. The fact that an Omni-Heat Thermal Electric jacket costs between $750 and $1,200 and a pair of gloves costs around $400 reflects the "higher-end" nature of this segment of the markets Columbia serves.[42]

Creating a Product Portfolio

Timely, appropriate, and effectively executed acquisitions account for a large part of Columbia Sportswear's growth. In fact, over the years, Columbia acquired major brands such as Sorel, Mountain Hardwear, Montrail, and OutDry. Each of these acquisitions created conditions through which Columbia has improved its performance. In September 2000, Columbia acquired Sorel for $8 million when that firm filed for bankruptcy.[43] The Sorel acquisition allowed Columbia to gain knowledge, as well as better footing, in the outdoor footwear category.[44] In January 2006, Columbia continued its acquisition of knowledge and reach in the footwear market when it acquired Montrail for $15 million.[45] The Montrail acquisition gave Columbia better insight into the lightweight footwear segment of the market, whereas the Sorel acquisition gave it superior knowledge in the cold-weather footwear market sector. See Exhibit 8 for sales generated by these acquisitions during 2010 and 2011.

Columbia's most recent acquisition – OutDry Technologies – was in 2010. OutDry created a patented membrane lamination technology that allowed it to create products that were "dryer, lighter and more

Exhibit 8 Columbia Brands

	Year Ended December 31,		
	2011	**2010**	**% Change**
	(In millions, except for percentage changes)		
Columbia	$1,391.5	$1,262.4	10%
Montrail Hardwear	142.3	121.9	17%
Sorel	150.3	89.7	68%
Other	9.9	9.5	4%
	$1,694.0	$1,483.5	14%

Source: Shareholder Information. *Columbia.* Accessed 20 Apr 2012 at http://investor.columbia.com/annuals.cfm.

comfortable for all outdoor enthusiasts."[46] Columbia plans to incorporate this technology into its apparel so it may better serve its customers. Notwithstanding these acquisitions, the largest (and probably most important) acquisition in Columbia's history was that of Mountain Hardwear.

Serious mountaineers hold Mountain Hardwear in great esteem and the demand for its products was growing quickly in 2003. To meet this demand, Mountain Hardwear needed to grow rapidly; however, it was unwilling to take on the massive amount of debt needed to fund its expansion. Columbia acquired Mountain Hardwear for $36 million in April 2003. Without question, this acquisition increased Columbia's knowledge of outdoor apparel. More importantly however, it allowed Columbia to vastly improve its knowledge of the outdoor accessories (such as tents and sleeping bags) market. When Columbia bought Mountain Hardwear, it used its excess cash to expand Mountain Hardwear's manufacturing and distribution capabilities, while simultaneously increasing Columbia's product line.[47] In each of these acquisitions, Columbia found a way to gain knowledge and insights while increasing its share of various markets including those of outdoor apparel, footwear, and accessories.

Columbia's Leadership Structure

Columbia has twenty members within its top management team with Timothy P. Boyle serving as President and CEO. Key individuals within the team include Michael W. Blackford as VP of Global Innovation, Thomas B. Cusick as VP of Finance and Chief Finance Officer (CFO), and Peter J. Bragdon as VP of Legal and Corporate Affairs and General Counsel and Secretary. Blackford, Cusick, and Bragdon's direct contributions to the firm's use of the balanced scorecard to assess its capabilities and areas in which improvement are needed are thought important to the firm's ultimate success. In this context, CFO Cusick represents the financial assessment portion of Columbia while Blackford represents assessment of innovation. As highlighted previously, Columbia's drive for innovation may lead to challenges in intellectual property compliance, calling for strong legal counsel from Bragdon.

Although it is a publicly traded company, Columbia has maintained a strong organizational culture rooted in the ideals established when it was a small family-owned company. The most logical reason for this lasting characteristic is the strong familial line of leadership that has guided the company since its establishment in 1937. Throughout its history, no other corporate leader embodied Columbia's hardworking and feisty spirit as well as Gertrude Boyle who unexpectedly had to assume the leadership role after the death of her husband. Her leadership and the succession of her son, current CEO and President, Tim Boyle, has guided the company through the tumultuous and competitive landscape of the outdoor apparel industry.

Among other actions, Tim Boyle and the top management team focus on maintaining Columbia's resources and capabilities. A key reason for this is that Columbia's success remains rooted in its ability to aggressively innovate and market its products to customers – old and new. There is no doubt that historically, Columbia's success is a product of the decisions made by the firm's strategic leaders. The continuity of the top management team members in turn has simultaneously contributed to continuity in the strategies the firm seeks to implement successfully.

The Board of Directors is comprised of nine individuals and chaired by the company's iconic leader and longest serving member, Gertrude Boyle, who has served since 1978. At 87 years old, Chairwoman Boyle is also the oldest serving member of the Board of Directors, which has an average age of 65 (Exhibit 9).

While Sarah Bany, Tim Boyle, and Gertrude Boyle have family ties, the board shows a diverse mix of members in that some are from outside the family and the firm itself. Additionally, the board's composition reflects a heterogeneous mix of industry specialists ranging from Edward George from the banking industry to John Stanton from the telecommunications industry. Points of concern for the board may include issues such as the time constraints and dedication of its directors, as only Edward George and Gertrude Boyle are retired and some members, such as Stanton and Klenz, serve on multiple boards. Lastly, while there have not been any ethical concerns related to the corporate governance of Columbia's board, with Gertrude Boyle being 87, there are implications concerned with succession and the future composition of Columbia's board of directors.

The Hike Ahead

As is the case for many organizations, numerous challenges face Columbia as it strives to achieve its goals and competitively dominate the outdoor activities apparel market. Effectively managing seasonal fluctuations, protecting the firm's intellectual property, and maintaining profitability through economically challenging times are three major challenges Columbia is facing. Although Columbia has the reputation as a leading innovator

Exhibit 9 Columbia Sportswear Board of Directors

Name	Title	Principal Occupation	Director Since
Gertrude Boyle	Chairwoman	Chair of the Board of Directors, Columbia Sportswear Company	1970
Timothy P. Boyle	Director	President and CEO, Columbia Sportswear Company	1978
Murrey R. Albers	Director	President and CEO, United States Bakery	1993
Stephen E. Babson	Director	Managing Director, Endeavour Capital	2002
Sarah A. Bany	Director	Co-owner and Executive Vice President of Brand Development, Moonstruck Chocolate Company	1988
Andy Bryant	Director	Executive Vice President of Technology, Manufacturing and Enterprise Services and Chief Administrative Officer, Intel Corporation	2005
Edward S. George	Director	Retired Director, First National Bank San Diego	1989
Walter T. Klenz	Director	Retired Managing Director, Beringer Blass Wine Estates	2000
John W. Stanton	Director	Private Investment, Trilogy Equity Partners and Trilogy International Partners	1997

Source: Shareholder Information. Board of Directors. Accessed 4 Dec 2012 at http://investor.columbia.com/directors.cfm

with cutting-edge technology and high quality outdoor activity products, the industry is highly competitive. Moreover, the increasing popularity of performance- and technology-driven outdoor activities apparel has increased the attractiveness of this sector of the market for several current and potential competitors. As noted earlier, another challenge for Columbia is associated with taking actions to protect the firm's intellectual property from competitors and any counterfeit operations that might surface to present customers with "fake" products that look similar to Columbia's offerings. Furthermore, retail distribution channels (including Dick's Sporting Goods, Sports Authority, and REI) account for the majority of Columbia's sales. As a result, managing profitable relationships and limiting the power of retailers is another challenge Columbia and its leaders face.

Seasonality and High Variability in Sales

Typical of the outdoor apparel market, Columbia consumers' seasonal trends typically influence customers' purchasing decisions. As temperatures around the world drop during the fall and winter seasons, the demand for Columbia's products increases, especially in the outerwear product category. Historically, outerwear is the highest selling product category contributing to the majority of Columbia's net sales. On average from 2008 to 2010, outerwear accounted for about 38 percent of Columbia's sales. Outerwear, by design, protects those wearing it from harsh, cold, and inclement weather conditions commonly encountered in the fall and winter seasons. Due to the nature of the product and market

volatility, the majority of outerwear sales take place during the fall and winter months.

In 2011, approximately 65 percent of our net sales and all of our profitability were realized in the second half of the year, illustrating our dependence upon sales results in the second half of the year, as well as the less seasonal nature of our operating costs.[48]

In terms of revenues, Columbia typically finishes the fiscal year strong and realizes most of its sales in its third and fourth quarters. However, because operating expenses occur throughout the year, sales skewed toward the fall and winter season create forecasting challenges. Columbia must determine if sales during the colder seasons will generate enough revenue to reach profit goals and cover operating costs throughout each year.

Because Columbia relies intensely on above average sales during the fall and winter seasons, historically, it faces periods of weaker growth after unseasonably warm winters. Weather phenomena, such as dramatic climate changes and the steadily increasing number of what appear to be unseasonably warm winters across the nation, are some of the most unpredictable challenges facing Columbia. An unseasonably warm winter not only results in a drop of demand for Columbia's products, but also creates hardships felt across the entire organization. For instance, in the past, unseasonably warm winters have created (1) excess inventory, (2) decisions to reduce the prices of the firm's products, (3) slow sales, (4) a drop in orders from retailers, (5) a reduction in workforce, and (6) dramatic decreases in future demand. According to the US Environmental Protection Agency,

...the average surface temperature of the Earth is likely to increase by 2 to 11.5 ° F by the end of the 21st century.... the average rate of warming over each inhabited continent is very likely to be at least twice as large as experienced during the 20th century. The warming will differ by season, with winters warming more than summers in most areas.[49]

Moving forward, the changing weather and all the issues it creates for Columbia will be an ongoing challenge for the organization and its leaders.

Columbia's sales skewing toward the fall and winter seasons also proves its product lines mostly appeal to consumers living in locations that traditionally experience colder seasons. This is a challenge because, due to the recreation and leisure connotation of Columbia's product lines, sales and consumer demand greatly depend on "consumers' discretionary spending patterns."[50] Similar to many other organizations, Columbia has witnessed a decrease in consumer discretionary spending attributable to the challenging economy that characterized many markets throughout the world from roughly 2007 through at least 2012. Evidence showed that during this time, consumers spent less and aggressively hunted for better bargains by abandoning brand loyalty behaviors and switching to private labels or store brands for lower prices and special offers.[51] Specifically, these trends present Columbia with key issues because the active lifestyle apparel market is one of the few growing sectors in retail and participation in outdoor activities is also on the rise. From 2009 to 2010 for example, participation in the United States in outdoor activities – such as triathlons, white water kayaking, and mountain climbing – were up 64 percent, 35 percent, and 20 percent respectively.[52] Growth in the outdoor and active wear markets coupled with Columbia product lines' one-dimensional appeal to consumers suggest the organization isn't reaching its full potential. Columbia's leaders must examine its position in the market and industry and move forward to increase market share in spite of economically tough times.

Intellectual Property

In recent years, innovative and highly technical products that enhance performance have come in high demand in the active lifestyle and athletic apparel market. For organizations competing on innovation and technology, differentiating one's products from those of competitors is imperative. As an industry leader in innovative outdoor active wear, Columbia has done just that, but not without

the challenge of protecting its technology and innovative designs from substitutes developed by competitors and counterfeit operations. The Outdoor Industry Association estimates Columbia's losses between $100 and $200 million a year due to counterfeit or "knock-off" Columbia products sold worldwide, accounting for an average of about 10 percent of Columbia's sales in 2010.[53] This sales percentage not only includes lost sales Columbia might have attained, but also the damages that low quality, counterfeit goods have on Columbia's image. Counterfeiting is an epidemic; popular Columbia products are reverse-engineered and reproduced to create products that fool consumers into thinking they are buying authentic Columbia brand products.

Although securing trademarks and patents to protect the technology and designs in Columbia's latest products would help Columbia create a niche in a highly competitive market, several key issues surround this challenge. In the United States, successfully securing a patent takes an average of 22 months. In the fast-moving cyclical world of apparel and fashion, 22 months might as well be a lifetime. Many second-movers in the apparel industry can develop substitutes in less time and quickly penetrate the market. Furthermore, Columbia's products may be innovative from the perspectives of consumers and industry participants, but that does not guarantee that the firm's designs and ideas are indeed sufficiently innovative to support receiving a patent as a means of protection.

Maintaining Profitability

Columbia is in a unique situation; although retailers account for a majority of its sales, several of these same retailers are also major competitors selling their own private label branded outdoor activities apparel. For instance, as noted earlier, REI sells its own popular brand of outdoor activity apparel that competes with Columbia's products. Columbia's products are sold everywhere from small independently operated sporting goods stores to international sporting goods chains and major department store chains. Many of these retailers have one thing in common that endangers Columbia's unique relationship with them: deep pockets full of ample resources. Columbia's overall profitability depends largely on retailers successfully selling its products to consumers. The power, money, and resources of retailers pose a major threat to Columbia. Retailers can use this combination to create their own products similar to Columbia's products. Moreover, retailers could leverage their power and place major demands on Columbia – such as special discount pricing. Furthermore, the threat retailers pose to

Columbia is more pressing given that the firm does not have a suitable direct-to-consumer operation in place. With only 114 physical locations and a website that the firm failed to launch until 2009, Columbia recognizes its lack of direct channels to consumers, publishing in its 2010 Shareholders' Annual Report, "the main purpose of this [direct-to-consumer] operation is to enhance consumer brand awareness, increase brand equity, and build a strong emotional connection with brand."[54]

Essentially, Columbia's dependence on retailers for the majority of its sales has created an unusually competitive environment. Its challenge moving forward is to maintain strong relationships with these fierce, but essential, competitors. The demand for e-commerce is another key issue Columbia's leaders will have to resolve. E-commerce is a growing part of the active apparel industry and quickly becoming a minimum expectation of consumers. Columbia will have to enhance its current IT technology and create integrative information systems. The e-commerce segment of its business will further challenge Columbia's unique relationship with its retailers. As online shopping grows in popularity, Columbia will have to find or determine the best way to present consumers with online shopping options through both retailers and its own website. Columbia faces successfully balancing pricing, product exposure, and expanding the business in the online space, while maintaining its relationships with and limiting the power of retailers. With all of these challenges, is Columbia's historic success threatened? What actions should the firm's leaders initiate to maximize the likelihood of continuing success for the firm established over eighty years ago?

NOTES

1. Ross, W. (27 Nov 2010). Behind the Gert Boyle Kidnap Attempt. *The Daily Beast*. Accessed 10 Apr 2010 at http://www.thedailybeast.com/articles/2010/11/27/how-gert-boyle-head-of-columbia-sportswear-foiled-a-kidnap-attempt.html.

2. Bella, R. (17 Nov 2010). Gert Boyle, the "One Tough Mother" of Columbia Sportswear, outwits armed robber. *OregonLive.com*. Accessed 10 Apr 2012 at http://www.oregonlive.com/west-linn/index.ssf/2010/11/gert_boyle_the_one_tough_mother_of_columbia_sportswear_outwits_armed_robber.html.

3. Ibid.

4. Ibid.

5. Ibid.

6. About Us. *Columbia*. Accessed 20 Apr 2012 at http://www.columbia.com/About-Us/About_Us_Landing,default,pg.html.

7. Columbia Sportswear Company. *Funding Universe*. Accessed 10 Apr 2012 at http://www.fundinguniverse.com/company-histories/Columbia-Sportswear-company-company-History.html.

8. Ibid.

9. Ibid.

10. Ibid.

11. Columbia's History. *Columbia*. Accessed 10 Apr 2012 at http://www.columbia.com/history/About_Us_History,default,pg.html.

12. Columbia Sportswear Company. *Funding Universe*. op. cit.

13. Columbia's History. *op. cit.*

14. Columbia Sportswear Company 2011 Annual Report to Shareholders. *Columbia.com*. http://www.shareholder.com/visitors/DynamicDoc/document.cfm?DocumentID=3026&CompanyID=COLM&zid=ed0392bc.

15. Columbia Sportswear Company 2010 Annual Report to Shareholders. *Columbia.com*. http://www.shareholder.com/visitors/dynamicdoc/document.cfm?documentid=2916&companyid=COLM&page=1&pin=&language=EN&resizethree=yes&scale=100&zid=07228b68.

16. Columbia Sportswear Company 2011 Annual Report to Shareholders. *op. cit.*

17. Molavi, J. (Mar 2011). Volatility per barrel Oil's Past, Present, and Future. *IBIS World*. http://clients.ibisworld.com/mediacenter/researchpapers.aspx?a=155#a155.

18. Thomas, S. (3 Mar 2011). Downstream Effects Petrochemical Reactions. *Financial Mail*. http://www.fm.co.za/Article.aspx?id=136125.

19. Cost to Import (US$ per container). *World Bank.org*. http://search.worldbank.org/data?qterm=cost%20to%20import%20a%20container&language=EN

20. Molavi, J. (Mar 2011) *op. cit.*

21. Fair Disclosure Wire. *ABI/INFORM Trade & Industry*. 2 2, 2012. http://search.proquest.com/abitrade/docview/921747180/1362758B63A17FFC1CE/1?accountid=7082.

22. Brettman, A. (14 Mar 2012). Columbia Sportswear expected to lay off about 80 employees. *The Oregonian*. http://impact.oregonlive.com/playbooks-profits/print.html?entry=/2012/0….

23. Lindsey, R. (13 Mar 2012). U.S. has fourth warmest winter on record; West & Southeast drier than average. *NOAA Climate Services*. http://www.climatewatch.noaa.gov/article/2012/u-s-has-fourth-warmest-winter-on-record-west-southeast-drier-than-average

24. 2011 Outdoor Recreation Participation Topline Report. *The Outdoor Foundation*.

http://www.outdoorindustry.org/research.php?action=detail&research_id=133

25. Ibid.

26. Ibid.

27. Siemers, E. (27 Mar 2012). Eugene company sues Columbia Sportswear over heated clothing technology. *The Portland Business Journal*. http://www.bizjournals.com/portland/news/2012/03/27/eugene-companysues-.

28. Columbia Sportswear Company 2011 Annual Report to Shareholders. *op. cit.*

29. Siemers, E. (27 Mar 2012). *op. cit.*

30. Nike NKE. *Morningstar.com*. http://search.morningstar.com/sitesearch/search.aspx?s=o&q=nike.

31. VF Corporation Profile. *Yahoo Finance*. Accessed 18 Apr 2012 at http://finance.yahoo.com/q/pr?s=VFC+Profile.

32. Investor Relations, Annual Reports. *VF*. http://phx.corporate-ir.net/phoenix.zhtml?c=61559&p=irol-reportsAnnual.

33. L.L. Bean, Inc. *Hoovers*. http://www.hoovers.com/company/LL_Bean_Inc/cftkri-1.html.

34. Ibid.

35. L.L. Bean Tops in Customer Service Survey. (1 Feb 2010). *Chain Store Age*. http://business.highbeam.com/410731/article-1G1-219654881/ll-bean-tops-customer-service-survey.

36. 2011 Company Fact Sheet. *llbean.com*. https://www.llbean.com/customerService/aboutLLBean/images/110531_LLB-Fact-Sheet.pdf

37. Recreational Equipment, Inc. *Hoovers*. http://www.hoovers.com/company/Recreational_Equipment_Inc/hcxjji-1.html.

38. Columbia Sportswear Company 2011 Annual Report to Shareholders. *op. cit.*

39. Ibid.
40. Brettman, A. (12 Mar 2011). Columbia Sportswear's Innovation Heats Up With Electric Jackets, Gloves and Boots. *Oregon Live*. Accessed 10 Apr 2012 at http://www.oregonlive.com/business/index.ssf/2011/03/columbia_sportswears_innovatio.html.
41. Ibid.
42. Ibid.
43. Columbia Sportswear Completes Acquistion of Sorel Brand. (22 Sep 2000). *Business Wire*. Accessed 10 Apr 2012 at http://www.thefreelibrary.com/Columbia+Sportswear+Completes+Acquisition+of+Sorel+Brand.
44. Columbia Sportswear Company 2004 Annual Report. *Columbia.com*. http://files.shareholder.com/downloads/COLM/2074879299x0x293549/7B6387CA-8000-4C84-85B5-8CB81A45ECCF/2004_annual_final.pdf.

45. Columbia Sportswear Company Announces Acquistion of Montrail, Inc. Footwear Brand. (26 Jan 2006). *Lexdon*. Accessed 10 Apr 2012 at http://www.lexdon.com/article/Columbia_Sportswear_Company_Announces_Acquisition/30375.html.
46. Columbia Sportswear Company Completes Acquistion of OutDry(R) Technologies. (1 Sep 2010). *Columbia*. Accessed 10 Apr 2012 at http://investor.columbia.com/releasedetail.cfm?ReleaseID=504184.
47. Fitch, S. (16 Apr 2003). Can Columbia Sportswear Scale This Mountain? *Forbes*. Accessed 10 Apr 2012 at http://www.forbes.com/2003/04/16/cz_sf_0416columbia.html.
48. Columbia Sportswear Company 2011 Annual Report to Shareholders. *op. cit.*
49. Global Buying Behaviour in the Recession. (5 Mar 2012) *Euromonitor International*. http://blog.euromonitor.com/2012/03/global-buying-behaviour-in-the-recession.html.
50. Columbia Sportswear Company 2011 Annual Report to Shareholders. *op. cit.*
51. Global Buying Behaviour in the Recession. (5 Mar 2012) *op. cit.*
52. AM Mindpower Solutions. (1 Feb 2012). The US Athletic Apparel and Footwear Industry Outlook to 2015 - Evolving Niche Segments in Sportswear. *MarketResearch.com*. http://www.marketresearch.com/AM-Mindpower-Solutions-v3771/Athletic-Apparel-Footwear-Outlook-Evolving-6846675/
53. Columbia Sportswear blazing intellectual property trail in China. (2 Mar 2010). *Outdoor Industry Association: CEO Brief*. Accessed 10 Apr 2012 at http://www.outdoorindustry.org/news.ceo.php?newsId=12085&newsletterId=118&action=display.
54. Columbia Sportswear Company 2011 Annual Report to Shareholders. *op. cit.*

Entrepreneurship is the pursuit of opportunity beyond the resources you currently control.

Howard H. Stevenson,
Sarofim-Rock Professor of Business Administration
Harvard Business School

After the latest round of discussions with a major real estate developer, Rosanne Haggerty – the founder of Common Ground and the current CEO of Community Solutions – returned to her office located in a building in Manhattan's Madison Square North Historic District. The building was also home to hundreds of formerly homeless New Yorkers. As she prepared for the strategy planning session the following week, she felt the urge to charter her top team to explore different revenue models to ensure the organization would have the financial strength to meet the growing client demands.

Common Ground, which developed and managed affordable supportive housing, had been consistently hailed as one of the best-run non-profit organizations in the U.S. It had received the Fast Company/Monitor Group Social Capitalist Award, the Rudy Bruner Award for Urban Excellence, the Peter Drucker Award for Non-Profit Innovation, and the World Habitat Award through the United Nations and the Building and Social Housing Foundation. Yet its spin-off organization – Community Solutions – was now attracting the most attention.

From its inception, Community Solutions targeted individuals who were chronically homeless under the existing social support system. The early successes of Community Solutions, including its famous "100,000 Homes Campaign," demonstrated that it was possible to mobilize disparate parties across the country to tackle locally based problems related to homelessness without draining enormous public resources. Community Solutions intentionally worked across sectors, weaving together the efforts of non-profits with government, philanthropy and business.

Although Rosanne was determined to keep the entrepreneurial spirit alive within the spinoff, she also worked to ensure that Community Solutions would be financially compensated for the numerous innovations it pioneered. (Refer to Exhibit 1 for a timeline of major organizational events.) Should Community Solutions, going forward, see itself as a consulting organization, or a product-service integrator? What would be the appropriate revenue model to capture its value added?

Homeless Problem in New York City

One of the ironies of New York City was the proximity between the haves and the have-nots. Times Square, an iconic tourist destination, historically had one of the highest densities of homeless individuals.

Common Ground was founded in 1990. It was one of many non-profit organizations in the city that addressed homelessness. Common Ground pioneered new housing models that offered homeless men and women an alternative to the city's congested shelters. Their buildings offered private, safe and affordable apartments linked to health, mental health and employment supports to

IMD Professor Howard Yu and Community Solutions' director Becky Kanis prepared this case as a basis for class discussion rather than to illustrate either effective or ineffective handling of a business situation.

© Vividfour / Shutterstock.com

Exhibit 1 Common Ground Timeline

individuals moving from shelters and the streets. As Rosanne explained:

For many homeless individuals, the mere idea of permanency – signing a lease and paying a monthly rent check – is daunting. Many of these individuals do not access the city's shelters, sometimes in resistance to rules and sometimes for reasons of fear or pride.[1]

Rosanne grew up outside Hartford, Connecticut, and at 17 had to help her mother take care of her seven younger siblings after her father died. As an undergraduate at Amherst College, she majored in American studies – her senior thesis was on Thomas Merton, the Trappist monk and social critic. After graduating, she volunteered at Covenant House – the homeless teens' charity – on 43rd Street in Times Square. There was a massive, derelict hotel next door that she could not get out of her mind. "The Times Square Hotel was so big and so visible," she recalled. The area was known mostly for peep shows and prostitutes. "My mind was drawn to what could be done with it."[2] For the next seven years, she worked with Catholic Charities, learning, among other things, how to apply the new Low Income Housing Tax Credit (LIHTC) to create housing for the homeless.

While working with the homeless, Rosanne learned that conditions at the Times Square Hotel had worsened dramatically and the city of New York was threatening to shut it down. "It was the largest single-room occupancy hotel in New York City," she said. "The building was on the verge of being condemned. It violated 1,700 serious building codes." Trash, mildew and crack vials were everywhere. Most of the remaining 200 residents were elderly or mentally ill, some were veterans. The building was in bankruptcy and had been carelessly managed by a string of court-appointed administrators. The potential loss of the hotel, however, as ramshackle as it might have seemed, would contribute to increased homelessness in the city and eliminate desperately needed, though badly maintained, affordable housing.

Rosanne further explained, "The typical squalor of these buildings (single room occupancy hotels) was really a management problem."[3] The ingredients she believed would make for a successful transformation of the building and create attractive accommodation were good design, committed on-site management and connecting residents with support needs, including services such as health care and job training.

LIHTC turned out to be a crucial funding source to redevelop the Times Square Hotel. "Part of it was timing," Rosanne explained. "It was a relatively new program and not a lot of people knew how to use it."[4] She proceeded to launch an association called Common Ground, making use of tax credits and obtaining subsidies from the federal, state and city governments to acquire and renovate the building. She also pulled together a group of investors that ran the gamut, from J.P. Morgan to Ben & Jerry's.

By the time the Times Square Hotel reopened in 1993, Common Ground had turned the 652-unit building into a state-of-the-art apartment building for homeless and low-income single adults. It was "supportive" in that it had onsite counseling services to help residents turn their lives around, as well as a garden roof deck, a computer lab, a beautiful lobby area with chandeliers, a tight security system, medical facilities, a dining room, a library and an art studio. It became a showcase for doing things differently.

Because of the success of The Times Square Hotel, Common Ground gained more access to government and commercial financing. Meanwhile, Rosanne had returned to graduate school in real estate finance and development, and tried out more sophisticated strategies with each new project. When renovating Common Ground's second residence – the Prince George Hotel – she knitted together 10 funding sources, including JPMorgan Chase, Fannie Mae, the Corporation for Supportive Housing and Deutsche Bank, to buy the building through a foreclosure and bankruptcy process.

When the Prince George reopened in 1999, it offered job-training counselors, health services, psychologists, therapists and even acupuncturists. "We make it easy for people to succeed," Rosanne said. And the luxury ballroom? "We organized a job-training collaboration with four other not-for-profit groups who restored the space."[5] Rosanne explained that this reduced the cost to $1.5 million. The ballroom became an event venue that generated $800,000 in annual rentals.

Before Common Ground purchased its third building, the infamous Andrews Hotel in lower Manhattan, it interviewed over 200 homeless individuals still living on the street and deemed "resistant" to housing by groups contracted to assist them. They asked individuals what type of housing would be attractive and appealing to them, and planned the Andrews to respond to their preferences. In 2003 Common Ground held an open design competition to translate the wishes of the homeless into a plan for the Andrews. Competitors were asked to design 19 prefabricated dwelling units per floor. These had to meet city codes and handicapped accessibility standards without the need to alter the building's basic structure or exterior walls. The budget per prefabricated unit was set at $5,000, manufactured, installed and furnished. The 189 entries from 13 countries ranged from individual applicants to architectural school teams to design firms. Jurors for the competition included design luminaries Steven Holl (architect and Professor of Architecture at Columbia University) and Toshiko Mori (Professor in Practice and Chair at Harvard Design School). The top five winning designs were implemented in 2005.

Along with external funding, Common Ground received government subsidies to support building operations and resident services of $18,000 per resident per year. The cost of housing a person in a homeless shelter in New York City was over $25,000 annually; the costs for the homeless in hospitals and jails could be between two and five times that amount.

A Bold Experiment

In 2003 Common Ground experimented with an outreach program. It began with a simple observation. After The Times Square Hotel had been up and running for a few years, Rosanne and her staff realized that many of those who had been homeless in the Times Square area before the project opened were still living on the street. Almost everyone living in The Times Square Hotel had come from homeless shelters. Those who refused shelters were simply assumed to be uninterested in help, and thus never made it to Common Ground's facilities.

To understand the root cause of the situation, Rosanne organized a midnight winter count to assess first-hand the size of this so-called service-resistant population, that is, homeless individuals who refused shelters even under the most severe weather conditions.

The identification of this population seemed puzzling. In New York City, dozens of organizations had designed programs to help the homeless in various ways. Hospitals provided emergency room and detoxification services; a large soup kitchen was located fifteen blocks away from Times Square; and faith-based organizations descended on the city from the suburbs to feed the homeless in the middle of the night. Yet a group of individuals continued to live on the streets off Times Square.[6]

Ending chronic homelessness was important from both a human and a financial standpoint because these individuals consumed enormous public resources. A classic example was Murray Barr, described by the *New Yorker Magazine* as "Million Dollar Murray." Practically a fixture on the streets of Reno, Murray cost Nevada's taxpayers a million dollars over 10 years in substance abuse treatment, emergency room visits and other services. Interestingly, not a dime had been spent on housing. "It cost us one million dollars not to do something," observed Officer O'Bryan of the Reno Police Department.[7] Research out of San Francisco also indicated that providing stable housing to a chronically homeless person reduced emergency room visits by 56%. University of California researchers tracked 15 chronically homeless individuals over 18 months and found that they cost taxpayers over $1.5 million in hospital and law enforcement bills. Across the United States, nearly two-thirds of high-cost Medicaid enrollees were homeless or unstably housed.

Convinced by first-hand observations, Rosanne put together a "Street-to-Home Initiative" that targeted the so-called service-resistant population. The goal was to identify who was living on the streets and what it would take to get them into housing. "You can comfortably walk past a nameless guy in Harlem, but once you know that it's Ed, a Vietnam vet with cancer, you can't be comfortable anymore."[8] Rosanne further described, "It occurred to me that we needed someone without preconceived ideas about the problem or the individuals who were homeless. I began looking for someone with a military background to get things done."[9] She hired Becky Kanis, a West Point graduate and former special ops commander with the army.

Becky swiftly took a team of third-party outreach workers out onto the streets and started interviewing homeless people and creating detailed profiles. She and her team asked the homeless if they needed food, medical assistance, financial support, a job, shelter, counseling or housing. Most importantly, the team sought to understand why people were not using services that already existed. During these interviews, people were eager to voice their displeasure with the shelter system and spoke at length about their dislike of traditional outreach workers. Some found the application process unfriendly and intimidating. Some felt the rules were arbitrary and disrespectful.[10] On the street, they had lots of problems – but they had freedom. And they deeply valued their independence. Again and again, they made their needs clear; they needed housing, not shelter.[11]

The staff of Street-to-Home then developed a simple, straightforward process. It aimed to cut through the bureaucracy that intimidated and alienated the homeless. The core task was to help the chronically homeless – individuals who had spent an average of seven-and-a-half years on the street – complete applications for subsidized or supportive housing. The process established by New York City government agencies involved several steps to verify eligibility for subsidized and supportive housing, including medical screening, a thorough psychiatric evaluation and proof of a source of income (i.e., welfare or disability benefits). Street-to-Home thus offered a simple proposition: to streamline and simplify the application process whenever possible. Staff also advocated fiercely for their clients with other service providers and government agencies that often discriminated against the chronically homeless.

Meanwhile, the newly renovated Andrews Hotel, unlike The Times Square and other Common Ground buildings that offered long term leases, was designed to provide temporary, short-term housing. Focusing on the needs of individuals who simply required a "first step" off the street to begin the process of moving back into housing, the Andrews Hotel was able to adopt a simpler intake screening procedure. The Andrews Hotel was also more tolerant of challenging behaviors. There was no sobriety requirement, and some who moved in directly from the street would arrive drunk and combative. To keep them on the path to housing, there were no curfews and no compulsion to enter into other rehabilitation and support services. Residents did not have to accept social services if they did not want to.

In the first year of operation, 43 homeless individuals who had previously refused shelters were placed directly into housing (in both the Andrews Hotel and elsewhere). These 43 people were referred by 13 independent outreach organizations, which asserted that the clients were long-term homeless persons from the neighborhood. Yet, despite the housing placements, the following midnight count revealed that street homelessness was actually **up** by 17% in Times Square! The troubling statistic brought the basic assumptions of the Street-to-Home initiative into question.

On a hunch that the initiative did not sufficiently target the long-term homeless, James McCloskey, Director of Street-to-Home at the time, made a radical decision. At 05:00 every morning for four consecutive weeks, he took his team out to canvas the streets and created a *by-name* roster with individual photos of all those who slept in the neighborhood. To their surprise, even though they counted an average of 55 people on the streets each morning, only 18 of them were there every day. All the others were only there intermittently.

Interestingly, some homeless advocates saw any counting exercise of the New York homeless as a flawed effort. Patrick Markee, senior policy analyst for the Coalition for the Homeless, argued repeatedly that tallying the city's homeless was an impossible task, destined to result in an inaccurate count. He complained that homeless people rarely remained in plain sight and often hid underground in subway tunnels and other places where the city's canvas of public spaces would miss them. Still, Rosanne contended that any one-time number that the city came up with was immaterial. "Doing multiple counts following the same methodology," she said, "gives you a high-level picture of whether the problem has changed or moved and, by extension, whether your homeless policy works."[12]

To concentrate its efforts, Street-to-Home stopped accepting referrals from third-party outreach teams – a very unpopular move at the time. These outreach organizations, which had previously been cooperative, responded with fierce protests. Freeing up its resources, however, meant that the Street-to-Home staff could focus exclusively on housing the 18 homeless individuals who were regularly in Times Square, even if they had drug, alcohol or medical problems. It turned out that the 18 had been homeless for an average of 14 years and were well known by Times Square business operators, police and homeless services agencies. All things considered, this group was the most difficult cohort on the street. Common Ground speculated that focusing on these iconic homeless individuals would demonstrate that the problem was solvable, which would potentially create a ripple effect, persuading others who had been on the street for shorter periods to accept help. Encouraging results began to emerge. Street-to-Home drove a 75% reduction of homelessness in Times Square over the next year, and cut that in half the following year, resulting in a total 87% sustained reduction (refer to Exhibit 2).

Going Beyond Street-to-Home

The scale and scope of Common Ground had undoubtedly contributed to the early success of the Street-to-Home initiative. At the time, critics said that the

Exhibit 2 Homelessness in Times Square

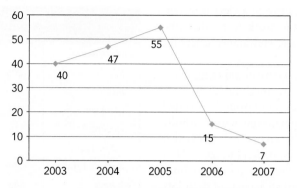

Source: Kanis, B. *Catalytic Innovations to Solve Homelessness.* Unpublished paper, The New School, New York, 2007.

Street-to-Home outreach program could be difficult to implement because some of the homeless were comfortable on the streets, the program did not focus enough on ending dangerous habits and it did not address the growing problem of homeless families. And above all, the goals were simply too ambitious.

To demonstrate to outsiders the feasibility of housing the chronically homeless, Rosanne led a change in the tenancy policies throughout Common Ground to prioritize the chronically homeless for available apartments, and in particular those moving from the street. The staff bristled at her directive at first, but they eventually complied. Rosanne, however, encouraged each housing facility to keep track of the impact of accepting Street-to-Home clients into the building. The organization also made a financial commitment to allocate additional resources to manage the impacts if the needs for support changed as a result of taking in this new population. After tracking the impact on building operations for 18 months, however, the new population was shown **not** to affect the operating demands or costs of Common Ground's housing. In the following fiscal year, both the housing facilities and Street-to-Home became jointly accountable for achieving ambitious targets of housing placements for the chronically homeless.

As Common Ground developed its reputation of being capable of housing the chronically homeless in Times Square, it influenced New York City to rethink its policies on street homelessness and the way it contracted for "outreach" services to the homeless. Common Ground's initial Street-to-Home program grew to eight employees and an annual budget of $350,000, which was funded by foundations and corporations. The program produced enough evidence to tip New York City toward a major overhaul of its outreach contracts and to include performance measured in outcomes (rather than activities) in new

contracts. In 2007 Common Ground received a $3.2 million contract from the city to extend the Street-to-Home Initiative beyond Times Square and reduce street homelessness by two-thirds in Brooklyn, Queens, and a more expansive area of Midtown (beyond Times Square). This represented a ten-fold increase in financial resources and a transition to a steady, reliable funding source. Later that year, Common Ground received another $6 million in federal funds from the U.S. Department of Housing and Urban Development (HUD). These additional funds represented five years of rent subsidies for over 130 formerly homeless residents moving from the streets into Common Ground buildings.

After two years of working as the first director of Street-to-Home, Becky was promoted to a new position: director of innovations. One of the innovations was the codification of what became the "vulnerability index." After seeing the benefits of identifying the chronically homeless by their names and faces, Becky's team expanded the Street-to-Home concept to incorporate information on medical conditions. After consulting Dr. Jim O'Connell of Boston's Healthcare for the Homeless, who had conducted the original research on causes of early mortality among homeless people living on the street, the team adopted eight markers that Dr. O'Connell had highlighted as putting the chronically homeless at more risk. By including these eight important markers[13] in the existing by-name roster, the vulnerability index became essentially a person-by-person record that allowed communities to create a health registry of those most at risk of dying on the street. The survey captured a homeless individual's health and social status and used risk factors and length of homelessness to identify and rank the most vulnerable in a community, turning the first-come, first-served notion on its head. The simplicity of the vulnerability index helped mobilize communities to act, recognize who was at risk of death with continued homelessness, provide a clear direction for prioritizing assistance, then work to re-align the housing and support resources to end homelessness for the most vulnerable first.

Meanwhile, to fulfill its mandate of reducing street homelessness by two-thirds throughout New York City (refer to Exhibit 3), Common Ground recruited and trained new staff and partnered with Catholic Charities in Brooklyn and Queens, which allowed it to increase its number of field workers by 20%. New members attended a three-week orientation boot camp where they learned about all aspects of their job, including available housing options, successful street outreach techniques, motivational interviewing and dealing with mental illness.

Yet, it was the external requests from outside New York that demanded new capacity development in the innovations team. Los Angeles County, Santa Monica, New Orleans, Washington, DC, Portland and Nashville had successively contacted Common Ground asking for support to emulate the Street-to-Home program in their local communities.

Although each local community's situation had unique features and required customization, they all followed the Community Solutions' approach in prioritizing housing for those identified as the most vulnerable and mobilizing local stakeholders such as public housing authorities, city and county elected officials and the business community. With the help of Common Ground's Innovation Team, Los Angeles County and city launched its Project 50; Washington, DC adopted its own program; and Phoenix implemented its Project H3. All of them were able to demonstrate that the Street-to-Home program was highly transferable to other communities. These new communities, without New York City's bureaucracy, demonstrated that individuals could be moved from the streets into supported housing in an average of 10 days.

A New Organization

As the innovations team developed various initiatives, Rosanne found it moving away from the core activities of Common Ground, even though these initiatives served the same mission of ending homelessness. By 2011 Common Ground had created nearly 3,000 units of permanent and transitional housing, primarily in New York City. Its housing portfolio included 10 buildings (plus 3 under construction), either owned or managed. Common Ground's integrated strategy – from building

Exhibit 3 Homelessness in New York City

	Estimate		
	2005	**2009**	**Change**
Surface Areas			
Manhattan	1805	777	−1028(−57%)
Bronx	587	164	−423(−72%)
Brooklyn	592	200	−392(−66%)
Queens	335	98	−237(−71%)
Staten Island	231	121	−110(−48%)
Surface Total	**3550**	**1360**	−2190(−62%)
Subways	**845**	**968**	123(+15%)
Total Unsheltered Individuals	**4395**	**2328**	**−2067(−47%)**

Source: Department of Homeless Services.

management to onsite social services – had been its primary approach. The innovations team, however, had become increasingly open in its operational approach. Its main objective was to build efficient local systems through partnership, not ownership.

The growing inconsistencies between the two operations prompted Rosanne to reorganize the innovations team and launch Community Solutions as an independent entity. Under the new setup, Common Ground continued in real estate development, housing management and street outreach in the New York City area, while Community Solutions focused on innovating on a national scale and advancing new models of homelessness prevention and community development. Recognizing the need to devote herself full-time to the ongoing development of Community Solutions, Rosanne recruited her own successor at Common Ground in 2008 before assuming the full-time role of Community Solutions' CEO. She further described her rationale:

I didn't want the previous success of Common Ground to limit our acknowledging the full potential of what we were pioneering through the innovations team. The people, processes and culture required for what we are now doing are fundamentally different from what we had at Common Ground. The spin-off enabled us to adopt a new strategy to match a very different theory of change than the one that informed our earlier work.

Value Creation, Value Capture

While Community Solutions had garnered professional accolades for its innovative approach, the organization was less certain about how to define a long-term revenue model. Top management understood well that without securing some form of recurring compensation for its pioneering work, relying on contributed resources alone would not be sufficient for Community Solutions to meet the growing demands from various constituencies.

Recent projects of Community Solutions could be classified into two broad categories: knowledge diffusion and in-depth co-development.

Knowledge Diffusion

The 100,000 Homes Campaign aimed to house the nation's 100,000 most vulnerable by July 2014. The goal was to engage and house the most vulnerable individuals throughout the country through a coordinated national movement led by Community Solutions. The effort aligned resources across multiple sectors including housing authorities, faith-based groups, public hospitals, local businesses, non-profits, landlords, property developers, philanthropists and concerned citizens.

Newly enrolled communities participated in a four-part online seminar that summarized the model for change and highlighted best practices, followed by a three-day intensive training on using the Vulnerability Index Survey. Communities then conducted a "registry week" to identify individuals on the streets and solicit the information and cooperation needed to link them to stable housing.

Campaign communities later attended a two-day intensive training during which quality improvement experts focused on eliminating unnecessary steps in the housing placement process by providing personalized coaching.

To diffuse new learning, mentors in all areas of best practice were identified and enlisted to volunteer in coaching and supporting colleagues across the country in implementing the Community Solutions model. Regular online seminars were held to disseminate new innovations in the field, and to share emerging issues and concerns. By November 2012, 173 communities had enrolled in the campaign, administrating over 35,000 Vulnerability Index surveys, helping over 22,000 individuals move back into stable housing. In total, 88% of tenants maintained their housing for a year or longer.

With growing interest across the nation, Community Solutions continued to enhance its free-to-use online database that allowed cities to score their surveys and produce reports on the most chronic and vulnerable on an ongoing basis. Because of information security, participating cities were only allowed to view their corresponding data at the city level; however, Community

Solutions' headquarters had access to information for the entire country. Rosanne explained:

By diffusing a proven approach and partnering with local stakeholders across the country, we have ended up with a unique view on homelessness in the U.S. If you want to understand certain patterns of homelessness around this country, we probably would have the answer.

In-Depth Co-Development

Community Solutions also saw strengthening local communities as another essential component in ending homelessness. Communities of concentrated poverty have the highest rates of unemployment, poor health, crime, family violence, low educational achievement and overcrowding. Such conditions made people vulnerable to losing their homes and community support. Community Solutions started creating new approaches to community development in these neighborhoods to demonstrate how to prevent homelessness at a common source.

Brownsville – Brooklyn, New York had one of the largest concentrations of public housing in the country and historically high rates of family homelessness. Community Solutions created the Brownsville Partnership to help vulnerable people remain stably housed and to improve their lives in the places they lived. The project sought to prevent homelessness before it occurred.

Community Solutions enlisted over a dozen leading non-profits and government agencies to bring new services and investment to Brownsville. The partners also pooled resources to make measurable progress on safety, health, education and economic opportunities. Local community leaders such as Greg Jackson, considered by many the unofficial mayor of Brownsville, turned the historic Brownsville Recreation Center into a welcoming haven for local families; Karrie Scarboro regularly organized her neighbors to monitor dangerous public space through walking groups and "neighborhood watch"-style events. Weekly coffee klatches drew out opinion leaders and inspired projects to improve the neighborhood. They also referred families to Brownsville Partnership case workers before an eviction or other crisis hit. Young people were organized to take part in community clean-ups every weekend.

"To make collaboration like this work, you need strong, local, authentic leaders like Greg," says Rosanne. "And you need people who know public policy, funding, and how to organize partners and resources in an efficient and targeted way. That's what we do."

Since it was launched in 2008, the initiative has assisted over 500 families with housing crises and prevented more than 350 evictions, avoiding approximately $12.6 million in public expenditures on emergency shelters. The effort has also connected more than 350 residents to job training.

In 2011, Community Solutions began a community development initiative modeled on the Brownsville Partnership in northeast Hartford, Connecticut.

As Rosanne reviewed the growing requests for Community Solutions, she focused on the need to identify an appropriate revenue model that the organization could rely upon as it sought to expand further. The Common Ground business model relied on property development and management fees. But Community Solutions' initiatives, though highly scalable, did not have a similar source of incremental income every year. Its core activities were building local problem-solving capability around the needs of vulnerable people; creating cost-efficient local services for high-need, high-cost users of public services; and creating collaborative efforts to weave together the efforts of non-profits with government, philanthropy and business. How can Community Solutions be adequately compensated for the numerous innovations it pioneers? Is there any way Community Solutions could capture a continuous revenue stream? Should the organization see itself as a consulting practice or a product-service integrator for local communities? Given the vast data that Community Solutions is accumulating, could there be an opportunity to partner with major technology firms such as IBM to jointly exploit its database systemically?

Community Solutions also needed to formulate new matrices to help track its "value added." Traditionally, many government agencies and private foundations awarded grants to service providers based on the actual activities delivered to homeless individuals. Community Solutions, however, was focusing on mobilizing disparate parties to tackle homelessness at the community level. How could it track successes and convincingly attribute the reduction of homelessness to its "indirect" services to other agencies?

Despite the increasing influence of Community Solutions across the country, Rosanne thought hard about the next year's priority that she would articulate in the strategy planning session the following week.

NOTES

1. "Common Ground Purchases The Andrews Hotel." *Common Ground Press Release*, 1 February 2002.

2. Gordon, Alastair. "Higher Ground." *WSJ Magazine*, 10 June 2010. http://magazine.wsj.com/hunter/donate/higher-ground/.

3. Hevesi, Dennis. "On the New Bowery, Down and Out Mix with Up and Coming." *New York Times*, 14 April 2002.

4. Gordon, Alastair. "Higher Ground." *WSJ Magazine*, 10 June 2010. http://magazine.wsj.com/hunter/donate/higher-ground/.

5. Ibid.

6. These men and women living on the street were often extensive users of government and not-for-profit services intended to help them. They repeatedly fell between the cracks, however, because the services themselves were not connected. After receiving treatment in a hospital or attending a program for alcohol detox and being discharged back to the street, these individuals often go through the process again within months.

7. Gladwell, M. "Million-dollar Murray." *The New Yorker*, 13 February 2006, 82(1) 96.

8. Gordon, Alastair. "Higher Ground." *WSJ Magazine*, 10 June 2010. http://magazine.wsj.com/hunter/donate/higher-ground/.

9. Fessler, Pam. "Ending Homelessness: A Model That Just Might Work." NPR, 7 March 2011. http://www.npr.org/2011/03/07/134002013/ending-homelessness-a-model-that-just-might-work.

10. Many were trapped in homelessness because of the extensive and unrealistic requirements of institutions, such as needing a copy of their birth certificate or showing proof of income or good credit in order to qualify for housing – an unlikely prospect for someone living on the streets for months or years.

11. Consider the case of Hasheem Muhammed, 23, who had been living on the streets for two years. He started sleeping on a beach after splitting up with his girlfriend. He lacked family who could take him in or means to get his own apartment. "I didn't have anywhere to go and I didn't want to go to a shelter," he said. Shelters in New York offered little respite from the dangers of the street, often featuring dank halls, urine smells, alcohol, drugs, and strangers in various states of coherence. Still, Hasheem found a community of street people who taught him where to find food, a weekly shower, and how to scrape out a living on the streets. Since then, he had been spending nights riding on the metro line and getting moved off by the police until he encountered Street-to-Home staff. (Kanis, B. *Catalytic Innovations to Solve Homelessness*. Unpublished paper, The New School, New York, 2007.)

12. Common Ground took inspiration from what London calls its Rough Sleepers Initiative. In 1998 when Londoners started doing regular counts, they found 621 "rough sleepers." In their 2001 count they found only 264 people. They had reduced homelessness by almost two-thirds in three years. And the way they did it was by getting all the outreach workers and service providers to cooperate with each other in networking and sharing information. (Lamb, Donna. "Counting the Homeless: First Step to Ending Homelessness." *The Greenwich Village Gazette*, 21 March 2003.)

13. The predictive markers included:
    • More than three hospitalizations or emergency room visits in a year
    • More than three emergency room visits in the previous three months
    • Aged 60 or older
    • Cirrhosis of the liver
    • End-stage renal disease
    • History of frostbite, immersion foot or hypothermia
    • HIV/AIDS
    • Tri-morbidity: simultaneous co-occurrence of any mental health disorder, any substance abuse disorder, and any significant chronic health condition such as diabetes, heart disease, or cancer.

Rev. Dr. Benita W. Harris
Asbury United Methodist Church

Frank Shipper, PhD
Perdue School of Business, Salisbury University

Karen P. Manz
Author and Researcher

Charles C. Manz, PhD
Isenberg School of Management, University of Massachusetts

Introduction

In 1983, Rink Dickinson, Jonathan Rosenthal, and Michael Rozyne were all recent college graduates and working for a food co-op warehouse in the Boston area. They began to question the system, asking questions such as, "What if food could be traded in a way that is honest and fair, a way that empowers both farmers and consumers? What if trade supported family farms' use of organic methods rather than methods that harm the environment?" Almost simultaneously, they started to hear about groups in Europe engaged in a concept called *fair trade*. The advocates of fair trade wanted to ensure that the producers of products such as coffee, tea, and chocolate would receive a better price for their crops while also providing support for improvements to their environmental, social, and political conditions. Dickinson, Rosenthal, and Rozyne liked the idea. According to Dickinson, they "…were basically food co-op people, interested in connecting small, local farmers with consumers to change the marketplace," however, it was not their intention to found a company. Instead, they took the idea to the board of directors of the co-op warehouse. Half the board supported the idea and half voted against it. It became apparent to them that if they were going to pursue their vision, they were going to have to do it themselves.

Over the next three years, they met once a month to develop their plan and raise the capital to establish their own organization. The three young entrepreneurs quickly learned that no institution – including organizations that specialized in high-impact social justice ventures – would lend them money. Thus, fundraising focused on family, friends, and their contacts. According to Dickinson, the general pitch was, "We want you to invest in this project and it is almost guaranteed to lose all of your money." On those terms, they were able to raise $100,000. While raising money, Dickinson said they used their jobs to learn about cooperatives, small farmers, entrepreneurship, marketing, and "making mistakes, right and left." The food co-op gave them "a great environment to learn some skills." In 1986, Dickinson, Rosenthal, and Rozyne were ready to launch Equal Exchange (EE). By that time, their ambition was "…to change the way food is grown, bought, and sold around the world."

EE embarked on its pioneering efforts to sell fair trade products in the U.S. with coffee from Nicaragua. From the beginning, EE has paid its producers, typically small farmers indigenous to their region, an above market price for their products out of a desire to help provide a better, more stable income and to more equitably distribute the proceeds of the final sales. EE prominently displays the company slogan on each product – "Small Farmers, Big Change."

Not content to just "...change the way food is grown, bought, and sold around the world," the founders of EE formally adopted a hybrid worker-owner co-op structure in 1990. They believed this ownership structure would make its employees feel valued and, in turn, they would invest their whole being in the organization. Key to this new structure was shared employee ownership. Each worker-owner buys one share of Class A voting stock; no one did, could, or can own more than one share of voting stock. Worker-owners can also buy unlimited shares of Class B, non-voting stock. This structure distributes power, and potentially leadership, equally across all worker-owners on a democratic one-person/one-share/one-vote basis.

2012

Twenty-seven years later not only is EE doing good – it is doing well (see Exhibits 1 and 2). EE sales have grown from zero in 1986 to $1 million in 1991 to $42.8 million in 2010.[2] In 2011, sales increased another 9 percent to $46.8 million and EE projected that sales would exceed $50 million in 2012. All EE products (coffee, tea, chocolate bars, cocoa, sugar, bananas, almonds, and olive oil) are fair trade and most products are organic as well.

Co-Executive Directors, Rink Dickinson and Rob Everts and the worker-owners of EE are still interested in changing the world through socially responsible business. Its mission statement reveals the heart of EE:

... to build long-term trade partnerships that are economically just and environmentally sound, to foster mutually beneficial relationships between farmers and consumers and to demonstrate, through our success, the contribution of worker co-operatives and fair trade to a more equitable, democratic, and sustainable world.

In 2006, EE announced, "Our Vision in 20 Years... [To build] a vibrant, mutually cooperative community of two million committed participants trading fairly one billion dollars a year in a way that transforms the world."

Functional Areas at EE

To fulfill its mission and vision, the founders developed a hybrid model that combined worker-ownership with a cooperative model to coordinate the functions. EE is a relatively small company. With approximately 100 worker-owners and geographically dispersed operations, worker-owners may fulfill multiple functions.

EE Governance Model

EE has a board of directors that is elected by the worker-owners. The worker-owners nominate candidates for the six *inside* board member positions and a joint, three-person committee – comprised of a worker-owner, a board member, and a member of the management committee – nominates candidates for the three *outside* seats. The worker-owners elect all nine seats, three each year.

In turn, the board of directors hires EE's Executive Director/s. Currently, the position is called "The Office of Executive Directors" as it is shared by Dickinson and Everts. They are mutually responsible for hiring employees

Exhibit 1 Sales Growth

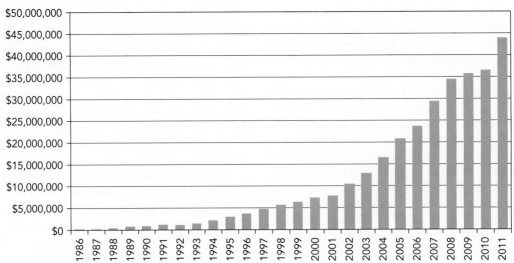

Source: This graph was constructed from financial data published by EE on the Web at http://www.equalexchange.coop/investing.

Exhibit 2 Profit/Loss (pre-tax)

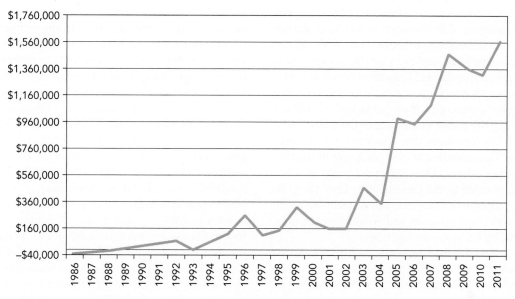

Source: This graph was constructed from financial data published by EE on the Web at http://www.equalexchange.coop/investing.

who, after significant input from the other worker-owners, may later become worker-owners themselves.

It is important to note that the Executive Directors are not board members. According to Lynsey Miller, Market Development Leader and a former board member, "They're at the board table, but they don't have votes. They are very active in that discussion and agenda setting." Thus, ultimately, the worker-owners who elect the board and hold two-thirds of the seats are responsible for hiring the Executive Directors.

All members of the board serve three-year terms. Instead of electing a new board every year and to promote board continuity, two inside directors and one outside director are elected each year.

This circular structure reinforces the following four concepts at the heart of the EE governance model:

1. the right to vote (one vote per worker-owner, not per share);
2. the right to serve as leader (e.g., board director, or other elected office);
3. the right to information;
4. the right to speak your mind.

EE provides the following elaboration of this model on its Web site:

A worker cooperative is an alternative for-profit structure based upon standard democratic principles. It is not designed to maximize profits, nor returns to investors, but rather to bring to the workplace many of the rights

and responsibilities that we hold as citizens in our communities. These principles include one-person/one-vote equality; open access to information (i.e., open-book management); free speech; and the equitable distribution of resources (such as income) …

The delegation of responsibilities is very much like that of conventional firms – which allows for efficiency – except that at EE those at the "bottom" of the organizational chart are, as owners, also at the "top" of the same chart.[3]

Everts describes the genesis of this governance model as follows:

From the beginning, it has been a culture in a context of participation and shared ownership of strong management. The founders were quite clear that ownership would be shared and that ultimately, accountability for the highest level decisions would be shared and that we would attempt to build a strong cultural of internal participation and democracy. There was no interest in having it be a collective.

One important position in this governance model is the Worker-Owner Coordinator. The worker-owners elect this individual, but this person is not a board member. The Worker-Owner Coordinator has many duties, the most public and demanding of which is facilitating the cooperative meetings that are held at least quarterly. Overall, the Coordinator is often akin to a police officer directing traffic; he or she does not make the rules of the cooperative, but is empowered by the cooperative to keep the system moving smoothly so necessary work may be completed. To do this, the Coordinator directs the jostling interests, opinions, and emotions of the members as best he or she can. One goal is to strike a balance between members' rights to ask questions, be heard, and press for changes with maintaining a safe, respectful, and constructive environment.

The Coordinator is automatically the representative of the worker-owners on certain "tripartite" committees, representing the board and management second. One example is the committee that nominates outside board members. The Coordinator also leads the 10-member worker-owner cabinet. The cabinet is a group of volunteers, accountable to the Coordinator. They carry out essential cooperative functions such as maintaining the internal education program and conducting the complex, multi-ballot, multi-site elections.

A secondary function for the Coordinator is to give the "State of the Cooperative" presentation at the annual meeting in May. This presentation provides an assessment of how well EE is functioning *as a cooperative*, not as a business per se. The worker-owners can call a meeting of the cooperative by presenting signatures of 10 percent of the worker-owners to the Coordinator. If a worker-owner wants to bring something to an upcoming meeting and has either the Coordinator's consent or the required number of signatures, the Coordinator is responsible for putting the individual on the agenda and working with that person so that her/his idea is well thought out and presented.

As can be seen by this description of the governance model, to be successful, EE must negotiate complex communication and coordination processes. Thus, recruiting, selecting, hiring, developing, and retaining employees who can operate within this governance model and flex with the needs of the organization is critical.

Human Resource Management

The worker-owners focus considerable attention on human resource management because, with the ownership culture that exists on a daily basis, worker-owners must be a good fit. Recruitment is probably EE's area of least worry. Whenever it does advertise an open position, it has multiple applicants. Because of its reputation, primarily spread by word of mouth, EE has no problem obtaining a significant and qualified applicant pool. The hiring process, outlined in Exhibit 3, is quite extensive and considered critical to the success of EE. Two unusual aspects of the hiring process include a three-stage interview and the fact that the hiring process is not considered complete until after the review process and after the new hire has been on the job for three months.

Once hired, new employees are matched with a mentor and put on probation for one year. New employee turnover during the first year is approximately 5 to 10 percent. After the first year, all worker-owners vote on whether to offer worker-ownership status to the employee (i.e., the opportunity to join the cooperative). Before the vote, the employee's mentor and the employee's supervisor circulate written statements on behalf of the candidate. With rare exceptions, only new employees who have fared well reach this point; new hires that have been poor employees or seem ill-suited for the co-op are generally weeded out by this time. Almost all worker-owner candidacy votes are taken online, but current worker-owners may also request an in-person meeting for a discussion and vote. In such a case, all worker-owners are free to discuss the individual's fit with EE before taking the vote. Worker-owners can vote "yes," "no," or "abstain." Unless 20 percent or more worker-owners vote "no," the candidate is welcomed into the co-op. Over 95 percent of employees who make it to the one-year point are accepted as worker-owners. Because of its infrequency, when one is not accepted, it can be a traumatic event for all.

During the probation period (first year of employment) the employee is expected to participate in a curriculum designed to teach about the mission and vision of EE, how they work, and to prepare the candidate for the responsibilities of worker-ownership and governance. The worker-owners feel it is very important to develop

Exhibit 3 Outline of Hiring Process

I. Executive Director Determines Need for Position
II. Executive Director and Chair of Hiring Committee Agree on Process
III. Hiring Committee Develops Tactics
IV. 100 Point Rating System (20 points for each category)
   a. Fit (mandatory)
   b. Team (mandatory)
   c. Communication (mandatory)
   d. Option 1 (e.g. skills, aptitudes)
   e. Option 2
V. Recruiting
   a. Defining Target Applicants
   b. Internal Posting
   c. Networks
   d. Previous Applicants
   e. External Advertising
VI. Essay Questions
VII. First Round Interviews – Conference Calls with Committee
VIII. Second Round Interview – In Person, or by Phone
IX. Third Round Interview – In-person Interview
X. Reference Checks
XI. Offer Letter – Delivered by Mail for Signature
XII. Three Month Review

Source: Condensed from company documents, 2005.

and strengthen its worker-ownership culture. To support the development of the culture, EE has developed an Owners' Manual that is over two hundred pages in length. To both support this effort for new employees and to reinforce the worker-ownership culture for all, "Exchange Time" is held every Thursday morning for one and a half hours. Exchange Time lectures and discussions cover topics such as fair trade, co-op history, and issues affecting EE's farmer partners, among others. New employees are essentially required to attend while all other employees are encouraged to participate. The discussions are recorded and shared with remote employees and regional offices via EE's intranet. Cody Squire, who joined EE right out of college a few years ago, enthusiastically described Exchange Time as:

It's one structured thing that you can depend on having every week just to learn about something new, to look deeper into something you already know about, or to hear from somebody who has just returned from working with farmer co-ops in Peru.

In addition to Exchange Time, EE has "10 percent time." Employees can use 10 percent of their work time for purposes unrelated to their core functions. This time can be used to cross-train, work on governance committees, or learn more about EE's products. For example, Miller used her 10 percent time to serve on the board of directors, where she helped create the 20-year vision for EE. Mike and his colleague in Quality Control, Danielle, led a program called "The Brew Crew," a year-long curriculum on coffee. People from other departments participate in coffee quality trainings every two weeks for a year.

To develop future leaders, EE uses an unusual 360 degree peer evaluation process in which peer, subordinate, superior, and self-evaluations are performed. The unusual aspect of EE's process is that all who provide feedback must sign their forms. In other words, the feedback is not anonymous. Alison Booth, Manager of EE's espresso bar in Seattle, Washington, described how it worked for her:

If I'm being evaluated, my supervisor and I will have access to them… Sometimes they are just nice to hear, but not terribly helpful; sometimes they're a little hard to hear. Most of the time, people are really careful to give constructive criticism, to give specific examples of things we could do better or things we did well.

Then, I do a self-evaluation and my boss does a supervisor's evaluation. He combines his thoughts with my evaluation and the peer evaluations and pulls them all together. We talk about what's working, areas for improvement, and what to focus on in the next year.

To further increase intellectual capital, EE maintains a library to which all employees have access. Mike described the library as, "Awesome … it's full of DVDs and books on anything from economics to feminism to fair trade to…." The worker-owners also have responsibility for the education committee, originally a board committee. EE identifies education as a "… vital function. In shifting accountability for this committee, Worker-Owners became more accountable for their own education and the orientation of new employees to our co-operative."[4]

The worker-owners staff many roles in this model and share in both profits and losses. Because EE operates as a worker cooperative, profit sharing is referred to as "patronage." "Patronage" is a common term used in cooperatives where co-op members receive a share of the profits, or bear a portion of losses, based on the extent they have participated in the co-op. At EE, all worker-owners who have worked a full year receive the same amount without regard to rank or seniority as all contributed the same amount of labor time. The total potential patronage distribution consists of 40 percent of net income after state taxes and preferred dividends are paid. Half of this distribution is reinvested in EE, and half is paid in cash. In years of losses, the Patronage rebates are charges against the retained distributions.

In terms of benefits, EE "is generous" according to Brian Albert, EE's Chief Financial Officer who joined EE after approximately thirty years with some well-known international firms. For example, it offers all employees twelve sick days each year. A worker-owner can use them for him/herself, to take care of a sick child, to attend a doctor appointment, or to spend time with a sick parent. Additionally, all worker-owners receive two weeks of vacation for the first two years. After that, they receive four weeks. After their eighth year, they receive five weeks. In addition, employees receive the standard holidays including the Friday after Thanksgiving.

EE is also generous in the area of pay, paying above average for novice level jobs, but below average for senior level management positions. It maintains a top-to-bottom pay ratio of four-to-one. It clearly states on its Web site that EE adopted this ratio to reflect the fair trade ethic inside the corporation.

Production

EE has not been content to be a single-product company. Its four major products and their percentage of sales are coffee (80.1 percent), chocolate (16.1 percent), tea (2.7 percent), and snacks (1.1 percent). Snacks include products such as Organic Tamari Roasted Almonds.

In 2010, EE increased its stake in Oke USA, an importer and seller of organic bananas, to 90 percent. Oke USA sales were $4.4 million in 2010. In 2011, EE introduced organic olive oil. Ninety percent of EE's coffees are certified organic and 100 percent of its tea, cocoa, chocolate, sugar, and bananas are certified organic.

To produce organic coffee, chocolate, tea, and its other products for sale to others, EE first secures the raw materials. The producers of these products come from around the world. EE buys raw product from four continents – North and South America, Africa, and Asia – and almost exclusively from developing countries (see Exhibit 4).

For example, coffee is grown largely in developing countries and is often the second most valuable commodity (after oil) exported by them, according to John M. Talbot, a sociology professor at the University of the West Indies in Jamaica.[i] The large multinationals typically buy their raw materials from either large plantations or large sellers of coffee. The large sellers depend on middlemen, often referred to as "coyotes," to buy coffee from small growers. According to an article in the April 25, 2011 issue of *Time* magazine, Ugandan coffee farmers receive 0.66 percent of the retail value of their product. In contrast, the U.S. Department of Agriculture estimated that U.S. farmers receive 12 percent of the retail value.

EE buys directly from cooperatives that represent small producers, thereby helping these co-ops to internalize the activity and profits formerly captured by the middlemen (see comparison of supply chains in Exhibit 5). EE buys raw materials from over forty small farmer cooperatives in twenty-five countries at prices higher than typical. In its 2009 annual report, EE defined it sourcing standards as:

- **Quality** - Find the best beans.
- **Flavor** - Select sweet beans with unique flavor characteristics.
- **Farmer Partners** - Trade with small farmer co-operatives that share our vision of community empowerment.
- **Direct Relationships** - Import directly from farmer co-operatives.
- **Fair Price** - Pay above the market price, often above fair trade prices.
- **Environment** - Support sustainable agriculture, the preservation of sensitive areas, and reforestation of degraded land.
- **Commitment** - Source all our coffee according to the quality of the beans and the quality of the source.

EE supports the cooperatives with both financial and technical assistance. In its 2008 Disclosure Document to Sell Class B Preferred Stock, the relationship with small farmers was described as follows, "Our Commitment: we pay a fair price to the farmer, trade directly with democratic co-ops, supply advanced credit, and support sustainable agriculture." In other words, EE goes beyond just paying a fair price; it pre-pays on its contracts with the cooperatives. It also provides assistance to the cooperatives to ensure they can provide a high quality product.

Mike Mowry, a quality control specialist, described what he did on a trip to Nicaragua as follows:

We do a lot of work going down and actually training about quality. Even with their quality departments, we do extensive training on how to roast samples and how to cup coffee.[5] The whole idea is collaborating with their tasters and our tasters.

Exhibit 4 Where EE Buys from Small Farmers by Country, 2010

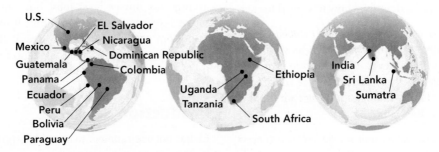

Source: Information taken from EE Web site at http://www.equalexchange.coop/farmer-partners.

---

i. Cacao, the key ingredient for chocolate, is also only exported by developing countries.

Exhibit 5 EE versus Conventional Supply Chain

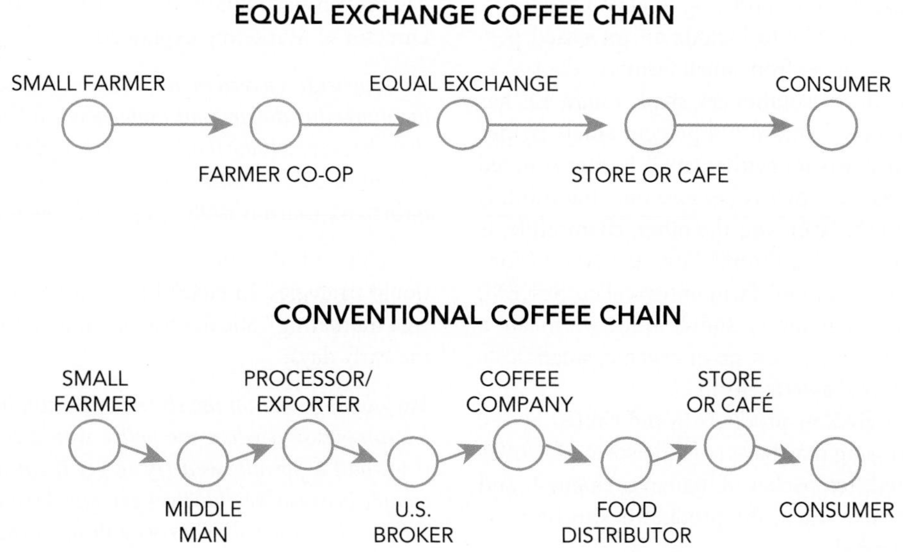

EQUAL EXCHANGE COFFEE CHAIN

SMALL FARMER   EQUAL EXCHANGE   CONSUMER

FARMER CO-OP   STORE OR CAFE

CONVENTIONAL COFFEE CHAIN

SMALL FARMER   PROCESSOR/ EXPORTER   COFFEE COMPANY   STORE OR CAFÉ

MIDDLE MAN   U.S. BROKER   FOOD DISTRIBUTOR   CONSUMER

Source: EE pamphlet.

EE maintains that "great" coffee can be obtained from many sources. What sets it apart is that it buys "great" coffee from "great" sources.

EE also provides assistance to the small farmer co-ops beyond food products. For example, it has provided assistance for training programs for women in Guatemala, an ecotourism project in Nicaragua, and new classrooms in El Salvador.

When all of the sourcing standards work well, quality product is shipped to EE for further processing. However, sometimes EE has to break off a relationship with a co-op for either quality-control reasons or compromised governance of the cooperative, such as not living up to expectations of accountability, transparency, and democratic governance.

Another difficulty with attempting to reach EE's production standards is illustrated with its history of bringing tea to market. In the 80s, when EE consisted of a small staff of five or six, tea was typically grown on large plantations; obtaining the product from small farmers was difficult. When EE first imported tea during the late 80s, the tea came from Sri Lanka and was a generic tea that may not have been from small farmers nor fair trade. At that time, there were no "fair trade" standards for tea; that would come later. However, EE did know the exporter, an exemplary, grassroots, non-profit, self-help organization called the "Sarvodaya movement." It still operates today. In fact, it was one of the key players in relief and reconstruction after the 2004 Indian Ocean tsunami. At that time, working in solidarity with this locally rooted, progressive, self-empowerment organization – that would also receive a sizable portion of the tea profits – was the moral equivalent of "fair trade." Unfortunately, that trade link was lost after approximately three years due to interruptions caused by the Sri Lankan civil war.

Around 1997, EE made a second attempt at procuring tea from a region of India famous for tea, Darjeeling. By then, formal fair trade standards had been created for tea. To EE's dismay, the standards focused on plantations. Even so, EE plowed ahead. A major hurdle for EE lay in the fact that there was no tea available that was fair trade certified *and* organic *and* high enough quality for EE's market *and* from small farmers. The market demanded the first three criteria, but not the fourth, which happened to be the most important to EE. With the help of key, even "ironic," allies in Darjeeling and Germany, EE began to create a path the firm thought gave it the best chance to eventually deliver a tea with all four characteristics. Rodney North, Spokesperson for EE, characterized its most important ally as "ironic" because it was a big tea plantation called TPI. In fact, it had been one of the model plantations for fair trade tea certification. The owners of TPI, the Mohan family, shared EE's aspirations to bring small farmers into the fair trade system. Thus, in the early years, 50 percent or more of the tea EE imported was from the TPI estates and TPI gathered the other 50 percent from co-ops of small farmers around them. TPI also assisted these co-ops with organic certification, fair trade certification, rehabilitating their tea bushes, and improving quality. Over time, TPI shifted its tea blends to include an increased percentage that was sourced from small farmers.

After many more evolutionary steps, today, EE has a line of twelve teas. Ten are 100 percent small-farmer tea leaf. The other two are neither small-farmer sourced nor traditional estate – that is because one, the mint, is sourced from a U.S. farm, and the other, chamomile, is from an exemplary philanthropic Egyptian NGO (nongovernmental organization) farm entity called SEKEM. "BUT, it is only a temporary source until we locate a suitable fair trade certified co-op of organic, small-scale chamomile growers," asserts North.

When EE receives its products in the United States, additional processing may have to be performed. Coffee has to be roasted, tea packaged, bananas ripened, and chocolate processed. Then, the product has to be marketed and distributed.

Marketing and Distribution

EE uses multiple channels to market and distribute its products: (1) retail outlets, (2) an interfaith network, (3) schools, (4) the Internet, and (5) EE cafés. Retail outlets – including health food stores, food co-ops, by-the-cup shops (i.e., cafés and restaurants), universities, and chain stores – account for approximately 72 percent of sales. The consumer-owned food co-ops were EE's first sales channel and remain the largest sales segment.

In contrast, selling to the larger grocery store chains has proven particularly difficult because, as the former Director of Marketing explained:

It is tougher to succeed in that channel, because we don't have the marketing dollars that major food companies have, and that's been something that's been a struggle to try to figure out how to succeed because you need to have a national brand awareness, which is really tough to do on a small budget.

Thus, EE developed some unconventional promotional strategies. In fact, Miller referred to them as "guerilla marketing." She described some of the marketing in the early days:

We would go out on the streets of Boston handing out coffee samples and when the police would come over to ask if we had a permit, we'd try to get them to have a coffee sample because we didn't get permits; kind of have to think on your feet and talk your way through challenges.

Another guerilla marketing tactic EE uses is grassroots events. Beside traditional in-store product demonstrations, EE staff members participate in public speaking events, organize consumer letter-writing campaigns to ask supermarkets to carry its products, and even go door-to-door to get its message across. Another example of EE's use of guerilla marketing is the type of coupon shown in Exhibit 6.

The interfaith channel is EE's second largest distribution channel with approximately 20 percent of sales.

Exhibit 6 Exclusive Coupon

EXCLUSIVE ONLINE COUPON
FOR THE EQUAL EXCHANGE CASE STUDY

Sample Equal Exchange's organic, Fair Trade products for yourself and save 10% off your order at our retail web store   http://shop.equalexchange.com

Coupon code: **dwdg10**

Coupon expires December 31, 2015

Source: EE Corporate Office – Marketing.

It includes a dozen formal partners: American Friends Service Committee, American Jewish World Service, Catholic Relief Services, Baptist Peace Fellowship of North America, Church of the Brethren, Disciples of Christ, Lutheran World Relief, Mennonite Central Committee U.S., Presbyterian Church USA, United Church of Christ, United Methodist Committee on Relief, and Unitarian Universalist Service Committee. The fair trade products distributed through these interfaith partnerships provide faith-based organizations with another opportunity to live in accord with their values and to discuss their connections and fellowship with those who grow and harvest food around the world. EE also provides materials to educate consumers on issues of economic justice, sustainable farming, and the effects of an increasingly industrialized food industry dominated by a small number of firms.

The development of the interfaith channel is a great example of entrepreneurship in action among the worker-owners at EE. Prior to the mid-90s, EE worked with congregations on an ad hoc, one-by-one basis. It was Timothy Bernard, a Lutheran minister, and Erbin Crowell, an EE salesperson that hit upon the idea of establishing formal relationships with faith-based communities. In North's words: "Erbin had to sell this idea internally to Dickinson and others and Timothy had to do likewise within the Lutheran community's leadership. Eventually, they created a pilot project which grew to be very successful."

Another example of entrepreneurship within EE was led by Virginia Berman. She began with fundraising opportunities with elementary, middle, and high schools; instead of selling items such as magazine subscriptions and popcorn, the schools would sell fair trade products from EE. Berman began to hear that the teachers wanted to help their students grasp the significance of fair trade. In response, Berman requested and received funding to create educational materials. Today, there is a flexible and engaging free-to-download curriculum targeted for late elementary through middle school age children on the EE Web site.

To reach the technologically savvy, EE has embraced social media such as Twitter, YouTube, and Facebook to communicate its message to current and potential consumers. Additionally, EE takes advantage of electronic media to provide e-newsletters and offers an unusually active, in-depth, and outspoken blog. All of these efforts are, as Miller said, "To try to connect with the public and consumers." The use of social media also reinforces its marketing efforts through retail stores and the interfaith network. Moreover, it leads to its fourth marketing channel, the Internet. In 2011, Internet sales to individual shoppers accounted for approximately two percent of sales. EE expects Internet sales to hit one million in 2012. Currently, EE is looking at how to expand its Internet sales. With over half of the interfaith sales previously discussed executed via online stores, approximately 12 percent of EE's sales come through the Internet.

EE's two cafés are its fifth form of marketing and distribution. EE started selling its products through cafés prior to the 2008 recession; one in Boston and the other in Seattle. Due to high capital costs and the challenge of winning new customers, it takes even popular cafés between 18 and 24 months to break even. For now, EE has placed the further addition of cafés on hold. Instead, it is trying a different way to reach out and touch customers.

In keeping with the EE tradition of thinking outside the box, it has developed cafés on wheels. They are described by Albert as follows:

We have two custom built tricycles very close to completion. They'll be in the Boston market probably within the next 30 to 60 days. They are stand alone. They have marine batteries and they carry all the supplies they need. They can brew coffee right there onsite. If you park it here in the morning and not much action, you can park it over there in the afternoon, yeah, that seems to be a better spot. It's kind of a brand building, and they have kind of a wow factor.[6]

EE is not alone in this endeavor; some independent cafés have also adopted a mobile approach to reach customers. For example, Common Grounds: A Fair Trade Coffee House in Salisbury, MD uses a converted trailer to reach customers at community events such as the West Wicomico Heritage Bike Tour and Salisbury University's Freshman Move-In Day.

As with all fair trade products, which tend to occupy the premium or gourmet segment of their categories, the pricing is above that charged by mass-marketers such as Maxwell and Kraft. This reflects the higher quality and the higher unit costs of a small firm, but it also supports the higher prices paid to the producers. Yet, the prices for EE products are still on par with much larger competitors such as Starbucks, Peet's, and Green Mountain, who offer comparable quality coffee. To persuade customers to buy its product without the aid of expensive marketing campaigns, EE uses a significant amount of informational marketing. For example, as stated earlier, on the packaging of every chocolate bar, tea bag or box, and every bag of coffee is the slogan, "Small Farmers, Big Change." In addition, information on how the product is grown, who grows it, where it was grown, and why it is different often appears on the packaging material. Sometimes pictures of growers also appear. To further differentiate the products, fair trade and USDA Organic seals are on the packaging materials, as well. EE tries to use every opportunity to get its message across and connect with the public and consumers.

Finance[7]

EE issues two forms of stock – Class A Common Stock and Class B Preferred Stock. Every worker-owner must own one share of Class A stock, and no more. No one else may purchase it. This ensures equal voting rights, one person-one vote, and to a larger degree, equal power among all worker-owners. Worker-owners purchase a share when they are elected into the company after completing their probationary first year. When originally issued in 1990, each share was worth $2000. In January 2011, each Class A share was worth $3,170.

To prevent the cost of stock ownership from being an obstacle to joining the cooperative, new worker-owners, once elected, are provided with an interest free loan to purchase their share. They have four years to repay the loan and can repay with the cash portion of the patronage distribution.

Both worker-owners and outsiders can own Class B Preferred Stock. Shares sell for $27.50. The board declares dividends annually usually in January; commonly, dividends are targeted at five percent. Originally, individual shares could be purchased. As Everts related, "Someone could buy a share for their grandchild for $27. We loved that type of thing, but we are operating under limits of 500 maximum outside shareholders. If you exceed that limit, then it is considered to be publicly traded." In 2011, preferred shares were sold only in lots equal to or greater than $10,000.[8]

Exhibit 7 Statements of Operations and Retained Earnings

	Years Ended December 31					
	2006	**2007**	**2008**	**2009**	**2010**	**2011**
SALES	$23,639,000	$29,370,480	$34,440,241	$35,832,510	$36,525,856	$46,819,829
COST OF SALES	$14,165,000	$18,866,940	$22,446,593	$23,075,260	$26,659,316	$33,617,786
GROSS PROFIT	$9,474,000	$10,503,540	$11,993,648	$12,757,250	$12,866,540	$13,202,043
OPERATING EXPENSES	$7,946,000	$8,646,241	$9,535,120	$10,771,023	$11,234,758	$11,350,116
INCOME FROM OPERATIONS	$1,528,000	$1,857,299	$2,458,528	$1,986,227	$1,631,782	$1,851,927
OTHER (EXPENSE) INCOME:						
Interest Expense	$(576,000)	$(737,131)	$(720,437)	$(622,848)	$(323,662)	$(387,182)
Reduction of Investment to Market Value			$(80,000)			
Bad Debt Expense – Loans		$(38,759)	$(80,000)			
Charitable Contributions Expense		$(5,296)	$(105,000)			
Interest Income		$22,118	$9,314	$3,754	$14,832	$7,346
Bad Debt (expense) Recovery, Net – Trade			$(14,265)			
		$(759,068)	$(990,388)			
INCOME BEFORE INCOME TAXES	$952,000	$1,098,231	$1,468,140	$1,367,133	$1,322,952	$1,472,091
PROVISIONS FOR INCOME TAXES:						
Current		$325,000	$435,000	$430,000	$484,000	$689,000
Deferred		$110,000	$165,000	$163,000	$94,000	$(40,000)
	$415,000	$435,000	$600,000	$593,000	$578,000	$649,000
NET INCOME	$537,000	$663,231	$868,140	$774,133	$744,952	$821,042
RETAINED EARNINGS, Beginning of Year	$1,255,725	$1,619,725	$2,069,068	$2,654,249	$3,174,783	$3,595,014
Less: Preferred Stock Dividends Paid	$(173,000)	$(213,888)	$(282,959)	$(253,599)	$(324,721)	$428,917
RETAINED EARNINGS, End of Year	$1,619,725	$2,069,068	$2,654,249	$3,174,783	$3,595,014	$3,987,139

Source: These 6-year consolidated financial statements were constructed from financial data published by EE on the Web at http://www.equalexchange.coop/investing.

Exhibit 8 Balance Sheet

	December 31					
	2006	**2007**	**2008**	**2009**	**2010**	**2011**
ASSETS						
CURRENT ASSETS:						
Cash and Equivalents	$480,150	$381,497	$212,717	$376,667	$823,699	$757,429
Accounts Receivable – Trade, Net of Reserve for Possible	$1,569,117	$1,973,098	$2,227,843	$2,185,768	$2,655,707	$2,849,063
Uncollectible Accounts of $50,000 in 2009 and 2008						
Notes Receivable – Other	$10,500	$34,174	$88,628	$324,996	$17,538	$34,800
Inventories	$6,983,311	$8,193,630	$10,839,429	$8,293,729	$8,290,646	$15,117,041
Prepaid Expenses, Advances in Inventory, and Other Current Assets	$381,538	$766,611	$928,227	$415,139	$535,330	$800,338
Deferred Income Tax Asset	$75,000	$77,000	$145,000	$115,000	$377,496	$367,496
TOTAL CURRENT ASSETS	$9,499,616	$11,426,010	14,441,844	$11,711,299	$12,700,386	$19,926,167
PROPERTY AND EQUIPMENT, NET	$6,497,284	$7,311,901	$7,473,243	$7,017,564	$6,653,683	$5,979,771
OTHER ASSETS:						
Intangible Assets, Net	$64,154	$49,194	$35,434	$28,994	$211,153	$182,212
Investments	$100,000	$151,326	$190,870	$381,861	$68,513	$43,360
Notes Receivable, Net of Current Portion	$128,233	$281,188	$234,473	$6,039	$38,501	$39,249
TOTAL ASSETS	$16,289,287	$19,220,219	$22,375,864	$19,145,457	$19,672,236	$26,170,759
LIABILITIES AND STOCKHOLDER EQUITY						
CURRENT LIABILITIES:						
Notes Payable – Lines-of-Credit	$3,006,846	$4,022,153	$5,164,438	$624,928	$567,952	$3,463,192
Capitalized Lease Obligations, Current Portion	$250,328	$420,470	$447,679	$432,124		
Mortgages and Other Notes Payable, Current Portion	$200,001	$319,677	$1,639,829	$550,639	$121,793	$1,253,534
Accounts Payable and Accrued Expenses	$1,219,767	$1,079,240	$940,158	$1,089,703	$1,539,374	$2,198,802
Accrued Expenses and Other Current Liabilities	$661,840	$660,063	$769,526			
Corporate Income Taxes Payable						$271,632
Patronage Rebates Payable	$228,036	$418,205	$255,255	$421,875	$147,000	$376,382
TOTAL CURRENT LIABILITIES	$5,566,818	$6,919,808	$9,216,885	$3,119,269	$2,376,119	$7,563,542
LONG-TERM LIABILITIES						
Capitalized Lease Obligation, Non-Current Portion	$886,058	$1,572,897	$1,125,216	$693,092	$ –	
Mortages and Other Notes Payable, Non-Current Portion	$3,238,671	$3,259,969	$2,875,097	$3,190,008	$3,228,784	$2,616,521
Deferred Income Taxes	$292,000	$404,000	$637,000	$770,000	$900,000	$850,000
COMMITMENTS AND CONTINGENCIES						
TOTAL LIABILITIES	$9,963,547	$12,156,674	$13,854,198	$7,772,369	$4,128,784	$3,466,521

(Continued)

Exhibit 8 (Continued) Balance Sheet

	December 31					
	2006	**2007**	**2008**	**2009**	**2010**	**2011**
STOCKHOLDERS' EQUITY:						
Preferred Stock; Authorized 299,800 Shares; Issued and Outstanding 390,116 Shares in 2011, 333,262 Shares in 2010, 290,429 Shares in 2009 and 206,864 Shares in 2008	$4,564,605	$4,829,986	$5,680,390	$7,978,429	$9,156,382	$10,728,960
Common Stock: Authorized 200 Shares; Issued and Outstanding, 108 Shares in 2011, 107 Shares in 2010, 99 Shares in 2009, 93 Shares in 2008, 85 Shares in 2007, 81 Shares in 2006	$222,165	$232,555	$260,903	$282,683	$313,343	$318,753
Less: Common Stock Subscriptions Receivable	$(80,755)	$(68,064)	$(73,876)	$(62,807)	$(60,682)	$(59,480)
Retained Earnings	$1,619,725	$2,069,068	$2,654,249	$3,174,783	$3,595,014	$3,987,139
TOTAL STOCKHOLDERS' EQUITY	$6,325,740	$7,063,545	$8,521,666	$11,373,088	$13,004,057	$14,975,372
TOTAL LIABILITIES AND STOCKHOLDERS' EQUITY	$16,289,287	$19,220,219	$22,375,864	$19,145,457	$19,355,278	$26,170,759

Source: These 6-year consolidated financial statements were constructed from financial data published by EE on the Web at http://www.equalexchange.coop/investing.

When EE offers its preferred shares, it does so in the following manner according to Everts:

We do have to be diligent and deliberate about talking to people and sharing. We have a very extensive disclosure document that everyone has to look at before they invest in us. There's got to be some connection to EE to get them here in the first place, whether it's a personal connection or whether they represent an account of ours; maybe they actually are a worker-owner and they want to be an investor, too. It has to be people who fundamentally know us and have direct access to the books and can see quite closely.

To assure direct access to financial information, EE practices an extreme form of open-book management. Privately or closely held firms such as EE are not required to make available to the public an annual report, but the company publishes each year's annual report on its Web site. The financial statements for 2006-2011 were extracted from those reports and are contained in Exhibits 7 and 8. EE goes further by putting all of its annual reports dating back to 1986 online and includes a Spanish language version for its suppliers in Latin America that represent 90 percent of EE's imports.[9]

Preferred shares are sold as a long-term investment. Preferred stockholders can redeem shares for their full price only after five years. Shares cannot be redeemed until after two years and then for only 70 percent of their value, 80 percent after three, and 90 percent after four.

There is a provision in the disclosure statement that the board of directors "… may postpone or delay a request for redemption" if the total debt to total equity ratio exceeds 2:1 or the redemption would cause it to exceed that ratio.

In addition, Class A Common Stock and Class B Preferred Stock have the following unusual restriction and explanation for that restriction on them in the disclosure document:

On the sale of all the assets, liquidation or dissolution of the corporation, any residual assets left after the payment of all debts shall be distributed first to the Class B shareholders in the amount equal to the balances in their internal accounts and then to the current members or, if said residual assets are insufficient, then on a pro rata basis in proportion to the relative balances in their internal accounts. Any assets remaining after said distribution shall be distributed to an alternative trading organization as so determined by the board of directors of the corporation.

Basically, if any capital gain as a result of the company's growth is ever realized through a sale, it stays within the fair trade community rather than being distributed to stockholders. According to North:

The mission purpose of this treatment is to remove the temptation that the Company would ever be sold for personal financial gain, and reflects that EE was created to do something quite specific, to carry out fair trade and to model a new approach to business, and not as vehicle to generate wealth for any one stakeholder. Therefore, the likelihood is that the company will remain independent, despite a steady stream of buy-out offers, and its mission remains intact. As the mission and the dividends, not the capital gain, are the basis for investment, this protects the stockholder's interest.

This version of a "poison pill" to prevent takeover by outsiders is uncommon. Some at EE call it the "No Exit Strategy." Albert related the following regarding this provision:

Anecdotally, I bumped into an attorney, she specializes in ESOP's and employee owned accounts ... she said that our by-laws are maybe a little over the top, but in the next breath said she's used them more than once as the model for others.

To raise additional working capital, EE uses an unusual method for debt financing. Anyone can buy an EE Certificate of Deposit (CD) through Eastern Bank of Massachusetts. The minimum for these CDs is $500. By 2012, EE had raised over $1 million via CDs. It also has received loans from the Calvert Foundation, Everance, religious institutions, and individual supporters. EE refers to these organizations and individuals as mission lenders. How the sources of capital have changed between 2005 and 2010 is shown in Exhibit 9. Although atypical, EE's financial policies collectively support its unusual governance model for a for-profit corporation.

The Industry

The industry consists of large multinationals that sell coffee, chocolate (i.e., Hershey, Nestle, and M&M/Mars), tea (i.e., Lipton), bananas (Dole and Chiquita) and other competitive products and small competitors. Everts says that EE is a victim of its own success. Since 1986, a number of fair trade firms have sprung up. Everts estimates that 700 or 800 other coffee roasters – large and small – are doing some amount of fair trade. For example, Starbucks now sells more fair trade coffee than EE, but it represents only a small percentage of Starbuck's total sales. The same is true of Dunkin' Donuts. In contrast, the U.S. companies deeply engaged in fair trade tend to be small. According to a 2009 study by the Fair Trade Federation (FTF), the average number of full-time employees in a fair trade company is fewer than 10.

In addition to other companies getting into fair trade, there are organizations competing to certify what is a fair trade product. Starting in 2012, Fair Trade USA (aka Transfair) will certify coffee, cocoa, and sugar grown on large-scale plantations and private estates as fair trade. Other terms such as "shade grown" applied in the industry to products sold by EE and others do not have a common definition.

Fair trade is growing rapidly. According to a 2012 report published by Fair Trade International, global sales

Exhibit 9 Sources of Capital 2005 and 2010

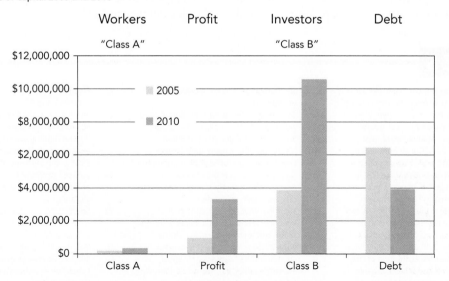

Source: This graph was constructed from financial data published by EE on the Web at http://www.equalexchange.coop/investing.

of fair trade certified goods were $6.6 billion in 2011, a 12 percent increase from 2010, and 44 percent over 2009 sales.[10] FTF estimated in 2008 the total market for fair trade products bought in the United States was $1.18 billion. North estimates that at retail, U.S. fair trade in 2011 was over $2 billion. In the same FTF report, increases in sales by product varied even for the same country. For example, fair trade coffee, the largest fair trade product, grew approximately 32 percent between 2010 and 2011 in the United States. In contrast, tea grew by 21 percent and cocoa grew by 67 percent in the same time period in the United States. Obviously, fair trade is growing more rapidly than non-fair-traded products. This growth is occurring in part because natural and fair trade products have gone mainstream.

In 2006 the Hartman Group reported, "Almost three-quarters (73 percent) of the U.S. population consume organic foods or beverages at least occasionally. Clearly, the conventional belief that all organic users are highly educated, high-income, Caucasian females should be put to rest." "LOHAS" is an industry term standing for Lifestyles of Health and Sustainability and may better serve as a moniker for those consumers who frequent outlets such as Whole Foods and food co-ops. According to North,

They are interested enough in being healthier and supporting environmental sustainability that they spend more time researching their purchases, they'll go out of their way, and they'll pay more (but not just any price). Some of them are also interested in matters of fairness and social justice – and will shape their purchases accordingly.

In a 2008 study by Alter Eco USA, 71.4 percent of U.S. consumers reported that they had heard the term "fair trade." However, less than 10 percent surveyed reported that they had recently purchased a fair trade item. This pattern may be changing. Researchers from the Massachusetts Institute of Technology, Harvard University, and the London School of Economics found "substantial consumer support for fair trade, although a segment of price-sensitive shoppers will not pay a large premium for the fair trade label."[11] The consumers who were already purchasing premium coffee were willing to pay an additional 8 percent for fair trade labeled premium coffee. The FTF expects the market to continue to grow if distribution widens and consumers can more easily identify fair trade products.

Challenges

Although EE is the largest company in the United States selling fair trade products exclusively and has continued to grow, Everts sees challenges ahead. One is the trend toward locally grown or prepared food. Obviously, coffee cannot be grown locally in the continental United States; but, it is increasingly locally *roasted*, a very popular selling point.

The significant challenge that Everts sees is "How does EE remain entrepreneurial?" As he said:

One challenge ahead is being prepared to take more risks, being prepared to reinvest in ourselves structurally, or whether it's to spin off cooperatives. We're contemplating this with the retail café sector. Being prepared to take risks and also how do we look at this thing, a big company succeeding in many local markets where we aren't necessarily based there, that's a challenge.

Given EE's leadership, worker-owners, culture, and history, changes do seem inevitable. The question is "What changes will they make?"

NOTES

1. The research on this company was partially supported by the Foundation for Enterprise Development. This case is copyrighted by the authors. Please address all questions to Frank Shipper at fmshipper@salisbury.edu, (410) 543-6333. The authors would like to thank the worker-owners of Equal Exchange who graciously shared their knowledge, experiences, and perspectives about the company. Their viewpoints were invaluable in ensuring that this case provides a true representation of the culture and practices of the company.

2. Sales figures for 2010, 2011, and 2012 were adjusted for the 2010 acquisition of Oke USA, an importer and seller of organic bananas. The Statement of Operations and Retained Earnings in Exhibit 7 is unadjusted.

3. Source: http://www.equalexchange.coop/worker-owned/. Accessed July 25, 2012.

4. Source: Internal document entitled, "Evolution of EE Governance: Worker-Owner Oversight of Education Committee."

5. "Cup coffee" is an expression used to describe the industry standard process to test the quality of coffee.

6. The trikes were introduced after this interview was conducted. To see a Boston Globe article about them go to http://www.boston.com/ae/food/restaurants/articles/2010/09/22/thanks_to_equal_exchange_trikes_its_one_whole_cafe_with_cream_and_sugar_to_go/.

7. Financial Statements can be found in Exhibits 7 and 8.

8. The JOBS Act of 2012 raised the limit from 500 to 2,000 investors before a company is to be publicly traded. This change is expected to be helpful to EE as well as other ESOP companies over the next 10 years.

9. Source http://www.equalexchange.coop/annual-reports/index.php. Accessed July 25, 2012.

10. Source: See: http://www.fairtrade.net/single_view1+M528a593be0f.html. Accessed July 26, 2012.

11. Hainmueller, J., Hiscox M., & Sequeira S. 2009. Consumer Demand for the Fair Trade Label: Evidence from a Field Experiment, Working Paper.

Matt Cook, Kathryn Hicks, Ricardo Rodriguez, Austin Rogers

Texas A&M University

Introduction

After going public in 2012, Facebook immediately experienced a fair amount of criticism and quite a bit of investor uncertainty. However, Mark Zuckerberg, Facebook's founder and CEO, was pleased to report that, as of one year later, on January 30, 2013, the firm had surpassed Wall Street's expectations. Moreover, in only eight years, Facebook's growth resulted in it becoming the largest social networking platform in the world.

Nevertheless, Zuckerberg and his top management team knew that they needed to consider how to adjust the firm's strategies to compete as a public company, partly in response to the belief among some users and analysts that Facebook was losing its ability to satisfy customers and shareholders simultaneously. In this regard, what should the firm do strategically to ensure its long-term and profitable growth? While Facebook's advertiser base is constantly looking to the firm for additional innovative means to target users, its investors are questioning its ability to monetize its user base. Relatedly, in a highly dynamic and competitive industry, how will Facebook out-innovate its rivals and retain customer "mind-share"? Along with his top management team, Zuckerberg concluded that the firm should focus on both worldwide and domestic market growth. With many recent product innovations and strategic changes, 2013 and the few years beyond were expected to defining ones for the young, public social networking firm.

Facebook's Timeline

At the age of eleven, Facebook founder's Mark Zuckerberg's orientation and actions hinted that he could become a successful entrepreneur. Born in 1984 as the only son to a psychiatrist and a dentist, he quickly gained a sense of reasoning and adaptability that allowed for complex, yet creative thinking. Growing up in New York, middle school offered excess spare time that Zuckerberg used to write software. After learning basic programming from his father, a private tutor – who constantly referred to Zuckerberg as a "prodigy" – was hired.[1] During high school at Phillips Exeter Academy, he created a music player as a product for sale by his newly founded company, Intelligent Media Group. Zuckerberg declined Microsoft and AOL's offers to purchase this firm.[2] Winning several awards in math, astronomy, and physics, Zuckerberg set his sights on Harvard University, claiming on his college application that he was fluent in French, Hebrew, Latin, and ancient Greek.[3] It was at Harvard that Zuckerberg's truly invigorating path began.

Getting Started

Given his early interests, the fact that Zuckerberg majored in computer science and psychology in college is perhaps not too surprising. He began his journey by writing a program called CourseMatch that allowed students to coordinate and strategically select their classes. Soon after this, he created Facemash. Facemash gave students the opportunity to rate others based on looks and then post these results online. Popularity for this site increased to the extent that campus networks were overwhelmed and malfunctioned, forcing Facemash to shut down.[4] Zuckerberg next embarked on creating a social network that he dubbed "Thefacebook." The young entrepreneur dropped out of Harvard during his sophomore year to develop his soon-to-be multibillion-dollar company.[5]

Working with his roommate Dustin Moskovitz, fellow investor, Peter Thiel, and former Napster employee,

Sean Parker, "Thefacebook" was renamed "Facebook." By 2007, Facebook Platform, which allowed programmers to create social applications within Facebook, was complete. The characteristic blue-colored website design stemmed from Zuckerberg's color-blindness, which limited him from clearly seeing the colors red and green, but allowed visual clarity with the color blue.[6] Later that year, Beacon was created as a social advertising foundation. This led to a massive increase in growth for Facebook as both students and companies could now derive value from the company. In August 2008, Facebook hired Sheryl Sandberg to be its Chief Operating Officer and, in an effort to reach new markets, in October 2008, in addition to its local headquarters in Palo Alto, California, Facebook set up its international headquarters in Dublin, Ireland. By July 2010, the company had over 500 million users and by the end of 2012, the user base totaled 1 billion.[7]

Earning Respect

In 2009, *Vanity Fair* magazine ranked Zuckerberg as the 23rd most influential person of the Information Age; in 2010, the magazine chose him as the most influential person.[8] *Fast Company* selected Facebook as the most innovative company of all in 2010 while *Glassdoor* indicated that employees identified the firm as the best place to work in both 2011 and 2013. Zuckerberg currently has an employee approval rating of 97 percent.[9] Mentors such as Apple's Steve Jobs and Netscape's CFO Peter Currie were serving as mentors for Zuckerberg regarding issues such as developing and using financing strategies and creating management teams.[10]

Expanding

Acquisitions have played a significant role in Facebook's success. Beginning in 2008 with ConnectU, Facebook has forged relationships with many influential companies over the years. The firm uses acquisitions to add products and technologies; but most importantly, to gain access to valuable human capital. Zuckerberg once elaborated on Facebook's acquisition strategy saying, "We have not once bought a company for the company. We buy companies to get excellent people."[11]

From 2008 to April 2013, Facebook acquired over 30 companies. The majority of these companies were never intended to survive as independent businesses. Facebook uses the acquired employees to improve Facebook capabilities and develop new businesses. It acquired companies such as Rel8tion, Beluga, Snaptu, Chai Labs, and ConnectU, as shown in Exhibit 1. Each acquired business brought knowledge to Facebook in a strategic area of weakness.

Exhibit 1 Acquisitions

Acquisition Date	Company	Business
23 Aug 2005	Facebook.com	AboutFace
19 Jul 2007	Parakey	Offline applications/ Web OS
23 Jun 2008	ConnectU	Social networking
10 Aug 2009	FriendFeed	Social networking aggregator
19 Feb 2010	Octazen	Contact importer
2 Mar 2010	Divvyshot	Photo management
13 May 2010	Friendster patents	Intellectual property
26 May 2010	ShareGrove	Private conversations/ Forums
8 Jul 2010	Nextstop	Travel recommendations
15 Aug 2010	Chai Labs	Internet applications
20 Aug 2010	Hot Potato	Check-ins/Status updates
29 Oct 2010	Drop.io	File hosting/sharing
15 Nov 2010	FB.com domain	American Farm Bureau Federation
25 Jan 2011	Relation	Mobile advertising
2 Mar 2011	Beluga	Group messaging
20 Mar 2011	Snaptu	Mobile app developer
24 Mar 2011	RecRec	ComputerVision
27 Apr 2011	DayTum	Information graphics
9 Jun 2011	Sofa	Software design
9 Jun 2011	MailRank	Email prioritization
2 Aug 2011	Push Pop Press	Digital publishing
10 Oct 2011	Friend.ly	Social casual Q&A service app
8 Nov 2011	Strobe	HTML 5 mobile apps, SproutCore
2 Dec 2011	Gowalla	Location based service
9 Apr 2012	Instagram	Photo sharing
13 Apr 2012	Tagtile	Customer loyalty app
5 May 2012	Glancee	Social discovery platform
15 May 2012	Lightbox.com	Photo sharing
21 May 2012	Karma	Social gifting
18 Jun 2012	Face.com	Face recognition platform
14 Jul 2012	Spool	Mobile bookmarking and sharing content
20 Jul 2012	Acrylic Software	RSS app "Pulp" and secure database app
24 Aug 2012	Threadsy	Social aggregator
28 Feb 2013	Atlas	Atlas advertiser suite
14 Mar 2013	Hot Studio	Design agency

Source: http://en.wikipedia.org/wiki/List_of_mergers_and_acquisitions_by_ Facebook

For example, in August 2009, Facebook acquired a news feed company called FriendFeed. Before the acquisition, Facebook's news feed required users to refresh the data manually and user posts that received comments did not move up to the beginning of the news feed. With the acquisition, Facebook leveraged FriendFeed's superior technology into the Facebook platform. However, the key to this and to the majority of Facebook's acquisitions was the knowledge and experience gained from the human capital that arrived with the acquisition. In the case of FriendFeed, Facebook gained four key employees that had previously played a major role in launching Google maps and Gmail as Google employees before starting FriendFeed.[12] The talent and experience of these talented individuals was the foundation for enhancing Facebook's ability to provide this type of functionality for its users.

In 2010, Facebook formed a strategic partnership with Zynga, one of the largest and most successful providers of web-based social games.[13] This partnership allowed Facebook to enter into the promising online gaming space while simultaneously attracting a younger user base. In return for helping Facebook, Facebook stated that it would help Zynga reach specific monthly growth targets and would give Zynga a portion of the revenues from ads placed on its game pages. In return, Facebook required that Zynga not launch its games on any other social platform.[14]

In March 2011, Facebook acquired Snaptu. Snaptu provides application software for services such as Facebook, Twitter, and LinkedIn that allows these services to be featured on phones. Snaptu's employees also became a part of Facebook.[15]

In 2012, Facebook faced competition in a major business unit: photo sharing. Instagram, a popular photo sharing application on iPhones, was gaining popularity and planning to launch an Android version. With analysts speculating it could rival Facebook in photo sharing,[16] Facebook evaluated the competitor and decided to complete a $1 billion dollar acquisition of Instagram. This acquisition, completed in September 2012, allowed Facebook and Instagram to share activities and core competencies and created additional value for users. It also helped strengthen Facebook's competitive advantage in photo sharing by gaining market power and economies of scope. The sharing of intangible and tangible resources between the two business units also created value for end users and helped strengthen Facebook's presence on mobile devices. Facebook's VP of Engineering,

Mike Schroepfer, explained the reasoning behind this acquisition:

So many of us at Facebook love using Instagram to share moments with our friends…and for so many people, sharing photos with friends is an important part of the Facebook experience. That's why we're so excited to bring Instagram to Facebook and see what we can create together.[17]

Facebook has since made Instagram available to all smart phones. Unlike its other acquisitions, the Instagram acquisition was the first major acquisition that involved the purchase of a product with already engaged users. This acquisition was also different in that Facebook allowed Instagram to operate as a standalone service and not incorporate into the Facebook mobile experience. Instagram benefited from the strong engineering team and infrastructure at Facebook and brought reciprocal experience by utilizing the seamless benefit of the Instagram mobile experience.[18] As of February 2013, Instagram had over 100 million Monthly Active Users (MAUs).[19]

Following the Instagram acquisition, Facebook acquired several additional companies including Spool, Acrylic Software, and Threadsy. In the case of Spool, which offered a mobile bookmarking service, Facebook decided to discontinue the product offering. However, Facebook will be utilizing Spool's five programmers to enhance the Facebook mobile experience.[20]

Facebook utilizes partnerships to help strengthen and enhance product offerings to customers. These strategic partnerships broaden and expand the Facebook experience and provide the firm's users with an engaging and complete product. In September 2011, Facebook chose to form partnerships with media companies Netflix and Spotify, thus allowing users to update their news feeds with information about what they were currently doing. Users could now seamlessly notify their connections about what they were listening to or watching.[21] In 2013, Facebook enhanced its partnership with Trend Micro, a global cloud security leader, and Rovi, an information database of movies, TV shows, and celebrities that can be tied to Facebook user profiles.[22] Facebook's partnership with Rovi will allow advertisers to advertise to specific customers groups that they want to target.[23] These strategic partnerships add value to the Facebook experience, which increases Daily Active Users (DAUs) and MAUs, leading to increased revenue.

Going Public

Facebook filed for its initial public offering on February 1, 2012. As detailed in the filing, Zuckerberg would retain a 22 percent ownership share and would own 57 percent of the voting shares. The shares were valued at $38/share, valuing the company at $104 billion, the largest valuation to date for a newly public company. One day before the IPO, Facebook announced it would sell 25 percent more shares than originally planned, raising the IPO to $16 billion. Trading began on May 18, 2012 at a price of $42.05; but by the end of the week, the stock had dropped 16.5 percent to $31.91. In less than four months, the price had declined to $17.55 and as of April 16, 2013, the share price was $26.92, representing one of the most disappointing IPOs in recent history.[24] More recently, Facebook's market cap exceeded $64 billion and showed a monthly growth rate around 2 percent.[25]

Inside Facebook

"Give people the power to share and make the world more open and connected." Facebook Mission Statement.[26]

Mission

After evolving for over four years from its original mission to "connect people through social networks at colleges," Facebook has transferred its focus from simply connecting college students to that of empowering all users. Facebook impacts the world by expanding the global user community, providing the most compelling user experience to increase user engagement, improving advertisement opportunities for businesses, creating engaging and easy-to-access mobile products, and developing a scalable infrastructure.[27] In a 2009 interview with *Forbes*, Mark Zuckerberg stated his vision in regard to the impact Facebook could have on the world:

Building a good economic engine is what allows all these other platform companies and advertisers and other partners to exist, and be a part of this ecosystem. Ultimately, what being … a company means to me, is … not being just that—building something that actually makes a really big change in the world.[28]

Although Facebook's scope has expanded, its purpose remains the same: giving people a way to share information in an easy and exciting way. Users are invited to share their photos, hobbies, educational backgrounds, friends, and just about every other piece of information about themselves. With the encryption of a powerful search engine, a continuously increasing number of companies, groups, and individuals establish connections within seconds.

Culture

Facebook itself operates under a developer-centered culture where the focus is less on the flashy features of a new product and more on the logistics behind products. Yee Lee provides a very important message in his article, "How Facebook Ships Code."[29]

Engineers [at Facebook] generally want to work on infrastructure, scalability, and "hard problems" — that's where all the prestige is. It can be hard to get engineers excited about working on front-end projects and user interfaces. This is the opposite of what you find in some consumer businesses where everyone wants to work on stuff that customers touch so you can point to a particular user experience and say, "I built that." At Facebook, the back-end stuff like news feed algorithms, ad-targeting algorithms, memcache optimizations, etc., are the juicy projects that engineers want.

These developers are referred to as the "offensive line" as they are the backbone of the Facebook team. One of the key aspects that sets Facebook apart is its celebration of its "offensive line." It ensures that the difficult jobs, those whose effects are less noticeable for the end user, are the ones that people at Facebook are most excited about doing. These jobs are the most highly respected occupations at Facebook and because of this, Facebook has managed to create a culture that would be challenging to duplicate or imitate.

Core Themes

An employee of Facebook for over three years, who previously worked for Google, cited four core themes at Facebook that countless others have echoed and confirmed.[30] The first is *Autonomy and Responsibility*, which enables all employees to govern their own work, resulting in a sense of ownership and pride. The second theme is *Focus on Impact*, which entitles developers and engineers to create whatever they want in their mission to have a positive effect on end users. As Facebook accumulated a significant user base, it focused on scaling horizontally, moving fast, and finding the right people. Facebook placed its engineers on small, independent teams and allowed them to make choices that had major impacts on the direction of their respective product lines. For example, historically, only three engineers have run Facebook's photo sharing service – the largest on the Internet. This type of control given to employees makes coming to work exciting and has created a culture at Facebook where changes designed to meet customers' needs can be quickly made.[31] The next theme is *Facebook is Run by Hackers*. What this tongue-in-cheek theme implies is that employees enjoy the ability to innovate and create new products based on extensive research into every small detail. The final theme is *Growth and Coaching*. A dominant culture that has evolved is described as "no fear of failure." This honors the concept that triumphs come out of failures, and this atmosphere plays a huge part in Facebook's success. Additionally, coaching allows for a constant embedding of continuous progression. With these motivations suggested by the four core themes, the source of much of Facebook's enthusiasm is obvious.

Outside Facebook

Social Networking

One of the most innovative creations in the twenty-first century is social networks. Connecting the world through schools, families, businesses, photos, and just about every other piece of information, social networks thrive on people sharing their life stories. In the last ten years, the most important networks have been Facebook, MySpace, Twitter, and LinkedIn, with several additional sites surfacing within the last few years. Facebook in particular is considered a disruptive innovation that has interfered with search engines such as Google and Yahoo!

Social networking sites serve three main purposes in addition to connecting people: advertising, employee and idea screening, and application development and gaming.

In September 2012, Facebook generated over $1 billion per quarter from advertising revenue. Facebook's advertisers range from Ford Motor Company and McDonald's to Dell and Nike. Procter & Gamble estimates that it generates $500 million in sales from Facebook advertisements. Over 3,800 Wal-Mart stores have their own Facebook page.[32]

These sites also provide a platform for employers to monitor current employees as well as find and screen possible new employees. With this screening, new information may lead to new social capital for a firm. Access to new ideas via social networking is critical to the innovation process. This process allows for a type of integration among suppliers and buyers that is difficult to find elsewhere.[33]

The last major source of innovative activity involves application, software, and gaming developers. Creations for Facebook apps and electronic platforms and operating systems have become especially popular. Zynga, a game development firm, developed the highest grossing online game on Facebook, FarmVille, and represented 12 percent of Facebook's total revenues.[34] Whether acting

as a hosting service, development platform, employment locater, or an innovation hub, "social networks" is a fascinating innovation with seemingly unlimited potential to identify and serve customers' needs.

The Industry

Facebook is influenced by several factors, most notably its customers. Customers can be divided into two categories: users and advertisers.

Users have tremendous power over Facebook as they constantly demand innovation and Facebook carefully listens to their needs, ever mindful that switching costs to another social network are relatively nonexistent. With every move Facebook makes, users send a signal—sometimes positive and sometimes negative. Small incremental innovations, such as tweaking the position of a box, may be seen as a positive or inconsequential change to users. Larger radical innovations, such as the creation of a personal "timeline" and reformatting an entire profile page, often cause the users to divide into two categories: those who appreciate the alteration and those who do not.

While user influence is high, the opposite is seen with advertisers. At first glance, one might conclude that advertiser power is high because Facebook depends on its advertisers for profit. This, however, is quite the contrary. Because Facebook supplies a lucrative customer base and despite speculation around the measurable impact of advertising on Facebook, the power held by advertisers is actually low. Placing advertisements on Facebook is incredibly targeted and effective. The COO of Facebook, Sheryl Sandberg, revealed that of the 60 studies conducted by Facebook in 2012 on how its advertisements impacted offline and online sales, 70 percent showed a ROI of better than three times, and 49 percent showed a ROI of better than five times. This large ROI for companies comes from Facebook's ability to target a narrow field of customers. For example, Facebook claims it can reach an 18- to 28-year-old woman with 90 percent accuracy. This compares to the industry average of approximately 35 percent.[35]

In April 2013, Facebook was testing an advertising feature that lets advertisers and agencies use Facebook Exchange (FBX) to take into account the browsing behaviors of Facebook users outside of Facebook.[36] This feature will provide advertisers the opportunity to display advertisements to users that have already browsed their sites or access information about the products or services it offers.[37] These advertisers will be able to describe a typical customer to Facebook and then utilize FBX to find those customers. This will significantly increase the ability of advertisers to interact directly with their most valuable customers. In 2012, Facebook brought in almost $5 billion in advertising revenue, accounting for 84 percent of total Facebook revenue.[38] This reliance on advertising revenue requires Facebook to ensure that advertisements are social, relevant, and well integrated with other Facebook content.[39]

There were over 6.8 billion mobile subscriptions worldwide at the end of 2012 and that number is expected to continue to grow.[40] Mobile platforms have quickly become one of the fastest growing segments of advertising. According to Gartner Research, spending in this space would likely reach $11.4 billion in 2013.[41] Recently, Facebook chose to allocate a large amount of its R&D to mobile products. Advertisers pay a premium to advertise to mobile users, which makes up for the lower volume of advertisements. Facebook's new approach to offering services to mobile devices involves its recent launch of Facebook Home. Facebook wants to interact with users continually throughout the day as they access their mobile devices. Facebook believes it can earn a significant amount of revenue by strategically placing advertisements that target specific mobile users. Home takes the Facebook application that many mobile phone users have installed and completely integrates it with the user interface of the phone. It was initially released on April 12, 2013 and will be preloaded on a new HTC smartphone.[42]

While some firms such as P&G claim results, others such as Coca-Cola are skeptical. With its 62 million followers on Facebook, Coca-Cola has publicly questioned Facebook's quantifiable effects on sales.[43]

Competitors

Facebook competes against direct competitors as well as others with the ability to attract its customers' "mindshare."[44] Twitter is an example of a direct Facebook competitor while Google examples one of Facebook's indirect competitors. The industry is growing rapidly, imitation costs are low, and it is difficult for firms to protect their competitive advantages for an extended period. In addition to Facebook, there are four main players in the social media industry: Google Plus, MySpace, LinkedIn, and Twitter. Comparisons of Facebook relative to a few of its competitors appear in Exhibit 2.

Google Plus
Google Plus, aggressively pushed by chief executive Larry Page, is a new social network leveraging the existing Google infrastructure to compete with Facebook.

Exhibit 2 Competitor* Comparisons (as of December 31, 2012)

	Google	LinkedIn	Facebook
Revenue	50.18B	972.31M	5.09B
Quarterly Revenue Growth	36.2%	81.0%	40.1%
Gross Profit	29.54B	846.79M	3.72B
EBITDA	16.28B	125.51M	1.19B
Net Income Available to Common Shareholders	10.79B	21.61M	32.0M
Market Cap	257.98B	19.63B	63.42B
Profit Margin	21.4%	2.2%	1.0%
Operating Margin	26.7%	5.9%	10.6%
Return on Assets	10.1%	3.2%	3.1%
Return on Equity	16.6%	2.8%	0.6%
Total Cash	48.09B	749.55M	9.63B
Total Debt	7.21B	0	2.36B
Current Ratio	4	2	11
Operating Cash Flow	16.62B	267.07M	1.61B

*As a private company, financial data for Twitter is not publicly available.

Source: Yahoo! Finance. http://finance.yahoo.com/

With nearly 100 million users utilizing various accounts and products such as email, profiles, and gaming, Google represents Facebook's largest competitor and seemingly has the capability to attract a substantial share of the social networking market. Google maintains a significant level of awareness among corporate users due to its popular Gmail service. It has begun to capitalize on this advantage by creating Google Plus for business. This service not only allows companies to establish their own social networking presence on Google Plus, but also integrates with Google's many features such as Google Search and Google Ads.[45] To expedite its growth and use, Google recently required all of its users to sign up for Google Plus. Competitors within the dynamic social networking space are rushing to create ways to differentiate themselves and increase their average revenue per user (ARPU). While Facebook accounted for 46 percent of logins for social media in recent times, the percentage of logins through Google is increasing.[46]

Twitter
This online "micro blogging" service was established in 2006 by Jack Dorsey. With over 200 million users and 1.6 billion "tweets" per day, Twitter has become one of the most iconic and visited websites on the Internet.[47]

The estimate of the firm's advertising revenues for 2013 was $583 million with the projection for 2014 being that this figure would double, surpassing $1 billion. The largest reason for growth is mobile ad revenues. Robert Hof from *Forbes* comments, "Unlike some leading online advertising companies such as Google and Facebook, which have been struggling to contend with lower mobile ad prices that have depressed their growth, Twitter has found mobile has been its key moneymaker."[48] Its quick and simple posts make mobile ads an ideal location and advertisers are flocking to exploit this channel.

MySpace

MySpace, engineered by Chris DeWolfe, implemented a strategy very similar to Facebook in its origination. This firm initially targeted the same audience as Facebook, had enormous capabilities, and was purchased by News Corporation, a large media corporation with professional management to lead its unique resources. Started in 2003, the site pioneered social networking and once boasted more users than any other social media site. However, its rise to popularity in the teenage and young adult category from 2005-2008 plummeted in 2009. Once a music-centered social platform, with the advent of Facebook, MySpace chose to reposition itself as a "social entertainment destination" and ultimately, alienated many of its followers.[49] While Facebook and other competitors focused on introducing a platform where developers could co-design, MySpace chose to build everything in-house. Although it designed many features, MySpace neglected to deepen its differentiating factors and in the end, other networks capitalized on this opportunity.[50]

LinkedIn

LinkedIn has differentiated itself by targeting working and employment seeking professionals. Used as a site to connect with future employers and employees, LinkedIn reports more than 200 million users in over 200 countries.[51] Founded by Reid Hoffman and managed by CEO Jeff Weiner, a previous Yahoo! executive, the firm has successfully managed to segment customers and compete alongside Facebook. LinkedIn's success stems from its creation of "connections" that allow people to maintain and discover relationships between many people and companies. The company went public in 2011, priced at $45/share. The value of a share of the firm's stock increased to just under $180 by mid-2013. It acquired several companies such as Rapportive and SlideShare, alongside several patents from additional companies.[52] With a focus on trust building and creation, LinkedIn

appears to have positioned itself to compete successfully with Facebook.

Out-Innovating the Competition

In comparison to its more profitable competitors who charge for their services such as LinkedIn, Facebook essentially gives away its social networking features at no cost. Creating a strategic subscription model is becoming the norm within the Internet services industry. While maintaining basic access and services with no fee, LinkedIn grants extra features to those who value its networking and job-search functionalities enough to pay a monthly fee. Other online services have begun offering the basics of their services for free and charging fees for premium features. The ability of subscription-based firms such as Netflix, Amazon Prime, and Dropbox Pro to attract lucrative users has started to attract investors. A recent study aimed at understanding the extent to which consumers value free online services calculated the amount customers would be willing to pay for different services. The results indicated that respondents between the ages of 23-33 maintain a significant level of willingness to pay for what have customarily been free services (see Exhibit 3).[53] With Google Search, Gmail, Wikipedia, and then Facebook topping the charts, this study revealed that subscription-based models have a promising future.

Strategic Leaders

Facebook's leaders have played a major role in making the company what it is today – the largest social network in the world.[54] Each leader has added essential values in creating a unique company. Facebook's team is not a result of luck; it is the result of Mark Zuckerberg's efforts to hire the best and most knowledgeable people in the industry.[55]

For Facebook, a major priority is to bring people on board who fit the culture and values of the company and who have the right attitude and skills to make strategic decisions. Individuals with visionary qualities help Facebook form and implement strategies for achieving strategic competitiveness and above average returns. Since 2008, Zuckerberg has hired a team capable of taking Facebook's growth to the next level. A list of key personnel at Facebook appears in Exhibit 4.

Mark Zuckerberg, Chairman of the Board and CEO

Mark Zuckerberg is the Chairman of the Board and CEO of Facebook Inc. He has been CEO since 2004 and Chairman of the Board since the company went public in 2012.[56]

Exhibit 3 Willingness to Pay for Services

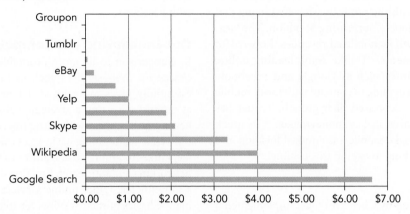

Source: Galston, E. (10 Mar 2013). *Are we in a subscription bubble?* Tech Crunch. http://techcrunch.com/2013/03/10/are-we-in-a-subscription-bubble/

Exhibit 4 Key Personnel

FOUNDERS	Mark Zuckerberg	Dustin Moskovitz	Eduardo Saverin	Chris Hughes	Andrew McCollum
BOARD	Mark Zuckerberg	Jim Breyer	Peter Thiel	Sheryl Sandberg	Mark Andreessen
	Erskine Bowles	Susan Desmond	Don Graham	Reed Hastings	
EXECUTIVE OFFICERS	Mark Zuckerberg Chairman & CEO		Sheryl Sandberg COO	David Ebersman CFO	Mike Schroepfer CTO

Wikipedia. *Facebook*. Accessed 20 May 2013. http://en.wikipedia.org/wiki/Facebook

As noted earlier, Zuckerberg's ability to innovate began at a young age and culminated with the inception of Facebook. Parts of the media sometimes paint an unattractive picture of Zuckerberg with respect to some of his actions over the years; however, his actions do not appear to support the media's occasional assertions related to behavior.[57] Indeed, Zuckerberg has been involved in various acts of charity and joined a new political organization that promotes venture and immigration reforms.[58]

David Ebersman, Chief Financial Officer

David Ebersman has been with Facebook since 2009. He started his career at Oppenheimer & Co., Inc. in 1991 where he worked as a research analyst. He later joined Genentech, a biomedical firm, from 1994 to 2009 where he had a brilliant career that ultimately contributed to his position as CFO of Facebook. Across Wall Street, investors consider him a truthful professional who works for the best interests of investors. Proof of this fact is the way he administered the takeover of Genentech by Roche, working tirelessly to generate the most value for Genentech's shareholders during the transaction. The value that Ebersman brings to Facebook is his expertise regarding public companies and his strong operational background. His

presence has resulted in a greater level of confidence for Facebook's team and its shareholders.[59]

Sheryl Sandberg, Chief Operating Officer

Sheryl Sandberg has been a very influential leader at Facebook since 2008. After graduating summa cum laude from Harvard University with an A.B. in Economics, Sandberg joined the World Bank to work on health projects in India.[60] After earning her MBA (also from Harvard), she held positions at McKinsey & Company, the U.S. Department of Treasury, and, most recently, Google. At Google, Sandberg is the VP of Global Online sales and Operations and was involved in the launch of Google's philanthropic arm, Google .org. As part of Facebook's top management team, her knowledge of international markets and finance is valuable as Facebook forms and implements its international strategy.

Theodore Ullyot, VP and General Counsel

Theodore Ullyot also started with Facebook in 2008. His academic background includes an A.B. in History from Harvard University and a J.D. from the University of Chicago.[61] Before Facebook, he was a partner at Kirkland & Ellis LLP where he focused on telecommunications and appellate law. Ullyot joined America Online and remained through its merger with Time Warner, ultimately becoming the Senior VP and general counsel for AOL Time Warner Europe. In January 2003, Ullyot began a two-year stint in the White House as associate counsel and deputy assistant to President George W. Bush and chief of staff to U.S. Attorney General Alberto R. Gonzales.[62] Ullyot's experience in government as well as public and private companies coupled with his telecommunications expertise and high-level connections make him a perfect fit for Facebook. Ullyot's current responsibilities include examining and addressing the rising concerns about data privacy among Facebook users.

Financial Results

In 2012, Facebook generated over $5 billion, mostly from advertising (Exhibit 5). Facebook relies heavily on advertising to generate positive cash flows. From 2010 to 2011, and 2011 to 2012, revenue increased 74 percent and 59 percent, respectively. This slowing of revenue growth is a concern for Facebook that must be accounted for and improved in order to continue to be a market leader in connecting advertisers to consumers. Net income from 2010 to 2011 increased 65 percent. However, from 2011 to 2012, net income decreased by a staggering 95 percent to only $53 million. This substantial reduction in income

Exhibit 5 Income Statement (summarized)

In Millions, except Per Share data, unless otherwise specified	12 Months Ended			% Change from 2010	% Change from 2011
	Dec. 31, 2012	Dec. 31, 2011	Dec. 31, 2010		
Revenue	$5,089	$3,711	$1,974	88%	37%
Costs and expenses:					
Cost of revenue	1,364	860	493	74%	59%
Research and development	1,399	388	144	169%	261%
Marketing and sales	896	393	167	135%	128%
General and administrative	892	314	138	128%	184%
Total costs and expenses	4,551	1,955	942	108%	133%
Income from operations	538	1,756	1,032	70%	−69%
Interest and other income (expense), net:					
Interest expense	−51	−42	−22	91%	21%
Other income (expense), net	7	−19	−2		
Income before provision for income taxes	494	1,695	1,008	68%	−71%
Provision for income taxes	441	695	402	73%	−37%
Net income	53	1,000	606	65%	−95%
Less: Net income attributable to participating securities	21	332	234	42%	−94%
Net income attributable to common stockholders	32	668	372	80%	−95%
Earnings per share attributable to Class A & B common stockholders:					
Basic	$0.02	$0.52	$0.34		
Diluted	$0.01	$0.46	$0.28		
Weighted avg. shares used to compute earnings per share attributable to Class A & B common stockholders:					
Basic	2,006	1,294	1,107		
Diluted	2,166	1,508	1,414		

Source: U.S. Securities and Exchange Commission. *Facebook Inc.* http://www.sec.gov/cgi-bin/viewer?action=view&cik=1326801&accession_number=0001326801-13-000003&xbrl_type=v#

was due to a 133 percent increase in total costs and expenses. Cash flows from operations and financing have been increasing each year to support cash out-flows used to purchase PPE and marketable securities (Exhibit 6). Facebook continues to emphasize R&D and, in 2012, the percentage spent on R&D increased by 261 percent, nearly $1.4 billion. Facebook hopes significant expenditures in 2012 will result in addi-tional revenue opportunities in the future. Another financial move occurred in preparation for its IPO when Facebook tried to eliminate short- and long-term debt (Exhibit 7).

Strategic Challenges

On January 30, 2013, Facebook announced that it had surpassed several milestones. Not only did the firm exceed 1.06 billion MAUs, it also tallied over 680 million monthly active *mobile* users[63] (Exhibit 8). However, the firm faces several unique challenges.

Monetizing Facebook's User Base

Facebook boasts an enormous user base, but finding a way to monetize its users is a significant challenge. User growth will likely not continue at the impressive rates it has seen in the past, which is why the firm needs to focus on long-term revenue growth. Social media monitors, such as SocialBakers, have reported concerns that Facebook's domestic growth has peaked. As a result, Facebook's ability to tie more revenue-generating ideas into the long-term strategy will be essential.

Facebook currently generates most of its revenue through two different methods: advertisements and roy-alties from third-party software developers.[64] As previ-ously discussed, advertising is the firm's primary source of revenue. Because of this, the advertisements on the site need to be effective enough to ensure advertiser satisfaction. Facebook posted a 37 percent increase in revenue from 2011 to 2012, but analysts are still worried. A closer look at the increase reveals that the primary driver behind the increase was a three percent advertise-ment price increase coupled with a 32 percent increase in the number of advertisements.[65] Put simply, Facebook's increase in revenue is merely a reflection of its increas-ing user base and does not appear to be a result of the firm's efforts to innovate. In a post-IPO world, investors want to see evidence that Facebook is working hard to create new avenues for revenue creation and bottom-line growth.

Exhibit 6 Consolidated Statements of Cash Flow (summarized)

(USD $)	12 Months Ended		
In Millions, unless otherwise specified Cash flows from operating activities	Dec. 31, 2012	Dec. 31, 2011	Dec. 31, 2010
Net income	$53	$1,000	$606
Adjustments to reconcile net income to net cash provided by operating activities:			
Depreciation and amortization	649	323	139
Loss on write-off of equipment	15	4	3
Share-based compensation	1,572	217	20
Deferred income taxes	−186	−30	23
Tax benefit from share-based award activity	1,033	433	115
Excess tax benefit from share-based award activity	−1,033	−433	−115
Changes in assets and liabilities:			
Accounts receivable	−170	−174	−209
Income tax refundable	−451	0	0
Prepaid expenses and other current assets	−14	−24	−38
Other assets	2	−5	−6
Accounts payable	1	6	12
Platform partners payable	−2	96	75
Accrued expenses and other current liabilities	160	37	20
Deferred revenue and deposits	−60	49	37
Other liabilities	43	50	16
Net cash provided by operating activities	1,612	1,549	698
Cash flows from investing activities			
Purchases of property and equipment	−1,235	−606	−293
Purchases of marketable securities	−10,307	−3,025	0
Sales of marketable securities	2,100	113	0
Maturities of marketable securities	3,333	516	0

(Continued)

Exhibit 6 Continued Consolidated Statements of Cash Flow (summarized)

(USD $)	12 Months Ended		
In Millions, unless otherwise specified Cash flows from operating activities	**Dec. 31, 2012**	**Dec. 31, 2011**	**Dec. 31, 2010**
Investments in non-marketable equity securities	−2	−3	0
Acquisitions of business-es, net of cash acquired, and purchases of intan-gible and other assets	−911	−24	−22
Change in restricted cash and deposits	−2	6	−9
Net cash used in investing activities	**−7,024**	**−3,023**	**−324**
Cash flows from financing activities			
Net proceeds from issu-ance of common stock	6,760	998	500
Taxes paid related to net share settlement of equity awards	−2,862	0	0
Proceeds from exercise of stock options	17	28	6
Proceeds from long-term debt, net of issuance cost	1,496	0	250
Repayments of long-term debt	0	−250	0
Proceeds from sale and lease-back transactions	205	170	0
Principal payments on capital lease obligations	−366	−181	−90
Excess tax benefit from share-based award activity	1,033	433	115
Net cash provided by financing activities	**6,283**	**1,198**	**781**
Effect of exchange rate changes on cash and cash equivalents	1	3	−3
Net increase (decrease) in cash and cash equivalents	872	−273	1,152
Cash and cash equivalents at beginning of period	1,512	1,785	633
Cash and cash equiva-lents at end of period	**2,384**	**1,512**	**1,785**

Source: U.S. Securities and Exchange Commission. *Facebook Inc.* http://www.sec.gov/cgi-bin/viewer?action=view&cik=1326801&accession_number=0001326801-13-000003&xbrl_type=v#

Exhibit 7 Consolidated Balance Sheets

(USD $)	Dec. 31, 2012	Dec. 31, 2011
In Millions, unless otherwise specified		
Current assets:		
Cash and cash equivalents	$2,384	$1,512
Marketable securities	7,242	2,396
Accounts receivable, net of allowances for doubtful accounts of $22 and $17 as of December 31, 2012 and 2011, respectively	719	547
Income tax refundable	451	0
Prepaid expenses and other current assets	471	149
Total current assets	**11,267**	**4,604**
Property and equipment, net	2,391	1,475
Goodwill and intangible assets, net	1,388	162
Other assets	57	90
Total assets	**15,103**	**6,331**
Current liabilities:		
Accounts payable	65	63
Platform partners payable	169	171
Accrued expenses and other current liabilities	423	296
Deferred revenue and deposits	30	90
Current portion of capital lease obligations	365	279
Total current liabilities	**1,052**	**899**
Capital lease obligations, less current portion	491	398
Long-term debt	1,500	0
Other liabilities	305	135
Total liabilities	**3,348**	**1,432**
Commitments and contingencies		
Stockholders' equity:		
Convertible preferred stock	0	615
Common stock value	0	0
Additional paid-in capital	10,094	2,684
Accumulated other com-prehensive income (loss)	2	−6
Retained earnings	1,659	1,606
Total stockholders' equity	**11,755**	**4,899**
Total liabilities and stockholders' equity	**$15,103**	**$6,331**

Source: U.S. Securities and Exchange Commission. *Facebook Inc.* http://www.sec.gov/cgi-bin/viewer?action=view&cik=1326801&accession_number=0001326801-13-000003&xbrl_type=v#

Exhibit 8 Mobile Monthly Active Users (in millions)

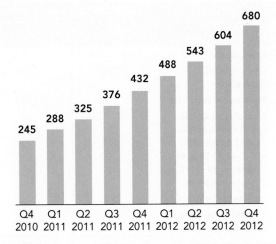

| Q4 2010 | Q1 2011 | Q2 2011 | Q3 2011 | Q4 2011 | Q1 2012 | Q2 2012 | Q3 2012 | Q4 2012 |
| 245 | 288 | 325 | 376 | 432 | 488 | 543 | 604 | 680 |

Source: MarketingCharts staff. (31 Jan 2013). *Facebook's Mobile User Base.*
Marketing Charts. http://www.marketingcharts.com/wp/direct/facebooks-
mobile-user-base-and-share-of-ad-revenues-keeps-growing-26610/

Future of Facebook

Although Facebook had a successful fiscal year in 2012, many analysts believe the company's level of meaningful growth is beginning to plateau. Further, Facebook's users, advertisers, and investors are anxious for the firm to develop more sustainable competitive advantages. With the introduction of Facebook Home, FBX, and Instagram, the firm has started to prove that it is capable of becoming much more than a basic social networking platform. Mark Zuckerberg and his team of strategic leaders have decided to invest a significant amount of R&D dollars to create additional value for customers. What financial results will Facebook generate in the years to come? Can Facebook find ways to generate value for demanding customers across time? How does the firm need to position itself relative to competitors to enhance its potential to earn above-average returns? Dealing with questions such as these and perhaps a host of others will affect Facebook's future.

NOTES

1. Vargas, J. A. (20 Sep 2010). *The Face of Facebook.* The New Yorker. http://www.newyorker.com/reporting/2010/09/20/100920fa_fact_vargas

2. Moore, D. (21 Apr 2003). *Machine Learning and MP3s.* Slashdot. http://news.slashdot.org/story/03/04/21/110236/machine-learning-and-mp3s

3. Grynbaum, M. M. (10 Jun 2004). *Mark E. Zuckerberg '06: The whiz behind thefacebook.com.* The Harvard Crimson. http://www.thecrimson.com/article/2004/6/10/mark-e-zuckerberg-06-the-whiz/

4. Grimland, G. (5 Oct 2009). *Facebook founder's roommate recounts creation of Internet giant.* Haaretz. http://www.haaretz.com/news/facebook-founder-s-roommate-recounts-creation-of-internet-giant-1.275748

5. Stone, B. (26 Jun 2008). *Judge Ends Facebook's Feud With ConnectU.* New York Times blog. http://bits.blogs.nytimes.com/2008/06/26/judge-ends-facebooks-feud-with-connectu/

6. Sutter, J. D. (20 Sep 2010). *Why Facebook is blue – six facts about Mark Zuckerberg.* CNN. http://www.cnn.com/2010/TECH/social.media/09/20/zuckerberg.facebook.list/index.html

7. Fowler, G. A. (4 Oct 2012). *Facebook Tops Billion-User Mark.* The Wall Street Journal (Dow Jones). http://online.wsj.com/article/SB100008723963900443635404578036164027386112.html

8. Deutschman, A., Newcomb, P., Siklos, R., McDonald, D. & Flint, J. (Oct 2010). *The Vanity Fair 100.* Vanity Fair.

http://www.vanityfair.com/business/features/2010/10/the-vf-100-201010

9. Glassdoor.com. (23 Apr 2013). *Facebook.* http://www.glassdoor.com/facebook

10. MacMillan, R. (1 Apr 2009). *Yu, Zuckerberg and the Facebook fallout.* Reuters. http://blogs.reuters.com/mediafile/2009/04/01/yu-zuckerberg-and-the-facebook-fallout/

11. Business Insider Interview. *Why Facebook Buys Startups.* http://www.youtube.com/watch?v=OlBDyltD0Ak

12. Kincaid, J. (20 Aug 2009). *Facebook Acquires FriendFeed.* Tech Crunch. http://techcrunch.com/2009/08/10/facebook-acquires-friendfeed/

13. Rao, L. (18 May 2010). *Facebook and Zynga enter into 5 year partnership. Expand use of Facebook credits.* Tech Crunch. http://techcrunch.com/2010/05/18/facebook-and-zynga-enter-into-five-year-partnership-expand-use-of-facebook-credits/

14. Gannes, L. (18 Jul 2011). *Zynga and Facebook exclusivity goes far beyond credits.* All Things D. http://allthingsd.com/20110718/zynga-and-facebook-exclusivity-goes-far-beyond-credits/?mod=ATD_iphone

15. Wauters, R. (20 Mar 2011). *Confirmed: Facebook Acquires Snaptu (For An Estimated $60-$70 Million.* Tech Crunch. http://techcrunch.com/2011/03/20/facebook-reportedly-acquires-snaptu-for-an-estimated-60-70-million/

16. Malik, O. (9 Apr 2012). *Here is Why Facebook bought Instagram.* Gigaom. http://gigaom.com/2012/04/09/here-is-why-did-facebook-bought-instagram/

17. Geron, T. (6 Sep 2012). *Facebook officially closes Instagram deal.* Forbes. http://www.forbes.com/sites/tomiogeron/2012/09/06/facebook-officially-closes-instagram-deal/

18. Etherington, D. (6 Sep 2012). *Facebook Closes Instagram Acquisition, Instagram Announces 5B Photos Shared.* Tech Crunch. http://techcrunch.com/2012/09/06/facebook-closes-instagram-acquisition-instagram-announces-5-billion-photos-shared/

19. Mansell, L. (n.d.) *Instagram Hits Over 100M monthly active users.* Geeks Hut. http://www.geekshut.com/instagram-hits-100m-monthly-active-users/8930

20. Protalinski, E. (14 Jul 2012). *Facebook acquires mobile-bookmarking service Spool.* Cnet. http://news.cnet.com/8301-1023_3-57472471-93/facebook-acquires-mobile-bookmarking-service-spool/

21. Bilton, N. (22 Sep 2011). *Facebook Announces Media Partnerships at Conference.* Bits. http://bits.blogs.nytimes.com/2011/09/22/at-facebook-f8-user-growth-and-a-facebook-timeline/

22. PR Newswire. (10 Apr 2013). *Trend Micro Expands Facebook Partnership Globally Providing Users Protection For Their Digital Lives.* Dark Reading. http://www.darkreading.com/end-user/trend-micro-expands-facebook-partnership/240152697

23. Yeung, K. (16 Apr 2013). *Facebook Partners with Rovi to Bring More in-depth Movie and TV content info to User Profiles.* The Next Web. http://thenextweb.com/insider/2013/04/16/facebook-partners-with-rovi-to-bring-more-in-depth-movie-and-tv-content-info-to-user-profiles/

24. Womack, B. & Thomson, A. (21 May 2012). *Facebook falls below $38 IPO price in second day of trading*. Bloomberg. http://www.bloomberg.com/news/2012-05-21/facebook-shares-drop-below-ipo-price-in-german-trading.html

25. Nasdaq (Apr 2013). Facebook, Inc. Stock Quote & Summary Data.

26. Reagan, G. (Jul 2009). *The Evolution of Facebook's Mission Statement*. New York Observer. http://observer.com/2009/07/the-evolution-of-facebooks-mission-statement/

27. Facebook Inc. 10-K for the fiscal year ending Dec 31, 2012. http://www.sec.gov/Archives/edgar/data/1326801/000132680113000003/0001326801-13-000003-index.htm

28. Kirpatrick, D. (16 May 2012). *Mark Zuckerberg, Social Revolutionary*. Forbes. http://www.forbes.com/sites/techonomy/2012/05/16/mark-zuckerberg-social-revolutionary/

29. Chambers, K. (4 Mar 2013). *The Best-Kept Secret at Facebook? The Offensive Line*. FullContact. http://www.fullcontact.com/blog/facebook-offensive-line/

30. Keyani, P. (Aug 2011). *Reflecting on 3 Years at Facebook*. Facebook. https://www.facebook.com/note.php?note_id=415679363919

31. High Scalability. (2 Aug 2010). *7 Scaling Strategies Facebook Used to Grow to 500 Million Users*. http://highscalability.com/blog/2010/8/2/7-scaling-strategies-facebook-used-to-grow-to-500-million-us.html

32. Edwards, J. (Sep 2012). *Meet the 30 Biggest Advertisers on Facebook*. Business Insider. http://www.businessinsider.com/the-30-biggest-advertisers-on-facebook-2012-9?op=1

33. Remneland-Wikhamn, B., Bergquist, M. & Kuschel, J. (2011). *Open Innovation, Generativity and the Supplier as Peer*. EconPapers. http://econpapers.repec.org/article/wsiijimxx/v_3a15_3ay_3a2011_3ai_3a01_3ap_3a205-230.htm

34. Johansmeyer, T. (1 Feb 2012). *Facebook's Financials Revealed [FACEBOOK S-1]*. business2community. http://www.business2community.com/facebook/facebooks-financials-revealed-facebook-s-1-0127737

35. Boorstin, J. (1 Oct 2012). *Facebook's Sandberg Details company's strategy*. USA Today. http://www.usatoday.com/story/money/business/2012/10/01/cnbc-sandberg-interview/1606601/

36. Veroneau, M. (19 Jun 2012). *Facebook Exchange: What Should You Know?* Digital Compass. http://blog.microsecommerce.com/index.php/social-marketing/facebook-exchange-what-should-you-know/

37. Kerr, D. (10 Apr 2013). *Facebook boosts ad targeting with partner categories*. CNet. http://news.cnet.com/8301-1023_3-57579009-93/facebook-boosts-ad-targeting-with-partner-categories/

38. Van Grove, J. (23 Feb 2012). *Facebook's ad revenue will hit $5B in 2012, but growth rates have peaked*. VB/Social. http://venturebeat.com/2012/02/23/facebook-ad-revenue-growth/

39. Boyd, E. (2 Feb 2012). *What is Facebook's Business?* Fast Company. http://www.fastcompany.com/1813498/what-facebooks-business

40. Staff. (May 2013). *Global mobile statistics 2013*. mobiThinking. http://mobithinking.com/mobile-marketing-tools/latest-mobile-stats

41. ABC7 News. (30 Jan 2013). *Facebook shifts focus to mobile platforms*. http://abclocal.go.com/kgo/story?section=news/business&id=8974840

42. Seifert, D. (4 Apr 2013). *HTC and Facebook announce the First smartphone with AT&T, arriving Apr 12th for $99.99*. The Verge. http://www.theverge.com/2013/4/4/4182302/htc-and-facebook-announce-the-first-smartphone

43. Hill, C. (21 Mar 2013). *Facebook's Big Problem*. The Motley Fool. http://www.fool.com/investing/general/2013/03/21/facebooks-big-problem.aspx

44. Madden, C. S. (Spring 1991). *Marketers Battle for Mind Share*. Baylor Business Review Vol. 9. 8-10.

45. Online Social Media. (16 Apr 2013). *Google Plus for business explained*. http://www.onlinesocialmedia.net/20130416/google-plus-for-business-explained/

46. Bowman, C. (8 Apr 2013). *Google Plus Gaining Ground on Facebook*. Mojo Creator. http://www.mojocreator.com/social-media/google-plus-gaining-ground-on-facebook/

47. Lunden, I. (30 Jul 2012). *Twitter Passed 500M Users In Jun 2012, 140M Of Them In US; Jakarta 'Biggest Tweeting' City*. TechCrunch. http://techcrunch.com/2012/07/30/analyst-twitter-passed-500m-users-in-june-2012-140m-of-them-in-us-jakarta-biggest-tweeting-city/

48. Hof, R. (27 Mar 2013). *Report: Twitter to Hit Nearly $1 Billion in Ad Revenues Next Year*. Forbes. http://www.forbes.com/sites/roberthof/2013/03/27/report-twitter-to-hit-1-billion-in-ad-revenues-next-year/

49. Hartung, A. (13 Jan 2011). *Why Facebook beat MySpace- and What you Should Learn*. The Phoenix Principle. http://www.thephoenixprinciple.com/blog/2011/01/why-facebook-beat-myspace-and-what-you-should-learn.html

50. Gillette, F. (22 Jun 2011). *The Rise and Inglorious Fall of Myspace*. Bloomberg Businessweek. http://www.businessweek.com/magazine/content/11_27/b4235053917570.htm

51. Nishar, D. (9 Jan 2013). *200 Million Users*. LinkedIn. http://blog.linkedin.com/2013/01/09/linkedin-200-million/

52. Clayton, N. (15 Jan 2013). *Now at 50m users, LinkedIn rival Viadeo acquires French startup Pealk and announces US innovation lab*. Wall Street Journal. http://blogs.wsj.com/tech-europe/2013/01/15/viadeo-announces-pealk-acquisition-and-u-s-lab-launch/

53. Galston, E. (10 Mar 2013). *Are we in a subscription bubble?* Tech Crunch. http://techcrunch.com/2013/03/10/are-we-in-a-subscription-bubble/

54. Facebook Current Report, Form 8-k, Filing Date Jul 26, 2012. http://pdf.secdatabase.com/700/0001193125-12-316895.pdf

55. Walter, E. (2013). *Think Like Zuck: The Five Business Secrets of Facebook's Improbably Brilliant CEO Mark Zuckerberg*. McGraw-Hill Professional.

56. Facebook Inc. (FB.O). People / Reuters.com. http://www.reuters.com/finance/stocks/companyOfficers?symbol=FB.O

57. The Social Network, Oct 1, 2012.

58. Gonzales, S. (8 Dec 2010). *Zuckerberg to donate wealth*. Silicon Valley Mercury News. http://www.mercurynews.com/breaking-news/ci_16813123?nclick_check=1

59. Diaz, S. (29 Jun 2009). *Facebook hires former Genentech exec as CFO*. ZDNet.com. http://www.zdnet.com/blog/btl/facebook-hires-former-genentech-exec-as-cfo/20421

60. Eldon, E. (25 Jun 2012). *Sheryl Sandberg, Facebook's Long Time COO, Becomes First Woman On Its Board of Directors*. TechCrunch.com. http://techcrunch.com/2012/06/25/facebooks-board-of-directors-adds-its-first-woman-sheryl-sandberg-its-long-time-coo/

61. Facebook Inc. (FB.O). op cit.

62. McCarthy, C. (29 Sep 2008). *Facebook hires D.C. lawyer as general counsel*. CNet. http://news.cnet.com/8301-13577_3-10053364-36.html

63. PR Newswire. (31 Dec 2012). *Facebook reports fourth quarter and full year 2012 results*. PR Newswire. http://www.prnewswire.com/news-releases-test/facebook-reports-fourth-quarter-and-full-year-2012-results-189078621.html

64. Isaac, A. (9 Sep 2012). *How much is Facebook worth?* Seeking Alpha. http://seekingalpha.com/article/855281-how-much-is-facebook-worth

65. Lu, Z. (19 Feb 2013). *Facebook, is it capable of more revenue?* Seeking Alpha. http://seekingalpha.com/article/1201931-facebook-is-it-capable-of-more-revenue

Glencore, Xstrata and the Restructuring of the Global Copper Mining Industry in 2012

"Now we have to educate the Xstrata investors, who don't understand Glencore: it ain't a black box, it ain't a bunch of guys sitting behind a screen speculating on commodity prices. It's a physical movement of tonnes around the world."

Ivan Glasenberg, Glencore CEO[1]

In early 2012, Glencore, one of the world's largest commodity traders, proposed to take over the mining company Xstrata. Stocks of both companies surged by more than 10% in the days following the announcement. Analysts noted the unprecedented nature of the deal: "Glencore provides the marketing and Xstrata the operational base. It could be a new model for the industry although it would be difficult to replicate by others."[2]

The management teams of both companies had a shared history. Ivan Glasenberg, Glencore's CEO, and Xstrata's CEO Mick Davis were both South African and had met at Witwatersrand University, where Davis taught accounting. Subsequently, Glasenberg had joined Marc Rich & Co., while Davis had entered the mining industry. In 2001, the pair reconnected. Davis had stepped down as head of finance for BHP Billiton after losing a succession battle; Glasenberg, who was hoping to spin off Xstrata, contacted Davis, suspecting he "might manage to do something" with the mining concern. Over a decade, "Big Mick" had transformed Xstrata from a nearly bankrupt US$250 million firm into a US$34 billion international giant.[3]

Ten years later, the two firms were set to combine. However, the deal had not yet been consummated, and shareholders Qatar Holding and Norges Bank were objecting to the transaction on the grounds that Glencore's bid was inadequate. Despite initially arguing that the deal was not a "must-do" and that the terms were "generous", Glencore sweetened its proposal.[4,5] Was this indeed the model of the future or was the merger misguided?

The case first provides an overview of a key commodity market and supply chain – copper – in which Glencore is active and Xstrata is a major player. Thereafter, the major competitors of Glencore and Xstrata are discussed. Finally, the strategy, position and issues of Glencore are reviewed.

Industry and Market Overview

Copper is used in many industrial and commercial products and is a key ingredient in alloys such as brass or bronze. One of copper's main properties is its conductivity of electricity and heat as well as its resistance to corrosion, making it useful for electrical wiring and heating pipes. The primary usage of copper is for electrical wiring (42% of total consumption) and construction (28%).[6]

At the turn of the millennium, demand for copper increased dramatically, driven by the development of markets such as China, the world's single largest consumer (36% of total usage).[7] New mining sites were expensive to develop and required substantial time to develop. Consequently, demand outstripped supply (Exhibit 1), causing prices to increase by 500% from 2002 to 2008. Thereafter, the financial crisis coupled with the global economic downturn eroded demand,

This case was written by Karel Cool, the BP Chaired Professor of European Competitiveness at INSEAD, Olivier Daviron (INSEAD MBA 12J), João Almeida D'Eça (INSEAD MBA 12J), João Mendes (INSEAD MBA 12J), Edoardo Vallardi (Consultant at The Boston Consulting Group and INSEAD MBA 12J), and Matthias Wefelnberg (Consultant at The Boston Consulting Group and INSEAD MBA 12J). It is intended to be used as a basis for class discussion rather than to illustrate either effective or ineffective handling of an administrative situation.

but by 2011 copper consumption had reached an all-time high (Exhibit 2).[8]

Worldwide output of copper mines ("primary production") was 15.9mn metric tons in 2010 (US$90.2 billion). Production and reserves were concentrated in the Americas (which accounted for 64.6% share in production), particularly the United States, Canada, and Chile. Asia Pacific was a distant second with 22.9% (Exhibit 3).[9] Since copper maintained its chemical and physical properties after recycling and could be repurposed, "secondary production" represented 18% of global consumption, or approximately 3.4mn metric tons.[10]

The market for copper was divided into an "addressable" and "non-addressable" market. The former represented the share of the total copper market in which international trading companies could operate, and was estimated at 14% or US$12.6 billion in 2010 (Exhibit 4).[11] The remainder was non-addressable because producers were vertically integrated, production was sold directly to consumers, or consumption occurred within the producer country. In recent years, an increasing number of large end-users and governments which supported them (notably China's) had acquired copper assets to become independent of multinational mining and trading companies by securing their own supply.[12]

Exhibit 1 Development of Copper Supply and Demand[13]

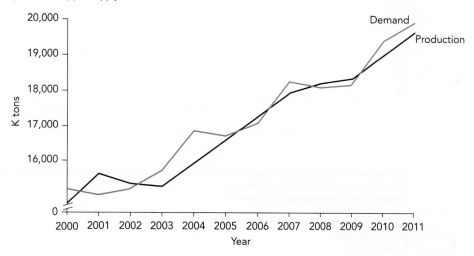

Exhibit 2 Historical Price of Copper[14]

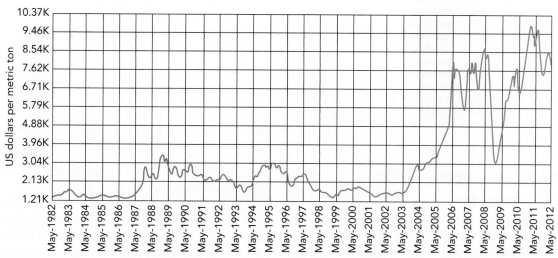

Description: Copper, grade A cathode, LME spot price, CIF European ports, US Dollars per Metric Ton

Exhibit 3 Mine and Smelter Production by Country[15]

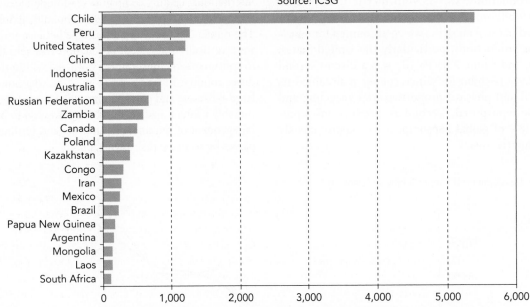

Copper Mine Production by Country: Top 20 Countries in 2009p
(Thousand metric tonnes)
Source: ICSG

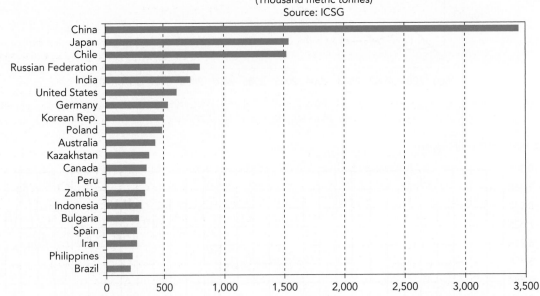

Copper Smelter Production by Country: Top 20 Countries in 2009p
(Thousand metric tonnes)
Source: ICSG

The Copper Supply Chain

Copper Production

Copper ore is mined in either open pits or below ground and typically contains less than 1% pure copper.[16] The ore has to be separated into its constituent parts through crushing and smelting. In the final refining process, copper is purified by removing any remaining sulphates.

The production process for recycled copper is shorter: scrap has to be smelted and refined.

The major players in the copper production industry were Codelco, BHP Billiton, Freeport-McMoRan, Xstrata, and Rio Tinto. These five accounted for 37% of total world primary copper production.[17] Compared to other commodity industries, however, the copper market was relatively fragmented (see Exhibit 5).

Exhibit 4 Overview of Market Shares by Glencore[18]

		Addressable market*	Total market
Metals and Minerals	Copper metal	50%	7%
	Copper concentrate	30%	4%
	Zinc metal	60%	13%
	Zinc concentrate	50%	10%
	Lead metal	45%	3%
	Lead concentrate	45%	10%
	Alumina	38%	8%
	Aluminum	22%	9%
	Nickel	14%	14%
	Cobalt	23%	23%
	Ferrochrome	16%	16%
Energy Products	Thermal Coal	28%	4%
	Met Coal	12%	4%
	Oil	3%	3%
Agricultural Products	Grains	9%	1%
	Oil & Oilseeds	4%	1%

Source: Company data.

* Note addressable market excludes 1) production in vertically integrated company, 2) production sold directly to end user and
3) production consumed in domestic country.

All of the major copper miners were also heavily involved in smelting and refining (Exhibit 6), a necessary step for transforming the commodity into ready-to-use outputs (such as wire) or alloys (such as brass and bronze). While copper production was centred in South America, most of the refining capacity was located in Asia. Refiners were paid a fixed margin over the intrinsic value of the commodity.[19] Therefore the profitability of this activity was typically lower and less volatile than that of the miners.

The copper industry had gone through a period of significant consolidation: between 2003 and 2007, nine of the 40 largest mining companies had been acquired.[20] Perhaps the best known was a transaction that ultimately never closed: BHP Billiton's offer for Rio Tinto. Announced in 2007, it would have been the third largest deal in history. A year later, the deal collapsed in the wake of the financial crisis and mounting opposition from regulators.[21]

The wave of acquisitions was driven by several factors. Scale was one consideration. Developing and operating a mine entailed a significant up-front investment. Few firms had the size required to independently finance

Exhibit 5 Market Concentration in Major Commodities (Herfindahl-Hirshman Index)

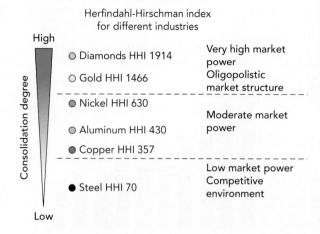

a project. To avoid concentrated exposure to one venture, mining companies often sought to invest in multiple new developments. Many were operated as joint ventures.

There were also benefits to horizontal integration: diversified firms could meet the many needs of end consumers through improved storage and transportation costs. Support functions such as procurement were also a source of leverage.[22] Chronic underinvestment further drove the wave of mergers and acquisitions. Due to decades of depressed copper prices, exploration and development had been limited. When copper prices increased, producers found themselves flush with cash; mergers and acquisitions became the expansion strategy of choice.

Another trend was the vertical integration of the major players into trading, marketing and logistics of their products. Companies like BHP Billiton and Rio Tinto were beginning to view this as a core activity.

Trading and Marketing

Trading referred to activities in two markets: i) the physical market (or "spot market"), which included the actors selling or buying physical commodities, and ii) the financial market (or "screen trading"), which included parties trading derivatives indexed to spot prices (such as forwards and futures).[23] Derivative contracts could be settled either in cash or by physically delivering the underlying commodity. These markets were used for a variety of purposes, from hedging to outright speculation.

Marketing was the bridge between producers and end consumers (Exhibit 7). Firms such as Glencore were responsible for developing customer relationships, negotiating supply contracts, and managing associated risks. For clients, marketers provided bulk breaking and product blending capabilities as well as global logistics.

Exhibit 6 Annual Production/Extraction of Top 10 Miners and Refiners[24]

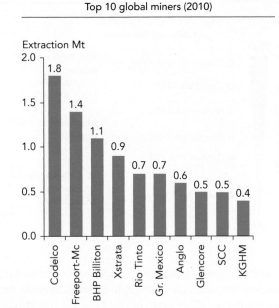

Top 10 global miners (2010)

Extraction Mt

Codelco 1.8
Freeport-Mc 1.4
BHP Billiton 1.1
Xstrata 0.9
Rio Tinto 0.7
Gr. Mexico 0.7
Anglo 0.6
Glencore 0.5
SCC 0.5
KGHM 0.4

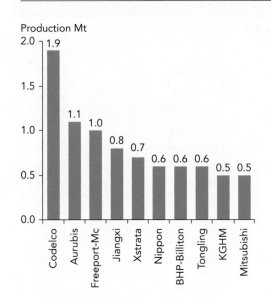

Top 10 global cathode producers (2010)

Production Mt

Codelco 1.9
Aurubis 1.1
Freeport-Mc 1.0
Jiangxi 0.8
Xstrata 0.7
Nippon 0.6
BHP-Billiton 0.6
Tongling 0.6
KGHM 0.5
Mitsubishi 0.5

Exhibit 7 The Role of a Commodity Marketer[25]

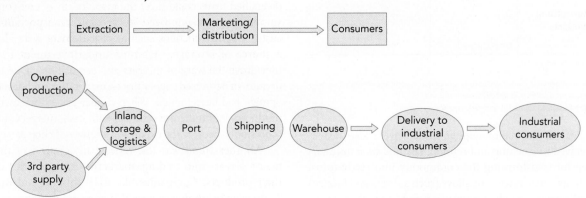

Extraction → Marketing/distribution → Consumers

Owned production → Inland storage & logistics → Port → Shipping → Warehouse → Delivery to industrial consumers → Industrial consumers

3rd party supply → Inland storage & logistics

Source: Company data.

They could also fulfill an inventory management function, helping producers reduce their working capital requirements and hedge their price risk exposure.[26]

Glencore's rise coincided with the development of the spot freight market. By the 1990s, 70% of freight traffic was spot chartered, compared with a mere 20% in the 1970s. In spite of the increased efficiency and transparency of the shipping market, Glencore had opted to operate a fleet of more than 200 vessels under a combination of long-term charter agreements and ownership stakes. Nick Hatch of the Royal Bank of Scotland explained: "Glencore's marketing business tends to benefit from high freight rates, not only due to greater shipping margins, but also because high freight rates tend to generate larger geographical price differentials – thus allowing Glencore

to leverage its in-house shipping capacity to capitalize on geographical arbitrage opportunities."[27]

Traders operated under two different agreements: agency and equity. As an agent, the marketer was a logistics provider, moving tonnage from producer to consumer for a fixed commission. According to Deutsche Bank, such agreements accounted for 7% of Glencore's marketing EBITDA contribution (Exhibit 8). Equity contracts involved taking possession of raw materials from producers and generating profits through arbitrage.

Trades typically fell into one of three categories. One was geographic arbitrage: traders sourced commodities in low-cost areas and sold them in regions where they could command a higher price. A second was product-related: traders could blend and refine a particular commodity in order to supply products that attracted higher prices. A product arbitrage opportunity might involve purchasing copper ore and refining it into either pure copper or copper alloy. Explained Glasenberg: "[Glencore is] able to play around and use its smelters for a better advantage, whereby you don't need to supply its high concentrate – high-quality concentrates into a smelter so you can get a price advantage by taking the higher concentrate – higher-quality concentrate and get a premium when a particular customer requires it, and put a lower-quality third-party concentrate through its smelters. This is what Glencore does."

Thirdly, trades could also be time-related, whereby marketers exploited the difference between the spot price of a commodity and its future price. An example of this was the "oil contango trade." Suppose a 12-month futures contract was at $85 a barrel, while spot oil was retailing at $80. In such a situation, a trader could purchase oil in the prompt market and sell long-term futures, locking in a profit.[28] Traders also made money from simple directional price bets on commodities. Analysts estimated that Glencore generated 10–20% of trading EBIT from such bets.

Trading was influenced by financial capabilities. Due to the size of its balance sheet and close relationships with lenders, Glencore could step in as a lender-of-last-resort during periods of high volatility. For example, in 2012, Greece's top refiner, Hellenic, found itself unable to finance oil purchases due to concerns over credit-worthiness. Glencore and Vitol, a competing trader, offered open financing in return for the right to sell oil at a sizeable premium.[29] Similarly, traders used periods of uncertainty to secure future supply. Ben Defay of JPMorgan explained: "… during the recent collapse in iron ore spot prices, Glencore agreed to take material on a spot basis from Rio Tinto and BHP Billiton, but only on the provision that they guarantee tonnage during 2012. Glencore also often arranged prepayment for material from new projects … in exchange for long-term off-take agreements."[30]

Financial liquidity had become increasingly important. The *Financial Times* estimated that in 2002, a trader could buy enough oil to fill a supertanker with less than US$50 million in credit lines; by 2012, skyrocketing oil prices meant that a similar purchase required more than US$200 million in working capital.

Due to the importance of funding costs, investment banks and other financial institutions had become involved in physical commodity trading. Morgan Stanley, one of the original "Wall Street refiners," entered the energy market in the 1980s. While most banks confined themselves to the financial commodity market by engaging in activities like derivative market making,

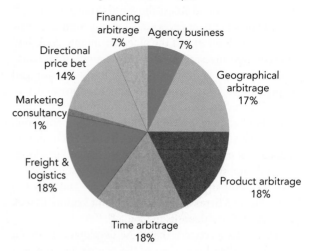

Exhibit 8 Marketing Contribution Analysis

- Financing arbitrage 7%
- Agency business 7%
- Directional price bet 14%
- Geographical arbitrage 17%
- Marketing consultancy 1%
- Product arbitrage 18%
- Freight & logistics 18%
- Time arbitrage 18%

Source: Deutsche Bank estimates

Morgan Stanley decided to become a physical trader. In the early 1990s, Olav Refvik became known as the "King of New York Harbour" after securing a dominant position in the transatlantic gasoline trade for the firm.[31] In 2008, revenues hit a peak of US$3 billion. By 2012, however, this number had fallen by 60% and the bank's management was contemplating selling at least part of the division due to heightened restrictions on proprietary trading.

As commodity markets deepened and became more transparent, it became easier for small trading firms and hedge funds to establish themselves. Private equity funds were also joining the fray.[32] For years, metal supply contracts had been negotiated as long-term agreements between parties. However, many markets had transitioned to spot prices, increasing price risk in the physical market and consequently creating demand for hedging instruments.[33]

Trades requiring large capital investments remained difficult for smaller firms and investors. Some investment banks viewed this as an opportunity. Both Goldman Sachs and JPMorgan entered the commodity warehousing industry in 2010, purchasing US-based Metro International and UK-based Henry Bath, respectively.[34] There were even more ambitious plans afoot. For example, JPMorgan was contemplating launching an exchange-traded fund that would allow investors to purchase physical copper. The vehicle could hold up to 61,800 tons of the metal, or 27% of the London Metal Exchange's global storage capacity.[35]

There were also a number of so-called "strategic buyers" which operated in the copper market. For example,

China had relentlessly stockpiled refined copper since 2009 and held around 40% of the world's known reserves.[36] Its rapid development necessitated vast quantities of raw materials (Exhibit 9) and the global economic crisis had allowed large investors to stockpile copper at advantageous prices. Its industrial policy actively discouraged copper exports by requiring government approval before sale.[37] China had also invested in commodity production.[38] For example, in 2009, China Development Bank, a state-owned financial institution, lent US$10 billion to Brazilian oil company Petrobras in exchange for a long-term oil supply commitment.[39] Similarly, state-owned resource company Chinalco held a large stake in Rio Tinto. The two firms also operated a joint venture to seek and exploit Tier 1 deposits in China.[40]

There was a concern that these developments might force the trading houses out of the market, but this was downplayed by Liberum Capital: "Whilst we suspect margins in trading for most market participants may be diminishing because of these trends, we feel Glencore's leading market position in supplier/customer relationships and the fact it is a physical as opposed to derivative based trader of commodities, should minimize the margin squeeze."[41]

Profitability along the Copper Supply Chain

Trading profitability varied across markets. Energy was a highly developed liquid market, and its margins of 1-2% reflected this. Metals, in contrast, were more difficult to move; margins were estimated at 4%. Agricultural commodities were complex and commanded margins of 7-10%.[42]

In the copper supply chain, many players were privately held or nationalized, and thus not obliged to report in detail their profitability. There remained few pure plays in metals production. Pure play miners such as First Quantum Minerals tended to be significantly smaller than their diversified peers and their financial performance reflected this: 13.2% return on equity versus 31.9% for their diversified peers, as did the share price (see Exhibits 10 and 11). Also, traders had lower ROE than mining companies and higher leverage. On average, they were valued less dearly than producers (1.2 price/book ratio versus 2.9 for diversified miners).

Key Competitors

Codelco

The government-owned company, founded in 1976 by order of the Pinochet administration, aggregated all the foreign mining companies previously nationalized in 1971. Codelco was the largest copper producer in the world with an annual production of 1.8mn tons (11% of global supply) in 2011. It owned around 20% of world copper reserves, as well as a large share of global refining capacity. Its assets were located in Chile but it sold its production all over the world. Copper revenues reached $15.7 billion

Exhibit 9 Consumption of Copper by Country[43]

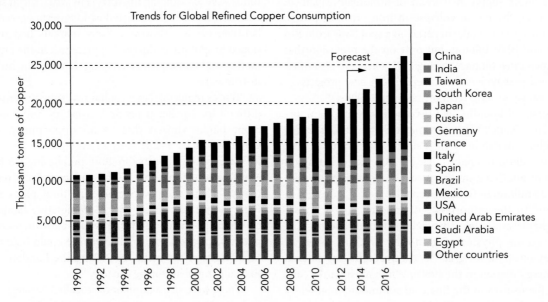

Source: A. Gonzalez, March 2012.

Exhibit 10 Sector Level Data

Data & Ratios as of FY 2010	Market Cap (in bns of US$)	Price/Earnings	Price/Book	Return on Equity	Return on Assets
Diversified Mining Companies					
BHP Billiton	$243.0	10.8	4.3	44.9%	24.7%
Rio Tinto	$144.8	9.6	2.4	27.9%	13.6%
Anglo American	$68.6	9.6	2.0	21.7%	10.6%
Xstrata	$69.6	14.6	1.7	12.7%	7.0%
Vale	$170.0	8.4	2.3	28.5%	15.3%
Weighted Average		**10.2**	**2.9**	**31.9%**	**16.9%**
Focused Mining Companies					
Antofagasta PLC	$24.8	23.6	4.0	18.3%	10.0%
First Quantum Minerals	$9.4	126.3	3.4	11.9%	6.4%
Norsk Hydro	$11.7	32.0	1.2	3.7%	2.3%
Weighted Average		**46.7**	**3.2**	**13.2%**	**7.3%**
Diversified Oil Companies					
Exxon Mobil	$368.7	11.8	2.5	23.7%	11.4%
Chevron	$183.6	9.8	1.7	19.3%	10.9%
Total	$124.5	8.4	1.5	18.7%	7.8%
ConocoPhilips	$100.1	8.8	1.1	17.4%	7.4%
Statoil	$74.9	11.6	2.0	18.2%	6.3%
		10.5	**2.0**	**20.8%**	**9.8%**
Trading/Logistics Companies					
Nobel Group	$10.2	16.7	2.6	17.5%	4.3%
Bunge	$9.5	16.0	0.8	23.5%	9.7%
Archer Daniels Midland	$19.2	9.9	1.1	12.2%	5.5%
Mitsui	$30.0	8.0	1.0	13.3%	3.6%
		10.9	**1.2**	**15.0%**	**5.1%**
Glencore (FY 2011)	$42.1	8.50	1.44	16.6%	4.9%

Source: Bloomberg

in 2011 versus $14.7 billion in 2010, while overall sales were $17.5 billion in 2011 (Exhibit 12). Profits before taxes peaked in 2007, reaching $8.5 billion, but fell by more than half over the two following years. Profitability recovered in subsequent years, reaching $7 billion in 2011.[44]

BHP Billiton

Created in 2001 through the merger of the Australian Broker Hill Proprietary Company (BHP) and the Anglo-Dutch Billiton, it was headquartered in Melbourne, and was one of the world's largest miners, with a market capitalization of $102.8 billion as of May 2012. It had extraction facilities all over the globe and covered a wide range of commodity products, including some interests in oil

and gas. For the year ending 30 June 2012, it had revenues of $71.7 billion and EBIT of $32 billion (Exhibit 13). Its net income of $23.9 billion made it one of the most profitable companies in the world. The company had a large presence in the copper market through its base metals division, which produced around 1.1mn tons in 2011. The division had total revenues of $14.2 billion, EBIT of $6.8 billion, and was among the most important producers of copper, lead, silver, gold, and zinc.

BHP's strategy was to own and operate "tier 1" assets diversified across different commodities, geographies, and markets. A "tier 1" is a large, expandable, long life mine with favorable mineralogy and geographic location and in the lower half of the cost curve.[45] BHP focused on

Exhibit 11 Sector Share Price Performance[46]

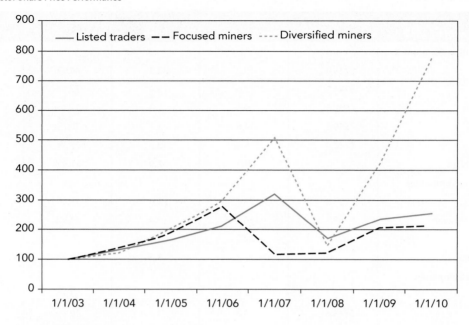

Exhibit 12 Codelco Financial Highlights

Codelco					
million $	FY 2011	FY 2010	FY 2009	FY 2008	FY 2007
Sales	17,515	16,066	12,148	14,425	16,988
EBITDA	6,667	5,945	5,779	6,588	9,382
EBIT	5,188	4,655	4,692	5,583	8,547
Net income	2,055	1,876	1,569	1,919	2,979
Assets	20,835	20,279	16,039	13,707	15,058
Market cap	-	-	-	-	-
Cash	1,576	1,069	630	387	2,074
Preferred equity + minorities	2	2	3	3	4
Total debt	8,039	9,108	4,791	4,824	4,434
Enterprise value	-	-	-	-	-
Cash flows from operations	2,650	3,262	2,999	3,243	4,687
Capex	−2,252	−2,309	−1,645	−1,975	−1,605
Free cash flow	399	952	1,354	1,267	3,082
Dividends	-	-	-	-	-

commodities with "deep cost curves," where the differential between the highest and lowest cost producer was significant. In 2010, Juan Correas of Santander estimated that BHP could produce copper at a cost 60-70% lower than the prevailing market price (Exhibit 14).[47] The firm's highly competitive cost structure was the result of economies of scale and investments in production technology. BHP had also been building its marketing function

since the 2001 merger: its efforts spanned supply chain optimization, working capital and cost control, product arbitrage, and agent and equity sales relationships with smaller producers.[48]

Rio Tinto

Rio Tinto PLC. (UK) and Rio Tinto Limited headquartered in Melbourne combined in February 2012 to become

Exhibit 13(a) BHP Billiton Income Statement[49]

BHP Billiton			
Income Statement			
	FY 2012	FY 2011	FY 2010
For the period ending	6/30/12	6/30/11	6/30/10
Revenue	72,226	71,739	52,798
Other Operating Revenue	28	27	12
Operating Expenses	46,046	39,369	33,775
Operating profit (loss)	26,208	32,397	19,035
Interest Expense	441	246	686
Foreign Exchange Losses (Gains)	(355)	1,074	112
Net Non-Operating Losses (Gains)	3,100	(178)	(1,335)
Pretax Income	23,022	31,255	19,572
Income Tax Expense	7,490	7,309	6,563
Income Before XO Items	15,532	23,946	13,009
Extraordinary Loss Net of Tax	-	-	-
Outside Equity Interests	115	298	287
Net profit (loss)	15,417	23,648	12,722
Total Cash Preferred Dividends	-	-	-
Other Adjustments	-	-	-
Net Inc Avail to Common Shareholders	15,417	23,648	12,722
Unusual Loss (gain)	6,670	157	(83)
Tax Effect on Abnormal Items	(2,781)	(2,126)	(18)
Normalized Income	17,158	21,684	12,469

Exhibit 13(b) BHP Billiton Balance Sheet[51]

BHP Billiton			
Balance Sheet			
	FY 2012	FY 2011	FY 2010
For the period ending	6/30/12	6/30/11	6/30/10
Assets			
Cash & Near Cash Items	4,781	10,084	12,456
Accounts & Notes Receivable	4,723	6,068	4,945
Inventories	6,233	6,154	5,334
Other Current Assets	4,714	2,974	2,399
Total Current Assets	20,451	25,280	25,134
LT Investments & LT Receivables	748	742	1,510
Net Fixed Assets	95,247	67,945	55,576
Gross Fixed Assets	135,833	101,968	85,145
Accumulated Depreciation	40,586	34,023	29,569
Other Long-term Assets	12,827	8,953	6,632
Total Long-Term Assets	108,822	77,640	63,718
Total Assets	129,273	102,920	88,852
Liabilities & Shareholders' Equity			
Accounts Payable	8,727	6,667	4,470
Short-Term Borrowings	3,531	3,519	2,191
Other Short-Term Liabilities	9,776	9,552	6,381
Total Current Liabilities	22,034	19,738	13,042
Long-Term Borrowings	24,799	12,388	13,573
Other Long-Term Liabilities	15,355	13,039	12,098
Total Long-Term Liabilities	40,154	25,427	26,481
Total Liabilities	62,188	45,165	39,523
Total Preferred Equity	-	-	-
Minority Interest	1,215	993	804
Share Capital & APIC	2,773	2,771	2,861
Retained Earnings & Other Equity	63,097	53,991	45,664
Total Equity	67,085	57,755	49,329
Total Liabilities & Equity	129,273	102,920	88,852

the Rio Tinto Group. The company had a combined 2011 market capitalization of $118.5 billion and assets such as open pits and underground mines, mills, refineries, smelters, and support facilities worth $95 billion. Rio Tinto's copper business was very diverse, comprising assets on all continents with the exception of Europe. In 2010 it produced around 700,000 tons of copper, with revenues of $7.6 billion and earnings of $1.9 billion. In 2011, earnings, EBITDA, and cash flows from operations reached record highs. Net earnings were 59% lower than in 2010, but this was primarily due to an $8.9 billion impairment charge to the aluminum business (Exhibit 15). Rio Tinto reported that in 2008, its Marketing Centre (responsible for all marketing functions) generated over $700 million in incremental cash flow; its total earnings in 2008 stood at US$10.3 billion.[50]

Freeport-McMoRan

The largest publicly traded copper producer in the world was headquartered in Arizona. Its assets were located across the globe and included the Grasberg mining complex in Indonesia, the world's largest copper and gold

Exhibit 13(c) BHP Billiton Segment Data[52]

BHP Billiton						
Segment Financial Data						
	FY 2012	%	FY 2011	%	FY 2010	%
For the period ending	6/30/12		6/30/11		6/30/10	
Revenue	72,226	100.00%	71,739	100.00%	52,798	100.00%
Iron Ore	22,601	31.40%	20,412	28.59%	11,139	21.40%
Petroleum	12,937	17.98%	10,737	15.04%	8,782	16.87%
Base Metals (Copper, Silver, Lead, Uranium & Zinc)	11,596	16.11%	14,152	19.82%	10,409	20.00%
Metallurgical Coal	7,576	10.53%	7,573	10.61%	6,059	11.64%
Energy Coal	6,022	8.37%	5,507	7.71%	4,265	8.19%
Aluminum	4,766	6.62%	5,221	7.31%	4,353	8.36%
Stainless Steel Materials	2,993	4.16%	3,861	5.41%	3,617	6.95%
Manganese	2,152	2.99%	2,423	3.39%	2,150	4.13%
Diamonds and Specialty Products	1,326	1.84%	1,517	2.12%	1,272	2.44%
Group and Unallocated Items	257	0.00%	336	0.00%	752	0.00%
Discontinued Operations, Net Unallocated Interest						
Carbon Steel Materials						
EBITDA	33,746	100.00%	37,093	100.00%	24,513	100.00%
Iron Ore	15,027	44.35%	13,946	37.26%	6,496	25.99%
Petroleum	9,415	27.79%	8,319	22.22%	6,571	26.29%
Base Metals (Copper, Silver, Lead, Uranium & Zinc)	4,687	13.83%	7,525	20.10%	5,393	21.58%
Metallurgical Coal	1,991	5.88%	3,027	8.09%	2,363	9.45%
Energy Coal	1,601	4.73%	1,469	3.92%	971	3.88%
Stainless Steel Materials	425	1.25%	990	2.64%	1,085	4.34%
Manganese	359	1.06%	780	2.08%	784	3.14%
Diamonds and Specialty Products	353	1.04%	779	2.08%	648	2.59%
Aluminum	25	0.07%	596	1.59%	684	2.74%
Group and Unallocated Items	(137)	0.00%	(338)	0.00%	(482)	0.00%
Operating Income	27,238	100.00%	31,980	100.00%	19,719	100.00%
Iron Ore	14,201	51.67%	13,328	41.15%	6,001	29.62%
Petroleum	6,348	23.10%	6,330	19.55%	4,573	22.57%
Base Metals (Copper, Silver, Lead, Uranium & Zinc)	3,965	14.43%	6,790	20.97%	4,632	22.86%
Metallurgical Coal	1,570	5.71%	2,670	8.24%	2,053	10.13%
Energy Coal	1,227	4.46%	1,129	3.49%	730	3.60%
Manganese	235	0.85%	697	2.15%	712	3.51%
Diamonds and Specialty Products	199	0.72%	587	1.81%	485	2.39%
Stainless Steel Materials	32	0.12%	588	1.82%	668	3.30%
Group and Unallocated Items	(248)	0.00%	(405)	0.00%	(541)	0.00%
Aluminum	(291)	−1.06%	266	0.82%	406	2.00%
Net Unallocated Interest						
Carbon Steel Materials						

Exhibit 14 BHP Billiton's Cost Structure Relative to Peers

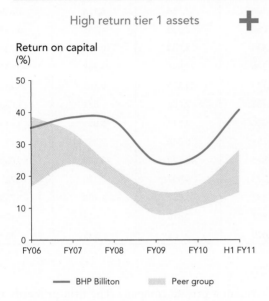

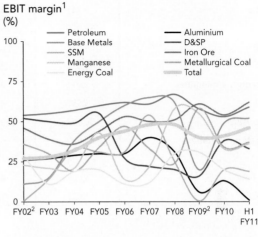

Note: Peer group Rio Tinto, Vale, Anglo American and Xstrata.
Source: Annual Reports, interim press releases and BHP Billiton analysis.

1. Calculated on the basis of UKGAAP for periods prior to FY05, except for the exclusion of PRRT from Petroleum's and BHP Billiton Group's results for all periods. All periods exclude third party trading activities. The Exploration and Technology business has been included in BHP Billiton Group's results from FY02 to FY05 and excluded from Diamonds and Specialty Products (D&SP).
2. Negative margins are not shown as the y-axis is set at zero. Stainless Steel Materials (SSM) had a negative EBIT margin in FY02 and FY09.

Exhibit 15 Rio Tinto Financial Highlights

Rio Tinto					
million $	FY 2011	FY 2010	FY 2009	FY 2008	FY 2007
Sales	60,537	56,576	41,825	54,264	29,700
EBITDA	26,657	22,748	10,920	18,964	11,050
EBIT	22,840	19,311	7,493	15,489	8,935
Net income	6,775	15,281	5,784	5,436	7,746
Assets	119,545	112,402	97,236	89,616	101,391
Market cap	90,742	136,960	200,654	42,748	274,975
Cash	10,255	10,469	4,693	1,298	1,972
Preferred equity + minorities	6,669	6,941	2,094	1,823	1,552
Total debt	21,804	14,341	23,002	39,758	11,061
Enterprise value	108,960	147,773	221,057	83,031	285,616
Cash flows from operations	20,578	18,734	9,622	15,231	8,659
Capex	−12,335	−4,591	−5,388	−8,574	−5,000
Free cash flow	8,243	14,143	4,234	6,657	3,659
Dividends	1,694	2,115	882	1,739	1,763

Exhibit 16 FCX Financial Highlights

Freeport-McMoRan					
million $	FY 2011	FY 2010	FY 2009	FY 2008	FY 2007
Sales	20,880	18,982	15,040	17,796	16,939
EBITDA	10,162	10,196	7,736	6,154	7,819
EBIT	9,140	9,068	6,599	4,255	6,555
Net income	5,747	5,544	3,534	-10,450	3,733
Assets	32,070	29,386	25,996	23,353	40,661
Market cap	34,877	56,743	34,525	9,385	39,235
Cash	4,822	3,738	2,656	872	1,626
Preferred equity + minorities	2,911	2,056	4,513	5,035	5,214
Total debt	3,537	4,755	6,346	7,351	7,211
Enterprise value	36,503	59,816	42,728	20,899	50,034
Cash flows from operations	6,620	6,273	4,397	3,370	6,225
Capex	−2,534	−1,412	−1,587	−2,708	−1,755
Free cash flow	4,086	4,861	2,810	662	4,470
Dividends	1,421	1,029	65	525	469

mine in terms of recoverable reserves.[53] The company's annual copper production was approximately 1.4mn tons in 2011, making FCX the second largest player in the sector. FCX grew both organically and through acquisitions. The firm had ties with Rio Tinto that began in 1993 with the acquisition of Atlantic Copper in Spain and were deepened in 1995 when a $1.4 billion strategic alliance with Rio Tinto in Indonesia was announced. In 2007, FCX became the largest publicly traded copper company in the world after acquiring Phelps Dodge. Revenues reached $20.9 billion in 2011 (Exhibit 16).

Vale

The Brazilian diversified metals and mining company had operations on every continent. It was the second largest mining company in the world and controlled 85% of Brazilian iron ore production. It had a small presence in copper: 302,000 tons in 2011. In February 2008, it entered into takeover talks with Xstrata but they were suspended in March as the parties could not agree on the price. Also, Glencore reportedly would only agree to a deal if it was allowed an equity stake in the combined entity and marketing rights to a significant part of the new firm's production.[54]

Trafigura

Trafigura was spun out of Marc Rich & Co. in 1993 following a management buyout, and had opted to

remain a private company. The firm primarily traded crude oil, petroleum products, non-ferrous concentrates, refined metals and coal. Trafigura maintained a portfolio of production, transport and refining assets, including storage terminals, service stations, metal warehouses and mines, worth up to $3.3 billion. In 2011, Trafigura generated profits of US $1.1 billion on revenues of $121.6 billion (Exhibit 17).[55] The company had been tainted by scandal, including illegal oil trading with Iraq and the dumping of toxic waste in the waters off Ivory Coast,[56] which left 15 people dead[57] and 108,000 seriously ill.

Glencore

The Early Years

It is impossible to discuss Glencore without mentioning Marc Rich. Born in Antwerp, Belgium, he and his family fled in 1941 after the Nazi invasion, and settled in New York. Rich attended New York University but left after one semester to join Philipp Brothers, an international commodity trading company where he learned the intricacies of the global metals market. Nominally a political conservative, Rich was a consummate dealmaker, doing business with both fascist Spain and communist Cuba.[58] In 1966, he married Denise Eisenberg, a songwriter and heiress to a New England shoe manufacturing fortune.[59]

Exhibit 17 Trafigura Financial Highlights

Trafigura					
million $	FY 2011*	FY 2010	FY 2009	FY 2008	FY 2007
Sales	121,600	79,242	47,269	73,166	50,861
EBITDA	-	-	-	-	-
EBIT	-	519	1,126	565	770
Net income	-	-	936	438	376
Assets	-	25,351	19,399	15,361	12,224
Market cap	-	-	-	-	-
Cash	-	1,489	1,404	1,177	1,052
Preferred equity + minorities	-	315	76	18	21
Total debt	-	-	10,113	7,650	6,047
Enterprise value	-	-	-	-	-
Cash flows from operations	-	-	−1,480	−949	−375
Capex	-	-	-	-	-
Free Cash flow	-	-	-	-	-
Dividends	-	-	-	-	-

*from Trafigura's corporate presentation

While Rich initially specialized in trading minerals, he was widely credited with inventing the spot market for crude in the early 1970s. In 1973, the Organization of Petroleum Exporting Countries (OPEC) declared an oil embargo. By 1974, the price of oil had quadrupled to $12 a barrel. Rich used his Middle Eastern contacts to buy oil cheaply from Iran and Iraq, which he subsequently resold to desperate Western oil companies for a handsome profit. In 1974, he and co-worker Pincus "Pinky" Green struck out on their own, forming Marc Rich & Co. AG in Zug, Switzerland.

The 1979 revolution in Iran presented another opportunity to Rich. Protests led to the cessation of exports from Iran. U.S. President Jimmy Carter's subsequent decision to ban imports from Iran caused a panic that drove oil prices to historic highs. On the 1st of February 1979, Ayatollah Khomeini returned to govern Iran. Simultaneously, one of Rich's closest business partners landed in Tehran, eager to cement ties with the new government. The relationship would endure for 15 years and was critical to Glencore's early success.[60] "We sold oil because it was available and the price was right," said Rich. "We didn't force anyone to either buy from us or sell it to us." His two most important clients were also embargoed nations: Israel and South Africa. He would later remark, "Business is neutral. You can't run a trading company based on sympathies."[61]

Using the proceeds from the Iranian oil trade, Rich began acquiring assets. In 1981, he purchased a Dutch grain trading company. He also expanded into coal,

increasing the scope of the firm's energy trading capabilities.[62] But Marc Rich & Co.'s success attracted the attention of the U.S. government. In 1983, Federal Prosecutor Rudolph Giuliani indicted Rich and Green on charges of racketeering, illegally trading with Iran, and tax evasion. The pair fled to Switzerland, earning them a place on the FBI's Top Ten Most Wanted Fugitives. Neither man is known to have set foot on United States soil since.[63]

Their trading company, however, continued to operate profitably. In 1987, Rich acquired the group's first industrial asset, a 27% stake in the Mt. Holly aluminum smelter in the United States, and purchased a controlling interest in a zinc/lead mine in Peru the following year. In 1990, Marc Rich & Co. acquired Südelektra AG, a Swiss infrastructure investment company that would be reinvented as a miner and rechristened Xstrata.

Management Change

When in 1992 Rich's attempt to manipulate the global zinc market failed, his firm was saddled with US$172 million in losses. Simultaneously, his marriage to Denise Rich was ending acrimoniously; the divorce would ultimately cost him US$365 million.[64] Under pressure from his partners, he agreed to be bought out of his 51% stake in Marc Rich & Co. and was succeeded as chairman and CEO by Willy Strothotte, a metals trader who had left the firm following a disagreement with Rich. The company rebranded itself as Glencore, supposedly shorthand for "Global Energy Commodities and Resources." Despite the name change, the company persisted with its founders' business practices, profiting from dealing with Saddam Hussein under the UN Oil-for-Food program.[65]

The company also continued acquiring industrial assets such as a zinc mine in Peru and the Colombian Coal Group in 1995.[66] In subsequent years, the trader purchased additional production assets on an opportunistic basis. According to Glasenberg, Glencore tended to avoid top-tier mines: "I'm very happy with getting tier-two or tier-three assets, putting them together, taking brownfield assets, putting them together, and creating not tier-one, but tier-two assets, which we bought cheaply from other people. Put them together, use the synergies and create a great asset that gives us a great return on equity, which we paid very little for." Marius Kloppers (INSEAD MBA'91D), CEO of BHP, had once criticized Glencore for never developing its own assets. Glasenberg had scoffed at the jibe: "That's great. Who the hell wants to build an asset if I can buy them cheaper than you can build them?"[67]

In its quest for cheap production, Glencore focused on politically risky regions where other mining firms

feared to tread; analysts estimated that 68% of the firm's industrial assets were located in such countries (Exhibits 18 and 19). A Morgan Stanley report assessed the danger of hold-up in these regions as follows: "… two factors provide comfort on this issue: a) Glencore's long track record of operating in such geographies, its pragmatic approach to relationships with the key stakeholders and institutional knowledge of the key players in these regions; and b) the asset portfolio is diversified across several geographies where the geopolitical risks are unlikely to be correlated (Kazakhstan, Colombia, DR Congo, Zambia, Peru, Bolivia, and Equatorial Guinea), thus reducing the impact of single-country risks."[68]

The Glasenberg Years

In 2002, Ivan Glasenberg officially succeeded Willy Strothotte as CEO. The former competitive race walker and chartered accountant had joined Marc Rich & Co. in 1984. To announce his reign, Glasenberg initially planned to float his firm's Australian and South African coal assets. But market volatility following the September 11th attacks made such a plan impractical.

Exhibit 18　An Overview of Glencore's Industrial Assets[69]

		Metals & Minerals			Energy products		Agricultural Products
		Zinc/Copper/Lead	Aluminium/Alumina	Ferroalloys/Nickel/Cobalt	Oil	Coal	Agricultural
Industrial assets relevant to the department		**Zinc** • AR Zinc 100% • Los Quenual es 97.1% • Portovesme 100% • Sinchi Wayra100% • Nyrstar 7.8% • Perkova 50.1% • Volcan 4.1% **Copper** • Katanga 74.4% • Mopani 73.1% • Cobar 100% • Pasar 78.2% • Punitaqui 100% • Mutanda 40% • Kansuki 37.5% **Polymetallic** • Kazzinc 50.7% • Xstrata 34.5% • Recyclex 32.2% • Polymet 9.3%	**Alumina** • Sherwin 100% **Aluminium** • Columbia Falls100% • Century Aluminium 44% **Integrated** • UC Rusal 8.8%	**Nickel and cobalt** • Murrin Murrin JV 82.4% **Cobalt** • Katanga 74.4% • Moparl 73.1% • Mutanda 40.0% • Kansuki 37.5% **Nickel, Cobalt and Ferrolloys** • Xstrata 34.5%	**Oil production and refining subsidiaries** • PossNett 40-99% Oil exploaration/development • West African E&P Assets (various shareholdings) **Shipping** • Various shipping assets **Oil storage and Logistics** • Various oil storage and logistics assets **Oil services/marketing** • Various oil storage and logistics assets	**Coal** • Prodeco 100% • Shanduka 70% • Xstrata 34.5% • Uncest 43.7% **Coal freight** • Various Logistics assests.	**Farms (27,000 ha)** • F8U: 198k ha; Australia: 63k ha; Paraguay: 9k ha **Orgination elevators/Silos** (4.8mt capacity) • F8u: 2.5mt; Australia: 0.8mt Europe: 0.5mt **Processing assets** • Oilseed/sunseed/Rapeseed crushing 2.6mt • Grain milling 0.5mt • Flour/rice milling 1.5mt • Biodiesel 1.5mt Port elevators/silos • F8U: 2 ports • Argentina: 2 ports • Europe: 3 ports
Mining Production	Processing	Yes	Yes	No	Yes	Yes	Yes	Limited	Blending	Limited	Blending	Farming-Yes but limited	Yes
Storage (own/rent)	Freight (own/charter)	Owned and leased	Chartered	Owned and leased	Chartered	Leased	Chartered	Owned and leased	Owned and leased	Owned and leased	Owned and leased	Some silo and port elevators owned	Chartered, some rail wagons
LME warehousing		Yes		Yes		Yes		N/A		N/A		N/A	

Source: Glencore, Deutsche Bank

Exhibit 19 Glencore Industrial Business NPV – Contribution by Country[70]

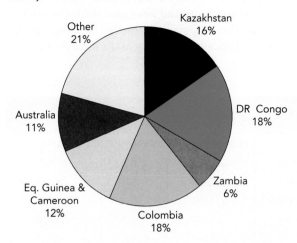

Source: Morgan Stanley Research.

The new CEO developed an alternative scheme: instead of floating the coal portfolio directly, Glasenberg would first spin off Xstrata, which would acquire the coal assets from Glencore for US$2.5 billion. Michael "Mick" Davis would head the mining group. Glencore would retain a 38.5% stake.[71]

Xstrata's public offering dramatically increased its financial flexibility, allowing Davis to initiate a multibillion-dollar acquisition spree. In June 2003, he purchased MIM Holdings for US$2.9 billion. In August 2005, Xstrata bought 19.9% of Falconbridge; the takeover was completed in November 2006 for US $16.9 billion.[72] Both deals greatly increased the miner's scale and geographic scope.

By 2012, Mick Davis had increased the company's revenues 18-fold since the IPO, from US$1.9 billion to US$33.9 billion. EBITDA had risen from US$0.4 billion in 2002 to US$11.6 billion in 2011. Total assets had surged from US$5.2 billion to US$74.8 billion (Exhibit 20) and it had become one of the top-15 miners globally by market capitalization (Exhibit 21). Xstrata was now the fourth largest copper producer in the world with operations in over 20 countries and a substantial presence in zinc, nickel, coal, and steel alloys. Its portfolio was primarily composed of "tier 2" assets that the company had purchased and improved; the miner had historically shied away from developing its own "tier 1" properties. Stated RBC: "XTA is currently a first quartile producer in coal, a second quartile producer of chrome, zinc, and nickel, and still an early third quartile producer in copper." A strong pipeline, however, would see the miner's copper production increase 52% by 2015, along with a reduction in unit production cost (Exhibit 22).[73]

The acquisition spree came at a price: as Xstrata's leverage increased, its solvency deteriorated. The U.S. financial crisis exposed weaknesses in the firm's capital structure, compelling management to announce a secondary offering in January 2009 (Exhibit 23). Glencore, however, was also suffering financial difficulties and lacked the liquidity to subscribe. Moreover, Glasenberg vehemently disagreed with the miner's decision to raise equity. Rather than dilute its principal shareholder, Xstrata compromised, accepting a portfolio of mining assets valued at US$2 billion in lieu of cash. Glencore further insisted that it be allowed to buy back the assets for US$2.25 billion at a future date. Smaller shareholders were livid and accused Xstrata of favoritism.

The incident illustrated the complex relationship between the two companies. While nominally separate, Xstrata and Glencore were deeply intertwined. The European Commission already viewed the pair as a single entity for regulatory purposes following Xstrata's acquisition of Falconbridge.[74] Glasenberg and Davis were fully aware that the status quo was unsustainable. In 2007, they had even agreed upon a valuation before other considerations derailed a deal.

IPO and Merger with Xstrata

Xstrata's rights issue and the financial crisis convinced Glasenberg to take Glencore public. A public offering would provide the capital required to complete the merger and obviate the need for a third-party valuation, a sticking point in previous discussions with Davis. In May 2011, Glencore completed its initial public offering but saw its share price fall almost immediately (Exhibit 24). RBS explained: "Since Glencore's IPO in London on 18 May, it has been a difficult time for equity markets, the mining sector, and Glencore in particular. After performing broadly in line with the mining sector during its first few weeks of trading, Glencore underperformed the sector following the release of its 1Q11 interim management statement on 14 June. [...] there are a number of contributory reasons [...]: lower-than-expected contribution to Glencore's earnings from associates mainly Xstrata; volatility in earnings and margins from Glencore's marketing (trading) operations (38% of 1Q11 EBIT)."[75]

The markets seemingly struggled to value Glencore; the firm's diverse mixture of activities and minority interests was perplexing to both analysts and investors (Exhibits 25 and 26). A JPMorgan Cazenove analyst report commented: "It is worth noting there is very little science in our predictions for the trading business – they are simply based on mean reversion and/or trend development based on GDP growth as well as in-house volume growth. Moreover there is no "spot" hard data that can provide one with a real time feel for earnings momentum as there is in the mining sector. This will continue to be a factor with Glencore we feel until at least two quarters of trading history and associated market reaction."[76] There was also concern over whether the firm's strategy of opportunistically purchasing assets in politically risky

Exhibit 20(a) Xstrata Income Statement[77]

Xstrata PLC					
Income Statement					
	FY 2011	**FY 2010**	**FY 2009**	**FY 2008**	**FY 2007**
For the period ending	12/31/11	12/31/10	12/31/09	12/31/08	12/31/07
Turnover	33,877	30,499	22,732	27,952	28,542
Cost of sales	22,245	20,113	13,098	16,001	15,544
Gross Profit	11,632	10,386	9,634	11,951	12,998
Operating Expenses	3,201	2,732	5,577	4,702	4,221
Operating profit (loss)	8,431	7,654	4,057	7,249	8,777
Interest Expense	452	620	754	832	969
Net Non-Operating Losses (Gains)	(169)	420	1,773	1,249	(319)
Pretax Income	8,148	6,614	1,530	5,168	8,127
Income Tax Expense	2,215	1,653	669	1,304	2,311
Income Before XO Items	5,933	4,961	861	3,864	5,816
Extraordinary Loss Net of Tax	-	-	-	-	(53)
Minority Interests	220	267	200	269	326
Net profit (loss)	5,713	4,688	661	3,595	5,543
Total Cash Preferred Dividends	-	-	-	-	-
Net Inc Avail to Common Shareholders	5,713	4,688	661	3,595	5,543
Exceptional L(G)	−3	593	2436	1433	−129
Tax Effect on Abnormal Items	75	−129	−324	−330	10
Normalized Income	5,785	5,158	2,773	4,698	5,371
Basic EPS Before Abnormal Items	1.99	1.77	1.05	2.77	3.17
Basic EPS Before XO Items	1.97	1.61	0.25	2.12	3.24
Basic EPS	1.95	1.61	0.25	2.12	3.27
Basic Weighted Avg Shares	2,931	2,911	2,647	1,694	1,695
Diluted EPS Before Abnormal Items	1.99	1.77	1.03	2.76	3.17
Diluted EPS	1.93	1.58	0.25	2.09	3.19
Diluted Weighted Avg Shares	2,969	2,964	2,699	1,728	1,742
Adjusted Basic EPS	1.97	1.77	1.05	2.77	3.17
Reference Items					
EBITDA	11,648	10,386	6,476	9,645	10,904
EBITDA Margin	34.38%	34.05%	28.49%	34.51%	38.20%
Gross Margin	34.34%	34.05%	42.38%	42.76%	45.54%
Operating Margin	24.89%	25.10%	17.85%	25.93%	30.75%
Profit Margin	16.86%	15.37%	2.91%	12.86%	19.42%
Dividends per Share	0.40	0.25	0.08	0.10	0.28

Exhibit 20(b) Xstrata Balance Sheet[78]

Xstrata PLC					
Balance Sheet					
	FY 2011	FY 2010	FY 2009	FY 2008	FY 2007
For the period ending	12/31/11	12/31/10	12/31/09	12/31/08	12/31/07
Assets					
Cash & Near Cash Items	1,948	1,722	1,177	1,156	1,148
Short-Term Investments	-	-	2,424	-	54
Accounts & Notes Receivable	3,037	3,930	2,856	1,570	2,451
Inventories	5,242	4,763	4,570	3,573	4,167
Other Current Assets	1,066	1,054	1,309	776	785
Total Current Assets	11,293	11,469	12,336	7,075	8,605
LT Investment & LT Receivables	1,001	861	712	231	301
Net Fixed Assets	51,454	45,884	39,397	36,141	33,242
Gross Fixed Assets	70,449	62,417	52,194	43,615	38,368
Accumulated Depreciation	18,995	16,533	12,797	7,474	5,126
Other Long-Term Assets	11,084	11,495	11,379	11,867	9,973
Total Long-Term Assets	63,539	58,240	51,488	48,239	43,516
Total Assets	74,832	69,709	63,824	55,314	52,121
Liabilities & Shareholders' Equity					
Accounts Payable	2,562	2,544	1,796	1,667	2,429
Short-Term Borrowings	1,566	2,318	206	794	1,118
Other Short-Term Liabilities	4,334	4,192	3,201	2,599	2,364
Total Current Liabilities	8,462	9,054	5,203	5,060	5,911
Long Term Borrowings	8,804	7,154	13,587	16,668	11,654
Other Long-Term Liabilities	11,865	11,480	10,115	9,187	9,342
Total Long-Term Liabilities	20,669	18,634	23,702	25,855	20,996
Total Liabilities	29,131	27,688	28,905	30,915	26,907
Total Preferred Equity	-	-	-	-	-
Minority Interest	2,037	1,745	1,637	1,636	1,386
Share Capital & APIC	16,940	16,960	16,565	10,796	10,384
Retained Earnings & Other Equity	26,724	23,316	16,717	11,967	13,444
Total Equity	45,701	42,021	34,919	24,399	25,214
Total Liabilities & Equity	74,832	69,709	63,824	55,341	52,121
Reference Items					
Net Debt	8,422	7,750	10,192	16,306	11,570
Net Debt to Equity	18.43	18.44	29.19	66.83	45.89
Current Ratio	1.33	1.27	2.37	1.40	1.46
Inventory – Raw Materials	1,677	1,493	1,386	1,353	1,451
Inventory – Work in Progress	2,350	2,285	2,238	1,350	1,763
Inventory – Finished Goods	1,215	985	946	870	953
Goodwill	6,495	6,508	6,538	7,146	7,336
Investments in Associated Companies	1,769	1,786	1,790	1,963	186

Exhibit 20(c) Xstrata Segment Data[79]

Xstrata PLC

Segment Financial data

For the period ending	FY 2011 12/31/11	%	FY 2010 12/31/10	%	FY 2009 12/31/09	%	FY 2008 12/31/08	%	FY 2007 12/31/07	%	FY 2006 12/31/06	%
Revenue	**33,877**	**100.00%**	**30,499**	**100.00%**	**22,732**	**100.00%**	**27,952**	**100.00%**	**28,542**	**100.00%**	**17,102**	**100.00%**
Copper	15,037	44.39%	14,004	45.92%	9,223	40.57%	11,464	41.01%	12,794	44.83%	7,007	40.97%
Coal	**9,981**	**29.46%**	**7,788**	**25.54%**	**6,749**	**29.69%**	**7,944**	**28.42%**	**4,201**	**14.72%**	**3,617**	**21.15%**
Coal-Thermal	8,057	23.78%	6,167	20.22%	5,762	25.53%	6,347	22.71%	3,614	12.66%	3,019	17.65%
Coal-Coking	1,924	5.68%	1,621	5.31%	987	4.34%	1,597	5.71%	587	2.06%	598	3.50%
Zinc Lead	3,756	11.09%	3,922	12.86%	3,450	15.18%	3,202	11.46%	4,726	16.56%	3,721	21.76%
Nickel	3,192	9.42%	2,738	8.98%	1,891	8.32%	3,105	11.11%	5,252	18.40%	1,678	9.81%
Ferroalloys	1,689	4.99%	1,894	6.21%	1,105	4.86%	1,733	6.20%	159	0.56%	199	1.16%
Technology	222	0.66%	153	0.50%	114	0.50%	235	0.84%	217	0.76%	120	0.70%
Chrome									1,064	3.73%	748	4.37%
Platinum					200	0.88%	269	0.96%	129	0.45%	12	0.07%
Operating Income	**8,431**	**100.00%**	**7,654**	**100.00%**	**4,315**	**100.00%**	**7,327**	**100.00%**	**9,042**	**100.00%**	**3,970**	**100.00%**
Copper	3,924	46.54%	3,820	49.91%	2,126	49.27%	2,297	31.35%	4,163	46.04%	2,058	51.84%
Coal	**2,810**	**33.33%**	**2,216**	**28.95%**	**2,041**	**47.30%**	**3,546**	**48.40%**	**687**	**7.60%**	**906**	**22.82%**
Coal-Thermal	1,921	22.78%	1,415	18.49%	1,695	39.28%	2,616	35.70%	544	6.02%	656	16.52%
Coal-Coking	889	10.54%	801	10.47%	343	7.95%	930	12.69%	143	1.58%	250	6.30%
Coal-other					3	0.07%	3	0.07%	3	0.03%	2	0.05%
Zinc Lead	814	9.65%	917	11.98%	506	11.73%	104	1.42%	1,517	16.78%	295	7.43%
Nickel	611	7.25%	503	6.57%	−18	−0.42%	341	4.65%	2,447	27.06%	614	15.47%
Ferroalloys	153	1.81%	353	4.61%	−47	−1.09%	907	12.38%	64	0.71%	105	2.64%
Unallocated	103	1.22%	−180	−2.35%	−282	−6.54%		0.00%	−194	−2.15%	−163	−4.11%

	1	%	2	%	3	%	4	%	5	%	6	%
Technology	27	0.32%	26	0.34%	22	0.51%	32	0.44%	43	0.48%	22	0.55%
Iron Ore	(11)	0.13%	(1)	−0.01%	(1)	−0.22%						
Share of Results from Associates					−56	−1.30%			15	0.17%	4	0.10%
Zinc Lead									12	0.13%	2	0.05%
Coal					3	0.07%			3	0.03%	2	0.05%
Chrome									266	2.94%	118	2.97%
Platinum					24	0.56%	100	1.36%	34	0.38%	11	0.28%
Assets	**74,832**	**100.00%**	**69,709**	**100.00%**	**63,824**	**100.00%**	**55,314**	**100.00%**	**52,249**	**100.00%**	**47,720**	**100.00%**
Copper	24,086	32.19%	22,264	31.94%	20,603	32.28%	18,050	32.63%	19,825	37.94%	19,262	40.36%
Coal	19,608	26.20%	18,302	26.25%	17,341	27.17%	11,998	21.69%	11,421	21.86%	8,908	18.67%
Nickel	14,187	18.96%	12,962	18.59%	11,788	18.47%	12,422	22.46%	9,402	17.99%	9,178	19.23%
Zinc Lead	8,185	10.94%	7,567	10.86%	7,179	11.25%	6,661	12.04%	7,150	13.68%	6,546	13.72%
Ferroalloys	5,487	7.33%	6,066	8.70%	1,612	2.53%	1,421	2.57%	159	0.30%	170	0.36%
Unallocated	1,685	2.25%	1,673	2.40%	1,403	2.20%	1,208	2.18%	666	1.27%	662	1.39%
Iron Ore	1,402	1.87%	721	1.03%	23	0.04%						
Technology	192	0.26%	154	0.22%	133	0.21%	124	0.22%	140	0.27%	104	0.22%
Discontinued											**1634**	**3.42%**
Aluminium											1634	3.42%
Chrome									1,292	2.47%	1,148	2.41%
Platinum					3,742	5.86%	3,430	6.20%	2,194	4.20%	108	0.23%

Exhibit 21 Top 15 Miners by Market Cap[80]

Company	Market Cap as of 10/15/12 (billions of US$)
BHP BILLITON PLC	$175.59
VALE SA-PF	$96.95
RIO TINTO PLC	$92.32
SABIC	$70.80
XSTRATA PLC	$46.04
ANGLO AMER PLC	$40.00
BARRICK GOLD CRP	$38.96
GLENCORE INT PLC	$38.27
FREEORT-MCMORAN	$38.10
GOLDCORP INC	$35.35
SOUTHERN COPPER	$29.72
NORILSK NICKEL	$29.57
NEWMONT MINING	$27.35
MITSUI & CO	$25.50
GRUPO MEXICO-B	$25.30

had made together, was announced on February 5, 2012. Glencore would offer 2.8 of its shares for every share of Xstrata, an 8% premium; the trading company would finish with a 55% stake in the mining group. The deal required the approval of 75% of Xstrata shares excluding Glencore's existing stake. As the trader controlled a third of the miner's equity, a mere 16.5% vote against would result in the transaction's collapse.

Management cited several potential synergies: the combined group's expanded capabilities and geographic footprint would allow for new arbitrage opportunities; scale in freight, logistics, and procurement would result in reduced expenses, as would the elimination of redundant functions and personnel. Xstrata's management forecasted an US$500 million increase in EBITDA, including US$50 million in cost synergies.[82] They also anticipated 11% annual top-line growth for the combined entity through 2015.[83] Analysts also argued that the companies' approaches to asset development were complementary: "Historically XTA has not concentrated on early stage M&A opportunities. Instead it has focused on acquiring producing assets, where commodity price risk has a very material effect on the probability of creating value. GLEN, by contrast, primarily buys earlier stage deals [and] executes roll-up/consolidation strategies or distressed assets, where the ability to make huge returns even in a weak commodity price environment is high."[84]

locales could persist following the IPO: "Part of the reason Glencore has been able to capitalize on investment opportunities is its private structure. A listed entity has many more stakeholders that need to be consulted and in some cases grant approval. Once listed, Glencore may not always be able to act on opportunities quickly."[81]

Glencore's collapsing equity valuation did not halt the merger talks. The transaction, codenamed "Everest" in reference to a Himalayan expedition the two CEOs

The Financial Times questioned whether many of these proposed benefits would actually be realized.[85] Several major shareholders expressed dissatisfaction with the terms of the agreement. Richard Buxton, head of UK equities at Schroders, stated: "This is a fabulous

Exhibit 22 XTA Copper Production Cost Curve[86]

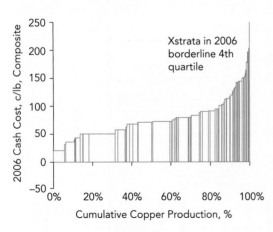

Xstrata's cost position in 2006

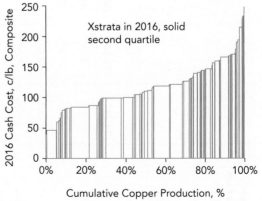

Xstrata's cost position in 2016e

Source: Brook Hunt, corporate reports and HSBC analysis

Exhibit 23 Xstrata and Peers–Stock Performance since IPO[87]

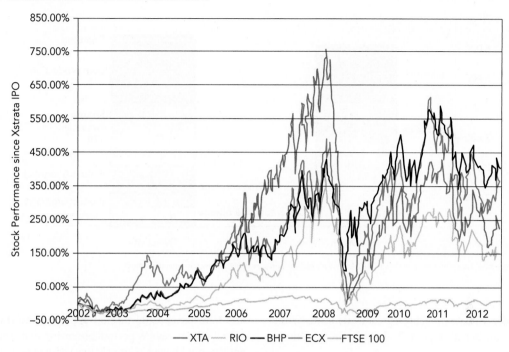

Exhibit 24 Glencore and Peers–Stock Performance since IPO[88]

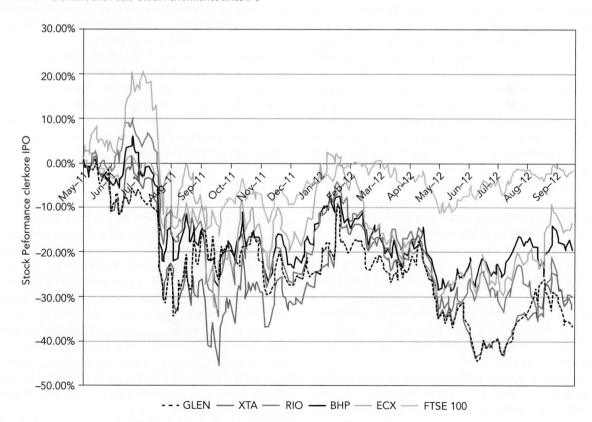

Exhibit 25 Breakdown of 2010 EBITDA[89]

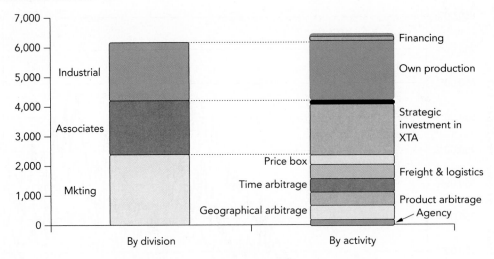

Source: Deutsche Bank, Financing is not included in EDITDA, but we believe it is an area in which Glencore generates a profit.

deal for Glencore, it's probably a great deal for the Xstrata management, but it's a poor deal for Xstrata's majority shareholders."[90]

As part of the merger agreement, Mick Davis would accede to the CEO job while Glasenberg would serve as President & Deputy CEO. Moreover, Xstrata's 65 most senior employees would receive retention packages totalling up to £254 million. The pay-out to the miner's management team was not linked to performance, a decision scorned by investors, pundits, and analysts alike.

Investor objections to the deal, however, carried no weight until Qatar Holding, an indirect subsidiary of the Qatar Investment Authority and owner of an 11% stake in Xstrata, sought improved merger terms. In the fund's view, "an exchange ratio of 3.25 would provide a more appropriate distribution of benefits of the merger."[91] In August, Norges Bank Investment Management, the manager behind Norway's oil-backed sovereign wealth fund, boosted its holdings of Xstrata and demanded better terms from Glencore.[92] While the trading house initially refused to budge, Glasenberg suggested a last minute compromise on September 7th: Glencore would grant a ratio of 3.05 if he were allowed to become CEO of the combined entity. Xstrata's board responded by stating that the new premium on offer was low for a takeover. Furthermore, removing Mick Davis created "significant risk around the retention of the Xstrata senior and operational management."[93]

The deal was still subject to approval from multiple regulators, a bureaucratic hurdle necessitated by the combined group's global reach. The Australian Competition and Consumer Commission approved the transaction after a 47-day review period, observing that "the merged entity would have a relatively low share of global production and would compete against a number of remaining substantial competitors."[94] In a surprising twist, however, the European Commission elected to investigate the merger, overruling its previous declaration that the two companies represented a single entity.

Meanwhile, on March 20, 2012, Glencore announced the takeover of Viterra, a Canadian grain trader, for C$16.25 a share, a 48% premium. The deal, valued at C$6.1 billion, was paid for entirely in cash. Analysts were skeptical about the strategic logic driving the deal. When questioned, a company spokesperson merely responded: "There will be synergies, significant synergies."

Outlook

Analysts and shareholders were meticulously combing through the operations, performance, and deals. Some governments were also raising concerns, and the objections by sovereign wealth funds to the merger terms could potentially kill the deal. While Xstrata management would come out rich, was this the best competitive move for Glencore? Would it be better off selling Xstrata? In 2009, Xstrata had proposed a merger with Anglo American, the primary shareholder of DeBeers, but they had snubbed the overture, saying they were focused on developing Tier-1 assets.[95] There might be other opportunities, however. And were the much-vaunted synergies illusive or was the Glencore-Xstrata combination indeed the model of the future?

Exhibit 26(a) Glencore Income Statement[96]

Glencore International PLC Income Statement						
	FS2 2011	**FY 2011**	**FY 2010**	**FY 2009**	**FY 2008**	**FY 2007**
For the period ending	12/31/11	12/31/11	12/31/10	12/31/09	12/31/08	12/31/07
Turnover	186,152	186,152	144,978	106,364	152,236	142,343
Cost of sales	181,938	181,938	140,467	103,073	146,893	136,068
Gross Profit	4,214	4,214	4,511	3,291	5,343	6,275
Operating Expenses	857	857	1,063	839	850	1,185
Operating profit (loss)	3,357	3,357	3,448	2,452	4,493	5,090
Interest Expense	1,186	1,186	1,217	854	1,135	1,301
Net Non-Operating Losses (Gains)	(1,833)	(1,833)	(2,109)	(369)	2,022	(3,204)
Pretax Income	4,004	4,004	4,340	1,967	1,336	6,993
Income Tax Expense	(264)	(264)	234	238	268	568
Income Before XO Items	4,268	4,268	4,106	1,729	1,068	6,425
Extraordinary Loss Net of Tax	-	-	-	-	-	-
Minority Interests	220	220	355	96	24	311
Net profit (loss)	4,048	4,048	3,751	1,633	1,044	6,114
Total Cash Preferred Dividends	-	-	-	-	-	-
Other Adjustments	-	-	2,460	650	677	5,006
Net Inc Avail to Common Shareholders	4,048	4,048	1,291	983	367	1,108
Exceptional L(G)	341	341	(99)	1,091	3,843	(809)
Tax Effect on Abnormal Items	-	-	-	-	(87)	-
Normalized Income	4,389	4,389	1,192	2,074	4,123	299
Basic EPS Before Abnormal Items	0.78	0.78				
Basic EPS Before XO Items	0.72	0.72				
Basic EPS	0.80	0.72				
Basic Weighted Avg Shares	6,940	5,658				
Diluted EPS Before Abnormal Items	0.72	0.72				
Diluted EPS	0.74	0.69				
Diluted Weighted Avg Shares	7,372	6,087				
Reference Items						
EBITDA	4,423	4,423	4,474	3,074	5,068	5,527
EBITDA Margin	2.38%	2.38%	3.09%	2.89%	3.33%	3.88%
Gross Margin	1.60%	2.26%	3.11%	3.09%	3.51%	4.41%
Operating Margin	1.18%	1.80%	2.38%	2.31%	2.95%	3.58%
Profit Margin	1.67%	2.17%	2.59%	1.54%	0.69%	4.30%
Dividends per Share	0.15	0.15				

Exhibit 26(b) Glencore Balance Sheet[97]

Glencore International PLC					
Balance Sheet					
	FY 2011	**FY 2010**	**FY 2009**	**FY 2008**	**FY 2007**
For the period ending	12/31/11	12/31/10	12/31/09	12/31/08	13/31/07
Assets					
Cash & Near Cash Items	1,305	1,463	860	826	658
Short-Term Investments	40	66	75	113	339
Accounts & Notes Receivable	15,903	12,663	9,156	9,617	11,408
Inventories	17,129	17,393	15,073	7,805	12,212
Other Current Assets	11,354	12,711	13,561	18,147	12,265
Total current Assets	45,731	44,296	38,725	36,508	36,882
LT Investments & LT Receivables	1,547	2,438	3,202	2,808	3,611
Net Fixed Assets	14,639	12,088	6,845	6,859	5,742
Gross Fixed Assets	18,858	15,494	9,268	8,958	7,147
Accumulated Depreciation	4,219	3,406	2,423	2,099	1,405
Other Long-Term Assets	24,248	20,965	17,504	15,136	13,720
Total Long-Term Assets	40,434	35,491	27,551	24,803	23,073
Total Assets	86,165	79,787	66,276	61,311	59,955
Liabilities & Shareholders' Equity					
Account Payable	14,523	12,450	8,162	7,445	8,835
Short-Term Borrowings	8,185	11,881	2,082	1,524	1,516
Other Short-Term Liabilities	8,768	12,507	20,337	21,737	24,116
Total Current Liabilities	31,476	36,838	30,581	30,706	31,467
Long-Term Borrowings	19,844	18,251	16,403	13,071	10,023
Other Long-Term Liabilities	2,510	2,191	1,348	1,223	1,894
Total Long-Term Liabilities	22,354	20,442	17,751	14,294	11,917
Total Liabilities	53,830	57,280	48,332	45,000	43,384
Total Preferred Equity	-	-	-	-	-
Minority Interest	3,070	2,894	1,258	906	900
Share Capital & APIC	26,866	46	46	46	46
Retained Earnings & Other Equity	2,399	19,567	16,640	15,359	15,625
Total Equity	32,335	22,507	17,944	16,311	16,571
Total Liabilities & Equity	86,165	79,787	66,276	61,311	59,955
Reference Items					
Net Debt	26,684	28,603	17,550	13,656	10,542
Net Debt to Equity	82.52	127.08	97.80	83.72	63.62
Current Ratio	1.45	1.20	1.27	1.19	1.17
Cash Conversion Cycle	35.54	43.30	46.91	29.30	
Other Inventory	13,979	17,393	15,073	7,805	12,212
Pure Retained Earnings	4,039	1,823	1,461	1,414	1,320
Investments in Associated Companies	18,858	16,766	14,881	13,221	11,822

Exhibit 26(c) Glencore Segment Data[98]

Glencore International PLC

Segment Financial Data

	FY 2011	%	FY 2010	%	FY 2009	%	FY 2008	%	FY 2007	%
For the perioding ending	12/31/11		12/31/10		12/31/09		12/31/08		12/31/07	
Revenue	**186,152**	**100.00%**	**144,978**	**100.00%**	**106,364.00**	**100.00%**	**152,236**	**100.00%**	**142,343**	**100.00%**
Metals & Minerals	51,984	27.93%	45,211	31.18%	35,391.00	33.27%	40,685	26.72%	48,152	33.83%
Energy Products	117,065	62.89%	89,349	61.63%	62,391.00	58.66%	98,157	64.48%	84,083	59.07%
Agricultural Products	17,103	9.19%	10,418	7.19%	8,582.00	8.07%	13,394	8.80%	10,108	7.10%
Cost of Revenue							**147,565**	**100.00%**	**136,068**	**100.00%**
Metals & Minerals							39,179	26.55%	43,720	32.13%
Energy Products							95,767	64.90%	82,749	60.81%
Agriculture Products							12,618	8.55%	9,595	7.05%
Corporate/Eliminations							1	0.00%	4	0.00%
Gross Profit							**4,671**	**100.00%**	**6,275**	**100.00%**
Corporate/Eliminations							(1)	-0.02%	513	8.18%
Agricultural Products							776	16.61%	(4)	-0.06%
Metals & Minerals							1,506	32.24%	4,432	70.63%
Energy Products							2,390	51.17%	1,334	21.26%
Operating Income	**5,398**	**100.00%**	**3,448**	**100.00%**	**2,452.00**	**100.00%**				
Metals & Minerals	2,599	48.15%	2,561	74.27%	1,051.00	42.86%				
Energy Products	1,072	19.86%	685	19.87%	1,358.00	55.38%				
Agricultural Products	(47)	-0.87%	717	20.79%	345.00	14.07%				
Corporate /Eliminations	1,774	32.86%	(515)	-14.94%	(302.00)	-12.32%				
Property/Plant/Equipment	**14,639**	**100.00%**	**12,088**	**100.00%**	**6,845.00**	**100.00%**	**6,859**	**100.00%**	**5,742**	**100.00%**
Metals & Minerals	9,367	63.99%	8,860	73.30%	5,672.00	82.86%	4,814	70.19%	4,345	75.67%
Energy Products	4,210	28.76%	2,489	20.59%	679.00	9.92%	1,580	23.04%	903	15.73%
Agricultural Products	1,062	7.25%	739	6.11%	494.00	7.22%	412	6.01%	250	4.35%
Corporate / Eliminations							53		244	
Assets	**86,165**	**100.00%**	**79,787**	**100.00%**	**66,276.00**	**100.00%**	**61,311**	**100.00%**	**59,955**	**100.00%**
Metals & Minerals	32,272	37.45%	29,708	37.23%	27,099.00	40.89%	35,597	58.06%	34,374	57.33%
Energy Products	25,627	29.74%	22,188	27.81%	16,845.00	25.42%	20,296	33.10%	18,841	31.43%
Agricultural Products	6,528	7.58%	6,967	8.73%	2,863.00	4.32%	2,943	4.80%	4,570	7.62%
Corporate / Eliminations	21,738	25.23%	20,924	26.22%	19,469.00	29.38%	2,475	4.04%	2,170	3.62%

Exhibit 27 Financial Performance Benchmarking: Xstrata vs. Peers[99]

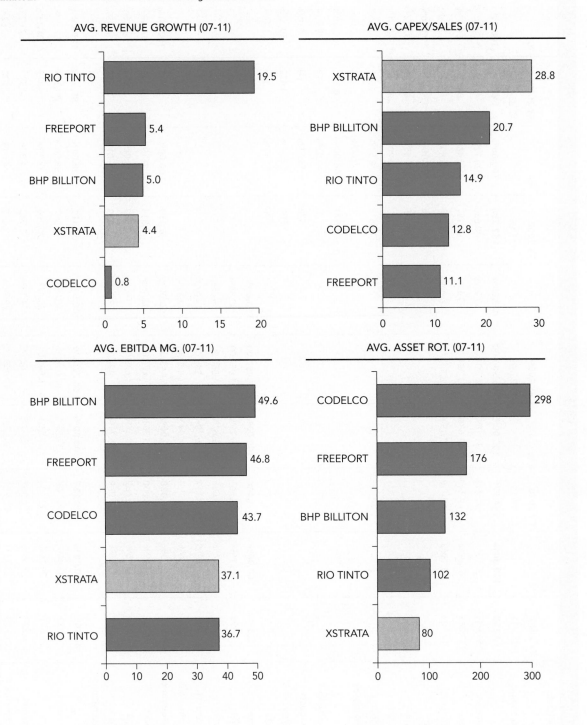

Exhibit 28 Bloomberg Analyst Projections for Glencore and Xstrata[100]

Glencore-Analyst Financial Projections 2012-2015									
USD millions	2007	2008	2009	2010	2011	2012	2013	2014	2015
Revenue	142,343	152,236	106,364	144,978	186,152	205,309	213,635	224,267	222,091
YoY Growth	-	*6.95%*	*−30.13%*	*36.30%*	*28.40%*	*10.29%*	*4.06%*	*4.98%*	*−0.97%*
EBIT	5,090	4,493	2,452	3,448	3,357	4,314	5,835	6,865	6,244
Margin	*3.58%*	*2.95%*	*2.31%*	*2.38%*	*1.80%*	*2.10%*	*2.73%*	*3.06%*	*2.81%*
Tax Rate(%)	8.12%	20.06%	12.10%	5.39%	-	-	-	-	-
Tax	568	268	238	234	(264)	0	0	0	0
NOPAT	4,522	4,225	2,214	3,214	3,621	4,314	5,835	6,865	6,244
Minority Interests	311	24	96	355	220	220	220	220	220
Margin	-	-	-	-	-	-	-	-	-
Capex	(1,577)	(1,823)	(1,088)	(1,657)	(2,606)	(2,395)	(3,123)	(3,742)	(4,708)
Margin	*1.11%*	*1.20%*	*1.02%*	*1.14%*	*1.40%*	*1.17%*	*1.46%*	*1.67%*	*2.12%*
Depreciation & Amortization	437	575	622	1,026	1,066	1,045	1,087	1,141	1,130
Margin	*0.31%*	*0.38%*	*0.58%*	*0.71%*	*0.57%*	*0.51%*	*0.51%*	*0.51%*	*0.51%*
Net Working Capital Change	-	(4,808)	6,090	1,539	903	1,689	1,758	1,845	1,827
Margin	*0.00%*	*3.16%*	*5.73%*	*1.06%*	*0.49%*	*0.82%*	*0.82%*	*0.82%*	*0.82%*
Free Cash Flow	3,071	7,761	(4,438)	689	958	1,055	1,822	2,199	618
Xstrata-Analyst Financial Projections 2012-2015									
USD millions	2007	2008	2009	2010	2011	2012	2013	2014	2015
Revenue	28,542	27,952	22,732	30,499	33,877	30,642	34,280	36,349	42,197
YoY Growth	*66.89%*	*−2.07%*	*−18.67%*	*34.17%*	*11.08%*	*−9.55%*	*11.87%*	*6.03%*	*16.09%*
EBIT	8,777	7,249	4,057	7,661	8,431	4,466	5,864	7,241	9,130
Margin	*30.75%*	*25.93%*	*17.85%*	*25.12%*	*24.89%*	*14.58%*	*17.11%*	*19.92%*	*21.64%*
Tax Rate(%)	28.44%	25.23%	43.73%	24.99%	27.18%	27.18%	27.18%	27.18%	27.18%
Tax	2,311	1,304	669	1,653	2,215	1,214	1,594	1,968	2,482
NOPAT	6,466	5,945	3,388	6,008	6,216	3,252	4,270	5,272	6,648
Minority Interests	326	269	200	267	220	220	220	220	220
Margin	-	-	-	-	-	-	-	-	-
Capex	(2,848)	(4,796)	(3,568)	(5,819)	(8,108)	(7,236)	(8,651)	(10,628)	(14,397)
Margin	*9.98%*	*17.16%*	*15.70%*	*19.08%*	*23.93%*	*23.62%*	*25.23%*	*29.24%*	*34.12%*
Depreciation & Amortization	2,127	2,396	2,419	2,732	3,217	2,751	3,077	3,263	3,788
Margin	*7.45%*	*8.57%*	*10.64%*	*8.96%*	*9.50%*	*8.98%*	*8.98%*	*8.98%*	*8.98%*
Net Working Capital Change	560	(713)	2,154	519	(432)	571	639	677	786
Margin	*1.96%*	*−2.55%*	*9.48%*	*1.70%*	*−1.28%*	*1.86%*	*1.86%*	*1.86%*	*1.86%*
Free Cash Flow	4,859	3,989	(115)	2,135	1,537	(2,024)	(2,162)	(2,990)	(4,967)

Exhibit 29 Profit Margins (2008) from Trading Activities for Different Players[101]

Net profit margin from trading activities
(%)

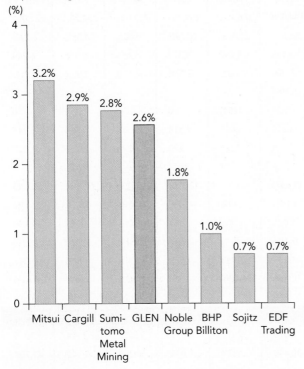

Appendix

Glossary of key terms

Arbitrage spread: The simultaneous purchase and sale of an asset in order to profit from a difference in the price. Arbitrageurs price differences of identical or similar securities or goods, on different markets or in different forms. Arbitrage exists as a result of market inefficiencies. The price differential captured by the trader is referred to as the arbitrage spread.

Derivative: Relates to financial derivatives. A financial derivative is a financial contract/product related to an underlying asset, i.e., the value of the derivative depends on the value of the asset. Derivatives come in different forms, such as forwards and options, and provide a way for market participants to hedge risks.

Directional bet: Speculation on a specific direction, i.e., rise or decline, of the market for an asset. A directional bet involves buying or selling the asset or trading associated derivatives.

Forward/future contracts: Contracts for future delivery of an underlying asset between two parties. The parties entering the contract have the obligation to deliver/pay according to the terms specified in the contract. For most assets, these contracts are settled financially instead of through physical delivery.

Hedging: Activity through which the holder or beneficiary of a certain asset can protect against potential losses, such as those arising from market fluctuations. Hedging can be achieved through a number of different instruments. In the case of the commodities market, the most common forms of hedging are forward and option contracts.

Market making: Intermediaries, e.g., banks or trading companies, provide price quotes and ensure liquidity in markets by buying and selling an asset they hold in inventory from its clients. Market makers typically make a profit on the bid-offer spread.

Option: The right to buy or sell an asset at an agreed upon price at a specified date or period in the future. In contrast to a forward/future contract, the holder of an option has the right and not the obligation to complete the associated transaction.

Proprietary trading: Trading of assets with a company's own funds, with the goal of making a profit for itself.

Prompt market: Another term for the spot market, i.e., a market in which all transaction take place with immediate effect.

Spot market: Market for assets at current prices for immediate delivery. This is in contrast to the forward market.

NOTES

1. Preliminary FY 2011 Presentation, Thompson Reuters
2. "Glencore and Xstrata would be 'unique'", The Financial Times, February 2, 2012.
3. "How Glencore and Xstrata nailed the $76bn deal", The Australian, February 6, 2012.
4. "Glencore chief's resolve hits deal hopes", Financial Times, August 21, 2012.
5. "Glencore softens Xstrata proposals", Financial Times, September 9, 2012.
6. "Usage of Copper": http://www.lme.com/copper_industryusage.asp
7. International Copper Study Group: "2010 World Copper Factbook", www.icsg.com
8. LME Copper Price Graph, http://www.lme.com/copper_graphs.asp
9. Datamonitor, Industry Profile Global Copper, March 2011, Reference code: 0199-0717.
10. International Copper Study Group: "2010 World Copper Factbook", www.icsg.com
11. "Glencore: Rome wasn't built in a day: Initiate at Neutral", JP Morgan Cazenove, Analyst Report, June 23, 2011.
12. "Chinese investors keen on copper, coal assets abroad 2012": http://resourceinvestingnews.com/34149-chinese-investors-keen-copper-coal-assets-abroad-2012-junior-miners-demand.html
13. World Copper Factbook.
14. Indexmundi, www.indexmundi.com
15. World Copper Factbook.

16. USEPA, Profile of The Nonferrous Metals Industry. EPA 310-R-95-010

17. "The 10 Biggest Copper Producers": http://metals.about.com/od/suppliersaz/tp/The-10-Biggest-Copper-Producers.htm

18. "Glencore: Rome wasn't built in a day: Initiate at Neutral", JP Morgan Cazenove, Analyst Report, 6/23/2011

19. Aurubis: Annual report.

20. "Record cash flows fund mining consolidation", The Financial Times, June 20, 2007.

21. "Rio and BHP Billiton: the biggest M&A dead-end in history?" Financial News, October 25, 2010.

22. "The Future Mine: Bigger is Better", Miningtechnology.com, October 2, 2009.

23. These and other technical terms are defined in the appendix to this case.

24. CRU, Aurubis company presentation.

25. "Glencore International PLC: A closer look at marketing", Credit Suisse, November 28, 2011.

26. 'Marketing Briefing', BHP Billiton, July 10, 2003.

27. "Glencore International: A unique business combination", Royal Bank of Scotland N.V., June 29, 2011.

28. "Profiting from a contango, not so easy", FT Alphaville, December 8, 2008.

29. 'Exclusive: Glencore, Vitol keep oil flowing to Greece', Reuters, May 30, 2012.

30. "Glencore: Lots of fingers in lots of pies - feedback from marketing day", JPMorgan Cazenove, December 1, 2011.

31. "Why Morgan Stanley's commodities empire is shrinking", The Economic Times, June 7, 2012.

32. "Private equity turns to commodities", The Financial Times, June 7, 2012.

33. "Iron ore swaps herald new opportunities globally", Norton Rose, July 2010 http://www.nortonrose.com/knowledge/publications/29384/iron-ore-swaps-herald-new-opportunities-globally

34. "Goldman and JPMorgan enter metal warehousing", The Financial Times, March 2, 2010.

35. "Copper ETF plan would 'wreak havoc'", The Financial Times, May 23, 2012.

36. "Chinese copper market accounts for 40% of global consumption", http://www.companiesandmarkets.com/News/Agriculture-Farming-Raw-Materials/Chinese-copper-marketaccounts-for-40-of-global-consumption/NI3430

37. "Hot Copper Shorts Burning Commodity Firms", Caixin Online, May 30, 2012, available at http://english.caixin.com/2012-05-30/100395560.html

38. "Chinese investors keen on copper, coal assets abroad 2012": http://resourceinvestingnews.com/34149-chinese-investors-keen-copper-coal-assets-abroad-2012-junior-miners-demand.html

39. "China Starts Investing Globally", The New York Times, February 20, 2009.

40. "Rio Tinto joins up with Chinalco to explore for copper", The Telegraph, November 25, 2011.

41. "Glencore: Unapologetically unique", Liberum Capital, June 29, 2011.

42. "Glencore: Polished?", MF Global, MF Global Company Note, June 16, 2011.

43. "Copper promises long-term value for commodities in vestors": http://www.dovecommunications.ca/copper-promises-long-term-value-for-commodities-investors/potential-mine-production-consumption-graph/

44. "CODELCO – CHILE", Consolidated Financial Statements, as of December 31, 2011.

45. Annual Report 2009, Anglo American.

46. Bloomberg.

47. "BHP Billiton PLC: Initiation of Coverage", Santander, January 18, 2010.

48. Marketing Briefing, BHP Billiton, October 2, 2007, available at http://www.bhpbilliton.com/home/investors/reports/Pages/Roll%20up%20Pages/Marketing%20BriefingCarbonsteel.aspx

49. Ibid.

50. 2008 Annual Report, Rio Tinto.

51. *Bloomberg.*

52. Ibid.

53. Freeport-McMoRan Copper & Gold Inc., 2011 annual report.

54. "Vale and Xstrata at impasse in talks", The Financial Times, February 14, 2008.

55. Javier Blas, "Trafigura profits soar above $1bn". The Financial Times, December 12, 2011.

56. Leigh, David "Papers prove Trafigura ship dumped toxic waste in Ivory Coast". London: The Guardian, May 19, 2009.

57. "Death toll from Ivory Coast pollution rises to 15". Reuters, February 19, 2007.

58. Silverstein, K., "A Giant among Giants". Foreign Policy. May/June 2012.

59. Daniel, A. (2009). The King of Oil: The Secret Lives of Marc Rich. New York: St. Martin's Press.

60. Ammann, D., "Iran Sanctions: The Sobering Lessons of Marc Rich". ABC News. March 22, 2010.

61. Ammann, D. (2009). The King of Oil: The Secret Lives of Marc Rich. New York: St. Martin's Press. ISBN 0-312-57074-0.

62. History. 2012. Glencore International. http://www.glencore.com/history.php

63. Rich and Green were pardoned by President Clinton on his last day in office on January 20, 2001.

64. "Book Talk: Daniel Ammann on Glencore Founder Marc Rich". Reuters, February 17, 2010.

65. Final Report. 2004. Iraq Survey Group. http://www.globalsecurity.org/wmd/library/report/2004/isg-finalreport/isg-final-report_vol1_rfp-02.htm

66. Annual Results Presentation. March 2008. Glencore International.

67. "Xstrata's untimely ambitions", Mining Journal Online, June 15, 2012.

68. "Glencore: Master of Commodity Flows", Morgan Stanley Research Europe, June 29, 2011.

69. "The Value in Volatility", Deutsche Bank, 6 June 2011.

70. "Glencore: Addressing key bottom-up issues", Morgan Staneley, June 29, 2011.

71. Global Offer, London & Zurich Listing. March 2002. Xstrata plc. http://www.xstrata.com/publications/acquisitionsandoffers/ipo/

72. History. Xstrata plc. http://www.xstrata.com/about/history/

73. "Xstrata PLC: Gearing approaching Falconbridge lows", RBC, January 6, 2011.

74. Commission of the European Communities, Case No COMP/M.4256 – XStrata / Falconbridge, July 13, 2006.

75. "Glencore International: 1H11 Results Preview", The Royal Bank of Scotland NV, August 17, 2011.

76. "Glencore: Rome wasn't built in a day; Initiate at Neutral", JPMorgan Cazenove, June 24, 2011.

77. Bloomberg.

78. Ibid.

79. Ibid.

80. Ibid.

81. "The Value in Volatility", Deutsche Bank, June 6, 2011.

82. "Xstrata plc. announces agreed amendments to Management Incentive Arrangements in all-share merger with Glencore International plc.", Press Release, Xstrata, June 27, 2012, available at www.xstrata.com/restricted/glencorexstrata

83. Annual Report 2011, Strategic Review, Xstrata, available at http://www.xstrata.com/assets/reports/ar11/strategic-review/ceo-strategic-review/glencore-merger/

84. "Glencore / Xstrata: In merger of equals talks: looks feasible at 2.70-2.80", Liberum Capital, February 3, 2012.

85. "Lex in depth: Glencore", The Financial Times, June 14, 2012.

86. HSBC, Xstrata, February 7, 2012, p 3.

87. Bloomberg

88. Ibid.

89. "The Value in Volatility", Deutsche Bank, June 6, 2011.

90. "Glencore-Xstrata could face blocking threat". The Financial Times, February 7, 2012.

91. "Glencore crunch meeting over merger", The Financial Times, June 27, 2012.

92. "Norway fund opposes Glencore merger", The Financial Times, August 28, 2012.

93. "Glencore softens Xstrata proposals", The Financial Times, September 9 2012

94. "Australia Regulator Won't Block Glencore-Xstrata Merger", Dow Jones Newswires, July 4, 2012.

95. Observers viewed Anglo American's response as a missed opportunity: "During three months of mining merger drama, Anglo American has played the part of an indignant duchess not acknowledging the existence of the vile commoner standing at her castle door and asking for an audience." "Anglo rejects Xstrata merger offer", The Financial Times, June 22, 2009.

96. Bloomberg

97. Ibid.

98. Ibid.

99. Ibid.

100. Ibid.

101. Value on top of intrinsic value of commodity (Source: Company reports, BCG).

Harley-Davidson: Strategic Competitiveness that Spans Decades

Guriqbal Cheema, Joel Cunningham, Pallavi Daliparthi, John Klostermann, Brian Rabe

Texas A&M University

"It's more than a brand. It's a culture."[1]

Kent Grayson
Professor of Marketing, Northwestern University

Introduction

Harley-Davidson is an American cultural and business icon on the level of Levi Strauss and Coca-Cola. Often imitated, but never duplicated, Harley-Davidson has managed to survive, and has, at times, thrived for many decades. Through depression, recessions, world wars, high technology developments, Japanese competition, and increasing government regulation, Harley-Davidson has maintained operations where over a dozen other U.S. motorcycle firms have failed. Harley-Davidson has even survived over a decade as a subsidiary of a bowling alley service firm. It has achieved this by essentially relying on designing, manufacturing, selling, and servicing a relatively static product: two wheels, a 45° V-Twin engine, and a set of handlebars.

How has Harley-Davidson managed to survive through these and other hardships in a motorcycle market that is dominated by leisure riders? How has it kept the doors open while its historic U.S. rival, Indian Motorcycles, is currently in its fourth incarnation? How has it maintained its attractiveness with outlaw bikers, investment bankers, and those who appear to be experiencing a "mid-life crisis" and who sometimes turn to the firm's products as a result? More importantly, what is this firm selling that keeps it as the industry leader in full-size motorcycles? The answer to these questions is not a 526-pound batch of steel with 250 feet of wiring, but rather the fact that Harley-Davidson is selling the American dream of freedom. How it is able to do this is a fascinating story.

The Challenge

With over 6,000 employees, 1,400 franchises, and nine production facilities, Harley-Davidson has managed to survive the economic downturn that was in full force in late 2007 and for the next few years; but the firm is not out of the woods yet. In fact, Harley-Davidson is struggling with three pivotal issues, the first of which is that the firm's products are viewed as leisure items. The other two issues are similar in nature in that they deal with the fact that managing the firm's target market is challenging, particularly as demand for its products is changing. Individually and collectively these issues pose a real challenge to the company's long-term success. Without addressing these issues, Harley-Davidson may lose its ability to create value for customers and to serve stakeholders' needs as a result.

As noted, the first issue Harley-Davidson must successfully address is the fact that consumers see the firm's products primarily as leisure items. This means that in many consumers' eyes, purchasing motorcycles, performance parts, and high-dollar apparel is a luxury rather than a necessity. Because of this, Harley's products must compete for funds from what at least sometimes can be volatile discretionary budgets for consumers. When economic conditions are challenging, the motorcycle market tends to experience difficulties in terms of generating adequate sales. While Harley-Davidson's revenue streams originate from several sources, very few of them appeal to a cost-sensitive consumer base.

© Vividfour / Shutterstock.com

Second, Harley-Davidson is challenged to effectively specify its target market as a first step to appropriately serving that market's needs. Historically, the firm's target market has been males between the ages of 29 and 55. However, in the last decade, Harley-Davidson has pursued younger riders and women as a means of expanding its target customer segments. But expanding the segments the firm serves with its products is not a risk-free decision or choice for the firm to make in that serving others might cause the firm to lose its ability to effectively serve the specific needs of the 29- to 55-year-old male (again, the historical target customer). This matter is considered more fully later in the case.

Third, demands and cost drivers for the motorcycle market are ever changing. Overseas competitors have shifted their focus from being the least expensive to being affordable *and* to providing a wider variety of motorcycles to customers as options to purchase. This competitive shift has put pressure on Harley-Davidson's key markets and has forced the firm to respond. With over 12 percent and 55 percent of the European and U.S. heavyweight motorcycle market respectively, Harley-Davidson has a substantial territory to defend.

History.[2] Harley-Davidson, Inc. has been a publicly traded firm since 1987. It has two primary divisions: Motorcycles and Related Products and Financial Services. The Financial Services Division provides credit to motorcycle buyers and dealerships as well as risk management and insurance services for all parts of the firm. The Motorcycles and Related Products Division currently operates through eight primary segments:

- Parts & Accessories (17.5 percent of net revenue in 2011)
- General Merchandise (5.9 percent of net revenue in 2011)
- Licensing ($43.2 million of net revenue in 2011)
- Harley-Davidson Museum
- International Sales (32 percent of net motorcycle revenue in 2011)
- Patents and Trademarks
- Other Services
- Marketing

In 1903, William S. Harley and Arthur Davidson founded Harley-Davidson Motor Company, known by enthusiasts as "the Motor Company," in order to fund their racing pursuits. Accordingly, their first motorcycles were merely contemporary bicycles with small engines retrofitted to the frame. It was Harley-Davidson's early success in motorcycle racing that fueled the demand for its early models, which were sold in dealerships as early as 1904. Because these turn of the century races were as much about endurance as speed, Harley-Davidson acquired invaluable knowledge pertinent to practicality and robust design. After significant success in road and endurance races, Harley-Davidson broke fresh ground with the introduction of the V-Twin engine design. Superior to large single-cylinder engines, the lighter V-Twin design allowed similar displacement in a lighter package with a shape that fit naturally into the bicycle-inspired frames of the early 1900s. Few suspected that this design would become so integral to modern motorcycles.

Having dedicated over a third of its production to the U.S. Army, Harley-Davidson sales exploded during World War I. With the advent of motorized warfare, the motorcycle proved itself to be far more than just a novel invention. In addition to proving itself to the Army, Harley-Davidson also proved itself to soldiers. After the war, soldiers returned home and became a loyal customer base for the young firm. Through the 1920s, Harley-Davidson continued to focus on design improvement and racing. It spent much of this decade fighting for market share with multiple medium and small competitors. During this time, firms producing automobiles, airplanes, bicycles, and industrial machinery also tried their hand at building motorcycles.

The 1930s were a unique time for the motorcycle industry. In the wake of the Great Depression, the public was looking for inexpensive, simple transportation. At the same time, unemployment and inflation shrank potential customers' purchasing power. It was during this time that many of the smaller motorcycle manufacturers dropped out of the industry. Most of these firms were subsidiaries of companies in related industries. These failed motorcycle firms had many of the capabilities needed to produce motorcycles, but lacked the corporate focus and support to continue production during such a difficult economic time. It was during this time that the U.S. domestic market shrank, with only Indian and Harley-Davidson remaining. With the market divided between only two domestic producers, Harley-Davidson's production held steady.

With the onset of World War II, Harley-Davidson found itself to be a major supplier for the Allied war effort. Again, war vaulted Harley-Davidson into a position of higher volume, improved reputation, and deeper loyalty with owners and soldiers. As the war came to an end, the United States was flooded with a surplus of Army WL45 motorcycles. Suddenly, this country was full of prospective riders who understood Harley-Davidson's product and appreciated how motorcycles could provide inexpensive, dependable transportation. At this point, only Indian Motorcycles was a competitor for Harley-Davidson. But in 1956, at the height of an economic recession, Indian Motorcycles declared bankruptcy and stopped producing motorcycles altogether, leaving only Harley as a major producer and seller of motorcycles.

As the sole U.S.-based motorcycle power, Harley-Davidson enjoyed great success. Nevertheless, the lack of competition nearly became its undoing. This market condition allowed Harley-Davidson to take more risk in the form of acquisitions, causing the firm to lose its tight focus on a single market. It began branching out to other leisure and motorized products such as off-road motorcycles, ski boats, and golf carts. At the same time, the bulk of Harley-Davidson's revenue stream was still coming from the sale of its heavy motorcycles. Many of the acquisitions the firm completed in the latter part of the 1950s and the early 1960s, such as the Tomahawk Boat Manufacturing Company in 1962, were in similar industries, but a poor fit with Harley nonetheless. The acquired companies were often in deep trouble when Harley-Davidson purchased them. In the end, Harley-Davidson was hobbled with losing ventures that diluted its focus and did not fit well with its core competencies. In 1969, the American Machine and Foundry Company (AMF – a longtime producer of leisure products such as tile bowling pins and ball returns) purchased the financially distressed Harley-Davidson.[3]

Most enthusiasts consider the AMF years as the "dark ages" of Harley-Davidson's history. AMF operated Harley-Davidson as a profit center, reducing allocations to the unit's marketing and research and development (R&D) functions as a result. For the next 13 years, Harley's aging product line remained essentially unchanged. In fact, its line was so static over the years that many of the parts from a 1937 model fit on the 1969 design. Harley-Davidson had just two motorcycles with different trim packages: the low-budget sportster, the sport bike of its day, and a full-size motorcycle available in two different models. In light of Honda and Kawasaki's entrance into the U.S. market, Harley-Davidson's stale product line was even more disappointing. Many did not see these imports as a threat given the prestige and heritage of the Harley-Davidson name. However, the Harley-Davidson image was deteriorating. Even with its products in desperate need of a facelift, AMF relied on Harley-Davidson's reputation to defend its competitive position; AMF plastered Harley-Davidson's name on products like snowmobiles and golf carts. While trying to capitalize on the value of Harley-Davidson's brand name,

quality became a serious problem; customers would have to return new motorcycles to a dealership multiple times to fix manufacturing problems. It was during this time that owners coined the saying "a Harley always marks its spot," a phrase referring to the machine's nearly universal oil leaks. This turned off many prospective customers, as they believed a Harley-Davidson would require constant owner maintenance. All the while, Japanese motorcycle companies enticed more and more riders looking for inexpensive, dependable transportation.

By 1981, Japanese motorcycles were established in the U.S. market not only as dependable transportation, but also as performance machines. Harley-Davidson's sales were in free-fall as its tired designs appealed to a narrowing market segment. It was selling to customers who liked classic style and dated functionality, and all for a high price. Finally, the employees and management of Harley-Davidson led a managed buyout of the company from AMF.[4] The new owners immediately took stock of the firm's strengths and vulnerabilities and increased its R&D and marketing budgets significantly. Because negative effects of AMF's past business decisions still hampered the new management team, sales remained low. In 1985, Harley-Davidson's top management team struggled to restructure the firm and divested itself of most of its unrelated assets. In 1987, Harley-Davidson became a publicly traded company, and none too soon as Harley-Davidson had revamped its product line into four motorcycle styles that were united by the introduction of a new engine. This was the turning point for Harley-Davidson. From this point forward, the firm's quality control was exponentially more effective. In addition, Harley-Davidson focused more on efforts to operate efficiently and effectively. Following the precepts of just-in-time techniques and enhancement to the logistics function were critical to the firm's attempts to enhance efficiency and effectiveness. At the same time, Harley shifted to three major initiatives:[5]

- ■ Improved manufacturing process, leveraging technology, robotics, and employee involvement
- ■ Restructuring business management to a modern system
- ■ Aggressive management of its brand name through dealership management, patenting activities, and careful licensing of related products

The modern Harley-Davidson fought back from the brink several times, each time seeming to evolve and adapt. What appears to be universal to each evolution of the company is that quality, promotion, and market focus have always been a priority.

How Harley Does It[6]

Harley-Davidson focuses on a subset of the motorcycle market featuring customers who value heritage, style, reputation, durability, and adaptability. Until 2000, Harley-Davidson's motorcycles sold at nearly a 25 percent premium. In the last decade, that premium has dropped to 5 to 10 percent, depending on the class of motorcycle. This is due to Japanese motorcycle manufacturers shifting to marketing and selling somewhat unique motorcycles for a better than average price. In comparison, Harley-Davidson uses the Sportster© line as an introductory product, but most of its motorcycles sell for over $15,000, with the average sale price of just over $16,893.[7] Harley-Davidson motorcycles provide a unique product at a price that its target customers deem acceptable or reasonable. While its competitors may have attempted to cut costs, Harley-Davidson has continued to invest in its products in ways that protect the quality of its brand image. Harley-Davidson's market focus is primarily males between the ages of 29 and 55. However, this has been changing.[8] Recently, it has targeted female customers.

What It Does Best[9]

In its modern incarnation (1987 to present), Harley-Davidson achieved success by doing what it does best. Granted, multiple firms make great motorcycles, and many of these firms have a dedicated following. However, through the actions the firm has taken over the years, Harley-Davidson has developed and maintained what is a unique position in the U.S. motorcycle market. Effectively managing its brand name, production or manufacturing simplicity, and a dedicated product following are the key sources of the firm's competitive strength.

Harley-Davidson's brand name is its most important asset. Cultivated through good times and bad, its brand name is a powerful motivator for current and prospective customers. For many Americans, Harley-Davidson is the American motorcycle. This belief is no accident. After being separated from AMF, Harley-Davidson's top management team decided to significantly increase the amount of resources being allocated to marketing and R&D. This appears to have been a wise decision in that Harley-Davidson now holds 55 percent of the entire U.S. motorcycle market, and an even higher share in the U.S. heavy motorcycle market. Strict protection of its brand name permeates every decision the firm makes. Its motorcycles, while occasionally deviating in style, generally follow traditional themes. Harley-Davidson only

makes a design change after witnessing a strong market trend.[10] For example, the custom portion of the motorcycle market has been designing machines with wide rear tires for nearly two decades; in 2007, Harley-Davidson launched a single model with a wide rear tire.

Harley-Davidson is also very selective about its franchise (dealership) opportunities, another method through which the firm protects its brand. Due to free-trade laws, Harley-Davidson is no longer able to insist that its dealerships sell only Harley products. However, it utilizes price incentives to encourage dealerships to stay "Pure-Harley."[11] Harley-Davidson is especially protective of its name and logo when it comes to licensed products, most of which are sold in its dealerships. If it is not the best quality, the product's license is revoked. Retailers can sell ladies' shirts at a 100 percent premium because they are of excellent quality and cannot be found anywhere. This aura of exclusivity is embedded in the very DNA of Harley-Davidson Inc., from the headquarters to the dealerships. This aspect of culture is an asset in that the notion of wanting to be seen as providing products that are somewhat "exclusive" in nature permeates the firm's decision processes as it seeks to serve its target customers' needs.

Harley-Davidson's production process is another important firm-specific asset. The key elements of the process are the melding of a JIT supply chain with team production management and part interchangeability.[12] When combined, the elements of Harley's production process are unique. Japanese manufacturers have used the same JIT concept for years, but have not stressed a limitation of key components. After 1987, Harley-Davidson updated its production facilities and design process. Its production facilities in Kansas City, Missouri and York, Pennsylvania are the best examples of modern robotics combined with team enablement. Interchangeable parts are the most important component of this asset. This concept simplifies all areas of the motorcycle production process; but it is perhaps most evident in the production of Harley's frames and engines. Harley-Davidson produces five unique frames for each motorcycle family: Sportster©, Dyna, Softail©, V-Rod©, and Touring. Even with 28 different models and seemingly limitless options, Harley-Davidson produces only three engines. Internal machining, displacement, and color coating are the only differences across the engines. The Sportster© line comes in two displacements: 883 and 1204 cubic inches. The Dyna, Softail©, and Touring lines all share the same Twincam© engine, available in 96 and 103 cubic inches. The V-Rod's© engine is only produced in one version.[13] This production approach with respect to interchangeable parts appears to be a competitive advantage in that it allows Harley to produce several models, subdividing its target market segments even further, while keeping production costs lower than if it produced 28 different frames and engines.

Loyalty to the brand is another important asset for Harley-Davidson. While its brand name protection applies primarily to prospective customers, its product following centers on existing customers, many of whom are repeat buyers of the firm's products. There are multiple examples of Harley's dedicated following. At the extreme for example, consider the fact that some private riding clubs only grant membership to those willing to tattoo the bar and shield logo on multiple locations of their body. For others, remaining committed to the firm's mantra that owning a Harley "is a journey, not a destination" and participating in company-sponsored events with others sharing this belief accounts for their loyalty. Regardless of the reason for it, customer loyalty to the Harley brand appears to influence these individuals to purchase Harley products other than motorcycles such as clothing and a wide range of product accessories. Historically, loyalty to the brand has resulted in a large percentage of Harley customers choosing to buy another Harley when it is time for a new motorcycle. However, the "graying" of Harley's customer base is potentially a problem as at some point, this group of customers will no longer be purchasing new products.[14]

Keeping It Simple[15]

In 2011, Harley-Davidson generated 88 percent of its revenues from a single business area (Motorcycles and Related Products) and 12 percent from its second primary segment (Financial Services). This composition of sales revenue is consistent with previous years and suggests that Harley may continue business as usual to help the firm reduce its idiosyncratic risk. It will also try to expand its business in other countries with a primary focus on providing quality product and services. Harley-Davidson has been able to earn positive returns while focusing on just two businesses because it has developed strengths that allow it to create value for customers. Moreover, there are fewer challenges in managing only two businesses. This approach allows Harley-Davidson to not only gain economies of scale, but also use its resources efficiently.

Marketing

Historically, males between the ages of 29 and 55 have been Harley-Davidson's target customer. However, this is changing.[16] Recently for example, the firm is also targeting female customers with motorcycle models that have a lower seat height and pink, purple, and light blue color schemes. Its marketing has also reflected an effort to attract more female riders. It has even tailored its riding classes (the Riders Edge Program©) to have all-female sessions and to make new women riders feel more comfortable. A woman could walk into a Harley-Davidson dealership having never sat on a motorcycle and within an hour purchase a motorcycle for as little as $8,000. She could then join a riding class that would grant a motorcycle endorsement on her driver's license.

Thus, Harley-Davidson is beginning to market to a multi-generational and multi-cultural audience. In this regard, the firm is working to attract a more diversified audience in terms of age, gender, and ethnicity.[17] Harley-Davidson is a market leader in the U.S. heavyweight segment. The average median household income of a Harley-Davidson purchaser is $89,000.[18] Harley-Davidson primarily uses advertising and promotional activities via television, print, radio, direct mailings, electronic advertising, and social media to market its product. Moreover, local marketing efforts in conjunction with dealers are highly encouraged. Harley-Davidson uses its customers' experience to continuously develop and introduce innovative products. The market is flooded with high quality, low price Japanese bikes. However, Harley-Davidson does not seek to imitate these bikes. Instead, it uses direct input from its customers to improve its product. Harley-Davidson modifies its product based on input generated through customer surveys, interviews, and focus groups. Thus, some believe that "The real power of Harley-Davidson is the power to market to consumers who love the product."[19]

In 2010, the company introduced "Creative Model" – a Web-based method for marketing its product. In this model, passionate fans are enabled for the purpose of helping Harley develop creative approaches for targeting new customers. Customer experience has traditionally been the main source of Harley-Davidson's marketing strategy. It all started in 1983, when the company introduced Harley Owners Group (H.O.G),[20] which has now grown to more than 1 million members worldwide.[21]

Harley-Davidson distributes its products through an independent dealer network that almost exclusively sells Harley-Davidson motorcycles. These dealerships are licensed dealers and fully authorized to sell and service new motorcycles. They can have secondary locations to provide additional service to the customers. These non-traditional outlets are an extension of the main dealership and consist of Alternate Retail Outlets (ARO) and Seasonal Retail Outlets (SRO). AROs are generally located in high traffic areas such as airports, vacation destinations, tourism spots, and malls and only sell parts, accessories, and general merchandise. SROs are also located in high traffic areas, but operate only on a seasonal basis. AROs and SROs are not allowed to sell new motorcycles. The parts and apparel orders from the dealer are not taken at face value. Harley-Davidson's forward-looking, market-driven allocation system restricts the number of units a particular dealer is able to order. In Canada, the company sells its products to one wholesale dealer, Deeley Harley-Davidson Canada/Fred Deeley Imports Ltd., which in turn sells to independent dealers.[22]

The European, the Middle Eastern and African (EMEA) region is managed from regional headquarters in Oxford, England. Harley-Davidson distributes its products through subsidiaries located in Austria, Dubai, Czech Republic, France, Germany, and Italy. In the EMEA region, Harley-Davidson distributes all products sold to independent dealers through its subsidiaries located in Austria, Czech Republic, United Arab Emirates, France, Germany, Italy, South Africa, Spain, Switzerland, Netherlands, Russia, and United Kingdom. A headquarters in Singapore manages the Asia Pacific regions with the company distributing its product to independent dealers in China, India, Australia, and Japan. The rest of Asia Pacific is managed through the U.S. operations.

Financial Services Segment

Harley believes that its Harley-Davidson Financial Services unit (HDFS) provides sufficient financing to independent distributors, dealers, and retail customers. HDFS provides financing to dealers and retail customers in the U.S. and Canada, but not in the EMEA, Asia-Pacific, and Latin America regions, although these regions do have access to financing through other financial services companies.

Competition

As is the case for many leisure and transportation industries, the U.S. motorcycle market is extremely competitive. Currently, Harley-Davidson competes with four classes of competitors with each group competing in a different market and in different ways. The four competing groups are commonly classified as Metric Cruiser, Metric Sport, U.S. Cruisers, and Custom Cruisers.

Metric Cruiser Competitors. The industry uses the term Metric Cruiser to denote motorcycles made outside the United States with traditional styling. Traditional styling is commonly reflected through an exposed engine

and non-integrated body panels. Japanese motorcycle makers such as Honda, Star (Yamaha), Suzuki, and Kawasaki dominate these models. It is important to note that not all metric cruiser competitors are considered to be heavy motorcycles (over 650 cubic centimeter displacement). These competitors compete with Harley-Davidson on price, but also use the individual model's unique features to garner a competitive advantage. Honda introduced the Fury©,[23] a regular production chopper based on the 1300 VTX power plant in 2009. In 2004, Kawasaki introduced the Vulcan© 2000[24] with a 2,053 cubic centimeter engine, the largest mass-produced V-Twin motorcycle ever. Most of these competitor models of similar size are comparable in features to Harley-Davidson models. The presence of smaller competitor models forces Harley-Davidson to keep entry-level models like the 883 cubic centimeter Sportster©. Smaller metric cruisers like the Suzuki Boulevard 40©, retailing at $2,600 less[25] than Harley-Davidson's least expensive model, keep downward pressure on introductory model prices.

Metric Sport Competitors. Metric Sport motorcycles are made outside the United States, mostly in Japan, and are race-inspired, high performance motorcycles with full body panels and excellent aerodynamic characteristics. Motorcycles like the Suzuki Hayabusa© and the Kawasaki Ninja© are examples of this competitor class. While these motorcycles do not directly compete with most Harley-Davidson models, they do appeal to younger prospective customers because of their breathtaking performance and relatively low prices. In general, metric sport customers are not attracted to most Harley-Davidson models.

Harley-Davidson has taken two key actions to attract young, performance-oriented riders from its sport motorcycle competitors. It introduced the V-Rod© line in 2002 with a high performance, liquid-cooled motor. Harley-Davidson also purchased Buell,[26] a sport motorcycle company using Harley-Davidson motors, in 1993. In 2003, Buell sport motorcycles became a full subsidiary with its models being sold through Harley-Davidson dealerships. Neither of these actions has resonated with the younger riders Harley sought to reach by taking them. As a result, Harley-Davidson opted to discontinue Buell in 2009 after slumping sales.[27] The V-Rod© still exists, but with a median price tag of $15,300 it has not done much to lower the age of the average Harley-Davidson rider.

U.S. Cruiser Competitors. Victory Motorcycles and Indian Motorcycle are the only U.S. Cruiser style motorcycle manufacturers. Victory, a subsidiary of Polaris and a relative newcomer to the motorcycle market, started production in 1998.[28] Polaris is best known for its high quality all-terrain vehicles and personal watercraft. In the last five years, Victory models have been selling at prices more closely comparable with Harley-Davidson. At the same time, Victory increased the number of models and styles; it even brought in famous motorcycle customizers Arlen and Corey Ness[29] to add style and street credibility to its entire product line. In 2009, Indian Motorcycle began its fourth incarnation in an effort to leverage its famous name and art-deco styling. After a shaky start, Indian was recently purchased by Polaris. This move is likely part of a strategy to position Victory and Indian in separate parts of the U.S. motorcycle market and to fulfill the needs of different types of customers. This approach is similar to the strategy General Motors used for decades of offering different products to different types of customers. The median price for an Indian motorcycle is $28,000. Its current tag line is, "Your great grandfather would be proud. Jealous, but proud."[30] Indian is targeting high-income earners with a love for classic motorcycle styling.

Custom Cruiser Competitors.

This class of competitors is comprised of small and medium firms that build highly customized motorcycles with large displacement motors. Firms such as Big Dog Motorcycles,[31] Big Bear Choppers,[32] and American IronHorse are the dominant competitors in this space.[33] These competitors have become far less of an issue for Harley-Davidson since the economic downturn of 2008. With their high levels of customization, these competitors' models come with a high price tag. As their target market shrunk in the recession, these firms thinned significantly; an estimated 60 percent have gone out of business or changed their core function to components production. Others, such as Darwin Motorcycles, now offer custom motorcycles for as little as $18,600.[34] These competitors will always pose a threat to Harley-Davidson. They force Harley-Davidson to continually innovate and customize its product. It is ironic that most of these motorcycle manufacturers use Harley-Davidson style or actual Harley-Davidson components in their production.

Strategic Leaders

"No one can accurately predict the future. What I can predict with the utmost confidence are the things that won't change at Harley-Davidson – namely, our commitment to providing more great motorcycles; to enhancing the

unparalleled Harley lifestyle experience, and to continuing to provide excellent financial performance."

– Jeff Bleustein
Annual Report 1997[35]

Although the strategic intent of Harley-Davidson has not changed much since 1997, the way it operates and leads has certainly adapted to reflect new ways of doing business.

Keith Wandell–Chairman and CEO. When Keith Wandell joined Harley-Davidson in 2009, many people were skeptical of his leadership due to his lack of motorcycle experience. However, his fresh perspective has allowed Wandell the opportunities and relationships needed to steer the company toward a sales gain for the first time in nearly five years. Wandell attributes this success to his dear colleague and now CEO at Ford, Alan Mulally. Wandell took some tough measures such as cutting labor contracts, closing plants, and overall "trimming the fat."[36] He has sold old investments and is trying to making Harley-Davidson more attractive to women and the younger generation. And, of course, Wandell is now an avid Harley-Davidson rider.

Executive Suite. Each member of the C-suite is highly qualified for his role. Each leader serves multiple roles within the organization and is an individual contributor as well as a team leader.[37] The CFO and Senior VP, John A. Olin, joined Harley-Davidson in May 2009 with over 25 years of leadership experience in finance. President and COO of Buell Motorcycle Company, Jon R. Flickinger, has grown within Harley-Davidson where he began his leadership role as a Director of Field Operations in January 1995. With over 30 years of experience in the commercial finance industry, it is appropriate that Lawrence G. Hund should serve as the President and COO of the Harley-Davidson Financial Services division. At 46, nearly 10 years younger than the other executive members, President and COO of Harley-Davidson Motor Company, Matthew S. Levatich, has made significant contributions at Harley-Davidson for the past 15 years.

Board of Directors. Each member of Harley-Davidson's board brings different experiences to the boardroom. This eclectic set of experiences facilitates the firm's efforts to position itself in the ever-growing market of the motorcycle business. Information regarding the age, title, and other boards each member serves on is provided in Exhibit 1.

Exhibit 1 Board of Directors

Board Member	Age	Title	Other Boards
Barry K. Allen	62	Senior Advisor to Providence Equity Partners President, Allen Enterprises, LLC	Fiduciary Management BCE Inc.
John Anderson	60	Former President and CEO, Levi Strauss & Co.	
Richard L. Beattie	71	Chairman of Simpson Thacher & Bartlett LLP	Heidrick & Struggles International Inc. Evercore Partners Inc.
Martha F. Brooks	51	Former President and COO, Novelis Inc.	Bombardier Inc.
George H. Conrades	73	Chairman, Akamai Technologies, Inc.	Akamai Technologies, Inc. Oracle Corporation Ironwood Pharmaceuticals, Inc.
Donald A. James	67	Co-founder, equity owner, Chairman and CEO of Deeley Harley-Davidson Canada/Fred Deeley Imports Ltd.	
Sara L. Levinson	60	Former Non-Executive Chairman of ClubMom, Inc.	Macy's Inc.
Thomas Linebarger	48	Chairman and CEO, Cummins Inc.	Cummins Inc.
George L. Miles Jr.	69	Executive Chair, Chester Engineers, Inc.	American International Group Inc. EQT Corporation HFF, Inc. WESCO International Inc.
James A. Norling	69	Chairman of the Board, GlobalFoundries Inc.	
Keith Wandell	60	Chairman, President and CEO, Harley-Davidson, Inc.	Constellation Brands, Inc. Dana Holding Corporation
Jochen Zeitz	48	Chairman of PUMA CEO of PPR Sport & Lifestyle Group and Chief Security Officer of PPR	Puma AG PPR

Source: Harley-Davidson Inc (HOG: New York). Insiders at Harley Davidson Inc. *Bloomberg Businessweek.* http://investing.businessweek.com/research/stocks/people/board. asp?ticker=HOG.

The current size of the Harley-Davidson board is slightly large when compared to the advised board size of six to seven.[38] However, each member brings significant diversity and experience to the board meetings.

Richard Beattie provides Harley-Davidson with several years of legal and military experience. His background helps Harley-Davidson deal with any corporate law or governance issues. Barry Allen serves the role of financial advisor at Harley-Davidson as well as that of a decision-maker at other corporations. Other board members incorporate their knowledge from the financial, retail, and technological boards they serve on to help the company gain strategic competitiveness in the industry.

International Growth

Any discussion of Harley-Davidson's future would not be complete without examining its expansion into India and China, the two BRIC economies with a strong history of motorcycle ownership and enough income growth to ensure viable target markets.[39] After all, moving from Harley-Davidson's current position of 32 percent of revenue from international sales to its stated goal of 40 percent by 2014[40, 41] will be challenging. Doing so will require a delicate balance in order to maintain the ethos of Harley-Davidson while simultaneously adapting to local customs and consumer preferences. Nevertheless, it could be argued that Harley-Davidson is already well on its way in this regard.

For example, just four months after officially entering the Indian market in July 2010, Harley announced it would build an assembly plant in northern India in order to reduce import tariffs by as much as 80 percent.[42] Previously, high tariffs resulted in its models costing twice as much as their U.S. equivalents.[43] By only assembling the motorcycles in India, Harley-Davidson is able to satisfy the desire of its customers in India to purchase an "American" motorcycle by sourcing all the parts from the United States while significantly increasing its competitive position through lower pricing.

Time will be required to see if Harley-Davidson's approach in India will achieve the success the firm seeks. Indeed, Harley-Davidson sold only about 1,000 bikes in India in its first 18 months of operations.[44] This level of sales should be considered though within the context of the fact that Harley's local assembly plant in India has only been operational for the past 12 months.[45] Accordingly, the Indian market has not been exposed to the lower pricing model for very long and may need some time to overcome the stigma associated with previously higher prices. For example a mid-level bike used to cost $27,000, prior to tariff reduction; now, the cost of this product is around $20,000.[46, 47] These prices, while still high by local standards, show that Harley-Davidson is making a concerted effort to cater to the needs of customers located in developing countries. Such a strategy is essential for long-term viability given global growth trends and the inevitable shift of income away from Harley-Davidson's more traditional western markets. In response to such growth, it has even committed to opening dealerships in cities like Jaipur and Kochi – cities outside the larger Indian metropolises.[48] In this manner, Harley-Davidson will be able to appeal to India's rural landowners who would like to ride Harley-Davidsons in the countryside.[49]

Unfortunately, Harley-Davidson's venture into China, the world's largest motorcycle market, has been less smooth and illustrates what can happen when a company enters a foreign market without sufficient background preparation. For example, China currently restricts the use of motorcycles on elevated highways and major thoroughfares in about 100 cities.[50] Import duties can also add as much as 30 percent to the price of a Harley-Davidson, resulting in high-end models costing the equivalent of a luxury sedan such as the Audi A4.[51] Perhaps more troubling is the admission by most in China that motorcycles are associated with utilitarian tasks like transportation to work, not leisure riding as is the case in developed economies such as the United States.[52] These realities increase the difficulty Harley-Davidson faces as the firm seeks to establish the level of success in China that is similar to what the firm has been able to accomplish in India.[53]

Regulation

Safety must always be at the forefront of Harley-Davidson's mind to avoid any unwanted attention. For example, when taking Harley-Davidson's "Rider's Edge" operation courses, all riders are required to wear protective gear, including a helmet, that meets Department of Transportation (DOT) regulations.[54] Skeptics might say

that Harley-Davidson is merely trying to minimize its liability. However, most would agree that increased injury rates from not wearing protective gear only serve to vilify motorcycle use. Indeed, Harley-Davidson even periodically issues communications to its customers encouraging riders to check the condition of their helmets.[55] Still, motorcycle riders in general have been affected by the recent loosening of helmet laws throughout the United States. "Two decades ago, 47 states required helmets for all riders. Today, 20 do. Twenty-seven states require helmets only for younger riders. Three — Illinois, Iowa and New Hampshire — don't require helmets at all."[56] Another safety-related concern is the fact that "in 1996, 5.6 motorcyclists were killed for every 10,000 registered motorcycles," according to DOT statistics. However, by 2006, the most recent data available, the rate had risen to 7.3…"[57] To be fair, such a study does not prove causality. Still, such studies can bring unwanted negative attention to the motorcycle industry and reinforce cultural stereotypes that motorcycle riders are risk-seeking freewheelers. To make its motorcycles appealing to a broader target market, Harley-Davidson must continue to espouse a culture of safety,[58] even in the face of decreasing safety regulations.

New EPA emission regulations could also affect Harley-Davidson's growth. Still, the last revision of motorcycle emission standards in 2003 did little to alter Harley-Davidson's growth trajectory and prompted the following promise.

Jim McCaslin, President of Harley-Davidson Motor Company, has stated that Harley-Davidson "plans to meet the requirements of the proposed EPA standards and still make the motorcycles true to the look, sound, and feel that you know and love" and that "the air-cooled V-Twin will continue to be the core of the Harley-Davidson motorcycle lineup for many years to come."[59]

The latter was especially welcome news to Harley-Davidson purists, but nevertheless is indicative of the regulation challenges facing Harley-Davidson's predominately air-cooled (as opposed to cleaner burning water-cooled) engines. If Harley-Davidson wishes to continue to operate in an increasingly environmentally sensitive market, it must continue to hone its ability to meet stricter pollutant regulations.

Financial Analysis

Harley-Davidson is currently climbing its way out of what were likely the worst financial times the company had faced since its inception in 1903. It peaked with nearly $6.2 billion in revenue in 2006, and then witnessed its revenue fall nearly 30 percent between 2007 and 2009.[60, 61] Harley-Davidson is in the recreation vehicles industry, making its products arguably among the most expensive of consumer discretionary items. As noted earlier, individuals find it difficult to justify purchases of these types of products when encountering challenging economic conditions. To compound the financial crisis in the United States between 2007 and 2010, Harley-Davidson's units-sold figures peaked at over 349,000 in 2006. Does the reduced number of units sold since 2006 potentially suggest that the overall demand for Harley-Davidson's products is declining?[62] Right now in its rebound, Harley-Davidson has managed to grow its revenue over 11 percent from its 2009 lows and bring its operating margin back up to 16 percent from a disappointing 4 percent in 2009.[63]

Going forward, work remains for Harley-Davidson to return to a strong financial position. To start, Harley-Davidson is currently highly leveraged as suggested by the firm's debt-to-equity ratio of 1.6. Historically, it has operated with this ratio well below 0.5.[64] Much of this new debt resulted from a decision to create capital for the firm's financing division. More specifically, this capital was to be used as a way of helping customers purchase a Harley-Davidson motorcycle. Because most of this debt is in the form of medium-term notes that do not require repayment until after 2014, and because Harley-Davidson has the necessary current free cash flow to pay its current liabilities, this debt is not a huge immediate concern. Even so, it is something the firm's leaders should monitor to make sure it does not get out of control.[65]

Furthermore, Harley-Davidson will have to make a concerted effort to control costs to get back to the 25+ percent operating margins it experienced during the boom years of 2004-2007. It is the case that part of the difference between Harley's current operating margin of 16 percent and the highly desirable operating margin of 25 or more percent is a factor of its fixed costs being allocated across fewer sales units. Nonetheless, keeping variable costs under control will be crucial to the firm's efforts to strengthen its operating margin until the number of units sold increases. Detailed financial data concerning Harley-Davidson is shown in Exhibits 2 through 6.

The Sum of All Parts

At the end of the day, Harley-Davidson cannot depend on its strong brand name to carry it through the twenty-first century. Between expanding its target consumer base beyond the stereotypical biker with his "old lady" sitting behind him, to successfully breaking free of the red tape and increased costs associated with international expansion, Harley-Davidson is potentially facing a challenging future. However, as one of the few motorcycle manufacturers focused exclusively on building motorcycles and without having to worry about cars, scooters, or snowmobiles, it stands to reason it should be able to lead the pack.

Exhibit 2 HOG Income Statement

Consolidated Statements of Operations (USD $)	12 Months Ended		
In Thousands, except Per Share data, unless otherwise specified	Dec. 31, 2011	Dec. 31, 2010	Dec. 31, 2009
Revenue:			
Motorcycles and related products	$4,662,264[ii]	$4,176,627[ii]	$4,287,130[ii]
Financial services	649,449	682,709	494,779
Total revenue	**5,311,713**	**4,859,336**	**4,781,909**
Costs and expenses:			
Motorcycles and related products cost of goods sold	3,106,288	2,749,224	2,900,934
Financial services interest expense	229,492	272,484	283,634
Financial services provision for credit losses	17,031	93,118	169,206
Selling, administrative, and engineering expense	1,060,943	1,020,371	979,384
Restructuring expense and asset impairment	67,992	163,508	224,278
Goodwill impairment			28,387
Total costs and expenses	**4,481,746**	**4,298,705**	**4,585,823**
Operating income	829,967	560,631	196,086
Investment income	7,963	5,442	4,254
Interest expense	45,266	90,357	21,680
Loss on debt extinguishment	9,608	85,247	
Income before provision for income taxes	792,664	390,469	178,660
Provision for income taxes	244,586	130,800	108,019
Income from continuing operations	548,078	259,669	70,641
Income (loss) from discontinued operations, net of tax	51,036	−113,124	−125,757
Net income (loss)	**$599,114**	**$146,545**	**($55,116)**
Earnings per common share from continuing operations:			
Basic	$ 2.35	$1.11	$0.30
Diluted	$2.33	$1.11	$0.30
Earnings (loss) per common share from discontinued operations:			
Basic	$0.22	($0.48)	($0.54)
Diluted	$0.22	($0.48)	($0.54)
Earnings (loss) per common share:			
Basic	$2.57	$0.63	($0.24)
Diluted	$2.55	$0.62	($0.24)
Cash dividends per common share	$0.48	$0.40	$0.40

[ii] Revenue is attributed to geographic regions based on location of customer.

Source: U.S. Securities and Exchange Commission. http://www.sec.gov/Archives/edgar/data/793952/000119312512074944/0001193125-12-074944-index.htm

Exhibit 3 HOG Balance Sheet

Consolidated Balance Sheets (USD $)			
In Thousands, unless otherwise specified	**Dec. 31, 2011**	**Dec. 31, 2010**	**Dec. 31, 2009**
Current assets:			
Cash and cash equivalents	$1,526,950	$1,021,933	$1,630,433
Marketable securities	153,380	140,118	39,685
Accounts receivable, net	219,039	262,382	269,371
Finance receivables, net	1,168,603	1,080,432	1,436,114
Variable interest entities' restricted finance receivables, net	591,864	699,026	
Inventories	418,006	326,446	323,029
Restricted cash held by variable interest entities	229,655	288,887	
Deferred income taxes	132,331	146,411	179,685
Other current assets	102,378	100,991	282,421
Total current assets	**4,542,206**	**4,066,626**	**4,341,949**
Finance receivables, net	1,754,441	1,553,781	3,621,048
Variable interest entities' restricted finance receivables, net	2,271,773	2,684,330	
Property, plant and equipment, net	809,459	815,112	906,906
Goodwill	29,081	29,590	31,400
Deferred income taxes	202,439	213,989	177,504
Other long-term assets	64,765	67,312	76,711
TOTAL ASSETS	**9,674,164**	**9,430,740**	**9,155,518**
Current liabilities:			
Accounts payable	255,713	225,346	162,515
Accrued liabilities	564,172	556,671	514,084
Short-term debt	838,486	480,472	189,999
Current portion of long-term debt	399,916		1,332,091
Variable interest entities' current portion of long-term debt	640,331	751,293	
Total current liabilities	**2,698,618**	**2,013,782**	**2,268,224**
Long-term debt	2,396,871	2,516,650	4,114,039
Long-term debt held by variable interest entities	1,447,015	2,003,941	
Pension liability	302,483	282,085	245,332
Postretirement healthcare liability	268,582	254,762	264,472
Other long-term liabilities	140,339	152,654	155,333
TOTAL LIABILITIES			
Shareholders' equity:			
Series A Junior participating preferred stock, none issued			
Common stock, 339,107,230 and 338,260,456 shares issued in 2011 and 2010, respectively	3,391	3,382	3,368
Additional paid-in-capital	968,392	908,055	871,100
Retained earnings	6,824,180	6,336,077	6,324,268
Accumulated other comprehensive loss	(476,733)	(366,222)	(417,898)
Stockholders equity before treasury stock	7,319,230	6,881,292	6,780,838
Less: Treasury stock (108,566,699 and 102,739,587 shares in 2011 and 2010, respectively), at cost	(4,898,974)	(4,674,426)	(4,672,720)
Total shareholders' equity	**2,420,256**	**2,206,866**	**2,108,118**
Total liabilities and shareholders' equity	**$9,674,164**	**$9,430,740**	**$9,155,518**

Source: U.S. Securities and Exchange Commission. http://www.sec.gov/Archives/edgar/data/793952/000119312512074944/0001193125-12-074944-index.htm

Exhibit 4 HOG Statement of Cash Flows

Consolidated Statements of Cash Flows (USD $)	12 Months Ended		
In Thousands, unless otherwise specified	Dec. 31, 2011	Dec. 31, 2010	Dec. 31, 2009
Consolidated Statements Of Cash Flows [Abstract]			
Net cash provided by operating activities of continuing operations (Note 2)	$885,291	$1,163,418	$609,010
Cash flows from investing activities of continuing operations:			
Capital expenditures	(189,035)	(170,845)	(116,748)
Origination of finance receivables	(2,622,024)	(2,252,532)	(1,378,226)
Collections on finance receivables	2,760,049	2,668,962	607,168
Collection of retained securitization interests			61,170
Purchases of marketable securities	(142,653)	(184,365)	(39,685)
Sales and redemptions of marketable securities	130,121	84,217	
Other, net			2,834
Net cash provided/used by inv. activities of cont. oper.	(63,542)	145,437	(863,487)
Cash flows from financing activities of continuing operations:			
Proceeds from issuance of medium term notes	447,076		496,514
Repayment of medium term notes	(59,211)	(200,000)	
Proceeds from issuance of senior unsecured notes			595,026
Repayment of senior unsecured notes		(380,757)	
Proceeds from securitization debt	1,082,599	598,187	2,413,192
Repayments of securitization debt	(1,754,568)	(1,896,665)	(263,083)
Net +/− in credit facilities & unsecured commercial paper	237,827	30,575	(1,083,331)
Net repayments in asset-backed commercial paper	(483)	(845)	(513,168)
Net change in restricted cash	59,232	77,654	(167,667)
Dividends	(111,011)	(94,145)	(93,807)
Purchase of common stock for treasury, net of issuances	(224,548)	(1,706)	(1,920)
Excess tax benefits from share-based payments	6,303	3,767	170
Issued common stock under employee stock option plans	7,840	7,845	11
Net cash provided/used by fin. activities of continuing oper.	(308,944)	(1,856,090)	1,381,937
Exchange rate effect on cash/cash equiv. of continuing oper.	(7,788)	4,940	6,789
Net increase/decrease in cash/cash equiv of continuing oper.	505,017	(542,295)	1,134,249
Cash flows from discontinued operations:			
Cash flows from operating activities of disc. oper.		(71,073)	(71,298)
Cash flows from investing activities of disc. oper.			(18,805)
Exchange rate effect on cash/cash equiv. of discont. oper.		(1,195)	(1,208)
Net cash used by discontinued operations, total		(72,268)	(91,311)
Net increase/decrease in cash/cash equivalents	505,017	(614,563)	1,042,938
Cash and cash equivalents:			
Cash and cash equivalents - beginning of period	1,021,933	1,630,433	568,894
Cash and cash equivalents of disc. oper. - period start		6,063	24,664
Net increase (decrease) in cash and cash equivalents	505,017	(614,563)	1,042,938
Less: Cash and cash equivalents of disc. oper. - period end			(6,063)
Cash and cash equivalents - end of period	**$1,526,950**	**$1,021,933**	**$1,630,433**

Source: U.S. Securities and Exchange Commission. http://www.sec.gov/Archives/edgar/data/793952/000119312512074944/0001193125-12-074944-index.htm

Exhibit 5 HOG Statement of Stockholder's Equity

Consolidated Statements Of Shareholders' Equity (USD $) In Thousands, except Share data, unless otherwise specified	Common Stock [Member]	Additional Paid-In Capital [Member]	Retained Earnings [Member]	Accumulated Other Comp. Income (Loss) [Member]	Treasury Balance [Member]	Total
Beginning Balance 12/31/08	$3,357	$846,796	$6,458,778	($522,526)	($4,670,802)	$2,115,603
Beg. Share Bal. 12/31/08	335,653,577					
Comprehensive income:						
Net income (loss)			(55,116)			(55,116)
Other comprehensive income/loss:						
Foreign currency translation adjustment				30,932		30,932
Amortization of net prior service cost, net of taxes				2,679		2,679
Amortization of actuarial loss, net of taxes				11,761		11,761
Pension & post-retirement plan funded status adj., net of taxes				29,111		29,111
Pension & post-retirement plan settlement & curtailment, net of taxes				32,197		32,197
Change in net unrealized gains (losses):						
Investment in retained securitization interests, net of taxes				13,600		13,600
Derivative financial instruments, net of tax benefit				(1,239)		(1,239)
Comprehensive income						63,925
Adj. to apply measurement date provisions of FSP 115–2, net of taxes			14,413	(14,413)		
Dividends			(93,807)			(93,807)
Repurchase of common stock					(1,920)	(1,920)
Share-based comp. & 401(k) match made with Treasury shares		27,363			2	27,365
Issued nonvested stock (in shares)	1,147,393					
Issuance of nonvested stock	11	(11)				
Tax benefit of stock options & nonvested stock		(3,048)				(3,048)
Ending Balance at 12/31/09	3,368	871,100	6,324,268	(417,898)	(4,672,720)	2,108,118
Ending Share Balance 12/31/09	336,800,970					
Comprehensive income:						
Net income (loss)			146,545			146,545

(Continued)

Exhibit 5 Continued HOG Statement of Stockholder's Equity

Consolidated Statements of Shareholders' Equity (USD $) In Thousands, except Share data, unless otherwise specified	Common Stock [Member]	Additional Paid-In Capital [Member]	Retained Earnings [Member]	Accumulated Other Comp. Income (Loss) [Member]	Treasury Balance [Member]	Total
Other comprehensive income (loss):						
Foreign currency translation adj.				9,449		9,449
Net prior service cost amort, net of taxes				925		925
Actuarial loss amort., net of taxes				20,944		20,944
Pension & post-retirement plan funded status adj., net of taxes				18,431		18,431
Pension & post-retirement plan settlement & curtailment, net taxes				1,549		1,549
Change in net unrealized gains (losses):						
Derivative financial instruments, net of tax benefit				(2,972)		(2,972)
Marketable securities, net of tax benefit				(133)		(133)
Comprehensive income						194,738
Adj. for consolidation of QSPEs under ASC Topics 810 & 860			(40,591)	3,483		(37,108)
Dividends			(94,145)			(94,145)
Repurchase of common stock					(1,706)	(1,706)
Share-based comp. & 401(k) match made with Treasury shares		26,961				26,961
Issued nonvested stock (in shares)	823,594					
Issuance of nonvested stock	8	(8)				
Exercise of stock options	6	7,839				7,845
Exercise of stock options (in shares)	635,892					
Tax benefit of stock options & nonvested stock		2,163				2,163
Ending Balance at 12/31/10	3,382	908,055	6,336,077	(366,222)	(4,674,426)	2,206,866
Ending Balance, shares at 12/31/10	338,260,456					
Comprehensive income:						
Net income (loss)			599,114			599,114

Other comprehensive income (loss):						
Foreign currency translation adj.				(5,616)		(5,616)
Net prior service cost amortization, net of taxes				(564)		(564)
Actuarial loss amort., net of taxes				23,584		23,584
Pension & post-retirement plan funded status adj., net of taxes				(146,768)		(146,768)
Pension & post-retirement plan settlement & curtailment, net taxes				174		174
Change in net unrealized gains (losses):						
Derivative financial instruments, net of tax benefit				18,219		18,219
Marketable securities, net of tax benefit				460		460
Comprehensive income						488,603
Dividends			(111,011)			(111,011)
Repurchase of common stock	473,240				(224,551)	(224,551)
Share-based comp. & 401(k) match made with Treasury shares		49,993			3	49,996
Issued nonvested stock (in shares)	5					
Issuance of nonvested stock		(5)				
Exercise of stock options	4	7,836				7,840
Exercise of stock options (in shares)	373,534					374,000
Tax benefit of stock options & nonvested stock		2,513				2,513
Ending Balance at 12/31/11	$3,391	$968,392	$6,824,180	($476,733)	($4,898,974)	$2,420,256
Ending Balance, shares at 12/31/11	339,107,230					

Source: U.S. Securities and Exchange Commission. http://www.sec.gov/Archives/edgar/data/793952/000119312512074944/0001193125-12-074944-index.htm

Exhibit 6 HOG Revenue and Net Income 2002–2011

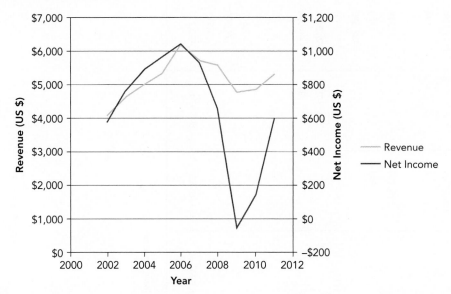

Source: Graph created from information from U.S. Securities and Exchange Commission. http://www.sec.gov/Archives/edgar/data/793952/000119312512074944/0001193125-12-074944-index.htm

NOTES

1. Weber, J. Harley Just Keeps On Cruisin'. 5 Nov 2006. *BloombergBusinessweek*. Web. 24 Apr 2012. http://www.businessweek.com/magazine/content/06_45/b4008069.htm

2. Various sources including 1) Barkley, M. K. A Business Plan for a Harley-Davidson Motorcycle. Web. http://ocls.cmich.edu/msa/projects/mbarkley06-05.pdf. 2) Harley-Davidson USA: History. Web. 22 Apr 2012. http://www.harley-davidson.com/en_US/Content/Pages/H-D_History/history.html. 3) P3naz89. History of Harley Davidson -Part 1. 17 Aug 2009. *YouTube*. Web. 22 Apr 2012. http://www.youtube.com/watch?v=79twzhOXlJQ. 4) Harley-Davidson History. *HowStuffWorks*. Web. 22 Apr 2012. http://auto.howstuffworks.com/harley-davidson-history1.htm. 5) Harley Davidson History Time Line. *Harley. Munising.com*. Web. 22 Apr 2012. http://harley.munising.com/.

3. Ibid.

4. Ibid.

5. Bruce, R. The Harley-Davidson Story. http://cobweb2.louisville.edu/faculty/regbruce/bruce/cases/harley/harley.htm.

6. Various sources including *op. cit.*

7. Harley-Davidson USA. *Harley-Davidson USA*. Web. 22 Apr 2012. http://www.harley-davidson.com/en_US/Content/Pages/home.html.

8. Harley Defies Stereotypes. 7 Mar 2012. *Dennis Kirk Powersports Blog*. Web. 22 Apr 2012. http://powersports-blog.denniskirk.com/1842/harley-davidson/harley-defies-stereotypes/.

9. Various sources including *op. cit.*

10. Weber, J. *op. cit.*

11. Harley-Davidson USA. *Harley-Davidson USA. op. cit.*

12. Gardiner, M. Harley-Davidson Motorcycle History. *op. cit.*

13. Harley-Davidson USA. *Harley-Davidson USA. op. cit.*

14. Hamner, S. 2009. Harley, you're not getting any younger. *New York Times* Online, March 22.

15. Various sources II including: 1) Harley-Davidson USA. *Harley-Davidson USA. op. cit.* 2) Hitt, M. A., Ireland, R. D., & Hoskisson, R. E. (2011). *Strategic Management - Competitiveness & Globalization - 10th Edition*. Mason, OH: South-Western CENGAGE Learning. 3) Bruce, R. *op. cit.* 4) Gamble, J. E., Schäfer, R. Case 21 Harley-Davidson. *Scribd*. Web. 22 Apr 2012. http://www.scribd.com/doc/19943405/Harley-Davidson-Case-Study. 5) Harley-Davidson. *Wikipedia*. Wikimedia Foundation. Web. 22 Apr 2012. http://en.wikipedia.org/wiki/Harley-Davidson. 6) Harley-Davidson 2011: Annual Report. *Harley-Davidson Website*. http://www.harley-davidson.com/en_US/Media/downloads/Annual_Reports/2011/HD_Annual2011.pdf.

16. Harley Defies Stereotypes. 7 Mar 2012. *Dennis Kirk Powersports Blog*. Web. 22 Apr 2012. http://powersports-blog.denniskirk.com/1842/harley-davidson/harley-defies-stereotypes/.

17. Demographic Headwinds Hitting Harley-Davidson. 17 Jul 2009. *Seeking Alpha*. Web.
22 Apr 2012. http://seekingalpha.com/article/149478-demographic-headwinds-hitting-harley-davidson.

18. Harley-Davidson USA. *Harley-Davidson USA. op. cit.*

19. Hitt, M. A., Ireland, R. D., & Hoskisson, R. E. 2011. *op. cit.*

20. Gardiner, M. Harley-Davidson Motorcycle History. *op. cit.*

21. Harley-Davidson USA: Harley Owner's Group. *Harley-Davidson Website*. Web. http://www.harley-davidson.com/en_US/Content/Pages/HOG/HOG.html.

22. Harley-Davidson USA: Who Can be a Dealer. *Harley-Davidson Website*. Web. 22 Apr 2012. http://www.harley-davidson.com/en_US/Content/Pages/Becoming_a_Dealer/Who_Can_Become_A_Dealer.html?locale=en_US

23. Honda: Street: Chopper. *Powersports. Honda.com*. Web. http://powersports.honda.com/street/chopper.aspx.

24. Korfhage, B. 2004 Kawasaki Vulcan 2000. 5 Dec 2003. *MotorcycleUSA.com*. http://www.motorcycle-usa.com/163/949/Motorcycle-Article/2004-Kawasaki-Vulcan-2000.aspx.

25. Suzuki: Motorcycles. *Suzuki Cycles*. Web. 22 Apr 2012. http://www.suzukicycles.com/Product%20Lines/Cycles.aspx?sc_lang=en.

26. Gardiner, M. Harley-Davidson Motorcycle History. *op. cit.*

27. Harley-Davidson to Discontinue Buell Sport Bikes. 15 Oct 2009. *New York Times - Wheels*. Web. 22 Apr 2012. http://wheels.blogs.nytimes.com/2009/10/15/harley-davidson-to-discontinue-buell-sport-bikes/.

28. American Motorcycles. Victory Motorcycles: Touring, Cruiser, Muscle, V-Twin & Wide-Tire. Web. 22 Apr 2012. http://www.polarisindustries.com/en-us/victory-motorcycles/Pages/Home.aspx.

29. Duke, K. 2004 Victory Vegas Comparison. 26 Nov 2003. *MotorcycleUSA.com*. http://www.motorcycle-usa.com/267/1040/Motorcycle-Article/2004-Victory-Vegas-Comparison.aspx.

30. Indian Motorcycles. Web. http://www.indianmotorcycle.com/en-us/pages/home.aspx.

31. Big Dog Motorcycles - Custom Motorcycles & Choppers, Motorcycle Apparel & Accessories - Homepage. *Big Dog Motorcycles*. Web. 22 Apr 2012. http://www.bigdogmotorcycles.com/.

32. Big Bear Choppers | Custom Chopper Motorcycles | Bike Kits | Kit Bikes. *Big Bear Choppers*. Web. 22 Apr 2012. http://www.bigbearchoppers.com/.

33. American IronHorse Motorcycles of Huntsville. *American IronHorse Motorcycles of Huntsville*. Web. 22 Apr 2012. http://www.americanironhorsehuntsville.com/.

34. Darwin Motorcycles. *Darwin Motorcycles*. Web. 22 Apr 2012. http://www.brassballsbobbers.com/.

35. Bleustein, J. L. Letter to Shareholders. *Harley-Davidson USA: Investor Relations*. http://www.harley-davidson.com/company/investor/ar/1997/leadership.htm.

36. Bhasin, K. Harley-Davidson's CEO is Trying to Save His Company by Copying Ford. 21 Nov 2011. *Business Insider – War Room*. http://articles.businessinsider.com/2011-11-21/strategy/30424435_1_harley-davidson-keith-wandell-ford-ceo.

37. Harley-davidson In (HOG: New York). *Bloomberg Businessweek*. http://investing.businessweek.com/research/stocks/people/people.asp?ticker=HOG:US.

38. Pozen, Robert C. The Case of Professional Boards. *Harvard Business Review*. 2010.

39. Lakshmi, R. Harley-Davidson Coming to India to Test a New Market. 31 Aug 2009. *Washington Post*. Web. 22 Apr 2012. http://www.washingtonpost.com/wp-dyn/content/article/2009/08/30/AR2009083002250.html.

40. Harley-Davidson Demographics. Update. 18 Feb 2011. *Cyril Huze Blog: World's Number One Magazine For Custom Motorcycle News*. Web. 22 Apr 2012. http://www.cyrilhuzeblog.com/2011/02/18/harley-davidson-demographics-update/.

41. Harley-Davidson looking beyond Indian metros for growth. 3 Jan 2012. *IBN Live*. Web. 22 Apr 2012. http://ibnlive.in.com/news/harleydavidson-looking-beyond-indian-metros-for-growth/218921-25-162.html.

42. Sidner, S. Harley-Davidson to Build Bikes in India. 4 Nov 2010. *CNN World*. Web. 22 Apr 2012. http://articles.cnn.com/2010-11-04/world/india.bikes_1_india-market-harley-davidsons-haryana?_s=PM:WORLD.

43. Bellman, E. Harley to Ride Indian Growth. 28 Aug 2009. *Wall Street Journal*. http://online.wsj.com/article/SB125135162394762877.html.

44. Harley-Davidson looking beyond Indian metros for growth. *op. cit.*

45. Harley-Davidson Introduces Two Bikes at Lower Price. 5 Jan 2012. *NDTV.com*. Web. 22 Apr 2012. http://www.ndtv.com/article/business/harley-davidson-introduces-two-bikes-at-lower-price-163887.

46. Ibid.

47. Currency Converter Widget. *XE: (—/—) — to — Rate*. Web. 22 Apr 2012. http://www.xe.com/ucc/convert/?Amount=1400000.

48. Harley-Davidson looking beyond Indian metros for growth. *op. cit.*

49. Our Motorcycles. *Harley-Davidson India*. Web. 22 Apr 2012. http://www.harley-davidson.in/harley-davidson-india-our-motorcycles.html

50. Harley-Davidson in China Encounters Barriers of Entry for Two Wheels: Cars. 18 Sep 2011. *Bloomberg*. Web. 22 Apr 2012. http://www.bloomberg.com/news/2011-09-18/harley-davidson-finds-milwaukee-beats-china-as-leisure-motorcycle-market.html.

51. Ibid.

52. Ibid.

53. Ibid.

54. Harley-Davidson USA: New Rider Course. *Harley-Davidson Web Site*. Web. 22 Apr 2012. http://www.harley-davidson.com/en_US/Content/Pages/learn-to-ride/new-rider-course.html?locale=en_US.

55. Harley-Davidson Press Release. Motorcyclists! Harley-Davidson encourages all to check their helmets. 2 Apr 2008. *Cycle Matters*. Web. 22 Apr 2012. http://www.cyclematters.com/motorcycle-blog/safety-training/harley-davidson-proclaims-april-check-your-helmet-month-2008.cfm

56. Yaukey, J., Benincasa, R. Motorcyclist deaths spike as helmet laws loosen. 27 Mar 2008. *USA Today*. Web. 22 Apr 2012. http://www.usatoday.com/news/nation/2008-03-26-bikehelmets_N.htm.

57. Ibid.

58. Johnson, R. When Heaven Is a Harley. 19 Dec 2011. *Wall Street Journal*. Web. http://online.wsj.com/article/SB10001424052970203537304577030113224587198.html

59. Summary and Analysis of Comments: Control of Emissions from Highway Motorcycles. Dec 2003. *U.S. EPA: Office of Transportation and Air Quality*. EPA420-R-03-016. Web. http://www.epa.gov/otaq/regs/roadbike/420r03016.pdf

60. Harley-Davidson Downshifts Profit Forecast. 7 Sep 2007. *Market Watch*. Web. 22 Apr 2012. http://articles.marketwatch.com/2007-09-07/news/30806235_1_harley-davidson-harley-davidson-shares-retail-sales.

61. Morningstar Analyst Report. 27 Feb 2012.

62. Harley-Davidson USA: Harley Owner's Group. *op. cit.*

63. Morningstar Analyst Report. *op. cit*

64. Ibid.

65. Harley-Davidson 2011: Annual Report. *op. cit.*

CASE 15

Herman Miller: An On-Going Case of Reinvention and Renewal[1]

Frank Shipper, PhD
Perdue School of Business, Salisbury University

Karen P. Manz, PhD
Author & Researcher

Stephen B. Adams, PhD
Perdue School of Business, Salisbury University

Charles C. Manz, PhD
Nirenberg Professor of Leadership, Isenberg School of Management, University of Massachusetts

At first glance Herman Miller would appear to be only a $1.65 billion dollar manufacturer of office furniture. Herman Miller is, however, a company that is known beyond furniture for its innovation in products and processes since D.J. De Pree became president over 90 years ago.[2] It is one of only four organizations and the only non-high technology one selected to *Fortune*'s 100 Best Companies to Work For and Most Admired Companies, and *FastCompany*'s Most Innovative Companies in both 2008 and 2010. The three high technology organizations selected were Microsoft, Cisco, and Google. Not usual company for a firm in a mature industry and definitely not for an office furniture company. Ever since D.J. De Pree became president, Herman Miller has followed a different path from most firms. It is one distinctively marked by reinvention and renewal.

This path has served it well. Early in its history it survived the Great Depression and multiple recessions in the 20th century. In the early part of the 21st century, it recovered from the dot.com bust. As it enters 2010, Herman Miller once again faces a turbulent economy. Will this path allow it to flourish once again?

Background

Herman Miller's roots go back to 1905 and the Star Furniture Company, a manufacturer of traditional style bedroom suites in Zeeland, Michigan. In 1909, it was renamed Michigan Star Furniture Company and hired Dirk Jan (D.J.) De Pree as a clerk. D.J. De Pree became president in 1919. Four years later D.J. convinced his father-in-law, Herman Miller, to purchase the majority of shares and renamed the company Herman Miller Furniture Company in recognition of his support.[3]

In 1927, D.J. De Pree committed to treating "all workers as individuals with special talents and potential." This occurred after he visited the family of a millwright who had died unexpectedly. At the visit, the widow read some poetry. D.J. De Pree asked the widow who the poet was and was surprised to learn it was the millwright. This led him to wonder whether the millwright was a person who wrote poetry or a poet who was also a millwright. This story is part of the cultural folklore at Herman Miller that continues to generate respect for all employees and fuels the quest to tap the diversity of gifts and skills held by all.

In 1930, the country was in the Great Depression and Herman Miller was in financial trouble. D.J. De Pree was looking for a way to save the company. At the same time, Gilbert Rhode, a designer from New York, approached D.J. De Pree and told him about his design philosophy. He then asked for an opportunity to create a design of a bedroom suite at a fee of $1000. When D.J. De Pree reacted negatively to such a fee, Gilbert Rhode suggested an alternative payment plan, 3% royalty on the furniture sold, to which D.J. agreed, figuring that there was nothing to lose.

A few weeks later, D.J. received the first designs from Rhode. Again, he reacted negatively. He "thought that they looked as if they had been done for a manual training school and told him so." Gilbert Rhode explained in a letter his design philosophy – first, "utter simplicity: no surface enrichment, no carvings, no moldings," and second, "furniture should be anonymous. People are important, not furniture. Furniture should be useful." Rhode's designs were antithetical to traditional designs, but D.J. saw merit in them and this set Herman Miller on a course of designing and selling furniture that reflected a way of life.

In 1942, Herman Miller produced its first office furniture – a Gilbert Rhode design referred to as the Executive Office Group. He died two years later and De Pree began a search for a new design leader. Based largely on an article in *Life* magazine, he hired George Nelson as Herman Miller's first design director.

In 1946, Charles and Ray Eames, designers based in Los Angeles, were hired to design furniture. In the same year, Charles Eames' designs were featured in the first one-man furniture exhibit at New York's Museum of Modern Art. Some of his designs are now part of the museum's permanent collection.

In 1950, Herman Miller, under the guidance of Dr. Carl Frost, Professor at Michigan State University, was the first company in the state of Michigan to implement a Scanlon Plan. Underlying the Scanlon Plan are the "principles of equity and justice for everyone in the company...." Two major functional elements of Scanlon Plans are the use of committees for sharing ideas on improvements and a structure for sharing increased profitability. The relationship between Dr. Frost and Herman Miller continued for at least four decades.

During the 1950s, Herman Miller introduced a number of new furniture designs including those by Alexander Girard, Charles and Ray Eames, and George Nelson. Specifically, the first molded fiberglass chairs were introduced and the Eames lounge chair and ottoman were introduced on NBC's *Home Show* with Arlene Francis, a precursor to the *Today Show*. Also in the 1950s,

Herman Miller began its first overseas foray, selling its products in the European market.

In 1962, D.J. became chairman of the board and his son, Hugh De Pree, became president and chief executive officer. D.J. had served for over 40 years as the president.

During the 1960s, many new designs were introduced both for home and the workplace. The most notable design was the Action Office System, the world's first open-plan modular office arrangement of movable panels and attachments. By the end of the 1960s, Herman Miller had formed a subsidiary in England with sales and marketing responsibility throughout England and the Scandinavian countries. Also, it had established dealers in South and Central America, Australia, Canada, Europe, Africa, the Near East, and Japan.

In 1970, Herman Miller went public and made its first stock offering. The stock certificate was designed by the Eames Office staff. In 1971, it entered the health/science market, and in 1976, the Ergon chair, its first design based on scientific observation and ergonomic principles, was introduced. In 1979, in conjunction with the University of Michigan, it established the Facility Management Institute that established the profession of facility management. Also, in the 70s, Herman Miller continued to expand overseas and introduce new designs.

By 1977, over half of Herman Miller's 2500 employees worked outside of the production area. Thus, the Scanlon plan needed to be overhauled since it had been designed originally for a production workforce. In addition, employees worked at multiple U.S. and overseas locations. Thus, in 1978, an ad hoc committee of 54 people from nearly every segment of the company was elected to examine the need for changes and to make recommendations. By January 1979, the committee had developed a final draft. The plan established a new organization structure based on work teams, caucuses, and councils. All employees were given an opportunity in small group settings to discuss it. On January 26, 1979, 96% of the employees voted to accept the new plan.

After 18 years Hugh De Pree stepped down, and Max De Pree, Hugh's younger brother, became chairman and chief executive officer in 1980. In 1981, Herman Miller took a major initiative to become more efficient and environmentally friendly. Its Energy Center generated both electrical and steam power to run its million square foot facility by burning waste.

In 1983, Herman Miller established a plan whereby all employees became shareholders. This initiative appeared to be a natural outgrowth from the adoption of the Scanlon Plan in 1950. Employees from 1983 forward shared in both the ownership and the profits of the firm.

In 1984, the Equa chair, a second chair based on ergonomic principles, was introduced along with many other designs in the 1980s. In 1987, the first non-family member, Dick Ruch, became chief executive officer.

By the end of the decade, the Equa chair was recognized as a Design of the Decade by *Time* magazine. Also, in 1989, Herman Miller established its Environmental Quality Action Team. It is to "… coordinate environmental programs worldwide and involve as many employees as possible."

In 1990, Herman Miller was a founding member of the Tropical Forest Foundation and was the only furniture manufacturer to belong. That same year, it discontinued using endangered rosewood in its award-winning Eames lounge chair and ottoman, and substituted cherry and walnut from sustainable sources. It also became a founding member of the U.S. Green Building Council in 1994. Some of the buildings at Herman Miller have been used to establish Leadership in Energy & Environmental Design (LEED) standards. Because of its environmental efforts, Herman Miller received awards from *Fortune* magazine and the National Wildlife Federation in the 1990s.

In the 90s, Herman Miller again introduced some ground-breaking designs. In 1994, it introduced the Aeron chair and almost immediately it was added to the New York Museum of Modern Art's permanent Design Collection. In 1999, it won the Design of the Decade from *Business Week* and the Industrial Designers Society of America.

In 1992, J. Kermit Campbell became Herman Miller's fifth CEO and president. He was the first person from outside the company to hold either position. In 1995, Campbell resigned and Mike Volkema was promoted to CEO. At the time the industry was in a slump and Herman Miller was being restructured. Sales were approximately 1 billion. Mike Volkema had been with Meridian, a company Herman Miller acquired in 1990, for seven years. So with approximately 12 years of experience with either Herman Miller or its subsidiary and at the age of 39, Mike Volkema became CEO.

In 1994, Herman Miller for the Home was launched to focus on the residential market. It reintroduced some of its modern classic designs from the 40s, 50s, and 60s as well as new designs. In 1998, hmhome.com was set up to tap this market.

Additional marketing initiatives were taken to focus on small and mid-size businesses. A network of 180 retailers was established to focus on small businesses and a 3-D design computer program was made available to mid-size customers. In addition, order entry was digitally linked among Herman Miller, suppliers, distributors, and customers to expedite orders and improve their accuracy.

The 2000s

The 2000s started off spectacularly with record profits and sales in 2000 and 2001. The Board of Directors approved a special one-time option grant of 100 shares to each nonexecutive, North American-based employee in June of 2000, and the Eames molded plywood chair was selected as a "design of the century" by *Time* magazine. Sales had more than doubled in the six years that Mike Volkema had been CEO.

Then the dot.com bubble burst and the events of September 11, 2001 occurred in the U.S. Sales dropped 34% from $2,236,200,000 in 2001 to $1,468,700,000 in 2002. In the same years profits dropped from $144,100,000 to losses of $56,000,000. In an interview for *FastCompany* magazine in 2007, Volkema said, "One night I went to bed a genius and woke up the town idiot."

Although sales continued to drop in 2003, Herman Miller returned to profitability in that year. To do so, Herman Miller had to drop its long-held tradition of life-long employment. Approximately 38% of the work force was laid off. One entire plant in Georgia was closed. Mike Volkema and Brian Walker, then President of Herman Miller North America, met with all the workers to tell them what was happening and why it had to be done. One of the workers being laid off was so moved by their presentation that she told them she felt sorry for them having to personally lay off workers.

To replace the tradition of life-long employment, Mike Volkema, with input from many, developed what is referred to as "the new social contract." He explains it as follows:

We are a commercial enterprise, and the customer has to be on center stage, so we have to first figure out whether your gifts and talents have a match with the needs and wants of this commercial enterprise. If they don't, then we want to wish you the best, but we do need to tell you that I don't have a job for you right now.

As part of the implementation of the social contract, benefits such as educational reimbursement and 401K plans were redesigned to be more portable. This was done to decrease the cost of changing jobs for employees whose gifts and talents no longer matched customer needs.

Sales and profits began to climb from 2003 to 2008. In 2008, even though sales were not at an all-time high, profits were. During this period, Brian Walker became president in 2003 and chief executive officer in 2004.

Mike Volkema became chairman of the board in 2004. They continue in these positions in 2012.

Then Herman Miller was hit by the recession of 2009. Sales dropped 19% from $2,012 billion in 2008 to $1,630 billion in 2009. In the same years profits dropped from $152 million to $68 million. In March 2012, Mark Schurman, Director of External Communications at Herman Miller, predicted that the changes made to recover from the 2001-2003 recession would help it better weather the 2007-2009 recession.

Herman Miller Entering 2012

Herman Miller has codified its long practiced organizational values and publishes them on its web site under a page entitled "What We Believe." These beliefs are intended as a basis for uniting all employees, building relationships, and contributing to communities. Those beliefs as stated in 2005 and remaining in effect in 2012 are as follows:

- **Curiosity & Exploration**: These are two of our greatest strengths. They lie behind our heritage of research-driven design. How do we keep our curiosity? By respecting and encouraging risk, and by practicing forgiveness. You can't be curious and infallible. In one sense, if you never make a mistake, you're not exploring new ideas often enough. Everybody makes mistakes: we ought to celebrate honest mistakes, learn from them, and move on.
- **Engagement**: For us, it is about being owners–actively committed to the life of this community called Herman Miller, sharing in its success and risk. Stock ownership is an important ingredient, but it's not enough. The strength and the payoff really come when engaged people own problems, solutions, and behavior. Acknowledge responsibility, choose to step forward and be counted. Care about this community and make a difference in it.
- **Performance**: Performance is required for leadership. We want to be leaders, so we are committed to performing at the highest level possible. Performance isn't a choice. It's up to everybody at Herman Miller to perform at his or her best. Our own high performance–however we measure it–enriches our lives as employees, delights our customers, and creates real value for our shareholders.
- **Inclusiveness**: To succeed as a company, we must include all the expressions of human talent and potential that society offers. We value the whole person and everything each of us has to offer, obvious or not so obvious. We believe that every person should have the chance to realize his or her potential regardless of color, gender, age, sexual orientation, educational background, weight, height, family status, skill level—the list goes on and on. When we are truly inclusive, we go beyond toleration to understanding all the qualities that make people who they are, that make us unique, and most important, that unite us.
- **Design**: Design for us is a way of looking at the world and how it works–or doesn't. It is a method for getting something done, for solving a problem. To design a solution, rather than simply devising one, requires research, thought, sometimes starting over, listening, and humility. Sometimes design results in memorable occasions, timeless chairs, or really fun parties. Design isn't just the way something looks; it isn't just the way something works, either.
- **Foundations**: The past can be a tricky thing–an anchor or a sail, a tether or a launching pad. We value and respect our past without being ruled by it. The stories, people, and experiences in Herman Miller's past form a unique foundation. Our past teaches us about design, human compassion, leadership, risk taking, seeking out change, and working together. From that foundation, we can move forward together with a common language, a set of owned beliefs and understandings. We value our rich legacy more for what it shows us we might become than as a picture of what we've been.
- **A Better World**: This is at the heart of Herman Miller and the real reason why many of us come to work every day. We contribute to a better world by pursuing sustainability and environmental wisdom. Environmental advocacy is part of our heritage and a responsibility we gladly bear for future generations. We reach for a better world by giving time and money to our communities and causes outside the company; through becoming a good corporate citizen worldwide; and even in the (not so) simple act of adding beauty to the world. By participating in the effort, we lift our spirits and the spirits of those around us.
- **Transparency**: Transparency begins with letting people see how decisions are made and owning the decisions we make. So when you make a decision, own it. Confidentiality has a place at Herman Miller, but if you can't tell anybody about a decision you've made, you've probably made a poor choice. Without transparency, it's impossible to have trust and integrity. Without trust and integrity, it's impossible to be transparent.

All employees are expected to live these values. In a description of the current processes that follow, numerous examples of these values in action can be found.

Management

Mike Volkema is currently the chairman of the board, and Brian Walker is the president and chief executive officer. Walker's compensation was listed by *Bloomberg Businessweek* as $693,969 in 2011. Compensation for CEOs at five competitors was listed by *Bloomberg Businessweek* to range from $777,923 to $973,154. Walker and four other top executives at Herman Miller took a 10% pay cut in January, 2009, and they took another 10% pay cut along with all salaried workers in March, 2009. The production workers were placed on a 9 day in two weeks work schedule, effectively cutting their pay by 10% as well. A little over one year later in June, 2010 most employees' pay cuts and furloughs were rescinded. That the executives would take a pay cut before all others and twice as much is just one way human compassion is practiced at Herman Miller.

By Securities and Exchange Commission (SEC) regulations a publicly traded company must have a board of directors. By corporate policy, the majority of the 14 members of the board must be independent. To be judged an independent, the individual as a minimum must meet the NASDAQ National Market requirements for independent directors (NASDAQ Stock Market Rule 4200). In addition, the individual must not have any "other material relationship with the company or its affiliates or with any executive officer of the company or his or her affiliates." Moreover, any "transaction between the Company and any executive officer or director of the Company (including that person's spouse, children, stepchildren, parents, stepparents, siblings, parents-in-law, children-in-law, siblings-in-law and persons sharing the same residence) must be disclosed to the Board of Directors and is subject to the approval of the Board of Directors or the Nominating and Governance Committee unless the proposed transaction is part of a general program available to all directors or employees equally under an existing policy or is a purchase of Company products consistent with the price and terms of other transactions of similar size with other purchasers." Furthermore, "It is the policy of the Board that all directors, consistent with their responsibilities to the stockholders of the company as a whole, hold an equity interest in the company. Toward this end, the Board requires that each director will have an equity interest after one year on the Board, and within five years the Board encourages the directors to have shares of common stock of the company with a value of at least three times the amount of the annual retainer paid to each director." In other words, board members are held to standards consistent with the corporate beliefs and its ESOP program.

Although Herman Miller has departments, the most frequently referenced work unit is a team. Paul Murray, Director of the Environmental Health and Safety explained their relationship as follows:

At Herman Miller, team has just been the term that has been used since the Scanlon Plan and the De Prees brought that into Herman Miller. And so I think that's why we use that almost exclusively. The department — as a department, we help facilitate the other teams. And so they aren't just department driven.

Teams are often cross-functional. Membership on a team is based on ability to contribute to that team. As Gabe Wing, Design for the Environment Lead Chemical Engineer, described it,

You grab the appropriate representative who can best help your team achieve its goal. It doesn't seem to be driven based on title. It's based on who has the ability to help us drive our initiatives towards our goal.

Teams are often based on product development. When that product has been developed, the members of that team are redistributed to new projects. New projects can come from any level in the organization. At Herman Miller leadership is shared. One way in which this is done is through Herman Miller's concept of "talking up and down the ladder." Workers at all levels are encouraged to put forth new ideas. As Rudy Bartels, Environmental Specialist said,

If they try something, then they have folks there who will help them and be there for them. And by doing that, either — whether that requires a presence of one of us or an email or just to say, "Yeah, I think that's a great idea." That's how a lot ... in the organization works.

Because the workers feel empowered, a new manager can run into some behavior that can startle them. As Paul Murray recalled,

I can remember my first day on the job. I took my safety glasses off ... and an employee stepped forward and said, "Get your safety glasses back on." At Company X, Company Y,[4] there was no way would they have ever talked to a supervisor like that, much less their supervisor's manager. It's been a fun journey when the work force is that empowered.

The beliefs are also reinforced through the Employee Gifts Committee, and Environmental Quality Action

Team. True to its practice of shared leadership the Employee Gifts Committee distributes funds and other resources based on employee involvement. As explained by Jay Link, manager of Corporate Giving, the program works as follows:

…our first priority is to honor organizations where our employees are involved. We believe that it's important that we engender kind of a giving spirit in our employees, so if we know they're involved in organizations, which is going to be where we have a manufacturing presence, then our giving kind of comes alongside organizations that they're involved with. So that's our first priority.

In addition, all employees can work 16 paid hours a year with the charitable organization of their choice. Herman Miller sets goals for the number of employee volunteer hours contributed annually to its communities. Progress toward meeting those goals is reported to the CEO.

The Environmental Affairs Team has responsibility for such areas as solid waste recycling and designing products from sustainable resources. It was formed in 1988 with the authorization of Max De Pree. One success that it has is in the reduction of solid waste taken to the landfill. In 1991, Herman Miller was sending 41 million pounds to the landfill. By 1994 it was down to 24 million pounds and by 2008 it was reduced to 3.6. Such improvements are both environmentally friendly and cost effective.

These beliefs are carried over to the family and community. Gabe Wing related how, "I've got the worst lawn in my neighborhood. That's because I don't spread pesticides on it, and I don't put fertilizer down." He went on to say how his wife and he had to make a difficult decision this the summer of 2009 because Herman Miller has a policy "to avoid PVC (polyvinyl chloride) wherever possible." In restoring their home, they chose fiber cement board over PVC siding even though it was considerably more costly. Gabe went on say, "Seven years ago, I didn't really think about it."

Rudy Bartels is involved in a youth soccer association. As is typical, it needs to raise money to buy uniforms. Among other fund raisers that it has done is collecting newspapers and aluminum cans. As he tells it, "When I'll speak they'll say, 'Yeah, that's Rudy. He's Herman Miller. You should — you know we're gonna have to do this.'"

These beliefs carry over to all functional areas of the business. Some of them are obviously beneficial and some of them are simply the way Herman Miller has chosen to conduct its business.

Marketing

Herman Miller products are sold internationally through wholly owned subsidiaries in various countries including Canada, France, Germany, Italy, Japan, Mexico, Australia, Singapore, China, India, and the Netherlands. Its products are offered through independent dealerships. The customer base is spread over 100 countries.

Herman Miller uses Green Marketing to sell its products. For example, the Mirra Chair introduced in 2003 with PostureFit Technology was developed from its inception to be environmentally friendly (cradle-to-cradle principles). These chairs are made of 45% recycled materials, and 96% of their materials are recyclable. In addition, they are assembled using 100% renewable energy. In 2003, *Architectural Record* magazine and *Environmental Building News* named the Mirra chair as one of the "Top 10 Green Products." Builders who use Herman Miller products in their buildings can earn points toward LEED's (Leadership in Energy & Environmental Design) certification.

In addition, Herman Miller engages in cooperative advertising with strategic partners. For example, at Hilton Garden Inns, some rooms are equipped with Herman Miller's Mirra chairs. On the desk in the room is a card explaining how to adjust the chair for comfort and then lists a Hilton Garden Inn web site where the chair can be purchased.

Herman Miller segments its markets into work, home, healthcare education, and government. Many products are marketed across segments.

To enhance its marketing analysis and promotions, Herman Miller also segments its markets geographically. The North American, Asian, European and Latin American markets are all tracked independently.

Production/Operations

Herman Miller is globally positioned in terms of manufacturing operations. In the United States, its manufacturing operations are located in Michigan, Georgia, and Washington. In Europe, it has considerable manufacturing presence in the United Kingdom, its largest market outside of the United States. In Asia, it has manufacturing operations in Ningbo, China.

Herman Miller manufactures products using a system of lean manufacturing techniques collectively referred to as the Herman Miller Performance System (HMPS) (Figure 1). It strives to maintain efficiencies and cost savings by minimizing the amount of inventory on hand through a JIT (Just in Time) process. Some suppliers deliver parts to Herman Miller production facilities five or six times per day.

Figure 1 The Herman Miller Production System

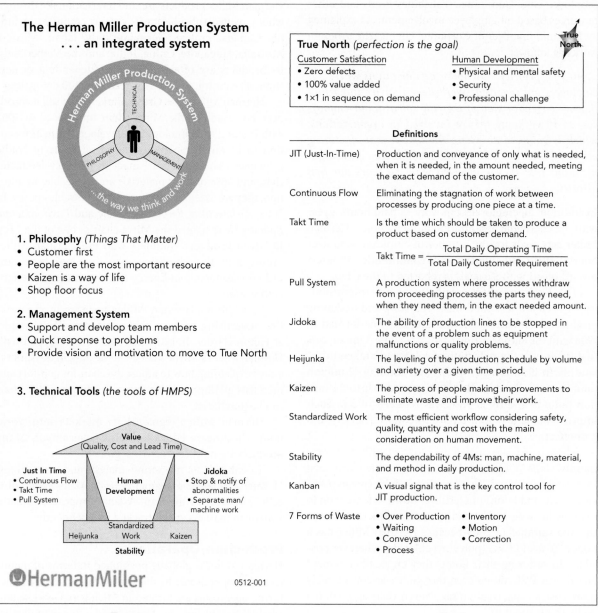

The Herman Miller Production System
. . . an integrated system

True North (perfection is the goal)

Customer Satisfaction	Human Development
• Zero defects	• Physical and mental safety
• 100% value added	• Security
• 1×1 in sequence on demand	• Professional challenge

Definitions

JIT (Just-In-Time)	Production and conveyance of only what is needed, when it is needed, in the amount needed, meeting the exact demand of the customer.
Continuous Flow	Eliminating the stagnation of work between processes by producing one piece at a time.
Takt Time	Is the time which should be taken to produce a product based on customer demand.
	$$\text{Takt Time} = \frac{\text{Total Daily Operating Time}}{\text{Total Daily Customer Requirement}}$$
Pull System	A production system where processes withdraw from proceeding processes the parts they need, when they need them, in the exact needed amount.
Jidoka	The ability of production lines to be stopped in the event of a problem such as equipment malfunctions or quality problems.
Heijunka	The leveling of the production schedule by volume and variety over a given time period.
Kaizen	The process of people making improvements to eliminate waste and improve their work.
Standardized Work	The most efficient workflow considering safety, quality, quantity and cost with the main consideration on human movement.
Stability	The dependability of 4Ms: man, machine, material, and method in daily production.
Kanban	A visual signal that is the key control tool for JIT production.
7 Forms of Waste	• Over Production • Inventory
	• Waiting • Motion
	• Conveyance • Correction
	• Process

1. Philosophy (Things That Matter)
• Customer first
• People are the most important resource
• Kaizen is a way of life
• Shop floor focus

2. Management System
• Support and develop team members
• Quick response to problems
• Provide vision and motivation to move to True North

3. Technical Tools (the tools of HMPS)

Value
(Quality, Cost and Lead Time)

Just In Time
• Continuous Flow
• Takt Time
• Pull System

Human Development

Jidoka
• Stop & notify of abnormalities
• Separate man/machine work

Standardized Work
Heijunka · Kaizen

Stability

HermanMiller   0512-001

Front   Back

Production is order-driven with direct materials and components purchased as needed to meet demand. The standard lead time for the majority of its products is 10 to 20 days. As a result, the rate of inventory turnover is high. These combined factors could cause inventory levels to appear relatively low in relation to sales volume. A key element of its manufacturing strategy is to limit fixed production costs by outsourcing component parts from strategic suppliers. This strategy has allowed it to increase the variable nature of its cost structure while retaining proprietary control over those production processes that Herman Miller believes provide a competitive advantage. Because of this strategy, manufacturing operations are largely assembly-based.

The success of the Herman Miller Performance System (HMPS) was the result of much hard work. For example, in 1996, the Integrated Metals Technology (IMT) subsidiary was not going well. IMT supplied pedestals to its parent company Herman Miller. Its prices were high, lead time long, and quality was in the 70% range. The leadership of the subsidiary decided to hire the consulting arm of Toyota, Toyota Supplier Support Center (TSSC). Significant improvements were made by inquiring, analyzing, and "enlisting help and ideas of everyone." For example, quality defects in parts per million decreased from approximately 9000 in 2000 to 1500 in 2006. Concurrently, on-time shipments improved from 80% to 100% and safety incidents per 100 employees dropped from 10 to 3 per year.

The organizational values mentioned earlier were incorporated into the design of The Greenhouse, Herman Miller's main production facility in Michigan. The building was designed to be environmentally friendly. For example, it takes advantage of natural light and landscaping. Native plants are grown without the use of fertilizers, pesticides, or irrigation. After the facility was opened, aggressive paper wasps found the design to their liking. Employees and guests were stung, frequently. In keeping with Herman Miller beliefs a solution was sought. Through research it was learned that honey bees and paper wasps are incompatible. Therefore, 600,000 honey bees and their 12 hives were co-located on the property. The wasps soon left. Two additional consequences were that due to pollination by the bees, the area around the facility blooms with wild flowers and a large amount of honey is produced. Guests to the home office are given a four-ounce bottle of the honey symbolizing its corporate beliefs.

Human Resource Management

Human resource management is considered a strength for Herman Miller. It is routinely listed on *Fortune's* 100 Best Companies to Work For, including 2010. It had approximately 278 applicants for every job opening. In the 2009 downturn, Herman Miller cut its workforce by more than 15%, reduced pay of the remaining workforce by at least 10%, and suspended 401(k) contributions. Employees praised management for "handling the downturn with class and doing what is best for the collective whole" according to *Fortune* magazine's February 8, 2010 issue. *Fortune* also estimated voluntary turnover to be less than 2%. On June 1, 2010, the time-and-pay cuts of 10 percent begun in the spring of 2009 were discontinued due to Herman Miller's quick turnaround.

Herman Miller practices "Business as Unusual" as pointed out many years ago by Hugh De Pree, former president, and it appears to pay off in both good and tough times. Herman Miller shares the gains as well as the pains with its employees especially in regards to compensation.

Pay is geared to firm performance, and it takes many forms at Herman Miller. As in other companies, all employees receive a base pay. In addition, all employees participate in a profit-sharing program whereby employees receive stock based on the company's annual financial performance. Employees are immediately enrolled in this plan upon joining Herman Miller and immediately vested. Profit sharing is based on corporate performance because as one employee explained:

The problem we see is you get to situations where project X corporately had a greater opportunity for the entirety of the business, but it was difficult to tell these folks that they needed to sacrifice in order to support the entirety of the business when they were being compensated specifically on their portion of the business. So you would get into some turf situations. So we ended up moving to a broader corporate EVA (Economic Value Added) compensation to prevent those types of turf battles.

The company offers an Employee Stock Purchase Plan (ESPP) through payroll deductions at a 15% discount from the market price. Also, all employees are offered a 401(k) where they receive a 50% match for the first 6% of their salaries that the employee contributes. Again, employees are immediately eligible to participate in this plan upon joining Herman Miller and immediately vested. The company match was suspended in 2009 due to the recession. Through the profit sharing and the ESPP, the employees own approximately 8% of the outstanding stock.

Furthermore, all employees are offered a retirement income plan whereby the company deposits into an account 4% of compensation on which interest is paid quarterly. Employees are immediately eligible to participate in this plan upon joining Herman Miller, but are required to participate for five years before being vested. Additionally, a length of service bonus is paid after 5 years of employment. Finally, the company pays a universal annual bonus to all employees based on the company's performance against Economic Value Added (EVA) objectives. EVA is a calculation of the company's net operating profits, after tax, minus a "charge" for the cost of shareholder capital. This is in addition to the other compensation programs, including profit sharing, with the same calculation used to determine both employee and executive bonus potential.

Thus, pay takes a number of forms at Herman Miller, but most all forms are at least partially, if not wholly, contingent on corporate performance. One employee summed up pay as follows, "You can dip into Herman Miller's pocket several times based on the performance of the company."

Other benefits also take many forms at Herman Miller. Employees are given a range of benefits, as they are in many organizations. Some are, however, quite different from those found in other organizations, such as a $100 rebate on a bike purchase. It is justified as "part of our comprehensive program designed for a better world around you." Other benefits that Herman Miller provides that are identified by the company as "unique" are,

- 100% tuition reimbursement
- Flexible schedules: job sharing, compressed work-week, and telecommuting options
- Concierge services: help in getting directions, dry cleaning, greeting cards or a meal to take home, these services make it easier for you to balance work and home life
- Employee product purchase discounts
- On-site services including massage therapy, cafeterias, banking, health services, fitness center, fitness classes, and personal trainers

Herman Miller in keeping with its beliefs offers extensive wellness benefits including fitness facilities or subsidized gym memberships, health services, employee assistance programs, wellness programs/classes, and health risk assessments. The other benefits that are offered that most large organizations also offer include health insurance, dental insurance, vision care plans, prescription plans, flexible spending accounts, short and long term disability, life insurance, accidental death and disability insurance, and critical illness/personal accident/long-term care. All benefits are also available to domestic partners.

When appropriate, Herman Miller promotes people within the organization. Education and training are seen as key to preparing employees to take on new responsibilities. For example, Rudy Bartels, Environmental Specialist, as well as multiple vice presidents, began their careers at Herman Miller on the production floor.

Three other benefits are unique to Herman Miller. First, every family that has or adopts a child receives a Herman Miller rocking chair. Second, every employee who retires after 25 years with the company and is 55 years or older receives an Eames lounge chair. Third, Herman Miller has no executive retreat, but it does have an employee retreat, The Marigold Lodge, on Lake Michigan. This retreat is available to employees for corporate related events, such as retirement parties and other celebrations, and in some instances includes invited family and guests.

Finance

During normal economic times, financial management at Herman Miller would be considered conservative.

Through 2006, its leverage ratio was below the industry average and its times interest earned ratio was over twice the industry average. Due to the drop-off in business, the debt to equity ratio rose precipitously from 1.18 in 2006 to 47.66 in 2008. To improve this ratio, over 3 million shares were sold in fiscal year 2009.[5] In the four previous fiscal years, Herman Miller had been repurchasing shares. The debt to equity ratio was reduced to 3.81 by the end of 2009. To improve short-term assets, dividends per share were cut by approximately 70% and capital expenditures were reduced to zero in 2009 (Financial statements for years 2006-2010 can be found in Tables 1 and 2.).

For fiscal year 2008, 15% of Herman Miller's revenues and 10% of its profits were from non-North American countries. In 2007, non-North American countries accounted for 16.5% of revenues and approximately 20% of Herman Miller's profits.

Financially, Herman Miller holds true to its beliefs. Even in downturns, it invests in research and development. In the dot.com downturn, it invested tens of millions of dollars in R & D. Inside Herman Miller this investment project was code named "Purple."

In the December 19, 2007 issue of *FastCompany* magazine commenting on this project, Clayton Christensen, Harvard Business School professor and author of *The Innovator's Dilemma*, is quoted as saying, "Barely one out of 1000 companies would do what they did. It was a daring bet in terms of increasing spending for the sake of tomorrow while cutting back to survive today."

Herman Miller continues to receive awards both for the design of its product and for its treatment of its employees. For example, in 2011, it was designated as one of ten design icons in Fast Company's "Thirty Companies That Get It," and in 2012, Herman Miller was recognized with the Huntington Pillar Award, given by the Women's Resource Center to companies that demonstrate outstanding dedication to empowering women in the workplace.

Accessories Team: An Example of HM's Strategy, Leadership, and Beliefs in Action

The Accessories Team was an outgrowth of project "Purple." One of the goals of this project was to stretch beyond the normal business boundaries. Office accessories is one area in which Herman Miller has not been historically involved even though it is a big part of what the independent dealers sell. Once identified, "Robyn was tapped to put together a team to really explore this as a product segment that we could get more involved

Table 1 Consolidated Balance Sheets (In millions, except share and per share data)

	May 28, 2011	May 29, 2010	May 30, 2009	May 31, 2008	June 2, 2007	June 3, 2006
Assets						
Current Assets:						
Cash and cash equivalents	148.6	$ 134.8	$ 192.9	$ 155.4	$ 76.4	$ 106.8
Short-term investments (Note1)		–	–	15.7	15.9	15.2
Marketable securities	11.1	12.1	11.3	–	–	–
Accounts receivable	193.1	144.7	148.9	209.0	188.1	173.2
Less allowances in each year	4.5	4.4	7.3	5.6	4.9	5.0
Inventories, net	66.2	57.9	37.3	55.1	56.0	47.1
Prepaid expenses and other	59.2	45.2	60.5	58.0	48.3	47.9
Total Current Assets	478.1	394.7	450.9	493.2	384.7	390.2
Property and Equipment:						
Land and improvements	19.9	19.4	18.8	19.0	18.9	20.9
Buildings and improvements	149.5	147.6	137.4	139.4	137.2	139.1
Machinery and equipment	531.0	546.4	552.0	547.4	543.3	523.8
Construction in progress	13.0	10.7	9.8	17.4	17.6	23.5
Gross Property & Equipment	713.4	724.1	718.0	723.2	717.0	707.3
Less: accumulated depreciation	(544.3)	(548.9)	(538.8)	(526.9)	(520.4)	(504.0)
Net Property and Equipment	169.1	175.2	179.2	196.3	196.6	203.3
Goodwill and indefinite-lived intangibles	133.6	132.6	72.7	40.2	39.1	39.1
Other amortizable intangibles, net	24.3	25.0	11.3	–	–	–
Other assets	9.3	43.1	53.2	53.5	45.8	35.4
Total Assets	814.4	$770.6	$767.3	$783.2	$666.2	$668.0
Liabilities and Shareholders' Equity						
Current Liabilities:						
Unfunded checks	6.4	4.3	3.9	8.5	7.4	6.5
Current maturities of long-term debt	–	100.0	75.0	–	3.0	3.0
Accounts payable	112.7	96.3	79.1	117.9	110.5	112.3
Accrued liabilities	153.1	112.4	124.2	184.1	163.6	177.6
Total Current Liabilities	272.2	313.0	282.2	310.5	284.5	299.4
Long-term debt, less current maturities	250.0	201.2	302.4	375.5	173.2	175.8
Other liabilities	87.2	176.3	174.7	73.8	52.9	54.2
Total Liabilities	609.4	690.5	759.3	759.8	510.6	529.4
Minority Interest	–	–	–	–	.3	.2
Shareholders' Equity:						
Preferred stock, no par value (10,000,000 shares authorized, none issued)	–	–	–	–	–	–

Continued

Table 1 (Continued) Consolidated Balance Sheets (In millions, except share and per share data)

	May 28, 2011	May 29, 2010	May 30, 2009	May 31, 2008	June 2, 2007	June 3, 2006
Common stock, $0.20 par value (240,000,000 shares authorized, 57,002,733 and 53,826,061 shares issued and outstanding in 2010 and 2009, respectively)	11.6	11.4	10.8	11.1	12.6	13.2
Additional paid-in capital	82.0	55.9	5.9	–	–	–
Retained earnings	218.2	152.4	129.2	76.7	197.8	192.2
Accumulated other comprehensive loss	(104.2)	(136.2)	(134.1)	(60.1)	(51.6)	(63.3)
Key executive deferred compensation	(2.6)	(3.4)	(3.8)	(4.3)	(3.5)	(3.7)
Total Shareholders' Equity	205.0	80.1	8.0	23.4	155.3	138.4
Total Liabilities and Shareholders' Equity	$814.4	$770.6	$767.3	$783.2	$666.2	$668.0

Table 2 Consolidated Statements of Operations (In millions, except per share data)

	May 28, 2011	May 29, 2010	May 30, 2009	May 31, 2008	June 2, 2007	June 3, 2006
Net sales	$1,649.2	$1,318.8	$1,630.0	$2,012.1	$1,918.9	$1,737.2
Cost of sales	1,111.1	890.3	1102.3	1,313.4	1,273.0	1,162.4
Gross margin	538.1	428.5	527.7	698.7	645.9	574.8
Operating Expenses:						
Selling, general, and administrative	366.0	317.7	330.8	395.8	395.8	371.7
Restructuring expenses	3.0	16.7	28.4	5.1	–	
Design and research	45.8	40.5	45.7	51.2	52.0	45.4
Total operating expenses	414.8	374.9	404.9	452.1	447.8	417.1
Operating earnings	123.3	53.6	122.8	246.6	198.1	157.7
Other Expenses (Income):						
Interest expense	19.9	21.7	25.6	18.8	13.7	14.0
Interest and other investment income	(1.5)	(4.6)	(2.6)	(3.8)	(4.1)	(4.9)
Other, net	2.4	1.7	.9	1.2	1.5	1.0
Net other expenses	20.8	18.8	23.9	16.2	1	10.1
Earnings before income taxes and minority interest	102.5	34.8	98.9	230.4	187.0	147.6
Income tax expense	31.7	6.5	31.0	78.2	57.9	47.7
Minority interest, net of income tax			(.1)	(0.1)		0.7
Net Earnings	**70.8**	**$28.3**	**$68.0**	**$152.3**	**$129.1**	**$99.2**
Earnings per share - basic	$1.24	$.51	$1.26	$2.58	$2.01	$1.4
Earnings per share - diluted	$1.06	$.43	$1.25	$2.56	$1.98	$1.45

Source: Herman Miller's 10_K's

with," according to Mark Schurman, Director of External Communications at Herman Miller.

In 2006, Robyn established the team by recruiting Larry Kallio to be the head engineer and Wayne Baxter to lead sales and marketing. Together, they assembled a flexible team to launch a new product in 16 months. They recruited people with different disciplines needed to support that goal. Over the next two years, they remained a group of six. Some people started with the team and then as it got through that piece of work, they went on to different roles within the company. The team during its first eight months met twice a week for half a day. Twenty months out it met only once a week.

The group acts with a fair amount of autonomy, but it does not want complete autonomy because, "We don't want to be out there completely on our own because we have such awesome resources here at Herman Miller," Robyn explained. The group reaches out to other areas in the company when different disciplines are needed for a particular product, and tap people that could allocate some of their time to support it.

Wayne described what happened on the team as follows:

We all seem to have a very strong voice regarding almost any topic; it's actually quite fun and quite dynamic. We all have kind of our roles on the team, but I think other than maybe true engineering, we've all kind of tapped into other roles and still filled in to help each other as much as we could.

Another member of the accessories team described decision making as follows:

If we wanted to debate and research and get very scientific, we would not be sitting here talking about the things that we've done, we'd still be researching them. In a sense, we rely upon our gut a lot, which I think is, at the end of the day, just fine because we have enough experience. We're not experts, but we're also willing to take risks and we're also willing to evolve.

Thus, leadership and decision making is shared both within the team and across the organization. Ideas and other contributions to the success of the team are accepted from all sources.

Out of this process has grown what is known as the "Thrive Collection." The name was chosen to indicate the focus on the individual and the idea of personal comfort, control, and ergonomic health. Products included in the collection are the Ardea® Personal Light, the Leaf® Personal Light, Flo® Monitor Arm, and C2® Climate Control. All of these are designed for improving the individual's working environment. Continuing Herman Miller's tradition of innovative design, the Ardea light earned both Gold and Silver honors from the International Design Excellence Awards (IDEA) in June, 2010.

The Industry

Office equipment is an economically volatile industry. The office furniture segment of the industry was hit hard by the recession. The AKTRIN Research Institute stated in a 2003 industry report, "…corporate profitability is one of the most forthright determinations for business office furniture acquisition." Neither the industry nor Herman Miller has returned to their sales peaks of 2007. Herman Miller's stock market value of $1,437,979 at the end of 2011 represented 10.79% of the total stock market value of the industry identified by Standard & Poor's Research Insight as Office Services & Supplies. Both figures represented increases from the ending 2009 market value of $1,095,322,000 and total stock market value of the industry of 7.3%. According to Hoover's, Herman Miller's top three competitors are Commercial Furniture Group, Inc., Flexsteel Industries, Inc., and HMU, LLC. All three of these are different than what Hoover's listed as the top three competitors for Herman Miller in 2009.

The industry has been impacted by a couple of trends. First, telecommuting has decreased the need of large companies to have office equipment for all employees. Some companies such as Oracle have a substantial percentage of their employees telecommuting. The majority of Jet Blue reservation clerks telecommute. Second, more employees spend more hours in front of computer screens than ever before. Due to this trend, the need for ergonomically correct office furniture has increased. Such furniture helps to decrease fatigue and injuries such as carpal tunnel syndrome.

As with most industries, the cost of raw materials and competition from overseas has had an impact. These trends tend to impact the low-cost producers more than the high-quality producers.

The Future

In a June 24, 2010, press release, Brian Walker, Chief Executive Officer, stated, "One of the hallmarks of our company's history has been the ability to emerge from challenging periods with transformational products and processes. I believe our commitment to new products and market development over the past two years has put us in a position to do this once again. Throughout this period, we remained focused on maintaining near-term profitability while at the same time investing for the future. The award-winning new products we introduced last week at the NeoCon tradeshow are a testament to that focus, and I am incredibly proud of the collective spirit it has taken at Herman Miller to make this happen." The financial results in 2011 appear to indicate that this strategy is working. However, in a press release accompanying the third quarter results for 2012, Mr. Walker stated, "Our financial results this quarter (see Tables 3, 4, & 5) reflect the continued strength of our international business, particularly within Asia and Latin America. These emerging markets remain an important point of emphasis in our growth strategy, and we are thrilled to announce the planned closing of the POSH

acquisition (a Hong Kong-based designer, manufacturer, and distributor of office furniture systems, freestanding furniture, seating, and filing and storage)."

Mr. Walker continued explaining, "Within North America, business levels in the quarter were constrained by a slowdown in sales and orders to the U.S. federal government and within the healthcare sector. We were, however, very encouraged to see solid year-over-year increases across most other North American customer groups as well as in our Specialty and Consumer segment. Given the momentum of our international operations, the acquisition of POSH, and the improving state of the broader U.S. economy, we are

Table 3 Herman Miller, Inc. Condensed Consolidated Statements of Operations (Unaudited) (Dollars in millions, except per share data)

	Nine Months Ended			
	March 3, 2012		February 26, 2011	
Net Sales	$1,303.5	100.0%	$1,207.7	100.0%
Cost of Sales	862.9	66.2%	815.3	67.5%
Gross Margin	440.6	33.8%	392.4	32.5%
Operating Expenses	332.8	25.5%	297.6	24.6%
Restructuring Expenses	–	–	3.0	0.3%
Operating Earnings	107.8	8.3%	91.8	7.6%
Other Expense, net	14.0	1.1%	16.1	1.3%
Earnings Before Income Taxes	93.8	7.2%	75.7	6.3%
Income Tax Expense	30.6	2.3%	21.9	1.8%
Net Earnings	$63.2	4.8%	$53.8	4.5%
Earnings Per Share – Basic	$1.09		$0.94	
Weighted Average Basic Common Shares	58,144,031		57,032,799	
Earnings Per Share – Diluted	$1.08		$0.77	
Weighted Average Diluted Common Shares	58,414,707		57,652,948	

Source: Herman Miller Reports Planned Strategic Investments, Strong Cash Flow in the Third Quarter of FY2012, Press Release, March 21, 2012

Table 4 Herman Miller, Inc. Condensed Consolidated Statements of Cash Flows (Unaudited) (Dollars in millions)

	Nine Months Ended		
	March 3, 2012	February 26, 2011	Percentage Change
Net Earnings	$63.2	$53.8	17%
Cash Flows provided by Operating Activities	82.4	52.5	57%
Cash Flows used for Investing Activities	(6.2)	(23.0)	−73%
Cash Flows used for Financing Activities	(0.6)	(4.3)	−86%
Effect of Exchange Rates	–	3.7	N/C
Net Increase in Cash	75.6	28.9	162%
Cash, Beginning of Period	$142.2	$130.5	9%
Cash, End of Period	$217.8	$159.4	37%

Source: Herman Miller Reports Planned Strategic Investments, Strong Cash Flow in the Third Quarter of FY2012, Press Release, March 21, 2012

Table 5 Herman Miller, Inc. Condensed Consolidated Balance Sheets (Unaudited) (Dollars in millions)

	March 3, 2012	May 28, 2011	Percentage Change
Assets			
Current Assets			
Cash and Cash Equivalents	$217.8	$142.2	53%
Marketable Securities	10.7	11.0	−3%
Accounts Receivable, net	154.9	193.1	−20%
Inventories, net	56.3	66.2	−15%
Prepaid Expenses and Other	50.7	59.2	−14%
Total Current Assets	490.4	471.7	4%
Net Property and Equipment	159.3	169.1	−6%
Other Assets	166.0	167.2	−1%
Total Assets	$815.7	$808.0	1%
Liabilities and Shareholders' Equity			
Current Liabilities			
Accounts Payable	93.2	112.7	−17%
Accrued Liabilities	129.1	153.1	−16%
Total Current Liabilities	222.3	265.8	−16%
Long-term Debt	250.0	250.0	0%
Other Liabilities	74.3	87.2	−15%
Total Liabilities	546.6	603.0	−9%
Shareholders' Equity Totals	269.1	205.0	31%
Total Liabilities and Shareholders' Equity	$815.7	$808.0	1%

Source: Herman Miller Reports Planned Strategic Investments, Strong Cash Flow in the Third Quarter of FY2012, Press Release, March 21, 2012

increasingly confident in the future growth prospects of our business."

Questions to address: Will the strategies that have made Herman Miller an outstanding and award-winning company continue to provide it with the ability to reinvent and renew itself? Will disruptive global, economic, and competitive forces compel it to change its business model?

NOTES

1. Many sources were helpful in providing material for this case, most particularly employees at Herman Miller who generously shared their time and viewpoints about the company to help ensure that the case accurately reflected the company's practices and culture. They provided many resources, including internal documents and stories of their personal experiences.

2. Corporate titles such as president and chief executive officer are not capitalized in this case because they are not capitalized in company documents.

3. At Herman Miller, people, including D.J. De Pree, are referred to by their first or nicknames or in combination with their surnames, but hardly ever by their titles or surnames alone.

4. The names of the two Fortune 500 companies were deleted by the authors.

5. Herman Miller's fiscal year ends on May 30th of the following calendar year.

CASE 16

Itaipu Binacional

Claudia Coser

Business School – PUCPR

Kleber Vanolli

Itaipu Binacional

History

Itaipu Binacional was created in 1974 to manage the construction of a hydroelectric plant (called the Itaipu Dam) that was structured as "an international company." Today, the Itaipu Dam is recognized as "the world's largest generator of renewable clean energy."

Initially, the Brazilian government was assigned to raise funds for the project, which was financed by short-term credit from private financial institutions and foreign government banks. The debt, which approximated $16 billion in U.S. dollars, is to be repaid by 2023 when the Itaipu Treaty is set to expire. The Itaipu Treaty is the legal instrument that was signed by Brazil and Paraguay in 1973 to permit the "exploitation" of the Paraná River by the two countries for the purpose of generating energy for the countries' needs. The Itaipu Treaty's origination coincided with the global crisis that surfaced because of the dramatic increase in oil prices that occurred in the early 1970s. At this time, research of renewable energy sources intensified in order to ensure the availability of energy sources in Brazil and Paraguay. The plant doubles the capacity of power generation in Brazil, meeting 26 percent of the country's power demand. Paraguay had an increase in its GDP, from only 5 percent in 1975 to 10.8 percent in 1978. The enhanced commercial activity increased Paraguay's demand for power.

The construction of the Itaipu Binacional hydroelectric power plant, also known as the Itaipu Dam, was likened to a labor of Hercules by the American magazine *Popular Mechanics*. Moreover, in 1994, the American Society of Civil Engineers chose the Itaipu Dam as "one of the seven modern Wonders of the World." During the actual construction process, the region where it was built became a beehive of activity. Between 1975 and 1978, more than 9,000 houses were built on both sides of the Paraná River at the border between Brazil and Paraguay to provide living residences for the men working in the project. At the time, the net result of the building activity was that the population of Iguassu Falls increased from roughly 20,000 to almost 102,000 inhabitants. In total, Itaipu Binacional created jobs for about 40,000 workers at the construction site and in support offices in Brazil and Paraguay.

The dam works were completed and the canal's gates closed in the late fall of 1982. In November of that year, the president of Brazil, João Figueiredo, and the president of Paraguay, Alfredo Stroessner, triggered the mechanism that lifted the 14 floodgates and released dammed water from the Paraná River. Releasing the water formally launched the operations of the world's largest hydroelectric dam.

Filling the reservoir affected the lives of thousands of people who lived on the banks of the Paraná River between Iguassu Falls and Guaira. The inhabitants of Iguassu Falls saw the empty river downstream of the dam because of the closure of the gates, while Guaira residents mourned the flooding of Seven Falls. Over the 170 km of land that was submerged between the two cities, a total of 8,519 urban and rural properties were flooded on the Brazilian side. The indemnities paid at the time to compensate residents for their losses totaled $209 million.

Itaipu as Part of Brazil's Energy Matrix: Institutional Regulatory Pressures

The Brazilian energy model (called the "energy matrix") is considered the cleanest in the world. According to the United Nations Program for the Environment (UNEP), almost 46 percent of all energy used in Brazil comes from clean sources including biomass, ethanol, wind, and solar. However, hydroelectric power generates over 75 percent of the electricity used in Brazil. The 46 percent of Brazil's energy use accounted for by clean sources is far superior to the average of 13 percent renewable sources in the world's industrialized countries (and falling to 6 percent within developing nations). Moreover, estimates are that the current amount of power generated by hydroelectric power in Brazil is roughly one third of its potential.

During the Conference of the World Summit on Sustainable Development in Johannesburg in 2002, scientists and other participants concluded that all hydroelectric power generation is renewable. This assessment was ratified in 2003 during the third World Water Forum that was held in Kyoto, Japan. The arguments for recognizing hydroelectricity as a highly desirable energy source include the following:

1. It is a renewable source of energy that uses the energy of flowing water with no reduction in the water's quantity.
2. It enables the use of other renewable energy sources, offering at the same time operational flexibility in response to fluctuations in the demand for electricity. The flexibility and storage capacity of hydroelectric power plants have made them the most efficient and economical in support of the use of intermittent sources of renewable energy such as solar or wind power.
3. It promotes energy security and price stability for a host nation, given that the water of the rivers is a domestic resource.
4. It contributes to the storage of drinking water. The hydroelectric plant reservoirs collect rainwater, which also can be used for consumption or irrigation.
5. Its lifecycle produces very small amounts of greenhouse gases (GHG).
6. Over the long term, the technologies used to produce hydroelectricity have become well known and are considered to be proven. In this regard, the effects of generating hydroelectricity are clearly understood, as are the techniques used to effectively manage those effects.
7. A hydropower plant has an average lifespan of 50 to 100 years. Within a plant's lifespan though, new technologies can be added for the purpose of enhancing the plant's efficiency and effectiveness. In contrast, a thermal plant's lifespan is far shorter at close to 30 years; incorporating the latest technological developments in these plants is more complicated compared to doing so in hydroelectric plants.
8. The hydroelectric projects that are developed and operated in an economically viable, environmentally sensible and socially responsible way represent sustainable development in its finest form. In fact, the World Commission on Environment and Development recognized in 1987 that effectively designed and established hydroelectric projects represent "development (that meets) the needs of people today without compromising the ability of future generations in meeting their own needs."[1]

As a hydroelectric plant, the Itaipu Dam produces an average of 90 million megawatt-hours of power annually. This output is equivalent to the daily production of 536,000 barrels of oil or 47 million m3 of gas, and is equal to 25 percent of the domestic oil production in Brazil. If the significant amount of energy produced by the Itaipu dam were generated through other, less environmentally friendly means such as oil, approximately 38 million tons of carbon dioxide (CO_2) would be released into the atmosphere annually. If the same amount of Itaipu-based energy were generated by coal, CO_2 emissions would reach 85 million tons per year. A person working in the construction industry once commented about the Itaipu Dam's output:

"God has been generous toward the Brazilians, and Saint Peter has cooperated greatly in recent years in keeping the reservoirs at enviable levels for the production of hydropower. But we should not count only on that. In order to grow at rates of 5 percent or 6 percent annually, Brazil has to do much more than it has done in the field of production and transmission of electricity. It is time to think about the future. We have been through several scares. In the late 1990s we had worrying blackouts and in 2001, we experienced a terrifying energy crisis. The country had to experience severe electricity rationing, which has succeeded only because of the extraordinary capacity of understanding and cooperation of our people."[2]

Still, roughly 72 percent of Brazil's hydroelectric potential remains untapped. Affecting the possibility of tapping more of this capacity in Brazil are the obstacles associated with the growing environmental and socio-economic restrictions toward new projects. A bottle-neck between the electrical and environmental planning delays implementation of hydropower projects. The critical path for many industry experts is the environmental licensing.

One reason for the delays is the fact that the electric sector in Brazil has experienced many changes over the past 15 years. Absolute control of the State was the reality until the early 1990s when privatization processes were initiated. Because of the power rationing that occurred in 2001, long-term planning became a priority in 2004 with the main goal of providing the country with alternatives to balance supply and demand, combining two ministries for the purpose of being able to do so: Mines and Energy (MME) and the Environment (MMA).

In part, these ministries were created to positively address the bureaucratic challenges as well as the increasing financial expenses associated with applying for and receiving environmental approval for licenses to develop new hydroelectric projects. Another reality was that the large state-owned power plants discourage hydroelectric investors who fear unfair competition, financing conditions, and high taxes.

Evidence shows that the process associated with the environmental licensing process for a hydroelectric plant is more complicated and time-consuming (up to 1200 days) than the process associated with a thermoelectric licensing process, which is only a few months. Thermoelectric power plants use plant oil, diesel, and coal; plants using gas and sugarcane pulp bagasse were considered to rely on alternative sources of energy.

The coal power plants and diesel engines negatively affect the atmosphere with pollution and produce very expensive energy due to the fuel price. The decisive factor is to select the thermoelectric plants with a more attractive cost/benefit outcome. This positive outcome can be reached by taking into account the investment cost and the additional cost when the plant operates, using fuel, to calculate costs and benefits. Brazil's energy matrix features a strong renewable component; at the same time however, the country fails to maintain appropriate operational standards, the result being that the thermal power plants operate at relatively low levels of efficiency.

Itaipu and Sustainability: The Normative Institutional Pressures

The 2002 World Summit on Sustainable Development established that sustainable development is built on "three interdependent and mutually supportive pillars:" Economic Development, Social Development, and Environmental Protection. The concept of sustainable development applied to the energy sector comprises the implementation of measures to meet the current demand for energy and to guarantee the availability of energy sources for future generations.

From a technological basis, Brazil holds the third largest hydropower potential functionality in the world, behind only China and Russia. It is also important to note that when considering the cost of hydropower as a means of competitively generating energy supplies, Brazil has a great potential for expansion of generation capacity via hydroelectricity. Many developing countries do not use hydropower. Nonetheless, hydroelectricity accounts for some level of power generation in 159 countries across the world. Five countries account for more than half of the global hydropower production: China, Canada, Brazil, the United States, and Russia.

Participants in the Symposium on Hydropower and Sustainable Development of the United Nations, held in October of 2004, took the following position:

"Having considered the social, economic and environmental benefits of hydropower and its potential contribution in achieving sustainable development goals, we firmly believe that there is a need to develop hydroelectricity which is economically, socially and environmentally sustainable."[3]

A "Guidelines for Sustainability" document was published by The International Hydropower Association (IHA) in 2004. These guidelines, which were actually presented during the UN Symposium, were built on the core values identified in the final report of the World Commission on Large Dams (November, 2000): equity, efficiency, participatory decision-making, sustainability and transparency (accountability). The purpose of the IHA Guidelines was to "promote greater consideration of environmental, social and economic sustainability in the evaluation of new hydroelectric projects and the management and operation of power plants."

While establishing a code of "effective or good" practices for the hydropower sector is important, more must be done to fully satisfy expectations. Indeed, the IHA has developed the Protocol of the Hydropower Sustainability Assessment, a tool that is used to objectively analyze proposed hydropower projects and evaluate the effectiveness and efficiency of existing plants. The Protocol was adopted as a working document in 2006. The Guidelines and Sustainability Assessment Protocol of the International Hydropower Association established an international reference standard for developing and operating hydropower and was based on the commitment of the members of the IHA to continuous improvement within the full context of sustainable development.

According to the Executive Technical Director of Itaipu:

"The thermoelectric and hydroelectric projects are different in important respects; for instance, thermal plants have a construction period of approximately 36 months, against deadlines of 50–60 months for hydropower. On the other hand, their lifespan is 15–20 years while hydropower plants often reach a hundred years." [4]

In the view of the former Minister of Mines and Energy:

"The positive aspect of the 1980s is that they kicked off the beginning of the growing recognition that economic development is only real and meaningful if it is pursued with an environmentally sustainable and socially responsible approach. But organizations and pressure groups, which at the time mobilized in defense of the environment, did not succeed in controlling the emissions of harmful gases such as carbon dioxide, which kept increasing. Unfortunately, these organizations mistakenly invested also against "large dams," pressing multilateral lending institutions–including the World Bank–that in response drastically diminished their support for hydropower projects, reaching full on poor countries of Asia, Africa and Latin America. Back then, it was not possible to predict that the 20th century would be ending with 1 billion, 600 million people without the benefits of electricity." [5]

Given these realities, Itaipu can be a point of reference for and study by other hydroelectric ventures. By assigning strategic relevance to sustainability in 2003, Itaipu started changing its definitions of mission and strategic objectives. From there, it took the lead in the field of hydropower in order to search for sustainable electricity. This strategic direction presented operational adjustments in several contexts. We explore these changes and their consequences next.

Itaipu and Strategic Redefinition: Mission and Strategic Objectives

Because of regulative and normative pressures, Itaipu leaders chose to undertake a full range of activities for the purpose of producing energy on a fully sustainable basis. The ultimate goal is to establish a viable industry from the various perspectives that different Itaipu stakeholders— governments, businesses, funding agencies, regulatory agencies, and community—hold and value. Thus, in agreement with the Ministry of Mines and Energy, Itaipu is committed to the following activities and expectations:

"The Ten-Year Plan for Energy Expansion for the period 2007-2016, approved by the Ministry of Mines and Energy in February 2008, with the program of works of short and medium term, there is a signal of an expansion of 50,000 MW, which is added to the average of 5,000 MW per year in power generation. Studies of energy scenarios for 2030 indicate the maintenance of the energy matrix with a share of renewable sources around 47 percent and the energy matrix with 83 percent." [6]

Among the full set of records and documents in Itaipu's files, some are prominent because of their strategic nature and value. We highlight some of these items in Table 1. To a certain degree, the specifications of the items in Table 1 reflect institutional pressures affecting Itaipu's efforts to formalize its direction and appropriate actions to take in light of those pressures. The appointment in 2003 of a new Brazilian General-Director (who earned a degree in agronomy) also influenced the formation of items shown in Table 1.

The alterations in perspective that are suggested by the changes to Itaipu's vision and mission statements regarding operations of the power plant highlight the fact that an organizational approach that had been focused on hydroelectric use was shifted to a focus on developing methods to generate electricity with sustainability in mind. The commitment to sustainability is emphasized by the changes to the vision statement that were formalized in 2012. To facilitate sustainability, decisions were made to operate the plant at least partly by using other forms of energy, such as biogas, for electricity-generating purposes.

Table 1 Definitions of Mission and Vision of Itaipu

Definition of the Mission until 2003
Hydroelectric use of water resources of the Paraná River, belonging to both countries as a consortium, from and including the Salto Grande de Sete Quedas or Salto de Guaira, to the stream mouth of the Iguassu River.
Definition of the Mission in 2003
Generate quality electric power, within the context of social and environmental responsibility, promoting economic development, tourism and technological development, in Brazil and Paraguay.
Addition to the Vision Statement in 2012
To be consolidated as a generator of clean, renewable energy by 2020, with the best operating performance and best sustainability practices in the world, promoting sustainable development and regional integration.

In the "Strategic Planning 2012-2016" document that describes Itaipu's commitments and operations, the basic principles associated with sustainability as well as additional key objectives are presented:

- Acknowledgment of the importance of water, raw material for hydropower generation, as a renewable natural resource, scarce, non-transferable, under public control, whose preservation should be a universal concern.
- The development of the societies of both countries should be sustainable, so that the use of natural resources by the present generation will not compromise this same resource for future generations.
- The understanding that universal access to energy with quality and compatible prices is one of the factors most relevant to the development of both countries and for the promotion of social welfare.

Supporting efforts to implement Itaipu's Strategic Plan and objectives is a set of Policies and Guidelines that were established in the organization for 2012-2016. These Policies and Guidelines are presented in Table 2.

The policies and guidelines of Itaipu communicate essential changes in the modus operandi of the organization. Until 2003, there was a predominance of essentially technical elements to generate electricity, with some degree of concern about environmental dimensions, in order to increase the life of the plant and socioeconomic development initiatives limited to the convergence with the business. Relations between Brazil and Paraguay are based on the contractual aspects of binationality.

In 2003, Itaipu became concerned with a number of issues including those of increasing the efficiency of the plant's operations while remaining committed to sustainability objectives. Participatory management models and techniques were identified at this time as a means to effectively address these two core issues. The managers of the binationality-focused plant also wanted to contribute to efforts aimed at integration of South America through how the plant designed and executed its operations.

For the 2012 to 2016 period, the increasing expectations of Itaipu with respect to corporate sustainability requirements were thought to be products of different sources of normative and cultural influences, at least to some degree. Concerns about various issues such as humanity, diversity, and harmony between business operations and the environment in which they are situated are examples of normative and cultural influences that yielded a focus on what some people call the *bio-civilization*. In this respect, the binationality associated with Itaipu was considered to be a potential model of

Table 2 Policies and Guidelines

Policies and Guidelines until 2003
1. Binationality (Brazil and Paraguay)
2. Institutional image: relationship between the two countries
3. Goals of the company defined at the strategic level
4. Financial economic optimization
5. Decision criteria at all levels when conducting cost-benefit analyses
6. Generation and supply of electric power with full accessibility and reduction of operating costs
7. Preservation of environmental conditions to control and treat the factors that may affect the life and performance of the plant as well as its ecosystem
8. The socioeconomic development of the region when initiatives converge with the company's interests
9. The administrative structure and workforce of the company always seeking operational and productivity efficiency
10. An effective legal department that is available to address potential legal liabilities

Policies and Guidelines Established in 2003
1. Binational integration: an instrument of integration of South America
2. Ethical values
3. Business efficiency as reflected in the tariffs
4. Democratic management: responsible, participatory and transparent
5. Development of human resources
6. Social commitment: active cooperation promoting its development
7. Environmental commitment: preservation, conservation and recovery leaving a better environment to future generations

Policies and Guidelines Defined for 2012-2016
1. Respect for the human being: recognize and respect the dignity of human diversity
2. Binational integration: harmonious coexistence, the seeking of joint solutions, constituting paradigm for the Latin American integration
3. Proactivity and innovation
4. Responsibility under the aegis of the agreement between Brazil and Uruguay
5. Recognition of the results of the efforts and work of the people
6. Corporate sustainability: initiatives that are socially just, environmentally and economically viable and culturally accepted, ensuring continuity
7. Regional sustainable development: socioeconomic development, social inclusion and improvement of environmental conditions.
8. Ethical values

Latin American integration for others to emulate. The Corporate Strategic Map (see Figure 1) reflects some of the normative and cultural influences Itaipu was experiencing. The focus of these influences is divided into three dimensions: stakeholders, internal processes, and learning and growth. In turn, these three dimensions yield a total of 16 strategic objectives that are part of Itaipu's efforts to reach its mission and vision (see Table 1)

primarily by adhering to and using the guidelines and following the principles shown in Table 2.

In 2013, the Itaipu workforce that had been formed to support Itaipu's efforts to reach its mission and vision totaled 1,424 employees in Brazil and 2,036 in Paraguay. Outcomes resulting from Itaipu's operations (as supported by its workforce) in light of the normative and cultural influences it was encountering are impressive.

Figure 1 Corporate Strategic Map 2012–2016

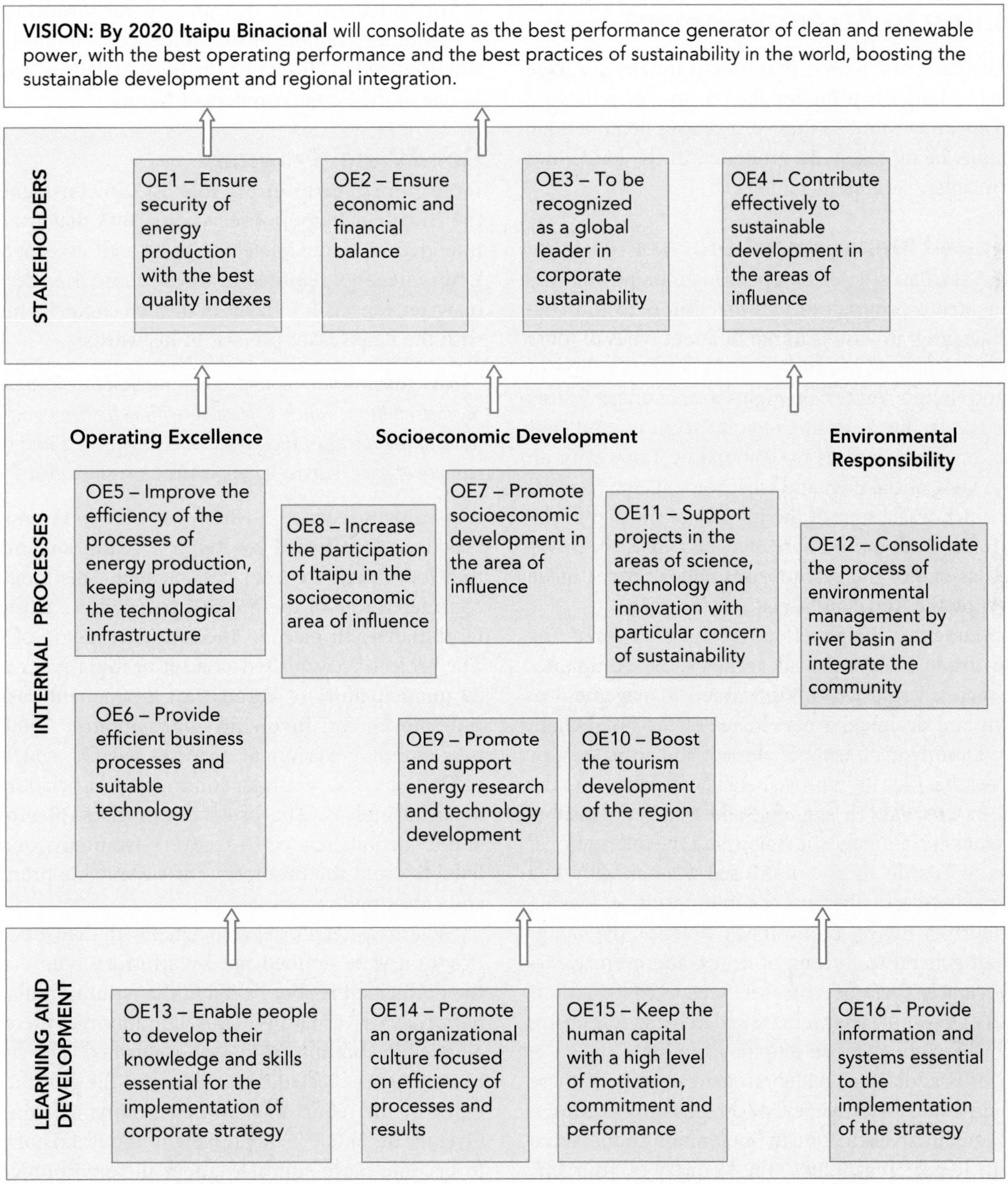

VISION: By 2020 Itaipu Binacional will consolidate as the best performance generator of clean and renewable power, with the best operating performance and the best practices of sustainability in the world, boosting the sustainable development and regional integration.

STAKEHOLDERS

OE1 – Ensure security of energy production with the best quality indexes

OE2 – Ensure economic and financial balance

OE3 – To be recognized as a global leader in corporate sustainability

OE4 – Contribute effectively to sustainable development in the areas of influence

INTERNAL PROCESSES

Operating Excellence

Socioeconomic Development

Environmental Responsibility

OE5 – Improve the efficiency of the processes of energy production, keeping updated the technological infrastructure

OE8 – Increase the participation of Itaipu in the socioeconomic area of influence

OE7 – Promote socioeconomic development in the area of influence

OE11 – Support projects in the areas of science, technology and innovation with particular concern of sustainability

OE12 – Consolidate the process of environmental management by river basin and integrate the community

OE6 – Provide efficient business processes and suitable technology

OE9 – Promote and support energy research and technology development

OE10 – Boost the tourism development of the region

LEARNING AND DEVELOPMENT

OE13 – Enable people to develop their knowledge and skills essential for the implementation of corporate strategy

OE14 – Promote an organizational culture focused on efficiency of processes and results

OE15 – Keep the human capital with a high level of motivation, commitment and performance

OE16 – Provide information and systems essential to the implementation of the strategy

In that year, for example, the Itaipu Dam generated 92.2 million MWh of electricity, an amount that supplied 17 percent of the Brazilian market for electricity and 73 percent of the Paraguayan demand. In that year, the payment of royalties for the generation of electricity was approximately $230 million per year for each country. In Brazil, the amount allocated to neighboring municipalities near the reservoir represented an average increase of 52 percent in revenues, benefiting about 600,000 people.

Itaipu and Biocivilization: From Planning to Accomplishment

Next, we discuss issues that illustrate or describe approaches Itaipu is using for the purpose of achieving its mission and vision. As these discussions demonstrate, the actions being taken are grounded in the guidelines and principles featured in Table 2.

Integrated Management Tourism

On the Brazilian side of its operations, Itaipu initially implemented a program of fees for visitors to tour the dam. This program also featured different types of tours and the presentation of entertainment (such as a show of lights and sounds) on certain nights to encourage visitors to tour the facilities. In this regard, Itaipu offered new tourism products such as the Panoramic Tours with an external view of the dam and what was called a "Special Tour," which was a tour of the interior of the plant. The Special Tour was quite impressive, and in 2010, it was selected as one of the best tourism opportunities made available by the Brazilian Ministry of Tourism.

Subsequently, Itaipu effectively implemented the tourism trade integrating all agencies and companies of the sector. Itaipu led the Integrated Management of Tourism and designed a new image of the hotel chain Iguassu Destiny in Brazil and abroad, and attracted private investment for its improvement and expansion in the region. As a result of these actions, the number of visitors to the Iguassu National Park, Itaipu, and the International Airport of Foz do Iguassu increased dramatically. The image of these areas became far more positive, leaving behind former images of too much violence, the smuggling and general trafficking of drugs, and even terrorism. Obviously, these benefits were seen as contributions to society as a whole and were viewed as being responsive to normative influences on Itaipu's operations.

There is additional evidence of the success of these efforts. In 2009, for example, Foz do Iguassu was chosen as the best tourist destination in Brazil among non-capital cities. In Report Brazil 2009, the Ministry of Tourism's survey on the competitiveness of 65 destinations that encourage regional tourism development, Foz do Iguassu was awarded the highest score in five dimensions: access, services and tourist facilities, marketing and promotion of the destination, entrepreneurship, and environmental aspects.

In order to ensure sustainability for the actions of Iguassu Destiny, the Iguassu Fund was created. This fund is maintained by voluntary contributions resulting from tour ticket sales and room tax fees charged by the hotels. This fund also promotes tourism regardless of leadership changes that may occur in the management of Itaipu, City of Foz do Iguassu, and state and federal governments.

Another example of the influence of Itaipu in tourism occurred in 2011 when the Iguassu Falls was selected as one of the Seven Wonders of Nature.

Good Water Program

Jorge Samek, early in his role as Director-General of the Brazilian Itaipu, observed in 2003 that water was intended to produce electricity as well as generate all kinds of energy required to those whose lives depended on water, especially citizens in the two countries involved with the Itaipu Dam project. In his words:

"That's exactly what we need: a new model of civilization tested on a miniature, which is feasible within the changing conditions of the Earth in the global warming process and growing scarcity of their resources, a new way for sustainability."[7]

Accordingly, relying on what was at the time a new perspective, as reflected by Itaipu´s vision and mission, the Good Water Program was created. This project was considered one of the greatest social and environmental initiatives in place in the southern region of Brazil. The project is comprised of a set of initiatives covering 29 municipalities of Paraná in a permanent participation movement, involving approximately 2000 partners among government agencies, NGOs, educational institutions, cooperatives, community associations, and local businesses. The project comprises 20 programs and 65 actions related to recovery from environmental liabilities and the promotion of sustainable production and consumption.

The areas/territories associated with the Good Water Program were defined not by arbitrary boundaries of the municipalities but by using the natural limits of the *hidrobacias* river basins. Thus, communities are created along with committees in each watershed. The communities that are created are products of the guidance provided by the requirements of environmental education. Overall, the interest was for many thousands of people to become more educated about the environment and ongoing efforts to effectively sustain it.

The Good Water Program seeks to reach objectives in multiple areas. For example, there is an interest to engage in activities for the purpose of recovery of micro-river basins. This is achieved primarily by planting and protecting the riparian areas and monitoring water quality. Other actions taken include those of promoting agro-ecological practices and disseminating healthy food items, taking actions to improve the quality of areas that have been degraded by agricultural activities, and evaluating the sustainability of indigenous communities. Collecting recyclable materials, trying to protect communities' biodiversity conditions or realities, and engaging in environmental education programs in schools are still other actions being taken under the guise of the Good Water Program.

The Agroenergy Condominium of Ajuricaba integrates 32 pig farmers from Marechal Cândido Rondon and is the first condominium in the country to produce electricity with biogas from the fermentation of manure, ensuring an income of R$270,000 per year with the thermal power generation, electric vehicles, and biofertilizers. The green belt, also called the Biodiversity Corridor (70 meters wide) connects the Iguassu National Park of the Big Island, the border between the Paraná and Mato Grosso do Sul, allowing the genetic flow of the regional flora and fauna. Once it is fully formed, this type of belt might be extended to other two state parks in Rio Grande do Sul and São Paulo.

According to Zilda Arns (2008), the projects developed by Itaipu, in conjunction with the Pastoral da Criança, other organizations and the local communities, encourage school education, volunteering, income generation, gender equity, as well as contributing to the prevention of sexual exploitation and child labor. Thus, a host of positive outcomes results from the projects Itaipu is undertaking.

Farmers migrated from grain production (soybeans) to fruit production, vegetables and organic vegetables in areas equivalent to a little more than two football fields, supplying markets in the region and school lunches of municipal education.

"Organic agriculture has transformed our lives. I was able to send two daughters to college," said one of the farmers.

Over 700 aquaculture cages are scattered around the Itaipu Lake with a potential of production of 6000 tons of fish a year. The natural barrier of the riparian forest that borders thousands of miles from the Itaipu Lake and its tributaries from the Brazilian side was reinforced by 24 million trees that were planted in the last ten years. Also, preventing livestock farming and silting up of rivers resulted in the recovery of the local flora which in turn brought back native species of fauna.

The implementation of the Federal University of Latin American Integration—UNILA—opens up a new perspective for tourism and the service sector. This university will help Foz do Iguassu to be consolidated as a tourist city, attracting students and families of all Latin American countries, not only because of the courses that will be offered, but also university events. The campus design was created by the architect Oscar Niemeyer. Some actions of the program, as long as they are sustainable, also prolong the life of the plant reservoir as well as the ability to store water which has been widely discussed in terms of energy in the country. Consumer groups have adopted a perspective of welfare rather than consumption.

In 2005, the Good Water Program received the Earth Charter (Earth Charter +5) award as presented in Amsterdam. Other awards that have been received include the Brazilian Environmental Benchmarking (2007 and 2011), and the Americas Award, the UNITAR in 2011. Such awards show that the Good Water Program represents development and participatory management in environmental projects that harmonize economic development with energy production and environmental preservation.

Final Considerations

Despite being one of the largest power plants in the world and being located in countries with the highest potential for renewable energy generation, those operating the Itaipu Dam face constant challenges. In part, these challenges find leaders seeking to satisfy what are often competing interests as expressed by different stakeholders. These realities are captured by the following statement as offered by a member of the International Hydropower Association (IHA) board:

"There is a growing global awareness that hydropower projects should provide the first portion of the water and energy benefits to local communities, especially those directly affected by the project. Hydropower produces a sixth of the world's electricity, and with the right investments, their contribution could be tripled."[8]

Also at least partly describing the challenges those involved with leading the Itaipu Dam project are comments from a physicist researcher located in Brazil:

At the moment, scientists and technicians, opinion leaders and decision makers, can be divided into two incompatible groups. One group includes those who do not feel any responsibility towards future generations, but who realize the importance of energy to the comfort and survival of homo sapiens. And another group who values sustainability as if humanity could do without energy.[9]

The challenges to be overcome by the power generation industry in Brazil are proportionally equivalent to the abundance of resources. On one hand, the country has abundant natural resources; on the other hand, tax

policies and the barriers they create increase the difficulty of efforts to integrate the nation's power generation capabilities for the purpose of satisfying citizens' needs. For these reasons as well as others mentioned herein, Itaipu is an interesting case of an organization that seeks to serve customers' needs within the context of the environmental conditions affecting its operations.[10]

NOTES

1. IHA–International Hydropower Association; NHA USA–USA National Hydropower Association; INHA–Indian National Hydropower Association; HA Nepal–Nepal Hydropower Association; CHA–Canadian Hydropower Association.
2. Itaipu. The great energy: multiple views on hydroelectricity / Social Communication Itaipu; Making Competence

Communication and Marketing, Graphic Design and Art Direction TAB Editorial Marketing. - Foz do Iguaçu: 2009.
3. Ibid.
4. Ibid.
5. Ibid.
6. Ibid.
7. Ibid.
8. Ibid.

9. Ibid.
10. In preparing several parts of this case, materials available from Itaipu Binacional's website (http://www.itaipu.gov.br/) was carefully studied. Insights from studying these materials subsequently informed the development of different parts of the case.

Will J. C. Penney Strike Gold with Its New Strategy?

John Coplen, Shawn Cozine, Jason Lee, Ophira Moses, Brendan Zanitsch

Texas A&M University

"We can become America's favorite store."

Ron Johnson
CEO of jcpenney

From Rocky Mountain Mine Store to "America's Favorite Store"

The history of J. C. Penney (JCP) spans more than a hundred years and begins with James Cash Penney in Evanston, Wyoming. Penney started his journey working in one of three Golden Rule stores during the mining boom at the turn of the last century.[1] After working for three years, he was promoted to third partner and opened his first store, the Golden Rule store in Kemmerer, Wyoming.[2] In 1907, Penney bought out his two partners and for the next six years, he opened stores throughout the mountain west. In 1913, he incorporated as "J. C. Penney Company, Inc." and moved the corporate operations to New York for better access to both manufacturers and suppliers.[3] His stores continued to be successful in western mining towns because he offered "one fair price." By 1915, Penney had 83 stores in operation.

During the Great Depression, JCP survived because of the firm's use of effective managerial and leadership practices and by offering lower priced goods, but still delivering high quality for the price.[4] JCP achieved this by primarily carrying private label brands. Private labels allowed Penney to control quality and provide lower prices to customers compared to the prices of most brand name items.[5] This successful approach to serving customers allowed the company to succeed despite difficult times and even grow to 1,496 U.S. stores by 1936. After the depression, JCP continued to grow with sales reaching $1 billion by its 50th anniversary in 1952.[6]

It was not until 1961 that JCP began transitioning from free-standing stores to establishing locations in shopping centers. JCP also expanded its selection of inventory when it moved into shopping centers. By the end of the 1960s, JCP locations not only sold appliances, sporting goods, garden merchandise, and auto parts, but also provided services such as beauty salons, portrait studios, restaurants, and auto centers.[7] The firm expanded its presence and customer services further by entering the catalog business in 1963 and by acquiring the Thrift Drug chain, which it continued operating along with other acquired drug stores until 2004.

JCP began with a general store approach similar to Sears Roebuck & Co. In essence, this approach found JCP wanting to sell a wide range of goods and services. The store chain also owned several non-core businesses, such as a bank and some drugstores. However, in its attempt to cater to the needs of all, JCP got caught in the middle with little customer interest in its products. During this period, JCP was neither a true mass merchandiser nor a department store. "We tried being all things to everyone, and we lost our identity," said Faust-Jones, who, in addition to being a JCP manager, wrote about the company for her master's degree project. "So we went back to our roots."[8]

As the company began to fight for customers with more distinctly focused department stores such as Macy's, Dillard's, Beall's, and Nordstrom in addition to mass merchandisers such as Sears, JCP decided in 1983 to begin phasing out auto services, hard line appliances, hardware, lawn and garden merchandise, and fabrics, and emphasize its apparel, home furnishings, and leisure lines. With the exception of its drugstores, this set of actions focused JCP as an apparel department store company with credit card and finance departments.[9] For the next ten years, JCP operations continued relatively unchanged. In 1996, JCP purchased Eckerd drugstores for $3.3 billion to expand its drugstore business and in 1998, JCP transitioned into a third sales channel: the Internet. At that time, JCP was operating a catalog business, bricks-and-mortar JCP stores, drugstores, credit card and finance operations, and its Internet store.

In 1999, JCP shifted the emphasis of its bricks-and-mortar stores to a "stores-within-a-store" model that highlighted JCP's top private label brands: Original Arizona Jean Company, St. John's Bay, and Worthington.[10] Entering into the new millennium, JCP realized that operating only in shopping malls was detrimental to its future growth and, after several decades without them, JCP began opening off-the-mall stores. JCP rearranged these new stores from the traditional two-story design into one-story formats and focused on convenience.[11] This location-related decision put JCP in areas that were easier to access, with additional foot traffic in the stores becoming a benefit of the new locations. Nevertheless, with the changing economy and trends, JCP would have to undertake still additional changes to survive another hundred years.

Transitioning to the New Millennium Market

During the first decade of the 21st century, JCP decided to divest Eckerd Drug. At the same time, JCP focused on increasing its Internet presence and Internet sales with Facebook campaigns, viral advertising, and a revamped Web site. To date, its Internet presence is achieving some success as suggested by the fact that the firm generated $376 million in Internet sales in the first quarter of 2011.[12] Additionally, in an attempt to soften its image and keep its customers in its stores longer, JCP began opening Seattle's Best Coffee bars in its department stores in 2009.

Around this time, JCP decided to target the middle class consumer by positioning itself as an alternative to mass merchandise stores such as Target. JCP continued its tradition of developing and marketing private label brands by working with well-known designers and product lines. These included the cosmetic company Sephora, chef Emeril Lagasse, designers Ralph Lauren, Kimora Lee Simmons, and Ryan Sheckler, and interior decorator Martha Stewart. JCP also revamped many of its successful labels such as Arizona Jeans and designs from Liz Claiborne.[13] More of the firm's older stores were transitioned to single-story venues with large parking lots and shopping carts. During this time, JCP was using a traditional pricing strategy with relatively high prices punctuated by hundreds of promotions and sales that occurred at different times during each year.[14]

Unfortunately, sales began to stagnate during the financial recession of 2007. Competition increased from both low-price discounters such as Walmart and, to a lesser degree, Target, and from higher end retailers such as Nordstrom. To a degree, JCP found itself in a virtual no man's land, unable to compete on price and without the product quality and selection to attract customers looking for more crisply differentiated products. JCP's new CEO, Ron Johnson, thought the stores looked tired and that customers were insulted by the higher-than-expected prices.[15] By the end of 2011, Johnson and others were prepared to initiate significant changes for the purpose of improving JCP's performance.

The Big Picture

The external environment, particularly in terms of individuals' level of disposable income and their spending patterns, significantly affects the ability of JCP and other retailers to generate sales as a foundation for competitive success. During the financial recession that began in earnest in 2007, JCP, along with many retailers, suffered a one-two combination punch — levels of disposable income fell quickly and willingness to spend followed suit.

An apparent reduction in the size of the middle and lower-middle classes in the United States was another economic factor affecting JCP during the recession. This was an issue in that historically, these groups were the target customer for JCP's goods and services. Simultaneously, the demand for luxury goods and for inexpensive and lower-quality products was growing. The net result of these consumer purchasing patterns was a decrease in the size of what had been JCP's core target customer–that is, the middle and lower-middle class consumers.[16]

Although the economy is slowly improving, consumer confidence is not consistently reflecting the same level of improvement. One reason for this may be that unemployment and *under*employment remains stubbornly high. Major volatility in the political arena has also contributed to the uncertainty of consumers. Many expect continuing uncertainty about at least the federal taxes they will pay if not their state and local taxes as well. When facing this type of financial uncertainty in terms of their disposable income, consumers tend to reduce their expenditures. In combination, these economic factors appear to generate an unfavorable forecast for firms such as JCP, at least in the short term.

A More Specific Picture

As noted above, an economic downturn drastically affects the retail industry and firms competing in it such as JCP. When consumer disposable income most recently fell, it put the survival of the retailers in jeopardy. Retailers took steps to counter the effects of the sputtering economy by redeploying, demoting, and laying off staff, reducing salaries and inventory, and cutting prices – and thus in many cases profits as well – to remain in business.

With the start of a seemingly severe recession in 2007 and the resulting increase in price consciousness among American consumers, retailers have increasingly decided to compete on price as a way to attract customers. JCP was one of the retailers that chose to engage in this type of competition. In recent years for example, 97 percent of JCP merchandise was sold at sale or promotion prices. Discount retailers such as Walmart and Target are able to weather recessions better due to their already existing low cost product lines and competencies in logistics. JCP does not have the capabilities necessary to compete solely on price with either Walmart or Target.

There were 14 apparel department stores (or retailers) with sales of at least $3 billion in the United States in 2011. (See Exhibit 1.) Typically, these retailers are grouped into various categories, one of which is as follows:

1. Luxury retailers such as Neiman Marcus
2. High-end retailers such as Nordstrom
3. Mid-tier retailers such as J. C. Penney, Macy's, Kohl's, Sears, and Dillard's
4. Off-price retailers such as Ross and TJ Maxx
5. Discounters such as Walmart and Target[17]

Perhaps especially during challenging competitive conditions such as those faced by today's mid-tier retailers, suppliers' costs can affect a firm's profitability. This is certainly the case for JCP. To positively address this issue, JCP has developed and uses a network featuring more than 2,500 suppliers.[18] With multiple suppliers, JCP's ability to reduce suppliers' power is enhanced. Its suppliers are located both domestically and internationally. JCP operates a central purchasing department in Plano, Texas as well as inspection offices in 15 foreign countries.[19] Another issue of note regarding suppliers is that JCP's private and exclusive brands accounted for 55 percent of the merchandise purchased in JCP stores during 2010 and 2011.[20]

As mentioned, JCP competes directly with several companies that provide similar products to a similar market. Both Sears and Kohl's, for example, have revenues that exceed $15 billion and have stores located in almost every state, with many of these stores located in the same shopping centers as one another and/or JCP. All three companies (JCP, Kohl's and Sears) have robust histories and a high degree of capability and desire to compete. Some of JCP's direct competitors are discussed next.

Sears

Sears is an American retail department store chain founded by Richard Warren Sears and Alva Roebuck. Sears is a large chain with a highly diversified portfolio of offerings for customers; it also has units in both Canada

Exhibit 1 U.S. Retail Apparel Sales Comparison 2011

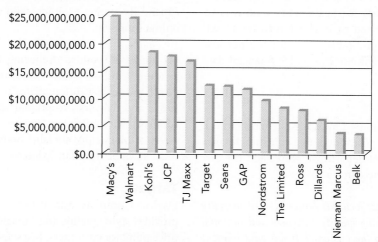

and Mexico. Sears is credited with creating the catalog retail business model.

In the early part of this century, and in light of declines in its market share, Sears decided to upgrade its selection and sell more expensive lines of clothing. However, its customer base preferred lower-cost clothing and shifted its business to other retail chains. Since making this shift in the merchandise it carries, Sears has been unable to recapture its previous market share. Additionally, the variety of products and services Sears offered to customers as a result of its shift in focus dulled some of its key customers' focus on apparel. A loss of customers interested in buying apparel to more specialized chains that are concentrating on apparel price or selection is an unintended consequence of not focusing on apparel to a degree that would allow Sears to effectively serve its core customers' needs.

In November 2004, Sears Roebuck and Kmart were merged; Sears Holding is the name of the newly-created firm. To date, this merger has not been the success envisioned by the firm's leaders and its investors. Increasing the combined firm's total market share and achieving profitably synergies were key goals associated with this merger. However, these positive outcomes have not been achieved, suggesting the possibility that it was poorly conceived and/or that too much debt was generated to complete the transaction of merging the two firms. It seems that the newly-created Sears made several other mistakes as well. For example, some believe that a decision in 2006 to restructure the firm's operations into units that were, most often, run by management with inadequate experience was a mistake.[21] Taken together, problems such as those of failing to generate anticipated synergies and to find an effective way to structure its operations have contributed to a cash flow problem for Sears. This serious issue is being partly addressed by a decision to try to sell some of Sears' most profitable stores for the purpose of generating cash.[22] Exhibit 2 provides financial data for Sears.

Kohl's

Kohl's was established in 1962 by Max Kohl in Brookfield, Wisconsin. Kohl's is positioned as a mid-tier retailer "between the high-end department stores and the discount stores." Kohl's mission statement is

To be the leading family-focused, value-oriented specialty department store offering quality exclusive and national brand merchandise to the customer in an environment that is convenient, friendly, and exciting.[23]

Women between the ages of 25 and 54 are Kohl's target customers. In 2005, Kohl's presented a new slogan to these customers – "Expect great things" – and made significant efforts to bring this statement to life. Working to provide valued and exclusive apparel at affordable prices, Kohl's has two strategic committees in place to oversee its "four strategic initiatives: merchandise content, marketing, inventory management, and in-store experience."[24] The "in-store experience" aims to achieve, "Every customer, Every time, Every store." Kohl's corporation has garnered support and created success by concentrating on a single business strategy without getting sidetracked by ineffective diversification projects.[25] Exhibit 3 provides financial data for Kohl's.

Macy's

Macy's is another mid-tier retailer against whom JPC competes directly. Currently operating 840 stores and with sales revenue of approximately $24 billion in 2010, Macy's was founded in 1858 in New York City.

Macy's actively uses social media to interact with the new generation of customers and follow the needs of its customers. It customizes 15 percent of its merchandise to cater to the specific market segment of each store; it constantly analyzes the demographics and changing preferences of its customers and works to incorporate new trends as they develop.[26] For example, a store with a largely Asian customer base carries more shoes in smaller sizes. This approach has produced profitable returns for Macy's at a time when many department stores are struggling.[27]

Macy's is also working to increase the amount of revenue it generates through online sales. Analysts expect the demand for online retailing to grow and Macy's is positioned to further tap its current customer base and expand its market to others who appreciate the ease of online shopping.

Macy's has a deep product portfolio of a variety of private label brands.[28] Believing that it is "recognized as a retail industry leader in developing private brand merchandise that differentiates the assortments in (its) stores and delivers exceptional value to the customer," ALFANT, bar iii, Belgiqe, Charter Club, and ideology are a few of Macy's private label brands. Financial data for Macy's can be found in Exhibit 4.

Target

Dayton Company established Target in 1962. Target provides style, quality, and the latest in fashion at a low price point for customers. In a sense, Target is sometimes thought of as having some characteristics associated

Exhibit 2 Sears Consolidated Statements of Operations

(USD $)	12 Months Ended		
In Millions, except Per Share data, unless otherwise specified	Jan 28, 2012	Jan 29, 2011	Jan 30, 2010
REVENUES			
Merchandise sales and services	$41,567	$42,664	$43,360
COSTS AND EXPENSES			
Cost of sales, buying and occupancy	30,966	31,000	31,374
Selling and administrative	10,664	10,425	10,499
Depreciation and amortization	853	869	894
Impairment charges	649		
Gain on sales of assets	−64	−67	−74
Total costs and expenses	43,068	42,227	42,693
Operating income (loss)	−1,501	437	667
Interest expense	−289	−293	−248
Interest and investment income	41	36	33
Other loss, net	−2	−14	−61
Income (loss) from continuing operations before income taxes	−1,751	166	391
Income tax expense	−1,369	−27	−111
Income (loss) from continuing operations	−3,120	139	280
Income (loss) from discontinued operations, net of tax	−27	11	17
Net income (loss)	−3,147	150	297
(Income) loss attributable to noncontrolling interests	7	−17	−62
NET INCOME (LOSS) ATTRIBUTABLE TO HOLDINGS' SHAREHOLDERS	−3,140	133	235
Amounts attributable to Holdings' shareholders:			
Income (loss) from continuing operations, net of tax	−3,113	122	218
Income (loss) from discontinued operations, net of tax	−27	11	17
NET INCOME (LOSS) ATTRIBUTABLE TO HOLDINGS' SHAREHOLDERS	($3,140)	$133	$235
Basic:			
Continuing operations	($29.15)	$1.09	$1.85
Discontinued operations	($0.25)	$0.10	$0.14
Earnings Per Share, Basic, Total	($29.40)	$1.19	$1.99
Diluted:			
Continuing operations	($29.15)	$1.09	$1.85
Discontinued operations	($0.25)	$0.10	$0.14
Earnings Per Share, Diluted, Total	($29.40)	$1.19	$1.99
Basic weighted average common shares outstanding	106.8	111.5	117.8
Diluted weighted average common shares outstanding	106.8	111.7	117.9

Source: Sears 10-K filing at sec.gov

with both mid-tier retailers and discounters. For example, Target's customers, who it refers to as "guests," are younger and more affluent than that of its direct discounter rival, Walmart and more price sensitive compared to Macy's typical customer.[29]

Specifically then, Target caters to the needs of price sensitive customers who prefer high-end apparel from notable designers under its private label brands. A recent survey showed that many customers shopping at Target first shop at other stores like Macy's, JCP, and Kohl's for

Exhibit 3 Kohl's Corp Income Statement

	2011	2010	2009
Net sales	18,804	18,391	17,178
Cost of merchandise sold (exclusive of depreciation shown separately below)	11,625	11,359	10,680
Gross margin	7,179	7,032	6,498
Operating expenses:			
Selling, general, and administrative	4,243	4,190	3,951
Depreciation and amortization	778	750	688
Operating income	2,158	2,092	1,859
Other expense (income):			
Interest expense	303	313	311
Interest income	(4)	(9)	(10)
Interest expense, net	299	304	301
Income before income taxes	1,859	1,788	1,558
Provision for income taxes	692	668	585
Net income	1,167	1,120	973
Net income per share:			
Basic	4.33	3.69	3.19
Diluted	4.30	3.66	3.17

Source: Kohl's 10-K filing at sec.gov

Exhibit 4 Macy's Consolidated Statements of Income

(USD $)	12 Months Ended		
In Millions, except Per Share data, unless otherwise specified	Jan 28, 2012	Jan 29, 2011	Jan 30, 2010
Income Statement [Abstract]			
Net sales	$26,405	$25,003	$23,489
Cost of sales	−15,738	−14,824	−13,973
Gross margin	10,667	10,179	9,516
Selling, general and administrative expenses	−8,281	−8,260	−8,062
Gain on sale of properties, impairments, store closing costs and division consolidation costs	25	−25	−391
Operating income (loss)	2,411	1,894	1,063
Interest expense	−447	−579	−562
Interest income	4	5	6
Income (loss) before income taxes	1,968	1,320	507
Federal, state and local income tax expense	−712	−473	−178
Net income (loss)	$1,256	$847	$329
Basic earnings (loss) per share	$2.96	$2	$0.78
Diluted earnings (loss) per share	$2.92	$1.98	$0.78

Source: Macy's 10-K filing at sec.gov

clothes before they come to Target. This indicates that there is an ample amount of cross shopping for apparel among mid-tier retailers and between mid-tier retailers and at least discounters. This fact complicates firms' efforts to identify and effectively serve a target customer group.[30] Exhibit 5 details financial data for Target.

JCP's Financials

With the increase in competitive convergence among mid-tier retailers in terms of goods and services offered and to a lesser degree the price points associated with them, JCP has experienced erosions in some of its margins and other financial ratios. From 2005 to 2011 for example, JCP's operating income fell from 7.12 percent to 4.68 percent. The drop was most pronounced between 2007 and 2011, falling from a high in 2007 of 9.66 percent

to a low of 4.68 percent in 2011 – a 48 percent drop in 5 years. It appears an increase in operating expenses from 31.63 percent to 34.51 percent of revenues drove the decrease.[31]

Since divesting Eckerd's in 2004, JCP's other operating ratios have deteriorated as well. Its cash conversion cycle has increased from 70 to 73 days, times earned interest has dropped from 5.0 to 2.5, current and quick ratios have decreased, and inventory to net worth has increased 28 percent. These financial results and conditions seem to suggest that JCP's strategy was not resonating with customers. Relative sales were down, it was taking JCP longer to turn inventory, short-term debt had

Exhibit 5 Target Consolidated Statements of Operations

(USD $)	12 Months Ended		
In Millions, except Per Share data, unless otherwise specified	**Jan 28, 2012**	**Jan 29, 2011**	**Jan 30, 2010**
Sales	$68,466	$65,786	$63,435
Credit card revenues	1,399	1,604	1,922
Total revenues	69,865	67,390	65,357
Cost of sales	47,860	45,725	44,062
Selling, general and administrative expenses	14,106	13,469	13,078
Credit card expenses	446	860	1,521
Depreciation and amortization	2,131	2,084	2,023
Earnings before interest expense and income taxes	5,322	5,252	4,673
Net interest expense			
Nonrecourse debt collateralized by credit card receivables	72	83	97
Other interest expense	797	677	707
Interest income	−3	−3	−3
Net interest expense	866	757	801
Earnings before income taxes	4,456	4,495	3,872
Provision for income taxes	1,527	1,575	1,384
Net earnings	$2,929	$2,920	$2,488
Basic earnings per share (in dollars per share)	$4.31	$4.03	$3.31
Diluted earnings per share (in dollars per share)	$4.28	$4	$3.30
Weighted average common shares outstanding			
Basic (in shares)	679.1	723.6	752
Diluted (in shares)	683.9	729.4	754.8

Source: Target 10-K filing at sec.gov

increased, and inventory was accounting for a larger portion of the firm's net worth.

An analysis of JCP's recent financial reports paints a very cloudy picture of the company's condition. The restructuring and rebranding of JCP during fiscal 2011 have skewed its operating statement.[32] It shows a negative net profit and negative operating income. JCP contends that this was to be expected, but there are other troubling signs. First and foremost is the increase of 5 percent in JCP's cost of goods sold. Additionally, operating expenses increased to an all-time high of 36.04 percent of revenue, most likely due to the cost of restructuring. But not all of the recent financial results are negative or discouraging; for instance, JCP reduced its debt to increase its times earned interest from 2.55 to 3.60 and debt-to-assets dropped from 62 percent to 58 percent. JCP's cash conversion cycle is remaining stable and a decrease in day's sales offset the decrease in days payable. Detailed financial data for JCP can be found in Exhibits 6a–6e.

In total, the financial-related conditions and results presented above can be interpreted as suggesting that JCP should change its strategy and/or the implementation of its strategy as a means of improving its performance. Details about these possibilities are presented later.

Industry Comparisons

JCP has a cash conversion cycle of 73 days compared to 61 days for Kohl's and 83 days for Macy's. Because Kohl's competes rather directly with JCP in terms of target customers the firms seek to serve, it appears that this firm is operating more efficiently compared to JCP, whereas Macy's cash conversion cycle is longer due to the slightly higher quality of its products compared to some other mid-tier retailers such as JCP and Kohl's.

JCP has a debt-to-asset ratio of 62 percent compared to 42 percent for Kohl's. JCP has maintained this higher leverage for several years but is beginning to reduce its debt. This reduces JCP's flexibility during challenging economic conditions. This is especially true of the times earned interest. Kohl's has a times earned interest of 13 compared to JCP's 2.55, reflecting a financial disadvantage for JCP relative to one of its main competitors.

JCP Leadership Team

Awareness of and careful study of the firm's deteriorating performance and its less-than-positive-future potential caused JCP's board of directors to conclude that changes had to be made quickly in order for the firm to better serve all stakeholders and certainly shareholders. And the board decided that a new strategy was required in

Exhibit 6a JCP Five Year Financial Summary

($ in millions, except per share data) Results for the year	2011	2010	2009	2008	2007
Total net sales	$17,260	$17,759	$17,556	$18,486	$19,860
Sales percent (decrease)/increase:					
Total net sales	(2.8)%	1.2%	(5.0)%	(6.9)%	(0.2)%[1]
Comparable store sales[2]	0.2%	2.5%	(6.3)%	(8.5)%	0.0%
Operating (loss)/income	(2)	832	663	1,135	1,888
As a percent of sales	*(0.0)%*	*4.7%*	*3.8%*	*6.1%*	*9.5%*
Adjusted operating income (non-GAAP)	536	1,085	961	1,002	1,791
As a percent of sales (non-GAAP)	*3.1%*	*6.1%*	*5.5%*	*5.4%*	*9.0%*
(Loss)/income from continuing operations	(152)	378	249	567	1,105
Adjusted income from continuing operations (non-GAAP)	207	533	433	484	1,043
Per common share					
(Loss)/income from continuing operations, diluted	$(0.70)	$1.59	$1.07	$2.54	$4.90
Adjusted income from continuing operations, diluted (non-GAAP)	0.94	2.24	1.86	2.17	4.63
Dividends declared	0.80	0.80	0.80	0.80	0.80
Financial position and cash flow					
Total assets	$11,424	$13,068	$12,609	$12,039	$14,331
Cash and cash equivalents	1,507	2,622	3,011	2,352	2,532
Long-term debt, including current maturities	3,102	3,099	3,392	3,505	3,708
Free cash flow (non-GAAP)	23	158	677	22	(269)

[1] Includes the effect of the 53rd week in 2006. Excluding sales of $254 million for the 53rd week in 2006, total net sales increased 1.1% in 2007.

[2] Comparable store sales are presented on a 52-week basis and include sales from new and relocated stores that have been opened for 12 consecutive full fiscal months and Internet sales. Stores closed for an extended period are not included in comparable store sales calculations, while stores remodeled and minor expansions not requiring store closures remain in the calculations. Our definition and calculation of comparable store sales may differ from other companies in the retail industry.

Source: J. C. Penney Corporation 10-K filing at sec.gov

lieu of merely extending efforts to find ways to improve the implementation of the current strategy. Given its conviction that a strategy that differed perhaps significantly from the one in place and perhaps even the strategies the firm had implemented historically, the board expressed an intention of hiring an individual to become the new CEO who possessed extensive retail experience and success with part of that person's success possibly being generated outside the apparel industry at some point during her/his career. JCP's board found such a person at Apple, Inc. Given a belief in his ability to turn JCP around, JCP's board selected Ron Johnson to become the firm's new CEO. Johnson seeks to establish a retailing revolution at the more than 100-year old retailer known as J. C. Penney. This objective is highlighted by the quote from Johnson opening the next section of material.

Ron Johnson

"I'm not here to improve, I'm here to transform."

> *Ron Johnson*
> *JCP CEO for less than two weeks*[33]

Ron Johnson began his tenure as CEO of JCP on November 1, 2011.[34] Prior to joining JCP, Johnson was Senior VP of the retail division of Apple. During his time at Apple, he launched Apple's retail stores and in 10 years turned those stores into the twenty-first largest retailer in the United States.[35] Seen by some as a visionary, Ron Johnson was responsible for the strategy that made Apple's retail stores the most profitable retail store on a per-square foot basis in the world. Before his time at Apple, he was the VP of Merchandising for Target. During his tenure, he was largely credited with creating

Exhibit 6b JCP Consolidated Statements of Operations

($ in millions, except per share data)	2011	2010	2009
Total net sales	$17,260	$17,759	$17,556
Cost of goods sold	11,042	10,799	10,646
Gross margin	6,218	6,960	6,910
Operating expenses/(income):			
Selling, general and administrative (SG&A)	5,109	5,358	5,410
Pension	121	255	337
Depreciation and amortization	518	511	495
Real estate and other, net	21	(28)	5
Restructuring and management transition	451	32	–
Total operating expenses	6,220	6,128	6,247
Operating (loss)/income	(2)	832	663
Net interest expense	227	231	260
Bond premiums and unamortized costs	–	20	–
(Loss)/income from continuing operations before income taxes	(229)	581	403
Income tax (benefit)/expense	(77)	203	154
(Loss)/income from continuing operations	(152)	378	249
Income from discontinued operations, net of income tax expense of $4 and $1, respectively	–	11	2
Net (loss)/income	$(152)	$389	$251
Basic (loss)/earnings per share:			
Continuing operations	$(0.70)	$1.60	$1.07
Discontinued operations	–	0.04	0.01
Net (loss)/income	$(0.70)	$1.64	$1.08
Diluted (loss)/earnings per share:			
Continuing operations	$(0.70)	$1.59	$1.07
Discontinued operations	–	0.04	0.01
Net (loss)/income	$(0.70)	$1.63	$1.08
Weighted average shares–basic	217.4	236.4	232.0
Weighted average shares–diluted	217.4	238.0	233.1

Source: J. C. Penney Corporation 10-K filing at sec.gov

the "chic" image that distinguished Target from Walmart, its main discounter competitor. This distinction contributed to Target's ability to earn above average returns for the past decade. Johnson received his MBA from Harvard and undergraduate degree from Stanford University.[36] Johnson quickly established a top management leadership team that he believes will be instrumental in efforts to transform the firm by to some degree transforming how customers shop. Kristen Blum, for example, is serving as Executive Vice President and Chief Technology Officer. We show three key members of this leadership team in Exhibit 7 and discuss these individuals next.

Prior to joining JCP, Ms. Blum served in the retail industry as the Chief Information Officer and Senior VP at Abercrombie & Fitch from 2006 to 2010. She was responsible for the strategic transformation of people, processes, and technology in support of international growth initiatives. Blum also served as a Director of Supply Chain Solutions and International Retail at Apple, Inc. for four years, overseeing technology supporting global operations and the development of systems to support Apple retail. She also held "merchandising, planning, and allocation roles at Planet Hollywood, Walt Disney, and Victoria's Secret." Blum received a B.A. from Ohio State University.[37]

Exhibit 6c JCP Consolidated Statements of Comprehensive (Loss)/Income

($ in millions)	2011	2010	2009
Net (loss)/income	$(152)	$389	$251
Other comprehensive (loss)/income, net of tax:			
Unrealized gain on investments, net of tax of $(29), $(27) and $(27), respectively	53	49	48
Net actuarial (loss)/gain, net of tax of $277, $(249) and $(94), respectively	(440)	391	151
Prior service credit adjustment, net of tax of $11, $9 and $9, respectively	(17)	(15)	(15)
Total other comprehensive (loss)/income, net of tax	(404)	425	184

Source: J. C. Penney Corporation 10-K filing at sec.gov

JCP named Mike Kramer as Chief Operating Officer in December 2011. Kramer has extensive experience in the retail industry. Most recently, he was the CEO of Kellwood, a company that designs, manufacturers, and markets a collection of premium fashion brands that seek to serve a broad range of customers. Sag Harbor, XOXO, and My Michelle are a few of the brands comprising the Kellwood portfolio. Prior to Kellwood, Kramer was Executive VP and CFO at Abercrombie & Fitch. His connection to Mr. Johnson is that he worked for Apple retail as that firm's CFO from 2000 to 2005. He earned a B.S. from Kansas State University in 1987 and is a Certified Public Accountant.[38]

Known for his ability to recruit retailing talent, Daniel E. Walker is serving as JCP's Chief Talent Officer. Walker held the same position at Gap Inc. and Apple Inc., and he is responsible for introducing Ron Johnson to Steve Jobs. In addition to carefully assessing the talent already housed with JCP, Walker is recruiting extensively to find talented people who can fill in gaps in the firm's current ranks of employees. He is seeking to hire passionate people who possess solid fundamental principles

Exhibit 6d JCP Consolidated Balance Sheets

($ in millions, except per share data)	2011	2010
Assets		
Current assets		
Cash in banks and in transit	$175	$169
Cash short-term investments	1,332	2,453
Cash and cash equivalents	1,507	2,622
Merchandise inventory	2,916	3,213
Income taxes	413	334
Prepaid expenses and other	245	201
Total current assets	5,081	6,370
Property and equipment, net	5,176	5,231
Prepaid pension	-	763
Other assets	1,167	704
Total Assets	$11,424	$13,068
Liabilities and Stockholders' Equity		
Current liabilities		
Merchandise accounts payable	$1,022	$1,133
Other accounts payable and accrued expenses	1,503	1,514
Current maturities of long-term debt, including capital leases	231	–
Total current liabilities	2,756	2,647
Long-term debt	2,871	3,099
Deferred taxes	888	1,192
Other liabilities	899	670
Total Liabilities	7,414	7,608
Stockholders' Equity		
Common stock[(1)]	108	118
Additional paid-in capital	3,699	3,925
Reinvested earnings	1,412	2,222
Accumulated other comprehensive (loss)	(1,209)	(805)
Total Stockholders' Equity	4,010	5,460
Total Liabilities and Stockholders' Equity	$11,424	$13,068

[(1)] Common stock has a par value of $0.50 per share; 1,250 million shares are authorized. At January 28, 2012, 215.9 million shares were issued and outstanding. At January 29, 2011, 236.7 million shares were issued and outstanding.

Source: J. C. Penney Corporation 10-K filing at sec.gov

Exhibit 6e JCP Consolidated Statements of Cash Flows

($ in millions)	2011	2010	2009
Cash flows from operating activities:			
Net (loss)/income	$(152)	$389	$251
(Income) from discontinued operations	–	(11)	(2)
Adjustments to reconcile net (loss)/income to net cash provided by operating activities:			
Restructuring and management transition	314	24	–
Asset impairments and other charges	67	8	48
Depreciation and amortization	518	511	495
Net (gains) on sale of assets	(6)	(8)	(2)
Benefit plans expense	55	197	276
Pension contribution	–	(392)	–
Stock-based compensation	46	53	40
Excess tax benefits from stock-based compensation	(10)	(2)	–
Deferred taxes	(153)	126	76
Change in cash from:			
Inventory	297	(189)	235
Prepaid expenses and other assets	(67)	27	36
Merchandise accounts payable	(111)	(93)	32
Current income taxes payable	(15)	33	(54)
Accrued expenses and other	37	(81)	142
Net cash provided by operating activities	820	592	1,573
Cash flows from investing activities:			
Capital expenditures	(634)	(499)	(600)
Proceeds from sale of assets	15	14	13
Proceeds from joint venture distribution	53	–	–
Acquisition	(268)	–	–
Cost investment, net	(36)	–	–
Net cash (used in) investing activities	(870)	(485)	(587)
Cash flows from financing activities:			
Proceeds from issuance of long-term debt	–	392	–
Payments of long-term debt	–	(693)	(113)
Financing costs	(20)	(14)	(32)
Dividends paid, common	(178)	(189)	(183)
Proceeds from issuance of stock warrant	50	–	–
Stock repurchase program	(900)	–	–
Proceeds from stock options exercised	18	8	4
Excess tax benefits from stock-based compensation	10	2	–
Tax withholding payments reimbursed by restricted stock	(45)	(2)	(3)
Net cash (used in) financing activities	(1,065)	(496)	(327)
Net (decrease)/increase in cash and cash equivalents	(1,115)	(389)	659
Cash and cash equivalents at beginning of year	2,622	3,011	2,352
Cash and cash equivalents at end of year	$1,507	$2,622	$3,011
Supplemental cash flow information:			
Income taxes paid	$91	$50	$130
Interest paid	227	258	264
Interest received	2	5	5
Significant non-cash transactions:			
Pension contribution of Company common stock	$ –	$ –	$340

Source: J. C. Penney Corporation 10-K filing at sec.gov

Exhibit 7 JCP Leadership Team

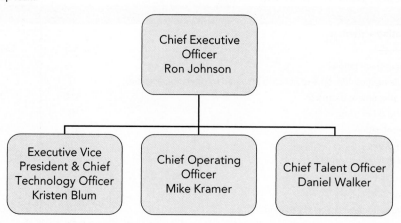

and a strong work ethic. Walker also seeks to hire people who want to learn and be a part of a productive team. In fact, he sees effective team work as critical to the firm's performance and to his goal of making JCP "America's favorite place to work."[39]

All Working Together to Bring About Change

A new strategy can be foreshadowed by the experience that comes with the people that a struggling company hires for key corporate level positions. As the brief discussions above show, the individuals forming a key part of JCP's new leadership team have critical experience with companies that have established a recognizable brand name or image. They have worked with companies that have done things differently and had success doing so. Whether it is experience with Apple, Target, Abercrombie & Fitch, or Kellwood, the key underlying commonality is that they all have knowledge in identifying and highlighting products and experiences for consumers.

The New JCP

The largest external influence affecting the retailing industry and the department store segment of that industry today is the weak economy. The prolonged downturn has increased consumers' sensitivity to prices. As a result, discounters such as Walmart and Dollar General have seen increases in their sales to consumers seeking what they perceive to be a true "bargain" when they shop. Largely because of consumers' sensitivity to price, retailers of all types are more aware of the prices of their products. An outcome of this awareness is more intense competition among all competitors on the price variable. Converging on a single competitive dimension

such as price makes it harder for firms to differentiate themselves in consumers' eyes. And in the long run, competing on the price variable only has the potential to harm a firm's ability to earn above-average returns unless that firm is capable of effectively implementing a cost leadership strategy.

The type of convergence discussed above has created increased rivalry among firms. Although the threat of new entrants and substitutes and the bargaining power of suppliers and buyers have not disappeared, firm rivalry has become increasingly intense during the recession. Johnson's new strategy is oriented to differentiating JCP from competitors in ways that create value for customers. Offering customers low and stable prices for goods and services is a key aspect of the strategy Johnson is implementing at JCP. Since he knows that JCP cannot outcompete discounters rivals such as Walmart by competing only on the basis of prices offered to customers, Johnson has decided to focus JCP's efforts (as a mid-tier retailer) on the price conscious middle- and upper-middle class consumer – a group of customers he believes is dissatisfied with products and experience offered by discounters such as Walmart and potentially by high-end retailers such as Nordstrom as well. In terms of the discounters, the hope is that customers are dissatisfied with services they receive while purchasing items at a low price. With respect to high-end retailers, the hope is that customers are dissatisfied with the price they are paying for differentiated goods and/or services. Johnson hopes the stability in his pricing scheme and JCP's new engaging atmosphere will persuade these customers to frequent JCP.

As mentioned, Johnson is upgrading the atmosphere of JCP's stores as a way of differentiating them from competitors. He hopes that fresh displays and layouts will limit the threat of online competitors by giving customers a place they enjoy shopping. JCP hopes that the new look along with the ability to physically see, touch, and try on clothes will give it an advantage over online retailers, who are an increasingly strong threat to JCP.

JCP is in a highly competitive market with competitors who share many similar resources. Fortunately, there are several segments of the retail department store segment that firms may choose to target. JCP for example believes that it can create value for the segment of customers wishing to purchase moderately-priced apparel that is of acceptable quality.

Due to the effects of the economic downturn, Johnson knew that JCP had to win back customers who had become dissatisfied with JCP and the goods and services it was offering and the venues in which they were presented. To signify that change was coming and that the change was intended to be significant, JCP announced in January of 2012 that it planned to become "America's Favorite Store."[40] The core of this plan is the firm's newly-designed "Fair and Square" pricing strategy. Johnson hopes this new approach to pricing his firm's products will appeal to consumers throughout each year – not just during promotions or sales. The "Fair and Square" pricing strategy aims to do away with promotions in favor of a simple three-tiered pricing scheme, which is as follows:

- *Everyday low price.* The firm will use sales data from the previous year to determine the everyday price. The intention is for these prices to be at least 40 percent lower.[41] For example, a pair of Arizona jeans priced at $40 would now have the everyday price of $24.
- *Fewer promotions.* There will be only 12 sales each year, with each one corresponding to the calendar months. The store will select items to put on sale for a "Month-Long Value." For example, "jewelry and Valentine's Day gifts" would go on sale in February, while Christmas decorations would be discounted in November. Poor-selling products would go on clearance and be tagged "Best Prices," letting consumers know that this is the lowest price possible.[42]
- *A new tag* to help the customer identify the "tier" in which a product is located. JCP used to cover the old price with the new sale price. Now, each time a product is allocated a new price, it receives a new tag to let customers know the value they are receiving. A red tag indicates an "Every Day" price, a white tag a "Month-Long Value," and a blue tag a "Best Price."

- *Haggle-free pricing.* The firm will use whole numbers in its prices. For example, instead of pricing an item at $19.99, it will be marked $20. Johnson believes customers are not fooled by the old pricing scheme and will appreciate the candor of up-front pricing.
- *New advertising.* Ellen Degeneres is the new face of JCP and TV ads will be aimed to inform and excite shoppers about its new pricing strategy and its benefits. The retailer will also send a freshly designed catalog (that refers customers to its bricks-and-mortar stores and/or online store) to some 14 million customers.[43]

While this strategy may seem similar to Walmart's everyday low cost prices, JCP is not attempting to price its products lower than the discounter Walmart. Instead, it hopes to provide a low, stable price for customers desiring to purchase higher-level quality merchandise than is offered by discounters such as Walmart.

Cash conversion cycles and inventory management are important performance measures for retailers. In the past, JCP primarily touted its styles and brands and made the majority of its sales when the merchandise was on sale or promotion. The new strategy of everyday low prices will make projecting sales volume more predictable and decrease the risk of items that do not sell or of having too much inventory of styles that are proving to be unpopular with customers. Overall, the firm's new pricing strategy is thought to be one with the potential to improve JCP's inventory management numbers and decrease the amount of net working capital and capital expenditure needed to sustain the company.

Johnson is also changing the look of JCP stores by freshening the exteriors, interiors, and logo. The interior will do away with the numerous racks and shelving units. Instead, JCP will merchandise its brands through *TheShops*™ centered on *TheStreet*™. This "Main Street" will comprise a series of approximately 80 "brand shops similar to the cosmetics shops it already has in stores. *TheSquare*™ will also be placed in the store to offer services and expert advice" – an attempt to mimic the Genius Bar at Apple stores. Johnson hopes this layout will draw more customers away from online shopping as well as from the firm's bricks-and-mortar competitors.[44]

JCP will advertise and promote less with the implementation of its new strategy. Out of the proposed $900 million in savings,[45] JCP will save $300 million by not running advertisements and promotions.[46] The new strategy is to return to "one fair price" and cut promotional selling. The hope is that customers will associate

JCP with cost savings at all times throughout each year. The savings in net working capital will increase the short-term value of the firm, but the long-term implications could have a devastating impact on market share. These actions will take time to evaluate; it is a risky proposition but, if successful, may generate a competitive advantage for JCP.

Competitors' Reactions

What remains to be seen is if this fundamental change in how JCP intends to compete in the mid-tier retailers' category will result in a competitive advantage for the firm relative to its rivals. Early on, the market seemed enthusiastic that JCP was heading in the right direction as suggested by the fact that the firm's stock price quickly increased from $34.32 a share to $41.52 – a 21 percent increase.[47] However, in January of 2013, the price of the firm's stock was hovering around $18 per share – a level reflecting investors' concerns as to whether JCP would have sufficient cash flow to support the firm while the hoped-to-be positive effects of changes to the firm's strategy come into play.

Of course, rivals are monitoring JCP's strategic changes and the results (especially the financial outcomes) associated with those changes. However, dramatic shifts by JCP's competitors are unlikely in the short term. The changes being taken at JCP appear to be bold, costly, and potentially risky. Moreover, as already suggested, time is needed to gauge customers' responses to JCP's efforts to create more value for them relative to the value being created by the firm's rivals. Moreover, Macy's experiences will be recalled by mid-tier retailers. In this regard, history suggests that after attempting to reduce sales and promotions, Macy's was forced to return to its old pricing structure following considerable protests by its core customers. Accordingly, competitors such as Sears and Kohl's will be hesitant to join JCP in attempting to compete in a manner that is somewhat similar to an approach with which Macy's was previously unsuccessful.[48]

JCP has already experienced or received some backlash from disenchanted stakeholders. A few salespeople feel they no longer have a job,[49] while some customers feel the new prices are not anything special. "I honestly didn't see anything to scream about," said Cheryl Cook of her latest shopping trip to JCP.[50] While these concerns are not without cause, JCP's strategic changes appear to be reinvigorating the brand – at least in the short term.

Conclusion

Johnson is making bold changes to JCP's strategy. Dealing in particular with pricing at least in the short term, the firm is concentrating on a consistent, low price with far fewer promotions that may confuse and potentially irritate customers. By using its new pricing strategy and enhancing the customer's shopping experience in its stores, JCP hopes to entice customers who are financially conscious while seeking a relatively high degree of differentiation and/or quality in the products they purchase. This strategy appears to be one with the potential to be viable in what remains a relatively weak economy, certainly in the United States.

Looking to and considering the future however, Johnson is confident that the economy will improve. Consequently, he is coupling JCP's new pricing strategy with an innovative new store design and shopping experience. Patterning JCP after a town square is an action Johnson and those working with him hope will draw customers into the firm's stores. Moreover, the hope is that once in the newly designed stores, customers will encounter a unique experience that will maintain and hopefully increase their interest in the goods (including its private-label merchandise) and services JCP is offering to them.

By pioneering what he believes is a unique store design at least for mid-tier department store retailers, Johnson hopes to set a new standard for retail shopping as a foundation for competing successfully against JCP's competitors – both its "bricks-and-mortar" competitors as well as the online shopping experience that is increasingly available to customers from an array of sources. In this regard, Johnson seeks to enhance and improve the shopping experience for customers to such an extent that potential online customers will be drawn to JCP's stores for the purpose of experiencing the firm's high levels of service and quality.

But there are questions or issues to consider. Will the actions Johnson is putting into place increase the flow of customers to JCP's stores? If so, will those customers result in increases in sales and profits? If not, what actions should be taken for the purpose of trying to improve JCP's ability to compete today as a giant, mid-tier retailer? And, will JCP have sufficient cash flow to support its operations over the period of time required to see if its new strategy will resonate with customers?

NOTES

1. JCP. (2012). *JCP 10-K*. Plano, Texas.
2. J. C. Penny Company, Inc. (2010). *Funding Universe*. Retrieved 15 Apr 2012 at http://www.fundinguniverse.com/company-histories/JC-Penney-company-Inc-company-History.html
3. JCP. (2012). *op. cit.*
4. Ibid.
5. Ibid.
6. Ibid.
7. Ibid.
8. Creno, C. (2012). *AZ Central*. Retrieved from www.azcentral.com/business/articles
9. JCP. (2012). *op. cit.*
10. Ibid.
11. Howell, D. (24 Nov 2011). JCPenney makes off-the-mall move: new, smaller test format adds trapping familiar to mass channel. *DSN Retailing Today*.
12. Hayes, K. (May 16 2011). *Investor relations at JCP*. Retrieved 15 Apr 2012, from http://ir.JCP.com/phoenix.zhtml?c=70528&p=irol-newscompany
13. JCP. (2012). *op. cit.*
14. Ibid.
15. D'Innocenzio, A. (25 Jan 2012). J.C. Penney simplifies its sales strategy. *Times Union*. Retrived from http://www.timesunion.com/business/article/J-C-Penney-simplifies-its-sale-strategy-2702233.php
16. Banjo, S., Tally, K. (5 Jul 2012). June Retail Sales Reflect Consumer Qualms. *WSJ*. Retrieved from http://online.wsj.com/article/SB10001424052702303962304577508443935757600.html
17. Banjo, S. & Talley, K. (12 July 2012). June Retail Sales Reflect Consumer Qualms. *The Wall Street Journal*. Retrieved from http://online.wsj.com/article/SB1000142405270230396230457750844 3935757600.html
18. JCP. (2012). *op. cit.*
19. Ibid.
20. Ibid.
21. Berman, B. (2010). Competing in Tough Times. *FT Press*.
22. Ibid.
23. About Kohl's. *Kohl's Press Room*. Retrieved from http://www.kohlscorporation.com/pressroom/PressRoom02A.htm
24. Kohl's Fact Book Quarter Ended May 2010. *Kohl's Corporation*. Retrieved from http://www.kohlscorporation.com/InvestorRelations/pdfs/FactBook/FactBookQ12010.pdf
25. McCaw, B. (25 Nov 2008). Kudos to Kohl's and its Exclusive Brand Strategy. *License to Brand*. Retrieved from http://licensetobrand.typepad.com/license_to_brand/2008/11/kudos-to-kohls-and-its-exclusive-brand-strategy.html
26. Schonberger, J. (20 Mar 2012). A Change in Business Strategy Proves Profitable for Macy's. *Kiplinger*. Retrieved from http://www.kiplinger.com/columns/picks/archive/change-in-business-strategy-proves-profitable-for-macys.html
27. The Workshop at Macy's. *Macys Inc.* Retrieved at http://www.macysinc.com/businessfashion/innovation/expertise/
28. Ibid.
29. R. Duane Ireland, R. E. Hoskisson, & M. A. Hitt (2009). Understanding Business Strategy: Concepts and Cases, 3rd edition. *Cengage Learning*.
30. Corporate. *Target*. Retrieved from http://www.target.com/
31. JCP. (2012). *op. cit.*
32. D'Innocenzio, A. (30 Mar 2012). Penney's pricing strategy takes a toll on sales. *Bloomberg Businessweek*. Retrieved from http://www.businessweek.com/ap/2012-03/D9TR26LO0.htm
33. Coleman-Lochner, L. (16 Nov 2011). J.C. Penney New CEO Johnson Reviews Products, Pricing Strategies. *Bloomberg Businessweek*. Retrieved from http://www.businessweek.com/news/2011-11-16/j-c-penney-new-ceo-johnson-reviews-products-pricing-strategies.html
34. Brossart, D. (14 Jun 2011). J. C. Penney Company Names Ron Johnson as Its Next Chief Executive Officer, Effective November 1. *J.C. Penney Investing*. Retrieved 15 Apr 2012 from http://ir.jcpenney.com/phoenix.zhtml?c=70528&p=irol-newsCompanyArticle&ID=1573712&highlight=
35. 2011 Top 100 Retailers. (Jul 2011). *Stores.org*. Retrieved 23 Apr 2012 from http://www.stores.org/2011/Top-100-Retailers
36. J.C. Penney Co Inc (JCP: New York) *Bloomberg Businessweek.com*. Retrieved from Ron Johnson bio at http://investing.businessweek.com/research/stocks/people/person.asp?personId=652443&ticker=JCP:US&previousCapId=255397&previousTitle=BEST%20BUY%20CO%20INC
37. J.C. Penney Co Inc (JCP: New York) *op. cit.*
38. Mike Kramer, Chief Operating Officer. *JCP Media Room*. Retrieved from http://www.jcpmediaroom.com/posts/8/Mike-Kramer
39. Halkias, M. (21 Jan 2012). J.C. Penney talent chief talks about new era. *The Dallas Morning News*. Retrieved from www.dallasnews.com/business/retail/20120121-j.c.-penney-talent-chief-talks-about-new-era.ece
40. JCP. (2012). *op. cit.*
41. Heller, L. (26 Jan 2012). Why JCP will be the most interesting retailer of 2012. *Forbes*. Retrived from http://www.forbes.com/sites/lauraheller/2012/01/26/why-jcpenney-will-be-the-most-interesting-retailer-of-2012/
42. D'Innocenzio, A. (2012). JCP simplifies its sales strategy. *op. cit.*
43. Ibid.
44. Ibid.
45. Talley, K. (11 Apr 2012). Penney's CFO to Step Down. *Wall Street Journal*. Retrieved from http://online.wsj.com/article/SB10001424052702304444604577337741914694860.html
46. JCP. (2012). *JCP 10-K*. Plano, Texas.
47. Bickle, M. (30 Jan 2012). JCPenny's Consumers Voice Opinions Regarding Sales. *Forbes*. Retrieved from http://www.forbes.com/sites/prospernow/2012/01/30/jcpenneys-customers-voice-opinions-regarding-sales/
48. Zmuda, N. (30 Jan 2012). JC Penny Reinvention Is Bold Bet, but Hardly Fail-Safe. *Advertising Age*. Retrieved from http://adage.com/article/news/jc-penney-reinvention-bold-bet-fail-safe/232406/
49. Rooneu, J. (14 Mar 2012). JCP's New Strategy: A tough sell on the sales floor. *Forbes*. Retrived from http://www.forbes.com/sites/jenniferrooney/2012/03/14/jc-penneys-new-strategy-a-tough-sell-on-the-sales-floor/2/
50. Ford, E. (2 Feb 2012). New strategy, pricing on display at JC Penney. *Salisbury Post*. Retrieved from http://www.salisburypost.com/News/020212-JCP-reveals-new-pricing-strategy-1-fact-box-attached-qcd

CASE 18

KIPP Houston Public Schools

Dane Roberts

Rice University Jones Graduate School of Business

Sehba Ali, the recently selected superintendent of KIPP (Knowledge Is Power Program) Houston Public Schools, prefers that people do not refer to KIPP as "a miracle." Yes, it has effectively quadrupled the rate at which its low-income students attend college compared to traditional public schools. Yes, it has created a new model for public education that has spread throughout the United States and beyond. And, yes, visitors to the schools are often astounded by the focus and character shown by its students—often called KIPPsters—in comparison to the chaos that sometimes prevails in other schools serving neighborhoods of high poverty. But Ali believes there is no magic or miracle to it.

Instead she attributes KIPP's success to "a lot of smart people working hard and being nice. It's about innovation. It's about creativity. It's about being as smart as we can and being willing to take risks and make change."[1]

Despite the organization's dedicated staff members and students, who have committed with their signatures to "do whatever it takes" to succeed, there is no guarantee the future will be an unqualified success. KIPP Houston has faced challenges finding enough qualified teachers and leaders to continue its plans for rapid expansion. Securing adequate funding for its programs and facilities is also a perennial challenge. Finally, some lapses in quality among the 21 elementary and secondary schools in the Houston metro area are forcing Ali and other KIPP Houston leaders to grapple with the trade-off between campus autonomy and top-down management.

Setting the Scene

KIPP Houston is a network of charter schools located in Houston, Texas, the fourth largest city in the United States. Charter schools are public, taxpayer funded, and open to all students; however, they operate independently of traditional school districts. The 21 schools KIPP Houston operates are among 125 nationally that use the KIPP name. While all KIPP schools have a high level of autonomy, they share the imprimatur of the KIPP Foundation in San Francisco, California, to whom they pay a licensing fee and which is responsible for the year-long leadership training program that all school principals attend before founding a new KIPP school.

KIPP schools also adhere to a set of common operating principles known as the "Five Pillars," which the KIPP Foundation describes as:

- HIGH EXPECTATIONS—KIPP schools have clearly defined and measurable high expectations for academic achievement and conduct that make no excuses based on the students' backgrounds. Students, parents, teachers, and staff create and reinforce a culture of achievement and support through a range of formal and informal rewards and consequences for academic performance and behavior.
- CHOICE & COMMITMENT—Students, their parents, and the faculty of each KIPP school choose to participate in the program. No one is assigned or forced to attend a KIPP school. Everyone must make and uphold a commitment to the school and to each other to put in the time and effort required to achieve success.
- MORE TIME—KIPP schools know that there are no shortcuts when it comes to success in academics and life. With an extended school day, week, and year, students have more time in the classroom to acquire the academic knowledge and skills that will prepare

them for competitive high schools and colleges, as well as more opportunities to engage in diverse extracurricular experiences.

■ POWER TO LEAD—The principals of KIPP schools are effective academic and organizational leaders who understand that great schools require great school leaders. They have control over their school budget and personnel. They are free to swiftly move dollars or make staffing changes, allowing them maximum effectiveness in helping students learn.

■ FOCUS ON RESULTS—KIPP schools relentlessly focus on high student performance on standardized tests and other objective measures. Just as there are no shortcuts, there are no excuses. Students are expected to achieve a level of academic performance that will enable them to succeed at the nation's best high schools and colleges.[2]

KIPP Houston's mission is to "develop in underserved students the academic skills, intellectual habits, and qualities of character necessary to succeed at all levels of pre-kindergarten through twelfth grade, college, and the competitive world beyond."[3] KIPP Houston takes the college attendance aspect of its mission very seriously. Getting all of its students "to and through college" is a mantra of the organization. They painstakingly track the outcomes of all their students to find out how many attend and matriculate through college. Some KIPP Houston employees work full time to prepare and support students in their college application process.

Within KIPP Houston Public Schools, Ali manages 8 elementary schools (grades pre-kindergarten to grade 4), 10 middle schools (grades 5 through 8), and 3 high schools (grades 9 through 12). In order to establish a strong school culture from the ground up, a school is typically founded with the earliest grade level first, then expands each year into the next grade level. In the 2012–13 school year, KIPP Houston employed 968 people and served about 8,500 students; some schools have not yet added all grade levels. (More student demographic information is found in Exhibit 1.)

Storied Beginnings

The founding of KIPP has become the stuff of legend in education circles. In 1992, Michael Feinberg and David Levin, fresh out of Ivy League colleges, joined Teach for America (TFA), which places top college graduates as teachers in neighborhoods of high poverty for a two-year commitment. After a summer of training, Feinberg

Exhibit 1 KIPP Houston 2013 Enrollment

Total	8584
Eligible for Free or Reduced-Price Meals	**7317**
American Indian/Alaskan	36
Asian	73
Black/African American	3083
Hispanic/Latino	5287
White	55
Hawaiian/Pacific Islander	2
Two or more	48
Limited English Proficiency	**2559**
Pre-Kindergarten	1247
Kindergarten	891
Grade 1	845
Grade 2	696
Grade 3	537
Grade 4	292
Grade 5	719
Grade 6	775
Grade 7	755
Grade 8	668
Grade 9	461
Grade 10	367
Grade 11	206
Grade 12	125
Male	4196
Female	4338

Source: Internal 2013 PEIMS reporting document used with permission.

and Levin started teaching fifth grade in two poorly performing schools in the Houston Independent School District (HISD).[4]

At first they struggled to control disruptive students and engage their classes in learning activities, but Levin soon discovered a mentor in Harriet Ball, a master teacher down the hall from his classroom. As often as possible he would meet with and observe her teaching. He soon began to adopt some of her unorthodox methods—including singing, chanting, and lots of body movement—which seemed to capture the students' attention, make lessons memorable, and led to higher achievement.

Levin shared these new methods with his roommate, Feinberg. Both teachers also began visiting students in their homes, which strengthened relationships with their families and reinforced their high behavioral expectations. By the end of their first year, Levin and Feinberg were succeeding with their improved teaching and determination to reach students.

In their second year, Levin and Feinberg met another legendary teacher named Rafe Esquith. Esquith's inner-city Los Angeles fifth graders would arrive at school as early as 6:30 am and often stayed late into the evening. They performed complete Shakespeare plays, practiced problem-solving and mental math, learned to play musical instruments, and took field trips to Utah's national parks and Washington, D.C. The classroom operated a token economy in which students earned "money" through various efforts and achievements and could spend it on rewards and privileges.

In 1994, at the end of their two-year commitment to Teach for America, feeling confident in the classroom, getting excellent results, and inspired by Esquith's achievements, Levin and Feinberg decided to work together to start a new program for HISD fifth graders called the Knowledge Is Power Program, or KIPP.

After struggling to recruit students and maneuver through the school district bureaucracy to get the program off the ground, Levin and Feinberg launched KIPP, co-teaching about 50 students in one classroom. The students arrived by 7:30 a.m. and stayed until 5 p.m., came for weekend enrichment classes, and were required to attend summer classes. Using a mixture of Ball's engaging teaching practices, Esquith's high expectations and motivational techniques (including the chance to earn a field trip to Washington, D.C., at the end of the school year), a continual emphasis on college attendance, and their own personal innovations, the two teachers succeed in leading 90 percent of their students to pass the state's math and reading tests, after a fourth grade year in which about half had passed.

Nationwide Growth

With the success of KIPP's first year under his belt, Levin moved to New York, his home city, to start another Knowledge Is Power Program in the Bronx. Hoping to continue the gains the KIPP fifth graders had achieved, Levin and Feinberg also decided to expand both programs to become full middle schools, adding grades 6 through 8 as the students moved up through the grades. This expansion brought a new challenge of finding excellent teaching talent to maintain the high academic and behavioral expectations, but both Levin and Feinberg were able to lead their schools to results that far surpassed the neighboring public schools.

The success of the schools began to attract attention. Dozens of Teach for America teachers visited

the schools to see the teachers and kids in action. The mayor of Houston and the HISD superintendent and future U.S. Secretary of Education, Rod Paige, dropped in. In the coming years, the two schools broke off from their school districts to become state-sanctioned charter schools, free from some of the constraints of operating in a school district bureaucracy.

In 1999, *60 Minutes* aired a 13-minute segment showcasing the success of the two KIPP middle schools. At the same time, Donald Fisher, who had co-founded the clothing retailer The Gap with his wife Doris, and his family were in the midst of a year-long search for an education-related philanthropic project. Fisher was impressed by what he saw on *60 Minutes* and donated $25 million to help found the KIPP Foundation, which was charged with training principals to start new KIPP schools that would replicate the success of the first two. "Fisher Fellowships" are still awarded each year to those who will train with the foundation before starting new schools.

In its original incarnation, the KIPP Foundation focused on finding the right high-caliber leaders and giving them free rein to start schools anywhere in the United States. In those first years, each individual KIPP school was governed by its own board of directors and operated completely autonomously. Around 2005, when Richard Barth became CEO of the KIPP Foundation, the strategy shifted to a regional model, where KIPP schools in the same city or geographical area were grouped together into regional networks. Today, there are 31 regional KIPP organizations in 20 states and the District of Columbia.

A Region Is Born

Houston got an early start in this regional reorganization effort, creating more middle schools and expanding into elementary and high schools, which made it possible for students to remain with KIPP from pre-kindergarten at age three until high school graduation.

After working for the new KIPP Foundation, Feinberg returned to Houston to serve as superintendent of the growing KIPP Houston district. Feinberg believed the traditional districts, such as the Houston Independent School District, would continue to underperform until they were directly challenged by a competitor capturing a larger share of student enrollment. Using the analogy of the U.S. Postal Service offering overnight mail service only after FedEx had captured a significant share of the market, Feinberg initiated an ambitious growth plan called "KIPP Turbo," which called for 42 KIPP schools in Houston by 2017.[5]

With the economic crisis of 2008, the Great Recession, and a subsequent $5.4 billion cut to education spending in 2011 by the Texas state legislature,[6] KIPP Turbo was scaled back. Instead of the original goal of 42 schools by 2017, KIPP Houston now plans to grow to 50 schools by 2033.[7] The budget shortfalls also led Feinberg to reconsider his role within the district. In 2011, Feinberg announced he would dedicate more of his time to fundraising and political advocacy, on behalf of both KIPP Houston and the KIPP network as a whole. Although he would still play a key role on KIPP Houston's board, Feinberg decided it was time to turn KIPP Houston over to a new leader.

In late 2011, Sehba Ali was announced as the sole finalist for the role of KIPP Houston superintendent, and in July of 2012 she took over the superintendency.[8]

Like Feinberg, Levin, and many other KIPP leaders, Ali started her education career with Teach for America. After her two-year commitment as an English teacher in a low-income Houston middle school, Ali taught for one year at another Houston charter outfit called YES Prep. She then attended Stanford, earning a master's degree in education in 2003. The KIPP Foundation awarded Ali the Fisher Fellowship, and in 2004 she founded KIPP Heartwood Academy, located in a low-income neighborhood near San Jose. The school went on to score among the highest 8 percent of schools in California on standardized achievement tests.[9] When hired, Ali was serving as the chief academic officer of the KIPP Bay Area region.

The "Target Market"

From its founding, KIPP has sought to serve students in high-minority, low-income communities. School leaders actively recruit students from Houston's low-rent apartment complexes and neighborhoods. Of KIPP Houston's roughly 8,500 students, 85 percent are low income (as measured by receiving federal free or reduced-price lunch assistance), 36 percent are African-American, and 62 percent are Latino. Thirty percent are classified as having limited English proficiency.[10]

The Gulfton neighborhood of Houston was among the first areas from which KIPP recruited students and is typical of the areas KIPP schools target. Many of its residents are immigrants, with 58 percent of residents born outside the United States. The median family income is $28,703, with more than half of children under 18 years old living below the poverty level. Of Gulfton residents aged 25 and older, 18 percent have attained a bachelor's degree or higher. Nearly half (47.1 percent) have not graduated from high school. By comparison, in the directly

adjacent, affluent neighborhood of Bellaire, 77 percent of residents have attained a bachelor's degree or higher and less than three percent have not graduated high school. The median family income is $184,600; 4 percent of children under 18 live under the poverty level.[11]

Although a bachelor's degree is increasingly necessary to secure a middle-class income in the United States, the socioeconomic realities of KIPP's target neighborhoods can make the attainment of higher education a daunting challenge for students. Many parents have limited education and cannot help their children with homework, let alone navigate the process of preparing for and applying for college admittance. Parents often work in jobs that require long hours or irregular schedules, making it difficult to help their children or hold them accountable for completing school assignments.

Crime is significantly higher in the denser low-income neighborhoods, and some children have to cope with exposure to violence and gang activity. Houston has become an active hub for gangs, with a reported 29 percent increase in the gang presence from 2010 to 2012.[12] Gangs actively recruit young people in neighborhoods of high poverty, primarily in middle school but as early as elementary school, offering camaraderie and protection.[13]

Studies have also found that students from low-income families generally come to school less well-prepared to succeed academically. Due in part to differences in parenting patterns between high-income and low-income parents, poor children have significantly lower vocabularies than the children of the professional classes. Two researchers who observed and quantified the verbal interactions between high-socioeconomic and low-socioeconomic parents found that professional parents directed 2,153 words per hour at their children compared to parents on welfare assistance, who used 616. This substantial gap in exposure to language resulted in a comparable gap in vocabulary when children entered school. Tests of language skill at the ages of 9 and 10 showed the discrepancy persisted, affecting students' readiness for higher-level academic work.[14]

Despite the challenges facing families in poverty, many parents in the target neighborhoods are eager to seize the opportunity KIPP offers to give their children a good education. In a typical recruitment visit, a KIPP teacher will sit in the home of a prospective student and explain exactly what the school requires of parents, students, and teachers. After answering questions, the teacher will ask the parents and student if they are willing to make these promises. If they answer in the affirmative, the student, parents, and teacher will sign the "Commitment to Excellence." The teacher usually takes a photo of the new KIPPster holding a KIPP sign to celebrate his or her decision.

The number of students desiring to "Commit to Excellence" at a KIPP school exceeds the network's current capacity. From those who sign up, KIPP Houston decides which students to enroll through a lottery. The only students not subject to this random selection are those who have siblings who attended or currently attend a KIPP Houston school. Students who are not selected in the lottery are placed on a waiting list. According to KIPP Houston, there are currently over 8,000 students on the waiting list.[15]

Rules of the Game

Efforts to grow the network to meet excess demand have to meet the regulatory constraints that govern charter schools. The law allowing charter schools in Texas was passed by the state legislature in 1995 and was designed to increase the level of choice for students and teachers, as well as improve student learning by encouraging innovation and performance accountability. The law lays out areas in which charter schools have flexibility and areas in which they must meet the same requirements as other public schools.[16, 17]

Staffing

- Not required to hire certified teachers. The minimum requirement to teach is a high school diploma. In practice, in order to qualify for federal funding, charter schools do require "highly qualified" status (a bachelor's degree and demonstrated competency in the area they teach) for teachers of core academic subjects. These qualifications are still less onerous to obtain than formal state certification.
- Not required to have any minimum qualifications for principals or superintendents
- Not required to establish written employment contracts with teachers
- Not required to follow the minimum salary schedules laid out in the Texas Education Code.

Curriculum and Operations

- Required to teach the learning standards set out in Texas law
- Required to follow regulations in relation to special education, bilingual education, and certain reading instructional programs
- Required to follow graduation standards set out in Texas law
- Required to administer the same yearly achievement tests as other public schools

- Required to follow the same rules for student discipline given in state law
- Required to report daily attendance to the state for the sake of computing average daily attendance (ADA), which determines funding levels
- Required to instruct students for at least four hours during a day in which students are counted for ADA purposes, but are not required to instruct students for at least seven hours like other public schools
- Not required to provide 180 days of instruction as are other public schools (though funding levels depend on days of instruction)
- Not required to follow limitations on student-teacher ratios and class sizes.[18]

The Money Gap

Despite the increased flexibility afforded to charter schools by the state code, KIPP Houston faces other obstacles arising from the way public money is disbursed to schools.

Public schools in the United States are primarily funded through a mix of local, state, and federal sources. Nationally, federal funding accounts for 10 percent of revenues, with the remaining 90 percent coming from a mix of local and state sources.[19] In Texas, most of this money is raised from local property taxes, which can be levied by school districts. Districts use two kinds of property tax: maintenance and operations, or M&O, which is used for staffing and operating costs, and interest and sinking, or I&S, which is used to service debt from bonds issued for facility construction or renovation. These tax revenues, however, are subject to reallocation by the state based on several criteria.

The state determines district M&O funding using formulas that essentially serve three purposes:

- Base funding on actual student attendance. Districts are required to submit attendance reports that are used to calculate the district's ADA, a key input in the funding formula.
- Even out spending across rich and poor districts. A portion of the tax revenue from wealthy districts is reallocated to other districts.
- Weight funding based on how many students in the district have special needs, like special education, bilingual education, and gifted and talented education.

Charter schools, however, do not have taxing authority. Instead of M&O taxes, they depend solely on state reallocations of tax revenues. In the 2010–11 school year, for each student reported as enrolled, they received

$7,945.46 in the form of this allocation, which was 77 percent of their government funding.[20, 21] Other state and federal grants amounted to a total of $13,905,811, which yields a total government contribution of $10,269 per enrolled student. (For KIPP Houston's most recent Statement of Financial Position, see Exhibit 2. For a breakdown of government revenues, see Exhibit 3.)

Beyond this funding for operational expenses, charter districts are entitled to none of the revenue from I&S taxes, which means they receive no state funding for facilities.[22]

KIPP Houston CFO John Murphy says the lack of funding for facilities is without a doubt the biggest financial challenge the district faces.[23] One independent study found that primarily due to this facilities funding discrepancy, in the 2009–10 school year, KIPP Houston received from government sources $966 per pupil less than Houston Independent School District.[24] At KIPP Houston's current enrollment level, that amounts to $8,292,144 per year.

KIPP Houston made up for the deficit through both fundraising and frugality with facilities. Many KIPP Houston schools are housed in low-cost modular buildings, and some have relatively little land and green space compared to other public schools. The facilities KIPP Houston has acquired have come primarily through philanthropy. In the fundraising drive to finance the KIPP Turbo expansion, individuals and foundations committed well over $40 million to KIPP Houston.[25] The KIPP Houston board of directors generally transfers these funds to the PHILO Finance Corporation, an independent nonprofit 501(c)(3), which helps charter schools secure financing by guaranteeing bond issues and issuing grants to repay debt. In 2012, KIPP Houston's total liability for bonds and notes payable was $125,787,976, with most bonds bearing interest rates between 4 and 6.4 percent.[26]

Not surprisingly, KIPP Houston's biggest expense is instruction-related costs, which, over the span of 2008 to 2010, made up about 42 percent of per pupil expenditures.[27] Of this share, the vast majority goes toward teacher salaries. In 2012, the average KIPP Houston teacher earned a salary of $46,883.[28] The next highest cost is school and district administration, which represents 23 percent of per pupil expenditures (2008–10). The district spends about 15 percent on student services (e.g., food services, transportation, and counseling), 9 percent on facilities maintenance and security, and 5 percent on facilities debt service. (For KIPP Houston cost allocations compared to Houston ISD and YES Prep, see Exhibit 4. For the KIPP Houston 2013 expected budget, see Exhibit 5.)

Exhibit 2 KIPP, Inc. Statements of Financial Position as of June 30, 2012 and 2011

	2012	2011
ASSETS		
Cash and cash equivalents (*Note 2*)	$7,690,223	$12,655,763
Receivables:		
Government agencies	14,688,117	11,556,734
Pledges, net (*Note 3*)	1,504,302	1,692,472
Other	1,032,677	170,908
Prepaid expenses	497,794	551,320
Investments in certificates of deposit	300,000	300,000
Capitalized bond issuance costs	3,205,296	3,322,465
Bond proceeds held in trust (*Note 5*)	12,731,572	21,531,419
Property and equipment, net (*Note 4*)	121,856,439	111,214,248
TOTAL ASSETS	$163,506,420	$162,995,329
LIABILITIES AND NET ASSETS		
Liabilities:		
Accounts payable and accrued expenses	$4,426,361	$2,665,970
Accrued payroll expenses	6,864,303	6,814,000
Due to PHILO Finance Corporation	170,310	2,664,143
Construction payable	1,514,245	4,026,309
Accrued interest	2,607,129	2,629,158
Refundable advances	101,656	75,185
Bonds and notes payable (*Notes 5 and 10*)	125,787,976	125,697,730
Total liabilities	141,471,980	144,572,495
Commitments (*Note 12*)		
Net assets (*Note 8*):		
Unrestricted	17,467,175	14,224,473
Temporarily restricted (*Note 7*)	4,377,265	4,008,361
Permanently restricted for scholarships	190,000	190,000
Total net assets	22,034,440	18,422,834
TOTAL LIABILITIES AND NET ASSETS	$163,506,420	$162,995,329

Source: Financial Statements and Independent Auditors' Report. KIPP, Inc., October 16, 2012. Accessed April 21, 2013. http://kipphouston.org/sites/default/files/file_attach/KHPS_Audit_Report_for_the_Year_Ended_June_30_2012.pdf.

Exhibit 3 2010–2011 Financial Statement – Note on Government Grants

NOTE 9 - GOVERNMENT GRANTS
KIPP is the recipient of government grants from various federal, state and local agencies. Government grants include the following:

	2011	2010
State grants:		
Texas Education Agency Foundation School Program Act	$47,561,540	$37,398,934
Pre-K Expansion Grant	674,260	661,036
Technology Allotment	162,459	127,801
Texas Science, Technology, Engineering, and Math Initiative	160,734	378,097
Intensive Summer Programs	144,770	159,233
Teacher Excellence Awards	117,891	168,164
Above and Beyond Grant	51,001	
SSI Intensive Math Initiative	47,042	96,953
FSP Investment Capital Fund	23,475	52,107
School Lunch Matching	19,469	15,288
Texas Fitness Now	10,297	26,309
APIB Technical Training	3,600	
21st Century Community Learning Centers		194,692
Texas Education Excellence Grant		122,863
Governor's Educator Excellence		21,146
KIPP Coastal Village		11,000
Grants for Student Clubs		7,345
Total state grants	48,976,538	39,440,968
Federal grants:		
U.S. Department of Education	8,267,172	5,389,299
U.S. Department of Agriculture	4,223,641	3,170,398
Total federal grants	12,490,813	8,559,697
Total government grants	$61,467,351	$48,000,665

Source: Financial Statements and Independent Auditors' Report. 2011 Audit Report. KIPP, Inc., October 27, 2011. Accessed April 21, 2013. http://kipphouston. org/sites/default/files/file_attach/KHPS_Audit_Report_for_the_Year_Ended_ June_30_2011.pdf.

Exhibit 4 Percentage of Expenditures Per Pupil (ADA), 2007–2010

Cost	Houston ISD	KIPP Houston[1]	YES Prep
Instruction	54.62%	42.31%	53.50%
Administration (Central and School)	10.24%	23.30%	18.49%
Student Services	7.07%	14.99%	14.27%
Plant Maintenance and Security	9.78%	9.88%	10.98%
Facilities and Debt Service	16.05%	5.47%	0.49%
Other	2.22%	4.04%	2.27%

[1] Due to accounting anomalies in 2007–08, KIPP Houston numbers are an average of 2008–09 and 2009–10.

Source: Analysis of McGee, Josh B. "Houston School Finance Report." Arnoldfoundation. org. Laura and John Arnold Foundation, January 18, 2013. Accessed April 20, 2013. www.arnoldfoundation.org/resources/houston-school-finance-report.

Exhibit 5 KIPP, Inc. Consolidated District Final Budget For the Year Ended June 30, 2013

Other Revenues from Local Sources	$9,635,525
State Program Revenues	60,998,666
Federal Revenues	11,149,111
Total Revenue	$81,783,302
Basic Instruction	$33,724,037
Instructional Resources and Media Services	62,510
Curriculum Development and Instructional Staff Development	859,936
Instructional Leadership	1,707,373
School Leadership	9,580,515
Guidance, Counseling & Evaluation Services	2,853,292
Social Work Services	637,097
Health Services	366,415
Student Transportation	4,624,577
Food Services	5,379,537
Extracurricular Activities	728,194
General Administration	6,976,854
Plant Maintenance and Operations	9,880,396
Security & Monitoring Services	1,121,375
Data Processing Services	2,794,611
Community Service	537,479
Debt Service	7,144,023
Fundraising	1,632,532
Total Expenses	$90,610,756
Net Contribution	−$8,827,454

Source: Consolidated District Final Budget. KIPP Houston Public Schools, n.d. Accessed April 21, 2013. http://kipphouston.org/sites/default/files/file_attach/ FY13_Functional_Budget_121114.pdf.

Organization: Bottom Up and Top Down

At the core of KIPP Houston's operations are its teachers. A typical KIPP Houston instructor teaches a single subject in a single grade level of 85 to 110 students. Most schools employ one of the grade-level teachers to be a grade-level chair, leading the culture (behavioral norms) and coordinating activities within the grade level in addition to their teaching duties. Some teachers are also given department chair responsibilities, which involves aligning the curriculum and instruction for one content area across the different grade levels.

Given the Power to Lead principle, much of the job descriptions of teachers, how they are trained, and the ongoing professional development they receive is determined at the school level by the principal, who is responsible for the safety and academic performance of the school. Principals have wide discretion in resource allocation, including personnel decisions (teachers are "at-will" employees). This autonomy leads to differences in school organization within KIPP Houston, and the delegation of a school's administrative responsibilities can vary from school to school. Some principals hire a Dean of Students, who heads up student culture and discipline, and a Dean of Instruction, who is responsible primarily for the professional development of teachers. Other principals hire assistant principals, whose job descriptions combine Dean of Student and Dean of Instruction roles but who might be assigned specific grade levels to manage.

The principal reports to a Head of Schools at KIPP Houston's regional office. According to Head of Schools Ken Goedekke, these four heads report to Superintendent Ali and manage a "feeder pattern," which, when fully built out, consists of two elementary schools, two middle schools, and the one high school they feed into. In the last two years, heads of schools have also been in charge of spearheading curriculum alignment, which is the process of ensuring that similar academic standards and performance benchmarks are being used across the region. Curriculum alignment has long been on the radar at KIPP Houston but it has received more emphasis and resources since 2011. Next year, the curriculum alignment responsibilities will be managed by a separate head of schools with the other heads focusing on managing their feeder patterns.[29]

In addition to the line of direct reporting from schools, Ali manages a central office that includes managers of bus transportation, food services, and facilities; HR and finance professionals; and curriculum and student-support specialists. One of Ali's first acts as superintendent was to change the name of this central office from KIPP Inc. to the Regional Services Team (RST) to reflect its role as a support center for the region's campuses.

According to Goedekke, who manages a feeder pattern in Southwest Houston, there has been something of a shift in organizational expectations in the last two or three years. In 2010, most schools were still led by their founding principal. These principals had been given wide latitude to create a school according to the unique visions they had developed during the Fisher Fellowship year. Principals expected to be regionally supported in logistics, such as facilities maintenance, food, and transportation, but did not expect to have curriculum and instructional decisions made at the region level.

"They were given the reins to build a school, and they did," Goedekke says. But in 2013, only one original school founder remains in the principal role, and the new crop of principals expects more regional alignment to take place.[30]

"The new school leaders have seen the benefits of alignment. They asked, 'Why are ten fifth grade math teachers all writing their own lesson plans?' Organizationally, we needed to do something different."[31]

Goedekke says that schools that get excellent results on assessments of student academic progress continue to get wide latitude to make site-based decisions.[32]

Not all schools are performing up to KIPP's high standards. One measure of school performance is the annual state achievement tests that the Texas Education Agency uses to give an "accountability rating" to each school. The ratings measure the percentage of students who meet minimum requirements and are (from highest to lowest): Exemplary, Recognized, Acceptable, and Unacceptable. In the 2010–11 school year (the last year for which ratings are available), of the 10 KIPP Houston middle and high schools that received ratings, two were Exemplary, four were Recognized, three were Acceptable, and one was Unacceptable. By comparison, another Houston charter school network, YES Prep, achieved an Exemplary rating for six of its seven schools, the other school receiving Recognized status.[33]

How does the Power to Lead principle fit with these discrepancies? Goedekke says that for schools not performing well, district leadership needs to delicately intervene by, for example, suggesting exemplary lesson plans that struggling teachers can use.[34]

Sehba Ali believes that the Power to Lead allows for a more entrepreneurial and creative spirit in KIPP schools and can lead to innovation. She does not believe schools should simply try to replicate best practices.

"School leaders have a responsibility to be creative and innovate. We can't just say, 'You're a replication school,'" Ali says. She cites the example of KIPP Courage, a recently founded school that is getting good results using more technology in instruction. Some of their new practices will be adopted by an older, exemplary-rated KIPP school. She believes that when school leaders see compelling evidence of an effective practice, they will make the decision to adopt it without the need for top-down management.

The People Problem

Another of Ali's initiatives as superintendent was to clarify KIPP Houston's niche in the national KIPP landscape. According to Chief People Officer Chuck Fimble (responsible for HR and recruiting), in an early leadership meeting, Ali pointed out that many KIPP regions have a unique emphasis or identity. Some are known for their instructional expertise; others for their academic alignment.

"What is our regional identity?" she asked.

"We couldn't come up anything other than being first and being big," Fimble says.[35]

The answer that was agreed to was that KIPP Houston would become a first-class leadership development organization. This emphasis on leadership development would be important not just for KIPP Houston's identity but, more essentially, for its successful expansion.

Although the brakes were put on KIPP Turbo partly due to the economic downturn, another critical bottleneck was in human capital.

"We're pretty convinced we can find the money and schools [to grow]. The problem is finding the people," Fimble notes.[36]

Ali agrees: "KIPP Turbo assumed an incredible bench depth of talent. It takes more to develop leadership than we thought… [Between funding shortages and the need for talent,] talent is the bigger barrier."[37]

Even though KIPP Turbo has been scaled back, it will still require a large infusion of talent, both in leadership and teaching. Based on growth projections, over the course of the next five school years, KIPP Houston will need to hire about 1,300 new teachers (see Exhibit 6).[38]

Nationally, 32 percent of KIPP teachers are alumni of Teach for America,[39] the same route through which Feinberg and Ali came to the profession, and KIPP Houston depends heavily on former TFA corps members. Other teachers are recruited from the Houston and other surrounding Independent School Districts, some go through Alternative Certification Programs (which are abbreviated routes to certification), and some come to KIPP straight from college education programs.

Whatever their pathway into teaching, all KIPP teachers sign the Commitment to Excellence, which lays out the responsibilities of being a teacher at KIPP:

- We will always teach the best way we know how and do whatever it takes for our students to learn.
- We will always make ourselves available to students and parents for any concerns they might have. [All teachers are issued a cell phone, which students can call in the evenings for help with homework.]
- We will arrive at KIPP by 7:15 a.m. on Monday through Friday.
- We will remain at KIPP until 5:15 p.m. on Monday through Thursday and 4:00 p.m. on Friday.
- We will teach at KIPP during summer school… [2 weeks.][40]

In addition to the 10-hour daily commitment, most teachers work additional hours in the evening and on the weekends to plan lessons and assess student work.

A second-year KIPP teacher reflecting on her first-year reports, "It was difficult. I think the Power to Lead principle trickles down to teachers, too, so you have to find and do everything on your own, especially because

Exhibit 6 Projected KHPS Instructional Staff Hiring Needs

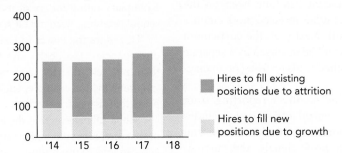

Source: Internal document used with permission.

as a region our curriculum wasn't aligned. Even if I tried to get help from other teachers, they would be teaching other things, so I couldn't use their resources."[41]

As a second-year teacher, she says things became easier. "I work from 7:00 a.m. to 6:00 p.m., plus about ten hours on the weekend, so about 65 hours per week. It's easier now that I have my curriculum from last year."[42]

Although the challenge of the work and KIPP Houston's social mission are both appealing to many young teachers, the heavy workload may be partly responsible for lower-than-average teacher retention rates. In the 2011–12 school year, KIPP Houston had a teacher retention rate of 58 percent, compared with 68 percent for YES Prep charter schools, and 83 percent for Houston Independent School District.[43] Over a longer time span, KIPP Houston reports a 72 percent retention rate, which is 6 percent below what charter management organizations nationally are getting.[44] The high turnover and dependence on Teach for America alumni give KIPP Houston a young teaching force, with a 2012 average of 3.8 years of experience, compared to a statewide average of 11.6 years.[45]

To help the organization better gauge job satisfaction and employee attitudes, KIPP Houston is using a "pulse survey," which KIPP Houston staff respond to twice annually. Many of the responses show high employee commitment. The three statements that employees most strongly agree with are "My team is committed to doing quality work," "The mission of KIPP makes me feel my job is important," and "I know what is expected of me at KIPP." The three statements that get the lowest scores are, "I would recommend my KIPP school/Inc. to a friend as a place of employment," "Leadership and school/department staff communicate with each other effectively," and "I plan to work at KIPP for at least three more years."[46] (See Exhibit 7 for pulse survey results.)

One way KIPP Houston hopes to engender longer-term commitments is through offering pathways to leadership. In addition to the Fisher Fellowship, KIPP Houston encourages talented teachers to apply for the Miles Fellowship, which is a two-year path to becoming a school founder, the first year spent as a resident leader in an established KIPP school and the second year as a Fisher Fellow (if accepted). Teachers can also remain in the classroom and attend KIPP Foundation—sponsored leadership programs for grade-level chairs and department chairs. In addition, KIPP Houston offers its own leadership classes from central office leaders, which take place after work hours.

Teachers who seek leadership positions are also signing up for a demanding role but one that comes with excellent support and the opportunity for high impact. One former Fisher Fellow who founded a higher-performing KIPP school reports that the Fellowship year prepared him well.

"The Fellowship was extremely flexible. I identified that I needed to learn Spanish, so they sent me to Mexico for a few weeks to learn it. There were a lot of things that I was able to work on—from a framework for evaluating teachers to mapping out curriculum—that set me up for a solid start."[47]

He explained that KIPP Houston was also a good place to found a school because of all the back office logistical support (e.g., in transportation, food services, and facilities) that allowed him to focus on curriculum and instruction.

With the support also came a lot of responsibility: "The workload was fairly intense—an average of eighty hours a week, with some times of the year approaching one hundred and others bottoming out at fifty....I think most school leaders leave because of burn out."[48]

No comprehensive research has been done on the employee attrition problem, so the issue of long hours is just one of many guesses concerning what is driving turnover. KIPP Houston plans to put together a committee to study the issue in the upcoming year.[49]

With the current KIPP Houston expansion plans, the region will need to fill about 40 new administrative positions in five years, but Fimble worries that KIPP Houston has lost its recruiting edge: "The talent exists. The number of teachers and leaders exists in the city as a whole. The problem is getting them to want to come to KIPP. What is our niche in the recruiting war? We used to be new, more entrepreneurial, and have better pay. Now we're not new, not as entrepreneurial, and the pay isn't much better, especially when looked at from a dollar-per-hour-worked perspective."[50]

To fill teaching roles for the upcoming school year the recruitment office has started new initiatives, including a social media campaign, billboards on Houston's highly trafficked freeways, recruitment events around the city, and the offer of a $1,000 referral bonus for anyone who successfully recruits someone to fill an instructional position.[51]

The Curriculum Conundrum

At the heart of the work KIPP Houston does is the curriculum: the learning standards that students are expected to master. In Texas, the elected, 15-member State Board of Education approves the curriculum for each subject in each grade level and schools are required by law to teach it.[52]

Exhibit 7

1. Region Snapshot *Updated on Feb 2013. Current through next reporting date of June 2013.*		Current Avt.	Change Year Over Year	Top % (Agree & Strongly Agree)	Bottom % (Disagree & Strongly Disagree)
	My team is committed to doing quality work.	4.27	−0.04	88%	3%
	The mission of KIPP makes me feel my job is important.	4.25	−0.07	88%	3%
	I know what is expected of me at KIPP.	4.21	0.06	90%	2%
	I have a trusted, personal friend at KIPP.	4.17	0.07	81%	6%
	My school leader/manager cares about me as a person.	4.16	0.03	83%	6%
	In the last six months my supervisor talked to me about my progress.	4.14	0.10	84%	7%
Top 6 Questions	There is someone at KIPP who encourages my development.	4.11	0.01	83%	7%
	I have opportunities at KIPP to learn and grow.	4.01	−0.01	78%	9%
	The leaders of my school/department live the values of the Freedom Tree.	3.96	0.03	76%	7%
	At work I have the opportunity to do what I do best every day.	3.89	0.00	75%	10%
	My colleagues live the values of the Freedom Tree.	3.89	0.05	73%	6%
	The regional leaders of KIPP Houston live the values of the Freedom Tree.	3.88	0.05	71%	5%
Bottom 6 Questions	In the last seven days, I have received recognition or praise for doing good work.	3.79	0.01	70%	16%
	At KIPP, my opinions seem to count.	3.70	0.00	66%	14%
	I have the resources I need to do my work well.	3.69	−0.01	68%	15%
	I would recommend my KIPP school/Inc. to a friend as a place of employment.	3.63	0.04	61%	16%
	Leadership and school/department staff communicate with each other effectively.	3.43	0.11	56%	22%
	I plan to work at KIPP for at least three more years.	3.38	0.07	49%	21%

Source: Internal document used with permission.

However, this process is not straightforward. There are so many learning standards—and many of them are so broad—that teachers have significant flexibility to decide what and how they teach, and most teachers believe it is not possible to teach all of them with any kind of depth and student understanding.

Sixth-grade social studies standard 6.2.B, for example, states that for the subject of history students should "evaluate the social, political, economic, and cultural contributions of individuals and groups from various societies, past and present."[53] One teacher may believe that learning about the Silk Road from China to Europe would be an excellent way to achieve this goal while another may teach it by studying the influence of the Aztec culture on modern Mexico.

This inherent flexibility has led to wide variations in curriculum, even among instructors teaching the same grade level and subject. For example, some KIPP schools used to focus on one section of the science standards each year to create an emphasis on earth science one year and life science the next, etc.; while other schools rotate through all areas of science every year.

In subjects and years that have state achievement tests, there tends to be less variation in curriculum because teachers generally align their classroom goals with the material that appears on the standardized assessment. To help schools and teachers more closely align their curricula and assess student learning, in the 2011–12 school year, KIPP Houston began writing and administering its own Common Assessments. These tests would be administered three times per year in each core academic subject. The effort has been led by both Heads of Schools and "Teacher Leaders" from each grade level and subject. Most subjects now have Common Assessments while other are yet to be developed.

To further complicate the curriculum puzzle, Texas is among the five states in the country that have chosen not to adopt a set of national standards called the Common Core.[54] The Common Core was developed as a cooperative effort by state governments seeking to clarify and benchmark national learning standards. While education leaders in Texas are free to ignore the Common Core, a study of nationwide state standards showed that what Texas considers "proficient" was the lowest in the nation and well below what national tests deem proficient.[55] While newer versions of the state achievement test are thought to be more rigorous, a school district that ignores the Common Core may risk failing to prepare its students to compete in the national market for college admittance.

"The Common Core standards are really good for preparing kids for college," Sehba Ali says. "We'll find the overlaps. We'll find the holes. We'll align to the Common Core and the TEKS [Texas learning standards]."[56]

One tool that many teachers have used to develop and share curriculum materials is BetterLesson. Adopted by KIPP schools nationwide in the 2010–11 school year, BetterLesson is a Web-based curriculum document storage and retrieval tool developed by a young Boston-based company.[57] Teachers can use the Web site to search for, download, and upload lesson plans, worksheets, PowerPoint presentations, and other curriculum materials. It connects KIPP educators across the country with each other and with teachers from other high-performing schools. With most teachers nationally aligning solely to the Common Core, however, KIPP Houston teachers may have less opportunity to leverage BetterLesson.

The Promise of Technology

Some see Web applications like BetterLesson as the tip of the iceberg when it comes to using information technology (IT) to improve school performance.

Harvard business professor Clayton Christensen predicts that digital learning will be a "disruptive innovation" that revolutionizes education in the coming decade.[58] Proponents of digital learning technologies herald its ability to give students immediate feedback and individualized learning experiences. Some Learning Management Systems (LMS) allow teachers to manage student assignments and track performance on one digital hub, cutting down on routine paper management and data analysis tasks.

Many teachers and schools are experimenting with various combinations of traditional and digital learning. These "blended learning" models can range from classrooms in which students rotate between computers, small group instruction, and independent work, to schools in which students self-manage larger blocks of time for online learning. KIPP first entered the world of blended learning in 2010, with the opening of KIPP Empower Academy in Los Angeles. KIPP Empower, an elementary school that will serve grades K–4 at full enrollment, uses a rotational blended learning model as a way to give students a highly personalized education with a small-group classroom feel.

Inspired by the success of KIPP Empower, educators in other KIPP regions, including KIPP Houston, have begun implementing elements of blended learning. For example, KIPP Courage, founded in Houston in summer 2012, incorporates blended learning in most of its classrooms. In addition to a computer lab where students use software to learn either Spanish or English or engage in individualized math practice problems, almost every classroom has a set of inexpensive netbooks, which students use to do research or access online learning activities. The principal, Eric Schmidt, says he combined the digital learning with practices he picked up from other KIPP schools during his Fisher Fellowship.[59]

Although it is a young experiment, Schmidt says it has helped a high percentage of their students reach their learning goals (see Exhibit 8). "One of the unintended consequences of this model has been our flexibility with human capital," Schmidt says. "We had two teachers call in sick unexpectedly, but we didn't have to request any substitute teachers because teachers or administrators who had planning times could cover the computer lab and still get their work done."[60]

Schmidt says the next step, which he hopes to accomplish before next school year, is to find an online Learning Management System to tie the disparate pieces of digital learning together into one system.

Matt Bradford, the Director of Knowledge Management, works within the IT department for KIPP Houston. Bradford and others in his department help support the back-end management of KIPP Houston IT initiatives; for example, by ensuring that the district's digital student rosters can interface with the various online programs. He sees potential in using IT resources to track student learning but says the big issues are which platform to use and standardization.[61]

"There's a lot of piloting of projects around the district without consistency from school to school. Schools might not agree to use similar systems, which makes it

Exhibit 8 Promotional Flyer for the KIPP Courage Blended Learning Model and Initial Results

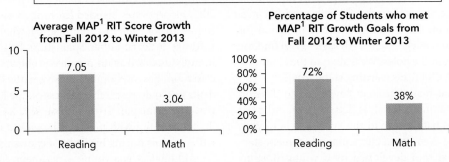

Phase I: Learning Lab

Two 30 minute Rotations:

30 minutes of *Rosetta Stone* in **English or Spanish Instruction**

30 minutes of **Math or Reading Intervention** with *Success Maker or Khan Academy*

30 minutes of "Explore Pod" with **Teacher-Created Blogs**

Phase II: Blended Reading Classroom

Two 30 minute Rotations:

30 minutes of **Independent Non-fiction Work on Chromebooks** with *Achieve 3000*

30 minutes of **Small Group Instruction** with a Teacher

30 minutes of **Group Work in a Fiction Book Club** with other Students

Average MAP[1] RIT Score Growth from Fall 2012 to Winter 2013

Reading: 7.05
Math: 3.06

Percentage of Students who met MAP[1] RIT Growth Goals from Fall 2012 to Winter 2013

Reading: 72%
Math: 38%

Source: KIPP Courage College Prep

difficult to support," Bradford says.[62] Sehba Ali believes the focus needs to remain on recruiting and developing excellent teachers, noting, "I come from the Bay Area, where the word on the street is that we will put a lot of computers in classrooms and that will solve all our problems. But technology is only good in the hands of great teachers." On the other hand, Ali sees potential for technology to enhance teacher effectiveness by, for example, providing minute-to-minute student performance data. This might indirectly alleviate the retention problem because "teachers who feel good about what they're doing in their classrooms tend to stay."[63]

Competitive Pressures

While KIPP Houston might have been the trailblazer in effective models of public schooling for low-income students, the competition is not sitting on its hands.

The Houston Independent School District has responded to the success of charter schools by attempting to replicate their most effective practices, including a longer school day, a college-bound culture, and one-on-two tutoring, in some of its underperforming schools.

The program, called Apollo 20, was launched in the 2010–11 school year.[64] After its first year, HISD reported math "gains [similar] to those seen in charter schools," especially in grades six and nine, in which students had received one-on-two tutoring,[65, 66] HISD has not been able to fund the program through its regular operating revenues, however, and has depended on philanthropic gifts for funding.[67]

YES Prep, the charter network with consistent "Exemplary" ratings, was founded in 1995 (the same year KIPP established its charter) by another TFA alum and friend of Michael Feinberg.[68] It has long been a friendly competitor but has had a slower growth trajectory and a different management philosophy. From the beginning, YES Prep's focus was less on leadership and more on defining curriculum and teacher expectations. New schools were opened by veteran leaders working side-by-side with less experienced leaders.[69] YES Prep schools aligned assessments of student learning years before KIPP, and they now use a common framework for evaluating, promoting, and compensating teachers.

Sehba Ali feels that KIPP Houston and YES Prep fill different niches in the education landscape:

"We're different. What we bring is innovation and creativity and autonomy for our leaders and teachers. There are people who are better suited for KIPP and people who are better suited for YES, but we have a lot to learn from each other."[70]

A newer and rapidly growing entrant into Houston's education space is Harmony Public Schools. Founded in 2001, Harmony already has 38 schools in Texas, including 12 in the Houston metro area, and over 24,000 students.[71] In 2010, 23 of its 25 campuses received Exemplary or Recognized ratings from the Texas Education Agency and the other two were rated Acceptable.[72] Harmony's schools were designed to make rapid replication possible, with highly defined management systems, a predefined curriculum from kindergarten to grade 12, and an online curriculum management system called CSCOPE.[73] It has been able to expand throughout the economic recession by employing a lean operational model that includes lower teacher salaries (almost $10,000 less than KIPP per average teacher), in part due to the practice of hiring Turkish teachers on H-1B visas.[74, 75]

The Next Chapter

The stakes for KIPP Houston are as high as ever. A 2011 study undertaken by the KIPP Foundation sought to determine the degree to which KIPP schools actually help their low-income students attend and complete college. Tracking students who had completed a KIPP middle school 10 or more years prior, they found that 33 percent had graduated from a four-year college. This means that KIPP's alumni are graduating from college at higher rates than the national average for all Americans (30.4 percent), and at close to four times the rate of students from the nation's lowest-income families. KIPP's goal is to increase the college completion rates of its alumni to match those of the nation's highest-income students—about 75 percent.[76]

The students in the study had attended Feinberg and Levin's original schools in Houston and the Bronx, which are well known for their excellence. The open question is whether or not an entire district can replicate that success, and KIPP Houston is at the forefront of answering that question.

Can the district find a sustainable model of public financing, or will philanthropy need to be a permanent part of the revenue mix? Will they find a way to recruit, develop, and retain enough teachers to sustain excellence and execute their planned growth? Can the district make good on its desire to blaze the trail in leadership development? Does KIPP Houston need to modify its organizational structure in order to provide consistent excellence for its KIPPsters? Finally, what role, if any, will technology play in addressing these strategic challenges?

Whatever choices Ali makes, she knows it will continue to require a lot of smart people working hard and being nice. And she knows it will involve no miracle or magic.

NOTES

1. Ali, Sehba. Personal interview. March 29, 2013.

2. "Five Pillars." *KIPP Public Charter Schools.* KIPP Foundation, n.d. Accessed April 21, 2013. www.kipp.org/our-approach/five-pillars.

3. "KIPP Houston Public Schools." KIPP Houston Public Schools, n.d. Accessed May 1, 2013. http://kipphouston.org.

4. This and the remainder this section and the next is drawn from Mathews, Jay. *Work Hard. Be Nice: How Two Inspired Teachers Created the Most Promising Schools in America.* Chapel Hill, NC: Algonquin of Chapel Hill, 2009.

5. Mathews, Jay. "Growing Up Fast." *Philanthropy 2008. Philanthropy roundtable.org.* Accessed April 17, 2013. www.philanthropyroundtable.org/topic/k_12_education/growing_up_fast.

6. Fernandez, Manny. "At Texas Schools, Making Do on a Shoestring." *New York Times.* April 9, 2012. Accessed April 17, 2013. www.nytimes.com/2012/04/09/us/

for-texas-schools-a-year-of-doing-without.html?pagewanted=all.

7. Fimble, Chuck. Personal interview. March 29, 2013.

8. KIPP Houston Public Schools. *New Superintendent: Sehba Ali. KIPP Houston Public Schools.* July 2012. Accessed April 17, 2013. http://kipphouston.org/node/227.

9. *KIPPBayArea.org.* KIPP Bay Area Schools, n.d. Accessed April 17, 2013. www.kippbayarea.org/schools/heartwood.

10. KIPP Houston data reported to the Texas Public Education Information Management System (PEIMS). January 15, 2013.

11. Based on 2010 United States Census. ZIP Codes 77081 and 77401. Incomes are in 2011 inflation-adjusted dollars. *American FactFinder.* United States Census Bureau, n.d. Accessed 19 Apr. 2013. http://factfinder2.census.gov/faces/nav/jsf/pages/index.xhtml.

12. Pinkerton, James. "Gangs on Rise, but Idea to Fight Them Raises Eyebrows." Chron.

com. *Houston Chronicle*, November 1, 2012. Accessed April 19, 2013. www.chron.com/news/houston-texas/houston/article/Solutions-differ-in-fight-to-curb-increasing-gang-4001924.php>.

13. "Information for Parents, Educators and Community Residents." *Stop Houston Gangs – Report Gang Crime Tips & Violence – Texas Gangs.* Stop Houston Gangs Task Force, n.d. Accessed April 19, 2013. www.stophoustongangs.org/default.aspx?act=frontpage.aspx.

14. Hart, Betty, and Risley, Todd R. "The Early Catastrophe: The 30 Million Word Gap by Age 3." General Services Administration, n.d. Accessed April 20, 2013. www.gsa.gov/graphics/pbs/The_Early_Catastrophe_30_Million_Word_Gap_by_Age_3.pdf.

15. "Past. Present. Future." *KIPP Houston Public Schools.* Accessed April 20, 2013. http://kipphouston.org/past-present-future.

16. "Charter Schools." Texas Education Agency, n.d. Accessed April 20, 2013. www.tea.state.tx.us/Charters.aspx.

17. The law provides for four different classes of charter school. In the following, "charter schools" refers to open-enrollment charters, such as KIPP Houston's schools.

18. "Charter Schools – Frequently Asked Questions." Texas Education Agency, n.d. Accessed April 20, 2013. www.tea.state. tx.us/index2.aspx?id=392.

19. "Revenues and Expenditures for Public Elementary and Secondary Education: School Year 2008–2009 (Fiscal Year 2009)." *National Center for Education Statistics.* Institute of Education Sciences, June 2011. Accessed April 20, 2013. http://nces.ed.gov/ pubs2011/2011329.pdf.

20. 2011 was the most recent year for which total student enrollment data was available. 5986 Students. PEIMS data from State of Texas. Texas Education Agency. *Snapshot 2011.* Accessed April 21, 2013. http://ritter.tea.state.tx.us/perfreport/ snapshot/2011/index.html.

21. Texas Education Agency Foundation School Program funding was $47,561,540 for year ended June 30, 2011. *Financial Statements and Independent Auditors' Report.* 2011 Audit Report. KIPP, Inc., October 27, 2011. Accessed April 21, 2013.

22. *School Finance 101: Funding of Texas Public Schools.* Rep. Texas Education Agency Office of School Finance, Jan. 2013. Accessed April 20, 2013. www.tea.state. tx.us/index2.aspx?id=7022&menu_id=645.

23. Murphy, John. Personal interview. April 17, 2013.

24. McGee, Josh B. "Houston School Finance Report." Laura and John Arnold Foundation, January 18, 2013. Accessed April 20, 2013. www.arnoldfoundation.org/resources/ houston-school-finance-report.

25. Mathews, Jay. "Growing Up Fast."

26. *Financial Statements and Independent Auditors' Report.* Audit Report. KIPP, Inc., October 16, 2012. Accessed April 21, 2013. http://kipphouston.org/sites/default/files/ file_attach/KHPS_Audit_Report_for_the_ Year_Ended_June_30_2012.pdf.

27. McGee, Josh B. "Houston School Finance Report." Laura and John Arnold Foundation, January 18, 2013. Accessed 20 Apr. 2013. www.arnoldfoundation.org/resources/ houston-school-finance-report.

28. Average of 715 teachers employed by KIPP Houston schools in 2012. *2011–12 AEIS Reports.* Rep. Texas Education Agency. Accessed April 21, 2013. http://ritter.tea. state.tx.us/perfreport/aeis/2012/.

29. Goedekke, Ken. Personal interview. April 18, 2013.

30. Ibid.

31. Ibid.

32. Ibid.

33. *2010–11 Academic Excellence Indicator System Campus Reports.* Rep. Texas Education

Agency. Accessed April 21, 2013. 2010–11 Academic Excellence Indicator System Campus Reports.

34. Goedekke, Ken. Personal interview. April 18, 2013.

35. Fimble, Chuck. Personal interview. March 29, 2013.

36. Ibid.

37. Ali, Sehba. Personal interview. March 29, 2013.

38. Internal document.

39. Frequently Asked Questions. *KIPP Public Charter Schools.* Accessed April 21, 2013. www.kipp.org/careers/applicant-faqs.

40. Internal document.

41. Personal interview. April 22, 2013.

42. Ibid.

43. *2011–12 AEIS Reports.* Rep. Texas Education Agency. Accessed April 21, 2013. http://ritter. tea.state.tx.us/perfreport/aeis/2012/.

44. Internal documents.

45. *2011–12 AEIS Reports.* Rep. Texas Education Agency. Accessed April 21, 2013. http://ritter. tea.state.tx.us/perfreport/aeis/2012/.

46. Internal documents.

47. Personal interview. April 21, 2013.

48. Ibid.

49. Fimble, Chuck. Personal interview. March 29, 2013.

50. Ibid.

51. Internal documents.

52. "SBOE State Board of Education." Texas Education Agency, April 4, 2013. Accessed April 22, 2013. www.tea.state.tx.us/index3. aspx?id=1156.

53. "19 TAC Chapter 113, Subchapter B." Texas Education Agency. Accessed April 22, 2013. http://ritter.tea.state.tx.us/rules/tac/ chapter113/ch113b.html.

54. "In the States." Common Core State Standards Initiative. Accessed April 22, 2013. www.corestandards.org/in-the-states.

55. Based on 8th grade reading in 2009. "Mapping State Proficiency Standards onto the NAEP Scales: Variation and Change in State Standards for Reading and Mathematics, 2005–2009." Institute of Education Sciences, 2009. Accessed April 22, 2013. http://nces.ed.gov/ nationsreportcard/pdf/studies/2011458. pdf.

56. Ali, Sehba. Personal interview. March 29, 2013.

57. "About BetterLesson." Accessed April 22, 2013. http://betterlesson.com/public/ about.

58. Christensen, Clayton M., Michael B. Horn, and Curtis W. Johnson. *Disrupting Class: How Disruptive Innovation Will Change the Way the World Learns.* New York: McGraw-Hill, 2008.

59. Schmidt, Eric. Personal interview. April 17, 2013.

60. Ibid.

61. Bradford, Matt. Telephone interview. March 27, 2013.

62. Ibid.

63. Ali, Sehba. Personal interview. March 29, 2013.

64. "Apollo 20 Program: A Strong Foundation for Success." Houston Independent School District, n.d. Accessed April 22, 2013. www.houstonisd.org/site/default. aspx?PageType=3.

65. "Study Shows Apollo 20 Academic Achievement Gains Match Top Charters." Houston Independent School District, October 6, 2011. Accessed April 22, 2013. www.houstonisd.org/site/default. aspx?PageType=3.

66. Fryer, Roland G., Jr. "The Impact of Apollo 20 on Student Achievement: Evidence from Year One." Rep. The Education Innovation Laboratory at Harvard University, n.d. Accessed April 30, 2013. www.houstonisd. org/site/handlers/filedownload.ashx?modu leinstanceid=95698&dataid=48186&FileNa me=ApolloResults.pdf.

67. "Donors Step up to Fund Apollo 20 School Turnaround Effort." Houston Independent School District, December 21, 2012. Accessed April 23, 2013. http:// blogs.houstonisd.org/news/2012/12/21/ donors-step-up-to-fund-apollo-20-school-turnaround-effort/.

68. "About YES" YES Prep Public Schools, n.d. Accessed April 22, 2013. http://yesprep.org/ AboutYES/topic/history/.

69. Phone interview. February 11, 2013

70. Ali, Sehba. Personal interview. March 29, 2013.

71. "Harmony Public Schools: About Us." Accessed April 22, 2013. www.harmonytx. org/AboutUs.aspx.

72. Radcliffe, Jennifer. "Harmony Charter Schools Beat Odds on Rise to the Top in Texas."*Houston Chronicle.* February 27, 2011. Accessed April 23, 2013. www.chron.com/ news/houston-texas/article/Harmony-charter-schools-beat-odds-on-rise-to-the-1585639.php.

73. "Course Descriptions." Harmony Public Schools, n.d. Accessed April 22, 2013. www. harmonytx.org/Portals/0/HPS-Course-Descriptions-2011-12.pdf.

74. "Frequently Asked Questions." *Harmony Science Academy.* Harmony Public Schools, n.d. Accessed Apr 22, 2013. www. hsagarland.org/?page=Category11.

75. *AEIS Reports.* Rep. Texas Education Agency, n.d. Accessed April 21, 2013. http://ritter.tea. state.tx.us/perfreport/aeis/2012/.

76. "The Promise of College Completion: KIPP's Early Successes and Challenges." KIPP Foundation, April 28, 2011. Accessed April 22, 2013. www.kipp.org/files/dmfile/ CollegeCompletionReport.pdf.

Krispy Kreme Doughnuts: Refilling the Hole in a Sweet Strategy

Arvind Chandran, Matt Lamoreux, Andrew Rice, Janice Seunsom

Texas A&M University

There is nothing quite like the melt-in-your-mouth experience of a fresh Krispy Kreme glazed doughnut dipped in a glass of cold milk. Roy Blount, Jr. of *New York Times Magazine* had it right when he said, "When Krispy Kremes are hot, they are to other doughnuts what angels are to people."[1] Impossibly sweet, addictive, and delicious, it can be hard to stop before devouring an entire dozen. As tempting as that may be, giving into instant gratification and gorging on a dozen of Krispy Kremes will only lead to overexpansion of the waistline and health problems down the road. Vitally important is moderation, which seems to be common sense for most people. However, the aggressive appetite for growth of their firm that Krispy Kreme's leaders displayed for a period of time also led to serious problems. Instead of aggressively seeking to increase sales revenues, Krispy Kreme likely would have been served better through actions oriented to achieving moderate and more manageable levels of growth over a period of time. Indeed, rapid growth that was too aggressive relative to competitive conditions as well as changes in the external environment resulted in a serious amount of overexpansion of the number of Krispy Kreme units. In turn, an excessive number of units resulted in significant challenges to the firm's efforts to operate profitably as the pathway to short- and long-term corporate success. Before describing the issues associated with rapid growth that led to difficulties, we first introduce Krispy Kreme as a firm and consider its initial almost meteoric success.

After the Internet bubble burst in the early part of the twenty-first century, many investors sought more tangible investments and very few stocks at the time seemed as promising as Krispy Kreme. Named "America's Hottest Brand" by *Fortune Magazine* in 2003,[2]

Krispy Kreme was growing rapidly following its decision in the late 90s to expand from its regional footprint in the Southeast United States. By late 2003, shares were trading at nearly $50, a substantial increase from their IPO value of $9 just three years prior.[3] The meteoric rise of Krispy Kreme in the early 2000s was followed shortly thereafter by its steep fall from grace. The trouble began with a series of accounting missteps and shortcomings within the corporate governance structure. When these troubles were combined with market saturation from overexpansion, changing trends in American diets, and misaligned incentives between franchisees and corporate headquarters, the company found itself on the brink of bankruptcy in 2005.[4]

However, Krispy Kreme is now showing signs of a possible resurgence. Implementation of "an emergency turnaround strategy" found the firm closing unprofitable stores, contributing to its ability to avoid filing for bankruptcy in the process of doing so. The company suffered huge losses from 2005 to 2008, but since then, stable leadership has emerged to implement initiatives that focus on improving operational effectiveness by streamlining retail operations and expanding and diversifying the firm's product lines.[5] These initiatives have yielded positive results, and the firm has been able to reduce its substantial debt as a foundation for continuously improving its performance. For the first time since 2005, the company experienced two consecutive years of profitability (2011 and 2012) and intended to open over 100 new stores in 2013.[6] This revamped plan shows that the firm has learned from the over-indulgent mistakes of its past and, potentially, that Krispy Kreme is poised to reclaim its standing as the sweetest doughnut company around.

Early History 1937-1994: The Birth and Growth of the "Original Glaze"

In 1933, a farmer in Paducah, Kentucky purchased a hand-written recipe from a New Orleans-born French pastry chef named Joe LeBeau. The recipe for yeast-raised doughnuts, believed to contain vanilla and potato flour, would become the foundation of the Krispy Kreme brand.[7] The farmer hired his nephew, Vernon Rudolph, to work as a door-to-door doughnut salesman in the fledgling business. After four years, Rudolph left his uncle's business seeking to make it on his own. He settled in the North Carolina town of Winston-Salem, and on July 13, 1937, opened a wholesale business selling doughnuts to local grocery stores.[8] Residents walking by the factory could not resist the intoxicating aroma of the doughnut making and soon began to demand hot, fresh doughnuts.[9] So, Rudolph "cut a hole in the factory wall and sold 'em out on to the street," and Krispy Kreme made its first foray into the world of retail.[10]

In the late 1940s, Krispy Kreme's expansion resulted in the firm becoming a regional chain. To ensure consistency, quality, and to safeguard the secret recipe, a central plant in Winston-Salem produced the doughnut mix before shipping it off to be cooked at the stores.[11] Within twenty years, there were thirty Krispy Kreme shops—a combination of company-owned and franchises—located throughout the Southeast. By the time of Vernon Rudolph's death in 1973, the thirty-six year old company had grown to ninety-four company stores and twenty-five franchises.[12]

Unfortunately, Rudolph did not adequately plan for his estate prior to his death, and Krispy Kreme had to be sold. Beatrice Foods, a highly diversified conglomerate based in Chicago, purchased Krispy Kreme in 1976 and changed the firm's strategic direction.[13] Former CEO, Scott Livengood, described the relationship between Krispy Kreme and Beatrice as a "horrible marriage" and said:

Beatrice didn't care so much if the stores made money, as long as we sold doughnuts to supermarkets. They didn't want to invest in stores or grow the company, they just wanted cash. Then they changed the logo to a tacky 70s look. And they actually messed with the doughnut formula![14]

The horrible marriage quickly ended in divorce when, in 1982, a group of 22 franchisees repurchased Krispy Kreme in a leveraged buyout. With the infusion of new leadership who cared deeply about the brand, the firm restored many of the values and strategies that had enabled its success in the firm's earlier years.

The most important element of Krispy Kreme's resurgence was a renewed focus on retail operations and the hot doughnut experience.[15] During the late 80s, Krispy Kreme implemented two innovative marketing activities that helped re-launch the brand into prominence. First, it created the concept of "Doughnut Theater.®" This concept exposed the doughnut-making equipment to customers so they could watch the doughnut production process. To this day, visitors can observe doughnuts cook for exactly 115 seconds in 365-degree vegetable shortening before travelling along the conveyor to pass through a glaze waterfall before curving around the counter where the salesperson plucks the hot, fresh doughnuts right off the line and puts them into customers' hands.[16] The second marketing innovation was the installation in every retail branch of the iconic "Hot Doughnuts Now" sign. Whenever hot doughnuts come fresh off the line, the neon sign turns on, letting customers know to come into the store to receive a free glazed doughnut, dependent upon the individual franchise's policy. The combination of these two clever marketing activities and the infusion of enthusiastic new owners set the stage for future success.

Recent History: Rapid Expansion, Brink of Collapse, and Resurgence

In 1995, Krispy Kreme moved into a new corporate headquarters, reshuffled its management team, and prepared to expand nationwide. To leverage the planned growth, the firm's leaders decided that the company should rely heavily on franchising instead of opening company-owned stores as a means of growing.[17] This choice would allow Krispy Kreme to receive a steady income flow from royalty fees, expand its customer base for mix and equipment via franchisees, and inflate its brand recognition. Launches in New York, Los Angeles, Boston, and Chicago were huge successes with devoted customers lining up around the block for a hot doughnut. By the end of 1999, the company's portfolio included 144 shops in 27 states, and revenues had climbed to $220 million – up 40 percent from just two years earlier.[18]

Still, the success of the initial nationwide expansion was accompanied by some major growing pains. When the original 21 franchisees purchased the company from Beatrice Foods in 1982, a governance-related decision was made indicating that financial decisions needed unanimous approval instead of a plurality. By the late 90s, "because of inheritances and gifting of stock, that group of 21 had mushroomed to 183 shareholders, each with veto power."[19] As then-CEO Scott Livengood put it,

"It was an absolute nightmare," and the company needed to restructure and go public.[20]

Krispy Kreme made its IPO in April 2000 with a split-adjusted price of $9.[25] Investors flocked to the company, and by the close of 2003, the stock was selling at a price just a bit over $49 per share. *Fortune Magazine* ran a cover story calling Krispy Kreme the "Hottest Brand in America." By the close of the 2003 fiscal year, the company had expanded to 433 stores, had reached $700 million in revenues, and had earned $88 million in operating profit.[21] This amounted to a four-year store growth of over 200 percent and revenue growth of about 220 percent. The company seemed to have the Midas touch, but the world was about to see the hole in Krispy Kreme's doughnut strategy.

As it turned out, the rapid expansion of the previous five years had not been carefully or effectively planned. The exponential growth in store locations yielded a huge revenue growth overall, but same-store sales were flat. As new franchises saturated the market and the novelty value of the firm's products faded, it became obvious that the early success of many stores was not sustainable.[22] Many of the once-profitable stores began to flounder and, in May 2004, Krispy Kreme experienced its first unprofitable quarter as a public company. Company leadership blamed the flat sales on low-carbohydrate diets, but it was clear to many that the Atkins Diet was not the only concern.[23]

The SEC launched investigations of improper buybacks of certain franchises, alleging that corporate leadership had made sweetheart deals to repurchase failing franchises. Additionally, franchisees filed suit alleging "channel stuffing" and accusing the corporate office of double shipping the usual amount of product at the end of quarters so the firm could achieve its revenue estimates.[24] Franchisees also alleged that corporate leadership was more concerned with maximizing overall revenue than with the well-being or success of the individual stores. A lawsuit filed by the Milberg Weiss law firm summed up many franchisee concerns, saying:

Rather than cultivate a steady customer based [sic], the Company instead attempted to capitalize on Krispy Kreme's "fad appeal" and adopted a business model and strategy for increasing sales that was predicated on the perpetual addition of new stores and the hyping of the Company's entry into new markets.[25]

As a result of these problems, long-time CEO Scott Livengood stepped down in 2004 and was replaced by turnaround specialist Stephen Cooper—who kept his other job as interim CEO of Enron—to end the downward spiral.[26] Cooper's first order of business was to secure over $225 million of financing to stave off potential bankruptcy and install capable financial managers. In the three years prior, Krispy Kreme had seen three different CFOs come and go, two of which had no experience as CFOs of large companies.[27] After putting the wheels to recovery in motion, Cooper handed the reins to Daryl Brewster, a former vice president at Kraft, to continue implementing the turnaround strategy he had designed.

Exhibit 1 U.S. Krispy Kreme Location Count

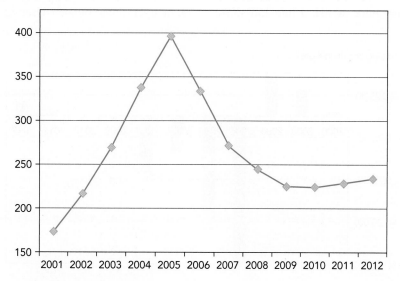

Source: Data for chart compiled from applicable Krispy Kreme 10-K filings.

In the main, the turnaround strategy called for Krispy Kreme to cut costs to a sustainable level as a path to prevent the firm's bankruptcy. One way cost cutting was undertaken is demonstrated by the decision to close over 240 stores as the company retrenched to its stronghold in the Southeast. These closings resulted in a cost to the firm of almost $300 million in impairment charges and lease termination costs.[28] See Exhibit 1 for a depiction in changes to the number of Krispy Kreme stores between the years 2001 and 2012.

As mentioned, another issue challenging Krispy Kreme in efforts to be successful was a change in the market with the rise of the health-conscious American consumer. In response to this development, Krispy Kreme introduced a variety of healthier doughnuts. A whole-wheat doughnut was introduced, and the entire product line was reformulated to eliminate trans-fats.[29]

Meanwhile, as domestic business plummeted, international business shouldered the load, adding over 400 franchises in twenty countries from 2004 through 2009, geographically diversifying the firm in the process.[30] In 2012, 66 percent of retail stores were located outside the United States[31] with management stating it would like to establish an international presence of 900 stores by the end of 2017.[32]

However, the firm as a whole continued to struggle under Brewster's leadership. When the stock price bottomed out at less than $4 a share in January 2008 due to the restructuring costs, Brewster was ousted in favor of James Morgan, the Chairman of the Board, who had over 25 years of management experience, including a stint as CEO of Wachovia Securities. Under Morgan's leadership, the firm implemented a number of new ideas, including a smaller factory store model, a hub-and-spoke

distribution system, increased coffee offerings, and an enhanced menu that included both healthier options and other product lines such as ice cream. These actions taken as a result of these ideas have positively affected the firm's performance; in fact, 2010-2011 marked the first consecutive profitable years since the firm reached its peak in 2004. Morgan noted that the recent success hinged upon the new actions the firm was taking, saying:

We are certainly pleased with these results, [but] more importantly, we are demonstrating the ability to execute on a strategic plan we believe will allow us to substantially increase revenue, improve margins, and expand the Krispy Kreme system over coming years.[33]

As revenue continued increasing at the end of 2012, Krispy Kreme looked to open as many as 100 new stores in the near term between domestic and international operations. However, Krispy Kreme seems to have learned its lesson from overexpansion. Morgan promised that going forward "expansion will come at a controlled rate. We have to crawl before we walk, and we may never try to run again."[34] See Exhibit 2 for a presentation of Krispy Kreme's net income over time.

Revenue Generation, Product Lines, and the Franchising Structure

Krispy Kreme generates revenue through four main business segments: Company Stores, Domestic Franchises, International Franchises, and the KK Supply Chain.[35] The company stores and domestic franchises operate in a similar fashion—generating revenues through retail operations and wholesaling to grocery stores,

Exhibit 2 Krispy Kreme Net Income (in millions)

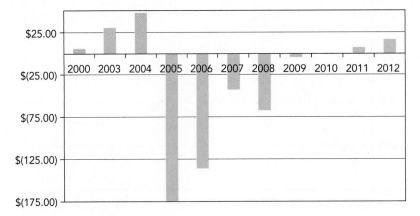

Source: Data for chart compiled from applicable Krispy Kreme 10-K filings.

convenience stores, and other large food service avenues. Over half of domestic sales occur through wholesaling channels. On the other hand, international franchises rely mainly on retail operations and do not generate significant revenues from wholesale activities.[36]

All three retail operations—company stores, domestic franchises, and international franchises—earn the majority of revenue through the sale of doughnuts. In fact, doughnut sales comprise over 88 percent of all retail sales while the remainder comes from selling beverage and complementary items.[37] Each Krispy Kreme branch offers a wide variety of doughnuts, including standard and seasonal varieties. The company realizes it is known as a specialty "sweet treat" producer; therefore, it does not offer bagels and breakfast sandwiches as other competitors have done.[38]

Krispy Kreme utilizes a variety of unique features to successfully sell a premium doughnut that devoted and loyal customers are willing to seek out and buy. While on the whole there is not a great deal of differentiation throughout the industry, Krispy Kreme is the exception. Unlike the cake-style doughnuts sold by most competitors, Krispy Kreme produces fluffy, yeast-based doughnuts that stand apart from the competition. The unique taste of a Krispy Kreme doughnut comes from a secret recipe that has remained within the company throughout its history. Additionally, "Doughnut Theater®" adds tremendous value to the consumer experience. It "provides customers with an entertainment experience and reinforces the commitment to quality and freshness by allowing them to see the doughnuts being made."[39]

As is the case with its competitors, Krispy Kreme has made a concerted effort as of late to expand revenues through coffee sales, but the dominant element of the Krispy Kreme business model continues to be doughnut sales. While Dunkin' Donuts generates approximately 60 percent of sales revenue from coffee and other beverages,[40] Krispy Kreme continues to lag far behind in that regard with only 4 percent of its sales coming from coffee.[41] Since the firm underwent national expansion, it has launched three different brands of coffee, but none has truly resonated with customers, preventing Krispy Kreme from becoming a significant competitor in the highly competitive coffee market. However, Krispy Kreme recently announced a re-emphasis on improving coffee sales. While, as noted, coffee only accounts for 4 percent of sales at the current time, Morgan recently told CNBC commentators that he wants to double that within the next two years.[42] This effort began with the launch of three new signature roasts in 2011, and has been bolstered by the introduction of a variety of

premium espresso-based drinks in 2012.[43] Morgan hopes to gain a better foothold in the competitive coffee market by first promoting Krispy Kreme's coffee to existing customers. Morgan says, "We've got to get them thinking coffee when they walk in our shops…right now we have a promotion where any size coffee is only 99 cents with the purchase of a dozen doughnuts."[44]

Krispy Kreme is working to improve current offerings by emphasizing products with a longer shelf life to reduce spoilage and decrease delivery costs. This is especially relevant to the wholesale sector, which accounted for over half of the revenues from domestic store locations in the 2012 fiscal year.[45] Krispy Kreme continues to be innovative with its other product selections. In this regard, the firm continuously experiments with new doughnut varieties including a wide array of crullers, doughnuts with fruit infused "kreme" filling, and seasonal/holiday-inspired doughnuts including doughnuts shaped like Christmas trees, Easter eggs, or footballs. It has experimented with ice cream and doughnut sundaes in some locations, lines of "chillers" (a version of a smoothie), and even doughnut milkshakes. But through it all, it has never lost contact with its identity as a doughnut company. In this way, it has always straddled the line between exploitation of its core product and a willingness to explore other products and areas of growth.

An interesting development that facilitated Krispy Kreme's international success was its focus on smaller-store footprints with a hub-and-spoke distribution model—a model it has recently started implementing in the domestic market. Historically, Krispy Kreme's domestic stores consisted of one type: the factory store. These stores' large footprints limit location options and are expensive to operate.[46] Utilizing a hub-and-spoke distribution system allows for two types of stores— factory stores and satellite shops. Today, factory stores serve as the hub and continue to function as they have in the past with full production capabilities that supply doughnuts for both retail and wholesale. Satellite shops, located in the same general vicinity of a factory store, serve as the spokes. Satellite shops do not make any doughnuts; instead, the factory store delivers fully cooked but unglazed doughnuts to its satellite locations. The unglazed doughnuts then undergo an abbreviated form of Doughnut Theater® by simply passing under the glaze waterfall. The new factory-satellite format allows Krispy Kreme to position smaller shops in more convenient locations (most are equipped with drive-thru windows for added convenience) and increase the utilization rates of the factory stores.[47]

Krispy Kreme's final business segment is the KK Supply Chain, which accounts for approximately 25 percent of the firm's revenues.[48] This segment generates revenue by selling the firm's doughnut mix and doughnut-making equipment to franchises. Other comparable firms use royalty payments as the foundation of the franchisor/franchisee relationship and allow firms to purchase supplies or ingredients at cost. However, this is not the case at Krispy Kreme. Its structure demands only a small royalty payment but requires that franchisees purchase doughnut mix and equipment at a mark-up with operating margins as high as 20 percent.[49] This structure led to a situation of misaligned incentives where maximizing overall corporate profits through increased KK supply chain revenue came at the expense of the individual franchisee. See Exhibit 3 for a presentation of sales accounted for by Krispy Kreme's four business segments.

Arenas in Which Krispy Kreme Competes

Krispy Kreme operates in two extremely competitive industries. It primarily competes in the Quick-Service Restaurant (QSR) segment of the restaurant industry. This segment is the industry's largest and has demonstrated steady growth over a long period of time.[50] Additionally, it competes on a wholesale level in the Baked Goods Production Industry. At present, both industries are experiencing relatively static growth. These industries are characterized by high fixed costs, low switching costs for customers, and relatively low product differentiation.

Both industries are extremely competitive and have a high concentration of competitive rivals. Dunkin' Donuts, Tim Hortons, Shipley's Do-Nuts, and countless smaller bakeries are Krispy Kreme's direct competitors in the QSR category. Despite having fourteen times as many stores as Krispy Kreme, Dunkin' Donuts is Krispy Kreme's closest competitor in sales (403.22M versus 628.2M, Krispy Kreme versus Dunkin' Donuts

Exhibit 3 Krispy Kreme Segment Revenue 2011

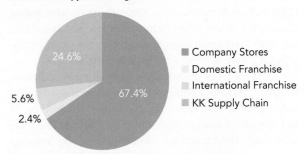

Source: Data for chart compiled from Krispy Kreme 2011 10-K filing.

respectively), product offerings, and worldwide presence (20 countries versus 30 countries). As shown in Exhibit 4, Krispy Kreme outpaces Dunkin' in many key metrics. The firm is able to generate higher ROA and ROE as compared to Dunkin' Donuts. Additionally, Krispy Kreme has a significantly lower leverage ratio as compared to Dunkin's extremely high 195 percent.

The firm also faces less direct competition from companies such as McDonald's, Starbucks, and coffee shops. The baked goods industry is equally competitive and populated by producers offering both fresh and pre-packaged goods. Pre-packaged goods with much longer shelf lives than Krispy Kreme include national brands such as Little Debbie, Hostess, and Sara Lee. Additionally, there are many freshly baked goods options provided by a myriad of local bakeries. Sales percentages for some firms are presented in Exhibit 5.

The threat of a new doughnut powerhouse emerging is not as worrisome as the problems individual Krispy Kreme stores face from mom-and-pop shop competitors. On a national scale, it would take an extremely large amount of capital to establish a network of stores and capture the economies of scale enjoyed by the QSR industry's largest firms. In addition, it would take significant investments of advertising dollars and time to develop the brand equity necessary to compete successfully on a national scale. In the wholesale market, distribution

Exhibit 4 Key Comparisons 2011

	Krispy Kreme	Dunkin' Donuts	Tim Hortons	Krispy Kreme (adj.)
Profit Margin	41.20%	5.50%	13.40%	7.50%
ROA	49.60%	1.10%	17.40%	9.10%
ROE	66.70%	4.60%	33.20%	12.20%
Debt/Equity	10.20%	195.50%	38.80%	10.20%

Sources: Data for table compiled from 2011 Annual Reports of Krispy Kreme, Dunkin' Donuts, and Tim Hortons.

Exhibit 5 Worldwide Market Share[†]

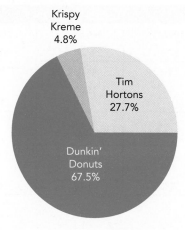

Krispy Kreme 4.8%

Tim Hortons 27.7%

Dunkin' Donuts 67.5%

[†]Data excludes market share from sources other than Krispy Kreme, Dunkin' Donuts, and Tim Hortons.

Source: Company Snapshot. *Dunkin' Donuts Official Website.* Accessed 3 Apr 2012. http://www.dunkindonuts.com/content/dunkindonuts/en/company.html; Krispy Kreme Doughnuts, Inc. 2012 Annual Report; About Us: Corporate Profile. *Tim Hortons Official Website.* Accessed 3 Apr 2012. http://www.timhortons.com/ca/en/about/profile.html

channels are extremely saturated and existing firms are well entrenched. Nevertheless, the capital requirements for an individual firm on a local business level are not high, and new entrants are a legitimate threat to the viability of individual Krispy Kreme stores.

In addition to the threat of a mom-and-pop shop becoming a sentimental favorite, there are many alternatives to the core doughnut product, which CEO James Morgan calls "an affordable indulgence."[51] Cakes, biscuits, bagels, muffins, breakfast sandwiches, or any other breakfast food option could replace the demand for doughnuts. One of the largest concerns in the overall competitive environment is the changing demands of consumers. As consumers become increasingly health conscious, the doughnut industry becomes more vulnerable to the threat of substitution, especially considering that each original glazed Krispy Kreme doughnut has 200 calories and 12 grams of fat.[52]

As for its customers, Krispy Kreme doughnuts appeal to individuals in all shapes and sizes, rendering a large but fragmented fan base. In fact, the managing editor of *Fortune*, Andy Serwer, claims that Krispy Kremes,

… are loved equally by 5-year-olds and 75-year-olds. By whites, blacks, Asians, and Hispanics. By New Englanders and Southerners. By Californians and New Yorkers. (Never mind by junkies and cops.) I say only three types of people claim they don't like Krispy Kremes: nutritionists (your basic glazed has 200 calories and 12 grams of fat), Dunkin'

Donuts franchisees, and compulsive liars. Fortunately for the company, that's not a large group.[53]

Because they represent such a large portion of Krispy Kreme's domestic business, the only buyers with the power to shake things up are firms in the wholesale sales channel. But even there, Krispy Kreme maintains wholesale contracts with a wide variety of grocery stores, convenience stores, and other large accounts—including Walmart, Kroger, and Sheetz—that shield it against being sunk by the withdrawal of any single large buyer.

Finally, suppliers hold little sway for the firm. Krispy Kreme's vertically integrated structure, the wide availability of necessary raw materials, the unlikelihood of suppliers entering the doughnut business, and low switching costs between vendors render the power of suppliers fairly moot.

Financial Results: Return to Profitability

Krispy Kreme has achieved two years of profitability after years of being in the hole for six. As discussed, this downturn led to the divestiture of many of the firm's domestic retail locations. Maintenance of consistent gross profit margins and modest revenue growth of 4.5 and 11.4 percent in 2009 and 2010, respectively, have allowed Krispy Kreme to contribute to its bottom line and return to profitability. In fact, Krispy Kreme showed net income of $166 million and a 41 percent profit margin in fiscal year ending January 2012. However, the majority of this increase stems from the $6.2 million sale of Krispy Kreme Mexico (30 percent interest) and the reversal of a deferred tax asset of $139.6 million, with an offsetting amount to the provision for income taxes.[54] (See Exhibit 6.)

It should also be noted that management appears to have initiated an aggressive debt retirement campaign and has shown a pattern of debt repayment. Much of this debt was prepaid stemming from the proceeds of sales of assets and discretionary use of cash.[55] All told, Krispy Kreme reduced its debt from $145 million in fiscal year 2005 to a much more manageable level of $27 million in 2011.

As noted above, Krispy Kreme was able to take advantage of a deferred tax asset; therefore, the metrics have been adjusted to remove this tax benefit. Despite this pro forma adjustment, Krispy Kreme appears to be in a healthy state in comparison to its primary competitors.

Exhibit 6 Krispy Kreme Key Figures

in millions	2011		2010		2009	
Revenue	403.22	100%	361.96	100%	346.52	100%
Cost of Revenue	346.43	86%	313.48	87%	297.86	86%
Gross Profit	56.79	14%	48.48	13%	48.66	14%
Other Operating Expense	31.22	8%	33.33	9%	36.89	11%
Operating Income	25.57	6%	15.15	4%	11.77	3%
Income Before Tax	30.36	8%	8.86	2%	0.42	0%
Net Income	166.27	41%	7.6	2%	−0.16	0%

Source: Data for table compiled from applicable Krispy Kreme 10-K filings.

Marketing

Interestingly, the manner in which Krispy Kreme doughnuts are consumed differs from how its competitors' doughnuts are consumed. The majority of Krispy Kreme doughnuts are purchased by an individual to be shared with friends, family, co-workers, or classmates. Research conducted by the company has shown that approximately 70 percent of doughnuts purchased at company-owned stores and franchises are for sharing occasions.[56] It should not be surprising then that over 55 percent of transactions are for a dozen or more doughnuts, signaling a high transaction value per customer.[57]

Knowing that so many Krispy Kreme's doughnuts are often purchased for the purpose of sharing the "eating" experienced with others has shaped Krispy Kreme's overall marketing approach: word-of-mouth. Despite the absence of a traditional advertising budget, Krispy Kreme enjoys over 65 percent brand recognition.[58] Social media has magnified that effect, and Krispy Kreme's ability to leverage this new form of media has been extremely important to the company's resurgence. With over 4.2 million Facebook fans, the company can reach its customers much faster and more efficiently than ever before in its history.[59] The company has even introduced its own smartphone app—"Hot Light"—that alerts customers when a Krispy Kreme location has hot doughnuts coming off the line and gives driving directions from the user's current location.[60]

The final unique aspects of Krispy Kreme lie in its philanthropic commitment to the community and ability to leverage the power of free. Krispy Kreme offers a wide array of fundraising opportunities through the sale of doughnuts and requires its franchisees to sponsor local charitable events. These efforts help build relationships within individual communities and contributed an estimated $30 million dollars to local charities during the 2012 fiscal year.[61] Furthermore, Krispy Kreme has a long-standing company tradition of leveraging the power of free, such as giving away a free hot doughnut. This drives store traffic and makes it difficult for many customers to resist purchasing at least an entire dozen as well. Additionally, whenever a new store location opens, instead of spending money on advertising, it sends dozens of free doughnuts to local television stations, radio stations, and newspapers, invariably garnering free publicity. A prime example of this tactic occurred when the company opened its first store in New York City. It sent dozens upon dozens of doughnuts to the Today Show and gained immense amounts of national publicity, including a ringing endorsement from Al Roker.[62]

Leadership

The importance of strong leadership cannot be overemphasized. A firm's ability to achieve an advantage and earn above-average returns is compromised when leaders fail to respond appropriately and quickly to changes in the complex global environment. Krispy Kreme has a strong set of leaders with its CEO, James Morgan, at its center.

James H. Morgan, Chairman—Chief Executive Officer

James Morgan began his career at Krispy Kreme as the Vice Chairman of the Board in 2004. In 2005, he was appointed Chairman of the Board and, after years of losing money, was named CEO. He has assumed duality, vesting in both CEO and Chairman of the Board positions. Morgan provides deep institutional knowledge and perspective regarding Krispy Kreme's strengths, challenges, and opportunities. He also brings extensive public company and financial services industry experience to the table. He has redirected the company's focus to small retail shops, a more diversified menu, and increasingly collaborative relationships with Krispy Kreme's franchisees. Upon Kenneth May's announcement that he was leaving the company for personal reasons in April 2012, Morgan also assumed the interim role of Chief Operating Officer (COO).

Douglas R. Muir—Executive Vice President and Chief Financial Officer (CFO)

After the quick turnover of three different CFOs between 2000 and 2004, it was crucial for the company to find a reliable and experienced CFO. Muir started with the company as a consultant in 2004 and was named Krispy Kreme's Chief Accounting Officer in June 2005. Prior to his career at Krispy Kreme, he held various senior financial management positions, including Audit Partner at Price Waterhouse Coopers and Executive VP and CFO at Oakwood Homes Corporation. He is also a certified public accountant. Muir became Krispy Kreme's Executive VP and CFO in June 2007.

G. Dwayne Chambers—Senior Vice President and Chief Marketing Officer

Chambers was appointed the Senior VP and Chief Marketing Officer of Krispy Kreme in September 2010.[63] In his own words, "As the Chief Marketing Officer, I am honored to oversee all aspects of branding, marketing, advertising, and communications for one of the greatest brands on the planet."[64] Taking the intangible aspects of Krispy Kreme into consideration, Chambers is primarily focusing on spending less on "traditional advertising and marketing" and instead focusing on social media to spread the word.[65] This approach also fits perfectly with the company's global expansion plans. Through Chambers' efforts, Krispy Kreme maintains a very active Twitter account and can be found on popular social networking sites including Facebook (with over 4.2 million "likes").

The Board

Krispy Kreme's board consists of nine members with each member bringing diverse and extensive backgrounds. Krispy Kreme's board includes former finance executives, former restaurateurs, and even a former Chief Accountant of the SEC. Most members are independent, have relevant industry experience, and serve on no more than two other boards. Qualifications for board members are individuals "who have achieved prominence in their respective fields and who have experience at a strategy/policy setting level or who have high-level managerial experience in a relatively complex organization."[66] Another key characteristic of the board is that while many firms do not form succession plans until their companies are in dire straits, part of Krispy Kreme's governance policies mandates an annual review of succession plans for the CEO and other key executives.

Rising to the Challenges

Health Concerns

The wild popularity of the low-carbohydrate Atkins diet that began in 2003 simply marked the beginning of healthier living in America. The decline in sales of the beloved Krispy Kreme doughnut was blamed on the success of the Atkins diet and other diets. Former CEO Scott Livengood stated, "It's impossible to predict if low-carb is a passing fad or will have a lasting impact."[67] Today it is clear that it was *not* a passing fad but, in fact, a paradigm shift being made by Americans toward healthier living despite that— or perhaps because—the United States is the most obese country in the world with 34 percent of the adult population classified as such.[68] Whatever the impetus, the "fad" of carb-counting diets and tracking the number of miles walked, run, or biked is now fully integrated into the lifestyles of many adults. This presents a significant challenge to Krispy Kreme given that its core products have a great deal of sugar, carbohydrates, and fat.

Today, there is a huge demand for all-natural, organic, gluten-free, low-cal, grass-fed, free-range, fresh water, locally grown food options. Clearly, Krispy Kreme does not fulfill any of these demands. Interestingly, despite this trend towards healthy options, by publicizing the quality of its coffee and offering a diverse menu of breakfast items in addition to doughnuts, Dunkin' Donuts' sales continue to increase. In 2009, Dunkin' Donuts stated, "We are paying attention to consumers' increased interest in low-carb foods."[69]

In its attempt to move away from the image of being extremely unhealthy, to date, Krispy Kreme has responded to this issue in only a limited manner. First, it has begun to offer alternative menu items to cater to the more health-conscious consumers. For instance, in addition to doughnuts, Krispy Kreme locations in Philadelphia now offer yogurt, oatmeal, soy milk, and Naked brand juices.[i,70] Other locations have begun selling mini-doughnuts. These small, bite-sized doughnuts cater to people who may be

---

[i] Juices stripped of artificial flavors, sugar, and preservatives.

budget conscious or who may appreciate help with portion control.[71] At this point, it is unclear how overall sales have been affected, but simply implementing these changes signals that Krispy Kreme is trying to overcome the stigma of offering an unhealthy product in a health-conscious world.

Restoring Stakeholder Trust in the Top Management Team

Overexpansion, accounting inaccuracies, disregard for franchisees, and issues with corporate governance left a bitter taste in the mouths of investors that the company has not been able to fully shake. While the leaders primarily responsible for Krispy Kreme's problems have moved on, high turnover and the issue of duality have made restoring confidence a continuing challenge for the firm.

Accounting problems surfaced in 2003 when Krispy Kreme began to reacquire failing franchises. Instead of recording the cost as an expense, Krispy Kreme recorded it as intangible assets under the name "reacquired franchise rights."[72] These improperly recorded expenses falsely inflated the company's value. The SEC launched an investigation in 2004 that forced the company to restate its financials from 2002 through 2004. Turnover and lack of experience were the likely culprits for these issues; between 2000 and 2004, the company employed three different CFOs, two with no prior experience as a CFO.[73] Ric Marshall, chief analyst at The Corporate Library, a governance watchdog, said the high CFO turnover rate raised red flags about the company's financial state.[74] Finally, in 2005, Douglas Muir was installed as the new Chief Accounting Officer (CAO) and was subsequently appointed as the firm's CFO in 2007. Through his work, Muir brought stability to the company's financial department, including a successful settlement to the 2009 SEC investigation.[75]

As if these accounting "mistakes" were not enough, Krispy Kreme had problems with lack of disclosure and insufficient corporate governance. During its first few years as a public company, many board members were holdovers from the firm's days as a private company. Some of these members were franchise owners.[76] This was a problem because it was alleged that the firm might have paid inflated prices for some of the franchises it bought back. These franchises were owned in part by a former Krispy Kreme board member and chairman as well as in part by another longtime director.[77] When pressed by analysts and asked why it paid such a high price for these acquisitions, the company never gave a concrete response and its lack of disclosure led to unfavorable speculation.[78]

Another sign of potential weak and/or ineffective governance was when former CEO Scott Livengood was given a hefty compensation package that was 20 percent higher than the median for similar-sized companies. After Livengood retired, the board also granted him a six-month consulting position that paid $275,000. According to Ric Marshall (as noted above, from the Corporate Library), this type of excessive compensation indicates that the board was not sufficiently independent. With most of the power bestowed upon the CEO, no one dared to question the aggressive accounting during the franchise buybacks, much less the CEO's compensation package. As Marshall summed up, "It was a classic governance failure."[79]

Fortunately, James Morgan's ascension to CEO in 2008 has provided stability and sound leadership for Krispy Kreme. Prior to his arrival, the firm had three different CEOs in less than three years. Morgan has overseen two consecutive years of profitability for the first time since 2004, and the firm has consistently reduced its considerable debt throughout his tenure.[80] However, because of the power he holds within the company, there are still plenty of reasons for investors to be concerned. Since 2008, Morgan has served dual roles as both the CEO and Chairman of the Board, and his influence was recently expanded to include the role of President. Due to the fact that Morgan has significant influence in both a management and an advisory role, effective monitoring by the firm's board of directors is required to ensure an alignment between an agent's and the principals' interests.

Overexpansion

One of the most significant challenges growing companies must overcome is increasing their size too quickly. At least for a period of time, Krispy Kreme failed to successfully manage this challenge. After going public in 2000, the company felt enormous pressure to sustain its growth. It decided that adding more locations would increase sales, but this move quickly oversaturated the market. J.P. Morgan analyst John Ivankoe stated that Krispy Kreme's "returns declined as [the] incremental appeal of each new retail store fell upon market penetration."[81] Increasing the number of store locations was not the only issue. On the wholesale front, the number of grocery stores, gas stations, and kiosks carrying its product grew exponentially and within a short amount of time, the company became ubiquitous.[82] In addition, while Krispy Kreme's "Doughnut Theater®" and neon "Hot Doughnuts Now" signs provided novel advantages, these features were absent at its offsite wholesale locations. The focus on the hot doughnut experience that reeled in drooling customers was forgotten and the novelty of a warm Krispy Kreme doughnut was lost.

Since James Morgan accepted the position as CEO in 2008, the company has acted aggressively to restructure the organization and the results have been positive. However, overexpansion issues have begun to occur on the international level. After teetering on the brink of bankruptcy and closing a number of stores in Australia, CEO and Director of Krispy Kreme Australia stated in December 2010:

The remaining retail outlets all have strong sales and customer support, and the company can now continue trading without underperforming stores adversely affecting the business... The process has demonstrated the strength of the Krispy Kreme brand and now that this period of restructuring is behind us, we will be focused on the ongoing development of the Krispy Kreme brand in Australia.[83]

Given that Krispy Kreme is on a promising path to recovery, a vital issue the company faces domestically and internationally is how to avoid its past mistakes of overexpansion. Krispy Kreme must carefully examine each site on an individual basis to ensure *every* site—both new and old—can be profitable.

Franchisor/Franchisee Relationships

Ironically, Krispy Kreme's revenues started declining when the firm began concentrating on growing revenues and profits at the parent-company level. The overemphasis on corporate profits caused many of its franchised outlets to struggle. When the company decided to expand nationwide in 1995, it made the decision to do so primarily through franchising instead of opening company-owned stores.[84] This allowed Krispy Kreme to more easily fund its ambitious growth plans while minimizing risk to the company.

The company's overexpansion was created in part by misaligned incentives between the franchisor and franchisees. A goal conflict always exists within franchisor/franchisee relationships: franchisors try to maximize sales made to franchisees while franchisees try to minimize expenses. Most franchisors maximize revenue from franchisees through royalty payments. For example, Dunkin' Donuts' CFO Kate Lavelle stated, "We have a strong royalty stream that is based solely on store sales... the franchisor is more likely to succeed by building profitable franchisees that can make royalty payments."[85] Krispy Kreme, on the other hand, not only collects franchise fees and royalty payments, but also requires that its franchisees buy doughnut-making equipment and its proprietary doughnut mix from headquarters at marked-up prices. Because the company was earning profits from its sales of raw ingredients and equipment, it was inclined to increase the number of stores (and thus, new customers for equipment and mix) without regard for the well-being of existing franchisees. Put simply, it got greedy, and its franchisor/franchisee relationships suffered as a result.

Today, the problems of misaligned incentives and unsupported franchisor/franchisee relations are still major concerns that Krispy Kreme is taking steps to address. In the company's latest 10-K report, it stated, "In fiscal 2013, we intend to add a Vice President of Franchise Development, a new role designed to lead our U.S. expansion efforts."[86] This statement indicates that the company recognizes its relationships with its franchisees are crucial to the company's growth and sustainable success. The 10-K also states that it is "committed to devoting additional resources and providing an even higher level of support to both our domestic and international franchisees."[87] Some of these resources include new and refined management tools, training manuals, and increased staffing. The company is sending a clear message that it is making an investment in its human capital, an asset that some argue is the most important a firm can have.

Conclusion

After posting huge losses from 2005-2008, Krispy Kreme began to stabilize under the leadership of James Morgan and posted only moderate losses in the 2009 and 2010 fiscal years. In 2011 and 2012, the champions of the Krispy Kreme brand persevered and were rewarded with profitability. Much of the turnaround can be attributed to how the leaders of this company recognized and responded to the mistakes made along the way.

NOTES

1. Foderaro, L. (25 Apr 1997). The Fans Face Off In New York's Great Doughnut Debate. *New York Times.* http://www.nytimes.com/1997/04/25/nyregion/the-fans-face-off-in-new-york-s-great-doughnut-debate.html?pagewanted=all&src=pm

2. Serwer, A. (7 Jul 2003). The Hole Story How Krispy Kreme became the hottest brand in America. *Fortune* via *CNN Money.* http://money.cnn.com/magazines/fortune/fortune_archive/2003/07/07/345535/index.htm

3. O'Sullivan, K. (1 Jun 2005). Kremed! The rise and fall of Krispy Kreme is a cautionary tale of ambition, greed, and inexperience. *CFO Magazine.* http://www.cfo.com/article.cfm/4007436.

4. Ibid.

5. Hoyland, C. (11 May 2009). Krispy Kreme CEO Confident in Brand Strategy. http://www.qsrweb.com/article/99038/Krispy-Kreme-CEO-confident-in-brand-strategy

6. McHugh, M. (26 Mar 2012). All's Forgiven: Krispy Kreme, Back from the Brink, Charms Investors. *YCharts*. http://ycharts.com/analysis/story/alls_forgiven_krispy_kreme_back_from_the_brink_charms_investors.

7. Krispy Kreme. International Directory of Company Histories, Vol. 61. St. James Press, 2004. http://www.fundinguniverse.com/company-histories/Krispy-Kreme-Doughnuts-Inc-company-History.html

8. Serwer, A. (7 Jul 2003). *op cit.*

9. *Ibid.*

10. *Ibid.*

11. Krispy Kreme. International Directory of Company Histories, Vol. 61. *op cit.*

12. *Ibid.*

13. Serwer, A. (7 Jul 2003). *op cit.*

14. *Ibid.*

15. Krispy Kreme Doughnuts Financial Information. 2011 Annual Report. *Krispy Kreme Official Website*. Accessed 3 Apr 2012. http://investor.krispykreme.com/phoenix.zhtml?c=120929&p=irol-reportsannual

16. Serwer, A. (7 Jul 2003). *op cit.*

17. Krispy Kreme. International Directory of Company Histories, Vol. 61. *op cit.*

18. *Ibid.*

19. Serwer, A. (7 Jul 2003). *op cit.*

20. *Ibid.*

21. Krispy Kreme Doughnuts Financial Information. 2006 Annual Report. *Krispy Kreme Official Website*. Accessed 3 Apr 2012. http://investor.krispykreme.com/phoenix.zhtml?c=120929&p=irol-reportsannual

22. O'Sullivan, K. *op cit.*

23. Serwer, A. (14 Jun 2004). A Hole In Krispy Kreme's Story. *Fortune* via *CNN Money*. http://money.cnn.com/magazines/fortune/fortune_archive/2004/06/14/372629/index.htm.

24. O'Sullivan, K. *op cit.*

25. Serwer, A. (14 Jun 2004). *op cit.*

26. *Ibid.*

27. O'Sullivan, K. *op cit.*

28. Krispy Kreme Doughnuts, Inc. *2012 Annual Report*. Winston-Salem, NC. http://www.sec.gov/Archives/edgar/data/1100270/000120677412001280/krispykreme_10k.htm

29. Wall Street Journal News Roundup. (8 Jan 2008). Krispy Kreme's CEO Resigns. *Wall Street Journal*. http://online.wsj.com/article/SB119974600162573205.html.

30. Krispy Kreme Doughnuts, Inc. 2012 Annual Report. *op cit.*

31. *Ibid.*

32. *Ibid.*

33. McHugh, M. *op cit.*

34. Mastrull, D. (10 Nov 2010). Krispy Kreme back in Philly with new business recipe. *Inquirer – philly.com*. http://articles.philly.com/2010-11-14/business/24955586_1_krispy-kreme-factory-stores-profit.

35. Krispy Kreme Doughnuts, Inc. 2012 Annual Report. *op cit.*

36. *Ibid.*

37. Krispy Kreme Doughnuts, Inc. 2012 Annual Report. *op cit.*, page 9

38. Hoyland, C. (11 May 2009). *op cit.*

39. *Ibid.*

40. Dunkin' Brands Financials: 2011 Annual Report. *Dunkin' Brands Official Website*. Accessed 3 Apr 2012. http://investor.dunkinbrands.com/financials.cfm

41. Beller, M. D. (22 Mar 2012). Krispy Kreme Moves Into Coffee as Others Move on. *CNBC.com*. Embedded Video. http://www.cnbc.com/id/46822929/Krispy_Kreme_Moves_Into_Coffee_as_Others_Move_on

42. Beller, M. D. *op cit.*

43. Coffees. *Krispy Kreme Official Website*. Accessed April 3, 2012. www.KrispyKreme.com/coffee

44. Beller, M. D. *op cit.*

45. *Ibid.*

46. Hoyland, C. (11 May 2009). *op cit.*

47. Krispy Kreme Doughnuts, Inc. 2012 Annual Report. *op cit.*

48. *Ibid.*

49. O'Sullivan, K. *op cit.*

50. Krispy Kreme Doughnuts, Inc. 2012 Annual Report. *op cit.*

51. Beller, M. D. *op cit.*

52. Nutrition Information. *Krispy Kreme Official Website*. Accessed 3 Apr 2012. http://www.krispykreme.com/nutri.pdf

53. Serwer, A. (7 Jul 2003). *op cit.*

54. Krispy Kreme Doughnuts, Inc. 2012 Annual Report. *op cit.*

55. *Ibid.*

56. *Ibid.*

57. *Ibid*

58. Krispy Kreme Doughnuts, Inc. 2012 Annual Report. *op cit.*

59. Adamson, A. (9 Feb 2012). For Krispy Kreme, Loyal Fans Have Been the Powerful Branding App of Choice For 75 Years. *Forbes: CMO Network*. http://www.forbes.com/sites/allenadamson/2012/02/09/for-krispy-kreme-loyal-fans-have-been-the-powerful-branding-app-of-choice-for-75-years/

60. Smith, G. (9 Mar 2012). Krispy Kreme gains social media appeal with Hot Light app. *Examiner.com*. http://www.examiner.com/article/krispy-kreme-gains-social-media-appeal-with-hot-light-app

61. Krispy Kreme Doughnuts, Inc. 2012 Annual Report. *op cit.*, page 22

62. Serwer, A. (14 Jun 2004). *op cit.*

63. RTT Staff Writer. Krispy Kreme Appoints Dwayne Chambers As SVP - Quick Facts. *RTT News*. Accessed April 3, 2012. http://www.rttnews.com/1420099/krispy-kreme-appoints-dwayne-chambers-as-svp-quick-facts.aspx

64. Dwayne Chambers: Chief Marketing Officer at Krispy Kreme. *Linked In*. http://www.linkedin.com/in/dwaynechambers

65. Morrison, M. (21 Mar 2011). Krispy Kreme's New CMO to Spend Less, Lean on Social Media. *Ad Age: CMO Strategy*. http://adage.com/article/cmo-interviews/krispy-kreme-s-cmo-spend-lean-social-media/149451

66. Corporate Governance Guidelines. *Krispy Kreme Official Website*. Accessed April 3, 2012. http://investor.krispykreme.com/phoenix.zhtml?c=120929&p=irol-govguidelines

67. Nowell, P. (11 Feb 2009). Is The Glaze Off Krispy Kreme? *CBS NEWS*. http://www.cbsnews.com/2100-201_162-617329.html

68. Reuters. Slideshow: Most Obese Countries. *Reuters*. http://www.reuters.com/news/pictures/slideshow?articleId=USRTXT3DK#a=7

69. Nowell, P. *op cit.*

70. Morrison, M. *op cit.*

71. Luna, N. (17 Oct 2008). Krispy Kreme launches first-ever mini-doughnut. *Orange County Register*. http://fastfood.ocregister.com/2008/10/17/krispy-kreme-launches-first-ever-mini-doughnut/4329/

72. Nowell, P. *op cit.*

73. O'Sullivan, K. *op cit.*

74. *Ibid.*

75. Lockyer, S. E. (4 Mar 2009). Krispy Kreme settles with the SEC. *Nation's Restaurant News*. http://nrn.com/article/krispy-kreme-settles-sec

76. O'Sullivan, K. *op cit.*

77. *Ibid.*

78. *Ibid.*

79. *Ibid.*

80. Hoyland, C. (15 Apr 2010). Krispy Kreme says it has 'firm foundation on which to build.' *QSRWeb.com*. www.qsrweb.com/article/95582/Krispy-Kreme-says-it-has-firm-foundation-on-which-to-build

81. O'Sullivan, K. *op cit.*

82. *Ibid.*

83. Thomson, J. (6 Dec 2010). Krispy Kreme out of administration, directors back in control. *Smart Company – Australia*. http://www.smartcompany.com.au/buy-or-sell-a-business/20101206-krispy-kreme-out-of-administration-directors-back-in-control.html

84. Krispy Kreme. International Directory of Company Histories, Vol. 61. *op cit.*

85. O'Sullivan, K. *op cit.*

86. Krispy Kreme Doughnuts, Inc. 2012 Annual Report. *op cit.*

87. *Ibid.*

Jim Kelly, Eric Ryza, Mark Herman, Norbert Forlemu, Swetha Manimuthu

Texas A&M University

Lockheed Martin takes flight in times of crisis.[1]

Introduction

It's a plane. It's a helicopter. Actually, it's the Lockheed Martin F-35 Lightning II, the most capable – and expensive – aircraft ever produced. Like a jet that can also hover, Lockheed's versatility is its greatest strength in times of crisis. Along with the escalation of conflicts in the Middle East and increased support for defense spending, Lockheed Martin's stock rose dramatically from a price per share of $31 in January 2001 to over $120 in mid-2008.[2] However, as of the end of 2011 and coinciding with the drawdown in Iraq and Afghanistan, Lockheed's stock dropped to $80.90. Nevertheless, Lockheed enjoyed an outstanding return on equity (ROE) of 112 percent in 2011. With four core business segments and a worldwide reputation for excellence, Lockheed *appears* well positioned to respond to changes in the market. However, fully 78 percent of Lockheed's total sales are from military arms[3] and 82 percent of total sales originate from within the United States. Simply put, Lockheed's dependence on U.S. defense spending has the potential to threaten the firm's longevity.

Lockheed Martin alone receives over 7 percent of total U.S. defense spending – that's one of every fourteen dollars paid by the Pentagon. Yet in times of economic crisis, this funding is threatened at all levels and has resulted in uneven cash flows and company-wide lay-offs. Recently, Lockheed downsized its workforce from 146,000 to 123,000,[4] reflecting the termination of key projects and a forecasted reduction in demand for both existing and new products. The early termination of the F-22 Raptor project in 2008 illustrates the potentially devastating effects of government budget constraints on the survivability of Lockheed. The F-35 Joint Strike Fighter currently in development has the potential to be the largest weapons project ever, with an estimated $1.51 trillion final tally.[5] However, production delays and the current political climate threaten to affect the scope of the project dramatically – a project at the core of Lockheed Martin's fiscal security.

Further, if Lockheed's fortunes improve in times of global unrest, reason suggests that the company suffers in times of peace and stability. Lockheed's challenge is delivering products with a 10- to 20-year development and production lead time that, ultimately, will be in uncertain demand (due to the impossible-to-predict state of flux in terms of world conflict) for customers with uncertain budgets. Lockheed's recent exploration into renewable energy and healthcare solutions adds an interesting dimension to its portfolio, as both are new business segments and outside the usual scope of its core competencies.

Taking Flight

Lockheed started when two brothers, Allan and Malcolm Loughead (pronounced "lock-heed"), handcrafted their first wooden planes in southern California in early 1913, mainly for hobbyists and as a military model. They were successful until the end of WWI left their business without a market and the company went bankrupt in 1921. Allan Loughead continued alone, collaborating with Fred Keeler to form the Lockheed Aircraft Company in 1926. Their first success was the Vega wooden monoplane, which made the first nonstop transcontinenal flight across the United States in 1928. This success inspired the Detroit Aircraft Corporation (DAC) to acquire the company in 1929. The new company thrived through WWII and produced multiple aviation legends such as the P-38 Lightning Fighter, the U-2 spy plane, and the SR-71 Blackbird. Lockheed also produced the XP-80 Shooting Star, the first American jet fighter, in only eight months.

In the 1960s, Lockheed attempted to enter the commercial jumbo jet market to compete with Boeing's then new 747 and the McDonnell-Douglas DC-10. As a late mover pitted against superior competition, Lockheed conceded defeat in 1972. On the brink of bankruptcy, Lockheed remained solvent through a $250 million loan guarantee from the U.S. government.[6] To add insult to injury, Lockheed's image was marred in the 1970s by a major bribery scandal. This scandal led to tougher U.S. anti-bribery laws and a new process called Total Package Pricing that is designed to make bidding more transparent and explicit.[7] Lockheed came out of the 1970s to prosper during the 1980s, winning new contracts for the F-117 stealth fighter and acquiring the division of General Dynamics responsible for producing the popular F-16.

Merger of Equals

The Martin Company was formed in 1917 by Glenn Martin who built his first airplane in 1909 and later merged with the Wright brothers. The company is notable for producing the first U.S.-constructed bomber, the B-29, as well as commercial and military flying boats.[8] The company produced missiles, electronics, and nuclear systems in the 1950s, and, in 1961, it merged with American Marietta Company, a construction materials and chemical company. The newly named Martin Marietta Corporation sold most of its businesses after incurring excessive debts to defend a hostile takeover, but in 1992, managed to purchase GE's aerospace business. In March 1995, the company merged with Lockheed to form Lockheed Martin, the largest defense contractor in the world. This so-called "merger of equals" was hailed by investors and others as a "rare instance of corporate synergy"[9] as the two companies were competitors, yet with minimal areas of overlap in specialties and capabilities.

The newly formed Lockheed Martin continued its expansion in 1996 by acquiring the Loral Corporation and COMSAT Mobile Communications. Because of low profits, the company then divested ten of its non-core technology operations and acquired a 30 percent stake in Asia Cellular Satellite to build its non-defense business. Shortly thereafter in 2000, Lockheed Martin was awarded a $3.97 billion contract by the Pentagon to develop an anti-missile system as well as a contract to supply 24 C-130J transports.[10]

Lockheed Martin continued to expand by acquiring the government technology services business of Affiliated Computer Services in 2003, and Sippican, a naval electronics company, in 2004. In the same year, it won a seven-year contract to provide information technology services to the Social Security Administration. The company had another successful year in 2005 when it was selected alongside Augusta Westland to build a new fleet of 23 presidential Marine One helicopters. It also acquired STASYS Ltd., a U.K.-based network communications company, and Systex Group, a provider of IT and technical support services to the U.S. government in the same year. In 2006, it acquired several businesses including ISX Corporation, Pacific Architects and Engineers, and Savi Technology. The company's Space Systems division also won the coveted Orion manned lunar spaceship contract from the National Aeronautics and Space Administration (NASA) that year. In 2007, Lockheed Martin combined its Information Technology and Global Services division with its Integrated Systems and Solutions division. Recognizing its limitations, the company collaborated with rivals Northrop Grumman and Alliant Techsystems to develop multirole weapons for Lockheed's F-22 Raptor and F-35 Lightning II.[11]

Despite Lockheed's efforts to build the capabilities necessary to fulfill its contracts, the F-22 Raptor was cancelled in late 2008 by the Secretary of Defense, Robert Gates, due to budget constraints. The F-22 was originally developed to combat Cold War threats by providing complete air superiority. At a cost of $354 million per plane,[12] however, this technology and capability was no longer justifiable. In addition, concerns about the acquisitions process as well as issues with program development and high costs led President Obama to cancel the VH-71 presidential helicopter contract in early 2009. To add to its woes, the future of the F-35 and Lockheed's relationships with eight partner countries[i] remains in jeopardy due to increasing costs and delays.

The Industry: Anything but Stable

Lockheed Martin has four business segments that primarily cater to customers in the defense segment: Aeronautics, Space Systems, Electronic Systems, and Information Systems and Global Solutions.[13]

---

[i]Britain, Australia, Italy, Turkey, Norway, Denmark, the Netherlands, and Canada.

Aeronautics

The aircraft industry comprises about 80 percent of the aeronautics industry. The growth of the airplane industry began with the Wright brothers' successful demonstration of wing dynamics to the American and European governments. After the successful use of aircraft in WWI, the U.S. government began to focus on military aircraft. This transformation led to the emergence and success of many entrepreneurs in the race for military aircraft superiority, most notably Boeing, Douglas, Loughead, and Martin. The conclusion of WWI and subsequent cancellation of over 90 percent of the defense contracts eliminated most of the smaller entrepreneurial ventures in this industry, leaving only the major players that have since grown to be leaders largely through mergers and acquisitions.

The aircraft industry consists of aircraft and aircraft parts for both military and civilian purposes, with aircraft sales accounting for 65 percent of the industry's revenues. Currently, Lockheed Martin is the industry leader for defense aircraft followed by Boeing and Northrop Grumman Corp.

The commercial aircraft industry tends to follow economic recessions and booms. On the other hand, the military aircraft industry is driven by international policies and conflicts that drive fiscal policies and defense budgets.

Accounting for 60 percent of revenue, government defense contracts strongly influence sales in the aeronautics industry. The emergence of this industry followed two historic incidents: the development of airborne missiles during WWII and the "race to space" of the U.S. and the U.S.S.R. After WWII, most aviation-focused companies began to develop missile technology. The growth of this industry closely follows occurrences of war and major political changes, such as the fall of the U.S.S.R.

The aeronautics industry has three segments: ballistic missiles, cruise missiles, and space vehicles. Because of the complexities of hardware and software involved, this industry is highly collaborative with one contractor sub-contracting to others.

Until the fall of the Iron Curtain, the market for missiles experienced strong growth. However, after the fall of the U.S.S.R, the demand for missiles dropped significantly as the expected need for both ballistic and aircraft-fired missiles declined. A major impact in this industry was the Strategic Arms Reduction Treaty between the U.S. and U.S.S.R., signed in 1991. According to the treaty, member nations would discontinue building guided and ballistic missiles and would destroy 30 percent of their respective ballistic missile stockpiles. The treaty was valid for 15 years with clear enforcement periods for reducing various missiles. This treaty was re-signed in 2010 and further reduced the number of warheads and launchers in deployment by each country. The industry experienced a significant growth spurt when the contracts for missiles grew in 2004 in relation to the war in Afghanistan and Iraq, but this growth slowed in the second half of the decade.

To ensure survival in the face of decreased business potential and in response to pressure to decrease costs, multiple mergers and acquisitions have occurred in the aeronautics industry. Additionally, multiple collaborative partnerships have been formed in this industry since the late 1990s as another path for industry participants to continue operating. The industry largely depends on the effect international tensions wield on defense spending, and to a smaller degree, economic conditions.[14,15]

Space Systems

The space system industry has three segments: space capsules with rocket boosters, re-entry vehicles, and satellites. Before the Iron Curtain's fall, the United States and the U.S.S.R. were competing on several space missions – most notably, launching satellites and sending a person to the moon. This industry grew with government spending to launch both communications satellites and the International Space Station into orbit in the 1990s. Manned missions slowed after the Challenger and Discovery tragedies. The industry now focuses on launch vehicles that put satellites into orbit, although this also leveled off around 2003.[16]

Electronic Systems

Perhaps surprisingly, the electronic systems segment of Lockheed Martin accounts for 31 percent of the company's total revenue, posting higher net sales, operating profits, inter-segment revenue, and international sales than the firm's other three divisions. Even so, Lockheed management felt that splitting the unit into two new divisions – Missiles and Fire Control (MFC) and Mission Systems and Training (MST) – would reduce costs and jump start revenue growth.[17] At present, this division provides avionics, training systems, communications systems, engineering support, integration support, and other support systems for naval, missile, nuclear, and aircraft systems. Lockheed announced the split would become effective at the end of 2012.

The electronic systems industry has a clear demarcation between government defense projects and commercial projects. The rules that govern the contracts of these two sets of customers vary considerably. Federal contracts involve different processes, accounting procedures, and conformance to several government norms for the suppliers. Consequently, the cost of executing a defense contract is substantially higher than that of a similar commercial contract. Government contractors have numerous agencies to satisfy, all of whom monitor the pricing, quality, and performance of the products, in addition to adherence to the various standards regarding implementation. Contractors are subject to several audits and are required to disclose their financial information in view of the former requirements.

Initially, the defense electronics industry negotiated electronics contracts separately from the larger, more comprehensive contracts. The average strike rate (how often a single contractor's bid is selected) for companies in this industry remains at 25 percent, a percentage the U.S. government has historically targeted. However, despite its efforts to reward contracts among the various contractors equally, some companies receive a larger share of the pie. These companies hold a stronghold in the defense market. As with the aeronautics industry, at one time there were many primary and secondary contractors in the electronics industry. However, with reductions to the defense budget since 1990, this has changed. Significant mergers among the larger companies put secondary contractors in a precarious situation. This merger activity, a preference for the larger companies, and government policies requiring a smaller and well-diversified contractor base, further reduced the number of the companies competing in this industry. Because of this reduction, the government now rewards contracts for whole systems instead of individual components and sub-systems using a competitive and transparent "request for proposal" bidding process.

Although investment in property, plant, and equipment required for this industry is low, because of government policies several deterrents for start-ups remain. Chief among these deterrents are specialized human resources, continuous facility improvements and cost reductions, intense national and international competition, and ongoing technology obsolescence.

Research and development (R&D) is integral to this industry, with funding for R&D coming explicitly from the contracts being awarded and government subsidies. This funding was implemented to ensure that a company could become the sole contractor for a proprietary technology and thereby capitalize on innovation. Despite the goal however, this funding began to decrease in the 1990s.

The industry grew in the early 2000s with the U.S. military initiative to integrate and upgrade its systems into what it called the Future Combat System. Another significant contribution to the growth of the industry was the increase in demand for Global Positioning Systems (GPS) in both the defense and commercial segments, with navigation systems first being utilized in a defense capacity during the Gulf War conflict in 1991. The launch of the GPS–2RM satellite by Lockheed Martin in 2005 increased the power available for existing signals and added additional frequencies for military and civilian GPS use. The third factor contributing to the growth of the electronics industry is the U.S. Army's recent development of a protection system for Stryker units that scans for and intercepts anti-tank missiles and grenades. As with the aeronautics and space systems segments and despite its growth in the civilian market, this industry is affected significantly by reductions in defense budgets.

Lockheed Martin is the industry leader for electronic systems. This is due to additional capabilities resulting from the merger of Lockheed and Martin and Martin's earlier acquisition of the GE Aerospace division. Raytheon is the second largest company in this industry, followed by AlliedSignal's recent acquisition – Honeywell. In addition, there are many other companies with well-diversified business portfolios operating in this industry.[18]

Information Systems and Global Solutions

Information systems and global solutions is the fourth industry and segment of Lockheed Martin. This business segment provides management services, information systems, and technology expertise to a wide variety of customer segments including biometrics, energy, financial services, human capital management, healthcare, transportation, and homeland security. This is a very competitive industry with large and small cap companies. With only 2 percent of this division's revenue originating from commercial customers in the United States and 5 percent from international customers, it is obvious that the purchases by the U.S. government account for the majority of the segment's revenues.[19]

How Lockheed Martin Competes

Lockheed Martin is committed to delivering superior shareholder returns while pursuing leading sustainability performance and good citizenship.

– Bob Stevens, CEO[20]

Lockheed Martin operates using four principles – Secure, Extend, Expand, and Enable.

- Secure our existing programs by performing with excellence. Additionally, we must continue to have candid dialogues with our customers and the highest degree of transparency on all our programs.
- Extend the value of our platforms by shaping follow-on business and tailoring our existing capabilities for new applications. We should also continue to seek and implement innovative business models.
- Expand our position within targeted segments with market-based strategies. This also means more pursuits internationally, and greater synergies between Lockheed Martin products.
- Enable meaningful growth through adjacent market opportunities. We want to focus on markets that will move the needle for us.[21]

Conditions in the external environment strongly influence the strategies Lockheed Martin uses in its Aeronautics, Space Systems, and Electronics Systems divisions. In this sense, these divisions have identified the technologies that will satisfy market demand and then use its resources, capabilities, and core competencies to satisfy those demands. In contrast, available resources and their relative uniqueness that are associated with the firm's Information Systems and Global Systems segment strongly influence how this particular segment competes. More specifically, Lockheed Martin identified the IT industry to be one in which the firm's capabilities and core competencies could be successfully applied in order to create value for customers. Accordingly, it now offers technology solutions to the energy, healthcare, and financial services sectors, among others, – which is a definitive move away from the U.S. defense budget (Exhibit 1).

Lockheed Martin provides aircraft and advanced technology solutions to its customers, primarily the U.S. government. The firm emphasizes innovation, human capital, and ethical practices as the foundation for serving customers' needs.

Over its life, Lockheed Martin has expanded its business operations and now operates well-diversified business segments. This diversification helps the firm weather economic downturns and defense-specific spending cuts. Diversification for Lockheed has primarily come through mergers and acquisitions, the most notable of which was the merger between Lockheed and Martin in 1995. Also of significant note was the acquisition of the advanced electronics company, Loral Corporation, in 1996.[22] Lockheed Martin's business segments share

Exhibit 1 Lockheed Martin Business Segment Basis

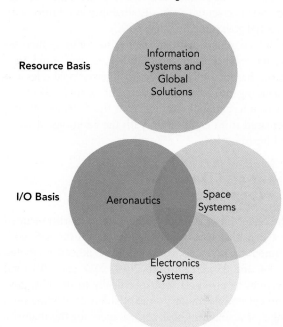

Source: Lockheed Martin Corporation. *Annual Report*. Bethesda, MD: Lockheed Martin Corporation, 2011. Retrieved 07 Mar 2012. http://www.lockheedmartin.com/content/dam/lockheed/data/corporate/documents/2011-Annual-report.pdf

capabilities and a culture defined by the executive leadership with a large amount of project-based cooperation between its aeronautics, space vehicle, and electronics business divisions.

Lockheed Martin enjoys its position as a leader in the defense sector; however, U.S. government dependent businesses do not operate or compete in a risk-free environment. Successful performance in this sector involves, for example, keeping costs at an acceptable level while adhering to the many rules and regulations governing the firm's operations. Lockheed Martin focuses on continued operational efficiency and cost-controlling measures to remain attractive to its customers and shareholders alike. In view of this, it works closely with its suppliers, anticipating raw material prices and planning accordingly. It believes that solid execution is important and works to stay on schedule in development and production, although this has been a particular point of contention in the F-35 program.

Innovation is the key to survival for any technology company and is an organizational activity to which Lockheed Martin devotes considerable resources. For example, anticipating the growth in demand for unmanned vehicles and global security services, Lockheed Martin is now investing heavily in the development of these types of systems and activities.[23] It is attuned to the behaviors of its customers and understands that managing costs is essential to its sustainability in a future with potential government budget cuts.

In accordance with an interest to continue increasing its revenues and profitability as well, Lockheed Martin has focused on increasing international sales and expanding into adjacent markets. For example, the number of international customers for the F-35 aircraft has increased from eight to ten with the additions of Israel and Japan.

Financial Data and Performance[24,25,26,27,28,29,30,31,32]

The 1995 combination of Lockheed and Martin resulted in a firm that was heavily dependent on the U.S. government for revenues. For example, Lockheed attributed 82, 84, and 85 percent of its 2009, 2010, and 2011 total revenues to products sold specifically to the U.S. government and its military allies (Exhibit 2). Relying on a single or a small number of customers for the majority of a firm's sales (as is the case for Lockheed) creates a dependence that is undesirable. The net profits of the company, totaling $2.66 billion in 2011, came from its four operating segments: Aerospace, Space Systems, Electronic Systems, and Information Systems and Global Solutions. Aerospace and Electronic Systems are the two dominant segments in the Lockheed portfolio, accounting for nearly 63 percent of the company's sales in 2011. Further, the Space Systems segment's only customers are NASA and the U.S. Department of Defense. Some Space

System products are sold internationally, but the transfer is facilitated and regulated by the U.S. government.

Given the aforementioned ties to the U.S. government's funding decisions relative to the firm's business segments, some might view Lockheed Martin as a risky investment. The long period of time that is commonly required for the firm's R&D investments to lead to revenue enhancements, coupled with the fact that the markets for its primary products are constrained by the political and legal external environment, could lead investors to believe there is relatively little room for growth in the company. According to Lockheed's financials, however, those investors would be wrong. Largely because of its ability to innovate and collaborate, Lockheed Martin has been at the forefront of many technologically significant aerospace breakthroughs. Its ROE for 2011 of 112.76 percent exceeds the performances of all of its main competitors, with the exception of Boeing, which posted a 127.94 percent ROE over the same period. In contrast, Northrop Grumman, which predominantly manufactures systems and platforms, such as the E-2 Hawkeye and the Global Hawk unmanned aerial vehicle used extensively in the war on terror, earned only a 17.73 percent ROE. Industry giant General Dynamics was only slightly better for 2011 with a ROE of 19.03 percent (Exhibit 3).

While many investors would be very satisfied by a firm's ability to earn a 112.76 percent return on its equity, analyzing Lockheed's capital structure yields additional and important insight about the firm's overall financial performance. In this respect, Lockheed Martin earned only a 5.7 percent profit margin due in large part to its

Exhibit 2 Percent of Revenue from U.S. Government Comparison

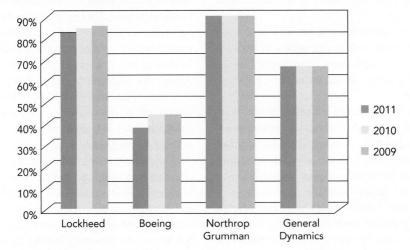

Exhibit 3 2011 Return on Equity Comparison

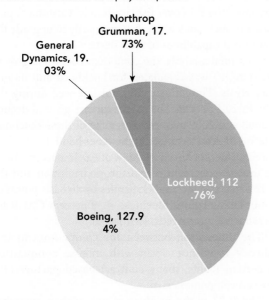

Source: 2011 10-K filings of companies listed via www.sec.gov

significant debt. Its debt to assets ratio is 645 percent, giving pause to investors contemplating the possibility of purchasing stock in Lockheed Martin. Further, because the U.S. government is its predominant customer, all requests for proposals are put out to bid in a static fashion. The U.S. government has moved away from awarding contracts on a component and sub-system basis, now preferring to award entire systems to one contractor. Because cost is a major consideration, the government specifies the technical requirements but refrains from dictating production and development techniques. All

bidders are expected to adhere to the technical requirements specified. Cost is considered only after a bidder's satisfactory compliance to all technical specifications.

Study of firms' financial situations suggests the possibility that there are no moderately financed companies in terms of capital structure within this industry, as both Lockheed Martin and Boeing are heavily leveraged, while General Dynamics and Northrop Grumman rely heavily on equity. The dichotomy between the two approaches is quite revealing. The two low-leverage companies, General Dynamics and Northrop Grumman, only have debt-to-asset ratios of 29.53 and 38.07 percent, respectively, which would be the reason for their "less-than-spectacular" return on equity.

Leading its competitors in this segment, Lockheed Martin shows the most stable per share earnings over a five-year period ending in 2011, ranging from $7.02 to $7.81 (Exhibit 4). This may be one reason that institutions own 91 percent of the company's stock. By comparison, earnings per share for General Dynamics have ranged from $5.10 to $6.94 over this period, while the EPS for Northrop's stock has varied from $4.12 to $7.52. Perhaps surprisingly, Boeing's earnings-per-share have been the most volatile over this particular five-year period, ranging from a low of $1.87 diluted EPS in 2009 to a high of $5.33 in 2011.

From an income statement perspective, the size and scope of Lockheed Martin can be quite difficult to comprehend fully. Lockheed Martin is a behemoth of an industry leader with annual revenues in excess of $40 billion for each of the last five years. The aerospace segment, only the second largest division in the company, had revenues in excess of $14 billion for 2011.

Exhibit 4 Net Earnings per Share (Diluted) Comparison

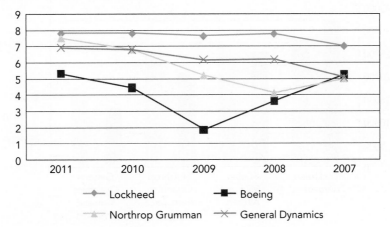

Source: 2011 10-K filings of companies listed via www.sec.gov

For a company such as Lockheed Martin, the backlog of orders is an indicator of a firm's health that investors examine. Lockheed had a tremendous backlog of orders in excess of $30.5 billion for 2011, up $3 billion from the previous year. This backlog compared favorably with those of its competitors. Boeing had a reported backlog of $24.1 billion, down from $25.1 billion in 2010, and Northrop Grumman and General Dynamics' Combat Systems division had a $19.2 and $11.4 billion backlog by comparison. This bodes well for Lockheed, as the majority of its backlog cannot be attributed to any one system. The F-35 program accounts for a significant percentage of the firm's backlog, but the C-130, F-16, and C-5 all have plenty of demand in waiting for the next several years (Exhibit 5).

With the high hopes of Lockheed for the program and the commitment from the U.S. government and some of its allies, the F-35 project is likely to be a long-lived program that sustains the company for decades to come. In fact, according to the Lockheed company analysis gathered from Business Source Complete, the program could generate revenues in excess of $1 trillion over the next several decades. Despite having been in production for several decades, several of the legacy programs including, for example, the F-16, still provide excellent returns for the firm. The C-130 program, along with all of the variant types manufactured, is seen on nearly every U.S. military installation and fulfills multiple roles for the different branches of the service. Additionally, the longer-lived programs, again referring to the F-16, commonly experience customers in addition to the U.S. government deciding to buy the firm's products. For example, given its performance capabilities, governments representing

Taiwan, India, and the United Arab Emirates have also purchased the F-16 over the last decade. Customers purchase products such as the F-16 primarily to upgrade the quality and capabilities of their fleets.

As a final analysis, the compounded annual growth rate (CAGR) was calculated for Lockheed and its primary rivals. The industry did not fare well during the 2007 to 2011 period. The stock market's general decline in 2008 and 2009 accounts for some of these outcomes in terms of growth rates. On the other hand, final calculations place Lockheed's CAGR at −6.37 percent, besting the −7.14 percent of Northrop Grumman and the −7.12 percent of General Dynamics by 80 basis points or so, but falling behind Boeing's −4.30 percent CAGR for the same five year stretch (Exhibit 6).

The interaction between the competitors in this industry is unique. Even with intense competition on certain fronts, many contract-based partnerships between companies exist.

The F-22 is the product of one such partnership among Lockheed Martin, Pratt and Whitney, and Boeing. Boeing was responsible for the wings, aft fuselage, avionics integration, life support system, training system, fire protection system, and 70 percent of the mission software. Pratt and Whitney supplied the two engines, and Lockheed Martin was responsible for program management and the remainder of the aircraft's components. The F-22 was launched in 2007 in a ceremony hosted by all three companies.[33]

These partnerships have become common in the industry, particularly with companies pursuing similar projects and products. Typically, these partnerships exist so each firm can use its core competencies to

Exhibit 5 Order Backlog Comparison (in millions)

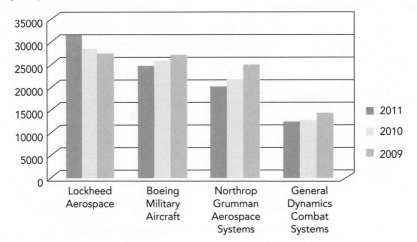

Source: 2011 10-K filings of companies listed via www.sec.gov

contribute to the mission specified within each individual project.

Ethics

The very nature of being a defense contractor means that the market is very narrow and a competitor's gain is another firm's loss. There have been several very high profile examples of corporate espionage, scheming, and illegal activities such as bribes throughout the history of the industry as firms vie for competitive advantage.

Lockheed itself was embroiled in scandal in the 1970s after paying several bribes to foreign officials and political organizations in exchange for receiving several aerospace contracts. This scandal tarnished the image of the company, which had been known at that time more for financial troubles than for innovation.[34]

Another instance involved an engineer from Boeing who Lockheed hired in 2005. The two firms were battling for a multibillion-dollar long-term contract to produce long-range missiles for the U.S. defense department. The engineer Lockheed hired brought with him over 25,000 pages of documents relating to the project in contention. Boeing initially brought the issue to light by saying there were only seven pages, but as the investigation into possible wrongdoing expanded, complete records in excess of 25,000 pages referring to the Lockheed bid, all of which were confidential, proprietary information, were found.[35]

Over the last few decades however, Lockheed has re-engineered itself into a competitive juggernaut of defense and has developed a reputation for ethical and transparent dealings. Lockheed's strategic leaders are working diligently to create a culture of accountability, ethical standards, and transparency. This direction has permeated the organization, and the company seems to be a beacon for the industry. As an example of the honesty and accountability of the firm, former CEO Robert Stevens took full responsibility for the cost overruns and production and development issues of the famed F-35 joint strike fighter program.[36] The program director, Dan Crowley, had come under scrutiny for the issues with the program, but Stevens stepped up and took full accountability, giving Crowley a vote of confidence rather than using him as a scapegoat.

The Pilots

Our business is built on integrity, and we will not risk compromising it.

– Bob Stevens, CEO[37]

Lockheed Martin is a large corporation by any reasonable measure. Of course, talented and effective strategic leaders are foundational to efforts for this firm to achieve strategic competitiveness and earn above-average returns. Overall, Lockheed Martin appears to have a top management team in place with the potential to help the firm successfully deal with the industry's challenges as well as the firm's challenges. Nonetheless, recent leadership-related upheavals have occurred within the firm.

Following the traditional patterns of large cap, multinational corporations, Lockheed coupled the role of Chairman of the Board and CEO and, from 2004 until his retirement as CEO in early 2013, had entrusted the firm's direction and welfare to Robert J. Stevens.[38] Stevens' Lockheed career started in 1993 and, based on Stevens' career trajectory at the nation's largest defense contractor and the firm's performance, it seems appropriate to give Stevens some credit for Lockheed's success. During his tenure at the helm, the corporation was awarded several billion-dollar government contracts, including the F-22 Raptor and the F-35 Lightning Stealth fighter programs and, along with the entire management team, he maintained Lockheed's position as a top defense contractor.

Simultaneous to Stevens' retirement announcement in April 2012 was the announcement of his successor – the then current Vice Chairman, President, and COO, Chris Kubasik. However, with less than 60 days before taking the post, Kubasik was forced to resign "after an internal ethics (investigation) found that he had a personal relationship with a subordinate that violated the company's code of ethics."[39] The board immediately promoted Marillyn A. Hewson, Executive VP of the

Exhibit 6 Compounded Annual Growth Rate Comparison, 2007 – 2011

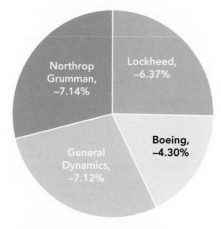

Source: 2011 10-K filings of companies listed via www.sec.gov

Electronics Systems division, to assume Kubasik's positions (in addition to her own) – including the early 2013 promotion to CEO. At the same time, Lockheed announced that Stevens would assume the position of Board Executive Chairman until the end of 2013 "to facilitate a smooth CEO transition."[40]

The Lockheed Martin Board of Directors includes some individuals who are well known and experienced. For example, three board members – Admiral (ret.) James Ellis, General (ret.) Joseph Ralston, and Admiral (ret.) James Loy – all served in distinguished positions in the Navy, Army, and Coast Guard, respectively. Additionally, all three had impressive and successful careers with organizations such as the Cohen Group and the Institute of Nuclear Power Operations. These individuals are key members of the board, largely because of their insights about the defense community and their contacts within that community (see Exhibit 7).

Chain of Command

Developing a strong managerial succession plan with respect to the firm's top management team is an important activity within Lockheed Martin. Lockheed's plan likely made it possible and even desirable for the firm to announce simultaneously Stevens' retirement and Kubasik's selection as his replacement. Subsequently, given the reported improper relationship with which Kubasik was involved, Lockheed relied on its succession plan to select Marillyn Hewson as the firm's new CEO.

STRATEGIC CHALLENGES

Declining Federal Defense Budget

The U.S. military spending as a percentage of GDP is expected to decline to an average of 4.0 percent over the

Exhibit 7 Lockheed Martin Board Members

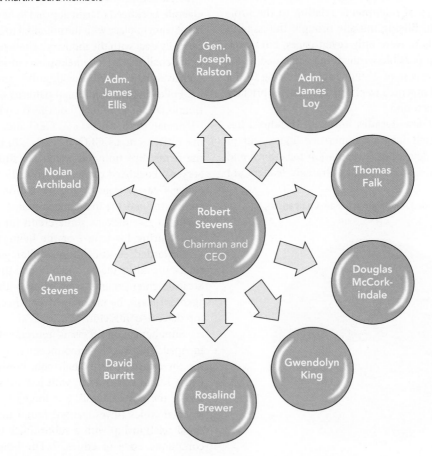

Source: Lockheed Martin: Who We Are. http://www.lockheedmartin.com/us/who-we-are/corporate-governance/board.html

next five years (2012-2016), down from 4.6 percent during the past five years (2007-2011).[41]

As a leader in the military aircraft segment, Lockheed's largest customer is the U.S. government, comprising 82 percent of 2011 sales.[42] Therefore, an uncertain future for the U.S. government's defense budget poses a unique challenge with regard to investing in and growing the business. This is especially challenging given long-term projects such as the F-35, a product that has been in development since 1994. This project alone has required over a decade of development and it will be several more years before customers receive their first orders.[43] Despite a temporary respite from worry when, in December 2011, Congress agreed to finance all U.S. government activities through September 30, 2012,[44] Lockheed's management team receives little relief from having to attempt to predict the future to make decisions about the firm's strategies as well as their implementation.

At the top of Lockheed's financial worries list is the Budget Control Act of 2011. This act can trigger automatic reductions in defense spending in January 2013 if Congress and the administration fail to reach a budget agreement.[45] As stated in Lockheed's 2011 annual report, "the resulting automatic across-the-board budget cuts in sequestration would have significant consequences to our business and industry."[46] While Lockheed is diversified to some degree, this diversification cannot fully mitigate the impact of budget reductions resulting from sequestration. The termination of large U.S. defense contracts would adversely affect its business and future financial performance.[47] Also on Lockheed's list of concerns are the steps being taken by the U.S. government to reduce its global commitments – as exemplified by its withdrawal from Iraq – this may further reduce the need for defense spending.

International Market Risks

Lockheed's international customers comprised 17 percent of 2011 net sales, and the firm plans to grow its international sales over the next several years[48] despite the fact that the unpredictable nature of the international market segment poses even more challenges than Lockheed's domestic market "due to the potential for greater volatility in foreign economic and political environments."[49] Because of the ongoing global economic recession, foreign governments, especially those in European countries, have proposed a variety of budget cuts and austerity measures that may result in defense budget reductions. Dealing in foreign markets also exposes the firm to currency exchange risks since a weakening foreign

currency can adversely impact profits when converted into U.S. dollars.

Exporting to foreign countries, especially in the defense market, requires adherence to stringent export control policies. If a violation were to occur, the responsible business unit – or potentially Lockheed Martin as a whole – may be restricted from exporting products for a period of time. Other penalties could occur from not complying with industrial cooperation regulations as part of international business contracts. These offset contract agreements could potentially include meeting in-country purchase and manufacturing levels, sometimes for several years.[50] Some opponents of this system argue that contract offsets are borderline bribes that promote corruption in foreign countries due to the lack of transparency, especially in the defense market where secrecy is mandated for national security reasons. "The U.S. Department of Commerce Trade Promotion Coordinating Committee Report of March 2000 claimed that the defense sector accounted for 50 percent of all bribery allegations over 1994-1999."[51] Nearly 130 different countries are estimated to use offset agreements, and the value of offsets has been increasing as a percentage of the main contract value.[52]

Regulation of the Defense Market

The defense market customer base is severely limited due to constraints imposed by the U.S. government. All U.S. firms selling products internationally deal with trade embargos and restrictions with certain countries; however, additional scrutiny applies to the defense market because of concerns over national security as dictated by the International Traffic in Arms Regulations (ITAR). "ITAR relates to Section 38 of the U.S.A.'s Arms Export Control Act (22 U.S.C. 2778), which authorizes the President to control the export and import of defense articles and defense services."[53] In addition to the cost of the lengthy contract approval process because of ITAR, these regulations may deter foreign countries from accepting bids from U.S. companies such as Lockheed. In April 2011, India excluded Boeing and Lockheed from bidding on its $11B defense project for a new fighter jet. Many speculated this was due to growing restrictions on U.S. export policies related to ITAR.[54] Even close U.S. allies such as the United Kingdom are becoming frustrated with the lengthy process ITAR imposes. However, conditions are improving with regard to a more efficient approval process for the United States' closest allies. "In 2004 the processing time for all U.K.-related ITAR licenses was 22 days, compared to 42 days a few years ago."[55]

Although Lockheed Martin is highly experienced in the defense industry, it has violated ITAR policies in the past:

In 2008, the Department of State charged Lockheed Martin with violations of the Arms Export Control Act and the ITAR for providing classified and unclassified technical data related to the sales of Hellfire missiles to the United Arab Emirates in 2003 through 2004.[56]

The outcome of these allegations resulted in Lockheed paying a $4 million civil fine. Despite this past violation, Lockheed's code of ethics clearly states its intentions to comply with the laws and regulations that govern its businesses.[57]

Controlling Costs

Perhaps the most pressing challenge facing Lockheed Martin is its failure to control costs, specifically within the F-35 program. Lockheed has succeeded in producing a unique product for a discerning set of customers; however, it has failed to maintain an acceptable cost for the F-35, as evidenced by continually rising program costs estimated at 1.51 trillion.[58] As a multi-role fighter with three distinct variants, the F-35 is slated to replace legacy fighters such as the F-16, F-18, A-10, and now fill the role of the forlorn F-22. Thus, the versatility demanded of the F-35 has carried significant costs. Lockheed Martin obviously underestimated the cost to develop such an aircraft and is struggling to provide the features required at an acceptable cost. As a result,

a number of partner countries have expressed concern over the per-unit cost of the F-35 and have threatened to cancel or reduce their contracts unless Lockheed meets certain milestones. Italy has already reduced its orders for the F-35 from an initial 131 to 90, largely due to austerity measures in the country, but also due to concerns about increasing costs.[59] With every cost revision of the F-35, Lockheed Martin must justify an increase in contract value to its customers.[60] Lockheed's inability to control costs with the F-35 program may hinder its ability to earn customers' trust with respect to price and time estimates for its other products.

The delays and cost overruns have plagued the aircraft industry as a whole, and this is especially true with tactical aircraft. Since the first plane produced by the Wright brothers, the costs to produce increasingly complex airplanes has increased exponentially. "By 2054, if that rate continues, the cost of a single combat airplane will equal the entire projected defense budget."[61] In fact, former Lockheed CEO Norman Augustine joked that the Navy and Air Force would have to share the jet for three and one-half days each per week[62] and provided a chart to show the exponential increase in costs over time. Many countries have considered prolonging or increasing the use of the F-16 as a low-cost, combat-proven alternative if the F-35 delays and increasing costs continue. Thus, as Lockheed Martin looks to the future, it faces challenges with respect to its current operations as well as a host of challenging decisions about how to best position the firm to succeed in the years to come.

NOTES

1. Hoover's Online. *Lockheed Martin Corporation Profile*. Retrieved 28 Feb 2012 from Hoover's Online.

2. "This Defense Company Has 24% Upside – Even with the Pentagon's Spending Cuts." *Money Morning*. Retrieved 08 Feb 2012. http://moneymorning.com/2012/02/08/this-defense-company-has-24-upside-even-with-the-pentagons-spending-cuts/

3. "The SIPRI Top 100 Arms-producing and Military Services Companies, 2010." *www.sipri.org*. Retrieved 03 Mar 2012. http://www.sipri.org/research/armaments/production/Top100

4. "Absolute Freedom." *Lockheed Martin. Supporting the Warfighter*. 22 Feb 2012. Retrieved 24 Mar 2012. http://www.lockheedmartin.com/us/news/speeches/022212-hewson.html

5. "Lockheed F-35 Cost Estimate by U.S. Increases 9% in Year." *Bloomberg*. 30 Mar 2012. Retrieved 03 Apr 2012.

http://www.bloomberg.com/news/2012-03-30/lockheed-f-35-fighter-estimate-increased-9-in-a-year-u-s-says.html

6. Terris, Daniel. *Ethics at Work: Creating Virtue in an American Corporation*. Waltham, MA: Brandeis UP, 2005.

7. Ibid.

8. Hoover's Online. *Lockheed Martin Corporation Profile*. op cit.

9. Terris, Daniel. *Ethics at Work: Creating Virtue in an American Corporation*. Waltham, MA: Brandeis UP, 2005. p. 69.

10. Hoover's Online. *Lockheed Martin Corporation Profile*. op cit.

11. Ibid.

12. "Catch F-22 for Obama." *The Christian Science Monitor*. The Christian Science Monitor, 04 Mar 2009. Retrieved 08 Mar 2012. http://www.csmonitor.com/Commentary/the-monitors-view/2009/0304/p08s01-comv.html

13. Lockheed Martin Corporation. *Annual Report*. Bethesda, MD: Lockheed Martin Corporation, 2011. Retrieved 07 Mar 2012. http://www.lockheedmartin.com/content/dam/lockheed/data/corporate/documents/2011-Annual-report.pdf

14. "Aircraft." *Encyclopedia of American Industries*, Online Edition. Gale, 2011. (SICs: 3721)

15. "Manufacturers of Guided Missiles and Space Vehicles." *Encyclopedia of American Industries*, Online Edition. Gale, 2012. (SICs: 3761)

16. Ibid.

17. Fryer-Biggs, Zachary. "Lockheed Martin Announces Split of Electronic Systems Division." *DefenseNews*. 8 Oct 2012. Retrieved 19 Mar 2013. http://www.defensenews.com/article/20121008/DEFREG02/310080003/Lockheed-Martin-Announces-Split-Electronic-Systems-Division

18. "Search, Detection, Navigation, Guidance, Aeronautical, and Nautical Systems and Instruments." *Encyclopedia of American Industries*, Online Edition. Gale, 2011. (SICs: 3812)

19. Lockheed Martin Corporation. *Annual Report*. op cit.

20. "Absolute Freedom." *Lockheed Martin · Our Leadership Commits*. Retrieved 24 Feb 2012. http://www.lockheedmartin.com/us/who-we-are/sustainability/leadership-commitment.html

21. Lockheed Martin Corporation. *Annual Report*. op cit.

22. Hoover's Online. *Lockheed Martin Corporation Profile*. op cit.

23. "Lockheed Martin Corporation, Company Profile." op cit.

24. "Lockheed Martin Corporation 2009 Form 10-K." U.S. Securities and Exchange Commission (Home Page). 25 Feb. 2010. Retrieved 8 Apr 2012. http://www.sec.gov/Archives/edgar/data/936468/000119312510040520/d10k.htm

25. Lockheed Martin Corporation. *Annual Report*. op cit.

26. "Lockheed Martin Corporation, Company Profile." op cit.

27. "Northrop Grumman Corporation 2009 Form 10-K." U.S. Securities and Exchange Commission (Home Page). 09 Feb 2010. Retrieved 08 Apr 2012. http://www.sec.gov/Archives/edgar/data/1133421/000095012310010126/v54508e10vk.htm

28. "Northrop Grumman Corporation 2011 Form 10-K." U.S. Securities and Exchange Commission (Home Page). 08 Feb 2012. Retrieved 08 Mar 2012. http://www.sec.gov/Archives/edgar/data/1133421/000119312512045323/d250683d10k.htm

29. "The Boeing Company 2009 Form 10-K." U.S. Securities and Exchange Commission (Home Page). 08 Feb 2010. Retrieved 08 Apr 2012. http://www.sec.gov/Archives/edgar/data/12927/000119312510024406/d10k.htm

30. "The Boeing Company 2011 Form 10-K." U.S. Securities and Exchange Commission (Home Page). 09 Feb 2012. Retrieved 08 Mar 2012. http://www.sec.gov/Archives/edgar/data/12927/000119312512048565/d255574d10k.htm

31. "General Dynamics 2009 Form 10-K." U.S. Securities and Exchange Commission (Home Page). 19 Feb 2010. Retrieved 08 Apr 2012. http://www.sec.gov/Archives/edgar/data/40533/000119312510034883/0001193125-10-034883-index.htm

32. "General Dynamics 2011 Form 10-K." U.S. Securities and Exchange Commission (Home Page). 17 Feb 2012. Retrieved 8 Apr 2012. http://www.sec.gov/Archives/edgar/data/40533/000119312512066385/d271667d10k.htm

33. "History - F22 Raptor." Boeing. Retrieved 10 Mar 2012. http://www.boeing.com/history/boeing/f22.html

34. "SCANDALS: Lockheed's Defiance: A Right to Bribe?" *Time Magazine U.S.* 18 Aug 1975. Retrieved 24 Mar 2012. http://www.time.com/time/magazine/article/0,9171,917751,00.html

35. Bowermaster, David. "Boeing Probe Intensifies over Secret Lockheed Papers." *The Seattle Times*. 09 Jan 2005. Retrieved 1 Apr 2012. http://seattletimes.nwsource.com/html/businesstechnology/2002146025_boeinglockheed09.html

36. Butler, Amy. "Lockheed CEO Stands By Company Leadership" *Aviation Week*. 04 Mar 2010. Retrieved 15 Mar 2012. http://www.aviationweek.com/aw/generic/story_generic.jsp?channel=aerospacedaily&id=news/asd/2010/03/05/04.xml&headline=Lockheed%20CEO%20Stands%20By%20Company%20JSF%20Leadership

37. "Absolute Freedom." op cit.

38. "CEO Profile of Robert Stevens." *Forbes*. Retrieved 12 Apr 2012. http:// people.forbes.com/profile/robert-j-stevens/49897

39. "Christopher Kubasik, Lockheed Exec Ousted Over Inappropriate Relationship, To Receive $3.5 Million." *Huff Post Business*. 12 Nov 2012. Retrieved 16 Mar 2013. http://www.huffingtonpost.com/2012/11/12/christopher-kubasik-separation-package_n_2117840.html

40. "Lockheed Martin Board Elects Marillyn Hewson CEO & President and Member of the Board." *Lockheed Martin, Press Releases, 2012, November*. 9 Nov 2012. Retrieved 16 Mar 2013. http://www.lockheedmartin.com/us/news/press-releases/2012/november/110912-corp-leadership.html

41. "The U.S. Defense Market 2012-2016: Market Opportunities & Challenges." *ICD Research*. 29 Feb 2012. Retrieved 7 Mar 2012. http://defense-update.com/20120229_the-u-s-defense-market-2012-2016-market-opportunities-challenges.html

42. Lockheed Martin Corporation. *Annual Report*. op cit.

43. "Lockheed F-35 Cost Estimate by U.S. Increases 9% in Year." *Bloomberg*. 30 Mar 2012. Retrieved 3 Apr 2012. http://www.bloomberg.com/news/2012-03-30/lockheed-f-35-fighter-estimate-increased-9-in-a-year-u-s-says.html

44. Lockheed Martin Corporation. *Annual Report*. op cit.

45. Ibid, p.9.

46. Ibid, p.9.

47. Ibid, p.9.

48. Ibid, p.11.

49. Ibid, p.11.

50. Ibid, p.11.

51. "Defense Offsets, Addressing the Risk of Corruption & Raising Transparency." *Transparency International*. Apr 2010. p. 14. Retrieved 11 Mar 2012. http://www.acrc.org.ua/assets/files/zvity_ta_doslidzhennya/TI_Defence_Offset_Report_20101.pdf

52. Ibid.

53. "UK Warns U.S.A. Over ITAR Arms Restrictions." *Defense Industry Daily*. 1 Dec 2005. Retrieved 17 Apr 2012. http://www.defenseindustrydaily.com/uk-warns-usa-over-itar-arms-restrictions-01549/

54. "U.S. Industry Loses Big in India: Is ITAR to Blame?" *National Defense Industry Association blog*. 28 Apr 2011. Retrieved 1 Apr 2012. http://www.freerepublic.com/focus/f-news/2712314/posts

55. "UK Warns U.S.A. Over ITAR Arms Restrictions." op cit.

56. "Navigating ITAR Compliance." *Melbourne Legal Team*. Retrieved 13 Apr 2012. http://www.melbournelegalteam.com/itar-compliance.html

57. "Setting the Standard, Code of Ethics and Business Conduct." *Lockheed Martin*. September 2011. Retrieved 12 Apr 2012. http://www.lockheedmartin.com/content/dam/lockheed/data/corporate/documents/setting-the-standard.pdf

58. "Lockheed F-35 Cost Estimate by U.S. Increases 9% in Year." op cit.

59. "Italy to Cut F-35 Fighter Jet Orders as Part of Defense Revamp." *Bloomberg BusinessWeek*. 16 Feb 2012. Retrieved 16 Apr 2012. http://www.businessweek.com/news/2012-02-16/italy-to-cut-f-35-fighter-jet-orders-as-part-of-defense-revamp.html

60. Lockheed Martin Corporation. *Annual Report*. op cit.

61. Kotter, J. "Leading change: Why transformation efforts fail." *Harvard Business Review* (Vol. 73, p. 175). 1995, Boston, MA: Harvard Business School Publication Corp.

62. "The cost of weapons: Defence spending in a time of austerity." *The Economist*. 26 Aug 2010. Retrieved 17 Mar 2013. http://www.economist.com/node/16886851

CASE 21

Logitech: Finding Success through Innovation and Acquisition

Alan N. Hoffman

Bentley University and Rotterdam School of Management, Erasmus University

Logitech is a long-standing company with a reputation for quality personal computing products offered at a reasonable price. Additionally, Logitech's reputation for being on the cutting edge of technology in the computer peripherals industry is second to none. This offers the company the enviable position of being at the top of its industry. However, the recent recession accompanied by the changing face of the personal computing industry offer significant challenges for the future. Logitech may have to find new ways to compete in a world where its products have become standard fare on most personal computing devices. With a reputation for leading the industry, will Logitech find new technologies to conquer, or will it find itself struggling to survive?

Company Background

Logitech, headquartered in Romanel-Sur-Morges, Switzerland, was the world's leading provider of computer peripherals in 2010. Personal computer peripherals were input and interface devices that were used for navigation, internet communications, digital music, home-entertainment control, gaming, and wireless devices. Derived from the French word *logiciel*, meaning "software," Logitech was originally formally established in 1981 as a software development and hardware architecture company by two Stanford graduate students in

Apples, Switzerland. Shortly after establishing itself as a quality software development company, Logitech saw a new hardware product opportunity that was emerging in the mid-1980s: the computer mouse. The mouse was standard equipment on the original MacIntosh computer launched in January 1984. Logitech viewed the mouse as a growth opportunity, and this became a turning point for the company's future. Logitech introduced its first hardware device, the P4 mouse, for users of graphics software. An OEM sales contract with HP followed, and in 1985, it entered the retail market, selling 800 units in the first month. In July 1988, Logitech's executives decided to take the company public to help finance its rapid growth.

In the early 1990s, while facing increasingly strong competition in the mouse business, Logitech identified a larger market opportunity for computer peripherals and began growing its business beyond the mouse. Throughout the next few years, Logitech introduced products such as: (1) computer keyboards, (2) a digital still camera, (3) a headphone/microphone, (4) a joystick gaming peripheral, and (5) a web camera on a flexible arm. While these new products were introduced under the Logitech name, the company also continued innovation in its core mouse business. New and revolutionary technologies developed by Logitech allowed it to continue as an industry leader in the mouse and keyboard business.

The author would like to thank Tyler Thompson, Heather Wooten, Meagan Foy, Samantha Louras, and Will Hoffman for their research and contributions to this case. Reprinted by permission of Dr. Alan N. Hoffman, Dept. of Management, Bentley University, 175 Forest St, Waltham, MA 02452. RSM Case Development Centre prepared this teaching case to provide material for class discussion rather than to illustrate either effective or ineffective handling of a management situation. The author has disguised identifying information to protect confidentiality.

In the mid 1990s, the PC market exploded due to the popularity of the Internet and new home/office software applications. The growth of the PC industry created increasing demand for the peripheral products that Logitech produced. The Internet allowed computer users to access new areas, such as music, video, communications, and gaming. From that point forward, Logitech continued to grow both organically and through acquisition, as new opportunities arose to expand their portfolio of products.

Between 1998 and 2006, Logitech made a number of significant acquisitions to expand its product portfolio. It acquired companies such as Connectix for its line of webcams, Labtec for its audio business presence, Intrigue Technologies for its "Harmony" remote controls, and Slim Devices for its music systems. All of these acquisitions were accomplished strategically to help Logitech position itself in all aspects of the personal peripherals world.

In addition to achieving significant growth through strategic acquisitions, Logitech also continued to innovate and grow its core business. Logitech made significant innovations in the area of cordless mice and keyboards. It also introduced the industry's first retail pointing device with Bluetooth wireless technology. Logitech then expanded its Bluetooth technology to many other products in the digital world, including cordless gaming controllers and a personal digital pen.

Logitech provided consumers cutting-edge innovation while maintaining its product quality. Logitech maintained its product leadership by combining continued innovation, award-winning industrial design, and excellent price performance with core technologies, such as wireless, media-rich communications, and digital entertainment.

Strategic Direction

Logitech is in the business of designing and selling the world's best personal peripherals. The company continues to expand both internally and through acquisition to grow their portfolio of peripheral products while maintaining the strength and quality of its core technologies. Logitech is "driving innovation in PC navigation, internet communications, digital music, home-entertainment control, and gaming and wireless devices" (Logitech, 2007).

Logitech strives to continually "deliver landscape changing technology, while keeping a focus on even the subtlest of design details that makes its products personal and its brand cherished by millions of customers worldwide. Logitech will continue to help make interaction

with the digital world more personal and rewarding for entertainment in the living room, communications on the go, and personal computing in the office" (Logitech, 2007).

As a publicly traded company on both the Swiss Exchange and the NASDAQ Exchange, the organization's overall corporate objectives are growth and earnings. Throughout its entire existence, Logitech has continuously grown through both innovation and acquisition, while maintaining positive earnings. To date, the company has done well at accomplishing its key objectives. Growing out of these main objectives, Logitech has set several additional objectives, including:

- Product leadership
- Continued innovation
- Award-winning industrial design
- Strong price performance

Logitech is extremely proactive when it comes to innovation. Along with incremental improvement of its core technologies and products, Logitech is also continuously, radically innovating new technologies in the peripherals industry. When Logitech sees a business or electronics industry that is growing rapidly or quickly gaining recognition, it finds ways to design and create innovative peripheral products to complement the products that make up the specific industry. For example, when the gaming industry began to experience recognition and rapid growth, Logitech designed and introduced its first gaming console controller in 2000 (the Logitech GT Force racing wheel for Playstation 2).

Another of Logitech's significant innovations was the Logitech io Personal Digital Pen. This invention "merges the use of a traditional pad of paper with the digital world." In today's business world, a significant amount of information and documentation is stored and archived electronically. This new platform – the digital pen – will "enable the automated transformation of handwritten data into archived information for both consumers and professionals" (Logitech, 2007).

Through new product developments such as these, it is clear that Logitech is very proactive when it comes to innovation. The company wants to be the number one provider of all personal peripheral products in the world, and it strives to be the first to introduce any new and exciting peripheral technologies.

Competitors

As a specialized company, Logitech is exclusively in the industry of personal peripherals, which it sells to retailers as well as major computer manufacturers. The demand of such an industry often depends strongly on the economic stability and income of its consumers, as well as the profitability of its business customers. This is because technology products like the ones offered by Logitech are often expensive, and individuals and companies are reluctant to buy them unless they have the income to do so. Within this industry, there are a number of factors that affect Logitech's competitiveness and price structure. With respect to market competition, Logitech has three major competitors: Creative Technology Ltd., Microsoft Corporation, and Royal Philips Electronics N.V.

Creative Technology Ltd. is one of the worldwide leaders in digital entertainment products for the personal computer (PC) and the Internet. Creative Technology was founded in Singapore in 1981, with the vision that multimedia would revolutionize the way people interact with their PCs (Creative Technologies Ltd., 2010). The Creative Technology product line includes MP3 players, portable media centers, multimedia speakers and headphones, digital and web cameras, graphics solutions, revolutionary music keyboards, and PC peripherals. Creative had a net profit margin of −29.58% in FY 2009 and −32.82% in the first quarter of 2010.

Microsoft Corporation provides software/hardware products and solutions worldwide. Founded in 1975 by Bill Gates and Paul Allen, Microsoft's core business is to create operating systems and computer software applications (Daily Finance, 2010; Rovi Corp., 2010). Microsoft has since expanded into markets such as mice, keyboards, videogame consoles, customer relationship management applications, server and storage software, and digital music players. In FY 2009, Microsoft Corporation had annual sales of $58.4 billion and a net income of $14.5 billion.

Royal Philips Electronics is a Netherlands-based company that focuses on improving people's lives through innovation. Philips is a well-diversified company with products in many different industries. Products offered by Philips include consumer electronics, televisions, VCRs, DVD players, and fax machines, as well as light bulbs, electric shavers and other personal care appliances, medical systems, and silicon systems solutions (Philips, 2010). With this diversified portfolio of products, Royal Philips had FY 2009 revenues of $30.76 billion and a gross profit of $11.59 billion (Yahoo! Inc., 2010).

Logitech is the only company of this group exclusively focused on personal peripheral products, whereas all of its competitors have products and resources invested in a wide variety of other industries.

Trends

Logitech implemented a strategy of innovation mixed with strategic acquisitions to enhance its products with the technologies and software of other companies in order to create the most advanced, innovative, and collaborative experience for their customers. As Logitech has always been on the forefront of mouse and keyboard technology, it has also been a leader in video conferencing technology since the early stages of its mountable computer camera development. Instead of following market trends, Logitech has often created them.

From 1998 to 2004, Logitech made many important strategic acquisitions in order to enhance future portfolios and expand the depth of its peripheral product lines. Its first acquisition was the video camera division, QuickCam PC, of Connectix Corporation. This led to an influx of peripherals, such as cameras and wireless cameras, and served as a very early introduction to Logitech's current video conferencing division. The second successful acquisition was the 2001 purchase of Labtec, Inc., an audio peripheral maker.

Following the Labtec acquisition, the company developed a hunger to expand its product focus. In 2004, Logitech acquired Intrigue Technologies, Inc. This acquisition positioned Logitech as a leader in advanced remote-control production. With this, peripherals suddenly were able to accommodate more than just computer and videogame uses. This positioned them for their next acquisition, Slim Devices in 2006, a manufacturer of music systems. Logitech used these two acquisitions to expand its multi-business unit corporation into a diverse and specialized company appealing to a large group of technology users. Finally, with its acquisition of Paradial AS, Logitech was able to combine their peripheral products with the software, video effects, and security features Paradial offered (Logitech Acquires Paradial, 2010). This allowed Logitech to deliver a complete and intuitive HD video conferencing experience for companies of any size.

Future industry trends revolve around content strategy and consumer expectations regarding mobile web and Smartphone applications. Content strategy involves decisions about what information and features to include in a product, including those that provide the most benefit or fulfill the most needs; for Logitech, anything else is just noise and dilutes the product. In terms of mobile web and smartphone application trends, Logitech has three options: (1) develop closed partnerships with specific platforms (iPhone or Blackberry); (2) produce apps for each platform; or (3) produce "platform-neutral" apps by using the mobile web.

Global Presence

As the global economy expands and becomes more reliant on technology, Logitech has seen an increase in the desire for ease of use when it comes to portable computers, games, and video conferencing technology. Logitech has consistently expanded its product offerings to satisfy this growing demand for computer peripherals. In FY 2009, 85% of its revenue came from retail sales of peripheral products, such as mice, keyboards, speakers, webcams, headsets, headphones, and notebook stands. Logitech has also seen global demand sharpen for devices designed for specific purposes, such as gaming, digital music, multimedia, audio/visual communication over the Internet, and PC-based video security. The company's products combine essential core technologies, continued innovation, award-winning industrial design, and excellent value that are all necessary to come out on top of a rapidly changing and evolving technological industry. Since its inception in 1981, Logitech has been a growing player in the technological product market and has distributed products to over 100 different countries.

For Logitech, opportunities arose as the desire for global communication increased. The trend of wireless and portable communication, such as Skype and Apple's Facetime, has opened a window of opportunity for new and more advanced products to enable video communication and conferencing.

As computers have aged, Logitech has been able to sell add-on peripherals for users who want to add newer applications to their older computers. Logitech successfully continues to sell products at the end of the product life cycle, such as mice and keyboards, and to generate profits to fund new product development, such as the new Logitech Revue with Google TV. As consumers become more globally conscious and connected, Logitech is able to tailor its products toward the many uses of video communication and high speed Internet capabilities.

Since its founding, Logitech has created a global presence and reputation for its brand and products. In 2009, Logitech's sales were distributed globally, with 45.3% in the Eastern European, Middle Eastern and North African regions; 35.6% in the Americas; and 19.1% in Asia Pacific. By expanding its presence globally, Logitech became the leading provider of personal peripherals in the world. In addition to being an innovator in its industry, Logitech also has maintained reasonably priced products. In 2009, 67% of their sales stemmed from products that were priced under sixty dollars. This innovative mindset, accompanied by reasonable prices, has contributed to booming sales, and in the end, Logitech's good financial health as a company.

Finance

The recession in 2008/2009 hit Logitech hard. For the full fiscal year 2010, sales dropped to $2.0 billion, down from $2.2 billion in fiscal 2009. Operating income was $78 million, down from $110 million, and net income was $65 million ($0.36 per share), compared to $107 million ($0.59 per share) in the prior year. Gross margin for fiscal 2010 was 31.9 percent compared to 31.3 percent in fiscal 2009. As a result of the economic downturn, Logitech found it necessary to restructure its workforce. In early 2009, Logitech reduced its salaried workforce globally by 15%.

Logitech's stock price spiked to $40 in late 2007 as a result of record sales and profits from its successful launch of iPod-capable peripherals. The iPod peripherals (speakers, docks, and headphones) made the increasingly popular iPod easier to use. But by 2009, Logitech's operating margin was 5.15%, far below its 2007 high of 12%, due to increasing price competition. Logitech did not issue dividends to shareholders; it needed to reinvest its net income back into R&D and product advertising, and also have available capital for strategic acquisitions.

Logitech has outlined very specific financial objectives that it seeks to achieve. It aims to realize sales growth between 13–19% with a gross margin between 32–34%. Logitech also intends to invest 5% of its sales revenue to R&D and 12–14% to marketing. By continuously investing resources in research and development, Logitech has taken a strategic approach to maintaining long-term growth and profitability.

Marketing

Logitech began manufacturing mice for Apollo Computers, and later, for HP. These relationships were built at industry trade shows and became particularly important for Logitech's growth and expansion because such clients were not buying just one or two mice at a time – they purchased 25,000. This gave Logitech strong sales right out of the gate. Logitech also developed a logo for its brand that became well known among both corporate customers and the general public as a symbol of innovation and quality within the personal peripherals industry.

In 2004, Logitech also signed an agreement with Global Internet Telephone Company and Skype to co-market and promote their products in the United States, Canada and Europe (Logitech and Skype Announce

Marketing Agreement, 2004). Pursuant to this agreement, a Logitech headset and 120 Skype minutes were bundled together into one package and offered to customers. In addition, the two companies also cross-promoted one another on their respective websites. This was a wise marketing decision for Logitech because it expanded the brand name and promoted its product to more users, as Skype was also a booming and expanding company.

Logitech has also made very strategic decisions regarding the marketing of specific products. Logitech recognized that women were a segment typically not targeted by technology fields in general, and it saw this as a prime opportunity for the Logitech Quick Cam product (Buchanan, 2005). In 2005, Logitech launched commercials for the Quick Cam that targeted businesswomen, showing a traveling mother using the Logitech Quick Cam product in her hotel room to say goodnight to her children and husband. Logitech recognized that women do, in fact, embrace technology when it fits their needs, and demonstrated in its commercials how its product could fit those needs.

On a smaller scale, Logitech also made a wise marketing decision by giving products a recognizable and memorable logo. The Logitech logo and branding is visible on all of its products and has become a recognizable symbol of quality and innovation in the peripherals and technology industries.

Logitech initially had a limited marketing budget when it first introduced its mouse in the early 1980s. This small budget limited promotional activities available to Logitech. However, the company made a few key marketing decisions early on that allowed it to wisely implement the budget it had. Logitech chose to position itself at industry trade shows, particularly at Comdex in Las Vegas. This allowed Logitech not only to get the Logitech name out within the industry, but gained it several key clients that allowed it to expand and grow.

Operations

One of the initial weaknesses Logitech faced regarding operations was that it had numerous manufacturing locations dispersed throughout the world. The problem with having so many locations was that these facilities were not cost effective. Many of the facilities were located in countries where it was expensive to operate, and the labor costs for qualified employees were high. Logitech realized in the early 1990s that the personal computer industry was becoming increasingly competitive. Logitech thus made two primary operations decisions that allowed it to significantly increase its competitiveness. First, Logitech consolidated manufacturing,

which was once widely dispersed throughout China. This helped the company maintain lower prices on its products, increasing its competitiveness. In addition to its China manufacturing facilities, Logitech established a second center for R&D in Cork, Ireland – a prime location for innovation in the technology and IT sectors. Second, Logitech also knew the industry was changing rapidly and that it would no longer be able to compete simply by manufacturing computer mice. Logitech thus made a strategic operational decision to expand its product line beyond the mouse and introduced a variety of products, including a handheld scanner, Fotoman (a digital camera), Audioman (a speaker/microphone), and Wingman (the first gaming peripheral).

These operational decisions not only helped Logitech remain innovative and competitive within the industry, but they also positioned the company for success during the personal computing industry boom in the mid- to late-1990s, when the Internet and online industries took off. Even by that time, Logitech was known as a leading personal peripheral provider. Logitech was both innovative, with more than 130 personal computer peripheral products, and reasonably priced. When the PC industry took off, Logitech was already established as an industry leader, and its sales soared along with the industry.

Logitech also has become a leader in the wireless peripherals sector. By closely following consumer trends, Logitech saw early on that the personal peripherals sector was moving into a new digital era, where wireless peripherals were becoming a new trend. Logitech created an entirely new product category with the Logitech Cordless Desktop, a wireless mouse and keyboard bundle. By staying on top of and leading consumer trends, Logitech sold over 100 million cordless mice and keyboards.

The Changing Landscape Ahead

Logitech became a leader in computer peripherals by developing innovative products and focusing on the consumer's experience. Between 2007 and 2010 alone, Logitech received eleven different awards for nineteen products and fourteen categories (see App. IV). In a market saturated with deep-pocketed competitors like Microsoft and Philips, Logitech has used innovation as its means of survival.

In 2010, however, Logitech faced significant challenge: The way people interacted with their devices had begun to change. The iPhone and iPad used touch screen technology with built-in accelerometers, eliminating the need for mice and Trackpads. Additionally, camera and higher quality speakers had become standard equipment built into the iPhone, iPad, and Windows laptop computers; Apple had introduced the "magic pad" to replace the mouse altogether. The need for consumers to buy add-on peripherals was slowly evaporating, as more peripherals became standard equipment designed into new mobile technologies.

As a consequence, Logitech could someday see its peripherals market disintegrate completely. Logitech must decide if it should invest more in video conferencing and television all-in-one remote controls, and/or focus on developing partnerships with computer and telecom manufacturers and mobile carriers such as ATT, Verizon, T-Mobile, and Sprint. Once again, the computer industry is changing, and Logitech will have to formulate new diversification strategies to ensure its long-term survival.

Appendix I – History Timeline

1981	Daniel Borel and Pierluigi Zappacosta incorporate in Switzerland the company that will eventually be called Logitech.
1982	The company introduces its first mouse, the P-4.
1985	The company enters the retail market with the introduction of the C7 mouse.
1988	Logitech International S.A. is taken public on the Bourse de Zurich; a handheld scanner, the firm's first non-mouse product, is introduced.
1991	Logitech introduces the first radio-based cordless mouse.
1994	The company opens its manufacturing facility in Suzhou, China.
1997	Logitech gains a listing on the NASDAQ and divests its scanner business.
1998	Guerrino De Luca takes over the CEO position from Borel, who remains chairman; the QuickCim PC video camera division of Connectix Corporation is acquired.
2001	Logitech acquires audio peripheral maker Labtec Inc.
2003	Logitech ships its 500 millionth mouse.
2004	Intrigue Technologies, Inc., maker of advanced remote controls, is acquired.

Source: Logitech, 2007

Appendix II – Market Segments

Selected 2009 worldwide retail value share by category			
Mice	**Webcams**	**PC speakers**	**Remotes**
40.1%	49.4%	34.1%	39.8%

Source: Logitech estimate based on available market data.

Appendix III – Global Economic Trend Analysis

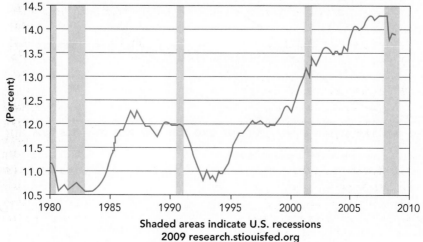

Household Debt Service Payments as a Percent of Disposable Personal Income (TDSP)
Source: Board of Governors of the Federal Reserve System

Shaded areas indicate U.S. recessions
2009 research.stiouisfed.org

Source: Yahoo! Finance, 2010

Appendix IV – List of Innovation Awards

- CES Innovations 2010 Honoree (7 categories)
- iF Product Design Award 2010 (1 product)
- CES 2009 Best of Innovations Category Winner (2 categories)
- CES Innovations 2009 Honoree (5 categories)
- 2009 red dot Design Award (1 product)
- Good Design Awards 2008 (4 products)
- CES 2008 Best of Innovations Honoree (1 product)
- CES Innovations 2008–Design and Engineering Showcase Honors" (6 products)
- iF Product Design Award 2008 (2 products)
- 2007 red dot Design Award (2 products)
- Good Design Award 2007 (2 products)

Appendix V – Internet Usage in China

Internet users
People with access to the Internet.

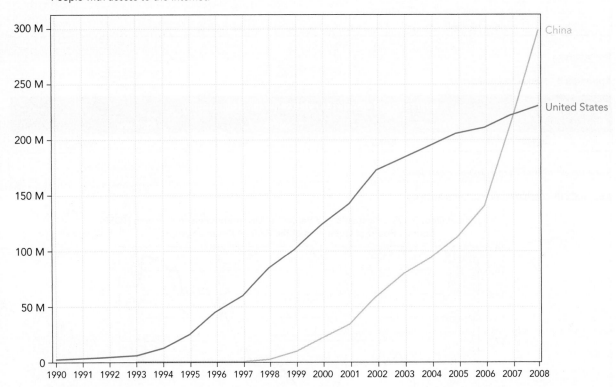

Data Source: World Bank, World Development Indicators. Last updated July 26, 2010

Appendix VI – Logitech Price Performance

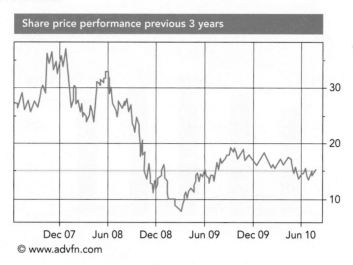

Source: ADVFN

Appendix VII – Logitech Six-Quarter Price Graph

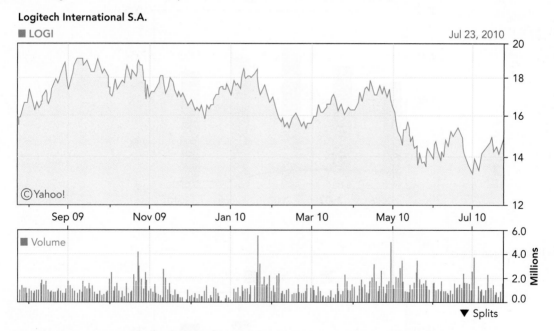

Source: Yahoo, http://finance.yahoo.com/q/bc?s=LOGI+Basic+Chart

Appendix VIII – Operating Margin

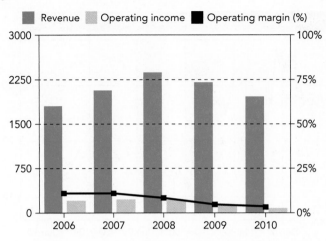

Appendix IX – Profit Margin

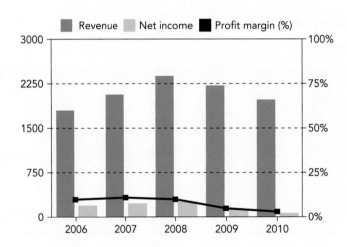

Appendix X – Debt-to-Assets

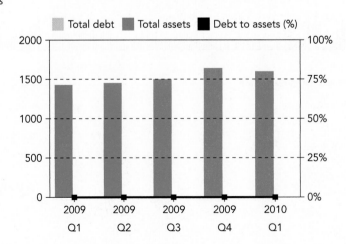

Appendix XI – Cash Position

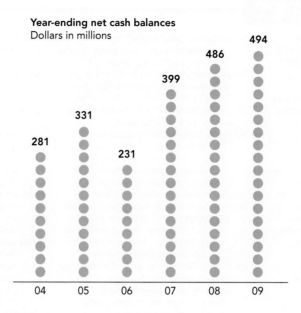

Year-ending net cash balances
Dollars in millions

281	331	231	399	486	494
04	05	06	07	08	09

Appendix XII – Logitech Solvency in 2010

SOLVENCY RATIOS	
SHORT-TERM SOLVENCY RATIOS (LIQUIDITY)	
Net Working Capital Ratio	22.09
Current Ratio	1.8
Quick Ratio (Acid Test)	1.2
Liquidity Ratio (Cash)	0.73
Receivables Turnover	9.6
Average Collection Period	38
Working Capital/Equity	35.3
Working Capital pS	2.02
Cash-Flow pS	0.78
Free Cash-Flow pS	−0.36
FINANCIAL STRUCTURE RATIOS	
Altman's Z-Score Ratio	4.35
Financial Leverage Ratio (Assets/Equity)	1.6
Debt Ratio	37.5
Total Debt/Equity (Gearing Ratio)	0.00
LT Debt/Equity	0.00
LT Debt/Capital Invested	16.0
LT Debt/Total Liabilities	0.0
Interest Cover	0.0
Interest/Capital Invested	

WORKS CITED

ADVFN. (2010). Logitech International S.A. Retrieved from http://www.advfn.com/p.php?pid=financials&symbol=NASDAQ%3ALOGI

Bardman, E. R. (2010). Logitech. [Slideshow Presentation]. Retrieved from http://www.bloobble.com/broadbandpresentations/presentations?itemid=3377

Buchanan, H. (2005, December 11). Logitech - Marketing Technology to Women. Retrieved from http://marketingtowomenonline.typepad.com/blog/2005/12/logitech_market.html

Business Wire. (2010, July 7). Logitech Acquires Paradial. Retrieved from http://www.businesswire.com/portal/site/home/permalink/?ndmViewId=news_view&newsId=20100707006829&newsLang=en

China Internet Watch. (2010, May 3). China Internet Users Reached 404 Million. Retrieved from http://www.chinainternetwatch.com/634/china-internet-usersreached-404-million/

Creative Technologies Ltd. (2010). Corporate Profile. Retrieved from http://www.creative.com/corporate/about/

Daily Finance. (2010, July 19). Microsoft Corp. - Company Description. Retrieved from http://www.dailyfinance.com/company/Microsoftcorporation/msft/nas/company-description

Eddy, N. (2009, November 11). Logitech Acquires LifeSize Communications. *eWeek.com*. Retrieved from http://www.eweek.com/c/a/Midmarket/Logitech-Announces-Acquisition-of-LifeSize-Communications-271671/

Fu, R. (2009, November 19). China Mobile Internet User Behavior Study 2009. *China Internet Watch*. Retrieved from http://www.chinainternetwatch.com/390/china-mobile-internet-user-behaviorstudy-2009/

FundingUniverse. (n.d.). Logitech Company History. Retrieved 20 July 2010 from http://www.fundinguniverse.com/company-histories/Logitech-International-SA-Company-History.html

Google Finance. (2010). Creative Technology Ltd. Retrieved from http://www.google.com/finance?q=SIN:C76

Google Finance. (2010). Logitech International S.A. Retrieved from http://www.google.com/finance?q=NASDAQ:LOGI&fstype=ii

Higginbotham, S. (2010, July 23). China has 420m Internet Users and a Need for Speed. GigaOm. Retrieved from http://gigaom.com/2010/07/23/china-has-420m-internet-users-and-a-need-for-speed/

Hollister, S. (2010, May 20). Logitech's Google TV Companion Box Includes Smartphone Apps, We Go Eyes-On. Retrieved from http://www.engadget.com/2010/05/20/logitechs-google-tv-companion-boxincludes-smartphone-apps-we/

Kirk, J. (2009, January 6). Mouse-Maker Logitech to Cut 525 Salaried Employees. *PC World*. Retrieved from http://www.pcworld.com/article/156397/mousemaker_logitech_to_cut_525_salaried_employees.html

Labrousse, J. (2009, November 11). Growth Opportunities Drive Product Strategy. Slideshow Presentation. Retrieved from http://www.bloobble.com/broadbandpresentations/presentations?itemid=3135

Logitech. (2004, November 17). Logitech and Skype Announce Marketing Agreement. Retrieved from http://ir.logitech.com/releasedetail.cfm?ReleaseID=174109

Logitech. (2007). iPod Capability. Retrieved from http://logitechviva.navisite.net/web/ftp/pub/pdf/speakers/ipod_custom_fit_adapors_enu.pdf

Logitech. (2007). Logitech History. Retrieved from http://www.logitech.com/lang/pdf/logitech_history_200703.pdf

Logitech. (2009). 2009 Annual Report. Retrieved from http://files.shareholder.com/downloads/LOGI/974346673x0x308649/2E8292E0-A5EF-4804-97A6-2273EFBA14D7/Logitech_2009_AR_Inv_Proxy_Webready_072309.pdf

Logitech. (2009). Logitech Advanced 2.4 GHz Technology with Unifying Technology. Retrieved from http://www.logitech.com/images/pdf/roem/Advanced_24_Unifying_FINAL070709.pdf

Logitech. (2010). Company Backgrounder. Retrieved from http://ir.logitech.com/overview.cfm?/&cl=us,en

Logitech. (2010). Key Ratios and Statistics. Retrieved from http://ir.logitech.com/financials-keyratios.cfm

Logitech. (2010). A Leader in Innovation and Design. Retrieved from http://www.logitech.com/en-us/175/482.

Logitech. (2010). The Logitech Story. Retrieved from http://www.logitech.com/enus/about/logitech-story

Logitech. (2010). Logitech's Swiss Origins. Retrieved from http://www.logitech.com/en-in/176/3708?WT.ac=pi%7C3814%7C%7Chp

Logitech and Skype Announce Marketing Agreement. (2004, November 17). Retrieved from http://ir.logitech.com/releasedetail.cfm?ReleaseID=174109

MISH. (2009, May 5). MISH's Global Economic Trend Analysis. [Graph image]. Retrieved from http://1.bp.blogspot.com/_nSTOvZpSgc/Sf1XZcpoJxl/AAAAAAAAGCk/Y38fyMUWmVM/s1600-h/debt+service+payments.png

Operating Margin. (2010). Investopedia ULC.

Philips. (2010). Company Profile. Retrieved from http://www.usa.philips.com/about/company/index.page

Profit Margin. (2010). Investopedia ULC.

Quindlen, G. P. (2009, November 11). Getting Back to Growth: Logitech. [Slideshow Presentation]. Retrieved from http://www.bloobble.com/broadbandpresentations/presentations?itemid=3134

Rovi Corp. (2010). Microsoft Corporation. Retrieved from http://www.allgame.com/company.php?id=915

Smith, G. (2010, January 12). Five User Experience Trends I'll be Watching in 2010. *nForm*. Retrieved from http://nform.ca/blog/2010/01/five-user-experiencetrends-il

Wikinvest. (2010). Logitech International SA (LOGI). Retrieved from http://www.wikinvest.com/stock/Logitech_International_S.A._(LOGI)

Yahoo! Finance. (2010). Logitech International S.A. (NMS). Retrieved from http://finance.yahoo.com/q/bc?s=LOGI+Basic+Chart

Yahoo! Inc. (2010). Royal Philips Electronics Company Profile. Retrieved from http://biz.yahoo.com/ic/41/41823.html

Jenna Beyer, Leon Faifman, Eric Ho, Miso Kezunovic, and Lance Olian

Texas A&M University

Love[i]

Rachael Fowler ran cross-country and played tennis in high school. In college, she successfully completed two full marathons. After college, she remained active and health conscious. Now a 37-year-old mother of two boys, Rachael maintains her physical fitness through gym sessions with a personal trainer and by attending yoga classes twice a week. At the end of one yoga session, a friend of hers suggested she purchase some yoga apparel from lululemon. Overhearing the two women talk, the class instructor added that she was a lululemon ambassador and began to rave about the quality and style of lululemon's products.

"This is how 80 percent of our guests come to know lululemon, through word-of-mouth. Guests are so pleased with the clothes we offer that they can't help but tell all their friends about it," explains Laci Levisay, a lululemon associate from a store in Austin, Texas.[1] Levisay continues, "For the other 20 percent who walk into lululemon stores with no previous knowledge, store employees look to find out as much as possible about the guests' lifestyle and then educate them on what products would best suit their needs."

Choose a Positive Thought

Based in Vancouver, Canada, lululemon athletica provides premium quality athletic apparel at a premium price. One of lululemon's signature items is its yoga pants, typically sold by competitors for between $25 and $50.[2] Yoga pants available in lululemon stores and online range between $78 and $128 with its most popular pair priced recently at $98 – two to three times rivals' prices.[3] However, lululemon's products sell and they sell fast. Demand for lululemon clothing is so high that stores have trouble keeping new lines in stock. Sheree Waterson, Lulu's chief product officer conveyed this example, saying, "A hot-pink color named 'Paris Pink' that launched in December (of 2011) was supposed to have a two-month lifecycle but sold out its first week."[4] The question then arises as to why customers, or "guests" as lululemon refers to them, are willing to pay high prices for high fashion items that are destined to be soaked in sweat!

It seems the answer to this question resides in lululemon's ability to connect with its guests on a deeper level than just the typical sales associate–customer relationship. After all, other companies such as Nike, Adidas, and Under Armour not only produce high-tech clothing with the same soft cotton feel, four-way stretch, and moisture-wicking technology that lululemon touts, but do so much less expensively for their end consumers. Ultimately, what competitors cannot duplicate is lululemon's culture. It is lululemon's deep understanding of its target market, close relationships with its communities, and an inimitable culture that transforms customers/guests into diehard loyalists.

This is not to say that lululemon does not uphold the highest quality standards in its products. Levisay states, "People will save up if they need to in order to afford our clothing because of the benefits they provide." She goes on to explain, "It's silly to spend that much on yoga

i. The majority of headers used in this case are quotes from the lululemon athletica manifesto.

pants if they're not going to live up to their promise."[5] Jennifer Black, president of an investment research firm confirms this sentiment saying, "lululemon won't put stuff in its store just to sell it. They don't compromise on quality."[6]

Friends Are More Important than Money

lululemon athletica's in-depth knowledge of its target audience is an important, firm-specific asset. "Rooted in yoga but expanded into any sweaty pursuit you may have, lululemon creates technical fabrics that work with you instead of against you. Plus, they look cute!" explains Levisay. The stores' "…guests comprise anyone living a physically active life that strives to achieve balance,"[7] although the majority of shoppers are female, have disposable income, and are in the 15- to 65-year-old range.[8] Fitness blogs confirm that lululemon "…recognizes this niche market and combines high performance material with attractive product design to create a committed brand following."[9]

One of the strongest examples of lululemon's focus on culture is the company manifesto, which appears on multiple lululemon products, from bags to water bottles. Explaining the company's perpetuation of its manifesto, Whitney, a store employee and lululemon blogger writes,

We are sharing a piece of our culture and inspiration as a company. We have traditionally printed our [bags] with the lululemon manifesto, which is a series of statements that embodies our company's vision, culture and beliefs… [as] a constant reminder of our vision to create components for people to live longer, healthier and more fun lives.[10]

Observe a Plant Before and After Watering

Each and every store employee at lululemon is considered a steward of the company's culture. From the beginning of the hiring process, throughout training, and continuing throughout employment, each employee is expected to reflect the company's mission and vision. lululemon athletica's "…success is reflected in everything within the store experience. The people who work there believe strongly in the lifestyle and what it represents."[11] A focus on employee development is a crucial component of the company's strategy. In general, a lot of money and effort is put into training store employees. Levisay comments,

Employees don't exist just to fold clothes or set up displays. They share their knowledge of the clothing and culture with every guest that walks through the door. They have the ability to explain functions of the clothing you would not necessarily recognize; items such as hidden pockets,

body support, material that protects against harmful UV rays, and special woven silver that makes the material antibacterial.[12]

Another employee, Samantha Baldwin, clarifies the link between employee and guest. "If your employees are happy and feel supported in their goals, your genuine nature comes across and this allows consumers to buy the experience, buy the product." This "caring-and-sharing" culture bolsters the high-quality products. Baldwin continues, "It wasn't just about selling stretchy pants. It was about connecting with people on an authentic level and finding out their story."[13]

This Is Not Your Practice Life

lululemon athletica was founded in 1998 by Dennis "Chip" Wilson in response to increased female participation in sports and in accordance with his belief in yoga as the optimal way to maintain athletic excellence into an advanced age. Wilson, an avid surfer and snowboarder, had previously parlayed his passions for these sports into building a successful company – Westbeach – that sold snowboarding and skateboarding apparel. After taking a yoga class, Chip fell in love with the practice. Once again melding his athletic passions with his acumen for producing high-end performance apparel, Chip saw the opportunity to produce higher-quality yoga attire.[14]

Wilson noticed that the cotton materials used in yoga apparel were inefficient for the demands placed upon them. He applied his knowledge of materials to design highly technical fabrics that would move and breathe better. Chip opened a design studio and retail store that doubled as a yoga studio at night to pay the rent. Yoga instructors at the studio became product testers, wearing Chip's designs while teaching, and providing feedback about the product.[15]

The first official lululemon store was opened in 2000 in Kitsilano, a beach neighborhood in Vancouver. The first store served as a community hub for multiple aspects of healthy living including nutrition, running, biking, and of course yoga. Realizing the potential for female-centric, high-quality athletic apparel, lululemon began to grow; expanding across Canada for the next couple of years and entering the U.S. market in 2003.

lululemon athletica continued to expand both in North America and overseas and announced its initial public offering in May 2007. In 2009, lululemon expanded its offerings by launching an e-commerce channel and ivivva, a subsidiary specializing in athletic gear for girls 4 to 14 years old.[16]

Dennis "Chip" Wilson

The success of lululemon is attributable to the vision of Dennis "Chip" Wilson. After taking the company public in 2007 and serving as Chief Innovation and Branding Officer, Chip officially turned over the reins in January 2012.[17] During his time with lululemon, he helped the company grow to 147 stores, transformed the brand into a cult following, and provided company focus by developing the lululemon manifesto.[18] He remains chairman of the board and continues to represent lululemon at investor meetings. His successor, Christine Day, has renewed the company's goals and assembled an exemplary "management team with a complementary mix of retail, design, operations, product sourcing, marketing and information technology experience from leading apparel and retail companies such as Abercrombie & Fitch Co., The Gap, Inc., Nike, Inc., and Speedo International Limited."[19]

Christine Day

Christine Day joined lululemon as Executive VP of Retail Operations in January 2008 and was promoted to CEO in June 2008.[20] Day was with Starbucks for 20 years, most recently serving as President of the Asia Pacific Group of Starbucks Coffee International.[21] Starbucks and lululemon are very similar in that both are high-growth, international companies focused on cultivating their culture and brand loyalty. Day will focus on brand expansion and developing long-term corporate- and business-level strategies.

John Currie

lululemon athletica's current Chief Financial Officer (CFO) joined the strategic leadership team in January 2007.[22] Currie has a long history as a financial leader within several companies including CFO of Intrawest Corporate and senior financial positions at a telecommunications service provider.[23] He helped Chip take lululemon public in July 2007 and actively communicates with investors every quarter.

Ten to Fifteen Friends Allows for Real Relationships

Of the nine individuals serving as members of lululemon's board of directors, seven are independent. These independent directors contribute a vast array of knowledge, including experience in retail markets, finance, and corporate structure. Several have worked with very high-growth companies and companies with strong corporate cultures. The combined skills and knowledge of this board will help guide lululemon through its growth and changes in its strategies. See Exhibit 1 for background information on additional leaders and board members.

Don't Trust that an Old Age Pension Will Be Sufficient

In terms of financial strength, lululemon athletica ("LULU") is positioned to weather declines in the economic environment. The company has a significant amount of cash, over 50 percent of assets and, although the company has a line of credit should it face an immediate liquidity need, lululemon holds no debt. Companies such as Adidas, Nike, and Under Armor all carry some debt and it is certainly noteworthy to see lululemon operate with none. lululemon athletica has experienced tremendous growth in both revenue and profitability over the last couple of years. As seen in its income statement, revenue grew by a compound annual growth rate of 41.47 percent from fiscal year (FY) 2009 to FY 2012. lululemon's net profit margin improved from 12.87 percent in 2010 to 18.39 percent in 2012, driven mainly by improvements in the gross margin and control over the growth in sales, general, and administration expenses. As expected by the growth in sales and profitability, both return on equity and return on assets also increased (Exhibit 2).

As seen in Exhibit 3, lululemon compares very favorably to some very well-known companies within the performance apparel clothing industry. Because lululemon operates primarily in a niche product market, it is able to compete against the likes of Adidas, Nike, and Under Armour and still generate above-average returns, principally by offering customers what it believes are higher-quality products. Historically, Adidas, Nike, and Under Armour did not offer separate apparel lines for yoga activities; however, all three have recently entered this particular market. Even so, lululemon is the only publicly traded company focused solely on the yoga apparel market. While lululemon does face competition from other companies with yoga apparel lines, none of these competitors can demand the premium that lululemon has on its products.

The Pursuit of Happiness Is the Source of All Unhappiness

At the beginning of FY 2013, lululemon was forecasting that its revenue and profit would continue to grow, albeit at a slower pace compared to the firm's recent growth rates. Management was forecasting that same-store sales would increase around 20 percent in FY 2013 and that earnings per share (EPS) would be between $1.50

Exhibit 1 Other lululemon Leaders

Delaney Schweitzer: Executive VP, Retail Operations North America

Delaney Schweitzer began her career at lululemon in 2002. Since her days as a lululemon educator then manager, Schweitzer has served in various capacities within lululemon, including Director of Training and Culture and Director of Original Intent. Prior to joining lululemon, Schweitzer spent 10 years in the hospitality industry as a general manager. She is a graduate of the Executive Advanced Management Program at Harvard Business School. (Source: *Forbes.com*. http://people.forbes.com/profile/schweitzer-delaney/142021. Apr 2012)

Sheree Waterson: Executive VP, Chief Product Officer

Sheree Waterson has served as Executive VP, General Merchandise Management and Sourcing since June 2008. Prior to joining lululemon, she served as President of Speedo North American, a Warnaco, Inc. brand, from January 2005 to June 2007. She was VP of Merchandising, Women's, for Levi Strauss & Co. from January 2002 to August 2004. From 1997 to August 2001, she served as CEO of Enfashion.com. She graduated from the University of California, Berkeley with a BA in Psychology. (Source: *Forbes.com*. http://people.forbes.com/profile/sheree-waterson/127405. Apr 2012)

Michael Casey: Director

Michael Casey has been a member of the Board since October 2007. He retired from Starbucks in October 2007, where he had served as Senior VP and CFO from August 1995 to September 1997, and Executive VP, CFO, and Chief Administrative Officer from September 1997 to October 2007. Subsequent to retirement, he served as a Senior Advisor to Starbucks from October 2007 to May 2008 and from November 2008 to present. Prior to joining Starbucks, Casey was Executive VP and CFO for Family Restaurant, Inc., and President and CEO of El Torito Restaurants, Inc. He is also a member of the board of directors of The NASDAQ OMX Group, Inc. Casey graduated from Harvard University with an AB degree in Economics and Harvard Business School with an MBA.

RoAnn Costin: Director

RoAnn Costin has been a member of the Board since March 2007. She has served as the President of Wilderness Point Investments, a financial investment firm, since 2005. From 1992 until 2005, she served as the President of Reservoir Capital Management, Inc., an investment advisory firm. Costin was a director and member of the audit committee of Toys "R" Us from 1995 to 2005. Costin received a BA in Government from Harvard University and an MBA from the Stanford University Graduate School of Business.

Brad Martin: Director

R. Brad Martin has been a member of the Board since March 2007. He served as the CEO of Saks Inc., a retail department store company, from 1989 until January 2006. He is a member of the board of directors of First Horizon National Corporation, a banking company, Dillard's, Inc., and FedEx Corporation. He also served on the board of directors of Gaylord Entertainment Company from November 2006 to May 2009, and on the board of directors of Ruby Tuesday, Inc. from April 2008 to June 2011. Martin received his BS in Political Science from the University of Memphis and an MBA from Vanderbilt University.

Marti Morfitt: Director

Martha A.M. (Marti) Morfitt has been a member of the Board since December 2008. She has served as the CEO of Airborne, Inc. since October 2009 and as a principal of River Rock Partners, Inc., a business and cultural transformational consulting firm, since 2008. She served as the President and CEO of CNS, Inc., a manufacturer and marketer of consumer healthcare products from 2001 through March 2007. From 1998 to 2001, she was COO of CNS, Inc. Morfitt currently serves on the boards of Graco, Inc., a fluid handling systems and components company of Life Time Fitness, Inc. She received her HBA (Honors Business Administration) from the Richard Ivey School of Business at the University of Western Ontario and an MBA from the Schulich School of Business at York University.

Rhoda M. Pitcher: Director

Rhoda M. Pitcher has been a member of the Board since December 2005. For the past 14 years, she has been the Founder and CEO of Rhoda M Pitcher Inc., a management consulting firm providing services in organizational strategy and the building of executive capability to *Fortune* 500 corporations, institutions, start-ups, and non-profits. From 1978 to 1997, Pitcher co-founded, built, and sold two international consulting firms. Pitcher holds a Master's degree in Organizational Development from University Associates.

Thomas G. Stemberg: Director

Thomas G. Stemberg has been a member of the Board since December 2005. Since March 2007, he has been the managing partner of Highland Consumer Fund, a venture capital firm. From February 2005 until March 2007, he was a venture partner with Highland Capital Partners. Stemberg co-founded Staples, Inc., an office supplies retailer, serving as its Chairman from 1988 to 2005, and as its CEO from 1986 until 2002. He serves on the board of directors of CarMax, Inc., PETsMART, Inc., and Guitar Center. He received an AB in Physical Science from Harvard University and an MBA from the Harvard Business School.

Emily White: Director

Since September 2010, White has been Senior Director of Local and now Mobile Partnerships at Facebook Inc. Prior to joining Facebook, White was at Google Inc., running the North America Online Sales and Operations channel from 2001 to 2007 and the Asia Pacific and Latin America business from 2007 to 2009. From 2009 through 2010, White ran the Local and Commerce monetization businesses. She serves on the boards of the National Centre for Women in I.T., a non-profit coalition working to increase the participation of girls and women in computing and I.T. She received a BA in Art History from Vanderbilt University.

Source, except where indicated: *lululemon.com*, http://investor.lululemon.com/management.cfm, April 2012.

Exhibit 2 Financial Metrics

	FY 2012	FY 2011	FY 2010
Revenue Growth	40.63%	57.14%	28.12%
Net Profit Margin	18.39%	17.12%	12.87%
Return on Equity	37.12%	39.09%	16.89%
Return on Assets	29.83%	30.21%	18.97%

Source: lululemon athletica inc: Competitors. Finance. *Yahoo.com*. Accessed 20 April 2012.

and $1.57. The EPS expectation translates into a 16 to 22 percent growth range for net profit in 2013, which is substantial given the economic condition of the United States.[24] Even so, these forecasts disappointed stock analysts that had expected the company would maintain its breakneck pace of growth at least throughout 2013.[25]

As the first – and sole – potential sign of trouble for the company, YE 2012 inventory increased nearly 85 percent from $57 million to $104 million. This growth in inventory combined with a lower sales growth forecast may reflect pressure from the economic environment, pressure that lululemon has historically weathered unscathed. Additionally, with the increased popularity of yoga and sustained above-average returns, new competitors are beginning to enter the market. For instance, in late 2011, Nike, Gap, and Nordstrom launched their own lines of yoga clothing to capture part of the growing market. The increased competition from these major apparel retailers will pressure lululemon and test its ability to continue generating desirable returns for shareholders as well as for other stakeholders such as employees.

Financial information regarding lululemon appears in Exhibits 4, 5, and 6.

Life Is Full of Setbacks

lululemon athletica has four primary competitors that operate in the same sphere of yoga apparel: Nike, Adidas, Under Armour, and VF Corp. Up to this point, lululemon has been able to successfully expand its business through focused and targeted marketing – but the firm's competitive environment is rife with potential threats and challenges.

Nike

Nike began with a handshake between two visionary Oregonians: Bill Bowerman and Phil Knight. This pair grew the company from a U.S.-based footwear distributor to a global marketer of athletic footwear, apparel, and equipment that is unrivaled in the world.[26] Headquartered near Beaverton, Oregon, a suburb of Portland, Nike now operates in more than 160 countries around the globe. Through its suppliers, shippers, retailers, and other service providers, Nike directly or indirectly employs nearly one million people. This includes more than 35,000 Nike employees across six continents, each of whom contributes to fulfilling Nike's mission statement: "To bring inspiration and innovation to every athlete in the world."[27]

The Nike brand is world-renowned and the company is characterized by strong operational and financial performance. For FY 2011, the company recorded $20.8 billion in revenues and $2.8 billion in income before taxes. Nike's balance sheet is strong and the company has

Exhibit 3 Direct Competitor Comparison

	lululemon	Adidas	Nike	Under Armour	Industry Average
Market Capitalization	$10.58B	$16.39B	$50.77B	$5.26B	$416.10M
Employees	5,807	40,637	38,000	1,800	2.59K
Quarterly Revenue Growth	51.4%	11.3%	15.1%	33.9%	14.7%
Revenue	$1.00B	$17.64B	$23.42B	$1.47B	$812.37M
Gross Margin	56.9%	47.5%	43.8%	48.4%	35.5%
EBITDA	$317.22M	$1.67B	$3.46B	$199.07M	$60.60M
Operating Margin	28.67%	7.57%	12.98%	11.05%	5.80%
Net Income	$184.06M	$887.06M	$2.27B	$96.34M	N/A
Earnings Per Share	$1.27	$2.12	$4.79	$1.85	$0.17
Price to Earnings	$58.03	$18.52	$23.11	$54.88	$13.88
Price to Earnings Growth	$1.56	$2.89	$1.72	$2.11	$1.01
Price to Sales	$10.47	$0.93	$2.14	$3.39	$0.51

Source: Lululemon Athletica, Inc: Competitors. Finance.*Yahoo.com*. Accessed 20 April 2012.

Exhibit 4 Consolidated Statements of Operations

(Dollars in Thousands)	Jan 29, 2012	Jan 30, 2011	Jan 31, 2010
Net revenue	$1,000,839	$711,704	$452,898
Cost of goods sold	431,569	316,757	229,812
Gross profit	569,270	394,947	223,086
Operating Expenses:			
Selling, general and administrative expenses	282,312	212,784	136,161
Provision for impairment and lease exit costs	–	1,772	379
Income from operations	286,958	180,391	86,546
Other income (expense), net	2,500	2,886	164
Income before provision for income taxes	289,458	183,277	86,710
Provision for income taxes	104,494	61,080	28,429
Net income	184,964	122,197	58,281
Net income attributable to non-controlling interest	901	350	
Net income attributable to lululemon athletica inc.	$184,063	$121,847	$58,281
Net basic earnings per share	$ 1.29	$ 0.86	$ 0.41
Diluted earnings (loss) per share	$ 1.27	$ 0.85	$ 0.41
Basic weighted-avg number of shares outstanding	143,196	70,860	70,251
Diluted weighted-avg number of shares outstanding	145,278	71,929	70,949

Source: lululemon athletica, Inc. Form 10-K for 2011. Accessed 14 Apr 2012.

approximately $4.6 billion in cash and short-term investments, representing over 30 percent of assets. Nike holds under $0.5 billion in debt, a minimal amount compared to its liquidity. In terms of financial strength, Nike has a substantial capacity to invest in new markets and ventures.

Nike recently launched its own line of yoga apparel to capture part of the growing market. Nike yoga products are typically part of Nike's Dri-Fit line and are priced less than lululemon's products. Nike tops are priced from $20 to $40 while its pants are priced from $40 to $70. The line was launched in late 2011 and it has yet to be seen whether its products will be attractive to lululemon's customers.

Adidas

Adolf ("Adi") Dassler was inspired by a single idea when he made his first shoes in 1920 at just twenty years of age: to provide every athlete with the best footwear for their respective discipline. This principle guided him and his company until his death in 1978. His first shoe, made from the few materials available in the difficult post-war period, was constructed using canvas. From the very beginning, Dassler, a passionate athlete himself, was in close contact with sporting event participants, and personally attended many important sporting events.[28]

On January 31, 2006, Adidas acquired Reebok International Ltd., providing the new Adidas Group

with a footprint of around €9.5 billion ($11.8 billion) in the global athletic footwear, apparel, and sports hardware markets. Today, the Adidas product range extends from footwear and apparel to accessories for all kinds of sports. Its key priority sports are running, soccer, basketball, and training.[29]

Similar to Nike, Adidas is a world-renowned brand and is characterized by solid operational and financial performance. For FY 2011, the company recorded €3.3 billion in revenues and €0.9 billion in income before taxes. Adidas' balance sheet is moderately strong; the company has approximately €1.3 billion in cash and short-term investments, representing over 12 percent of assets. Adidas holds under €1.3 billion in debt, a moderate amount compared to its liquidity. Based on these metrics, Adidas has the capacity to invest in new markets and ventures.

Though Adidas does have yoga apparel, its line is very limited. The firm's styling is significantly different from lululemon's, suggesting that Adidas is targeting a different market compared to lululemon.

Under Armour

Founded in 1996 by former University of Maryland football player Kevin Plank, Under Armour started with the simple plan to make a superior tee shirt; one that

Exhibit 5 Consolidated Balance Sheets

(Dollars in Thousands)	Jan 29, 2012	Jan 30, 2011	Jan 31, 2010
ASSETS			
Current assets			
Cash and cash equivalents	$409,437	$316,286	$159,573
Accounts receivable	5,202	9,116	8,238
Inventories	104,097	57,469	44,070
Prepaid expenses and other current assets	8,357	6,408	4,529
	527,093	389,279	216,410
Property and equipment, net	162,941	70,954	61,591
Goodwill and intangible assets, net	31,872	27,112	8,050
Deferred income taxes	8,587	7,894	15,102
Other non-current assets	4,141	4,063	6,105
	$734,634	$499,302	$307,258
LIABILITIES AND STOCKHOLDERS' EQUITY			
Current liabilities			
Accounts payable	$14,536	$6,659	$11,028
Accrued liabilities	34,535	25,266	17,583
Accrued compensation & related expenses	22,875	16,872	10,626
Income taxes payable	8,720	18,399	7,742
Unredeemed gift card liability	22,773	18,168	11,699
	103,439	85,364	58,678
Other non-current liabilities	25,014	19,645	15,472
	128,453	105,009	74,150
Stockholders' equity			
Undesignated preferred stock	–	–	–
Exchangeable stock	–	–	–
Special voting stock	–	–	–
Common stock	551	534	511
Additional paid-in capital	205,557	179,870	158,921
Retained earnings	373,719	189,656	67,809
Accumulated other comprehensive income	21,549	20,329	5,867
	601,376	390,389	233,108
Non-controlling interest	4,805	3,904	–
	$734,634	$499,302	$307,258

Source: lululemon athletica inc. Form 10-K for 2011. Accessed 14 Apr 2012.

provided compression, wicked perspiration off your skin rather than absorbing it, and worked with your body to regulate temperature and enhance performance.[30] Under Armour's mission is to "Make all athletes better through passion, design, and the relentless pursuit of innovation."[31]

For FY 2011, the company recorded $1.47 billion in revenues and $0.16 billion in income before taxes. Under Armour's balance sheet is strong and the company has approximately $175 million in cash and short-term investments, representing over 19 percent of assets. The company holds approximately $78 million in debt, a relatively minimal amount compared to its liquidity. Under Armour has the capacity required to invest in new markets and ventures, but not to the degree that Nike and Adidas

Exhibit 6 Consolidated Statements of Cash Flows

(Dollars in Thousands)	Jan 29, 2012	Jan 30, 2011	Jan 31, 2010
Cash flows from operating activities			
Net income attributable to lululemon athletica inc	$184,063	$121,847	$58,281
Net income attributable to non-controlling interest	901	350	–
Net income	184,964	122,197	58,281
Items not affecting cash			
Depreciation and amortization	30,259	24,614	20,832
Stock-based compensation	10,340	7,273	5,616
Provision for impairment and lease exit costs	–	1,772	379
Derecognition of unredeemed gift card liability	(1,775)	(1,406)	(2,183)
Deferred income taxes	(693)	11,234	387
Excess tax benefits from stock-based compensation	(5,750)	(7,863)	3,858
Gain on investment	–	(1,792)	–
Other, including net changes in other non-cash balances	(13,730)	23,966	30,790
Net cash provided by operating activities	203,615	179,995	117,960
Cash flows from investing activities			
Purchase of property and equipment	(116,657)	(30,357)	(15,497)
Investment in and advances to franchise	–	–	(810)
Acquisition of franchises	(5,654)	(12,482)	–
Net cash used in investing activities	(122,311)	(42,839)	(16,307)
Cash flows from financing activities			
Proceeds from exercise of stock options	9,614	5,836	1,209
Excess tax benefits from stock-based compensation	5,750	7,863	(3,858)
Net cash provided by (used in) financing activities	15,364	13,699	(2,649)
Effect of exchange rate changes on cash	(3,517)	5,858	3,772
Increase in cash and cash equivalents	93,151	156,713	102,776
Cash and cash equivalents, beginning of year	$316,286	$159,573	$56,797
Cash and cash equivalents, end of year	$409,437	$316,286	$159,573

Source: lululemon athletica inc. Form 10-K for 2011. Accessed 14 Apr 2012.

possess. The company has grown rapidly over the years, but remains significantly smaller than Nike and Adidas.

The Under Armour brand is strong in the United States; however, it lacks the worldwide awareness that Nike and Adidas possess. Nevertheless, the company has strong operations and financial performance and has marketed its products very aggressively in the United States. Under Armour recently launched its own line of yoga apparel to capture part of this expanding, growing market. Under Armour's yoga products are priced from $40 to $100 and its pants are priced from $70 to $100. The Under Armour yoga line has styling similar to lululemon yet has a limited selection as, to date, the company has focused on other apparel lines.

VF Corp.

VF Corporation, organized in 1899, is a worldwide leader in branded lifestyle apparel, footwear, and related products. VF is a highly diversified apparel company with multiple brands, product categories, channels of distribution, and geographies. Included in the VF Corp. portfolio are brands such as The North Face, Vans, Timberland, Jansport, Wrangler, 7 For All Mankind, and Nautica. It markets its products to consumers shopping in specialty stores, upscale and traditional department stores, national chains, and mass merchants located in different parts of the world.[32]

Among its brands, VF Corp. is the owner of lucy, a women's active wear brand that most closely compares to lululemon's dedicated yoga apparel brand. lucy is a relatively young company, founded only a year after lululemon. "The styles are designed and developed by women who do the activities we design for: yoga, running, training, exploring the outdoors, and traveling to your favorite destination."[33]

For FY 2011, VF Corp. recorded $9.4 billion in revenues and $1.2 billion in income before taxes. Of the lululemon competitors, VF Corp.'s balance sheet is the weakest. The company has approximately $341 million in cash and short-term investments, representing just over 3 percent of assets. VF Corp. holds over $2.1 billion in debt, a relatively large amount compared to its liquidity. Based on these metrics, VF Corp. has a very limited capacity to invest in new markets and ventures.

VF's lucy is not well known within the United States and represents only a small portion of the VF Corp. brand portfolio. lucy yoga products are typically priced less than lululemon's products with a similar styling. lucy tops tend to be priced from $35 to $80 while its pants are priced from $35 to $90. lucy is the closest brand to lululemon in terms of product and customer focus, but the brand is one of the smallest in a large portfolio of the parent firm's brands.

That Which Matters the Most Should Never Give Way to that Which Matters the Least

The general environment is particularly interesting for lululemon due to the niche nature of its product offerings (yoga, and more recently, running gear). Although lululemon offers products for males and even for children as young as four years old,[34] its target is females between the ages of 15 and 65. Given this broad, targeted band of the female population, the potential market for lululemon's products is over 105 million women in the U.S. alone,[35] representing over two-thirds of the U.S. female population. Not even considering men, children, and international customers, it is evident that the potential customer base for lululemon is substantial. Of course, other factors, such as the medium to high price of its products and the fact that not all potential customers need or want yoga apparel, cull from this potential customer base.

The geographic footprint of lululemon is growing every day. The company currently has 47 stores in Canada, 108 in the United States, 18 in Australia, and 1 in New Zealand.[36] Through distribution centers in the United States and Canada, and the 2009 addition of its e-commerce business, the company has been able to serve an increasing number of international markets.[37] Since its customer base encompasses such a large number of people, the ethnic mix of its customers is quite diverse. Based on its product pricing, lululemon targets higher income clientele.

Given the global economic downturn, consumers worldwide have cut their discretionary spending. The company's bottom line would be expected to decrease due to the high priced, :discretionary" nature of its products; surprisingly, lululemon's sales have continued to grow for the past twelve quarters.[38] At this point however, it is unknown how the long-term effects of the changing global economy will affect the firm's profitability.

Uncertainties in political and legal areas also affect lululemon. The company has manufacturing facilities in the United States and Canada, but it also relies heavily on its factories in China, Taiwan, South Korea, Peru, Israel, Cambodia, Thailand, and Vietnam.[39] International and country-specific rules and regulations play a significant role in getting the company's products to market in a timely manner. Ensuring compliance with lululemon's internal, international, and country-specific policies is a time- and capital-intensive effort.

Recently, the company has had to deal with the California Transparency in Supply Chains Act of 2010. This law requires retailers and manufacturers doing business in California to disclose their efforts to eliminate human trafficking and slavery from their direct supply chains.[40] This is just one example of the many legal hurdles that lululemon must address to operate effectively both domestically and globally while relying on foreign production facilities. Any potential changes in international trade laws could have a detrimental effect on lululemon's operations. Additionally, changes in international tax regulations and country-specific tax laws play a large role in the variability of the company's earnings and are an area that the company must continue to carefully evaluate.

Technology has played a surprisingly important role in lululemon's operations. Many of its product features are technology driven, including its use of silver thread in select products.[41] Technology has also played a key role in lululemon's expansion. The introduction of e-commerce in April 2009 has made it possible for the company to reach customers outside of its traditional bricks-and-mortar locations.[42, 43]

Virtually all of the company's employees, ambassadors, and guests participate in yoga and/or running. Collectively, they provide a considerable amount of valuable feedback on how to improve existing products and create potential product line extensions. Guests are given the opportunity to provide feedback in stores and online. Ambassadors are local athletes and yoga instructors recruited by lululemon to help promote the brand and apparel. They are the focal point of the company's unique "grassroots marketing" campaign, but are not paid by the company. Ambassadors are given products to test so they can provide crucial feedback for the company. In turn, they become fans of lululemon's products and encourage potential customers to visit a store.[44]

Finally, lululemon's physical environment is taken into consideration in the company's operations. Whether it is reducing paper use or packaging waste at its corporate offices or gathering fabric remnants at its factories, lululemon is constantly striving to reduce its environmental footprint.[45]

Creativity IS Maximized When You Are Living in the Moment

lululemon athletica constantly scans its external environment to identify potential key issues, including new trends that the firm might be able to serve by developing product line extensions and/or entering new markets. Scanning keeps lululemon alert with respect to identifying new potential competitors.

After a thorough environmental scanning, lululemon continues to monitor the environment and attempts to filter out the "noise" in an effort to identify what is actually important. Upon identifying potential issues, lululemon develops projections of anticipated outcomes should a potential issue become a real problem.[46] Finally, lululemon conducts an assessment of the timing and importance of environmental changes and trends it observes.[47]

The implementation of this comprehensive analysis process led the company to introduce its running apparel segment and develop the ivivva brand for children. It also contributed to lululemon adding its e-commerce option to serve its global customer base. This process also keeps the company aware of potential competition, including the multiple entrants into its product field since the company's founding in 1998.[48]

Jealousy Works the Opposite Way You Want It to

The threat of new entrants within the yoga apparel industry is very high, and this poses a threat to lululemon's continuous efforts to succeed. Virtually every company that has any semblance of active wear in its product lines and manufacturing capabilities is an actual or potential competitor. As noted previously, leading global companies, such as Nike and Adidas, and regional powerhouses such as Under Armour, have joined the market.[49] The ease of

market entry has also opened the door for retailers such as GAP, Nordstrom, Eddie Bauer, Macy's, and many others in recent years. These new entrants bring additional capacity that, theoretically, should reduce lululemon's profits, especially in an industry where switching costs are very low. As a testament to the power of its brand and culture, this has yet to become a reality for lululemon.

The company has high standards for its suppliers and this requires a large investment of lululemon's time to ensure they are up to standards. In a retail setting, timing is very important. Because lululemon champions product exclusivity as a main component of its popularity, having an adequate and timely supply of product is crucial. In addition, lululemon does not own any of its manufacturing facilities. In fact, more than 36 percent of its product offerings are produced by 5 of its 45 manufacturers. If something were to happen to any one of these five manufacturers, it would have devastating effects on lululemon's supply chain. Additionally, 90 percent of its products are produced in Asia, with 49 percent produced solely in China.[50] Any global political or environmental events that affect this part of the globe would have material ramifications on lululemon's product supply.

The vast number of similar products available from many different brands means that buyers have multiple choices available to them. Additionally, lululemon's products are on the high end of the price spectrum. A change in buying habits or a large decrease in discretionary spending could affect lululemon's ability to operate as profitably as the company desires. Surprisingly, lululemon has continued to grow at an admirable pace in spite of the global economic downturn and decline in discretionary spending. Not only is it charging more than some, if not most, of its competitors, but it is selling more than it ever has. Its brand equity combined with extremely loyal customers and a highly successful grassroots marketing campaign have made lululemon a force in the industry.

Dance, Sing, Floss, and Travel

lululemon athletica uses a clear set of strategies to achieve the company's vision – "To be a community hub to provide our guests with knowledge, tools and the components for people to live longer, healthier and more fun lives."[51]

Listen, Listen, Listen

The company relies on its ability to maintain the value and reputation of its brand by successfully anticipating and adjusting to customer preferences and changing needs.[52] lululemon concentrates on providing an active and comfortable communication relationship with its customers. One example is the fact that executives go into the stores and observe customer behavior. Further examples include yoga instructors providing frequent and detailed inputs to the firm's research and development process, sales staff treating their customers as guests rather than buyers, and apparel folding stations located near the dressing rooms so employees can overhear and respond to comments and complaints.[53]

By building relationships with its customers, lululemon is better able to design and produce products that satisfy their needs. For instance, the design team "identifies trends based on market intelligence and research, proactively seeks the input of our guests and our ambassadors" to develop products in conjunction with suppliers.[54] This process ensures that its products are of the highest quality and able to perform according to customer preference.

Goal Setting Triggers Your Subconscious Computer

The company concentrates on creating value through its grassroots marketing, superior service, and communication with customers. Supply-chain activities also play an interesting role in lululemon's strategy. The company creates artificial scarcity through limited production runs and purposely seeks to maintain low levels of inventory. This strategy keeps the already sought-after clothing at a demand level that exceeds supply. As a result, lululemon rarely has leftover inventories, which serves as an advantage in the ever-changing retail industry. When new lines are released to the public, excitement is generated, and these lines typically sell out before their anticipated expiration date. According to the *Wall Street Journal*, this creates a "feeling of scarcity that increases the psychological need to purchase the products."[55]

Your Outlook on Life Is a Direct Reflection of How Much You Like Yourself

The company relies on its unique capability to design and create technologically advanced products and market those unique products to a particular/targeted group of individuals. The company indicates that it may expand its product variety and target new market segments that share the same interests as the target market: healthy lifestyles and stylish performance wear.[56]

Sweat Once a Day

The vast majority of lululemon's revenues come from product sales in its stores located throughout the world; but a small portion comes from sales at the five ivivva branded stores. The company notes that ivivva's clothes are for very seriously active girls. The products are designed with inputs from several parties including ice skaters, gymnasts, and dancers. At least in the near term, if not the mid-term as well, revenue growth is expected to come from newly established lululemon locations, increases in ivivva's sales, and from additional online sales activity. Finally, two percent of total revenues come from wholesale operations. Revenue from wholesale operations – originating in premium yoga studios, health clubs, and fitness centers – are not expected to grow dramatically. Wholesale operations are viewed as offering "an alternative distribution channel that is convenient for our core consumer and enhances the image of our brand."[57]

Do It Now, Do It Now, Do It Now

The company's success has been built on lululemon's ability to deliver quality products that are carefully and successfully tailored to address customers' preferences. The company has been able to create these products through input received from customers and through its grassroots marketing that utilizes ambassadors, such as local athletes and yoga instructors. As the company grows in size and continues to expand globally, can it maintain the community-centered and symbiotic relationships it has historically relied on for success?

International growth is another issue for lululemon to consider. To date, lululemon has expanded internationally into various countries such as the United States, Australia and New Zealand. These developed countries share common languages and have similar cultures, meaning that the barriers to expansion in these countries are lower than the barriers in emerging markets such as China and India. With further expansion, will the company be able to replicate its success in countries with significantly different cultures?

NOTES

1. Levisay, L. (19 Apr 2012). Interview with Laci Levisay. (L. Olian, Interviewer)
2. Mattioli, D. (22 Mar 2012). Lululemon's Secret Sauce. Retrieved 16 Apr 2012, from *Wall Street Journal*. http://online.wsj.com/article/SB100014240527023038129045772958 82632723066.html
3. Women's: Pants. Retrieved 14 Apr 2012, from *lululemon.com*. http://shop.lululemon.com/products/category/women-pants?mnid=mn;women;bottoms;pants
4. Mattioli, D. *op. cit.*
5. Levisay, L. *op. cit.*
6. Stettner, M. (4 Mar 2011). Lululemon's Bags Reinforce A Distinctive Culture. Retrieved 12 Apr 2012, from *Investors.com*.
7. Levisay, L. *op. cit.*
8. lululemon athletica inc. (2011). *lululemon athletica inc. Annual 10-K.*
9. Maggie. (8 Oct 2009). Lululemon Puts The CULT In Culture. Retrieved 18 Apr 2012, from *The Fit Post*. http://thefitpost.com/2009/10/08/lululemon-puts-the-cult-in-culture/
10. Whitney. (22 Apr 2010). Carry on and spread love! Retrieved 15 Apr 2012, from *lululemon.com*. http://www.lululemon.com/community/blog/carry-on-and-spread-love/
11. Ip, A. (2 Dec 2011). Lululemon Athletica a carefully cultivated culture. Retrieved 14 Apr 2012, from *The Calgary Journal*. http://www.calgaryjournal.ca/index.php/ourcity/politics-a-money/387-lululemon-athletica-a-carefully-cultivated-culture
12. Levisay, L. *op. cit.*
13. Ip, A. *op. cit.*
14. Our Company History. Retrieved 19 Apr 2012, from *lululemon.com*. http://www.lululemon.com/about/history
15. Ibid.
16. Our frequently asked questions. Retrieved 20 Apr 2012, from *lululemon.com*. http://www.lululemon.com/faq
17. Dreier, F. (2 Feb 2012). Lululemon CEO: Wilson Knew It Was Time To Go. Retrieved 15 Apr 2012, from *Forbes*. http://www.forbes.com/sites/freddreier/2012/02/02/lululemon-ceo-wilson-knew-it-was-time-to-go/
18. The World's Billionaires. (Mar 2012). Retrieved 15 Apr 2012, from *Forbes*: http://www.forbes.com/profile/chip-wilson/
19. lululemon athletica inc. (2011). *op. cit.*
20. Officers and Directors: Christine Day. Retrieved 15 Apr 2012, from *lululemon.com*. http://investor.lululemon.com/biodisplay.cfm?ubioid=19073
21. Peer, M. (3 Apr 2008). Christine Day Breathes New Life Into Lululemon. Retrieved 15 Apr 2012, from *Forbes*. http://www.forbes.com/2008/04/03/day-christine-lululemon-face-markets-cx_mp_0402autofacescan03.html
22. Officers and Directors: John E. Currie. Retrieved 15 Apr 2012, from *lululemon.com*. http://investor.lululemon.com/biodisplay.cfm?ubioid=16216
23. John E. Currie. Retrieved 15 Apr 2012, from *Forbes*. http://people.forbes.com/profile/john-e-currie/50244
24. lululemon athletica inc. (2012). Lululemon Athletica, Inc. announces fourth quarter and full year fiscal 2011 results. Acquire Media.
25. Martell, A. (22 Mar 2012). Lululemon profit rises, outlook disappoints. Retrieved 20 Apr 2012, from *Reuters*. http://www.reuters.com/article/2012/03/22/us-lululemon-idUSBRE82L0L120120322
26. Nike Inc. Retrieved 21 Apr 2012, from *NikeInc.com*. http://nikeinc.com/pages/about-nike-inc
27. Ibid.
28. Adidas. Adidas Group. Retrieved 21 Apr 2012, from *Adidas Group*. http://www.adidas-group.com/en/ourgroup/assets/History/pdfs/History-e.pdf
29. Ibid.
30. Under Armour. *Under Armour*. Retrieved 21 Apr 2012, from *Under Armour*: http://www.uabiz.com/company/about.cfm
31. Ibid.
32. VF Corporation. (2012). *VF Corporation 10-K.* VF Corporation.
33. Lucy Activewear. *Lucy Activewear*. Retrieved 21 Apr 2012, from *Lucy Activewear*. http://www.lucy.com/About/ABOUT_US,default,pg.html
34. Our frequently asked questions. *op. cit.*
35. Profile of General Population and Housing Characteristics. (2010). Retrieved 15 Apr 2012, from *U.S. Census Bureau*. http://factfinder2.census.gov/faces/tableservices/jsf/pages/productview.xhtml?pid=DEC_10_DP_DPDP1&prodType=table
36. Lululemon: Profile. (20 Apr 2012). Retrieved 20 Apr 2012, from *Yahoo! Finance*. http://finance.yahoo.com/q/pr?s=LULU+Profile
37. Our frequently asked questions. *op. cit.*
38. Mattioli, D. *op. cit.*
39. Our factories. Retrieved 16 Apr 2012, from *lululemon.com*. http://www.lululemon.com/community/legacies/factories
40. Ibid.
41. Fabrics and Technology. Retrieved 15 Apr 2012, from *lululemon.com*: http://www.lululemon.com/education/info/fabricsandtechnologies
42. (Jan. 2011). *ICR XChange: lululemon athletica inc.*
43. lululemon athletica inc. (2011). *op. cit.*
44. Grassroots actions. Retrieved 16 Apr 2012, from *lululemon.com*. http://www.lululemon.com/education/info/fabricsandtechnologies
45. Our focus. Retrieved 16 Apr 2012, from *lululemon.com*. http://www.lululemon.com/legacies/focus
46. Hitt, M. A., Ireland, R. D., & Hoskisson, R. E. (2012). Strategic Management: Competitiveness & Globalization. Mason, OH: South-Western.
47. Ibid.
48. Competitors. (20 Apr 2012). Retrieved 20 Apr 2012, from *Yahoo! Finance*. http://finance.yahoo.com/q/co?s=LULU
49. Ibid.
50. lululemon athletica inc. (2011). *op. cit.*
51. Chip. (30 Mar 2009). The lululemon vision. Retrieved 18 Apr 2012, from *lululemon.com*. http://www.lululemon.com/community/blog/the-lululemon-vision/
52. lululemon athletica inc. (2011). *op. cit.*
53. Mattioli, D. *op. cit.*
54. lululemon athletica inc. (2011). *op. cit.*
55. Mattioli, D. *op. cit.*
56. lululemon athletica inc. (2011). *op. cit.*
57. Ibid.

Brett P. Matherne

Georgia State University

Steve Gove, David Thornblad

Virginia Tech

It is apt that 2012's top grossing film was *The Avengers* for movie studios and exhibitors sought to avenge a dismal prior year at the box office. Domestic box office receipts climbed 6% from 2011 to a record setting $10.8 billion.[1] Three films, *The Avengers*, *The Dark Knight Rises*, and *Skyfall* grossed more than $1 billion *each* in global ticket sales (Exhibit 1). Behind the scenes, the success, even the fundamental health of the exhibition industry, is far less clear. Consider these contradictions:

- Domestic ticket revenues grew 6% in 2012, but that volume ranks just 13th since 1980. The 1.364 billion tickets sold is down 13% from the most recent high in 2002 of 1.575 (Exhibit 2).
- 2012's record revenues resulted from ticket price increases, not more attendees. At $7.94, the average ticket price has risen 24% since 2005. But over the long term, prices keep pace with inflation, raising questions about the creation of differentiated value (Exhibit 3).
- The long-term per-capita trend is negative. In 2012, the average number of films seen per capita was 3.9.[2] In 1946, the peak of moviegoing in America, the industry sold 4 billion tickets and the typical American went to 28 films per year at the theater.
- Movies are more widely available than ever, creating new substitutes for where, when, and how to view movies.

Exhibitors are especially anxious for moviegoers to return to the theater as the industry has invested an estimated $1.6 billion to convert theaters from film to digital projection since 2005 (Exhibit 4). The main promises of digital projection are decreased distribution costs, 3D capability, and the potential to show alternative content. Despite the sizable investment, financial benefits have yet to materialize for exhibitors. Attendance decreased in 5 of the 8 years since conversion began.

Which represents the current and future state of the movie exhibition industry: The bright lights of a red carpet Hollywood premiere or a dimly lit marquee?

The Motion Picture Value Chain

The motion picture industry value chain consists of three stages: studio production, distribution, and exhibition – the theaters that show the films. All stages are undergoing consolidation and technological changes, but the basic three-phase structure is largely unchanged since the 1920s.

Studio Production

The studios produce the life blood of the industry: they create motion picture content. Content drives attendance and studios are highly concentrated. The top six studios in 2012 created 17% of the films for the year, but these films accounted for 76% of the box office gross (Exhibit 5). The top 10 studios constitute over 90 percent of box office receipts. This concentration, coupled with highly differentiated content, gives the studios considerable negotiating and pricing power.

Exhibit 1 Top 25 Releases of 2012

Movie	3D	3D %	Studio	Genre	MPAA Rating	Prod. Budget (mil.)	Domestic Gross (mil.)	Domestic %	Domestic Rank	International Gross (mil.)	International %	International Rank	Total Gross (mil.)	Total Rank
The Avengers	Yes	52%	Buena Vista	Act Adv.	PG-13	$220.0	$623.4	41%	1	$888.4	59%	1	$1,511.8	1
The Dark Knight			Warner Bros.	Act Thrl	PG-13	250.0	448.1	41%	2	632.9	59%	4	1,081.0	2
The Hunger Games			LGF	Act Adv.	PG-13	78.0	408.0	59%	3	278.5	41%	12	686.5	9
Skyfall			Sony	Act	PG-13	200.0	300.9	29%	4	737.6	71%	2	1,038.5	3
Twilight: Brk. Dawn 2	Yes	49%	Summit	Rom	PG-13	120.0	290.8	35%	5	532.5	65%	6	823.3	6
The Hobbit	Yes	44%	Warner Bros.	Fant	PG-13	175.0	288.7	31%	6	632.2	69%	5	920.9	4
Amazing Spider-Man	Yes	44%	Sony	Act Adv.	PG-13	230.0	262.0	35%	7	490.2	65%	8	752.2	7
Brave	Yes	32%	Buena Vista	Anim	PG	185.0	237.3	44%	8	298.1	56%	10	535.4	11
Ted			Universal	Comedy	R	50.0	218.8	43%	9	289.4	57%	11	508.2	12
Madagascar 3	Yes	45%	Para. - DrmWrks	Anim	PG	145.0	216.4	29%	10	525.7	71%	7	742.1	8
Dr. Seuss - Lorax	Yes	50%	Universal	Anim	PG	70.0	214.0	61%	11	134.8	39%	19	348.8	17
Wreck-It Ralph	Yes	38%	Buena Vista	Anim	PG	165.0	181.4	51%	12	173.4	49%	17	354.8	16
Men in Black 3	Yes		Sony	Sci-F Com	PG-13	225.0	179.0	29%	13	445.0	71%	9	624.0	10
Lincoln			Buena Vista	Hist. Drama	PG-13	65.0	161.9	98%	14	3.3	2%	25	165.2	25
Ice Age: Cont. Drift	Yes	35%	Fox	Anim	PG	95.0	161.2	18%	15	714.0	82%	3	875.3	5
Snow White & the Huntsman			Universal	Adv	PG-13	170.0	155.3	39%	16	241.3	61%	14	396.6	14
Hotel Transylvania	Yes	?	Sony	Anim	PG	85.0	146.6	46%	17	173.8	54%	16	320.4	18
Taken 2			Fox	Act	PG-13	45.0	139.5	38%	18	232.0	62%	15	371.6	15
Django Unchained			Weinstein	West	R	100.0	139.4	74%	19	48.4	26%	24	187.8	23
21 Jump Street			Sony	Act Com.	R	42.0	138.4	69%	20	63.1	31%	23	201.6	21
Les Miserables			Universal	Musc	PG-13	61.0	131.8	47%	21	150.5	53%	18	282.3	19
Prometheus	Yes	25%	Fox	Sci-Fi Act	R	130.0	126.5	31%	22	276.9	69%	13	403.4	13
Safe House			Universal	Act Thrl	R	85.0	126.4	61%	23	81.7	39%	20	208.1	20
The Vow			Sony / Sc. Gems	Drama	PG-13	30.0	125.0	64%	24	71.1	36%	21	196.1	22
Argo			Warner Bros.	Drama Thrl	R	45.0	115.3	62%	25	69.3	38%	22	184.5	24
Total for Top 25						$2,891.0	$5,536.3			$8,184.1			$13,720.4	
Average for Top 25		41%				$115.6	$221.5	47%		$327.4	53%		$548.8	

Notes: Data from Boxofficemojo.com, MPAA, NATO, and author estimates. 3D revenues is based on opening weekend. Genres as follows: Act = Action; Adv. = Adventure; Anim = Animation; Com = Comedy; Drama = Drama; Fant = Fantasy; Hist = Historical; Musc – Musical; Rom = Romance; Sci-F = Sci-Fi; Thrl = Thriller; West = Western. Some production budgets estimated.

Exhibit 2 Domestic Box Office Receipts & Ticket Sales, 1980-2012

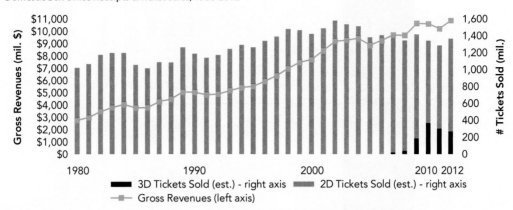

Data Source: Boxofficemojo.com and author estimates. 3D ticket volume estimated based on reported 3D revenues with ticket prices estimated as 30% premium over 2D. Portion of 2012 3D revenue and ticket volume is estimated.

Exhibit 3 Ticket Prices 1980 - 2012

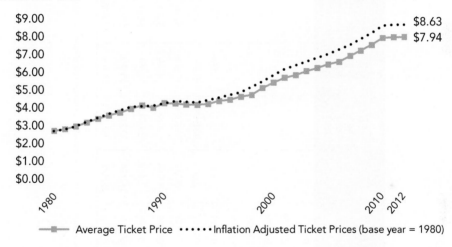

Studios are increasingly managed as profit centers in large corporations. Management is risk averse, as investments are large and a formula for success elusive. Consider the fate of two films inspired by comic books in 2011. Warner Bros.'s *Green Lantern* was considered a flop, grossing $219 million ($116 million domestic, $103 internationally) and ending plans for a series. That same year Paramount's *Thor* grossed $449 million ($181 domestically, $268 internationally), giving the green light to a sequel.

Studios focus on 14- to 24-year-olds, consistently the largest audience for movies. At just 15% of the U.S. population, this group purchases 21% of all tickets. More narrowly, 10% of the population are "frequent" moviegoers who attend more than one movie per month and are responsible for half of all ticket sales.[3] Studios target this audience with PG and PG-13 fare including 19 of 2012's top 25 releases. However, domestic demographic trends are unfavorable. While the U.S. population will increase 42% by 2050, this core audience will increase just 35% (19 million) or 475 per existing screen (Exhibit 6).

The risks for studios are significant as production costs are considerable (see Exhibit 1). Studios invested $1.6 billion for the 10 films which ranked among 2012's highest grossing ($165 million per film). Costs have increased faster than inflation. In 1980, the production budget for the highest grossing films averaged just $11 million. In the 1990s, films turned to special effects and costs reached $102 million (up 827%). Today, special effects alone can top $100 million for a major production. These investments are considerable, yet no guarantee for success: *Green Lantern*, the flop, was made for $200 million while the successful *Thor* cost $150 million.

Domestic exhibitors were once the sole distribution channel for films. This has changed dramatically. Films

Exhibit 4 U.S. Theater Screens 2000-2011

Year	Total Screens #	Change from Prior Year	Analog Screens #	Change from Prior Year	As % of Total Screens	Digital Screens #	Change from Prior Year	As % of Total Screen	Est. Digital Invest. (mil.)	D Digital 3D #	Change from Prior Year	As % of Total Screens	As % of Digital	Est. 3D Invest. (mil.)
2000	37,396		37,396		100.0%									
2001	36,764	–1.7%	36,764	–1.7%	100.0%									
2002	35,280	–4.0%	35,280	–4.0%	100.0%									
2003	36,146	2.5%	36,146	2.5%	100.0%									
2004	36,594	1.2%	36,594	1.2%	100.0%									
2005	38,852	6.2%	38,862	6.2%	100.0%	200		0.5%	$10					
2006	38,415	–1.1%	36,412	–6.3%	94.8%	2,003	901.5%	5.2%	$100					
2007	38,974	1.5%	34,342	–5.7%	88.1%	4,632	131.3%	11.9%	$256	986		2.5%	21.3%	$74
2008	38,843	–0.3%	33,319	–3.0%	85.8%	5,515	19.1%	14.2%	$311	1,427	44.7%	3.7%	25.9%	$107
2009	39,233	1.0%	31,815	–4.5%	81.1%	7,418	34.5%	18.9%	$453	3,269	129.1%	8.3%	44.1%	$245
2010	39,547	0.8%	23,773	–25.3%	60.1%	15,774	112.6%	39.9%	$985	7,837	139.7%	19.8%	49.7%	$588
2011	39,641	0.2%	14,020	–41.0%	35.4%	25,621	62.4%	64.6%	$1,606	13,001	65.9%	32.8%	50.7%	$975

Notes: Based on author estimates and MPAA reports on # screens. Estimated investments (cumulative) based on estimated cost of digital screen ($50,000 per installation) and digital 3D ($75,000 per installation). Digital screen counts include digital 3D.

Exhibit 5 Top 6 Studios / Distributors 2012

Studio / Distributor	2012				2000				% Change 2000-2012	
	Rank	$ Share	Total Gross	# Films	Rank	$ Share	Total Gross	# Films	Total Gross	# Films
Sony / Columbia	1	16.6%	$1,792	25	7	9.0%	$682	29	163%	−14%
Warner Bros.	2	15.4%	$1,665	36	3	11.9%	$905	22	84%	64%
Buena Vista	3	14.3%	$1,551	18	1	15.5%	$1,176	21	32%	−14%
Universal	4	12.2%	$1,324	17	2	14.1%	$1,069	13	24%	31%
20th Century Fox	5	9.5%	$1,025	19	6	9.5%	$723	13	42%	46%
Paramount / Dream Works	6	8.5%	$914	21	4	10.4%	$791	12	16%	75%
Total for Top 6			$8,273	136			$4,664	81	77%	68%
Industry Total			$10,835	795			$7,661	478	41.4%	66.3%
Top 6 as % of Industry			76.3%	17.1%			61.4%	16.9%	24.3%	1.0%

Source: Author calculations based on data from boxofficemojocom.

Exhibit 6 U.S. Demographic Trends

Segment	% of Movie Tickets Purchased (2011)	# in 2010 (mil.)	% of Population (2010)	# in 2050 (mil.)	% of Population (2050)	# Increase	% Change
Under 5 years		21.1	7%	28.1	6%	7.0	33%
5 to 13 yrs	15%	37.1	12%	50.7	12%	13.6	37%
14 to 17 yrs	9%	17.0	5%	22.7	5%	5.7	34%
18 to 24 yrs	12%	30.7	10%	39.5	9%	8.8	29%
25 to 44 yrs	28%	83.1	27%	110.9	25%	27.8	33%
45 to 64 yrs	24%	81.0	26%	98.5	22%	17.5	22%
65 yrs+	11%	40.2	13%	88.5	20%	48.3	120%
Total (mil.)		310.2		439.0		128.8	42%

Source: Data: US Census (2008), Table 2. Projections of the Population by Selected Age Groups and Sex for the United States: 2010 to 2050 (NP2008-T2), MPAA Theatrical Statistics, and author estimates.

must increasingly cross cultural and language boundaries and appeal to the global market. Over 70% of U.S. studio revenues are now international (Exhibit 7). Studios see this as the primary opportunity for growth. While domestic receipts increase on flat ticket sales, both ticket sales and dollar volume are rising rapidly internationally. From 2000 to 2012, domestic receipts grew at an average of just 3% while international growth averaged 13% annually. The studios are also changing their perspective on ticket prices in large population markets. In India, for example, attendees paid an average of just $0.50.[4] However, Indian exhibitors sold 3.3 billion tickets in 2008. At current growth rates, the attendance volume increase each year in India alone equals total current U.S. annual admissions.[5]

This trend of content internationalization shows no signs of abating. While the drama of *Argo* and the humor of *Ted* cost less to produce, they are risky in international markets. Franchise films, with known characters, made in 3D and laden with special effects, present the least content risk internationally. Yet these films carry their own risk due to large budgets. The special effects alone for a major film may exceed $100 million. *The Avengers*, *The Dark Knight Rises*, and *Skyfall* all rank in the top 10 for worldwide gross. Combined, they constitute an investment of $670 million in production costs.

As studios shift their focus to the international market they are less dependent on domestic exhibitors. This increases the threat of disintermediation through alternative distribution channels. Studios increase revenues through product licensing, DVD sales, and international expansion; at the same time exhibitors – movie theaters – have seen their business decline.

Exhibit 7 Domestic & International Box Office Receipts ($ bil.)

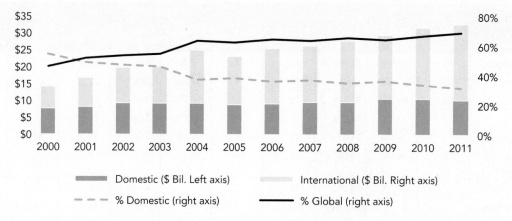

Distribution

Distributors are the intermediaries between the studios and exhibitors. Distribution entails all steps following a film's artistic completion including marketing, logistics, and administration. Distributors either negotiate a percentage of the gross from the studio for distribution services or purchase rights to films, profiting the box office directly. Distributors select and market films to exhibitors' booking agents. They handle collections, audits of attendees, and other administrative tasks. There are over 300 active distributors, but most is done by a few majors, commonly a division of a studio. Disney Pixar, for example, produced *Brave* while distribution was done by Disney's Buena Vista.

Until 2005, the distribution of all motion pictures in the U.S. entailed the physical shipment of reels of 35mm film, a process little changed from the 1940s. Each theater would receive a shipment of physical canisters containing a "release print" of a film. These prints cost $20,000 – $30,000 in up-front costs and $1,000 – $1,500 for each print. Print costs for a modern major picture opening on 3,500 screens costs $3.50 – $5.25 million. This is borne by the studios and exhibitors, but paid for by movie attendees.

Beginning in 2006, distributors and studios encouraged exhibitors to transition to digital projection technology. The technology works by using high powered LCD projectors to cast the movie onto a specialized screen. In lieu of film, the movies are delivered on reusable hard drives or via satellite or high speed internet. The threat of piracy is a major concern for the industry so all files are encrypted. The cost savings of digital distribution over film are considerable: The cost of each hard drive is $150, just 10% of the cost of physical film. Additionally, digital projection allows for consistently high quality images as there is no physical wear to the film, and enables the exhibition

of "alternative content" – images other than motion pictures that are obtained outside of the studio system.

The transition to digital projection involves considerable capital investment. Each digital projection system can serve a single screen and costs $50,000 to $75,000, including the projector, computers and hardware, and a specialized screen. To encourage the transition, distributors offered rebates in the form of virtual print fees (VPSs) for each film received digitally. These fees, as much as 17% of rental costs, will expire in 2013.

Exhibition

Exhibitors offer a location where audiences can view a motion picture. The basic business model of exhibitors (using movies as the draw and selling concessions to make a profit) has changed little since the time of touring motion picture shows that would set up in town halls and churches. As the popularity of motion pictures expanded, permanent local theaters were established. Studios soon recognized the potential profit in exhibition and vertically integrated, allowing control over audiences and capturing these downstream profits. This practice ended in 1948 with the Supreme Court's ruling against the studios in *United States v. Paramount Pictures*.

Theaters were divested by studios, leaving the two to negotiate film access and rental fees. Single theater and single screen firms' exhibitors fared poorly as studios retained the upper hand in setting rental rates. Exhibitors sought to increase bargaining power and economies by consolidating, multiplying the bargaining power of individual theaters by the number of screens managed.

This reached its zenith in the 1980s with the mass rollout of the multiplex concept. Maximizing both bargaining power based on multiple screens while minimizing labor and facility costs, exhibitors constructed large entertainment complexes, sometimes with two dozen or more screens. Most of the original local single screen theaters that survived were doomed as they were unable to compete on cost or viewing experience and were unable to gain access to the capital needed to construct multi-screen locations. Today, the typical exhibitor location has 7–12 screens and is likely to be operated by Regal, AMC, Cinemark, or Carmike. These four operate 1,061 theaters in the U.S. (just 19%), but control 45% of the screens (Exhibit 8). This market concentration provides exhibitors with negotiating power for access to films, prices for films, prices for concessions, and greater access to revenues from national advertisers. However, the real power continues to remain with the studios due to differentiated content, the ability to play rival exhibitors against each other, and the increasing potential for disintermediation.

The Business of Exhibition

Exhibitors have three main revenue sources: box office receipts, concessions, and advertising (Exhibit 9). Managers have low discretion; their ability to influence revenues and expenses is limited. Operating margins average a slim 15 percent; net income may fluctuate wildly based on the tax benefits of prior losses. Overall, the business of exhibitors is best described as loss leadership on movies: the firms make money selling concessions and showing ads to patrons who are drawn by the movie.

Box Office Revenues

Ticket sales constitute two-thirds of exhibition business revenues. The return, however, is quite small due to the power of the studios. For large exhibitors, film costs average 53% of box office receipts. For smaller circuits, average costs are higher. Rental fees are based on the size of the circuit and the time and seat commitment made to a film. The revenues retained by the theater increase with each week following an opening. On opening weekend an exhibitor may pay the distributor 80–90% of the box office gross, retaining only 10–20%. In subsequent weeks the exhibitor's portion increases. The record-setting revenues at the box office have been the result of increases in ticket prices, the majority of which has flowed back to the studios.

The complexity of booking is increasing. The majority of revenues historically comes from opening weekend. In industry terminology the "multiple" (the percentage coming after opening weekend) has been declining steadily, falling 25% since 2002,[6] putting exhibitors at increasing risk. While exhibition used to be a question of which movie to show, it now also involves decisions as to how many theaters to allocate to analog versus digital and 2D versus 3D. All these factors plus the "make or break" nature of opening weekend complicate the exhibitor's operations.

Concessions

Moviegoers frequently lament the high prices for concessions. Concessions average near 30% of revenues. Direct costs of just 15% make concessions the largest and sometimes sole source of exhibitor profit. These profits are influenced by three factors: attendance, pricing, and material costs. The most important is attendance: more attendees = more concession sales. Per-patron sales are influenced by prices – a common moviegoer complaint is high concession prices. The $4.50 and $8.00 price points for the large soda and popcorn are not accidental, but the result of market research and profit maximization calculation. Costs are influenced by purchase volume with larger chains able to negotiate better prices on everything from popcorn and soda pop to cups and napkins.

Exhibit 8 Leading U.S. Circuits 2012

Circuit	Total Screens	Total Theaters	Screens / Theater	Analog (% Screens)	Digital (% of Screens)	Digital 3D (%Screens)
AMC (AMC, Loews)	5,128	346	14.5	55.1%	44.9%	31.3%
Carmike (Carmike)	2,254	237	9.5	5.6%	94.4%	33.0%
Cinemark (Cinemark, Century)	3,878	297	13.1	0.0%	100.0%	48.0%
Regal (Regal, United Artists, Edwards)	6,614	527	12.6	28.6%	71.4%	42.1%
Total for 4 Largest Circuits	17,874	1,061	12.4	27.1%	72.9%	39.1%
4 Largest Circuits as % of Industry Total	45.1%	18.6%				
Industry Total	39,641	5,697	6.9	35.4%	64.6%	32.8%

Notes: Data from SEC filings, MPAA, NATO, and author estimates, based on screens entering fiscal 2012.

Exhibit 9 Typical Revenue & Expenses Per Screen at an 8-Screen Theater

REVENUES		
Box office ($285,650/$7.94 = 35,975 admissions; 691/week/screen)	$ 285,650	65%
Concessions (135,250/35,975 admissions = $3.75/admission)	$ 135,250	31%
Advertising ($21,500/35,975 admissions = $0.60/admission)	$ 21,500	5%
Total Revenues ($12.29/admission)	$ 442,400	100%
EXPENSES		
Fixed		
Facility	$ 50,000	11%
Labor	$ 40,000	9%
Utilities	$ 50,000	11%
Other SG&A	$ 60,000	14%
Total Fixed Costs	$ 200,000	45%
Variable		
Film Rental	$ 155,000	54%
Concession Supplies	$ 21,650	16%
Total Variable Costs	$ 176,650	40%
Total Expenses	$ 376,650	85%
OPERATING INCOME	$ 65,750	15%

Advertising

The low margins derived from ticket sales cause exhibitors to focus on other sources of revenue. The highest margin, therefore the most attractive, is advertising. Since 2002, advertising revenues, and the time devoted to them at the start of every feature, has increased dramatically, climbing from $186 to $644 million.[7] Exhibitors also generate revenue through pre-show and lobby advertising. Though this constitutes just 5 percent of exhibitor revenues, it is highly profitable (i.e.,

revenue with no direct monetary costs) and growing. Advertising revenues for exhibitors averaged $16,245 per screen.[8] Audiences, however, express dislike for advertising at the theater. Balancing the revenues from ads with audience tolerance is an ongoing struggle for exhibitors (Exhibit 10).

The Major Exhibitor Circuits

Four "circuits" dominate the domestic exhibition market, serving different geographic markets in different ways.[9] Regal, which operates its namesake Regal Theaters as well as United Artists and Edwards theaters, is the largest with 6,614 screens in 527 domestic theaters. Regal focuses on mid-size markets using multiplex and megaplexes that average 12 screens per location, with an average ticket price of $8.90. AMC, operating as AMC and Loews chains, is the second largest domestic exhibitor with 5,128 screens in 346 theaters. Averaging nearly 15 screens per location, AMC leads the industry in the operation of large multiplexes. They do so by concentrating on urban areas near large population centers such as those in California, Florida, and Texas. By focusing on 3D, IMAX, and other premium viewing experiences, AMC achieves the highest ticket prices, averaging $9.04. Cinemark is the third largest player with 3,878 screens in nearly 300 domestic locations under Cinemark and Century brands. Cinemark serves smaller markets, operating as the sole theater in over 80 percent of its markets. Their average ticket price of $6.72 in 2012 was the lowest of the major chains. Carmike concentrates on small to mid-sized markets, targeting populations of less than 100,000 that have few alternative entertainment options. They do so with fewer screens at each location. With 237 theaters, they have just 2,254 screens, an average of 9.5 per location. Carmike's ticket price averaged just $6.85 (Exhibit 11).

While ticket prices vary considerably, differences in net profit margins are due mostly to differences in utilization and the costs of facilities, labor, and utilities.

Exhibit 10 Exhibitor Advertising Revenue ($ mil.)

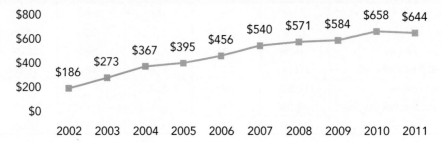

Source: NATO press releases 2005-2012.

Exhibit 11 Select 2012 Carmike, Cinemark & Regal Financials

	Carmike	Cinemark **	Regal
Theater and Attendance Information			
Screens (U.S. only)	2,502	3,916	6,880
Theaters (U.S. only)	249	298	540
Screens per Theater (U.S. only)	10	13	13
Total U.S. Attendance (in thousands)	50,357	163,639	216,400
Avg Ticket Price	$ 6.85	$ 6.72	$ 8.90
Avg Concessions	$ 3.10	$ 3.34	$ 3.46
Avg Attendance per Screen	20,127	41,787	31,453
Avg Admission Revenue per Screen	$ 137,130	$ 280,797	$ 279,811
Income Statement ($ mil.)			
Revenues			
Admissions	$ 343.10	$ 1,099.60	$ 1,925.10
Concessions*	$ 172.58	$ 546.20	$ 748.40
Other Income*	$ 23.62	$ 50.10	$ 150.70
Total Revenues	$ 539.30	$ 1,695.90	$ 2,824.20
Admissions as % of Revenues	64%	65%	68%
Concessions as % of Revenues	32%	32%	26%
Other as % of Revenues	4%	3%	5%
Expenses			
Exhibition	$ 186.00	$ 610.50	$ 1,000.50
Concessions	$ 23.20	$ 71.10	$ 101.10
Building, Wages, Utilities & Other Operating Costs	$ 211.70	$ 548.20	$ 1,120.30
Total Cost of Operation	$ 484.60	$ 1,229.80	$ 2,490.00
Operating Income	$ 54.70	$ 466.10	$ 334.20
Operating per admission	$1.08	$ 2.85	1.54
Operating Income as % total revenue	10%	27%	12%
Exhibition Costs as % of Admission Revenues	54%	56%	$52%
Concessions Costs as % of Concession Revenues	13%	13%	14%
Buildings, wages, utilities & other costs as % of Total Revenues	39%	32%	40%
Buildings, wages, utilities & other costs per attendee	$ 4.20	$ 3.35	$ 5.18
Net Income*	$ 96.30	$ 171.42	$ 144.80
Net Profit Margin	18%	10%	5%
Balance Sheet (dollars in millions)			
Total Assets	$ 712.70	$ 3,862.41	$ 2,209.50
Total Debt	$ 434.70	$ 1,914.18	$ 1,995.20
Debt : Assets Ratio	0.61	0.50	0.90

Notes: Data source: SEC filings & author estimates

* Carmike reports aggregated concession and advertising revenues. Amounts are estimated.

** Theater, screen and revenue, expense data for Carmike's U.S. operations. Net income, assets and debt figures are consolidated (dom. and intl.).

*** Net income may include carryover of substantial tax benefits from losses.

Despite considerable size differences, the actual cost of content for these circuits varies little among the major circuits. Regal's is lowest at 52% of admission revenues, followed by AMC (53%), Carmike (54%), and Cinemark (56%). While the rental costs for these circuits is similar, it is lower than for smaller circuits.

The circuits' ability to efficiently utilize their facilities varies considerably. Cinemark's average of 41,787 attendees per screen is nearly double Carmike's 22,032 per screen. The differences in utilization combined with differences in the underlying costs of facilities, wages and other expenses result in high variability in their costs on a per-ticket basis. At $5.18, Regal's cost per attendee is the highest, followed by Carmike ($4.20), and Cinemark ($3.35).

Despite the trend toward internationalization by studios, exhibitors have until recently been exclusively domestic firms. Cinemark has had the largest international presence with 167 theaters (1,324 screens) in Mexico and seven Central and South American countries. In 2012, AMC was acquired by the Chinese conglomerate Dalian Wanda Group Corp. for a reported $2.6 billion.[10] Wanda, with interests in property, entertainment, and tourism owns and operates 730 screens in China, responsible for 15% of the Chinese box office with plans to expand to 2,000 screens. The deal will make AMC the largest global exhibition company.

Overall, while the major circuits focus on different geographic locations, there is little differentiation in the offerings of exhibitors within individual markets. Prices differ little, the same movies are shown at the same times, and the food and services choices are nearly identical. Competition between theaters within markets often comes down to distance from home, convenience of parking, and proximity to restaurants.

Challenges for Exhibitors

Exhibitors are faced with an increasing number of challenges in their operating environment.

Benefitting from Digital Investments

Exhibitors have made considerable investments in digital projection technology. At the start of 2012, two-thirds of the 39,641 screens in the U.S. had been converted to digital with the remainder expected to be converted by 2014. The total investment by exhibitors is $1.6 billion. The benefits of this conversion should manifest themselves in lower exhibitor costs and increased revenues. To date, these do not appear to have accrued to exhibitors.

On the cost side, digital distribution dramatically reduces distribution costs when compared to physical film.

Digital distribution is expected to save $1 billion annually on print costs and distribution. Yet there is little evidence to date that these savings will accrue to the exhibitors. Film rental fees, which include distribution costs, have held steady despite the transition to digital. On the revenue side, exhibitors have seen significant additional per-ticket revenues from surcharges for enhanced viewing experiences, primarily 3D. 3D content requires the cooperation of studios and exhibitors. For studios, 3D adds 15–20% to the cost of production. For exhibitors, 3D requires conversion to digital projection and the added costs for 3D-capable equipment. Among domestic digital projection systems about half are 3D capable. The planned 2009 release of *Avatar* was used to spur digital installations. The film grossed $750 million domestically, with an estimated 82% from 3D viewings. The film was a critical and box office success, introducing audiences to a new age of 3D movies and projection. *Avatar's* success led to an increase, perhaps excess, of 3D releases.

The portion of opening weekend receipts from 3D movies averaged 63% from 2009 to 2011 (Exhibit 12). Today the 3D portion of major releases shows a worrisome trend. In 2011, only 45% of *Kung Fu Panda 2's* box office gross came from 3D and Disney's *Pirates of the Caribbean* had just 47%.[11] In 2012, the average across all 3D films released declined to 45%. 3D may be an aspect of the theater experience which audiences are only occasionally willing to pay for. Some industry observers caution that the future opportunity to capitalize on 3D-driven revenues may be limited. "Certain movies are doing well in 3D and others failing terribly," Bob Greenfield said. "People are getting a lot choosier. I would be surprised if in 2013 and 2014 we didn't see a more reduced slate that focuses on the films that deserve it."

Declining 3D attendance is a serious concern for exhibitors. With an average investment of $75,000, the payback period for 3D may be more than 3 years. The extent to which the conversion to digital will benefit exhibitors through cost reductions and revenue enhancement will be determined in the coming years as rental costs and 3D viewership rates are better established.

Countering the Declining Allure of the Theater

Traditionally, the draw of the theater may have been far more important than what film was showing. Moviegoers describe attending the theater as an experience, with the appeal based on:[12]

■ the giant theater screen
■ the opportunity to be out of the house
■ not having to wait to see a particular movie on home video

Exhibit 12 3D as Percentage of a Film's Opening Weekend Receipts

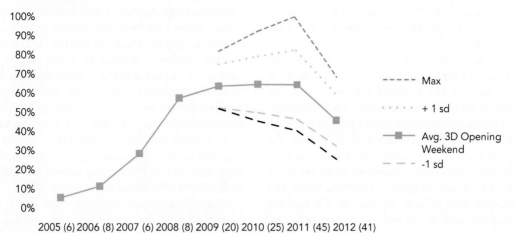

Notes: Based on news reports and author estimates. Numbers in parentheses are the number of 3D releases in a year.

- the experience of watching the movies with a theatrical sound system
- the theater as a location option for a date

The ability of theaters to provide these above what audiences can achieve at home appears to be diminishing. Of the reasons why people go to the movies, only the place aspects — the theater as a place to be out of the house and as a place for dating — seem immune to substitution. Few teenagers want a movie and popcorn with their date at home with mom and dad.

The overall "experience" currently offered by theaters falls short for many. Marketing research firm Mintel reports the reasons for not attending the theater more frequently are largely the result of the declining experience. Specific factors include: the overall cost, at-home viewing options, interruptions such as cell phones in the theater, rude patrons, the overall hassle, and ads prior to the show.[13] A recent *Wall Street Journal* article reported on interruptions ranging from the intrusion of soundtracks in adjacent theaters to cell phones. "The interruptions capped a night of moviegoing already marred by out-of-order ticketing kiosks and a parade of preshow ads so long that, upon seeing the Coca-Cola polar bears on screen, one customer grumbled: 'This is obscene.'"[14] Recounting bad experiences is a lively topic for bloggers. A typical comment: "I say it has gotten worse. I hate paying $9.00 for a ticket and the movie is 90–100 minutes long, people are talking on cell phones, the people who work at the theaters look like they are bored, and when you ask them a question, the answer is very rude."[15]

The time allocated to pre-show ads can be eye opening, even for industry insiders. Toby Emmerich,

New Line Cinema's head of production, faced a not-so-common choice: attending opening night in a theater or in a screening room at actor Jim Carrey's house. Said Emmerich in an *LA Times* article "I love seeing a movie with a big crowd, but I had no idea how many obnoxious ads I'd have to endure – it really drove me crazy. After sitting through about 15 minutes of ads, I turned to my wife and said, 'Maybe we should've gone to Jim Carrey's house after all.'"[16]

The Home Viewing Substitution

For many, home viewing is growing as a viable substitute to theater attendance due to rapid improvements and cost reductions in home viewing technology and the widespread availability of timely and inexpensive content. The unique value proposition offered by movie theaters' large screens, the long wait for DVD release, and advantages of theatrical sound systems are also fading.

Home Viewing Technology

The average home television set is increasingly a large, high-definition set coupled with an inexpensive yet impressive audio system. Compared to home equipment options of the past, at-home technology increasingly represents a significant substitute for moviegoing. Prior to 2009, television transmissions were formatted as 480 interlaced vertical lines (480i) of resolution, the standard since the 1950s. FCC-ordered changes resulted in all broadcasters converting digital broadcasts by February 2009, setting the stage for high definition (HD) digital broadcasts providing up to 1080 vertical lines of resolution (1080p).[17] This transition started a consumer movement to upgrade televisions. The transition also reduced the difference between home technology and the giant theater screen and sound system offered by theaters.

The average size of TVs has increased dramatically: from 23 inches in 1997 to 36.8 inches in 2012. As LCD technology became the standard for both computer and television screens, manufacturing costs declined. Wholesale prices for televisions fell 65 percent from the late 1990s to 2007.[18] Between 2011 and 2012 alone, the average retail price of a 32-inch TV declined from $546 to $435.[19] Consumers, however, spend more on every television, consistently electing to purchase larger and more advanced sets. In 2012 the average TV sold for $1200.[20] Features such as 3D, internet connectivity, and applications for Netflix, Hulu and others are becoming common and add little to retail prices. Sharp, a leading TV manufacturer, predicts that by 2015 the *average* screen will reach 60 inches.[21] Home viewing technology may be reaching its apex. While technologically image size and quality can continue to increase, they are limited by practical realities. The ideal distance for viewing a 42″ TV is 5′3″. A 70″ screen should be viewed from 8′9″. The adoption and benefit of 80″+ sets will require a viewing distance that exceeds the size of most living rooms they would be installed in.

Large screen televisions, low cost high-definition DVD players, and audio and speaker components are commonly packaged as low cost home theaters. The average Bluray DVD player now costs under $125 and 3D players under $150. Bundled home theater systems offer a movie experience that rivals many theaters, all for under $1,500. Mike Gabriel, Sharp's head of marketing and communications, stated, "People can now expect a home cinema experience from their TV. Technology that was once associated with the rich and famous is now accessible to homes across the country."[22]

Content Availability & Timing

The best hardware offers little value without content. Channels for renting or purchasing movies are increasing. "We're seeing a cultural shift occurring where people are consuming their entertainment from Netflix, the iPad, Hulu," said Paul Dergarabedian, president of Hollywood.com's box-office division. "There's more competition for the eyeballs of consumers."[23]

Since the 1980s, studios have relied on VHS, then DVD sales to fuel profits. DVD sales peaked at $13.7 billion in 2006.[24] This revenue stream fueled studio profits, but are in decline. In 2011, studio revenues from physical and digital sales totaled $9.5 billion.[25] Physical DVDs

are widely available, but are now exceeded by digital purchases (e.g., Apple's iTunes and Amazon). To spur sales, studios have been consistently reducing the time period between the theatrical and the DVD release. This "release window" declined from 166 days in 2000 to 120 days in 2012. Exhibitors express concern that these declines cannibalize theater sales. Studios, meanwhile, continue to seek ways to stem declining DVD sales and increase their return on each film. Decreased sales also result in lower prices for content. DVDs average $25 with upgrades to Blu-ray HD adding $5, and 3D and a digital copy for tablet or PC viewing adding another $3 each. Each sale nets the studio $12 to $15.[26]

Both studios and exhibitors are facing pressure from streaming and rental services. Once dominated by physical stores, movie rentals expanded into physical DVD channels with subscription (e.g., Netflix and Blockbuster) and one-up (e.g., Redbox and Blockbuster) options as well as subscription streaming (e.g., Netflix and Hulu). These offer very attractive prices for consumers, but have been identified by studios as a contributing factor for declining DVD sales. Studios net about $1.25 per DVD sold to a rental company.[27] This allows Netflix to offer a physical DVD subscription service of 2 DVDs out at a time for under $15 per month. RedBox's kiosk-based rentals are attractive to occasional viewers, costing as little at $1.25 per night.

Content-streaming services grew from $992 million in 2011 to $2 billion in 2012.[28] Streaming is among the most cost effective for viewers and providers. Estimates put Netflix's average streaming cost at $0.51 per viewing. This is offset by fewer content options. Apple's iTunes provides perhaps the greatest selection, but with rentals at $4 to $6 per viewing, emphasizes selection and HD quality over Netflix's low cost. Streaming sufficiently cannibalized DVD sales to the point that studios imposed a 28-day delay from DVD sales to the availability of streaming. Exhibitors expressed strong encouragement when several studios expressed a desire for a 56-day delay to increase DVD sales.

Studios are seeking to increase their share of the rental market, putting them increasingly in direct competition with exhibitors. For the studios, each current video on demand (VOD) showing contributes $3.50 in revenue, far less revenue than DVD sales.[29] Studios continue to develop premium VOD as an alternative. The main feature of Premium VOD (P-VOD) is a decreased release window, including simultaneous release on films in theaters and through P-VOD. Exhibitors threatened a boycott due to Universal's plan for a P-VOD release of *Tower Heist* just three weeks after it opened in theaters.

The plan was scrapped due to the threats. While exhibitors won the battle, the potential revenues from the planned $59.99 premium VOD will remain attractive to the studios.

Premium cable networks (e.g., HBO, Starz, etc.) offer both a programmed line-up of movies, albeit at scheduled times and with monthly subscriptions, but at low per-viewing rates. All major cable and satellite providers offer VOD services and carry multiple channels focusing on films. Overall, the availability of content and the visual and audio experience available in the home is rapidly converging with the offerings available at a movie theater. As a blogger on the movie fan site Big Picture posted:

I used to go to the movies all the time – even my blog is called the Big Picture. Then I started going less – and then less still and now – hardly at all. My screen at home is better, the sound system is better, the picture is in focus, the floors aren't sticky and the movies start on time. My seat is clean. And there's no idiot chattering away 2 rows behind me, and (this is my favorite) THERE'S NO CELL PHONES RINGING. EVER.[30]

Recent Exhibitor Initiatives

Exhibitors are well aware of the increasing number of ways in which to view motion pictures. They have a long tradition of adopting innovations that increase attendance or reduce costs. Exhibitors were among the first commercial adopters of air conditioning, which perhaps drew in as many customers as a refuge from summer heat as for entertainment. Advanced projection systems, screens, and sound systems have been continuously adopted to improve the viewing experience. Other innovations increase experience quality while also lowering costs. Stadium-style seating, now ubiquitous, was originally viewed as an experience differentiator, but equally beneficial is a reduction in the square footage needed per seat. This reduces the size and cost of facilities. Exhibitors continue to pursue a number of strategic initiatives aimed at increasing attendance, increasing the viewer's willingness to pay, and lowering costs.

Technological Innovations

The conversion to digital projection and roll-out of 3D are not the only projection innovations being pursued. Some directors are opting to increase image quality by doubling the number of frames per second (fps) of film from the long established standard of 24 to 48. Peter Jackson's 2012 The Hobbit was shown in the 48 fps format on a limited number of screens with the required projection technology. The increased frame rate results in an especially crisp image with no blurring that, while jarring to some, is said to create a sense of being part of live action.

Several circuits offer extra-large scale screens as a feature.[31] Traditionally located only in specially constructed dome-shaped theaters in science museums, the original IMAX format utilized film that was 10 times the size of that used in standard 35mm projectors. IMAX now operates more than 600 screens. These circuit-based IMAX digital screens are far smaller than the original IMAX screens, but can be much larger than the typical theater screen. Located within Regal or AMC theater complexes, the screens are often booked and operated by IMAX. Action films, usually in 3D, are a staple. To capture more of this differentiated revenue, several circuits have begun creating their own super-size screens.

Sound systems are also being upgraded. In the 1980s, theaters impressed viewers with 7.1 sound systems – two rear channels (left and right), two channels mid-screen, two near the screen, one under the screen, and a sub-woofer channel for bass. Such systems have long been available for homes. To keep theater sound as a differentiator, Dolby® Laboratories has created Atmos™[32], a full surround system with up to 64 individual channels for speakers in a theater, including multiple ceiling speakers that can truly immerse the audience in sound. Given the number of speakers involved, this may be a technology that is viable in very few homes. For those seeking still more, there is motion seat technology.[33] The heavy footsteps of a dinosaur, for example, are simultaneously seen on the screen, heard through the sound system, and felt through a motion seat that rumbles as if being shaken by the footsteps. Both IMAX and motion seats are offered as upgrades, commonly at premiums of $3 to $7 per ticket.

Alternative Content

Exhibitors' transition to digital projection is an enabling technology for alternative content, which consists of virtually any content that is not a motion picture. Revenues for this totaled $112 million in 2010[34]. Some estimate this will reach $1 billion annually – 10% of current box office.

Events have included concerts, live concerts and theater, sporting events, television series premiers and finales, even virtual art gallery tours such as 2012's *Leonardo Live*[35] that was broadcast one night only in 500 U.S. movie theaters.[36] The *Metropolitan Opera* is the most successful alternative content. Now in its seventh season, the series features 12 live events on Saturday afternoons, broadcast to nearly 700 domestic theaters. A distribution network for alternative content has emerged with companies such as National Cinemedia providing a single contract point for a variety of music, sports, television, and other alternative content. Having a large scale intermediary for a distributor is essential for exhibitors, as the cost of pursuing and licensing content is cost prohibitive for all but the largest exhibitor circuits.

Most exhibitors seek to incorporate alternative content in ways that attract new attendees during off-peak times, particularly Monday through Thursday when only 5% of theater seats are occupied.[37] Bud Mayo, CEO of Digiplex Digital Cinema Destinations, describes the approach: "What happens with those [alternative content] performances is that a single event will outgross certainly the lowest-grossing movie playing that theater that day. The relationship has averaged more than 10 times the lowest-grossing movie for the entire day."[38] In marginal dollar terms, alternative content can be a boon on otherwise slow nights. A recent Wednesday showing of Broadway's *West Side Story* at a Digitech theater had an average ticket price of $12.50 and grossed $2,425. In comparison, screens showing films that night grossed just $56 to $73. The alternative content also brought in nearly 200 additional potential customers for concessions.[39]

Dynamic Pricing

Movie theaters are among the minority of entertainment outlets that have not incorporated differentials based on content, schedule, and seating options. Most events have multiple pricing levels based on seating, night versus day, and weekday versus weekend. Movie theaters, partly due to existing exhibition contracts, commonly have limited flexibility. Matinee and youth and senior discounts are the primary pricing tiers. Ticketmaster, a leader in event ticket sales, is developing a "dynamic pricing" system that incorporates demand into pricing models.[40] This could mean radical changes with lower ticket prices for off-time and poorly attended movies and increased prices for prime seats at peak times on opening weekend. Thus far, no studio or exhibitor will acknowledge investigating the technology.[41]

Concession Initiatives

Expanding beyond the standard concession stand offers exhibitors opportunities to capture new revenue streams. Three main formats for concessions have emerged.

Expanded In-Lobby. Many theaters have expanded the concession counter beyond candy, popcorn and soda. This expanded in-lobby dining causes many theater lobbies to resemble mall food courts. In- and off-lobby restaurants operated or licensed by the exhibitor allow for pre-theater dining. Taking a page from restaurants where a primary profit center is often the bar, some theaters now configure the lobby around a bar, with expanded and upscale fare, beer, and alcohol service.

In-Theater Dining. Many theaters have adopted an in-theater dining format where orders are placed from the seat in the theater by a wait staff. Chunky's Cinema Pub, with three New England locations, locates theaters in lower cost, underutilized former retail locations. The format combines burger, salad, and sandwich options with beverages, including beer. The format is flat theater with banquet style tables. The seating is unique: old car seats on casters that allow for easy cleaning. Alamo Drafthouse Cinemas takes a similar approach using a stadium seating configuration. A single bar-style table in front of each row of seats serves as a table for customers' orders. In comparison to traditional theaters, these formats see significant increases in food and beverage sales.

Upscale Within-Theater Dining. Several circuits are targeting the high end of the theater market, focusing on the experience of the theater with luxurious settings and upscale food. In addition to its standard theaters, AMC has developed Dine-In Theaters with two theater configurations. Its Fork & Screen theaters are much like the Alamo Drafthouse Cinema with enhanced stadium theater seats and in-theater wait service on an expanded menu. Its Cinema Suite theaters make the experience more intimate. Customers, only 21 and older, purchase tickets for specific seats in smaller theaters with reclining lounge chairs with footrests and in-theater wait service.

Theater chain iPic offers perhaps the most luxurious theater experience available outside of a private screening room, complete with reclining leather chairs, pillows, and blankets. Lobbies resemble stylish high-end hotels and feature a cocktail lounge and full restaurants. Complete with a membership program, the theaters operate more like social clubs than traditional theaters. Tickets, $16–$27 per seat, are purchased not from a ticket booth but from a concierge.

Advertising Initiatives

Exhibitors are keen to expand advertising revenues, but must do so in ways that do not diminish the theater experience. Revenues are generated from advertisements both on- and off-screen. Off-screen advertising such as promotional videos, lobby events, and sponsored concession promotions are 9% of revenues. The majority, 91%, comes from on-screen ads for upcoming releases, companies, and products that play before the feature presentation. Both exhibitors and advertisers seek ways to make on-screen ads more palatable to audiences. Many ads are produced in 3D with production quality rivaling a studio release. Theaters are also incorporating innovative technologies such as crowd gaming into ads where the movement or sound of the audience controls on-screen actions. In October of 2008, audiences in the U.K. attending Disney's *Ratatouille* "drove" an on-screen Volvo XC70 through an obstacle-laden course, waving their arms while scoring points for avoiding obstacles. Results were ranked in real-time to audiences in other theaters.[42] What equipment was required? A wireless video camera placed above the screen, a web-enabled laptop containing the game linked to the developer's website, and specialized motion-sensing technology. These were linked to the theater's digital projector.

More interactive approaches are on their way: fans at a Formula One race in Singapore played the videogame Angry Birds, controlling in-game slingshots used to fling birds at the rivals, pigs based on voice volume. The louder the crowd, the further the birds were launched.[43] Making ads enjoyable, rather than loathed, may create an opportunity to increase this small but high-margin component of exhibitor revenues.

Bright Lights and Red Carpet or Dimly Lit Marquee?

Are these initiatives enough to return people to the local movie house? Is the future of the movie exhibition industry a return to red carpet glamor? Or will the lights on the marquee dim?

WORKS REFERENCED

1. All ticket sales and box office data in this section is from: www.boxofficemojo.com.
2. MPAA 2011 Theatrical Statistics.
3. MPAA 2011 Theatrical Statistics.
4. Thakur, A. (2009, July 29, 2009). India dominates world of films. *The Times of India*. Retrieved from Factiva.
5. Ibid.
6. Fritz, B., & Kaufman, A. (2011, December 30, 2011). Solid start, fast fade for movies, *LA Times*. Retrieved from latimes.com/entertainment/news/movies/la-fi-ct-box-office-wrap-20111230,0,2205189.story
7. NATO press releases, Cinema Advertising, 2005-2012.
8. Ibid.
9. Data on the firms, theaters and screens, location, etc. from web sites and SEC filings.
10. Kung, M., & Back, A. (2012). Chinese conglomerate buys AMC movie chain in U.S. *Wall Street Journal*, p. 2.
11. Boorstin, J. (2011, May 31, 2011). Huge Upside and Ominous Underbelly From a Big Weekend Box Office. Retrieved from http://www.cnbc.com/id/43228469/.
12. Mintel Report, Movie Theaters - US - February 2008 - Reasons to Go to Movies over Watching a DVD.
13. Mintel Report, Movie Theaters - US - February 2008 - Reasons why Attendance Is not Higher.
14. Kelly, K., Orwall, B., & Sanders, P. (2005). The Multiplex Under Siege. *Wall Street Journal*, December 24, 2005, P. 1.
15. blog comment on Cinema Treasures | Over the past ten years, the movie theater experience has ...; http://cinematreasures.org/polls/22/,accessed 12/11/2008
16. Incident reported in Patrick Goldstein, 2005, Now playing: A glut of ads, *Los Angeles Times*, July 12, 2005 in print edition E-1; http://articles.latimes.com/2005/jul/12/entertainment/et-goldstein12; accessed December 5, 2008.

17. DuBravac, S. (2007) Connecting tomorrow's consumer: Consumer technology trends to watch, presentation at Fleck Connection Conference, http://www.fleckresearch.com/fcc2007.
18. Ibid.
19. Tuttle, B. (2012). TV prices shrink — Yet average TV purchase costs more. *Time Magazine*.
20. Ibid.
21. Average TV size up to 60-inch by 2015 says Sharp, *TechDigest*, http://www.techdigest.tv/2008/01/average_tv_size.html; accessed 2008/12/11.
22. Ibid.
23. Verrier, R. (2012, December 30, 2011). U.S. theater owners get lump of coal at box office, *LA Times*. Retrieved from latimes.com/entertainment/news/movies/la-fi-ct-theaters-20111230,0,7228622.story.
24. Kung, M. (2012, May 10, 2012). Movie Magic to Leave Home For? *Wall Street Journal*, pp. D1-D2.
25. Snider, M. (2012, 1/9/2012). Blu-ray grows, but DVD slide nips home video sales. *USA Today*.
26. Jannarone, J. (2012, February 6, 2012). As Studios Fight Back, Will Coinstar Box Itself Into a Corner? *Wall Street Journal*, p. C6.
27. Ibid.
28. Zeitchik, S., & Horn, J. (2013). Sundance darlings eye alternative distribution platforms, *LA Times*. Retrieved from http://touch.latimes.com/#section/641/article/p2p-74047654/
29. Jannarone, J. As Studios Fight Back, Will Coinstar Box Itself Into a Corner?
30. The Big Picture | Why is Movie Theatre Revenue Attendance Declining? http://bigpicture.typepad.com/comments/2005/07/declining_movie.htm. Accessed 12/11/2008.

31. Dodes, R. (2012, April 19, 2012). IMAX Strikes Back, *Wall Street Journal*. Retrieved from http://online.wsj.com/article/SB10001424052702304299304577347940832511540.html?KEYWORDS=IMAX+strikes+back.
32. Dolby Laboratories. (2013) Dolby Atmos: Hear The Whole Picture. http://www.dolby.com/us/en/professional/technology/cinema/dolby-atmos.html, Accessed: 1/5/2013.
33. Kung, Movie Magic to Leave Home For?
34. Sony. (2011). Alternative Content for Theatres. *Sony Digital Cinema 4K*, 1.
35. Schubin, M. (Writer).(2012). Alternative content at a theater near you. You Tube: SchubinCafe.
36. Smith, R. (2012, February 15, 2012). Leonardo's London Blockbuster: The Movie, *NY Times*. Retrieved from Factiva.
37. Cinedigm. (2012). Investor Presentation: Jefferies 2012 Global Technology, Media & Telecom Conference. Cinedigm. Retrieved from http://files.shareholder.com/downloads/AIXD/2302444840x0x567367/4a213e2c-11ae-4cdc-8dd1-970919ac80ac/CIDM%20IR%20deck%20050712%20Short.pdf
38. Ellingson, A. (Oct. 15, 2012). Who's stressed about digital cinema? Not Digiplex's Bud Mayo. *The Business Journal - LA*.
39. Ibid.
40. Lazarus, D. (2012, April 26, 2012). Movie tickets: Now how much would you pay?, *LA Times*.
41. Ibid.
42. Audience Entertain. (2009). AE Case: Volvo XC70 Launch, Retrieved from http://www.youtube.com/watch?v=HYVuLGLnyAM.
43. Reuters. (Sept. 22, 2011). Angry Birds to Swoop on Formula One Track, *CNBC*. Retrieved from http://www.reuters.com/article/2011/09/22/us-angrybirds-idUSTRE78L1IY20110922.

CASE 24

Phase Separation Solutions (PS2): The China Question

Hill Paul J. Hill School of Business

IVEY | Publishing

In early 2008, Paul Antle, president and chief executive officer (CEO) of Phase Separation Solutions (PS2), received a call from the State Environmental Protection Agency of China, expressing interest in PS2's Thermal Phase Separation (TPS) technology. PS2 was a small, Saskatchewan-based environmental solutions company that had grown, under Antle's entrepreneurial direction, to become a North American leader in the treatment of soil, sludge and debris impacted with various organic contaminants. The company specialized in the cleanup of two waste streams using its TPS technology. The first was the remediation of soil contaminated with persistent organic pollutants (POPs), such as pesticides and polychlorinated biphenyls (PCBs). The second was recovering usable oil from industrial sludge generated in various industries, such as the oil and gas industry.

Despite Antle's initial concerns that the call had been a scam, he soon visited China to learn more about the market in China and to build relationships. The Chinese inquiries were sincere. By mid-2010, nearly one and a half years after Antle's first visit, potential cooperative opportunities had emerged with two separate Chinese organizations: one in soil remediation, and the other in oil recovery from oil sludge. The two potential opportunities were attractive to PS2. The international geographic diversification would transform PS2 from a domestic player to an international player, and in so doing, would significantly improve its growth potential.

The PS2 management team was no stranger to international markets. The TPS technology had been successfully employed in 14 countries in the past 15 years. However, the modes of international involvement had been on a non-equity basis, in the forms of equipment exporting, licensing and service contracts. Although the cooperative opportunities in China would bring PS2 to a higher level of internationalization, the decision was not to be taken lightly. A series of questions needed to be answered. Should PS2 enter the Chinese market? Which of the two opportunities should it pursue? Would it be feasible to pursue both? Did PS2 possess the required resources and capabilities to pursue an equity-based entry? What ownership levels should PS2 assume for each option? How would PS2 staff its Chinese operation(s) if PS2 decided to pursue the opportunities in China?

Company Overview[1]

PS2 was founded in 2004 by a group of Canadian entrepreneurs who believed that the key to the safe management of environmental liability was the proper application of advanced clean technology, such as their TPS technology. By combining their extensive experience in the fields of hazardous waste management, remedial technology development and environmental engineering, they created PS2 to take advantage of the new opportunities in the Canadian environmental market. In the Government

This case was written with generous financial assistance from the Hill-Ivey Case-Writing Fund.

George Z. Peng and Paul W. Beamish wrote this case solely to provide material for class discussion. The authors do not intend to illustrate either effective or ineffective handling of a managerial situation. The authors may have disguised certain names and other identifying information to protect confidentiality.

Version: 2012–03–30

of Canada's 2004 budget, it had pledged \$3.5 billion[2] over the following 10 years for environmental cleanup.

In 2005, after securing an investment of \$3 million from Golden Opportunities Fund Inc.[3] in the form of senior secured debentures, the company constructed a fixed soil reclamation facility in Wolseley, Saskatchewan. This facility was capable of treating a wide variety of soil contaminated with POPs, industrial sludge and waste pharmaceuticals. The location was chosen so that PS2 could target the markets in both Eastern and Western Canada, and in the United States. The facility, which had a capacity of 20,000 tons per year, was permitted to treat a wide variety of pollutants. It was one of only three fixed facilities in Canada permitted to treat PCB and dioxin/furan-impacted soil. In late 2005, the facility became operational and started generating revenue. It was fully commissioned in early 2006.

PS2 generated revenue by securing service "contracts" for the treatment of contaminated soil or on a "fee-for-service basis," wherein small quantities of contaminated soil were accepted from customers. Its customer base comprised environmental service companies, utility companies and general industry. The number and size of contracts obtained each year for contaminated soil varied and depended on the funding that customers had budgeted for remedial projects.

PS2 went public in 2007 through a reverse merger with West Mountain Capital Corporation (WMT), a capital pool company (see more information in a later section). The reverse merger brought PS2 to an advanced level of growth by introducing more funds and professional management expertise.

In early 2008, PS2 diversified into pharmaceutical waste management by acquiring an Ontario firm. Later that year, however, PS2 decided to divest it to focus its resources on the Wolseley facility, in response to the contaminated soil market that had opened up significantly since the acquisition. The soil treatment market in Canada received a big boost in late 2008 when the federal government introduced new regulations that established deadlines for ending the use and long-term storage of both PCBs and products containing PCBs. The new regulations also required that these products be sent for destruction by the end of 2009 (later extended to 2011). Such a policy change resulted in a strong demand for PS2's TPS technology; subsequent to this announcement, PS2 secured contracts for 2009 and into 2010, utilizing 80 percent of its capacity at its Wolseley facility.

As a result of the new regulations in 2008, PS2 posted record revenues of \$5.88 million and net profits of \$2.51 million in 2009 (see Exhibits 1, 2 and 3 for PS2's

Exhibit 1 Phase Separation Solutions Income Statements (in Canadian Dollars)

	2007	2008	2009	2010E	2011E
Revenue	255,633	–	5,884,361	4,900,000	7,233,333
Cost of goods sold	257,473	103,323	2,009,746	1,760,000	2,893,333
Gross profit expenses	(1,840)	(103,323)	3,874,615	3,140,000	4,340,000
General & administrative	415,567	608,493	886,620	822,312	904,543
Stock-based compensation	19,488	91,555	71,244	98,000	144,667
EBITDA	(436,895)	(803,371)	2,916,751	2,219,688	3,290,790
Amortization	335,609	393,091	420,941	407,448	361,331
EBIT	(772,504)	(1,196,462)	2,495,810	1,812,240	2,929,459
Interest & bank charges	31,783	17,682	9,745	8,980	3,417
Earnings from operations	(804,287)	(1,214,144)	2,486,065	1,803,259	2,926,042
Interest income	5,661	21,386	–	–	–
Interest on long-term debt	(368,161)	(44,484)	(106,948)	–	–
EBT	(1,166,787)	(1,237,242)	2,379,117	1,803,259	2,926,042
Discontinued operations, net of income taxes	(345,983)	(193,516)	129,030	–	–
Taxes	–	–	–	–	907,073
Net earnings for the period	(1,512,770)	(1,430,758)	2,508,147	1,803,259	2,018,969

Source: Fundamental Research Corp., "West Mountain Capital Corp. (TSXV: WMT)–Initiating Coverage—Thermal Treatment of Soil, Sludge and Other Waste Streams," March 23, 2010, http://www.baystreet.ca/articles/research_reports/fundamental_research/WestMountainCapital040110.pdf.

Exhibit 2 Phase Separation Solutions Balance Sheets (in Canadian Dollars)

Assets	2007	2008	2009	2010E	2011E
Cash and cash equivalents	1,253,446	783,993	3,255,003	5,072,250	7,432,087
Accounts receivable	117,725	155,344	681,075	696,499	1,028,166
Income tax receivable	–	177,861	–	–	–
Assets related to discontinued operations	–	141,988	–	–	–
Prepaid expenses and deposits	2,750	12,094	9,144	8,843	13,053
Current assets	**1,373,921**	**1,271,280**	**3,945,222**	**5,777,592**	**8,473,306**
Restricted cash	145,301	167,383	217,394	217,394	217,394
Capital assets	2,970,732	2,982,937	2,716,322	2,408,874	2,147,543
Other assets	51,216	46,096	41,904	41,904	41,904
Total assets	**4,541,170**	**4,467,696**	**6,920,842**	**8,445,763**	**10,880,146**
Liabilities & shareholders' equity					
Bank loan	–	107,000	–	–	–
Accounts payable & accrued liabilities	296,207	299,658	864,972	509,952	838,331
Deferred revenue	184,409	393,798	–	–	–
Convertible debentures	–	–	474,203	–	–
Liabilities related to discontinued operations	–	184,903	38,732	38,732	38,732
Current portion of obligations under capital lease	5,570	56,412	61,318	97,631	–
Current liabilities	**486,186**	**1,041,771**	**1,439,225**	**646,315**	**877,063**
Obligations under capital lease	–	158,652	97,631	–	–
Convertible debentures	–	464,274	–	–	–
Shareholders' loans	–	–	–	–	–
Long-term debt	–	–	–	–	–
Asset retirement obligations	93,431	102,775	113,052	153,052	193,052
Shareholders' equity					
Share capital	6,915,817	6,935,817	6,935,817	7,459,213	7,459,213
Contributed surplus	90,141	181,696	252,940	350,940	495,607
Equity component of convertible debentures	–	57,874	49,193	–	–
Deficit	(3,044,405)	(4,475,163)	(1,967,016)	(163,757)	1,855,212
Total liabilities & shareholders' equity	**4,541,170**	**4,467,696**	**6,920,842**	**8,445,763**	**10,880,146**

Source: Fundamental Research Corp., "West Mountain Capital Corp. (TSXV: WMT)–Initiating Coverage—Thermal Treatment of Soil, Sludge and Other Waste Streams," March 23, 2010, http://www.baystreet.ca/articles/research_reports/fundamental_research/WestMountainCapital040110.pdf.

financial statements). In 2010, PS2 was expected to fulfill the contracts it had secured in 2008 and 2009. However, PS2's ability to secure new contracts and source new business for its unused treatment capacity in 2010 and future years could be affected by the economic climate of the day. For example, if the economy was poor, potential customers might need to suspend their remedial projects, which could lead to delays in securing revenue.[4] In addition, recent regulatory changes with regard to PCBs would provide PS2 with only a short-term momentum as PCB treatment was a declining market.

By mid 2010, the management team comprised Antle, Stephen Clarke as vice-president of Business Development and Paul Coombs as chief financial officer (see Exhibit 4 for a biography of Antle). The company had 15 employees.

The Thermal Phase Separation (TPS) Technology[5]

The TPS technology is an indirectly heated thermal desorption process that adopts a closed-loop system

Exhibit 3 Phase Separation Solutions Statements of Cash Flows (in Canadian Dollars)

	2008	2009	2010E	2011E
Operating activities				
Net earnings for the period	(1,430,758)	2,508,147	1,803,259	2,018,969
Discontinued operations, net of income taxes	193,516	(129,030)	–	–
Items not involving cash				
Asset retirement obligations	18,992	48,868	40,000	40,000
Amortization	390,017	410,664	407,448	361,331
Gain on settlement of debentures	–	(5,621)	–	–
Stock-based compensation	91,555	71,244	98,000	144,667
	(736,678)	**2,904,272**	**2,348,708**	**2,564,967**
Changes in non-cash operating working capital	168,894	(173,404)	(370,143)	(7,499)
Cash from (used in) operating activities - discontinued operations	(630,629)	24,847	–	–
Cash from (used in) operations	**(1,198,413)**	**2,755,715**	**1,978,565**	**2,557,468**
Financing activities				
Cash acquired on reverse takeover	–	–	–	–
Repayment of long-term debt	–	–	–	–
Proceeds from bank loan	107,000	–	–	–
Repayment of bank loan	–	(107,000)	–	–
Payment of capital lease obligations	(48,483)	(56,115)	–	–
Proceeds (repayment) of debentures – net	500,000	(31,722)	–	–
Proceeds from issuance of common share & exercise of stock options	20,000	–	–	–
Cash provided by (used in) financing activities	**578,517**	**(194,837)**	**–**	**–**
Investing activities				
Increase in restricted cash	(22,082)	(50,011)	–	–
Purchase of capital assets	(322,076)	(139,857)	(61,318)	(97,631)
Capital expenditures	–	–	(100,000)	(100,000)
Cash provided by investing activities – discontinued operations	494,601	100,000	–	–
Cash provided by (used in) investing activities	**150,443**	**(89,868)**	**(161,318)**	**(197,631)**
Increase (decrease) in cash	(469,453)	2,471,010	1,817,247	2,359,837
Cash beginning of period	1,253,446	783,993	3,255,003	5,072,250
Cash end of period	**783,993**	**3,255,003**	**5,072,250**	**7,432,087**

Source: Fundamental Research Corp., "West Mountain Capital Corp. (TSXV: WMT)–Initiating Coverage—Thermal Treatment of Soil, Sludge and Other Waste Streams," March 23, 2010, http://www.baystreet.ca/articles/research_reports/fundamental_research/WestMountainCapital040110.pdf.

using non-incineration engineering principles. The mechanism of the technology is akin to a household clothes dryer, which is indirectly heated, vaporizing the water from laundry. In a TPS unit, the contaminated soil is indirectly heated to boil off the hazardous contaminants, which are subsequently captured as a vapor. The vapor is then re-condensed into a liquid so the contaminants don't escape to the environment. The TPS technology was the only technology capable of extracting up to 90 percent of oil (by volume) from industrial sludge. It

was also capable of separating hydrocarbons with boiling points up to 550°C. The technology had been internationally proven and was recognized as being world-class for its performance, lack of harmful air emissions, mobility and reliability. The technology had been used to treat hundreds of thousands of tons of contaminated material worldwide at many high-profile projects, such as the Sydney, Australia's 2000 Olympic Games Site Restoration Project. The technology had been used or was permitted to be used in more than 10 countries.

Exhibit 4 Paul Antle, the Serial Entrepreneur: A Biography

Paul G. Antle, B.Sc., M.Eng., CCEP, was the president and chief executive officer of Phase Separation Solutions, Inc. A recognized leader in the Canadian environmental and waste management industries, he had over 25 years of experience and had started, operated, grown and sold numerous businesses.

Antle was born in St. John's, Newfoundland and Labrador. He graduated from Memorial University in 1985 with a B.Sc. degree in Chemistry. With no desire to do research or teach, he went on to the University of New Brunswick (UNB) to pursue a master's degree in Chemical Engineering, with an aim to apply his chemistry background in a practical application. Antle graduated from UNB with a master's degree at the age of 22 in 1987. With résumés in hand and an eagerness for work, he journeyed to Toronto, Ontario. However, he was not successful in landing a job he wanted. Antle returned to Newfoundland, empty handed but not discouraged.

Two months later, Antle was hired to kick-start a newly opened waste management division for a local construction company that had encountered PCBs at its construction site. After working for the company for nine months and achieving all his goals, Antle determined that it was time for a new challenge. Armed with a bank loan and helped by some friends, he hung out his own shingle as an entrepreneur on July 14, 1988, when he founded the SCC Environmental Group (SCC) in Newfoundland and Labrador.

From its meager beginnings, SCC grew during the first half of the 1990s to become known for its advanced site remediation and integrated hazardous waste management. The company employed 150 Newfoundlanders and worked on four continents. In 1994, SCC launched the TPS Technology. The reputation of SCC grew to such a point that Stratos Global Corp., a satellite communications company, purchased SCC in September 1996 for $3.2 million.

Stratos Global invested in the TPS technology and financed the promotion of it to the international oil and gas sector. SCC soon started dealing in international contracts. During 1997/98, however, Stratos Global refocused its business and decided to divest any interests that were not related to telecommunications. Antle decided to buy the company back, and the transaction was completed on July 13, 1998. He then sold it to MI Drilling Fluids of Houston, Texas, on December 14, 1999, for $10.0 million. MI Drilling Fluids used the TPS technology for the treatment of drilling mud and cuttings generated by the oil and gas industry. Antle served as the president and CEO of SCC from 1988 to 1999, as vice president of Stratos Global Corporation from 1996 to 1998, and as vice president of Thermal Operations at MI Drilling Fluids from 1999 to 2001.

In 1995, Antle founded Island Waste Management Inc., which he sold for $5.6 million in August 2006. He joined PS2's management/ownership team in 2005 to oversee its growth into a public company and its diversification into pharmaceutical waste management. Antle holds a majority equity interest in PS2 and runs it as president and CEO.

Antle was inducted into the Academy of Entrepreneurs in September 1995; was a finalist for Atlantic Canada's Entrepreneur of the Year Award in 1995; received a World Young Business Achiever Award in 1997; was recognized for his contribution to the Newfoundland and Labrador Environmental Industry in 2002; in August 2002 was part of Canada's official delegation to the United Nations World Summit on Sustainable Development held in Johannesburg, South Africa; in May 2003 was named one of Canada's Top 40 Under 40™; and in November 2003 was named Alumnus of the Year for Gonzaga High School.

TPS technology was originally developed as a mobile, onsite remedial technology. However, because of its modular design, it could be easily deployed at a fixed facility if required due to cost considerations (e.g., to take advantage of economies of scale or to avoid prohibitive transportation costs). Compared with the traditional means of treating contaminated soil and industrial sludge, such as incineration or land filling, TPS technology had a series of advantages. First, the TPS process produced safe soil with an 85 percent decrease in volume that could be returned to the environment. This process was a better alternative to burying contaminated soil in landfills, which was only a temporary solution, as it did not destroy or remove contaminants. Second, the TPS process not only enabled the recovery of oil and other hydrocarbons for reuse or resale but also generated its own fuel source to fire the system. Third, compared with incineration and land filling, TPS technology produced no harmful air emissions and no land and water pollutants. Fourth, compared with incineration, the TPS process produces significantly fewer greenhouse gas emissions.

Although the TPS technology had significant advantages over the traditional technologies, the TPS technology could compete only in applications and regions where it was cost-competitive compared with the traditional technology, or where government regulations required the proper treatment of waste.

The PS2 management team launched the Thermal Phase Separation (TPS) technology in 1994 from the firm they had founded. The technology and company were sold to Stratos Global Corp. in 1996 and bought back again in 1998, only to be resold to MI Drilling Fluids of Houston, Texas, in 1999. Since the acquisition, MI Drilling Fluids had used the TPS technology exclusively for the treatment of drilling mud and cuttings generated by the oil and gas industry.

In 2002, the founders of PS2 licensed the technology from MI Drilling Fluids, wherein PS2 received exclusive rights to use the technology, in Canada and the

United States, for the decontamination treatment of all types of hazardous waste streams, until 2012. In return, PS2 paid an initial licensing fee of $61,460 and agreed to start paying a royalty of US$10 per ton of material processed, after the first 15,000 tons. PS2 also agreed to pay US$0.10 million for each TPS unit installed subsequent to the first unit. Although the company had yet to reach its first 15,000 tons of production, PS2 had started paying royalties in October 2008, after the license was renegotiated to extend the expiration date to 2019. In 2009, MI Drilling Fluids granted PS2 the exclusive rights to use the technology in China.

All the patents associated with the TPS technology were set to expire in 2019, after which the company would not need to renew its license. This patent deadline implied that competition would increase after 2019, when potential competitors would be able to more easily adopt the TPS technology.

The Market for Persistent Organic Pollutants and Industrial Sludge in Canada[6]

PCB Market

Due to their fire resistance and chemical stability, PCBs had been primarily used as insulating fluids and coolants in electrical equipment and machinery since the early 1900s.[7] However, PCB production had been banned in North America since the 1970s, due to their harmful effects on humans and the environment. Despite the ban on production, PCBs still persist in the environment due to their resistance to environmental degradation. According to the United Nation's 2001 Stockholm Convention on Persistent Organic Pollutants (POPs), PCBs were considered one of the 12 most persistent organic pollutants.

Even though the TPS technology could be used to treat oil sludge and a variety of POPs and other organic contaminants, the main focus of PS2 was the PCB-contaminated soil treatment market in Canada. The PCB market was believed to have high entry barriers due to high start-up costs, difficulty in sourcing and securing friendly locations for facilities and a minimum of two to three years of environmental assessment and regulatory evaluation.[8] In addition, this market was a niche market that needed special expertise that could only be developed through many years of immersion in the industry. PCB soil remediation in North America was a declining market because PCB production had been banned since the 1970s. PS2's Wolseley facility was one of only three plants in Canada with the environmental certification to service the PCB market.

Although PS2 also had the exclusive rights to use the technology in the United States, it was banned from transporting PCB-contaminated soil from the United States to Canada. All other types of contaminated soil, however, were allowed to be transported to Canada for treatment. Because the U.S. market for contaminated soil was highly competitive, PS2 did not have any immediate plans to establish a fixed facility there. However, an entry through licensing by granting the use of the TPS technology to an American company might be considered.

Market Size. In 2008, the known amount of PCB-contaminated soil in Canada was only approximately 200,000 tons. Even though many believed that several additional sites potentially contained unknown amounts of PCB-contaminated soil, the future prospects for the industry were not good. In addition to limited sustainable future revenue, past revenues for the industry in Canada had been highly volatile.

Competitors and Strategies. The Canadian PCB market was an oligopoly, with PS2 and Bennett Environmental (BEV) as the main competitors. BEV provided solutions for soil contamination problems throughout Canada and the United States, using a technology called thermal oxidation, essentially an incineration technology.[9] BEV had a market capitalization of $81 million. Compared with PS2, BEV was the major player with a capacity of 80,000 tons, four times the capacity of PS2's 20,000 tons. Because both PS2 and BEV had similar cost structures, they competed on the basis of the locations of their facilities relative to project sites because transportation costs played a significant role in the economics of such projects. PS2's facility was located in Saskatchewan, whereas BEV's facility was located in Quebec. As such, BEV had an advantage in Quebec, and in most of Ontario, whereas PS2 clearly had an advantage in Western Canada. The majority of PCB-contaminated soil was located in Ontario and Quebec, with British Columbia a distant third.

Although BEV had recently entered into a contract to remove and treat approximately 10,500 tons of PCB-contaminated soil located in southern Ontario (which was estimated to be worth $7 million to $9 million), the remaining amount of PCB-contaminated soil available for removal and treatment was in decline.[10]

Due to limited growth potential in the PCB treatment market (i.e., the "known" amounts of PCB-contaminated soil in Canada was only approximately 200,000 tons, or approximately two years of production at PS2 and BEV's combined capacity), BEV had been seeking opportunities for geographical diversification and product diversification to reduce volatility in revenues and improve efficiency through continuous operations. It had diversified into the treatment of contaminated construction debris.

Industrial Sludge Market in Canada

Industrial sludge referred to the residual, semi-solid waste generated as a result of an industrial production process. Although industrial sludge could be of different types, PS2's target was hydrocarbon-based sludge with more than 50 percent hydrocarbons. Conventionally, such sludge either ended up in man-made lagoons or landfills, or was incinerated. Landfills and incineration were much less expensive than PS2's TPS technology; however, such methods created environmental liabilities due to their potential impacts on subsoil, groundwater and air.

As a result of the general public's ever-increasing environmental awareness, the conventional disposal method of using landfills was under siege. For example, in September 2008, the Ontario government had initiated regulatory changes to its Land Disposal Restrictions (LDR), which required proper pre-release treatment of industrial sludge. Under the new regulations, land disposal of untreated hazardous wastes was prohibited, and treated wastes were required to meet specific treatment standards before being disposed of. Such treatment requirements were specified as either concentration-based numerical levels or as specified treatment methods.

Such regulatory changes created demand for technologies that could meet the environmental regulation, such as PS2's TPS technology. One potential target identified by PS2 in the industrial sludge sector was paint sludge. According to data from Stewardship Ontario,[11] the collection target of Ontario for paint and coatings contents and containers was 10,573 tons per year, or 47 percent of available for collection. Based on PS2 management's estimation that the paint sludge market represented about 7 percent to 10 percent of the industrial sludge market, the 2009 industrial sludge market in Ontario was, at most, approximately 150,000 tons. Assuming that Ontario's GDP was 40 percent of Canada's GDP, and that paint waste generation would be proportional to GDP, the total industrial sludge in Canada was estimated to be at 375,000 tons in 2009.

Despite the potential size of this market appearing to be of a decent size for small firms such as PS2, the market was still at an emerging stage. The prohibition against dumping sludge into landfills might simply create more opportunities for other conventional disposal methods, such as incineration. The real market potential for firms

such as PS2 would largely depend on their comparative cost advantages over other conventional disposal methods, and on future regulatory evolution, which was a slow process. The potential of this market for PS2 was also limited due to the distance between Ontario and PS2's facility in Saskatchewan. PS2 had yet to break into the industrial sludge market in Canada.

PS2 Strategic Moves

The vision of PS2 was to become a fully integrated environmental service company.[12] As such, the company was always seeking opportunities to expand both organically and through acquisition for the purpose of transforming itself into a more integrated and more diversified waste management company. On the domestic front, PS2 had gone through the following strategic moves.

Diversification into Pharmaceutical Waste Management[13]

Given the limited growth potential in soil remediation and oil recovery from industrial sludge, PS2 was searching for growth opportunities. It ventured into the pharmaceutical waste treatment market by acquiring a pharmaceutical waste-processing firm, Pharma Processing, on March 17, 2008. Pharma Processing was a well-known pharmaceutical waste management service provider that processed hazardous and non-hazardous pharmaceutical waste at its facility in Brampton, Ontario. Pharma Processing had been in operation since 1994. The acquisition was completed on July 23, 2008. The rationale behind the acquisition included geographic diversification, product diversification and scope economies.[14]

The pharmaceutical waste stream was 49.6 percent plastic packaging comingled with pharmaceuticals. Because of the co-mingling, the plastic in this waste stream was not readily recyclable. Thus, pharmaceutical wastes were typically incinerated. Using a modified version of its TPS technology, PS2 patented a process to depolymerize the plastic and deactivate the pharmaceutical ingredients. Using this process, PS2 was able to generate up to 44 litres of No. 2 fuel oil and up to 20 cubic meters of "synthetic" natural gas from 1 cubic meter of pharmaceutical waste, while producing only 60 kilograms (kg) of carbon dioxide per metric ton (CO_2/mT). In comparison, incineration not only cost more but also produced more than 300 kg CO_2/mT of waste without offering any recovery value.

Despite PS2 having succeeded in developing and commercializing its pharmaceutical waste business unit, the company decided, in October 2008, to exit this business to free capacity at the Wolseley facility for the soil market, which had increased since the acquisition. The decision was made as a result of the slower than projected growth rates and the higher per-unit transportation costs of pharmaceutical waste, which typically had a much lower density than contaminated soil. On December 12, 2008, the unit was acquired by an undisclosed firm. The pharmaceutical waste unit was sold at a profit, and the patent resulting from this business remained the property of PS2. Thus, the door was left open for PS2 to enter the business in the future.

Going Public through Reverse Acquisition of West Mountain Capital Corp.

Because PS2 was a small growth company, it needed to raise money to fund the various growth strategies required to realize its vision. In the absence of further venture capital financing, going public was a necessary strategy. However, an initial public offering (IPO) in its own name might not be appropriate for several reasons. First, the IPO market was not strong enough during a time of recession. Second, the company was at too early a stage for a broadly distributed regular IPO. Third, and most importantly, a traditional IPO might not allow the company founders to retain higher ownership levels, whereas at the company's current stage of development, the technical expertise of the strong founder-manager team was critical.

PS2 resorted to TSX Venture Exchange (TSXV), the public venture capital marketplace in Canada, which provided growth companies with access to capital and offered investors a venture investment market. TSXV offered a unique listing vehicle, the Capital Pool Company® (CPC)[15] program, which provided an alternative, two-step introduction to the capital markets that would meet PS2's requirements. The CPC program identified entrepreneurs whose development and growth-stage companies required capital and public company management expertise and introduced them to investors who had financial market experience. Unlike a traditional IPO, the CPC program enabled seasoned directors and officers to form a CPC with no assets other than cash and no significant commercial operations. They could then list the CPC on TSXV and raise a pool of capital. The CPC then used these funds to seek out an investment opportunity in a growing business. Once the CPC had completed its "qualifying transaction" and acquired an operating company that met TSXV's listing requirements, its shares continued trading as a regular listing on the TSX Venture Exchange. Alternatively, an existing operating company could reverse acquire the CPC. The use of CPCs not only provided a going-public process that had more certainty, greater flexibility and allowed for greater control by the operating company but also removed the company's risk from the going-public process.

PS2 reverse acquired West Mountain Capital (TSXV: WMT), a CPC that was incorporated in 2005 with its headquarters in Calgary, Canada.[16] As a CPC, it did not have commercial operations. It intended to identify and evaluate entrepreneurial companies with a view to completing a "qualifying transaction" to become integrated with an existing company satisfactory to its evaluation. In December 2007, based on the strength of PS2's technology and the recognized expertise of its executive team, WMT decided to be taken over by PS2 in a reverse takeover. In so doing, PS2 went public on the TSXV and, by April 2010, had grown to a market capitalization of $12.67 million. In the newly integrated corporate structure, PS2 became the only wholly owned subsidiary of WMT, the parent firm. The new vision and mandate of West Mountain Capital was to evaluate and seek complementary acquisition in the environmental services industry with a view to building a fully integrated environmental services firm focused in Western Canada.[17]

Other Potential Future Moves

Consistent with its vision of building a fully integrated and diversified environmental services firm, WMT also had plans for geographical diversification. Its Wolseley facility had an annual treatment capacity of 20,000 tons (which could be expanded to 60,000 tons, subject to regulatory approval, at a relatively low capital expenditure of $2 million). However, because the Wolseley facility was a fixed facility, and all the contaminated material needed to be transported there, transportation costs played a huge role in the viability of the company's business model. The company could establish a second facility in Ontario (the largest market in Canada) if and when demand exceeded the current plant capacity of 20,000 tons.

The Chinese Market

China has seen rapid economic development since its opening up to the outside world three decades earlier. Real GDP per capita rose from $220 in 1980 to $2,883 in 2010,[18] or an annual growth rate of approximately 9 percent from 1980 to 2010. However, this economic achievement had been made at the cost of the environment. Residents in big cities rarely saw a clear sky due to ubiquitous smog resulting from industrial pollution, coal-based power generation, and transportation exhaust.

Environmental pollution was becoming a big issue in China due to its many negative consequences. Smog affected worker attendance and productivity rates in many cities. Various types of pollution also placed a big burden on the country's medical system. An estimated 410,000 Chinese people died each year as a result of pollution.[19] Environmental pollution had also become a social issue. For example, in recent years, the number of mass protests caused by environmental issues had grown by an annual rate of 29 percent.

The social pressure became even more urgent after the 2008 Beijing Olympics. To prepare for the games, the Chinese government had taken a series of measures to reduce pollution in the participating Chinese cities, including restricting vehicle use, reducing coal combustion and closing some pollution-emitting factories. As a result of these measures, city dwellers saw a clear sky for the first time in decades. The 2008 Beijing Olympic Games not only provided China with an opportunity to showcase its beauty, history and power but also presented the Chinese people with a new perspective on the relationship between economic development and environmental protection. A consensus emerged in China that environmental protection needed to become a priority in the country's agenda. The Chinese government now regarded environmental protection as a "basic state policy."

Since 2008, the Chinese government had stepped up its involvement and commitment in environmental protection. In 2009, the environmental expenditure by the Chinese State Environmental Protection Agency was at $162.5 billion, up from $75 billion in 2005.[20] The government had also sped up its implementation of the Stockholm Convention on Persistent Organic Pollutants (POPs), an international environmental treaty that aimed to eliminate or restrict the production and use of POPs for their damage to human health and the environment.

POPs Market in China

PCB Market Size. PCB production had been banned in China since the 1980s. Prior to the ban, approximately 10,000 tons of PCBs had been produced, some of which were released into the environment. The total amount of high-density PCB waste (>500 parts per million [ppm]) in China was estimated to be 50,000 tons, and the total amount of low-density wastes (50–500 ppm) was estimated to be 500,000 tons.[21] This amount was three times the Canadian PCB market size. Assuming a treatment cost of ¥3,000,[22] the Chinese PCB market was ¥1.65 billion, or approximately $255 million.

The PCB-contaminated soil was spread in numerous PCB-contaminated sites, which were difficult to identify.

Zhejiang and Liaoning provinces alone had 83 sealed PCB-contaminated sites. Based on the distribution of PCB use in China, China might have as many as 800 PCB-contaminated sites.[23]

POPs Market Size in General. In addition to the 550,000 tons of soil contaminated with PCBs (which was one of many POPs), an additional 1 million tons of soil was contaminated with other POPs.[24] Assuming a similar treatment cost to that of PCBs, of ¥3,000,[25] the POPs market size was estimated to be ¥3.00 billion, equivalent to approximately $470 million. Experts estimated that China might have as many as 300,000 to 600,000 sites contaminated with POPs.[26]

Because PS2's technology could be applied regardless of the types of POPs to be treated, it would compete in a market of $725 million. Even this number may have been conservative and would probably rise as the Chinese government improved its environmental protection measures. Furthermore, the ongoing rapid industrialization and urbanization in the country would probably continue to generate POP wastes.

Current Market Situation. The Chinese government was strongly committed to the Stockholm Convention on Persistent Organic Pollutants. It also had a strong resolve to tackle the issue of POP contamination. In 2010, the Chinese government announced that it would invest more than US$3 billion in soil investigation and soil remediation over the next five years, beginning in 2011.

Compared with developed countries, the management of POP-contaminated soil in China was still at an early stage. China lagged behind with respect to research capabilities, policies, procedures and techniques for safely managing and disposing of its enormous POPs contamination. As such, in 2006, the Chinese government embarked on the China PCBs Management and Disposal Demonstration Project, which was jointly funded by the Global Environment Facility Trust Fund (through the World Bank). The project was to be implemented in Jiangsu and Liaoning provinces, with the specific objective to help China establish and strengthen its policies, regulations and standards for PCB management and disposal. It also aimed to establish and enhance China's capability in PCB waste monitoring, treatment and disposal.[27] The successful PCB management and disposal experience from this project would then be disseminated across the country.[28] Launched in 2006, the project had been progressing well. In 2009, a successful trial run was conducted on the Shenyang PCBs High Temperature Incineration Facility in Liaoning Province.

Under the same demonstration project, an indirect Thermal Desorption Unit (TDU) was to be procured to dispose of PCB-contaminated soil and to carry out the cleanup, treatment and disposal of PCB equipment storage sites in the two demonstration provinces. After following the World Bank's international competitive bidding procedures, the consortium of Beaudin Consulting (U.S.), BRISEA Group, Inc. (U.S.) and Beijing Construction Engineering Group won the bid in early 2009 at the price of $3,732,453. The TDU would take up an area of about 5,000 square meters and would have a daily capacity of treating 70 tons of soil contaminated with PCBs up to 20,000 ppm. Contaminated soil would be transported to the TDU facility for treatment. After treatment, the PCB level in treated soil would be less than 1.0 ppm. The TDU unit had been delivered to Jiangsu Province in China after its fabrication in the United States. However, no information was available about whether the TDU unit worked to specification and expectations.

PS2's Advantage. Even though a TDU unit had been procured from another contractor for the PCB demonstration project, PS2 and its TPS technology would provide the Chinese market with a competitive alternative for the Chinese market for several reasons. First, the TPS technology had originally been developed as a mobile, onsite remedial technology. This attribute would prove to be attractive to the Chinese market, which had numerous small contaminated sites. PS2's TPS-PS model had a handling capacity of 50 kg per hour, whereas the smallest model from Beaudin Consulting, which had been used in the demonstration project, was in the range of 2 to 3 tons per hour.[29] Although the TDU unit also claimed to be capable of being easily installed and dismantled,[30] the TPS technology had higher mobility. Second, PS2 had been seriously considering China, as was demonstrated by its involvement with the Chinese market in the past one and a half years of relationship building and market research. Many other environmental firms were still locked in the mentality of creating an entry mode through equipment export and service contracts.

PS2's TPS technology was likely to be embraced in a market such as China, where hundreds of thousands of contaminated sites were widely dispersed across the country. In the demonstration project, the contaminated soil would need to be transported to the TDU for treatment, and the desorbed POPs would need to be further transported to a high-temperature incineration facility. This approach might not be sustainable in the longer run for several reasons. First, soils contaminated with POPs could not be easily transported because of their bulk. Second, new laws and regulations were expected to ban the importation of waste containing POPs from province to province, in response to public pressure.

Oil Sludge Market in China

Three to five percent of crude oil becomes sludge, which is unusable if not further treated.[31] When sludge is transported in oil tankers or stored in storage tanks, it settles to the container bottom, where it cannot be drained but must be removed and hauled away at considerable expense. Oil sludge is caused by oil solidifying or gelling in a storage tank, often as a result of an excess of water in the oil.[32] Sludge can cause major problems in oil storage tanks if not cleaned regularly. Typical crude oil tank bottoms contain more than 50 percent by weight oil, 30 to 45 percent water and 5 to 20 percent solids.[33]

The Chinese petrochemical industry generated approximately 5.67 million tons of oil sludge each year, based on its processing of domestic production.[34] China's oil import dependence ratio surpassed 55 percent in early 2010 and was forecasted to reach 60 percent in 2015. Thus, more sludge would likely be generated from oil imports. China imported 4.08 million barrels of crude oil per day (BPD), or 1.49 billion barrels on a yearly basis in 2009.[35] Based on a BPD to tons per year conversion ratio of 49.8,[36] China imported 203.2 million tons of oil in 2009. Assuming a conservative ratio of 3 percent of oil sludge to oil, China would need to treat 6.1 million or more tons of oil sludge as a result of its annual oil imports. Much of the huge amount of oil sludge would need to be treated at facilities close to coastal oil terminals or oil reserve bases in China.

Traditionally, oil sludge in China had been dumped directly into the environment (e.g., into unlined, earthen pits), buried without treatment or incinerated. This situation could not be continued as new regulations in some provinces enforced proper treatment, in response to the environmental awareness of the general public. As such, an emerging industry was oil sludge treatment. However, the industry was still in its infancy, and the market was very fragmented. This fragmentation was in part because of the spread of oil sludge generation in many oil fields and port facilities.

Pharmaceutical Waste Market

In 2006, China produced 570,000 tons of pharmaceutical waste, most of which were incinerated, generating up to 1176.3 grams of toxic equivalents (g TEQ) of dioxins, or 11 percent of total dioxin release in China.[37] The amount of pharmaceutical waste would continue to increase because of an aging Chinese population that would lead to greater future spending on health care. The Chinese government had decided to offer basic medical care to farmers in rural areas. Although the pharmaceutical waste market was not a priority for PS2, compared with the other two waste streams of POP-contaminated soil and oil sludge, PS2 could still consider it as a market to diversify into in the future, especially when considering the absolute size of the pharmaceutical waste market and PS2's past experience in pharmaceutical waste management in Canada.

The Options in China for PS2

Option 1: Remediation of POP-Contaminated Soil

The first option required the cooperation of the Nanjing Institute of Environmental Sciences (NIES) of the State Environmental Protection Agency, Ministry of Environmental Protection for the People's Republic of China. Located in Nanjing, the capital city of Jiangsu Province, NIES was a key technical provider for policies, legislation, action plans and technical guidelines on biodiversity conservation in China. Its research areas included rural environmental protection, nature conservation and biodiversity protection. NIES employed more than 200 scientific and technical staff, who carried out research on rural ecology, nature conservation, pollution prevention of township and village enterprises, and agriculture chemicals. NIES undertook key national research programs and scientific research projects on the rural environment. It also provided the scientific basis and technical support for the management of rural environments and nature and of ecological conservation while assisting in the formulation and implementation of relevant action plans.

In the NIES option, a joint venture (JV) would be established between PS2 and NIES on a mutually beneficial date. In addition, NIES would act as an agent for PS2's TPS technology in China. The JV would construct a mobile TPS unit in China and use it in a demonstration project for the treatment of 2,000 to 3,000 tons of POP-contaminated soil. (The TPS unit had a capacity to treat approximately 30,000 tons of soil per year). This task would cause no concern to PS2 because its TPS technology had originally been a mobile, onsite remedial technology. PS2 also had extensive experience in applying its mobile technology on numerous contaminated sites around the world.

After the success of the demonstration project, the JV would subsequently use its TPS technology to design, plan, launch, bid for, operate and participate in various remediation projects throughout China. To use its technology in this way, the JV would need to design, engineer, manufacture and market TPS units in China for use in various parts of China. The JV was also proposed to provide solutions and consulting services for environmental remediation issues.

The JV would need an investment of approximately $3.0 million. This option offered several attractive advantages. First, NIES was a government agency, which significantly reduced the risk of the project. Second, NIES had extensive remedial experience and expertise. Third, NIES had identified and inventoried more than 300 sites in just three provinces. The sites ranged in size from 3,000 tons to 2,000,000 tons of contaminated soil. Fourth, the project was a demonstration project, which not only had a lower risk level but also acted as a free advertising campaign for PS2's technology. Being involved in a demonstration project also implied that PS2 was an early entrant into the emerging environmental market in China and would most likely enjoy certain first-mover advantages.

Option 2: Oil Recovery from Oil Sludge

The second option was to cooperate with Zhoushan Nahai Solid Waste Central Disposal Co. Ltd. (Nahai) in Zhejiang Province. Established in September 2009, Nahai was a private company and was the largest and only solid waste management company in the Zhoushan area of Zhejiang. It covered a land area of 33,700 square meters, and the investment was ¥62.35 million (approximately Cdn$9.8 million).[38] Despite Nahai's short history, it had become a leader in the management of hazardous waste and oil sludge in the Zhoushan area. The company had an excellent infrastructure, including an oil storage facility (capacity of 2,500,000 tons), a waste oil recovery facility (capacity of 1,000,000 tons per year), bilge water treatment process (capacity of 20,000 tons per day) and a solid waste destruction facility (capacity of 20 tons per day). Nahai possessed the only waste management processing permit in Zhoushan.

Zhoushan comprised a group of islands located at the opening of the Yangtze River, just south of Shanghai. It was in the center of the world's largest four fisheries and had been ranked as the ninth largest harbor among Chinese coastal harbors and the biggest commercial petroleum transit base in China. Many oil storage facilities were located in this region due to its accessibility to the traditional shipping lanes. For example, Zhoushan was home to the Aoshan Oil Terminal, China's largest oil transshipment base, and Zhoushan National Oil Reserve

Base Co., Ltd. (one of China's 12 state strategic crude oil reserve bases).

The cooperation with Nahai would be in the form of a JV. The JV was proposed to establish a fixed facility in Zhoushan, which would be capable of processing 10,000 tons of oily sludge per year and expandable to 100,000 tons per year. The facility would process and recover oil from the oily sludge waste generated from oil storage operations and oil tanker cleaning activities in the region. PS2's management team was well suited for this task due to their global experience. The JV would also further define and develop other technologies to complement the oily sludge treatment process, provide solutions and consulting services with respect to oil recovery issues, and explore opportunities of applying the oily sludge treatment technology to other parts of China.

The JV would need an investment of approximately $3.0 million. This option was attractive for several reasons. First, Nahai's owner was an accomplished entrepreneur, similar to Paul Antle. The two entrepreneurs had identified with each other from the beginning. Throughout their interactions, a solid trust had been developed. Second, Nahai had solid assets and had obtained a wide range of permits. Third, Nahai was located in a region that generated approximately 180,000 tons of oily sludge waste per year.[39] This amount was about 3 percent of the total amount of oil sludge

China generated in 2009 (6.1 million tons as previously shown) from its oil imports.

The Decision

The environmental market in China presented PS2 with both challenges and opportunities. For a small entrepreneurial firm such as PS2, the cooperative opportunities with NIES and Nahai in such a large market would not only affect the metrics of the company but would also strain corporate resources and the organizational structure. The China entry would also mark an important stage along its internationalization path. Although the entrepreneurial leadership at PS2 had been successful in the past and was eager to achieve even higher goals, this situation differed from its past projects in the international market, which had been based on the export of equipment and service contracts.

After careful deliberation, PS2 had arrived at a point where a series of decisions needed to be made. Any delay might open opportunities for competitors. Should PS2 enter the Chinese market? Should PS2 pursue the NIES option or the Nahai option? Would it be feasible to pursue both? What ownership levels should PS2 assume for each option? How would PS2 staff its Chinese operation(s)? Antle needed to use a thorough analysis of market situation and PS2's resources and technical and organizational capabilities to arrive at some answers.

NOTES

1. Summarized from: Phase Separation Solutions Inc., http://www.phaseparation.com/index.html; Fundamental Research Corp., "West Mountain Capital Corp. (TSXV: WMT)–Initiating Coverage—Thermal Treatment of Soil, Sludge and Other Waste Streams," March 23, 2010, http://www.baystreet.ca/articles/research_reports/fundamental_research/WestMountainCapital040110.pdf; "Investment Fund Sees Gold in Clean Dirt," Daily Commercial News and Construction Record, December 19, 2005, http://dcnonl.com/article/20051219300. All web links in this case were accessed in February and March 2012.

2. All currency amounts shown in Canadian dollars unless otherwise specified.

3. Golden Opportunities is a labor-sponsored investment fund (LSIF) corporation under Saskatchewan's Labor-sponsored Venture Capital Corporations Act. An LSIF, or simply retail venture capital (RVC), is a fund managed by investment

professionals that invests in small to mid-sized Canadian companies. The Canadian federal government and some provincial governments offer tax credits to labor-sponsored venture capital corporation (LSVCC) investors to promote the growth of such companies. Golden Opportunities is the largest provincial RVC fund in Saskatchewan.

4. "Management's Discussion and Analysis of Financial Position and Results of Operations for West Mountain Capital Corp. for the Three Months and Year Ended December 31, 2009," http://ca.hotstocked.com/docs/west_mountain_capital_corp/management_s_discussion_analysis/20091231mda.pdf.

5. Summarized from Phase Separation Solutions Inc., "Patented Thermal Phase Separation (TPS) Technology," http://www.phaseparation.com/links/techt.html; Fundamental Research Corp., "West Mountain Capital Corp. (TSXV: WMT)–Initiating Coverage—Thermal Treatment

of Soil, Sludge and Other Waste Streams," March 23, 2010, http://www.baystreet.ca/articles/research_reports/fundamental_research/WestMountainCapital040110.pdf; http://www.sunrisepublish.com/common/pdfs/publications/SaskBusiness_Magazine/SB_JanFeb2012_web.pdf; West Mountain Capital Corp., "Phase Separation Solutions Expands License to Cover China," news release, August 10, 2009, http://www.phaseparation.com/images/pdf/aug10.pdf

6. Based on Fundamental Research Corp., "West Mountain Capital Corp. (TSXV: WMT)–Initiating Coverage—Thermal Treatment of Soil, Sludge and Other Waste Streams," March 23, 2010, http://www.baystreet.ca/articles/research_reports/fundamental_research/WestMountainCapital040110.pdf and other sources as specified.

7. "The History of PCBs," http://www.foxriverwatch.com/monsanto2a_pcb_pcbs.html.

8. Phase Separation Solutions Inc., "Elevating the Thinking in Waste Management," http://www.phaseparation.com/images/pdf/Golden%20Opportunities%20Presentation.pdf.

9. Bennett Environmental Inc., www.bennettenv.com.

10. Fundamental Research Corp., "West Mountain Capital Corp. (TSXV: WMT)–Two Joint Ventures to Be Established in the Chinese Waste Management Market," August 11, 2010, http://www.phaseparation.com/images/pdf/WMT%20-%20Aug%202010%20Master.pdf.

11. Stewardship Ontario, Final Consolidated Municipal Hazardous or Special Waste Program Plan, Volume 1, July 20, 2009, https://ozone.scholarsportal.info/bitstream/1873/15214/1/295182.pdf.

12. Jordan Luy, "TSX Venture 50 Spotlight: West Mountain Capital Corp.," http://www.tmxmoney.com/en/news/interviews/Apr6-2011_WMT.html.

13. Summarized from: Westcap Mgt. Ltd., "Golden Opportunities Fund's Investee Company—Phase Separation Solutions Inc. Enters into Agreement to Acquire Pharma Processing," news release, March 17, 2008, http://www.westcapmgt.ca/news/news_details.php?news_id=33; "West Mountain Completes Pharma Processing Acquisition," news release, July 23, 2008, http://www.stockwatch.com/swnet/newsit/newsit_newsit.aspx?bid=Z-C:WMT-1514767&symbol=WMT&news_region=C; http://www.neia.org/file/d569e488-b451-4310-b444-ff0eaf728d39.pdf; Phase Separation Solutions Inc., "Elevating the Thinking in Waste Management," http://www.westmountaincapital.com/pdf/Golden%20Opportunities%20Presentation.pdf; West Mountain Capital Corp,, "Consolidated Financial Statements, June 30, 2010 and 2009," http://ca.hotstocked.com/docs/show/west_mountain_capital_corp/financial_statements/q22010fs.pdf.

14. Westcap Mgt. Ltd., "Golden Opportunities Fund's Investee Company—Phase Separation Solutions Inc. Enters into Agreement to Acquire Pharma Processing," news release, March 17, 2008, http://www.westcapmgt.ca/news/news_details.php?news_id=33.

15. Refer to [TSX Inc., "Capital Pool Company Program," http://www.tmx.com/en/pdf/CPCBrochure.pdf] for a description of the Capital Pool Company® program, a two-step introduction to the Canadian capital market at TSX Venture Exchange.

16. Company Overview of West Mountain Capital Corp, Prior to Reverse Merger with Phase Separation Solutions, Inc., Bloomberg Businessweek, http://investing.businessweek.com/research/stocks/private/snapshot.asp?privcapId=26000232.

17. West Mountain Capital, "Portfolio," http://www.westmountaincapital.com/links/portfolio.html.

18. "Real Historical Gross Domestic Product (GDP) Per Capita and Growth Rates of GDP Per Capita for Baseline Countries/Regions (in 2005 Dollars) 1969–2011," www.ers.usda.gov/Data/Macroeconomics/Data/HistoricalRealPerCapitaIncomeValues.xls.

19. The Common Language Project, "China Fact Sheet," http://clpmag.org/article.php?article=China-Fact-Sheet_4.

20. West Mountain Capital Corp., "Phase Separation Solutions Expands License to Cover China," news release, August 10, 2009, www.phaseparation.com/images/pdf/aug10.pdf.

21. The People's Republic of China, "National Implementation Plan for the Stockholm Convention on Persistent Organic Pollutants," April 2007, http://www.pops.int/documents/implementation/nips/submissions/China_NIP_En.pdf.

22. http://www.infzm.com/content/64914; http://nf.nfdaily.cn/nfzm/content/2011-11/18/content_33440330.htm

23. Authors' estimates based on the project document for "Building the Capacity of the People's Republic of China to Implement the Stockholm Convention on POPs and Develop a National Implementation Plan," 2004, http://www.thegef.org/gef/sites/thegef.org/files/repository/China_-_POPs.pdf.

24. http://www.cenews.com.cn/xwzx/hq/qt/200802/t20080214_220144.html. This number may be extremely conservative.

25. This number may be conservative. See Ralph S. Baker et al., "In-pile Thermal Desorption of Soil and Sediment," 2006, http://www.terratherm.com/pdf/white%20papers/paper7-11-6-09.pdf.

26. "Soil Pollution Poisons More than Farmland," China Daily, March 10, 2011, http://www.china.org.cn/environment/2011-03/10/content_22098214.htm.

27. "Project Progress," POPs Action in Canada, September/October 2009, pp. 2–3,http://en.mepfeco.org.cn/Resources/Periodicals/PAIC/201009/P020100908629022960445.pdf.

28. "Project Document on a Proposed Grant from the Global Environment Facility Trust Fund in the Amount of USD 18.34 Million to the People's Republic of China for a PCB Management and Disposal Demonstration Project," April 25, 2005, http://www.thegef.org/gef/sites/thegef.org/files/repository/China_-_PCB_Mgmt_Disposal_Demopdf.

29. http://www.ygnfilcore.com/content.asp?id=44&menuId=72|6; Beaudin Consulting webpage, http://www.beaudins.com/.

30. Hangzhou DADI Environmental Protection Engineering Co., Ltd., "Thermal Desorption System," http://www.dadiep.com/en/jishu.aspx?id=8.

31. "Oil-sludge-processing Industry Overview," Russian-American Business, October 19, 2010, http://russianamericanbusiness.org/web_CURRENT/articles/654/1/Oil-sludge-processing-industry-overview.

32. LianDi Clean Technology Inc., "LianDi Clean Technology Inc. Announces Landmark Strategic Alliance with Leading Japanese Oil Sludge Company," news release, September 13, 2010, http://www.china-liandi.com/September%2013%20-%20Liandi%20Landmark%20Agreement%20with%20SKK.html.

33. Dee Ann Sanders, "Pollution Prevention and Reuse Alternatives for Crude Oil Tank-Bottom Sludges," ipec.utulsa.edu/Conf2001/sanders_123.pdf.

34. Authors' calculation is based on China's crude oil production in 2009 of 3.79 million barrels per day and the assumptions later in the paragraph.

35. Reuters Africa, "UPDATE 2–China 2010 Crude Oil Imports up 17.5 pct to Record High," January 10, 2011, http://af.reuters.com/article/energyOilNews/idAFTOE70607320110110.

36. "How Many Barrels of Crude Oil in One MT?" http://www.onlineconversion.com/forum/forum_1058197476.htm.

37. Ministry of Environmental Protection of the People's Republic of China, Foreign Economic Cooperation Office, POPs Action in China, July 2009, http://en.mepfeco.org.cn/Resources/Publications/201009/P020100908621278591698.pdf.

38. "Environmental Impact Assessment," http://app.zjepb.gov.cn/UpLoad/xzxksb/201081290007.doc.

39. Fundamental Research Corp., "West Mountain Capital Corp. (TSXV: WMT)–Two Joint Ventures to Be Established in the Chinese Waste Management Market," August 11, 2010, http://www.phaseparation.com/images/pdf/WMT%20-%20Aug%202010%20Master.pdf.

Stephani Angelina, Rob Hammel, Julian Kahn, Jeff Morris, Humayun Naqvi

Texas A&M University

Research in Motion launched the business world's most recognizable gadget – the BlackBerry – but today faces a mounting pile of problems amid operational stumbles and a tumbling stock price.

– Wall Street Journal

Research in Motion Ltd. (RIM)[i] is the maker of the BlackBerry wireless device and the email services that accompany it. The Canadian-based company, headquartered in Waterloo, Ontario, designs, manufactures, and markets wireless solutions for the worldwide mobile and telecommunications market. Its portfolio includes the BlackBerry wireless devices, software development tools, and various other software and hardware development offerings.[1] Mike Lazaridis and Douglas Fregin, two engineering students with a penchant for data transmission and wireless solutions, co-founded the firm.[2, 3] Since expanding from pagers into the wireless telecommunications market, RIM has been popular with government and corporate buyers for its data encryption capabilities. In spite of this popularity, RIM has essentially failed in its efforts to strongly penetrate the mainstream consumer market.[4, 5] Moreover, over time, the lucrative public and private sector contracts that had been the bread and butter of RIM for so long became targets of major competitors, most notably Apple. From RIM's humble beginnings, to its role as a dominant player in handheld devices, it was unimaginable to analysts and stakeholders alike that what was once a multimillion-dollar corporation with multinational ties could succumb so quickly and thoroughly to the pressures of an increasingly complex marketplace. The rates at which business cycles

have increased within the telecommunications industry have led RIM to multiple acquisitions of developers and manufacturers, all of which were intended to diversify RIM's offerings and enhance its users' experience. Yet the trappings of competitiveness on a global scale have led to missed opportunities and nearly insurmountable errors. From patent disputes and threatened international distribution restrictions on usage to severe service outages, the competitive marketplace has taken a crippling toll on RIM. The company that laid claim to launching the world's most recognizable electronic wireless device – the "Crackberry," as it was affectionately known – faces mounting pressure from competitors such as iPhone and Google Android smartphones.[6] How can RIM, a company with an ailing product line but high global brand recognition, quickly make up for lost time and lost market share? Can it once again become a dominant player in the telecommunications industry, or will it become a story of a firm's failed strategic actions that were taken in a highly competitive market?

History

The consulting business co-founded by Mike Lazaridis and Douglas Fregin financed RIM's early growth. It was not until 1992 however, when Harvard Business School graduate Jim Balsillie joined RIM as a partner, that the company really gained traction.[7] By 1995, the Inter@ctive Pager, a revolutionary two-way pager, was completed and brought to market, kickstarting a deluge of investments. After its IPO in January 1998, RIM was able to introduce the first BlackBerry: essentially, a handheld computer with wireless capabilities.[8] It subsequently signed contract agreements with BellSouth and

---

i. Since the writing of this case study, RIM changed its name to BlackBerry and now trades on the Nasdaq as BBRY and as BB in Toronto.

IBM, among others, to provide wireless services and the ability to browse news, stock market data, and weather information via a handheld device. At the time, being able to engage in these search activities via a handheld device was revolutionary. RIM was able to inject additional funds when public offerings on the NASDAQ exchange raised $250 million, propelling RIM into the next millennium.[9, 10]

By 2004, RIM had already sold a million BlackBerry devices globally and – with its unmatched QWERTY keyboard, email, and web-browsing capabilities – fast became the darling of the public and private sectors (see Exhibit 1 for 2012 product offerings).[11] In 2007, with the launch of Apple's iPhone, a product targeting private consumers rather than the corporate market then long dominated by BlackBerry, the playing field changed. Lazaridis dismissed the iPhone's "severe limitations," believing that the customer wanted a simple, efficient, compact, and secure wireless device with a tactile keyboard.[12] And, in ways, Lazaridis' conclusion was understandable in that at the time, BlackBerry was not losing market share. In fact, the firm's stock was selling at a

then-record price of over $140 per share. Partly influencing this price was the fact that RIM achieved a growth rate of 84 percent in earnings per share over the three previous years. Additionally, in 2009, *Fortune* magazine identified RIM as the fastest growing company in the world.[13, 14] In the meantime, Apple was allowing users to customize their phone for their needs, and Google soon followed into the market with the introduction of the Android.

Challenges of Lazaridis' assumption soon surfaced. First, the launch of the BlackBerry PlayBook tablet in April 2011 was criticized in large part to its lack of email capability. RIM then experienced a second setback in its efforts to satisfy shareholder confidence. On October 10, 2011, according to RIM, "a transition to a back-up switch did not function as tested, causing a large backlog of data." This mishap meant that millions of BlackBerry users all over the world experienced service outages for over 72 hours.[15] With the confidence of consumers waning and intense pressure from shareholders reeling from a drop in stock price of almost 75 percent in one year, co-CEOs Mike Lazaridis and Jim Balsillie decided

Exhibit 1 RIM's BlackBerry Smartphone and Tablet Portfolio for Fiscal 2012

BlackBerry Bold series
BlackBerry Bold 9900 and 9930
The thinnest BlackBerry smartphones to date and the first to offer the union of a high performance keyboard and touch display integrated within the iconic BlackBerry Bold design.
BlackBerry Bold 9790
Full featured smartphone with touch display and keyboard built with premium materials and finishes, but in a more compact form factor than the BlackBerry Bold 9900 and 9930 series.
BlackBerry Torch series
BlackBerry Torch 9810
A new and higher performance version of the BlackBerry Torch 9800, running BlackBerry 7 OS.
All-Touch BlackBerry Torch 9850 and 9860
The BlackBerry Torch 9850 and 9860 new all-touch design, running BlackBerry 7 OS.
BlackBerry Curve series
BlackBerry Curve 9350/9360/9370
Designed to address a large segment of the global phone market by providing customers with an affordable, easy-to-use, full-featured and socially connected smartphone.
All-Touch BlackBerry Curve 9380 Smartphone
The first all-touch smartphone in the BlackBerry Curve family.
The BlackBerry PlayBook tablet
The BlackBerry PlayBook tablet features the new BlackBerry PlayBook OS 2.0 based on technology resulting from the Company's acquisition of QNX in fiscal 2011. The BlackBerry PlayBook offers a 7-inch high definition display, a dual core 1GHZ processor, dual high-definition cameras, true multitasking and a powerful and fast web browsing experience that supports Adobe Flash.

Source: Research in Motion Limited, Form 40-F, for the fiscal year ended March 3, 2012, p. 19. http://ca.blackberry.com/content/dam/bbCompany/Desktop/Global/PDF/Investors/Documents/2012/2012rim_ar_40F.pdf

to step down. Thorsten Heins, RIM's Chief Operating Officer and former Chief Technology Officer of Siemens AG, replaced the co-CEOs.[16] Pondering what to do with a company whose stock price had fallen below $14 per share, whose market share had suffered significantly, and whose consumer confidence was in the doldrums was a key challenge facing the new CEO.[17]

Competitors and Competing Products

Short product lifecycles coupled with intense competition with regard to innovation characterize the telecommunications industry. Since 2007, the industry has seen unprecedented growth due to the improvements in technology with regard to wireless data speed and increased access to reliable wireless service. As the user base continues to grow and with more options than ever before available to consumers, companies operating in all areas of the industry have to ensure their products are innovative, reliable, and able to meet customers' current and future needs at an affordable cost to them.

As handset software and hardware providers jockey for the top position in the industry, wireless providers are searching for ways to increase their subscriber base, with one widespread method being the notion of "handset exclusivity." As discussed in a U.S. House of Representatives Subcommittee in May 2008, at the time, "…eight of the ten most popular smartphones are available to only one carrier. Popular phones, particularly innovative smartphones, drive growth in the market for wireless services and offer the best chance for wireless carriers to survive and grow."[18] The most visible – and arguably successful – example of this was AT&T's agreement with Apple to be the exclusive carrier of the iPhone upon the device's launch in 2007. Future generations of the iPhone became available on multiple wireless carriers. However, many viewed AT&T's original agreement as a brilliant move in that embracing the iPhone allowed the firm unprecedented access to new customers and has continued to contribute to record sales for the company year after year.[19] With wireless providers well aware of the potential financial windfall the next "killer device" can bring, one can expect the competition to be the "exclusive home" of said device to increase as time goes on.

Apple, Inc. – iPhone

On January 9, 2007, Steve Jobs, then-CEO of Apple, fundamentally changed the telecommunications industry when he unveiled his company's latest innovation: the iPhone.[20] Introduced to the market in June of 2007, Apple's iPhone has been an unprecedented success for the company; as of fiscal 2012, Q1 revenue attributed to the iOS platform (both from the iPhone and its sister product, the iPad) accounted for 72 percent of Apple's total revenue – astonishing considering that the product line did not exist a mere five years earlier.[21]

Before the introduction of the iPhone, "smartphones" all possessed some combination of a keypad coupled with a low-resolution screen that required the end-user to use the device utilizing the keypad or an included stylus. The main innovation present in the iPhone was the absence of a traditional keypad. In its place was a 3.5-inch scratch-resistant multi-touch glass display that allowed "users to control [an] iPhone with just a tap, flick or pinch of their fingers."[22] It also leveraged the success of Apple's most successful peripheral product at the time, the iPod, by integrating its functionality into the iPhone. Instantly, a user's music and videos purchased via the iTunes store (since 2008, the largest music retailer in the United States[23]) was accessible through one's iPhone.

As of April 2011, the total numberof iOS device sales (all iPhone and iPad devices since their respective introductions) totaled 189 million.[24] As of Q4 2011, the global market share claimed by the iPhone stood at 23.8 percent of all smartphones.[25] In the United States alone, as of January 2012, there were 101.3 million U.S. smartphone subscribers, with Apple's iPhone devices accounting for 29.5 percent of that number (almost 30 million subscribers).[26]

Google – Android OS

Android began as a small start-up company (Android, Inc.) founded in late 2003 in Palo Alto, California. Twenty-two months later, in August 2005, Google quietly acquired the company and made it a wholly owned subsidiary.[27] While not known with certainty at the time, this acquisition was the key catalyst of Google's intention to move into the mobile device market as part of its strategy to expand its advertising platform (Google's main source of revenue) across a burgeoning market.[28]

After years of development, Google officially launched Android on September 23, 2008.[29] Several standard features highlighted this launch; a customizable user experience coupled with real-time synchronization of Google services (such as Gmail, Calendar, and Contacts) were the key features designed to "woo" customers away from the iPhone.[30]

Over the last several years, and through four full versions, Android has grown to become the world's most-used smartphone platform, capturing nearly 50 percent of the global smartphone market by Q2 2011.[31] As of January 2012, Android held a 48.6 percent share of total smartphone subscribers (about 49.2 million) in the United States.[32] According to Andy Rubin, Senior VP of Mobile at Google and co-founder of Android, Inc., as of February 2012, there were over 850,000 Android phones and tablets activated each day.[33]

Android's rapid adoption among smartphone users was due in no small part to Google's innovative licensing strategy. First, unlike Apple or RIM, Google does not manufacture its own devices. Instead, it licenses third-party manufacturers to install Android on their own devices. In addition, Google has made Android available as open-source software. As such, Google does not charge a licensing fee for manufacturers that choose to utilize Android OS on their devices.[34] In other words, Google is providing a free operating system for cell phone manufacturers. Because Google does not publicize direct or indirect revenues attributable to Android, it is difficult to determine just how successful Android has been to the company.

Microsoft – Windows Phone

Launched on October 21, 2010 in Europe and on November 8, 2010 in the United States and Canada,[35] the Windows Phone OS was the successor to the software giant's previous mobile platform, Windows Mobile.[36] Microsoft's strategy behind Windows Phone was to differentiate itself from its competitors by offering a "glance and go" experience. Microsoft used this competitive approach to underscore its design and marketing strategy for the platform.[37] Microsoft's proprietary user interface dubbed "Metro" is the most visible dimension of how the firm competes in this space.[38] The central feature(s) of the Metro UI are "Live Tiles" that

...continuously update the phone's start screen with information customized by the user...the tiles provide at-a-glance updates from features such as...Facebook updates, contact information, [email and entertainment].[39]

The adoption of Windows Phone has been slow in relation to its competitors. As of Q4 2011, Windows Phone accounted for only 1.3 percent of all smartphone consumers.[40] However, in February 2011, Microsoft announced a major strategic partnership with Nokia,[41] the world's largest manufacturer of mobile phones at the time.[42] This announcement surprised some in that Nokia had developed its own mobile OS, dubbed "Symbian" that, as recently as 2010, had been the global leader in market share among mobile communication devices.[43] As Nokia and Microsoft noted however, their partnership

would allow each company to focus on its core competencies (Nokia: hardware; Microsoft: software) and "... work together to integrate key assets and create completely new service offerings, while extending established products and services to new markets."[44] Nokia launched its first Windows Phone equipped device, the Nokia Lumia 900, on April 8, 2012 in the United States.[45] The product received positive reviews initially (albeit relative to other Windows Phone devices).[46] As with Google, Microsoft does not offer sales figures directly attributable to Windows Phone.[47]

App Stores

The App store accounts for a large part of the success of Apple with its products. The runaway success of the App Store even caught Apple by surprise;[48] its users had downloaded over two billion apps by 2009,[49] with that number growing to 25 billion by March 2012.[50] The App Store includes a wide variety of free-to-use, fee-based, and ad-supported apps. Both Google and Microsoft have launched their own versions of the App Store, named Google Play Store and Windows Marketplace, respectively. Each store shares similar offerings available through Apple's App Store as well as apps that are exclusive to each mobile platform.

The Competitive Arena

The wireless industry has consolidated with regard to the variety of mobile platforms available to consumers, with the "Big 4" operating systems (BlackBerry, iOS, Android, and Windows Phone) accounting for roughly 80 percent of all active smartphone devices on a global basis (Nokia's OS, Symbian, held 15 percent. However, this platform has since been abandoned in favor of Windows Phone).[51]

A growing trend within the industry is the increasing amount of litigation involving patents related to mobile technology. Since 2006, mobile handset related lawsuits have increased 25 percent year-over-year.[52] A byproduct of this trend has been the increase in acquisitions by companies within the wireless industry. These acquisitions are taking place to enhance a firm's patent portfolios, limiting litigation exposure as a result of doing so. For example, Google acquired Motorola Mobility for $12 billion dollars in late August 2011 to secure the roughly 17,000 patents possessed by Motorola, thereby further protecting itself from patent litigation.[53]

The increase in litigation over patents is not necessarily to block competitors from utilizing the technology in question, but rather to ensure that patent holders receive compensation for what is used. For example, it is estimated that Microsoft, while struggling to cement its Windows Phone platform's place in the market, earned $444 million in licensing agreements in 2012 alone for its arsenal of Android patents.[54]

As RIM has experienced firsthand, any judgment against a company can be disastrous, not only from a technological standpoint, but also from a financial one. In early 2006, RIM reached a settlement with a small Virginia-based firm over a patent dispute to the tune of $612.5 million.[55] Interestingly, this figure was on the low end of analysts' expectations, particularly considering that RIM avoided having to pay future royalties to the firm.[56]

Since the introduction of the BlackBerry, one of RIM's strengths has been enterprise services, highlighted by its proprietary BlackBerry Enterprise Server (BES). Coupling its ease of integration within firms' existing IT infrastructure with unparalleled data security, RIM carved its place as the go-to standard for enterprise users within a short amount of time and, for the better part of the first decade of the 21st century, this position was unchallenged.[57]

Recently however, RIM's position within this market segment has not only been challenged, but is now in serious jeopardy, as more and more users are migrating from their BlackBerry phones to other mobile platforms, most notably Apple's iPhone and its iOS platform. In fact, a report published in fall 2011 showed that the iPhone had become the top smartphone for enterprise use, with its market share increasing from 31 percent in 2010 to 45 percent in 2011, while BlackBerry's share dropped from 35 percent to 32 percent over the same period.[58]

This dramatic shift has presented two realities of the enterprise user market. First, as smartphones have continued to evolve into entertainment hubs capable of running a wide variety of applications while still meeting the needs of traditional "work phones," the value placed on overall user satisfaction is higher than the value placed on data security.[59] Secondly, companies are increasingly allowing employees to use their existing mobile devices as their "work phones," with one study showing that, "…58 percent of the companies are now provisioning smartphones to their employees [in 2011] as against an estimated 66 percent [in 2010]."[60] Additional studies predict as many as 30 percent of existing BlackBerry users in large enterprises will switch to another mobile platform in 2012.[61]

Customers

As evidenced with the shift away from BlackBerry devices among enterprise users, consumers (residential and commercial) will not be pigeonholed into buying a device that does not meet their needs. Furthermore, while mobile OS providers have tried to offer services that increase the likelihood that a customer remains within her/his mobile ecosystem, cross-platform integration is steadily increasing (e.g., syncing an iPhone with Gmail), resulting in reduced switching costs and less incentive for one to stick with a particular mobile operating system.

In addition to BES, another benefit associated with the BlackBerry OS is its BlackBerry Messenger service (BBM). This proprietary service is available to over 50 million active users and allows BlackBerry owners instant messaging capabilities that do not draw against one's text messaging plan.[62] Those using this service are passionate and vocal about its benefits as shown by a plethora of fan sites dedicated to the service. However, as with BES, this capability may not be the draw it once was to lure users into the BlackBerry ecosystem, as is evidenced by widespread rumors and speculation that the BBM service may be ported to other mobile OSs in the near future.[63, 64]

Any company error can have disastrous ramifications, as was demonstrated by the consumer reaction to the temporary service outage experienced by RIM in October 2011. Over a three-day span, BlackBerry service was temporarily unavailable due to a "hardware error" that was not remedied by the backup system in place, affecting users across the globe.[65] Even after service was restored, as many as one in five Blackberry phone users polled indicated that they were considering switching to another mobile OS because of the outage. Among another set of BlackBerry users, seven out of ten indicated that they would "…need some reassurance from the manufacturer as they would be put off by the recent problems," and "four out of five consumers said they were put off choosing a handset from a manufacturer that has experienced major service problems."[66]

Suppliers

Many of the suppliers of materials and labor related to the manufacture of mobile devices reside in and around China and depend on the high-volume orders placed by the aforementioned companies in order to survive. Most companies do not list these suppliers by name. Under pressure from various labor groups over concerns of an unsafe factory work environment, Apple only recently disclosed the details of its relationship with Foxconn Technology Group[67] (investigations of the allegations against Apple discovered that most were fabricated).[68] Additionally, many of the suppliers have agreements with multiple companies; it stands to reason that any perceived difficulty with one company dealing with a supplier could have significant negative ramifications to the supplier's business as other manufacturers could take notice and contract with another supplier.

Previously, RIM noted that while it does its best to negotiate favorable terms with various suppliers, it is critical to meet the volume projections promised to suppliers, as any excess materials retained by suppliers significantly increase suppliers' costs and may result in less favorable future negotiations.[69]

Internal Conditions

As of early 2012, RIM was debt free with over $1.5 billion in cash.[70] This financial mix offered RIM the opportunity to execute strategic initiatives and invest in projects that boost its bottom line in the near and distant future.

RIM also holds intangible assets valued at almost $3.3 billion dollars.[71] These assets are comprised mainly of patents and the value placed on them by companies wishing to license them from RIM. The most recent additions to this portfolio include "those relating to 3G and 4G technologies... as well as agreements with third parties for the use of intellectual property, software, messaging services, and other BlackBerry related features."[72]

RIM participates in many strategic alliances throughout the world and is an active participant in numerous associations within the industry (see Exhibit 2).[73] RIM has developed critical capabilities such as end-to-end security, extensive geographic coverage, and competitive

pricing through these arrangements.[74] With regard to the latter two factors, RIM recently launched a BlackBerry in India.[75] With this focus to grow BlackBerry services among global subscribers by "leveraging the BlackBerry platform, brand, and other assets," RIM hopes to create additional value for its stakeholders.[76]

Competing Internationally

At year-end 2012, RIM intended to unveil a new operating system – BlackBerry 10. With this unveiling comes the opportunity to focus on what specifically the firm uses to compete in established and emerging markets.[77] RIM has outlined four principles that it believes will provide the foundation for above average returns for stakeholders in both the short and long term (see Exhibit 3).

RIM has decided to compete in both the handheld and tablet market. To do so it must overcome the increased complexities of the telecommunications industry. Economic and cultural conditions – not to mention increased hostility in global markets through competition – must be handled tactfully, yet aggressively. The mobile device market, being as competitive as it is, has conditioned customers to have high expectations. In this regard, they search for superior value at a price where differentiated features are paramount to success and perceived value must rationalize the purchase.[78] Apple's iPhone and iPad offerings have essentially cornered the high-end market, allowing the firm to charge a premium for the brand and for the user interface experience. RIM, however, has recognized that emerging markets

Exhibit 2 Industry Associations

RIM is an active participant in numerous industry associations and standards bodies including:	
• 4G Americas	• Alliance for Telecommunications Industry Solutions (ATIS)
• American National Standards Institute	• Bluetooth SIG
• CDMA Development Group	• Consumer Electronics Association
• European Telecom Standards Institute	• GlobalPlatform
• GSM Association	• IEEE (Professional Support Services for P1725)
• International Imaging Industry Association (I3A)	• JEDEC
• MIDI	• MIPI: Mobile Industry Processor Interface
• NGMN (Germany)	• Open Mobile Alliance
• Telecommunications Industry Association (TIA)	• TIA 3rd Generation Partnership Project 2
• UPnP Forum (Universal Plug and Play)	• Wholesale Applications Community (WAC)
• Wi-Fi – Alliance	• WiMAX Forum
• Wireless World Research	

Source: Research in Motion Limited, Form 40-F, for the fiscal year ended March 3, 2012, p. 24. http://ca.blackberry.com/content/dam/bbCompany/Desktop/Global/PDF/Investors/Documents/2012/2012rim_ar_40F.pdf

Exhibit 3 Key Principles

- Ensuring a successful launch of the BlackBerry 10 platform and the timely launch of the first BlackBerry 10 products
- Leveraging the BlackBerry platform, brand, and other assets to drive global subscriber growth and create value for RIM's stakeholders
- Implementation of broad efficiency programs across all functions in the organization
- A realignment of the Company's organization to reduce complexity and increase accountability.

Source: Research in Motion Limited, Form 40-F, for the fiscal year ended March 3, 2012, p. 15. http://ca.blackberry.com/content/dam/bbCompany/Desktop/Global/PDF/Investors/Documents/2012/2012rim_ar_40F.pdf

are still relatively untapped. Growth in BRIC[ii] countries has created demand for high quality handheld devices. Furthermore, although average income in these countries is significantly lower than in the West, the global economic downturn allows for the possibility of a successful outcome.[79] With more than 77 million global subscribers as of fiscal 2012, BlackBerry still leads in many markets. That, and the 55 million BBM users around the world, signal to RIM that there is a demand within the professional and private international community for both a user friendly "…experience and cost effectiveness for both carriers and customers."[80] On the other hand, although RIM has recently enjoyed particularly rapid growth in East Asian and Latin American markets, it still needs to address consumer preferences, as it has seen its overall global market share decline significantly over the past several years in relation to Android-based smartphones and Apple's iOS operating system. With a deluge of Android-based competitors entering the market, RIM is expecting to launch its first 4G (technically called an LTE) device late in 2012.[81] The 4G RIM offering will be part and parcel of the new BlackBerry 10 smartphone and will satisfy the growing desire for "faster download speeds…and higher-value data plans."[82]

Trend toward Emerging Markets

RIM has expanded its focus to international markets where, despite its abysmal market share, it has experienced substantial growth in the past five years (see Exhibit 4). The rapid growth comes mainly from the emerging markets such as China, India, Indonesia, the UAE (United Arab Emirates), and South Africa. With distribution channels in more than 175 countries, the growing BlackBerry subscriber base outside North America accounted for 70 percent of RIM's revenues in

ii. Brazil, Russia, India, and China

fiscal 2012 compared to 54 percent in fiscal 2011,[83] suggesting that the firm's international strategies are critical to its efforts to achieve competitive success and reducing its reliance on sales in North America alone. In fact, current management believes that the global smartphone and tablet markets are still in their infancy. Accordingly, RIM aims to increase its focus in these key market segments by leveraging its brand equity and capabilities as the foundation for increasing subscriber growth and gaining market share.[84]

RIM recognizes that price will be the biggest challenge, especially in markets such as China, India, and Indonesia where the average yearly income is less than $5,000.[85] To obtain global efficiency, RIM outsources the majority of its manufacturing to specialized global electronic manufacturing services (EMS) companies who position themselves in ways that allow them to meet RIM's volume, scale, cost, and quality requirements.[86] On the other hand, it has decentralized some of its operations to respond quickly to local market environments, such as providing low-cost pre-paid plans, financing, half-price devices, and free applications. In the highly regulated market of the UAE, RIM has reached an agreement with the government to allow local officials to monitor and access customer data for national security reasons.[87] Patrick Spence, global head of sales at RIM, said that while smartphone sales grew 61 percent globally in 2011, sales revenue increased by 97 percent in India.[88] With more than 3,500 outlets in 80 cities, RIM launched the BlackBerry Curve 9220 on April 19, 2012 in India. The device represented the most affordable smartphone for customers in India and provided many conveniences and applications as well as the longest lasting battery life.[89] On April 24, RIM launched the BlackBerry Curve 9220 in Indonesia, one of its most lucrative markets with more than 4,000 stores.[90]

Unlike in developed countries where RIM's primary market is the business segment, customers in emerging markets see RIM's BlackBerry as a social-networking device as well.[91] The primary differentiation of RIM lies in its BBM, which targets not only young working professionals, but also college and high school students. According to Nupur Raval, a student in India, this was a winning combination. "If I were to take an iPhone, it wouldn't suit my budget. With the Curve, I can chat on the BBM, send files to anyone across the globe, and it is all free. Its plans are within my budget."[92]

The growing importance of international markets exposes RIM to both political and economic risks when doing business outside of its domestic markets. As demand has risen, so has the opportunity to smuggle in

Exhibit 4 Global Smartphone Market Share and RIM Revenue Source

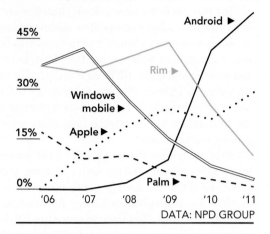

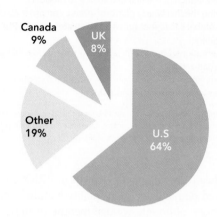

RIM Revenue Source 2006

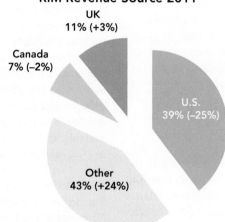

RIM Revenue Source 2011

Sources: Bloomberg BusinessWeek, S&P Capital IQ

devices from subsidized countries, a development that pushes prices down.[93] In company documents, RIM acknowledges some of the significant risk factors it faces in the global market, including restrictions on import and use of the firm's products and services in certain countries, foreign exchange risks, litigation in foreign court systems, and the potential impact of copyright levies. In 2010, the relationship between RIM and the UAE became rocky as the government threatened to block services on BlackBerry devices unless RIM came in line with UAE telecommunication regulations.[94] Had both parties not reached an agreement, RIM would have lost about half a million customers in the region. Since then, shipments of the device to the Middle East have more than doubled and RIM initiated negotiations for a lease on a flagship store in Dubai.[95]

Customers and Markets

Although RIM must compete for a share of the global market, it must remain aware of who its core customers are and have always been. Although RIM remains a leader in enterprise mobility with over 90 percent deployment in *Fortune* 500 companies, it is losing its ability to maintain relationships with those customers. RIM has always been at home in the corporate world, yet its grasp is slipping as employers increasingly allow employees to connect their personal smartphones to corporate networks. Due in large part to competitive pressure exerted by the likes of Apple, this trend also reveals RIM's inability to maintain customer relationships with corporations who formerly used BlackBerry almost exclusively. Although RIM considers its 4,800 full-time marketing, sales, and distribution network's customer relations to be critical to its success, those working in customer relations seem to have failed to extol RIM's key advantage: security.[96] For many years, customers viewed the BlackBerry platform as an "end-to-end solution with comprehensive security specifically for enterprise access to email, PIM, and other corporate information from a single wireless device."[97] Security or, more specifically, data encryption, is the reason it was so successful in acquiring government and corporate contracts during its extraordinary growth over the last decade. RIM's R&D innovations, such as the recently developed BlackBerry Smart Card Reader, further enhance BlackBerry device security for a wide range of government users. In fact, leading security agencies have tested the "BlackBerry Enterprise Solution" and found it to be secure enough to be the first mobile platform to achieve Common Criteria EAL 4+ certification.[98] With the increased demands on RIM to both fulfill demand and meet the individual customer's needs, it is imperative that, with the severe pressures facing RIM today, it focus on its best customers. It must therefore attempt to provide superior perceived value to governments and corporations while simultaneously continue to "focus on providing manageability and scalability solutions to BlackBerry users."[99, 100]

By focusing on its security benefits while concurrently satiating the appetite for a faster, more user-friendly operating system, RIM is able to differentiate its products from Apple and Android devices that aren't made specifically for privacy. Furthermore, by extolling the virtues of security and providing customer support functions to maintain expectations, it is possible for RIM to create higher perceived value for its customers at a lower price point than its competitors. Therefore, RIM allows for not only private users in emerging markets to reap the benefits of the BlackBerry operating system and the BBM platform, but from a global perspective, a growing number of companies and professionals will see the distinct benefit of a secure data package.[101]

Choosing the Markets in Which RIM Will Compete

Fiscal 2012 was a defining time for RIM. It introduced ten new smartphones and launched a multitude of software updates for both its smartphone and tablet offerings, proving it was willing to diversify its product line and tap into various markets.[102, 103] After laying off 11 percent of its workforce in the summer of 2012, RIM believed the launch of the BlackBerry PlayBook would mark a new beginning. The PlayBook was RIM's answer to the highly vetted iPad; the firm's hope was that the

product would help it reverse its increasingly dour market performance.[104] However, as much as diversification can sometimes help increase a firm's market flexibility and reduce fluctuations in its profit, improperly executed diversification can harm consumer and shareholder confidence, as reflected in the case of the BlackBerry PlayBook.[105] At the time of the product's launch, it did not have an email application and required a synchronized BlackBerry smartphone to realize its full potential. These oversights were seen as a major reason for the sharp decline in RIM's share price following the launch of the PlayBook.[106] As of fiscal year 2012, fourth quarter sales of RIM's smartphones fell 21 percent from the previous quarter, marking the first time in six years that it recorded a decline in smartphone sales – and a significant one at that.[107] This sales drop was accompanied by a net loss of $125 million.[108,109]

The job of co-CEOs Jim Balsillie and Mike Lazaridis was to specify how RIM was to gain competitive advantage, help select new strategic positions, and deliver value to the firm's stakeholders. As reflected in sales, it was clear that Balsillie and Lazaridis had failed.[110] Of course, taking competitive actions in the telecommunications industry, perhaps especially during a global economic downturn, is not without risk. Looking forward, RIM's stakeholders expect RIM's management team, headed by new CEO Thorsten Heins, to identify new ways to create value for all stakeholders and especially for the firm's shareholders. Revenue from BlackBerry smartphones via network carrier sales represented approximately 62 percent of revenue for fiscal 2012, compared to approximately 74 percent of revenue for fiscal 2011. These data seem to suggest that RIM is attempting to position BlackBerry smartphone sales as its dominant business with the remainder of sales coming from the PlayBook.[111] Furthermore, one should expect to see the features and functionalities developed by RIM's recent acquisitions – including companies such as The Astonishing Tribe, NewBay, Torch Mobile, and Tungl – to be shared across vertically integrated business units specializing in various software and hardware developments and integrated into RIM's new smartphone offerings and PlayBook.[112] RIM's willingness to transfer technological knowledge across its two major product offerings shows that the firm is willing to assume some risks[113] in that poor performance in one product area could negatively affect the performance in the other product area in light of efforts to integrate efforts to produce and sell both products. Approaching the two major product offerings in this manner is consistent with one of RIM's four major principles, that being the "implementation of broad efficiency programs across all functions of the organization."[114]

Financial Performance

RIM generates revenue from two operating segments: hardware and software. The hardware segment is the primary source of earnings and accounts for approximately 80 percent of RIM's total revenue. From 2007 to 2010, RIM enjoyed rapid revenue growth, rising from $6 billion to $19.9 billion. The increase in revenue was attributed primarily to an increase in hardware sales from $4.9 billion to $16.4 billion (see Exhibit 5). In these years, RIM was able to maintain steady profit margins at 18 percent on average and its stock performance was moving very closely with its competitors.

Beginning in 2011 however, RIM faced a grim outlook and a steep decline in its stock price. The introduction of the Apple iPhone and Windows Phone substantially affected sales, especially in the hardware segment. By the end of 2011, RIM's revenues had dropped 7.4 percent from $19.9 billion to $18.4 billion. Although the software segment increased by more than 26 percent, RIM's larger hardware segment sales decreased by about 15 percent, thus negatively impacting overall performance (see Exhibit 6a, 6b).

As cost of sales and operating expenses increased, RIM's profit margins shrunk from 17.13 percent in 2010 to 6.3 percent in 2011. In the meantime, Apple, Google, and Microsoft maintained, on average, 25 percent plus profit margins. In fact, Apple experienced above average returns and its stock price soared more than 62 percent in 2011. Among the four major players, RIM was the only company in the industry to experience negative growth in 2011 (see Exhibit 7).

Strategic Alliances and Relationships

RIM believes that strategic alliances and the relationships associated with them will drive the successful execution of its short- and long-term plans.[115] To continue to explore and exploit its competitive advantages, RIM recognizes it is critical to broaden its scope by developing new partnerships and relationships with technology leaders possessing skills that are complementary to RIM's. Currently, the areas of strategic alliances and relationships include, but are not limited to, software application developers and companies, global telecommunication carriers, intranet and Internet applications, social networking providers, microchip and other tech manufacturers, and global systems integrators.[116] In the markets in which RIM competes, time-to-market is critical and by maximizing learning and value creation in its partnership, RIM hopes to be able to develop new

products and services relatively quickly compared to its competitors. In 2010, RIM invested $100 million in a joint venture with China Broadband Capital Partner, creating an independent company called BlackBerry Partners Fund China, which focuses on mobile Internet and mobile cloud technologies.[117]

RIM also seeks to use partnerships to minimize costs and improve supply chain models. As mentioned above, RIM outsources the majority of its manufacturing to specialized global EMS companies on a contractual basis (non-equity strategic alliance). RIM strives to reduce risks by having various partners located in key geographical areas and by regularly auditing these facilities.[118]

In the past, close business relationships with various telecom executives propelled RIM's growth. However, the competitive landscape has changed and RIM's competitors now have the ability to develop similar cooperative relationships with carrier partners, sales channel partners, suppliers, and other parties that RIM had previously enjoyed exclusively. The loss of this exclusivity has limited RIM's ability to promote its products and services.[119]

Leadership

For years, RIM had an unusual corporate structure comprised of co-CEOs who also served as the co-chairmen of the board. As RIM's smartphone market share came under attack from rivals Apple Inc. and Google Inc., and RIM's share price tumbled last year, the structure became a lightning rod for criticism by shareholders and analysts.[120] For many years, RIM defended the firm's leadership structure until such time that a few shareholders threatened to bring the issue to shareholder vote. To avoid the vote, RIM agreed to review its structure and eventually separated the role of CEO and Chairman.[121] The new Chairman of the board is Barbara Stymiest. Prior to this shift, the two men who had a major influence on the company and made the majority of important decisions were Michael Lazaridis and Jim Balsillie.[122]

Michael Lazaridis

Michael Lazaridis is a Canadian innovator and the founder of RIM. He is currently the Vice-Chairman of the board of directors, but previously served as the co-CEO and co-Chairman of the Board alongside Jim Balsillie until January 2012.[123] Lazaridis dropped out of college a month before graduation and founded RIM alongside childhood friend Douglas Fregin.[124] Fregin stayed behind the scenes at RIM but remains active in product development and design for the BlackBerry

Exhibit 5 Financial Performance

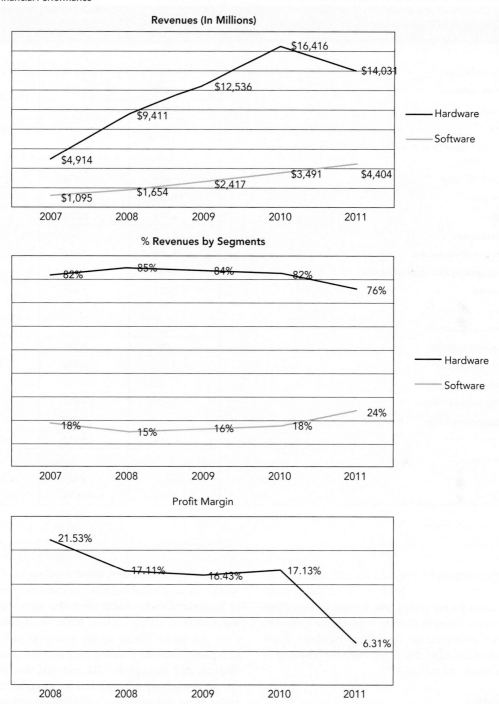

Revenues (In Millions)

$16,416

$14,031

$12,536

$9,411

$4,914

$1,095 $1,654 $2,417 $3,491 $4,404

2007   2008   2009   2010   2011

— Hardware
— Software

% Revenues by Segments

82%   85%   84%   82%

76%

18%   15%   16%   18%   24%

2007   2008   2009   2010   2011

— Hardware
— Software

Profit Margin

21.53%

17.11%   16.43%   17.13%

6.31%

2008   2008   2009   2010   2011

Source: http://www.sec.gov/Archives

line.[125] Lazaridis, on the other hand, was active in RIM's development and played an integral role on the creative side of the company. He was involved in product strategy, R&D, and manufacturing. Lazaridis was the major driver of activities taken to create the BlackBerry and worked for years on the idea of bringing "together the technology of pagers and computers to send emails over a wireless network."[126]

Exhibit 6a Consolidated Statements of Operations (in millions)

Consolidated Statements of Operations (USD $)	12 Months Ended		
In Millions, except Per Share data, unless otherwise specified	Mar 03, 2012	Feb 26, 2011	Feb 27, 2010
Revenue			
Hardware and other	$14,031	$16,416	$12,536
Service and software	4,404	3,491	2,417
Total Revenue	**18,435**	**19,907**	**14,953**
Cost of sales			
Hardware and other (includes a fiscal 2012 inventory provision of $502 million)	11,217	10,516	7,979
Service and software	639	566	390
Total cost of sales	**11,856**	**11,082**	**8,369**
Gross margin	**6,579**	**8,825**	**6,584**
Operating expenses			
Research and development	1,559	1,351	965
Selling, marketing and administration	2,604	2,400	1,907
Amortization	571	438	310
Litigation			164
Impairment of goodwill	355		
Total operating expenses	5,089	4,189	3,346
Income from operations	1,490	4,636	3,238
Investment income, net	21	8	28
Income before income taxes	1,511	4,644	3,266
Provision for income taxes	347	1,233	809
Net income	$1,164	$3,411	$2,457
Earnings per share			
Basic	$2.22	$6.36	$4.35
Diluted	$2.22	$6.34	$4.31

Source: http://www.sec.gov/Archives

The predecessor to the BlackBerry was a large interactive pager. Once Lazaridis realized that a small keyboard could be integrated into a small device effectively, he moved closer to creating what is now known as BlackBerry.[127] Following the BlackBerry PlayBook debacle, Lazaridis decided to step down from his positions as the co-chairman and co-CEO.[128]

Jim Balsillie

Jim Balsillie joined RIM in the early 1990s when Lazaridis received a critical contract from Rogers Cantel Mobile Communications to develop wireless digital networks. Lazaridis, well equipped with the creative mindset required within the industry, needed someone to take care of the business side of things. The need became even

stronger when RIM developed wireless local area networks. Lazaridis met Balsillie, an executive VP and CFO at Sutherland and Schultz, when that firm was hired for a job. In 1992, Balsillie joined RIM, invested money, and even put up his house up for mortgage to finance the company. Balsillie focused on business development, finance, and strategy at RIM and said that his job was "to get the money. Mike's job is to spend it."[129] After faltering from the pressure of RIM's competitors, Balsillie joined Lazaridis and stepped down from his co-CEO and co-chairman posts. Balsillie remained a director until the board vetoed his plan to reinvent RIM.[130]

One cause of BlackBerry's failure was its design that called for the product to send messages over a secure network but did not offer a full-fledged web browsing

Exhibit 6b Consolidated Balance Sheet (in millions)

Consolidated Balance Sheets (USD $)	Mar 03, 2012	Feb 26, 2011
In Millions, unless otherwise specified		
Current		
Cash and cash equivalents	$1,527	$1,791
Short-term investments	247	330
Accounts receivable, net	3,062	3,955
Other receivables	496	324
Inventories	1,027	618
Income taxes receivable	135	
Other current assets	365	241
Deferred income tax asset	197	229
Total current assets	7,056	7,488
Long-term investments	337	577
Property, plant and equipment, net	2,748	2,504
Goodwill	304	508
Intangible assets, net	3,286	1,798
Total Assets	**13,731**	**12,875**
Current		
Accounts payable	744	832
Accrued liabilities	2,382	2,511
Income taxes payable		179
Deferred revenue	263	108
Total current liabilities	3,389	3,630
Deferred income tax liability	232	276
Income taxes payable	10	31
Total liabilities	3,631	3,937
Commitments and contingencies		
Capital stock and additional paid-in capital		
Preferred shares, authorized unlimited number of non-voting, cumulative, redeemable and retractable		
Common shares, authorized unlimited number of non-voting, redeemable, retractable Class A common shares and unlimited number of voting common shares issued - 524,159,844 voting common shares (2/26/11 – 523,868,644)	2,446	2,359
Treasury stock March 3, 2012 – 8,711,010 (February 26, 2011 – 2,752,890)	−299	−160
Retained earnings	7,913	6,749
Accumulated other comprehensive income (loss)	40	−10
Total shareholders' equity	10,100	8,938
Total liabilities and shareholders' equity	**$13,731**	**$12,875**

Source: http://www.sec.gov/Archives

experience. To remedy this, Jim Balsillie developed a radical plan to reinvent RIM:

He wanted RIM to let North American and European network operators use its proprietary network to offer messaging and social networking services to low-end smartphones, *including RIM's popular BlackBerry Messenger. Balsillie's vision was that this would allow carriers to offer smartphones with less expensive data packages attached to them. Volume would make up for the lower cost of the service. The board rejected the idea, and Balsillie resigned as a director as a result.[131]*

Exhibit 7 Financial Data and Outcomes Comparison

Key Statistics				
	RIMM	**AAPL**	**MSFT**	**GOOG**
	RESEARCH IN MOTION LIMITED	**APPLE INC**	**MICROSOFT CORP**	**GOOGLE INC**
Market Cap USD Mil	6,880	534,230	272,030	193,900
% of Institutional Ownership	65.6	70.2	65.5	81.8
Forward Dividend Yield (Annualized)	N/A	N/A	2.6	N/A
Enterprise Value USD Mil (Apr 20, 2012)	5,170	517,560	222,310	153,340
Beta	2.18	1.00	1.00	1.19
Price Performance (Last 52 weeks)	−74.79	62.31	26.59	13.52
Forward P/E	7.45	11.27	10.74	11.76

Financials				
	RIMM	**AAPL**	**MSFT**	**GOOG**
	RESEARCH IN MOTION LIMITED	**APPLE INC**	**MICROSOFT CORP**	**GOOGLE INC**
Revenue USD Mil	18,435	127,841	73,031	37,905
EBITDA USD Mil	3,490	45,450	29,990	14,800
Net Income USD Mil	1,164	32,982	23,344	9,737
EPS USD	2.22	35.14	2.76	29.76
Dividends	N/A	N/A	0.72	N/A
Shares Mil	524	939	8,513	327
Operating Cash Flow USD Mil	2,912	45,310	29,891	14,565
Working Capital USD Mil	3,667	17,018	46,144	43,845
Free Cash Flow USD Mil	−207	37,692	27,566	11,127
Total Debt (mrq)	0	0	12,800	7,710

Profitability				
	RIMM	**AAPL**	**MSFT**	**GOOG**
	RESEARCH IN MOTION LIMITED	**APPLE INC**	**MICROSOFT CORP**	**GOOGLE INC**
Gross Margin %	3.1	42.4	77.7	65.21
Profit Margin %	6.31	25.8	31.96	27.09
Operating Margin %	10.69	33.87	38.04	32.11
Asset Turnover (Average)	1.39	1.13	0.67	0.58
Return on Assets %	8.75	29.26	21.44	14.93
Return on Equity %	12.23	45.58	38.23	18.66

Thorsten Heins

Upon the resignations of Lazaridis and Balsillie, Thorsten Heins became RIM's new CEO. He was tasked with the responsibility of turning around the company. At the time of his appointment, he was a relatively unknown company insider who joined RIM four years prior as a senior VP for the handheld business unit. As of mid-2011, he had been become one of the firm's two COOs. According to company sources, Heins was previously responsible for hardware and software engineering while also playing a major role in sales and in creating RIM's product portfolio. Heins is a native of Germany and

Exhibit 7 (Continued) Financial Data and Outcomes Comparison

Growth				
	RIMM	**AAPL**	**MSFT**	**GOOG**
	RESEARCH IN MOTION LIMITED	**APPLE INC**	**MICROSOFT CORP**	**GOOGLE INC**
Revenue %				
Year over Year	−7.39	65.96	11.94	29.28
3-year Average	18.55	42.4	5	20.26
5-Year Average	43.48	41.16	9.57	29.01
Operating Income %				
Year over Year	−67.86	83.79	12.71	13.11
3-Year Average	−18.2	59.5	6.49	20.98
5-Year Average	13.1	68.97	10.52	27.03
Net Income %				
Year over Year	−65.88	84.99	23.4	14.49
3-Year Average	−14.96	61.81	9.4	32.07
5-Year Average	13.05	67.11	12.94	25.91
EPS %				
Year over Year	−64.98	82.71	28.1	13.11
3-Year Average	−12.38	72.85	12.89	30.76
5-Year Average	15.01	64.90	17.52	24.52

Liquidity/Financial Health				
	RIMM	**AAPL**	**MSFT**	**GOOG**
	RESEARCH IN MOTION LIMITED	**APPLE INC**	**MICROSOFT CORP**	**GOOGLE INC**
Current Ratio	2.08	1.58	2.94	5.92
Quick Ratio	1.61	1.35	2.69	5.7
Financial Leverage	1.36	1.54	1.72	1.25
Debt/Equity	0	0	0.17	0.05

Numbers in trailing twelve months unless otherwise noted

Source: Morningstar and Yahoo Finance

worked at Siemens for almost 24 years prior to joining RIM. At Siemens, he worked in R&D, sales and product management, customer service, and most recently served as the CTO.[132]

Unlike Balsillie, Heins initially believed that RIM did not need to initiate major changes to bounce back. After the poor returns in the first quarter of 2012, Heins revised this belief. Recently Heins did some house cleaning and the COO, the CTO, and ex-CEO Jim Balsillie left the company. According to Heins,

The company will step back from it [the consumer market] in order to focus on the business products that made it a

juggernaut in the first place. It's also considering licensing its software and isn't ruling out the possibility of selling the whole business.[133]

Although Heins acknowledges the difficulties in the current business, he is also optimistic about RIM's future and "he argues that contrary to widespread perception, RIM remains on strong footing. The company is debt-free and sits atop $2 billion in cash."[134]

Board of Directors

Barbara Stymiest, a director since March 2007, is RIM's new chairperson of the board. She is not part of the

RIM management team but works for the Royal Bank of Canada and is currently in charge of the overall strategic direction of the company. Removing the CEO duality was a major move for RIM and shows that a shift in strategy was needed for RIM to move in a different direction. With Stymiest's experience at the Royal Bank, she brings a unique perspective to reevaluate the future direction of the company under Thorsten Heins.

RIM's board is comprised of individuals from various companies and the only person on the board from the management team is Thorsten Heins (see Exhibit 8). Michael Lazaridis is also part of the board but is no longer actively involved in the firm's management structure, despite being the founder of the company and ex-chairman of the board. High-level executives from companies such as Sun Life Financial Inc., Fairfax Financial Holdings, Zero Footprint Software Inc., and Credit Suisse Group are also present on the board. Individuals' backgrounds include accounting, finance, strategy, physics, and engineering.[135] With a heterogeneous board and new management, RIM hopes to be able to implement a new strategy to revive the company and compete with its fast growing competitors.

Issues and Challenges

At a basic level, RIM must re-evaluate and give detailed attention to actions the firm should take to succeed today while planning for what it should do to remain successful in the future. After its original entrance into the market, RIM has simply failed to deliver products with significant new features. Some call an inability to innovate across time an "entrepreneurial failure."[136] In this regard, it may be that while Google and Apple were targeting new markets, RIM appeared to be "resting on its laurels."[137] Rather than providing fresh offerings, RIM relied on incremental improvements to drive sales growth and wound up overtaken by the speed of technology. Given the recent unrest and upheaval of the company, the challenge moving forward lies in where to allocate resources so the firm can improve its performance.

Better understanding competitors and their actions may be a path through which RIM can make progress toward performance improvements. From the beginning, RIM dismissed Apple's iPhone as inferior. By ignoring the iPhone as a competitive threat, RIM fell behind. As other companies developed security features that were comparable to RIM, the company's ability to create unique value for customers disappeared.[138] With email "no longer a key differentiator," the BlackBerry began to lose its luster.[139] No longer the sole provider of superior data security, companies began to abandon not only BlackBerry, but also the practice of providing employees with company-issued phones. At the end of the day, the popularity of BYOD (bring your own device) practices has driven down the prevalence of B2B transactions in this industry.[140]

In the midst of its challenge to reinvigorate innovation, January 2012 saw the rise of a new CEO, Thorsten

Exhibit 8 Board of Directors

Name	RIM Board Member Start	Current or Former Position and Employer
Barbara Stymiest (Chair since January 2012)	March 2007	Group Executive, Royal Bank of Canada (former)
Mike Lazaridis (Vice Chair)	1984	Co-Chairman and Co-CEO, RIM (former)
Timothy Dattels	July 2012	Senior Partner, TPG Capital, LP (current)
Thorsten Heins	January 2012	President and CEO, RIM (current)
David Kerr	July 2007	Managing Partner, Edper Financial Corp (current)
Claudia Kotchka	July 2011	VP of Design Innovation & Strategy, Procter & Gamble, Inc. (former)
Richard Lynch	February 2013	President, FB Associates, LLC (current)
Roger Martin	July 2007	Dean and Professor of Strategy, Rotman School of Management (current)
Bert Norberg	February 2013	President and CEO, Sony Ericsson (former)
John E. Richardson	2003	Senior Partner, Clarkson Gordon & Co. (former)
Prem Watsa	January 2012	Chairman of the Board and CEO, Fairfax Financial Holdings Limited (current)
John Wetmore	March 2007	President, CEO, and CFO, IBM Canada (former)

Source: http://ca.blackberry.com/company/investors/corporate-governance/board-of-directors.html

Heins. Typically, selecting a new CEO from inside the firm results in a continuation with the existing strategies. [141] Heins began by focusing on BlackBerry 10 and signaled there would be no "seismic changes." [142] However, after roughly ten weeks as RIM's new CEO, Heins initiated a major strategic review of the firm and its operations. Even trying to sell the firm became part of the comprehensive review Heins ordered. [143]

Given the leadership changes and confusion regarding direction, formalizing a plan and instilling confidence in the competence of the new leaders is essential. Even before the recent upheaval, stakeholders had called leadership into question. In the summer of 2011, an anonymous letter posted to BGR[iii] received publicity, as its alleged author was a high-ranking RIM employee. The letter bemoaned the structure, culture, and focus of the company, called on RIM's leaders to

streamline operations, and offered detailed recommendations. [144] Without question, RIM's leaders must address the lagging morale that is apparent to both insiders and outsiders. [145] Moreover, the listed risk factors in RIM's most recent AIF[iv] increased from 10 to 36 pages. The first risk (which was a warning that "RIM may not be able to enhance its current products and services, or develop new products and services, in a timely manner or at competitive prices") does nothing to restore stakeholder confidence. [146] These risk factors appear to highlight the challenge RIM faces in an increasingly complex competitive environment. What strategic decisions have the greatest potential to help RIM improve its performance? How should the firm's strategic leaders approach all of the challenges now facing the firm? The quality of answers RIM develops to these and related questions will influence its ability to be a strong competitor in the markets in which it has chosen to compete.

---

iii. BGR is a leading online destination for news and commentary focused on the mobile and general consumer electronics markets.

iv. Canadian equivalent to an Annual Report.

NOTES

1. Form 40-F: Research in Motion Limited. For fiscal year ended March 3, 2012. (2012). Retrieved 20 Apr 2012, from http://ca.blackberry.com/content/dam/bbCompany/Desktop/Global/PDF/Investors/Documents/2012/2012rim_ar_40F.pdf

2. Funding Universe. *Research in Motion Ltd.* (2003). Retrieved 20 Apr 2012, from http://www.fundinguniverse.com/company-histories/research-in-motion-ltd-company-history.html

3. CBC News. (2008). *In Depth: Research in Motion.* Retrieved 20 Apr 2012, from http://www.cbc.ca/news/background/rim/

4. Funding Universe. op cit.

5. Form 40-F: Research in Motion Limited. (2012). op cit.

6. Ibid.

7. CBC News. (2008). op cit.

8. Funding Universe. op cit.

9. CBC News. (2008). op cit.

10. Funding Universe. op cit.

11. White, D. (3 Apr 2012). *Warning: Research in slow motion.* Retrieved 20 Apr 2012, from Financial Review at http://afr.com/p/technology/warning_research_in_slow_motion_qyySqdneJwsEdeEk5d2wrM

12. Libbenga, J. (8 Nov 2007). *BlackBerry boss blows raspberries at iPhone.* Retrieved 20 Apr 2012, from The Register at http://www.theregister.co.uk/2007/11/08/why_iphone_is_no_threat_to_blackberry/

13. Funding Universe. op cit.

14. CNN. (2009). *100 Fastest-Growing Companies.* Retrieved 20 Apr 2012, from CNN Money at http://money.cnn.com/magazines/fortune/fortunefastestgrowing/2009/snapshots/1.html

15. Prodhan, G., & Sandle, P. (11 Oct 2011). *BlackBerry Problems Hit Four Continents.* Retrieved 20 Apr 2012, from Reuters at http://www.reuters.com/article/2011/10/11/us-rim-idUSTRE79A3JU20111011

16. Miller, H. (16 Dec 2011). *RIM Shares Tumble on Delayed Blackberry.* Retrieved 21 Apr 2012, from Bloomberg at http://mobile.bloomberg.com/news/2011-12-15/rim-forecast-misses-analyst-estimates?category=%2Fnews%2Ftechnology%2F

17. Yahoo! Finance. (21 Apr 2012). *RIM.TO.* Retrieved 21 Apr 2012, from http://finance.yahoo.com/q?s=RIM.TO.

18. U.S. House of Representatives Subcommittee. (2008). *Competition in the Wireless Industry.* Washington, D.C.: U.S. House of Representatives Subcommittee.

19. Whitney, L. (7 Dec 2011). *iPhone to help AT&T grab record smartphone sales this quarter.* Retrieved 15 Apr 2012, from CNET News at http://news.cnet.com/8301-1023_3-57338461-93/iphone-to-help-at-t-grab-record-smartphone-sales-this-quarter/

20. Wong, K. (10 Jan 2007). *The Introduction of the iPhone From an Apple First-Timer's Perspective.* Retrieved 15 Apr 2012, from abc News at http://abcnews.go.com/Technology/Business/story?id=2783651&page=1#.T5M6fKZYudC

21. Wingfield, N. (24 Jan 2012). *Apple's Profit Doubles on Holiday iPhone 4S Sales.* Retrieved 15 Apr 2012, from The New York Times at http://www.nytimes.com/2012/01/25/technology/apples-profit-doubles-as-holiday-customers-snapped-up-iphones.html?pagewanted=all

22. Apple, Inc. (18 Jun 2007). *iPhone Delivers Up to Eight Hours of Talk Time.* Retrieved 15 Apr 2012, from Apple Press Info at http://www.apple.com/pr/library/2007/06/18iPhone-Delivers-Up-to-Eight-Hours-of-Talk-Time.html

23. Apple, Inc. (3 Apr 2008). *iTunes Store Top Music Retailer in the US.* Retrieved 15 Apr 2012, from Apple Press Info at http://www.apple.com/pr/library/2008/04/03iTunes-Store-Top-Music-Retailer-in-the-US.html

24. Yin-Poole, W. (21 Apr 2011). *Total Apple iOS sales: 189 million.* Retrieved 15 Apr 2012, from Eurogamer at http://www.eurogamer.net/articles/2011-04-21-total-apple-ios-sales-189-million

25. Gartner. (15 Feb 2012). *Gartner Says Worldwide Smartphone Sales Soared in Fourth Quarter of 2011 With 47 Percent Growth.* Retrieved 15 Apr 2012, from Gartner Newsroom: http://www.gartner.com/it/page.jsp?id=1924314

26. Staff, A. (8 Mar 2012). *iOS, Android increase smartphone market share while all others lose ground*. Retrieved 15 Apr 2012, from appleinsider.com at http://www. appleinsider.com/articles/12/03/08/ios_ android_increase_smartphone_market_ share_while_all_others_lose_ground.html

27. Elgin, B. (17 Aug 2005). *Google Buys Android for Its Mobile Arsenal*. Retrieved 15 Apr 2012, from Businessweek at http://www. businessweek.com/technology/content/ aug2005/tc20050817_0949_tc024.htm

28. Sharma, A., & Delaney, K. J. (2 Aug 2007). *Google Pushes Tailored Phones To Win Lucrative Ad Market*. Retrieved 15 Apr 2012, from The Wall Street Journal at http://online.wsj.com/ article_email/SB118602176520985718- lMyQjAxMDE3ODA2MjAwMjlxWj.html

29. Morrill, D. (23 Sep 2008). *Announcing the Android 1.0 SDK, release 1*. Retrieved 15 Apr 2012, from Android Developers at http:// android-developers.blogspot.com/2008/09/ announcing-android-10-sdk-release-1.html

30. Android Open Source Project. (2008). *Release features - Android 1.0*. Retrieved 15 Apr 2012, from Android Open Source Project at https://sites.google.com/a/ android.com/opensource/release- features—android-1-0

31. Swallow, E. (2 Aug 2011). *Android Captures Nearly 50% of Global Smartphone Market*. Retrieved 15 Apr 2012, from Mashable at http://mashable.com/2011/08/02/android- market-share/

32. Flosi, S. (6 Mar 2012). *comScore Reports Jan 2012 U.S. Mobile Subscriber Market Share*. Retrieved 15 Apr 2012, from comScore at http://www.comscore.com/Press_Events/ Press_Releases/2012/3/comScore_Reports_ Jan_2012_U.S._Mobile_Subscriber_Market_ Share

33. Rubin, A. (27 Feb 2012). *Walking around Mobile World Congress and seeing the Android ecosystem…* Retrieved 15 Apr 2012, from Andy Rubin Google+ Page at https://plus.google. com/u/0/112599748506977857728/posts/ Btey7rJBaLF

34. Open Handset Alliance. (5 Nov 2007). *Industry Leaders Announce Open Platform for Mobile Devices*. Retrieved 15 Apr 2012, from Open Handset Alliance at http://www. openhandsetalliance.com/press_110507. html

35. Hollister, S. (26 Sep 2010). *Microsoft prepping Windows Phone 7 for an Oct 21st launch? (update: US on Nov. 8?)*. Retrieved 15 Apr 2012, from engadget at http://www. engadget.com/2010/09/26/microsoft- prepping-windows-phone-7-for-an-Oct- 21st-launch/

36. Miniman, B. (10 Feb 2010). *Thoughts on Windows Phone 7 Series (BTW: Photon is Dead)*. Retrieved 15 Apr 2012, from pocketnow.com at http://pocketnow.com/ thought/thoughts-on-windows-phone-7- series-btw-photon-is-dead

37. Wilcox, J. (15 Dec 2011). *What Windows Phone 'glance and go' means to you [contest winner]*. Retrieved 15 Apr 2012, from betanews at http://betanews. com/2011/12/15/what-windows-phone- glance-and-go-means-to-you-contest- winner/

38. Kindel, C. (18 Mar 2010). *Windows Phone 7 Series UI Design & Interaction Guide*. Retrieved 15 Apr 2012, from The Windows Phone Developer Blog at http:// windowsteamblog.com/windows_ phone/b/wpdev/archive/2010/03/18/ windows-phone-7-series-ui-design-amp- interaction-guide.aspx

39. Microsoft. (19 Nov 2010). *Windows Phone 7 launches*. Retrieved 15 Apr 2012, from Microsoft Advertising at http://advertising. microsoft.com/uk/windows-phone-7- launches

40. Nielsen. (18 Jan 2012). *More US Consumers Choosing Smartphones as Apple Closes the Gap on Android*. Retrieved 15 Apr 2012, from nielsenwire at http://blog.nielsen. com/nielsenwire/consumer/more-us- consumers-choosing-smartphones-as- apple-closes-the-gap-on-android/

41. Nokia. (10 Feb 2011). *Nokia and Microsoft Announce Plans for a Broad Strategic Partnership to Build a New Global Mobile Ecosystem*. Retrieved 15 Apr 2012, from Microsoft News Center at http://www. microsoft.com/en-us/news/press/2011/ feb11/02-11partnership.aspx

42. Gartner. (11 Aug 2011). *Gartner Says Sales of Mobile Devices in Second Quarter of 2011 Grew 16.5 Percent Year-on-Year; Smartphone Sales Grew 74 Percent*. Retrieved 15 Apr 2012, from Gartner Newsroom at http://www. gartner.com/it/page.jsp?id=1764714

43. Pettey, C., & Tudor, B. (10 Sep 2010). *Gartner Says Android to Become No. 2 Worldwide Mobile Operating System in 2010 and Challenge Symbian for No. 1 Position by 2014*. Retrieved 15 Apr 2012, from Gartner Newsroom at http://www.gartner.com/it/ page.jsp?id=1434613

44. Nokia. (10 Feb 2011). op. cit.

45. Chen, B. X. (26 Mar 2012). *Nokia's Lumia 900 Gets a Price and Release Date*. Retrieved 15 Apr 2012, from Bits Blog (The New York Times) at http://bits.blogs.nytimes. com/2012/03/26/lumia-900-price/

46. Ionescu, D. (4 Apr 2012). *Nokia Lumia 900: A Review Roundup*. Retrieved 15 Apr 2012, from PCWorld at http://www.pcworld.com/ article/253192/nokia_lumia_900_a_review_ roundup.html

47. Bright, P. (19 Apr 2012). *Microsoft's record 3rd quarter revenue: Windows grows, Entertainment staggers*. Retrieved 19 Apr 2012, from ars technica at http:// arstechnica.com/microsoft/news/2012/04/ microsoft-posts-record-3rd-quarter- revenue-windows-resumes-growth- entertainment-back-in-the-red.ars?utm_ source=rss&utm_medium=rss&utm_ campaign=rss

48. Foresman, C. (21 Dec 2009). *App Store success several times what Apple likely expected*. Retrieved 15 Apr 2012, from ars technica at http://arstechnica.com/apple/ news/2009/12/app-store-success-surprised- even-apple.ars

49. Bangeman, E. (28 Sep 2009). *Over 2 billion served: App Store passes another milestone*. Retrieved 15 Apr 2012, from ars technica at http://arstechnica.com/apple/ news/2009/09/over-2-billion-served-app- store-passes-another-milestone.ars

50. Moyer, E. (3 Mar 2012). *Apple's App Store: 25 billion downloads*. Retrieved 15 Apr 2012, from CNET News at http://news.cnet. com/8301-13579_3-57390111-37/apples-app- store-25-billion-downloads/

51. Aune, S. P. (15 Nov 2011). *Android Grabs 52.5% of Global Mobile OS Market*. Retrieved 15 Apr 2012, from TechnoBuffalo at http://www. technobuffalo.com/companies/google/ android/android-grabs-52-5-of-global- mobile-os-market/

52. Mack, E. (6 Nov 2011). *Mobile Patent Wars: A Closer Look at How Everyone Loses*. Retrieved 15 Apr 2012, from PCWorld at http://www.pcworld.com/article/239873/ mobile_patent_wars_a_closer_look_at_ how_everyone_loses.html

53. Albanesius, C. (14 Feb 2012). *DOJ Approves Google's Acquisition of Motorola Mobility*. Retrieved 15 Apr 2012, from PCMag at http://www.pcmag.com/ article2/0,2817,2400226,00.asp

54. Mack, E. (6 Nov 2011). op. cit.

55. CBS News. (11 Feb 2009). *Settlement Ends BlackBerry Patent Suit*. Retrieved 15 Apr 2012, from CBS News at http://www.cbsnews. com/2100-205_162-1368894.html

56. AP. (3 Mar 2006). *Settlement reached in BlackBerry patent case*. Retrieved 15 Apr 2012, from msnbc.com at http://www. msnbc.msn.com/id/11659304/wid/11915829#. T5PdgaZYudB

57. Enterprise Management Associates. (19 Oct 2011). *New EMA Research Shows BlackBerry on Sharp Decline*. Retrieved 15 Apr 2012, from PRWeb at http://www.prweb.com/ releases/2011/10/prweb8890404.htm

58. Agarwal, A. (17 Nov 2011). *Blackberry Losing The Enterprise Smartphone Market Share To iPhone!* Retrieved 15 Apr 2012, from Trak.in at http://trak.in/tags/business/2011/11/17/ blackberry-loosing-enterprise-smartphone- market-iphone-android/

59. Rosati, J. (16 Nov 2011). *iPhone nabs even more of Blackberry's marketshare, now top ranked in business world*. Retrieved 15 Apr 2012, from Today's iPhone at http://www. todaysiphone.com/2011/11/iphone-nabs- even-more-of-blackberrys-marketshare- now-top-ranked-in-business-world/

60. Agarwal, A. (17 Nov 2011). op. cit.

61. Eddy, N. (19 Oct 2011). *BlackBerry Market Share Declining: Report*. Retrieved 15 Apr 2012, from eweek.com at http://www. eweek.com/c/a/Midmarket/BlackBerry- Market-Share-Declining-Report-786023/

62. RIM. (2012). *BlackBerry Messenger*. Retrieved 15 Apr 2012, from Blackberry Developers at http://us.blackberry.com/developers/blackberrymessenger/

63. Geller, J. S. (3 Mar 2011). *Exclusive: BlackBerry Messenger will launch on Android and iOS*. Retrieved 15 Apr 2012, from BGR.com at http://www.bgr.com/2011/03/03/exclusive-blackberry-messenger-will-launch-on-android-and-ios/

64. Kee, E. (13 Apr 2012). *BlackBerry Messenger caught on Android*. Retrieved 15 Apr 2012, from ubergizmo at http://www.ubergizmo.com/2012/04/blackberry-messenger-on-android/

65. Pepitone, J. (13 Oct 2011). *BlackBerry service restored after worst outage ever*. Retrieved Feb 15, 2012, from CNNMoney at http://money.cnn.com/2011/10/13/technology/blackberry_outage/index.htm

66. The Telegraph. (14 Oct 2011). *One in five BlackBerry users considering switching to new supplier after service problems*. Retrieved 15 Apr 2012, from The Telegraph at http://www.telegraph.co.uk/technology/blackberry/8827016/One-in-five-BlackBerry-users-considering-switching-to-new-supplier-after-service-problems.html

67. Bloomberg. (15 Feb 2012). *FLA's checks of Apple's suppliers start at Foxconn*. Retrieved 15 Apr 2012, from Taipei Times at http://www.taipeitimes.com/News/front/archives/2012/02/15/2003525509

68. This American Life. (16 Mar 2012). *460: Retraction*. Retrieved 15 Apr 2012, from thisamericanlife.org at http://www.thisamericanlife.org/radio-archives/episode/460/retraction

69. Form 40-F: Research in Motion Limited. (2012). op cit.

70. RIM. (3 Mar 2012). *Research in Motion Limited Balance Sheet*. Retrieved 15 Apr 2012, from Yahoo! Finance at http://finance.yahoo.com/q/bs?s=RIMM+Balance+Sheet&annual

71. Ibid.

72. Form 40-F: Research in Motion Limited. (2012). op cit.

73. Ibid.

74. Ibid.

75. Wagstaff, J. (18 Apr 2012). *Analysis: In Asia, BlackBerry's RIM sees a glimmer of hope*. Retrieved 19 Apr 2012, from Orlando Sentinel at http://articles.orlandosentinel.com/2012-04-18/features/sns-rt-us-rim-asiabre83h0cb-20120418_1_blackberry-platform-blackberry-messenger-blackberry-s-rim

76. Form 40-F: Research in Motion Limited. (2012). op cit.

77. Hitt, Ireland, & Hoskisson. (2011). *Competitiveness & Globalization - Strategic Management*. Mason: South Western.

78. Ibid.

79. *The World Fact Book*. (2012). Retrieved from CIA at https://www.cia.gov/library/publications/the-world-factbook/

80. Form 40-F: Research in Motion Limited. (2012). op cit.

81. Ibid.

82. Ibid.

83. Form 40-F: Research in Motion Limited. (2012). op cit.

84. Ibid.

85. *The World Fact Book*. (2012). op cit.

86. Form 40-F: Research in Motion Limited. (2012). op cit.

87. Whitney, L. (8 Mar 2010). *RIM averts BlackBerry ban in UAE*. Retrieved 30 Mar 2012, from cnet at http://news.cnet.com/8301-1009_3-20019011-83.html?tag=mncol;txt

88. Market Watch. (18 Apr 2012). *RIM seeking to shore up market share*. Retrieved 19 Apr 2012, from The Wall Street Journal at http://www.marketwatch.com/story/rim-seeking-to-shore-up-market-share-2012-04-18

89. *RIM Press Release*. (2012). Retrieved from RIM: http://press.rim.com/release.jsp?id=5759

90. Wagstaff, J. (18 Apr 2012). *In Asia, BlackBerry's RIM sees a glimmer of hope*. Retrieved 19 Apr 2012, from Reuters at http://www.reuters.com/article/2012/04/18/uk-rim-asia-idUSLNE83H00Y20120418

91. *CBCNews*. (31 Oct 2011). *VIDEO: Why Indonesia is BlackBerry nation*. Retrieved 19 Apr 2012, from CBC at http://www.cbc.ca/news/technology/story/2011/10/31/technology-indonesia-rim-blackberry.html

92. Ghosh, A. (18 Oct 2011). *BlackBerry's Success in India*. Retrieved 20 Apr 2012, from *Forbes India* at http://forbesindia.com/printcontent/29132

93. Wagstaff, J. (18 Apr 2012). op cit.

94. Kerr, D. (12 Apr 2012). *RIM plans to open its first Middle East retail store in Dubai*. Retrieved 19 Apr 2012 from cnet at http://news.cnet.com/8301-1035_3-57413450-94/rim-plans-to-open-its-first-middle-east-retail-store-in-dubai/

95. Miller, H. (11 Apr 2012). *RIM Plans Middle Eastern Retail Push With Dubai Store*. Retrieved 19 Apr 2012, from Bloomberg at http://www.bloomberg.com/news/2012-04-11/rim-plans-middle-eastern-retail-push-with-dubai-store.html

96. Ibid.

97. Ibid.

98. Ibid.

99. Ibid.

100. Hitt, Ireland, & Hoskisson. (2011). op cit. p. 104.

101. Ibid. p. 107.

102. Form 40-F: Research in Motion Limited. (2012). op cit.

103. Hitt, Ireland, & Hoskisson. (2011). op cit. p. 165.

104. Ibid. 179.

105. Ibid. 165.

106. Williams, C. (30 Mar 2012). *BlackBerry beats a shambolic retreat*. Retrieved 21 Apr 2012, from The Telegraph at http://www.telegraph.co.uk/technology/blackberry/9176416/BlackBerry-beats-a-shambolic-retreat.html

107. Sharp, A. (30 Mar 2012). *RIM posts loss as new CEO begins to clean house*. Retrieved 21 Apr 2012, from Reuters at http://www.reuters.com/article/2012/03/30/us-rim-idUSBRE82S1DD20120330.

108. Williams, C. (30 Mar 2012). op cit.

109. Sharp, A. (30 Mar 2012). op cit.

110. Hitt, Ireland, & Hoskisson. (2011). op cit.

111. Form 40-F: Research in Motion Limited. (2012). op cit.

112. Ibid.

113. Hitt, Ireland, & Hoskisson. (2011). op cit. p. 171.

114. Form 40-F: Research in Motion Limited. (2012). op cit.

115. Form 40-F: Research in Motion Limited. (2012). op cit.

116. Ibid.

117. Ko, M. (28 May 2010). *BlackBerry joint venture to invest $100M in China's mobile industry*. Retrieved 20 Apr 2012, from InfoWorld at http://www.infoworld.com/d/mobilize/blackberry-joint-venture-invest-100m-in-chinas-mobile-industry-439

118. Form 40-F: Research in Motion Limited. (2012). op cit.

119. Ibid.

120. Connors, W. (30 Jan 2012). *RIM Publishes Promised Corporate Governance Report*. Retrieved 19 Apr 2012, from The Wall Street Journal at http://online.wsj.com/article/SB100014240529702046529045771937828059 63226.html

121. Connors, W. (30 Jan 2012). op cit.

122. Bloomberg. (n.d.). *Research in Motion*. Retrieved 19 Apr 2012, from Bloomberg Businessweek at http://investing.businessweek.com/research/stocks/people/board.asp?ticker=RIMM:US

123. Bloomberg. (n.d.). *Research in Motion: Michael Lazaridis*. Retrieved Apr 16, 2012, from Bloomberg Businessweek: http://investing.businessweek.com/research/stocks/people/person.asp?personId=399964&ticker=RIMM:US

124. Encyclopedia of the World. (n.d.). *Jim Balsillie and Mike Lazaridis*. Retrieved 15 Apr 2012, from NotableBiographies: http://www.notablebiographies.com/newsmakers2/2006-A-Ec/Balsillie-Jim-and-Mike-Lazaridis.html

125. Bloomberg. (n.d.). *Research in Motion - Douglas Fregin*. Retrieved 16 Apr 2012, from Bloomberg Businessweek at http://investing.businessweek.com/research/stocks/people/person.asp?personId=399968&ticker=RIM:CN&previousCapId=399960&previousTitle=RESEARCH%20IN%20MOTION

126. Encyclopedia of the World. op cit.

127. Ibid.

128. Perez, M. (22 Jan 2012). *A look at RIM's downfall – Where does RIM go from here?* Retrieved 16 Apr 2012, from Intomobile at http://www.intomobile.com/2012/01/22/does-rim-go-now/

129. Encyclopedia of the World. op cit.

130. Perez, M. (22 Jan 2012). op cit.

131. Zeman, E. (14 Apr 2012). *Balsillie's Secret Plan to Save RIM: Crazy Or Smart?* Retrieved 16 Apr 2012, from InformationWeek at http://www.informationweek.com/news/mobility/smart_phones/232900301

132. Reuters. (23 Jan 2012). *Thorsten Heins: a few facts about the new RIM CEO*. Retrieved 16 Apr 2012, from The Guardian at http://www.guardian.co.uk/technology/2012/jan/23/thorston-heims-new-rim-ceo

133. McCracken, H. (29 Mar 2012). *Maybe RIM's Thorsten Heins Isn't So Clueless After All*. Retrieved 16 Apr 2012, from Time: Techland at http://techland.time.com/2012/03/29/maybe-rims-thorsten-heins-isnt-so-clueless-after-all/

134. Gillette, F. (5 Apr 2012). *Thorsten Heins: Into RIM's Ring of Fire*. Retrieved 16 Apr 2012, from Bloomberg Businessweek at http://www.businessweek.com/articles/2012-04-05/thorsten-heins-into-rims-ring-of-fire#p1

135. Research in Motion. (19 Apr 2012). *Board of Directors*. Retrieved 19 Apr 2012, from RIM at http://www.rim.com/investors/governance/boardofdirectors.shtml

136. Mourdoukoutas, P. (1 Apr 2012). *The Entrepreneurial Failure of Research in Motion*. Retrieved 20 Apr 2012, from Forbes at http://www.forbes.com/sites/panosmourdoukoutas/2012/04/01/the-entrepreneurial-failure-of-research-in-motion/

137. Gustin, S. (23 Jan 2012). *New RIM CEO Fails to Impress as Shares Tank After Shakeup*. Retrieved 20 Apr 2012, from TIME: Business at http://business.time.com/2012/01/23/new-rim-ceo-fails-to-impress-as-shares-tank-after-shakeup/

138. Taylor, P. (30 Mar 2012). *Chief needs to say goodbye to old RIM way*. Retrieved 20 Apr 2012, from Financial Times at http://www.ft.com/cms/s/0/b6a98f4c-7831-11e1-b237-00144feab49a.html#axzz1scDiUusF

139. Miles, S. (30 Mar 2012). *Opinion: The Challeges Facing BlackBerry Maker, RIM*. Retrieved 20 Apr 2012, from CNN at http://www.cnn.com/2012/03/30/opinion/stuart-miles-rim-blackberry

140. Berkow, J. (7 Feb 2012). *Halliburton abandons BlackBerry, Picks up iPhone*. Retrieved 20 Apr 2012, from Financial Post at http://business.financialpost.com/2012/02/07/halliburton-abandons-blackberry-picks-up-iphone/

141. Hitt, Ireland, & Hoskisson. (2011). op cit.

142. Connors, W. (24 Jan 2012). *RIM's New CEO Sticks with Strategy, Investors Don't Take Kindly to BlackBerry Maker's News; Shares Fall 8.5%*. Retrieved 20 Apr 2012, from The Wall Street Journal at http://online.wsj.com/article/SB1000142405297020380650457178660064171778.html

143. Taylor, P. (30 Mar 2012). op cit.

144. Geller, J. S. (30 Jun 2012). *Open letter to BlackBerry bosses: Senior RIM exec tells all as company crumbles around him*. Retrieved 20 Apr 2012, from BGR at http://www.bgr.com/2011/06/30/open-letter-to-blackberry-bosses-senior-rim-exec-tells-all-as-company-crumbles-around-him/

145. Connors, W., Das, A., & Chon, G. (30 Mar 2012). *RIM Weighs Bleak Options*. Retrieved 20 Apr 2012, from Wall Street Journal at http://online.wsj.com/article/SB10001424052702303816504577313952155314034.html

146. Silcoff, S. (13 Apr 2012). *The Risk Factor Rises at RIM*. Retrieved 20 Apr 2012, from The Globe and Mail: http://www.theglobeandmail.com/news/technology/tech-news/the-risk-factor-rises-at-rim/article2402188/

IVEY | Publishing

It was April 11, 2011, and the merger between Canadian Satellite Radio Holdings Inc. (the parent company of XM Canada) and SIRIUS Canada Inc. (SIRIUS Canada) had received the approval of the CRTC (Canadian Radio-television and Telecommunications Commission). This approval had been the last obstacle standing in the way of Mark Redmond, who had been appointed president and chief executive officer (CEO) of the new organization. Redmond had been given plenty of time to prepare for this merger, which had first been announced in November of 2010. However, with only a few months before the launch of the implementation plan, Redmond was once more reviewing the proposal he had prepared. The merger of XM Canada and SIRIUS Canada would not be easy. Both organizations had been fierce competitors, and their survival was clearly dependent on a successful merger. Redmond's plan needed to address the makeup of the management team, the consolidated marketing strategy, the integration of the operations and information systems, and the financing of all these activities.

Satellite Radio

In 1992, the FCC (Federal Communications Commission) had approved the Digital Audio Radio Service (DARS) that designated certain segments of radio frequency for satellite broadcast on radio. Through an auction process, two companies had been awarded a license to use these frequencies. The first, American Mobile Radio (later to become XM Radio), had paid $93 million for its licence, and the second company, CD Radio (later to become SIRIUS Satellite Radio), had paid $89 million.[2]

Then, in the spring of 2001, XM Radio launched two satellites into orbit: "Rock" and "Roll." By September, XM Radio was broadcasting in two markets, Dallas and San Diego. Before the end of 2001, its service had gone nationwide.[3]

SIRIUS Satellite Radio launched its service in February of 2002 in four markets: Denver, Houston, Phoenix and Jackson. By the summer of 2002, it too had gone nationwide.[4]

The competition was intense. Both companies were in a race to sign up as many consumers as possible to their subscription models. For as little as US$12.95 per month, subscribers nationwide could enjoy digital-quality music, news, sports, talk and more. However, the fixed costs for each of XM Radio and SIRIUS Satellite Radio were overwhelming. Each satellite launched into orbit cost an estimated US$1.5 billion.[5] In addition, the existing radio equipment in homes, cars, boats and motorhomes was not capable of receiving a satellite radio signal. Both XM Radio and SIRIUS Satellite Radio offered subsidized radio upgrades to make the purchasing decision easier on the consumer. Both companies had also started paying automotive manufacturers to install satellite radio equipment in each car and

The Richard Ivey School of Business gratefully acknowledges the generous support of the National Bank in the development of these learning materials.

Professors David Wood and Craig Dunbar wrote this case solely to provide material for class discussion. The authors do not intend to illustrate either effective or ineffective handling of a managerial situation. The authors may have disguised certain names and other identifying information to protect confidentiality.

Version: 2011-12-08

Exhibit 1 Satellite Radio by Manufacturer

XM Radio	SIRIUS Satellite Radio
Acura	Aston Martin
Buick	Audi
Cadillac	Bentley
Chevrolet	BMW
Ferrari	Chrysler
GMC	Dodge
Harley Davidson	Ford
Honda	Jaguar
Hyundai	Jeep
Infiniti	Kia
Kawasaki	Land Rover
Lexus	Lincoln
Nissan	Maybach
Porsche	Mazda
Saab	Mercedes Benz
Scion	Mercury
Subaru	MINI
Suzuki	Mitsubishi
Toyota	Rolls Royce
	Subaru
	Volvo
	VW

Source: Satellite Radio USA. "Satellite Radio in Your New Car," http://satelliteradiousa.com/satellite_radio_in_your_car.html, accessed on November 15, 2011.

then offered up to a year of free service to each new car owner (see Exhibit 1). Despite their efforts, the conversion rates were poor. In the fourth quarter of 2009, automotive manufacturers sold 2,619,518 new cars in the United States that were equipped with a satellite receiver. However, a year later, new satellite radio subscribers totalled only 257,028.[6]

The reasons for poor satellite radio market penetration were varied. Some argued that when the alternative is free, a subscription model at any price is too expensive. Others blamed the introduction of portable digital mp3 players and the popular iPod. Whatever the reason, it was clear that something had to change. By 2006, both companies had accumulated large losses. Between 2001 and 2006, XM Radio and SIRIUS Satellite Radio had a combined loss of US$3.8 billion on sales of not much more than US$1.6 billion.[7] On November 14, 2007, the shareholders of XM Radio and SIRIUS Satellite radio agreed to merge the two companies.

Sirius XM Radio Inc.

Although the proposed US$11.4 billion merger had many critics (not least of which were the U.S. regulators), the merger finally closed on July 29, 2008.[8] Although customers would reap some benefits, including greater selection and access to exclusive content, the merger was primarily driven by synergies. By the company's own estimates, US$425 million in synergies could be realized in 2009, and even greater synergies were likely in 2010. Mel Karmazin, the CEO of SIRIUS XM Radio Inc., commented:

As the economy has softened, we have been able to leverage what we expect will be more than $425 million in synergies for 2009 – a number that we expect to see grow through 2010 and beyond. The ability to introduce new programming packages – an option that would not have been available to us absent the merger – has opened new avenues for growth. At a time when many companies struggle to begin to streamline their operations and refine their product offerings, we have already done both and are reaping the benefits of the merger.

We moved quickly to integrate our teams. Senior management for the combined company was up and running within days of closing the merger. Our offering to advertisers has been streamlined to cover both platforms and is being heavily marketed. As contracts with our vendors and others have come up, we have been able to realize efficiencies and are confident this trend will continue.

SIRIUS and XM have long been the hallmarks of the best in audio entertainment and one of the most exciting aspects of the merger has been the opportunity to bring new programming options to the market. Our long awaited "Best of" options, which allow listeners to access both the SIRIUS and XM platforms for additional $4 a month, have been well received. This kind of organic growth is a great example of how our stockholders and listeners are benefiting from the merger.

In addition to "Best of" options, we introduced our a la carte programming option. We also have options for music lovers; new programming tailored for listeners who are focused on sports, news and talk; and channel packages that are strictly family friendly. For our most devoted listeners, we now have an interoperable radio, the Mirge, which can deliver both platforms in their entirety through one device. The SIRIUS and XM $12.95 per month packages remain our most popular options and, for pennies a day, continue to be a great value.

Although we have not made all the gains that we would like to see, we have made incredible financial progress *at SIRIUS XM. We posted positive pro forma adjusted income from operations in the fourth quarter for the first time in the history of SIRIUS and XM. This is dramatic considering we had a loss of $224 million one year ago.*[9]

In 2009, the first full year since the U.S. merger, SIRIUS XM Radio Inc. was starting to see some very encouraging results. Both free cash flow and EBITDA (earnings before interest, taxes, depreciation and amortization) had turned positive in 2009. Growth, although slower, remained positive as new subscribers were added. In addition, the APRU (average revenue per user) had increased from $10.65 in 2008 to $10.92 in 2009.[10]

In addition to having increased its revenues, SIRIUS XM Radio Inc. had also been able to reduce its operating expenses. In 2009, the SAC (subscriber acquisition cost) was $64, a significant drop compared with SACs of $70 in 2008 and $83 in 2007. The decrease in SAC was primarily due to lower OEM (original equipment manufacturer) subsidies, lower chip set costs and lower after-market acquisition costs, which had been partially offset by higher after-market inventory-related charges. Due to lower operating expenses and greater labor efficiencies in the customer support center, the customer service and billing expenses also dropped from $1.18 in 2008 to $1.06 in 2009.[11]

However, the cost to realize these synergies was not trivial. SIRIUS XM Radio Inc. had recorded a restructuring expense of US$10.4 million in each of 2008 and 2009, in addition to an impairment expense of US$22.3 million, which related to obsolete satellite equipment.

By 2010, business had continued to improve. Revenue and subscribers were growing, while operating costs on a per-subscriber base were dropping (see Exhibit 2 for additional income statement details). However, the Canadian subsidiaries of SIRIUS Satellite Radio and XM Radio remained two separate entities. Because of Canadian regulations, both Canadian subsidiaries were required to have Canadian ownership, and their previous negotiations to merge had failed.

Canadian Satellite Radio Holdings Inc.

XM Canada (a wholly owned subsidiary of Canadian Satellite Radio Holdings Inc.) was established in 2002 to provide satellite radio in Canada. Canadian Satellite Radio Holdings Inc. was a publicly traded company; however, 58 percent of the equity was owned by John Bitove, 23 percent was owned by XM Radio Inc. (now SIRIUS XM Radio Inc.) and 19 percent was publicly traded on the Toronto Stock Exchange (TSX). As the

exclusive licensed provider of XM Radio in Canada, XM Canada leveraged the existing satellite network and technology, the XM brand and distribution relationships. XM Canada was primarily focused on selling through the OEM automotive network, but relied on self-paying subscribers. As a result, the strategy of XM Canada was focused on selling to consumers through the automotive channel.

By 2010, XM Canada had 589,700 subscribers for its lineup of up to 130 channels, which included 13 Canadian content channels that had been designed and developed by XM Canada. Content was also available through receivers installed in cars and had also expanded to include providing content through both the Internet and mobile devices, including iPhone, BlackBerry and Android devices. In addition to the exclusive content that was developed internally or in partnership with XM Radio, XM Canada also had an exclusive agreement with the National Hockey League.

XM service was available as standard equipment or as a factory-installed option in more than 150 different vehicles for model year 2010, including cars manufactured by General Motors, Honda/Acura, Toyota/Lexus, Nissan/Infiniti, Hyundai, and Porsche. XM radios were also available under Pioneer, Audiovox and other brand names at such national consumer electronics retailers as Best Buy, Future Shop, Canadian Tire, Wal-Mart Canada and other national and regional retailers.[12]

However, despite subscriber growth and a recent initiative to control marketing costs and subscriber acquisition costs, XM Canada was still losing money. Given the success of the merger between XM Radio and SIRIUS Satellite Radio in the United States, there was significant pressure to follow a similar merger strategy in Canada.

Sirius Canada Inc.

SIRIUS Canada Inc. (SIRIUS Canada) was started in 2004 to serve the Canadian market, both with content from the parent company, SIRIUS Satellite Radio, and with Canadian content through the two other investors, the Canadian Broadcasting Corporation (CBC) and Slaight Communications. SIRIUS Canada was the exclusive licensee of SIRIUS Satellite Radio and leveraged the satellite network, technology, and brand of SIRIUS Satellite Radio. SIRIUS Canada focused on the OEM automotive market by selling subscriptions to the automotive manufacturers for a limited period of time for each new car. SIRIUS also put a strong emphasis on selling direct to consumers through the after-market

Exhibit 2 Sirius XM Radio Inc. Income Statement

	Unaudited Pro Forma		
	For the Years Ended December 31,		
	2009	**2008**	**2007**
		(In thousands)	
Revenue:			
Subscriber revenue, including effects of rebates	$2,334,317	$2,258,322	$ 1,888,709
Advertising revenue, net of agency fees	51,754	69,933	73,340
Equipment revenue	50,352	69,398	57,614
Other revenue	90,280	39,087	38,945
Total revenue	2,526,703	2,436,740	2,058,608
Operating expenses:			
Satellite and transmission	82,170	99,185	101,721
Programming and content	370,470	446,638	401,461
Revenue share and royalties	486,990	477,962	403,059
Customer service and billing	232,405	244,195	217,402
Cost of equipment	40,188	66,104	97,820
Sales and marketing	232,199	342,296	413,084
Subscriber acquisition costs	401,670	577,126	654,775
General and administrative	181,920	267,032	271,831
Engineering, design and development	36,152	52,500	62,907
Depreciation and amortization	203,145	245,571	293,976
Restructuring, impairments and related costs	32,807	10,434	—
Share-based payment expense	78,782	124,619	165,099
Total operating expenses	2,378,898	2,953,662	3,083,135
Income (loss) from operations	147,805	(516,922)	(1,024,5 27)
Other expense	(583,157)	(381,425)	(221,610)
Loss before income taxes	(435,352)	(898,347)	(1,246,137)
Income tax expense	(5,981)	(3,988)	(1,496)
Net loss	$ (441,333)	$ (902,335)	$(1,247,633)

Source: *SIRIUS XM Radio Inc. 2009 Annual Report*, page 11.

retail channel. As a result, SIRIUS was dominant in the retail market, but lagged the competition in the OEM automotive market.

In 2010, SIRIUS Canada offered 120 full-time channels that provided commercial-free music, news, talk, sports, and children's programming. Of the 120 channels, 12 were focused on Canadian content, including six channels that were provided by the CBC. Content was available primarily through "plug-n-play" aftermarket receivers sold at national and regional consumer electronics retailers, including, among others, Best Buy, Future Shop, Visions Electronics, The

Source, Costco, Wal-Mart, Canadian Tire, and Home Hardware. Content could also be heard through receivers installed in new cars through one of the multiyear distribution arrangements with several automobile OEMs, including, among others, Ford, Chrysler, BMW, Mazda, Mercedes-Benz, Subaru, Toyota, Volkswagen, Audi, Kia, and Mitsubishi.[13]

Despite SIRIUS Canada's improved financial performance and its growing subscriber base, no one could ignore the potential synergies that could be achieved through a merger with XM Canada, especially in terms of marketing, information systems and operations.

Canadian Merger

After several years of discussion, XM Canada and SIRIUS Canada Inc. (SIRIUS Canada) agreed to a merger on November 24, 2010. Under the terms of the agreement, the new company would be owned 22.7 percent by Canadian Satellite Radio Holdings Inc. (the publicly traded Canadian company), 37.1 percent by SIRIUS XM (the U.S. parent), 15.0 percent by the CBC, 15.0 percent by Slaight Communications, and 10.2 percent by other investors. The objectives of the merger were similar to the objectives in the United States: to improve the product offering to customers, to reduce operating expenses and to maximize revenue through a unified market strategy.

The Company believes that the combined company will have a total subscriber base of over 1.7 million. In the most recently reported quarter ending November 30, 2010, the combined company will have pro forma revenues of approximately $55 million and pro forma Adjusted EBITDA of approximately $5.5 million, and currently expects to have total debt of approximately $150 million. On a trailing 12-month basis, the combined company will have pro forma revenues of approximately $200 million, and pro forma Adjusted EBITDA of approximately $3.7 million. The Combination Transaction is currently expected to yield synergies of approximately $20 million (on an annualized basis) within 18 months after Closing by allowing the combined company to better manage costs through improved efficiencies and greater economies of scale.[14]

Although the shareholders had overwhelmingly approved the transaction, Redmond knew that many challenges remained ahead.

The integration of the Company and SIRIUS requires the dedication of substantial management effort, time and resources. There can be no assurances that management of the combined business will be able to integrate the operations of each of the businesses successfully or achieve any of the synergies or other benefits that are anticipated as a result of the Combination Transaction. Any inability of management to successfully integrate the operations of the Company and SIRIUS could have a material adverse effect on the business, financial condition and results of operations of the combined company. The challenges involved in the integration may include, among other things, the following:

- *addressing possible differences in corporate and management philosophies;*
- *integrating and retaining personnel from different companies;*

- *retaining key personnel, partners and clients during the period between execution of the Purchase Agreement and Closing, including addressing the uncertainties of key employees regarding their future;*
- *integrating information technology systems and resources; and*
- *performance shortfalls relative to expectations at one or both of the companies as a result of the diversion of management's attention to the Combination Transaction.*

It is possible the integration process could result in the disruption or interruption of, or the loss of momentum in, ongoing business or inconsistencies in standards, controls, procedures and policies, any of which could adversely affect the Company's ability to maintain relationships with clients and employees or its ability to achieve the anticipated benefits of the Combination Transaction, or could reduce its earnings or otherwise adversely affect the business and financial results of the combined business. In addition, the integration process may strain the Company's financial and managerial controls and reporting systems and procedures.[15]

Management Team

The first and most pressing concern for Redmond was the new management structure. XM Canada and SIRIUS Canada had been bitter rivals for many years; thus, picking the right mix of executives would be critical to a successful integration. Redmond wanted to ensure the management team had good representation from both XM Canada and SIRIUS Canada, but he also needed to ensure he selected the most qualified candidates from the following:

Michael Moskowitz – President and CEO (XM Canada): Moskowitz had served as the chief executive officer and president of XM Canada since January 1, 2008. Moskowitz was responsible for overseeing all aspects of XM Canada's operations from OEM and aftermarket sales to programming, marketing, partnership development, finance and operations. He had worked more than 15 years in the Canadian communications and technology industries. He had been a "Top 40 Under 40" award recipient in 2004 and held an honors degree from York University and an MBA from Dalhousie University.[16]

Michael Washinushi – Chief Financial Officer (CFO) (XM Canada): Washinushi was chief financial officer, treasurer, and secretary of XM Canada. Prior to joining the company in 2005, Washinushi had served as the director of Development and Acquisitions for KIT Limited Partnership, where he had been responsible for managing the firm's real estate portfolio. Washinushi held a Bachelor of Arts degree in Economics from York University.[17]

Mark Knapton – Vice-president Operations (XM Canada): Knapton was vice president – Call Centre & Retention of XM Canada. In his role, Knapton was responsible for managing Listener Care activities and customer operations, including the repeater network and customer service strategies to drive sales and manage churn. He had more than 24 years of experience in customer care environments in both the airline and telecommunications industries.[18]

Janet Gillespie – Vice-president Marketing (XM Canada): Gillespie had been vice president, Marketing of XM Canada, since January 2008. Gillespie played an integral role in strengthening XM Canada's marketing. She had more than 20 years of experience in marketing and sales from a variety of leading technology and communications firms, including the past eight years at Palm Canada Inc. Prior to working at Palm, she had held account management and marketing positions at several leading global technology firms, where Gillespie had built her management experience in strategic communications and public relations, channel marketing, and building advertising and direct marketing strategies.[19]

Sherry Kerr – General counsel (SIRIUS Canada): Kerr had joined the company in 2006 to assist with regulatory matters, in particular the CRTC. Prior to joining SIRIUS Canada, Kerr had been a lawyer with McCarthy Tétrault, specializing in copyright law and communications regulations in Canada.

Jason Redman – CFO (SIRIUS Canada): Redman had been with the company only seven months when the merger was announced. Redman had earned an accounting degree from the University of Waterloo, an MBA from Kellogg School of Management and was a chartered accountant. Prior to joining SIRIUS Canada, Redman had worked as the CFO at Look Communications Inc. for four years.[20]

Paul Cunningham – Vice-president Marketing (SIRIUS Canada): Cunningham had been with SIRIUS Canada since the beginning, working in marketing and penetrating the retail market. Prior to joining SIRIUS Canada, Cunningham had worked at Thompson Electronics in retail marketing.

John Lewis – Vice-president Programming (SIRIUS Canada): Lewis had been with SIRIUS Canada since the beginning in his current capacity. Prior to joining SIRIUS Canada, Levin had worked at CBC.

Al McNevin – Vice-president Customer Relations (SIRIUS Canada): Since the inception of SIRIUS Canada, McNevin had run the customer service center and the loyalty program. Converting the OEM customers to paid subscriptions had been an important part of McNevin's duties.

In addition to picking the right people, Redmond needed to address differences in compensation. Although the total compensation package offered to executives at XM Canada and SIRIUS Canada were equivalent, the XM Canada executives had a long-term stock option program that was not available to SIRIUS Canada executives. Further complicating matters were the provisions for share ownership, options and change of control held by many key executives at XM Canada. For example, CEO Michael Moskowitz, CFO Michael Washinushi, Vice-president of Customer Operations Mark Knapton and Vice-president of Marketing Janet Gillespie all held shares, and their employment contracts included change of control provisions totaling $3.2 million.[21] No such change of control provision was included in the employment contracts of SIRIUS Canada executives.

The two organizations also had organizational structure differences. XM Canada operated as an independent business that was separate and distinct from XM Radio Inc. SIRIUS Canada, however, focused primarily on marketing and customer service and relied on SIRIUS Satellite Radio Inc. for support services. These differences in structure therefore needed to be considered when selecting the new management team.

Finally, Redmond had to concern himself with the retention of key employees. If one of the executives or senior managers was not willing to stay, should that individual be offered a retention bonus or other incentive?

The success of the Combination Transaction will depend in part on the Company's ability to retain key personnel currently employed by either of the Companies and SIRIUS. It is possible that certain members of the 39 management team may decide not to remain with the combined business while it works to complete the Combination Transaction or after the Combination Transaction has been completed. If key executives or employees terminate their employment, the future success of the combined business might be adversely affected.[22]

Information Systems and Operations

Synergies in operations and information systems were one of the primary reasons for the merger in the first place. Combining accounting functions, customer care and the call center were all viable options. However, other functional areas were more complicated. To start with, at XM Canada, the Canadian content was developed internally, whereas SIRIUS Canada relied on its investors, Slaight Communications and CBC, to provide Canadian content. SIRIUS Canada also supplemented satellite coverage with a terrestrial repeater network of 12 repeaters, which were maintained by CBC (repeaters were deployed in the largest Canadian cities to improve coverage and reduce interruptions by buildings or other obstacles). In addition, XM Canada had been established as a standalone business. As a result, it maintained its own information systems infrastructure. SIRIUS Canada, on the other hand, had relied on the information systems infrastructure of SIRIUS Satellite Radio Inc. for day-to-day operations, for which it paid a royalty to SIRIUS Satellite Radio Inc.

The synergies presented in the shareholder circular considered only the most conservative estimates.

Therefore, a more aggressive approach to consolidating the operations and information systems of XM Canada and SIRIUS Canada might enable Redmond to exceed the synergy target, but at what cost and with how much additional risk?

Marketing

Marketing presented the greatest opportunity for both reducing operating costs and increasing additional revenue. Approximately three-quarters of the $20 million in proposed synergies would result from a reduction in marketing expenditures. Unlike the synergies from operations and information systems, the savings from marketing would not require any reduction in staff or severance payments.

Exhibit 3 XM Canada and Sirius Canada Pro Forma Income Statements
Pro forma consolidated statement of loss year-ended August 31, 2010 (unaudited)

	CSR August 31, 2010	Sirius August 31, 2010	Financing Pro Forma Adjustments	Acquisition and other Pro Forma Adjustments	Notes(s)	Pro Forma Combined Group
Revenues	$ 56,611,828	$145,899,082	$ —	$(2,942,537)	2(f)	$199,568,373
Operating Expenses						
Cost of revenue	32,210,480	43,831,468	—	(1,554,485)	2(b), (c), (d)	74,487,463
Reversal of part II license accrual	(1,186,832)	—	—	1,186,832	2(c)	—
General and administrative	16,293,938	10,022,864	—	2,942,906	2 (c), (d)	23,373,896
Stock based compensation	2,088328	—	—	—		2,088,328
Marketing	17,158,757	77,572,771	—	3,310,559	2(b)	98,042,087
Amortization of intangible assets and property and equipment	24,764,414	2,420,902	—	6,385,455	2(f)	33,570,771
Total operating expenses	91,329,085	133,848,005	—	6,385,455		231,562,545
Operating profit (loss)	(34,717,257)	12,051,077		(9,327,992)		(31,994,172)
Interest revenue	(47,702)	(97,188)	—	—		(144,890)
Interest expense	19,703,051	—	(31,913,591)	—	2(j)	16,509,460
Debt repurchase	(7,076,232)	—	—	—		(7,076,232)
Revaluation of derivative	196,473	—	—	—		196,473
Foreign exchange (gain) loss	(2,757,319)	87,924	2,291,055	—	2(k)	(378,340)
Net earnings (loss)	$(44,735,528)	$ 12,060,341	$ 902,536	$9,327,992		$(41,100,643)
Basic and diluted loss per share	$ (0.88)				3	$ (0.33)

The related notes form an integral part of the unaudited pro forma financial information.

Note: Canadian Satellite Radio Holdings Inc., *Notice of Annual and Special Meeting of Shareholders to be held February 17, 2011 and Management Information Circular*, page H-4.

Exhibit 4 XM Canada and Sirius Canada Pro Forma Balance Sheet

Pro forma consolidated Balance Sheet as of November 30, 2010 (unaudited)

	CSR November 30, 2010	Sirius September 30, 2010	Financing Pro Forma Adjustments	Acquisition and other Pro Forma Adjustments	Note(s)	Pro Forma Combined Group
Assets						
Cash and cash equivalents	$ 4,111,766	$ 49,278,899	$21,553,000	$ (43,685,252)	2(p)	$ 31,258,413
Accounts receivable	2,219,430	7,228,780	—	—		9,448,210
Inventories	—	279,885	—	—		279,885
Prepaid expenses and other current assets	3,131,401	1,398,228	—	—		4,529,629
Restricted investment, letter of credit	4,000,000	—	—	—		4,000,000
Current assets	13,462,597	58,185,792	21,553,000	(43,685,252)		49,516,137
Long term prepaids and other assets	916,000	36,720	—	—		952,720
Property and equipment net	9,261,142	2,752,894	—	—		12,014,036
Identifiable intangible assets, net	164,682,982	4,003,169	—	49,072,914	2(e)	217,759,065
Good Will	—	—	—	143,330,259	2(e)	143,330,259
Total Assets	**$ 188,322,721**	**$ 64,978,575**	**$ 21,553,000**	**$ 148,717,921**		**$423,572,217**
Current Liabilities						
Accounts payable and accruals	$ 24,149,223	$ 26,937,999	—	$ 700,000	2(m)	$ 51,787,322
Due to related parties	—	19,977,262	—	(13,172,252)	2(l)	6,805.010
Future tax liability	—	1,093,647	—	—	2(o)	1,093,647
Interest payable	3,881,028	—	—	400,000	2(a)	3,481,028
Deferred leasehold inducement	—	42,890	—	—		42,980
Deferred revenue	29,425,373	84,319,295	—	(2,942,538)	2(e)	110,802,130
	57,455,624	132,371,093		(15,814,790)		174,011,927
Long term Debit	118,748,889	—	24,608,927	5,635,409	2(j)	148,993,225
Deferred revenue	7,184,720	13,604,272	—	(718,472)	2(e)	20,070,520
Future tax liability	—	—	—	18,750,000	2(o)	18,750,000
Other long term obligation	11,032,385	207,304	—	734,078	2(e) (iii)	11,973,767
Total liabilities	**194,421,618**	**146,182,669**	**24,608,927**	**8,586,225**		**373,799,439**
Shareholders' equity deficiency						
Share Capital	334,152,570	36,000,100		(334,152,570)	2 (q)	
				157,146,913	2 (a), (e)(i)	
				(734,078)	2 (e) (iii)	
				(26,013,000)	2(l)	166,399,935
Contributed Surplus	29,886,938	—		(29,886,938)	2 (q)	
				2,311,115	2 (e) (ii)	2,311,115
Deficit	(370,138,405)	(117,204,194)		370,138,405	2 (q)	
				(734,078)	2(e) (iii)	
			(3,055,927)	3,055,927	2 (g) (i)	
				(1,000,000)	2 (m), (n)	(118,938,272)
Total shareholders' equity (deficiency)	**(6,098,897)**	**(81,204,094)**	**(3,055,927)**	**140,131,696**		**49,772,778**
Total liabilities and shareholders' equity (deficiency)	**$ 188,322,721**	**$ 64,978,575**	**$21,553,000**	**$ 148,717,921**		**$ 423,572,217**

The related notes form an integral part of the unaudited pro forma financial information.

Source: Canadian Satellite Radio Holdings Inc., Notice of Annual and Special Meeting of Shareholders to be held February 17, 2011 and Management Information Circular, page H-5.

Exhibit 5 XM Canada and Sirius Canada Select Pro Forma Adjustments

j) The effect of the adjustments to debt and interest expense as a result of the proposed refinancing transactions described in adjustments g), h) and i) are as follows:

	Actual			Pro Forma		
	Debt outstanding at November 30, 2010	**Interest expense for 3 months ended November 30, 2010**	**Interest expense for 12 months ended August 31, 2010**	**Debt outstanding at November 30, 2010**	**Interest expense for 3 months ended November 30, 2010**	**Interest expense for 12 months ended August 31, 2010**
9.75% New Senior notes	—	—	—	$130,000,000	$ 3,168,750	$12,675,000
12.75% US$ Senior notes	$ 71,865,335	$2, 274,778	$11,151,187	—	—	—
8% convertible notes	17,104,816	614,585	2,375,961	18,993,225	$ 474,831	1,899,322
Promissory notes I	1,094,934	92,639	323,959	—	—	—
Promissory notes II	1,291,850	114,080	381,528	—	—	—
XM credit facility	27,391,954	1,266,496	3,608,686	—	—	—
	$118,748,889	4,362,578	17,841,321	$ 148,993,225	3,643,581	14,574,322
Interest on other obligations		493,883	1,861,730		493,883	1,861,730
Pro forma adjustment on promissory notes note (2)(e)(iii)		—	—		18,352	73,408
Total interest expense		**$4,856,461**	**$19,703,051**		**$4,155,816**	**$16,509,460**

The effective interest rate of the new Senior Notes is estimated to be 9.75%. A variation 1/8 % in the stated interest rate on the new Senior Notes would increase or decrease interest expense by $0.2 million. The fair value of the new Senior Notes has been estimated to be equivalent to the face amount at issuance.

The fair value of the 8% convertible notes has been determined to be $19.0 million as at November 30, 2010 based on market conditions for similar convertible notes with similar remaining term of maturity as the notes. As required by CICA Handbook section 3863, *Financial Instruments—Presentation*, the fair value of the convertible debt has been allocated between a financial liability and equity components based on determining the fair value of the liability element, the most easily measurable component and the residual was assigned to the equity element. As a result, the effective rate on the convertible debt is 10.0%. The pro forma interest expense has been adjusted to reflect the revised estimate of the effective interest rate.

Source: Canadian Satellite Radio Holdings Inc., *Notice of Annual and Special Meeting of Shareholders to be held February 17, 2011 and Management Information Circular*, page H-12.

In addition to being optimistic about the savings, Redmond was also optimistic that the newly merged Canadian business would be able to increase revenues. Although the Competition Bureau of Canada was expected to restrict any increase in prices, it did not prevent new products and services from being offered to existing customers for additional revenue. In the United States, the "best of both worlds" campaign had proved that some subscribers would pay an additional fee to have access to both XM and SIRIUS channels.

The final marketing decision facing Redmond related to distribution and sales. XM Canada had primarily focused on selling subscriptions to new car buyers through the automotive manufacturers. SIRIUS Canada, on the other hand, had targeted the automotive manufacturers to purchase prepaid subscriptions and after-market consumers to purchase their subscriptions through retail outlets. Redmond needed to determine whether all three sales strategies were equally successful and whether all three could coexist under one company. Redmond also knew that segmenting each channel with a different brand was not an option as SIRIUS XM Radio Inc. had already made the decision to co-brand all products and services under the "SIRIUS XM" brand.

Financing

Finally, Redmond needed to consider the financing of the new corporation. In addition to the debt held by both

Exhibit 6 Comparable Capital Financing Information

XSR Comparable Companies Analysis

(in local currency millions, except where denoted and per share amounts)

Company	Price 11-Apr-11	Mkt. Cap. (mm)	E.V. (mm)	LTM Sales (mm)	BV of Debt (mm)	Interest Expense LTM	BV of Equity (mm)	Credit Rating S&P	Dividend Yield %	Fwd. Sales Growth[2][3] FY1 - FY2
Astral Media Inc.	C$37.75	$2,073	$2,622	$977	$579	$25	$1,401	-	2.0%	4.5%
Corus Entertain-ment Inc.	C$21.07	$1,735	$2,449	$785	$723	$54	$990	BB+	3.6%	2.0%
SIRIUS XM Radio Inc.	US$1.78	$11,466	$13,784	$2,817	$2,892		$208	BB	-	10.5%
IMAX Corporation	US$30.43	$2,085	$2,072	$248	$18	$2	$158	-	-	11.6%
Median										**7.5%**
Canadian Satellite Radio Holdings Inc.[1]	**US$3.15**	**$387**	**$513**	**$239**	**$152**	**$14**	**$47**	**-**	**-**	**8.5%**

[1] Pro forma figures for Canadian Satellite Radio.
[2] Forward figures as per street estimates.
[3] Forward figures calendarized to August 31 year end.

XSR Comparable Companies Analysis

(in local currency millions, except where denoted and per share amounts)

Company	EV/ Sales[2][3]			EV/EBITDA[2][3]			P/E[2][3]			Net Debt	
	LTM	FY1	FY2	LTM	FY1	FY2	LTM	FY1	FY2	LTM EBITDA	Total Cap.
Astral Media Inc.	2.7x	2.6x	2.5x	9.0x	8.0x	7.6x	12.5x	11.6x	10.8x	1.9x	28.2%
Corus Entertainment Inc	3.1x	2.9x	2.8x	9.6x	8.5x	8.1x	18.3x	12.8x	11.5x	2.7x	41.0%
SIRIUS XM Radio Inc	4.9x	4.2x	3.8x	17.2x	15.6x	12.5x	NM	NM	23.5x	2.9x	91.3%
IMAX Corporation	8.3x	7.7x	6.9x	NM	17.8x	15.5x	20.2x	28.5x	27.2x	0.0x	0.0%
Median	**4.0x**	**3.5x**	**3.3x**	**9.6x**	**12.0x**	**10.3x**	**18.3x**	**12.8x**	**17.5x**	**2.3x**	**34.6%**
Canadian Satellite Radio Holdings Inc.[1]	**2.1x**	**2.1x**	**2.0x**	**19.4x**	**19.4x**	**10.6x**	**NM**	**NM**	**NM**	**4.7x**	**72.6%**

[1] Pro forma figures for Canadian Satellite Radio.
[2] Forward figures as per street estimates.
[3] Forward figures calendarized to August 31 year end.

Note: Mkt. Cap. = market capitalization; E.V. = enterprise value; LTM sales = last 12 months' sales; BV of debt = book value of debt; BV of equity = book value of equity; mm = millions; FY = fiscal year; EBITDA = earnings before interest taxes, depreciation and amortization; P/E = profit/earnings

Source: National Bank

XM Canada and SIRIUS Canada, the proposal included additional debt to finance the business. In aggregate, the debt was significant:

If the Combination Transaction and the Refinancing are completed as currently contemplated, the anticipated total indebtedness of the Company after giving effect to the Combination Transaction and the Refinancing is currently anticipated to be approximately $150 million. This level of indebtedness could reduce funds available for investment in research and development and capital expenditures or create competitive disadvantages compared to other audio entertainment companies with lower debt levels.[23]

Although the pro forma financial statements showed some improvements in income and cash flow, the proposal also suggested refinancing and taking on additional debt (details of the pro forma consolidated financial statements for XM Canada and SIRIUS Canada are in Exhibits 3, 4 and 5). This new proposed debt (maturing in 2018) had some advantages. If Redmond was able to secure the finances as proposed, the interest charges would decline despite the higher debt.

The transaction completed in the United States had gone through a similar refinancing during the merger, but it had not been easy. At the time the merger was completed in the United States, the credit markets had tightened and the merger was at risk. Because the Canadian merger also required debt refinancing, any delay in bond issuance would put a merger in jeopardy.

The proposed debt financing offered some options. Redmond could revisit the capital structure and consider the option of issuing equity, convertible debt or some combination of the two. Other players in the communications and broadcasting industry had much lower debt financing costs and had elected to take on less debt in relation to their equity (Exhibit 6 includes comparable capital structure details). If the deal was financed with debt as proposed, many financing considerations would continue to remain going forward. Assuming the combined entity was able to generate the anticipated cash flows, Redmond needed to decide how quickly to pay down the debt and to what target level. Some analysts believed the company could start to pay dividends as early as 2014. Redmond needed to consider the company's future dividend policy. Finally, liquidity for Canadian Satellite Radio Holdings Inc. shares would likely remain a challenge because of its small public float (3.3 million shares out of a total of 122.8 million shares outstanding). Redmond would need to consider which strategies to follow to improve share liquidity, including future equity offerings.

Conclusion

As the closing date approached, Redmond's level of excitement and anxiety grew. He knew he had only one opportunity to get it right. There were management dynamics to be considered, operation and information systems synergies to plan, marketing strategies to deliberate, and finally, financing to structure.

Over the next few weeks, the board would be meeting to review Redmond's plan. This schedule left little time to make any final changes or additions to the plan. Perhaps just as important, this plan was Redmond's first opportunity to prove that the board had not made a mistake in appointing him the new CEO of SIRIUS XM Canada.

NOTES

1. This case has been written on the basis of published sources only. Consequently, the interpretation and perspectives presented in this case are not necessarily those of SIRIUS Canada Inc. or any of its employees.
2. Satellite Radio USA, "The History of Satellite Radio," *Satellite Radio USA*, http://satelliteradiousa.com/satellite_radio_history.html, accessed on November 15, 2011.
3. Ibid.
4. Ibid.
5. Ibid.
6. Brian Newman Rayl, "Sirius XM (NASDAQ: SIRI) Q4 Subscriber Preview," *Satellite Radio Playground*, February 2, 1011, http://satelliteradioplayground.com/tag/conversion-rate/, accessed on November 15, 2011.
7. Sirius XM Radio Inc. 2007 Annual Report and Proxy Statement.
8. Dawn Kawamoto, "Sirius and XM Close Merger," *CNET News*, July 29, 2008, http://news.cnet.com/8301-1035_3-10001299-94.html, accessed on November 15, 2011.

9. Mel Karmazin, *SIRIUS XM Radio Inc. 2008 Annual Report*, p. 1.
10. SIRIUS XM Radio Inc. 2009 Annual Report, p. 3.
11. Ibid.
12. Canada Satellite Radio Holdings Inc. 2010 Annual Report.
13. Canadian Satellite Radio Holdings Inc., *Notice of Annual and Special Meeting of Shareholders to be held February 17, 2011 and Management Information Circular*, p. F-1.
14. Canadian Satellite Radio Holdings Inc., *Notice of Annual and Special Meeting of Shareholders to be held February 17, 2011 and Management Information Circular*, p. 7.
15. Canadian Satellite Radio Holdings Inc., *Notice of Annual and Special Meeting of Shareholders to be held February 17, 2011 and Management Information Circular*, p. 39.
16. Bloomberg BusinessWeek, "Executive Profile: Michael Moskowitz,"http://investing.businessweek.com/research/stocks/people/person.asp?personId=39825885&ticker=XSR:CN, accessed on November 21, 2011.
17. Reuters, "Canadian Satellite Radio Holdings Inc. (XSR.TP)," http://

www.reuters.com/finance/stocks/companyOfficers?symbol=XSR.TO, accessed on November 21, 2011.
18. Ibid.
19. Bloomberg BusinessWeek, "Canadian Satellite Radio-A (XSR Toronto)," http://investing.businessweek.com/research/stocks/people/person.asp?personId=40084593&ticker=XSR:CN, accessed on November 21, 2011.
20. "Jason Redman," *LinkedIn* entry, http://www.linkedin.com/pub/jason-redman/26/973/233, accessed on November 23,2011.
21. Canadian Satellite Radio Holdings Inc., *Notice of Annual and Special Meeting of Shareholders to be held February 17, 2011 and Management Information Circular*, p. 54.
22. Canadian Satellite Radio Holdings Inc., *Notice of Annual and Special Meeting of Shareholders to be held February 17, 2011 and Management Information Circular*, p. 39.
23. Canadian Satellite Radio Holdings Inc., *Notice of Annual and Special Meeting of Shareholders to be held February 17, 2011 and Management Information Circular*, p. 39.

CASE 27

Tata Motors Limited: Ratan's Next Step

DARDEN
BUSINESS PUBLISHING
UNIVERSITY of VIRGINIA

On January 10, 2008, Ratan Tata, chairman of Tata Motors Limited (Tata Motors), drove onto the stage at the New Delhi Auto Expo in the world's cheapest car. As he parked next to two other models of the Nano, he thought back on the day several years prior when he had promised the world an affordable car that could be bought for under $2,500.[1] At the time, India was an emerging economy that had begun to invest millions of dollars in transportation infrastructure. Ratan saw the influx of roads and new prosperity for Indians as the perfect environment to debut a car that could be purchased by almost anyone. Like his personal hero, John F. Kennedy, Ratan challenged the people around him to design and produce something that had previously been unthinkable.

Ratan's ability to deliver on such a bold aspiration instilled in his investors and him the confidence that Tata Motors was capable of competing in the international automobile market. The Nano's production was made possible by a wide range of capabilities within the Tata Group, which, along with Tata Motors, owned 98 other companies operating in 80 countries. Such a diverse and complete range of resources made Tata's future bright.[2]

And even as Ratan stood on the stage introducing his accomplishment, he wondered what the next step ought to be to move his company forward. A lifelong interest in automobiles and an appreciation of the Western car market led Ratan to believe that he would have to establish a firm foothold in the United States and the United Kingdom to be considered a contender in the global automotive industry. His mind turned to the ongoing bid and negotiations to acquire Jaguar Land Rover (JLR) from Ford Motor Company (Ford). Establishing a luxury brand would go a long way toward separating Tata Motors from regional automotive firms. Yet he had to think about whether the firm was well positioned to execute the acquisition if it won the bid. Or was organic growth a safer route to the same end?

Global Automobile Landscape

The automobile industry was a revolving door of brand ownership and development among a limited number of conglomerates. Underlying the swapping and bargaining of various marques between companies was a tone of nationalism. Traditional American firms such as General Motors (GM) and Ford pitted themselves against foreign competitors, particularly those in the Far East, where automotive production was growing at a tremendous rate: Between 2005 and 2008, U.S. motor vehicle production declined 13%, while China's production increased 63%, and India's jumped 51%.[3]

The disparity between the Eastern and Western car markets reflected a global economic slowdown, which favored cheaper and more efficient vehicles. Ford, which had been pouring money into its fledgling Premier Automotive Group (PAG), had determined it would be more cost-effective to dismantle the sector altogether, raise capital, and reinvigorate its mainstay marques to form a cohesive and unified campaign. A return to core

© Vividfour / Shutterstock.com

brands for Ford meant eliminating luxury models, which had experienced a significant decline from 2004 to 2006.[4]

Luxury brand or not, without two raw materials—steel and aluminum—auto production lines would be idle. Steel was at the heart of the car manufacturing process. The prices of those resources were either a threat or benefit to a firm's operating costs. In 2006, Tata faced downward pressure on its margins when the price of aluminum ingot rose 23% and steel increased $9 per ton over the previous year.[5] Auto production was highly dependent upon the steel and aluminum industries.

The main factors in being able to produce automobiles on a mass scale across different vehicle types were R&D, manufacturing capability, and access to successful platforms. Most major auto companies used platforms to produce varying types of vehicles while saving on design particulars. A dashboard display, for instance, could be used for multiple vehicles. In addition to aesthetic nuances to vehicles, platform technology incorporated features under the hood including engines and chassis. Platform technologies were valuable for companies because when one was developed, it could be applied to multiple vehicles of the same class to produce identical internal components while allowing for multiple body designs.

In addition to platform production, most auto companies were focused on building brands that would be familiar to consumers. In general, automobiles were big-ticket items for consumers, and when faced with such a large purchasing decision, many buyers were swayed by their comfort with the brand. For that reason, particular brand names were especially valuable in the global automotive market—Jaguar and Land Rover were primary examples of universally recognized brands.

Jaguar was originally known as the Swallow Sidecar Company until World War II, when the similarity of its initials to those of Hitler's elite guard, the Schutzstaffel (SS), drew negative connotations. In 1968, almost 25 years after the name change, Jaguar merged with British Motors Company (BMC) and deepened its ties to England. Jaguar's cars were known for having a sporty look and were driven by the aristocracy of England. After collaborating with Ford throughout the late 1970s and 1980s, Ford finally purchased Jaguar outright in 1989 for $2.5 billion.

Land Rover's image and reputation was also built in the United Kingdom. The two automakers even shared the same parent company in the 1960s when they were owned by British Leyland Company, which became BMC. Land Rover spun off from BMC and operated independently in the United Kingdom until being acquired by Bayerische Motoren Werke AG (BMW) in 1994. It was then sold to Ford in 2000.

Tata Motors' Market in India

Ratan had always had a personal interest in automobiles and even considered applying his Cornell architecture degree to the field of auto design following graduation from college. Instead, he spent two years working on the floor of Tata Steel and gained an intimate understanding of the business and its capabilities. Throughout his ascension to the top of Tata Motors, he won traction with Indians by catering to their price sensitivity, but he did so with the long-term goal of extending the company's reach outside India's borders. He believed, however, that it was necessary to establish a sufficient base in India before expanding to Europe and the Americas.[6]

As Ford was experiencing a fluctuating market in the West (Exhibit 1), Tata Motors was capitalizing on an emerging automotive market in India (Exhibit 2). In an attempt to compete with China as an up-and-comer in the global automotive industry, the Indian government passed massive legislation—called the National Highways Authority of India (NHAI) Act—that would fund the creation of highways and other domestic travel infrastructure. The increased ease of transportation would not only broaden the company's capabilities to transport goods around the country but also increase demand for the automobile among Indian citizens.

Before the NHAI Act was passed in 1988, the majority of Indians owned a two-wheel vehicle. Construction associated with the act was scheduled to be completed between 2005 and 2007, which coincided with Ratan's unveiling of the Nano; analysts called the timing a stroke of brilliance.

The task of building "The People's Car," as the Nano was sometimes called, began with Ratan's directive to Tata Motors that it was in a time of great opportunity and it had to capitalize. There was competition from other firms to supply a car to the Indian consumer that could be safe and reliable. The auto firm Mahindra & Mahindra had recently begun to distribute the Maruti 800, which

Exhibit 1 Ford's Revenues 2003–2007

Year	Automotive Revenues (in billions of U.S. dollars)	Growth
2003	138.2	
2004	147.1	6.44%
2005	153.5	4.35%
2006	143.3	−6.64%
2007	154.4	7.75%

Data source: Ford Motor Company annual reports, 2003–2007.

Exhibit 2 Tata Motors Financials 2003–2007

Sources of Revenue				
	2003–04	**2004–05**	**2005–06**	**2006–07**
Domestic Vehicle Sales	85.70%	85.14%	80.88%	82.80%
Exports	6.75%	7.35%	9.86%	8.55%
Vehicle Spare Parts	4.26%	3.79%	4.05%	3.77%
Dividend	0.38%	0.80%	1.19%	0.76%
Hire Purchase	0.90%	0.77%	1.78%	n/a
Other	2.04%	1.87%	2.23%	4.12%

Uses of Revenue				
	2003–04	**2004–05**	**2005–06**	**2006–07**
Materials	57.05%	59.77%	60.23%	61.78%
Taxes & Duties	17.93%	17.16%	16.45%	16.23%
Operation & Other Expenses	10.87%	9.43%	9.53%	9.29%
Employees	5.67%	5.03%	4.71%	4.26%
Reserve	3.16%	3.49%	3.96%	3.85%
Shareholders	1.81%	2.20%	2.05%	1.80%
Depreciation	2.46%	2.18%	2.04%	1.82%
Interest	1.04%	0.75%	0.93%	0.97%

Data source: Tata Motors Limited annual report, 2007.

had more features than the Nano—including air conditioning, sun visors, and radio—but it was still roughly twice the price. Ratan rode the wave of India's infrastructure growth by becoming strongly leveraged in domestic vehicle sales. In 2006, 81% of Tata Motors' revenue came from domestic vehicle sales.[7]

Even though car sales in India were robust, Tata Motors faced some brawny competitors—Maruti Udyog Limited (also known as Maruti Suzuki) and Korean-owned Hyundai Motor Company (see Exhibit 3 for key 2007 comparison data).

To produce vehicles in line with regulations and with international appeal, Tata Motors would have to devote a major amount of capital and resources to R&D, and even then, recognition and trust would be granted sparingly. Tata Motors had certainly been successful in joint ventures and acquisitions to expand internationally, but those achievements were largely made by selling generic vehicles on large contracts to governments and other public entities.

Competing globally for luxury buyers would put Tata in the company of four premium brands that dominated the market: BMW, Mercedes, Audi, and Volvo (85% in 2006).[8] And it would require becoming attractive to a distinct group of car owners, a majority of whom were 55 years and older (Exhibit 4).[9] Several other factors

Exhibit 3 Competitor Data, 2007 (in millions of U.S. dollars except as noted)

	Hyundai	**Maruti Udyog**	**Tata**
New car market share, India	17.3%	55.3%	20.6%
Luxury brands	Genesis (concept car 2007)	SX4 Grand Vitara XL7	None
Revenues	74,418.6	3,688.0	6,717.2
Net income	1,711.2	377.7	650.5
Profit margin	2.3%	10.2%	9.7%
Total assets	89,650.6	1,850.3	2,820.7
Total liabilities	70,310.1	604.9	1,159.7

Sources: Scott Gibson, "Asian Action Pack; Equities," Abnam. Ambro Research, December 14, 2006; Datamonitor, "New Cars in India," December 2007 (0102-0358); Datamonitor, "New Cars in India," December 2008 (0102-0358).

made this cohort unique. Luxury car owners tended to buy used cars more than new (although the chances of purchasing a new luxury car increased with age and income; see Exhibit 5 for the geographic distribution of the world's richest people), were more likely to pay in cash, were markedly more inclined to see foreign nameplates as more prestigious than domestic, and were less influenced by gas mileage or environmental benefits.[10]

Exhibit 4 U.S. Luxury Car Owner Profile

Race/Ethnicity	% Purchased New
White	92
Black	2
Asian	6
Hispanic	7
Age	
18–24	2
25–34	13
35–44	11
45–54	20
55–64	22
65+	32
Marital Status	
Married	71
Not married	29
Household Income	
Under $25K	12
$25K–$49.9K	12
$50K–$74.9K	18
$75+	57

Data source: "Auto Market: Sport & Luxury Cars, United States, January 2003," Mintel Oxygen database, August 30, 2011.

Exhibit 5 Global Wealth Overview

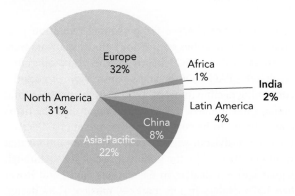

Source: Credit Suisse Research Institute, Global Wealth Report, October 2010, http://piketty.pse.ens.fr/fichiers/enseig/ecoineg/EcoIneg_fichiers/DaviesShorrocks 2010(CSGlobalWealthReport).pdf (accessed September 1, 2011).

Despite the competition, acquiring JLR would put Tata in a niche market and make it one of the truly global players in the automobile industry. The company also had a favorable rating from its customers—a 2006 Customer Satisfaction Study placed Tata at the top of its market for customer satisfaction.[11] That kind of service

would be expected in the luxury brand market and the company would no doubt benefit from it.

Previous Acquisitions

Tata Motors was somewhat of a pioneer in foreign automobile acquisition. In 2004, it became the first India-based automobile firm to make an overseas acquisition when it bought Daewoo Commercial Vehicles. The move was a calculated attempt to meet the company's public goal of increasing its revenue stream from other countries by 10% to 15% over the three-year period of 2004–2007. At the time, Tata Motors was nearing maximum capacity at 200,000 units annually, 85% of which were being sold domestically in India. As a leading South Korean automobile company, Daewoo offered a low-risk means of entering the global auto market for a modest price of $116 million.[12]

The acquisition allowed Tata Motors to combat domestic overexposure because Daewoo had significant markets in South Korea and Pakistan. The deal was also in line with Tata Motors' aggressive global expansion goal. According to Praveen Kadle, executive director of finance, "We acquire a company only if it gives us a new technology, new markets, new products, new customer bases, or a new product development capability. The deal must also make financial sense."[13]

To convince Daewoo that its new Indian owner was capable of a smooth transition, Tata Motors translated all its literature into Korean for the board and hired professional translators to facilitate communication. Tata Motors' management also interacted directly with Daewoo employees and assured them that they would all retain their positions after the acquisition, a promise they would eventually keep. In a poignant tone, Tata Motors' managing director Ravi Kant explained, "We are connected to the local society and want to add value to it. It's not a question of thrusting ourselves. That is one thing, which we are strictly avoiding, anywhere we are going."[14]

In another concerted effort to increase its international presence, Tata Motors acquired a portion of the Spain-based bus company Hispano Carrocera SA (HC) in 2005. The deal gave Tata Motors rights to 21% of HC's shares, technology, and brand rights. Tata Motors was primarily interested in HC's large commercial vehicle platforms and in replicating its compliance with safety and emissions standards. In an act of forward thinking, Tata Motors stipulated in the deal that the remaining 79% of HC could be purchased in the future if both companies came to agreeable terms.

The deal allowed Tata Motors to simultaneously enter the bus market and develop a presence internationally.

Exhibit 6 Tata Motors Vehicle Types 2003–2007

	2003	**2004**	**2005**	**2006**	**2007**
Passenger					
Percent	50%	48%	48%	46%	42%
Number	104,000	140,000	179,000	189,000	228,000
Commercial					
Percent	50%	52%	52%	54%	58%
Number	106,000	152,000	190,000	215,000	299,000

Data source: Tata Motors Limited annual report, 2007

HC produced high-end public transportation buses, which were in high demand in Middle Eastern countries; similar demand was emerging in India as the government's infrastructure overhaul began.

In both the Daewoo and HC acquisitions, Tata Motors was intent on obtaining platform technologies for new vehicle types so it didn't have to engineer new components to generate new categories of vehicles (see Exhibit 6 for vehicle types). As a result of its experience with these two foreign acquisitions (among others), Tata Motors had realistic expectations and confidence pursuing a potential deal with JLR. Kadle said, "The most important thing in acquisitions is human integration. Employees from shop floor workers to senior management must be comfortable about working with us."[15]

Ford and the Premier Automotive Group

The PAG housed Ford's most luxurious and expensive brands: Jaguar, Land Rover, Aston Martin, Volvo, and Lincoln. Formed in 1999, the PAG was intended to separate Ford's marquee brands from its mass-production vehicles. Originally, the group incorporated Volvo, Aston Martin, Jaguar, and Lincoln. Land Rover was added to the group in 2000 when Ford purchased the firm for $2.7 billion. The brands produced anemic returns over the next several years and forced Ford to reevaluate their status and place within the company (Exhibit 7). In 2006, Ford unveiled its "The Way Forward" campaign, which opened discussion about selling off particular brands to avoid further losses. Particularly Jaguar, and to a lesser extent Land Rover, had experienced significant declines in production and sales. In addition to those losses, Ford had continued to invest in marketing and advertising with JLR over the previous six years, which resulted in estimated losses of up to $10 billion.

On the cost side of JLR operations, several factors contributed to what the firm described as *unfavorable earnings*—an increase impairment charge for long-lived assets, costly currency exchange rates (mostly related to

Exhibit 7 Jaguar and Land Rover Financial Data (in millions of U.S. dollars except as noted).

	CY2006	**CY2007**	**CY2008E**
Revenue	12,969	14,942	13,336
Cost of sale	10,909	11,871	10,802
Gross profit	2,060	3,071	2,534
MKTG and selling expense (% to revenue)	8.2	7.2	6.5
R&D expense (% to revenue)	5.3	5.5	5.8
General and admin expense (% to revenue)	2.8	2.4	2.5
EBITDA (prior to adjustment)	26	1037	700
Depreciation	383	387	333

Data source: Data source: Vaishali Jajoo, "Commercial Vehicles Sector Update," Angel Broking, December 2008

hedges), higher charges for personnel-reduction programs, and warranties on previous model year cars were noted as problematic.[16] Based on the year's operating results, the PAG 2006 business plan review projected a continuing decline in net cash flows in the next year and perhaps beyond. There was talk of refocusing the firm's commitment to its core automotive operations. Because PAG was a division within Ford, there were unions that would be affected by the potential sale of JLR. Although Jaguar had 871 dealers in 64 markets, and Land Rover had 1,376 dealers in 138 markets, most of JLR's design and production took place in the United Kingdom; if the brands were sold, it was feared that jobs would be shipped out of the United Kingdom (see Exhibit 8 for dealers, sales, and locations). JLR's presence in the United Kingdom was also due to the fact that a majority of sales took place there and in the United States.

Ford formally decided to sell the JLR brands in June 2007. Over the next several months, Ford accepted bids from a variety of companies including

Exhibit 8 Jaguar and Land Rover Dealers and Sales, 2005–2007

Jaguar			
	2005	**2006**	**2007**
Dealers	880	871	859
Vehicles Sold	89,802	74,593	60,485
Europe	53%	55%	59%
N. America	36%	29%	27%
Asia-Pacific	7%	10%	9%
Rest of World	4%	6%	5%

Land Rover			
	2005	**2006**	**2007**
Dealers	1,400	1,376	1,397
Vehicles Sold	185,120	193,640	226,395
Europe	60%	51%	60%
N. America	26%	26%	23%
Asia-Pacific	7%	8%	7%
Rest of World	7%	15%	10%

Data source: Ford Motor Company annual reports, 2005–2007.

Capital Management LLC, TPG Capital, Mahindra & Mahindra, One Equity, and Tata Motors. By November, Ford had narrowed the offers down to three preferred bidders: One Equity, Mahindra & Mahindra, and Tata Motors. JLR trade union members feared that the buyer would not ultimately be able to maintain the prized and celebrated iconic branding of JLR; to address those union concerns, each bidder would be given the opportunity to present its plan directly to the UK trade unions.

Terms of the Deal

Negotiations between Ford and its suitors dated back to June 2007. Throughout that period, Ford had refined what it was actually selling in addition to the JLR brands. Included in the sale would be access to JLR's R&D departments and ownership of their respective intellectual property. The inclusion of these terms ensured that JLR's new owner would gain ownership of the platforms used to produce all JLR's vehicles.

The sale of JLR was part of a portfolio restructuring Ford was undergoing. Ford had lost $15 billion the previous two years and had decided to dismantle PAG in an attempt to revive its core business. Ford believed that the strength of the entire company rested on the value of the brands under the PAG umbrella, but after 2004, a major

decline in the global automotive industry had begun to diminish that value.

The strategy was part of Ford's "The Way Forward" campaign. It was inefficient to try to maintain such a variety of marques when they were so unprofitable. Ford had spent 15 years and approximately $17 billion to establish and maintain the PAG division. In 2005, Jaguar produced 85,000 vehicles—a 20% reduction from the 100,000 vehicles sold in 2001. And there had been a 37% drop in sales in the same time period. The dismantling of Ford's PAG had begun in 2006 when it put the niche brand Aston Martin up for sale. "As part of our ongoing strategic review, we have determined that Aston Martin may be an attractive opportunity to raise capital and generate value," said Bill Ford, chairman and CEO.[17] By the time Ford decided to sell Jaguar in 2007, the company was not able to cover the fixed production costs. And it had posted losses of $282 million in the first quarter of the year. Part of the conclusion reached by the consultants was that adverse economic conditions in the West had greatly decreased demand for luxury cars (Exhibit 4).

A major obstacle for any company bidding on JLR would be the unions, which represented a large portion of the work force. They complicated the bargaining process by demanding that the new owner keep jobs and plants in the United Kingdom. JLR had strong ties there; its departure would mean many lost jobs and also be a blow to national pride.

When the three bidders presented their proposals to union members, Tata Motors came away a clear favorite because it planned to continue the incumbent business strategy through 2011 using the existing team. Its plans included expanding its presence in emerging markets and keeping management in place. In fact, Tata Motors intended to let all of JLR's 16,000 UK-based employees stay put.[18]

The unions were also concerned that the other two bidders, each backed by private equity firms, did not have the same capabilities to maintain JLR. Tata Motors, however, already had supply chain logistics in place for distribution and would therefore be able to use some of the money saved in those areas to bid higher for JLR.

The financial terms of the deal stipulated that for $2.3 billion, Ford would transfer the entire businesses of JLR to the winning bidder. But none of JLR's debt would be transferred; that included $600 million that Ford agreed to pay into union pensions. Furthermore, Ford would continue to supply the acquirer with various supports and services associated with and tied to the brands. Supplemental support came in the form of accounting services, powertrain supply, vehicle stamping, vehicle components, and technological support.[19]

If Tata Motors won the bid, it would be able to secure the money for the acquisition by obtaining a bridge loan of $3 billion from Citigroup and JPMorgan. Taking on a large loan of short duration during a global financial crisis had analysts skeptical about the Tata Motors deal— especially for a potentially difficult brand to manage. Citing a major decline in JLR's major markets of the United States and United Kingdom and Ford's inability to make a profit on Jaguar in 10 years, S&P threatened to seriously consider downgrading Tata Motors' rating from its lofty B+ status.

In addition to the challenge of taking on large debt, many people were interested in how Tata Motors would go about advertising high-end products that stood in stark contrast to its current line of cars, including the Nano. Tata Motors was also facing new emissions standards litigation from the European Union that all JLR vehicles would have to comply with in the future.[20]

With respect to synergies that could be realized upon the completion of the deal, Ratan was excited about the opportunity to combine his company's stable of sport utility vehicles with Land Rover's lineup. Ratan was prepared to use Land Rover technologies to upgrade his own models and hoped to reduce the cost of Land Rover vehicles with technologies developed during production of the Nano. The upside of Tata Motors' array of products was that there would not be an overlap in competing market segments.

If Ratan made the deal, there would be an immediate need to begin working on a marketing strategy because both Jaguar and Land Rover had promising vehicles in their respective pipelines. Jaguar was moving in the direction of producing performance vehicles: The XFR and XKR, both upgrades from current models, were slated to roll off the assembly line in 2009 (the X-type car had a price tag in the mid-30K range in 2006).[21] Land Rover was in the process of updating the aesthetics of its models by giving their bodies face-lifts and redesigning the interiors of the Range Rover and the Range Rover Sport, which would be unveiled in 2009 (the Range Rover SUV had a price tag in the low-60K range in 2006).[22]

Conclusion

The crowd cheered as Ratan Tata finished speaking and made his way backstage. He was excited and wondered what would come next. If Ford did not choose Tata Motors as the preferred bidder for JLR, Ratan would either have to wait for another brand to be up for sale or try to figure out a way to grow the current Tata Motors brands to enter overseas markets. His stomach churned as he thought of the time and energy it would take to research foreign markets, tailor products to their individual needs, and then find ways to affordably distribute Tata Motors' vehicles.

NOTES

1. Richard S. Chang, "Tata Nano: The World's Cheapest Car," January 10, 2008, Wheels, *New York Times*, http://wheels.blogs.nytimes.com/2008/01/10/tata-nano-the-worlds-cheapest-car/ (accessed December 3, 2010).

2. Christabelle Noronha, "View from the Top," *Tata.com*, http://www.tata.com/aboutus/articles/inside.aspx?artid=DB7yGg47wW4= (accessed December 3, 2010).

3. Datamonitor, "Global Automobiles & Components: Industry Profile," April 2008.

4. John Paul McDuffie, "Should Tata Motors Buy Jaguar and Land Rover?," *Knowledge@Wharton*, September 20, 2007, http://knowledge.wharton.upenn.edu/india/article.cfm?articleid=4226 (accessed December 3, 2010).

5. Datamonitor, "Tata Motors Limited SWOT Analysis," February 8, 2011.

6. http://www.tata.com/aboutus/articles/inside.aspx?artid=DB7yGg47wW4=.

7. Tata Motors Limited annual report, 2006.

8. Bernstein Research, "The E and F Segments," *European Autos: Segmentation and Margins*, 2007.

9. "Auto Market: Sport & Luxury Cars-US-January 2003," via Mintel, (August 30, 2011).

10. Ibid.

11. Datamonitor, "Tata Motors Limited SWOT Analysis," February 2011, 5.

12. Ian Rowley and Nandini Lakshman, "Can Tata Rev Up Jaguar?," *BusinessWeek.com*, March 26, 2008, http://www.businessweek.com/globalbiz/content/mar2008/gb20080326_384146.htm (accessed January 26, 2011).

13. Cynthia Rodrigues, "On the Fast Track: Tata Motors Takes the Inorganic Route to Growth in Its Mission to Go Global," *Tata.com*, April 2006, http://www.tata.com/company/Articles/inside.aspx?artid=zyxxMQvwTA0= (accessed December 3, 2010).

14. http://www.tata.com/company/Articles/inside.aspx?artid=zyxxMQvwTA0=.

15. Ibid.

16. Ford Motor Company 10-K, 2007, 44–6.

17. Sharon Silke Carty, "Will Ford Make the Leap and Sell Jaguar? Aston Martin Is on the Block," *USA Today*, August 31, 2006, http://www.usatoday.com/money/autos/2006-08-31-jaguar-usat_x.htm (accessed January 26, 2011).

18. Heather Timmons, "Ford Reaches Deal to Sell Land Rover and Jaguar," *New York Times*, March 27, 2008.

19. John Neff, "Officially Official: Tata Buys Jaguar Land Rover for $2.3 Billion," *Autoblog*, March 26, 2008, http://www.autoblog.com/2008/03/26/officially-official-tata-buys-jaguar-land-rover-for-2-3-billio/ (accessed December 3, 2010).

20. "Tata Sons to Lend Support for Financing the Deal," *Economic Times* (India), March 27, 2008, http://economictimes.indiatimes.com/news/news-by-industry/auto/automobiles/tata-sons-to-lend-support-forfinancing-the-deal/articleshow/2902766.cms (accessed January 26, 2011).

21. Edmunds website, "Jaguar X-Type Review," http://www.edmunds.com/jaguar/x-type/ (accessed September 1, 2011).

22. Jerry Flint, "Ford's Premier Automotive Goof," *Forbes.com*, July 27, 2004, http://www.forbes.com/2004/07/27/cz_jf_0727flint.html (accessed January 26, 2011) and Edmunds website, "2006 Land Rover LR3 True Cost to Own," http://www.edmunds.com/land-rover/lr3/2006/tco.html?style=100604445&ps=used (accessed September 1, 2011).

Principled Entrepreneurship and Shared Leadership: The Case of TEOCO [The Employee Owned Company][1]

Prof. Thomas Calo, Ed.D.
Perdue School of Business, Salisbury University

Prof. Olivier Roche, PhD
Perdue School of Business, Salisbury University

Prof. Frank Shipper, PhD
Perdue School of Business, Salisbury University

Introduction

Fairfax, October 6, 2009. Atul Jain, founder of TEOCO, a provider of specialized software for the telecommunications industry, had been meeting all day to finalize a partnership agreement with TA Associates, a private equity firm. For Atul, the pace of activities had been relentless on this special day.[2] By all accounts, the last 12 hours had been hectic, but the closing of the transaction was a success. The event had started with back-to-back meetings between TEOCO's senior management and their new partner's representatives and had culminated with the usual press conference to mark the occasion. The senior management teams of both organizations announced to the business community that TA Associates [TA] had made a minority equity investment of $60 million in TEOCO. It was indeed a memorable day, the culmination of intense and uneven negotiations between two organizations that did not have much in common except for deep industry knowledge and a shared interest in seeing TEOCO succeed.

This new partnership marked the end of a marathon, but Atul did not feel the excitement that usually comes with crossing the finish line. It was late and he was tired. Back in the quiet of his office, he reviewed, once again, the draft of the press release relating the day's event. As he read the various statements captured from the meetings, he still had the uneasy feeling that comes with making life-changing decisions when one does not have all the required information. There were so many unknowns. Partnering with the right investor, like many other entrepreneurial endeavors, was not a decision made in a vacuum. It was all about good timing, cold analysis, gut feeling and luck; the latter was last but by no means least. Despite all the uncertainty, Atul felt that this was a worthy endeavor.

Atul had come a long way since his humble beginnings in India and a lot was at stake, not only for him but also for the 300 employees of the company. The TEOCO enterprise had been a successful business endeavor and at the same time a very personal journey. What had begun as a result of frustration with his old job in Silicon Valley 15 years ago had become one of the fastest growing businesses in the telecom software industry; the fast pace of the company's development had not gone unnoticed. For quite some time now, TEOCO had been on the "radar screen" of investors looking for high-growth opportunities. However, Atul had never cultivated a relationship with potential external investors; he had remained congruous with his long-held business beliefs that an alliance with external financiers was rarely in the best interest of a company and its employees.

Atul [CEO & Chairman]: "I am often asked why we didn't approach an investor for money or seek venture capital. I have two answers to this question. My first answer is: that's not our way of doing business. I believe that every entrepreneur must aspire to be debt-free and profitable from the very first day. My second answer is: nobody would have given me the money even if I had asked! I also had a fear – that external investment might impact the culture and values that I wanted TEOCO to promote and cherish. I wanted to steer the TEOCO ship along a very different course. My dream was to set up an enterprise based on a model of shared success. TEOCO's success wouldn't just be my success; it would be our success. TEOCO wouldn't just have one owner; it would be owned by each of its employees – who would therefore be called employee owners."

But several months earlier, events had taken an unexpected turn; unsolicited financiers approached TEOCO once again, this time offering to invest a substantial amount of capital. Still, Atul was reluctant to engage in negotiations with a party that, as far as he knew, did not share TEOCO's values.

Atul: "[In the early days]we took a conscious decision not to accept venture capital. I have always had a healthy disdain for venture capital because it numbs the entrepreneur's competitive edge and enfeebles him. I still remember TEOCO's early battles with [competitors] Vibrant and Broadmargin and how difficult it was for us to compete with all that extra money flowing into the rivals' coffers. But we took the hard road – and survived….What, then, went wrong with Broadmargin or Vibrant? If I have to over-simplify, I'd say that both were done in by venture capital. VC is an impatient master; it forces you to always go for the home run, and always push hard on the gas. With certain kinds of businesses this works; indeed, it might be the only way. Think of Google: their business space is so vast that only continuous and unbridled growth can sustain the venture. But TEOCO's space is very different; there is no exponential growth here that everyone can go chasing…I would guess that the size of the telecom Cost Management business is no larger than $100 million per year; so to survive you have to be patient and play your cards carefully. This isn't the place to be if you are in a tearing hurry to grow…. While this strategy of focusing on niche markets significantly limits our market potential, it does keep the sharks away. The big companies are not bothered by niche products for telecom carriers; they don't want to swim in small ponds."

Atul's comment reflected the situation a few years ago; TA's recent partnership offer was made in a new context. In this rapidly changing industry, there are constantly new directions in technology and the landscape continually shifts. The industry, consolidating quickly, required that in order to remain a viable player, TEOCO would have to change gears – sooner rather than later.

Until now, the primary focus of the company had been on the North American telecom carriers. However, with the anticipated consolidation of the telecom industry in North America, TEOCO needed to focus on international expansion. In addition, to leverage TEOCO's deep expertise in cost, revenue and routing, the company would soon need to fish "outside the pond" and enter the global business support system / operations support system (BSS/OSS) market. Here, TEOCO could find itself in competition with much larger players, and it would be valuable to have a strong financial partner.

Indeed, the company had reached an important threshold in its organizational development. But if TEOCO was at a crossroads, so was its founder. Atul was in his late forties and he was not getting any younger. In this industry Atul had known many entrepreneurs who, like himself, had rapidly grown their businesses only to find out that "you are only as good as your last call." For a few of these entrepreneurs, one or two poor decisions had triggered a descent that had been as swift as their earlier ascent, and they ended up with very little to show for their efforts. These were the intangibles. During rare moments of quiet reflection, Atul realized that his "risk return profile" had changed imperceptibly over time. Having all his eggs in the same basket and going for all or nothing had been fun in his mid-thirties when everything was possible, but it would be much less so in his early fifties when starting from scratch would be a very unappealing scenario for Atul and his family. Furthermore, he felt an obligation to create liquidity for the employees who had supported him on this fifteen - year journey and had their own dreams and goals. At the end of the day, any business has only three exit options: it could get listed, be sold or go bankrupt! And the latter option is not particularly appealing.

It was in this context and mindset that he had agreed to listen to what TA Associates had to offer. Founded in 1968, TA had become one of the largest private equity firms in the country. The company was managing more than $16 billion in capital by 2009, and it had an extensive knowledge of the industry. Atul was impressed by TA's approach, its willingness to take a minority position, and Kevin Landry, Chairman and the "spirit" of TA. This private equity firm not only managed capital; it also had an impressive network of relationships. In addition, TA executives had been adamant that Atul remain in charge, and he was keen on continuing as the controlling shareholder. The fund would appoint two board members (see Appendix 1), but TEOCO's current management team would still lead the company as it had in the past.

Reviewing the details, Atul could not spot any flaws in the logic of the transaction. It was neither a marriage of love nor a "shotgun wedding," just a pragmatic alliance between two companies with complementary skills and resources at a time when such an alliance was valuable to both parties: TA looking for a good investment and TEOCO shareholders looking for partial liquidity. As Atul re-read the press release and a few of his quotes, he reflected that he meant every word.

Atul: *"We are pleased to welcome TA as our first institutional investor. As a company that has avoided external capital for 15 years, we are delighted to find a partner that will strengthen TEOCO without changing the culture of our organization. We see this as the beginning of a new phase in TEOCO's history where we look to add even greater value to communications service providers worldwide."*

This was definitely a new era and there would be no turning back. For better or for worse, this partnership had to work. Atul made minor corrections to the wording of the document and authorized its release.

Company Background and Activities

TEOCO's predecessor, Strategic Technology Group (STG), was founded as an S corporation in 1994. The company's initial focus was to provide high quality consultancy for IT projects. STG's first clients included Mobil, Siemens, Cable & Wireless, SRA, TRW and Freddie Mac. The company started operations in April 1995 and three years later, in March 1998, the company name was changed to TEOCO (The Employee Owned Company). At the same time, TEOCO made the strategic decision to shift its business from consultancy to product development and to focus on the telecommunications industry. This was achieved through the acquisition of a fledgling software product that processed invoices of telecom payables. BillTrak Pro would ultimately become TEOCO's best-selling network cost management software.

Subsequently, the company grew rapidly. As the number of employees exceeded 75, the maximum numbers of shareholders an S corporation can have, the company changed its status to a C corporation to enable a broad-based employee ownership. Over the years

preceding the burst of the "Dot.com" bubble, TEOCO not only expanded its client base for its basic products but also invested substantial amounts of capital in three startups. These entities were: *netgenShopper.com* for online auctions; *Eventrix*, an event planning portal; and *AppreciateYou.com* to support employee retention. These internet startups functioned as separate entities, each at their own location, with their own business goals and core values, managed by different entrepreneurs/managers; at the same time, they each relied on TEOCO's cash flow for their development.

Ultimately, none of these ventures emerged as viable businesses and this left TEOCO in a difficult financial situation. As a result, TEOCO registered its first year of losses in 2000.

Atul: *"This failure was devastating, but also a humbling experience. I learned the hard way that no entrepreneur can survive inside a technology incubator. We had to pay a price for all these transgressions…Our revenues were still impressive, but the money in the bank was dwindling rapidly… We were truly caught in deep and dangerous waters. I have often wondered what went wrong. It wasn't as if we made one big mistake….I guess we just took our eyes off the ball. Somewhere along the way, we lost our focus; we tried to do too many things at the same time and ended up getting nothing right. We had to quickly get back to our knitting. The question was: how?"*

Under Atul's leadership, TEOCO made the judicious decision to refocus its activities on its core industry expertise and its largest clients. To achieve this, the organization solidified its position in the telecom sector by improving its services and developing new products. In 2004, research and development efforts resulted in the patented XTrak technology which today represents the core of the company's invoice automation solution. In addition, TEOCO was able to migrate from software licensing to the far more lucrative software-as-a-service model. Instead of a fixed licensing fee, the company charged a recurring monthly fee based on the volume of data processed for each client. As the recurring revenue model took hold, it became much easier to grow revenues from year to year and improve the company's profitability.

In 2006, TEOCO acquired Vibrant Solutions, bringing in cost management and business intelligence assets with its 24 employees. Ultimately this resulted in the important development of TEOCO's SONAR solution for cost, revenue and customer analytics. Finally, in 2008, Vero systems was acquired, adding routing management and its 36 employees to the repertoire of communication service provider solutions.

This stream of acquisitions and internal development left TEOCO with a staff of about 300 employees and a portfolio of three major activities: cost management, least cost routing and revenue assurance.

Cost Management

Cost management solutions include invoice automation and payable processing. Powered by XTrak, TEOCO's invoice automation solution processes over 1,000,000 invoices annually. This facilitates the audit and analysis of billions of dollars in current billings due to each telecom company. While the usual scanning of paper bills relies on optical character recognition technologies that routinely require hands-on intervention to correct misrepresented characters on complex invoices, the XTrak technology mines the original formats which produced the paper to create files for loading into cost management solutions. By eliminating the tedious, costly and error-prone task of manual invoice data entry, telecom companies increase productivity and reduce costs by increasing the number of disputes filed and resolved and by reducing late-payment charges. In addition, TEOCO also processes "payables" on behalf of clients by managing the full life-cycle of invoice payment, including account coding, management review and payment reconciliation. TEOCO's employees audit client invoices, comparing rates, inventory and usage with other source data to identify and recover additional savings. Finally, the company manages disputed claims on behalf of its clients from creation through resolution. TEOCO has the technical capability to capture all correspondence between parties and can review and track every claim to resolution.

With regard to cost management, it is worth noting that the Sarbanes-Oxley Act of 2002 requires every listed company to implement a reliable reporting system. TEOCO's services support this compliance by improving the details and timeliness of the reports generated by/for telecom companies. TEOCO's rapid development in this area coincided with a market need that was augmented by the legal requirements imposed by the Act.

Least Cost Routing

TEOCO's routing solutions help telecom companies determine the optimal route between two customers with regard to cost, quality of service and margin targets. Capable of supporting multiple services and various networks, the company is able to monitor CDRs (Call Detail Records) in near real time to identify bottlenecks, re-route traffic and improve the quality of services for greater satisfaction of its clients' customers.

Revenue Assurance

Communications service providers can lose 5-15% of gross revenue due to revenue leakage. TEOCO's SONAR solution is an industry first in supporting switch-to-bill reconciliation. TEOCO combines its specialized industry expertise with high-capacity data warehouse appliances to create a unified CDR and makes a high volume of current and historical CDR data available on a single platform for in-depth analysis. This helps telecom companies uncover billing discrepancies, detect fraudulent behavior, reveal usage patterns, understand customer profitability, conduct margin analysis, and determine the financial viability of reciprocal compensation agreements.

Industry Landscape: Continuous Change

Competitors

TEOCO operates in a fragmented and highly competitive industry. Appendix 2 lists its competitors in each of the three major business segments. TEOCO operates mostly in North America; therefore, the main competitors in the cost management segment are Razorsight, Connectiv and Subex. These same companies compete for revenue assurance, as well as others such as cVidya and Wedo. Finally, in the least cost routing segment, TEOCO faces a different set of competitors: Pulse Networks, Global Convergence Solutions and Telarix.

Brian [Marketing & Communications Department]: "So [from the customer's point of view] what we bring to the table is just end-to-end solutions that reach all of these different categories. While we still compete with certain people, it's on a specific product; not across the board."

Indeed, with the possible exception of Subex, none of the above competitors operates in the same three business segments as TEOCO, and Subex does not provide a domestic least cost routing in North America. Since TEOCO derives 50% of its revenue from cost management and 25% from revenue assurance, Razorsight and Subex could be considered TEOCO's main business competitors. Faye summarizes TEOCO's current market position.

Faye [General Manager/Account Management]: "In North America, we dominate the cost management space. We've got a decent lock on least cost routing, which is a very operational and technical function that bridges between network and finance."

One of the ways TEOCO differs from most of its VC-backed competitors is its focus on internal cost management. This manifests itself in two different ways. The management begins the year by making a conservative revenue plan for the year. The company then manages its expenses to be a fixed percentage of the projected revenues. Investments in Sales, Marketing, and R&D are adjusted throughout the year to ensure that expenses stay within the pre-defined limits. The second way cost management manifests itself is how the cost of each individual transaction is closely managed and monitored, whether it be purchasing hardware, leasing office space, renewing supplier contracts, recruiting new employees, or planning business travel.

One of the consequences of this strong discipline of cost management is that TEOCO is consistently profitable, something most of its competitors struggle to accomplish. This enables the company to focus its energy on clients and innovation.

Clients

TEOCO operates in an industry where clients are known and clearly identifiable. One of the key reasons clients buy from TEOCO is because its solutions have a strong ROI (Return on Investment). In other words, TEOCO's products quickly pay for themselves and then begin to generate profits for the companies that subscribe to them.

Faye: "The telecommunication space is who we sell to exclusively, and within that space, we have a relatively known and discrete customer list or target list, if you will. We don't sell cookies. Not everybody's going to buy what we're selling...I know who those customers are and I can identify groups within that addressable market that fall into natural tiers. So either because of their size or because of the market that they cater to themselves, whether they're wireless or wire line or whether they're cable companies, I can identify who they are and then try to focus products and services that I think will best meet their needs."

There are four telecom companies that drive about 65% of TEOCO's domestic revenue: Verizon, Sprint, AT&T and Qwest; these are the "platinum" accounts. For obvious reasons, they get a lot of attention from both the engineering and product delivery standpoints. Thirty-five other companies, including Cricket, Global Crossing, Metro PCS, Level 3 and Bell Canada, account for the remaining balance of revenues.

TEOCO, like most of its competitors, is client-centered. Smooth customer interactions are not only critical to increase sales and garner new relationships but also to develop new products. Over the years, most of the ideas

for new products or improvements to existing products have come out of discussions with customers.

Hillary [Marketing & Communications Department]: "Our number one avenue for receiving customer feedback is our TEOCO summit, our annual user meeting... where customers are able to talk one-on-one with not only TEOCO representatives but also with other customers to learn what they are doing...and then circling back with TEOCO."

Initially, TEOCO used its generic products, either developed in-house or brought in via acquisitions, to start relationships with new clients. More recently, however, the company has innovated solutions driven by specific clients. These, in turn, are adjusted to suit the needs of other clients. Dave describes this "evolutionary loop."

Dave [Software Architect]: "With our first product [BillTrak Pro], we sold it to a number of different carriers resulting in a broad footprint of wireline and wireless carriers. Then we had account managers engage with our customers, and it's through conversations with our existing customers, generally, that the ideas for the next set of products come out... More recently, I'd say that most of our products are customer-driven, so what will happen is we'll have someone in the company that will identify a need at a specific customer. Then, we'll enter into some kind of partnership with them, whether we'll develop the application specifically to their needs and then work to resell that and make it useful to other customers as well."

Growth Strategies

TEOCO's Product Strategy: "Spidering" through Clients' Organizations

Since the number of clients is limited, two other ways to grow the business are cultivated. A company like TEOCO can either "productize" its current services or acquire a competitor with a different client base and cross-sell its products.

Faye: "But for the products we're selling, if we have two new sales a year, that's significant ... maybe you could squeak out a third in a good year. So the majority of the sales growth really comes from existing accounts...most of the growth though is coming from those large platinum accounts. Those are the ones that have money to spend and where we're driving products, driving solutions, trying to help them tell us or help them identify where they have needs. The other way to grow the business is to acquire companies that have a different business and then cross-sell services. For instance, with the Vero acquisition, we added another 'vertical' line of business [least cost routing]…And then Vero had a relatively separate client base… so we were able to cross-sell products into each other's companies' portfolio of clients [i.e., TEOCO's clients buying least cost routing services and Vero's clients buying cost management products]."

Faye joined the company in March 2010, a few months after TA's investment in TEOCO with a charter to grow TEOCO's revenues with its smaller customers. With Faye in position, the company became more market-driven and far more aggressive in cross-selling its services and products among the three main lines of business. As well, it adopted a more cohesive approach to expand the client base, including leveraging its reputation for excellence and for having the technical ability to solve problems across various business segments.

Faye: "We're 'spidering' through [our clients'] organizations. With each additional organization that we enter into, the stickier we become. Our software products run the gamut from mission critical to nice-to-have. And the more mission criticals and nice-to-haves we get, the stickier we are in that organization, in all the organizations…. [For instance]…I'm not going outside AT&T, but I have – instead of two customers at AT&T, I now have ten. And they're distinctly different sales each time."

TEOCO's Acquisition Strategy

For the first ten years of TEOCO's existence, Atul had built the business based on the premise that growth had to be organic and financed through internal cash flow. To some extent, his views on acquisition were consistent with his opinions about external financing from VCs and private funds. For Atul, acquisition and growth financed by external funds represented a risky development strategy that could dilute a company's culture.

However, as noted earlier, internal growth through innovation had been slow and limited in scope. Cross-selling products between vertical lines of business coming from acquired companies with a different client base offered far more potential for the organization's growth. Therefore, it was just a matter of time before TEOCO would decide to "experiment" with acquisitions:

Atul: "When we started building TEOCO, I was very focused on organic growth. I felt that acquisitions tend to dilute culture and values. But then we happened to acquire a company called Vibrant Solutions (in 2006) and that acquisition went so phenomenally well, it gave us a lot of encouragement. The people were great, the product was solid and the client relationships were very valuable. They integrated well into our company and into our culture. We felt it made TEOCO a much stronger company. We had just broadened from cost management into revenue management before we acquired Vibrant, but I don't believe we would have been as successful in delivering on that without the expertise of the people that came from that acquisition."[3]

The subsequent acquisition of Vero in 2008 brought TEOCO closer to the network and strengthened its position in the marketplace, particularly with the larger customers. This reinforced TEOCO's belief that acquisition of carefully selected targets should be a key component of its overall growth strategy.

Atul: "So at the end of that I said to myself maybe my narrow-minded thinking about acquisition diluting the culture was wrong, that in fact, if you do it right, you have an opportunity to strengthen the culture."[4]

From these two positive experiences, Atul established guidelines for the kinds of companies to target when scanning the market for future acquisitions. TEOCO would look for companies that:

- Had people with deep industry expertise;
- Offered solutions/products that the marketplace valued;
- Had a solid customer base that had been established over time;
- Offered potential synergies with current products/services offered by TEOCO;
- Had not been able to develop their full potential due to poor management;
- Had a manageable size to facilitate their integration into TEOCO's current businesses.

Atul: "One thing you will see in the companies we acquire is that before the acquisition those companies were not running that smoothly. If they were, perhaps they wouldn't be up for sale or be affordable. We tend to acquire companies that present a challenge but also an opportunity for us to improve the business and make it much stronger and more valuable."[5]

What enabled TEOCO to successfully integrate Vibrant and Vero into its business? TEOCO brought to the table: 1) a solid core business that generated a positive and stable cash flow; 2) a well-established strength in cost management (not only for its clients but also for itself); and 3) a disciplined approach to the management of human resources. Indeed, TEOCO is conservatively managed, and Atul is recognized by employees for his ability to select and retain the best while optimizing the use of the organization's human resources. TEOCO core strengths, when applied to the business of Vibrant and Vero, resulted in a bigger and better company.

TTI Acquisition Rationale: Going Global and Getting "Closer to the Network"

In December 2009, TEOCO began to consider the acquisition of the company that would become in 2010 its biggest acquisition ever – TTI Telecom. TTI was an Israel-based global supplier of service assurance solutions to communications service providers. The company had 300 employees and was listed on NASDAQ (TTIL). Through this acquisition, TEOCO would gain access to a wide array of intellectual property including a Mediation Platform, Fault Management and Performance Management Systems, and valuable expertise in 4-G and data-centric networks. Service assurance is important in a data environment because it reduces jitter and packet loss during the delivery of high value data transfer. To some extent, TEOCO's existing portfolio of services and products would expand on TTI's well-recognized expertise in the next generation network (i.e., 4-G). In addition, TTI had an international client base that offered the potential to cross-sell TEOCO's existing product lines. In August 2010, TEOCO completed the acquisition, thus taking a big step in a new direction which, as of this writing, has yet to show conclusive results, but is considered a positive move.

Atul (at the time of the TTI acquisition): "Our last acquisition was Vero Systems (in October, 2008) and that brought us one step closer to the network. We were doing least cost routing and in that world you are trying to help determine how to terminate calls in the most cost-effective manner. The Vero solution got us working with network players and got us into the switches. It became clear that the closer we got to the network, the better business value we could create. So we started looking for companies that have intellectual property and an international client base that would bring us even closer to the network. TTI [Telecom] really fit that bill for us. TEOCO has traditionally been focused on North America so we thought acquiring a company with an international client base was of value to us. Their solutions in fault management, performance management and service management all bring us closer to network and assuring Quality of Service. We are good at handling large volumes of data and deriving intelligence out of that data. And we convert that intelligence into business value. A lot of people can derive intelligence from data but they aren't able to create actionable intelligence that creates bottom line value. We think we will be able

to improve the economics of the data TTI collects for our customers. It may be a little into the future, but we believe this acquisition positions us to get to that future."[6]

TTI Acquisition Challenges

From a technical and marketing point of view, the acquisition of TTI represented a very logical move that would allow TEOCO to expand its business while remaining focused on telecom carriers. It fit many of the acquisition criteria that Atul had laid out (see prior section), but it also represented a substantial departure from previous acquisitions in three critical aspects: its size, its location and culture, and the means of its acquisition.

1. **The Size of the Target Company:** In terms of revenues, TTI was four to five times larger than the last acquisition made by TEOCO, and this purchase effectively doubled the size of the organization. On that point, Atul was the first to recognize that TEOCO was entering uncharted territories.

    Atul: "All the other acquisitions were small. We bought a company with 24 employees, we bought a company with 36 employees, and this time we bought a company with 300 plus employees. So, this is going to present a completely different challenge and I don't know what that is going to be because I haven't dealt with it. So, it's yet to come."

    From the outset, and unlike prior acquisitions, TTI remained an entity that was managed separately. Therefore, one of the key issues to be addressed in the short to medium term would be the degree of integration between the two companies.

2. **The Location and Culture of the Target Company:** TEOCO had essentially been operating in the U.S., whereas TTI was located in Israel and was far more international in its operations. This created tremendous opportunities for marketing synergies and for cross-selling products to a different client base.

    Faye: "So I see leveraging a lot of the existing sales and marketing resources in Israel. I mean they have a strong presence in Israel, but they're really European. EMEA is big. But also CIS, they do a lot in Russia. … MTS is one of their customers, which is just a huge, huge Russian company. Internationally, it's a brand new client base into which we can cross-sell the least cost routing and probably not the cost management products because they don't translate outside of North America as well. But certainly the least cost routing products. Taking their products into the North American base is definitely something we can do. And as far as clients' crossover versus new, they have about ten North American customers, only four of whom are existing customers of ours."

At the same time, however, it also exposed TEOCO's business to a pool of larger competitors that competed on a global basis. TTI was "swimming in a different pond" in which blue chip companies with well-recognized brands and deep pockets were aggressively marketing their services.

Faye: "We participate in a handful of shows, and again, that's expanding quite a bit this year because of the international presence and customer base…it's further complicated, though, by this acquisition of TTI because … they are a very sales and marketing-centric company, and it's going to be interesting to see how the cultures meld. … I see a lot of Advil for me between now and then. We're going to have to get there. Traditionally, TTI has gone to a lot of shows and they like to build brand new booths and spend hundreds of thousands of dollars for each of these shows on their presence there, and [at TEOCO] we don't do that."

Indeed, TEOCO's management was cost conscious and not prepared to invest heavily in shows and other marketing activities where Return on Investment (ROI) is difficult to measure. It was not evident how the two cultures would merge. TTI management might argue that substantial resources would be needed to compete in their market segment while TEOCO's management would probably take the position that overspending on marketing and poor cash-flow management were the reasons for TTI's financial problems prior to its acquisition.

3. **The Means of Acquisition:** One cannot understand the acquisition of TTI without first understanding how the alliance with TA changed the company's and CEO's ways of doing business, as well as their risk/return profile. To some extent TA gave TEOCO's management both the means and the incentives to take more risks. TA's involvement provided TEOCO with the credentials to approach financial institutions and increase the company's financial leverage to acquire a large target. It is one thing when a US$50 million company approaches a bank to finance the acquisition of another company of equivalent size. It is quite another when a US$16 billion equity firm with a substantial stake in the acquirer approves the transaction at the board level. Following TA's equity participation, no one ever asked TEOCO if they had the means to acquire TTI and complete the

transaction. The legitimacy provided by TA's participation was essential for the financing of the acquisition of a listed company where time is of the essence.

Avi Goldstein [CFO]: "Before TA came on board, taking debt was something that was not on the table. And when TA came on board and they asked us, 'Are you willing to take debt to finance acquisitions?' and we said, 'Yes'… And maybe without TA we wouldn't go after TTI because of the debt, not so much because of the size of TTI."

While providing the means to be more aggressive in TEOCO's growth strategy, the partnership with TA also reduced Atul's aversion to risk. It was the TA "push-and-pull" strategy (i.e., providing the financial means while reducing the acceptable risk threshold) that allowed this transaction to materialize.

Atul: "I haven't fully understood how the TA transaction has changed us. I think, over time, I will understand how it has changed us. All I can tell you is that I feel a degree of financial independence and I personally feel that it is more important for me to focus on making a greater difference for the world. I don't know that I could have supported this acquisition if I hadn't gotten liquidity because this acquisition had a much higher risk profile."

Company Culture and Philosophy

The background and evolution of TEOCO provide the context for exploring the unique way in which the organization functions, which in turn explains the basis for its success. Three different lenses provide the focus for this understanding: shared leadership; a culture of employee ownership; and human resources as a strategic function. These three characteristics have combined to contribute to TEOCO's success, as well as its competitive advantage.

Shared Leadership

The shared leadership team is comprised of three leaders of the organization with distinctly different, but complementary, skills and responsibilities. These leaders are Atul Jain (Chairman and CEO), Philip M. Giuntini (Vice Chairman and President) and John Devolites (Vice President and General Manager). (See Appendix 3.)

Atul is the central figure in the story of TEOCO. By understanding Atul's background, philosophy of life, vision and style, the organization and its unique culture create a cohesive portrait.

Atul was born in India in the early 60s. He has an older sister and an older brother. His father was a mid-level civil servant in India, now retired. Both of his parents live with him and his family, which is customary in Indian culture. Atul is married and has three children. His intellect and abilities were identified at an early age. When he was a teenager, he was invited to attend the prestigious Indian Statistical Institute, known as one of the best schools in India for the study of statistics, which required that the young Atul move away from home to live in another part of the country.

Atul was raised in the Indian religion of Jainism, an important aspect of his background that shaped his view of people and organizations. While he does not wear his religion "on his sleeve," it is evident that his religious beliefs and upbringing have had a significant impact on his leadership style and the culture he has shaped within TEOCO. Atul does not go to temple and does not even pray, so in that sense he does not consider himself to be a religious person. On the other hand, he expressed that he has internalized the culture and religion and that it manifests in his thinking about business. Jainism is an ancient but minority religion in India,[7] yet its influence far exceeds its size, as Jains represent some of the wealthiest Indians. Among its core beliefs are a philosophy of non-violence toward all living things, vegetarianism, a strong belief in self-help and self-support, and a continual striving toward the liberation of the soul. These tenets can be seen in Atul as he believes that everyone is an "independent soul," and that consequently he "can't make you do anything that you don't want to do." What stands out is that this type of thinking is very uncharacteristic for a leader.

Atul: "As a CEO of the company, I understand that I have no control over anybody. I can't get anybody to do anything...so I don't spend my time trying to control people... what I try to do is to conduct myself in a manner that may encourage people to work in a certain way. I can try to create an environment that is encouraging, an environment in which people wish to excel."

When he came to the United States it was not to be an entrepreneur but to study for a doctorate degree in Probability and Statistics. He describes himself as an "accidental entrepreneur." A disillusioning experience working for a Silicon Valley firm led him to reconsider his options. When commitments regarding future assignments and compensation were not honored, and he felt disrespected by the company's CFO, he became motivated to take the risk to establish his own company to prove that "you don't have to be an *&%$# in order

to succeed in business." At the same time, this experience impressed upon him the importance of treating his future colleagues with fairness and respect.

Atul's personal leadership style, which is reflected by the organization overall, is quite atypical, especially for an entrepreneur. Atul openly admits his shortcomings. While manifesting many of the traits of an entrepreneur, he sets himself apart by claiming that one of his greatest strengths is that he knows what he does not know. In fact, he even says, "I know that I don't know how to run a business." In conjunction with his perceived shortcomings, he also believed that you create joy at work by sharing the decision making with others in the organization. The end result was his desire to establish a structure of shared leadership within TEOCO. He demonstrated this by establishing a "Steering Committee" of the senior employees within one year of the existence of the company, much prior to his association with Philip and John.

While there has been much discussion in the management literature on the potential value of shared leadership, few organizations have attempted it, and even fewer have utilized it successfully. In many respects, the notion of shared leadership is quite contrary to traditional beliefs about leadership in U.S. organizations, which have strongly followed the military model of command and control. Atul's personal background and beliefs, coupled with a unique confluence of circumstances, have made shared leadership a major factor contributing to the success of TEOCO.

To understand why shared leadership at TEOCO was both possible and successful requires an understanding of the unique combination of personalities, leadership strengths and styles, along with the career and life circumstances – not only of Atul, the founder and CEO, but also the other two members of the leadership team: Philip, President; and John, General Manager.

Philip was a very successful, retired executive. Atul read an article in the *Washington Post* in September, 1998, that profiled Philip's retirement from American Management Systems (AMS) after 28 years. He contacted Philip, established a relationship with him, and eventually persuaded him to become a member of TEOCO's Board of Advisors. Within a year, Philip agreed to come out of retirement to serve as the Vice Chairman and President.

John followed a path similar to Philip's. He served as President of Professional Services for Telecordia. His earlier career experiences included executive positions at PriceWaterhouseCoopers, American Management Systems (AMS), and Booz Allen Hamilton. He became a member of the board in 2000, and in February 2004 he joined the company as a senior executive. In January 2005, he assumed the role of General Manager of its Telecom Business unit.

Personalities: In contrast with these two veteran executives, Atul was an entrepreneur with little or no experience in running a sizable business. However, he was a leader with a vision, strong intellect and a passion to build a successful company. In explaining why shared leadership works at TEOCO when it has not worked at many other organizations, Atul says that "I recognize that Philip and John are far more seasoned business professionals than me…. I go to them for guidance and advice and I will rarely do things that they do not agree with." That said, Atul acknowledged that there are many challenges to shared leadership.

Atul: "The single biggest thing it requires on my part is to give up a ton of decision-making authority, and most people in a CEO chair are not willing to do that. I have to be subservient to John and Philip, and I'm happy to be … I feel that it is not in my personality to be authoritative… being forced to conduct myself in an authoritative manner is offensive to my soul."

John underlined the importance of personality in ensuring the success of shared leadership. While working at consulting firms, he had studied this concept and he commented, "I will tell you that when you look at the situation, it comes back to the individuals and the egos that they have. And if they have large egos, this would not work." When first asked about describing shared leadership at TEOCO, he responded by suggesting, "How about shared fate?"

Complementary Management Skills: The skill sets of these leaders are very complementary, and together form a powerful combination for organizational success. This was described separately, and consistently, by each of them. Atul excels at cost management and judging people.

Atul: "I really see my role as primarily focusing on culture and values and candidly I own all the decisions related to the ownership structure and internal management. However, I don't build anything and I don't sell anything."

Referring to Atul's strengths in cost management and people management, as opposed to direct customer interface, John noted that Atul rarely has customer interface, as Atul entrusts this responsibility to him. John's own skills and interests are focused on creativity and client relations. He sees his job as assembling people around clients and projects, and keeping customers happy. Finally, Philip is the one who makes it all happen. He is

skilled at running a business that will endure, and has the organizational skills to free up Atul and John to do what they do best. As Philip describes, "We are all strong in a different place. Collectively, when we are together, we basically combine our strengths and eliminate our weaknesses…we do not compete with each other in our strong areas, and I think that is the key to it." John adds, "We would not be as successful if one of the other two of us weren't here." Atul shares the same view but from a different angle.

Atul: "I understand that I have certain strengths, and I tend to focus on playing to those strengths, and I have an understanding of what I'm not. … I think incompetence can be valuable, if you know it. If you recognize that you don't know what to do, you're forced to ask others and the resulting collaborative environment has a power of its own."

Career and Life Circumstances: While personality and skills are important factors, it appears as well that life circumstances were a necessary pre-condition to the effectiveness of the collaborative model at TEOCO. In their own way, each of these leaders acknowledged that at a different time and place, shared leadership would not necessarily have been a model they would have liked or one with which they would have been successful. As John described, "I think you have to be at a point in your life where you're pretty comfortable with who you are." All three of these men, as a result of their career circumstances, have done well in their professional lives. All of them have "builder" personalities; they derive a great deal of satisfaction from growing a business. For these leaders, the journey of growing TEOCO into a successful enterprise is as important as the end result.

Culture of Employee Ownership

Atul has shaped the culture of TEOCO and ensures that it is continuously reinforced. This culture is founded upon the core values of the company. As he expresses it, "I define success as 'living up to your values.'" Those values are rooted in a business philosophy he calls "principled entrepreneurship," which he defines as "a business where you have a set of values and you commit to living up to those values while trying to create business success." He further specifies, "They have to be a clear set of articulated values." In describing his success, he says that "what motivates me is to make as big a difference as I can for as many people as I can. And I was never in it solely for the money."

TEOCO has a clearly articulated set of core values (see Appendix 4) and a very distinct culture. Atul explains that the former were established even before he knew what the words "core values" meant. The initial slogan for the company was: "We'll take care of our employees, they'll take care of our clients, and that will take care of the business." He says that the actual articulation of and focus on "core values" began after he read a 1999 *Inc. Magazine* article based on the book *Built To Last: Successful Habits of Visionary Companies,*[8] which caused him to ask, "*Who* are we?" rather than focusing primarily on "*What* do we want to be?"

A hallmark of TEOCO is the ownership culture that is embedded in the company. As an employee owned company, Atul wants all employees to buy and own TEOCO stock. Yet consistent with his overall philosophy of life, he does not believe he can make anybody buy the stock; he can only give them information and the opportunity to make that decision. He strongly believes that the environment created by employee ownership leads to better organizational performance and stronger employee commitment.

Atul: "I believe in the model of shared success. And I believe that if you share your success with the people that actually influence it and create it, then you create [something] extremely powerful. So, I'm fond of saying that TEOCO is a difficult company to beat – not because we are so good, but because it's tough beating a bunch of employee owners that feel so passionately about what they do."

He and the leadership team continuously seek to create and reinforce an "ownership culture" and have employees take an active part in ownership. Carrie (Director of Human Resources) has worked for TEOCO for seven years; previously she had worked for other organizations with stock programs that create an ownership stake in the company.

Carrie: "I would say that TEOCO is the first company I've worked for where it is as big a deal. And we make it such a large component of the culture and we spend a ton of time from an HR perspective making sure people understand all the different elements of ownership, why we feel it's important to us, what different programs and mechanisms are out there to provide ownership and allow them to have an ownership stake in the company."

Hillary is an employee who has worked for TEOCO for five years in various professional positions, but has not worked at any other companies. She said she realized how much she appreciates the overall work environment at TEOCO when she compared her circumstances with friends. To describe the differences that may exist in working for an employee owned company as opposed to a traditional company, she said, "I think the employees here at TEOCO have a lot more knowledge about what's going on."

Dave, one of the earliest and longest-serving employees, when asked what employee ownership meant to him, said, "I've got a stake in the game. My kid's college education is riding on this whole thing. There are no two ways about it…. I think a lot of the people in the company think that way."

Additionally, John, General Manager, explains further,

"It's keeping people motivated. It's keeping them focused. I think employee ownership helps us with some of those things…. [It's] a very powerful ally when you're in a market that's got a lot of competition in it."

In addition to the organization's core values and corporate culture, the sense of ownership is reinforced through three distinct types of mechanisms: 1) Employees' involvement in the decision-making process; 2) Bonus and Stock Ownership; and 3) A Philosophy of Total Compensation.

Employee Involvement in the Decision-Making Process

The secret to making it work, according to Atul, is that "you have to create a culture of sharing in the decision-making process." The core values of TEOCO are manifested in the degree of employee involvement within the organization, as well as in the many significant ways employees contribute.

All Hands Meeting: At 11:00 a.m. on the first Thursday of every month, an "all-hands meeting" is held for all employees. This is a standing meeting, never moved or cancelled for any reason – one for U.S.-based employees and one for employees in India. For those U.S.-based employees who are geographically dispersed from corporate headquarters, a video feed goes out and an audio feed comes back so that questions can be posed from off-site locations. Each meeting lasts from 60 to 90 minutes and concludes with a pizza lunch.

These meetings have a structured format so that employees know what to expect. First, new employees are introduced; next, employee service anniversaries are acknowledged and celebrated (five, ten and 15 years' service awards are presented); and then there is a monthly drawing for the TeoStar Award. The second half of the meeting more formally introduces its principal objective: leadership providing a business update, as well as any news of particular interest to employees.

Once per quarter the meeting is devoted to detailed financial updates. This is described as an "open book" presentation; there is a review of the balance sheet and client revenues, an update from each line of business, and a discussion of new business prospects. Avi, CFO, elaborated that it is "not only one page of the P & L and one page of the balance sheet; it's pretty extensive." Based on his prior experiences as a CFO, he said this is "like having a shareholder's meeting every quarter." Further, he specified that the company practices "open book management" and that the employees can see the books at any time.

The February meeting each year is devoted to a presentation on the year-end financials, and employees are informed what percent of their target bonus they will receive. As of 2011, all employees with 3+ years of service have received more than 100% of their target bonus for the last several years. Miscellaneous presentations are also made on topics of relevance, such as an update on the internal stock market.

Every meeting concludes with an open segment called "benefits and concerns." First, employees are encouraged to discuss any benefits received or positive experiences that have happened in the company. Mutual support and a form of company "cheerleading" is adopted. This is followed by a unique opportunity for any employee to raise any issue of concern. No question is considered out of bounds, and senior management is expected to respond openly and fully. The only ground rule is that every question must be phrased in the format of "I wish I knew…." For example, "I wish I knew why our financials were not as good this quarter," or "I wish I knew why we do not have a benefit such as…." Atul said that this protocol ensures that concerns are presented in an impersonal and non-offensive manner; rather than being a challenge, each question focuses on looking for an explanation. He said that this approach has been "a game changer," "has really changed the tone of the meetings," and reflects the way in which owners would treat each other.

The A-Team: In addition to the opportunity to raise issues at the all-hands meeting, a standing group of employee representatives meets each month. TEOCO's Advisory Team, simply called the A-Team, serves as an interface between the employee owners and the leadership team. The team is comprised of 12 people: eight full-time members and four alternates. Any employee can bring any issue to the A-Team, and the A-Team can bring any issue they choose to the leadership of the company. Similarly, the leadership can bring any issue to the A-Team. This is considered a mechanism to involve employees in the governance of the business; its chief function is to provide a voice to the employee-owners.

The membership rotates each year, and outgoing members choose the incoming team. By design it is not intended to be composed of management, and the majority of the members are lower-level employees. As well, it intentionally includes a cross-section of members: single, married, from all geographic areas and from different levels within the organization.

Bonus and Stock Ownership

All employees receive an annual cash bonus. The program seems to function more like a traditional profit sharing plan, as it is not individual performance-related. The bonus pool equals 15% of pre-tax and pre-bonus profit of the company for the calendar year. The plan is designed to be entirely transparent. Each employee has a target bonus of 8% of base salary. The eligibility for the bonus percentage increases as the employee rises to different organizational levels, as follows:

20-40% - Executive Leadership;
20% - Vice President;
16% - Senior Principal;
12% - Principal;
8% - all other employees.

Titles have no meaning at TEOCO in the traditional sense of their relationship to a level of job responsibility. Rather, titles are determined on the basis of the employee's value to the company. There is a vice president, for example, who does not manage anyone.

In addition to bonuses, employees can purchase stock or receive stock options. At the initial founding of TEOCO in 1994, the only ownership vehicle was for employees to purchase stock outright. At the beginning of the company, Atul offered employees a specific number of shares to purchase, and he claims that every employee took full advantage of this opportunity. However, by 1999-2000, the value of the stock had risen to a level that Atul explains made it difficult for employees to purchase outright, so traditional stock options were awarded, instead of requiring employees to fully purchase the shares at the time of the grant. While acknowledging that options are necessary, Atul strongly believes that "option holders are not the same as shareholders," because he believes that the mere granting of options does not create ownership.

With regard to purchasing stock, it should be noted that employees have the option of taking their annual bonus in stock up to a maximum of 60%. The remaining 40% is intended for use in paying taxes.

The stock plan also provides for repurchase rights. If an employee terminates, the company has the right to repurchase the stock, with two exceptions. If an employee worked for the company for at least five years and owned the stock for a minimum of three years or if an employee worked for the company for ten years and owned the stock for at least a year, they may retain the stock, with the rationale that since they contributed many years of service to the success of the company, they should be able to continue to benefit. However, for others the stock is typically repurchased by the company.

Starting in January, 2007, the company decided to replace its 401K match with an ESOP. When the ESOP was implemented, it was both a bold and controversial decision. Atul came to the reluctant conclusion that if he wanted to create a broad-based ownership, an ESOP was needed as an involuntary mechanism. This was a difficult decision for him as it risked making existing employees unhappy, but he finally realized that it "was the only method to create broad-based ownership [because] educating and cajoling and encouraging was never going to work broadly enough."

His struggle with the ESOP was further complicated by the fact that Philip and John were not initially supportive. Their resistance delayed implementation for a year or two. This issue put the shared leadership model to a test; still, he said that even though he is the CEO, "there are times I know the right answer and they just don't see it, and I accept their decision." Only when these two had fully embraced it was the ESOP adopted. In the end, ESOP became very successful. While some employees were initially unhappy, they eventually saw how the TEOCO stock has outperformed the market since its inception in 2007.

Despite his belief in the need for the ESOP, Atul maintains that it does not create "ownership culture" in the same way that voluntarily investing one's own money to buy shares does. However, he wanted to achieve a broad-based ownership which, in his opinion, would not have been possible otherwise. From his perspective, ownership means wealth and the real benefit would be realized if the company was sold or went public. A successful and attractive company, especially one in the high tech field, can expect to sell at a high multiple of the price-to-earnings ratio, which would result in an impressive return for employees, rewarding them for their exemplary performance and company loyalty.

A Philosophy of Total Compensation

Atul's philosophy of compensation is that base salaries should be in the range of 0-10% below the going market rate. He believes that employees can accept this as a trade-off for a supportive and respectful work environment, a sizable bonus, along with the benefits of employee ownership. He even prefers it when a new employee takes a modest pay cut to join TEOCO, because he believes it is "a very resounding affirmation that they believe in our company and in our core values."

Atul: "We work our hardest if we are happier, if we enjoy our work and if we feel that we belong. That's why TEOCO has chosen to be an employee owned company; you don't work for an employer here, you work for yourself."

Since every TEOCO employee owns some company stock and receives an annual bonus and generous benefits, he feels that they are not underpaid. This full range of benefits seems to be highly valued and appreciated by employees. Hillary, for example, said that these make it difficult for her to consider leaving to work at another company. In comparing TEOCO's benefits with those her friends receive at other organizations, she is especially appreciative; three weeks instead of two weeks of vacation, the casual work environment and the flexible schedule were all cited.

Finally, TEOCO never misses an opportunity to recognize employees' commitment to the company, as well as their performance, by distributing awards. These awards reinforce the core values of the company: excellence, dedication and team work. It should be noted that these are peer-to-peer awards in which fellow employees are recognized for actions that exemplify one of the core values. (See Appendix 5 for an exhaustive list of TEOCO benefits and awards.)

Human Resources as a Strategic Function

In addition to shared leadership and employee ownership programs, the third component of TEOCO's competitive advantage is the way the senior executive team emphasizes the importance of managing TEOCO's main asset: its human resources. In many organizations, Human Resources is seen as a necessary cost of doing business; the HR function typically operates at a functional level or, at best in far fewer companies, at the executive level.[9] At TEOCO, however, Atul has elevated HR to the strategic level. While there is a dedicated human resources director, Atul effectively serves as the organization's Chief Human Resources Officer.

For most organizations, the human resource policies and practices are transactional in nature. At TEOCO, the HR function has become the principal means of cultural transmission and reinforcement. In addition, Atul devotes strategic focus on HR because of his belief in the potential of an empowered work force. To some extent, part of the company's overall strategy is working from the "bottom up." The company relies on the abilities of its employees to understand what the market needs and develop new products. An example of how the empowered workforce functions at TEOCO was related by Dave [Software Architect]:

We are not structured in a way that we have a team for incubating products … it's through conversations with our existing customers, generally, that the ideas for the next set of products come out.

Meanwhile, it is the shared leadership model that provides the opportunity for Atul to be so strongly and strategically focused on HR while depending on John, Faye and others to bring in the revenues. In an organization whose principal assets and competitive advantage are its human and intellectual capital, Atul and the shared leadership team have recognized the strategic importance of HR to its success.

The culture at TEOCO revolves singularly around the principle of employee ownership; it is embedded in the language, the policies and practices, the daily activities and even the rituals at TEOCO. There is a formal HR policy manual which is kept continuously current. While the manual is comprehensive in its scope, it is somewhat limited in specific details. Atul's stated philosophy of a policy manual is that "less is more," and the existing manual is larger than he would prefer. His rationale for not wanting to embed detailed procedures into the policy manual is that he prefers to have as few rules as possible. He believes that every employee will always want to do what is in the best interest of the company, and to reinforce the culture at TEOCO he believes that doing the right thing might at times require violating a policy.

TEOCO's articulated core values, and the resulting organizational culture, are evident in the working environment as well as in the HR policies and practices. The overall environment could be described as one of collegiality and mutual respect. Atul's background and beliefs support his desire for peace at the office, wanting employees to respect one another and not wanting employees to feel insecure about their jobs. Hillary validated this perception when she said "I think the environment is one of my favorite things about TEOCO." She claims that Atul comes by her office every week, and she thinks it is the same for many other employees as well. She described that "he walks around" and is very interactive. Brian independently said that "I get high-fives from Atul probably four days a week." He noted that many new employees, especially those who come from larger organizations, often comment on how surprised they are that the CEO recognizes them, let alone that they see

him come down to their floor. Further, Brian mentioned that interpersonal relationships are very important at TEOCO. For many employees some of their best friends work there, and "that's a really big benefit that isn't on any paperwork or on any contract."

The socialization process at TEOCO begins at new employee orientation and is continuously reinforced through the HR policies and practices. Carrie (Director of HR) believes that the principal mission of HR is to help shape employee perceptions, especially as it relates to employee ownership, and to impress upon every employee the core value of "driving for progress through ownership."

The HR policies and practices, themselves, demonstrate their critical importance through the resulting work environment. Taken together, the culture of employee ownership, combined with the strategic focus on HR, serve to recruit, motivate and retain the TEOCO workforce.

The importance of human assets to the company's success is highlighted by the active involvement of its CEO and chairman in the hiring process. He interviews every applicant before a hiring decision is made. As he says, "Nobody gets hired without meeting me, and nobody gets hired without getting my nod." The two areas in which he exercises tight-fisted control are hiring and cost management. He believes he has developed unique expertise to know "who to hire and what to look for." His focus is not only on technical competence, but on "cultural fit" as well. In many ways Atul could be described as the keeper of the culture. He gets so deeply involved in the hiring process that he says he is sometimes asked if he doesn't have anything better to do, and he responds by saying that there is nothing more important because the hiring process is so vital to the company's continued success.

TA, TTI and the Future of TEOCO

How will the story of TEOCO unfold with the investment by TA and the acquisition of TTI? From a purely business perspective, these decisions were justifiably necessary and defensible. However, each of the three distinctive characteristics of TEOCO's model of success, the shared leadership model, the culture of employee ownership and the resulting HR policies and practices, are being challenged in this post-acquisition environment.

Impact on Shared Leadership
The scope of the combined enterprise presents challenges that may strain the shared leadership model. TA's

investment already added two influential directors to TEOCO's board. While directors usually have a "nose in, hands out" approach to management, the representatives of investment funds appointed to a company's board tend to be far more proactive in their dialogues with the senior team managing their investment. The subsequent acquisition of TTI added a fourth executive, Eitan Naor, into the leadership mix and in the last two years, Avi (TEOCO's CFO) has also become a key member of the Executive Leadership Team. Considering the distance between TEOCO and TTI, as well as their respective nearly equal sizes, it remains to be seen how the strengths and weaknesses of each leader will play out in the management of this new entity. For instance, Atul's well-recognized skills in hiring and motivating employees on a daily basis may not prove as beneficial or essential for TTI.

Impact on the Culture of Employee Ownership

Avi claims that the cultures have nothing in common. Yet the senior management team seems adamant that the culture of TEOCO has not and will not change. Faye says, "I don't think there's been significant change." Still, she acknowledged the inevitability that an aggregated culture will arise in which each organization impacts the other. But she adds, "I can see [Atul] sitting in that chair right now saying, 'It's not going to happen.'"

These statements are not surprising, as it is nearly universal that in this situation company executives proclaim that their acquisition will not change the corporate culture. Yet some degree of change is inevitable, and change has already occurred. These events will inevitably impact business activities and decision-making. The TTI acquisition and the investment of TA enhance the likelihood that within the next three years TEOCO may be acquired by a larger corporation, go public or require some other fundamental organizational realignment. Before agreeing to the TA investment, Atul says that he went to the employees for their consent. He believes the employees were comfortable with the transaction or he would not have done it; he says that the employees are aware of its positive impact as well as the potential outcome.

Atul is determined to continue on the same path as before these major events. He points out that a condition of TA's investment in TEOCO was that he retain the role of CEO because he is so essential to the culture of the company. The bank, as a condition of the loan for the purchase of TTI, had the same requirement. Meanwhile,

Atul is intent on TA receiving a good return on their investment in TEOCO.

Atul: "But I will no longer do that with a sense of obligation; I will do that with a sense of joy. You know, if you do something out of joy, you do it differently than when you do it out of a sense of obligation."

An immediate impact is that these two events place a strain on employee ownership. The ownership mix shifted significantly with the TA investment. Prior to this equity transaction, Atul controlled 75% of the shares, while employees owned 25% from all combined sources. Post-TA, the employee share was halved as they were offered approximately 60% liquidity on their previous ownership. Given Atul's ownership, and his intention to maintain a controlling interest in the company, coupled with TA's sizable equity stake, an issue that arises is whether there is any meaningful future opportunity to expand employee ownership. This is further compounded by the near doubling of the total number of employees.

An interesting paradox, according to Atul, is that despite the lower total employee ownership, there is a perception that the TA liquidity has strengthened the culture of ownership. He said that he "predicted that post-TA our payroll deductions [to purchase stock] would go down. It has increased … because [the employees] see a success story," even though the stock purchase price has since increased. Atul attributes this pattern to the fact that employees witnessed other employees making significant sums of money from the TA transaction. He claims that now they truly understand and value ownership. As he says, "Once you've made money out of ownership, it changes you forever. And until you do, you don't believe it." Atul felt a very deep sense of gratitude to his long-term employees for their loyalty and sacrifice in creating value for TEOCO. The TA transaction allowed him to fulfill his commitment that one day they would get a return on their investment of time and money into TEOCO.

While these events will inevitably bring about changes in the way the company is managed, John believes that these will not dilute the culture. The TA investment "allowed TEOCO to preserve something that I think is pretty important to the way we operate, which is having employee ownership in the business, and that employees have a piece of it." A firm believer in employee ownership, he has "worked at the world's largest employee-owned company, for Telecordia, which was owned by SAIC." He claims that TEOCO is heavily modeled after SAIC in terms of employee ownership as a mechanism.

John: "*If you're just paying people to show up to work and they get an annual bonus – those are two factors. But if you introduced the third factor of employee ownership – why wouldn't you treat that as a means to motivate the employees beyond just simply giving them a salary and giving them a bonus? … And that's what Dr. Beyster [the founder of SAIC] figured out before anybody else figured it out.*"

These perceptions by senior management were validated by Carrie, HR Manager. When asked about the relatively small percentage of total stock owned by employees, she claims that the perception of employee ownership continues to be important, and that all employees still have the opportunity to build additional equity. She cited, for example, that every new employee is granted a certain amount of ownership rights; they determine how much stock they want to purchase either through payroll deduction or the internal stock market. Brian validated this further when he said that once employees realize the benefits of being invested in the company, it changes their perspective. Like Atul, he underlined that this reality became clear for many employees when they witnessed others cashing out a portion of their equity with the TA investment. As he said, "Once that clicks in, it builds on it."

It remains to be determined if the employees of TTI will become owners, and whether they will embrace the culture of ownership. It is also uncertain how TEOCO's employee perceptions may change in terms of the growing price of ownership and the potential diminished opportunity for share availability.

Impact on Human Resources as a Strategic Function

The TTI acquisition will strain Atul's role as the organization's chief human resources officer as someone who has been intimately and deeply involved in all HR-related decisions of the company. Dave describes Atul's current role in HR activities.

Dave: "*Atul is very, very, very engaged at the staffing and who's working on what and the hiring process. It's personnel stuff. Personnel and costs are the two things he focuses on… it blows my mind the level of detail and recollection he has on individual people and what's going on in the company.*"

As the company continues to grow, and as the complexity of issues expands, it will become increasingly difficult to maintain this level of involvement in details. A further challenge will be the issue of the standardization and consistency of application of HR-related policies and practices. Atul has a strong aversion to formal policies, preferring instead to have maximum flexibility and discretion in deciding HR issues.

Atul: "*Life is all about making decisions and the reason management exists is to use judgment. Too many people want to make too many rules and they don't want to use judgment, and I feel that if judgment doesn't exist then management doesn't have a job.*"

Given the increasingly litigious and regulated work environment for organizations, such a philosophy can create challenges for HR. When asked about Atul's philosophy of a policy manual where "less is more," HR Director Carrie admitted that there are some policies "that do cause me a little heartburn just because it's a little tough to administer without having something solid." One example she cited is that the sick leave policy is administered on an honor system. The only way to monitor abuse, she says, is indirectly by the impact such abuse may have on employee performance. As the company gets larger, she believes it would be easier if there were specific guidelines to turn to in a dilemma, to be able to say, "Here's the policy." Yet despite the lack of specifications, she claims there appears to be a high degree of consistency in the administration of HR policies.

Whether HR will continue to be viewed as a strategic function and receive the executive focus that it has had will be tested as well in the new corporate environment.

Impact on TEOCO's Core Competencies

While Atul believes that corporate culture and philosophy have played "key roles in our success," he says "that without its distinctive core competencies the company could not have been successful." Whether the core competencies that TEOCO has built can carry over in the post acquisition environment is an unanswered question. That TTI is similar in size to TEOCO and that they are geographically separated are two factors that will pose challenges in transferring specialized expertise from the acquiring company to the acquired company and vice versa. Also, given that the two companies had different cultures at the time of acquisition, additional work will have to be done to ensure successful transference of core competencies.

Conclusion

The challenge for any organization with a strong culture and a loyal work force is to sustain them and adapt them in the face of organizational change. Over a very short period of time, TEOCO has changed its capital structure and expanded its business. How and to what extent TEOCO manages these changes will determine whether it maintains its competitive advantage and, finally, what will be its overall fate.

Appendix 1: Board of Directors

In addition to John Devolites, Philip M. Giuntini and Atul Jain, TEOCO's board is composed of a majority of outside board members with deep telecom industry expertise:

Gabriel Battista, Former Chairman, Talk America Gabe Battista formerly served as Chairman of the Board of Directors of Talk America, where he previously served as CEO. Prior to joining Talk America in January of 1999, Mr. Battista served as CEO of Network Solutions, Inc. Before joining Network Solutions, Mr. Battista served as CEO, President and COO of Cable & Wireless, Inc. He also held management positions at US Sprint, GTE Telenet and The General Electric Company. He serves as a director of Capitol College and Systems & Computer Technology Corporation (SCTC).

Brian J. Conway, Managing Director, TA Associates Mr. Conway heads TA Associates' Boston office Technology Group, focusing on recapitalizations, buyouts and minority growth investments of technology-based growth companies. He is also a member of TA Associates' Executive Committee. Prior to joining TA Associates, Mr. Conway worked with Merrill Lynch in Mergers and Acquisitions and Corporate Finance. He serves on the Board of Directors for Epic Advertising, IntraLinks, and Numara Software.

Hythem T. El-Nazer, Senior Vice President, TA Associates Mr. El-Nazer's focus at TA Associates is on recapitalizations, management-led buyouts, and growth capital investments in telecommunications, media and other technology-based services companies. Prior to joining TA Associates, Mr. El-Nazer worked with McKinsey & Company and Donaldson, Lufkin & Jenrette - Investment Banking. He serves on the Board of Directors for eSecLending, Radialpoint, and is Board Observer at Orascom Telecom Holding S.A.E. and Weather Investments S.p.A.

Robert J. Korzeniewski, Former Executive Vice President, VeriSign As VeriSign's Executive Vice President, Corporate Development and Strategy, Mr. Robert Korzeniewski is responsible for providing a consistent strategy and focus for investments and merger and acquisition activity. Mr. Korzeniewski served from 1996–2000 as CFO of Network Solutions, Inc., which was acquired by VeriSign in June 2000. Mr. Korzeniewski came to Network Solutions from SAIC, where from 1987 to 1996, he held a variety of senior financial positions.

Source: TEOCO's website

Appendix 2: Industry Landscape / Major Competitors

1) Least Cost Routing

Vendors	Regions					Market Segments	
	NA	CALA	EMEA	APAC	OVERALL	Mobile	PSTN
Ascade	P	–	NP	NP	NP	NP	NP
Connective-Sol	NP	–	–	–	P	NP	P
GCS	NP	–	–	–	NP	NP	NP
OrcaWave	NP	–	P	–	P	P	NP
Prime Carrier	P	–	P	P	P	P	P
Pulse Networks	NP	–	–	–	NP	NP	NP
Subex	–	NP	–	–	–	–	–
Telarix	ML	P	ML	–	ML	ML	ML

2) Revenue Assurance

Vendors	Regions					Market Segments	
	NA	CALA	EMEA	APAC	OVERALL	Mobile	PSTN
Connectiva	P	P	NP	NP	NP	NP	NP
Connectiv	NP	–	–	–	P	NP	P
Cvidya	NP	–	–	NP	–	–	NP
Razorsight	P	–	–	–	P	P	P
Subex	NP	P	ML	ML	ML	ML	ML
Qosmos	P	–	P	P	P	P	P
Wedo	NP	–	ML	NP	ML	ML	ML

3) Cost Management

Vendors	Regions					Market Segments	
	NA	CALA	EMEA	APAC	OVERALL	Mobile	PSTN
Connectiv	P	–	–	–	P	P	P
Martin Dawes	–	–	NP	–	P	NP	P
Razorsight	ML	–	–	–	NP	NP	NP
Subex	P	NP	ML	ML	ML	ML	ML

Source:
TEOCO Marketing Department: NA = North America; CALA = Central America & Latin America; EMEA = Europe, Middle East, and Africa; APAC = Asia & Pacific. PSTN = Public Switched Telephone Network.

P = has a presence in the market
NP = has a notable presence in the market
ML = is a market leader

Appendix 3: TEOCO / TTI Leadership

Atul Jain, Chairman and CEO: Atul Jain founded TEOCO Corporation in 1994. Prior to starting TEOCO Corporation, Mr. Jain was with a Silicon Valley firm called TIBCO for seven years. At TIBCO, Mr. Jain's focus was to work with Fortune 500 clients to design and build state-of-the-art software solutions leveraging the company's trademark TIB platform.

Philip M. Giuntini, Vice Chairman and President: Philip M. Giuntini joined TEOCO in February 2000 as Vice Chairman and President. Prior to joining TEOCO, Mr. Giuntini was President and on the Board of Directors of American Management Systems, Inc. (AMS), a $1B international business and information technology consulting firm headquartered in Fairfax, Virginia.

John Devolites, Vice President and General Manager: John Devolites is currently the Vice President and General Manager at TEOCO focusing on solutions for the communications service provider industry. Previously, Mr. Devolites served as President of Professional Services for Telcordia. His other work experiences include executive positions at PricewaterhouseCoopers, E-Commerce Industries, Andersen, American Management Systems (AMS), Alexander Proudfoot PLC, and Booz Allen Hamilton.

Avi Goldstein, Chief Financial Officer (CFO): Avi Goldstein joined TEOCO in October 2008 and was nominated TEOCO's CFO on April 2009. Prior to joining TEOCO, Mr. Goldstein co-founded several startup companies as well as provided consulting services in the Telecom arena with a strong focus on Mergers and Acquisitions. Prior to that Mr. Goldstein served as an Executive Vice President and CFO of ECtel Ltd. (NASDAQ: ECTX) from its establishment until 2005. Mr. Goldstein led ECtel to a successful IPO as well as private placements and M&A activities.

Eitan Naor, General Manager and CEO of TTI: Eitan Naor joined TEOCO in August 2010 and brings more than 25 years of leadership and experience in the global telecom and service assurance markets. Prior to joining TEOCO, Mr. Naor served as President and CEO of Magic Software (NASDAQ:MGIC), where he led a significant restructure of the business and regained focus in its worldwide network of partners, resulting in a significant increase in sales and a return to profitability in less than one year. Mr. Naor also had great success in his other professional roles, including President and CEO of ECTEL (NASDQ: ECTX), Division President at AMDOCS, and Vice President with ORACLE Israel.

Source: TEOCO's website

Appendix 4: TEOCO's Core Values & Value Proposition

At TEOCO, The Employee-Owned Company, we are driven by our core values. These values are our guiding principles in all business initiatives:

- **Alignment with Employees, Clients, and Community**: We act in the best interest of our employees, clients and community, consistently seeking partnership and mutual benefit.
- **Integrity, Honesty, and Respect**: We value our reputation and conduct our business with integrity, honesty, and respect for each individual.
- **Acting with Courage**: We demonstrate a willingness to take risks, while conducting our business in a responsible manner.
- **Drive for Progress through Ownership**: We are committed to a relentless pursuit of excellence, never being satisfied with the status quo. We are a team whose sum is greater than its parts and devoted to constant innovation.

TEOCO sets standards of excellence that others strive to emulate in our areas of focus – cost management, routing and revenue management. TEOCO's value proposition is as follows:

- **Innovation:** TEOCO's committed emphasis on one industry allows us unparalleled customer focus. We commit a significant share – up to 30% – of our annual revenues to research and development to address your precise needs.
- **Stability**: TEOCO is the only firm in our industry segment that is financially sound, debt free, and employee owned. You can rest assured that we are responsive to your needs and will be there tomorrow.
- **Integrity**: At TEOCO, acting with integrity is one of our essential core values. We focus intensely on developing mutually beneficial, trust-based relationships with customers and communicating honestly in every situation.
- **Deep Industry Expertise**: Our team includes experienced professionals, many of whom have substantial telecommunications experience and/or have worked directly in service provider cost management organizations.

Source: TEOCO's website

Appendix 5: TEOCO's Benefits and Awards

Flexible Schedule: Flexible working hours occur on an informal basis and vary from job to job and department to department. While there is no formal HR policy on flexible working hours or working from home, this approach is consistent with its performance-driven culture in that what ultimately matters is employee performance. Even though employees may be permitted flexibility with schedules and working from home, employees are expected to be available nights, weekends and even vacations when there are pressing deadlines or problems to troubleshoot.

Snacks and Beverages: Company-provided snacks, coffee and other beverages are made available throughout the day for all employees.

"Splash Vacation:" After completing five years of service (and on every subsequent fifth-year anniversary) employees are provided with an extra week of paid vacation. They are also provided with a reimbursement of up to $2,000 for expenses incurred (transportation, lodging, etc.) in taking a vacation for themselves and their family to any place of their choosing.

ACE Award: ACE stands for Attitude, Commitment and Excellence. This is TEOCO's version of an "Employee of the Year" award, and is given annually to the employee who best exemplifies these three qualities. The winner, who receives stock and a cash award, is chosen by a committee which is comprised of previous winners of the ACE Award.

MVP Award: The Most Versatile Player Award, similar in concept to the ACE Award, is given annually to an employee who may not rise to that level of excellence, but who contributes to the organization in multiple ways. The winner receives stock and a cash award. Like the ACE Award, the winner is chosen without any management involvement, and the selection committee is comprised of previous winners of the award.

TEOCO Star Award: This is a peer-to-peer award in which employees recognize fellow employees for doing something that exemplifies one of the core values. This award would be TEOCO's version of a "spot bonus," with the exception that it is peer-to-peer rather than given by a supervisor. For example, one employee being helpful to another on a project might garner them a recommendation for the award. At the monthly "all-hands meeting," there is a drawing amongst all those nominated that month, and the winner receives a $150 Amex gift card as well as official acknowledgement.

One-Year Service Award: All new employees, on their first anniversary of employment, are given a plant, a balloon and a card signed by other employees to acknowledge their first anniversary.

NOTES

1. The authors would like to thank the employee owners of TEOCO who graciously shared their knowledge, experiences and perspectives about the company. Their viewpoints were invaluable in ensuring that this case provides a true representation of the culture and practices of the company.

2. All employees are referred to in this case by their first name including the CEO because that is standard practice at TEOCO.

3. http://www.billingworld.com/articles/2010/09/teoco-ceo-reversal-on-acquisitions-complete.aspx

4. Ibid.

5. Ibid.

6. Ibid.

7. Jainism is the least populous of the Indian religions; comprising approximately 0.5% of the population (Hindus represent approximately 80%, Muslims approximately 12% and Christians approximately 3%).

8. James C. Collins and Jerry I. Porras. "Built to Last: Successful Habits of Visionary Companies," New York: Harper Collins Publishers, 1994.

9. As Peter Drucker said, "All organizations now say routinely, 'people are our greatest asset.' Yet few practice what they preach, let alone believe it." "*The New Society of Organizations*," *Harvard Business Review*, Sept/Oct, 1992.

Christina Ehrler, James Gillis, Michael Huesemann, Marco Sandoval, Leslie Turckes

Arizona State University

Tesla Motors

Since its inception in 2003, Tesla Motors has made significant breakthroughs in the electric vehicle (EV) market with its proprietary power-train technology. Its first Roadster model provided a driving experience that was on par with a traditional gas engine and was the precursor for considerable success in the automobile market over the last few years. However, as the production of the most recent Roadster model winds down, Tesla is faced with a challenging situation that might determine the future direction of the company and ultimately its survival.[1]

In July 2012, Tesla released its EV family sedan, the Model S, priced at the upper range of the luxury vehicle market.[2] This sedan represents Tesla's first foray into the family segment of the automobile market, providing a significant opportunity for company growth. Tesla currently takes only limited orders for the vehicles and expects the production capacity to be built up over the next few years. This model is intended to serve as a good introduction of Tesla's EV capabilities to the public and allay concerns about performance and reliability of EVs before its Model X crossover is introduced into the market.[3] The Model X will not be ready for delivery until 2014, but it will be the first mid-sized vehicle produced by Tesla. Between these two vehicles, Tesla has an impressive product pipeline lineup that has the potential to appeal to middle-class consumers and to expand Tesla's current consumer base comprising high-net worth early adopters. However, Tesla is not the only manufacturer looking to develop EVs. Most automobile manufacturers have developed or are in the process of developing their own EVs—the Chevy Volt being the most well known.

Toyota is developing an all-electric version of its RAV4 as part of a contract with Tesla.[4] Currently, Tesla's vehicles have greater range and offer better performance, but these major automakers represent a significant threat to the viability of Tesla.

Tesla is thus confronted with two issues: How to move forward and in which direction? Tesla could maintain its status as a niche manufacturer of high-quality, high-performance EVs, or it could seek to leverage its first mover advantage and therefore gain market share with expanded, affordable access to EVs in the greater automobile market. Tesla is limited in its ability to manufacture vehicles due to its size and access to resources, which puts it at a disadvantage in comparison to other automakers. However, if Tesla fails to act in a decisive way, it risks losing its technological advantage and opens the door for other manufacturers to develop their own EV models and crowd Tesla out of the lucrative automobile market. How will Tesla maintain its technological lead over its competitors? How will Tesla shift from targeting early adopters to reaching the larger consumer market—and should it? How will it deal with the lack of infrastructure to support these new vehicles? Finally, how will Tesla deal with the environmental effects of more EVs on the road and will these effects ultimately conflict with its founding principles?

Company History

Tesla Motors Inc., a Silicon Valley-based company founded in 2003, designs, manufactures, and sells zero-emission electric cars and power train parts, such as lithium-ion battery packs. These power train components are then bought and used by other carmakers, such as Toyota.[5] Tesla's vision is to "create the most compelling car company of the 21st century by driving the world's transition to electric vehicles."[6] Tesla's mission has three elements: to build and sell its own EVs, to sell patented electric power train parts to other car manufacturers, and to serve as a role model to speed the transition to EVs. Thus far, Tesla is uniquely positioned to be the only company that sells "pure electric" vehicles.[7] Its first model, the Tesla Roadster sports car, has been on the market since 2008, followed by Tesla S and X sedans in 2012 and 2014, respectively.[8] Tesla investors include Daimler ($76 million), Toyota ($50 million), Panasonic ($30 million), and the U.S. Department of Energy ($464 million).[9] Through its initial public offering (IPO) on June 29, 2010, Tesla raised $226 million in capital.[10] Tesla currently has more than 1,200 employees, a new 5 million square-foot factory in Fremont, CA, and 18 showrooms in the United States and Europe.[11,12]

Leadership Team

Tesla Motors' executive and management team has guided the company through the design and production of its first vehicle and its expansion into the larger automobile market and has played an important role in shaping the strategic vision of the company. Some team members have been with the company since its inception.

Elon Musk – Chairman, Product Architect, and CEO

As co-founder of Tesla Motors, Musk has been a force to reckon with. During the company's initial founding, Musk was appointed chairman and product architect (responsible for design vision and execution), while Martin Erberhard was named CEO, and JB Straubel was the CTO (chief technology officer).

During his time as chairman and product architect, Musk had a significant role in designing the Tesla Roadster, for which he won an Index and Global Green Award in 2008. In addition to leading the development of the Tesla Roadster, Musk was also the initial controlling investor in the company. He worked to secure additional investments from a wide variety of firms ranging from Google to Daimler. With Daimler, Musk was able to establish a strategic partnership in 2009, which included $50 million in investments. In 2008, Musk took on the additional role of CEO. Musk has continued spearheading changes within the company's products, including the development of the company's newest vehicle, the Model S sedan. In 2011, Musk was named Innovator of

the Year in Technology by the *Wall Street Journal*.[13] Musk is also the CEO of SpaceX and chair of SolarCity.[14]

JB Straubel – Chief Technology Officer

Straubel has been the CTO of Tesla since its inception. As a co-founder of the company, Straubel has played a guiding role in the company's technical and production divisions beginning with the Tesla Roadster and continuing down to the latest sedans, the Model S and Model X. Together with a team of engineers, he developed the Roadster to prove EVs can provide just as much power as a traditional high-performance sports car.[15] He is involved with every stage of production—from the preliminary design stages through vehicle systems testing, which he manages directly. Straubel also evaluates new technologies for the company and interfaces with key vendors to ensure that the best products and technologies are integrated into Tesla's vehicles.

Deepak Ahuja – Chief Financial Officer

Ahuja became the CFO of Tesla in 2008. Then-CEO Ze'ev Drori said, "Deepak's experience as CFO of multibillion dollar business units with global sourcing and manufacturing operations makes him the ideal person to lead our finance organization through the company's next period of rapid growth."[16] Ahuja's experience in the automotive industry ranges from composites engineering to finance. Ahuja was the controller of Small Cars Product Development for Ford, which had the goal of bringing fuel-efficient cars to North America. Prior to this, he was the CFO for Ford in South Africa. He worked as a composites engineer for Kennametal, in Pittsburgh, before he joined Ford.[17]

Since Ahuja joined Tesla, he has helped the company accumulate $660 million in liquid assets, acquire a new manufacturing facility in California, and guide the company's financial team with a target of manufacturing 20,000 cars per year, the level at which the company expects to report a net profit from its operations.[18]

In addition, many of Tesla's senior executives have had prior experience with other automakers (see Exhibit 1). Aside from Ahuja, who came from Ford, company executives include Franz von Holzhausen, Chief Designer, who previously designed cars for Mazda, Volkswagen, Audi, and GM; Gilbert Passin, VP Manufacturing, who had previously worked at Toyota; Peter Rawlinson, VP and Chief Engineer, who came from Jaguar; and John Walker, VP North American Sales, who was previously employed by BMW, Audi, and GM. Apart from providing expertise and unique "know-how" related to EV technologies, the experience of the top management team in

Exhibit 1 Tesla's Management Team

Elon Musk **CEO, Product Architect** Spacex Solar City PayPal	JB Straubel **CTO** MIT Innovator of the Year	Deepak Ahuja **CFO** Ford Kennametal	Franz von Holzhausen **Chief Designer** Mazda Audi General Motors
Arnnon Geshuri **VP, Human Resources** Google	Greg Reichow **VP, Powertrain Operations** SunPower	Gilbert Passin **VP, Manufacturing** Toyota Mack Trucks	Peter Rawlinson **VP & Chief Engineeer** Corus Jaguar Lotus
Jim Dunlay **VP, Hardware** Hewlett Packard Sun Microsystems	George Blankenship **SVP, Sales** Apple Gap	John Walker **VP, N. American Sales** BMW Audi General Motors	Jérôme Guillen **Director, Model S** Daimler Mercedes-Benz

Source: Tesla Motors Company Overview, Summer 2011, "World Class Applied Tech & Auto Experience," http://files.shareholder.com/downloads/ABEA-4CW8X0/1459391711x0x494001/dd297293-ec2d-4dc5-8db4-63d491fb6bd0/Company_Overview_Q3_2011.pdf

the automobile industry provided Tesla with significant institutional knowledge and credibility in the market.

Social and Economic Trends Influencing Tesla's Business Model

Tesla's innovation and focus is driven by a strong concern for the environment. In particular, the looming threat of global climate change has significant implications for the widespread acceptance of its products.[19] The company believes that environmentally conscious and well-informed consumers will become more and more interested in environmentally friendly products. These products include zero-carbon emission EVs that can be recharged using electricity from renewable sources such as wind and photovoltaics.[20]

Public concern over global climate change is likely to cause concomitant changes in political and legal trends, such as government mandates to significantly decrease greenhouse gas emissions. For example, by 2020 the United States has pledged to reduce greenhouse gases by 28 percent, and Europe is planning to supply 20 percent of its energy via renewable sources.[21] Furthermore, a number of countries have already enacted a carbon tax,[22] and more are likely to follow suit, which will give Tesla's EVs a competitive advantage over fossil-fuel–powered automobiles. In addition, some countries (including Japan) offer zero or low taxes and green subsidies for EVs, thereby increasing their appeal to consumers.[23] Since 2010, the United States has provided a federal tax credit of $7,500 toward the purchase of pure EVs.[24]

Continuous and rapid improvements in lithium-ion battery technology are also vital in reducing the cost of EVs while increasing their driving range (per charge). It has been claimed that lithium-ion batteries will be the preferred choice in the twenty-first century.[25] Recently, Stanford University researchers discovered that they can increase the lifespan of lithium-ion batteries by 10 times.[26] Although Tesla Motors is not waiting for this technology to be developed, it is actively involved in a partnership with Panasonic to accelerate the development of high-efficiency nickel-based lithium-ion battery cells specifically designed for EVs.[27]

Global changes in consumer demographics are also likely to significantly increase the demand for emission-neutral vehicles. Global population growth, particularly in India and China, together with economic development have increased worldwide demand for automobiles. The number of passenger vehicles has exhibited rapid growth, from 53 million in 1950 to 622 million in 2008, and is expected to increase.[28] Furthermore, because of the sociocultural and political/legal trends mentioned earlier, the composition of the world's automobile fleet is expected to change to include more emission-neutral EVs. These two factors—population growth and a shift in consumer preference—are said to create a significant growth in the global market for EVs.

In addition, increasing crude oil prices have increased interest in renewable sources of energy as well as in conservation of energy. Such interest has led nations and governments to consider alternative modes of transportation such as bicycling and/or investing in public transport such as buses, subways, and trains. These choices represent different cost-benefit analyses at societal levels and could pose a significant threat to the auto industry in general. However, increased fuel prices are more likely to affect traditional gasoline-based automobiles, potentially shifting personal auto demand toward EVs. Thus there is considerable uncertainty as to how increased fuel prices might affect demand for the auto industry and, in particular, for EVs.

Finally, global economic trends, particularly changes in currency exchange rates and free trade agreements, while currently not of prime concern to Tesla Motors, may determine how the company expands its operation and sales in Europe, Asia, and elsewhere, in the future.

Key Suppliers and Customers

Like all other car manufactures, Tesla Motors depends on a large number of global suppliers for automobile parts.[29] Critical to Tesla's operations are the suppliers of components, such as lithium-ion battery packs. In order to protect its proprietary battery technology and at the same time outsource the mass-production of a battery pack consisting of 18,650 cells, Tesla formed a partnership with Panasonic to develop the next-generation EV battery system.[30] Panasonic invested $30 million for the collaboration in battery cell development.[31]

Tesla customers include both the individuals purchasing a Tesla EV as well as the other automakers who procure Tesla EV power train components. Individual customers have a wide range of options in this market. While a pure electric high-performance sports car such as the Roadster has no equivalent models (see Exhibit 2), the newer models such as Model S or Model X have a wide range of potential competitors that include hybrids and traditional gasoline-powered vehicles. Even within the hybrid or pure electric segments, many companies such as BMW, Daimler, Lexus, and Cadillac have these competing options (see Exhibit 2).

As an original equipment manufacturer (OEM), Tesla has entered into partnerships with Daimler and Toyota to enable the development of EV components. Daimler has incorporated Tesla's battery packs and chargers into Daimler's electric smart cars, while Toyota, as noted earlier, invested $50 million in a collaborative partnership with Tesla to develop and mass produce an electric version of the Toyota RAV4 in 2012.[32] Both these partnerships have significant implications for Tesla's growth. On the one hand, it could increase future demand for Tesla EV components and expertise. On the other, it could create potential competitors who have deeper pockets and wider reach and thereby inhibit Tesla's growth in an individual market.

Key Competitors

Toyota Motor Company

Toyota Motor Company is a large multinational based in Japan and is currently the world's largest automobile manufacturer based on sales and production volume.[33] The company also owns the luxury brand Lexus. Japan and North America account for the bulk of Toyota's sales with 26 percent and 28 percent, respectively, and Asia and Europe account for 11 percent and 17 percent, respectively.[34] While it is a global company, Toyota's focal market is Japan, where its goal is to achieve 40 percent of market share.[35] Toyota primarily seeks to "localize global operations with targeted regional strategies; promote key initiatives globally; diversify into automotive-related business sectors; maintain financial strength; and focus on shareholder value."[36] The company has also sought to expand research and development, increase efficiency, and focus on financing operations.[37] Toyota has been consistently profitable and is usually the most profitable automobile company based on net income.[38]

Toyota has a partnership with Tesla for procuring EV power train components for its RAV4. The Toyota RAV4 is one of Toyota's first all-EV along with another offering based on its small IQ car model; both were introduced into the market in 2012.[39,40] These models, however, are designed for short commutes and have limited ranges. The RAV4 has a base price of $50,610 ($43,110 net after the federal rebate), but it is expected to have a range of only 100 miles.[41]

General Motors

General Motors (GM) is the world's second largest manufacturer by volume and is still the largest automotive company in the United States.[42] Its brands include Chevrolet, GMC, Buick, and Cadillac after discontinuing or selling its Hummer, Pontiac, Saab, and Saturn brands.[43] GM recently emerged from bankruptcy protection, which it had filed for in 2009 after becoming insolvent during the 2008 financial crisis. GM's primary market is North America; however, it has seen tremendous growth in China, where it recently surpassed sales of 2 million units in a year.[44] GM also expects to see sales grow by 25 percent in South America over the medium term[45] and has seen significant growth of 21 percent in the Middle East as of October 2011.[46] GM's strengths tend to be in the broad range of trucks and SUVs.

GM's most recent offering for the EV market is the Chevy Volt. However, the Volt is not a "pure electric" vehicle and is more of a hybrid. Its battery range is only 35 miles but has a total range of 407 miles when its gas

Exhibit 2 Tesla's Market Position

	Internal Combustion	Hybrid Electric	Plug-in Hybrid	Pure Electric
Performance Vehicles	Porsche Aston Martin Ferrari Mercedes-Benz Corvette		Fisker	Roadster
Premium Vehicles	BMW Mercedes-Benz Lexus Audi	BMW Mercedes-Benz Cadillac Lexus	Fisker BMW	Model S Model X
Small Premium Vehicles	BMW Mercedes-Benz Volkswagen Audi	Lexus Mercury		Gen III
Family Vehicles	Toyota Nissan Ford Hyundai	Toyota Nissan Ford Honda	Toyota Chevrolet BYD Volkswagen	Nissan BYD Ford
Subcompact/City Vehicles	Volkswagen Suzuki Toyota Honda			Mini Mitsubishi Smart BMW

Source: Tesla Motors Company Overview, Summer 2011, "Uniquely Positioned in Large Market," http://files.shareholder.com/downloads/ABEA-4CW8X0/1459391711x0x494001/dd297293-ec2d-4dc5-8db4-63d491fb6bd0/Company_Overview_Q3_2011.pdf

range is included[47] and is priced at $31,645.[48] GM has had trouble meeting sales goals for the Volt and has recently come under investigation for fires associated with the Volt's battery.[49] GM also plans to develop a pure EV as part of a Chinese joint venture with the Shanghai Automotive Industry Corporation, to take advantage of its market position in China.[50]

Ford Motor Company

Ford Motor Company is North America's second largest manufacturer of cars and trucks and produces many of its own subcomponents.[51] Like GM, Ford's primary market is in the United States; however, its international business is not as large as GM's. Recently, Ford has been challenged by increasing competitive pressures, primarily from Asian manufacturers.[52] As a result, Ford has focused on trimming its product lines by focusing more on its Ford and Lincoln brands while discontinuing or selling its controlling shares in Mercury, Mazda, Land Rover, and Jaguar.[53]

Early in 2011, Ford unveiled plans for its first pure electric car, the Focus Electric. The Focus Electric is said to be competitive in terms of range with the Nissan Leaf and the Chevy Volt which would be in the range of 50 to 100 miles.[54] It features a regenerative braking system and a braking coach to maximize driving efficiency.[55] It is also priced slightly higher than its competitors, at $39,990.[56] Ford also has an all-electric minivan, the C-Max, which has been rolled out to market. By 2020, Ford expects 25 percent of its fleet to be EVs.[57]

Honda Motor Company

Honda is a large multinational company based in Japan and is a diversified manufacturer of automobiles, motorcycles, and power products.[58] Automobile sales accounted for 76 percent of total sales with 79 percent of its net sales coming from outside Japan.[59] Honda vehicles are known for their efficiency and durability and have seen significant growth around the world, with over 10 percent of the U.S. vehicle market share.[60]

In late 2010, Honda introduced an EV concept based on its existing Fit model.[61] The Fit EV is expected to have a range of 100 miles and features a three-mode electric drive system that allows drivers to select between economic, sport, and normal modes to adjust the driving experience to allow for different levels of performance or conservation.[62] The Fit EV launched in 2012[63] was priced lower than the Nissan Leaf, at around $29,900.[64]

Nissan Motor Company

Nissan is a Japanese auto manufacturer that has experienced significant growth over the last decade. Recently, it launched a global initiative called "Nissan Power 88" that calls for "accelerated growth across new markets and segments" over the next six years.[65] By 2017, Nissan aims to have a global market share of 8 percent with a sustainable operating profit of 8 percent.[66] The company expects to have a global portfolio of 66 vehicles that cover 92 percent of all markets.[67] Currently, Japan, North America, and Europe account for 15 percent, 33 percent, and 17 percent of unit sales, respectively, and overall sales were up by 23 percent in 2011.[68]

The company has increased its focus on EVs and expects to sell 1.5 million EVs by 2017.[69] Recently, Nissan introduced its first EV Leaf, which has performed well by selling over 20,000 units. In addition to acceptance in the market, Leaf has won several awards—the Japan Car of the Year award in 2011–2012, the 2011 European Car of the Year, and the 2011 World Car of the Year.[70] The Nissan Leaf features a range of 100 miles, seats five people, and is priced at $33,000.[71] Nissan is aggressively pursuing the EV segment[72] and has an ongoing partnership with Renault to continue manufacturing EVs.

Other Motor Companies

The automobile market is highly competitive, and many other auto manufacturers have a significant presence in the United States and abroad. Companies such as Hyundai and Daimler have yet to field an EV but have announced plans to do so over the next few years. Many manufacturers are introducing hybrid vehicles, but these companies look to be late entrants into the EV segment. While pure EV players like Tesla are relatively rare in this market because of the need for significant capital requirements, the range of current and potential EV options available to customers (hybrid electric, plug-in hybrid, pure electric) from these existing conventional automobile manufacturers indicates that competition in this segment is likely to increase over the next few years. In addition, these competitors are well-established automobile companies with extremely large-scale operations, significant brand equity, and established customer loyalty. In addition, access to financial resources may be the most significant advantage that these firms have over smaller companies like Tesla, as they not only have

significant cash reserves but also because they can leverage their positions to issue debt and raise more cash. Finally, most of these firms have extensive dealership and service networks. Smaller firms and newer entrants such as Tesla in contrast have a very limited distribution and service network at present.[73] Replicating such networks takes significant time and cost to develop for a company like Tesla. Thus, the competitive environment for Tesla provides significant challenges for Tesla as well as others looking to enter the automobile industry.

Tesla's Operations

Given the significant challenges in its competitive environment, Tesla has focused on positioning itself as a different kind of automobile company. Tesla views itself as a Silicon Valley company focused on technology disruption that is leading the technological revolution in the automobile industry. Tesla's co-founder, Elon Musk, considers Tesla to be more aligned "to an Apple, or Google, than a GM or Ford," while describing Tesla as a "technology velociraptor."[74] What Tesla is doing, Musk continues, "is mind-blowing for the car business, but par for the course in Silicon Valley."[75] It has sought to promote an image that is considered innovative, smart, and cool. It is this vision of an innovative technological revolutionary that has driven many of Tesla's choices and decisions across several elements of its operations in order to separate itself from the status quo of traditional automobile manufacturers.

Technology

As one of the pioneers in the field of EV, Tesla has developed a comprehensive, integrated, proprietary electric power train technology (see Exhibit 3) consisting of lithium-ion cells with a unique chemistry and high-energy density, an actively cooled battery pack, a compact set of software-controlled power electronics, a highly efficient A/C induction motor, and a high RPM single-gear gear box. Both the motor and gear box are manufactured in-house. Each of these power train components are synergistically integrated to provide superior performance in terms of range and cost (see Exhibit 4). The ranges of the Tesla Model S and the Tesla Roadster are 300 and 245 miles, respectively, much greater than the ranges of competitors, such as the Ford Focus EV (100 miles), Nissan Leaf (73 miles), and Chevy Volt (35 miles). Furthermore, Tesla also leads the market in low-priced batteries, at about $400 per kWh, compared to the average of its competitors of $650 per kWh (see Exhibit 4).

Exhibit 3 Tesla's Power Train Technology

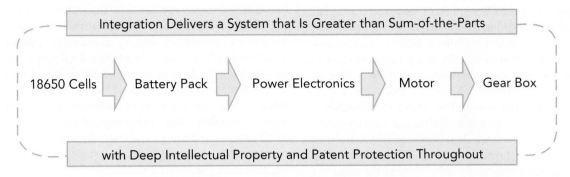

Integration Delivers a System that Is Greater than Sum-of-the-Parts

18650 Cells ⟹ Battery Pack ⟹ Power Electronics ⟹ Motor ⟹ Gear Box

with Deep Intellectual Property and Patent Protection Throughout

- Unique Chemistry
- Proprietary Cathode Geometry
- Automotive-Grade Construction
- Passive Safety Features
- Modified Cell Case

- High Energy Density
- Active Cooling
- Mfg Trade Secrets
- Charge Balancing
- Active Safety Features

- Power Mgmt Software
- 2 Way Inverter
- Charge Mgmt Software
- On Board Charger
- Flux Phasing & Mgmt
- Compact Design
- Thermal Mgmt Software

- Instant Peak Torque
- A/C Induction Motor
- No Rare Earth Metals
- 87% Avg Efficiency
- In House Mfg

- Proprietary Design
- Up to 18,000 RPM
- No Shifting
- In House Mfg

Source: Tesla Motors Company Overview, Summer 2011, "Comprehensive, Proprietary Technology", http://files.shareholder.com/downloads/ABEA-4CW8X0/1459391711x0x494001/dd297293-ec2d-4dc5-8db4-63d491fb6bd0/Company_Overview_Q3_2011.pdf

Exhibit 4 Tesla's Electric Vehicle Leadership on Range and Cost

1. Tesla Leads on Range (maximum miles per single charge)

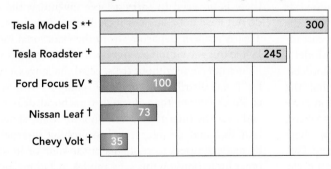

Tesla Model S *+	300
Tesla Roadster +	245
Ford Focus EV *	100
Nissan Leaf †	73
Chevy Volt †	35

* - Estimated
+ - EPA 2-cycle city/highway test
† - EPA derived 5-cycles test

2. Tesla Leads on Cost (battery pack cost in $/kWh)

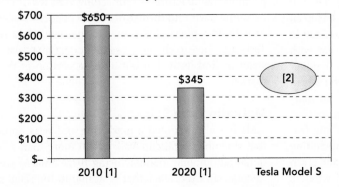

2010 [1]	2020 [1]	Tesla Model S
$650+	$345	[2]

[1] Cost Survey: Roland Berger Study
LiB Value Chain and Cost Model (March 2010)

[2] Tesla Model S – Projected cost not disclosed. Includes all cells, electronics, packaging, and labor costs

Source: Tesla Motors Company Overview, Summer 2011, "EV Leadership on Range and Cost," http://files.shareholder.com/downloads/ABEA-4CW8X0/1459391711x0x494001/dd297293-ec2d-4dc5-8db4-63d491fb6bd0/Company_Overview_Q3_2011.pdf

Product-Market Approach

As a pioneer in the EV segment of the market, Tesla has adopted a three-pronged approach to increase the number and variety of EVs available to mainstream consumers: by selling its own vehicles in a growing number of company-owned showrooms and online; by selling its patented electric power train components to other automakers so that they may get their own EVs to customers sooner; and by serving as a catalyst and positive example to other automakers, demonstrating that there is an overwhelming demand for vehicles that are both fun to drive and environmentally safe.[76] Part of the objective in selling power train components to other automakers was to leverage its technology to cover its operating costs while also moving forward with its personal car-building objective so that, eventually, it can become a BMW of EVs—with a target of 15 percent profit margins.[77]

Tesla's first EV model was the Roadster. The Roadster was a pioneering EV in many dimensions—performance: 0 to 60 MPH in 3.7 seconds; range: 245 miles; development cost: $125 million; and time: launched three models in two years.[78] It was targeted at the high-performance, high-end segment of the EV market. At a base price of $89,000, the Roadster prompted media criticism that the company was catering exclusively to affluent consumers. While Tesla's goal is to sell EVs to mainstream consumers at more affordable prices, Tesla purposely aimed its first production vehicle at "early adopters" so that the company could optimize the technology before cascading it down to less-expensive vehicles. Tesla's Model S sedan, launched in 2012, was priced at a more affordable $49,900 after tax credits,[79] which was roughly half the price of the Roadster. Such a dramatic reduction in price seems to be following an approach adopted by Silicon Valley firms and the global technology industry, where prices for cellular phones, laptop computers, and flat-screen televisions drop dramatically every product cycle. However, this approach has been rare in the global auto industry, where the prevailing business model has been one of mass production in assembly plants optimized to build hundreds of thousands of vehicles per year with comparatively low sticker prices.[80] With the introduction of the Model S sedan at a lower price, Tesla began making a strategic shift from a targeted high-end market segment to reach the broader family sedan market. The Model S sedan also has several distinguishing features to enable it to compete in this segment, including more cargo room than any other sedan, five-star crash rating, 17-inch touchscreen computer and 4G wireless connectivity, performance up to 300 miles per charge, 45-minute quick charge, rapid 1-minute battery swap,

0 to 60 MPH in less than six seconds, and exceptional handling.[81] Tesla already has more than 6,000 orders for the all-electric sedan that will sell anywhere between $57,400 and $77,400 depending on the range and trim level.[82] Tesla plans to provide additional offerings using the Model S platform as it targets different customers with different needs in the family sedan market. Thus, it hopes to launch a number of other cars ranging from sedans, cabriolets, vans, crossovers, and SUVs based on its adaptable common power train. Building each one may take little additional investment since Tesla is building each from the Model S platform.[83]

Distribution Network

Tesla has developed a different distribution network driven by an ambitious effort to take control of its own sales and service operations and capture the revenue and customer feedback that traditional auto manufacturers cede to a network of dealers. It has developed a storefront approach to automotive sales and delivery versus the more traditional dealer network. In Musk's view, the current automotive distribution system is extremely inefficient—it puts dealers at odds with the OEMs regarding service and inventory. Instead of having tens of thousands of cars on dealer lots, Tesla uses a just-in-time delivery system with cars being made to order.[84] Since there is no need to carry a large inventory, the stores do not have to be large or include extensive floor space. That is a major departure from the traditional model.[85] While this revolutionary approach has many advantages, it does not come without risks. Legal challenges lie ahead for Tesla's distribution model of selling its own vehicles at stores (rather than through franchised dealerships) and over the Internet. As Tesla notes, "Many states have laws that may be interpreted to prohibit internet sales by manufacturers to residents of the state or to impose other limitations on this sales model, including laws that prohibit manufacturers from selling vehicles directly to consumers without the use of an independent dealership or without a physical presence in the state." As a result, Tesla may have to change its sales model for at least some states or find itself shut out of a big portion of the U.S. market.[86]

Marketing and Sales

Tesla has also adopted a marketing and sales approach that resembles a Silicon Valley firm more than a traditional automobile manufacturing firm. Tesla is seeking to create an experience that is similar to the retail strategy used by Apple with its storefronts. To accomplish this, the firm hired George Blankenship as VP of Sales and Ownership Experience. Blankenship, who was previously the architect of the Apple retail model, introduced his ideas into Tesla stores using top-notch technology. As Blankenship says, "Tesla stores are designed to let people explore and learn about Tesla's technology for themselves. You'll never see a 'Don't Touch' sign in a Tesla store. We want everyone—from kindergartners to grandparents—to come in and see for themselves why driving electric is the future."[87] Tesla's mission is to reinvent the way people buy cars. Breaking from the traditional dealership model, Tesla stores seek to entice, inform, and engage prospective customers with innovative touchscreen interfaces, knowledgeable product specialists, and a virtual design studio where they can customize their own premium Model S sedans.[88]

A key enabler in achieving this store experience is Tesla's use of cutting-edge software integrated into the many touchscreens located around the sales floor. Design Studio is a software tool that allows consumers to customize, view, and share their own Tesla EVs on the Web, on their smartphones and iPads, and at Tesla stores. Using HTML5 for cross-platform compatibility, the Design Studio makes the buying experience flexible, engaging, and interactive.[89] "The Design Studio's goal is to personalize the Tesla experience," said George Blankenship. "It's the most advanced configuration any automaker has come up with, letting you choose exactly what you want, look at it from every angle, and see it in the wild."[90] All of this technology may or may not impact customers; besides, Tesla product specialists are also equipped with iPads when they walk prospective customers through the process and explore their options. Tesla's new Santana Row showroom also offers the capability for customers to "throw" their design to a large screen at the back of the store with a swipe of their hand.[91] Not only has Tesla tried to alter the experience inside the store from the traditional dealership, but they have also pushed this progressive model out to the exterior appearance and location.

Since opening its first American showroom in Santa Monica, California, in 2008, Tesla has targeted high foot-traffic retail locations across the country to better acquaint casual shoppers with its electric cars.[92] Tesla's retail locations are more like galleries than stores and are not dealerships in the traditional sense. All of them have a Model S sedan and hands-on exhibits highlighting what Tesla has to offer—a kind of place where a wealthy customer shopping the likes of Tiffany and Gucci will wander in and get a taste of what Tesla is all about.[93] The firm currently operates 16 stores in the United States, 2 in Canada, 13 in Europe, and 3 in Asia/Pacific with an ambitious expansion targeting a 50-showroom global network coinciding with the launch of the Model S sedan in 2012.[94]

By integrating distribution, marketing, and sales in this way, Tesla believes that it will be "able to better control costs of inventory, manage warranty service and pricing, maintain and strengthen the Tesla brand, and obtain rapid customer feedback."[95]

Service

An example of customer feedback driving additional value into Tesla's operations is the mobile service concept that the firm has adopted. Tesla relied on customer feedback when putting together its service strategy, as did online shoe retailer Zappos.com and the Best Buy computer repair service "Geek Squad." Similar to the Best Buy concept, the Tesla retail stores are the service hub for mobile service rangers that provide house calls to perform annual inspections and firmware upgrades.[96] The service costs $1 per mile each way, with a $100 minimum. The fee will not cover its expenses, but Tesla says surviving the loss is cheaper than building more service centers.[97]

By adopting this overall model, Tesla believes it "will avoid the conflict of interest in the traditional dealership structure inherent to most incumbent automobile manufacturers where the sale of warranty parts and repairs by a dealer are a key source of revenue and profit for the dealer but often are an expense for the vehicle manufacturer."[98]

Corporate Culture

A significant part of creating a different kind of company has been the focus on building a corporate culture that emphasizes the values and vision espoused by the leadership team. The culture Tesla strives to create starts from the type of people it seeks to hire, as the front page of the career section on its Web site proclaims. "Do you question tradition and constantly think of ways to improve the status quo? Do you thrive in environments where brilliance is common and challenge is the norm?" the Web site asks. "Are you excited by challenge because you're among the best in your field? If so, you'd be in good company at Tesla Motors."[99] For the task of building this entrepreneurial startup-like culture, the firm turned to Arnnon Geshuri, who was successful in building a similar culture at Google. Geshuri has a good track record in assembling great teams and putting people to work. His reputation as a Silicon Valley legend in the realm of staffing and recruiting was cemented at Google, where he managed a recruiting staff of 900 employees who fielded

Exhibit 5 Balance Sheet

Tesla Motors, Inc. Consolidated Balance Sheets (in thousands, except share and per-share data)		
	December 31, 2012	December 31, 2011
Assets		
Current assets		
Cash and cash equivalents	$201,890	$255,266
Short-term marketable securities	—	25,061
Restricted cash	19,094	23,476
Accounts receivable	26,842	9,539
Inventory	268,504	50,082
Prepaid expenses and other current assets	8,438	9,414
Total current assets	524,768	372,838
Operating lease vehicles, net	10,071	11,757
Property, plant and equipment, net	552,229	298,414
Restricted cash	5,159	8,068
Other assets	21,963	22,371
Total assets	$1,114,190	$713,448
Liabilities and Stockholders' Equity		
Current liabilities		
Accounts payable	$303,382	$56,141
Accrued liabilities	39,798	32,109
Deferred revenue	1,905	2,345
Capital lease obligations, current portion	4,365	1,067
Reservation payments	138,817	91,761
Long-term debt, current portion	50,841	7,916
Total current liabilities	539,108	191,339
Common stock warrant liability	10,692	8,838
Capital lease obligations, less current portion	9,965	2,830
Deferred revenue, less current portion	3,060	3,146
Long-term debt, less current portion	401,495	268,335
Other long-term liabilities	25,170	14,915
Total liabilities	989,490	489,403
Commitments and contingencies (Note 14)		
Stockholders' equity:		
Preferred stock; $0.001 par value; 100,000,000 shares authorized; no shares issued and outstanding	—	—
Additional paid-in capital	1,190,191	893,336
Accumulated other comprehensive loss	—	(3)
Accumulated deficit	(1,065,606)	(669,392)
Total stockholders' equity	124,700	224,045
Total liabilities and stockholders' equity	$1,114,190	$713,448

(continued)

Exhibit 5 (continued) Balance Sheet

Tesla Motors, Inc. Consolidated Balance Sheets (in thousands, except share and per-share data)		
DOE Loan Facility draw-downs have been as follows (in thousands):		
	Loan Facility Available for Future Draw-downs	**Interest Rates**
Beginning balance, January 20, 2010	$465,048	
Draw-downs received during the three months ended March 31, 2010	(29,920)	2.9%–3.4%
Draw-downs received during the three months ended June 30, 2010	(15,499)	2.5%–3.4%
Draw-downs received during the three months ended September 30, 2010	(11,138)	1.7%–2.6%
Draw-downs received during the three months ended December 31, 2010	(15,271)	1.7%–2.8%
Remaining balance, December 31, 2010	393,220	
Draw-downs received during the three months ended March 31, 2011	(30,656)	2.1%–3.0%
Draw-downs received during the three months ended June 30, 2011	(31,693)	1.8%–2.7%
Draw-downs received during the three months ended September 30, 2011	(90,822)	1.0%–1.4%
Draw-downs received during the three months ended December 31, 2011	(51,252)	1.0%–1.5%
Remaining balance, December 31, 2011	188,797	
Draw-downs received during the three months ended March 31, 2012	(84,267)	0.9%–1.6%
Draw-downs received during the three months ended June 30, 2012	(71,274)	1.0%–1.3%
Draw-downs received during the three months ended September 30, 2012	(33,256)	1.0%–1.2%
Remaining balance, December 31, 2012	$	—

Source: Tesla Motors. "Quarterly Report Form 10-Q." Financial Statements. November 14, 2011, p. 3.

2.5 million job applications in one year.[100] The brand of creative energy and drive for innovation created at Tesla is said to be different, something that sets it apart from the established competition in Detroit and elsewhere in the United States. As in most Silicon Valley companies, there are no walls within the company's working area. Tesla strives for an open work environment to foster a creative, cooperative, and idea-driven workforce.[101]

Tesla Financials

Due to Tesla's current state of development and the high costs associated with the research and development of electric power trains and vehicle designs, Tesla has realized significant losses since its inception in 2003. From 2003 to December 2012, total losses were $1.065 billion (see Exhibit 5),[102] including a reported loss of $396.3 million or $3.69 per share for year 2012 (see Exhibit 6). In the summer of 2010, Tesla entered into a loan facility from the Department of Energy program designed for Advanced Technology Vehicles Manufacturing in the amount of roughly $465 million.[103] Since then Tesla has had consistent draw-downs on the debt facility to cover operations; and as of December 31, 2012, had availed

itself completely of this loan facility (see Exhibit 7). However, Tesla ended the year with $221 million cash on hand (see Exhibit 5), and with the recent announcement that it would report a profit for the first time, for the first quarter 2013 operations, Tesla seems to have sufficient cash on hand to sustain operations for some time.

Tesla also has significant cash flows coming from a developmental contract with Toyota for electric power trains for an electric version of the Toyota RAV4. The total contract is worth $60 million of which Tesla has received $35.5 million through September 30, 2011.[104] The rest of the contract will be paid as the contract nears completion and will serve as a source of cash flow over the next few years. For the second phase of the agreement, Tesla expects to receive roughly $100 million from Toyota between 2012 and 2014 based on delivery of power train components.[105] Between this contract and sales of the Model S, Tesla has the potential to experience significant growth in sales over that timeframe.

Strategic Challenges

Tesla Motors is presently positioned as the sole manufacturer of fully electric vehicles in the automobile

Exhibit 6 Income Statement

Tesla Motors, Inc. Consolidated Statements of Operations (in thousands, except share and per-share data)			
	Year Ended December 31,		
	2012	**2011**	**2010**
Revenues			
Automotive sales	$385,699	$148,568	$97,078
Development services	27,557	55,674	19,666
Total revenues	413,256	204,242	116,744
Cost of revenues			
Automotive sales	371,658	115,482	79,982
Development services	11,531	27,165	6,031
Total cost of revenues	383,189	142,647	86,013
Gross profit	30,067	61,595	30,731
Operating expenses			
Research and development	273,978	208,981	92,996
Selling, general and administrative	150,372	104,102	84,573
Total operating expenses	424,350	313,083	177,569
Loss from operations	(394,283)	(251,488)	(146,838)
Interest income	288	255	258
Interest expense	(254)	(43)	(992)
Other expense, net	(1,828)	(2,646)	(6,583)
Loss before income taxes	(396,077)	(253,922)	(154,155)
Provision for income taxes	136	489	173
Net loss	$(396,213)	$(254,411)	$(154,328)
Net loss per share of common stock, basic and diluted	$(3.69)	$(2.53)	$(3.04)
Weighted average shares used in computing net loss per share of common stock, basic and diluted	107,349,188	100,388,815	50,718,302

Source: Tesla Motors. "Quarterly Report Form 10-Q." Financial Statements. November 14, 2011, p. 4.

industry. It has enjoyed first-mover advantage with the Tesla Roadster sports car, and Tesla hopes to enjoy future success with its Model S sedan and Model X crossover. These two vehicles will allow Tesla to gain a new customer base beyond the more affluent individuals who were targeted for the Roadster. With environmental concerns and the rising price of gasoline, an electric car does fulfill the needs of a niche market looking for an environmentally friendly car. However, Tesla competes against a large number of automobile makers who have access to a much larger resource pool and market share. Tesla's range and better performance of its EV may not be enough to compete successfully.

With a commitment to developing a car that is better for the environment, Tesla may also take into consideration how the lithium-ion batteries will affect the environment over time and if it will conflict with one of its founding principles. The public concern over global climate change is likely to lead to more government mandates concerning carbon emissions. This could provide Tesla an advantage over other automobile makers. The partnership with Panasonic to develop high-efficiency nickel-based lithium-ion battery cells will definitely provide Tesla with future opportunities. By providing Tesla EV parts to companies such as Daimler and Toyota, Tesla has a large future growth potential as well. Being a young company and competing against larger, established companies may force Tesla to make some hard decisions regarding its product and whether it should diversify its portfolio. Also, the threat of potential newcomers into the EV market is high, especially since manufacturers like Toyota, Chevrolet, Ford, Honda, Nissan,

Exhibit 7　Department of Energy Loan Facility

DOE loan facility draw-downs have been as follows (in thousands):	Loan Facility Available for Future Draw-downs	Interest rates
Beginning balance, January 20, 2010	$465,048	
Draw-downs received during the three months ended March 31, 2010	(29,920)	2.9%–3.4%
Draw-downs received during the three months ended June 30, 2010	(15,499)	2.5%–3.4%
Draw-downs received during the three months ended September 30, 2010	(11,138)	1.7%–2.6%
Draw-downs received during the three months ended December 31, 2010	(15,271)	1.7%–2.8%
Remaining balance, December 31, 2010	393,220	
Draw-downs received during the three months ended March 31, 2011	(30,656)	2.1%–3.0%
Draw-downs received during the three months ended June 30, 2011	(31,693)	1.8%–2.7%
Draw-downs received during the three months ended September 30, 2011	(90,822)	1.0%–1.4%
Draw-downs received during the three months ended December 31, 2011	(51,252)	1.0%–1.5%
Remaining balance, December 31, 2011	188,797	
Draw-downs received during the three months ended March 31, 2012	(84,267)	0.9%–1.6%
Draw-downs received during the three months ended June 30, 2012	(71,274)	1.0%–1.3%
Draw-downs received during the three months ended September 30, 2012	(33,256)	1.0%–1.2%
Remaining balance, December 31, 2012	$	—

Source: Tesla Motors. "Quarterly Report Form 10-Q." Financial Statements. November 14, 2011, p. 14

and Daimler are already in contention in the EV market. Tesla would not have the economies of scale to compete, not to mention the resources to do so, in comparison to the vast resources these companies can bring to any development project.

Tesla has financed much of its business through debt. This leaves the company operating with a continued negative net income. High sales volume will be needed to make a profit and pay down some of the debt. It is a concern whether Tesla is capable of generating sufficient profit in order to lower its debt. Overall, demand for the fully electric car is relatively low. Tesla faces the challenge of increasing the demand for its cars over the cars of the larger rival automobile companies. To create demand, Tesla must demonstrate that its cars compete favorably on the basis of performance, driving range, price, safety, and durability. There are other pressing issues that Tesla needs to address as well. Should Tesla continue to compete in the automobile market, or should they allow itself to be bought out? As it stands, Toyota already owns a significant amount of the firm's shares. If it does choose to compete, would a different approach provide the company with a better market share and position within the industry, as compared to a focus on the relatively high-end and environmentally conscious segment of the market? Can a firm with a Silicon Valley approach succeed in the more traditional automobile sector? Should Tesla expand its focus to include trucks and SUVs, or stick to just high-performance and luxury cars? What market segments should it pursue? And, to combat the debt and increase sales, how should Tesla pursue its expansion on the retail side of things? Is complete control of the stores better than franchising to dealerships? Another issue the key decision makers, such as CEO Elon Musk, face is how to address the maintenance of the cars, the network it would require, and how that fits in with the firm's strategy.

Tesla's future direction and ultimately its success or failure will rely on how management answers these questions over the next few years.

NOTES

1. Tesla Motors. "Quarterly Report Form 10-Q." Financial Statements. November 14, 2011, p. 6.
2. Ibid.
3. Ibid.
4. Ibid., p. 17.
5. Cholia, Amy. "Tesla and Toyota's RAV4 EV and now a Tesla-Daimler Partnership." September 14, 2010. Accessed December 4, 2011. http://alttransport.com/2010/09/tesla-and-toyotas-rav4-ev-and-now-a-tesla-dailmer-partnership.

6. Tesla Motors, Inc. 2011. Shareholder. com. November 13, 2011. http://files. shareholder.com/downloads/ABEA-4CW8X0/1404747030x0x494001/dd297293-ec2d-4dc5-8db4-63d491fb6bd0/Company_Overview_Q3_2011.pdf.

7. Ibid.

8. Ibid.

9. Ibid.

10. Scholer, Kristen and Lee Spears. "Tesla Posts Second-Biggest Rally for 2010 U.S. IPO." June 29, 2010. www.businessweek. com/news/2010-06-29/tesla-posts-second-biggest-rally-for-2010-u-s-ipo.html, accessed December 4, 2011.

11. Tesla Motors, Inc. 2011. Shareholder. com. November 13, 2011 http://files. shareholder.com/downloads/ABEA-4CW8X0/1404747030x0x494001/dd297293-ec2d-4dc5-8db4-63d491fb6bd0/Company_Overview_Q3_2011.pdf.

12. Reuters Fundamentals. TSLA. November 5, 2011.

13. Tesla Motors. "Elon Musk Named Innovator of the Year in Technology by WSJ Magazine" [Online]. October 28, 2011. [Cited December 9, 2011.] www.teslamotors.com/about/press/releases/elon-musk-named-innovator-year-technology-wsj-magazine.

14. Tesla Motors. Executive Bios [Online]. 2011. [Cited December 9, 2011.] www.teslamotors. com/about/executive-bios.

15. Bullis, Kevin. "Technology Review's Annual List of 35 Innovators Under 25 – JB Straubel." 2008. Technology Review published by MIT. December 14, 2011. www.technologyreview. com/tr35/profile.aspx?TRID=742.

16. Tesla Motors. "Deepak Ahuja, Seasoned Auto Industry Finance Executive, Joins Tesla Motors as CFO" [Online]. August 4, 2008. [Cited December 11, 2011.] www. teslamotors.com/about/press/releases/deppak-ahuja-seasoned-auto-industry-finance-executive-joins-tesla-motors-cfo.

17. Tesla Motors. Elon Musk Named Innovator of the Year in Technology by WSJ. Magazine. [Online]October 28, 2011. [Cited December 9, 2011.] www.teslamotors.com/about/press/releases/elon-musk-named-innovator-year-technology-wsj-magazine.

18. Conway, Gavin. "5 minutes with… Deepak Ahuja, Tesla Motors' finance boss." October 6, 2011. The Charging Point. December 14, 2011. www. thechargingpoint.com/entertainment/5-minutes-with-Deepak-Ahuja-Tesla-Motors-finance-boss.html.

19. Gallup Poll, "Americans Global Warming Concerns Continue to Drop," March 11, 2010, www.gallup.com/poll/126560/americans-global-warming-concerns-continue-drop. aspx, accessed December 6, 2011.

20. Greening Business, www.earthshare. org/greening-business.html, accessed December 6, 2011.

21. Tesla Motors, Go Electric – Environment, www.teslamotors.com/goelectric/environment, accessed December 6, 2011.

22. Carbon Tax Center, "Where Carbon is Taxed," July 21, 2011, www.carbontax.org/progress/where-carbon-is-taxed/, accessed December 6, 2011.

23. Tesla Motors Press Release, "Tesla Announces Japan Will be First Destination in Asia," April 21, 2010, www.teslamotors. com/de_DE/about/press/releases/tesla-announces-japan-will-be-first-destination-asia, accessed December 6, 2011.

24. Federal Tax Credit for Electric Vehicles, www.fueleconomy.gov/feg/taxevb.shtml, accessed December 7, 2011.

25. Buchmann, I. "Will Lithium Ion Batteries Power the New Millenium?," Cadex Electronics, Inc., September, 2008, www. buchmann.ca/Article5-Page1.asp, accessed December 6, 2011.

26. Serpo, Alex. "A Ten-fold Improvement in Battery Life," CNET News, January 15, 2008, http://news.cnet.com/A-tenfold-improvement-in-battery-life/2100-1041_3-6226196.html, accessed December 6, 2011.

27. Reuters. "Tesla, Panasonic Partner on Electric Car Batteries," January 7, 2010, www.reuters.com/article/2010/01/07/tesla-panasonic-idUSN0721766720100107, accessed December 6, 2011.

28. Worldwatch Institute Report VST111, "Vehicle Production Rises, But Few Cars are Green," 2011, www.worldwatch.org/node/5461, accessed December 7, 2011.

29. Tesla Motors, Wikipedia article, http://en.wikipedia.org/wiki/Tesla_Motors, accessed December 7, 2011.

30. Reuters, January 7, 2010, "Tesla, Panasonic Partner on Electric Car Batteries," www.reuters.com/article/2010/01/07/tesla-panasonic-idUSN0721766720100107, accessed December 7, 2011.

31. Tesla Motors Company Overview, Summer 2011, "Uniquely Positioned in Large Market", http://files.shareholder.com/downloads/ABEA-4CW8X0/1459391711x0x494001/dd297293-ec2d-4dc5-8db4-63d491fb6bd0/Company_Overview_Q3_2011.pdf, accessed December 7, 2011.

32. Tesla Motors Company Overview, Summer 2011, "EV Leadership Validated By…", http://files.shareholder.com/downloads/ABEA-4CW8X0/1459391711x0x494001/dd297293-ec2d-4dc5-8db4-63d491fb6bd0/Company_Overview_Q3_2011.pdf, accessed December 7, 2011.

33. Standard & Poor's. "Toyota Motor Company." Stock Report. 2011.

34. Ibid.

35. Ibid.

36. Ibid.

37. Ibid.

38. Ibid.

39. Valdes-Depena, Peter. "Toyota Announces 6 New Hybrids, Electric Cars." September 14, 2010. CNN Money. Accessed December 10, 2011. http://money.cnn. com/2010/09/14/autos/toyota_new_hybrids/index.htm.

40. Murphy, John. "Toyota Plans Electric Vehicle in 2012." January 11, 2009. Wall Street Journal. December 10, 2011. http://online.wsj.com/article/SB123168046746371557.html.

41. Ibid.

42. Standard & Poor's. "General Motors." Stock Report. 2011.

43. Ibid.

44. Rana, Omar. GM's sales in China surpassed 2 million in Oct. 2011. November 9, 2011. Accessed December 11, 2011. www. egmcartech.com/2011/11/09/gms-sales-in-china-surpassed-2-million-in-oct-2011.

45. Team, Trefis. "GM Stock Set For 30 Percent Gain As South American Strength Offsets Weakness Elsewhere." November 11, 2011. Forbes. Accessed December 11, 2011.

46. General Motors. "GM Middle East Q3 Sales Increase 21 Percent." October 11, 2011. GM News. December 11, 2011. http://media. gm.com/content/media/us/en/gm/news. detail.html/content/Pages/news/us/en/2011/Oct/1011_GMME.

47. General Motors. Chevy Volt Electric Car Features. 2011. Accessed December 11, 2011. www.chevrolet.com/volt-electric-car/features-specs.

48. Chevrolet. 2010 Volt. Accessed December 15, 2011. www.chevrolet.com/volt-electric-car/.

49. Terlep, Sharon. "Slow Sales Dogged Volt Before Fires." December 5, 2011. Wall Street Journal. Accessed December 11, 2011. http://online.wsj.com/article/SB10001424052970204903804577078692310067200.html.

50. Bradsher, Keith. "G.M. Plans to Develop Electric Cars With China." September 20, 2011. New York Times Online. Accessed December 11, 2011. www.nytimes. com/2011/09/21/business/global/gm-plans-to-develop-electric-cars-with-chinese-automaker.html.

51. Standard & Poor's. "Ford Motor Company." Stock Report 2011.

52. Ibid.

53. Ibid.

54. Fox News. "Ford Unveils Its First Electric Car." January 7, 2011. Fox News.com. Accessed December 11, 2011. http://www.foxnews. com/leisure/2011/01/07/ford-unveils-electric-car.

55. Ibid.

56. Plugin Cars. Detailed Price Information for Ford Focus Electric. December 15, 2011. www.plugincars.com/ford-focus-electric/price.

57. Lichterman, Joseph. "Ford Plugs Electric Cars." 2011. MSN Autoweek. Accessed December 11, 2011. http://editorial. autos.msn.com/article.aspx?cp-documentid=1185287.

58. Standard & Poor's. "Honda Motor Company." Stock Report. 2011.

59. Ibid.

60. Ibid.

61. Honda Motors. "World Debut of Honda Fit EV Concept Electric Vehicle and Plug-in Hybrid Platform at Los Angeles Auto Show."

November 17, 2010. Honda News Releases. Accessed December 11, 2011. http://world. honda.com/news/2010/4101117Fit-EV-Concept-Los-Angeles-Auto-Show.

62. Ibid.

63. Ibid.

64. Addison, John. "New Honda Fit EV likely to cost less than Nissan LEAF." November 30, 2011. CleanTech Blog. Accessed December 15, 2011. www.cleantechblog.com/2010/11/ new-honda-fit-ev-likely-to-cost-less-than-nissan-leaf.html.

65. Standard & Poor's. "Nissan Motor Company." Stock Report. 2011.

66. Ibid.

67. Ibid.

68. Ibid.

69. Ibid.

70. AFP News. "Nissan Leaf electric wins Japan car of the year." December 4, 2011. Yahoo News. Accessed December 11, 2011. http:// ph.news.yahoo.com/nissan-leaf-electric-wins-japan-car-185552497.html.

71. Chambers, Nick. "Nissan LEAF." October 8, 2010. Plugin Cars. Accessed December 11, 2011. www.plugincars.com/nissan-leaf/review.

72. Standard & Poor's. "Nissan Motor Company." Stock Report. 2011.

73. Tesla Motors Company Overview, Summer 2011, "Tesla-Owned Distribution and Service," http://files. shareholder.com/downloads/ABEA-4CW8X0/1459391711x0x494001/dd297293-ec2d-4dc5-8db4-63d491fb6bd0/Company_Overview_Q3_2011.pdf.

74. Yarow, Jay. "Revealed: Tesla's IPO Roadshow." June 22, 2010. Business Insider. Accessed December 12, 2011. www. businessinsider.com/teslas-ipo-roadshow-2010-6#tesla-is-a-technology-company-not-a-car-company-1.

75. Ibid.

76. "Corporate Strategy Tesla Motors." October 11, 2011. Online Automotive News Update. Accessed December 12, 2011. www.otpnews. info/corporate-strategy-tesla-motors.html.

77. DeBord, Matthew. "Could Tesla Lead Electric Car Business? Maybe." August 3, 2011. CBS Moneywatch. Accessed December 12, 2011. www.cbsnews.com/8301-505123_162-48741282/could-tesla-lead-electric-car-business-maybe.

78. Yarow, Jay. "Revealed: Tesla's IPO Roadshow." June 22, 2010. Business Insider.

Accessed December 12, 2011. www. businessinsider.com/teslas-ipo-roadshow-2010-6#tesla-is-a-technology-company-not-a-car-company-1.

79. Tesla Motors. Tesla Model S Facts. Accessed December 14, 2011. www.teslamotors.com/ models/facts.

80. "Corporate Strategy Tesla Motors." October 11, 2011. Online Automotive News Update. Accessed December 12, 2011. www. otpnews.info/corporate-strategy-tesla-motors.html.

81. Yarow, Jay. "Revealed: Tesla's IPO Roadshow." June 22, 2010. Business Insider. Accessed December 12, 2011. www. businessinsider.com/teslas-ipo-roadshow-2010-6#tesla-is-a-technology-company-not-a-car-company-1.

82. DeBord, Matthew. "Could Tesla Lead Electric Car Business? Maybe." August 3, 2011. CBS Moneywatch. Accessed December 12, 2011. www.cbsnews.com/8301-505123_162-48741282/could-tesla-lead-electric-car-business-maybe.

83. Yarow, Jay. "Revealed: Tesla's IPO Roadshow." June 22, 2010. Business Insider. Accessed December 12, 2011. www. businessinsider.com/teslas-ipo-roadshow-2010-6#tesla-is-a-technology-company-not-a-car-company-1.

84. Boslet, Mark, and Eric Weshoff. "Tesla Targets 50 Auto Showrooms With an Apple Twist." July 9, 2010. Greentech Media. Accessed December 12, 2011. www. greentechmedia.com/articles/read/tesla-targets-50-auto-showrooms-with-an-apple-twist.

85. Ibid.

86. Garthwaite, Josie. "Tesla IPO: 12 Things You Should Know." January 31, 2010. GigaOM. Accessed December 12, 2011. http://gigaom. com/cleantech/tesla-ipo-12-things-you-should-know-about-tesla.

87. Tesla Motors. "Tesla Puts Model S Technology On Display." November 23, 2011. Accessed December 12, 2011. http://ir.teslamotors.com/releasedetail. cfm?ReleaseID=626357.

88. Ibid.

89. "Tesla Takes Auto Retail High-Tech With Digital Design Studio." April 20, 2011. The Auto Channel. Accessed December 12, 2011. www.theautochannel.com/ news/2011/04/20/528894-tesla-takes-auto-

retail-high-tech-with-digital-design-studio. html.

90. Ibid.

91. Ibid.

92. Sweeney, Brigid. "Tesla Showroom Coming to Oakbrook Center." November 3, 2011. Chicago Business. Accessed December 12, 2011. www.chicagobusiness.com/ article/20111103/BLOGS01/111109889/tesla-showroom-coming-to-oakbrook-center.

93. LeBeau, Phil. "Tesla's High-End Boutiques are Spreading." November 3, 2011. CNBC. Accessed December 12, 2011. www.cnbc. com/id/45152857/Tesla_s_High_End_Boutiques_are_Spreading.

94. Boslet, Mark, and Eric Weshoff. "Tesla Targets 50 Auto Showrooms With an Apple Twist." July 9, 2010. Greentech Media. Accessed December 12, 2011. www. greentechmedia.com/articles/read/tesla-targets-50-auto-showrooms-with-an-apple-twist.

95. Ibid.

96. Squatriglia, Chuck. "Tesla's Repair 'Rangers' Make House Calls." October 6, 2009. Autopia. Accessed December 12, 2011. www.wired.com/autopia/2009/10/tesla-housecalls/.

97. Ibid.

98. Boslet, Mark, and Eric Weshoff. "Tesla Targets 50 Auto Showrooms With an Apple Twist." July 9, 2010. Greentech Media. Accessed December 12, 2011. www. greentechmedia.com/articles/read/tesla-targets-50-auto-showrooms-with-an-apple-twist.

99. Hull, Dana. "The Man to See About a Job at Tesla." December 10, 2011. Mercury News. Accessed December 12, 2011. www. mercurynews.com/business/ci_19501138.

100. Ibid.

101. Ibid.

102. Tesla Motors. Fourth Quarter & Full Year 2012 Shareholder Letter. www.sec.gov/Archives/edgar/ data/1318605/000119312513067177/ d462441dex991.htm. "Quarterly Report Form 10-Q." Financial Statements. November 14, 2011, p. 6.

103. Tesla Motors. "Quarterly Report Form 10-Q." Financial Statements. November 14, 2011, p. 14.

104. Ibid, p. 17.

105. Ibid, p. 22.

CASE 30

Yahoo! Inc.: Marissa Mayer's Challenge[1]

At 12:45 a.m. on August 25, 2012, Marissa Mayer, the recently appointed chief executive officer (CEO) of Yahoo! Inc. (Yahoo), sent an e-mail to all employees of the company. The e-mail exhorted them to continue to work hard and keep up their spirits, given the many challenges the company faced.[2] The email indicated to the employees that their CEO, pregnant and due to deliver her first child in early October, was hard at work at that late hour. Mayer was due to meet Yahoo's board in mid-September at Yahoo's headquarters in Sunnyvale, California, in order to present her strategy to turn the company around. The board meeting, originally scheduled for New York City, had been moved to its current location given Mayer's advanced stage of pregnancy. In recent months, Yahoo had reconstituted its board to admit three members who represented an activist shareholder, seen the departure of its previous CEO amid embarrassing circumstances, suffered the loss of key senior executives, and faced the phasing out of its investment in Alibaba, a Chinese Internet company. After a highly secretive search, Yahoo's board had convinced Mayer to move from Google (where she was the company's twentieth hire) to take over the leadership position at Yahoo.[3] The Yahoo board, the investment community, and Yahoo's employees were all eagerly waiting for Mayer's vision for confronting the company's challenges.

The Internet Consumer Services Industry[4]

The Internet was a vast network of interconnected smaller networks of computers, supported by both tangible infrastructure (physical hardware) and intangible infrastructure. In 2012, the Internet was the essential medium for communication and content and its importance to everyday life was regarded as higher than that of the telephone, television, and computer. Companies that provided the intangible infrastructural support to the Internet were clustered into segments whose boundaries were rapidly changing and dissolving. Of these clusters, companies such as Google and Yahoo comprised the content and electronic commerce segment. This segment consisted of players that offered search engines and portals to enter and navigate the Internet, as well as a wide gamut of destinations for information and shopping. These players sought to monetize the traffic that passed through their offerings via advertising and transaction fees. Players in this segment often expanded to other Internet segments in order to consolidate their competitive position.

Search sites allowed users to find relevant information on the Internet. The quest for companies in this sub-segment was to use technology to offer accuracy and

Case 30: Yahoo! Inc.: Marissa Mayer's Challenge

397

speed to users as a way of differentiating themselves from others. In March 2012, the top three players in terms of market share were Google (66.4 percent), Microsoft (15.3 percent), and Yahoo (13.8 percent). While Google had held onto its leadership position, Microsoft's Bing (launched in 2009) had taken market share away from Yahoo and a host of smaller players. As per an agreement reached between Microsoft and Yahoo, Bing was to power all of Yahoo's search offerings by mid-2012. Search sites monetized traffic through banner (display) and keyword advertising.

Portals were sites that aggregated content (some of which was their own, while the vast majority belonged to others) in a unified way and were often the starting point for users' Internet activity. Microsoft, Yahoo, and AOL were the leading portals. However, Google, which was essentially a search site because of its simple interface, offered iGoogle, a customizable portal. Like search sites, portals obtained revenue through advertising, although many of them received transaction fees from several fee- or subscription-based sites that were accessed through the portal.

Players in the portal segment attempted to offer an array of destination sites for information, entertainment, and electronic commerce. The goal of these players was to drive traffic to the myriad sites and monetize the traffic via display and click-through advertising, as well as by selling several fee- or subscription-based services. In this sub-segment, competition was intense between pure portal sites and search sites that offered various destination options. The key metric to measure traffic to these sites was the number of unique visitors for a specific period (see Exhibit 1). In recent times, however,

advertisers looked at the average time spent by users at a site as a key measure of advertising rates. In this area, social networking sites such as Facebook and Twitter had a distinct advantage over portals and search sites. A 2012 study reported that the average time spent by a user on Facebook was 405 minutes a month and that Facebook alone accounted for nearly 15 percent of the time users spent online, compared to 10.6 percent for all of Google's sites, and 8.6 percent for Yahoo's sites.

Internet advertising revenues in the United States were $31.7 billion in 2011[5] (compared to $38.5 billion for broadcast television and $30 billion for cable television), representing an increase of 22 percent over 2010. An industry expert explained the significance of crossing the $30 billion mark:

This historic moment, with an especially impressive achievement in mobile, is indicative of an increased awareness from advertisers that they need to reach consumers where they are spending their time — in digital media. Pushing past the $30 billion barrier, the interactive advertising industry confirms its central space in media. Across search, display, and digital video, digital provides a wealth of opportunity for brands and consumers. With the proliferation of smartphones and tablets, it is likely that the tremendous growth in mobile will continue as these screens become even more crucial to the marketing mix.[6]

The fastest-growing segment of Internet advertising was mobile advertising, which totaled $1.6 billion in 2011, an increase of 149 percent over 2010. An industry expert commented on mobile advertising:

The year 2011 saw mobile advertising become a meaningful category. By combining some of the best features of the Internet, along with portability and location-based technology, mobile advertising is enabling marketers to deliver timely, targeted, relevant, and local advertisements in a manner that was not previously possible. It is for these reasons that we see strong growth to continue with mobile advertising.[7]

In 2011, the 10 leading search and portal companies accounted for 71 percent of total online advertising revenues, while the next fifteen accounted for 11 percent. Search revenues of $14.8 billion (up from $11.7 billion in 2010) made up 46.5 percent of total revenues (up from 44.8 percent in 2010), while display-related advertising was $11.1 billion (versus $9.6 billion in 2010) or 34.8 percent. Of the two prevalent pricing models, performance-based pricing (cost per click-through) had been the dominant model since 2006 and accounted for 65 percent of all advertising in 2011.[8]

Exhibit 1 U.S. Internet Traffic Data for January 2012 (Top Five)

Site[1]	Unique Visitors (Millions)[2]	Reach Percentage[3]
Google	187.368	85.1
Microsoft	179.220	81.4
Yahoo!	177.249	80.5
Facebook	163.505	74.3
Amazon	109.997	50.0

[1] Includes various sites owned by the specific company.

[2] This represents the number of times a site was opened; page views indicates the number of pages opened by a visitor in a site and is also used as a traffic metric. For example, Yahoo reported over 700 million page views in January 2012.

[3] The percentage of Internet-active individuals who visit the site (one of all the sites owned by a company) at least once during the month.

Source: Standard & Poor's Industry Surveys: Computers: Consumer Services & The Internet, April 5, 2012.

As reported in *Standard & Poor's Industry Surveys*, there were around 613 million websites worldwide in February 2012, a significant increase from 285 million in 2011. Several factors were responsible for the growth of the Internet. Chief among them were the increasing affordability of computers and increasing Internet penetration rates. In a virtuous cycle, as component prices fell rapidly, PC manufacturers passed on the price decreases to customers, who in turn increased the demand for PCs, leading to lower prices due to manufacturers' economies of scale and purchasing power savings. For example, nearly 80 percent of U.S. households owned a PC in 2012, up from 63 percent in 2000, and the vast majority of users had bought a PC or a similar device for Internet connectivity. In 2011, North America had the largest Internet penetration rate of 78.6 percent, followed by Oceania/Australia with 67.5 percent, and Europe with 61.3 percent. However, the fastest-growing market in percentage terms was Africa, and the fastest-growing market in absolute terms was Asia, which had over a billion Internet users in 2011 versus 114,300 in 2000. While the average worldwide Internet penetration rate was 32.7 percent, Asia's was only 26.2 percent (only higher than Africa's 13.5 percent),[9] indicating the growth potential of this region (Exhibit 2 provides a profile of worldwide Internet usage).

Yahoo's Company Background[10]

In February 1994, two graduate students at Stanford University in California, David Filo and Jerry Yang, wanted to find a way to keep track of their favorite websites on the Internet. As the list of websites became larger each day, they began categorizing them into groups and subgroups. They developed a website to capture their categorization method and called it Yahoo!, naming it after the dictionary definition of the word: "rude, unsophisticated, uncouth." Housed in their two computers in a campus trailer, their search engine began to attract the attention of their friends and soon others who needed a way to find websites of interest on the Internet. By the fall of 1994, Yahoo recorded its millionth user hit and Filo and Yang realized that they had chanced upon a business opportunity. They obtained venture capital funding and appointed Tim Koogle (a Motorola veteran and Stanford graduate) as the company's first CEO. Yahoo went public through an initial public offering (IPO) in April 1996. The company offered the first online navigational guide to the World Wide Web and monetized this opportunity by selling advertising space on its site. Soon after its IPO, Yahoo formed Yahoo! Japan and Yahoo! Europe to offer search services to Internet users worldwide. The company grew organically and via acquisitions, to both broaden its reach and generate additional revenue streams.

When Terry Semel replaced Tim Koogle as CEO in 2001, Yahoo had 3,000 employees, 24 global properties, and annual revenues of over $717 million. During this time, it had dropped Inktomi as its search engine provider and moved to using the then-startup Google. Semel continued Yahoo's push to seek new revenue sources by getting into music, blogging, and photo sharing and posting.

Jerry Yang, one of Yahoo's co-founders, replaced Terry Semel as CEO in 2007. Yahoo faced intense competition from Google in the Internet advertising space, and the two companies competed with each other to acquire complementary businesses. A combination of intensifying competition and the global economic slowdown resulted in Yahoo's first employee layoffs in early 2008 and a second round at the end of the same year. In 2008, Microsoft made a second bid to acquire Yahoo,

Exhibit 2 Worldwide Internet Usage as of December 21, 2011

Region	Internet Users	Percentage of Total Worldwide Internet Users	Internet Growth Rate Percentage (2000–2011)	Penetration (Percentage of Total Population)
Africa	139,875,242	6.2	2,988.4	13.5
Asia	1,016,799,076	44.8	789.6	26.2
Europe	500,723,686	22.1	376.4	61.3
Middle East	77,020,995	3.4	2,244.8	35.6
North America	273,067,546	12.0	152.6	78.6
Latin America/Caribbean	235,819,740	10.4	1,205.1	39.5
Oceania/Australia	23,927,457	1.1	214.0	67.5

Source: Internet World Stats, www.internetworldstats.com/stats.htm, accessed August 28, 2012.

Case 30: Yahoo! Inc.: Marissa Mayer's Challenge

399

after its 2006 bid had been rejected. Jerry Yang and Roy Bostock (Yahoo's board chairman) convinced the company's board to reject Microsoft's offer, considering it as undervaluing Yahoo.

Carol Bartz replaced Jerry Yang as CEO in 2009. She was charged with turning around the company and toward that goal she announced a search engine partnership with Microsoft, sold several underperforming acquisitions, and discontinued certain services. In addition, Bartz expanded Yahoo's global presence by making key acquisitions in regions such as the Middle East. However, Yahoo's revenues declined for the third consecutive year in fiscal 2010, and the company announced further employee layoffs to cut costs. Bartz was fired by Yahoo's board in late 2011 after failing to turn around the company. She was replaced on an interim basis by Tim Morse, the company's chief financial officer.

In January 2012, the board announced that Scott Thompson, then the president of PayPal, would become the company's new CEO. Thompson's tenure was short as he was forced to step down on May 13, 2012, after it was revealed that he had falsified his educational background on his resumé. During Thompson's tenure, Daniel Loeb, who controlled the hedge fund Third Point LLC, became an activist investor at Yahoo and demanded sweeping changes at the board and top management levels.

After Thompson's departure, Roy Bostock and two other board members stepped down, and Fred Amoroso became board chairman. Yahoo appointed Ross Levinsohn (who headed the company's media business) as interim CEO and began an intense search for a permanent leader. At the July 12, 2012, annual stockholders' meeting, Daniel Loeb and two of his nominees were elected to Yahoo's board. On July 16, 2012, the board announced that Marissa Mayer, a senior executive at rival Google, was to be Yahoo's new CEO. Ross Levinsohn, who had fully expected to be named Yahoo's permanent CEO, resigned from the company after Mayer's appointment.[11]

Corporate Governance at Yahoo

The Microsoft Bid

On February 1, 2008, Microsoft made an unsolicited bid to acquire Yahoo by offering (in cash and stock) $31 per share, valuing the company at $44.6 billion. Yahoo's stock price had closed at $19.18 the previous day. When Yahoo's board rejected the offer, Microsoft increased its bid price to $33 per share.[12]

Once again, Yahoo rejected the bid, demanding $37 per share (valuing Yahoo at $47.5 billion). In a letter

to Steve Ballmer, Microsoft's CEO, offering the rationale for rejecting the bid, Yahoo stated:

Our Board… unanimously concluded that it (the bid) was not in the best interests of Yahoo! and its stockholders. Our Board cited Yahoo!'s global brand, large worldwide audience, significant recent investments in advertising platforms and future growth prospects, free cash flow and earnings potential, as well as its substantial unconsolidated investments, as factors in its decision.… We are not opposed to a transaction with Microsoft if it is in the best interests of our stockholders. Our position is simply that any transaction must be at a value that fully reflects the value of Yahoo!, including any strategic benefits to Microsoft, and on terms that provide certainty to our stockholders.[13]

Carl Icahn's Proxy Fight

After Microsoft withdrew its offer on May 3, 2008, activist investor Carl Icahn (who had invested in Yahoo earlier and owned 4.98 percent of Yahoo's common stock) launched a proxy fight to replace all 10 board members with his own nominees at the upcoming stockholders' meeting. Icahn's intention was to force the sale of Yahoo to Microsoft upon gaining control of the board.[14] On July 21, 2008, Yahoo announced that it had settled with Icahn by appointing him to the board and giving board seats to two of his nominees. In return, Icahn agreed to withdraw his proxy fight. He eventually resigned from Yahoo's board in October 2009 and in 2010 began to rapidly decrease his investment in the company.

Third Point LLC's Activism[15]

Daniel S. Loeb, who headed the hedge fund Third Point LLC, began accumulating Yahoo shares in 2011 and by March 2012 held 5.8 percent of the company's outstanding shares. He began to actively campaign for changes after several unfruitful meetings with CEO Scott Thompson. Loeb was firm in demanding that Yahoo's strategic direction should be to find ways to monetize the millions of site visitors per month. Rather than focus on pushing Yahoo into new businesses, which was Scott Thompson's vision, Loeb wanted Yahoo to focus on its media business. He argued that in hiring two executives to the board with a technology background (which Yahoo had done in February 2012), Yahoo was moving away from the media business. In addition, Loeb demanded that the company sell its Alibaba stake as well as its 35 percent stake in Yahoo Japan and use the capital to strengthen its core advertising business. Loeb filed a proxy statement to gather support for his four nominees (three of whom had advertising backgrounds, the fourth was himself) to replace the more technology-oriented Yahoo board members.

"Resumégate"

On May 3, 2012, a Silicon Valley website reported that Daniel Loeb had written to Yahoo's board about a possible discrepancy in CEO Scott Thompson's educational background. Loeb had alleged that Thompson had inaccurately indicated that he had graduated with dual degrees in accounting and computer science, whereas in reality he had graduated with just an accounting degree. Since Yahoo had reported Thompson's educational background in regulatory filings, this error amounted to a misrepresentation of facts.[16] Yahoo's board admitted that Loeb was correct in his accusations and after an internal investigation, Thompson resigned from the company. Patti S. Hart, a member of Yahoo's board who took the lead role in vetting Thompson at the time of his appointment, resigned following Thompson's departure.

At the July 12, 2012, annual stockholders' meeting, Daniel Loeb and two of his nominees were elected to the company's board. His fourth nominee voluntarily took himself out of the running after Third Point and Yahoo reached an agreement. Exhibit 3 lists Yahoo's board members.

Yahoo's Business Operations[17]

Products and Organization. In 2012, Yahoo was a global digital media company that attracted visitors to its website by offering personalized content and experiences and monetized the visits via advertising (81 percent of total revenues in 2011) and transaction fees.

Exhibit 3 Yahoo's Board Members

Name	Member Since
Alfred Amoroso (Board Chairman)	February 2012
John Hayes	April 2012
Sue James	January 2010
David Kenny	April 2011
Peter Liguori	March 2012
Daniel Loeb	May 2012
Marissa Mayer (CEO and President)	July 2012
Thomas McInerney	April 2012
Brad Smith	June 2010
Maynard Webb	February 2012
Harry Wilson	May 2012
Michael Wolf	May 2012

Source: "Board of Directors," Yahoo!, Inc., http://investor.yahoo.net/directors.cfm, accessed May 2, 2012.

The company's online properties and services (called Yahoo! Properties) were classified into three categories: Communications and Communities, Search and Marketplaces, and Media.

Products in the Communications and Communities category included Yahoo! Mail, Yahoo! Messenger, Yahoo! Groups, Yahoo! Answers, Flickr, and Connected TV, and were aimed at enabling users to "organize into groups and share knowledge, common interests, and photos."[18] While some of these services were free of charge and supported by advertising revenue, other services were fee- or subscription-based.

Offerings such as Yahoo! Search, Yahoo! Local, Yahoo! Shopping, and Yahoo! Travel in the Search and Marketplaces category were "designed to quickly answer users' information needs by delivering innovative and meaningful search, local, and listings experiences on the search results pages and across Yahoo!"[19] In December 2009, Yahoo entered into a ten-year agreement with Microsoft whereby Microsoft would get a 12 percent share of search revenues and would provide Yahoo with the technology that ran its search engine. The agreement discontinued Yahoo's existing relationship for this purpose with Google. Yahoo generated revenues from this category via listing fees and transaction fees in addition to advertising.

Products such as Yahoo! Homepage, Yahoo! News, and Yahoo! Finance formed the cornerstone of the Media category, whose goal was to engage users with "compelling content."[20] While the majority of revenues for this category came from advertising, Yahoo! Sports services such as Yahoo! Fantasy Football were fee-based. Exhibit 4a provides a breakdown of Yahoo's revenues.

Yahoo managed its global business geographically, reporting financial results by three segments — Americas, EMEA (Europe, Middle East, and Africa), and Asia Pacific (Exhibit 4b reports financial results per geographic segment). Yahoo sites were in 45 languages in 60 countries.

Sales, Marketing, and Product Development.

Since advertising was the primary revenue driver, Yahoo organized its sales team into three categories based on the type of customer served. The field advertising sales channel sold display and search advertising to leading advertisers and agencies. The mid-market channel sold advertising to medium-sized businesses, and the reseller/small business channel sold it to regional and small business advertisers. While Yahoo employed its own sales teams in the United States, it used a combination of internal salespeople and external sales agencies in international markets. The marketing team ensured that the

Case 30: Yahoo! Inc.: Marissa Mayer's Challenge

401

Exhibit 4 Yahoo! Inc. Revenue Breakdown

Ex. 4a Revenue Sources ($) in thousands			
	2009	**2010**	**2011**
Display	1,866,984	2,154,886	2,160,309
Search	3,396,396	3,161,589	1,853,110
Other[1]	1,196,935	1,008,176	970,780
TOTAL	**6,460,315**	**6,324,651**	**4,984,199**

[1] Listings-based services revenue, transaction revenue, and fees revenue.

Ex. 4b Revenues by Geographic Segment ($) in thousands			
	2009	**2010**	**2011**
Americas	4,852,331	4,425,457	3,302,989
EMEA[1]	598,300	579,145	629,383
Asia Pacific	1,009,684	1,320,049	1,051,827
TOTAL	**6,460,315**	**6,324,651**	**4,984,199**

[1] Europe, Middle East, and Africa.

Source: Yahoo! Form 10-K, Annual Report, http://yhoo.client.shareholder.com/secfiling.cfm?filingID=1193125-11-50000, accessed May 2, 2012.

Yahoo! brand name continued to be widely recognized and drew traffic to the company's various properties. Yahoo used a combination of organic and acquisition-driven paths to product innovation. It spent $1 billion in internal product development in 2011 (versus $1.1 billion in 2010 and $1.2 billion in 2009), employing a team of software engineers and forming alliances with universities to improve existing products and create new ones.

Human Resources. When Yahoo announced cuts to its workforce of 2,000 employees in April 2012, it was the sixth major round of layoffs in the last four years. The company's employee headcount in September 2012 was around 12,000, spread out in 25 countries. Depending on their tenure and position in the organization, employees were compensated by salary, bonuses, commission, and stock options. The vast majority of the employees worked in the product development area, followed by sales and marketing, administration, and operations. Yahoo used a matrix structure where products such as Messenger, Mail, and Yahoo! Finance were the "verticals," and support functions such as public relations and legal were the "horizontals." The structure was created during former CEO Terry Semel's tenure (2001–2007).

Finances. Exhibit 5 provides Yahoo's financial statements for a three-year period, while Exhibit 6 contains summary stock prices for the company. Yahoo had not declared a dividend in its history. A $100 investment in Yahoo stock on December 29, 2006, would have resulted in an investment value of $59 on December 30, 2011, in comparison to $140 for the NASDAQ 100 Index, $99.50 for the S&P 500, and $137 for the S&P North American Technology-Internet Index.

Enter Marissa Mayer

Early Actions. Prior to joining Yahoo, Marissa Mayer had a 13-year career at Google, where she held a variety of positions. She was responsible for launching

Exhibit 5 Yahoo! Inc. Financial Statements Consolidated Statements of Income (Condensed for Year Ending December 31 in $ Thousands)

	2009	**2010**	**2011**
Revenue	6,460,315	6,324,651	4,984,199
Cost of Revenue	2,871,746	2,627,545	1,502,650
Gross Profit	**3,588,569**	**3,697,106**	**3,481,549**
Operating Expenses:			
Sales and Marketing	1,245,350	1,264,491	1,122,302
Product Development	1,210,168	1,082,176	1,005,090
General and Administrative	580,352	488,332	495,804
Amortization of Intangibles	39,106	31,626	33,592
Restructuring Charges, net	126,901	57,957	24,420
Total Operating Expenses	**3,201,877**	**2,924,582**	**2,681,208**
Income From Operations	386,692	772,524	800,341
Other Income, net	187,528	297,869	27,175
Earnings in Equity Interests	250,390	395,758	476,920
Net Income (after provision for taxes and income attributable to non-controlling interests)	**597,992**	**1,231,663**	**1,048,827**

(Continued)

Exhibit 5 (Continued) Yahoo! Inc. Financial Statements Consolidated Statements of Income (Condensed for Year Ending December 31 in $ Thousands)

	2010	2011
ASSETS		
Current Assets:		
Cash and Cash Equivalents	1,526,427	1,562,390
Short-term Marketable Debt Securities	1,357,661	493,189
Accounts Receivable, net	1,028,900	1,037,474
Prepaid Expenses and Other Current Assets	432,560	359,483
Total Current Assets	**4,345,548**	**3,452,536**
Long-term Marketable Securities	744,594	474,338
Property and Equipment, net	1,653,422	1,730,888
Goodwill	3,681,645	3,900,752
Intangible Assets, net	255,870	254,600
Other Long-term Assets	235,136	220,628
Investments in Equity Interests	4,011,889	4,749,044
Total Assets	**14,928,104**	**14,782,786**
LIABILITIES & EQUITY		
Current Liabilities:		
Accounts Payable	162,424	166,595
Accrued Expenses & Other Current Liab.	1,208,792	846,044
Deferred Revenue	254,656	194,722
Total Current Liabilities	**1,625,872**	**1,207,361**
Long-term Deferred Revenue	56,365	43,639
Capital Leases & Other Long-term Liab.	142,799	134,905
Deferred & Other Long-term Liabilities	506,658	815,534
Total Liabilities	**2,331,694**	**2,201,439**
Stockholders' Equity	12,596,410	12,581,347
Total Liabilities and Equity	**14,928,104**	**14,782,786**

Yahoo! Inc. Summary Statements of Cash Flow (In $ Thousands for Year Ended December 31)			
	2009	2010	2011
Net Cash Flow Provided by Operating Activities	1,310,346	1,240,190	1,323,806
Net Cash (Used in) Provided by Investing Activities	(2,419,238)	509,915	202,362
Net Cash (Used in) Provided by Financing Activities	34,597	(1,501,706)	(1,455,958)
Effect of Exchange Rate Changes on Cash & Cash Equivalents	57,429	2,598	(34,247)
Net Change in Cash & Cash Equivalents	(1,016,866)	250,997	35,963
Cash & Cash Equivalents at Beginning of Year	2,292,296	1,275,430	1,526,427
Cash & Cash Equivalents at End of Year	**1,275,430**	**1,526,427**	**1,562,390**

Source: Adapted from Yahoo! Inc. 2011 10-K. Yahoo! Form 10-K, Annual Report, http://yhoo.client.shareholder.com/secfiling.cfm?filingID=1193125-11-50000, accessed May 2, 2012.

Exhibit 6 Yahoo! Inc. Selected Stock Price Data ($ at Close of Market)

Date	Price
Jan. 2, 2008	19.18
Jan. 2, 2009	11.73
Jan. 4, 2010	15.01
Jan. 3, 2011	16.12
Jan. 3, 2012	15.47
Sept. 4, 2012	15.74

Source: Yahoo! Finance, http://finance.yahoo.com/, accessed May 2, 2012.

more than 100 products at Google and was a key player in developing Google's home page. Her last position at the company was Vice-President of Local, Maps, and Location Services, where she led the product management, engineering, design, and overall strategy for the Google Maps suite of products.[21]

One of the first things that Mayer did at Yahoo was to announce that she would review every hire that the company made, a practice similar to that done at Google by the company's two co-founders. While this slowed down hiring at Yahoo, one anonymous company employee was quoted as saying:

It's gotten a little frustrating. But I can't say that I blame her. The problem at Yahoo in the past couple of years has been "B-players" hiring "C-players" who were not fired up to come to work and were tolerated too long. I mean nobody good wanted to come to Yahoo. If I am inheriting a mess like that, I'd want to review all the talent that comes in the doors, too.[22]

She quickly instituted a number of changes at the company. Principal among them were a weekly all-employee meeting every Friday afternoon, free food in the company cafeteria, replacement of employees' Blackberry phones with a choice of iPhones or Android-based phones, and the launch of a program termed "PB&J," an acronym for Process, Bureaucracy, and Jams. The PB&J program was to solicit employee input on a variety of things, including improving the work culture and increasing productivity. One employee reacted to Mayer's actions:

While the free food and iPhones are nice, it was the midnight email that finally won my heart. Redundant processes and policy, and bureaucracy are the worst enemies to innovation and efficiency. Of course, change will not happen overnight. There are so many things that need to improve in order to get us back in the same league as Google

and Apple. But I have faith in the company and Marissa. And I truly hope the company will be great again.[23]

Challenges. The privately owned Alibaba Group was one of China's biggest Internet companies specializing in electronic commerce. In 2005, Yahoo invested $1 billion in Alibaba for a 40 percent equity share. It also handed over the responsibility of operating its Yahoo! China website to Alibaba. The two companies began negotiations in 2010 on the future of Yahoo's investment. Softbank, a Japanese Internet and telecommunications company, had also invested in Alibaba. In addition, Softbank had a 65 percent stake in Yahoo! Japan, with Yahoo owning the rest. Alibaba and Softbank wanted to buy out Yahoo's stake in Alibaba as well as its stake in Yahoo! Japan. While Yahoo agreed to the Alibaba divestment (it had made no decision on the Yahoo! Japan issue), the bone of contention was in structuring the deal to minimize Yahoo's tax bill on the capital gains. In late August 2012, Yahoo announced that it would sell half its Alibaba investment immediately for $7.6 billion (resulting in after-tax cash of $4.3 billion) and the rest when Alibaba was expected to go public in 2015.[24] The key challenge to Mayer in this area was how to use the proceeds of the Alibaba investment. Early on, she had indicated that she would use the proceeds to make critical acquisitions, but pressure from shareholders had caused her to back off from this position.

In addition to the Alibaba issue, Mayer faced the main strategic challenge of establishing Yahoo's identity as a company. While it had started out as a technology firm, its principal revenue source was currently advertising. However, many Yahoo insiders still regarded themselves as working for a technology company that had a presence in media. Daniel Loeb's insistence that Yahoo's best bet was to find a way to monetize its visitor traffic indicated that he wanted Yahoo to morph into a media company. Given Mayer's technology background and experience at Google, would this morphing play to her strengths? The growing markets were Asia and Africa, regions where Yahoo had only a weak presence. Should Yahoo acquire companies to benefit from growth in these markets? In addition, the Internet was moving to a mobile platform where Yahoo had only a marginal presence. While the mobile platform was showing tremendous growth (albeit from a small base), it was not clear whether it would support traditional revenue sources. Management faced these issues prior to meeting with the company's board in September.

NOTES

1. This case has been written on the basis of published sources only. Consequently, the interpretation and perspectives presented in this case are not necessarily those of Yahoo! Inc or any of its employees.

2. Nicholas Carlson, "Marissa Mayer Sent a Late Night Email Promising to Make Yahoo 'The Absolute Best Place to Work,'" August 27, 2012, www.businessinsider.com/marissa-mayer-sent-a-late-night-email-promising-to-make-yahoo-the-absolutebest- place-to-work-2012-8, accessed September 22, 2012.

3. Yahoo! Press Release, July 16, 2012, http://files.shareholder.com/downloads/YHOO/2435053555x0x583265/6948e13b-7b6c-49d8-9011-a7220229460e/YHOO_News_2012_7_16_General.pdf, accessed September 22, 2012.

4. Standard & Poor's Industry Surveys: Computers: Consumer Services & The Internet, April 5, 2012.

5. IAB Internet Advertising Report, April 2012, www.iab.net, accessed September 24, 2012.

6. Ibid.

7. Ibid.

8. Ibid.

9. Internet World Stats, www.internetworldstats.com/stats.htm, accessed September 24, 2012.

10. Yahoo! Inc. Company Information, www.hoovers.com/company-information/cs/company-profile.Yahoo!_Inc.7fdc8a9aba94345b.html, accessed May 2, 2012; "The History of Yahoo! - How It All Started…" Yahoo! Media Relations, http://docs.yahoo.com/info/misc/history.html, accessed September 18, 2012

11. Kara Swisher, "Exclusive — Ross Levinsohn Departs Yahoo," http://allthingsd.com/20120730/as-expected-ross-levinsohndeparts-yahoo/, accessed May 2, 2012.

12. "Microsoft Makes Unsolicited Bid for Yahoo," NBCNEWS.com, www.msnbc.msn.com/id/22947626/ns/businessus_business/t/microsoft-makes-unsolicited-bid-yahoo, accessed September 18, 2012.

13. Yahoo! Press Release, April 7, 2008, http://files.shareholder.com/downloads/YHOO/2435053555x0x185760/ab576752-f008-457a-b678-186098240468/YHOO_News_2008_4_7_General.pdf, accessed May 2, 2012.

14. David Litterick, "Yahoo! Rejects Microsoft and Carl Icahn Bid," The Telegraph, July 14, 2008, www.telegraph.co.uk/finance/newsbysector/mediatechnologyandtelecoms/2793196/Yahoo-rejects-Microsoft-and-Carl-Icahnbid.html, accessed September 18, 2012.

15. Evelyn M. Rusli, "Activist Investor Charts Plan to Revitalize Yahoo," The New York Times, March 9, 2012, pp. B1, B5; and proxy statements filed by Third Point LLC, http://files.shareholder.com/downloads/YHOO/2435053555x0xS899140-12-176/1011006/filing.pdf, accessed May 2, 2013 and http://files.shareholder.com/downloads/YHOO/2435053555x0xS899140-12-204/1011006/filing.pdf, accessed May 2, 2012.

16. Poornima Gupta, "Yahoo CEO Scott Thompson's Resume is Faked, Third Point Alleges," The Huffington Post, www.huffingtonpost.com/2012/05/03/scott-thompson-resume-yahoo_n_1475700.html, accessed September 18, 2012.

17. This section was based on the following sources: Yahoo! Inc. 2011 10-K; "Yahoo! Inc. Company Information, www.hoovers.com/company-information/cs/company-profile.Yahoo!_Inc.7fdc8a9aba94345b.html, accessed May 2, 2013; Nicole Perlroth, "Revamping at Yahoo to Focus on its Media Properties and Customer Data," The New York Times, April 11, 2012, p. B4.

18. http://files.shareholder.com/downloads/YHOO/2435053555x0xS1193125-12-86972/1011006/filing.pdf, accessed May 2, 2012.

19. Ibid.

20. Ibid.

21. "Board of Directors," Yahoo!, http://investor.yahoo.net/directors.cfm, accessed September 19, 2012.

22. Nicholas Carlson, "Marissa Mayer Reviews Every New Hire at Yahoo," September 4, 2012, www.businessinsider.com/marissa-mayer-is-reviewing-every-single-new-hire-at-yahoo-2012-9, accessed September 19, 2012.

23. Nicholas Carlson, "Marissa Mayer Sent a Late Night Email Promising to Make Yahoo 'The Absolute Best Place to Work,'" August 27, 2012, www.businessinsider.com/marissa-mayer-sent-a-late-night-email-promising-to-makeyahoo-the-absolutebest-place-to-work-2012-8, accessed September 19, 2012.

24. Charles Arthur, "Yahoo Sells Chunk of Alibaba Stake," The Guardian, September 19, 2012, www.guardian.co.uk/technology/2012/sep/19/yahoo-efinance, accessed September 24, 2012.

Company Index